THE OXFORD HANDBOOK OF

BRITISH AND IRISH WAR POETRY

THE OXFORD HANDBOOK OF

BRITISH AND IRISH WAR POETRY

Edited by

TIM KENDALL

OXFORD
UNIVERSITY PRESS

OXFORD
UNIVERSITY PRESS

Great Clarendon Street, Oxford OX2 6DP

Oxford University Press is a department of the University of Oxford.
It furthers the University's objective of excellence in research, scholarship,
and education by publishing worldwide in

Oxford New York

Auckland Cape Town Dar es Salaam Hong Kong Karachi
Kuala Lumpur Madrid Melbourne Mexico City Nairobi
New Delhi Shanghai Taipei Toronto

With offices in

Argentina Austria Brazil Chile Czech Republic France Greece
Guatemala Hungary Italy Japan Poland Portugal Singapore
South Korea Switzerland Thailand Turkey Ukraine Vietnam

Oxford is a registered trade mark of Oxford University Press
in the UK and in certain other countries

Published in the United States
by Oxford University Press Inc., New York

British Library Cataloguing in Publication Data

Data available

Library of Congress Cataloging in Publication Data

Data available

Typeset by Laserwords Private Limited, Chennai, India
Printed in Great Britain
on acid-free paper by
Biddles Ltd., King's Lynn, Norfolk

ISBN 978−0−19−928266−1

1 3 5 7 9 10 8 6 4 2

Acknowledgements

I am grateful to Andrew McNeillie for his unstinting support during the development of this book. I have also profited from the advice and expertise of Eva Nyika, Tom Perridge, Jacqueline Baker, and Jean Van Altena. The contributors suffered my cajoling emails with good grace. My final and largest debt is to my wife, Fiona.

TK

CONTENTS

PART III ENTRE DEUX GUERRES

PART IV THE SECOND WORLD WAR

PART V CONTINUITIES IN MODERN WAR POETRY

PART VI 'POST-WAR' POETRY

PART VII NORTHERN IRELAND

LIST OF CONTRIBUTORS

Dawn Bellamy is a Visiting Fellow in the Department of English at the University of Bristol. She has recently been awarded a Ph.D. for her thesis 'Keith Douglas and Influence'.

Matthew Bevis is a Lecturer in Nineteenth-Century Literature at the University of York. He has recently published articles on a range of Victorian writers, and a book on Tennyson for the Pickering & Chatto series, *Lives of Victorian Literary Figures* (2003). He is now completing a monograph on the relations between oratory and literature, *The Art of Eloquence: Byron, Dickens, Tennyson, Joyce* (2007), and editing a collection of essays, *Some Versions of Empson* (2007).

Fran Brearton is Reader in English at Queen's University, Belfast. She is author of *The Great War in Irish Poetry* (2000) and *Reading Michael Longley* (2006), and gave the 2004 British Academy Chatterton Lecture on Robert Graves's poetry.

Tara Christie is a Ph.D. candidate at Emory University, where she specializes in twentieth-century British and Irish literature and seventeenth-century Metaphysical poetry. Her essay 'Seamus Heaney's Hardy' appears in the Summer 2004 issue of *The Recorder: The Journal of the American Irish Historical Society*. She is currently working on a dissertation entitled 'Modernism, the Metaphysical Poets, and the First World War'.

Sarah Cole is an Associate Professor in the Department of English and Comparative Literature at Columbia University, where she teaches courses on twentieth-century British literature and culture. Her first book, *Modernism, Male Friendship, and the First World War* (2003), focuses on institutions of masculine intimacy in the late Victorian and early modernist period. She is currently working on a project about violence and aesthetics in the twentieth century.

Brendan Corcoran is an Assistant Professor in the Department of English at Indiana State University, where he teaches courses in twentieth-century Irish and British poetry. A biographical essay on Seamus Heaney is forthcoming in the *Dictionary of Literary Biography* volume *Nobel Laureates in Literature* (2006). He is working on a project examining the elegy in twentieth-century Irish poetry.

Santanu Das is currently a British Academy Postdoctoral Fellow at Queen Mary, University of London, and a former Research Fellow at St John's College, Cambridge.

He is the author of *Touch and Intimacy in First World War Literature* (2005). He is presently working on a monograph on India and First World War writing, and an anthology that brings together Commonwealth responses to the First World War.

Rainer Emig is Professor of British Literature at the University of Regensburg. His main areas of teaching and research are nineteenth- and twentieth-century literature and culture. His publications include *Modernism in Poetry* (1995), *W.H. Auden* (1999), and *Krieg als Metapher im zwanzigsten Jahrhundert* (War as Metaphor in the Twentieth Century) (2001). He has recently completed a monograph entitled *Eccentricity: Culture from the Margins* and co-edited a collection of essays on *Hybrid Humour*.

Simon Featherstone works in the School of English, Performance, and Historical Studies at De Montfort University, Leicester. His recent publications include *Postcolonial Cultures* (2005).

Stacy Gillis is Lecturer in Modern and Contemporary Literature at the University of Newcastle. She has published widely on feminist theory, cybertheory, First World War studies, and popular fiction. Forthcoming work includes a collection on the First World War and popular culture and a monograph on twentieth-century British detective fiction.

Helen Goethals teaches Commonwealth history at the University of Lyon 2, and her research is centred on the interaction of poetry and politics. The articles she has published on the Second World War discuss the work of W. H. Auden, Philip Larkin, John Jarmain, and George Orwell.

David Goldie is a Senior Lecturer and Director of Undergraduate English in the Department of English Studies at Strathclyde University. He is the author of *A Critical Difference: T. S. Eliot and John Middleton Murry in English Literary Criticism, 1919–1928* (1998) and co-editor of *Beyond Scotland: New Contexts for Twentieth-Century Scottish Literature* (2004) and the forthcoming *Scotland in the Nineteenth-Century World* (2006). His main areas of research and publication are English and Scottish early twentieth-century literature, criticism, and popular culture. He is currently working on a monograph on the Scottish literature and popular culture of the First World War.

Hugh Haughton teaches English at the University of York. He has recently completed *Derek Mahon and Modern Irish Poetry* (forthcoming, 2007). He is the editor of *The Chatto Book of Nonsense Poetry* (1985), *John Clare in Context* (with Adam Phillips, 1994), *Alice in Wonderland and Through the Looking-Glass* (1998), *Sigmund Freud: The Uncanny* (2003), and *Second World War Poems* (2004). He is currently co-editing (with Valerie Eliot) *T. S. Eliot: The Letters*.

Geoffrey Hill was born in Bromsgrove, Worcestershire, in 1932. He is the author of a dozen books of poetry and three books of criticism. Since 1988 he has lived and taught in Massachusetts, as a University Professor and Professor of Literature and Religion at Boston University. He is also Honorary Fellow of Keble College, Oxford; Honorary Fellow of Emmanuel College, Cambridge; Fellow of the Royal Society of Literature; and Fellow of the American Academy of Arts and Sciences. His *Collected Critical Writings* is under contract with Oxford University Press.

Daniel Karlin is Professor of English at the University of Sheffield. He previously taught at University College London and Boston University. He edited *The Jungle Books* for Penguin Classics and the Oxford Authors volume of Kipling's stories and poems, and has published numerous articles on Kipling.

Tim Kendall is Professor of English Literature at the University of Exeter. He has published a book of poems, *Strange Land*, and full-length studies of Muldoon and Plath. From 1994 until 2003 he edited the international poetry magazine *Thumbscrew*. His latest monograph is *Modern English War Poetry* (2006), and his next is a study of Robert Frost.

John Lee is Senior Lecturer at the University of Bristol. His main research interests lie in the field of English Renaissance literature. Recent publications include 'Refrains and Echoes: Spenser's *Amoretti and Epithalamion*', *Poetica* (2006); 'Reanimating Criticism: Towards a Materialist Shakespeare', *English* (2004); 'Twins and Doubles as an Aspect of Shakespeare's Pluralism', *International Shakespeare Yearbook* (2004); and 'Kipling's Shakespearean *Traffics and Discoveries*', *Shakespeare Studies* (2003).

Edna Longley is a Professor Emerita at Queen's University Belfast. She is the author of *Poetry & Posterity* (2000), and editor of *The Bloodaxe Book of 20th Century British and Irish Poetry* (2000). Her edition of Edward Thomas's poems, *The Annotated Edward Thomas*, will appear in 2007.

John Lyon teaches English Literature at the University of Bristol. He has published on Shakespeare, seventeenth-century poetry, George Eliot, Henry James, Joseph Conrad, Rudyard Kipling, D. H. Lawrence, elegy, influence, and contemporary poetry, particularly Geoffrey Hill.

Alan Marshall is Head of American Studies at King's College London, and has just completed a book on American poetry and democratic thought. He previously held a lectureship at the University of York. His essays, poems, and reviews have appeared in various books and journals.

Peter McDonald is a poet and critic. He is editor of Louis MacNeice's *Collected Poems* (2006), and the author of, among other books, *Serious Poetry: Form and Authority from Yeats to Hill* (2002). He has published four volumes of poetry, most recently *Pastorals* (2004) and *The House of Clay* (2007). He works in Oxford, where he is Christopher Tower Student and Tutor in Poetry in the English Language at Christ Church.

Vivien Noakes is the editor of the definitive variorum edition of *The Poetry and Plays of Isaac Rosenberg* (2004), and of *Voices of Silence: The Alternative Book of First World War Poetry* (2006). She has published extensively on the life and work of the nonsense poet and painter Edward Lear, and was Guest Curator of the major exhibition 'Edward Lear: 1812–1888' at the Royal Academy of Arts, London, and the National Academy of Design, New York (1985). She was formerly a Lecturer at Somerville College, Oxford, and is a Fellow of the Royal Society of Literature.

Cornelia D. J. Pearsall is Associate Professor of English at Smith College. Her book *Tennyson's Rapture* is forthcoming from Oxford University Press. Other book-length projects include 'Tennyson and the Federation of the World', on the laureate and imperial expansion; 'Loved Remains', on the materialization of mourning in Victorian Britain; and a collection of essays on war poetry from Tennyson to Plath. She has published articles on such subjects as Browning's dramatic monologues, the funeral of the Duke of Wellington, and Auden's post-war poetry.

Marjorie Perloff is the author of many books on modern poetry, including *The Poetics of Indeterminacy: Rimbaud to Cage* (1981), *The Futurist Moment* (1986), *Radical Artifice* (1992), *Wittgenstein's Ladder* (1996), and most recently, *Differentials: Poetry, Poetics, Pedagogy* (2004). She has frequently written on Yeats, beginning with *Rhyme and Meaning in the Poetry of Yeats* (1970). She is Sadie Dernham Patek Professor Emerita of Humanities at Stanford University and currently Scholar-in-Residence at the University of Southern California.

Adam Piette is Professor of Modern English Literature at the University of Sheffield, and author of *Imagination at War* (1995) and *Remembering and the Sound of Words* (1996). He has worked at the universities of Paris XIII, Lausanne, Geneva, and Glasgow, and is currently completing a project on Cold War writing.

Ralph Pite's biography of Hardy, *Thomas Hardy: The Guarded Life*, appeared in 2006; he has also published *Hardy's Geography: Wessex and the Regional Novel* (2002). He is Professor of English Literature at Cardiff University, and has written extensively on Romanticism, modern poetry, and Victorian literature. He is author of a book of poems, *Paths and Ladders* (2003).

Mark Rawlinson is Senior Lecturer in English at the University of Leicester. He is the author of *British Writing of the Second World War* (2000). He is currently finishing a book on the Second World War in fiction after 1945, writing a monograph on Pat Barker, and researching the cultural significance of camouflage.

Gareth Reeves is Reader in English at Durham University. He is the author of *T. S. Eliot: A Virgilian Poet* (1989); *T. S. Eliot's 'The Waste Land'* (1994); two volumes of poetry, *Real Stories* (1984) and *Listening In* (1993); and, with Michael O'Neill, *Auden, MacNeice, Spender: The Thirties Poetry* (1992); as well as essays on, among others, Wallace Stevens, W. H. Auden, Donald Davie, Thom Gunn, Seamus Heaney, Robert Lowell, and Charles Tomlinson.

Peter Robinson is Professor of English and American Literature at the University of Reading. He has published many books of poetry, including *Selected Poems* (2003), *Ghost Characters* (2006), and *There are Avenues* (2006). Three volumes of literary criticism have appeared, the latest being *Twentieth Century Poetry: Selves and Situation* (2005). His books of translations include *The Greener Meadow: Selected Poems of Luciano Erba* (2007) and, with Marcus Perryman, *Selected Poetry and Prose of Vittorio Sereni* (2006).

Vincent Sherry is Distinguished Professor of English at Villanova University. His publications include *The Uncommon Tongue: The Poetry and Criticism of Geoffrey Hill* (1987); *Ezra Pound, Wyndham Lewis, and Radical Modernism* (1993); *James Joyce; ULYSSES* (1995); and *The Great War and the Language of Modernism* (2003). He has edited the *Cambridge Companion to the Literature of the First World War* (2005). He is currently writing a biography of Ezra Pound and a book-length study of English modernism and pan-European decadence.

Stan Smith holds the Research Chair in Literary Studies at Nottingham Trent University. He has published two books on *W. H. Auden* (1985, 1997) and edited *The Cambridge Companion to W. H. Auden* (2004). Other books include *Inviolable Voice* (1982), *Edward Thomas* (1986), *W. B. Yeats* (1990), *The Origins of Modernism* (1994), and *Irish Poetry and the Construction of Modern Identity* (2005). He is at present completing a study of Early Modern English Poetry, 1890–1940 for the Longman History of Literature in English series.

Jon Stallworthy is a Fellow of the British Academy and of the Royal Society of Literature. Formerly Professor of English Literature at Oxford University, he has published seven books of poetry, and is the biographer of Wilfred Owen and Louis MacNeice. His *Anthem for Doomed Youth* appeared in 2002. He has edited Owen's *Complete Poems and Fragments* (1983), Henry Reed's *Collected Poems* (1991), and several anthologies, including *The Oxford Book of War Poetry* (1988).

Claire M. Tylee is Senior Lecturer in English Literature at Brunel University, having formerly taught at Málaga University and the University of Leicester. She has published widely on war writing by women, and is best known for *The Great War and Women's Consciousness* (1990) and *War Plays by Women* (1999). Her edited collection of essays *In the Open: Jewish Women's Writing and Twentieth-Century British Culture* is in process, and she is currently researching Holocaust literature in Britain.

Paul Volsik is Professor of British Poetry at the University of Paris 7 Denis-Diderot. After a Ph.D. in French literature at the University of Sussex, he wrote a French doctoral thesis on Dylan Thomas and has since published on nineteenth-

and twentieth-century British and Irish poets (most recently Philip Larkin, Eavan Boland and Medbh McGuckian, Ted Hughes, Thomas Hardy, William Barnes) as well as on translation theory.

April Warman is currently at Pembroke College, Oxford, where she is researching a D.Phil. on modern poetry's relation to the dead. She specializes in the work of Paul Muldoon, Michael Longley, and Geoffrey Hill.

Roderick Watson teaches literature at the University of Stirling, where he is also Director of the Stirling Centre for Scottish Studies. He has been General Editor of the Canongate Classics since the start of the series and editor of *The Poetry of Scotland* (1995). His books include *Hugh MacDiarmid* (1976, 1985); *The Poetry of Norman MacCaig* (1989); *Into the Blue Wavelengths* (poetry, 2004); and *The Literature of Scotland* (1984; revised in 2 vol. 2006).

David Wheatley lectures in English at the University of Hull. His first collection of poetry, *Thirst* (1997), was awarded the Rooney Prize for Irish Literature; *Misery Hill* appeared in 2000, and a third, *Mocker*, in 2006. He has published articles and reviews in many journals and edited collections, and was a founder editor of *Metre*. He has also edited the work of James Clarence Mangan, and is writing a book on contemporary British poetry for Cambridge University Press.

Gerwyn Wiliams is a Professor and Head of the School of Welsh, University of Wales, Bangor. He has published widely, mainly on twentieth-century literature, and among his publications are *Y Rhwyg* (1993), a study of Welsh poetry about the First World War; *Tir Neb* (1996), a study of Welsh prose and the First World War; and more recently, *Tir Newydd* (2005), a study of Welsh literature and the Second World War. He is also an accomplished poet, having won the Crown in the 1994 National Eisteddfod; his latest collection, *Tafarn Tawelwch*, was published in 2003.

INTRODUCTION

TIM KENDALL

The term 'war poetry' has become so familiar that its internal tensions often go unnoticed. Yet it seems hard to imagine two human activities more unlike each other than experiencing a war and writing a poem. One suggests destruction, the other creation; one chaos, the other order; one pain, the other pleasure. War poetry accommodates binary oppositions, most notably life and death: if poetry is, as Louis MacNeice claims, '*always positive*', so that even 'a poem in praise of suicide is an act of homage to life',[1] then a war poem must be at war with itself, its affirming flame illuminating a dark subject-matter. Some critics, such as John Lyon in this present volume, consider the mismatch to be fatal: better to fall silent than to write a poem which, by making formal sense out of war's violent nonsense, betrays the facts. Truth is a weapon to which soldier-poets during the twentieth century often lay claim. Nevertheless, according to its detractors, war poetry may be true neither to war nor to poetry.

Theodor Adorno, the modern philosopher most often associated with these debates (and not merely because of what he is supposed to have said about poetry after Auschwitz), raises a similar concern in relation to Holocaust art: 'The so-called artistic representation of the sheer physical pain of people beaten to the ground by rifle-butts contains, however remotely, the power to elicit enjoyment out of it.'[2] Adorno's mistake is to idealize art: his 'so-called' has already judged the case, disqualifying as unworthy of the name any art which refuses to behave as decorously as he would wish. Adorno ignores the horrific possibility that delight

---

[1] Louis MacNeice, 'Broken Windows or Thinking Aloud', in *Selected Prose of Louis MacNeice*, ed. Alan Heuser (Oxford: Clarendon Press, 1990), 138.

[2] Theodor Adorno, 'Commitment', trans. Francis McDonagh, in Ernst Bloch *et al.*, *Aesthetics and Politics* (London: NLB, 1977), 189.

is an essential component of sympathy. But the best war poets always know that they involve themselves in a monstrous negotiation between artistic pleasure and human suffering, and that there is readerly enjoyment to be elicited from a choking gas-victim or a three-week-dead enemy corpse. War poetry is attracted to pain, and makes artistic capital out of it; after all, as David Bromwich pithily argues, 'what is simply repellent simply repels'.[3] Small wonder that so much war poetry should be guilt-ridden. When a distraught fellow soldier tells Ivor Gurney how he had heard in the distance the 'infernal, silly' call of a cuckoo as he held a dying friend in his arms, the poet finally repents of having sensed an opportunity: 'I became aware of shame at the unholy joy that had filled my artist's mind.'[4] Gurney's awareness is conspicuous because, for once, the shame seems to have won out. A war poem represents the partial victory of unholy joy over shame.

MacNeice's grandiose (and, it ought to be confessed, almost meaningless) claim that art is necessarily a homage to life therefore requires careful revision. The war poem pays homage only to the impulse which, against all odds and at whatever cost, produced it. During the First World War, Owen, Gurney, and Sassoon wrote poems explicitly stating the need to forget events on which the poems themselves dwell: 'I try not to remember these things now,'[5] Owen states in 'The Sentry', having just lingered lovingly over them. He writes the poem as if against his own volition, not only to create a drama of self-sacrifice, but because he wants to distance himself from unholy motives: like the Ancient Mariner, he is (apparently) compelled to repeat a story from which he wishes to be freed. He cannot be seen to profit, and must even suffer for his art. Yet, although a war poem may seek to justify itself as a warning, or a bearing witness, or an act of compassion or catharsis or redress, its primary motivation is to celebrate (even, as in Owen's case, at the expense of healing) its own achievement.

Gurney's 'unholy joy' is especially apt to describe the war poet's enterprise, because, like 'war poetry' itself, it verges on the oxymoronic, oxymoron being the natural figure for a poetry which binds opposites. This understanding is not confined to the soldier-poets. Yeats's refrain in 'Easter, 1916'—'A terrible beauty is born'[6]—comments on the changed world of Irish politics, but it is also self-reflexive: the poem *is* the terrible beauty, born out of the suppression of the Easter Rising. War poetry, like Holocaust art of the kind Adorno attacks, beautifies the terrible. One may cavil at Yeats's deliberate provocation, in an essay on J. M. Synge,

[3] David Bromwich, 'How Moral Is Taste?', in *Skeptical Music: Essays on Modern Poetry* (Chicago: University of Chicago Press, 2001), 240.

[4] Ivor Gurney to Catherine Abercrombie, ? June 1916, in *Collected Letters*, ed. R. K. R. Thornton (Ashington and Manchester: MidNag/Carcanet, 1991), 91.

[5] Wilfred Owen, 'The Sentry', in *The Complete Poems and Fragments*, i: *The Poems*, ed. Jon Stallworthy (London: Chatto & Windus, Hogarth Press, and Oxford University Press, 1983), 188.

[6] William Butler Yeats, 'Easter, 1916', in *The Poems*, ed. Daniel Albright (London: Dent, 1990), 228–30.

that 'All noble things are the result of warfare',[7] but the essays in this Handbook offer eloquent testimony to the extent to which modern poetry (and art more widely) is indebted to war. This may be 'terrible' to accept; yet, when Seamus Heaney quotes Coventry Patmore's belief that *The end of art is peace*,[8] such an admirable vision does not seem altogether enticing. For who, among the many poets studied by the contributors to this collection of essays, would ever want art to end?

Yeats, 'J. M. Synge and the Ireland of His Time', in *Essays and Introductions* (Basingstoke: Macmillan, 1961), 321.

Seamus Heaney, 'The Harvest Bow', in *Opened Ground: Poems 1966–1996* (London: Faber, 1998), 184.

PART I

BEGINNINGS

CHAPTER 1

....

FIGHTING TALK: VICTORIAN WAR POETRY

....

MATTHEW BEVIS

Victorian war poetry is often engaged in conflict with its own form, rather than with an external enemy. Browning's *Dramatic Lyrics* (1842) begins with a series of apparently belligerent 'Cavalier Tunes', but readers approach them armed with a note from the volume's advertisement. There the poet observes that most of the poems are 'though for the most part Lyric in expression, always Dramatic in principle, and so many utterances of so many imaginary persons, not mine'.[1] 'Cavalier', then, may be a lyrical-dramatic pun: the soldier-singers are proud to be voicing their support for Charles I, but the poet who creates these voices asks us to consider whether they are themselves cavalier. A later poem in the collection, 'Incident of the French Camp', focuses on the potential consequences of such fighting talk. The speaker recalls a moment when Napoleon's army, pursuing the Austrians, stormed Ratisbon under the command of one of the Emperor's most renowned generals, Jean Lannes. Napoleon looks on:

> Just as perhaps he mused 'My plans
>   That soar, to earth may fall
> Let once my army-leader Lannes
>   Waver at yonder wall,'
> Out 'twixt the battery-smokes there flew

[1] Robert Browning, quoted in *The Poetical Works of Robert Browning*, iii, ed. Ian Jack and Rowena Fowler (Oxford: Clarendon Press, 1988), 178.

> A rider, bound on bound
> Full-galloping; nor bridle drew
>   Until he reached the mound.
> Then off there flung in smiling joy,
>   And held himself erect
> By just his horse's mane, a boy:
>   You hardly could suspect—
> (So tight he kept his lips compressed,
>   Scarce any blood came through)
> You looked twice ere you saw his breast
>   Was all but shot in two.[2]

The enjambed lines in the first stanza work with the rider to accentuate his pace, but in the second they shift from stridency to hesitancy. We are asked to glance back even as we move forward. 'And held himself erect' initially sounds proud, but the next line, in telling us how he did so, comes as a shock (the 'rider' also becomes a more vulnerable 'boy'). You 'hardly could suspect' him, this boy, 'So tight he kept his lips compressed' (a soldierly example to others of tight-lipped trustworthiness)—until, that is, you come to suspect something else as the sentence makes its inexorable progress. The penultimate line makes one last grasp at a dignified diction ('ere', 'breast') before the close of the stanza brings the incident into clearer focus. The poem ends when we are told that 'the boy fell dead'; while Napoleon was dwelling on whether his plans might fall to earth, the poem was contemplating another kind of falling.

The Victorians are not often credited with an attentiveness to the realities of warfare. They have frequently been taken to task for keeping their own lips compressed and for refusing to dwell on the bloodier side of conflict. Their war-tunes have been heard as cavalier, and critical study has been focused instead on the rude awakenings of the twentieth century. Never such innocence again. Lytton Strachey's *Eminent Victorians*, published in the final year of the Great War, marks the divide. Strachey's father had been a general in the army, but the son was a conscientious objector, and such objections can be heard in the icy briskness of his book's final sentence. Recalling how General Gordon's death in Khartoum was avenged by Kitchener's army at Omdurman in 1898, Strachey observes: 'it had all ended very happily—in a glorious slaughter of 20,000 Arabs, a vast addition to the British Empire, and a step in the Peerage for Evelyn Baring'.[3] This parody of a happy ending is meant as the final nail in the coffin of Victorian imperial confidence, and Strachey's view has held sway in subsequent literature. As Samuel Hynes observed more recently, the Great War 'brought to an end the life and values of Victorian and Edwardian England'.[4]

---

[2] Browning, 'Incident of the French Camp', ibid. 197.

[3] Lytton Strachey, *Eminent Victorians* (Harmondsworth: Penguin, 1986; 1st pub. 1918), 266.

[4] Samuel Hynes, *A War Imagined: The First World War and English Culture* (London: Bodley Head, 1990), p. ix.

This general judgement has been echoed in appreciations of war poetry. As the First World War comes to be seen as heralding a break between Victorian and modern conceptions of conflict, so a series of neat poetic oppositions emerges—the glorious versus the gruesome, the heroic versus the hellish, the romantic versus the realistic. One need not deny the differences between writing before and after the First World War without feeling that such oppositions do a disservice to the complexities of both nineteenth- and twentieth-century war poetry, to the former in particular. Victorian war poetry has frequently been belittled or ignored by critics, usually by way of dismissive references to Tennyson serving as prelude to discussion of the poets of the Great War.[5] Even Malvern Van Wyk Smith, in what remains the only book-length study of the subject, confines himself to the Anglo-Boer War, and closes with the assertion that 'after the Boer War, war poetry could no longer be merely a sub-department of patriotic verse'.[6] But war poetry was not 'merely' this before the Boer War. Such statements have not helped to generate interest in the subject. It is not given attention in essay collections,[7] and a recent study of Victorian war literature sidelines poetry on the grounds that 'so much of it seems little more than a string of patriotic slogans'.[8] This sense of Victorian war poetry as a synonym for victorious war poetry needs to be reconsidered. Like the speaker in Browning's poem, whose responsible gaze insists on looking twice, Victorian poets often require us to see double.

I

In *Fifteen Decisive Battles* (1851), Edward Creasy noted that 'It is an honourable characteristic of the Spirit of this Age, that projects of violence and warfare are regarded among civilized states with increasing aversion. . . . Yet it cannot be denied that a fearful and wonderful interest is attached to these scenes of carnage.'[9] The interest was reflected in sales of Creasy's book (a Victorian best-seller, it was reprinted thirty-eight times before 1894). The 'scenes' were not merely

[5] See e.g. Jon Silkin, *Out of Battle: The Poetry of the Great War* (Oxford: Oxford University Press, 1972), 26–7, and Bernard Bergonzi, *Heroes' Twilight: A Study of the Literature of the Great War*, 2nd edn. (London: Macmillan, 1980), 16.

[6] M. Van Wyk Smith, *Drummer Hodge: The Poetry of the Anglo-Boer War* (Oxford: Clarendon Press, 1978), 310.

[7] 'War poetry' is not accorded a chapter (or even an index citation) in either Joseph Bristow (ed.), *The Cambridge Companion to Victorian Poetry* (Cambridge: Cambridge University Press, 2000), or Richard Cronin, Alison Chapman, and Anthony H. Harrison (eds.), *A Companion to Victorian Poetry* (Oxford: Blackwell, 2002). Instead, the emphasis is on patriotism; see Tricia Cootens, 'Victorian poetry and patriotism', in Bristow (ed.), *Cambridge Companion*, 255–79.

[8] John Peck, *War, the Army and Victorian Literature* (Basingstoke: Palgrave, 1998), p. xiii.

[9] Edward Creasy, *Fifteen Decisive Battles of the World: From Marathon to Waterloo*, i (London: Bentley, 1851), pp. iii–iv.

historical; every year of Victoria's reign, her soldiers were fighting a series of 'little wars' in some part of the world.[10] The perplexed Victorian fascination with warfare is also evident in a group of phrases that, according to the *OED*, made their way into the language during the period. In addition to 'war-footing' (1847), 'war-code' (1853), 'war-news' (1857), and 'war-machines' (1881), the *Dictionary* cites a collection of words that 'denote works of art, etc., of which the subject is war': 'war-ballad' (1854), 'war poem' (1857), 'war story' (1864), 'war pictures' (1883), 'war artist' (1890), 'war-plays' (1896), 'war films' (1897). The interest in war did not preclude a critical engagement with it; even the advent of the Victoria Cross (the first medal in England to recognize acts of bravery independent of rank[11]) raised some awkward questions. When Wilfred Owen snapped, 'The Victoria Cross! I covet it not. Is it not *Victorian*? yah! pah!',[12] he was not the first to announce a refusal to be beguiled by that age's pageantry. On hearing the news of its introduction in 1855, *Punch* offered its own commentary by having two shivering soldiers on the front line in the Crimea discuss the VC: ' "Well, Jack! Here's good news from Home. We're to have a medal." "That's very kind. Maybe one of these days we'll have a coat to stick it on?" '[13]

The unsettling aspects of war found their way into poetic theory and practice even as Victorian writers sought to distance themselves from the fray. In his inaugural lecture in the Oxford Poetry Chair in 1857, Matthew Arnold observed that one of the chief characteristics of 'a *modern* age, of an age of advanced civilization, is the banishment of the ensigns of war and bloodshed from the intercourse of civil life. . . . Wars are still carried on; but within the limits of civil life a circle has been formed within which man can move securely, and develop the arts of peace uninterruptedly.'[14] Accompanying this modern spirit is 'the supreme characteristic of all: the intellectual maturity of man himself; the tendency to observe facts with a critical spirit'.[15] As an early example of such reflective, unwarlike modernity, Arnold cites Grecian society and its expressive flowering in Thucydides' *History of the Peloponnesian War*. However, as Arnold continues, the 'arts of peace' are not allowed to remain uninterrupted:

In the case of Thucydides I called attention to the fact that his habit of mind, his mode of dealing with questions, were modern; that they were those of an enlightened, reflecting man among ourselves. . . . The predominance of thought, of reflection, in modern epochs is not without its penalties . . . it has produced a state of feeling unknown to the less enlightened

---

[10] See Robert Giddings, *Imperial Echoes: Eye-Witness Accounts of Victoria's Little Wars* (London: Cooper, 1996), p. xvi.

[11] See Max Arthur, *Symbol of Courage: A History of the Victoria Cross* (London: Sidgwick & Jackson, 2004).

[12] Wilfred Owen, quoted in Hynes, *A War Imagined*, 246.

[13] *Punch*, 28 (17 Feb. 1855), 64.

[14] Matthew Arnold, 'On the Modern Element in Literature', in *The Complete Prose Works of Matthew Arnold*, i, ed. R. H. Super (Ann Arbor: University of Michigan Press, 1960), 23.

[15] Ibid. 24.

but perhaps healthier epochs—the feeling of depression, the feeling of *ennui*. Depression and *ennui*; these are the characteristics stamped on how many of the representative works of modern times![16]

This passage echoes Arnold's argument in his 1853 Preface, where modernity's reflective powers lead to the disabling 'dialogue of the mind with itself'.[17] If the civilizing process paradoxically creates the conditions in which it may not be able to flourish, then those 'ensigns of war' are not quite banished, but become part of the warring psyche. War is not, then, what modern life avoids, but part of a description of what it embodies. 'Dover Beach' (1851) tries to form a circle within which man can move securely, outside the realm of war, yet from its opening this lyrical 'art of peace' is haunted by its demons as the speaker addresses his interlocutor: 'On the French coast the light/Gleams and is gone; the cliffs of England stand.'[18] In the 1850s, this light was not only part of a picturesque scene, but also a glint of menace (as the invasion scares of that decade would show). The poem ends:

> And we are here as on a darkling plain
> Swept with confused alarms of struggle and flight,
> Where ignorant armies clash by night.

The source for this passage is Thucydides' description of the Battle of Epipolae in his *History of the Peloponnesian War*, where he recounts a night battle in which the Athenians became disoriented and came to blows with one another. The source that, for Arnold, was meant to enshrine 'that noble serenity which always accompanies true insight'[19] is harnessed here to express a sense of the modern mind's loss of bearings. The speaker's aim is to draw attention to a bower sheltering him and his beloved from the warring world outside, but 'swept' might refer to 'we' as well as to the 'plain'. That is, the poem closes not just with the sense that 'it's us against them', but also with the more disturbing suggestion that the couple may be swept up in it all by being against each other. Like many Victorian lyrics, 'Dover Beach' is a war poem of sorts, not only because the threat of war hovers in and around its edges, but also because war is part of the fabric of its most intimate human imaginings.

The complex debt that Arnold owes to Thucydides bears on the question of the classical inheritance of Victorian war poetry. This inheritance has often been cited as another marker of the Victorian/modern divide. Victorian poetics is seen as responsive to an epic tradition that is said to endorse militaristic values, while twentieth-century war poetry is, as Matthew Campbell puts it, 'a poetry which no longer feels that it can sing in celebration of arms and the man'.[20] There is

---

[16] Ibid. 32.

[17] Arnold, 'Preface to the First Edition of *Poems*' (1853), in *The Poems of Matthew Arnold*, ed. Miriam Allott, 2nd edn. (London: Longman, 1979), 654.

[18] Arnold, 'Dover Beach', ibid. 254.

[19] Arnold, 'On the Modern Element in Literature', 28.

[20] Matthew Campbell, 'Poetry and War', in Neil Roberts (ed.), *A Companion to Twentieth-Century Poetry* (Oxford: Blackwell, 2003), 65.

some truth in this distinction, but it should also be noted that the celebrations of classical epic are themselves equivocal. When Arnold in his Preface advocated a return to the classical simplicity of the Greek tradition and style as an escape from the luxuriant disease of modernity, he prescribed an avoidance of 'contemporary allusions' and an emphasis on 'action' rather than on appeals to 'our transient feelings and interests'.[21] The work that was meant to exemplify these critical principles was *Sohrab and Rustum* (1853), and—as many contemporary reviewers noted—the poem frequently borrowed from the structure and the style of the *Iliad*. Yet, Arnold's borrowings give voice not to a Homeric championing of war, but to that side of Homer that Simone Weil so sensitively described. Speaking of 'those few luminous moments, scattered here and there throughout the poem', Weil observes:

The tradition of hospitality persists, even through several generations, to dispel the blindness of combat. . . . [M]oments of grace are rare in the *Iliad*, but they are enough to make us feel with sharp regret what it is that violence has killed and will kill again . . . Whatever is not war, whatever war destroys or threatens, the *Iliad* wraps in poetry; the realities of war, never.[22]

Weil notes that 'the brief evocations of the world of peace are felt as pain',[23] and these evocations are at the heart of Arnold's debt to Homer. When Rustum mortally wounds his son Sohrab, the latter lies dying and announces that he pities his mother for her loss. As Rustum listens, combat gives way to thoughts of hospitality:

> he listened, plunged in thought:
> And his soul set to grief, as the vast tide
> Of the bright rocking Ocean sets to shore
> At the full moon; tears gathered in his eyes;
> For he remembered his early youth,
> And all its bounding rapture; as, at dawn,
> The shepherd from his mountain-lodge descries
> A far, bright city, smitten by the sun,
> Through many rolling clouds—so Rustum saw
> His youth; saw Sohrab's mother, in her bloom;
> And that old king, her father, who loved well
> His wandering guest, and gave him his fair child
> With joy; and all the pleasant life they led,
> They three, in that long-distant summer-time . . .[24]

The first simile makes grief feel like a homecoming, as if grief itself were a source of rest to a mind that has for so long attempted to resist it. The second, in comparing the warrior to the shepherd, evokes a dream of the pastoral world in which the only

---

[21] Arnold, 'Preface', 657 and 659.

[22] Simone Weil, *The Iliad, or The Poem of Force*, trans. Mary McCarthy (Wallingford, Pa.: Pendle Hill, 1956), 27, 29, 31.

[23] Ibid. 31.   [24] Arnold, *Sohrab and Rustum*, in *Poems of Matthew Arnold*, 345–6.

thing that smites is the sun ('smitten' here, with its suggestion of being enamoured, serves to bathe martial action in romantic yearning). Both similes are lingering dreams—precarious digressions from the realization that awaits the father, forlorn attempts to stay the flow of the action, for it is action that has brought the losses Rustum contemplates. These similes are emblems of the luxuriant modern style that Arnold wished to avoid, and such luxuries (and the brooding which accompanies them) frequently punctuate *Sohrab and Rustum*, turning it into a 'modern' poem in its willingness to dwell on 'the dialogue of the mind with itself' that war can produce. Indeed, the setting of the poem (two armies of Eastern troops, the Tartars and the Persians, face each other on the plains of the Oxus) is not as remote from 'contemporary allusions' and 'transient feelings and interests' as Arnold might wish to suggest. As Isobel Armstrong notes: 'what could be more modern than this? The historical context of Arnold's writing was the collapse of the Ottoman empire, the insecure status of Afghanistan and the new alignments of Britain, France and Russia, *the* nineteenth-century problem. The Crimean war was two years away, but the eastern question already cast shadows at the beginning of the 1850s.'[25] Those shadows can be glimpsed in *Sohrab and Rustum*, a poem chastened by its own mixed allegiances, and enriched by its debt to a classical tradition that dwelt on the cost as well as the honour of war.

The fertile ambiguities of Arnold's principles and practice cast their own shadows across the writing of the period, and the Crimean War was not one of those contemporary events or transient interests that poets felt themselves at liberty to pass over. In many ways, the Crimean conflict was a new kind of war. It was the first time that commissioned war artists accompanied a British army into the field, and the first conflict of European military powers to be recorded by camera. These developments encouraged a verisimilitude in battle painting and other genres, fostering a shift from older heroic depictions to a more realistic portrayal of the battlefield.[26] The war was also the first to make use of the telegraph, and to call upon the art of the war correspondent (unlike those in the Great War, these correspondents were subject to very little censorship[27]). William Howard Russell, correspondent for *The Times*, proclaimed: 'The only thing the partisans of misrule can allege is that we don't "make things pleasant" to the authorities, and that, amid the filth and starvation and deadly stagnation of the camp, we did not go about "babbling of green fields", of present abundance, and of prospects of victory.'[28] Much of Russell's writing sets itself against babble, and reads like a description of the front line in the First World War: 'the skies are black as ink—the wind is

---

[25] Isobel Armstrong, *Victorian Poetry: Poetry, Poetics and Politics* (London: Routledge, 1993), 216.

[26] See Matthew Paul Lalumia, *Realism and Politics in Victorian Art of the Crimean War* (Ann Arbor: UMI Research Press, 1984).

[27] See Andrew Lambert and Stephen Badsey, *The War Correspondents: The Crimean War* (Stroud: Alan Sutton, 1994).

[28] William Howard Russell, in *The Times*, 12 Feb. 1855, 9.

howling over the staggering tents—the trenches are turned into dykes . . . men are out for twelve hours at a time . . . not a soul seems to care for their comfort or even for their lives.'[29]

As both these quotations suggest, *The Times* was a forum for many criticisms that would later be echoed during the Great War (for two criticisms in particular: the mismanagement of the army by an incompetent aristocracy and the neglect of the rank-and-file by a corrupt officer class). Indeed, the war correspondents—described by one contemporary as 'poetic writers of prose'[30]—might be seen as England's first soldier-poets. In a note to his poem *The Death-Ride: A Tale of the Light Brigade*, Westland Marston observed: 'the masterly Records of the War which now appear in our crowded journals—records which are at once histories and poems—leave to formal poetry only this task—to adopt their descriptions and to develop their suggestions; to comment, as it were, upon their glorious texts'.[31] These texts were 'glorious' because they attended to something more than glory, and poets who adopted and developed newspaper copy were responding to a form of expression that questioned heroic conceptions of war even as it acknowledged a regard for their enduring value. Nowhere is this development more apparent than in the responses of Russell and Tennyson to one of the most renowned military blunders of the period, the charge of the Light Brigade.[32]

T. S. Eliot once praised Herbert Read's war poetry as 'neither Romance nor Reporting . . . it has emotion as well as a version of things seen'.[33] The first sentence of Russell's report on the charge of the Light Brigade treads a fine line between romance and reporting: 'If the exhibition of the most brilliant valour, of the excess of courage, and of a daring which would have reflected lustre on the best days of chivalry can afford full consolation for the disaster to-day, we can have no reason to regret the melancholy loss which we sustained in a contest with a savage and barbarian enemy.'[34] The 'If' announces that this romantic vocabulary is under pressure; an 'excess' of courage is not only courage, but also foolhardiness, and the progress of the sentence gives readers reasons to feel unconsoled (one might not regret a 'loss', but it is harder not to regret a '*melancholy* loss'). Tennyson famously adapted *Times* reports when composing 'The Charge of the Light Brigade', but he kept their dual depiction of war as both ennobling and horrifying. As Trudi Tate has recently suggested, although 'often regarded as a simple-minded piece of patriotism', the poem 'is in fact a subtle and even anguished reflection upon the

---

[29] Russell, in *The Times*, 25 Nov. 1854, 9.

[30] 'War and Poetry', *Edinburgh Review*, 196 (July 1902), 53.

[31] Westland Marston, *The Death-Ride: A Tale of the Light Brigade* (London: Mitchell, 1855), 8.

[32] See Geoffrey Regan, *Someone Had Blundered: A Historical Survey of Military Incompetence* (London: Batsford, 1987), 192–208.

[33] T. S. Eliot, quoted in Dominic Hibberd (ed.), *Poetry of the First World War: A Casebook* (London: Macmillan, 1981), 52.

[34] Russell, in *The Times*, 14 Nov. 1854, 7.

Crimean war'.[35] Around the time of composition, the poet admitted that, despite his official position as Victoria's Laureate, he was unable to sympathize 'at this hour with any song of triumph when my heart almost bursts with indignation at the accursed mismanagement of our noble little army, that flower of men'.[36] This indignation can be glimpsed in his poem:

> 'Forward, the Light Brigade!'
> Was there a man dismayed?
> Not though the soldier knew
>   Some one had blundered:
> Theirs not to make reply,
> Theirs not to reason why,
> Theirs but to do and die:
> Into the valley of Death
>   Rode the six hundred.
>
>   .   .   .   .   .
>
> When can their glory fade?
> O the wild charge they made!
>   All the world wondered.
> Honour the charge they made!
> Honour the Light Brigade,
>   Noble six hundred.[37]

The soldiers made a charge, not a reply, and Tennyson's poem, as if to make some form of reparation, does the opposite. The soldiers followed orders and asked no questions; the poem gives orders and poses questions ('Was there a man dismayed?' does not quite manage to be rhetorical). Part of its strength comes from the way in which Tennyson does not make the soldiers' suffering feel like a mere inevitability ('Some one had blundered'), even though it acknowledges that the men had no choice ('Theirs but to do and die'). The poem is at once drawn to honour the sacrifice they made and angered by the necessity of having to honour this event at all, hence the reference to the 'wild' charge, which is similar to Russell's 'excess of courage' (somewhere between a rebuke and a compliment), before the adjective is dropped a couple of lines later for the sake of good form. *Contra* Wilfred Owen, this war poetry does not reside 'in the pity', for Tennyson is aware that to invite only pity may be to invite complacency. Rather, when we are told to 'honour' the Light Brigade, the imperative signals not only the need for remembrance, but also for an answering action (to 'honour' as one would honour a debt).

---

[35] Trudi Tate, 'On Not Knowing Why: Memorializing the Light Brigade', in Helen Small and Trudi Tate (eds.), *Literature, Science, Psychoanalysis, 1830–1970: Essays in Honour of Gillian Beer* (Oxford: Oxford University Press, 2003), 166.

[36] Tennyson to unknown recipient [probably Sydney Dobell], 23 Jan. 1855, in *The Letters of Alfred Lord Tennyson*, ii, ed. Cecil Y. Lang and Edgar F. Shannon (Oxford: Clarendon Press, 1987), 104.

[37] Tennyson, 'The Charge of the Light Brigade', in *Poems of Tennyson*, ii, ed. Christopher Ricks, 2nd edn. (London: Longman, 1987), 511–13.

The poem is one such action, and honours the men by refusing to stay silent about blunders. The piece was built on an adaptation of *The Times* report, which had referred to 'some hideous blunder'; Tennyson reshaped it to 'Some one had blundered' and explained that 'the line kept running in my head, and I kept saying it over and over till it shaped itself into the burden of the poem'.[38] This 'burden'—meaning both 'that which is borne' and 'the refrain or chorus of a song' (*OED*)—weighs heavy on the poem, for so insistent was this sound, and this military error, that the Laureate rhymed it with words that deviated from the Queen's English (according to Tennyson's friend, W. F. Rawnsley, 'hundred' is pronounced 'hunderd' in Lincolnshire).[39] What we hear in these sounds, and in sounds that drum through the poem ('thund*ered*', 'soldi*er*', 'sab*res*', 'gunn*ers*', 'shatt*ered*', 'sund*ered*'), is a ghost of the words 'err' and 'erred'. These whispers are the poem's burden, words uttered under its breath, and echoed again in the line 'All the world wondered', where 'wondered' condenses the poem's mix of awestruck admiration and perplexed incredulity. It also carries within it the sound of the poem's pride for the men alongside its awareness of the pointlessness of their death ('won', 'erred'). An exemplary Victorian war poem, 'The Charge of the Light Brigade' sounds war's heroism, but it also sounds it out. In doing so, the poem demands an admiring spectatorship even as it remains wary of turning war into a spectator sport.

The progress of the Crimean War was marked by much poetry that sang of arms and the man in a less equivocal fashion—Gerald Massey's *War Waits* (1855) and James Friswell's anthology *Songs of the War*, both of which emphasized 'that fund of patriotism which is the safeguard of any kingdom, however mismanaged or misgoverned'.[40] Yet many poets who supported the war were intent on highlighting the messiness of the business: Martin Tupper's 'The Van and the Rear' begins 'Brilliant troops in proud array, | Thrilling trumpets, rattling drums', before the rear quickly makes itself heard in the next stanza: 'Mangled wretches, horrors dire, | Groans and curses, wounds and woes.'[41] Moreover, writers who opposed the war were raising their voices in collections like Ernest Jones's *The Battle-Day and Other Poems* (1855), Alexander Smith and Sydney Dobell's *Sonnets on the War* (1855), and Dobell's *England in Time of War* (1856). Even *The Times*, so often critical of the war, grew impatient with these poetic developments: 'Aeschylus fought at Marathon, Milton was the secretary of Cromwell, Goethe a minister of state. Instead of this, what have we now? Poets hiding themselves in holes and corners.'[42] This comment is from a review of one of the most important war

---

[38] Tennyson, quoted in Matthew Bevis (ed.), *Lives of Victorian Literary Figures: Tennyson* (London: Pickering & Chatto, 2003), 84.

[39] W. F. Rawnsley, quoted in Bevis (ed.), *Lives*, 83.

[40] James Friswell (ed.), *Songs of the War* (London: Ward & Lock, 1855), p. ii.

[41] Martin Tupper, 'The Van and the Rear', in *A Batch of War Ballads* (London: Bosworth, 1854), 6.

[42] *The Times*, 25 Aug. 1855, 8. *Punch* echoed such criticisms; see 'The War Poets', *Punch*, 28 (13 Jan. 1854), 17.

collections of the period, Tennyson's first volume of poetry since taking up the mantle of Poet Laureate, *Maud and Other Poems* (1855).

The *OED*'s earliest example of the term 'war poem' is a reference to *Maud*. The example comes from a letter by John Addington Symonds in which he recalled a lecture he attended: '[The speaker] chiefly talked about the two Lushingtons & Maud which he considers a true war poem & praises highly.'[43] 'True' hints at a debate over values, and the volumes of Henry and Franklin Lushington (friends of Tennyson) offer one side of the argument. In their work, the war poem is an incitement to decisive action: 'For a moment, dearly as we love him, let Hamlet stand aside: he has but too much to say in Germany: we want Fortinbras just now.'[44] Such positions echoed the views of Carlyle, who in his lecture on 'The Hero as Poet' (1841) had explained that 'the Poet who could merely sit on a chair, and compose stanzas, would never make a stanza worth much. He could not sing the Heroic warrior, unless he himself were at least a Heroic warrior too.'[45] Tennyson was frequently drawn to this classical model of the poet-warrior, and to a conception of poetry as a form of martial action; as he observed in his Epilogue to *The Charge of the Heavy Brigade at Balaclava*, 'The song that nerves a nation's heart | Is in itself a deed.'[46] Likewise, the speaker of his monodrama takes up Fortinbras's tone when he feels able; *Maud* opens with the protagonist calling for 'loud war by land and sea' (I. i. 47),[47] echoes language and arguments from poems by the Lushingtons and other pro-war collections (war as antidote to domestic commercial greed, as heroic endeavour, as Christian crusade), and ends when he signs up for the army.

Yet Tennyson was not content to 'let Hamlet stand aside'. He saw *Maud* as 'akin to *Hamlet*',[48] and although the poem's speaker talks a good fight, he also expresses a need to escape the fighting talk: 'let a passionless peace be my lot, | Far-off from the clamour of liars belied in the hubbub of lies' (I. iv. 151–2). The poem does not merely reiterate the views of the Lushingtons and the pro-war contingent; it frames them in a dramatic form that asks readers to consider the paucity of the 'clamour' alongside the probity of the speaker's own chatter. Indeed, the speaker's longing for a critical distance often leads him towards a pointed critical engagement. When, gazing down on a nearby village, he mutters to himself that 'Jack on his ale-house bench has as many lies as a Czar' (I. iv. 110), he draws a comparison between a

[43] John Addington Symonds to Charlotte Symonds, ? May 1857, in *The Letters of John Addington Symonds*, i, ed. Herbert M. Schueller and Robert L. Peters (Detroit: Wayne State University Press, 1967), 105.

[44] Henry and Franklin Lushington, 'Preface', in *La Nation Boutiquière & Other Poems Chiefly Political and Points of War* (Cambridge: Macmillan, 1855), p. xxv.

[45] Thomas Carlyle, *Heroes, Hero-Worship and the Heroic in Literature* (London: Dent, 1908), 312.

[46] Tennyson, 'Epilogue', in *Charge of the Heavy Brigade at Balaclava*, in *The Poems of Tennyson*, iii, ed. Christopher Ricks, 2nd edn. (London: Longman, 1987), 97.

[47] Tennyson, *Maud*, in *Poems of Tennyson*, ii. 513–84.

[48] Tennyson, in conversation with James Knowles, quoted in Gordon N. Ray, *Tennyson Reads Maud* (Vancouver: University of British Columbia, 1968), 23.

member of the British public and a Russian leader with whom that public was at war. Nicholas I was widely condemned in the British press as a liar because of his claim to be fighting a holy war, not a war of aggression. But the same might be said of the speaker's homeland: the pretext for the war was that Britain was protecting the rights of the Greek Christians in Turkey against Russian invasion; the subtext was that Turkey was a key strategic location for Britain's imperial commercial holdings in the East.[49] As speaker in *Blackwood's* remarked: 'Above all, let us eschew cant in giving our reasons for the war. We go to war because Russia is becoming too powerful.'[50] War insists upon differentiation, but *Maud* is also listening out for discomforting alliances.

Tennyson's little Hamlet is a 'true' Victorian war poem because it acknowledges and explores the warring claims that make the speaker's own pronouncements part of the viewpoint he criticizes. When he comes across Maud singing 'a passionate ballad . . . a martial song' (I. v. 165–6), he hears her

> Singing of men that in battle array,
> Ready in heart and ready in hand
> March with banner and bugle and fife
> To the death, for their native land.
>
> (I. v. 169–72)

Their land, not our land. The accents of Fortinbras are overheard by an alienated listener, who then begs 'silence, beautiful voice', for 'you only trouble the mind | With a joy in which I cannot rejoice, | A glory I shall not find' (I. v. 180–3). This moment encapsulates the predicament and the achievement of the most enduring Victorian war poetry—a speaker drawn to, yet distrustful of, martial fervour, who aspires to be included in the battle march, yet senses the limits of its rhythms (hence the rich tonal ambiguity of 'I shall not find', which sounds at once envious, lonely, critical, and proud). What he finds instead, and what we find through him in the poem's feverish repetitions and echoes, is a disturbing confluence of the language that explores his romantic engagement with Maud with that which charts his public engagement with the war (the name 'Maud' itself means 'war' or 'battle'). Erotic and martial vocabularies frequently overlap, as in the polysemic nature of 'dying', so that we begin to see the speaker's love for Maud as a kind of death-wish, and his final willingness to 'die' for his country not only as an ennobling sacrifice for a cause, but also as a desperate attempt to conduct a courtship by other means. The first glimmer of the speaker's love-in-madness comes in the poem's second line when he tells us of the lips of the hollow 'dabbled with blood-red heath' (I. i. 2); at the end of the poem, when he talks of the 'blood-red blossom of war' (III. vi. 53), we sense that he is still seeing red. *Maud*'s final lines contain a strangely enervated

---

[49] See Trevor Royle, *Crimea: The Great Crimean War 1854–1856* (London: Little, Brown and Company, 1999).

[50] G. C. Swayne, 'Peace and War: A Dialogue', *Blackwood's Edinburgh Magazine*, 76 (1854), 592.

music even though the speaker agrees to march to the death. 'Their native land' becomes 'my native land':

> We have proved we have hearts in a cause, we are noble still,
> And myself have awaked, as it seems, to the better mind;
> It is better to fight for the good than to rail at the ill;
> I have felt with my native land, I am one with my kind,
> I embrace the purpose of God, and the doom assigned.

(III. v. 55–9)

'We have hearts in a cause' might sound both full- and half-hearted ('a cause' is finally something he can stand for, yet 'a' cause, not 'the' cause, suggests that any cause will do). During the 1850s and 1860s attention was turning towards enlistment, and, as one official report noted, 'few enlist from any real inclination for military life.... Enlistment is, for the most part, occasioned by want of work—by pecuniary embarrassment—by family quarrels—or by any other difficulties of a private nature.'[51] The private difficulties and embarrassments of *Maud*'s speaker are occasion for the poem's ending. What we are observing is the progress from private grief to civic responsibility, and—more disturbingly—a link between a patriotic fervour and a pathological fever, and the rhymes in the stanza provide insight into the mental status of a speaker in favour of war at all costs: 'still/ill'. Contemporary reviewers disagreed about what position Tennyson was taking in *Maud*, some arguing that the Laureate was for the Peace Party since he allowed a madman to speak in defence of war, others insisting that the war passages were evidence of his support of England's involvement in the Crimea.[52] But Tennyson's dramatic form is investigating positions, not taking them. His poem is an echo of a war-cry, an echo of questionable fidelity that provokes rather than distils thought.

　　Maud's ghost, and the ghost of the Crimean conflict, haunted collections of Victorian poetry after the war. In *The Defence of Guenevere, and Other Poems* (1858), William Morris set himself to challenge traditional conceptions of chivalry by mingling a focus on warlike emblems with an attentiveness to another kind of detail. 'Concerning Geffray Teste Noir', for example, begins with a speaker recalling 'The dancing trumpet sound, and we went forth; | And my red lion on the spear-head flapped', but its progression marks a shift from collective battle charges to isolated waverings, as the earlier excitement of those repeated 'and's turns sour:

> And I, being faint with smelling the burnt bones,
> And very hot with fighting down the street,

[51] *Report of the Commissioners Appointed to Inquire into the Present System of Recruiting in the Army* (London, 1861), p. xvii.
[52] See Edgar Shannon, 'The Critical Reception of Tennyson's *Maud*', PMLA, 68 (1953), 397–417.

> And sick of such a life, fell down, with groans
> My head went weakly nodding to my feet.[53]

The journey from the spear-head to the weakly nodding head is one which has taken account of the publicized horrors of the Crimean War. Similarly, in Morris's 'The Wind', his old knight's romantic reminiscences are interrupted when 'in march'd the ghosts of those that had gone to the war':

> I knew them by the arms that I was used to paint
> Upon their long thin shields; but the colours were all grown faint,
> And faint upon their banner was Olaf, king and saint.[54]

To recognize the soldiers by the emblems on their shields might imply that their physical injuries render them unrecognizable, as the men carry the scars of battle with them into the world beyond. These dead do not rest easy with their sacrifice, and their march heralds not a glorious remembrance, but a kind of beleaguered trooping of the colours. George Meredith's 'Grandfather Bridgeman', which he deemed important enough to stand at the head of his collection *Modern Love* (1862), contains a similar sense of fading splendour. A grandfather reads a letter from his soldier-grandson in the Crimea, lauding his victories and turning to the assembled family to note, 'You'll own war isn't such humbug: and Glory means something, you see'.[55] What they eventually see, though, is another ghost; the letter turns out to be several weeks old, and Tom has been severely wounded during the interim. At the end of the poem he makes his entrance: 'Wheeled, pale, in a chair, and shattered, the wreck of their hero was seen; | The ghost of Tom drawn slow o'er the orchard's shadowy green.' This shattering, at once physical and emotional, frequently makes itself felt in post-Crimean War poetry, as touchable ghosts hover in the margins of the verse to remind readers of how war might re-figure and disfigure the body.

Beyond the Crimean War lay the Indian Mutiny, an event that further tested Victorian confidence in its imperial project and the violence that accompanied it. As Gautam Chakravarty has noted, the poetry of the Mutiny (unlike novelistic or historical explorations) tended to excise the sequence of causes that led to the popular insurgency and to focus instead on the sufferings of the British.[56] This focus again took its bearings from the press. The Cawnpore massacre was covered by *The Times* in leaders which dwelt on war-torn bodies with unprecedented directness:

The women having been stripped naked, beheaded and thrown into a well; the children having been hurled down alive upon the butchered mothers, whose blood yet reeked on

---

[53] William Morris, 'Concerning Geffray Teste Noir', in *The Collected Works of William Morris*, ed. May Morris, i (London: Longmans, Green, 1910), 76 and 78.

[54] Morris, 'The Wind', ibid. 110.

[55] George Meredith, 'Grandfather Bridgeman', in *The Poetical Works of George Meredith* (London: Constable, 1912), 125.

[56] Gautam Chakravarty, *The Indian Mutiny and the British Imagination* (Cambridge: Cambridge University Press, 2005), 107.

their mangled bodies. . . . Children have been compelled to eat the quivering flesh of their murdered parents, after which they were literally *torn asunder* by the laughing fiends who surrounded them.[57]

Victorian war poets have been accused of being irresponsibly squeamish about the effects of conflict, yet many poets who responded to the Indian Mutiny could be charged with not being squeamish enough, for their use of the press reports led to poems in which salacious detail served only as an excuse for hysterical cries of retribution. Mary E. Leslie borrowed *The Times*'s gratuitous 'quivering' when drawing attention to 'a common grave | Heaped high with quivering, crushed humanity',[58] while Martin Tupper's poems dwelt on atrocity in order to countenance an equally violent revenge: 'Who pulls about the mercy?—the agonized wail of babies hewn piecemeal yet sickens the air.'[59] Even before the Cawnpore incident, John Nicholson had suggested 'a Bill for the flaying alive, impalement, or burning of the murderers of the women and children at Delhi'. After the atrocities, the tone became even more vindictive, and, as one historian has pointed out, 'the Cawnpore massacre gave sanction to a retributive savagery which is one of the most shameful episodes in British history'.[60] The sanction was upheld by poems like Leslie's and Tupper's, although there were other voices that resisted this kind of grimly gleeful baiting. Christina Rossetti's 'In the Round Tower at Jhansi, June 8, 1857', as its title implies, tries to get close to the action and dates itself journalistically; yet, after an initial reference to how 'The swarming howling wretches below | Gained and gained and gained',[61] the focus turns to the last moments of the Skene family inside the tower as they decide to take their own lives rather than die at the hands of the mutineers. The emphasis is on the creation of a desperate dignity, rather than the incitement of a bloodthirsty revenge. Indeed, Rossetti kept the poem in the volume even after she found out that Captain Skene and his wife were actually captured and killed by the sword.[62] The violence of the Mutiny is also handled with sensitivity in Tennyson's first volume of *Idylls of the King* (1859), a collection which sold more than any previous volume of his work, and which dwelt on how imperial aggression might be seen as both the model and the catalyst for the violence it deplored in its colonies.[63]

---

[57] *The Times*, 17 Sep. 1857, 9.

[58] Mary E. Leslie, 'Massacre at Cawnpore, 1857', in *Sorrows, Aspirations, and Legends from India* (London, 1858); repr. in Donald Thomas (ed.), *The Everyman Book of Victorian Verse: The Pre-Raphaelites to the Nineties* (London: Dent, 1993), 161.

[59] Tupper, quoted in Sashi Bhusan Chaudhuri, *English Historical Writing on the Indian Mutiny 1857–1859* (Calcutta: World Press, 1979), 259.

[60] Ronald Hyam, *Britain's Imperial Century 1815–1914: A Study of Empire and Expansion* (London: Batsford, 1976), 224.

[61] Christina Rossetti, 'In the Round Tower at Jhansi, June 8, 1857', in *The Complete Poems of Christina Rossetti*, i, ed. R. W. Crump (Baton Rouge, La.: Louisiana State University Press, 1979), 26.

[62] See *The Times* report on 11 Sept. 1857, 7. Rossetti added a note to the poem in 1875 to acknowledge the factual inaccuracy.

[63] See Matthew Bevis, 'Tennyson's Civil Tongue', *Tennyson Research Bulletin*, 7/3 (Nov. 1999), 113–25.

Tennyson has frequently been cited as the formative influence on a late Victorian hymning of empire, but the continuation of his *Idylls of the King* leads to poems that stage within themselves imperial anxieties as Arthur's rule is subjected to searching questions. Herbert Tucker has recently observed that 'saddest of all Victorian epics, the *Idylls* in their gloomy analytic coherence shadow with equal plangency the losses that empire exacts and the downfall that awaits it'.[64] This plangency can be sensed in 'The Last Tournament' (1871), in which Arthur's imperial project meets with an imperious disobedience; the King insists that his knights do not seek revenge for a mutinous uprising, but they disobey his orders. Looking to the East, the horrors of the Indian Mutiny are recalled; only now it is the imperial state's violence that is given prominence:

>   [they] roared
> And shouted and leapt down upon the fallen;
> There trampled out his face from being known,
> And sank his head in mire, and slimed themselves:
> Nor heard the King for their own cries, but sprang
> Through open doors, and swording right and left
> Men, women, on their sodden faces, hurled
> The tables over and the wines, and slew
> Till all the rafters rang with woman-yells,
> And all the pavement streamed with massacre:
> Then, echoing yell with yell, they fired the tower,
> Which half that autumn night, like the live North,
> Red-pulsing up through Alioth and Alcor,
> Made all above it, and a hundred meres
> About it, as the water Moab saw
> Come round by the East, and out beyond them flushed
> The long low dune, and lazy-plunging sea.
>
> So all the ways were safe from shore to shore,
> But in the heart of Arthur pain was lord.[65]

The sprawling first sentence insists on showing us what Victoria's little wars might involve. The breathless pace of the violence, accentuated by verbs at the end of run-on lines ('sprang', 'hurled', 'slew', 'saw', 'flushed'), is matched by its savagery. Like the other verbs, we initially expect 'slew' to be transitive, but the grammatical shock as we veer into the next line gives gruesome voice to the indiscriminate nature of the killing. What we are asked to dwell on, though, is the monosyllabic drag of the last two lines, isolated on the page, for it is here where imperial supremacy counts the cost of the safety it creates. The callous efficiency of 'So' is almost parodic ('so they all lived happily ever after'), before the 'But' records a heartbeat that has become distempered by the order it has established.

---

[64] Herbert Tucker, 'Epic', in *A Companion to Victorian Poetry*, 32.
[65] Tennyson, 'The Last Tournament', in *Poems of Tennyson*, iii. 521–2.

Timothy Lovelace has recently attended to Tennyson's meditations on the double-edged nature of battle wrath (both its honourable and its destructive potential), and noted that 'the glories of battle often appear on the perimeters of Tennyson's pictures, his center of focus is usually rusting swords, vales of bones, or failing kingdoms'.[66] This focus was to become an increasingly central aspect of late Victorian poetry, as the glories of battle gave way to a more sustained look at the complex figure of the soldier. Often labelled as a career for malcontents or misfits, soldiering had a long history of stigma. Pay and conditions were very poor, and the iniquity of the purchase system was one of many reflections of class prejudice operating at all levels of the military life.[67] Wellington referred to his men at Waterloo as 'the scum of the earth', and the rank-and-file were frequently associated with alcoholism and sexual licentiousness (brothels provided cheap spirits; by 1862, a third of home-based troops were hospitalized on account of venereal disease[68]). At mid-century, Robert MacDonald recalled his experience as a recruiter: 'it was only in the haunts of dissipation or inebriation, and among the lowest dregs of society, that I met with anything like success'.[69]

After the Crimean War and the Indian Mutiny, the dregs were invested with a new dignity. An enthusiastic reporter for *The Times* noted: 'Any hostility which may have existed in bygone days towards the army has long since passed away. The red coat of the soldier is honoured throughout the country.'[70] This is overpitched, but it highlights a shift. Samuel Smiles honoured the redcoat in his own way by ending *Self-Help* (1859) with examples of the soldier as 'the true gentleman', referring to the rank-and-file as 'rough, gallant fellows' and pointing out that in the war and the Mutiny 'even the common soldiers proved themselves gentlemen under their trials'.[71] Smiles's vocabulary hovers between old and new conceptions of the soldier, but his sense of the figure's 'trials' was shared by many, and growing calls for army reform and improvement of the soldier's lot culminated in the abolition of the purchase system in 1871. These revaluations found their way into poetry; Francis Hastings Doyle, who in 1867 succeeded Arnold as Professor of Poetry at Oxford, wrote a number of poems on the nameless men who fought in Victoria's name, and his 'The Private of the Buffs', like many other pieces, focused on the soldier as an individual, rather than as part of a collective—'poor, reckless, rude, low-born,

---

[66] Timothy Lovelace, *The Artistry and Tradition of Tennyson's Battle Poetry* (New York and London: Routledge, 2003), 165.

[67] See Peter Burroughs, 'An Unreformed Army? 1815–1868', in David Chandler and Ian Beckett (eds.), *The Oxford Illustrated History of the British Army* (Oxford: Oxford University Press, 1994), 160–88, and John R. Reed, 'Military', in Herbert Tucker (ed.), *A Companion to Victorian Literature and Culture* (Oxford: Blackwell, 1999), 183–93.

[68] See Edward M. Spiers, *The Army and Society 1815–1914* (London: Longman, 1980), 77 and 162.

[69] Robert MacDonald, *Personal Narrative of Military Travel and Adventure in Turkey and Persia* (Edinburgh: Black, 1859), 296.

[70] *The Times*, 22 Oct. 1856, 6.

[71] Samuel Smiles, *Self-Help*, ed. Peter Sinnema (Oxford: Oxford University Press, 2002), 331.

untaught, | Bewildered, and alone'.[72] Like Smiles's 'rough gallant', this 'low-born' but 'untaught' hero came to stand as a kind of synecdoche for war itself: savage yet chivalric, uncivilized yet the defender of civilization.

These developments intersected with the proselytizing tenor of British imperial rhetoric as Christian militarism captured the public imagination and helped to produce a new kind of soldier-hero.[73] Embracing the purpose of God and the doom assigned became a recurring feature of the poetry of soldiering. Military adventure was fused with religious narratives, and prominent figures like Havelock and Gordon came to embody a cluster of virtues with roots in nineteenth-century evangelical imperialism.[74] This diverse range of vocabularies (soldier as degenerate malcontent, as stoic victim, as Christian hero) permeates Gerard Manley Hopkins's sonnet 'The Soldier' (1885). It begins by asking, 'Yes. Why do we all, seeing of a soldier, bless him? Bless | Our redcoats, our tars? Both these being, the greater part, | But frail clay, nay but foul clay.'[75] The move from 'frail' to 'foul' is a gesture to earlier conceptions of the soldier, but the answering voice is swift:

> Mark Christ our King. He knows war, served this soldiering through;
> He of all can reave a rope best. There he bides in bliss
> Now, and seeing somewhere some man do all that man can do,
> For love he leans forth, needs his neck must fall on, kiss,
> And cry 'O Christ-done deed! So God-made-flesh does too:
> Were I come o'er again' cries Christ 'it should be this.'

To envisage life as a form of 'war' and 'soldiering', and the job as a representation of 'all that man can do', is to see the soldier as both Everyman and Christ-like martyr. The act of soldiering on is accorded a transcendental dignity, for the soldier's death (hinted at in talk of a 'rope' and 'his neck') now intimates resurrection. The journey of 'foul clay' in this sonnet is the rite of passage of the soldier in Victoria's reign: from dens of prostitution to stages of pilgrimage, from inebriation to incarnation.

II

The century's closing decades witnessed a different kind of soldierly apotheosis, one of the most enduring bequests from Victorian poets to twentieth-century writers.

---

[72] Francis Hastings Doyle, 'The Private of the Buffs', in Edmund Clarence Stedman (ed.), *A Victorian Anthology, 1837–1895* (Boston: Houghton Mifflin, 1895).

[73] See Olive Anderson, 'The Growth of Christian Militarism in Mid-Victorian Britain', *English Historical Review*, 86 (Jan. 1971), 46–72.

[74] See Graham Dawson, *Soldier Heroes: British Adventure, Empire and the Imagining of Masculinities* (London: Routledge, 1994), 79–155.

[75] Gerard Manley Hopkins, in 'The Soldier', in *Poems and Prose*, ed. W. H. Gardner (Harmondsworth: Penguin, 1953), 60.

When Rudyard Kipling's soldier in 'The Instructor' notes that *'There's one above is greater than us all'*,[76] he is referring not to God, but to the bullet that flies just above his crouching body. This war poetry breathes a different air; the soldier is no longer, technically speaking, a redcoat (Hopkins's poem was written in the last year that red coats were worn in battle),[77] but wears khaki for protective colouration. The soldier comes of age in Victorian poetry and culture as the methods of warfare themselves reach a terrifying maturity, and the figure now enjoys a new kind of privilege as he completes the metamorphosis from scapegoat to underdog. This focus on the soldier was due again, in part, to the progress of the newspapers and to the public's hunger for news of war in particular (between 1880 and 1900 the number of newspapers doubled, and during the Franco-Prussian War alone the circulation of the *Daily News* trebled). As one correspondent recalled, the demand for war reports was also a demand for news of the 'sweating, swearing, grimy, dirty, fearless and generous Tommy'.[78]

Tommy Atkins was heard as well as seen. The Victorian music-halls were, as J. A. Hobson argued in *The Psychology of Jingoism*, 'a very serviceable engine for generating military passion';[79] but they were also a space in which imperial jingoism and the official line on war might be questioned. The term 'jingoism' was the outgrowth of a popular music-hall song by G. W. Hunt (sung by G. H. Macdermott) from 1878, the chorus of which ran:

> We don't want to fight, but by Jingo if we do,
> We've got the ships, we've got the men, and got the money too.
> We've fought the bear before, and while we're Britons true,
> The Russians shall not have Constantinople.[80]

Voices like this were common, but recent work on the music-hall has pointed to other tones that need to be heard alongside them in order to appreciate the complexity of late Victorian imaginings of war. Macdermott's rival, Herbert Campbell, often performed another song on the same bill, this one written by Henry Pettit, with the chorus:

> I don't want to fight, I'll be slaughtered if I do!
> I'll change my togs and sell my kit and pop my rifle too!
> I don't like the war, I ain't no Briton true
> And I'd let the Russians have Constantinople.[81]

---

[76] Rudyard Kipling, 'The Instructor', in *The Definitive Edition of Rudyard Kipling's Verse* (London: Hodder & Stoughton, 1989; 1st pub. 1940), 472.

[77] See Philip Warner, *Dervish: The Rise and Fall of an African Empire* (London: Macdonald, 1973), 134.

[78] Melton Prior, *Campaigns of a War Correspondent* (London: Arnold, 1912), 287.

[79] J. A. Hobson, *The Psychology of Jingoism* (London: Grant Richards, 1901), 2.

[80] G. W. Hunt, 'Macdermott's War Song', repr. in *The Music Hall Songster* (London: Fortney, 1893), n. p.

[81] Henry Pettit, quoted in Peter Davison, 'A Briton True: A Short Account of Patriotic Songs and Verse and Popular Entertainment', *Alta* (Spring 1970), 216.

This emphasis on the 'I' lurking inside the 'We', and on a man who insists on being representative only of feelings of isolation, can be heard in different ways. Steve Attridge suggests that this speaker gave audiences a chance to laugh at the unwilling recruit, thereby offering 'tangential support for the strident imperial tone of Macdermott's act';[82] but he might also be heard as a spokesman for the disaffected, a man who has the courage to say what others are thinking, and who questions a military ethos even as he feels compelled to submit to it.[83] Late Victorian war songs often manage to combine a sense of the 'we' and the 'I'; they have something of the swagger of military marches, but the burdens of their refrains start to feel like solitary whistlings in the dark as the century nears its close. The soldier's pluck was no longer to be condescended to as a reason to avoid his disconsolate pleadings. J. B. Booth acknowledged the significance of these voices when he observed: 'Tommy moaned all through his sing-songs.'[84]

The most accomplished translation of Tommy's moaning into metre was effected by Kipling, and for more than thirty years after its publication his *Barrack-Room Ballads, and Other Verses* (1892) was the most popular book of verse in the English-speaking world. Not against war, but against complacency about what war entails, his dramatic monologues took their lead from the music-hall to breathe new life into Atkins. Situating himself between wholly dignified and derogatory vocabularies, his 'Tommy' insisted: 'We aren't no thin red 'eroes, nor we aren't no blackguards too | But single men in barricks, most remarkable like you.'[85] One contemporary anthologist summed up the remarkable Tommy as 'humanly full of discontent and grievance, with no more love than stay-at-home folk for blistering marches and an empty belly, fonder of life than most, he is a great and honourable fighter, gay in the face of a soldier's death, and a broad humorist in time of peril', before noting that 'Kipling handles honour and glory with no hint of awe'.[86] Kipling was responsibly wary of awe, of the way it can act as a refusal to dwell on what honour and glory can cost its recipient, but he was also cognizant of how the 'broad humorist' might offer a certain kind of disingenuous consolation, whereby the soldier becomes a mere clown, somebody whose joking might deflect attention from his suffering or lead some to reflect that he exists solely for their entertainment. Accordingly, his Tommies have a rueful wit, a trench humour that is burdened by an awareness of what war can inflict even as it refuses to bow under the strain of that burden.

[82] Steve Attridge, *Nationalism, Imperialism and Identity in Late Victorian Culture* (Basingstoke: Palgrave, 2003), 30.

[83] The working-class inflection of this voice is also important, as Attridge explains: 'A growing recognition of Tommy Atkins's background grew contemporaneously with an awareness of the effects of material deprivation among the working class. . . . The soldier figure is both accommodated and distanced, supported and derided, an expression of unity and of class antagonism' (ibid. 69 and 43).

[84] J. B. Booth, *A Pink 'Un Remembers* (London: Laurie, 1937), 123.

[85] Kipling, 'Tommy', in *Rudyard Kipling's Verse*, 399.

[86] John Macleay, in *idem* (ed.), *War Songs and Ballads of Martial Life* (London: Scott, 1900), pp. xxvi–xxvii.

This tone is frequently heard in the soldiers' chorus, where the traditional sense of the form as a collective utterance is permeated by a dissentient isolation, an elegiac moan that runs through the sing-song. In 'That Day' (1895), for instance, the chorus becomes a form of torment:

> Now there ain't no chorus 'ere to give,
>   Nor there ain't no band to play;
> An' I wish I was dead 'fore I done what I did,
>   Or seen what I seed that day![87]

Daniel Karlin has astutely observed that 'solidarity with one's kind is the most precious gift in Kipling's world. . . . But Kipling's emblem is the Cat that Walked by Himself.'[88] Kipling's soldier is awkwardly positioned between solitude and solidarity. Very much his own man, yet also fearful of betraying or dishonouring his comrades, he frequently speaks with regret about what collective endeavour might encourage in war, even as he acknowledges the longing for community that war creates. These divided impulses are heard here, in a chorus that laments the lack of a chorus, and in lines that express both a loneliness and a need to be alone.

Kipling's poems often bring into prominence a particular strength of Victorian war poetry: a desire to dispel illusions, alongside an attempt to keep disillusion at bay. One means of effecting such a balance is through the double-jointed nature of the dramatic monologue, which allows us to sense another kind of eloquence and viewpoint operating behind the speaker. 'The Young British Soldier' is a characteristic example of Kipling's dexterity; spoken by an old soldier to a new recruit going out to India, the poem ends:

> When you're wounded and left on Afghanistan's plains,
> And the women come out to cut up what remains,
> Jest roll to your rifle and blow out your brains
>   An' go to your Gawd like a soldier.
>   Go, go, go like a soldier,
>   Go, go, go like a soldier,
>   Go, go, go like a soldier,
>   So-oldier *of* the Queen![89]

On the one hand, Kipling's ingenuity with accent helps to accentuate the old man's uncompromising perspective. 'Jest roll' turns 'just' into 'jest', as if to suggest that in this arena justice has become a joke, while 'your Gawd' whittles down heavenly comfort by pairing a local pronunciation with a disturbingly localized pronoun—'*your* Gawd' seems oddly uncollaborative (even question begging) at such a crucial juncture. On the other hand, the poet's craft hints at the limits of

---

[87] Kipling, 'That Day', in *Rudyard Kipling's Verse*, 437.
[88] Daniel Karlin, in *Rudyard Kipling: A Critical Edition of the Major Works*, ed. Daniel Karlin (Oxford: Oxford University Press, 1999), p. xxi.
[89] Kipling, 'The Young British Soldier', in *Rudyard Kipling's Verse*, 418.

this perspective: '*so-old*ier' drags it out of him, for 'so old' is this soldier that his scepticism about war has degenerated into a luxurious cynicism, as instanced by the first word of the stanza: 'When' should read 'If' (after all, this speaker has survived). The silent young auditor of this dramatic monologue might be forgiven for feeling that the experienced old-timer is parading his worldliness, showing off while showing him the ropes.

The imperative to 'go like a soldier' also manages to hover between a sardonic and an ennobling tone. The speaker can be heard as a disillusioned commentator here, drawing attention to how a soldier's dying for his country is often an expedient, messy suicide. In contrast to a classical emphasis on the importance of a proper burial, we are left lingering on 'remains', a gruesome decaying from verb to noun. Yet, Kipling's form contains within it another sound: the thrice-repeated 'Go, go, go like a soldier' (itself containing a set of three) might also be heard as a dignified burial ritual of sorts, the repetitions aligning themselves with the three volleys traditionally fired over a soldier's grave by his comrades. And that final metrical swooping on '*of*' is a commitment to the pride of belonging. Like so many of Kipling's war poems, the speaker's very insistence on keeping a stiff upper lip is what lends the piece its air of vulnerability. Such richly compounded accents bespeak a poetic fighting talk that, although it may include patriotic and militaristic zeal, also moves beyond it.

Kipling was an important influence on war poetry of the 1890s, although many poets tended to take their cue from his general defences of the Empire, rather than from the more provocative insinuations of his soldier-speakers.[90] The 1890s saw the publication of more anthologies of popular war poetry than any previous decade, and much of the writing in these collections does not ring true to the complex achievements of the age.[91] Henry Newbolt's 'Vitaï Lampada' was much anthologized, and its refrain, 'Play up! play up! and play the game!'[92] is representative of the kind of imperial tub thumping that spoke of war as a public school cricket match in the colonies: 'There's a breathless hush in the Close tonight— | Ten to make and the match to win—.' Yet despite this 'breathless hush' and the aspiration towards indefatigable grandeur in the refrain, there is something disconcertingly shrill in the tone of this poem and others like it, as if the poet doth protest too much about the nobility and gentlemanliness of war. At the beginning of the new century the *Edinburgh Review* looked back over the Victorian period and suggested that recent attempts to glorify war were actually reactionary responses

[90] For a representative selection, see Elleke Boehmer (ed.), *Empire Writing: An Anthology of Colonial Literature 1870–1918* (Oxford: Oxford University Press, 1998).

[91] See e.g. William Ernest Henley (ed.), *Lyra Heroica: A Book of Verse for Boys* (London: David Nutt, 1892), which focuses exclusively on 'the beauty and blessedness of death, the glory of battle and adventure, the nobility of devotion' (p. vii).

[92] Henry Newbolt, 'Vitaï Lampada', in *Admirals All and Other Verses* (London: Mathews, 1897); repr. in Boehmer (ed.), *Empire Writing*, 287.

to a much more widespread phenomenon in poetry and culture: an increasingly modern nervousness about how and whether war could be justified. Questioning a 'forcible-feeble kind' of war poetry, and contrasting the present time with 'a hundred years ago [when] poets were satisfied with the simple motive of their country's triumph', the reviewer explained that there was now a desire to search for the grounds of war:

This is perhaps one of many signs of an increasing contradiction between the fact of war and the conscience of civilized humanity.... The actual vision of battle does not seem to inspire poetry.... The poet who devotes himself to celebrate acts of war, although his art may be redeemed if he can reveal the soul of good in things evil, does nevertheless choose a lower region when he might inhabit a higher.[93]

This higher region is what many Victorian poets had been trying to inhabit for some time, a poetic domain in which an 'actual vision of battle' is complemented by an attentiveness to what occurs in and around the battle's edges, and in which celebration is complicated by meditation. This reviewer was writing when 'the fact of war' was highly prominent; the Boer War (the longest, bloodiest, and most expensive war ever fought by the Victorian army) had just ended, and had given rise to unprecedented modern 'evils'—civilian casualties, guerrilla warfare, and concentration camps.[94]

The 'forcible-feeble' brigade was quick to support the war. Swinburne's sonnet 'The Transvaal' was published in *The Times* a day after war was declared, and ended with the cry: 'Strike, England, and strike home.'[95] William Ernest Henley followed suit; the first poem in his next collection, 'Remonstrance', borrowed Swinburne's line for its own ending.[96] But this line contains within it an unwitting pun as if in remonstration (to 'strike home' may also be to strike *at* home), and other writers were increasingly drawing attention to the way in which a tyrannical militarism abroad was not only at odds with how modern liberal Britain wished to perceive itself, but also an emblem of the true state of the country.[97] W. H. Colby accordingly took Swinburne's line in another direction in his poetic contribution to the debate: 'Where are the dogs agape with jaws afoam? | Where are the wolves? Look, England, look at home.'[98] The emphasis on the material and moral damage inflicted upon those who waged and won wars (as well as upon those who lost them) was pronounced. As Van Wyk Smith notes, 'opponents of war managed to put their case more volubly, more insistently, and to a much larger

---

[93] 'War and Poetry', 40, 50–1, 53–4.
[94] See Denis Judd and Keith Surridge, *The Boer War* (London: John Murray, 2002).
[95] A. C. Swinburne, 'The Transvaal', *The Times*, 11 Oct. 1899, 7; repr. in *Swinburne's Collected Poetical Works*, ii (London: William Heinemann, 1935), 1223.
[96] William Ernest Henley, 'Remonstrance', first published in *For England's Sake: Verses and Songs in Time of War* (London: David Nutt, 1900); repr. in Boehmer (ed.), *Empire Writing*, 283.
[97] See e.g. J. A. Hobson, *Imperialism: A Study* (London: Nisbet, 1902).
[98] W. H. Colby, *The Echo*, 13 Oct. 1899.

audience . . . than in any previous war'.[99] This is undoubtedly true, but two of the most distinguished war poets of the late Victorian period (Thomas Hardy and A. E. Housman) were intent on forging a tone that expressed something other than voluble insistence. When Hardy complained that bellicose war poetry tended to 'throw into the shade works that breathe a more quiet and philosophic spirit',[100] he was not defending anything as simplistic as 'anti-war poetry'. Rather, he was defending the need for another kind of accent in poetry about war. When poems against war themselves take on a warring tone (Colby's lines above are an example of this; his poetic questions are merely rhetorical), they might be said to become part of the problem they anatomize. Hardy and Housman were more circumspect about the seductive pull of fighting talk, and were aware of the ease with which it could generate an oppositional voice that was implicated in the stridency it condemned.

Hardy's war poetry takes another kind of breath; in his poems one feels that marching rhythms might at any time be given their marching orders. In 'Embarcation', the first in his series of 'War Poems' to be included in *Poems of the Past and Present* (1901), we learn that 'deckward tramp the bands'.[101] 'Tramp', not 'march'—even the soldiers seem unable to pick up their feet, and Hardy's metrical feet frequently display a similar recalcitrance. An article in the *Quarterly Review* in 1900 noted that patriotic poetry had been changing its tune. From Tennyson onwards, Victorian poetry 'has, perhaps, here and there a somewhat uncertain sound, as though feeling its way . . . the patriotic fervour of our forefathers, is exchanged for a limping jolt'.[102] This uncertain sound resonates throughout Hardy's work. Rather than absorbing themselves *in* battle, his war poems tend to dwell on scenes of anticipation or aftermath, either gathering a kind of reluctant breath for what is to come or stuttering over a past that refuses to go away. Take the close of 'The Man He Killed' (1902), where a soldier dwells on the whys and wherefores of battle:

> 'I shot him dead because—
>   Because he was my foe,
> Just so: my foe of course he was;
>   That's clear enough; although
>
> 'He thought he'd 'list, perhaps,
>   Off-hand like—just as I—

---

[99] Van Wyk Smith, *Drummer Hodge*, 122.

[100] Thomas Hardy, quoted in Kathryn R. King and William W. Morgan, 'Hardy and The Boer War: The Public Poet in Spite of Himself', *Victorian Poetry*, 17 (1979), 66–84.

[101] Hardy, 'Embarcation', in *The Complete Poems*, ed. James Gibson (London: Macmillan, 1976), 86.

[102] 'English Patriotic Poetry', *Quarterly Review*, 192 (1900), 526 and 536. For another contemporary review which noticed a change in tune, see J. A. R. Marriott, 'The Imperial Note in Victorian Poetry', *Nineteenth Century*, 48 (1900), 236–48.

Was out of work—had sold his traps—
  No other reason why.

'Yes; quaint and curious war is!
  You shoot a fellow down
You'd treat if met where any bar is,
  Or help to half-a-crown.'[103]

Class solidarity across a national divide is part of what makes war, rather than the 'foe', feel like the enemy here. Despite the speaker's awareness of division, the internal and terminal rhymes in the first stanza ('because/because/he was/he was', and 'foe/so/foe/although') give voice to a will that strives to locate its identity within partnerships. The doubled-up grammar echoes this feeling, as the phrase 'Was out of work' looks back to the 'I' of the previous line, and forward to the man who sold 'his' traps, not fully able to distinguish between the two men even as a distinction is being formulated. The final stanza is characteristic of Hardy's eerie end-games: its release from the broken rhythms of the previous stanzas should come as something of a relief, yet the acquired ease of the lines is precisely what is disturbing about them. The speaker could sound chirpy, uttering his conclusion with a shrug of the shoulders rather than with a belaboured sigh. Indeed, 'quaint' and 'curious' seem oddly cosy, as if the speaker is working too hard to suppress other kinds of adjective. It is as though his killing during the war has desensitized him, rendered him unable to weigh up the significance of his actions. This is a portrait not of the soldier as *either* victim *or* victor, but of the victor himself as a victim—seeking a numbness in rhythm and a shelter in euphemism. Hardy's war poems frequently end with this kind of blank stare; war has inflicted itself on the fabric of the poem's attenuated form, rather than being something that the form describes.

A. E. Housman was another who was intent on shaping poems that were not straightforwardly pro- or anti-war, but that could muster the poise to count costs alongside blessings. Even before the Boer War, he was mulling over what it might mean to fight for Queen and country. '1887', the opening poem of *A Shropshire Lad* (1896), plumbs the depths of the phrase 'God save the Queen' in order to consider the need for the soldiers, those other kinds of saviour 'who shared the work with God'.[104] Such wry observations do not quite toe the patriotic line, but nor do they mock it. In Housman's work, the call of battle is neither wholly championed nor belittled; 'XXXV' in *Shropshire Lad* is representative of the poet's divided allegiances, and of those of Victorian war poetry more generally, so I quote it in full:

On the idle hill of summer,
  Sleepy with the flow of streams,

---

[103] Hardy, 'The Man He Killed', in *Complete Poems*, 287.
[104] A. E. Housman, '1887', in *A Shropshire Lad*, in *Collected Poems and Selected Prose*, ed. Christopher Ricks (Harmondsworth: Penguin, 1988), 23.

Far I hear the steady drummer
    Drumming like a noise in dreams.

Far and near and low and louder
    On the roads of earth go by,
Dear to friends and food for powder,
    Soldiers marching, all to die.

East and west on fields forgotten
    Bleach the bones of comrades slain,
Lovely lads and dead and rotten;
    None that go return again.

Far the calling bugles hollo,
    High the screaming fife replies,
Gay the files of scarlet follow:
    Woman bore me, I will rise.[105]

In his study of the literature of war, Andrew Rutherford quotes Arnold Kettle's assertion that 'the refusal to be heroic may be very human, but it is also less than human' before noting that 'literature which explores this paradox deserves more critical attention than it currently receives'. The endorsement of the quiet life in the pastoral code should not play down the heroic life of action, he explains, because 'heroic virtues are needed to protect the innocence of the pastoral world from the violence and evil which would otherwise destroy it'.[106] Victorian war poetry is often responsive to this insight, and Housman's speaker on the idle hill acknowledges even as he would seem to resist it. The poem is a rich compound of competing voices; the lines 'Dear to friends and *food for powder*, | Soldiers marching, *all to die*', for instance, play off two of the most renowned commentators on war's absurdity and its necessity, Falstaff and Hotspur. The first allows room for Falstaff's sense of the hollowness of war in his comment on the soldiers as mere 'food for powder', yet the second is perhaps responsive to Hotspur's sense of the honour of war in his call to the men, 'die all, die merrily'.[107] Neither voice is fully persuasive (Falstaff can sound expediently unprincipled, and Hotspur blithely inhumane), but their dialogue stages questions that Housman is frequently intent upon asking about war. Like the speaker of *Maud*, haunted by the march 'with banner and bugle and fife', this speaker's move to rise manages to sound both decided and exhausted, and the call of the bugles is itself rendered ambiguous as Housman's arch rhyme ('hollo/follow') gets to work on it; within the greeting 'hollo' one begins to hear something 'hollow'. Indeed, it is not clear what the speaker's 'rising' portends—rising up to join the soldiers, or rising against them by moving further away.

[105] Housman, 'XXXV', in *A Shropshire Lad*, ibid. 59.
[106] Andrew Rutherford, *The Literature of War: Five Studies in Heroic Virtue* (London: Macmillan, 1978), 2 and 9.
[107] William Shakespeare, *The First Part of King Henry IV*, iv. ii. 62 and iv. i. 135.

Geoffrey Hill has questioned the achievement of Wilfred Owen's war poetry by suggesting that it 'applies a balm of generalized sorrow at a point where the particulars of experience should outsmart that kind of consolation'.[108] One of the strengths of Housman's poem is that it breathes an air of 'generalized sorrow' without feeling complacent or merely luxurious. His speaker may perhaps be envious of the sleep of those dead who are unperturbed by noises in their dreams, but 'Lovely lads and dead and rotten' also conveys both pity and anger, a feeling that the particulars of experience are not to be tidied up into wholly consolatory patterns. This poem, and the one by Hardy, were both immensely popular in the trenches during the First World War; as Paul Fussell has argued, the work of these two poets in particular 'anticipates [and] even helps to determine the imaginative means by which the war was conceived'.[109] But the richness of this work owes much, in turn, to the searchings of earlier Victorian war poetry, a poetry that—in its refusal to provide a ringing endorsement of war even as it remained wary of the dangers of that refusal—offered itself as bequest and as monitory force.

[108] Geoffrey Hill, ' "I in Another Place": Homage to Keith Douglas', *Stand*, 6/4 (1964–5), 7.
[109] Paul Fussell, *The Great War and Modern Memory* (Oxford: Oxford University Press, 1975), 282.

CHAPTER 2

....

'GRAVER THINGS...BRAVER THINGS': HARDY'S WAR POETRY

....

RALPH PITE

Hardy's novels of 'Character and Environment' and his 1912–13 poems continue to dominate his reputation, and none of them seem to have much to do with war. The few military characters in the well-known novels, such as Sergeant Troy in *Far From the Madding Crowd* (1874), align themselves with other seductive and deceitful men—Edred Fitzpiers in *The Woodlanders* (1887) and Alec d'Urberville in *Tess of the d'Urbervilles* (1891)—suggesting greater interest in the male stereotype than the military one. The exception to this rule is *The Trumpet-Major*, Hardy's 1879 historical novel set during the Napoleonic Wars; the book is not highly regarded, however, and has even been dismissed as a minor aberration. *The Dynasts* (1904–8), Hardy's 'Epic-Drama' of Napoleon, has usually been treated, until recently at least, as a major aberration. Although Hardy made frequent allusions in his ghosted autobiography, *The Life of Thomas Hardy* (1928, 1930) to his long-standing fascination with the Napoleonic Wars, the low critical reputation of *The Dynasts* has made it easy to assume he was being protective towards his most significant artistic failure.[1]

---

[1] This is an anachronistic view, since *The Dynasts* was a success in Hardy's lifetime, particularly during the war years when he wrote his *Life*.

Current work to reclaim *The Dynasts*, and the broader effort to draw attention to previously neglected parts of Hardy's output, have gradually made it more difficult simply to disparage or set aside his interest in war.[2] Particularly between the late 1890s and the end of the First World War—between *Wessex Poems* (1898) and *Moments of Vision* (1917)—he became visibly preoccupied with contemporary and historical wars. *Moments of Vision* includes 'Poems of War and Patriotism'; *Poems of the Past and the Present* (1901), his second collection, has a sequence entitled 'War Poems'; and in *Wessex Poems*, there are several Napoleonic pieces—'Valenciennes', 'San Sebastian', 'Leipzig', 'The Peasant's Confession', 'The Alarm', plus at one remove 'The Dance at the Phoenix'. In the same collection, 'The Casterbridge Captains' arises out of the North-West Frontier wars of the mid-nineteenth century, and, in total, nearly one-third of the book could be defined as war poetry. Similarly, *The Dynasts* takes up almost all of two volumes in the five-volume edition of the *Complete Poetical Works*.[3]

If the received idea of Hardy does not sit comfortably with his production of so much war poetry, neither do his war poems conform to what is expected of the genre. Typically (and this is to generalize), the best war poetry is seen as arising out of the grand disillusion of the First World War. Paul Fussell's influential *The Great War and Modern Memory* (1975) reinforced this narrative, in which the horrors of the trenches, and especially the Somme, shattered belief in England's cause, creating at once bitterness and nostalgia. Sassoon's contempt for the officer class, Owen's pity for friend and foe alike, and Edward Thomas's hesitant but resolute attachment to the English countryside, all variously condemn Rupert Brooke's overwrought ardour for self-sacrifice. Brooke's 1914 sonnets may be viewed as genuinely idealistic, as co-opted by the Establishment or as opportunistic themselves; whichever position is taken, the war's progress (through fervour, catastrophe, and attrition towards exhaustion and a victory finally achieved by new and unheroic tactics) is seen repeating itself in a poetic development from empty-headed enthusiasm towards the grittier, battle-weary wisdom of the true war poets. That development neatly aligns itself with the replacement of the patriotic and imperial delusions of the Victorian world by the sober realism of modernity.

---

[2] For recent considerations of *The Dynasts*, see G. Glen Wickens, *Thomas Hardy, Monism, and the Carnival Tradition: The One and the Many in* The Dynasts (Toronto: University of Toronto Press, 2002), and Charles Lock, 'Hardy Promises: *The Dynasts* and the Epic of Imperialism', in Charles P. C. Pettit (ed.), *Reading Thomas Hardy* (Basingstoke: Macmillan, 1998), 83–116. Examples of work on neglected parts of Hardy's *œuvre* include Peter Widdowson, *Hardy in History: A Study in Literary Sociology* (London: Routledge, 1989); Joe Fisher, *The Hidden Hardy* (London: Macmillan, 1992); Roger Ebbatson, *Hardy: The Margin of the Unexpressed* (Sheffield: Sheffield Academic Press, 1993); and M. R. Higgonet (ed.), *The Sense of Sex: Feminist Perspectives on Hardy* (Urbana, Ill.: University of Illinois Press, 1993).

[3] Thomas Hardy, *The Complete Poetical Works of Thomas Hardy*, 5 vols., ed. Samuel Hynes (Oxford: Clarendon Press, 1982–95).

In some respects it is an alarmingly heroic story, even though it presents heroism as attained by seeing through received ideas of heroism. The 'lions-led-by-donkeys' version of the First World War—of lion-hearted Tommies sent to needless death in their thousands by incompetent commanders—is repeated in Owen and Sassoon. Though of the officer class themselves, both poets are on the side of the ordinary soldiers, first in the way they led their troops, and secondly in their writing—in specific poems that praise the lower ranks or attack the generals, and through a style that discards the ornate mellifluousness of late Victorian poetry. This is especially true of Sassoon and of Charles Sorley, and it is frequently noted as an aspect of the war's poetry generally.[4]

War poetry is thus understood within a sequence of feeling in which naivety gives way to disillusionment and mature understanding; in that process, rhetoric, idealism, and unreflecting nationalism are left behind, and respect for the established hierarchy loses out to admiration for the ordinary man, now seen as one's equal.[5] This is all very well except that it rescues war itself, making the trenches a crucible in which fantasy is refined away. Rosenberg's question—'What in our lives is burnt | In the fire of this?'[6]—is given too swift an answer: hypocrisy is burnt away, illusions shattered. Rosenberg meant nothing so straightforward, and his lines are reduced by a normative understanding of what war poetry should express. War shows people the futility of war, so it is not absolutely futile.

This contradiction within the received idea of war poetry emerges more clearly if you consider an advocate for war such as John Ruskin, who saw conflict as morally beneficial:

First, the great justification of this game [war] is that it truly, when well played, determines *who is the best man*; who is the highest bred, the most self-denying, the most fearless, the coolest of nerve, the swiftest of eye and head. You cannot test these qualities wholly, unless there is a clear possibility of the struggle ending in death.[7]

These views seem absolutely opposed to Wilfred Owen's poetry or Ivor Gurney's (if not to Sassoon's), yet the idea of warfare as a test of mettle—which was passed by Owen and Sassoon, but failed by Brooke—persists unacknowledged within the literary history we bring to the appraisal of their work. Jon Silkin, in the introduction to his anthology *The Penguin Book of First World War Poetry* (1979), puts the case most schematically, outlining in four 'stages of consciousness' the emergence of

---

[4] Some of the stylistic changes may be due to Hardy's example, especially his manner in the sequence 'Satires of Circumstance' from 1912, which is cited by Sassoon as an influence.

[5] Martin Stephen's 'Preface' to his anthology *Never Such Innocence: Poems of the First World War* (London: Dent, 1988), pp. vii–xvii, carefully considers these models of understanding the poetry.

[6] Isaac Rosenberg, 'August 1914', in *The Poems and Plays of Isaac Rosenberg*, ed. Vivien Noakes (Oxford: Oxford University Press, 2004), 130.

[7] John Ruskin, *The Crown of Wild Olive: Three Lectures on Work, Traffic and War* (London: Smith, Elder & Co., 1866), 167. Daniel Pick discusses the period's attitudes to war in his *War Machine: The Rationalization of Slaughter in the Modern Age* (New Haven: Yale University Press, 1993).

scepticism from innocence that was brought about by the Great War. According to this model, Hardy's war poetry fails; and Silkin, in his widely read study *Out of Battle*, condemns Hardy for responding 'so inertly to the First World War'. His poems were, Silkin says 'neither indictments of war nor ... tentative gropings for a position in which the demands of war and the compunctions of killing may be, if not reconciled, at least held in tolerable equilibrium'.[8] Unlike *The Dynasts* and Hardy's Boer War poems, Hardy's First World War poetry typically becomes, according to Silkin, 'declamatory propaganda in the pejorative sense of the word'.[9] These judgements are not accurate about or attentive to the poems Hardy wrote during the Great War, and Silkin condemns Hardy's work simply because it does not voice the required, disillusioned attitude. Moreover, the complexity of Hardy's various poetries of war reveals the narrowness of Silkin's critical focus and its historical blindspots.

When Hardy was growing up, Dorchester was an army town 'made colourful by the constant presence of the red-coated and splendidly accoutred soldiery of those days',[10] and the county was filled with stories of the war fever of forty years before. The English fleet had been at anchor just off Weymouth in 1804 amid widespread fears of a French invasion; these culminated on 1 May in a general panic and mobilization. Hardy returned again and again to this incident, in his poem 'The Alarm', in *The Trumpet-Major*, and in Part 1 of *The Dynasts* (ii. iv–v); he alluded to it again in *The Return of the Native* (1878), in his short story 'A Tradition of Eighteen Hundred and Four' (1882), and in his poem 'One We Knew'. It is a peculiarly compulsive preoccupation. 'The Alarm' was written 'In Memory of one of the Writer's Family who was a Volunteer during the War with Napoleon', Hardy's paternal grandfather, who had been one of the 'Bang-up Locals' and marched on Weymouth to repel the invader.[11] Similarly, Hardy always pointed out to visitors Captain Hardy's monument on Blackdown Hill, visible through the windows of Max Gate. This Hardy, not directly related to Thomas Hardy, had been Nelson's flag captain at Trafalgar and is portrayed admiringly in the Trafalgar scenes of *The Dynasts* (Part 1, v. ii and iv).

Hardy himself was condemned to remain a non-combatant—not born during the Napoleonic Wars, too young for the Crimean War, and far too old for the wars at the end of the century. This exclusion from glory bred a fear that he fell short because his qualities, as Ruskin might put it, had never been wholly tested. In addition, Hardy was particularly alert to the pitfalls of non-combatant status

---

[8] Jon Silkin, *Out of Battle: The Poetry of the Great War* (Oxford: Oxford University Press, 1972), 37.

[9] Ibid. 44.

[10] Michael Millgate, *Thomas Hardy: A Biography Revisited* (Oxford: Oxford University Press, 2004), 51.

[11] Hardy, 'The Alarm', in *The Complete Poems of Thomas Hardy*, ed. James Gibson (London: Macmillan, 1976), 35. For further details about the Dorset Volunteers, see George Lanning, 'Thomas Hardy and the Bang-up Locals', *Thomas Hardy Journal*, 16/2 (May 2000), 54–8.

because he had seen others fall into them. When the Franco-Prussian War broke out in the summer of 1870, he was working in London for the architect Raphael Brandon (1817–77), in his offices in St Clement's Inn, 'an old-world out-of-the-way corner',[12] as Hardy later described it. Brandon seemed to have escaped from the business of self-promotion and self-advancement that Hardy disliked in London's architectural world, but his serenity vanished in the face of war. The conflict proved to be 'a cause of much excitement to Brandon', who bought all the papers and read them avidly, including the 'leading articles on the war'. Hardy's close friend Horace Moule had written many of these, and he too became feverishly involved in this foreign conflict. In 1865, Moule gave Hardy a copy of the *Thoughts of the Emperor M. Aurelius Antoninus*, inscribing it with a quotation from the book: 'This is the chief thing: Be not perturbed: for all things are according to the nature of the universal.' Plainly, though, Moule and the other-worldly Brandon were both highly perturbed by the outbreak of war; for a while Hardy was as well. He grew, he said later, 'as excited' as his friends and visited the Waterloo veterans in Chelsea Hospital, though what he found there disappointed him: 'tattered banners mended with netting and . . . the old asthmatic and crippled men'.[13]

Later in the 1870s, Moule and Brandon committed suicide—Moule in 1873, Brandon four years later—and the rest of Hardy's life was troubled by their fate. It was not so much that war had revealed the shallowness of their stoicism, or simply that their excitement in 1870 glamorized the violence of imperial might (ignoring the 'old asthmatic and crippled' veterans), although Hardy's later writings show that he was alert to both these possible mistakes. Instead, Brandon and Moule typified for Hardy the danger of not finding an equivalent to the heroic endeavour supplied to warriors by battle. His friends' vicarious involvement in the 1870–1 war was unhealthy, because it compensated for the drifting uncertainty of their own lives. Brandon's kindliness masked a despairing sense of failure, after the eminence he had attained in the 1840s, and Moule's career was running into the sand, amidst increasingly frequent depressive and alcoholic episodes.[14] War became the intoxicating and terrifying reminder of what you had failed to achieve in your civilian life, if you were someone like Brandon or Moule, so that, in turn, war fever became a kind of denial—an immersion in struggle to disguise your own acquiescence.

Hardy consistently presented himself as an unambitious person, stoical, fatalistic, and disinterested, and he took Moule's quotation from Marcus Aurelius as his motto in life. Yet not only was he far more driven and energetic than this image suggests

---

[12] Hardy, *The Life and Work of Thomas Hardy by Thomas Hardy*, ed. Michael Millgate (London: Macmillan, 1984), 81.

[13] Ibid. 82. See Millgate, *Thomas Hardy: A Biography Revisited*, 84.

[14] Hardy, who knew Edmund Gosse well, notices in his friends the unexpected jingoistic fervour that Gosse observed in his father during the Crimean War and recorded in *Father and Son* (1907), a book that Hardy read.

(the evidence of his intentness is everywhere), he was also concerned to intervene. His novels all possess a polemical element, whether directed against the divorce laws, class privilege, tourist complacencies, intellectuality, masculine self-importance, or the sexual double standard, and (in retrospect at least) he saw his novel-writing career as an attempt to reform the novel. He wrote in 1891, soon after the triumphant success of *Tess*:

Ever since I began to write—certainly ever since I wrote 'Two on a Tower' in 1881—I have felt that the doll of English fiction must be demolished, if England is to have a school of fiction at all...the development of a more virile type of novel is not incompatible with sound morality.[15]

The sense of being dedicated to a manly task supported Hardy as he followed a career his family disliked and his Dorset compatriots thought either disreputable or trivial. Keeping in mind a sense of mission also defended him against the rudderless melancholy from which Brandon and Moule had suffered so badly. He learnt the attitude in part from Leslie Stephen, whom he befriended soon after Moule's traumatizing death, and may have been drawn to Stephen by the firmness he appeared at least to embody.

War for Hardy possessed, then, a fatal glamour that revealed a psychological need. Having that need revealed could be destructive, sometimes fatally so, but the need for heroism could not be denied. Hardy's response was to establish routines and principles, strict habits of both activity and engagement, even though his world-view told him that human action achieved nothing and even though he saw himself as, by temperament, passively inclined. He went out to battle in his novels, taking on, through them, the forces of the English Establishment, and he did something similar in his war poetry.

When the Boer War broke out in October 1899, English public opinion was carried along on a wave of patriotic feeling partly generated by the poets, Swinburne included:

> scourge these dogs, agape with jaws afoam,
> Down out of life. Strike, England, and strike home.[16]

This is from Swinburne's 'The Transvaal', published right at the beginning of the war; in 'Reverse', which appeared four weeks later, the abuse of the enemy is more violent still.

> But loathing more intense than speaks disgust
> Heaves England's heart, when scorn is bound to greet
> Hunters and hounds whose tongues would lick their feet.[17]

[15] Hardy to H. W. Massingham, 31 Dec. 1891, in *The Collected Letters of Thomas Hardy*, i: *1840–1892*, ed. Richard Little Purdy and Michael Millgate (Oxford: Oxford University Press, 1978), 250.

[16] A. C. Swinburne, 'The Transvaal', *The Times*, 11 Oct. 1899, 7; repr. in *Swinburne's Collected Poetical Works*, ii (London: William Heinemann, 1935), 1223.

[17] Swinburne, 'Reverse', in *Swinburne's Collected Poetical Works*, ii. 1224.

Hardy congratulated George Gissing for attacking the bloodthirsty jingoism of such poems in a review of 4 November 1899.[18] His own rejoinder came via poems he wrote in the course of that autumn and winter and published in newspapers and periodicals: the *Daily Chronicle, The Graphic, Literature, Westminster Gazette, The Sphere*, the *Cornhill*. This medium of dissemination was a departure for Hardy, certainly as a poet (only one of the *Wessex Poems* had been printed before it appeared in the collection). His choice of outlet shows that he was making a decisive attempt to speak to the nation (an endeavour continued by the mainstream features of *Poems of the Past and the Present* when it appeared two years later). As he did so, he began at once to voice reservations about the war and the poetry it had led to.

In the first of the poems, 'Embarcation', there are, among the soldiers setting sail, 'None dubious of the cause, none murmuring'; on the other hand, Hardy points out that these battalions, which resemble Henry V's army when he set out to conquer France, will

> argue in the selfsame bloody mode
> Which this late age of thought, and pact, and code,
> Still fails to mend.[19]

'Departure', a companion piece and (like Swinburne's poems) another sonnet, is more outspoken:

> When shall the saner softer polities
> Whereof we dream, have sway in each proud land
> And patriotism, grown Godlike, scorn to stand
> Bondslave to realms, but circle earth and seas?[20]

Hardy reserved 'Departure' for his next collection two years later; the poem he published at the time made the more cautious remark, 'Still fails to mend', which can be taken as more resigned than critical. Nonetheless, the contrast with Swinburne's tone is glaring, while the formal similarity and the moments of shared vocabulary ('scorn', for instance) encourage comparison. Likewise, the emphasis in Hardy's poem on speech ('argue' in 'Embarcation', and 'the seeming words that ask and ask again' of the soldiers in 'Departure') counters Swinburne's repeated insistence that the time for talking was over (his 'loathing more intense than speaks disgust' echoes his 'Speech and song / Lack utterance now for loathing' in 'The Transvaal'). All these aspects suggest a conscious riposte on Hardy's part to the pro-war writing he was surrounded by.

With the disagreement comes a shift of focus from the soldiers to those they leave behind. 'Embarcation' ends with the 'Wives, sisters, parents' who wave and smile, 'As if they knew not that they weep the while'; 'Departure' watches the ships

---

[18] Hardy to George Gissing, 5 Nov. 1899, in *Collected Letters*, ii: *1893–1901*, ed. Richard Little Purdy and Michael Millgate (Oxford: Oxford University Press, 1980), 235.
[19] Hardy, 'Embarcation', in *Complete Poems*, 86.   [20] Hardy, 'Departure', ibid. 87.

'smalling slowly to the gray sea-line', as 'each significant red smoke-shaft pales' and, plangently, 'Keen sense of severance everywhere prevails'. Just and only at that moment, according to the poem, you can make out the questioning protest of the soldiers. Likewise, 'The Going of the Battery' is the 'Wives' Lament', 'A Wife in London' hears of her husband's death and the following day receives his last letter, while the 'Song of the Soldiers' Wives and Sweethearts' and 'The Souls of the Slain' both look forward (though with different feelings) to returns and reunions. The poetry's near-exclusive concern is with those left behind—with their anxieties and vulnerabilities—and it makes no reference to the fighting itself or to the campaign's vicissitudes, although Hardy followed events closely. It is as if he wants his readers to reconsider the vocabulary of war mongering itself by showing them how and where the war will inevitably 'strike home'.

'Home' is a word Hardy often uses in these poems. The soldiers' wives hope eagerly for their partners' 'nearing home again, | Dears, home again';[21] the souls of the slain, as they land on Portland Bill, 'say "Home!" ';[22] they are heading, they say, 'homeward and hearthward' in hope of acclaim, and at the end of the poem those 'whose record was lovely and true . . . Bore to northward for home'; they are allowed back into the paradise that is England, however, not because of their feats in battle but because of 'old homely acts' of kindness to friends and family, 'the long-ago commonplace facts | Of our lives—held by us as scarce part of our story, | And rated as nought!' Likewise, Drummer Hodge, in one of Hardy's finest Boer War poems, came to the war 'Fresh from his Wessex home', and in what appears a foreshadowing of Rupert Brooke, the 'portion of that unknown plain' where he is buried 'Will Hodge for ever be'.[23] Brooke, though, has rewritten Hardy, perhaps deliberately. In 'Drummer Hodge', some corner of this foreign field has not been made 'for ever England' by Hodge's death; the English soldier has instead been taken up into the 'unknown plain'; his grave will be watched in eternity by the southern stars—the 'foreign constellations', that are renamed 'strange-eyed constellations' at the poem's end. His 'homely Northern breast' will 'Grow to some Southern tree'.[24]

Homely, in the sense of unsophisticated, unadorned, or unpolished, is 'Sometimes approbative, as connoting the absence of artificial embellishment; but often apologetic, depreciative' (*OED*). The returning souls of the slain depreciate their 'Deeds of home', valuing instead 'glory and war-mightiness', as war encourages them to do. Similarly, Victorian culture repeats a version of the *Bildungsroman* in which foreign travel and imperial adventure turn the homely into the experienced, the pale and gentle boy into the swarthy, toughened man. Dickens in *Great Expectations* and Hardy himself in *A Pair of Blue Eyes* employ this narrative

---

[21] Hardy, 'Song of the Soldiers' Wives and Sweethearts', ibid. 97.
[22] Hardy, 'The Souls of the Slain', ibid. 93.   [23] Hardy, 'Drummer Hodge', ibid. 91.
[24] Hardy took up the same idea again in 'Transformations', and made it more encouraging; see *Complete Poems*, 472.

pattern, following it and challenging it at the same time. Drummer Hodge is a further instance of the same subtle realignment; it would, in other words, be more consoling to the bereaved and more encouraging to an empire-building point of view if Hodge were transformed by war or if in his death he set a heroic example and inspired his fellows. Yet none of this takes place; he just turns into 'some Southern tree' after 'They throw in Drummer Hodge, to rest | Uncoffined—just as found'.[25]

The poem hinges on the 'Yet' which begins the third stanza, a change of direction that appears (quite conventionally) to offer consolation amidst loss. Hodge has died an unheroic death and been buried quickly (stanza 1); worse still (stanza 2) he had no understanding of what he was fighting for, 'yet' (stanza 3) the plain harbours him, a tree grows out of him, and 'strange-eyed constellations reign | His stars eternally'. There seems something lasting here ('for ever' and 'eternally' both occur in the final stanza), and something uplifting too, a hint that Hodge is coming home in Africa because Africa accepts him, as Nature in its indifference takes up everything, and because the strange stars, whose meaning he could never work out while he was alive, now 'reign | His stars' after death. A familiar poetic structure conforms to a familiar pattern of feeling, which is then redirected by the resistances offered by the diction of the last stanza. Sympathy for the dead man does not glorify either him or his role in the larger purpose of war; sympathy persists, like the stars' gaze, disdainful of whatever cause may have led to Hodge's death. The purposelessness of the death, similarly, does not disturb compassion; rather, the poem suggests that you need to remain undistracted by questions of praise or blame, profit or loss, if you are to mourn Hodge as he deserves.

This approach means that writer and reader are performing a 'deed of home' in thinking about the war dead. When the souls of the slain are divided at the end of the poem of that title, each sets off to its destination—the condemned to oblivion in the 'fathomless regions' of the sea, the virtuous 'homing . . . Like the Pentecost Wind'. They leave behind, the speaker says, 'in the gloaming | Sea-mutterings and me'. The mutterings of the resentful souls, consigned to the depths, combine with the noises audible as Hardy wakes from his dream-like experience: the noises of the waves slapping and gurgling, 'muttering' in the hollows of the rocks around Portland Bill. Lingering in the air too, however, is the muttering, the suppressed grumbling of a poet unconvinced about the war, drawn to protest and withholding or moderating that protest out of pity for those who have suffered directly. Many of his Boer War poems were prompted, he said, by particular losses known to him, and throughout the conflict he had Arthur Henniker and his wife Florence in his mind. Hardy had been in love with Florence Henniker in the mid-1890s, and remained a close friend; her husband was a professional soldier who had sailed away on one of

[25] I am grateful to Roger Ebbatson for his discussion of Hardy's use of 'home' in the Boer War poems, in his *An Imaginary England: Nation, Landscape and Literature, 1840–1920* (Aldershot: Ashgate, 2005), 99–108.

the troopships from Southampton.[26] Not until the war was over and Henniker had come safely home did Hardy feel it appropriate to write more openly about what his age still failed to mend; and even then, his protest found ways of acknowledging the actuality of both war's slaughter and war's bravery.

News of the peace treaty that brought the war to a close reached Max Gate on 2 June 1902, Hardy's birthday, and he set a flag flying in celebration. Almost at once, he began working on *The Dynasts*. Between July that year and September 1903, he completed the six acts that made up the first part, which was published in January 1904. This connection between the Boer War and *The Dynasts* has been observed before. Jon Silkin aligned the 'final didactic and anti-war emphases' of Hardy's work with general post-war disillusionment in the early years of the twentieth century,[27] and Kenneth Millard saw the same atmosphere prompting Kipling's turn from writing poetry, such as the *Barrack-Room Ballads* (1892), to writing prose: 'following the Boer War . . . there was little public interest in poetry of the services'.[28] It was then in oddly unpromising conditions that Hardy began his epic of Napoleon. After the war in South Africa had reached an avowedly ignominious conclusion, amidst widespread doubts about the 'methods of barbarism' employed by the British Army, he embarked upon his fullest exploration of military life.[29]

One motive may have been, once more, the chance of addressing contemporary concerns.[30] Stories of Britain being invaded, for instance, were popular in the first decade of the twentieth century, and *The Dynasts* begins with the threat of Napoleon's landing. These Edwardian thrillers pitted England against Germany, conflicts among a number of European powers being reduced to a duel between these two. Hardy composed *The Dynasts*, he said, intent upon correcting the imbalance in all the current histories of the period:

But the slight regard paid to English influence and action throughout the struggle by so many Continental writers who had dealt with Napoléon's career, seemed always to leave room for a new handling of the theme which should re-embody the features of this influence in their true proportion. (1, Preface)

---

[26] See his letters written around Christmas 1899 to Florence Henniker and Winifred Thomson, in *Collected Letters*, ii. 240–3.

[27] Silkin, *Out of Battle*, 33; M. Van Wyk Smith also notes a link between *The Dynasts* and the Boer War in his excellent *Drummer Hodge: The Poetry of the Anglo-Boer War* (Oxford: Clarendon Press, 1978), 145.

[28] Kenneth Millard, *Edwardian Poetry* (Oxford: Clarendon Press, 1991), 13. David Trotter analyses this moment in Kipling's career in his 'Kipling's England: The Edwardian Years', in Phillip Mallett (ed.), *Kipling Considered* (Basingstoke: Macmillan, 1989), 58 ff.

[29] See Paula M. Krebs, *Gender, Race, and the Writing of Empire: Public Discourse and the Boer War* (Cambridge: Cambridge University Press, 1999), 33–54. Campbell-Bannerman, then leader of the Opposition, used the phrase 'methods of barbarism' in Parliament, on 17 June 1901, during discussion of Emily Hobhouse's report into the British concentration camps in South Africa.

[30] Charles Lock asserts that an 'allegorical reading' of *The Dynasts*, which shows 'how the epic of the Napoleonic Wars can be interpreted in terms of the Edwardian sense of power and imminent decline of the British Empire . . . is certainly possible' (Charles Lock, 'Hardy Promises: *The Dynasts* and the Epic of Imperialism', in Pettit (ed.), *Reading Thomas Hardy*, 84).

Accordingly, not only are the great British-led victories of Trafalgar and Waterloo culminating points in the work, but Napoleon also complains repeatedly that the Russian and Austrian armies are funded by English money.[31] The detailed historical accuracy of *The Dynasts* is remarkable, but within it, nonetheless, Edwardian anti-German feeling is discernible. Hardy presents the wars as a clash between a sea-based power and a land-based one, so that his new handling encourages the reader to see something of Bismarck in Napoleon.

Similarly, Samuel Hynes has drawn attention to the post-Boer War desire for national regeneration, typified by Baden-Powell, a hero of the war, and his founding of the Scout movement in 1908.[32] *The Dynasts* is in many respects an inspiriting and patriotic work. George Orwell, who complained about the 'debunking version of war' endemic among left-wing intellectuals during the 1920s—'the theory that war is all corpses and latrines and never leads to any good result'—also grumbled that Hardy's writing, like A. E. Housman's, was 'not tragic, merely querulous'; 'one ought', he did however concede, 'to make an exception of *The Dynasts*.'[33] Orwell, during a war, singles out this part of Hardy's *œuvre* for praise, convinced of the encouragement it offers to those enduring wars. Harley Granville-Barker responded to the same quality in it when he put on a version of *The Dynasts* in the West End during the first winter of the Great War. This openness to patriotic feeling has helped to make *The Dynasts* appear suspect to those still wedded to 'the debunking version of war'; equally, its links with Edwardian nation building make it look worryingly at odds with Hardy's otherwise pronounced dislike of war mongering, of military conflict—'the old & barbarous' way, as he called it, of 'settling disputes'[34]—and his suspicion of nationalist allegiances.

Yet *The Dynasts* is nothing like an Empire Day pageant, not least because it presents such a strikingly nuanced picture. Nelson may be an unambiguously noble figure, and Wellington the epitome of phlegmatic English resolve. Prime Minister Pitt, though, is caught up with George III, otherwise a genial and unpretentious monarch, in a master–servant relationship that wears Pitt down, consigning him to an early grave. On the other side, Napoleon, even if lawless and vain, is never the monster of legend. Hardy makes fun, in fact, of the English wish to believe in a baby-eater across the Channel. Increasingly, instead, Napoleon speaks of himself as powerless. When he is watching his army setting out in 1812 to invade Russia, for instance, he wonders at what is taking place:

---

[31] 'What cares England . . . | Her gold it is that forms the weft of this | Fair tapestry of armies marshalled here!', and 'Even here Pitt's guineas are the foes: | 'Tis all a duel 'twixt this Pitt and me' (*The Dynasts*, 1, IV. v. 40, 42–3 and VI. i. 78–9).

[32] See Samuel Hynes, *The Edwardian Turn of Mind* (Princeton: Princeton University Press, 1968), 26–9.

[33] George Orwell, 'Looking Back on the Spanish War' (1943) and 'Inside the Whale' (1940), in *The Penguin Essays of George Orwell* (Harmondsworth: Penguin, 1984), 217 and 114.

[34] Hardy to Florence Henniker, 11 Oct. 1899, in *Collected Letters*, ii. 232.

> Since Lodi Bridge
> The force I then felt move me moves me on
> Whether I will or no; and oftentimes
> Against my better mind . . . Why am I here?
> —By laws imposed on me inexorably!
> History makes use of me to weave her web.
>
> (Part 3, I. i. 64–9)

Byron's *Manfred* is in the background here, and the vast questions of personal destiny and historical determinism are answered in Byron's throwaway manner with a shrug—'Well, war's my trade.' The same thought had been Napoleon's recourse earlier, in 1805, when the Austrians surrendered at Ulm:

> I tell you frankly that I know not why
> Your master wages this wild war with me.
> I know not what he seeks by such injustice,
> Unless to give me practice in my trade—
> That of a soldier—whereto I was bred:
> Deemed he my craft might slip from me, unplied?
>
> (Part 1, IV. v. 11–16)

He is more disingenuous in his triumphant youth than in his wearied decline; even so, his claim is made resonant by the incompetence of his opponents. Not until Wellington begins to wage the Peninsular campaign (late in Part 2) does Napoleon begin to confront a strategist to rival him.

Wellington succeeds through solid planning and obstinate resolve, and the second of these qualities is paralleled in Napoleon's Russian nemesis, General Kutúzof. Before the battle of Austerlitz, Kutúzof is, like Pitt and even Nelson elsewhere in Part 1, already 'old and weary'. He is 'nodding, waking, and nodding again' (Part 1, VI. ii stage directions), and cannot resist either Napoleon's cleverness or the bad advice of his own officers. Seven years later, Kutúzof has been transformed into a '*strange, one-eyed, white-shakoed, scarred old man, / Ruthlessly heading every onset made*' (Part 3, I. ix. 40–2). In the stage directions, he 'presents a terrible appearance now bravely serving though slowly dying, his face puffed with the intense cold, his one eye staring out as he sits in a heap in the saddle, his head sunk into his shoulders' (Part 3, I. xi, stage directions). Napoleon cuts a similar figure after Waterloo. His 'head droops lower and lower as he sits listless in the saddle' (Part 3, VII. ix, stage directions), though by now he is the less impressive of the two, 'listless' where Kutúzof is relentless, his single eye 'staring out'.

Napoleon, then, is less a revolutionary figure in *The Dynasts* (threatening or inspiring, according to your politics) than someone unusually good at their job. His exceptional craft exposes the feebleness of the existing powers, but later comes up against people equally skilled and more determined. In *The Dynasts*, Napoleon seems to represent the life force itself, rather than a particular historical or political moment; he is a disruptive energy that decays slowly over time into the rigid forms of old age, obsessed with self-perpetuation as his powers fade. Because there is, as it were, nothing to Napoleon beyond his military talent, it is inevitable that he should come to impersonate what he overthrows, setting up monarchies in the countries he liberates and preoccupied by the need to establish a dynasty. On the other side, Kutúzof seems less to symbolize retributive justice or Mother Russia's power of resistance than to embody an elemental defiance of death; similarly, the Battle of Waterloo is won by endurance alone.[35] What commands, Wellington's aide asks him, would he want carried out if he were killed. 'These simply', Wellington answers, 'to hold out unto the last' (Part 3, VII. vii. 38). When another officer arrives asking for 'some relief, however temporary', Wellington can offer none—'he, I, every Englishman afield | Must fall upon the spot we occupy, | Our wounds in front' (Part 3, VII. vii. 48–50). Defeat for the French comes, accordingly, with Wellington's cry, 'Aha—they are giving way!' (Part 3, VII. viii. 74).

This means that there is a nihilist undercurrent to the work's resignation about politics. The world is run by tired, elderly men, whose age renders them small-minded, but they are only young men aged; they show that youthful hopes and ideals will always peter out in disappointment. It is in the nature of the young to set out to change the world, and in their nature, too, to become old—first complacent, then weary, and then frightened. Napoleon recognizes something of this after Waterloo:

> I found the crown of France in the mire,
> And with the point of my prevailing sword
> I picked it up! But for all this and this
> I shall be nothing.
>
> (Part 3, VII. ix. 38–41)

'Great men are meteors', he says, a few lines later, 'that consume themselves | To light the earth. This is my burnt-out hour.' He is echoing his arch-enemy, Pitt, who also died convinced he had achieved nothing:

> So do my plans through all these plodding years
> Announce them built in vain!
> His heel on France, monarchies in chains
> To France, I am as though I had never been!
>
> (Part 1, VI. vi. 46–9)

Ambition seems to be broken against forces of obstinate resistance as desire is thwarted by experience. At this point a patriotic celebration of English resilience—

---

[35] The earlier victory at Trafalgar mirrors Napoleon's, because the French navy is 'rotten': 'Demoralized past prayer is the marine— | Bad masts, bad sails, bad officers, bad men,' as Admiral Villeneuve acknowledges (Part 1, II. ii. 11–12). Natural justice early on in the campaign, as talent sweeps aside corruption, is replaced, after the stalemate of Borodino and amidst the 'damn close-run thing' of Waterloo, by a feeling that war tests the survival instinct.

the nation's 'tough, enisled, self-centred, kindless craft' (Part 3, VII. ix. 57) that Napoleon believes has undone him in the end—comes into alignment with a conviction that wars can never be won, only endured and not lost. Nothing comes of war in *The Dynasts*; there is nothing to celebrate at battle's end except battle's end. Moreover, in Napoleon's case there is something lamentable about the way his faults of character have allowed the old monarchical powers to reassert themselves so totally. By the time Napoleon the liberator is snuffed out by the dynasts, he has turned into a dynast himself, and that knowledge can offer comfort to liberal regret. Even so, there is no positive advance to hold on to afterwards and to use to justify the carnage or console oneself for the suffering. In 1815, we are back where we started, exactly and entirely. It is as though Napoleon and Pitt had never been.

Hardy cultivated an ambiguity about whether to pronounce *The Dynasts* with a long or short 'i'—'Die-nasts' or 'Dinnasts'. There is a similar doubt about 'Christminster' in *Jude the Obscure*, which Hardy probably pronounced with a short 'i', as in 'Christine', though usually it is spoken with a long 'i' (as in Christ Church). Your decision over this hints at your allegiances, either to Establishment religiosity (long 'i'), which is probably hypocritical, or the common people's carelessness about religion (short 'i'), which is both more honest and more kindly. Something of the same question is raised in *The Dynasts*, because those who view these powers respectfully will tend to lengthen the vowel. The prominence of this ambiguously sounding word draws attention to the two possibilities, die and din—the din of dying and the dying away of the din, both of which are highlighted in the work. Scenes end by fading out, as figures are lost in haze, enveloped in smoke, or disappear into mist, rain, and snow. At the end of the Battle of Jena:

The crossing streams of fugitives strike panic into each other, and the tumult increases with the thickening darkness till night renders the scene invisible, and nothing remains but a confused diminishing noise, and fitful lights here and there.

The fog of the morning returns, and curtains all. (Part 2, I. iv, closing stage direction)

There is an elegiac feeling here (that echoes 'the withdrawing roar' of the sea on Matthew Arnold's Dover Beach and in Tennyson's 'Morte d'Arthur', where 'the wailing died away' on the mere); simultaneously, the perspective seems to be rising above elegy in search of indifference or calm.

The shifts of perspective in *The Dynasts* are probably the most famous thing about it. In the 'Spectacle . . . presented to the mind's eye', Europe is seen from on high, as if from orbit:

as a prone and emaciated figure, the Alps shaping like a backbone, and the branching mountain-chains like ribs, the peninsular plateau of Spain forming the head. . . . The point of view then sinks downwards through space, and draws near to the surface of the perturbed countries, where the people . . . are seen writhing, crawling, heaving, and vibrating in their various cities and nationalities. (Part 1, Preface and Fore Scene)

Hardy's scene endings evidently continue this alternation of viewpoint. For the same reasons, he offers a series of disruptively discordant similes for the grand armies of the campaigns—marching columns of men look like caterpillars, their ships are moths, weaponry glitters 'like a display of cutlery at a hill-side fair', and aides rushing to and fro are 'like house-flies dancing their quadrilles' (Part 3, VII. i, stage directions and, VII. ii, stage directions). The grotesqueness of these comparisons appears to betray a wish to demean their subjects. At moments of highest intensity, and when Hardy's English readership is likely to be at its most fervently patriotic, he introduces these reminders of a perspective from which wars, like all human activity, appear infinitely trivial.

The similes may appear, initially at least, to share and endorse the perspective of the Spirit of the Years, soberly concerned to deflate human self-importance. The curious achievement of *The Dynasts*, however, is to make such elevation above events continuous with pity. From on high, Europe appears like one weakened human being, and as, time and again, the reader is immersed in carnage only to be released from it at the end of a scene, the difference between participating and witnessing is felt more keenly. Seeing it whole is made part of learning to pity it all, every single person involved and the historical catastrophe.

For Hardy, then, though war can achieve nothing, perhaps war poetry can achieve something. He ends *The Dynasts*, famously, on a note of wider optimism.

> But—a stirring thrills the air
> Like to sounds of joyance there
>   That the rages
>   Of the ages
> Shall be cancelled, and deliverance offered from the darts that were,
> Consciousness the Will informing, till It fashion all things fair!
>
> (Part 3, After Scene, 105–10)

There is just the possibility that the universe will one day operate more justly and kindly than at present. Hardy expressed the same tentative hope in 'The Darkling Thrush' and one or two other pieces in *Poems of the Past and the Present*.[36] In *The Dynasts*, the source of hope lies in Pity (it is the Chorus of the Pities which speaks the final lines), and the consciousness that they foresee informing the will is compassionate. '[M]ust not Its heart awake,' they ask, 'Promptly tending | To Its mending | In a genial germing purpose, and for loving-kindness' sake?' (Part 3, After Scene, 96–9). *The Dynasts* is written in such a way that it can take part in, and even perhaps bring forward minutely, this transformation of things.

More usually, Hardy's war poetry offers no such hope. The wives, waiting for their husbands to return in 'The Going of the Battery', resist despair by believing in Providence, and then discover that that belief is precarious:

---

[36] It is a recurrent sentiment, though never again put as ardently as in *The Dynasts*. Compare 'God's Education', in *Complete Poems*, 278–9.

—Yet, voices haunting us, daunting us, taunting us,
Hint in the night-time when life beats are low
Other and graver things . . . Hold we to braver things,
Wait we, in trust, what Time's fulness shall show.[37]

The taunts are grave, graver and more serious than hoping that 'some Hand will guard their ways' (as the previous stanza imagines), but in response to that, after the line's hiatus, the women take courage. The lines carry traces of *In Memoriam*, and they dissent from Tennyson's trust in the larger hope. To wait 'in trust' in Hardy's poem seems to mean not panicking even while you recognize that you are in the hands of something blind and undiscriminating. The most terrible ending could be in store, but still you 'trust', you do not give way. The poems ends with these lines, at the point when the women, after the pause in the penultimate line, are resolving to go forward and, almost it seems, preparing for battle themselves. That respect for the bravery of the non-combatant is typical of Hardy's war poetry and it mirrors—it is mirrored by—the fortitude of his own writing.

This story, though, has an unhappy ending. Two of Hardy's most famous war poems, 'In Time of "The Breaking of Nations"' and 'Men Who March Away', were written about the First World War, and, as in 1899, Hardy again supplied patriotic poetry for the periodicals in 1914–15. Nonetheless, his best poetry during the Great War and afterwards is restricted to pieces in which he despairs of himself and of his work. 'I Looked Up from My Writing' finds the world so hideous that it makes no sense to compose poetry about it any longer. 'Quid Hic Agis?' accuses the poet himself of being a coward and a failure because the horrors of the war have silenced him. That accusation does contain an element of challenge (addressed to the reader, the conscientious objector, or the reluctant conscript), and Hardy composed further responsibly heartening poems for *Moments of Vision*. He wrote, for instance, of an old psalm tune heard again, 'Here in these turmoiled years of belligerent fire | Living still on—and onward, maybe, | Till Doom's great day be!',[38] and about Shakespeare, whose writings have lasted and will last 'In harmonies that cow Oblivion, | And, like the wind, with all-uncared effect | Maintain a sway'.[39] These, though, are strained attempts to discover and provide solace amidst misery; they lack the conviction of, say, 'To the Moon' and 'A Backward Spring', both of which acknowledge despair, and they are attempts to suppress the self-disdain that surfaces elsewhere, in 'The Pedigree' or 'Old Furniture'.

The butchery of the Western Front was, to Hardy, literally unendurable, and not being able to bear it made him feel ashamed. Not only did the First World War disappoint his faint hope that humanity might slowly be advancing, and that ultimately consciousness would inform the will, and not only was there no

---

[37] Hardy, 'The Going of the Battery', ibid. 89.
[38] Hardy, 'Apostrophe to an Old Psalm Tune', ibid. 432.
[39] Hardy, 'To Shakespeare', ibid. 439–40.

glory (still less romance) in a war fought with machine-guns, but more absolutely disheartening than these was Hardy's fear that the latest war just could not be borne, not at least in the same way that earlier ones had been. *The Dynasts* had shown people learning doggedness, and had even suggested that the moment of battle could be welcomed because it demanded resolve, realizing a power latent within individuals and communities. St Paul wrote that 'Suffering breeds endurance, endurance breeds character, character breeds hope' (Rom. 5: 4), and Hardy in *The Dynasts* articulates something roughly similar to this: 'character breeds pity, pity breeds hope' is perhaps the extra stage he introduces. The destructive forces confronting soldiers in the First World War proved too overwhelming, however; the conflict could not breed endurance even if it could be (and was being) endured somehow. At least, Hardy found that he could not 'Hold . . . to braver things' any longer. Out of that dejection arose a different kind of war poetry and, in the post-war years, an impressive desire to help the veterans. Hardy opened his home to Sassoon, Blunden, T. E. Lawrence, and many others, welcoming and discreetly counselling those soldiers in particular whose belief in the possibility of courage had been tested to breaking-point.[40]

[40] Similarly, Hardy responded quickly and generously to requests for help designing war memorials, whether they came from Dorchester or from Dudley. See William W. Morgan, 'Verses Fitted for a Monument: Hardy's Contribution to the Dudley War Memorial', *Thomas Hardy Journal*, 1/1 (Jan. 1985), 25–31.

CHAPTER 3

FROM DARK DEFILE TO GETHSEMANE: RUDYARD KIPLING'S WAR POETRY

DANIEL KARLIN

In 1920 George Saintsbury dedicated *Notes on a Cellar-Book* to Kipling, not as a fellow wine-lover but as 'the best poet and taleteller of his generation'. Of course he didn't need much excuse; wine and verse have a long-standing (or long-staggering) association. But Saintsbury gave his genial literary compliment a polemical edge. Kipling was not merely 'the best poet and taleteller of his generation', but 'one than whom no living Englishman has done more to foster the spirit that won in 1914–18'.[1] If we remember, however, the less agreeable meaning of 'taleteller', we might think of Kipling's own look in the mirror, in the most anguished of the *Epitaphs of the War*, 'Common Form':

> If any question why we died,
> Tell them, because our fathers lied.[2]

---

[1] George Saintsbury, *Notes on a Cellar-Book* (London: Macmillan, 1920). For Kipling's response, see *The Letters of Rudyard Kipling*, v: *1920–1930*, ed. Thomas Pinney (Basingstoke: Macmillan, 2004), 7 and 22–3.

[2] Rudyard Kipling, *Epitaphs of the War*, in *The Definitive Edition of Rudyard Kipling's Verse* (London: Hodder & Stoughton, 1989), 390. *Epitaphs of the War* was first published in *The Years Between* (1919), with the title *Epitaphs*. The 'Definitive Edition' was first published in 1940; it does not always give the original provenance of poems, and does not consistently follow an order of composition or publication.

Kipling had lost his only son, killed at the Battle of Loos in 1915. Was he one of these lying fathers? As a 'living Englishman' he carried the burden of survival. Saintsbury's tribute suggests that Kipling's whole career had been leading up to '1914–18', and 'Common Form' seems like an acceptance of responsibility, though not for 'the spirit that won'. But perhaps there is a flaw in this teleological design. Perhaps the story is less clear-cut, whether for good or ill; Kipling may be neither the architect of victory nor the spinner of death-dealing lies. The gravitational pull of the Great War draws the preceding fifty years into itself; writings on war itself are doubly likely to be judged in this way, and those of Kipling, who wrote so much about war and over so long a period, are no exception. But the journey whose destination seemed so clear to Saintsbury in 1920 had started from a point at which '1914–18' was not only unforeseen, but unimaginable.

This essay will follow two lines of argument. The first takes account of Kipling's origins as a writer in order to understand his attitude to war, and to trace both the continuities and changes in the way he wrote about it. The second takes issue with Saintsbury's assumption that Kipling's vocation as a writer was instrumental—that he had been engaged, all his life, in a literary form of nation building. I think this is only half the story, and that Kipling's war poetry, in particular, is marked by impulses towards different kinds of truth telling: one voices experience, the other advocates ideas; one sings, the other prophesies in song. The best of Kipling, whether in prose and verse, is the product of a divided self; and the 'two sides to his head' were not always at peace with each other.[3]

I

A scrimmage in a Border Station—
  A canter down some dark defile—
Two thousand pounds of education
  Drops to a ten-rupee jezail—
The Crammer's boast, the Squadron's pride,
Shot like a rabbit in a ride!

---

[3] The phrase comes from 'The Two-Sided Man', a poem whose first stanza formed one of the chapter headings in *Kim*: 'Much I owe to the Lands that grew— | More to the Lives that fed— | But most to Allah Who gave me two | Separate sides to my head' (*Rudyard Kipling's Verse*, 587).

These lines come from 'Arithmetic on the Frontier', published in Kipling's first collection of poems, *Departmental Ditties and Other Verses*, in 1886.[4] Compare them to the following lines from 'The Children', published in 1917:

> That flesh we had nursed from the first in all cleanness was given
> To corruption unveiled and assailed by the malice of Heaven—
> By the heart-shaking jests of Decay where it lolled on the wires—
> To be blanched or gay-painted by fumes—to be cindered by fires—
> To be senselessly tossed and retossed in stale mutilation
> From crater to crater. For this we shall take expiation.
> *But who shall return us our children?*[5]

The contrast between these two poems measures the distance Kipling had travelled in his experience—or better say, since he was never personally in combat, his apprehension—of war. In 1886 he was 21 years old—the same age as 'the Crammer's boast, the Squadron's pride'. In 1917 he was mourning the loss of his son, who was barely 18 when he was killed. 'Arithmetic on the Frontier' makes no mention of parents; 'The Children' makes no mention of school. The German shell which abolished the (more than) 'two thousand pounds of education' invested in John Kipling was, in all likelihood, cheap to manufacture. But in 'The Children' Kipling thinks not of education but of nurture—'That flesh we had nursed'. It is not a matter of public policy but of the most intimate human touch. 'Shot like a rabbit in a ride!' That has bite and lilt, and an apt heartlessness. But in 'The Children' the body takes on a 'heart-shaking' parodic life, 'lolling' and 'gay-painted', as though it were still a child fond of idleness and dressing up. In a final pun it is 'senselessly tossed', both because it is, itself, without sensation, and because its fate is beyond reason. There is no 'arithmetic on the front line'.

The contrast between the two poems extends further. The jaunty knowingness of the earlier one tells us about something more than a young man's ignorance of what it means to father, and lose, a child. It derives from a world-view that had become untenable in 1917, whether one was a parent or not. Towards the end of 'Arithmetic on the Frontier' Kipling adopts the first-person plural, referring to 'our messmates' being killed, as though he were one of the young men concerned; it is on this note that the poem concludes.

> With home-bred hordes the hillsides teem.
> The troopships bring us one by one,
> At vast expense of time and steam,
> To slay Afridis where they run.

---

[4] Kipling, 'Arithmetic on the Frontier', in *Rudyard Kipling's Verse*, 45. The 'Frontier' is the North-West Frontier, between part of British India (now Pakistan) and Afghanistan. A 'jezail' is a long-barrelled Afghan musket.
[5] Kipling, 'The Children', ibid. 523.

> The 'captives of our bow and spear'
> Are cheap, alas! as we are dear.[6]

It may be absurd for an empire to conduct itself like this, but the absurdity itself is a guarantor of imperial status. The tone is rueful, not shocked or scandalized; the speaker has an insider's confidence both that things will continue to be mismanaged and that the troopships will keep coming. In turn, we can imagine readers wryly acknowledging the truth of the observation, but not feeling threatened or moved; to take pleasure in the poem, you have to digest its callousness, make it your own; if it makes you truly indignant, you have misread it. 'The Children', by contrast, is meant to make you feel wretched, and at odds with the order of things that has produced this wretchedness. The loss of a son disaffiliates his parents. At the same time they bear collective responsibility for the very conditions which have caused their anguish. The untroubled 'we' of 'Arithmetic on the Frontier' has suffered an irreconcilable split. 'These were our children who died for our lands,' the poem begins; 'We have only the memory left of their home-treasured sayings and laughter.' But in the following stanzas a different 'we' appears, separated from the children by more than death: 'They believed us and perished for it. Our statecraft, our learning | Delivered them bound to the Pit and alive to the burning.' As we have seen, Kipling reiterated this self-accusation in *Epitaphs of the War*. It was 'common form' for the 'Crammer's boast' to die on the frontier, too, but what made that acceptable has ceased to function. The fathers lie, and are wounded by the terrible reflux of their falsehood.

II

The 'scrimmage in a Border Station' typified war to Kipling's generation. He was born in 1865, in the middle of a century of unparalleled peace—the century between Waterloo and Ypres. During this period the British Army fought no battle on European soil, the first such century since the Middle Ages. In the same period France went through two revolutions (1830 and 1848), a *coup d'état* (1851), invasion and defeat by Prussia (1870), and the blood-bath of the Paris Commune (1871). Of course, conflicts such as the Crimean War (1853–6), the Indian Mutiny (1857), the Afghan and Sudanese campaigns in the 1880s, and above all the Boer War (1899–1902), seemed bloody, protracted, and costly enough at the time, but even the Boer War was not, as Kipling thought, 'a first-class dress-parade for Armageddon'.[7] When Armageddon came, it was on an inconceivably greater

---

[6] The phrase 'Captives of our bow and spear' derives from Jer. 6: 23, which has 'bow and spear' in a passage referring to conquest.

[7] The phrase is attributed to a general in Kipling's 'The Captive' (in *Traffics and Discoveries*, first published in 1904). 'The Song of the Old Guard', subtitled 'Army Reform—After Boer War' (*Rudyard Kipling's Verse*, 313–14) is less optimistic, satirizing the diehard conservatives who cling to privilege and place, and whose dead hand won't slacken its grip 'Till Armageddon break our sleep'.

scale, and it was close to home. What Robert Lowell, in 1965, foresaw as America's imperial future — 'small war on the heels of small | war' — was the reality of Britain's imperial past.[8] (Nor did the small wars demand large forces. At its height the entire Indian Army would barely have filled a week's draft headed for the Somme. There was no conscription, and neither Army nor Navy were 'representative' of society. The generic 'Tommy' of *Barrack-Room Ballads* (1892) is a social derelict; he is not 'working-class' and is indeed despised by all ranks of respectable society; if he is not low in one sense, he is so in another, a 'gentleman-ranker' who has fallen from his social position through crime or debauchery.[9] Only the officers who led this motley crew could claim a recognized social status, an irony of which 'Arithmetic on the Frontier' is acutely conscious.

Military conflict in the outposts of Empire was very much as Kipling describes it in this and a score of other poems and stories: haphazard, intermittent, local. During his time as a reporter, working for the *Civil and Military Gazette* in Lahore and its larger sister paper, the Allahabad *Pioneer*, he heard innumerable anecdotes of such engagements, and was able to record details of speech and behaviour with an immediacy which still strikes home; he became a kind of verse chronicler of different branches of the 'Service', and a spokesman for its habit of mind. But the inwardness of the fiction and poetry from this period which deals with war is not simply a product of diligent, or even imaginative, 'reporting'. It is bound up with his grasp of the mentality of imperial service, which locates honour and authenticity on the frontier, and defines the metropolitan centre in terms of its folly and ignorance. On the Border, you can expect the infallible judgement of your peers; at home, public opinion is swayed by politicians and the press. 'I'll see you in the *Times*', one departing Viceroy says to his successor:

> A quarter-column of eye-searing print,
> A leader once a quarter — then a war;
> The Strand a-bellow through the fog: — 'Defeat!'
> ''Orrible slaughter!'[10]

Yet there is no question of subverting this ritual of misrepresentation; if anything, the opposite is the case: what would be truly disconcerting to the hard-bitten 'proconsul' would be to have his actions reported objectively, in quiet tones, on the streets of a London divested of fog and glamour.

---

[8] Robert Lowell, 'Waking Early Sunday Morning', in *Collected Poems*, ed. Frank Bidart and David Gewinter (London: Faber, 2003), 386. 'I have been on the Border in eight wars, not counting Burma,' says the Sikh narrator of 'A Sahibs' War' (*Traffics and Discoveries*, first published in 1904). 'The first Afghan War; the second Afghan War; two Mahsud Waziri wars (that is four); two Black Mountain wars, if I remember right; the Malakand and the Tirah. I do not count Burma, or some small things'.

[9] Kipling, 'Gentlemen-Rankers', in *Rudyard Kipling's Verse*, 424–5.

[10] Kipling, 'One Viceroy Resigns', ibid. 72. The speaker is Lord Dufferin, who retired as Viceroy in 1888; he is giving the benefit of his wisdom to Lord Lansdowne.

If people buying newspapers in the Strand are ignorant in one way, those making the news by suffering, or inflicting, the "Orrible slaughter' are so in another; but this allows them to speak more than they know, as in the poem's final lines:

> 'What was the end of all the show,
>   Johnnie, Johnnie?'
> Ask my Colonel, for I don't know,
>   Johnnie, my Johnnie, aha!
> We broke a King and we built a road—
> A court-house stands where the Reg'ment goed.
> And the river's clean where the raw blood flowed
>   When the Widow give the party.
>   (*Bugle*: Ta—rara—ra-ra-rara!)[11]

Law and trade, the court-house and the road, encapsulate the imperial mission (Kipling has no time for the Church). Yet the establishment of this new order rests on violence: 'We broke a King'. This may be an imperialist act, but it has its roots in English history, in the Revolution and the beheading of Charles I, and further back still, the 'breaking' of King John and his enforced acceptance of Magna Carta.[12] Not that the agent of this regenerative violence knows anything of its 'end', whether aim or outcome: 'Ask my Colonel, for I don't know'. What he knows is suggested by something else—the something which makes Kipling a poet and not merely a skilled apologist. 'We *broke* a King and we *built* a road' balances destruction of the old authority with creation of the new. But a road is also for marching, for marching away. 'A court-house *stands* where the Reg'ment *goed*': another kind of balance opposes the stable to the mobile, the permanence of Law to the transience of Force. Then comes the third line, which doesn't countenance the neat summing-up of the couplet—'And the river's clean where the raw blood flowed', as though a river could wash its hands of bloodshed. The light from this terrible phrase glares back at the 'court-house', standing not just where the 'Reg'ment goed' but where 'the raw blood flowed'. It returns us to the visceral lines earlier in the poem which evoke with brutal jollity the catering arrangements at the Widow's party:

> 'What did you do for knives and forks,
>   Johnnie, Johnnie?'
> We carries 'em with us wherever we walks,
>   Johnnie, my Johnnie, aha!

---

[11] Kipling, 'The Widow's Party', ibid. 422. The 'Widow' is Queen Victoria.

[12] Kipling's 'The Old Issue' (ibid. 296–8), published on the outbreak of the Boer War in 1899, reminds us that 'All we have of freedom' was gained by violent resistance to monarchical tyranny: 'Lance and torch and tumult, steel and grey-goose wing, | Wrenched it, inch and ell and all, slowly from the King.' Magna Carta is invoked in this poem, as well as the execution of Charles I. See also 'The Reeds at Runnymede' (ibid. 715–16), one of the poems which Kipling contributed to C. R. L. Fletcher's *A History of England* (1911).

> And some was sliced and some was halved,
> And some was crimped and some was carved,
> And some was gutted and some was starved,
> When the Widow give the party.

What, then, of the sound of the bugle, the poem's last 'word' which is not a word? Is it triumphant, melancholy, ironic? It is all these; language can do for music what music cannot do for itself. The bugle's note also blends the two 'voices' in the poem, that of its sophisticated maker and its other-knowing speaker. The first knows about old ballads, and King John, and could tell you what the Colonel thought; the second knows about 'raw blood'.

Many of the poems of *Barrack-Room Ballads* have to manage such conflicting voices. One solution is formal, visible on the page, as in 'The Widow at Windsor' where a parenthesis punctuates, and punctures, each boastful or militant quatrain:

> There's 'er nick on the cavalry 'orses,
>   There's 'er mark on the medical stores—
> An' 'er troopers you'll find with a fair wind be'ind
>   That takes us to various wars.
>   (Poor beggars!—barbarious wars!)
> .   .   .   .
> We 'ave 'eard o' the Widow at Windsor,
>   It's safest to leave 'er alone:
> For 'er sentries we stand by the sea an' the land
>   Wherever the bugles are blown.
>   (Poor beggars!—an' don't we get blown!)[13]

In other poems this formal poise is absent, and the reader is left to make sense of clashing perspectives. ' "Snarleyow" ' tells the story of a horse-drawn artillery battery moving into position during one of those 'barbarious wars': first the horse of the title, and then one of the artillerymen, the 'Driver's Brother', is mortally wounded. When 'Snarleyow' gets tangled in the limber of the gun, the Driver's Brother pleads for the team to be halted: ' "Pull up, pull up for *Snarleyow*—'is 'ead's between 'is 'eels!" ' But the Driver refuses:

> The Driver 'umped 'is shoulder, for the wheels was goin' round,
> An' there ain't no 'Stop, conductor!' when a batt'ry's changin' ground;
> Sez 'e: 'I broke the beggar in, an' very sad I feels,
> 'But I couldn't pull up, not for *you*—your 'ead between your 'eels!'
>
> 'E 'adn't 'ardly spoke the word, before a droppin' shell
> A little right the batt'ry an' between the sections fell;
> An' when the smoke 'ad cleared away, before the limber-wheels,
> There lay the Driver's Brother with 'is 'ead between 'is 'eels.

[13] Kipling, 'The Widow at Windsor', in *Rudyard Kipling's Verse*, 413–14.

> Then sez the Driver's Brother, an' 'is words was very plain,
> 'For Gawd's own sake get over me, an' put me out o' pain.'
> They saw 'is wounds was mortial, an' they judged that it was best,
> So they took an' drove the limber straight across 'is back an' chest.[14]

The wounding of 'Snarleyow' and that of the Driver's Brother are analogous—the parallelism of the gruesome phrase "is 'ead between 'is 'eels' makes that clear. Yet the Driver's Brother first begs the Driver to 'pull up', and then to drive on; to show the wounded animal mercy by not finishing him off, and to mercifully finish off the wounded man. Concerning the horse the Driver is implacable: though he himself 'broke the beggar in', now that the horse is literally broken ('almost tore in two'), he shrugs all sentiment away. But he behaves differently with his brother. To begin with, his responsibility is shared with other members of the gun team: '*They* saw 'is wounds was mortial, an' *they* judged that it was best', not *He saw . . . he judged*; and the implication must be that, had his wounds not been 'mortial', *they* might have judged differently. But then what? Logically the Driver should fulfil his statement of ruthless intent—'I couldn't pull up, not for *you*'—by driving over his brother's body, not in mercy but in pursuance of his duty. Does Kipling let him off the hook? The poem's last two quatrains deepen the problem rather than resolve it:

> The Driver 'e give nothin' 'cept a little coughin' grunt,
> But 'e swung 'is 'orses 'andsome when it came to 'Action Front!'
> An' if one wheel was juicy, you may lay your Monday head
> 'Twas juicier for the niggers when the case begun to spread.
>
> The moril of this story, it is plainly to be seen:
> You 'aven't got no families when servin' of the Queen—
> You 'avent got no brothers, fathers, sisters, wives, or sons—
> If you want to win your battles take an' work your bloomin' guns![15]

These two stanzas seem at odds. In the first, the Driver does his job better for the horror of what happened to his brother; his 'little coughin' grunt' is both an expression of self-control and an intimation of vengeful rage. The word 'coughin' ' looks forward via its homophone 'coffin' to the 'case' which the Driver will unleash on the 'niggers' (who have themselves been linguistically degraded; they were 'a native army-core [corps]' earlier). In the economy of the poem the Driver keeps in his emotions in one form in order to 'spread' them in another. The second stanza, however, knows nothing of this; it proposes an absolute disavowal of human family ties, let alone those which relate us to animals. (Snarleyow, who gives his name to the poem, disappears from it half-way through.) 'Bloomin' ' is a euphemism for 'bloody', so the phrase 'bloomin' guns' may remind us of the wheel which is literally

---

[14] Kipling, ' "Snarleyow" ', ibid. 412–13.
[15] Ibid. 413. 'Monday head' suggests a hangover after the weekend's drinking (cf. 'Monday mice', a euphemism for black eyes). 'Case' ('case-shot') is a form of ammunition used against infantry, in which bullets loaded into a metal canister spread on impact.

bloody, 'juicy' with the Driver's Brother's blood; but then we are exhorted not to care about this one way or the other. The 'moril' is anything but 'plainly to be seen'; it shifts, depending on our standpoint in the poem.

In *Barrack-Room Ballads* such ambivalence is inseparable from the evocation of war in all its particularity and complicatedness; but it does not extend to the causes, or ideals, or political calculations, which lie behind the 'barbarious wars'. These 'larger' issues are taken for granted, or simply ignored. In 'Fuzzy-Wuzzy' the origins of the war in the Sudan against Muslim rebel tribes led by the Mahdi are summed up in one line: 'Our orders was to break you, an' of course we went an' did.' The speaker is more interested in paying his rollicking tribute to the fact that the Sudanese dervishes had done some breaking of their own:

> Then 'ere's *to* you, Fuzzy-Wuzzy, an' the missis an' the kid;
> Our orders was to break you, an' of course we went an' did.
> We sloshed you with Martinis, an' it wasn't 'ardly fair;
> But for all the odds agin' you, Fuzzy-Wuz, you broke the square.[16]

The 'square'—the famous infantry formation against which Ney's cavalry had foundered at Waterloo—may be symbolic of order, of British courage and discipline, but it is not reducible to a symbol (and it is not courage which triumphs, but superior fire-power). For the speaker it is less a national-historical matter than one of professional pride (or chagrin); to put it another way, thoughts of Waterloo are at the reader's discretion, and are not enforced by the poem's rhetoric. The limitation in point of view which Kipling imposed on himself served him well; it made possible the truths of *Barrack-Room Ballads*, which still retain their scandalous, or even (in respect of modern pieties) blasphemous force. The framework for this understanding and voicing of the soldier's mentality cracked with the Boer War and disintegrated in 1914–18.

III

When the Boer War broke out in October 1899, Kipling and his wife Carrie had still not settled in a permanent home; in the month it ended, in June 1902, they bought Bateman's, near Burwash in Sussex, where they remained for the rest of their lives. Although Kipling spent a good deal of time in South Africa during the war, he was no longer a local reporter; his primary focus shifted to England herself,

---

[16] Kipling, 'Fuzzy-Wuzzy', ibid. 401; the 'square' was breached at the Battle of Tamanieb, 13 Mar. 1884. 'Martinis' are Martini-Henry rifles; their proximity with 'sloshed' makes the line a bit ludicrous today, but Kipling had probably not come across the cocktail (the first *OED* citation is 1897), and could not foresee that 'sloshed' would come to mean 'drunk' (first citation 1946); he is using it as a euphemism for 'slaughtered'.

the war's effect on her people, above all the political and moral lessons to be drawn both from the disastrous beginning of the conflict and its sobering resolution.

England as a nation struck Kipling as unprepared, and indeed unfit, for war. Even a poem such as 'The Absent-Minded Beggar', written to support a charitable appeal for relief of soldiers' families, opens with a scornful dig at the people who are being asked to stump up:

> When you've shouted 'Rule Britannia', when you've sung 'God Save the Queen',
>   When you've finished killing Kruger with your mouth,
> Will you kindly drop a shilling in my little tambourine
>   For a gentleman in khaki ordered South?[17]

The internal rhyme between 'killing' and 'shilling' is apt because the 'shilling' is such a military coin (recruits 'take the Queen's shilling'; 'Shillin' a Day' is the title of a Barrack-Room Ballad about the miserly military pension); the civilians who are aping military valour are challenged to put their money where their mouth is. There was too much mouth about the business for Kipling's liking, too much national complacency and boasting; he pointed the moral by a deliberate anachronism, placing 'Recessional', the warning poem he had written for Queen Victoria's Diamond Jubilee in 1897, at the end of his Boer War 'Service Songs'.[18] 'England' viewed from India or Burma might be exasperatingly feckless in its conduct of the Empire, but that very quality was part of its charm; in England itself the charm was broken, or rather had to be conjured anew, using the spell not of distance but of proximity. That helps to explain Kipling's concentration, in the period following the Boer War, on stories and poems about England and the English, epitomized by *Puck of Pook's Hill* (1906) and *Rewards and Fairies* (1910). But this effort at 'rebuilding' England was only partially successful; the psychic wound which Kipling suffered in the Boer War was healed, but as often with old wounds, never quite lost its ache.

Many of the Boer War poems are therefore 'condition-of-England' poems as much as they are poems about the events and experiences of the war itself. Or rather, Kipling uses these events and experiences as a lens through which 'England' is seen and judged by the soldiers, who in earlier poems would have taken metropolitan inefficiency and mismanagement in their marching stride. 'Chant-Pagan', the opening poem of 'Service Songs', announces this theme:

> Me that 'ave been what I've been,
> Me that 'ave gone where I've gone,

---

[17] Kipling, 'The Absent-Minded Beggar', ibid. 459.

[18] 'Recessional' kept this position in the 3-vol. *Poems 1886–1929*, the last collected edition published in Kipling's lifetime; in the *Definitive Edition* the poem shifted forward in time again, appearing on pp. 328–9 between 'The Question' (1916) and 'For All We Have and Are' (1914). 'Service Songs' was not published as a separate volume, but appeared as a section of *The Five Nations* (1903), which also includes other poems relating to the Boer War.

> Me that 'ave seen what I've seen—
>   'Ow can I ever take on
> With awful old England again,
> An' 'ouses both sides of the street,
> And 'edges both sides of the lane,
> And the parson an' gentry between,
> An' touchin' my 'at when we meet—
>   Me that 'ave been what I've been?
> Me that 'ave watched 'arf a world
> 'Eave up all shiny with dew,
> Kopje on kop to the sun,
> An' as soon as the mist let 'em through
> Our 'elios winkin' like fun—
> Three sides of a ninety-mile square,
> Over valleys as big as a shire—
> *'Are ye there? Are ye there? Are ye there?'*
> An' then the blind drum of our fire . . .
> An' I'm rollin' 'is lawns for the Squire,
>   Me![19]

The sublime is here pressed into service against the servility of 'awful old England'. The man who has risen to the height of 'Kopje on kop' sinks back in the social scale; his pained exclamation, ''Ow', is absorbed into ''ouses', and muffled; 'three sides of a ninety mile square' have shrunk to those sharp-edged ''edges both sides of the lane'. 'Both sides' plays against 'three sides'; England's boundaries close in on you, while in South Africa vistas are possible.

As a work of social criticism in verse, 'Chant-Pagan' is artfully done, but as a poem it is lessened by that very quality. A small slip—one that Kipling would not have committed in *Barrack-Room Ballads*—has the speaker wobbling in lines 6–9 between 'An'' and 'And', as though his register were shifting between demotic and educated. There is social criticism in *Barrack-Room Ballads* too, but it comes naturally to the speakers and stays in character; in 'Chant-Pagan' Kipling is too eager to prompt. Poetry becomes a platform for exhortation, and the expression—however passionate, however witty—of opinions rather than feelings. Even in the poems of 'Service Songs' which strive to be most like the old *Barrack-Room Ballads*, this deflection of imaginative sympathy into salesmanship is evident. 'The Parting of the Columns' wants to convey the message of imperial solidarity between the 'rank an' file' of Britain and her dominions, and succeeds only in an embarrassingly unconvincing ventriloquism:

> We've seen your 'ome by word o' mouth, we've watched your rivers shine,
> We've 'eard your bloomin' forests blow of eucalyp' and pine;
> Your young, gay countries north and south, we feel we own 'em too,
> For they was made by rank an' file. Good bye—good luck to you!

---

[19] Kipling, 'Chant-Pagan', in *Rudyard Kipling's Verse*, 461.

> We'll never read the papers now without inquirin' first
> For word from all those friendly dorps where you was born an' nursed.
> Why, Dawson, Galle, an' Montreal—Port Darwin—Timaru,
> They're only just across the road! Good-bye—good luck to you![20]

The same slight inconsistency as in 'Chant-Pagan'—'north and south', 'rank an' file'—suggests a larger uncertainty, as though Kipling had lost faith in his gift, not for 'word o' mouth' but for words from the horse's mouth. But he still had the gift; it is there in 'Lichtenberg', where the smell of wattle brings 'all Australia' to a horseman from New South Wales:

> There was some silly fire on the flank
>   And the small wet drizzling down—
> There were the sold-out shops and the bank
>   And the wet, wide-open town;
> *And* we were doing escort-duty
>   To somebody's baggage-train,
> And I smelt wattle by Lichtenberg,
>   Riding in, in the rain.
>
>   .   .   .   .   .   .
>
> And I saw Sydney the same as ever,
>   The picnics and brass-bands;
> And my little homestead on Hunter River
>   And my new vines joining hands.
> It all came over me in one act
>   Quick as a shot through the brain—
> With the smell of the wattle round Lichtenberg,
>   Riding in, in the rain.[21]

'Fire' in line 1 is both the opposite of 'wet' in line 2, yet a different thing; a *silly* thing, too, as irritating as a drizzle, yet perfectly capable of killing you—'Quick as a shot through the brain'—rather than just making you wet and uncomfortable. And the small word 'And' is beautifully deployed in the two stanzas: first to suggest how the monotony and drudgery which are intrinsic to war can be suddenly, magically undone (they were firing at us, and it was raining, and the town was just like all other towns, *and* we were bored stiff—and I smelt wattle . . .); and then the beautiful linking together of memory in which *and* joins the scenes like the 'new vines joining hands'.

---

[20] Kipling, 'The Parting of the Columns', ibid. 469–70. A 'dorp' is a (South African) Dutch word for a village or small town.

[21] Kipling, 'Lichtenberg', ibid. 476. The 'small wet drizzling down' may have been suggested by the medieval lyric 'Westron wynde', 'Westron wynde when wyll thow blow, | The small rayne downe can rayne— | Cryst, yf my love wer in my armys | And I in my bed agayne!' (this text from Christopher Ricks (ed.), *The Oxford Book of English Verse* (Oxford: Oxford University Press, 1999), 14). Kipling's poem has erotic longing as well as longing for homeland; the last three lines have the exclamation 'Ah, Christ!' and rhyme 'again' with 'rain'.

The struggle in Kipling's Boer War poems between an inwardness of feeling which produces (as though spontaneously) images of authentic experience, and the desire to bully or jolly 'public opinion' into adopting a particular point of view, is complicated by Kipling's attitude to the Boers themselves. Unlike every other colonial war of the nineteenth century, the Boer War was, as the title of one of the stories in *Traffics and Discoveries* puts it, 'A Sahibs' War': that is, a war between white men. There are Kipling stories which take seriously the interplay of racial politics and economic interests in different parts of South Africa, from British-ruled Natal, the Cape Colony with its population of doubtfully loyal Afrikaners, to the Boer republics of the Transvaal and the Orange Free State; but there are also poems in which these issues dissolve into the simplified figure of the Boer farmer and fighter, who had taught England her lesson, but with whom the English soldier could fraternize and be reconciled after the war (the speaker of 'Chant-Pagan' intends to leave 'awful old England', and return to South Africa to work for his former enemy). In 'Piet' a soldier voices respect for the fighting qualities of his enemy, as had the speaker of 'Fuzzy-Wuzzy'; but where racial difference in the earlier poem is integral to its convincing us that an English soldier would indeed feel and speak as he does (in other words, that the respect being shown is truthful), in the later poem racial kinship has the opposite effect, blighting the poem's atmosphere and making the feeling sound confected and false:

> I've 'eard 'im cryin' from the ground
>   Like Abel's blood of old,
> An' skirmished out to look, an' found
>   The beggar nearly cold.
> I've waited on till 'e was dead
>   (Which couldn't 'elp 'im much),
> But many grateful things 'e's said
>   To me for doin' such.[22]

If the dying Boer is Abel, then the Englishman who has slain his brother is Cain; yet it is God, not Cain, who hears the voice of Abel's blood crying from the ground.[23] In this strange version, God-like Cain goes looking for Abel, and finds him, and behaves indeed as his brother's keeper, and receives his brother's blessing for doing it. The speaker of 'Fuzzy-Wuzzy' is more cynical and succinct about his fallen foe: ''E's generally shammin' when 'e's dead.' There seems to be no question that 'Piet' might be 'shammin'', though the treachery, or trickery, of the Boers is a constant theme of other poems and stories. Kipling is in a muddle here; the Great War cleared up the muddle, but brought something worse in its place.

---

[22] Kipling, 'Piet', in *Rudyard Kipling's Verse*, 480.

[23] Gen. 4: 9–10: 'And the Lord said unto Cain, Where is Abel thy brother? And he said, I know not: Am I my brother's keeper? And he said, What hast thou done? the voice of thy brother's blood crieth out to me from the ground.'

IV

....

'Piet' opens with a sentiment which Kipling was to disavow a decade later:

> I do not love my Empire's foes,
>   Nor call 'em angels; still,
> What *is* the sense of 'atin' those
>   'Oom you are paid to kill?

This temperate outlook belongs, as the poem's subtitle tells us, to a 'Regular of the Line'; in 1914 this 'Regular' would have been serving in the 'Army of Mercenaries' which in 1914–15, as A. E. Housman put it, 'saved the sum of things for pay'.[24] The thousands of men (John Kipling among them) who volunteered in this period joined what was still thought of as a professional fighting force; but already the face of war was changing, and in January 1916 it altered decisively with the advent of conscription. The struggle between an 'Empire' and its 'foes' was replaced, in Kipling's eyes, by a death struggle between civilization and barbarism. In this light, the lack of preparedness, the conservatism, and the sloth which had angered him at the time of the Boer War took on a different dimension, as did the guilt and shame of those who had colluded in the sacrifice of 'The Children'. The poems of the Boer War are marked by an impulse to make speeches in the voices of soldiers, rather than voicing soldiers' speech, and the Great War exacerbated this impulse; at the same time, the relationship between those fighting the war and those responsible for it (responsible for its conduct, but also for its having come about in the first place) appears poisoned beyond remedy. 'War poetry' now had to bear the strain of a judgement which turned outward towards a 'foe' defined in new terms, as absolute evil, and inward towards the 'fathers' who had temporized with that foe and mistaken it for human.

It makes sense to hate the Germans, as opposed to the 'Empire's foes', because they are beyond the pale of human fellowship. The feeling is specific to Germany, and does not apply to her allies. 'One of the reasons . . . why we shall be good friends with the Turk again is that he has many of our ideas about decency,'[25] Kipling remarks in *Sea Warfare*. The remark is prompted by a description of how the crew of a submarine operating in the Sea of Marmara relish the opportunity to wash

---

[24] A. E. Housman, 'Epitaph on an Army of Mercenaries', in *Collected Poems and Selected Prose*, ed. Christopher Ricks (Harmondsworth: Penguin, 1988), 138. The poem was first published in *The Times*, 31 Oct. 1917, under a leading article on 'The Anniversary of Ypres'. On 21 Dec. 1935, a month before he died, Kipling wrote of it as 'the high-water mark of all War verse. . . . Only eight lines but absolutely *perfect*' (Kipling to James Barry, in *The Letters of Rudyard Kipling*, vi: *1931–1936*, ed. Thomas Pinney (Basingstoke: Macmillan, 2004), 417).

[25] Kipling, 'Tales of "The Trade" ', in *Sea Warfare* (London: Macmillan, 1916), 126. *Sea Warfare* collected the newspaper articles which Kipling wrote at the behest of the Admiralty in 1915 and 1916, with accompanying poems, including 'Mine Sweepers' (in *Rudyard Kipling's Verse*, 631), ' "Tin Fish" ' (ibid. 648), and 'My Boy Jack' (ibid. 216).

themselves and their clothes; it is connected, not literally but metaphorically, with the comment of a submariner in another section of the book: 'Oh, if Fritz only fought clean, this wouldn't be half a bad show. But Fritz can't fight clean.'[26]

In 'The Beginnings', Kipling claimed that hatred of Germany was both a national and a novel phenomenon:

> It was not part of their blood,
>   It came to them very late
> With long arrears to make good,
>   When the English began to hate.[27]

The rhyme 'blood/good' is not a 'true' rhyme; the English haven't, in the past, had the good of hatred, but they are going to make good that lack; they are going to make 'blood' and 'good' rhyme in earnest. There is little if any objective evidence for this notion, and it is more likely that Kipling was projecting onto his country a feeling he could no longer keep himself from voicing. He could not conceive of a civilized German, let alone feature one in his writing; the word he adopted and made famous, 'Hun', is like a savage amputation of 'human'.[28] There can be no respect, and no mercy, for the German as enemy; there are no poems which record the valour, endurance, or suffering of German soldiers, no genial tribute to 'Fritz' or hope of sharing a stein of beer with him after the War is over.

Kipling's hatred, in its purity and absolutism, was inimical to large strategic or political aims, since these always involve an element of compromise, more or less ignoble. The politicians who negotiated the Armistice believed that Britain's national interest would best be served by weakening Germany but not annihilating her; Kipling took the opposite view. Again, the contrast with the Boer War is revealing. In 'Piet' there is an indulgent recognition of the cleverness of the Boers in getting their conquerors to put them back on their feet as part of the peace settlement:

> Ah, there, Piet! with your brand-new English plough,
>   Your gratis tents an' cattle, an' your most ungrateful frow,

[26] Kipling, 'The Fringes of the Fleet', in *Sea Warfare*, 59.

[27] Kipling, 'The Beginnings', in *Rudyard Kipling's Verse*, 673. The poem was first published with Kipling's most hate-filled (if not hateful) story, 'Mary Postgate', in *A Diversity of Creatures* (1917); when the poem was separately reprinted after the War, in *Poems 1886–1929*, it was, like 'The Children', given the misleading subtitle '1914–18'.

[28] The Germans had only themselves to blame for 'Hun'; the *OED* cites Kaiser Wilhelm II's speech to German troops being sent to China, exhorting them to behave as mercilessly as Huns (speech reported in *The Times*, 30 July 1900). In 1902 Kipling denounced the proposal that Britain should join Germany in a naval blockade of Venezuela, in a poem whose concluding lines reject an alliance 'With the Goth and the shameless Hun!' ('The Rowers', in *Rudyard Kipling's Verse*, 284). In the context of the Great War, he first used the word in 'For All We Have and Are', published in *The Times*, 2 Sep. 1914: 'Stand up and take the war. | The Hun is at the gate!' (in *Rudyard Kipling's Verse*, 329).

You've made the British taxpayer rebuild your country-seat—
I've known some pet battalions charge a dam' sight less than Piet.[29]

The pun on *charge* maliciously reflects on the less-than-zealous performance of some self-regarding Army units; 'pet' falls short of 'Piet', so the Boers get the best of it in both peace and war. Such concessions are unimaginable in Kipling's writings about the Great War. The spirit of unreconciled hatred is embodied in 'Justice', a poem written shortly before the Armistice, in October 1918. The justice Kipling claims is a kind of wild revenge, going beyond the 'normal' bounds of retribution, proposing the annihilation of the German polity:

> That neither schools nor priests,
>   Nor Kings may build again
> A people with the heart of beasts
>   Made wise concerning men.
> Whereby our dead shall sleep
>   In honour, unbetrayed,
> And we in faith and honour keep
>   That peace for which they paid.[30]

As with 'Piet', there is a pun in the last line about money, but the humour of it is sour. 'That peace for which they paid' means 'that peace which our dead bought with their lives', but it also means 'that peace for which they, the Germans, paid'. Kipling has in mind more than crushing war reparations that would prevent Germany physically from rebuilding her strength. In a letter written four days before the Armistice, he glossed the lines 'A people with the heart of beasts | Made wise concerning men' as

a people with such an outlook on life as would be possessed by animals who had been laboriously instructed in the baser side of humanity and also the higher—a sort of were-wolf people in fact. (And it's curious that out of the Hun country comes the best and fullest story of the were-wolf who disguises itself as man or woman. . . . Every race betrays itself in its legends, don't you think?)[31]

Such a people must not be allowed normal human institutions—education, religion, authority—because these would foster an unnatural '[wisdom] concerning men', which the 'beast' would take advantage of when the time came round again.

This view of Germany is axiomatic in Kipling's public poetry of the War; it licenses both the minatory tone of 'For All We Have and Are', with its denunciation

---

[29] Kipling, 'Piet', 481. '[F]row' is the German 'Frau', i.e. wife.
[30] Kipling, 'Justice', in *Rudyard Kipling's Verse*, 394.
[31] Kipling to John Powell, 7 Nov. 1918, in *The Letters of Rudyard Kipling*, iv: *1911–1919*, ed. Thomas Pinney (Basingstoke: Macmillan, 1999), 519. The image of Germany as the 'were-wolf' recurs in many letters of the 1920s and 1930s as Kipling raged against German reconstruction and rearmament. The phrase 'who disguises itself' is a 'Freudian' slip, leaving the werewolf grammatically suspended between human and non-human identity.

of the 'crazed and driven foe', and the vengeful widow's pleasure at manufacturing artillery shells in 'The Song of the Lathes' ('Shells for guns in Flanders! Feed the guns!').[32] It vitiates even some of the *Epitaphs of the War*, particularly those dealing with women.[33] Indeed, the best of the *Epitaphs* avoid speaking of the enemy altogether, or only in the most neutral terms; what happens to 'The Beginner' does not happen because the enemy is evil, but simply because he is there:

> On the first hour of my first day
> In the front trench I fell.
> (Children in boxes at a play
> Stand up to watch it well.)[34]

The wit of the parallel is not adverse to its pathos, but is the very condition of it. But Kipling can be heartless too; he makes 'The Sleepy Sentinel' pick his way through an intricate pattern of rhyme and word-play, as though to remind him of his lack of alertness:

> Faithless the watch that I kept: now I have none to keep.
> I was slain because I slept: now I am slain I sleep.
> Let no man reproach me again, whatever watch is unkept—
> I sleep because I am slain. They slew me because I slept.[35]

'They slew me' carries no special animus; the poem is quite properly absorbed by its reflexive dance, and doesn't waste its energy implying that it was somehow wicked of the Germans to take advantage of the sentinel's carelessness. Indeed, with these poems the heretical thought occurs that they are not denominated as 'English' at all.

> My son was killed while laughing at some jest. I would I knew
> What it was, and it might serve me in a time when jests are few.

The father who stumbles so forlornly along the path of the old 'fourteener' is English by right of rhythm, but not of feeling. 'The Coward', 'The Refined Man', the victim of 'Shock'—none of these, from within the words he is given, disavows his counterpart on the other side of the trenches. Is ' "Tin Fish" ', the briefest and most fearful of the War poems outside the *Epitaphs*, the boast of 'us' or 'them'?

> The ships destroy us above
> And ensnare us beneath.
> We arise, we lie down, and we move
> In the belly of Death.

---

[32] Kipling, 'For All We Have and Are' and 'Song of the Lathes', in *Rudyard Kipling's Verse*, 330 and 310.

[33] See e.g. 'Raped and Revenged' (ibid. 391), in which the 'used and butchered' woman expresses satisfaction that 100 lives have been taken for her one. 'V. A. D. (Mediterranean)', which, until *Poems 1886–1929*, was the concluding poem of the *Epitaphs*, has a similar theme: the nurse's death is avenged by the sinking of 'certain keels for whose return the heathen look in vain' (ibid. 392).

[34] Kipling, 'The Beginner', ibid. 389.   [35] Kipling, 'The Sleepy Sentinel', ibid. 389.

> The ships have a thousand eyes
>   To mark where we come . . .
> But the mirth of a seaport dies
>   When our blow gets home.[36]

I think the ellipsis is the track of a torpedo through the water; certainly Kipling never made a grimmer play on words than the phrase 'gets home', which is just what the drowned sailors will never do. But the seaport might be Portsmouth or Cherbourg as much as Hamburg or Rostock.

I do not mean that such poems are colourless; they are not the conception of a neutral, but of an embattled and tormented Englishman; they breathe their Englishness in form and diction. But they do not—cannot, in their very integrity—deny that they might be transposed, translated. 'Gethsemane', to take a last example, is bred-in-the-bone English, drawing its name magic from the English Bible, its lilt from a ballad tradition going back 500 years, its word-play from a poem by Christina Rossetti; you couldn't substitute 'German' for 'English' in the fourth line without doing violence to the poem (not to mention that the Germans would not have been welcomed by pretty girls in Picardy); even the observation of social difference has a native English ring.[37] Yet despite all this—through it all—the poem is not one-sided, does not hug its suffering to its national self. Beside it, poems like 'Justice' or 'The Beginnings' seem pinched and thin, linguistically and spiritually malnourished:

> The Garden called Gethsemane
>   In Picardy it was,
> And there the people came to see
>   The English soldiers pass.
> We used to pass—we used to pass
>   Or halt, as it might be,
> And ship our masks in case of gas
>   Beyond Gethsemane.
>
> The Garden called Gethsemane,
>   It held a pretty lass,

---

[36] Kipling, ' "Tin Fish" ', 648.

[37] Kipling, 'Gethsemane', ibid. 98; 1st pub. in *Twenty Poems by Rudyard Kipling* (1918). It is oddly placed in the *Definitive Edition*, coming between two unrelated (and jarring) pieces, 'The Broken Men' (1902, about genteel bankrupts fleeing abroad) and 'The Song of the Banjo' (1894). Jesus prays in Gethsemane: 'O my Father, if it be possible, let this cup pass from me' (Matt. 26: 39); Kipling's tact suppresses the remainder of the verse—'nevertheless not as I will, but as thou wilt'—which would sound false in the speaker's mouth. Christina Rossetti's 'May' begins, 'I cannot tell you how it was; | But this I know: it came to pass— | Upon a bright and breezy day | When May was young, ah pleasant May!', followed by this mournful turn: 'I cannot tell you how it was; | But this I know: it did but pass. | It passed away with sunny May, | With all sweet things it passed away, | And left me old, and cold, and grey' (in *The Complete Poems of Christina Rossetti*, ed. R. W. Crump, 3 vols. (Baton Rouge, La.: Louisiana State University Press, 1979), i. 51).

But all the time she talked to me
    I prayed my cup might pass.
The officer sat on the chair,
    The men lay on the grass,
And all the time we halted there
    I prayed my cup might pass.

It didn't pass—it didn't pass—
    It didn't pass from me.
I drank it when we met the gas
    Beyond Gethsemane!

Beyond Gethsemane lies Calvary. He is English, this soldier-Christ; but no man, and no nation, claims exclusivity in the Crucifixion. Kipling's art reaches beyond its author's grasp, implying the fellowship his hating soul repudiated. This greatest of all Kipling's poems of the War casts a German, because a human, shadow.

PART II

THE GREAT WAR

CHAPTER 4

WAR POETRY AND THE REALM OF THE SENSES: OWEN AND ROSENBERG

SANTANU DAS

In 'The Storyteller', Walter Benjamin observes the strange phenomenon that the soldiers returned from the First World War have grown silent—'not richer, but poorer in communicable experience'—unable to articulate the 'truth of war' with any more coherence or force than Owen's soldier could utter the lie.[1] This was often literally the case as one of the most common symptoms of shell-shock (or neurasthenia, as it was then known) was mutism. Along with nightmares, tremors, and mutism, the war issues of the British medical journal *The Lancet* reported cases of blindness and deafness, resulting from what the eyes and ears had witnessed.[2] A month before his death, Wilfred Owen wrote to Siegfried Sassoon about his servant Jones, 'shot through the head, [who] lay on top of me, soaking my shoulder, for half

---

[1] Walter Benjamin, 'The Storyteller', in *Illuminations*, trans. Harry Zohn, ed. Hannah Arendt (London: Jonathan Cape, 1970), 84.

[2] See F. W. Mott, 'The Effects of High Explosives upon the Central Nervous System', *The Lancet*, 12 and 26 Feb., 11 Mar. 1916, 331–8, 441–9, 545–53; and the anonymously authored 'Neurasthenia and Shell Shock', *The Lancet*, 18 Mar. 1916, 627. For recent discussion of 'shell-shock', see Ben Shephard, *A War of Nerves* (London: Jonathan Cape, 2000).

an hour'. He goes on to elaborate: 'Catalogue? Photograph? Can you photograph the crimson-hot iron as it cools from the smelting? This is what Jones's blood looked like, and felt like. My senses are charred.'[3] Owen here struggles with the paradoxical notion of sense experience: on the one hand, it is intensely private and stubbornly resists translation, and on the other hand, for it to be shared and communicated, it has to create a retrospective narrative. In order to evoke the judder of the moment, he has recourse here to certain literary devices: images, alliteration, and metaphor. The process carries historical traces too: the word 'crimson' points to the world of *fin-de-siècle* literature as one decadent aesthete writes to another, both well versed in Wilde and Swinburne. Owen at once invokes and throws away the allusion to photography, showing his essential difference from his 'visually submissive' friend and mentor; instead, it is the imagined bodily contact with the 'crimson-hot iron' that for him captures the moment, bringing in its wake the phrase 'My senses are charred'. What does Owen mean here, and what implications does it have for poetry which not only partakes in the realm of the senses but aims to produce, as one of its most influential Romantic practitioners noted, 'excitement in co-existence with an over-balance of pleasure'?[4]

If the shadow of John Keats looms over much trench poetry, his craving for a 'life of Sensations rather than of Thoughts'[5] seems to have achieved its perverse validation in the world of the trenches. 'Our youth', recalled Robert Graves, 'became all-flesh and waived the mind.'[6] The trench experience was one of the most sustained and systematic shattering of the human sensorium: it stripped man of the protective layers of civilization and thrust his naked, fragile body between the ravages of industrial modernity, on the one hand, and the chaos of formless matter, on the other. Consider the following two extracts from the Imperial War Museum archives, suggesting the range of sensory devastation:

The shell came and killed the chap on my left & wounded the other on my right & it blew up [?] overhead. It shook me up terrible & we had orders to run in twos to the finished dugout. So we went & as I went round the corner I put my hands in poor G. Kentish brains. I may add that his head was completely off his body. As we arrived at the dugout another shell came over & killed 2 Lon [?] Irish Rifles.[7]

Now the mud at Passchendaele was very viscous indeed, very tenacious, it stuck to you. Your puttees were solid mud anyway. When you took your puttees off you scraped them and hoped for the best . . . . It got into the bottom of your trousers, you were covered with

[3] Wilfred Owen to Siegfried Sassoon, 10 Oct. 1918, in Wilfred Owen, *Collected Letters*, ed. Harold Owen and John Bell (London: Oxford University Press, 1967), 581.

[4] William Wordsworth, 'Preface to *Lyrical Ballads*' (1802), in *William Wordsworth*, ed. Stephen Gill (Oxford: Oxford University Press, 1984), 609.

[5] John Keats to Benjamin Bailey, 22 Nov. 1817, in *The Letters of John Keats*, ed. Robert Gittings (Oxford: Oxford University Press, 1970), 37.

[6] Robert Graves, 'Recalling War', in *The Complete Poems of Robert Graves*, ed. Beryl Graves and Dunstan Ward (London: Penguin, 2003), 359.

[7] C. T. Abbot, entry for war diary, 29 June 1917, Imperial War Museum, 83/31/1.

mud. The mud there wasn't liquid, it wasn't porridge, it was a curious kind of sucking kind of mud. When you got off this track with your load, it 'drew' at you, not like quicksand, but a real monster that sucked at you.[8]

What was traumatically modern about the war, as is evident from the first extract, was its mechanized nature: the triumph of material over men, the invisibility of the enemy and randomness of death. The conjunction of underground trench warfare and industrial weaponry severed the link between space, vision, and danger which has been used to structure perception in conventional warfare: life now depended on the arbitrary direction of a shell, robbing the soldiers of any sense of agency or purpose. Arthur Graeme West describes the front line soldiers cooped up in their subterranean 'funk-holes' as 'hens in cages', 'shivering a little as a shell draws near'.[9] If Tennyson's 'The Charge of the Light Brigade', with its combination of chivalry, motion, and spectacle, underpinned notions of warfare for a particular class, the soldiers soon realized that they were not, as Brooke had envisaged, 'swimmers into cleanness leaping' but rather, as Wyndham Lewis noted, 'houseflies on a section of flypaper'.[10] The constant barrage by the artillery tore up the Western Front, and combined with rain, turned it into a giant cesspool amidst which the soldiers stood, floundered, and occasionally even drowned. Owen refers to 'an octopus of sucking clay'.[11] But there lay a deeper anxiety that the second extract hints at: the world might not only regress into primordial slime, but might actually draw man into its glutinous ooze.

The absence of vision is a source of bewilderment in war writings. Burgoyne in his war diaries describes the trenches as 'dark as Hades and wet'.[12] In *The First Hundred Thousand* (1915), Ian Hay notes, 'The day's work in the trenches begins about nine o'clock the night before'; Ferdinand Céline corroborates: 'Everything that's important goes on in the darkness.'[13] As I have argued elsewhere, the visual topography of everyday life was replaced by the haptic geography of the trenches: in the dark, subterranean world of the Western Front, men navigated space not through reassuring distance of the gaze but through the tactile immediacy of their bodies.[14] *Creep, crawl, burrow, worm* are regular verbs in trench narratives,

---

[8] J. Dillon, Imperial War Museum Sound Archives, AC4078.

[9] Arthur Graeme West, *The Diary of a Dead Officer* (London: Allen & Unwin, 1919), 67.

[10] Rupert Brooke, 'Peace', in *The Poetical Works of Rupert Brooke*, ed. Geoffrey Keynes (London: Faber, 1960), 19; Wyndham Lewis, *Blasting and Bombardiering: An Autobiography (1914–16)* (London: John Calder, 1982; 1st pub. 1937), 161.

[11] Owen to Susan Owen, 16 Jan. 1917, in *Collected Letters*, 427.

[12] Gerald Achilles Burgoyne, *The Burgoyne Diaries*, ed. Claudia Davidson (London: Thomas Harmsworth, 1985), 10.

[13] Ian Hay, *The First Hundred Thousand: Being the Unofficial Chronicle of a Unit of 'K 910'* (London: William Blackwood, 1915), 245; Ferdinand Céline, *Journey to the End of the Night*, trans. Ralph Manheim (London: John Calder, 1988; 1st pub. 1932), 62.

[14] I have argued this point at length in my book *Touch and Intimacy in First World War Literature* (Cambridge: Cambridge University Press, 2005). I have drawn on some common material here.

suggesting the shift from the visual to the tactile. After three weeks at the Front, Owen writes to his mother, 'I have not seen any dead. I have done worse. In the dank air, I have *perceived* it, and in the darkness, *felt*' (Owen's emphases).[15] Touch, for Owen, becomes the ground of both testimony and trauma. Eric Leed in his study *No Man's Land: Combat and Identity in World War I* (1979) has explored the changes in the perceptual processes of the soldiers resulting from 'war in the labyrinth', focusing on the exaggerated role of sound and how it broke down rational structures of thought.[16] 'You couldn't; you can't communicate noise,' noted Robert Graves in an interview; 'Noise never stopped for one moment—ever'; and we have Sassoon's soldier 'going stark, staring mad because of the guns'.[17]

Darkness, guns, mud, rain, gas, bullets, shells, barbed wire, rats, lice, cold, trench foot: these images which have formed the 'modern memory' of the war are largely culled from the trench poetry of Owen, Sassoon, Graves, and Rosenberg—to name only a few—just as discussions of war poetry have tended to be assimilated into a historical doctrine expressing the 'truth of war'. Indeed, Owen, in his famous preface, actively sought this conflation. Consequently, historical and literary narratives often become interchangeable, as if war poetry was the transparent envelope of sense experience: the seared senses of the war-torn soldier which become the most powerful form of testimony, altering the very meaning of the term 'war poetry' in the twentieth century. Consider 'A Working Party', 'written while in the Front Line during my first tour of trenches'[18] on 30 March 1917:

> Three hours ago he blundered up the trench,
> Sliding and poising, groping with his boots;
> Sometimes he tripped and lurched against the wall
> With hands that pawed the sodden bags of chalk.
> He couldn't see the man who walked in front;
> Only he heard the drum and rattle of feet
> Stepping along barred trench-boards, often splashing
> Wretchedly where the sludge was ankle-deep.
>
> Voices would grunt 'Keep to your right—make way!'
> When squeezing past some men from the front line:
> White faces peered, puffing a point of red;
> Candles and braziers glinted through the chinks
> And curtain-flaps of dug-outs; then the gloom

[15] Owen to Susan Owen, 19 Jan. 1917, in *Collected Letters*, 429.

[16] Eric Leed, *No Man's Land: Combat and Identity in World War I* (Cambridge: Cambridge University Press, 1979), 126–31. See also Paul Fussell, who powerfully evokes the physical nature of trench warfare—mud, sunrise, bird-song—in his classic study *The Great War and Modern Memory* (Oxford: Oxford University Press, 1975), 36–74.

[17] Robert Graves, 'The Great Years of their Lives', *The Listener*, 86 (15 July 1971), 74; Siegfried Sassoon, 'Repression of War Experience', in *Collected Poems 1908–1956* (London: Faber, 1984), 90.

[18] Siegfried Sassoon, note appended to 'A Working Party', in *The War Poems*, ed. Rupert Hart-Davis (London: Faber, 1983), 27.

> Swallowed his sense of sight; he stopped and swore
> Because a sagging wire had caught his neck.[19]

This is characteristic First World War verse in the way that the body of the individual soldier is used to challenge the abstract heroism of the epic: poetry is refashioned as missives from the trenches. Sassoon's poem is also acutely diagnostic of the altered phenomenology of the trenches: what the series of verbs in the first stanza—sliding, groping, tripping, lurching—suggests is that space is no longer experienced through a pair of eyes but through articulate flesh. 'If it is true that I am conscious of my body via the world', writes Merleau-Ponty in *Phenomenology of Perception* (1962), the body is also 'the unperceived term in the centre of the world'.[20] Here, darkness and sludge combine to alter this assumed relation, challenging the vertical organization of the human bodily gestalt and marking a regression to the horizontal movements ('groping', 'paw') of the beast. Different geographies of sense intersect in Sassoon's poem in the way the focus moves from the claustrophobia of the chalk bags to the rattle of feet and grunts of men to the glowing 'point of red' until chaos is come again with the darkness, and the surrounding world suddenly contracts and impinges on the flesh as 'sagging wire'. Yet, it was this sensory verisimilitude that Middleton Murry used to question Sassoon's literary claim while reviewing *Counter-Attack and Other Poems* (1918) for *Nation* on 13 July 1918: 'They are not poetry but verse . . . . They touch not our imagination, but our sense.'[21]

This essay argues how the distinction between 'sense' and 'imagination' begins to blur in the most powerful First World War verse as the inchoate cry of the senses—'the chaos of immediate sensation' which Murry deplored in Sassoon's verse—is evolved into a lyric voice at once rich and strange. In few periods of literary history are actual physical experience and artistic production as contiguous as in First World War verse, and such poetry loses much of its power without the touch of historical reality. But even the crudest war lyric is not the unmediated transcription of immediate sensation: between the sensate body and the printed voice, between experience and expression, come language and linguistic form. In poems such as Thomas's 'Rain' or Rosenberg's 'Returning, we hear the lark', sense impressions lead to an imaginative reconfiguration of nature that in turn develops into an existential questioning of life without ever abandoning the immediate experience; at the same time, both writers negotiate their relation with the Romantic lyric, particularly with John Keats.[22]

---

[19] Sassoon, 'A Working Party', 19.

[20] Maurice Merleau-Ponty, *Phenomenology of Perception*, trans. Colin Smith (London: Routledge, 1962), 94.

[21] John Middleton Murry, 'Mr Sassoon's War Verses', *Nation*, 23 (13 July 1918), 398.

[22] See Edna Longley, 'The Great War, history and the English lyric', in Vincent Sherry (ed.), *The Cambridge Companion to the Literature of the First World War* (Cambridge: Cambridge University Press, 2005), 65–6.

How is the sense experience of the trenches translated into the sensuousness of poetic form—depending on available contemporary models of literary language and genre—and what are the pleasures and dangers of such a process? The war poets refashioned lyric poetry as political testimony, yet poeticizing can also introduce ethical problems, something that made Plato exclude poets from the republic. But there is also a strong tradition of art as therapy, something that made Owen's doctor Arthur Brock encourage his shell-shocked patient to write, and to edit *Hydra* at Craiglockhart: in an atmosphere where the senses are 'charred', verse may provide a space at once to soothe and rekindle the senses and wrest form out of the formless. I shall examine some of these issues by looking at the works of two soldier-poets: Wilfred Owen, the young aesthete turned officer-poet, and Isaac Rosenberg, the Jewish East Ender painter-poet turned private soldier. In the foreword to Rosenberg's *Collected Works*, Sassoon, singling out 'Break of Day in the Trenches' for special praise, notes, 'Sensuous frontline existence is there, hateful and repellent, unforgettable and inescapable.'[23] With reference to both poets, I shall explore this 'sensuous frontline existence' and how, in their works, it is evolved into a complex relation between perception, emotion, and language.

OWEN: LIMIT EXPERIENCES

In a 'queer, ironic'[24] tale by D. H. Lawrence entitled 'The Blind Man', the blind but robust war veteran Maurice encounters his wife's civilian friend Bertie in the darkness of the barn. Suddenly inspired by the 'passion of friendship', the blind man stretches out his 'naked' hand and feels Bertie's face—'touching the small nose and the nostrils, the rough, short moustache, the mouth, the rather strong chin'—'in the soft travelling grasp'.[25] He finally takes Bertie's fingers, pressing them on his own war-blinded eye sockets, 'trembling in every fibre'. Tenderness, eros, and violence are combined in the scene, all mediated through the rhythmic beat of Lawrence's prose. For that moment in the text, the four bodies—of Maurice and Bertie as well as of the narrator and of the reader—are compacted through an act of visceral tightening.

Such responses often characterize our reading of the poetry of Owen as he repeatedly dwells on similar moments of perilous intimacy that go beyond his

---

[23] Sassoon, 'Foreword', in *The Collected Works of Isaac Rosenberg*, ed. Ian Parsons (London: Chatto & Windus, 1984), p. ix.

[24] D. H. Lawrence to Katherine Mansfield, 5 Dec. 1918, in *The Letters of D. H. Lawrence*, iii: *October 1916–June 1921*, ed. James T. Boulton and Andrew Robertson (Cambridge: Cambridge University Press, 1984), 303.

[25] Lawrence, 'The Blind Man', in *England, My England* (Cambridge: Cambridge University Press, 1990), 61–2.

celebrated cult of 'pity' and touches us on that fragile spot where distinctions blur. Through the most caressive of lyric voices, he draws us into moments of extreme sense experience, weaving linguistic-tactile fantasies around them: moments when the body is violated ('slashed bones bare', 'shaved us with his scythe'), the flesh gets exposed ('shatter of flying muscles', 'Ripped from my own back | In scarlet shreds', 'limped on, blood-shod') or the mouth starts bleeding ('I saw his round mouth's crimson deepen as it fell').[26] A Georgian aesthete in the pre-war years, especially in France, where he came under the influence of the Decadent pacifist poet Laurent Tailhade—he thought of writing a book of sonnets entitled 'Sonatas in Silence' and to have it bound in purple and gold[27]—Owen brings with him not only the vocabulary but the sensibility of the Decadents, at once charred and sharpened by the war. The power and the peril of his verse lie in the precise fact that it is never wholly 'modernist' while registering the ravages of modernity, that the decadent investment in sound and the senses continues into his descriptions of historical violence, and the pleasure principle is forever threatening to get out of hand.

Consider the following extract from his early poem, 'Greater Love':

> Your slender attitude
> Trembles not exquisite like limbs knife-skewed,
> Rolling and rolling there
> Where God seems not to care;
> Till the fierce love they bear
> Cramps them in death's extreme decrepitude.
>
> .   .   .   .
>
> Heart, you were never hot
> Nor large, nor full like hearts made great with shot;
> And though your hand be pale,
> Paler are all which trail
> Your cross through flame and hail:
> Weep, you may weep, for you may touch them not.[28]

Instead of the implied ironic contrast with Swinburne's 'Before the Mirror', there seems to be almost an intertextual aural contagion: the point of the juxtaposition

---

[26] Owen, 'Apologia pro Poemate Meo', 124; 'The Next War', 165; 'A Terre', 178; 'Dulce et Decorum Est', 140; '[I saw his round mouth's crimson deepen]', 123; all in *The Complete Poems and Fragments, i: The Poems*, ed. Jon Stallworthy (London: Chatto & Windus, Hogarth Press, and Oxford University Press, 1983).

[27] See Dominic Hibberd, *Owen the Poet* (Basingstoke: Macmillan, 1986), 33.

[28] Owen, 'Greater Love', in *Complete Poems and Fragments*, i. 166. Also see Jon Stallworthy, *Wilfred Owen* (London: Oxford University Press, 1973); and Hibberd, *Owen the Poet*, and idem, *Wilfred Owen: A New Biography* (London: Weidenfeld & Nicolson, 2002). Recent critical works include Desmond Graham, *The Truth of War* (Manchester: Carcanet, 1984); Douglas Kerr, *Wilfred Owen's Voices: Language and Community* (Oxford: Oxford University Press, 1993); and Adrian Caesar, *Taking It Like a Man: Suffering, Sexuality and the War Poets: Brooke, Sassoon, Owen and Graves* (Manchester: Manchester University Press, 1993). For a good overview, see Simon Featherstone (ed.), *War Poetry: An Introductory Reader* (London: Routledge, 1995), 7–115.

gets lost in the cascade of sound as the rhymes, assonance, and labials set our spirits, like the soldiers in 'Apologia pro Poemate Meo', 'surging light and clear'.[29] The swinging metre makes the syntax strangely palpable, turning words almost into things in our mouth and blinding us to the visual horrors. We momentarily forget that the adjectives ('large', 'full', 'great'), the rhyme ('hot/shot'), and the phrase 'pale', occurring in Swinburne's poem, are all tied to real-life carnage, to knife wounds, death cramps, and ruptured hearts. Mutilation is the stuff this poem is made of. Moreover, in a poem initially addressed 'To any Woman', what is the connection between mutilated male flesh and the aroused female body except in a context of eroticism, on the one hand, and misogyny, on the other? The word 'trembles' in fact shows the contradictory impulses at the heart of the poem: it comes from the *fin-de-siècle* world of exquisite pain, of Swinburne's Proserpine whose 'breasts tremble with tenderer breath',[30] but within the more immediate context, it summons up the whole world of neurasthenia, as in Owen's description of '50 strong men trembling as with ague, for 50 hours'.[31] This clash of associations, whether inadvertent or not, is perverse, and the eroticization of violence continues not only in his decadent poems such as '[Has your soul sipped]', 'The Rime of the Youthful Mariner', and '[I saw his round mouth's crimson]', but in late mature work where the language gets leaner. Thus, amidst the satiric realism of a poem as late as 'Disabled', there is a sudden eruption of a lush visual imagination ('leap of purple spurted from his thigh'[32]) that ends up fetishizing an amputation and mires the anti-war politics in a homoerotic aesthetic. Is this disjunction a result of his literary inheritance—an overdose of Georgian aestheticism, the lessons of Swinburne and Wilde filtered through the lens of war—or does it suggest a more private, morbid sensibility?

Owen's first encounter with 'the actualities of war' occurred in a hospital in France which he had gone to visit with his friend Doctor Sauvaiture. He writes to his brother Harold about the experience in striking detail:

First I saw a bullet, like this ⬤▬▬▷ cut out of a Zouave's* leg. Then we did the round of the wards; and saw some fifty German wretches: all more seriously wounded than the French. The Doctor picked out those needing surgical attention; and these were brought on stretchers to the Operating Room; formerly a Class room; with the familiar ink-stains on floor, walls and ceiling; now a chamber of horrors with blood where the ink was. Think of it: there were eight men in the room at once, Germans being treated without the slightest distinction from the French: one scarcely knew which was which. Considering the lack of appliances—there was only one water-tap in the room—and the crowding—and the fact that the doctors were working for nothing—and on Germans too—really good works was

[29] Owen, 'Apologia pro Poemate Meo', in *Complete Poems and Fragments*, i. 124.

[30] Algernon Charles Swinburne, 'Hymn to Proserpine', in *The Poems of Algernon Charles Swinburne*, i (London: Chatto & Windus, 1904), 68.

[31] Owen to Susan Owen, 19 Jan. 1917, in *Collected Letters*, 429; see Owen, 'Asleep', in *Complete Poems and Fragments*, i. 152.

[32] Owen, 'Disabled', in *Complete Poems and Fragments*, i. 175.

done. Only there were no anaesthetics—no time—no money—no staff for that. So after that scene I need not fear to see the creepiest operations. One poor devil had his shin-bone crushed by a gun-carriage-wheel, and the doctor had to twist it about and push it like a piston to get out the pus. Another had a hole right through the knee; and the doctor passed a bandage thus:

Another had a head into which a ball had entered and come out again.

This is how the bullet lay inthe zouave. Sometimes the feet were covered with a brown, scaly, crust—dried blood.

I deliberately tell you all this to educate you to the actualities of the war.[33]

The letter is marked by qualities we usually associate with Owen's verse—realism, pity, writing as testimony—but at the same time, there is a complete absorption with the body in pain. More disturbingly, there is also a narrative *jouissance* as distended body parts are evolved into child-like sketches or verbal witticism: 'push it like a piston to get out the pus'.

Both the drawings and the alliteration, however, go back to Owen's pre-war letters which dwell obsessively on illness and pain: lumps on the gum, headache, impaired vision, granulated pharynx, sore throat, boils on the neck, fever, or 'a most dervishy vertigo'.[34] Repressed homoeroticism, coupled with a rigorous Protestant ethic, may partly explain what Harold Owen calls his brother's 'morbid absorption' in his own health in his youth.[35] Thus, in 'Lines Written on my Nineteenth Birthday', a bout

[33] Owen to Harold Owen, 23 Sept. 1914, in *Collected Letters*, 285.
[34] Owen to Mary Owen, 16 Nov. 1912, ibid. 169.
[35] Harold Owen, *Journey from Obscurity*, i (Oxford: Oxford University Press, 1975), 161.

of indigestion makes him fantasize that he is being strangled by the 'tightening hand of Pain' and pricked by '*Torture's needles in the flesh*'.[36] If pain, as Elaine Scarry has argued in *The Body in Pain*, is a condition that defies 'objectification in language',[37] this was a crisis that Owen had learnt to overcome quite early in his life. Even in the letters, there is a strong urge to communicate the experiences through linguistic experiments ('It was the Enter: I—tis I that killed it') or little diagrams to describe that 'dervishy vertigo' or a headache:[38] it is in this context that the above illustrated extract has to be understood rather than as a straightforward case of 'sadomasochistic' aesthetic. The strange combination of an over-articulate sensuousness and a latent masochistic impulse reaches its fruition in his war poetry, where these twin impulses facilitate an acute—almost visceral—empathy with the body in pain. 'I shall stay in you, friend, for some few hours | You'll feel my heavy spirit chill your chest, | And climb your throat, on sobs . . .', notes the mutilated soldier-narrator in 'Wild with All Regrets'.[39]

'Sounds and colours', Sassoon writes about Owen's verse, 'were mulled and modulated to a subdued magnificence of sensuous harmonies and this was noticeable even in his everyday speaking.'[40] Sound and colour were fundamental to Sassoon's imagination; Owen's affinities are more with Keats, in that in both, there is an overriding concern with touch and texture, a palpable intimacy with the body. An unfettered lyric gift and physical empathy constitute the body in pain in Owen's poetry, hovering around moments when we no longer know where the *is* ends and the *was* begins. Are they men or shadows, asks the first line of 'Mental Cases'. But instead of the irony of Sassoon's 'Repression of War Experience' or the delicate pathos of Gurney's 'Strange Hells'—two other poems on neurasthenia—what we have in Owen is an obsessively corporeal imagination:

> Therefore still their eyeballs shrink tormented
> Back into their brains, because on their sense
> Sunlight seems a blood-smear; night comes blood-black;
> Dawn breaks open like a wound that bleeds afresh.[41]

Like Keats, he immerses himself—and his readers—in the sensuous world of his subjects, but in the context of war, an over-investment in the senses at once produces poetry and madness: while it enables him to transmit the paroxysm of pain, it also creates a fevered consciousness. Synaesthesia and neurasthenia are combined in lines such as 'on their sense | Sunlight seems a blood-smear'; or, in

---

[36] Owen, 'Lines Written on my Nineteenth Birthday', in *Complete Poems and Fragments*, i. 12.

[37] Elaine Scarry, *The Body in Pain: The Making and Unmaking of the World* (Oxford: Oxford University Press, 1985), 5.

[38] Owen to Susan Owen, 16 Nov. 1913, in *Collected Letters*, 212; Owen to Susan Owen, 20 May 1912, ibid. 137; Owen to Mary Owen, 16 Nov. 1912, ibid. 169.

[39] Owen, 'Wild with All Regrets', in *Complete Poems and Fragments*, i. 356.

[40] Siegfried Sassoon, *Siegfried's Journey, 1916–1920* (London: Faber, 1945), 62.

[41] Owen, 'Mental Cases', in *Complete Poems and Fragments*, i. 169.

'The Sentry', where vision, through proximity, assumes a threatening physicality: 'eye-balls, huge-bulged like squids', | Watch my dreams still'.[42] Similarly, Gurney, in 'To His Love', is haunted by that 'red wet | Thing' that he somehow must—and cannot—'forget'.[43] On the other extreme lies the anaesthesia, the 'insensibility' of those who 'cease feeling | Even themselves or for themselves'.[44] One is reminded of Septimus's lack of feeling at the time of Evans's death in Woolf's *Mrs Dalloway* (1925), or of Stanhope in Sherriff's *Journey's End* (1929). In the letter narrating the traumatic death of his servant Jones, Owen momentarily envisages such a condition—'I cannot say I suffered anything, having let my brain go dull'—but soon he adds—'I shall feel again as soon as I dare'.[45] Here lies the strange double bind for the war poet: poetry and aesthetics, by their very nature, are mired in feeling and in the senses, and the soldier-poet thus must at once experience traumatic reliving and creative ecstasy, retrieving and modifying the original experience through language. I shall briefly concentrate on three poems in each of which Owen pushes both sense experience and language to their limits—a gas attack, prolonged exposure to frost, and finally an offensive.

Consider 'Dulce et Decorum Est', which he referred to as 'a gas poem',[46] the title intended as an ironic allusion to Horace:

> Bent double, like old beggars under sacks,
> Knock-kneed, coughing like hags, we cursed through sludge,
> Till on the haunting flares we turned our backs
> And towards our distant rest began to trudge.
> Men marched asleep. Many had lost their boots
> But limped on, blood-shod. All lame went; all blind;
> Drunk with fatigue; deaf even to the hoots
> Of tired, out-stripped Five-nines that dropped behind.
>
> Gas! Gas! Quick, boys!—An ecstasy of fumbling,
> Fitting the clumsy helmets just in time;
> But someone still was yelling out and stumbling,
> And flound'ring like a man in fire or lime...
> Dim, through the misty panes and thick green light,
> As under a green sea, I saw him drowning.
>
> In all my dreams, before my helpless sight,
> He plunges at me, guttering, choking, drowning.
>
> ·   ·   ·   ·   ·   ·   ·   ·   ·   ·
>
> If you could hear, at every jolt, the blood
> Come gargling from the froth-corrupted lungs,

[42] Owen, 'The Sentry', ibid. 188.
[43] Ivor Gurney, 'To His Love', in *Collected Poems*, ed. P. J. Kavanagh (Manchester: Carcanet, 2004), 21.
[44] Owen, 'Insensibility', in *Complete Poems and Fragments*, i. 145.
[45] Owen to Siegfried Sassoon, 10 Oct. 1918, in *Collected Letters*, 581.
[46] Owen to Susan Owen, n.d. [?16 Oct. 1917], in *Collected Letters*, 499.

> Obscene as cancer, bitter as the cud
> Of vile, incurable sores on innocent tongues,—
> My friend, you would not tell with such high zest
> To children ardent for some desperate glory,
> The old Lie: Dulce et decorum est
> Pro patria mori.[47]

Owen here manages to play three central experiences of the war—night march, a gas attack, and traumatic neurosis—along almost a single, vertical bodily axis, gradually moving from the bloodied feet to the bloodied mouth. The opening phrase acts like the lens of the camera, bringing the body into the field of vision: against the surreal backdrop of the gas flares and the sound of the 'Five-nines', the soldiers limp on with their blood-shod feet, as iambs and trochees straggle within the pentameter to keep up with the somnambulist rhythm of the march. If the regular end-rhymes—'sacks/backs', 'sludge/trudge', 'boots/hoots'—suggest the crushing monotony of the routine, there is a more intimate sound pattern that evokes the body in pain. This is the wail of vowels where language breaks down—the 'e', 'o', and 'u' sounds (knock-kneed, coughing, cursed, sludge, our, trudge, lost, blood-shod, even, outstripped, dropped) in the opening stanza—which culminates in the noises of the retching body in the final lines. Mustard gas corrodes the body from within. The testimony of the gas attack moves from visual impressions to visceral processes, registering Owen's difference from his mentor Sassoon: from sounds produced between the body and the world—fumbling, stumbling, flound'ring, drowning—to sounds within the body: guttering, choking, writhing, gargling. Indeed, sound plays a particularly important role in a poem that climaxes on a savage contrast between tongues: the lacerated tongue of the soldier and the grand polysyllabic sound of the Latin phrase as he plays on the two meanings of 'lingua' (in Latin, it means both tongue and language).

The second stanza hurls the narrator and, with him, the readers into the very 'thick' of a gas attack. In Owen's poem, as in Sargent's painting *Gassed* (1918–19), which was done after witnessing the victims of a gas attack, the light seems to thicken and congeal; it creates a liquid, almost tactile, space in which the soldier drowns, the whole drama being witnessed through the thickness of a gas-mask lens. The moment is at once horrific and uncanny, hovering somewhere between perception, memory, flashback, and nightmare as the lyric 'I' is finally introduced. But why is there an 'ecstasy' of fumbling? Sassoon put a question mark beside the line. Coming from the Greek word *ekstasis*, literally meaning 'a standing outside of oneself' (*ek*—out of, *stasis*—a position, a standing), does it suggest the sense of transport inherent in a moment of frenzy, or does the narrator make a quick shift from participant to an observer over the medial pause in the line? Or is the distance temporal, inherent in the act of verse making, which explains the

---

[47] Owen, 'Dulce et Decorum Est', i. 140.

detachment? A psychological explanation hinting at a state in which ecstasy and horror meet through extremity may be sought in Owen's letter where he describes the exhilaration of going over the top. On the other hand, Freud in one of his essays on sexuality notes that 'feelings of apprehension, fright or horror' have a 'sexually exciting effect', and that 'all comparatively intense affective processes, even terrifying ones, trench upon sexuality'.[48] Yet, in a poem that explores the complicity of language in violence—the dangers of Horace's 'sweet' phrase[49]—'ecstasy' seems to suggest, almost inadvertently, the perverse narrative impulse itself: poetic language, asked to describe violence, touches itself instead through alliteration and echo (ecstasy/clumsy/misty) and experiences exhilaration, replacing real-life horror with linguistic rapture. Owen, while criticizing the 'sweetness' of a particular poetic tradition, seems to be seduced by the 'sweetness' of the lyric form itself: in the use of 'ecstasy', is there an inkling of the central problem of lyric testimony to violence, as opposed to other forms of writing—particularly when coupled with a Decadent aesthetic, in poems as late as 'The Kind Ghosts'? The melody of the rhyme, interwoven with the labials of the stanza, thralls us, stretching the verbs beyond their bounds so that an extra foot is left 'hanging' at the end of the lines (fumbling/stumbling/drowning): it creates a diffuse auditory realm analogous to the spectral space generated around the floundering body by its nervous movements. However, the compulsive rhyme of the gerundive '-ing' is also highly disturbing, evoking the classic tense of the trauma victim who, as Freud noted in *Beyond the Pleasure Principle* (1920), is doomed to a compulsion to repeat past experiences as the present.

If 'Dulce et Decorum Est' shows a disjunction between war realism and an unchecked lyric impulse, 'Exposure' inscribes this problem in the very consciousness of the participants. The poem is based on Owen's experiences in the early months of 1917: 'The marvel is that we did not all die of cold . . . only one of my party actually froze to death.'[50] Through eight stanzas, Owen evokes the sensuous geography of the trenches—winds, gas flares, wire, guns, rain, frost, bullets, mud—but instead of Sassoon's realism, or Blunden's ironic contrast, the war landscape is evolved into one of the most sustained explorations of the relation between sense experience, consciousness, and language. If the 'vile, incurable sores on innocent tongues' in 'Dulce et Decorum Est' is a rewriting of Keats's 'palate fine',[51] here, through the very opening phrase, Owen transmutes the quintessential expression of romantic

---

[48] Sigmund Freud, 'Infantile Sexuality', in *The Standard Edition of the Complete Psychological Works of Sigmund Freud*, vii, trans. James Strachey (London: Hogarth, 1953), 203.

[49] In the letter describing the poem to his mother, Owen writes, 'The famous Latin tag [from Horace, *Odes*, iii. ii. 13] means of course It is sweet and meet to die for one's country. Sweet! And decorous!'; to Susan Owen, 16 Oct. 1917, in *Collected Letters*, 499–500.

[50] Owen to Susan Owen, 4 Feb. 1917, in *Collected Letters*, 430.

[51] John Keats, 'Ode on Melancholy', in *The Complete Poems*, ed. John Barnard (Harmondsworth: Penguin, 1973), 349.

agony ('My heart aches'[52]) into collective sense experience ('Our brains ache'). Yet, like the poem's world of half-light ('drooping flares', 'flickering gunnery', 'sunken fires'), or its half-rhymes (silent/salient, wearied/worried, snow-dazed/sun-dozed), or the half-known faces at the end, Owen's poem is only half in parody of Keats's ode. The power of the poem lies in the way it teeters between irony and sensuousness, nature and nostalgia, sun and snow. This is particularly evident in stanza 7:

> Pale flakes with fingering stealth come feeling for our faces—
> We cringe in holes, back on forgotten dreams, and stare, snow-dazed,
> Deep into grassier ditches. So we drowse, sun-dozed,
> Littered with blossoms trickling where the blackbird fusses,
>   —Is it that we are dying?[53]

Here, we have a state of bodily extremity but the seductive music—the assonance, the alliterative 'f' woven with the labials and sibilance (perhaps a lesson learnt from the 'faery lands forlorn' of Keats's 'Ode to a Nightingale'), the long lines and the half-rhymes—turns the experience of being exposed into a long, lingering caress. A partly cancelled line from a related poem—'Fastening of feeling fingers on my wrist'—connects the unknown hands that had been laid on Owen's arm 'in the night, along the Bordeaux streets' with the sensuous threat of snow in the poem.[54] Is it Owen's shimmering homoeroticism that colours the experience, or is it one more example of a decadent aesthete struggling to portray harsh reality through the Victorian language of sensation? Or is it, like the word 'ecstasy' in 'Dulce et Decorum Est', another hint towards the misprision of language often inherent in the act of retelling which makes possible the history or the poetry of the senses? Language here can also be said to serve as a carapace against exposure as he relives the experience, lulling him with the memory of romance. But perception and hallucination are fused and confused in the stanza quoted above, as the Keatsian bower with its blossoms and blackbird surfaces not as inappropriate aesthetic from the poet-narrator but as nostalgia on the part of the soldiers themselves, a reverie so powerful that it dissolves the surrounding reality and whirls the poem and its participants into another space, another time. But such a move is politically deeply troubling—in fact, reprehensible—especially when read in conjunction with the letter. For, unlike Keats's 'vision or a waking dream', this is a historical experience involving extreme hardship and death, a collective experience which is not only transformed into a fantasy of desire and language but is then projected on to the

---

[52] Keats, 'Ode to a Nightingale', in *the Complete Poems*, 346.
[53] Owen, 'Exposure', in *Complete Poems and Fragments*, i. 185.
[54] Owen, 'It was the noiseless hour', in *The Complete Poems and Fragments*, ii: *The Manuscripts and Fragments*, ed. Jon Stallworthy (London: Chatto & Windus, Hogarth Press, and Oxford University Press, 1983), 460; Owen to Susan Owen, 14 Feb. 1914, in *Collected Letters*, 234. For the complex sources of the poem, see Hibberd, who makes this connection in *Owen the Poet*, 78; see also Graham's acute analysis of the 'conscious and highly-wrought texture' of this poem (*Truth of War*, 57).

soldiers themselves. 'Exposure', partly because it is based on real-life experience, powerfully bears witness to a central conflict that runs throughout Owen's verse: the relation between a sensuous, masochistic imagination and his responsibility as a war poet. This constant tension makes his poetry fascinating—linguistically, psychologically, as well as historically—but at the same time ethically disturbing, defying attempts at any consistent, progressive political reading.

'An experience', Foucault notes, 'is, of course, something one has alone; but it cannot have its full impact unless the individual manages to escape from pure subjectivity in such a way that others can I won't say re-experience exactly—but at least cross paths with it or retrace it.'[55] The process seems to be partly bared in the origin and composition of 'Spring Offensive'—his last poem—as Owen draws our attention to 'the very limits of limit experience'.[56] Two letters are helpful in this context. In a letter written to his brother Colin, Owen recounts the assault at Savy Wood in April 1917 on which 'Spring Offensive' is loosely based, describing the 'extraordinary exultation in the act of slowly walking forward, showing ourselves openly':

Then we were caught in a Tornado of Shells. The various 'waves' were all broken up.... When I looked back and saw the ground all crawling and wormy with wounded bodies, I felt no horror at all but only immense exultation at having got through the Barrage.[57]

A second letter, written to his mother after the composition of 'Spring Offensive', is also illuminating: 'I can find no word to qualify my experiences except the word SHEER.... I lost all earthly faculties, and fought like an angel.'[58] The fitting of such extreme experience into verse and wresting order out of chaos must require a monumental effort. The manuscript version is one of the most rewritten and illegible of all his papers, particularly the extraordinarily compacted stanza describing the actual offensive:

~~Glorious Lightly~~ So, soon   raced
~~Proudly~~   ~~went~~
~~Splendid~~, ~~Bright-faced~~   ~~ran~~
~~Turning~~, they topped the hill, and ~~walked~~ together
    ~~Down~~   stretch ~~green~~herbs
Over an open ~~plain~~ of ~~wind~~ and heather
    Exposed. And instantly the whole sky burned
                    set sudden cups
                ~~and c [?]~~ and
                set [?] and

[55] Michel Foucault, 'How an "Experience-Book is Born"', in *Remarks on Marx: Conversations with Duccio Trombadori*, trans. R. James Goldstein and James Cascaito (New York: Semiotext(e),1991), 40.

[56] Martin Jay, 'The Limits of Limit-Experience: Bataille and Foucault', in *Cultural Semantics: Keywords of Our Time* (Amherst, Mass.: University of Massachusetts Press, 1998), 62.

[57] Owen to Colin Owen, 14 May 1917, in *Collected Letters*, 458.

[58] Owen to Susan Owen, 4/5 Oct. 1918, ibid. 580.

> With ~~fl~~ fury against them; ~~and that easy slope~~
>   earth ~~hell~~
> ~~Opened To catch their blood~~ In thousands for their blood; and the green slope . . . .[59]

This is a stanza rooted in unthinkable horror, but what the cancelled words—'splendid', 'bright faced', or 'Glorious Lightly'—as well as the accelerating rhythm of the run-on line climaxing in 'Exposed' convey is the sense of exhilaration that Owen mentions in the letters. Is the exhilaration a subsequent emotion, contingent on having survived the offensive? Or is it Owen's unflinching fidelity to the truth of bodily sensation, hinting at something that Freud placed at the very heart of *Civilization and Its Discontents* (1929): 'in the blindest fury of destructiveness, we cannot fail to recognize that the satisfaction of the instinct is accompanied by an extraordinarily high degree of narcissistic enjoyment.'[60]

Owen is the quintessential pacifist poet of the First World War. Yet, the power of some of his most celebrated lyrics lies neither in realism nor in pity (both of which nonetheless inform his poetry in abundant measure), but in his sensuous evocation of certain limit experiences where eros, violence, and sound are combined. Whether these impulses inform the original experience or its retrospective fictionalization written *après coup* is open to debate. But this plunges us headlong into the relation between the aesthetics and ethics of representation: how politically responsible or aware is such poetry that seeks to represent extreme sense experiences and ends up transforming them through its own *jouissance*? Is it a problem of a specific historical inheritance—the *fin de siècle* which preceded the war—that inflects both the vocabulary and the sensibility; or is it endemic to lyric poetry, where the music and sensuousness put an anodyne over the unrest and the ugliness? Wordsworth noted that 'there can be little doubt but that more pathetic situations and sentiments, that is, those which have a greater proportion of pain connected with them, may be endured in metrical composition, especially in rhyme, than in prose'.[61] This partly explains the popularity of Owen and trench poetry more generally—over, for example, nursing memoirs which often make more depressing reading—but there is an essential difference. The situations Owen describes are not only 'pathetic' but based on real-life violence, and any extension of Wordworth's concept of aesthetic 'pleasure' must stop short of narrating or understanding historical carnage. Yet, pleasure is a key element in Owen's poetry at the semiotic level, which makes it at once deeply disturbing and affective: the sensuousness which mires it ethically has also, paradoxically, made it one of the most powerful and effective forms of protest poetry from the Second World War to Iraq, turning it into an important political

---

[59] Owen, 'Spring Offensive', in *Complete Poems and Fragments*, ii. 378.

[60] Freud, *Civilization and Its Discontents*, in *Standard Edition*, xxi. 121. Freud's observations are congruent with some of the experiences and emotions that Ernst Jünger recalls in *Storm of Steel*, and, more recently, with some revisionist accounts of war, as in Niall Ferguson's *The Pity of War* (Harmondsworth: Penguin, 1998), which has a section on 'The Joy of War', 357–66.

[61] Wordsworth, 'Preface to *Lyrical Ballads*', 610.

tool. However, if we interrogate our responses closely, we realize that at times we are even made party to the violence we seem to be repudiating. In 'Apologia pro Poemate Meo', Owen writes about an offensive: 'For power was on us as we slashed bones bare | Not to feel sickness or remorse of murder.'[62] Through his linguistic energy, he often transfers the 'power' on to us, the readers: Owen at least owns the experience he evokes; we do not.

ROSENBERG: 'WARM THOUGHT'

If sound and sense carry us through Owen's verse with their breath-taking fluency, the poetry of Rosenberg records the reverse process: a constant struggle and wrestling with ideas, images, and language. In a letter to Edward Marsh on 4 August 1916, he writes: 'You know how earnestly one must wait on ideas, (you cannot coax real ones to you) and let as it were, a skin grow naturally round and through them.' When the ideas come 'hot', the artist must 'seize them with the skin in tatters raw, crude, in some parts beautiful in others monstrous'.[63] In contrast to Owen's 'words bleeding-fresh',[64] it is ideas that come to Rosenberg with temperature and texture. The description is at once indicative of the quality of 'warm thought'[65] that characterizes his poetry as well as his deeply fraught relation with the English literary tradition. 'Scriptural and sculptural', Sassoon famously said, 'are the epithets I would apply to him':[66] the near-repetition neatly captures the intimate connection between the racial and the linguistic in the works of this Anglo-Jewish poet-painter from the East End of London. For there is a definite Hebraic and visual imagination at work in his poems as he tries to 'model' words in the English language.

Rosenberg, with his sparkling metropolitan wit and irony, remains something of an oddity in the canon of First World War poetry, refusing to be assimilated just as he was an outsider in the military by dint of his class, race, and height. Yet, this might reflect the way in which First World War verse has privileged a rhetoric of piousness and pity that excludes the playful, corroborating, perhaps

[62] Owen, 'Apologia pro Poemate Meo', i. 124.

[63] Isaac Rosenberg to Edward Marsh, 4 Aug. 1916, in *The Collected Works*, 239. See also *The Poems and Plays of Isaac Rosenberg*, ed. Vivien Noakes (Oxford: Oxford University Press, 2004), p. xviii. For details about Rosenberg's life, see Jean Liddiard, *Isaac Rosenberg: The Half-Used Life* (London: Victor Gollancz, 1975) and Jean Moorcroft Wilson, *Isaac Rosenberg: Poet and Painter* (London: Cecil Woolf, 1975). Also see D. W. Harding, *Experience into Words: Essays on Poetry* (Cambridge: Cambridge University Press, 1963), 91–103; Dennis Silk, 'Isaac Rosenberg (1890–1918)', *Judaism*, 14 (Fall 1965), 462–74; Jon Silkin, *Out of Battle: Poetry of the Great War* (Oxford: Oxford University Press, 1972), 249–314.

[64] Owen, 'The Poet in Pain', in *Complete Poems and Fragments*, i. 111.

[65] Rosenberg, '[A warm thought flickers]', in *Poems and Plays*, 106.

[66] Sassoon, 'Foreword', in Rosenberg, *Collected Works*, p. ix.

more than any other genre, Eliot's claim about the 'dissociation of sensibility'.[67] Apart from David Jones, Rosenberg was perhaps the only soldier-poet who had a 'direct sensuous apprehension of thought'.[68] 'Every space brimful of meaning; touched with adumbrations of some subtly felt idea':[69] his pronouncements on Italian painting can equally be applied to his own art. His pre-war verse, such as '[We are sad with a vague sweet sorrow]', '[Wistfully in pallid splendour]', or '[Sacred, voluptuous hollows deep]', is marked by a lush sub-Keatsian vocabulary, its 'low murmur'[70] and 'pale flower'[71] reminiscent of the early verse of Sassoon and Owen. Yet his love lyrics also combine sensuality with playfulness in a way that aligns him with a different tradition:

> Even now your eyes are mixed with mine.
> I see you not, but surely, he—
> This stricken gaze, has looked on thee.
> From him your glances shine.
>
> Even now I felt your hand in mine.
> This breeze that warms my open palm
> Has surely kist yours . . . [72]

If Victorian aestheticism leaves its mark on the war poets from Brooke to Owen, Rosenberg's affinities are with the Metaphysicals: he carried a book of Donne's poems with him to the war. While an excess of affect at the surface of language and images often characterizes both Decadent and First World War verse, in Rosenberg the affect is located in the texture of thought.

Compare the following extracts, in which each soldier-poet mourns his comrade in terms of his voice:

> 'Your voice sings not so soft—
> Though even as wind murmuring through raftered loft—
> Your dear voice is not dear,
> Gentle and evening clear,
> As theirs whom none now hear'.[73]
>
> (Owen, 'Greater Love')

> Who died on the wires, and hung there, one of two—
> Who for his hours of life had chattered through
> Infinite lovely chatter of Bucks accent . . . [74]
>
> (Gurney, 'The Silent One')

[67] T. S. Eliot, 'The Metaphysical Poets', in *Selected Essays* (London: Faber, 1951), 288.
[68] Ibid. 286.   [69] Rosenberg, 'Art', in *Collected Works*, 292.
[70] Rosenberg, 'Love To Be', in *Poems and Plays*, 26;
[71] Rosenberg, '[Like some fair subtle poison]', ibid. 40.
[72] Rosenberg, '[Even now your eyes are mixed in mine]', ibid. 68.
[73] Owen, 'Greater Love', in *Complete Poems and Fragments*, i. 166.
[74] Gurney, 'The Silent One', in *Collected Poems*, 250.

> Untuned air shall lap the stillness
> In the old space of the voice—
>
> The voice that once could mirror
> Remote depths
> Of moving being,
> Stirred by responsive voices near,
> Suddenly stilled forever.[75]

(Rosenberg, 'In War')

The lushness of Owen's lament ends up hushing the voice being mourned for; Gurney, quieter and perhaps more shrewdly observant, evokes the voice in all its delicate chatter through one powerful regional detail. What attracts Rosenberg, by contrast, is the sensuousness of the idea: the imagined passage of the wind or the voice, moving across, creating or vacating space as air replaces the voice, both invested with palpable materiality. Unlike in Owen, rhyme does not intrude on the silence, nor does the wind murmur: 'untuned' (implying a contrast with the 'musical' voice), the air partakes of the very 'stillness' which it now caresses, building up almost an architectonics of silence; there is also a hint of an underlying aquamarine imagery ('lap . . . stillness . . . mirror . . . depths') which ballasts the spatial metaphor. Touch, sight, and sound are all intrinsic to the idea as Rosenberg evolves synaesthesia into an intellectual apparatus without losing any of its immediacy; there is great tenderness and intimacy in the image of the voice mirroring the 'remote depths' or vibrating in playful response. While Owen sensuously enacts moments, in Rosenberg we have the investigation and analysis of the senses. While lines and whole stanzas of Owen spring to the tip of our tongue without the least bidding—and the 'Infinite lovely chatter of Bucks accent' is perhaps as difficult to forget for the readers as it was for the narrator—the irregular length and quirky rhythm of Rosenberg's lines resist easy memorization: this is perhaps one of the surest tests of not only how the sensory axis changes as we pass from Owen or even Gurney to Rosenberg, but of how war poetry registers the shock of a more radical modernist aesthetic.

Rosenberg's background may partly explain his divergence from the dominant vocabulary and poses of the *fin de siècle*. The son of immigrant Jews from Lithuania and growing up amidst poverty in the working-class surroundings in the East End of London, Rosenberg could not lay claim on the English language with the ease and felicity of the 'officer-poets', bequeathed to them largely by their public school education. Instead, as he writes, 'nobody ever told me what to read, or ever put poetry in my way'.[76] However, the lack of formal training, coupled with his Jewish background, left him free from the levelling influence of middle-class English prose, its tradition and pressures. 'I am rough now, and new, and will have no tailor' reads a line from 'Moses'; in a letter to Edward Marsh in 1914,

---

[75] Rosenberg, 'In War', in *Poems and Plays*, 131–2.
[76] Rosenberg to Miss Seaton, n.d. [1911], in *Collected Works*, 181.

Rosenberg writes, 'In literature, I have no judgement—at least for style. If in reading a thought has expressed itself to me, in beautiful words; my ignorance of grammar etc. makes me accept that.'[77] It is this absence of what Adam Phillips calls 'the official grammar of association'[78] which results in the striking originality of his thought and language, making it rich with the 'coarseness engrained' that he so valued among the 'great poets of the earth'.[79] Phrases such as 'cosmopolitan rat', 'gargantuan fingers', 'incestuous worm', 'limbs as on ichor-fed', 'blood-dazed intelligence', or 'Essenced to language' open up new worlds in English poetry, yoking acute details with a metaphoric imagination.[80] The last phrase is particularly resonant, given Rosenberg's awareness of the nature of the sign: 'Snow is a strange white word', he writes in 'On Receiving News of the War: Cape Town'.[81] At the same time, perhaps more than any other poet, he evokes the sensuous world of the trenches—the changing light over the parapets, a rat touching the hand, the sudden burst of lark song, the ritual of louse hunting, the crunch of wheels over the unburied dead—and these details are, in turn, used to explore certain social, political, and personal questions.

Rosenberg was one of the few soldier-poets who joined the Army for financial reasons. At the time of enlisting, he writes, 'I would be doing the most criminal thing a man can do.'[82] He had one of the longest stretches in France, serving almost uninterruptedly for twenty-one months from June 1916 till his death during a wiring patrol on 1 April 1918. During this period, the rigours of trench life were compounded with him being a Jewish private in an English battalion marked out by physical difference:

I could not get the work I thought I might so I have joined this Bantam Battalion (as I was too short for any other) which seems to be the most rascally affair in the world. I have to eat out of a basin together with some horribly smelling scavenger who spits and sneezes into it etc. . . . Besides my being a Jew makes it bad amongst these wretches.[83]

Rosenberg's letters expose aspects of trench life missing from the letters of the officer-poets: the desperate plea for a pair of new boots or a cake; writing poetry on lavatory paper or measuring his letter by the candle-light; sleeping on damp floors and 'coal-fatigueing all day (a most inhuman job)'.[84] But, unlike in Owen, the war-torn body is seldom the theme or evolved into a lyric voice; bodily details punctuate his poetry, but, like the ear with the poppy in 'Break of Day' or the

---

[77] Rosenberg, 'Moses', in *Poems and Plays*, 189; Rosenberg to Edward Marsh, n.d. [May–June 1914], in *Collected Works*, 202.

[78] Adam Phillips, 'Isaac Rosenberg's English', in *On Flirtation* (London: Faber, 1995), 186.

[79] Rosenberg, 'Emerson' [?1913], in *Collected Works*, 288.

[80] Rosenberg, 'Break of Day in the Trenches', 128; 'Louse Hunting', 136; '[A worm fed on the heart of Corinth]', 126; 'Dead Man's Dump', 140 and 141; all in *Poems and Plays*.

[81] Rosenberg, 'On Receiving News of the War: Cape Town', ibid. 83.

[82] Rosenberg to Mr Schiff, 8 June 1915, in *Collected Works*, 216.

[83] Rosenberg to Mr Schiff, n.d. [Oct. 1915], ibid. 219.

[84] Rosenberg to Edward Marsh, n.d. [postmarked 5 Jan. 1916], ibid. 229.

lidded eye in 'Dead Man's Dump', they are introduced in a matter-of-fact manner, absorbed into a broader argument or idea. As in Imagist poetry, a physical detail can work as an 'emotional and intellectual complex',[85] revealing fresh connections through the force of juxtaposition with other images. In the following extract, it reveals the nexus between social inequality, industrial modernity, and war:

> Iron are our lives
> Molten right through our youth.
> A burnt space through ripe fields
> A fair mouth's broken tooth.[86]

The East End Jew cannot lay claim to the 'ripe fields' of England in the way Thomas or Blunden can; nor does the war make the mouth the legitimate site of *l'amour impossible*, as in Owen; the 'iron', on the other hand, carries traces of the world of the 'fiendish mangling-machine' to which Rosenberg felt 'chained' at the age of 14 when he apprenticed to learn engraving and plate making.[87] The images here suggest what Edgell Rickword notes in his essay 'Poetry and Two Wars' two decades later: 'to the majority of inhabitants, war only accentuates miseries which are part and parcel of their daily lives.... war is the result of the same human will that condemns the people to low and precarious standard of life whether engaged with an external foe or not'.[88] While the socialist apects of Owen's poetry are better known—the plight of the soldiers on whom the 'shutters and doors' of society are 'all closed, on us the doors are closed'[89]—Rosenberg is alert to that huge section of the immigrant population to whom the doors of English society have never opened at all, whether in war or in peace.

Rosenberg was particularly fortunate in having some wealthy Jewish women as patrons who funded his education at the Slade. However, trained as an artist, Rosenberg could not make up his mind whether he was a poet-painter or a painter-poet. The painter's eye informs his verse, evident in the title of one of his war poems, 'Marching—as seen from the left file':

> My eyes catch ruddy necks
> Sturdily pressed back—
> All a red brick moving glint.
> Like flaming pendulums, hands
> Swing across the khaki—
> Mustard-coloured khaki—
> To the automatic feet.

---

[85] Ezra Pound, 'A Few Don'ts by an Imagiste', in Peter Jones (ed.), *Imagist Poetry* (Harmondsworth: Penguin, 1972), 130.

[86] Rosenberg, 'August 1914', in *Poems and Plays*, 130.

[87] Rosenberg to Miss Seaton, n.d. [before 1911], in *Collected Works*, 180.

[88] Edgell Rickword, 'Poetry and Two Wars', in *Literature in Society: Essays and Opinions*, ii: *1931–1978*, ed. Alan Young (Manchester: Carcanet, 1978), 158–9.

[89] Owen, 'Exposure', 185.

> We husband the ancient glory
> In these bared necks and hands.
> Not broke is the forge of Mars;
> But a subtler brain beats iron
> To shoe the hoofs of death,
> (Who paws dynamic air now).
> Blind fingers loose an iron cloud
> To rain immortal darkness
> On strong eyes.[90]

The twofold movement is characteristic: the march is painted in imagistic detail, which is unobtrusively developed into a critique of war; but this critique is then traced with all the warmth of the observed detail. In the first stanza, even within the visual field, the focus shifts from the ruddiness of the necks to the angled precision of the backs to the 'moving glint'. While the image of the 'flaming pendulums' introduces the theme of time, crucial to both poetry and the march, it also suggests the reduction of the human body to a clockwork mechanism: for an instant we are not sure to whom the 'hands' belong. Sound is joined to sight as the hands complete their swinging arc across the line, but the oppressive monotony of the march—particularly loathsome to one who was always being told off for his absent-mindedness—is now suggested through the trochaic beat, the repetition of 'khaki' as well as the adjective 'automatic'. The theme of mechanized warfare is developed most fully in the final six lines: adjectives such as 'subtler' or 'blind', now harnessed to the body of war rather than to that of the soldier, no longer suggest colours, but carry forward the idea of dehumanization. But this critique is filtered through a sensuous, mythic lens as the impersonal war machine is imagined as some sort of Amazonian brood, pawing air, like the 'Daughters of War', with their ruddy limbs.

In his essay 'The Pre-Raphaelites and Imagination in Paint', Rosenberg notes: 'Poetry and music achieve that end [of beauty] through the intellect and the ear; painting and sculpture through the eye.'[91] If 'Marching' is a painter's poem we realize his awareness of the difference between the two media when we contrast his pre-war painting *Hark, Hark the Lark* (1912) with his war poem, 'Returning, we hear the larks', which clearly draws on the former. In the painting, we see a number of seemingly 'primitive' figures—gaunt, elongated—listening with 'upturned . . . faces'. The poem, however, opens with pitch darkness as Rosenberg goes on instead to create one of the most haunting soundscapes in English poetry:

> But hark! joy—joy—strange joy.
> Lo! heights of night ringing with unseen larks.
> Music showering our upturned list'ning faces.[92]

---

[90] Rosenberg, 'Marching—as seen from the left file', in *Poems and Plays*, 123–4.
[91] Rosenberg, 'The Pre-Raphaelites and Imagination in Paint', in *Collected Works*, 298.
[92] Rosenberg, 'Returning, we hear the larks', in *Poems and Plays*, 139.

The song of the lark was one of the regular anomalies of trench life. A sergeant notes, 'The ecstasy of the lark.—That is inseparably connected with "stand-to" in the trenches.'[93] If in Blunden's *Undertones of War*, the pastoral is always threatened by the war, in the poem trench life is suddenly intruded upon by the pastoral, and Rosenberg transforms it into a moment of transcendent beauty: 'But hark!'. However, as we strain to listen, it is neither song nor death that at first drops from the dark, but rather the emotion of the listener. 'Joy' points beyond Rosenberg's essay 'Joy' to Blake's 'Infant Joy',[94] but here the sound is as important as the allusion: the repetitive incantation creates its own strange music, gathering the word, like the lark's song, into the spell of the sensuous. On the other hand, the phrase 'heights of night' is an acute piece of trench realism: cooped up in the bowels of the earth, the soldiers experience space vertically rather than horizontally—as height rather than volume—now resonant 'with unseen larks'. Indeed, touch and sound are fused in the 'shower' of music on the 'upturned list'ning faces', the word 'upturned' showing the poem's residual links with the painting, completing the circuit of synaesthesia. And yet the moment of sensuousness is laced with danger as a shell could easily accompany the song. This combination of beauty and menace is developed through the celebrated final similes—first, the blind man's dreams, and then the image of a girl's dark hair. The latter image is a recurring one, going back to his pre-war lyrics—the 'nestling hair of the night' caressing the cheek or a woman's 'soft dark hair' breathing like a prayer[95]—showing how certain images persisted in his mind and were harnessed to the new circumstances, here adding a sense of mystery and eroticism.

This precarious relation between sensuousness and seriousness is pursued further in 'Break of Day in the Trenches' and 'Louse Hunting'. Both sparkle with a shrewd ironic wit—something rare in First World War poetry—creating a certain *frisson* with the grimness of the subjects, and unsettling any stable response from the reader. Behind both poems, one can detect echoes of Donne's 'The Flea': whereas the mingling of blood is replaced by the touching of hands in the former, the killing of the flea gets brilliantly transposed into the ritual of delousing as Donne's conceit of 'self-murder'[96] is invested with an immediate and ominous significance. The opening line of the first poem—'The darkness crumbles away'[97]—captures the act rather than the object of perception: to the soldiers in their muddy, subterranean world, the enclosing walls of the trenches are conflated with the encompassing darkness which in turn seems to gain materiality. Looking forward to Barbusse's

---

[93] Unnamed sergeant, quoted in Fussell, *Great War and Modern Memory*, 242.

[94] William Blake, 'Infant Joy', in *Complete Writings*, ed. Geoffrey Keynes (Oxford: Oxford University Press, 1966), 118.

[95] Rosenberg, 'Night', in *Poems and Plays*, 107; 'Heart's First Word [II]', ibid., 112.

[96] John Donne, 'The Flea', in *The Complete English Poems*, ed. A. J. Smith (Harmondsworth: Penguin, 1996), 58.

[97] Rosenberg, 'Break of Day in the Trenches', in *Poems and Plays*, 128.

'parois de l'ombre' in *Clarté* (1919) and David Jones's 'walled darkness' in *In Parenthesis* (1937), Rosenberg goes one step further as he describes not the congealed darkness but the breaking of light.[98] The core of the poem, however, is the touching of the narrator's 'English hand' by the 'queer sardonic rat' which will soon cross no man's land and 'will do same to a German'. The action accretes intensities of meaning as different impulses jostle with each other: realism and satire, wit and wish-fulfilment, comedy and pathos. The abject creature of the trenches is exalted to an enlightened emissary of peace, joining the warring hands in a phantasmatic handshake as Rosenberg subverts a standard anti-semitic trope through brilliant irony. A few years later, we have T. S. Eliot's notorious lines: 'The rats are underneath the piles. | The jew is underneath the lot.'[99] If the link between the migratory rat and the immigrant Jew is hard to deny—one of the first poems Rosenberg wrote after joining the Army was 'The Jew'—it is also just possible that the two emphatically differentiated hands in fact beat with common Jewish blood. For, like the 'cosmopolitan rat' or the 'rootless'[100] poppy, the homeless Jew, as Rosenberg would surely have been aware, could be found on both sides of no man's land, making this European war a horrible fratricide for them. In Germany, when war was declared, around 96,000 Jews volunteered to fight for the country: 12 per cent of these were volunteers, 77 per cent served at the Front, and casualty rates ran at 12 per cent.[101] In France, by August 1914, 8,500 out of 30,000 Jewish immigrants had joined the French Army.[102]

In 'Louse Hunting', on the other hand, a daily trench activity is turned into a grotesque pageant: 'Nudes—stark and glistening, | Yelling with lurid glee'.[103] These statuesque figures are soon evolved into a phantasmagoria of movement and action, but we see only their projection on the walls of the dug-out:

> Then we all sprang up and stript
> To hunt the verminous brood.
> Soon like a demons' pantomime
> The place was raging.
> See the silhouettes agape,

---

[98]   Henri Barbusse, *Clarté* (Paris: Flammarion, 1919), 106; David Jones, *In Parenthesis* (London: Faber, 1963; 1st pub. 1937), 16.

[99]   T. S. Eliot, 'Burbank with a Baedeker: Bleistein with a Cigar', in *The Complete Poems and Plays* (London: Faber, 1969), 41. See also Anthony Julius, *T. S. Eliot: Anti-Semitism and Literary Form* (Cambridge: Cambridge University Press, 1995), 22.

[100]   The word occurs in the typed draft of the poem, reproduced in Rosenberg, *Poems and Plays*, 129.

[101]   The statistics are taken from Ulrich Sieg, 'Judenzählung', in Gerhard Hirschfeld, Gerd Krumeich, and Irina Renz (eds.), *Enzyklopädie Erster Weltkrieg* (Munich: Ferdinand Schöningh, 2004), 600. See also George L. Mosse, *The Jews and the German War Experience, 1914–1918* (New York: Leo Baeck Institute, 1977).

[102]   Emmanuel Le Roux, 'Exhibition honours Jewish soldiers in First World War', in *Le Monde* (rep. in *The Guardian*), 24 Oct. 2002, <http://www.aftermathww1.com/parisexpo.asp>

[103]   Rosenberg, 'Louse Hunting', in *Poems and Plays*, 136.

> See the gibbering shadows
> Mixed with the battled arms on the wall.
> See gargantuan hooked fingers
> Dug in supreme flesh
> To smutch the supreme littleness.

The exaggerated theatricality of the scene pushes it towards the mock-heroic, infecting the grotesque with humour and endangering our relation to the grimness of the situation. While the poem is predominantly visual, reiterated by the epanaphoric 'See', the magnification lends it almost a tactile quality, the bodies evoked by words such as 'flesh', 'fingers', 'hooked', 'pluck', and 'smutch'. Discussing modernist visual technology, Walter Benjamin notes:

With the close-up, space expands; with slow motion, movement is extended. The enlargement of a snapshot does not simply render more precise what in any case was visible, though unclear: it reveals entirely new structural formations. . . . The camera introduces us to unconscious optics as does psychoanalysis to unconscious impulses.[104]

Through size and projection, a daily trench ritual becomes an exposure of the murderous impulses of the soldiers—a reading of war psychology that we come across in Freud's 'Thoughts for the Times on War and Death': 'If we are to be judged by our unconscious wishful impulses, we are ourselves, like primaeval man, a gang of murderers.'[105] Moreover, for the son of Eastern European Jews, the imagery of delousing might have an added charge, being part of the contemporary anti-Semitic discourse. In 1882, German regulations were introduced, requiring the delousing of Eastern Jews before they entered the country; train carriages bringing them had to be steamed after every journey.[106] In France, *Le Rappel*, the organ of the radical Left, noted in November 1920: 'We must, as we have said, prohibit barracks where twenty Jews spread their lice and their blemishes.'[107] Given his general education, his 'cosmopolitan' exposure, and his acute consciousness of racial discrimination, it is unlikely that the symbolic undertones of 'louse hunting'—for the menace of the pogrom is not too far away—would be lost on him: in any case, as he himself once wrote, in a 'vital composition', 'one's own private thought, too secret even to reveal to ourselves, were suddenly shown to us from outside'.[108] Yet, the symbolic ramifications are never allowed to intrude into the poem, where comedy and menace are held in fine balance.

However, it is 'Dead Man's Dump' that inhabits most fully the geography of the trenches—flames, corpses, explosions—but develops it into a profound questioning of the relation between the living and the dead. In a letter to Marsh

---

[104] Benjamin, 'The Work of Art in the Age of Mechanical Reproduction', in *Illuminations*, 238–9.
[105] Freud, 'Thoughts for the Times on War and Death', in *Standard Edition*, xiv. 297.
[106] See Jack Wertheimer, *Unwelcome Strangers* (New York: Oxford University Press, 1987), 25–6.
[107] *Le Rappel*, quoted in Leon Poliakov, *The History of Anti-Semitism: Suicidal Europe, 1870–1913*, trans. George Klin (Oxford: Oxford University Press, 1985), 289.
[108] Rosenberg, 'Art', 291.

dated 8 May 1917, Rosenberg writes: 'I've written some lines suggested by going out wiring, or rather carrying wire up the line on limbers and running over dead bodies lying about.'[109] As the poem opens, 'the wheels lurched over the sprawled dead'.[110] The visceral shock produced by what Silkin calls 'the painful, exact verb'[111] is, however, evolved into a problem of consciousness: 'But pained them not, though their bones crunched'. Similarly, later, we have the image of a man's brains 'splattered on | A stretcher bearer's face', the shudder suggested through a single detail—'His shook shoulders slipped the load'—but almost immediately the realism gets coupled with a sense of spiritual desolation: 'The drowning soul was sunk too deep | For human tenderness.' How can souls 'drown' any more than silences 'sink' or wars 'blot' or hearing 'darken'? What the adjectival and adverbial phrases in 'Dead Man's Dump' do—and this is perhaps where the power of Rosenberg's verse lies—is to yoke together realism and metaphor, sense and symbol. Consider the penultimate stanza of the poem, where the focus narrows to the perspective of a dying soldier:

> Here is one not long dead;
> His dark hearing caught our far wheels,
> And the choked soul stretched weak hands
> To reach the living word the far wheels said,
> The blood-dazed intelligence beating for light,
> Crying through the suspense of the far torturing wheels
> Swift for the end to break,
> Or the wheels to break,
> Cried as the tide of the world broke over his sight.

Here, as in Owen's 'Futility', is a soldier 'full-nerved, still warm',[112] but it is not the moment of pain that attracts Rosenberg; nor does he use a language of desire. Instead, he delves into the perceptual and spiritual world as the soldier struggles between life and death. In narrative terms, the poem comes full circle with the reappearance of the limber, but the 'dark hearing' hints, beyond the distance of the wheels, at lyric closure, at a world fast closing over both sound and sight. The physical and the metaphysical are poignantly joined in the image of the 'choked soul' stretching 'weak hands | To reach the living word the far wheels said'. The image of the soul refers back to the previous description of the dead body as 'soul's sack | Emptied of God-ancestralled essences', pointing to the Hebraic sensibility, and with it comes the urgency of the question: 'Who hurled them out? Who hurled?' The sense of being *hurled out*—of being cast away—is powerful and personal: Rosenberg, the isolated Jewish infantryman, re-enacts the condition of his race in being hurled out as were his ancestors repeatedly in European history.

[109] Rosenberg to Edward Marsh, 8 May 1917, 'Art', 254.
[110] Rosenberg, 'Dead Man's Dump', in *Poems and Plays*, 139.
[111] Silkin, *Out of Battle*, 282.
[112] Owen, 'Futility', in *Complete Poems and Fragments*, i. 158.

In his essay 'On Lyric Poetry and Society', Adorno refers to the lyric as 'the most delicate, the most fragile thing', and observes that 'the ideal of lyric poetry, at least in the traditional sense, is to remain unaffected by the bustle and commotion'[113]—an assumption he then goes on to dismantle. First World War verse was one of the major realignments of this traditional relation as lyric poetry—that most intimate of genres—was not only refashioned as social protest but made to register the 'bustle and commotion' of the most terrifying forms of violence. Yet, in the works of both Owen and Rosenberg, there is a persistence of what Adorno calls 'the priority of linguistic form'[114] as the chaotic cry of the senses—interpenetrated, as we have seen, by the social and the personal—is evolved into the sensuousness of verse. 'The highest lyric works', Adorno continues, 'are those in which the subject, with no remaining trace of matter, sounds forth in language until language itself acquires a voice.'[115] Unsurprisingly, Sassoon remembers Owen by the timbre of his voice, which, in the account, blends seamlessly with his lyric gift as well as with his literary heritage: '[there was] the velvety quality of his voice, which suggested the Keatsian richness of his artistry with words. It wasn't a vibrating voice. It had the fluid texture of soft consonants and murmurous music.'[116] His comments on Rosenberg are an illuminating contrast: 'His experiments were a strenuous effort for impassioned expression; his imagination had a sinewy and muscular aliveness; often he saw things in terms of sculpture, but he did not carve or chisel; he modelled words with fierce energy and aspiration.'[117] Sassoon's accounts are at once affective and critically astute. Coming from two distinct literary-religious backgrounds—Owen with his decadent aestheticism and Evangelical upbringing, and Rosenberg with his metropolitan wit and Hebraic sensibility—they remain not only two of the most extraordinary of the First World War poets, but take English poetry in two highly original and powerful, yet wholly different, directions in the early years of the twentieth century. In one, we have the strength and sweetness of the Romantic-Decadent lyric tradition, being brought to bear witness to the horrors of industrial modernity and pouring forth as an aria for the death of the European bourgeois consciousness; the other reaches beyond Romanticism to the Metaphysical poets, and tries to forge a radical modernist aesthetic to suit his playful imagination and record the 'extraordinary conditions of this life'.[118] Yet, by the end of the War, both were dead, and it was left to Sassoon, Graves, and Blunden to mourn and ruminate.

---

[113] Theodor Adorno, 'On Lyric Poetry and Society', in *Notes to Literature*, trans. Shierry Weber Nicholson, ed. Rolf Tiedemann, i (New York: Columbia University Press, 1991), 37.

[114] Ibid. 43. For an illuminating discussion of how 'the story of form at the wartime moment is the story of how traditional forms internalize history', see Longley, 'The Great War, history and the English lyric', 77.

[115] Adorno, 'On Lyric Poetry and Society', 43.   [116] Sassoon, *Siegfried's Journey*, 62.

[117] Sassoon, 'Foreword', in Rosenberg, *Collected Works*, p. ix.

[118] Rosenberg to Laurence Binyon, n.d. [Autumn 1916], in *Collected Works*, 248.

CHAPTER 5

'MANY SISTERS TO MANY BROTHERS': THE WOMEN POETS OF THE FIRST WORLD WAR

STACY GILLIS

The critical as well as the popular literary history of the First World War is unique, in that the experience of war has been rendered through a small group of male poets. The influence and reproduction throughout the twentieth century of the war poetry by Rupert Brooke, Siegfried Sassoon, Wilfred Owen, and Isaac Rosenberg can only be partly ascribed to the particular confluence of the myths of the Edwardian idyll, of the young sacrificed male, and the terrors of technological trench warfare.[1] Joanna Scutts neatly summarizes this, arguing that to 'perceive in the history of

---

[1] While an examination of the ways in which these myths are inextricably linked with class structures is beyond the remit of this essay, we do need to remind ourselves that the characterization of the First World War as horrific would have been true only for a certain proportion of the soldier body: 'These writers generally came from pre-war environments which were leisured, comfortable and secure.

British culture in the early twentieth century a narrative arc of prewar innocence to postwar experience is both convenient and convincing'.[2] The ways in which the arc has been circumscribed, articulated, and poetized has largely been the result of this small group of male poets and their proponents. As Martin Gray points out, the 'war may be (and usually is) approached through the work of a few poets chosen by critics as poetically skilful, or self-selected by their ambitious sense of themselves as "poets"'.[3] While the reasons for the resonance of these myths surrounding the literary output of the war have been the subject of much work, what has received less attention is the way in which the myths surrounding these literary figures have resulted in the exclusion of other accounts of the war, accounts which spoke to other kinds of experiences and traumas. Drawing attention to the exclusion of a specific group—on the basis of gender, race, class, sexuality, and/or nationality—from an accepted canonical literary history is a fairly standard critical *modus operandi*; however, while it is not a remarkably innovative argument to make, it is one which, nevertheless, needs to be repeatedly foregrounded. It is particularly relevant when considering the poetry of the First World War, which was, from the opening shots of the war until the 1980s, considered a masculine group enterprise.

For some, like John H. Johnston, this 'natural' grouping is a result of the *kind* of war: 'These poets form a natural group by virtue of the fact that they were the first to deal with the kind of war peculiar to modern civilization; they were the first to attempt some assessment of the physical and spiritual effects of that kind of war.'[4] The understanding of this poetry as a response to the material conditions of war is one which has marked much of the criticism. For others, the exclusion of other voices is partly to do with the personal myth-making of the poets: 'Their group identity is, to an extent, part of the myth that they themselves create. Both during and after the war the poets are drawn together into loose fellowships, united by their common desire to come to terms with the traumatic experience of the trenches.'[5] While Gray here emphasizes the commonality of experience, he also rightly identifies how those war poets who survived were complicit in the act of myth making. Gray, however, also draws attention to the cultural afterlife of the myth and the importance of the war

---

War exposed them to hardship, squalor, insecurity, loss of control over their circumstances and the proximity of death and injury. They were understandably horrified. But one might reasonably ask how much of this would have been *as* shocking to slum dweller and coal miners in 1914' (Adrian Gregory, 'Goodbye to All That? The First World War and the Making of the Twentieth Century', *Bridges: An Interdisciplinary Journal of Theology, Philosophy, History and Science*, 12/1–2 (Spring–Summer 2005), 124).

[2] Joanna Scutts, 'A Breaking Point? The Position of the First World War in Literary History', *Bridges: An Interdisciplinary Journal of Theology, Philosophy, History and Science*, 12/1–2 (Spring–Summer 2005), 79.

[3] Martin Gray, 'Lyrics of the First World War: Some Comments', in Gary Day and Brian Docherty (eds.), *British Poetry: 1900–1950: Aspects of Tradition* (London: St Martin's Press, 1995), 57.

[4] John H. Johnston, *English Poetry of the First World War: A Study in the Evolution of Lyric and Narrative Form* (Princeton: Princeton University Press, 1964), p. ix.

[5] Gray, 'Lyrics of the First World War', 51.

poetry anthology in this enterprise: 'the poetry of the First World War was perceived as a homogeneous poetic kind from very early on in its history, and . . . publication in anthologies was both cause and consequence of this way of perceiving it'.[6] An account of how the figure of the male war poet came to represent the First World War in literary history is not the subject of this essay, although it will necessarily be touched on in passing. Rather, this essay is concerned with one group of poets which has been often excluded from our understanding of the war. I will first discuss the gendering of literary history of the First World War, before moving on to a wider discussion of women, war, and writing, and concluding with an account of how we might read the women war poets in light of current theories about mourning and within the current renaissance in First World War studies.

(En)Gendering the Literary History of War

Until recently, women's poetry has been largely absent from the literary accounts of the First World War. The numerous poetry anthologies published both during the war and through to the late 1970s were unanimous in their sustained championing of a fairly small group of male poets, a 'brotherhood of "Those who were there"—on the Western Front. Those who had not been there were presumed to be incapable of understanding what the experience had been like, and what it had meant.'[7] While the membership has fluctuated somewhat, at the centre are Owen, Rosenberg, Brooke, and Sassoon, with Charles Sorley, Julian Grenfell, Robert Graves, and Edmund Blunden slightly more subject to the vagaries of taste. These anthologies have been firm in their purpose of providing a 'voice' for the supposedly new kind of war waged between 1914 and 1918 and the impact on combatants, both at war and once they returned home. As such, the anthologies serve as one more form of memorial to the war. For example, Brian Gardner states that his anthology of (male) war poets is 'intended as a tribute to those who fought, and died, in the First World War. There have been many accounts of that unparalleled tragedy, and here is yet another: one written by the men who experienced it.'[8] This account of the war perpetuates a myth of authenticity surrounding the male poet—one whose voice has been authenticated through (masculine) experience. The first academic monograph on the war poets, Johnston's *English Poetry of the First World War: A Study in the Evolution of Lyric and Narrative Form* (1964), similarly drew attention

---

[6] Gray, 'Lyrics of the First World War', 48.

[7] Brian Gardner, 'Introductory Note', in *idem* (ed.), *Up the Line to Death: The War Poets, 1914–1918* (London: Eyre Methuen, 1976), p. xx.

[8] Ibid., p. xix.

to the war poets as worthy of particular consideration, perpetuating the notion of a traffic between masculinity, poetics, and war: 'their names remain firmly attached to the First World War, and their figures are inseparable from the circumstances that inspired the poetry by which—in most cases—they are best known'.[9]

Johnston goes on to argue that the 'mission' of the poet was to 'communicate his sense of the reality of war to the millions at home who would not or could not appreciate the magnitude of the experiences and sacrifices of the common soldier'.[10] This idea of a 'mission' is key to understanding how women's poetry of the First World War has been excluded from more canonical literary histories of the war. If the purpose of war was to win the battles fought in the trenches, then this excluded other kinds of experiences, whether the experiences of the munitions worker or those of the mourner. Gray, although somewhat resistant to the myths surrounding the war poet, still argues that a '[p]erusal of war poetry reveals that the poems are very often constructed out of an image-hoard of common, shared perceptions'.[11] The valorization of the 'authenticity' of certain experiences over others has been echoed in the numerous war poetry anthologies, which draw upon another strongly persuasive myth, that of successive groups of male poets sharing a common aesthetics and politics, something entrenched in Paul Fussell's oft-cited *The Great War and Modern Memory* (1975). This pattern is repeated in later texts: there are no women poets, for example, in John Silkin's *The Penguin Book of First World War Poetry* (1979), and he explicitly makes a connection between the war poets and the Romantic poets.[12] This approach necessitates an exclusionary tactic on the basis of various categories, but largely that of gender. Although Dominic Hibberd could point out, in 1981, that 'a precise definition has never been agreed' for the term 'war poet' and that changing tastes reflect who is in vogue, his case-book of war poetry criticism published in that year was still concerned with the group of male war poets (although some of the critics included are women) which has dominated the literary history of the war.[13]

Not until the 1980s was it begin to be widely recognized that women might have actually had something to say about the First World War. The publication of Elaine Showalter's *A Literature of their Own: British Women Novelists from Brontë to Lessing*

---

[9] Johnston, *English Poetry of the First World War*, 20. The self-perpetuating dialectic of masculinity, poetics, and war has, of course, valorized a reading of war poetry over non-war poetry, as Gray identifies: 'Foregrounding the factuality of war experience, while generating strong feelings in the reader, may lead to ignorance or circumvention of formal considerations. The poems cease to be poems, but just pegs on which to hang preconceptions about the nature of war, and the First World War in particular' (Gray, 'Lyrics of the First World War', 61).

[10] Johnston, *English Poetry of the First World War*, 12.

[11] Gray, 'Lyrics of the First World War', 54.

[12] Jon Silkin, 'Introduction', in *idem* (ed.), *The Penguin Book of First World War Poetry* (Harmondsworth: Penguin, 1979), 12, 21–7, 35–48. This is a particularly apposite comparison, as nowhere else in Anglo-American literary history—aside from these two points—have two very small groups of male writers come to represent a much wider political and aesthetic shift.

[13] Dominic Hibberd, 'Introduction', in *idem* (ed.), *Poetry of the First World War: A Casebook* (London: Macmillan, 1981), 11.

(1977) and Sandra M. Gilbert and Susan Gubar's *The Madwoman in the Attic: The Women Writer and the Nineteenth-Century Literary Imagination* (1979) was crucial in the gendered reconsideration of literary history, broadening its perspective to include women's writing. Since then, both the representation of women in literature and the works of women writers have come under increasing scrutiny. Nosheen Khan's *Women's Poetry of the First World War* (1988), Claire M. Tylee's *The Great War and Women's Consciousness: Images of Militarism and Womanhood in Woman's Writings, 1914–1964* (1990), Dorothy Goldman's collection *Women and World War 1: The Written Response* (1993), Sharon Ouditt's *Fighting Forces, Writing Women: Identity and Ideology in the First World War* (1994), and Trudi Tate and Suzanne Rait's collection *Women's Fiction and the Great War* (1997) are the best-known examples of the research which has emerged on women and the First World War in the last twenty-five years. Ouditt summarizes the ways in which the war opened up opportunities for women which had previously existed only for those located within a particular confluence of class and wealth:

[T]he war, even if it was a manifestation of a particularly brutal kind of masculine madness, created space for women to work, think and practise as artists. It helped to reveal the futility of a social and political pact that made men and women play infantile games with each other, and to over-invest in definitions of 'femininity' and 'masculinity' which rendered the bond unbreakable.[14]

These works have all dissected the relationship between gender politics, aesthetics, and the war, identifying how women could and did respond to the war in ways which moved beyond traditional expectations. To be considered alongside these works is the only anthology of women's First World War poetry, Catherine Reilly's *Scars Upon My Heart: Women's Poetry and Verse of the First World War* (1981).[15] The publication of this work and the fact that women's war poetry is the sole subject of Khan's work are indications of the range and depth of poetry produced by women during the war.

However, as Gill Plain has noted, the 'rediscovery of women's poetry of the First World War has been greeted more with alarm than with enthusiasm'.[16] As I have shown above, the valorization of the 'authenticity' of the (masculine) trench experience and the demarcation of this experience as the particular domain of a small group of front line soldiers is key to understanding how the canonization of

---

[14] Sharon Ouditt, *Fighting Forces, Writing Women: Identity and Ideology in the First World War* (London: Routledge, 1994), 217.

[15] This is the only anthology of women's First World War poetry, and it has been out of print for many years. It was reissued, combined with Catherine Reilly's later collection *Chaos of the Night: Women's Poetry and Verse of the Second World War* (1984), as *The Virago Book of Women's War Poetry and Verse* (1997). The current renaissance of First World War studies is clearly indicated, however, by the reissue of the original, *Scars Upon My Heart*, by Virago in 2006.

[16] Gill Plain, 'Great Expectations: Rehabilitating the Recalcitrant War Poets', in Vicki Bertram (ed.), *Kicking Daffodils: Twentieth-Century Women Poets* (Edinburgh: Edinburgh University Press, 1997), 25.

First World War poetry has functioned. The lack of 'a single, coherent vision of life on the home front'[17] problematizes both the valorization and the demarcation of the figure of the 'war poet'. There were more than 500 women writing and publishing poetry during the war, but most of them resist the easy designation of 'war poet'. From Teresa Hooley's 'A War Film', which details the new 'telecommunicating' of war by cinema—'As in a dream | Still hearing machine-guns rattle and shells scream, | I came out onto the street'[18]—to Jessie Pope's 'War Girls', which recounts how women had taken over traditionally masculine employment opportunities—'There's the girl who clips your ticket for the train, | And the girl who speeds the lift from floor to floor'[19]—to Mary H. J. Henderson's 'An Incident', which engages with the tropes of the young male sacrifice—'And the boy turned when his wounds were dressed, | Held up his face like a child at the breast'[20]—these poems do not sit easily within any one kind of war experience, and thus cannot be easily categorized. Although this poetry may have been written by a certain segment of the population—one which was largely based on class, education, and wealth—it is not reasonable to assume that it is all the same sort of poetry: ' "Women in the First World War" are often referred to as though they are a clearly defined, coherent group. It cannot be reiterated too often that the experiences of women differed dramatically between geographical areas, trades, age groups and classes.'[21] It is this lack of conformity to the insistence on (masculine) unanimity of experience during the war to which I will now turn.

WOMEN WRITING WAR

The war offered women a creative space in which to engage with these new identities; as Ouditt argues, the war allowed women to 'work, think and practise as artists'.[22] However, this notion of the woman artist must also be understood within the context of class—if private wealth meant that middle-class women had the luxury of volunteering their services, then it also meant that they had the luxury of time to write, a luxury not possible for the hundreds of thousands of working-class women war workers. Indeed, the *lack* of luxury—that is, luxury of a material kind—is often referenced in women's war poems as a way of demonstrating both a break with the past and an acknowledged sacrifice. In Helen Dircks's 'After Bourlon Wood' there

---

[17] Ibid.

[18] Teresa Hooley, 'A War Film', in Catherine Reilly (ed.), *The Virago Book of Women's War Poetry and Verse* (London: Virago, 1997), 56.

[19] Jessie Pope, 'War Girls', ibid. 90.   [20] Mary H. J. Henderson, 'An Incident', ibid. 52.

[21] Gail Braybon, 'Women and the War', in Stephen Constantine, Maurice W. Kirby, and Mary B. Rose (eds.), *The First World War in British History* (London: Arnold, 1995), 145.

[22] Ouditt, *Fighting Forces, Writing Women*, 217.

are several references to some semiotics of luxury which are clearly absent in war-time London:

> In one of London's most exclusive haunts,
> Amid the shining lights and table ware,
> We sat, where meagre Mistress Ration flaunts
> Herself in syncopated music there.[23]

Allusions to moments of luxury which are used to highlight the incongruity of the wartime setting are also to be found in Jessie Pope's 'The Nut's Birthday', in which the gifts of past birthdays—'Some ormulu, grotesquely chased | A little bronze Bacchante'—are compared with the infinitely more useful birthday gifts for a soldier: 'Some candles and a bar of soap, | Cakes, peppermints and matches, | A pot of jam, some thread (like rope).'[24] The emphasis on items of use may be extended to how women were considered during the war—as items of use in the large machinery of war.

One root of a pervasive gendering of the Home Front female is the fact that during the war, women were often doing what needed to be done everywhere else aside from the trenches. While the figures of the plucky working-class female munitions worker and the upper-middle-class VAD who overcomes her initial squeamishness are now just as much a part of the mythological afterlife of the war as the aristocratic officer whose 'play up and play the game' ethos is disabused, the circulation of these figures in the popular imagination does, in part, testify to the ways in which women used the space of the war to carve out new identities, however transitory, for themselves. With the need for manual labourers, women moved into factories, shipyards, railways, and on to the land. These sorts of opportunities were largely taken up by those previously in domestic service, as Nina MacDonald's 'Sing a Song of War-Time' details:

> Mummie does the house-work,
> Can't get any maid,
> Gone to make munitions,
> 'Cause they're better paid.[25]

The middle classes and above moved into volunteer positions—albeit ones which merely brought into a public domain those activities often associated with women—as Jenni Calder identifies: 'women's organizations [were] set up within an established middle- and upper-class tradition of volunteer work and fundraising...although efforts were made to give these organizations status and authority, relished by many of the women, often the work they did was much

---

[23] Helen Dircks, 'After Bourlon Wood', in Reilly (ed.), *Virago Book of Women's War Poetry and Verse*, 29.
[24] Jessie Pope, 'The Nut's Birthday', ibid. 89.
[25] Nina MacDonald, 'Sing a Song of War-Time', ibid. 69.

the same as traditional female domestic tasks.'[26] While these new identities were indubitably marked by class in terms of their availability, they all provided women with opportunities rarely available before the war.

These new employment opportunities—and, more tacitly, the social freedoms contained therein—are the subject of several poems, largely written by middle-class women, some endorsing and others opposing these freedoms. For Madeline Ida Bedford, the title of her poem 'Munition Wages' gives some indication of how the new economic freedoms of the largely working-class female munition workers were perceived:

> Earning high wages? Yus,
> Five quid a week,
> A woman, too, mind you,
> I calls it dim sweet.
> Ye'are asking some questions—
> But bless yer, here goes:
> I spends the whole racket
> On good times and clothes.[27]

While the speaker goes on to say that part of this spending spree is because the munitions worker might find herself 'Tomorrow—perhaps dead', the tone of the poem is condemnatory. Tensions surrounding duty and responsibility are often undercurrents of the poems about work. Mary Gabrielle Collins's 'Women at Munition Making' provides a much more sanctified version of the munitions worker, decrying the ways in which women have had to leave behind the traditional work of mothering to work in factories:

> Their hands should minister unto the flame of life,
> Their fingers guide
> The rosy teat, swelling with milk,
> To the eager mouth of the suckling babe.[28]

The nurturing hands of mothers becoming the killing hands of the munitions workers are, in this poem, antithetical to the 'natural' order of things: 'But this goes further, | Taints the fountain head, | Mounts like a poison to the Creator's very heart.' That women were being paid for this sort of work is positioned as both not 'playing the game' properly but also as disruptive of the natural social order.

No such recrimination is cast upon those working in a nursing or providing capacity. The reasons for this are various, but are linked with class and gender

---

[26] Jenni Calder, 'World War and Women—Advance and Retreat', in Barbara Korte and Ralf Schneider (eds.), *War and the Cultural Construction of Identities in Britain* (Amsterdam: Rodopi, 2002), 164.

[27] Madeline Ida Bedford, 'Munition Wages', in Reilly (ed.), *The Virago Book of Women's War Poetry and Verse*, 7.

[28] Mary Gabrielle Collins, 'Women at Munition Making', ibid. 24.

expectations. As some VADs were not paid for their work, they must have had private means. They were also providing care in a way which mapped on to traditional accounts of gender relations. Mary H. J. Henderson's 'An Incident' speaks to these constructions of gender and class, recounting an evening of nursing duty and taking care of gravely ill patients: 'And I fed him...Mary, Mother of God, / All women tread where thy feet have trod.' Similarly, the canteen helper in 'Y.M.C.A.' references traditional mothering strategies when speaking of her duties:

> Some linger for a friendly chat,
> Some call me 'Mother'—Think of that!
> And often, at the magic word,
> My vision grows a little blurred—
> The crowd in khaki disappears,
> I see them through a mist of years:
> I see them in a thousand prams—
> A thousand mothers' little lambs...[29]

The reference to Christian sacrifice in the last line, and the maternal overtones, are explicit in their referencing of such female war workers as sustaining the natural order of things and ensuring that the social fabric remains intact for a post-war world. A similar tone runs throughout the musings of Aelfrida Tillyard's 'A Letter from Ealing Broadway Station', in which the speaker is very conscious of the role her duties in guarding the railway station play in the overall war. Despite exhaustion and thoughts of her comfortable rooms at Newnham College, she thinks of the bombing of Antwerp and says:

> I'd like to feel that I was helping
> To send the German curs a-yelping,
> Well, if I serve the Belgian nation
> By guarding Ealing Broadway station,
> I'll guard it gladly, never fear.[30]

The woman is here positioned as treating her wartime job as a duty and thinking only of those whose lives she will save. Moreover, in referencing her previous life, she is endorsing a return to that life, rather than an engagement with the new freedoms open to women during the war. These sorts of poems can verge on the elegiac in their appropriation of traditional understandings of female activity.

Elegiac overtones are also present in accounts of England and Englishness. Drawing on the long history of the pastoral in English poetry, England was often configured in war poetry—by both men and women—as a place of redemption and healing. In Lilian M. Anderson's 'Leave in 1917', the pilot on leave wends his way across the English landscape, and initially 'his England was no England' as

---

[29] C.A.L.T., 'Y.M.C.A.', in *The Virago Book of Women's War Poetry and Verse*, 108.
[30] Aelfrida Tillyard, 'A Letter from Ealing Broadway Station', ibid. 114.

his thoughts are on 'towns | Crouched slumbering beneath the threat of death'.[31] Travelling south-westward to Devon, he is gradually brought back to life by the springtime fecundity of the English landscape: 'Here was the slated threshold of his home, | And here his lighted hearth; here daffodils | Shone amber in the firelight.' The safety of the hearth here is heightened by the pilot's waiting wife, who embraces him, drawing him back into the light of the hearth and back to England. Rose Macaulay juxtaposes the guns of France with the English countryside in 'Picnic':

> And life was bound in a still ring,
> Drowsy, and quiet, and sweet . . .
> When heavily up the south-east wind
> The great guns beat.[32]

The 'Flanders mud' is 'muffled and far away', as the walls of England protect those within. The poem ends with the words 'should break . . .' repeated twice, and the ellipses allow a note of warning to enter this pastoral vision of the Surrey hills. Notes of warning are ignored in Alice Meynell's 'Summer in England, 1914', which clearly endorses the pre-war innocence/post-war experience arc described by Scutts. 1914 is characterized in this poem as one of unparalleled harvest: 'The hay was prosperous, and the wheat; | The silken harvest climbed the down: | Moon after moon was heavenly-sweet.'[33] Christian imagery is used throughout this poem to emphasize the sacrifices made to protect this land of bliss and fruitfulness.[34] Certainly, an abrupt discontinuity caused by the war is foregrounded in most of these poems, which draw upon the elegiac to stress how much England—and Englishness—has to lose if the war is lost.

Some of the most provocative, and consequently problematic, poems produced by the women war poets are those which either take on the voice of a soldier or imagine life in the trenches. This can, at times, result in poems which are mawkishly sentimental in their account of soldiering, drawing heavily upon religious imagery. For example, while in 'Over the Top' Sybil Bristowe uses some remarkable imagery to describe fear—'It's like as if a frog | Waddled round in your inside'[35]—she falls back on religious sentiment to conclude the poem as the soldier heads over the top. Winifred M. Letts provides a more realistic account of life on the wards in recounting the death of a soldier:

> They put the screens about his bed;
> We might not play the gramophone,

---

[31] Lilian M. Anderson, 'Leave in 1917', ibid. 3.   [32] Rose Macaulay, 'Picnic', ibid. 66.

[33] Alice Meynell, 'Summer in England, 1914', ibid. 73.

[34] In this poem, Joan Montgomery Byles argues, the 'themes of nature and nurture are constantly contrasted with the martial values . . . One is whole, the poet suggests, only when the soul is in harmony with the landscape' (Byles, 'Women's Experience of World War One: Suffragists, Pacifists and Poets', *Women's Studies International Forum*, 8/5 (1985), 481).

[35] Sybil Bristowe, 'Over the Top', in Reilly (ed.), *The Virago Book of Women's War Poetry and Verse*, 13.

> And so we played at cards instead
> And left him dying there alone.[36]

The white of the counterpane juxtaposes with the red of the screens in this poem to evoke the gendered models of care within the hospital—it is the female nurse who puts up the screens to hide his death, whilst the male patients play cards. Once the patient has died, the poem ends with the assertive claim that they will 'make the row we did before' before tritely amending this by saying 'But—Jove!—I'm sorry that he's dead.' While Nosheen Khan argues that the 'light-hearted tone of the poem's conclusion does not stem from any shallowness of emotion, but reflects the veneer of indifference assumed by those who tended the dying as a safeguard that enabled them to cope with such tragedies',[37] there is certainly a slight tone of resentment at the curtailed activities here. In short, the living resent the dying for imposing strictures upon their activities. Margaret Postgate Cole uses the figure of the badly wounded soldier, but to different effect. The blinded and abandoned soldier in Cole's poem speaks of how 'all the nightmares of each empty head | Blew into air'.[38] The irony of the title—'The Veteran'—emerges in the final lines when the soldier reveals that he is not yet 19.[39] Jane Dowson argues that the women war poets 'projected themselves into male roles in order to engage imaginatively with the men at the Front'.[40] These poems demonstrate that there was no unanimity of creative engagement, whether in terms of form, style, or subject. What does mark them all, however, is the way in which they attempt to engage with loss.

War losses form the subject-matter of many of the other poems produced by women during and after the war. These poems are also elegiac in tone, but are usually more visceral in their account of loss. For Marian Allen, 'It seemed impossible that you should die',[41] a sentiment which is echoed by many other women. Vera Brittain's poems 'Perhaps—' and 'To my Brother', written for her fiancé and brother, respectively, should certainly be understood as memorials; but more poignant is the line which ends her poem 'The Superfluous Woman': she asks, '*who will give me my children?*'[42] The myth of a lost generation resonates throughout many of these poems.[43] In Nora Griffiths's 'The Wykhamist', the

[36] Winifred M. Letts, 'Screens', in *The Virago Book of Women's War Poetry and Verse*, 62.

[37] Nosheen Khan, *Women's Poetry of the First World War* (London: Harvester, 1988), 125.

[38] Mary Postgate Cole, 'The Veteran', in Reilly (ed.), *The Virago Book of Women's War Poetry and Verse*, 22.

[39] Khan argues that this poem 'fails to impress, being marred by its moralizing tones which stem from the writer's pacifist sympathies' (*Women's Poetry of the First World War*, 26).

[40] Jane Dowson, *Women, Modernism and British Poetry: 1910–1939* (Aldershot: Ashgate, 2002), 41.

[41] Marian Allen, 'The Raiders', in Reilly (ed.), *Virago Book of Women's War Poetry and Verse*, 1.

[42] Vera Brittain, 'The Superfluous Woman', *in Testament of Youth: An Autobiographical Study of the Years 1900–1925* (London: Virago, 1978), 535.

[43] For more on the myth of the lost generation, see Robert Wohl, *The Generation of 1914* (London: Weidenfeld & Nicolson, 1980).

speaker recounts activities of a year ago before ellipses mark a break in the poem: '...You..."died of wounds"...they told me | ...yet your feet | Pass with the others down the twilit street.'[44] The enclosing of the cause of death in quotation marks reminds us of the formalities of the war death, yet also introduces an ironic tone, one which is aggravated by the use of ellipses. These moments of anger and sorrow punctuate poems which often, otherwise, sound a note of resignation and Christian sacrifice. Even May Wedderburn Cannan's 'Lamplight'—in which, as Khan points, the 'private empire has to make way to the stronger claims of the national empire'[45]—and which is both sentimental and imperialistic, has one quiet line which speaks to a broader experience: 'And I think my heart was broken by the war.'[46] While these poems often draw upon the traditional forms of the English elegy and, for Janet Montefiore, rarely escape 'the Victorian and Georgian tradition, itself deeply imbricated with patriotic ideology',[47] the ways in which the gender politics of the early twentieth century both enabled and constrained these woman poets must form the focus of more research.

TRAUMA AND LOSS: ENDINGS

It is precisely the reliance upon these traditional forms of poetry that Plain is talking about when she argues that the critical resistance to women's war poetry can be ascribed to the fact that it 'fails to conform to a cultural demand for ahistorical, transcendent, and "difficult" writing'.[48] That women's war poetry does not fit within the parameters of what is expected of the genre makes a compelling argument for the processes of canonization. In his work on the male poets of the war, Johnston claims that the new kinds of technological violence available in this war had, as a 'natural consequence', a 'tentative, episodic, disconnected, emotional kind of writing, a desperate insistence on the shocking facts of life and death, a compulsive focus on the obscene details of crude animal needs and reactions, on wounds, death, and decomposition'.[49] This emphasis on the 'episodic' and the 'disconnected' is best understood within the context of the debates surrounding modernist versus Georgian poetics. It is well known that the war marked the demise of the positive reception of the Georgian poet; the post-war emphasis was on

---

[44] Nora Griffiths, 'The Wykhamist', in Reilly (ed.), *Virago Book of Women's War Poetry and Verse*, 44.

[45] Khan, *Women's Poetry of the First World War*, 168.

[46] May Wedderburn Cannan, 'Lamplight', in Reilly (ed.), *Virago Book of Women's War Poetry and Verse*, 16.

[47] Janet Montefiore, '"Shining Pins and Wailing Shells": Women Poets and the Great War', in Dorothy Goldman (ed.), *Women and World War*, i: *The Written Response* (Basingstoke: Macmillan, 1993), 55.

[48] Plain, 'Great Expectations', 26. [49] Johnston, *English Poetry of the First World War*, 13.

modernist experimentation. That modernism has been considered a keystone of innovative and ground-breaking literary work throughout the twentieth century has surely played a part in how the more traditional forms of women's war poetry have been excluded from histories of the war. Furthermore, as Deborah Tyler-Bennett argues, 'recognized ideas of what constitutes a "war poem" do not appear to be geared to embrace abstract or allegorical poems by women'.[50] The categories of war and women sit uncomfortably together in the critical and lay consciousness; adding the category of poetry exacerbates the tension even more.

The question of the quality of these poems has been a matter of some concern even for feminist critics. Discussing Reilly's anthology in *Feminism and Poetry* (1987), Montefiore criticized the poems for 'their often uncritical handling of War, Sacrifice, Poetry, and Religion: there is no professional finish to disguise thought and feeling'.[51] In a later work, she qualified this, claiming that although women's war poetry is 'incompetent and/or reactionary' and she is concerned with 'problems of value that this sets for the feminist critic',[52] she is wary of outright dismissal. Indeed, she goes on to say that 'such a dismissal means leaving unasked and unthought the ways in which the poems are problematic, which is only partly a matter of amateurishness and conventionality'. Dorothy Goldman struggles with the same conundrum—how not to dismiss these poems on the basis of their apparent conventionality: 'It was not simply their lack of first-hand military experience that inhibited women's poetry, but the inheritance of worn-out and inappropriate modes and language without the catalyst which the experience of the War provided in forcing more shocking and brutal forms of expression.'[53] Indeed, while, as I have shown, many of these poems use traditional motifs and styles and do not engage with the new poetic forms circulating in other arenas during the war, they are all engaging with the *conditions* of war. To put in another way, as Plain argues, many of these poems should be understood in terms of grief psychology: 'This process is evident in the considerable number of wartime and postwar poems that revisit places previously shared with a lost lover, or which focus on an activity or ideal associated with the lost person.'[54] A more complex interrogation of these poems provides a broader understanding of the relationship between women and war, as well as literature and war.

---

[50] Deborah Tyler-Bennett, ' "Lives Mocked at by Chance": Contradictory Impulses in Women's Poetry of the Great War', in Patrick J. Quinn and Steven Trout (eds.), *The Literature of the Great War Reconsidered: Beyond Modern Memory* (Basingstoke: Palgrave, 2001), 68.

[51] Montefiore, *Feminism and Poetry: Language, Experience, Identity in Women's Writing* (London: Pandora, 1987), 69. See Dowson for more on these debates: 'Such verdicts universalize the poetry from the weakest work and imply that realist modes, the intersection of historical and literary relevance or the wrong ideology were pertinent only to women's poems' (Dowson, *Women, Modernism and British Poetry: 1910–1939*, 37).

[52] Montefiore, ' "Shining Pins and Wailing Shells" ', 54.

[53] Dorothy Goldman, 'Introduction', in *idem* (ed.), *Women and World War*, i. 7.

[54] Plain, 'Great Expectations', 30.

In the preface to *Scars Upon My Heart*, Judith Kazantzis refers to how much of the critical and lay knowledge of the war comes from the poetry of soldiers like Sassoon and Owen. She goes on to say that we 'know little in poetry of what that agony and its millions of deaths meant to the millions of English women who had to endure them—to learn to survive survival'.[55] The poems in Reilly's anthology are one aspect of the various ways in which women testified to this process. They also give voice to the ways in which women found new identities in the war, ones which were as vital to the war effort as the trench soldier. Ouditt claims that it 'is likely that women's most commonly articulated (or unspoken) desire during the First World War was that justice be done to women and that their part in the war, whether as crusading nurse, desolated lover or pacifist activist, be acknowledged'.[56] The difficulty in articulating these desires was that it had to be done through traditional modes of expression if they were to be heard. All of the various forms of resistance and mourning contained within the traumas and losses of the war must be acknowledged.[57] The recent renaissance in First World War studies—including numerous conferences, books, television shows, and films—clearly indicates that the war has not lost its grip on the Anglo-American cultural imagination. This 'new' war is no untold story, but it must be appreciated that it was partly articulated by women.

[55] Judith Kazantzis, 'Preface', in Reilly (ed.), *Scars Upon My Heart*, repr. in Reilly (ed.), *Virago Book of Women's War Poetry and Verse*, p. xxi.

[56] Ouditt, *Fighting Forces, Writing Women*, 2.

[57] For an example of the current revision of First World War studies, see my 'Consoling Fictions: Mourning, World War One and Dorothy L. Sayers', in Patricia Rae (ed.), *Modernism and Mourning* (Lewisburg, Pa.: Bucknell University Press, 2006), 185–97. This piece is concerned with the ways in which popular fiction in the 1920s and 1930s synchronized with the forms and processes of mourning which dominated signifying practices, particularly modernism, after the war.

CHAPTER 6

··

WILFRED OWEN

··

MARK RAWLINSON

Wilfred Owen's cultural prominence is obvious, but also extraordinary, and it requires an effort of estrangement to begin to analyse its basis and its implications. The most famous and praised of a band of 'cultural heroes', 'his name has become synonymous with "war poetry" '.[1] Owen is an iconic victim and scapegoat: 'It was the war experience, the unanticipated horror of trench-combat, that turned him into the poet we now value so highly and respond to with such gratitude—gratitude because, more than any other poet of a century darkened by two mighty wars, he was able to tell us what war felt like and would feel like.'[2] Owen's reputation is not limited but guaranteed by his association with the war. It has been claimed, uncharitably, that in English schools today, poetry just is war poetry.[3] Some historians fear that Owen has become, by default, the primary authority on 1914–18, the pointsman in literary criticism's supposed campaign to wrest the First World War from the military historians.[4] But if our general and pedagogic culture has made of Owen an accessible modern, and an absolute historical witness, his normative status threatens to reduce his poems to convergent paraphrases and memorable epigrams. (Owen's most famous lines are a quoted, and rejected, Latin

---

[1] Adrian Caesar, *Taking It Like a Man: Suffering, Sexuality and the War Poets* (Manchester: Manchester University Press, 1993), 1 and 115.

[2] Ian Hamilton, *Against Oblivion: Some Lives of the Twentieth-Century Poets* (London: Penguin, 2003), 103.

[3] By the history editor of the *Times Literary Supplement*. See David Horspool, 'Back to Battle Stations', *The Guardian*, 21 Apr. 2001, Saturday Review, 9.

[4] The American critic Paul Fussell is singled out as the von Schlieffen behind this territorial *coup*. See Ian Beckett, 'The Military Historian and the Popular Image of the Western Front, 1914–1918', *The Historian*, Spring 1997, 11; and Brian Bond, *The Unquiet Western Front: Britain's Role in Literature and History* (Cambridge: Cambridge University Press, 2002), 88.

tag—as if Eliot could be sampled for effect by repeating '*Poi s'ascose nel foco che gli affina*'.)

This fate is marked by some obvious ironies. A poet who appeared to deprecate poetry in order better to resist social amnesia is now lord of the modern Parnassus, apotheosized as a witness to historical horror and even as a fictional character. His work is misremembered or misrecognized as a kind of attenuated and graphic combat story; and his lines are widely valued, in defiance of the evidence, for their refusal or transcendence of the merely poetic. As the archetypal 'poetry as witness', Owen's writing is beyond faulting: the absence of his verse from W. B. Yeats's *Oxford Book of Modern Verse* (1936) and Yeats's studied refusal of the emergent category of the war poet—'passive suffering is not a theme for poetry'[5]—have widely been viewed as a perversity. In the words of Seamus Heaney, 'what we might call his sanctity is a field of force which deflects anything as privileged as literary criticism. His poems have the potency of human testimony, of martyr's relics, so that any intrusion of the aesthetic can feel like an impropriety.'[6] But Desmond Graham has argued persuasively that Owen's poems deserve more exacting readings, the product of critical attention with its attendant improper questions:

This is partly because, used to other, more apparent obscurities we tend to read Owen slackly, assuming that we already know what he is saying; and it is partly the result of a general familiarity with the Great War and the anti-war spirit it engendered. The familiarity is especially dangerous as it encourages us to absorb both Owen's poetry and the war itself back into clichés of attitude. The once fresh exposé of the lies of militarism can live in our minds as a commonplace.[7]

Where recent scholarship has attempted this, it has done so largely by restoring the poems to Owen and to the historical contexts of their creation.[8] And in doing so, it might be said, Owen's poems have had to be reclaimed from his readers, as if to endorse Yeats's remark to Dorothy Wellesley: 'There is every excuse for him but none for those who like him.'[9]

For, as Graham suggests, Owen's poems have been appropriated as vehicles for familiar and anachronistic attitudes. The future pacifist John Middleton Murry

---

[5] W. B. Yeats, 'Introduction', in *idem* (ed.), *The Oxford Book of Modern Verse* (Oxford: Oxford University Press, 1936), p. xxxiv. Meanwhile, Michael Roberts, in *The Faber Book of Modern Verse* (1936) was celebrating the vowel cadences of Owen's half-rhymes.

[6] Seamus Heaney, 'The Interesting Case of Nero, Chekhov's Cognac and a Knocker', in *The Government of the Tongue: The 1986 T. S. Eliot Memorial Lectures and Other Writings* (London: Faber, 1988), p. xiv.

[7] Desmond Graham, *The Truth of War: Owen, Blunden, Rosenberg* (Manchester: Carcanet, 1984), 24.

[8] With no claim to inclusivity, one can highlight in this respect the work of Dominic Hibberd, building on the editorial and biographical scholarship of Jon Stallworthy, and the exegesis offered by Douglas Kerr, *Wilfred Owen's Voices: Language and Community* (Oxford: Oxford University Press, 1993).

[9] W. B. Yeats to Dorothy Wellesley, 26 Dec. 1936, in *Letters on Poetry from W. B. Yeats to Dorothy Wellesley*, ed. Kathleen Raine (Oxford: Oxford University Press, 1964), 113.

began one of the earliest appreciations of Owen's poetry, a review of the 1920 *Poems*, with an acknowledgement of their estranging qualities: 'I still remember the incredible shock of that encounter.'[10] James Fenton, eighty years later, revelling in the easy targets provided by the poet's juvenilia, reports instead the impact of Owen-the-war-poet's reversions to the borrowed idioms of 'Poesy', which attest to the 'oddity and uncertainty of the poet's development': 'Owen only shocks me [by] wilful nippings-back in style.'[11] Owen has become so familiar that he unsettles when he is himself and not his public image.

But to show signs of being disturbed or prostrated by Owen's poetry perhaps risks being mistaken for a jingo. Vietnam veteran Philip Caputo's memoir speaks on one level of the failure of Owen's warning, his goal of weaning future generations off the bellicist illusion:

After I came home from the war, I was often asked how it felt, going into combat for the first time. I never answered truthfully, afraid that people would think of me as some sort of war-lover. The truth is I felt happy. . . . I had read all the serious books to come out of the World Wars, and Wilfred Owen's poetry about the Western Front. And yet, I had learned nothing.[12]

But this passage is also eloquent about the stigma of appearing to be a 'war-lover', and a desire to present a mind clean of militaristic fetishes, a form of political correctness that can explain some misreadings of Owen's work.

It is now normal for English schoolchildren to read Owen and selected contemporaries in secondary school, some time between the age of 11 and 18. In a 'firmly pacifist' analysis of the literature with which teachers might challenge the idealization of war and violence, Winifred Whitehead writes that children should be introduced to books which 'firmly counter "the old lie"'. War poetry is efficacious in anti-war pedagogy, its 'freshness of experience' given added resonance by the 'poignancy' of authorial death.[13] It is deemed meet that schoolchildren should be confronted with 'the horror of war', though it remains unclear whether war sweetens the study of poetry, or vice versa. Owen himself precedes us in this respect, though as paternalistic elder brother rather than poet: 'I deliberately tell you all this to educate you to the actualities of war,' he wrote to Harold Owen about the sketches of war wounds he sent from his employers' villa in the Pyrenees two years and more before he went up to the line in an altogether different part of France, the British sector of the Western Front.[14]

---

[10]   John Middleton Murry, 'The Poet of the War', *The Nation and Athenaeum*, 28/21 (19 Feb. 1921), 705.

[11]   James Fenton, *The Strength of Poetry* (Oxford: Oxford University Press, 2001), 38.

[12]   Philip Caputo, *A Rumor of War* (London: Arrow, 1982), 81.

[13]   Winifred Whitehead, *Old Lies Revisited: Young Readers and the Literature of War and Violence* (London: Pluto, 1991), 70.

[14]   Wilfred Owen to Harold Owen, 23 Sept. 1914, in *Collected Letters*, ed. Harold Owen and John Bell (London: Oxford University Press, 1967), 285.

If it is hard to conceive of an adult today first opening Owen, it is not because such adults must have been persistent truants, but because this implies an unlikely innocence, the kind that Philip Larkin imagined was last to be seen in ranks of soberly dressed volunteers *circa* MCMXIV. The kinds of shock that Owen's poems can deliver today are connected with their construction of what Jahan Ramazani calls a 'guilty' audience.[15] This, I take it, is the undercurrent of Ted Hughes's Sassoonian homage (a rewriting of 'Blighters') to Owen's political authority. 'Wilfred Owen's Photographs' is about ostensive definition; hence it is a poem which resigns itself to the triumph of presence, sight, and touch over verbal signs. The poem describes a Commons debate hostile to legislation to abolish the cat-o'-nine-tails. But then the object in question is produced: 'Whereupon . . . quietly, unopposed, | The motion was passed.'[16] The guilty audience never includes us: Hughes's poem invites us to imagine brandishing Owen's verse, 'like the cat', at bearers of the 'old school tie' (often associated with the 'old lie'), a scenario that may indeed be more palatable than serving him up to children who can barely fix their own tie knots. The relationship Hughes sets up between poem and photograph resonates with the curious status of Owen's poems as artefact and witness, as verbal structures contrived to please with forms and fictions, and to disturb with gruesome rhythms and depictions.

Wilfred Owen's photographs are the ones recalled by Edinburgh University librarian Frank Nicholson, in a short memoir appended to Edmund Blunden's 1931 edition of the poems:

It was really the only occasion on which he had an opportunity of speaking freely to me, and it was then that I got a hint of the effect that the horrors he had seen and heard of at the Front had made upon him. He did not enlarge upon them, but they were obviously always in his thoughts, and he wished that an obtuse world should be made sensible of them. With this object he was collecting a set of photographs exhibiting the ravages of war upon the men who took part in it—mutilations, wounds, surgical operations, and the like. He had some of these photographs with him, and I remember that he put his hand to his breast-pocket to show me them, but suddenly thought better of it and refrained.[17]

Owen's first biographer, Jon Stallworthy, glosses Owen's second thoughts in a way that reminds us of the curse of bellophilia in Philip Caputo's memoir: 'his friend had no need of that particular lesson in reality'.[18] Nicholson, however, was loath to assert that modern ideological identity with the poet, noting that while 'perhaps'

[15] Jahan Ramazani, *Poetry of Mourning: The Modern Elegy from Hardy to Heaney* (Chicago: University of Chicago Press, 1994), 81.

[16] Ted Hughes, 'Wilfred Owen's Photographs', in *The Collected Poems*, ed. Paul Keegan (London: Faber, 2003), 79.

[17] Frank Nicholson, 'Memoir', in *The Poems of Wilfred Owen*, ed. Edmund Blunden (London: Chatto & Windus, 1933), 134.

[18] Jon Stallworthy, *Wilfred Owen* (Oxford: Oxford University Press, 1988), 222.

Owen thought 'such methods of propaganda were superfluous in my case', 'no doubt he felt the sight of them would be painful to me'.[19]

Owen's urge to assault the senses of the 'obtuse' with graphic renditions of hurt here precedes the poems which would become culturally acceptable forms of hurtful confrontation (an offensive interaction sometimes crudely dramatized in Sassoon's sonnets, like 'The Glory of Women'). If poetry served political protest against the war, because it could get past the censors, it also gets past another kind of censorship, which is more readily offended by graphic images of physical trauma, as both sources of disgust and of (disgusting) pleasure. (By analogy, we might compare the reception of a notorious *Guardian* front-page photograph of the charred corpse of an Iraqi tank commander from the First Gulf War, with that of Tony Harrison's poem on this image, 'A Cold Coming'.[20])

The conundrum of Owen's status as poet is compounded by something akin to but not quite the guilty paradox of 'saccharined . . . death' which Seamus Heaney unearths in reassessing his poetry of the Troubles in 'Station Island'.[21] With Owen it is a question of the persistence with which readers and critics have read against the grain and insisted on excluding the aesthetic, except where it can be reinscribed as history, in line with Louis MacNeice's notion of an 'impure poetry . . . conditioned by the poet's life'.[22]

OWEN MAKES HIMSELF A WAR POET

A further issue in evaluating Owen is the posthumousness of his public literary career. From this point of view, he is identical with his reception and publication histories, not differentiated from them and the uses to which he has been put (as in the case of Keats or Bob Dylan). Notably, the poet was revealed to his growing public in a process which reversed his poetic development, a factor which has perhaps given renewed life to the legend of the poet made by the war, which his early death helped to cement. In his lifetime, Owen published four poems: 'Song of Songs', an exercise in pararhyme which did not refer to the war (first in *The Hydra*, the Craiglockhart journal that Owen edited, then as a competition runner-up in *The Bookman*), 'Miners', 'Hospital Barge', and 'Futility' (all in *The Nation* during 1918).

---

[19] Nicholson, 'Memoir', 134–5.
[20] Kenneth Jarecke's photograph in *The Guardian*, 18 Mar. 1991, 1. On the first day of the 'War, Art and Medicine' conference, University College London/National Portrait Gallery, Oct. 2002, similar unease was evident in discussion following the public reproduction of the pastel sketches of the torn faces of servicemen made by Henry Tonks for the Great War plastic surgeon Harold Gillies at Queens Hospital Sidcup.
[21] Seamus Heaney, 'Station Island', in *Opened Ground: Poems 1966–1996* (London: Faber, 1998), 261.
[22] Louis MacNeice, *Modern Poetry: A Personal Essay* (Oxford: Oxford University Press, 1968), 79.

None of these poems corresponds to the figure of Owen as realist or satirical poet, though they are fairly representative of the broad characteristics of his *œuvre*, both formally and thematically. Seven further poems were included in Edith Sitwell's 1919 edition of the anthology *Wheels*, which she dedicated to the memory of Owen ('Strange Meeting', 'The Show', 'A Terre', 'The Sentry', 'Disabled', 'The Dead Beat', 'The Chances'). Her edition of *Poems by Wilfred Owen* (1920), remembered for Sassoon's introduction and for the inclusion of Owen's preface, added 'Futility' and fifteen further poems, including 'Dulce et Decorum Est', 'Insensibility', 'Spring Offensive', and 'Mental Cases'. Edmund Blunden's 1931 'New Edition', included pre-Craiglockhart poems for the first time, and printed Owen's 'table of contents'. The next edition, C. Day Lewis's *The Collected Poems of Wilfred Owen*, appeared in 1963, dividing a further enlarged corpus into an opening section of 'war poems' followed by 'other poems, and fragments' (to which 'Miners' was relegated) and 'minor poems and juvenilia'. Hibberd's edition of *War Poems and Others* (1973) interleaved extracts from letters amongst fifty-three poems sequenced according to date of composition. The most recent, and still the standard, edition was the fourth by a poet. Jon Stallworthy ordered the poems by date of final revision. ('Strange Meeting' is the last poem in Blunden, the first in Day Lewis, the third from last in Hibberd, and rather anonymously mid-table-of-contents in Stallworthy.) While the amount of data about Owen in circulation has increased, the war poet has not receded. Having read the first biography, Larkin told Robert Conquest that his much-admired Owen now 'seems rather a prick, really'; 'yet the poems', seven of which were printed in Larkin's revisionist *Oxford Book of Twentieth-Century English Verse* (1973), 'stay good'.[23]

Familiarity or facility with symbols of the Great War can make for presumptuous readers, not least through tacit invocations of an ideal type or generic war poet (a tendency reinforced, in James Campbell's analysis, by the way in which 'war poetry critics have protested the sufferings of *their* subjects',[24] substituting apology for criticism). Owen's own war was iconic, but in significant ways atypical, not just because he was a poet before he was a soldier. Most of Owen's war poems are based on his experiences in the first five months of 1917. During that time he was in hospital for six weeks, on a course in the base area for four weeks, and in action for only about thirty days. His front line service was unusually concentrated and varied. After helping to defend shattered positions that had hardly moved for more than a year, he took part in a few days of fast-moving, open warfare, virtually the only such moment anywhere on the British front between October 1914 and March 1918. He was never physically wounded, and he endured very little of what is thought of as the standard Western Front experience, the ghastly monotony of routine trench

---

[23] Philip Larkin to Robert Conquest, 9 Jan. 1975, in *The Letters of Philip Larkin*, ed. Anthony Thwaite (London: Faber, 1992), 519.

[24] James Campbell, 'Combat Gnosticism: The Ideology of First World War Poetry Criticism', *New Literary History*, 30 (1999), 210.

duty.[25] Owen's death, during an offensive crossing of the Oise-Sambre canal a week before the Armistice, was read from the start as a terminal irony of war, potent enough to help obscure a now 'forgotten victory'.[26]

At the end of April 1917, more than a week after his battalion of the Manchesters had been taken out of the line, Owen was dispatched to a Casualty Clearing Station specializing in the treatment of shell-shock (using William Brown's abreaction therapy.)[27] Evacuated across the Channel in June, Owen was boarded unfit for Home Service and transferred to Craiglockhart Hospital in Edinburgh. His treatment there by the 'ergotherapist' A. J. Brock continued until the end of October. Brock urged Owen to write, and in *Health and Conduct* (1923) he offered one of the earliest commentaries on the 'war poems' as a literal mastering of 'the phantoms of the mind'.[28]

At the end of January 1918 Owen was boarded for light duties, but he was not posted to the vast Northern Command Depot at Ripon until March, days before Ludendorff's break-out from the Hindenberg Line. A letter to his mother Susan at the beginning of October represents France as the elective destiny of the vatic poet: 'I came out in order to help these boys—directly by leading them as well as an officer can; indirectly, by watching their sufferings that I may speak of them as well as a pleader can.'[29] But while Field Marshal Haig's 'backs to the wall' Order of the Day for April 11—'each one of us must fight on to the end'[30]—made a return to France seemingly inevitable, Owen continued to pursue the possibility of home postings which would dramatically increase his chances of surviving the war to fulfil his poetic ambitions. C. K. Scott-Moncrieff, a new friend from Robert Ross's Poetry Book Shop circle, and the future translator of Proust, was employed at the War Office, whence he had helped get Robert Graves a 'safe' posting in Wales. Now a published poet, Owen also sought to build on his first contacts in metropolitan literary society. A note titled '*Projects*. (May 5. 1918. Ripon)' maps out a future including 'blank-verse plays on old Welsh themes', a return to the 'invented mythology' of a work in progress titled *Perseus*, and a collection of the juvenilia from which, it has often been claimed, the war had cut him free. As James Fenton notes, this plan wrecks the received story, the 'handy teleologies, which would have led us to construct an Owen shocked into the twentieth century by the war'.[31]

---

[25] See Dominic Hibberd, *Wilfred Owen: A New Biography* (London: Weidenfeld & Nicolson, 2002), p. xvii.

[26] Dan Todman, *The Great War: Myth and Memory* (London: Hambledon, 2005), 173.

[27] For an account of the rival therapies and the management of 'shell-shock', see Ben Shephard, *A War of Nerves: Soldiers and Psychiatrists 1914–1994* (London: Jonathan Cape, 2001).

[28] A. J. Brock, quoted in Hibberd, *Wilfred Owen*, 254–5.

[29] Owen to Susan Owen, 4/5 Oct. 1918, in *Collected Letters*, 580.

[30] Field Marshal Haig, quoted in Gary Sheffield, *Forgotten Victory: The First World War: Myths and Realities* (London: Review, 2002), 229; Hibberd, *Wilfred Owen*, 314.

[31] Fenton, *Strength of Poetry*, 37.

At the same time Owen was planning a collection entitled 'Disabled and Other Poems'. From April, in a cottage in Ripon acquired for the purpose, until June, when, boarded fit for active service, he was posted back to his unit, he revised all the war poems he had written since the previous summer, and composed a dozen new ones, including 'Strange Meeting', 'Mental Cases', and 'Futility'. Notwithstanding plans for a writing life after the Army, the sequence in Stallworthy's edition underlines Owen's immediate efforts to determine a publishable state for his war poems in the spring of 1918.

'DISABLED AND OTHER POEMS': THE ARCHITECTURE OF OWEN'S POETRY

Stephen Spender registered the freshness and strangeness of Owen before he became familiar, attributing to him a 'deeper human understanding' than to the 'aristocratic' Yeats, and making him a touchstone of 'pity for human suffering' by which we might place the early Eliot; but, most interestingly, he characterized Owen's *œuvre* (in Blunden's edition) by its heterogeneity. There is a conception of a 'whole edifice' in Owen's plans for 'Disabled and Other Poems', but Spender was obliged to note 'how very different all his poems are from each other. Each poem takes an entirely different aspect of this war, centred always in some incident, and builds round it.'[32] How much more serviceable is this appreciation of the emotional, rhetorical, and intellectual angularity of Owen's writing than the innocence to experience model of the Great War and its cultural impact, a model that flatters those born into hindsight, and flattens concrete experience.

Before he sought out the poems in *The Old Huntsman*, Owen knew Siegfried Sassoon, who was sent to Craiglockhart in July 1917, as the author of a 'too plain-spoken' letter to the 'Higher Command' (the text published in *The Times* that month as 'A Soldier's Declaration' is commonly known, in a tacit analogy with Luther's theses on Church corruption, as 'Sassoon's Protest').[33] Sassoon studiously dissociated himself from a critique of tactics and strategy (of the kind characteristic of post-war excoriations of staff incompetence from Basil Liddell Hart to Alan Clark and beyond):

I am not protesting against the military conduct of the War, but against the political errors and insincerities for which the fighting men are being sacrificed.

On behalf of those who are suffering now, I make this protest against the deception which is being practised on them. Also I believe that it may help to destroy the callous complacence

---

[32] Stephen Spender, *The Destructive Element: A Study of Modern Writers and Beliefs* (London: Jonathan Cape, 1935), 219.

[33] Owen to Susan Owen, 15 Aug. 1917, in *Collected Letters*, 485.

with which the majority of those at home regard the continuance of agonies which they do not share and which they have not sufficient imagination to realise.[34]

Sassoon altered Owen's sense of his past and future as a writer. Sassoon's 'The Redeemer', with its image of soldier as Christ crucified, was the poem, Owen now wrote, 'I have been wishing to write every week for the last three years',[35] as if he would backdate his identity as war poet to the outbreak of war (he joined up in October 1915, and wrote his first war poem, 'Inspection', in August 1917). Additionally, Sassoon's declaration of dissent mapped out the social co-ordinates of a discourse that Owen would explore in the next months, one which ventriloquized the mute suffering soldiery and harrowed the insensitive civilian.

The British Library sketch of contents for 'Disabled and Other Poems' opens with ten poems linked by a brace to the reiterated and underlined word 'Protest', the last of which is 'The Dead-Beat', the first verses that Owen wrote in 'Sassoon's style'.[36] The earliest version of this poem is in quatrains, and describes soldierly insensibility ('clot of meat') in juxtaposition with the Home Front discourses about the war which are supposed to provoke it—Caxton Hall (venue of a series of political lectures, a 'fashionable focus for resistance to the war', in which Bertrand Russell opposed the Military Service Act[37]), *Punch*, Bruce Bairnsfather (the invalided soldier who created the cartoon character 'Old Bill'), and Hilaire Belloc's weekly commentaries on the war in *Land and Water* (a continuation of *The Country Gentleman*).[38]

The revised version excises these deictical traces to create a starker myth (in line with the remark in the draft preface about the omission of 'proper names'): the dead-beat is sent mad not by the remains of dead comrades but by a vision of 'Blighty' and those who prosper there. (Blighty here is not the life-saving wound, 'a blighty', wished for by the speaker in 'The Chances', but one pole in a mind-wrenching dissonance that divides soldier and civilian.) 'The Dead-Beat' is an imitation, but with its callous 'Doc' rejoicing at the happy resolution ('"That scum you sent last night soon died"') of a diagnostic problem (is the 'unwounded' soldier 'crazed' or 'malingering'?), the poem is unmistakably a working through of Owen's own predicament as a visibly whole soldier not in France but in hospital.[39]

'Protest', for Owen, designated poems confronting the war's negations: 'Unrecognition', 'unnaturalness', 'inhumanity', 'lies', and madness. The volume was to

---

[34] Siegfried Sassoon, quoted in Jean Moorcroft Wilson, *Siegfried Sassoon: The Making of a War Poet* (London: Duckworth, 1999), 374.

[35] Owen to Mary Owen, 29 Aug. 1917, in *Collected Letters*, 489.

[36] See Owen's lists of contents, in *The Complete Poems and Fragments*, ii: *The Manuscripts and Fragments*, ed. Jon Stallworthy (London: Chatto & Windus, Hogarth Press, and Oxford University Press, 1983), 538–40; Owen to Leslie Gunston, 22 Aug. 1917, in *Collected Letters*, 485.

[37] Ray Monk, *Bertrand Russell: The Spirit of Solitude* (London: Jonathan Cape, 1996), 450.

[38] Owen, *Complete Poems and Fragments*, ii. 299.

[39] Owen, 'The Dead-Beat', in *The Complete Poems and Fragments*, i: *The Poems*, ed. Jon Stallworthy (London: Chatto & Windus, Hogarth Press, and Oxford University Press, 1983), 144.

open with 'Miners', in which posterity's neglect (conventionally a poet's jibe at future non-readers) is applied to dead colliers, colliers conscripted to work 'dark pits of War', and soldiers in general. The injunction of the official culture of remembrance—'lest we forget'—lay in the future, but it is scorned in advance with a vision of a 'soft-chaired' post-war which complacently fails to recall 'poor lads, | Left in the ground' (the triumphalism of Brooke's 'corner of a foreign field' is bathetically collapsed into household fuel).[40] 'On Seeing a Piece of Our Heavy Artillery Brought into Action' and 'Arms and the Boy' draw respectively on Owen's nineteenth-century tastes for variations on the sonnet and for decadent eroticism to elaborate on the theme of 'the unnaturalness of weapons'. The latter metalizes desire in the form of bayonet and bullet, 'famishing for flesh' and 'long[ing] to nuzzle in the hearts of lads', but the former metamorphoses the 'Great Gun' into a body part—'long black arm', 'dark arm'—which must, once 'that Arrogance which needs thy harm' is beaten down, be cut away.[41]

The masculine rhyming couplets of 'The Chances' (a poem begun at Craiglock-hart) underline the colloquial authority of a soldier 'who was in the know' about the kind of things 'as can happen' in a show.[42] The cadence is then held up with a quatrain that concludes on a stark and unhypocritical label for the 'misfortune' of being 'wounded, killed, and pris'ner': 'Jim's mad'. The more recently drafted 'Mental Cases', by contrast, dispenses with rhyme in a Dantean extension of the cosmology of 'Strange Meeting': 'Surely we have perished | Sleeping, and walk hell; but who these hellish?'[43] In the revised version of 'The Dead-Beat', the idea of being driven mad by the thought of others' safety is attributed to a private sol-dier. 'Mental Cases' associates its aetiology of madness with a first-person plural pronoun; we are interpellated as latter-day Virgils and made to walk the wards of some institutional inferno. The mad are mentally 'ravished' by the dead, a verb that blends the sense of military seizure with connotations of sexualized violence. This dissolution of categories is the key to the poem's rhetoric, which is directed at making us recognize that it was 'us who dealt them war and madness'. Psychiatric patients are corpse-like ('skulls' teeth', 'fretted sockets'). War is remembered as a phantasmagoria out of Bosch: 'sloughs of flesh', 'treading blood', 'flying muscles'. Nature is irremediably stained by this murder (shades of *Macbeth*): 'Sunlight seems a blood smear . . . | Dawn breaks open like a wound' (the poem further integrates the conceit in 'Inspection', next but one in the contents list, with its play on blood, dirt, and whitewash). The last distinction to fall in 'Mental Cases' is the one preserved by the readers' implied illusions of immunity, as the hands of the 'set-smiling corpses' come 'snatching after us who smote them'.

---

[40] Owen, 'Miners', ibid. 135–6; Rupert Brooke, 'The Soldier', in *Poetical Works of Rupert Brooke*, ed. Geoffrey Keynes (London: Faber, 1960), 23.
[41] Owen, 'Arms and the Boy', in *The Complete Poems and Fragments*, i. 151; 'On Seeing a Piece of Our Heavy Artillery Brought into Action', ibid. 154.
[42] Owen, 'The Chances', ibid. 171.   [43] Owen, 'Mental Cases', ibid. 169.

The devices of 'Inspection' (a private soldier's projection of 'Field Marshall God')[44] and 'The Last Laugh', which reprises the choric ordnance of 'Anthem for Doomed Youth' to mock the last words of the dying ('the Gas hissed')[45] are associated by Owen with the 'Inhumanity of War'. This is literally the case in the poems' alienation of war (via the agency of the supernatural or inanimate). 'Dulce et Decorum Est', by contrast, insists that the inhumanity of war is the want of humanity on the part of those who represent it as a desirable and proper state of affairs.

Owen carefully recorded the 'motives' of the poems he was collecting, presumably as an aid to their ordering and selection.[46] These bald, sometimes instrumental, paraphrases emphasize the didactic thrust of the volume (as do the poems he labels doubtful, such as '1914', 'Greater Love', and 'Identity Disc'): 'willingness of the old to sacrifice the young' (his powerful recasting of Abraham and Isaac), 'the insupportability of war' ('S.I.W.', a multifaceted narrative which gives the lie to the self-inflicted wound), 'vastness of losses', 'horrible beastliness of war' (an oddly apposite description for the allegorizing of 'The Show'), 'foolishness of war' (there is more to 'Strange Meeting' than that). Grief is represented by 'Anthem for Doomed Youth', the Tennysonian Arthurianism of 'Hospital Barge' and 'Futility', which are gathered after poems labelled 'cheerfulness'. Alongside a group dealing with 'the soul of soldiers', the latter are an aspect of Owen's complication of his portrait of the serviceman. The scheme in which he prepared his poems for the public brings out the variousness of his perspectives on the war, but it also promoted the political at the expense of the poetic. However, as Murry noted in 1920, in the new writing he was doing in 1918, 'there is no more rebellion, but only pity and regret, and the peace of acquiescence'.[47] Like the famous draft preface, 'Disabled and Other Poems' is an attempt to straighten out some of the contradictions in his evolving poetry of war.

Owen and the Poetry of War

'Apologia pro Poemate Meo', Dominic Hibberd has suggested, represents a distancing from Sassoon ('Poetry with him is become a mere vehicle of propaganda') at the behest of Robert Graves, who urged him that 'a poet should have a spirit above wars'.[48] It also transforms Owen's didacticism into something else, with which readers and critics have been less comfortable (even where they have been

[44] Owen, 'Inspection', in *Complete Poems and Fragments*, 95.
[45] Owen, 'The Last Laugh, ibid. 168.
[46] See Owen's lists of contents, in *Complete Poems and Fragments*, ii. 539.
[47] Murry, 'Poet of the War', 706.
[48] Hibberd, *Wilfred Owen*, 293–4; Owen to Leslie Gunston, 30 Dec. 1917, and Robert Graves to Wilfred Owen, *c.*22 Dec. 1917, in *Collected Letters*, 520 and 596.

able to recognize it). The distance which separated the civilian from the soldier—a failure of imagination, of responsibility—is turned into the privileged remoteness of a realm which is at once traumatic and enchanted. While the former is in practice often recoded by readers as an index of their own separation from bellicist ideologies, the latter does not fit into binary schemes of war and civility. We can chart this development of a poetry which locates positive value in 'the inwardness of war',[49] as Owen called it in 1918, towards his last poem, 'Spring Offensive', via the poem which has been presented as his *summa*, 'Strange Meeting'.

John Bayley once observed of Owen's bearding of his readers for their obtuseness, 'Amazing how it works, for nothing is more tiresome than to be told that one is utterly deficient in feeling for and understanding of something which one was not there to understand.'[50] We may recognize Bayley's experience, also that of the wedding guest in 'The Rime of the Ancient Mariner', but few of Owen's poems directly defy or affront the reader in this way. 'Dulce et Decorum Est' is one, and it wishes on its addressee 'some smothering dreams', like the nightmare about a gassed soldier it has just re-enacted. This desire to inflict battle trauma on those who have never been there approximates to the Sassoonian curse (the tank-in-the-music-hall fantasy of 'Blighters'), but its primary meaning is an unsatisfied condition for truth telling, the condition that the addressee, 'my friend', evidently fails to fulfil for as long as they repeat 'The old Lie'.[51] But the poem had earlier been addressed not to a reader but a writer, the poet Jessie Pope, who had imagined the infantry 'on tour':

> They'll take the Kaiser's middle wicket
> And smash it by clean British Cricket.[52]

Owen rejected two epigraphs—'To Jessie Pope, etc.', then 'To a Certain Poetess'—to leave the identity of those whose sleep is uninterrupted by war dreams unspecified.[53] But it is debatable how many readers feel themselves arraigned in this coda, rather than identifying with the poem's hostility to a jingoism which corrupts children (with 'incurable sores on innocent tongues').

'Apologia pro Poemate Meo', with its dogmatic insistence that because you do not 'share' in hell you are fit to be abased, supplies a pattern, but it is, in confirmation of Spender's observation of Owen's difference from himself, one which goes unrepeated:

> You shall not hear their mirth:
> You shall not come to think them well content

---

[49] Owen to Susan Owen, 31 Mar. 1918, in *Collected Letters*, 543.

[50] John Bayley, 'But for Beaumont Hamel . . .', *The Spectator*, 4 Oct. 1963, 419.

[51] Owen, 'Dulce et Decorum Est', in *Complete Poems and Fragments*,. 140.

[52] Jessie Pope, 'Cricket', in Dominic Hibberd and John Onions (eds.), *Poetry of the Great War: An Anthology* (Basingstoke: Palgrave, 1986), 58.

[53] See Owen's drafts for 'Dulce et Decorum Est', in *Complete Poems and Fragments*, ii. 294 and 296.

By any jest of mine. These men are worth
Your tears. You are not worth their merriment.[54]

.ve here is in fact a counterweight in a poem which started out as
ɔ, for the negativity of his war poems and turned into a risky exhibition of
. s compensations and thrills.

'Apologia pro Poemate Meo' might appear to be a deliberate exercise in reversing
the tropes of a Craiglockhart poem such as 'Dulce et Decorum Est': the curses of
'beggars' are transformed into the 'glee' of exultant warriors. Owen had anticipated
this new way of understanding the soldier's experience, an advance on the broader
ironies of *Wipers Times*-style black humour of the trenches, in another Craiglockhart poem, 'Insensibility'. Those soldiers who 'lose imagination' are released from
entanglements, 'their spirit drags no pack', and they can 'laugh among the dying'.[55]
The poem explicitly curses 'dullards whom no cannon stuns' for electing a different
kind of insensibility, denial not adaptation—'By choice they made themselves
immune | To pity'. In contrast, soldiers' insensibilities are forms of moral and intel-
lectual cauterization—the cessation of compassion, empathy, perspective—which
symbolize the usurpation of their humanity by war: 'some cease feeling | Even them-
selves or for themselves'. Here, 'happy' is the ironic (and Housmanesque) good
hap or fortune of unawareness, a felicity or fitness for circumstance in the loss
of faculties. But this phenomenology of front line duty (compare 'Exposure') is
at odds with the way in which Owen's imagination was animated to create new
conceptions of war experience.

'Apologia pro Poemate Meo' revalues the passivity (the picture of war stamping
out the autonomous individual) of 'Insensibility' into an active glorification of
battle: 'power was on us as we slashed bones bare'. The poet sails his unencumbered
spirit to enact a new kind of witness, passing out of a landscape of hopes strewn
in the 'sludge' ('Dulce et Decorum Est') or 'slime' ('The Sentry'[56]) into the realm
of a spirit (both an aspect of deity and a kind of morale) which shines through
the mud that masks faces. 'Anthem for Doomed Youth', whose refusal of the
consolations of Christian culture has been deconstructed many times since Jon
Silkin's 1972 reading, mimicked a cacophony of military noise which provided an
unmocking music of committal (its plangency drowns out the tones of consolatory
mourning). If Owen is unequal to keeping compensating myths at bay in this
poem,[57] in 'Apologia pro Poemate Meo' he embraces them with weird relish, now
deploying the language of Christian ritual and symbolism to elevate camaraderie
to an almost absurd spiritual plane. Countering the deafening soundings of a
battlefield purified of piety in 'Anthem for Doomed Youth', aesthetic sensation

[54] Owen, 'Apologia pro Poemate Meo', in *Complete Poems and Fragments*, i. 125.
[55] Owen, 'Insensibility', ibid. 145.   [56] Owen, 'The Sentry', ibid. 188.
[57] See Ramazani, *Poetry of Mourning*, 69–70.

now brings stillness—'beauty', 'music', and 'peace'—to the 'shell-storms'.[58] His men are transfigured into seraphs, curses and scowls at resented authority replaced by a passion for sacrifice.

The reversals of 'Apologia pro Poemate Meo' appear excessive. Here, surely, is a send-up of Pope's inflated rhetoric of soldier-tourists, boys eager to be matched with death in the ultimate test (that Owen recognized the psychological force of these concepts and feelings is witnessed by his narrative of delusion in 'Disabled').[59] But this reaction—and how often is Great War poetry read ironically when it goes against the grain of latter-day received opinion—is a mark of the disconcerting qualities of Owen's fascination with insensibility's Romantic antithesis, afflatus. War can be represented in terms of the civilian's ignorance (a mode employed by critics, notably Paul Fussell, as much as by poets) but also in terms of the soldier's inspiration. As Hibberd has come to stress in his painstaking reassessment of Owen's life and work, what singles Owen out is his mastery both of the kinship of pleasure and abomination (in rhythm, rhyme, and image) and of the convergence between his conception of the poet's relations to the oracular (out of Keats's *The Fall of Hyperion*) and the secrets into which soldiers are initiated.[60]

'Smile, Smile, Smile', a late poem written in France, attempts to bring these perspectives into alignment, and it does so with a novel representation of the reader, this time a figure for the soldier, not the civilian. A group of wounded men, 'head to limp head', are hectored by yesterday's *Mail*, which preaches unending war (also a war of generations, in the manner of 'The Parable of the Old Man and the Young'): 'Peace would do wrong to our undying dead.'[61] A fight to the finish is represented as the only monument to those who 'kept this nation in integrity', but in the poem the readers of this blague have no need to challenge it:

> The half-limbed readers did not chafe
> But smiled at one another curiously
> Like secret men who know their secret safe.

In Remarque, and in Benjamin, war brings on muteness. Owen, who had kept nothing about the Front secret from his mother Susan, his chief correspondent, imagines instead a conspiracy of silence, a brotherhood of privileged knowledge (issues of knowing and not knowing—both sides of the military's 'in the know'—are more consistent and complex reference points in Owen's poetry than is pity). Owen's figures for the unsayable are a link between the Romantic sublime and the Holocaust of Lanzmann and Lyotard. It is significant that Owen specifies what this knowledge is here ('Apologia pro Poemate Meo' begs to withhold what it has revealed):

---

[58] Owen, 'Apologia pro Poemate Meo', in *Complete Poems and Fragments*, i. 124.
[59] Amongst Owen's legatees, the Oxbridge writers of the 1930s, notably the autobiographical Isherwood, but also Auden and Spender, would labour under the moral burden of a missed test.
[60] See Hibberd, *Wilfred Owen*, 294.
[61] Owen, 'Smile, Smile, Smile', in *Complete Poems and Fragments*, i. 190.

> (This is the thing they know and never speak,
> That England one by one had fled to France,
> Not many elsewhere now, save under France.)

This is not only a richly ironic version of two nations politics: it is a gesture of dissociation which appropriates the foreign field as the true home (not 'Cheap Homes' for heroes) of English soldiery. This is a general form of the specific escape in 'Strange Meeting', the poem in which Owen attempted to integrate afflatus (OED: 'miraculous communication of supernatural knowledge', 'the imparting of an over-mastering impulse'), brotherhood, and violence.

'Strange Meeting' is consciously a departure from 'war poetry' as a rendition of experience or traumatic memory. This is a dream vision, a constructed landscape in which Owen sets in motion a figure derived from the earlier 'Earth's wheels run oiled with blood'. This poem argued that 'we' should 'fall out' (Sassoon was about to report to his regiment) and that he and Sassoon should dedicate themselves instead to poetry:

> Wisdom is yours and you have mastery.
> Beauty is mine, and I have mystery.[62]

This brotherhood in verse is transposed in 'Strange Meeting' to a *rapprochement* in 'Hell' (the dead man's 'dead smile' is not the mark of muzzle on mouth, as in 'S.I.W.', but an anticipation of the secret society of 'Smile, Smile, Smile').[63]

A key to the poem is the 'piteous recognition' of the 'strange friend' (a 'German conscript' in draft[64]), piteous recognition being what Owen has sought both to provoke and to deny in his audience. Significantly, this is not a recognition of the violence done *to* but *by* an individual: the poet extends his hands 'as if to bless' the dreamer whose blows he had vainly parried. Thus the dreamer is the proximate reason why 'men will go content with what we spoiled': namely, what is unsaid because of the poet's death. Keith Douglas's version of this poem, '*Vergissmeinnicht*', simplifies the scenario: it is the killer who recognizes the corpse 'almost with content'.[65] The form of 'Strange Meeting', by contrast, makes it possible for the silencing of the poet to be the occasion of reconciliation (in contrast to the failed touch of the sun in 'Futility').[66]

However, we would expect the dream vision to end with a waking back to reality, with a return on the trip (the epistemic content of the vision). The poem is incomplete in this sense (and editors have urged we regard it as unfinished): 'Let

---

[62] Owen, 'Earth's wheels run oiled with blood', in *Complete Poems and Fragments*, ii. 514.

[63] Owen, 'Strange Meeting', in *Complete Poems and Fragments*, i. 148.

[64] Owen, *Complete Poems and Fragments*, ii. 307.

[65] Keith Douglas, '*Vergissmeinnicht*', in *The Complete Poems*, ed. Desmond Graham (London: Faber, 2000), 118.

[66] See Santanu Das, *Touch and Intimacy in First World War Literature* (Cambridge: Cambridge University Press, 2006), 159–62.

us sleep now . . .' Crucially, the 'truth untold' remains unsaid, the oracular vision cannot be brought back. 'Strange Meeting' does not so much describe war as escape it (as Blunden or Sassoon, in their memoirs, always remark when leaving the line for rear areas; only their destination is bucolic, and this is hell). The poem's central concern is the fate of the poetic vision, which is here to be interred far from mortal sight (compare the buried 'voices' of the coal in 'Miners').

'Spring Offensive' reconfigures this myth of the 'truth untold' in the context of rapine soldiers rather than poets, thus developing the dialectic between the figures in 'Strange Meeting':

> But what say such as from existence' brink
> Ventured but drave too swift to sink,
> The few who rushed in the body to enter hell,
> And there out-fiending all its fiends and flames
> With superhuman inhumanities,
> Long-famous glories, immemorial shames—
> And crawling slowly back, have by degrees
> Regained cool peaceful air in wonder—
> Why speak not they of comrades that went under?[67]

These overmen are survivors, and unlike the dreamer and many of their fellow soldiers, they have made it back. Why do they not speak? Well, they are not poets. But like the soldier-newspaper-readers of 'Smile, Smile, Smile', they are conspirators in silence, guardians of a knowledge that cannot be communicated.

The distance between Owen's 'war poetry' and the works in which he attempts to find ways of expressing the poetry in war may be measured in a comparison of 'The Show', drafted at the end of 1917 and drawing on Henri Barbusse's novel *Le Feu* (1916), and the landscape of war in 'Spring Offensive'. The former is transitional, already departing from psychologistic and documentary frameworks for war experience and, like 'Strange Meeting', employing the device of distance from the battlefield: here, 'My soul looked down from a vague height.'[68] The poem is an experiment in representing the repellent—from on high the battlefield looks like a corpse covered in insects (another motif that Douglas revises in 'Vergissmeinnicht'), and the movements of these ramping caterpillars—'I saw their bitten backs curve, loop, and straighten'—are a disturbing reversal of the pathetic fallacy (more commonly the image of the human swarm is associated with right-wing authoritarian discourses on war).[69] The vision is completed with Death showing the speaker his face on the severed head of such a 'worm' with 'the feet of many men'. 'Spring Offensive' transforms the 'slimy' battlefield with its 'foul openings' into a different kind of space. (Back in the 1930s, I. M. Parsons drew

[67] Owen, 'Spring Offensive', in *Complete Poems and Fragments*, i. 193.
[68] Owen, 'The Show', ibid. 155.
[69] See Klaus Theweleit, *Male Fantasies*, 2 vols. (Cambridge: Polity, 1987–9); and Mark Rawlinson, *British Writing of the Second World War* (Oxford: Clarendon Press, 2000), 64 and 192.

on Rupert Brooke and I. A. Richards when he characterized the impact of Owen's work as 'a sense of release, as from some clogging mental medium into a cleaner and more firmly grasped state of mind'.[70]) The violence of combat—barrage, small arms, hand-to-hand engagement—is presented with a significant variant of Owen's iconography of weaponry, making the soldier's body the object of sacrifice and transubstantiation. Whereas the earth is rent, bodies are put into motion, 'went up' or 'plunged and fell away'. They are not torn, and their blood is cupped. As they 'breast' the 'surf of bullets', these soldiers may recall the leaping swimmers in Brooke's sonnet 'Peace', but they are closer to the Innocents of Yeats's 'News for the Delphic Oracle', or indeed the bodies, poised between elation in nakedness and vulnerability to harm, in F. T. Prince's Second World War poem 'Soldiers Bathing' (set on one of Scarborough's beaches).

Owen's protest was succeeded by a phase of creation, of which the burden was no longer the urgent need to communicate knowledge but instead a concern to find adequate emblems for the 'inwardness of war' which cannot be broadcast. In this he was abetted by his youthful investment in Romantic myths of oracular inspiration, a device that resurfaces in his later poems as a form for revealing that which must remain outside the ken of mortals.

His draft of a preface for his war poems (composed around May 1918) reveals unease with the direction his writing had taken. It draws on the language of 'Strange Meeting' (as well as that of William Wordsworth's Preface to *Lyrical Ballads*) to distance his work from the very poetic mythology that that poem renews, and this is part of the reason for its verbal familiarity. The visual cohesion of letterpress invites us to collude in supplying logical relations amongst Owen's notes, but this is to gloss over significant aporia which are the traces of Owen's argument with himself, rather than his argument with warmongers.[71] To paraphrase, with Owen's cancellations in square brackets, and my commentary in round ones: the poet doesn't write about heroes (because) English poetry is 'not yet fit' to speak of heroes. The volume is about War, but not concepts of war: ['battle'], glory, honour, and so on (the implication here seems to be that the category of heroes, by contrast, is non-idealizing). All this is secondary to the poet's abjuring Poetry (if poetry is not yet fit to speak of heroes, some other idiom must be employed). Even if Poetry is impossible, there is still a task for the poet. His subject is war (and nothing but war) and the pity of war. (Because the poet is not concerned with poetry, and the reader cannot be expected to ignore all evidence of the senses) what poetry there is must be in the pity of war. These elegies ('English Elegies' was a provisional title) will not console his ['a bereaved'] generation, but they may console the next generation. Today's poets can only warn (an address to the future), therefore ['War'] Poets

---

[70] I. M. Parsons, 'The Poems of Wilfred Owen', *The Criterion*, 10/41 (July 1931), 660.

[71] Jon Stallworthy transcribes Owen's draft preface, with its excisions and variant readings, in *The Complete Poems and Fragments*, ii. 535–6.

must be truthful. The book will be ephemeral, so the poet does not specify names and places. But if the spirit of the book survives Prussia (militarism in general, or German militarism?), the poet's ambition and the names of the heroes of whom he cannot speak—another secret—will be transported from the fields of Flanders (Elysium). (Those names would in fact be inscribed on the monumental masonry of Flanders war cemeteries, because the authorities did not want to repatriate English corpses.[72])

'The Poetry is in the pity' further underwrites the legend of the poet made by war. Larkin, though wary of Yeats's 'fatuous' dismissal of a poetry of 'reaction', thought it fair, in response to Day Lewis's edition of Owen in 1963, to describe 'not only what [Owen] wrote but how he wrote it' as 'historically predictable'.[73] It is not weakened by 'historical limitations', because it was not a poetry of pacifist protest (made obsolete or unpalatable by a second, 'necessary' world war) but a poetry of compassion (Larkin's synonym for Owen's 'pity'). The continuation of war and suffering, and hence of the necessity for compassion, 'makes him the only twentieth-century poet who can be read after Hardy without a sense of bathos'.[74]

Compassion is a late sense of pity, from the Latin *pietas*—piety—and is now normally distinguished from the latter's meaning of piousness, devotion, mindfulness of duty. Owen's work is certainly deeply antithetical to *pietas*, 'the dutiful respect owed . . . to parents and fatherland and gods'.[75] The *OED* distinguishes two chief modern senses of pity. One is an attribute of a person regarding others, 'a feeling or emotion of tenderness aroused by the suffering, distress or misfortune of another, and prompting a desire for its relief; compassion, sympathy'. The second is a transferred sense, an attribution to an occurrence or situation: 'A ground or cause for pity; a subject of condolence, or (more usually) simply of regret; a regrettable fact or circumstance; a thing to be sorry for.'

'The Poetry is in the pity.' But is it in the feeling elicited by misfortune or in the 'thing to be sorry for', the occasion of that misfortune? Some have been happier to fudge Owen's elision of the aesthetic, as Dennis Welland, in the first substantial study of the poet, does when he substitutes a more tractable formulation: 'The pity which is in the poetry'.[76] The proper reaction to suffering is compassion, which carries the implication of remedy, if not in practice, then in fantasy. This is a relation in which literature implicates its readers in vicarious empathy.[77] But 'the thing to be sorry for' carries with it no such compulsion, and regret may be a reflex at best: 'after we have paid our tribute of regret to the affair considered as a calamity,

---

[72] See J. M. Winter, *Sites of Memory, Sites of Mourning* (Cambridge: Cambridge University Press, 1995).

[73] Larkin, 'The War Poet', in *Required Writing: Miscellaneous Pieces 1955–1982* (London: Faber, 1983), 159.

[74] Ibid. 163.   [75] Michael Grant, *History of Rome* (London: Faber, 1978), 60.

[76] D. S. R. Welland, *Wilfred Owen: A Critical Study* (London: Chatto & Windus, 1960), 119.

[77] For a discussion of literature and compassionate empathy, see e.g. Martha Nussbaum, *Cultivating Humanity: The Literary Imagination and Public Life* (Boston: Beacon Press, 1995).

inevitably, and without restraint, we go on to consider it as a stage spectacle,' wrote Thomas De Quincey of the Drury Lane fire.[78] Some of Owen's poems arraign non-combatants and readers for their failure of pity, but others discover in war as a regrettable circumstance the possibility of quite other compensations than those of Christianity and national or class politics. One way of understanding Owen's later work, the poems which are (improperly?) concerned not only with war but with the possibility of poetic vision, is as pessimism or fatalism—he imagines the extermination of a generation, and there being no one left except those who deny anything exceptional is going on—ameliorated by a brotherhood in truth. Insisting that he is not concerned with poetry, Owen was countering this fatalism with an optimism of the political will, the logic of his warning. Though, as the draft preface relates, this will have to wait for the next generation. His was under France.

The next generation would make him a type of the revolutionary leader. Spender, who claimed Owen to be 'the most useful influence in modern verse', elected his shade to the school of pylon poets: 'if it had not been the War, it might have been the industrial towns, and the distressed areas'.[79] And long before Pat Barker drew on Bell's edition of the *Collected Letters* to create the correspondence of Billy Prior, the fascinatingly anachronistic subaltern whose fictional life converges on Owen's real one in the coda of the *Regeneration* trilogy, Auden, the main inheritor of Owen's alliterative revival, had used him as a model for his (Fascist) airman, 'hands in perfect order', in *The Orators*.[80]

But as the example of Billy Prior suggests, the refraction of the culture of the Great War through our own can make the war seem closer than it is. Juliet Barker recently described the Wordsworths, in 1820, escorted by a veteran to the field of Waterloo: 'it was the equivalent of a trip today to the killing-fields of the Somme.'[81] Only 1916 was ninety, not five, years ago (and 'killing fields' was not then a commonplace for Pol Pot's ruralization and extermination of Cambodians). Our own complex relationship to war, especially in Britain, which was victor in name, if little else, in the war that made the Great War only the First, and which put civilians in the bombardiers' sights, is a crucial factor in the way we understand Owen and his contemporaries. The British, unlike the German, French, or Japanese, have scarcely begun to examine, rather than rehearse, their memory of the Second World War; while there seemed to be little that the victors would rather have forgotten, this complacence may have seemed plausible. But the stringency of the values we attribute to the trench poets (not least issues of political pacifism) is a measure of

---

[78] Thomas De Quincey, 'Postscript' (1854) to 'On Murder Considered as one of the Fine Arts', in *The Collected Writings of Thomas De Quincey*, xiii, ed. D. Masson (London: A. & C. Black, 1897), 72.

[79] Spender, *The Destructive Element*, 220–1.

[80] Pat Barker, *The Ghost Road* (London: Viking, 1995), 254; W. H. Auden, *The Orators*, in *The English Auden: Poems, Essays, and Dramatic Writings 1927–1939*, ed. Edward Mendelson (London: Faber, 1977), 94.

[81] Juliet Barker, *Wordsworth: A Life* (London: Penguin, 2001), 370.

the difficulty we have in making sense of our implication in twentieth-century wars (the allegedly futile ones and the necessary ones, the clinically executed—'who dares wins'—and the incompetent). Owen should be of less importance to us as a historian than as a poet, a poet who did not just 'tell us what war was like' (and just why do we still set so much store by this?) but who strived to connect feelings about war and its negations with the values by which he lived his life.

....

CHAPTER 7

SHAKESPEARE AND THE GREAT WAR

....

JOHN LEE

24. The Disciplines of the Wars. Cf., as in other places, Shakespeare's 'Henry V'. Trench life brought that work pretty constantly to the mind.[1]

To be reminded of Shakespeare is to experience the Great War. That belief plays a significant role in David Jones's *In Parenthesis*. The re-creation of the experience of thinking of the present through a Shakespearean analogue is one of the poem's aims; the poem re-creates the poet's experience of the war by re-creating what were, for him, the war's literary allusions. One phrase above all characterizes this process and, through its recurrence, gives the Shakespearean and distinctively trench life experience at its fullest: 'the disciplines of the wars'. Lance-Corporal Aneirin Lewis, marching towards the Front, sings 'in a low voice . . . because of the disciplines of the wars' (*IP*, 42). John Ball, the quasi-protagonist of the poem, overhears soldiers warming to the discussion of 'tactics and strategy and | the disciplines of the wars—like so many Alexanders' (*IP*, 78). 'Old Sweat Mulligan' worries, like the High Command, over what will happen to Fred Karno's new conscript army, when and if it attempts a war of movement: 'where's the discipline | requisite to an offensive action?' (*IP*, 117). During the final attack of the poem, 'For the better discipline of the living', a green-gilled corporal speaks like a textbook, but with bravery, and

[1] David Jones, *In Parenthesis* (London: Faber, 1963; 1st pub. 1937), 196; subsequently abbreviated to *IP* in the text.

keeps the musketry under control (*IP*, 172). As the line wavers elsewhere and looks to fall back in disarray, Captain Cadwaladr 'restores | the Excellent Disciplines of the Wars' (*IP*, 181). 'The Queen of the Woods', at the poem's close, having given berries and flowers to all the dead, carries to Lewis, killed almost before the attack had begun, a 'rowan sprig', and whispers something over his dead body; what it is cannot be heard, 'because she was careful for the Disciplines of the Wars' (*IP*, 186). The Queen of the Woods's caution recalls that of the Lance-Corporal when he sang in low voice; Aneirin Lewis, like all the soldiers we see, lives and dies within the myriad disciplines of the wars, for war is disciplines—the ordering of the lives and bodies of men in order to achieve the production and regulation of force. To example war, as Jones conceives that task, is to example its disciplines, for it is those disciplines, so shockingly new to volunteer and conscript armies, which gave the war its parenthetical status, as an area or time of life operating under a different grammar.

Yet 'the Disciplines of the Wars' are not new in themselves, either in practice or description. With his endnote 24, quoted above, Jones takes care to ensure that his readers recognize the Shakespearean nature of the phrase on its first occurrence. Captain Fluellen, a Welshman, uses it some six times in Act 3 Scene 2 of *Henry V* as he questions the competence of the command of Captain Macmorris, an Irishman. To Fluellen the phrase opens up long perspectives of time, placing the wars in France in a continuum of wars and war writing. Such a view is in no way idiosyncratic *per se*, though perhaps only Fluellen would enjoy the chance to debate the precise nature of the disciplines in the middle of an attack on a French town. Niccolò Machiavelli, in his *Art of War*, had discussed how Roman techniques and strategies might best be adapted to the modern realities of European warfare in the sixteenth century. In doing so, he demonstrated a strategic sophistication which Carl von Clausewitz would later admire.[2]

The phrase also establishes more intimate relationships with *Henry V*. Lewis's singing low is glossed by Fluellen's later warning to Gower not to speak loudly, lest the noise give aid to the enemy.[3] The soldiers who discuss strategy, 'perfect in the great commanders' names' (*IP*, 78) and mocking each other's claims to military learning, seem themselves to be modern-day versions of Fluellen and Macmorris. Lewis, in fact, almost seems to ventriloquize Fluellen when, in Alice's *estaminet*, he lectures a man from Rotherhithe who distrusts the French: 'I tell you your contentions is without reason, it is indeed a normality in the vicissitudes of the blutty wars—moreover his Intelligences is admirable, the most notorious in all the world' (*IP*, 113). Captain Cadwaladr's restoration of the disciplines of the wars replays the scene in *Henry V* where Fluellen arrives to drive the malingering

---

[2] Niccolò Machiavelli, *Art of War*, trans. Christopher Lynch (Chicago: University of Chicago Press, 2003). Lynch mentions Clausewitz's appreciation of Machiavelli in the introduction, p. xxvi.

[3] Shakespeare, *Henry V*, IV. i. 64–82.

Bardolph, Pistol, and Nym back into the attack. 'The Disciplines of the Wars' exemplifies that peculiarly intense 'consciousness of the past' which Jones states in his preface that he found definitive of his experience of the Great War (*IP*, p. xi). Jones gives other, less intense Shakespearean examples: he tells us how he saw his companions as 'the children of Doll Tearsheet', heard in their talk ' "the pibble pabble in Pompey's camp" ', and believed the kisses he and they exchanged with their loved ones on Victoria platforms *en route* for France to have been essentially the same as Bardolph's marching kiss for Pistol's ' "quondam Quickly" ' (*IP*, pp. x, xi, xv). Within *In Parenthesis*, allusion may generate argument, contrasts as well as comparisons being set in motion. Aneirin Lewis may be imagined as a Fluellen-like figure, but, unlike Fluellen, he lies dead before the final battle; that battle will be quite unlike Agincourt, which was rendered almost magical by the lack of English casualties. The relationships with the Shakespearean text may be ironic and disturbing, as well as comic and conservative. To understand, or begin to understand, what made the disciplines of the wars which Captain Cadwaladr restored 'excellent' is to understand the poem's emotional and intellectual range: the disciplines may ennoble, degrade, and destroy the lives of those who live among them. They establish community, allow self-expression, but serve the ends of kings and states. They may give much, but take away everything. For David Jones, to be reminded of Shakespeare is to explore the nature of the Great War.

Some of us ask ourselves if Mr. X adjusting his box-respirator can be equated with what the poet envisaged, in 'I saw young Harry with his beaver on'. (IP, p. xiv)

One of the great and lasting achievements of Paul Fussell's *The Great War and Modern Memory*, first published in 1975, was to insist on the importance of the interaction between literature and life. For much subsequent writing on the war, the key question has been not what the war was, but how it was experienced; the Great War ceased to be a historical event, and became a phenomenon, essentially a mental landscape, within which much of the twentieth century subsequently occurred. Shakespeare was central to Fussell's account of that landscape; it was the possession of Shakespeare above all that led to the British soldier's distinctive theatricalization of the experience of the war.[4] Correcting Bernard Bergonzi's sense of the absence of myth, Fussell argued that the life of the trenches demonstrated 'Renaissance and medieval modes of thought and feeling' more than it did those of the eighteenth and nineteenth centuries.[5] One might assume, then, that Fussell would be receptive to, and take support from, the importance Jones accords Shakespeare in *In Parenthesis*. Yet Fussell is remarkably hostile to the poem—an 'honourable miscarriage', as one of his chapter subsections terms it—and his

---

[4] Paul Fussell, *The Great War and Modern Memory* (Oxford: Oxford University Press, 1975), 197.
[5] Ibid. 115.

hostility centres precisely on the presence of Shakespeare.[6] Seizing on Jones's wondering whether an officer adjusting his gas mask 'can be equated with that the poet envisaged in "I saw young Harry with his beaver on"', Fussell insists that it cannot. The very act of locating *In Parenthesis* within a tradition of war writing shows Fussell that Jones has misunderstood a fundamental truth about the Great War, which is that it was a war unlike any other before it.[7] The Great War, put simply, is a war outside tradition, a founding moment in a century of crisis and rupture. Shakespeare, as the greatest exemplar of tradition, is the last person who should be mentioned.

The mix of a modernist narrative of twentieth-century history with a neoclassical sense that the poet must tell the truth as it should be, and not as it is, is a little peculiar; yet one should still be grateful for Fussell's recognition of the Shakespearean aspects of the experience of the war. For, since Fussell, the silence on Shakespeare has been remarkable. One could argue that Modris Eckstein's *Rites of Spring: The Great War and the Birth of the Modern Age*, published in 1989, is concerned particularly with what the war led to, and would therefore be unlikely to mention Shakespeare.[8] Similarly, Samuel Hynes's *A War Imagined: The First World War and English Culture*, published in 1990, is interested primarily in the forms of radical discontinuity that went to make up the 'Myth of the War', and which helped to bring to a close the patterns of thinking and behaviour which constituted the Victorian and Edwardian eras.[9] But that neither of these long books which consider how the war was experienced mention Shakespeare even once is, at the very least, surprising. Sarah Cole's *Modernism, Male Friendship, and the First World War*, published in 2003, is, as its title suggests, a more subtle and detailed account of a particular area of war experience, male friendship, and its portrayal in literary works.[10] Often when Cole describes the troubled and complicated nature of such organizations of intimacy, one is reminded of Shakespeare's Sonnets. Indeed, can any good male poet write a sonnet to or about another man or group of men, without being conscious of the play between male friendship, sexual love, and the threat of loss that animates the Sonnets? Certainly, the title of one of Owen's most famous, 'Anthem for Doomed Youth', reads like a compressed paraphrase of the subject of the sonnets to the young man, and gains pathos by doing so. Within 'Anthem', 'The shrill, demented choirs of wailing shells' of the second quatrain asks to be compared to the 'Bare ruin'd choirs where late the sweet birds sang' of Shakespeare's Sonnet 73, itself a sunset lament for the passing of youth, and

---

[6] Ibid. 144.   [7] Ibid. 153.

[8] Modris Eckstein, *Rites of Spring: The Great War and the Birth of the Modern Age* (Boston: Houghton Mifflin, 1989).

[9] Samuel Hynes, *A War Imagined: The First World War and English Culture* (London: Bodley Head, 1990), p. xi.

[10] Sarah Cole, *Modernism, Male Friendship, and the First World War* (Cambridge: Cambridge University Press, 2003).

possibly for the dissolution of the civilization represented by the monasteries.[11] Moreover, one may hear Ophelia's 'orisons' in those of the stuttering rifles, and see in that allusion Owen's typical feminization of his soldiers at work, and wonder if the 'no prayers nor bells' of the next line is meant to lead one's thoughts on to the 'maimed rites' of Ophelia's funeral.[12] Such allusions would certainly be apt, but one cannot be sure; for there is a real sense in which no one escapes the influence of Shakespeare. The 'sad shires' in Owen's sonnet, for example, may have a Housmanesque ring to them, but it is difficult to read the Housman of *A Shropshire Lad* without hearing 'Fear no more the heat o'th' sun' from *Cymbeline*, a song sung over what is imagined to be the dead body of a young boy, although it is in fact the drugged body of a young girl: 'Golden lads and girls all must | As chimney-sweepers, come to dust'.[13] More biographically, Robert Graves's earliest recollection was of a fear of Shakespeare; his first memory was of the despondent terror he felt when a nursery cupboard was accidentally opened to reveal octavo volumes of Shakespeare piled to the ceiling. Given that this anecdote comes in *Goodbye to All That*, it may well not be true; yet it is still significant that Graves chose to tell it.[14] Edward Thomas held that *Hamlet* had been written expressly for him; and Ivor Gurney, sadly, came to believe that he was William Shakespeare.[15] Cole, one feels, might have mentioned Shakespeare at least once in a book on the literary depiction of male friendship.

The modernist narrative of the Great War, forward-looking, posited on an abrupt break with the past, became something of a cultural truth in the last quarter of the twentieth century. Over the same period, however, that modernist narrative has begun to be challenged in a variety of other fields. In social history, studies have increasingly argued that the imagery of remembrance and mourning with which English cultures responded to the Great War was overwhelmingly traditional, and that these traditional languages were remarkably successful in mediating grief and sustaining bonds of community. On this view, the Great War perhaps represents the apotheosis of classical and Romantic understandings of war and sacrifice. Jay Winter, in his 1995 *Sites of Memory, Sites of Mourning: The Great War in European Cultural History*, describes the Great War as the last nineteenth-century war, seeing the Second World War as far more distinctively 'modern'.[16] Perhaps the sharpest

---

[11] Wilfred Owen, 'Anthem for Doomed Youth', in *The Complete Poems and Fragments*, i: *The Poems*, ed. Jon Stallworthy (London: Chatto & Windus, Hogarth Press, and Oxford University Press, 1983), 99.

[12] Shakespeare, *Hamlet*, v. i. 213.   [13] Shakespeare, *Cymbeline*, IV. ii. 259–60.

[14] Robert Graves, *Goodbye to All That: An Autobiography* (London: Jonathan Cape, 1929), 14.

[15] The detail about Edward Thomas is from William Cooke, *Edward Thomas* (London: Faber, 1970), 189. It is quoted in David Gervais, *Literary Englands: Versions of 'Englishness' in Modern Writing* (Cambridge: Cambridge University Press, 1993), 53. For Gurney, see Michael Hurd, *The Ordeal of Ivor Gurney* (Oxford: Oxford University Press, 1978), 158.

[16] Jay Winter, *Sites of Memory, Sites of Mourning: The Great War in European Cultural History* (Cambridge: Cambridge University Press, 1995), 178.

attack on the modernist myth and its effects, though, has come from military and political historians. In *The Unquiet Front: Britain's Role in Literature and History* (2002), Brian Bond draws together recent work to argue for a picture of a war fought, on the British side, by skilled commanders, leading men whose morale always remained generally high. In a short time this army emerged as the most capable in British history, winning a remarkable victory. Such a picture reverses the view of the vast majority of modernist literary studies, but then that view, among military historians, is generally regarded as hopelessly inaccurate.[17] Of course, the failure of the social and political claims of the modernist narrative does not undermine that narrative's literary claims, which were, in any case, much the most interesting and important. But perhaps it may also be the time to return Shakespeare, and so the literary past, to the mental landscape of a less exceptional Great War.

Then came the War; and the dream of the world's brotherhood to be demonstrated by its common and united commemoration of Shakespeare, with many another fond illusion, was rudely shattered.[18]

The year 1916 was meant to have been Shakespeare's year. A committee had been formed as far back as 1904, in order to consider appropriate ways to commemorate the tercentenary of Shakespeare's death. Israel Gollancz was the committee's secretary; as he wrote, the committee sought a memorial that would 'symbolize the intellectual fraternity of mankind in the universal homage' accorded to the genius of Shakespeare, the greatest Englishman (*BHS*, p. vii). The committee decided on the building of a new theatre. Plans were drawn up, and a site purchased; and 'then came the War'. The year of 1916 would be remembered instead as one of the years of the Great War and especially, from a British perspective, as the year of the Battle of the Somme. Neither celebrations of international brotherhood nor the raising of funds for theatres were suitable for the changed times. Yet, while future dreams of world brotherhood might be in crisis, there was no rupture with the past; the need to commemorate the tercentenary was still felt, and so Gollancz took on the reduced aim of editing a commemorative volume of prose and verse, to be representative of the 'ubiquity of the poet's mighty influence'—if only among allied and neutral nations (*BHS*, p. viii). The result was *A Book of Homage to Shakespeare: To Commemorate the Three Hundredth Anniversary of Shakespeare's*

---

[17] Brian Bond, *The Unquiet Front: Britain's Role in Literature and History* (Cambridge: Cambridge University Press, 2002), 13. For an example that may be taken as representative of the problem with modernist accounts, see Robin Prior and Trevor Wilson, 'Paul Fussell at War', *War in History*, 1/1 (1994), 63–80.

[18] Israel Gollancz, 'Preface', in *idem* (ed.), *A Book of Homage to Shakespeare: To Commemorate the Three Hundredth Anniversary of Shakespeare's Death MCMXVI* (Oxford: Oxford University Press, 1916), p. vii; subsequently abbreviated in the text as *BHS*.

Death MCMXVI. Gollancz assembled 166 more or less distinguished contributors from around the world, whose contributions were published in more than thirty languages (*BHS*, p. viii).

Within this collection lies one of the very earliest anthologies of war poetry, and perhaps the first such international anthology. For, as is suggested by the title given within the book—*1916 | A Book of Homage to | Shakespeare*—many of the contributions, and most of the poetry in English, were more concerned with Shakespeare's relationship to the events of the Great War than with the arrival of the tercentenary itself. In this very conscious meditation on the uses of Shakespeare and literature in times of war, a number of tropes quickly become apparent in the writings of English poets. Typically, Shakespeare is cast as a repository and guarantor of moral value. Laurence Binyon's 'England's Poet' has the 'world-winning music' of Shakespeare's poetry rising above the chaos and murdering roar of the present time (*BHS*, 21). G. C. Moore Smith and Ronald Ross both write sonnets reworking Shakespeare's Sonnet 116, 'Let me not to the marriage of true minds': Shakespeare's works have become the 'ever fixèd mark | That looks on tempests and is never shaken'.[19] For Moore Smith, Shakespeare is seen as a force for international good, the mutual love of his works offering a way of holding nations together when 'bonds of statecraft snap and cease' (*BHS*, 237). John Drinkwater's 'For April 23rd, 1616–1916' strikes a more realistic note, hoping that the future will show the war to have been fought to guarantee 'the happy-willed | Free life that Shakespeare drew' (*BHS*, 30). Such a prayer for retrospective justification betrays an uncertain and doubting quality in Drinkwater's patriotism. Others use Shakespeare to question wars in general. Alfred Noyes, in a story entitled 'The Shadow of the Master: 1916', has Shakespeare appear to him in a dream, reading a history book whose account runs up to modern times. Noyes asks him if he sees 'any light in those pages': '*I am a shadow, he said, and I see none*' (*BHS*, 116). Shakespeare then goes on to condemn the 'dark book' of history he loved as a young man, but which he now sees as tending to the glorification of war: in place of his childish love of the 'glorious colouring of each pictured age' has come his recognition of 'how thumbed with innocent blood is every page' (*BHS*, 117). What there are not, however, amongst English poets, are poems that question Shakespeare's ability to survive or be present in the war. It is left to an American academic, Frederick Morgan Padelford, to question Shakespeare's continued relevance. In 'The Forest of Arden', he imagines that wood fallen on evil days, filled with the 'shriek of shell', the birds having 'ceased to haunt the air' (*BHS*, 361). That the war could take over the Shakespearean landscape, it seems, is an imaginative leap that English minds were not willing to make.

The poems discussed so far are of interest more for their conscious meditation on the use of Shakespeare in time of war than for their poetic qualities; one would

---

[19] The titles are, respectively, '1916' and 'Shakespeare, 1916' (*BHS*, 237 and 104).

not want to make significant claims for them, though most have their moments. The one poem which begins to generate poetic effects from the relationships it establishes with Shakespeare is Thomas Hardy's 'To Shakespeare after 300 Years'. Here are the opening two stanzas:

> Bright baffling Soul, least capturable of themes,
> Thou, who display'dst a life of commonplace
> Leaving no intimate word or personal trace
> Of high design outside the artistry
> > Of thy penned dreams,
> Still shalt remain at heart unread eternally.
>
> Through human orbits thy discourse to-day,
> Despite thy formal pilgrimage, throbs on
> In harmonies that cow Oblivion,
> And, like the wind, with all-uncared effect
> > Maintain a sway
> Not fore-desired, in tracks unchosen and unchecked.

> > > > (*BHS*, 1)

With the use of the capitalized 'Soul', Hardy invokes Ben Jonson's prefatory poem to the First Folio, 'To the Memory of My Beloved, the Author Mr William Shakespeare: And What He Hath Left Us'. There, Jonson had famously called Shakespeare the 'Soule of the Age'. Indeed—and whether this was Hardy's intention, or the result of Gollancz's shrewd editing, or chance—the physical placement of Hardy's poem at the volume's proper opening reinforces this literary relationship. Hardy's poem is also rather Jonsonian in the problems it creates for the poems that follow it. Hardy's sense that Shakespeare's 'Bright baffling Soul' is the 'least capturable of themes' sits awkwardly with Binyon's assertion that Shakespeare is a 'soul-transfigured sign' promising success; similarly, Hardy's sense that Shakespeare's immortality lies in the Shakespearean harmonies that are to be found blowing like a wind within mankind's discourse 'in tracks unchosen and unchecked' renders tenuous, or draws attention to the vague nature of, Binyon's claim to place and know what the Shakespearean music stands for. It also offers the proper and poetic repudiation of Fussell's desire to use Shakespeare as a kind of litmus test to ascertain whether or not the poet has properly understood the nature of the Great War; the Shakespearean presence can be neither checked, nor 'fore-desired'.

At least, it cannot in any simple way be 'fore-desired'. For, as Hardy well knows, the Shakespearean wind can be conjured and invoked, and that is what Hardy himself does here, as he delicately places his poem in the context of the Great War. The poem invokes the war as the 'Oblivion' that threatens, if ineffectively, Shakespeare's works. At the same time, the Great War as 'Oblivion' is to be understood in particularly Shakespearean terms, as it is a particularly Shakespearean word. Shakespeare uses 'oblivion' most significantly in *Troilus and Cressida*, a play concerned with exploring the question of 'what's aught but as 'tis valued?'[20] Throughout the play, value threatens to collapse into valuation, and various images of the transience of mortality and mortal achievements are given. The most famous, perhaps, occurs as Ulysses attempts to persuade Achilles to return to the battlefield. He urges him to understand that his past deeds and glory count for little, since 'Time hath, my lord, a wallet at his back, | Wherein he puts alms for oblivion, | A great-sized monster of ingratitudes'.[21] Agamemnon repeats something similar to Hector. The past and future are, for him, both 'strewed with husks | And formless ruin of oblivion'; words are only genuine in their moment of utterance; time will drain them of their meaning.[22] Hardy, in seeing the Great War as threatening oblivion, insists that Shakespeare's works are no such 'alms' or 'husks'; Shakespeare's works now have an existence independent of human valuation, and hence Hardy's depiction of them as an elemental force like the wind.

That wind may itself be felt blowing through Hardy's poem at this point, as *Troilus and Cressida* offers to characterize Hardy's conception of the war. The play is generally categorized as a 'problem play', a term that had been adopted by Frederic Boas in 1896, in part as a response to the play's relationship to tradition. This relationship Boas found barely understandable:

That the creator of a Prince Henry and a Hotspur should bring on the stage in travestied form the glorious paragons of antiquity, an Achilles and an Ajax, is at first sight one of the most startling phenomena in literature. It looks as if Shakespeare, conscious that he was wrestling with Homer for the supreme poetic crown of all time, thought to secure victory by heaping ridicule upon his rival. But for such a view there is not the slightest solid foundation.[23]

Such a view, however, makes good sense of a play in which the story of the fall of Troy, one of the founding narratives of the Western literary tradition, is reduced to the story of 'a whore and a cuckold'.[24] Fussell, in upbraiding David Jones, had insisted that the tradition of war writing 'contains, unfortunately, no precedent for an understanding of war as a shambles and its participants as victims'.[25] It is a remarkable statement, because so untrue; here again the violence that Fussell's commitment to a modernist ideology is doing to his critical acumen is to be felt. Shakespeare, in *Troilus and Cressida*, offers a far better, more incisive, and more intelligent characterization of war as a meaningless butcher's house than any Great War poet. The *Henriad* does a far more sophisticated job of undermining notions of glory than anything achieved by Sassoon or Owen. More particularly, Falstaff's abuse of the King's press to raise 'food for powder', as he calls his men, and money for himself, goes quite beyond any depiction of Great War injustices by English

---

[20] Shakespeare, *Troilus and Cressida*, ii. ii. 52.   [21] Ibid. iii. iii. 145–7.

[22] Ibid. iv. v. 166–7.

[23] Frederic Boas, *Shakespeare and his Predecessors* (London: John Murray, 1896), 377.

[24] Shakespeare, *Troilus and Cressida*, ii. iii. 68.

[25] Fussell, *Great War and Modern Memory*, 147.

combatants, as does his subsequent leading of his 'ragamuffins where they are pep-per'd; there's not three of my hundred and fifty left alive, and they are for the town's end, to beg during life'.[26] The danger of invoking tradition lies not in the constraints that might be placed on the Great War poet, but in the threat that Shakespeare's greater sophistication and literary power pose to poetry that so often relies on the Romantic claim to truth of subjective experience. Hardy, with a masterful humility, invokes the Shakespearean analogue, and then lets the wind blow.

A Book of Homage to Shakespeare is, and is not, a war work; Shakespeare is seen both as a support to the war effort and as a symbol of liberal values which see recourse to war as failure. Such a stance should not be thought to be radical or anti-war in its large outline; it is, rather, essentially conservative, and typifies how the British sought to depict the war to themselves and to others.[27] Perhaps here, however, such a con-servative liberalism can be seen at its best, as it insists on celebrating as well as it can an intellectual fraternity in which a love of Shakespeare unifies a diversity of positions and beliefs. Yet such liberalism is perhaps easier on the Home Front. The poets, the Georgian group of Drinkwater, Ross, and Davies, with Hardy as father figure, flanked by earlier established figures such as Noyes and Binyon, had little experience of the war. Binyon is the main exception; famous as the author of 'For the Fallen', a poem written very soon after the war's outbreak, Binyon had by 1916 had direct experience of the Front, having left his post at the British Museum and gone to serve, at the age of 46, as an orderly in France. He was, in fact, a very remarkable man. One of the foremost experts on Asian art, he presided over a literary circle in London, providing help to artists such as Pound, who would later, along with Eliot, come to admire deeply Binyon's translation of Dante. But then, many amongst Gollancz's contrib-utors were remarkable. Ross, for example, was the first British winner of the Nobel prize for science. This was, in other words, a Home Front of the great and the good, and *A Book of Homage* essentially offers us the Establishment's sense of the continued relevance of Shakespeare in time of war. But was Shakespeare similarly present to, and a resource for, the frontline soldier? For the private and the officer?

Probably the fiftieth anniversary of the strange outburst of the 'Kaiser-War' will be the occasion of various retrospects of the 'Soldier-Poets' (it was almost a technical term) who for some reason flourished awhile in England. I have a poor memory, but I believe one of them had the name and rank Captain William Shakespeare.[28]

Looking back from the late 1950s, after a post-war lifetime spent teaching and writing about literature, Edmund Blunden, opening his short survey, *War Poets:*

---

[26] Shakespeare, *1 Henry IV*, iv. ii. 63 and v. iii. 34–8.

[27] The difference between an avant-garde and modernist Germany and a conservative Britain appealing to tradition and international law is one of the fundamental distinctions that Modris Eckstein seeks to establish in *Rites of Spring*, esp. 116–17.

[28] Edmund Blunden, *War Poets: 1914–1918* (London: British Council, 1958), 37.

1914–18, devotes the first of the book's four sections to dismissing previous ages' writing on war as the more or less fantastic product of armchair soldiers; never, it seems to Blunden, prior to the Great War, had the soldier in the emplacement 'noticeably sung himself'. The only other place that Blunden can begin to hear the true voice of the soldier is in 'Elizabethan plays and poems here and there'. He names Tourneur, Webster, and Sidney, but above all Shakespeare; although his army identity disc has never been found, 'the author of *King Henry V, Cymbeline, Coriolanus, Macbeth* and *Othello* knew very well what happens to men and round them in real war; he is exact in all points'.[29] So exact, in fact, that one may consider Shakespeare not only a war poet, but a poet of the Great War: 'Captain William Shakespeare'.

Blunden's commissioning of Shakespeare comes at the end of his book, and is intended mainly as a way of elevating the literary value of the soldier-poets; he has little interest in exploring the analogy he sets up. Others had been less reticent. E. B. Osborn, the literary critic and editor of, among other works, the very successful 1917 war anthology *The Muse in Arms*, published, in 1919, *The New Elizabethans: A First Selection of the Lives of Young Men who Have Fallen in the Great War*. For Osborn, all the fallen, and those that remain, are Elizabethans, but the most explicitly Elizabethan of the fallen, due to their articulacy, turn out to be the soldier-poets; in their lives and writing Osborn detects an Elizabethan instinct of brotherliness which made them insist on remaining regimental officers with their men, an Elizabethan worship of Gloriana, here figured as England herself, and an Elizabethan and classless sense of adventure.

Osborn's literary judgement of others' writings and his own writing are poor; he believes that Robert Nichols is clearly the greatest of the war poets, and turns circles in the effort to portray the pre-war society of poets such as Brooke as morally clean. His points, though, are valid, as might be expected from their very generality. As has been mentioned, the homosocial element, bordering on the homoerotic, in Great War poetry is extremely marked, does ask to be compared with similarly intense male–male relationships depicted in the Elizabethan period, and may be a factor in the popularity of the sonnet as a form. Similarly, much war poetry, especially given its Georgian heritage, does focus on celebrations of and laments for England and the English countryside. It is Osborn's belief in the classless nature of the Great War, however, that drives his use of the Elizabethan analogy. He points, with some measure of truth, to 'the arrival, by every social path, of the New Elizabethans. These golden lads . . . come from every class and vocation, are of all ranks in the new army'.[30] He hopes, when those still alive return from the war, that middle-aged and old men will get out of their way, and let them build something 'more like than

---

[29] Edmund Blunden, *War Poets: 1914–1918* (London: British Council, 1958), 10–11.
[30] E. B. Osborn, *The New Elizabethans: A First Selection of the Lives of Young Men Who Have Fallen in the Great War* (London: John Lane, The Bodley Head, 1919), 1.

unlike that visionary *Civitas Dei*, which is the only home of mankind's aspirations and inspirations'.[31]

Osborn's political hopes are impractical and utopian, largely driven by the guilt which he acknowledges he feels as a middle-aged onlooker at the war; the political aspects of his Elizabethan analogy, however, are shared by many. They have already been seen in Drinkwater's hope that the present sacrifice will be for a properly Shakespearean future. Rupert Brooke has a similarly backward-looking hope. In 'Peace', one of the sonnets in *1914 and Other Poems*, he talks of young men turning gladly 'from a world grown old and cold and weary' filled with 'half-men, and their dirty songs and dreary', while in 'The Dead' the speaker talks of how 'holiness' has returned, and 'Honour has come back, as a king, to earth'.[32] Brooke's own style was consciously Elizabethan, as might be expected from a man who won a Cambridge fellowship with a dissertation on John Webster and Elizabethan drama.[33] Yet perhaps the poet most bound up in what might be termed the Elizabethan myth is Ivor Gurney. Gurney saw not only the period, but other soldiers and himself, in Elizabethan terms, thus, in a way, offering a poetic parallel to Osborn's prose accounts. In 'Poets' he lamented that of the 'hundred poets stood to welcome in day | In a Company's front', only he—excepting those 'put past wonder by pain' and those others who 'died in dreadfullest brute thunder'—has refused 'the immemorial tame set decrees | Of bed-and-breakfast, office and life by degrees', and has instead followed Ben Jonson's example.[34] The collection from which the poem comes, *Rewards of Wonder*, is packed full of Gurney's musical, historical, and literary heroes, the latter two categories being predominantly Elizabethan. It becomes clear that the fault of the present is its lack of communion with the Elizabethan past. In 'If Ben Jonson Were Back', modern poets are at fault as they 'Never talk of Elizabethans [and] follow not his ways',[35] while 'Friendly Are Meadows' worries over an England which has begun to be the 'admirer of the strange false thing', to an extent that threatens the possibility that Elizabethans will 'be no more remembered for plain truth and glory'.[36]

By the time of *Rewards of Wonder*, Gurney's schizophrenia had resulted in his being institutionalized, and the density and degree to which his powers live in the Elizabethan past, imagining pub conversations with dramatists, claiming brotherhood particularly with Ben Jonson—on the particular grounds that he,

[31] Ibid. 7.

[32] Rupert Brooke, 'Peace' and 'The Dead', in *Poetical Works of Rupert Brooke*, ed. Geoffrey Keynes (London: Faber, 1960), 19 and 21.

[33] Adrian Caesar suggests that the Elizabethan and Jacobean dramatists had an important influence on various areas of Brooke's life and work. See *Taking It Like a Man: Suffering, Sexuality and the War Poets* (Manchester: Manchester University Press, 1993), ch. 2. The sonnets of *1914 and Other Poems* ask to be read with John Donne's 'Holy Sonnets' in mind.

[34] Ivor Gurney, 'Poets', in *Rewards of Wonder: Poems of Cotswold, France, London*, ed. George Walter (Ashington and Manchester: MidNag/Carcanet, 2000), 74.

[35] Gurney, 'If Ben Jonson Were Back', ibid. 70.   [36] Gurney, 'Friendly Are Meadows', ibid. 94.

unlike Shakespeare, did have his identity discs, and was happy to boast of killing Spaniards in the Low Countries—is in large part a sign of his madness. Yet, Gurney's imaginative world had always been largely Elizabethan. His great success as an artist lies in music, where he has always held a very high reputation as a setter of songs. Here he made his name before the war, in a setting of five Elizabethan songs, some from Shakespeare, which he called his 'Elizas'.[37] In this Elizabethan imagination he was not atypical in kind, if he was in degree. The British world of the early twentieth century was dominated by Shakespeare and other Elizabethan figures in a way that is hard to comprehend now. That the clerk in Virginia Woolf's *Mrs Dalloway*, Septimus, goes 'to France to save an England which consisted almost entirely of Shakespeare's plays and Miss Isabel Pole in a green dress walking in a square' is comic but not incredible.[38] This was a time of mock-Tudor country houses. Lady Randolph Churchill (by this time Mrs Cornwallis-West) had, in 1912, managed to secure guarantees for £50,000, a huge sum, in order to mount an exhibition entitled 'Shakespeare's England'. An early example of a theme park, the underlying interest of this was seen to reside in the notion that the Edwardian present relied on a past of Elizabethan enterprise and exploration.[39] Rudyard Kipling, in *Puck of Pook's Hill* and *Rewards and Fairies*, had used Shakespeare's 'merry wanderer' as the figure through which to bring together and offer a vision of the British past to sustain the Britain of the future.

Kipling's sense of England as a single, if complex, entity was at this time unusual, as David Gervais has argued.[40] Yet the shadow of Kipling's Shakespearean England may lie more heavily on Great War poetry than has been recognized. Edward Thomas is typically a regional poet of a fragmented England, distinguished by his refusal to employ the vague pastoral conventions of which his Georgian contemporaries made use to conjure up a notion of England and Englishness. His poetry is above all a poetry of accurately observed places and times, leavened with the chronologically unspecific magic of place-names, or with the actions of seasons. The war, however, often pushed him towards larger, more unifying statements; this is perhaps most obvious in 'This is no case of petty right or wrong', where Thomas offers England as his explanation for why he fights: 'She is all we know and live by . . . And as we love ourselves we hate her foe.'[41] Offered as an explanation, the simple assertiveness of this is unsatisfactory; the reader wants to know what England

---

[37] The songs are 'Opheus', 'Tears', 'Under the greenwood tree', 'Sleep', and 'Spring'. They are available on a CD—titled *Severn Meadows: Songs by Ivor Gurney*.

[38] Virginia Woolf, *Mrs Dalloway* (London: Hogarth Press, 1925), 95.

[39] These details concerning 'Shakespeare's England' are taken from Marion F. O'Connor, 'Theatre of the Empire: "Shakespeare's England" at Earl's Court, 1912', in Jean E. Howard and Marion F. O'Connor (eds.), *Shakespeare Reproduced: The Text in History and Ideology* (New York: Methuen, 1987), 68–98.

[40] Gervais, *Literary Englands*, 8.

[41] Edward Thomas, 'This is no case of petty right or wrong', in *Collected Poems*, ed. R. George Thomas (London: Faber, 2004), 93.

is, or how and why she is loved. Far more successful is Thomas's 'Lob'.[42] 'Lob', like Kipling's Puck, has lived through many ages and places; but whereas Kipling enfranchises Puck from Shakespeare's plays, Thomas, in a move more suitable to a poet, puts Lob in dialogue with Shakespeare. The reader is told that once, when called Tom, Lob spoke 'with Shakespeare in the hall . . . when icicles hung by the wall'. The quotation from *Love's Labour's Lost* was important to Thomas; in a prefatory note to his anthology *This England*, Thomas had given that line and the song that it began as the particular example of those 'most English poems' around which the rest of the anthology was built. Such poems were to Thomas 'some of the echoes called up by the name of England'.[43] 'Lob' dramatizes that statement. From Lob's Shakespearean conversation onward, the poem asks to be read as a rewriting of *King Lear*. Lob as Tom becomes Mad Tom on the heath. Shakespeare's and Thomas's Mad Toms have both been many men, of many social stations. They have been the poor, the socially excluded, and the rebellious, as well as the rich and the sexually satisfied. They have been the English, in their varieties. And for Thomas's Mad Tom the answer to Lear's question of 'What hast thou been?' ends in a short history of the English wars: 'good Lob' is finally 'One of the lords of No Man's Land', who,

> Although he was seen dying at Waterloo,
> Hastings, Agincourt, and Sedgmoor, too,—
> Lives yet. He never will admit he is dead
> Till millers cease to grind men's bones for bread.

Lear's heath has become a 'No Man's Land', spreading back through history; it is a rich metaphoric proposition. Thomas celebrates the English resistance to tyrannic millers at the same time as he laments the lives lived out of sight by the English poor, only called into history for service in the wars of their kings.

The Damned Spot

Edmund Blunden's commissioning of Shakespeare as a captain is apt to the facts. The majority of soldier-poets who are still read were probably captains, as it was typically the rank to which an officer commissioned at the start of the war rose, given the necessary longevity and some ability—without which longevity there tended to be no poetry at all. For all of Osborn's praise of the classlessness of his New Elizabethans, it is still the classlessness of an officer class: of his twenty-four examples, eleven turn out to have been captains, and ten, Lieutenants. Moreover, the soldier-poets who were not commissioned were hardly typical privates: Gurney, for instance, had left a scholarship at the Royal College of Music to join the Army;

[42] Thomas, 'Lob', ibid. 57–62.
[43] Thomas, prefatory note, in *idem* (ed.), *This England: An Anthology from her Writers* (London: Oxford University Press, 1915), p. iii. The note is mentioned in Gervais, *Literary Englands*, 49.

Rosenberg had studied at the Slade School of Fine Art. Francis Colmer raises the obvious question in his tercentenary contribution, *Shakespeare in Time of War*. In the preface, Colmer declares Shakespeare to be the 'one and only *national poet*' of England; but he also believes that this is not generally recognized. Noting that all the brave schemes to celebrate the tercentenary have come to nothing, bar a few performances of the plays, he wonders whether this is 'altogether a matter for regret', since 'to the great mass of his fellow-countrymen Shakespeare is little more than a name'.[44] To Colmer, Shakespeare's works are the possession of a narrow educated élite; in such a situation, any large-scale celebration would be a hollow mockery.

Modern critics tend to share Colmer's view of Shakespeare's popularity. George Parfitt, for example, finds Wilfred Owen's attempt to write as from the ranks unconvincing. The judgement is correct, but the particular evidence he adduces is not. In Owen's 'Inspection', there is a reference to a 'damnèd spot' which, discovered on parade, has confined a ranker to camp. Parfitt argues that this reference is to be understood as the officer's after-the-fact, literary description of the soldier's later explanation that the dirt on his uniform was his blood.[45] I would argue, however, that this is the only place in the poem where the soldier's voice may conceivably be heard at all; the soldier's directly quoted words, 'The world is washing out its stains . . . It doesn't like our cheeks so red',[46] are so transparently Owen's as to make the poem's attempt at dialogue rather embarrassing. To argue thus is to insist on the popularity of Shakespeare. This is not unreasonable; according to Jonathan Rose, in *The Intellectual Life of the British Working Classes*, nineteenth-century popular culture 'was dominated by Shakespeare', and, as he says, 'Victorian "Bardolatry" was driven largely by working-class demand.' Shakespeare's popularity was such that theatre companies could go on tour intending to pick up actors for the smaller roles from amongst their audiences. Moreover, this popularity was not in deference to middle-class tastes; Shakespeare was a 'proletarian hero', and his plays provided a language of 'radical political mobilization'. The Shakespeare Chartist Association of Leicester quickly attracted some 3,000 members after its constitution.[47]

One might well, then, expect a particular private to have a detailed knowledge of Shakespeare. Colmer may not have known this, because he had little contact with working-class culture. Underlying much of Bernard Porter's *Absent-Minded Imperialists* is his argument that Britain 'was a truly *multi*-cultural society' in

---

[44] Francis Colmer, 'Preface', in *Shakespeare in Time of War: Excerpts from the Plays Arranged with Topical Allusion* (London: Smith, Elder & Co, 1916), p. xv.

[45] George Parfitt, *English Poetry of the First World War: Contexts and Themes* (New York: Harvester, 1990), 64.

[46] Owen, 'Inspection', in *Complete Poems and Fragments*, i. 95.

[47] Jonathan Rose, *The Intellectual Life of the British Working Classes* (New Haven: Yale University Press, 2001), 122–3.

the later nineteenth and early twentieth century, 'albeit with the cultures in this instance being mainly predicated on class'.[48] Porter constantly insists on the vast divide between English cultures; in effect, there were different, and remarkably rich, cultural worlds. That richness, and its commonness, can be glimpsed in another of Gurney's poems, 'First Time In'. The poem records a group of soldiers arriving for the first time at the front, fearing what they might meet, particularly in the light of the tales they have been told. As it happens, they meet a group of Welsh-speaking soldiers, who

> Sang us Welsh things, and changed all former notions
> To human hopeful things. And the next day's guns
> Nor any Line-pangs ever quite could blot out
> That strangely beautiful entry to War's rout.[49]

A little later in the poem, the poet commemorates the songs themselves: ' "David of the White Rock" '—the song that Aneirin Lewis had sung—and 'the "Slumber Song" so soft, and that | Beautiful tune to which roguish words by Welsh pit boys | Are sung'. It is a poem, of course, that is a part of the transformation it describes, and it shares in the particular mixture of precision and lyrical release that marks many of Gurney's finest poems: the 'former notions' are not changed to 'human things', but 'human hopeful things', a distinction that forces acknowledgement that the war is a human thing itself, if perhaps a human hateful thing; while that 'beautiful tune' remains unnamed, though located in the world of the poverty and wit of the mines. Also, and what is strangely beautiful to the ear, it is 'war's rout' that is 'blotted out'. What Gurney does not mention in the poem is what else he spoke of with the Welsh: in a letter to Catherine Abercrombie (the wife of Lascelles, the Georgian poet, academic, and at that time munitions' examiner) he tells of how one amongst his fears was of meeting a 'rather rough type' in the trenches. The Welsh, however, delighted him not only with their songs, but also with their conversation: they talked of 'Welsh folksong, of George Borrow, of Burns, of the RCM; of—yes—of Oscar Wilde, Omar Khayyam, Shakespeare and the war: distant from us by 300 yards'.[50]

Yet there is a great difference between the possession of a rich cultural tradition and the ability to produce literature, which demands a sophisticated knowledge of literary convention. According to Partridge and Brophy, song was the distinctive cultural product of the private soldier. In their collection, *Songs and Slang of the British Soldier: 1914–1918*, there seem to be no Shakespearean relationships of significance. (The editors themselves do draw Shakespearean parallels. Brophy sees

[48] Bernard Porter, *Absent-Minded Imperialists: Empire, Society, and Culture in Britain* (Oxford: Oxford University Press, 2004), 20.

[49] Gurney, 'First Time In', in *Rewards of Wonder*, 62.

[50] Gurney to Catherine Abercrombie, n.d. [probably 7 June 1916], quoted in Hurd, *Ordeal of Ivor Gurney*, 72.

in the songs an 'ironic method of outwitting misfortune' which can be traced back to Williams, a foot-soldier in *Henry V*.[51]) To find the Privates' use of Shakespeare, one might have to look for different, less literary uses. Some of these were more or less liturgical; as Fussell noted, there were the soldiers who went over the top repeating endlessly to themselves lines of Shakespeare, as reassuring tokens of a pre-war culture.[52] In Owen's poem, quoted above, the soldier's categorizing of his blood as a 'damnèd spot' allows him the dignity of self-observation, as well as insisting on a comic perspective. Such dark humour could itself seem Shakespearean. Edmund Blunden, in 'Trench Nomenclature', celebrated the 'sharp Shakespearean names' the troops gave to the trenches. 'Genius named them, as I live!', declares the poem's speaker in opening, since 'What but genius could compress | In a title what man's humour said to man's supreme distress?'[53] A list of trench names follows, such as *Jacob's Ladder*, *Brock's Benefit*, and *Picturedome*. Geoffrey Hill has noted how, when Cymbeline bids 'the crooked smokes climb' from the altars to the gods, he is attempting to suggest a control he does not have, for whether the smoke rises straight or crooked is not within his command.[54] The naming that Blunden's poem observes makes a similar attempt to control the uncontrollable. For, as well as the ironic recontextualization of the horrors that the names provide—in which the comedy is a measure of the individual's freedom from his material situation—there is the suggestion that it is the act of naming itself that has produced the horrors. This is logically incoherent; no one, after all, would want to call such horrors upon their own heads. Yet it is emotionally helpful, since it may be better to be the master of one's own destiny than to be the passive sufferer of what one is subjected to.

War, in fact, is not only about the dead and the processes of dying; it is also a celebration of life. Often that is seen best in the comedy of juxtapositions; Gurney is particularly good at giving the comedy of these bathetic contrasts: 'True, the size of the rum ration was a shocker | But at last over Aubers the majesty of the dawn's veil swept.'[55] For David Jones, the celebration of life becomes something very close to the celebration of language; reading *In Parenthesis*, one gains the sense of how lovely language is, and how lovely it is to live in language and so within history. At one point in the poem, a sergeant responds to one Watcyn's complaint that he is soaked through (and bound for pneumonia, piles, and disorders of the juices) with a brisk command to wring his shirt dry, and an order to the corporal to get hold of some Veno's medicine. Or thus goes the summary; the words themselves are much richer, for in amongst the sergeant's commands nestle lines from Amiens's

---

[51] John Brophy, in *idem* and Eric Partridge (eds.), *Songs and Slang of the British Soldier: 1914–1918* (London: Eric Partridge at the Scholartis Press, 1930), 7.

[52] See Fussell, *Great War and Modern Memory*, 198–9.

[53] Edmund Blunden, 'Trench Nomenclature', in *The Poems of Edmund Blunden* (London: Cobden-Sanderson, 1930), 173–4.

[54] Geoffrey Hill, ' "The True Conduct of Human Judgment": Some Observations on *Cymbeline*', in *The Lords of Limit: Essays on Literature and Ideas* (London: André Deutsch, 1984), 65.

[55] Gurney, 'Serenade', in *Collected Poems*, ed. P. J. Kavanagh (Manchester: Carcanet, 2004), 240.

'Under the greenwood tree' in *As You Like It*. The sergeant says: 'Wring your vest man, there is no enemy here. | Veno's corporal—cures for rough weather' (*IP*, 71). And faintly the echo is heard: 'Here shall he see | No enemy | But winter and rough weather.'[56] Amiens's song may sound from within the sergeant's words in part because 'cures for rough weather' was an advertising slogan of Veno's; if that is so, it does nothing to lessen, but rather increases, our appreciation of the thickness and liveliness of a culture in which Shakespeare's words constantly recur like an unchecked and unchosen wind (in Hardy's terms). In Jones's poem, death becomes more than anything the loss of a linguistic community; our sorrow at the death of Corporal Aneirin Lewis is in large part a sorrow at his loss of voice. Gurney remembers the 'Infinite lovely chatter of Bucks accent' of one 'Who died on the wires';[57] Jones is very good at giving us the chatter itself, and so the sense of language as a personal possession, something carried up to the front line along with, perhaps, a photograph, and some luxury like a candle, and a final letter. Shakespeare was a part of that language, part of the issue of kit to the British, to be used as the situation demanded, and sometimes sounding out by chance.

The individual's relationship with tradition, and with Shakespeare, may have suffered a crisis, but there was no general rupture in the Great War. Shakespeare was used in many ways—analytically, liturgically, expressively, politically, in commemoration and celebration. Those outside direct experience of the war, and those experiencing the war directly, both used Shakespeare to orientate themselves and to try to understand how the Great War was affecting their lives and their world. It could not have been otherwise, as Britain's own picture of itself and its history was strongly Elizabethan and Shakespearean. Tradition, and Shakespeare, are a vital part of the experience of the Great War, and need to be part of our attempt to understand that mental landscape and the art that constitutes part of that landscape. For Paul Fussell, such attempts would be pointless, as they would be pursuing 'bad' or 'false' art. Fussell wanted to deny poets recourse to tradition because, when poems sited themselves within literary tradition, one question above all others thrust itself upon him. What frightened Fussell about David Jones's allusions was the possibility that soldiering was a universal experience. To Fussell, this was unacceptable, because it was immoral: 'But the problem is, if soldiering is universal, what's wrong with it?'[58] One might praise Fussell's intention here, but the logic of his argument is confused. Soldiering obviously is a fairly universal experience. The hopeful fantasies spread by Margaret Mead and others about the pacific nature of tribal societies have been thoroughly rejected by subsequent studies; in the long anthropological view of history, twentieth-century Europe is a time of abnormal peace.[59] The point is that universality, normality, and naturalness

<hr />

[56] Shakespeare, *As You Like It*, ii. v. 6–8.   [57] Gurney, 'The Silent One', in *Collected Poems*, 250.
[58] Fussell, *Great War and Modern Memory*, 150.
[59] See Stephen Pinker, *The Blank Slate: The Modern Denial of Human Nature* (London: Penguin, 2003), 56–7. Pinker is here quoting the work of Lawrence Keeley.

are not definitions of morality. War is to be avoided because of the various kinds of damage and loss it inflicts on societies, not because inflicting such kinds of damage and loss are abnormal; they are not. Fussell's and others' well-intentioned fictions of a pacific mankind, and of the complete meaninglessness of wars, are to be rejected not because they are fictions, but because they set themselves against, and seek to replace, a body of far more interesting and culturally productive fictions, central to which is Shakespeare. Those fictions may be more troubling to face, acknowledging, as they do, the necessity and occasional glory of war, as well as nurturing the horror that may be felt at war's meaningless destructiveness. That doubleness is a great part of what made Shakespeare a living resource to those who, in their various ways, experienced and went on experiencing the Great War.

CHAPTER 8

WAS THERE A SCOTTISH WAR LITERATURE? SCOTLAND, POETRY, AND THE FIRST WORLD WAR

DAVID GOLDIE

In 1919, with the First World War barely nine months in the past, an obscure young poet-critic called T. S. Eliot penned a review for the *Athenaeum* that appeared to pose a rather impertinent question in its title. 'Was There a Scottish Literature?', it asked—the use of the past tense exacerbating what might already seem a rather presumptuous interrogation by a 30-year-old American. But Eliot's question, based as it was on a survey of Scottish literature by G. Gregory Smith, was a good one. Although his analysis takes a long perspective, following Gregory Smith in tracing the gradual absorption of Scottish into English literature back to the Renaissance, it also has a more immediate context: the poetry of the First World

I gratefully acknowledge the assistance of the Arts and Humanities Research Council and the University of Strathclyde for funding a period of study leave during which this article was written.

War.[1] Eliot's contention, that Scottish literature had evolved from an equivalent status to its English counterpart to a point at which it could no longer claim even provincial status within that literature, might seem a hard blow to Scottish cultural nationalism—although it was an attitude that helped spark a literary revival centred on Hugh MacDiarmid in the years that followed—but it is perhaps warranted by the literary experience of the war years.[2] In looking at a broad range of the poetry written and published in Scotland during the war, much of it written by unheralded and subsequently neglected poets, this essay will attempt to prove and perhaps qualify Eliot's contention. In emphasizing the extent to which Scottish poetry was subsumed in a generic British response to the war, the argument is not intended to undermine the strong, self-conscious literary revival that followed; rather, it is to explore the state of affairs that that revival sought to address.

THE POETRY OF ANGLO-SCOTLAND

Charles Hamilton Sorley has a good claim to be considered the best-known Scottish poet of the First World War. But in claiming him for Scotland, critics have tended to overlook quite how problematic this ascription of nationality actually is.[3] For, though he was born in Aberdeen and spent his early childhood there, Sorley was plainly formed in a milieu that might more properly be thought of as British. The son of an eminent academic (himself educated at Birkenhead, Edinburgh, Germany, and Cambridge), Sorley was schooled wholly in England and Germany (King's College Choir School, Marlborough College, and the University of Jena). When war came, he deferred his scholarship to University College, Oxford, and served in the Suffolk Regiment. His connection with Scotland, in other words, was little more than one might expect from any well-travelled middle-class Briton of the time. His pre-war poetry, too, fits more easily into a standard pattern of early-century English public school verse than it does into any conceivable Scottish model. The many literary references in his letters suggest a grounding

---

[1] T. S. Eliot, 'Was There a Scottish Literature?', *Athenaeum*, 4657 (1919), 680–1. The book under review was by G. Gregory Smith, *Scottish Literature: Character and Influence* (London: Macmillan, 1919).

[2] For a useful collection of texts relating to this revival, see Margery Palmer McCulloch, *Modernism and Nationalism: Literature and Society in Scotland, 1918–1939: Source Documents for the Scottish Renaissance* (Glasgow: Association for Scottish Literary Studies, 2004). The key work of this revival that shows the deepest influence of Eliot is Edwin Muir's *Scott and Scotland: The Predicament of the Scottish Writer* (London: Routledge, 1936).

[3] Sorley is, for example, included unproblematically in Trevor Royle (ed.), *In Flanders Fields: Scottish Poetry and Prose of the First World War* (Edinburgh: Mainstream, 1990). The Scottish Arts Council also assisted in the publication of Hilda D. Spear's edition of *The Poems and Selected Letters of Charles Hamilton Sorley* (Dundee: Blackness Press, 1978).

in, and enthusiasm for, Shakespeare, Housman, Hardy, and what he described as the 'honest Saxon words' of Masefield, as well as German poetry and philosophy. Above all in his pre-war letters, he stresses his affiliation to the writer he considers his 'countryman', and 'the greatest of English visionaries', Richard Jefferies. Indeed, Sorley imbibed so much of Jefferies and of the atmosphere of Marlborough that he was more than content, as he put it, to 'count myself as Wiltshire'.[4] This connection dominates the poetry in both its form and its content. His posthumous collection of verse, *Marlborough and Other Poems* (1916), contains along with its small clutch of brilliantly wry, disenchanted war poems a preponderance of verses on the English landscape exhibiting in varying degrees the thematic and formal influence of Meredith, Housman, Hardy, Masefield, and the Georgians.[5] While it might be nice, from a Scottish point of view, to claim such bitterly incisive poems as 'All the Hills and Vales Along' and 'When You See Millions of the Mouthless Dead' for Scotland, the poems themselves plainly refuse such an identification.

Sorley's Scots credentials are tenuous, but he is not, in fact, very different in experience and attitude from many other less problematically Scottish writers of the war. Take, for example, the case of Robert W. Sterling, who was born in Glasgow and educated at Glasgow Academy, Sedbergh School, and Pembroke College, Oxford. When war came, he was commissioned in the 1st Battalion Royal Scots Fusiliers, which suggests a positive gestural identification on his part with the land of his birth and early schooling. His poetry, however, shows few signs of such national allegiance, and bears instead many of the hallmarks of genre and caste that mark it as the work of a British public school and university man. His posthumously collected *Poems* is a moving testimony to his potential and his technical ability—he had won the Newdigate prize in 1914 and made an impressive attempt to revive the Saxon epic form in his long poem 'Maran'—but also a confirmation of his rootedness in the same English landscape tradition that inspired Sorley, as well as Edward Thomas, Ivor Gurney, and Edmund Blunden. Sterling was denied the time to develop and individualize this voice, however, and as a consequence his poems offer a fascinating record—like those, say, of Roland Leighton—of a tremendous but rather unfocused idealism. His writing is skilful, graceful, and passionate, but it is tied too closely to the assumptions and models of the British public school tradition from which it comes. The result is that his work, as a poem like 'To Pembroke College' illustrates, is seldom able to free itself from the self-dramatizing lyricism of undergraduate ennui:

> Full often, with a cloud about me shed
> Of phantoms numberless, I have alone

---

[4] Charles Sorley, *The Letters of Charles Sorley: With a Chapter of Biography*, ed. W. R. Sorley (Cambridge: Cambridge University Press, 1919), 34, 241, and 201.
[5] See Charles Sorley, *The Collected Poems of Charles Hamilton Sorley*, ed. Jean Moorcroft Wilson (London: Cecil Woolf, 1985).

> Wander'd in Ancient Oxford marvelling:
> Calling the storied stone to yield its dead:
> And I have seen the sunlight richly thrown
> On spire and patient turret, conjuring
> Old glass to marlèd beauty with its kiss,
> And making blossom all the foison sown
> Through lapsèd years.[6]

As a poem of education this clearly owes a great deal more to Arnold's 'Scholar Gypsy' than to the Scottish idea of the 'lad o' pairts': it is, in other words, unreconstructedly British rather than self-consciously Scottish.[7]

Similar observations might be made about the poetry of Hamish Mann and Alexander Robertson, both former pupils of George Watson's College in Edinburgh. Mann, a 2nd lieutenant in the 8th Black Watch, who was killed (like Edward Thomas) at Arras in 1917, was not educated in England, but the poems of his *A Subaltern's Musings* have much in common with those of Sorley and Sterling. Several are even more fervidly self-dramatizing than anything found in Sterling ('sometimes I would have my own eyes melt | With the infinitely dear sadness of my songs'[8]). But apart from a couple of experiments in the style of Burns, his poetry, as seen in 'Britain is Awake', 'Weep Not for Me', 'Rupert Brooke', and 'The Poet' ('They do not know my deep, poetic soul, | That sometimes heaves tempestuous and fierce'[9]), could be mistaken—as these titles alone suggest—for that of any sensitive, poetically inclined British public schoolboy of the era. Robertson had time to acquire the life experience that was denied to Mann, but his life and work are similarly inflected with the characteristic attitudes of the educated British middle class. Educated at Edinburgh and Oxford universities, Robertson was 32 and a lecturer in history at Sheffield University at the outbreak of war. He enlisted as a private in the 12th Battalion York and Lancaster Regiment, the 'Sheffield Pals', and along with many of their number was killed attacking Serre on the first day of the Somme. Robertson was a highly cultured poet, as can be seen from his wide range of reference to English and European authors and in some excellent burlesques such as 'Spencer loquitur: Moi, j'écoute en riant'. He was a promising Scottish historian, writing two well-received historical biographies, but it is only with a great deal of effort that he can be thought of as a principally Scottish poet. Looking at poems such as 'To my Comrades—12th York and Lancasters', 'On Passing Oxford in a Troop Train', and (again) 'Rupert

---

[6] Robert W. Sterling, 'To Pembroke College', in *The Poems of Robert W. Sterling* (London: Oxford University Press, 1915), 45.

[7] In fact, the short memoir published in his *Poems* makes no mention of Sterling's Scottish origins. It does, however, make a great deal of his Sedbergh and Oxford days, and of the fact that he died on St George's Day, 1915—coincidentally, the day on which Rupert Brooke died. See *Poems of Robert W. Sterling*, pp. v–xv.

[8] Hamish Mann, 'The Ideal', in *A Subaltern's Musings* (London: John Long, 1918), 10.

[9] Mann, 'The Poet', ibid. 36.

Brooke', what one finds is an uncomplicated attitude towards the Englishness that he had clearly embraced. He talks unhesitatingly in his poetry of 'this our England',[10] and clearly, as in 'Survivors', is content to identify its familiar landscape as home:

> We are survivors. We have reached the day,
> Desired for so long, scarce hoped for. We could pray
> For naught more blessed than this blessed hour,
> For see! The welcoming cliffs of England tower,
> White, radiant from the waves. Crowded we stand,
> With eyes insatiate towards that lovely land;
> Her homes appear and o'er the downs the roads
> Climb, white and tortuous, to unseen abodes,
> While, from the distance seen, her fields of corn
> Stand motionless on this unrivalled morn.[11]

The register and vocabulary here are as solidly English as any historical vignette by Arthur Bryant—bearing as they do a set of assumptions about a blessed countryside and its moderate, resolute people that runs in lines of iambic pentameter from Shakespeare's John of Gaunt to the speakers of Rupert Brooke's poems. But it is a register that Robertson employs as to the manner born, as do many of his fellow middle-class Scots.

Similar sentiments can be found in much of the poetry written by Scots educated, not at Oxbridge, but at the Scottish universities. John Stewart was a graduate of Glasgow University and a pre-war schoolteacher who enlisted in 1914 as a private in the Highland Light Infantry. Much more characteristic than Sterling of the Scottish type of the 'lad o' pairts'—that of the young man from humble beginnings who rises to eminence through a combination of native intelligence and formal education—Stewart moved swiftly through the ranks and was commanding the 4th Battalion South Staffordshire Regiment as lieutenant-colonel when he was killed in April 1918, aged 29. The poems in his *Grapes of Thorns* (1917), however, inhabit the same affective and intellectual terrain as that of his more ostensibly Anglicized peers. Stewart does show a knowledge of, and concern for, the voice of dialect poetry in the one vernacular poem in the collection, 'Left her Lane', which attempts to come to terms with the suffering of the war's bereaved:

> Aiblins she thocht he'd hap her doon
> In the old kirk-yaird ayont the toon
> Whaur the kirkspire shadows his faither's stane—
> But she maun tak' that gait her lane
>
> For at the mirk on yon hill-face
> They dug for him a resting-place

---

[10] Alexander Robertson, 'To the Kindly Ladies of Ripon', in *Last Poems of Alexander Robertson* (London: Elkin Matthews, 1918), 29.

[11] Robertson, 'Survivors', in *Comrades* (London: Elkin Matthews, 1916), 31.

> Whaur the grass is wat wi' the red-warm rain
> And she maun tak' her gait her lane.[12]

This is plainly a poem in the Scottish tradition, not only in its register and vocabulary but in its use of the tetrameters of folk poetry. Stewart, though, is perhaps guilty here of making a common assumption of much ersatz Scottish folk poetry: that the vernacular only really comes into its own in expressing the simple, if affecting, sentiments of the common folk—that dialect is the vehicle of simple emotion rather than complex ideas. When Stewart writes poems of education and formation, as in 'Alma Mater', in which he apostrophizes Glasgow University as 'Grey Mother on the windy hill',[13] or poems about literary ideas, such as 'Of the Poet', it is to standard Edwardian English that he turns. Similarly, the more reflective and moving poems in his collection—the elegies for dead friends and the valedictions on his own anticipated death—employ a high literary English. 'If I Should Fall upon the Field' is typical:

> If I should fall upon the field
>   And lie among the slain,
> Then mine will be the victory
>   And yours the pain;
> For this in prospect comforts me
>   Against all sadd'ning fears
> That, dying so, I make myself
>   Worthy your tears.[14]

The fact that his most personal poems are also the ones that are most conservative and conventional in their language and tone—that when he writes most directly out of his own experience it is English he reaches for—is perhaps significant. There remains something profoundly moving, given the particularly fraught circumstances under which they were written, about poems such as 'If I Should Fall upon the Field' which makes a probing, formal critical analysis seem somehow intrusive and inappropriate. But it is perhaps not impertinent to point out that this poem, like so many of its kind, gathers strength not from its originality, or its expression of a particularly personal feeling, but rather from its very commonplaceness. A strongly conventional poetry like this arguably gains its effect not only from the contexts that render its sentiments singularly compelling, but also from its close similarity to the many other poems of its type. In cases such as this, conventionality is not so much a sign of the poet's inability to master his form—though this may also be an issue—but a guarantee of the authenticity of its sentiments. One might go so far as to suggest that in war, the rules governing the distaste for cliché are suspended: a familiar, even perhaps rather hackneyed phrase or trope can be allowed to stand, beyond the reach of possible embarrassment, as it does on a war

---

[12] J. E. Stewart, 'Left her Lane', in *Grapes of Thorns* (London: Erskine MacDonald, 1917), 22.
[13] Stewart, 'Alma Mater', ibid. 33.   [14] Stewart, 'If I Should Fall upon the Field', ibid. 46.

monument or in the inscriptions of a reassuring, familiar phrase repeated endlessly on the gravestones in a war cemetery.

This quality of reassuring commonplaceness, in which even the most personal poetic expression is subject to the conventions of a common style and a settled frame of reference, is fundamental to much of the popular poetry of war—among which this British public school or university verse can be placed. This is to conceive of popular poetry not so much as an unimaginative practice desperately in need of the shake-up of a self-appointed avant-garde (in the way Pound or Eliot might look at it), but as a social practice that works with the consent and shared consolation of a wider readership—a poetry that is less the expression of extraordinary individuality than the statement of a commonplace social and experiential communality.

The poetry examined so far is, admittedly, governed by the concerns and particular experiences of a narrow class grouping that qualify any claim it might make to be popular in any fully meaningful sense. It might be argued, in particular, that the commonplaceness of the verse, and its manifest lack of a distinct Scottish perspective in the way of diction, setting, and form, can be explained simply by the fact of the relative immaturity and overwhelmingly Anglocentric formation of the poets featured so far. But in moving to the popular poetry published in Scottish newspapers and journals, one sees a perhaps unexpected congruence. There is, it should be said, a little more dialect poetry in these types of publication, but there is also a surprisingly large amount of the kinds of rather normative standard English poetry already discussed. What this suggests, perhaps, is that the argument about commonality versus particularity can be extended tentatively into the sphere of national expression: that in the prevailing climate of the war the need to express Scottish exceptionalism or particularity was less pressing than the demands of articulating a wider British solidarity.

NEWSPAPERS AND POPULAR POETRY

It is not surprising that the Edinburgh-based, Unionist *Scotsman* newspaper greeted the war with poetry in English that stressed British unanimity. Printed on the paper's leader page a week and a half into the conflict, 'British Bugles' is a standard piece of imperial trumpeting in the manner of Alfred Austin or Henry Newbolt, employing the usual high diction and heavily rhymed quatrains of that genre. The poem's message was one of reassurance that the subaltern nations (even perfidious Ireland) looked set to answer the call of the British bugle. The poem concludes:

> Every island, every last stretch,
> Where the ancient banner flies,
> Hears the braying of the bugles,
> And with one accord replies—

> Answers straightaway, 'we are ready,
> We are with you, Motherland,
> Though the strife be long and deadly,
> Armageddon be at hand.'

> Which from Erin, late divided,
> Racked by discord, sore dismayed,
> Thunders forth the glad assurance,
> 'We are one; be not afraid!'[15]

More surprising, perhaps, was the literary response of Scotland's most popular weekly paper, the Dundee-based *People's Journal*. This had for a long time been a radical liberal newspaper that had, especially in the 1870s and 1880s, promoted an extensive use of dialect Scots.[16] By the 1890s it was claiming a weekly readership of one million, making it not only Scotland's best-selling paper, but one of the United Kingdom's most popular weeklies.[17] The *People's Journal* had a long tradition of reader participation and, unlike the *Scotsman*, had been in the habit of publishing verse regularly before the war. So when war came, the *People's Journal* naturally responded with frequent and wide-ranging popular verse responses. Those published on Boxing Day 1914, under the heading 'Poems from our People: War Verses by Journal Readers', offer a representative snapshot.[18] Among the five poems, one is a parody of a Scottish poem written in cod German, one is a Scots dialect poem, and three are types of standard-English imperial poetry.[19] The first, 'The Kaiser's Prayer', is a parodic version of Robert Burns's 'Holy Willie's Prayer', in which the Kaiser's perceived hypocrisy and arrogance are entertainingly, and tellingly, compared to the self-deceiving Calvinism derided in Burns's original. The three poems in English are typical, in language, metre, and tone, of Edwardian popular verse. M. A. Cameron's 'The Defence of the Bridge' ('They guarded the bridge, a noble few') and H. C. McDonald's 'Follow Me' ('The Scots and English, side by side | With Welsh and Irish stem the tide, | And French and Indians closely vie | For roll of honour—do or die!') are types of martial verse exhorting conquest and heroism that could have been written of virtually any imperial campaign since

---

[15] 'A. B.', 'British Bugles', *The Scotsman*, 15 Aug. 1914, 10.

[16] For an excellent account of this, see William Donaldson, *Popular Literature in Victorian Scotland: Language, Fiction and the Press* (Aberdeen: Aberdeen University Press, 1986).

[17] *How a Newspaper Is Printed: Being a Complete Description of the Offices and Equipments of the Dundee Advertiser, People's Journal, Evening Telegraph, and People's Friend* (Dundee: John Leng & Co, n.d. [1891]), 18–19. This figure would mean that the paper would be read by more than one in four of all Scottish adults.

[18] The typicality of this type of verse can be seen by consulting Hilda D. Spear and Bruce Pandrich (eds.), *Sword and Pen: Poems of 1915 from Dundee and Tayside* (Aberdeen: Aberdeen University Press, 1989). Of the 100 poems they have collected from Dundee newspapers in 1915, only nine use dialect in any sustained way.

[19] 'Poems from Our People: War Verses by Journal Readers', *People's Journal* (*Dundee Edition*), 26 Dec. 1914, 3.

Waterloo. Similarly, 'The Red Cross Heroines' by 'A. P. of Dundee' ('The Praise of Tommy Atkins is singing in the air, | The plaudits of the Red Cross nurse are ringing everywhere') has the stilted quality of much Edwardian popular poetry. 'Tae Scotsmen' by 'G. M. C. of Cowdenbeath' sets out to strike a national tone in its use of the vernacular, but it too cannot escape the content and form of what F. S. Flint would describe as the 'tumpty-tum of hurdy-gurdy verses' that characterized British Edwardian popular poetry:[20]

> Ay, here the Scotsman's made it plain
> That the Kaiser's men can never drain
> Or sap the blood o' freedom's vein
> Frae plucky Scotty.

This tendency for popular vernacular poetry to echo, or even give itself over wholesale to, the dominant style of English martial poetry can be seen in the work of the *People's Journal*'s most celebrated poet, Joseph Lee.[21] Lee's formation was quite different from the poets discussed so far. Dundee-born, he had left school aged 14 and had pursued an adventurous and chequered career—not unlike that of W. H. Davies, Patrick MacGill, or Robert Service—which included several voyages as a casual seaman and a year as a cowpuncher in Canada. By the time war broke out, he had settled into a career in popular journalism and was a news editor at the *People's Journal*. In spite of this senior position and his age (38 years), Lee enlisted in the ranks of the local regiment, the Black Watch. He served in France and Flanders with its 4th Battalion before, in 1917, accepting a commission and serving with the King's Royal Rifle Corps. Lee had, in 1910, published a collection, *Poems: Tales o' Our Town*, that was characterized by a humorous, boisterously democratic tone plainly modelled on Burns and the ballads. During the war he continued to write poems for the Dundee papers, and published two collections, *Ballads of Battle* (1916) and *Work-A-Day Warriors* (1917). These contain a number of moving lyrics alongside many humorous observations of trench life, in which can be seen a number of continuities with his earlier poetry. What are more interesting, however, are the differences that appear as a consequence of his war experience. For one thing, his poems become shorter and less expansive. This may be due simply to the demands on his time made by war, but it might also be seen as characteristic of a wider contemporary British movement from Edwardian orotundity to Imagistic concision. The poems of *Tales o' Our Town* had often taken a loose narrative or comic form, dealing in a free-wheeling way with historical incident or folk observation. They were often entertaining and skilfully wrought, as in the humorous satire on Dundee politics of 'The Waukrife Wyverns':

[20] F. S. Flint, 'The Appreciation of Poetry' (1940), quoted in J. B. Harmer, *Victory in Limbo: Imagism 1908–1917* (London: Secker & Warburg, 1975), 17.

[21] For a useful account of Lee's career, and his great popularity, see Bob Burrows, *Fighter Writer: The Eventful Life of Sergeant Joe Lee, Scotland's Forgotten War Poet* (Derby: Breedon Books, 2004).

> 'O lang and lang I've lookit doon
> On bonnie, dirty Dundee toon,
> And seen i' Council knave and clown,
>   But sic a crew
> O' rowdy, rantin', roarin' fellows—
> Sae scant o' sense, sae sound o' bellows—
>   I never knew.'[22]

This expansive, extroverted attitude persists in some of the poems in Lee's war writing, as does some of his earlier McGonagallesque awkwardness.[23] But more characteristic, especially of the better work like 'The Green Grass', is a directness and simplicity of diction that is largely absent from his pre-war writing:

> The dead spake together last night,
>   And one to the other said:
>   '*Why are we dead?*'
>
> They turned them face to face about
>   In the place where they were laid;
>   'Why are we dead?'
>
> 'This is the sweet, sweet month o' May,
>   And the grass is green o'erhead—
>   Why are we dead?
>
> The grass grows green on the long, long tracks
>   That I shall never tread—
>   Why are we dead?'[24]

Another new appearance in Lee's war writing—as in Kipling's—is the short, Imagistic aphorism. One of several mordant examples of this is 'The Bullet', which reads in its entirety:

> Every bullet has its billet;
>   Many bullets more than one:
> God! Perhaps I killed a mother
>   When I killed a mother's son.[25]

The other salient fact about Lee's war writing, visible in these examples, is its movement away from Scots dialect. Lee had from the beginning, in common with almost all Scottish writers of the time, tended to use a standard poetic English in

---

[22] Joseph Lee, 'The Waukrife Wyverns', in *Poems: Tales o' Our Town* (Dundee: George Montgomery, 1910), 49.

[23] See e.g. 'Back to London: A Poem of Leave': 'But one short day since I had left | A land upheaved and rent, | Where Spring brings back no bourgeoning, | As Nature's force were spent; | Yet now I travelled in a train | Through the kindly land of Kent!' (Lee, *Work-a-Day Warriors* (London: John Murray, 1917), 22).

[24] Lee, 'The Green Grass', in *Ballads of Battle* (London: John Murray, 1916), 22.

[25] Lee, 'The Bullet', ibid. 21.

dealing with elevated or serious themes. While the great majority of the poems in *Tales o' Our Town* were written in the dialect of Dundee, a minority—the ones that dealt with serious historical ideas, such as 'The Greys at Waterloo' and 'St Mary's Tower', and lyrical poems of memory, like 'Compensations' and 'David Macrae: In Memoriam'—were written in the more orthodox register of Edwardian poetic English. The poems of *Ballads of Battle* and *Work-A-Day Warriors*, in contrast, are almost wholly in English, even when they deal with explicitly Scottish themes. Where the presiding genius of the earlier collection was Burns, the background voices that can be heard here are the more contemporary ones of British imperial poetry. One influence, perhaps not surprisingly, given Lee's nautical background, is Henry Newbolt. Poems such as '1815–1915: One Hundred Years Ago To-day', 'A Ballad of Dead Loves', and 'Requiem' (When the Last Post is blown, | And the last volley fired, | When the last sod is thrown, | And the last Foe retired, | And thy last bivouac is made under the ground— | Soldier, sleep sound!'[26]) trumpet a Newbolt-like imperial theme and concern with martial history, while others such as 'The Sea' and 'When the Armada Sailed from Spain' compare fairly directly with the sentiments and style of the poems in Newbolt's *Admirals All* (1897).

Arguably, though, the major voice underlying Lee's martial verse is that of Rudyard Kipling. Again, this is hardly surprising, given the omnipresence of Kipling's influence on the British popular poetry of the time. When Lee writes about the day-to-day life of the trenches, he lapses into the distinctive soldier's argot of Kipling's *Barrack-Room Ballads* and the stories of *Soldiers Three*. Poems like 'The Penitent' that deal with the forgivable recidivist tendencies of the Tommy, or 'Pick and Spade', 'Carrying Party', and 'Stand-to!' ('I was just a-dreamin' of 'Ome Sweet 'Ome, | A-top of a fevver bed'[27]) offer the reader, in a characteristic Kiplingesque mockney, a reassuringly familiar view of cheerful military stoicism in the face of military routine. Others, like 'Piou-Piou: The British Tommy Atkins to the French' and 'Tommy and Fritz', sound a recognizable note of manly admiration for the qualities of friend and foe alike. In 'Piou-Piou' the foreigner is, as in Kipling, an object first of comedy and then of admiration:

> Your trousies is a funny red,
>   Your tunic is a funny blue,
> Your cap sets curious on your 'ead—
>   And yet, by Gawd, your 'eart sits true,
>   Piou-piou![28]

'Tommy and Fritz' sounds a similarly Kiplingesque note in considering the merits of the enemy:

> He hides behind his sand-bag,
>   And I stand back o' mine;

---

[26] Lee, 'Requiem', ibid. 101.   [27] Lee, 'Stand-to!', ibid. 25.   [28] Lee, 'Piou-Piou', ibid. 84.

> And sometimes he bellows, 'Hullo, John Bull!'
>   And I hollers, 'German swine!'
> And sometimes we both lose our bloomin' rag,
>   And blaze all along the line.[29]

Just as Kipling had used dialect—especially cockney, Irish, and Scots—as a rhetorical device to emphasize cross-cultural, cross-class imperial consensus, so too Lee employs a range of dialect voices to similar ends, especially in his second wartime collection, *Work-A-Day Warriors*. In this volume there are many more poems in cockney than in Scots. But there are also, in poems such as 'War, Some Reflections by Corporal Richard Crew of the Canadians', 'Saint Patrick's Day in the Mornin': The Love Lilt of Corporal Patrick Mullohoy of the Connaught Rangers', 'The Australian', and 'Tik, Johnnie!', a range of voices and subject-matters that all seem designed to show the harmonic relations within and between the white and brown races of the Imperial Army—an impression reinforced by Lee's illustrations for the volume.

What may be going on in this movement of Lee's poetry from the influence of Burns to that of Kipling is a realignment of allegiance. In moving his primary idiom from demotic Scots to a range of demotic Englishes, Lee is registering a common effect of war service among many poets: the broadening of sympathy beyond the local and even the national. A poem which perhaps offers the clearest instance of this is 'Ancestry', from *Work-A-Day Warriors*—a poem that takes him a long way from the Dundee of *Tales o' Our Town*:

> I am one with the ancient Roman,
>   pressing on the great phalanx;
> I am one with the Spartan, the Trojan,
>   and the Grecian's steel-clad ranks;
> They with their Horse, Heaven-sent,
>   and I with my earth-born 'tanks';
> As I move to attack, with my kit on my back,
>   And my bombs and my steel-tipped gun,
>   They and I are One![30]

This might be seen to anticipate the attempts of David Jones in *In Parenthesis* (1937) to place the experiences of the war in a meaningful, long historical perspective.[31] But whereas Jones would use this perspective to construct new myths of Welsh and British nationhood, Lee appears to employ it in the opposite way. The ancestry that Lee proclaims in this poem is grounded not in a common heritage but in a shared experience: his proper subject is not the expression of the Scottish experience of war so much as the expression of war itself.

---

[29] Lee, 'Tommy and Fritz', ibid. 78.   [30] Lee, 'Ancestry', in *Work-a-Day Warriors*, 16–18.
[31] See also David Jones, 'Art in Relation to War', in *The Dying Gaul* (London: Faber, 1978), 123–66.

The Scottish poetry written for more overtly propagandistic purposes shares many of the emphases of Lee's work. Several Scottish writers operated in the characteristic semi-official capacity favoured by the War Propaganda Bureau at Wellington House, and later the Ministry of Information, in support of the war effort. Among them were John Buchan and R. W. Campbell—both independent writers, best known as popular novelists, who also happened to be employed by the British military establishment. Campbell's series of *Spud Tamson* books sold well during the war, and offered a reassuring portrait of Roman Catholic integration within the Scottish regiments, as well as Scottish integration into the larger British effort.[32] Buchan was the author of the huge and much acclaimed serial *Nelson's History of the War* (1915–19), as well as the creator of the Scots-South African agent Richard Hannay, hero of *The Thirty-Nine Steps* (1915), *Greenmantle* (1916), and *Mr Standfast* (1919). Both were also active, popularizing poets. Campbell, in particular, followed Lee in celebrating Scots wartime achievement in the mode of Kipling and British Imperial poetry. His 'Abdul the Sniper', 'Our Football Fools', and 'The Lowland Fuzzies', for example, all trade in immediately recognizable Kipling tropes. Campbell is even willing, in 'The Border Breed', to call on his master directly, invoking 'the style of Kipling, the touch that Tennyson made, | To write of the Border gallants who served in a Scots Brigade'.[33]

While Campbell preferred, like most Scottish popular poets, to employ standard English in preference to dialect Scots, Buchan was inclined to experiment in the dialect of his childhood in the Scottish Borders. The influence of Kipling was very strong in his fiction, but Buchan was more self-conscious about the construction of a poetry that drew on the Scottish ballad tradition from which writers like Lee had begun to move away.[34] Buchan was in some ways a typical émigré Scot—as he makes clear in his autobiography, his passion for Scottish culture had developed fully only after he had left the country.[35] But once developed, that passion manifested itself—as it had in the cases of his exemplars Burns and Scott—in the collection and writing of traditional Scots dialect poetry. His *The Northern Muse: An Anthology of Scots Vernacular Poetry* (1924) would give an important impetus to the post-war Scottish literary renaissance, kick-started in 1920 with the publication of the first series of Hugh MacDiarmid's anthology, *Northern Numbers*. But Buchan's dialect poetry of the war, published in *Poems, Scots and English* (1917), remains tied to the pious, rural Scotland of sentimental Victorian poetry. Whereas the narrative prose voice of both his historical fiction and his 'shocker' popular fiction is immaculately urbane, even cosmopolitan, his vernacular poetic voice is more

---

[32] See R. W. Campbell, *Private Spud Tamson* (Edinburgh: William Blackwood & Sons, 1915) and *Sergeant Spud Tamson, VC* (London: Hutchinson, 1918).

[33] R. W. Campbell, 'The Border Breed', in *The Making of Micky McGhee: And Other Stories in Verse* (London: Allen & Unwin, 1916), 53.

[34] Kipling was, of course, influenced in his own popular poetry by the Scots Border ballads.

[35] See John Buchan, *Memory Hold-the-Door* (London: Hodder & Stoughton, 1940), 80–1.

narrowly that of the country manse. Poems of the war, such as 'On Leave', come near to achieving a brooding, Housman-like resonance in their depictions of a death-haunted landscape:

> I saw a thoosand hills,
>   Green and gowd i' the licht,
> Roond and backit like sheep,
>   Huddle into the nicht.
>
> But I kenned they werena hills,
>   But the same as the mounds ye see
> Doun by the back o' the line
>   Whaur they bury oor lads that dee.
>
> They were juist the same as at Loos
>   Whaur we happit Andra and Dave.—
> There was naething in life but death,
>   And a' the warld was a grave.
>
> A' the hills were graves,
>   The graves o' the deid langsyne,
> And somewhere oot in the Wast
>   Was the grummlin' battle-line.[36]

Too often, however, they find resolution in an easy recourse to rural piety: in this case the double blow of the death of the speaker's comrades and his child is softened by a simple prayer:

> I flang me doun on my knees
>   And I prayed as my hert wad break,
> And I got my answer sune,
>   For oot o' the nicht God spake.
>
> As a man that wauks frae a stound
>   And kens but a single thocht,
> Oot o' the wind and the nicht
>   I got the peace that I socht.[37]

SCOTTISH DIALECT POETRY AND THE WAR

Buchan was not alone in this attempt to revive the dialect poetry of Scotland during the war—and perhaps not alone in creating vernacular speakers markedly less sophisticated than their creators. A mixed group consisting mainly of émigrés and indigenous gentry, among them Charles Murray, Violet Jacob, J. B. Salmond, and Mary Symon, published work before and during the war that attempted to

---

[36] John Buchan, 'On Leave', in *Poems, Scots and English* (London: T. C. & E. C. Jack, 1917), 56–7.
[37] Ibid. 58.

articulate the experience of north-east Scotland in its distinct Doric dialect voice. While poetry such as this undoubtedly assisted in a self-conscious revival of regional literary confidence, and contributed several moving poems on the war's effects on the Home Front, such as Violet Jacob's 'The Field by the Lirk o' the Hill' and Charles Murray's 'When will the War be by?', it is difficult to argue that it really extended very far the expressive range of British popular poetry. While it might occasionally capture the linguistic vitality of a rich oral culture, the tonal range of wartime Scots dialect poetry rarely stretched beyond pawky humour, simple rural piousness, and sentimental monologue—though it did, characteristically, add the odd exhortation to recruitment based on local regional pride.[38] George Abel, a United Free Church minister from Aberdeenshire and occasional contributor of 'Fireside Cracks' to the *People's Journal*, was perhaps not the best of these dialect writers, but his wartime collection *Wylins fae my Wallet* (1915) exhibits many of that genre's characteristic impulses and attitudes: from its retelling of biblical stories in Doric settings, through the mawkish sentiment of 'The Fairmer's Fairweel to His Commandeered Nag', to the ironic comedy of 'The Tiff, An' Efter'. In this poem, a termagant wife is paid back for her nagging when her husband returns to her from the war a deaf mute. It concludes with a rather characteristic moral:

> He'll never hear my ill-hung tongue
> File we're abeen the sod,
> But he sall ken it's better hung
> Fin we gyang hame to God.
>
> Oh, sirs, tak' tent afore it's late,
> An' min' yer teens an' tongues,
> Ye'll think upo' the whack we've gat,
> An' hae nae tiffs an' bungs.[39]

Abel is not above a little tub thumping, too. A recruiting poem like 'Mair Men!' adopts a stance that is typical in much dialect poetry of the war in attempting to employ its assumed closeness to the folk to talk them into enlisting in the wider cause:

> Sons o' Scotlan'! Hardy Northmen!
> Men o' breed, an' men o' brawn!

---

[38] See e.g. Jacob's 'Jock, to the First Army' and 'The Kirk Beside the Sands', in *More Songs of Angus, and Others* (London: Country Life and George Newnes, 1918), 15 and 26, and Murray's 'Ye're Better Men', 'Wha Bares a Blade for Scotland?', and 'A Sough o' War'—the latter welcoming the opportunity of war to prove its refrain that 'Auld Scotland counts for something still' (Charles Murray, *A Sough O' War* (London: Constable, 1917), 9, 15, 13–14). For a more positive assessment of this revival of Doric poetry, see Colin Milton, 'A Sough O' War: The Great War in the Poetry of North-East Scotland', in David Hewitt (ed.), *Northern Visions: Essays on the Literary Identity of Northern Scotland in the Twentieth Century* (East Linton: Tuckwell, 1995), 1–38.

[39] George Abel, 'The Tiff, An' Efter', in *Wylins Fae My Wallet* (Paisley: Alexander Gardner, 1916), 103.

> Hearken to yer country's priggin'!
> Are ye deaf, or are ye thrawn?
>
> .   .   .   .   .   .
>
> Men are wintet fae the Northlan',
> Men wi' shanks to weer the kilt,
> Men wi' Bannockburn's memory,
> Men 'at winna warp nor wilt.[40]

In the hands of a writer like Abel, dialect verse is not so much the means of adding a distinctive regional voice to a diverse and complex Britishness. It is instead the articulation of a more or less common and straightforward British attitude translated into the language of its regions. This is not to cast blame on Abel, but is rather to illustrate the powerful centripetal forces exerted during wartime: the threat of a common enemy was plainly a powerful force for the expression of unified rather than dissident opinion.

Such a centripetal tendency does, however, hold other benefits for the poetry of the British regions or subaltern nations. Once such literatures are accepted as assenting rather than dissentient literatures, once they are accepted as literatures that augment rather than threaten the dominant literature, then they become available as a stylistic or rhetorical resource to those who have been formed outside or at the margins of their traditions. The best way in which this might be illustrated is to look at the poetry of Alan Mackintosh. A popular and brave officer in the Seaforth Highlanders, and a bagpipe-player and Gaelic speaker, Mackintosh was clearly a more self-conscious Scot than Sorley, Sterling, or Brown, although, like them, he was a distinctive product of the British public school system and of Oxford. Part of Mackintosh's lineage was Highland Scottish, deriving on his father's side from Inverness and Ross-shire. Mackintosh, though, was born in Brighton, and had strong roots in English Nonconformist liberalism on his mother's side. After attending Brighton College, he went to St Paul's School and then to Christ Church, Oxford, on a Classical Scholarship. The Scottish attributes for which he would be remembered—the concerns with Scottish music and literature and with the Gaelic language—appear to have developed fully (as was the case with Buchan) only during his time at Oxford. It was there that this otherwise ostensibly English public schoolboy first manifested his highland identity in consistent way: cultivating, as his tutor John Murray put it, 'above all, the sentiments and the arts of the Highlands'.[41] In other words, Mackintosh's 'Scottishness' was less the product of an informing national culture, absorbed in the long process of formation, than a consciously acquired allegiance to a land of which he had only partial direct knowledge. His national identity was, in this sense, elective rather than involuntary—the result of an act of choosing rather than of cultural submersion or interpellation.

---

[40] Abel, 'Mair Men!', ibid. 75–6.

[41] John Murray, 'Memoir', in E. A. Mackintosh, *War, the Liberator and Other Pieces* (London: John Lane, 1918), 4.

His notion of the identity and the tradition to which he elects to belong is perhaps most clearly articulated in 'The Remembered Gods', a four-act Highland verse drama written during Mackintosh's two years at Oxford. This story, dealing with the contention between Christianity and the old, wilder gods of Morven, is, technically and lyrically, a very assured piece of work. Ostensibly, the play celebrates the Christian virtue of self-sacrifice, in the character of Mairi, over the dark temptations of pagan belief, manifested in her lover, Alastair. Its more powerful and memorable elements, however, are the vivid evocations of folk belief, heard in the alluring songs of Angus, Alastair, and Ian:

> The bitter gods, the beautiful white gods,
> That will be walking on the darkened cliffs,
> Lior the haunter of the roaring tides,
> Whose emerald eyes the drowning sailors see
> For one sweet instant, and are swallowed up.
> And Balor panoplied in shining rain,
> And armoured with the lightnings of the hills
> That fire our hearts to war. And chief of all,
> Angus the white-foot conqueror of men,
> The mist that would destroy the moon with love
> If she could hold him, the eternal mist
> That wanders still within our quiet hearts,
> Stirring the bitter love we may not sate
> Save with his own white beauty. These are they
> That were your father's gods in the old days.[42]

The Gaelic world that the play evokes is one of savage passionate grandeur and romantic loneliness sprinkled with liberal amounts of Yeatsian faery dust. It is, in other words, a conveniently timeless and generically evocative landscape into which Mackintosh can meld a range of personal fantasies—a suitable objective correlative for the passionate confusions of late adolescence. As in much of his other poetry, the world of the Gael functions not only as a kind of land of heart's ease into which the troubled individual retreats from the pressures of the urban, workaday world, but also as an Ossianic world of heroic, turbulent endeavour. The evolution of this idea in Mackintosh's poetry can be seen by looking at two poems. In the first, 'Return', written while Mackintosh was at school in London, the restorative landscape is the Sussex Downs. In the poem the retreat described is—as might be expected from a Brighton lad at large in the metropolis—to a nurturing downland countryside associated with childhood:

> So when our hearts are bitter,
> And smirched with blot and stain,
> And fruit has turned to ashes,

---

[42] Mackintosh, 'The Remembered Gods', ibid. 57–8.

> And all our joy is pain,
> Thank God upon the Downland
> We're children once again.[43]

In the year that he went up to Oxford, however, Mackintosh wrote 'Mallaig Bay', in which the emphasis is markedly different. Now, the South Downs of childhood are rejected for a more bracing and challenging landscape:

> I am sickened of the south and the kindness of the downs,
>   And the weald that is a garden all the day.
> And I'm weary for the islands and the Scuir that always frowns,
>   And the sun rising over Mallaig Bay.
>
> I am sickened of the pleasant down and pleasant weald below,
>   And the meadows where the little breezes play,
> And I'm weary for the rain-cloud over stormy Coolin's brow,
>   And the wind blowing into Mallaig Bay.
>
> I am sickened of the people that have ease in what they earn,
>   The happy folk who have forgot to pray,
> And I'm weary for the faces that are sorrowful and stern,
>   And the boats coming into Mallaig Bay.[44]

The Highland world portrayed here, then, becomes the signifier of a more strenuous way to the truth. It is recognizably a turn from the picturesque to the sublime; from a simple reassuring ideal of southern beauty to a more exquisite northern one in which awe and fear and sorrow are intertwined.[45]

When it came to war, then, Mackintosh's choice of a Scottish regiment was perhaps unsurprising. He was, as the evidence of his poetry and the facts of his biography suggest, still feeling his way tentatively towards a defining adult experience. In this situation, the combination of Celticism and military struggle was, no doubt, extremely alluring—as it was to many romantically inclined young Anglo-Scots and Englishmen. Mackintosh would, tellingly, reveal a little of this sentiment later in his poem 'The Volunteer':

> I took my heart from the fire of love,
>   Molten and warm not yet shaped clear,
> And tempered it to steel of proof
>   Upon the anvil-block of fear.[46]

---

[43] Mackintosh, 'Return', quoted in Colin Campbell and Rosalind Green, *Can't Shoot a Man with a Cold: Lt. E. Alan Mackintosh MC 1893–1917, Poet of the Highland Division* (Glendaruel: Argyll, 2004), 23.

[44] Mackintosh, 'Mallaig Bay', in *A Highland Regiment* (London: John Lane, 1917), 59.

[45] In this regard it is perhaps possible to see the allure of an austere, character-forming Scotland as analogous to the contemporary British fascination with the polar extremities that is admirably outlined in Francis Spufford, *I May Be Some Time: Ice and the English Imagination* (London: Faber, 1997).

[46] Mackintosh, 'The Volunteer', in *A Highland Regiment*, 47.

For Mackintosh, then, war held out the promise of sublime, character-forming experience, and the addition of a Celtic perspective could not help but sharpen and sweeten this promise. The way he consequently employs a Highland Scottish sensibility to wring the last drops of poignancy from war's tragedy can be seen in a poem such as 'Cha Till MacCruimein' in which he draws, perhaps a little opportunistically, on traditions of Highland fatalism and lamentation.[47] Written in Bedford in February 1915, before he went out to France, the poem describes the departure for the Front of the 4th Camerons:

> And every lad in his heart was dreaming
> Of honour and wealth to come,
> And honour and noble pride were calling
> To the tune of the pipes and drum;
> But I was hearing a woman singing
> On dark Dunvegan shore,
> 'In battle or peace, with wealth or honour,
> MacCrimmon comes no more.'[48]

To suggest that he uses Highland traditions opportunistically is not to accuse Mackintosh of mendacity or dishonesty. It is to suggest, rather, that he regards that culture as a useful source of the literary tropes and attitudes within which he can structure and articulate a deeply felt set of personal responses. He adopts a Highland literary sensibility precisely because it has, since Romanticism, developed such powerful, resonant mechanisms for evoking sublime mournfulness. It is a trope that other writers of a Scottish background exploited, too. Hamish Mann's 'A Scotsman's Reply to an Offer to Transfer to the R.W.F.' was also written in 1915 in Bedford prior to its author's departure for France:

> O, I'm dreaming of a mountain-side where torrents leap and roar,
> And the skirling of the pipes upon a barren, rocky shore,
> Where the sad-faced Scottish lassies pray for lads they'll see no more
>   In the 42nd Highlanders (Black Watch).
>
> Yes, I'm longing for the heather moor, the murmur of the Tilt,
> The wild and rugged places where red Highland blood's been spilt.
> So, if I must die fighting, I'll die fighting in the kilt
>   Of the 42nd Highlanders (Black Watch).[49]

What is perhaps more significant than this opportunistic adoption of a Highland sensibility, however, is that it is only one of several sources upon which poets like Mackintosh and Mann feel they can legitimately draw. Mackintosh, like so many of

---

[47] This is a poem which Vera Brittain knew and valued, having been sent a copy of *A Highland Regiment* at Christmas 1917. See Vera Brittain, *Testament of Youth: An Autobiographical Study of the Years 1900–1925* (London: Virago, 1978), 416.

[48] Mackintosh, 'Cha Till MacCruimein', in *A Highland Regiment*, 16.

[49] Hamish Mann, 'A Scotsman's Reply to an Offer to Transfer to the R.W.F.', in *A Subaltern's Musings*, 26.

his peers, tends to use standard-English lyric forms for poems of intimacy—as in the moving 'To Sylvia', 'Farewell: To Sergeant H. Fraser and L.-Sergeant G. M'Kay', and 'From Home'—while employing a more self-consciously Scottish idiom for poems of exhortation and humour. This suggests that the 'Scottish' persona of several of his poems is only one of several available to him; that it is a rhetorical function as much as a pledge of identity.

It should be noted, though, that this is not necessarily a bad thing for Scottish poetry. While it threatens any claims such a poetry might wish to make to 'authenticity'—an arguably spurious contention in any case—it also opens up its literary and cultural resources to the use of others. The general myth of the Scottish soldier was a very productive one in the First World War. Many young Englishmen as well as Scots were drawn to serve in Scottish regiments by the allure of the Highland martial tradition, and British culture more generally was happy to accept the Scottish regiments, not just as colourful additions to the war effort but as central to—and perhaps even typical of—it. For young men of many backgrounds, as one observer would put it, 'the glamour of the kilt was irresistible'.[50] The son of an Anglo-Scottish London publisher like John Murray might choose a Scottish regiment, but so too did the son of the Englishman J. M. Dent. English publishers pushed out histories of the Highland regiments for the general reader, while crusty old literary campaigners like Sir William Watson acclaimed 'the spirit perfervid of the heroic Scot' with its 'ancient native prowess unforgot, | Valour undrooped, and manhood undecayed'.[51] The makers of the pioneering documentary film *The Battle of the Somme* (1916) actively sought out kilted soldiers, and its distributors were keen that it be screened with bagpipe accompaniment.[52] The extent of this lionization of the Highland regiments was so strong that it prompted one rather jaded Englishman working in the Scottish book trade to complain to the *Publishers' Circular* that the English were tending to 'make altogether too much fuss about the kilted regiments'.[53] When British soldiers—and later the British population more generally—needed a sentimental New Year song, they might turn to Burns's 'Auld Lang Syne'. C. E. Montague would quote Burns approvingly in *Disenchantment* (1922), taking a fragment from 'Auld Lang Syne' as the book's epigraph, and using Burns as one of his exemplars of the British virtues of uncomplicatedness, tolerance, and good humour shown by the ordinary soldiers in the war.[54] Wilfred Owen, similarly, found no difficulty in employing a Scottish perspective, as when

[50]   From a Cameron Highlander's diary, quoted in Lieutenant-Colonel J. Stewart and John Buchan, *The Fifteenth (Scottish) Division 1914–1919* (Edinburgh: Blackwood, 1926), 3.

[51]   Sir William Watson, 'To a Scottish Friend' (1915), in *Selected Poems of Sir William Watson* (London: Thornton Butterworth, 1928), 224.

[52]   See S. D. Badsey, 'Battle of the Somme: British War Propaganda', *Historical Journal of Film, Radio and Television*, 3/2 (1983), 109.

[53]   Henry R. Brabrook, 'If It's Scotch It's Scotch; If It's English It's—British', *Publishers' Circular*, 29 July 1916, 89.

[54]   C. E. Montague, *Disenchantment* (London: Chatto & Windus, 1922), 6–12.

in 'Disabled' he gave a bitter twist to the sentiments of Housman's 'To an Athlete Dying Young' in his description of a Scottish soldier: an amputee betrayed by the allure of looking 'a god in kilts'.[55]

What this suggests is not that there wasn't a Scottish literature in the First World War, but rather that such a category had ceased to be an exclusive one. It was not a matter of great consequence that Joseph Lee's poetry took on an increasingly English voice, just as it made little difference whether a poet like Alan Mackintosh was Scottish by birth or by his own election. The fact that Mackintosh chose a predominantly Scottish persona in his poetry was enough to show the continuing vitality and relevance of aspects of that tradition. T. S. Eliot had been astute enough to note that it might 'be an evidence of strength, rather than of weakness, that the Scots language and the Scottish literature did not maintain a separate existence'. The Scottish poetry of the war was perhaps not always as strongly individual as it might have been, but that may just bear out Eliot's contention that by 'throwing in its luck with English', Scottish literature 'has not only much greater chance of survival, but contributes important elements of strength to complete the English'.[56]

---

[55] Wilfred Owen, 'Disabled', in *The Complete Poems and Fragments*, i: *The Poems*, ed. Jon Stallworthy (London: Chatto & Windus, Hogarth Press, and Oxford University Press, 1983), 175. Owen, of course, spent a significant part of his wartime service at Craiglockhart Hospital near Edinburgh, where he met Siegfried Sassoon.

[56] Eliot, 'Was There a Scottish Literature?', 681.

CHAPTER 9

WAR POETRY, OR THE POETRY OF WAR? ISAAC ROSENBERG, DAVID JONES, IVOR GURNEY

VIVIEN NOAKES

Writing in 1937, David Jones states of *In Parenthesis*: 'I did not intend this as a "War Book"—it happens to be concerned with war.'[1] Although the world in which he was writing gloomed under the shadow of another war, there was no longer the urgency that had prompted Sassoon in his protest against the way in which the First World War was being deliberately prolonged, or the compelling need to inform and to warn that had guided Owen. But this disclaimer reflects more than immediate concerns: it denotes a difference in kind.

As the Great War progressed, war poetry as a genre underwent profound change. Years of attrition in which men endured subhuman conditions, endless cold and wet, and empty boredom fraught with constant danger, sudden, capricious death, and slow, agonized dying, affected not only the bodies and minds but also the

[1] David Jones, 'Preface', in *In Parenthesis* (London: Faber, 1963; 1st pub. 1937), p. xii.

souls of those who witnessed and experienced it. Some poets—in particular those who believed that they had a responsibility to try to influence the course of events—responded with the irony and satire of anger; Owen did so with pity. Many survived through a philosophy of resignation touched with humour: these were not the 'smiling Tommies' of the newsreels so disliked by the fighting soldiers, but men whom F. W. Harvey—a subaltern in the Gloucestershire Regiment and Ivor Gurney's closest friend—described in his poem 'To the Makers of Laughter' as 'seeing, clear, life's sorrow, | Yet [they] mock it down, and borrow | Strong courage of despair'.[2] Others drew this courage from interior worlds of imagination and memory, from the beauties they could still find in the world around them, and from the respect and admiration they felt for the men in whose lives they shared.

In his preface to *In Parenthesis*, Jones writes that 'We find ourselves privates in foot regiments. We search how we may see formal goodness in a life singularly inimical, hateful, to us.'[3] He served for long periods on the Western Front, and he loathed war and its destructive consequences; but he was not alone among the war poets in believing that, for all its horror, there was in war a vitality, even a beauty, that could transcend the immediate experience. This reaching for transcendence is not a characteristic that one normally associates with war poetry, but it was central to the work of the three poets whose work I shall be considering.

Ralph Waldo Emerson, whose poetry Isaac Rosenberg admired for being 'always near a brink of some impalpable idea, some indefinable rumour of endlessness',[4] believed that 'within man is the soul of the whole . . . the universal beauty'.[5] This idea is less remote from the experience of war than might at first appear. Jones suggests in his essay 'Art in Relation to War' that the soldier is more able to perceive war's hidden beauties than those who are ignorant of its realities:

I believe it can be said that all art, as such, has beauty for its end, without qualification, both the art of war and the arts of peace. . . . It . . . is left to the soldier . . . to keep his charity and to practise his art . . . [B]oth art and charity behave themselves in an analogous manner: they tend, both of them, to nose out the abstract 'goods' and 'beauties' behind the detestable accidents.[6]

But this beauty does not present itself easily. It must be searched for, as Ivor Gurney suggests in a letter to Marion Scott from France in December 1916:

The Artist must learn to feel the beauty of all things, and the sense of instant communion with God that such perception will bring. 'To feel Eternity in an hour.' Blake knew

---

[2] F. W. Harvey, 'To the Makers of Laughter', quoted in Anthony Boden, *F. W. Harvey: Soldier, Poet* (Gloucester: Alan Sutton, 1988), 340.

[3] Jones, 'Preface', p. xiii.

[4] Isaac Rosenberg, 'Emerson', in *The Collected Works of Isaac Rosenberg*, ed. Ian Parsons (London: Chatto & Windus, 1979), 289.

[5] Ralph Waldo Emerson, 'The Over-Soul', in *Emerson's Prose and Poetry*, ed. Joel Porte and Saundra Morris (New York: Norton, 2001), 164.

[6] David Jones, 'Art in Relation to War', in *The Dying Gaul*, ed. Harman Grisewood (London: Faber, 1978), 143 and 147.

that to attain to this height, not greater dexterity, but greater humility and beauty of thought were needed . . . After all, my friend, it is better to live a grey life in mud and danger, so long as one uses it—as I trust I am now doing—as a means to an end. Someday all this experience may be crystallized and glorified in me; and men shall learn . . . what thoughts haunted the minds of men who watched the darkness grimly in desolate places.[7]

The need to be soaked in the experience of war, and then to allow time for a full understanding of its significance to be realized before it could be adequately expressed, was felt also by Isaac Rosenberg, writing to Laurence Binyon in the autumn of 1916: 'I am determined that this war, with all its powers for devastation, shall not master my poeting; that is, if I am lucky enough to come through all right. I will not leave a corner of my consciousness covered up, but saturate myself with the strange and extraordinary new conditions of this life, and it will all refine itself into poetry later on.'[8]

For Rosenberg, who was killed on 1 April 1918, there was no 'later on'. For David Jones—who, like Rosenberg, had trained as an artist—it was different, although it was not until many years after the war that he developed as a poet: *In Parenthesis* began as a plan 'to do a lot of illustrations with long "captions" of a sort'.[9] Rosenberg, by contrast, was a long way down the road of his poetic development before war broke out, and he carried the central concerns of this earlier work into his trench poetry.

The pre-war Rosenberg was part urban poet, part mystic, and in his Jewishness he was above all a poet of exile. Central to his vision is the idea that man has been banished from his spiritual base, cut adrift in a world in which he can never feel at home, exiled from an existence of which he, Rosenberg, was only dimly aware but of whose reality he had no doubt, and for which, all his life, his soul longed. Night is the time when the physical senses sleep and the soul can awaken: in the light of dawn the poet's vision fades. He saw man living this daily life caught in a body which, with Donne, he called a 'soul's sack'.[10] 'How can I burst this trammel of my flesh', he wrote in 1912, 'That is a continent 'twixt your song and me? | How can I loosen from my soul this mesh | That dulls mine ears and blinds mine eyes to see?'[11] His longing was for a parallel existence, what he called 'an indefinitent 'twixt ideal; the haunting desire for that which is beyond the reach of hands'.[12] For him,

---

[7] Ivor Gurney to Marion Scott, 15 Dec. 1916, in *Collected Letters*, ed. R. K. R. Thornton (Ashington and Manchester: MidNag/Carcanet, 1991), 171.

[8] Rosenberg to Laurence Binyon, n.d. [Autumn 1916], in *Collected Works*, 248.

[9] Jones, quoted in Jonathan Miles, *Backgrounds to David Jones: A Study in Sources and Drafts* (Cardiff: University of Wales Press, 1990), 80.

[10] Rosenberg, 'Dead Man's Dump', in *The Poems and Plays of Isaac Rosenberg*, ed. Vivien Noakes (Oxford: Oxford University Press, 2004), 140. The image is from Donne's 'Elegy IX: The Autumnal', in *Complete English Poems*, ed. C. A. Patrides (London: Dent, 1985), 154.

[11] Rosenberg, 'Night and Day', in *Poems and Plays*, 47.

[12] Rosenberg to Miss Seaton, n.d. [1911], in *Collected Works*, 184.

true reality was invisible to the human eye but present in the soul. Only there, he believed, could man's spirit soar freely, for it is there that true beauty and joy exist, a beauty that 'sings and teaches her fair song | Of the Eternal rhythm',[13] and joy that is a recurring theme in his work. In a statement that applies equally to his poetry, he wrote: 'My ideal of a picture is to paint what we cannot see. To create, to imagine. To make tangible and real a figment of the brain. To transport the spectator into other worlds where beauty is the only reality.'[14] This idea was central to his ambition to write 'Simple *poetry*—that is where an interesting complexity of thought is kept in tone and right value to the dominating idea so that it is understandable and still ungraspable.'[15]

In Rosenberg's early work we find a benevolent creator where 'love is the radiant smile of God'.[16] But this mood of orthodox acceptance is not sustained. Instead, he came to see the Godhead as an uncaring tyrant, the architect of a world in which man is trapped, played with like a toy, in which his vision is dulled and his vitality trampled out, a world of banishment from all that is most beautiful, all he most craves, as the jealous God who created man abandons him to his fate. By the time he wrote his poem 'God' in late 1914 or 1915—after the outbreak of war but before he had enlisted—we find an uncompromising bitterness:

> In his malodorous brain what slugs and mire
> Lanthorned in his oblique eyes, guttering burned!
> His body lodged a rat where men nursed souls . . .
> On fragments of a skull of power,
> On shy and maimed, on women wrung awry,
> He lay, a bullying hulk, to crush them more . . .
> Ah! this miasma of a rotting God![17]

In this deepening mood he wrote some of his most powerful poems, as his earlier passivity in exile, a longing for that other, unattainable world, becomes a rebellious contempt for the force that delights in destroying exiled man. It is a voice that finds expression in lyric beauty as it combines a quiet, mystical awareness with passionate protest at a situation over which he has no control.

In June 1914 Rosenberg was in South Africa staying with his sister, and there, in August, he wrote 'On Receiving News of the War'. The first two stanzas describe the coming of winter into a summer land:

> Snow is a strange white word.
> No ice or frost
> Have asked of bud or bird
> For Winter's cost.

---

[13] Rosenberg, 'Night and Day', 56.   [14] Rosenberg, 'Rudolph', in *Collected Works*, 277.
[15] Rosenberg to Gordon Bottomley, n.d. [postmarked 23 July 1916], ibid. 238.
[16] Rosenberg, 'Night and Day', 56.   [17] Rosenberg, 'God', in *Poems and Plays*, 117.

> Yet ice and frost and snow
> From earth to sky
> This Summer land doth know.
> No man knows why.[18]

There are stages in this coming. As the snow stands in isolated passivity, it is the word, with its suggestion of untouched purity, that Rosenberg emphasizes. But this innocence does not last. With the arrival of ice and frost comes the harshness that was always there, waiting. The word 'asked' suggests that bud and bird have a choice, that winter's cost is not inevitable. But that is an illusion; with their coming the whiteness that had seemed benign combines to create a blanket of winter that will destroy those symbols of promise and freedom as it reaches out to envelop the earth.

In the third and fourth stanzas he turns from a scene of encompassing whiteness to the blood-red atavism that hides beneath the kiss of betrayal. Here God is still able to mourn for his creation; he is not yet the malevolent power he is soon to become in his poetry:

> In all men's hearts it is.
> Some spirit old
> Hath turned with malign kiss
> Our lives to mould.
>
> Red fangs have torn His face.
> God's blood is shed.
> He mourns from His lone place
> His children dead.

But then, in the final stanza, he seems to suggest that the war itself will offer the possibility of redemption, as man's bellicosity turns to create a purging, purifying power that will cleanse and re-create the world:

> O! ancient crimson curse!
> Corrode, consume.
> Give back this universe
> Its pristine bloom.

This was an image that represented for him the urgency and vitality that he both celebrated and mistrusted in the new art of Marinetti and the Futurists. 'Art is now, as it were a volcano', he wrote in 1914. 'The roots of a dead universe are torn up by hands, feverish and consuming with an exuberant vitality—and amid dynamic threatenings we watch the hastening of the corroding doom,' adding wistfully, 'the reign of Blake is yet to begin'.[19] His own role as an artist will be different. As Europe steps into its bath of blood, he 'will be waiting with beautiful drying towels

---

[18] Rosenberg, 'On Receiving News of the War: Cape Town', ibid. 83–4.
[19] Rosenberg, 'Art', in *Collected Works*, 294.

of painted canvas, and precious ointments to smear and heal the soul; and lovely music and poems'.[20]

This poem has in it something of the idea that we see in Rupert Brooke's swimmers 'into cleanness leaping'[21]—an idea, incidentally, that was shared by more than just poets[22]—but which is here approached quite differently. The poet whose work these images of winter in summer recall most closely is Wilfred Owen: 'War broke: and now the Winter of the world | With perishing great darkness closes in.'[23] But whereas Owen turns in the final lines to 'the need | Of sowings for new Spring, and blood for seed'—blood of the young men who will die—with Rosenberg it is the corrosive power of the curse itself that must re-create the pristine bloom that was destroyed by the malign kiss. Even after enlisting, Rosenberg still expressed a belief in the possibility of personal re-creation through war: 'One might succumb[,] be destroyed—but one might also (and the chances are even greater for it) be renewed, made larger, healthier.'[24] It was an idea that Gurney, much later in the war, was to echo, though unwillingly: 'when more dross is burnt out of me, perhaps then I shall see Beauty clearly in everything. Yet O, that this purification should come by war! Obscene and purely dreadful!'[25]

In June 1915 Rosenberg wrote to Sydney Schiff: 'I am thinking of enlisting if they will have me, though it is against all my principles of justice—though I would be doing the most criminal thing a man can do.'[26] He thought of joining the R.A.M.C., 'as the idea of killing upsets me a bit',[27] but he was too small, and it was as part of the 11th Battalion of the King's Own Royal Lancaster Regiment that he was sent to France at the beginning of June 1916. His poem 'The Troop Ship', describing the Channel crossing, is the 138th of his 158 surviving poems; we can see how considerable his poetic output had been before he reached the front line. In France, although he would later write that 'Sometimes I give way and am appalled at the devastation this life seems to have made in my nature',[28] he would suffer no shattering disillusionment, for this financially impoverished, but intellectually and spiritually enriched, private soldier had no illusions to shed. His best trench poetry would be a development, a maturing, of what had gone before.

[20] Rosenberg to Edward Marsh, n.d. [Oct.–Nov. 1914], ibid., 206.
[21] Rupert Brooke, 'Peace', in The Poetical Works, ed. Geoffrey Keynes (London: Faber, 1960), 19.
[22] e.g. Lieut.-General Sir Reginald C. Hart, 'A Vindication of War', Nineteenth Century and After, 414 (Aug. 1911), 238–9: 'Peace is a disintegrating force, whereas war consolidates a people. War is no doubt a dreadful ordeal, but it clears the air, and refines the race as fire purifies the gold and silver in the furnace. Nations, like individuals, ultimately benefit by their chastenings—this is one of the mysteries of Nature.' I am grateful to Paul Laity for drawing my attention to this.
[23] Wilfred Owen, '1914', in The Complete Poems and Fragments, i: The Poems, ed. Jon Stallworthy (London: Chatto & Windus, Hogarth Press, and Oxford University Press, 1983), 116.
[24] Rosenberg to Sidney Schiff, n.d. [Nov. 1915], in Collected Works, 221–2.
[25] Gurney to Marion Scott, 31 Oct. 1917, in Collected Letters, 361.
[26] Rosenberg to Sidney Schiff, n.d. [8 June 1915], in Collected Works, 216.
[27] Rosenberg to Sidney Schiff, n.d. [early Nov. 1915], ibid. 221.
[28] Rosenberg to Miss Seaton, 14 Feb. 1918, ibid. 268.

I spoke of Rosenberg's belief—expressed in many of his pre-war poems—that man's existence is one of exile, and how he saw, in the darkness of night, when the senses shut down and the eyes of the soul were opened, an escape from his quotidian banishment. In this vision there are the border states of dawn and twilight, and it is in one of these that he places his poem 'Break of Day in the Trenches', written in June 1916 during one of his first tours in the line. Here, the darkness of night is giving way to the inevitability of day, 'the same old Druid Time as ever'.[29] We know from his earlier work that as dawn breaks he is bringing us back into the world of imprisoned exile; but now a new, more violent, form of imprisonment has been added to the old. He is no longer tidily caged in earth: now he is 'Sprawled in the bowels of the earth, | The torn fields of France'. His companion, who leaps as he pulls the parapet's poppy—a poppy 'whose roots are in man's veins', already a symbol of transience and eventually of course of the fallen of the war—is his old adversary, sardonic, bitter, scornful, the God whose 'body lodged a rat where men nursed souls' and who taunts both friend and foe:

> Now you have touched this English hand
> You will do the same to a German
> Soon, no doubt, if it be your pleasure
> To cross the sleeping green between.

Man may believe himself to be superior to the rat—and, indeed, to the malign godhead—but it is the rat who has the freedom to move while the soldier is trapped in his trench. And as it moves, it seems to revel not only in the breaking of strong young bodies on which, in time, it will feast, but also in the terror it can see in the eyes of the men who are condemned to die:

> It seems, odd thing, you grin as you pass
> Strong eyes, fine limbs, haughty athletes,
> Less chanced than you for life,
> Bonds to the whims of murder,
> Sprawled in the bowels of the earth,
> The torn fields of France.
> What do you see in our eyes
> At the shrieking iron and flame
> Hurl'd through still heavens?
> What quaver—what heart aghast?

But for now the rat, and its feasting, must wait. Though death, and the return to earth, are as inevitable as the dropping of the petals of the poppy, at daybreak that earth is no more than a white dusting in the half-light of dawn. It is a portent, for in Rosenberg whiteness is synonymous with death.

In 'Returning, we hear the larks'—written in the following year, 1917—we have moved from dawn into night, but this is no longer the time of spiritual awakening

---

[29] Rosenberg, 'Break of Day in the Trenches', in *Poems and Plays*, 128–9.

that he had once welcomed. At the Front, darkness brought with it the constant threat of death, particularly from the shelling of those going into or coming out of the line:

> Sombre the night is.
> And though we have our lives, we know
> What sinister threat lurks there.
>
> Dragging these anguished limbs, we only know
> This poison-blasted track opens on our camp—
> On a little safe sleep.[30]

The sinister threat is reminiscent of the Judas kiss that presaged war. But then, suddenly, it all changes. The mood is shattered by a beauty that pours from the night sky, that music of joy that we find so often in his poetry, speaking directly to exiled man and sustaining him in his suffering:

> But hark! joy—joy—strange joy.
> Lo! heights of night ringing with unseen larks.
> Music showering our upturned list'ning faces.

This is the beauty, 'music's secret soul | Creeping about man's senses',[31] that he writes of in 'The Unicorn', the poetic play on which he was working in France at this same time, a play in which he wanted to put all his innermost experience 'to symbolize the war and all the devastating forces let loose by an ambitious and unscrupulous will'.[32]

Then comes the poem's final stanza as his wonder at this beauty fades into a realization of inevitability:

> Death could drop from the dark
> As easily as song—
> But song only dropped,
> Like a blind man's dreams on the sand
> By dangerous tides,
> Like a girl's dark hair for she dreams no ruin lies there,
> Or her kisses where a serpent hides.

The beauty of the music of the unseen larks, though real, is also an illusion: the song of birds may fill the sky, but it will not always be so. Just as the winter snow in 'On Receiving News of the War' turns from innocence to destruction, so will those tides engulf the man who does not know that they are there, and the serpent ruin the trusting girl. For now they may dream, but inevitably will come that betrayal which is the certain consequence of unguarded innocence, that reality which earlier

---

[30] Rosenberg, 'Returning, we hear the larks', ibid. 138–9.
[31] Rosenberg, 'The Unicorn', ibid. 253.
[32] Rosenberg to Miss Seaton, n.d. [8 Mar. 1918], in *Collected Works*, 270.

destroyed both bud and bird. Then the song of the larks will be silenced, and shells bringing death will drop effortlessly, casually from the dark.

In 'Dead Man's Dump' we can see—as well as vivid, powerful images of war and war's futility—both Rosenberg's sense of exile and his understanding of man's nobility and tenderness as he confronts the horror of the forces that are so carelessly destroying him. Its title speaks of the casualness of the disposal of the dead, but the poem itself reveals the nobility of men who must daily confront this thoughtless abandonment. It expresses the mystery of sudden, violent death with a deep compassion:

> A man's brains splattered on
> A stretcher-bearer's face;
> His shook shoulders slipped their load,
> But when they bent to look again
> The drowning soul was sunk too deep
> For human tenderness.[33]

Into this violence, where the air is loud with death as shells go crying over the shrieking pyre, comes a stanza of absolute stillness:

> None saw their spirits' shadow shake the grass,
> Or stood aside for the half used life to pass
> Out of those doomed nostrils and the doomed mouth,
> When the swift iron burning bee
> Drained the wild honey of their youth.

Man's days are as grass, and as the wind passes over it, it is gone.[34] They leave no trace behind, and it is the very creator of the sweetness of their youth who has destroyed them.

The third and fourth stanzas were initially a separate poem entitled 'The Young Dead'. They place the inevitability of the death within a context that transcends the war itself:

> Earth has waited for them
> All the time of their growth
> Fretting for their decay:
> Now she has them at last!
> In the strength of their strength
> Suspended—stopped and held.

Now the earth can reclaim the strong young bodies that will soon, like the other, older dead, be burnt black by strange decay. But what of man's noblest, most enduring, aspect?

> What fierce imaginings their dark souls lit
> Earth! have they gone into you?

---

[33] Rosenberg, 'Dead Man's Dump', 139–42.   [34] Cf. Ps. 103: 15–16.

Somewhere they must have gone,
And flung on your hard back
Is their soul's sack,
Emptied of God-ancestralled essences.

Even as he poses the question, we know that he does not believe it to be true. The earth may claim the emptied body—that mesh which encompassed the living man, denying him the powers of true perception—but his most potent, powerful aspect has escaped its grasp. The unknown, that which is beyond man's ability to reach but for which he strives in his endless search for the hidden reality, that indefinite ideal which is the poet's goal—it is there that their dark imaginings have gone.

There is, though, a realization in this poem that man is not only the victim of such wilful destruction: he is also brutish, the destroyer, the inheritor of that malign kiss. For, as the limber hurtles forward towards the wounded man lying in its path, it is *we* who crash round the bend as the choked soul stretches 'weak hands | To reach the living word the far wheels said', *we* who hear his weak scream, his very last sound as the wheels of our plunging limber graze his dead face. In the end, war is the creation of man. Man can no longer blame a tyrannical, jealous God for his suffering; nor—despite the crown of thorns, the sceptres old—can he control the forces of destruction that he has himself unleashed.

Rosenberg returns to the idea of the release of the soul from the body in 'Daughters of War', the poem that he considered to be his most significant exploration of war. Certainly it is his most abstracted, as the Daughters dance and call to the spirits of the dead before their last cries fade among the boughs of the tree of life. He told Marsh that he was trying to get 'that sense of inexorableness the human (or inhuman) side of this war has[.] It even penetrates behind human life.'[35] It reaches down, deep into the 'underside of things | And shut from earth's profoundest eyes',[36] and rises up into the huge embraces of the waiting Daughters, mighty Amazonians who sigh with longing for the souls that will be released as their human lovers are slain. And as they die, as the earth-men's earth falls away clean of the dust of old days, these earthly forms and days are burned to a grey ash that drifts in the wind as they move into timelessness, all human love now faded.

The achievement of these extraordinary poems is even greater when one realizes the conditions under which they were written. As a private, Rosenberg suffered the greatest of privations and the most exposed of trench experiences, and he had no one with whom to share his thoughts, except by letter. 'I believe if I met anybody with ideas I'd be dumb,' he wrote at the beginning of 1918. 'No drug could be more stupefying than our work . . . and this goes on like that old torture of water trickling, drop by drop unendingly, on one's helplessness.'[37] That he responded to

[35] Rosenberg to Edward Marsh, n.d. [postmarked 30 July 1917], in *Collected Works*, 260.
[36] Rosenberg, 'Daughters of War', in *Poems and Plays*, 142.
[37] Rosenberg to Gordon Bottomley, n.d. [postmarked 26 Feb. 1918], in *Collected Works*, 268.

this helplessness with a sense of growing, almost unsupportable, despair is clear from a letter he wrote to Edward Marsh at the end of January 1918, two months before his death, in lines cancelled by the censor: 'what is happening to me now is more tragic than the "passion play". Christ never endured what I endure. It is breaking me completely.'[38]

Rosenberg wrote of the artist's attempt 'to connect the inner with the outer by means of a more spontaneous and intelligent understanding of the actual'.[39] To an even greater extent this is true of the work of David Jones. In the post-war years, before he wrote *In Parenthesis*, he was much influenced by the writings of the French Thomist philosopher Jacques Maritain, whose works were first translated into English, under the auspices of Jones's friend Eric Gill, in 1923. In *The Philosophy of Art* Maritain wrote:

Art, in so far as ordered to Beauty, does not, at least when its object permits, stop at forms or at colours, nor at sounds, nor at words taken in themselves and *as things*, but it takes them also as making known other things than themselves, that is to say *as signs*.[40]

Jones saw man, from earliest times, as a sign-maker 'whose nature is to make things' that 'are of necessity the signs of something other'.[41] He believed painting and poetry to be sacramental acts which show forth, under another form, existing realities, making the universal shine out from the particular. Creating a single artefact, a whole, from the chaos that is modern war presented huge problems, for he was 'faced with the profoundest contradictions and he must resolve them all, not losing one, and still create delight'.[42] In order to bring unity to confusion, he turned to what T. S. Eliot called 'the mythic method', a means of 'controlling, of ordering, of giving shape and a significance to the immense panorama of futility and anarchy which is contemporary history'.[43]

Jones believed that the creations of the past lived still within the culture of a people in a line of unbroken artistic interpretation. By weaving the threads of this shared culture—dense in association—through the texture of his poem, he was able to re-present to his modern readers artistic riches that were their inheritance, drawing on earlier interpretations of warfare, courage, endurance and loss in order to throw light on the present situation and to reveal how this was not new, but part of a continuum of human experience. There was an added urgency in drawing

---

[38]   Rosenberg to Edward Marsh, n.d. [postmarked 26 Jan. 1918], in Berg Collection of English and American Literature, New York Public Library, Astor, Lennox, and Tilden Foundations.

[39]   Rosenberg, 'Art', 293.

[40]   Jacques Maritain, *The Philosophy of Art: Being "Art et Scholastique" by Jacques Maritain*, trans. Revd. John O'Connor (Ditchling: St Dominic's Press, 1923), 83–4.

[41]   Jones, 'Art and Sacrament', in *Epoch and Artist: Selected Writings*, ed. Harman Grisewood (London: Faber, 1959), 150.

[42]   Jones, 'Art in Relation to War', 141.

[43]   T. S. Eliot, '*Ulysses*, Order and Myth' (1923), in *Selected Prose of T. S. Eliot*, ed. Frank Kermode (London: Faber, 1975), 177.

on these sources, for he saw that the continuity they represented was breaking down. 'In the late nineteen-twenties and early' rubthirties', he wrote, 'among my most immediate friends there used to be discussed something that we christened "The Break" . . . [I]n the nineteenth century, Western Man moved across a rubicon.'[44] 'We saw, with varying degrees of clarity . . . the technological, scientific advances which, one way or another and whether beneficent or otherwise, were destructive of immemorial ways of life, of rooted cultures of all sorts.'[45] The technology that gave a particular character to modern warfare was also bringing about the destruction of the cultural inheritance on which he drew, giving both poignancy and relevance to its use.

With *In Parenthesis* Jones set out to explore some of the things that he had seen, felt, and been a part of between December 1915 and early July 1916, as he shared in the daily life of small groups of men who 'bore in their bodies the genuine tradition of the Island of Britain, from Bendigeid Vran to Jingle and Marie Lloyd'. He wanted to make 'a shape in words, using as data the complex of sights, sounds, fears, hopes, apprehensions, smells, things exterior and interior, the landscape and paraphernalia of that singular time and of those particular men'.[46] By drawing on the shared inheritance, he was able to show that their experience went beyond the singular and particular of their own lives into something wider and more universal. In broad sweeps and small, vivid detail, with echoes of *Y Gododdin*, *The Battle of Brunanburh* and *Chanson de Roland*, of Chaucer, Malory, Shakespeare and Hopkins, of the Bible and Catholic liturgy and much more, Jones built up his image of this particular war. The allusions he offers are not glorious or romantic: they speak of ancient treachery and madness, of fabled insult and of women seeking their husbands' long-decayed once-bodies. They speak of the extremes of daily hardships, of cold so deep that it 'hurts you in the bloody eyes, it grips chill and harmfully and rasps the sensed membrane of the throat'[47] calling back frozen regions of the Celtic underworld, of men sleeping in the rain and the mud as soldiers through centuries had done before them. Through their experience they could share in the emotions of those other generations, for they too could understand what it had meant to be a foot-soldier at Crécy. John Ball echoes Edward Thomas's Lob, who, 'Although he was seen dying at Waterloo, | Hastings, Agincourt, and Sedgmoor, too, — | Lives yet.'[48]

As John Ball prepares to go up the line for the first time, he realizes that the ordinary is about to become the extraordinary: 'there was in this night's parading, for all the fear of it, a kind of blessedness, here was borne away with yesterday's remoteness, an accumulated tedium, all they'd piled on since enlistment day: a whole unlovely order this night would transubstantiate, lend some grace to'.[49] 'I do

---

[44] Jones, 'Preface to *The Anathemata*', in *Epoch and Artist*, 113.
[45] Jones, 'Notes on the 1930s', in *The Dying Gaul*, 46.   [46] Jones, 'Preface', *In Parenthesis*, p. x.
[47] Jones, *In Parenthesis*, 61.
[48] Edward Thomas, 'Lob', in *Collected Poems*, ed. R. George Thomas (London: Faber, 2004), 62.
[49] Jones, *In Parenthesis*, 27.

not imply that this *should* be so', Jones wrote many years later, 'but I do assert that it *was* so.'[50] In the darkness, these novices stumble down the dark, muddy trenches:

> The repeated passing back of aidful messages assumes a cadence.
> Mind the hole
> mind the hole
> mind the hole to the left
> hole right
> step over
> keep left, left.
> One grovelling, precipitated, with his gear tangled, struggles to feet again:
> Left be buggered.[51]

As the rhythmic mellifluousness is shattered by the commonplace of the soldier's expletive, Jones brings us back to the reality of the soldiers' experience. Yet this too is part of the poetry. Through generations, soldiers' discourse has been built around 'impious and impolite words'. He is hampered in giving full expression to these by the sensibilities of the convention within which he is published, something he regrets, for he sees that in the circumstances of war they can acquire a dignity and, in their repetition, an almost liturgical quality: 'the "Bugger! Bugger!" of a man detailed, had often about it the "Fiat! Fiat!" of the Saints'.[52]

Once in the line, the men inhabit a border state as they 'sit in the wilderness, pent like lousy rodents all the day long; appointed scape-beasts come to the waste-lands, to grope; to stumble at the margin of familiar things—at the place of separation',[53] scarcely knowing why they are there but resigned to their unknowingness, for they have no other choice. Now Jones is concerned above all with the quiet heroism of the ordinary soldiers as they struggle to make the best of this chaotic, unlovely order. There are cowards, and there are those who swing the lead, but there is also stoicism and humour in the shared life of protracted awfulness: epic heroism exists in the grace of daily living. There are times when the men sink deep into their private thoughts, and times when they sing, sometimes quietly, almost to themselves—'David of the White Stone',[54] Welsh Calvinist Methodist hymns, 'O, O, O, it's a lovely war', even rugby songs.

As night comes on, John Ball experiences 'the deepened stillness as a calm, cast over us—a potent influence over us and him—dead-calm Sargasso dank, and for the creeping things. | You can hear the silence of it.' This eerie, death-laden silence is broken only by another eerie sound, the 'scrut, scrut, sscrut' of rats in no man's land as they enjoy their 'night-feast on the broken of us'.[55] The description of dawn that follows is perhaps the most desolate of any in First World War literature. At

---

[50] Jones, quoted in Miles, *Backgrounds to David Jones*, 81.   [51] Jones, *In Parenthesis*, 36.
[52] Jones, 'Preface', p. xii.   [53] Jones, *In Parenthesis*, 70.
[54] Ibid. 42. Translating from the Welsh, Jones does not give the more usual title, 'David of the White Rock'.
[55] Ibid. 53–4.

'stand-to', the men, stiff-boned, dead-eyed, and ashen-faced with tiredness and December cold, gaze out over no man's land with its grey bundles of the dead:

> [T]hey had barely slept—and a great cold to gnaw them. Their wet-weighted gear pulled irksomely, soaking cloth impeded all their action, adhered in saturate layers when they stood still . . . Their vitality seemed not to extend to the finger-tips nor to enable any precise act; so that to do an exact thing, competently to clean a rifle, to examine and search out intricate parts, seemed to them an enormity and beyond endurance.[56]

This, without histrionics or glory, is what it meant to be a private soldier on the Western Front.

Much later, they move forward into the battle of Mametz Wood, in a description that Bernard Bergonzi describes as 'unsurpassed for energy and exactitude anywhere in the literature of the war'.[57] As they cross no man's land, one by one the line gaps as they are picked off. The bodies of the fallen will become food for those scrutting rats, or will merge into the sodden clay as the remains of earlier warriors did in their time, as the bodies of 'the sweet brothers Balin and Balan | embraced beneath their single monument'.[58] This recalling of unintentional fratricide in Arthurian legend, reminiscent of Owen's 'Strange Meeting', is echoed on the last page of *In Parenthesis* in the shared burial place of a German and a British soldier who 'Lie still under the oak | next to the Jerry | and Sergeant Jerry Coke'.[59]

John Ball survives, though injured. Following the Somme battles of 1916, things changed, as the war, 'hardened into a more relentless, mechanical affair, took on a more sinister aspect', wrote Jones. 'The wholesale slaughter of the later years, the conscripted levies filling the gaps in every file of four, knocked the bottom out of the intimate, continuing, domestic life of small contingents of men, within whose structure Roland could find, and, for a reasonable while, enjoy, his Oliver.'[60] Jones, too, was injured in July 1916. He returned to France in October that year, and remained on the Western Front until February 1918. Of his early experiences he would write: 'I think the day by day in the Waste Land, the sudden violences and the long stillnesses, the sharp contours and unformed voids of that mysterious existence, profoundly affected the imaginations of those who suffered it. It was a place of enchantment.'[61] But on his return to France, the enchantment had gone. The new ways of mechanized warfare did not offer themselves to mythology and shared history: it had now become a war unlike any other.

Had he gone on to explore that later war, there is little doubt that Jones's deep respect for the ordinary soldier would not have wavered. It is a sentiment endorsed by Ivor Gurney, who, writing to Marion Scott in January 1918 in words that echo

---

[56] Ibid. 64–5.

[57] Bernard Bergonzi, *Heroes' Twilight: A Study of the Literature of the Great War*, 2nd edn. (London: Macmillan, 1980), 199.

[58] Jones, *In Parenthesis*, 163.   [59] Ibid. 187.   [60] Jones, 'Preface', p. ix.

[61] Ibid. p. x.

Rosenberg, asserted that 'the human race often seems to shame God, for even the most wise Deity and most pitiful could hardly refrain from triumph and shame to see how nobly men endure in schemes far beyond their comprehension'.[62] For Gurney, the ability to endure came from three things: the courage and comradeship of ordinary men with whom he shared his life; the strange natural beauties he could still find in the ravaged countryside around him; and the remembered beauties of his native Cotswold. These provide the subject-matter for many of his trench poems.

He experienced the love of comrades, 'Whose laughing spirit will not be outdone',[63] on his first night in the line. Then the relieving troops had been made welcome by the outgoing men, Welsh pit boys who sang 'their own folksongs with sweet natural voices. I did not sleep at all for the first day in the dugout—there was too much to be said, asked, and experienced . . . It was one of the notable evenings of my life.'[64] 'That strangely beautiful entry to War's rout',[65] which echoes Jones's sense of the extraordinary in his first going into the line, was the subject of two poems, both entitled 'First Time In'. Here, the horror they had expected to find was masked not just by the welcome they received, but even more by that singing whose beauty was thrown into relief by the harsh noise of the guns.

This counterpoise is characteristic of many of Gurney's war poems. He speaks of the additional joy that can be experienced by those who live in shadows as he delights in the shimmering summer heat and blue autumn mists at Laventie, in the rosy mist that mingles with the afterglow of sunset at Crucifix Corner, in the clear golden stars at which he gazes, half-dead with tiredness, in the 'relief of first dawn, the crawling out to look at it, | Wonder divine of Dawn, man hesitating before Heaven's gate'.[66] Whereas Rosenberg found beauty in an abstract, parallel existence, Gurney looked around him to seek out all that was good. And beyond that, he would retreat into the pleasant places of his faithful dreams, the hills and woods and wide water-meadows of his native Gloucestershire.

But on the other side of the balance is the pain that is a recurring theme, particularly in his first volume of poems, *Severn & Somme*, published in 1917. Just as horror gave added power to beauty, so that very awareness of beauty made the pain more difficult to endure: 'Pain, pain continual; pain unending; | Hard even to the roughest, but to those | Hungry for beauty . . . '[67] Reading the works of Edward Thomas in 1917, Gurney recognized the same torment of mind from which he suffered, and which prevented serenity for any but the shortest time. When the war was over, he would look back and know that it was 'Out of the heart's sickness

---

[62] Gurney to Marion Scott, 10 Jan. 1918, in *Collected Letters*, 391–2.
[63] Gurney, 'Servitude', in *Collected Poems*, ed. P. J. Kavanagh (Manchester: Carcanet, 2004), 16.
[64] Gurney to Marion Scott, 7 June 1916, in *Collected Letters*, 86.
[65] Gurney, 'First Time In', in *Rewards of Wonder: Poems of Cotswold, France, London*, ed. George Walter (Ashington and Manchester: MidNag/Carcanet, 2000), 62. The other poem entitled 'First Time In' appears at pp. 97–8.
[66] Gurney, 'Laventie', ibid. 34.   [67] Gurney, 'Pain', in *Collected Poems*, 15.

the spirit wrote. | For delight, or to escape hunger, or of war's worst anger.'[68] Like Rosenberg, his wish had been to use his experiences by crystallizing them into works of art—both poetry and music—so that others could understand what thoughts had haunted the minds of men in those desolate days. But in peacetime England he found a country that had no comprehension of what men had endured and no wish to understand, that took for granted the suffering and sacrifice it had demanded. In France he had found ways to sustain his spirit, but now the balance shifted beyond his control. In 1922 he was confined in an asylum where he remained until his death in 1937, 'a silent witness to the hideous crime perpetrated upon the spirit of man by modern war'.[69]

So what of war poetry? Hibberd and Onions have said that the 'more conventional authors' of 1914 'were in no doubt that the war poet's duty was the ancient one of calling men to the colours, celebrating the character of the Happy Warrior, and commending the national cause'.[70] As the war progressed that responsibility shifted, and as it did so it became more complex, spread out along a continuum of response. Whilst some poets had a new and powerful message about the nature of modern warfare that must be swiftly and urgently understood by those at home, others pursued a more abstract quest for its meaning. Possibly it was because they served in the ranks that neither Rosenberg nor Jones nor Gurney believed that they could influence the course of events, or perhaps it was because this had never been their purpose in writing. Jones made it clear that he 'had *no intention* whatever to "philosophise" about the rights and wrongs of war'.[71] He believed that 'the artist does not determine the nature of his society, he accepts whatever is to hand from his environment and conditions, he "illustrates" in the strict meaning of that word [making illumined, bringing light to bear upon], and keeping in mind its origin, what his particular culture and time makes available to him'.[72] What sets these three writers apart from some others of the war poets is that they did not move from the war to the poetry. Poetry, as a way of thought and expression through which they could search for abstract, universal beauties, was their starting-point. What war did was to offer them awesome material in their quest for new understandings of timeless truths.

---

[68] Gurney, 'War Books', ibid. 258.

[69] William Curtis-Hayward, quoted in Jon Silkin, *Out of Battle: The Poetry of the Great War* (Oxford: Oxford University Press, 1972), 122.

[70] Dominic Hibberd and John Onions, 'Introduction', in *idem* (eds.), *Poetry of the Great War: An Anthology* (Basingstoke: Palgrave, 1986), 27.

[71] Jones, quoted in Miles, *Backgrounds to David Jones*, 80.

[72] Jones, 'Art in Relation to War', 127; the definition is on p. 137.

CHAPTER 10

....

THE GREAT WAR
AND MODERNIST
POETRY

....

VINCENT SHERRY

'I think the day by day in the Waste Land, the sudden violences and long stillnesses, the sharp contours and unformed voids of that mysterious existence, profoundly affected the imaginations of those who suffered it. It was a place of enchantment. It is perhaps best described in Malory, book iv, chapter 15—that landscape spoke "with a grimly voice".'[1] So David Jones invokes the landscape he witnessed on the Western Front, where he served as an infantryman in the Royal Welch Fusiliers from 1915 to 1918. Here, in the preface to his book-length poem *In Parenthesis* (1937), he turns the terrain of his combat experience into a rich crypt of literary history. Inscribing a bibliography of his own affective memory, his record comprises, but exceeds, the reference to that landmark work of poetic modernism, Eliot's *The Waste Land*. If the moods of disillusion in that poem are attributed usually to the conditions of post-war ennui, Jones's citation reaches further back to establish his imaginative companionship in representing the event. The whole tradition of urban modernity in verse—stemming from the proto-modernism of mid-nineteenth-century French poetry, extending from Baudelaire and Gautier through Wilde and other 1890s poets to Eliot—is brought into the present tense of Jones's own service in war-torn

---

[1] David Jones, 'Preface', in *In Parenthesis* (London: Faber, 1963; 1st pub. 1937), pp. x–xi;. hereafter abbreviated in the text as *IP*. The introductory note by Eliot to the 1963 edition, recalling his own major part in soliciting the work for publication by Faber in 1937, supplies context and literary history for the continuities he perceives between his own work and Jones's.

France: the enchantments of depravity or disaster, the somewhat narcotic calm of shock and horror, all in all the ruined and ruinous beauty that is the muse of the mainstream tradition of modernist poetry over the long turn of the century.

It is not surprising, then, to find in Jones's poem a kind of history-in-miniature of literary modernism. The practices and attitudes of that now accomplished literary tradition—discontinuous or episodic narratives, verbal textures that mix idiomatic concision with dense allusive references, a cast of dramatic characters-in-voice that matches the range of speakers in *The Waste Land*—serve in Jones's work to represent his memory of the event that stands indeed as the signal instance of 'The Break', the watershed catastrophe that marks off the old and new worlds and so provides the ground, a more than nominal provocation, for the novelties of modernism. So it is surprising, equally, to find that Jones's work is really the only major modernist poem to come out of the actual experience of combat. If this assertion might be contested by critics who have argued for an expansion of the classificatory category of modernism, it is still true that, at least among the established canonical male modernists—Joyce, Pound, Lawrence, Yeats, Jones, Wyndham Lewis—only Lewis, whose most important work was not in poetry, saw service in France (Hulme, who died in Flanders in 1917, had written no poems since 1911). This dearth of 'combat modernist verse' might be taken as one more grim statistic of war dead—how many proto-modernist poets perished in the trenches?—but the other major modernist poets who lived out the war in London, specifically Pound and Eliot and Yeats, provide a coherent and revealing engagement with the cultural experience of this moment in history. Variously in discursive and personal prose, in the technical incentives as well as the local references of their verse, these poets record the profound impact that this Great War had on political and cultural and literary traditions, and so recover in deep detail the main lines of crisis and change that define the war's meaning in modern British history.

If the awareness these writers shared results in the main work of poetic modernism in English, as typified by *The Waste Land*, it is perhaps best to start this consideration with a reading of *In Parenthesis*. This work is obviously influenced by Eliot's poem, but conditioned equally strongly, and indeed immediately, by the reality of the experience that establishes the main historical conditions of literary modernism. We may then turn to a reading of the wartime writings of Pound and Eliot, who witness the political and cultural upheaval in the British capital, marking this watershed and assimilating its impact in the fabric of their own imaginative language. We may conclude by sounding the record of this same historical experience in the verse of Yeats, who was embroiled at this moment in the struggles for Irish independence, and attempt to assess the significance of the difference that his own Irish concerns make in his representation of the event of this World War. We may thus provide some comprehensive coverage of the major verse of literary modernism in Britain and Ireland in contact with the circumstances that provide for its timely import and resonance.

I

'You bunch together before a tarred door. Chalk scrawls on its planking—initials, numbers, monograms, signs, hasty, half-erased, of many regiments. Scratched out dates measuring the distance back to antique beginnings' (*IP*, 22). Here, in Part 2 of *In Parenthesis*, whose narrative follows the six-month course of Jones's early experience of the war, beginning with embarcation to Flanders in late December 1915 and ending on the first day (1 July 1916) of the disastrous Battle of the Somme, the vocal protagonist speaks his way into a collective memory, some conjured sense of martial legend and tradition, as he passes through this highly charged port of entry into the trench system. An initiation, an unmaking and remaking of a prior private identity, this moment takes its place in the typical sequence of stages in the combat memoir. Yet, in its pointed details, it also recalls one of the salient sites of the modernist imagination, as, say, in the opening poem of Pound's *Cantos*—where the ritual invocation of the gods of poetry includes the digging of the 'ell-square pitkin' and the imagining of access to the underworld, which, in Pound's mythological geography, stands as world-cultural and world-historical museum.[2] Pound and Jones provide different instances of a single riddle, a generative tension in literary modernism, a sensibility which, in its acute sensitivity to the pressures of the modern, the contemporary, the present day, opens understandably if paradoxically to the blandishments of the past. These appeals range from the more grandiose iterations of the value of 'tradition', which affords some sense of formal order to the chaos of living so intensely in the present, to the obvious nostalgia for other days, sometimes calmer but always better, richer, more significant days.

Jones's poem (really a verse-with-prose experiment, an initiative that this painter-writer can indulge in part because his education at Art School spared him the restrictions of the standard literary curriculum) turns a good deal of its innovations and imaginative action around this typically modernist challenge of 'making it new'. Most obviously, he adapts Joyce's signal instance of the technique that Eliot named 'the mythic method'.[3] For each of his narrative's seven parts he provides an epigraph from the early medieval Welsh bardic epic *Y Gododdin*. The older poet's account of the mustering, march, preparation, and consummation of the Battle of Catraeth, fought between local Britons (under the leadership of the putative model for the legendary Arthur) and invading Saxons, affords one of the available analogues for this modern Welsh regiment meeting the new German Army in 1916. Contemporizing the legend is not just the enabling challenge, it is the daunting

---

[2] Ezra Pound, *The Cantos* (London: Faber, 1986), 3.
[3] The phrase provides the main interpretive argument throughout Eliot's review of Joyce's novel, '*Ulysses*, Order and Myth' (1923), in *Selected Prose of T. S. Eliot*, ed. Frank Kermode (London: Faber, 1975), 175–8.

problematic in this work. Jones's imaginative ambition to insert his experience in the great tradition of romantic martial literature, extending from the Old English heroic poems through ancient Welsh legend to the Arthurian chronicles of Malory and beyond, is a project fraught with the difficulty of fit, of fittingness, in so far as the conditions and motivations of warfare in the early–late medieval period obviously differ considerably from those of the new technological century. It is nonetheless the substantial dare this poem takes on.

Consider the piece that stands at the ostensible centre of the heroic imagination of Jones's poem—in fact, at the exact midpoint of *In Parenthesis*, in the centre of Part 4. This is Jones's recasting of the ancient heroic boast. His new hero is a soldier garbed in (and named after) the standard-issue trench wear, 'Dai Great-Coat', at once the main type of the commons-in-arms in this current mass war and a sort of universal soldier. He tells of his part in the major campaigns of Western history and myth and legend, but configures this soldierly condition in terms of a most timely paradox, in a series of enigmatic images, like these:

> I was the spear in Balin's hand
> > that made waste King Pellam's land . . .
> I the fox-run fire
> > consuming in the wheat-lands . . .
> And I the south air, tossed from high projections by his Olifant . . .

> > > > > > (*IP*, 79–80)

This Dai is not Balin wielding the spear, he is the weapon itself; he did not set the consuming blaze, he is the fire set; he did not sound the trumpet that called men to action and glory or death, he is the air blown by the soldier sounding the heroic horn. While he is passive in each instance, he is also performing an action, at least in an instrumental way. This riddling role of the passive agent can be seen to depict the condition of soldiering in the modern arena of mass technological warfare, where any single man's strength is subordinate to the power of the new weaponry, and where individual martial prowess, which offers the source of the distinctive heroic action, is subordinate to the co-ordinate force of massed infantry. On the one hand, of course, this imaginative figure takes the ancient conceits of hero-making into the deflating circumstance of modern technological atrocity; but, on the other, it projects the contemporary pathos back into the ennobling pose of the heroic stance, whose values seem to be claimed here, at least as incipient possibility.

Again and again, in his appropriation of the older ethos, Jones elaborates this tension between ethical criticism and imaginative heightening in his representation of the modern martial experience. 'For the old authors', he remarks in the preface, 'the embrace of battle seemed at one with the embrace of lovers. For us it is different. There is no need to labour the point, nor enquire into the causes here' (*IP*, p. xv). Where those 'old authors' might claim the same physical strength as the basis of distinction in love and war, when individual power was expressed equally in each of these activities, this ancient compact is both invoked nostalgically and disclaimed rhetorically. And in the imaginative fabric of the poem, in the verbal possession and representation of the meaning of Jones's experience, this conceit is not foregone but deployed in an extraordinary compound of criticism and mythopoesis, each rhythm lifting and reinforcing the other—as in this depiction of the ground in front of Mametz Wood, the target of assault for Jones's division on the Somme front:

And you saw the whole depth of the advance and gauged the nature of the contest yard by yard, and made some estimate of the expenditure and how they'd bargained for each hundred feet with Shylock batteries. You marked how meshed intricacies of wire and cunning nest had played sharp tricks on green and eager plaintiffs. They lay heaped for this bloody suing. (*IP*, 148)

'You', the everyman-speaker in Jones's chronicle of modern mass war, takes note appropriately of the dimensionality of this event and, in a sort of inverse ratio to that, elaborates the pathos of the individual suitors slain in their courting of this all-too-huge contemporary Mars. This passage might be taken to focus the main interpretive problem in Jones's poem, at least in the major challenge of its modernist ambitions. In his attempt to recover a framework perspective on the present from the 'tradition', does he implement a resonant critique of the new conditions, or does he indulge some desperate pretence in maintaining the foregone order? Whatever response one makes to such questions, it may be affirmed that an imaginative energy is being directed centrally to an intellectual questioning of the relation of past and present, of Now to Then.

This heightening of the identity of the modern moment in contrast to or collusion with precedent is the quintessentially modernist awareness. One may thus emphasize the obvious in the word and meaning of modern*ism*: to the experience of being chronologically modern the suffix adds a sense of self-consciousness about the experience of being 'modern'. Most accurately, then, the word conveys a feeling of belonging to a particular moment of history, a specified Now, a *special* present, which is made more intense by virtue of some self-conscious difference from what went before. And where this Great War inscribed a manifold line of divide between centuries new and old, it will not be surprising to find the other major modernists defining the differences in ways that enable and enrich the most timely poetry of the event, even if it comes from the civilian war.

II

Political London presents one of the liveliest sites in the global picture of this World War. A crisis internal to the governing party of Britain defined this moment in local political time. English Liberals had to maintain support for a war which, by precedent and convention, by partisan tradition and policy principle, they ought to have opposed. This contradiction, which locates one of the major value watersheds in the traditions of liberal modernity, provides the formative ground for the most important modernist verse of the occasion.

The lines of opposition in the 1914 crisis may be drawn from the major division within the Liberal Party on the question of war in general. On one side, the memory of the great Victorian Prime Minister W. E. Gladstone preserved the ethic and method of moral rationalism. This liberal tradition of Public Reason maintained that armed force required an informed act of logical conscience, a choice reasoned freely and in public and in accord with the loftiest moral values.[4] On the other side, Liberal imperialists proceeded under the operative standards of *realpolitik*. In this way of thinking, the British military served as an instrument of security: its power could be parleyed through agreements with other European nations; these alliances could require involvement in hostilities, but these engagements could hardly be appealed to the codes of Gladstonian probity—the imperialists tended to negotiate English interests within a frame of global reference that put practical or local advantage and commercial concerns first.[5] Since 1906, the most powerful positions within the majority government were held by Liberal imperialists—Prime Minister H. H. Asquith and his Foreign Secretary Sir Edward Grey—but the logic of foreign policy was still controlled in its public discussions by Gladstonian protocols. In this situation, Asquith and Grey needed to keep private their alliance building with France and Russia. Officially, they continued to deny the existence of these 'secret agreements' (so dubbed by an already suspicious public), at least until early August 1914, when the network of European connections was activated.[6] At this moment, as Britain paused before the awful prospect of a Continental war, these rival traditions within Liberalism were evidenced in tensions that anticipated, in substantial detail, the major crisis that this developing event would present to partisan—and national—life.

The Foreign Secretary's speech before Parliament on 3 August provided the loftiest expression of the Liberal rationale for war, arguing the moral cause of a righteous defence of France in view of the imminent German incursion into

---

[4] The best representation of this salient value and its comprehensive practice in Western political tradition comes from John Rawls, *Political Liberalism* (New York: Columbia University Press, 1996), esp. pp. xxiv, xxvi–xxviii, xxx, 47–59, 212–27.

[5] A good contemporary reference on the ideas and values of political and intellectual Liberalism comes from L. T. Hobhouse, *Liberalism* (London: Williams & Norgate, 1910), a volume aimed at the broad-based readership of the series in which it appeared, the Home University Library of Modern Knowledge. The rival values and practice of Gladstonian and imperial Liberalism may be found on pp. 104 and 221.

[6] The existence of these 'secret agreements' and the influence they exerted on British policy and action constitute the subject of the major exposé by the founding director of the Union of Democratic Control (of foreign policy), E. D. Morel, in *Truth and the War* (London: National Labour Press, 1916), esp. 35–41, 273–300. A Liberal MP who resigned his seat in protest at the outbreak of war, Morel used his influence to access government archives to provide material support for his case.

neutral Belgium.[7] But other pressures—the commitments hidden in the 'secret agreements'—were also coming to bear on the Liberal government. The tension between these rival frames of partisan reference is reflected in the editorial reports on Grey's address in the two leading Liberal dailies on 4 August.

The *Manchester Guardian* holds true to the standard of reason at liberty, which, in this instance, the writer depicts as a compromised principle. This report protests that citizens and Parliament have not been given information sufficient to 'form a reasoned judgment on the current of our policy'. In Grey's conclusion that Britain must go to France's aid, even when Germany has vowed not to move on any undefended areas, the writer accurately intuits that the Secretary is being compelled by forces that exceed those of the moral rationale he has claimed. 'His reasons are extraordinary,' the editorial demurs. 'Is it rational? Can it be deduced, we will not say from the terms of the Entente, but from the account of secret conversations which was given yesterday? Can it be reconciled with any reasonable view of British policy? It cannot.'[8]

The especially strenuous effort of 'reconcil[ing]' these eventualities with a 'reasonable view of British policy' may be evidenced in the language of the news leader in the *Westminster Gazettte*, which offers this narrative—and argumentative—paraphrase of Grey's speech:

Sir Edward Grey passed to the consideration of the present position of the French fleet in the Mediterranean which *evidently* sprang out of the plans for co-operation. The French fleet was in the Mediterranean *because of the feeling of confidence* between the two countries. *Hence it followed* that if a foreign fleet came down the channel we could not stand aside and see it attack the defenceless coast of France. *The House was brought to the conclusion* that we had a definite obligation to defend the coast of France from attack, and, generally speaking, it showed that it was prepared to support the government in taking action. France was *therefore* entitled to know and know at once that she could depend on British support.[9]

Tellingly, this report of 'The House and Sir Edward Grey's Statement' bears the subtitle 'Logic of Events'. Complying entirely with Grey's own rationalistic stratagems, the report pays special attention to inserting those conjunctions that establish cause and reasoned transition in the argument. This language of analytical and ethical reasoning is obviously imposed on a resistant circumstance, however. The second-thought, second-hand, overlaid nature of this rhetoric of ethical reasoning is the one conclusion that may be safely drawn from this passage.

'Reason in all things' is a poetics, ethically addressed but aesthetically prepared, and the fact that it springs into service already and immediately witnesses quite evidently its established, well-endowed power. But if Anglo-American modernists

---

[7] The text of the speech was printed in all the major dailies on 4 Aug.; e.g. 'Sir E. Grey's Speech', *Manchester Guardian*, 7–8.

[8] 'Peace or War', *Manchester Guardian*, 4 Aug. 1914, 6.

[9] 'A Dramatic Scene: The House and Sir Edward Grey's Statement: Logic of Events', *Westminster Gazette*, 4 Aug. 1914, 10; my italics.

write their English, as Hugh Kenner has quipped, like a foreign language, handling it with the care of relative aliens, the outsider status that Pound and Eliot share in wartime London helps to account for their ability to reiterate the Liberal idiom, with a difference. It is the difference that takes the measure of that profound contradiction in the language of high partisan culture, which, all in all, witnesses the discrediting of the great tradition of moral rationalism within Liberalism. This dissonance provides, as it were, the tuning fork for the major modernist poetry of the moment. An auditing of this new literary language may begin with a listening to the least discrete critic of the established language of English liberalism.

In 'Studies in Contemporary Mentality', a twenty-part series published throughout 1917 in the *New Age*, Ezra Pound conducted a review of literary and political journalism in wartime Britain. The dominant quality in this verbal culture proves to be an indomitable 'reasonableness', a trait that appears nonetheless, in its service to the current war effort, in heavy duress. Pound pronounces this consolidating insight when he finds a defining standard for British political idiom in the distinguished literary weekly, the *New Statesman*:

I knew that if I searched long enough I should come upon some clue to this mystery. *The magnetism of this stupendous vacuity! The sweet reasonableness, the measured tone, the really utter undeniability of so much that one might read in this paper!* . . . The 'New Statesman' is a prime exemplar of the species, leading the sheltered life behind a phalanx of immobile ideas; leading the sheltered thought behind a phalanx of immobile phrases. This sort of thing cannot fail. Such a mass of printed statements in every issue to which no 'normal, right-minded' man could possibly take exception![10]

A 'reasonableness' that consists of 'measured tone' only, and so coalesces into the merest feeling of rationality; a logic as hollow as it is polished in presentation, well-managed indeed in all its impressive 'vacuity', its 'stupendous' emptiness: these are the sounds of contemporary Liberalism at war, a linkage Pound clinches with the metaphors of mobilization and the images of military formation. This sensibility stands exposed at the extremity of his ridicule in its vapid sagacity and absurd sententiousness. 'That is really all there is to it,' he summarizes, but tauntingly: 'One might really learn to do it oneself.'

How might Pound do it himself? How parley the rational inanities of official war discourse into new words, in verse? Pound's boast locates the main project and major dare of his emergent enterprise. But his mimic initiative proves a good deal more difficult—and so, potentially, more significant—than his vaunt might concede. The extent of the strength in the majority power's ownership of the common language may be witnessed by the fact that Pound's first substantial poetic challenge to it had to travel outside the home domain, to ancient Rome, where the task of rendering ancient Latin poetry opens up the possibility of an

---

[10] Ezra Pound, 'Studies in Contemporary Mentality', iv: 'The "Spectator"', *New Age*, 6 Sept. 1917, 407; my italics.

alternate voice within his own literary English. This opportunity locates the motive for the otherwise idiosyncratic labour of 'Homage to Sextus Propertius' (1919), the (highly) creative translation Pound undertook as his main poetic endeavour through the second half of the war.[11]

This Roman poet was chosen also for reasons beyond Pound's imaginative interests in linguistic difference. In his *Elegiae*, Propertius presents himself as a poet desiring to write of love when conventional expectation pressures him to proclaim a martial-minded verse. A poet of this moment is supposed to celebrate the imperial aims and military campaigns of the Augustan dynasty. His crafty engagement with those rules shows his persona making his evident requests for permission to sing about 'Cynthia', but addressing instead, more interestingly and slyly, quietly and indeed devastatingly, the attitudes and practices of an imperial poetics.[12] The mock-heroic diction of his *Elegiae*, his parodic Virgilisms, the hollow triumphalism and empty finishes of those all-too-heavily laboured martial cadences, which turn Augustan verse convention into august inanities: Propertius provides Pound with a model for echoing the times against the times. This is a pattern that the modern poet adapts to the syntax and vocabulary of his own political present.

The opening verse paragraph of Pound's poem recasts its Latin original in an extensive interpolation, which, in the guise of a poet's invocation of his Roman muse, acknowledges the deity reigning over the discourses of the current war:

> Out-weariers of Apollo will, as we know, continue their Martian generalities,
>   We have kept our erasers in order.[13]

Liberal divinity, god of logic as well as music and poetry, Apollo has been suborned to the work of current verse, worn out not by generals but by the 'generalities' of war, by political abstraction, by ideological argument. How, Propertius-like, might he play along with and pull against this existing linguistic condition?

The verbal art special to 'Propertius' features an interplay between an archly rationalist syntax and a wittily impenetrable vocabulary. On one side, the persona of the classics translator demonstrates a declarative knowingness about the *materia poetica*, here the site of ancient history and myth. Moving easily through this range of reference, Pound's speaker builds a progression of apparently factual statements as logical, common-sensible propositions of obvious knowledge. On the other side,

---

[11] In a letter to Iris Barry, 27 July 1916, Pound refers to a project of translating Propertius as a Roman poet of especially timely interest and relevance (in *Selected Letters of Ezra Pound, 1907–41*, ed. D. D. Paige (New York: New Directions, 1971), 90). Humphrey Carpenter quotes an unpublished letter by Pound to his father, 3 Nov. 1918, as likely evidence that the poem has been completed recently (Carpenter, *A Serious Character: The Life of Ezra Pound* (London: Faber, 1988), 324).

[12] An account of Propertius's address to contemporary verse conventions is provided by J. P. Sullivan, *Ezra Pound and Sextus Propertius: A Study in Creative Translation* (Austin, Tex.: University of Texas Press, 1964), 58–64, 75–6.

[13] Pound, 'Homage to Sextus Propertius', in *Personae: The Shorter Poems of Ezra Pound*, ed. Lea Baechler and A. Walton Litz (New York: New Directions, 1990), 205.

however, Pound's reader frequently experiences allusions to chronicle legend and literary fable that are fetched from the depths of Mediterranean antiquity and featured, it seems, for their very unfathomability. Consider, in this representative catalogue, the interaction between the local knowingness of Pound's persona and the distant incomprehensibility of these citations, which, one by one, and with the help of a classics manual, might be identified, but which, as substantial parts of a single imaginative narrative, challenge almost any reader's grasp of what the story is, of what is actually going on here:

> For Orpheus tamed the wild beasts—
>   and held up the Threician river;
> And Cithaeron shook up the rocks by Thebes
>   and danced them into a bulwark at his pleasure,
> And you, O Polyphemus? Did harsh Galatea almost
> Turn to your dripping horses, because of a tune, under Aetna?
> We must look into the matter.[14]

Who, most of us must ask, was Galatea? And how close did she get when she 'almost' turned to the horses of Polyphemus? That specifying adverb is Pound's interpolation,[15] whose blank space in the Latin original reveals the hollowness of his own (carefully) concocted knowledgeability. There is a particularly *pseudo*-logical quality to this tone, as indicated by another interpolated word, the first 'For'. This conjunction establishes the expectation of cause-and-effect sequence, the impression that some logical proposition is in process. It builds some presentiment of common-sense meanings, one that Pound complements with those reassuring words of common speech. He steadily undercuts this promise, however, by enforcing the awareness that we do not know these mythological personages very well, if at all. 'We must', the next interpolation goes, 'look into the matter'; but when we do, we see through the easy loquacity, the familiarizing fiction of inserted words like these, and find reason-seemingness as the aim and intended effect. Pound's new conceit echoes to the background sound of these times, and the immense pressure this moment exerts on his verse is shared as the working conditions of his conational and modernist accomplice.

III

Eliot's arrival in London in early August 1914 (having fled Germany, where, at Marsburg, in early summer, he had begun a year of study abroad) coincides with

---

[14] Ibid. 206.

[15] The relevant texts of Propertius's Latin and a standard prose translation are provided helpfully by K. K. Ruthven, *A Guide to Ezra Pound's 'Personae' 1926* (Berkeley: University of California Press, 1969); this is arranged by the alphabetized sequence of Pound's poem's titles.

the beginning of an identifiably dry time in his young poetic life, punctuated as such by his emergent acquaintance with Pound. Whatever causes are offered to explain the relative silence of these first two and more years,[16] it is revealing that the main way out of this condition lies in the same kind of action that Pound undertook in his engagements with the other tongue of literary Latin. For Eliot, it is French. The freeing effect does not represent escape but, like humour, works through a sort of transforming exaggeration, which amplifies the bizarre capacities that the language of the English political moment is demonstrating, where a native sense has become a stranger indeed to its own verbal reason. Eliot's poetic language reads as English, just in French.

'Petit Epître' is the first of the spring 1917 efforts:

> Ce n'est pas pour quo'on se dégoute
> Ou gout d'égout de mon Ego
> Qu'ai fait des vers de faits divers
> Qui sentent un peu trop la choucroute.
> Mais qu'est ce que j'ai fait, nom d'un nom,
> Pour faire ressortir les chacals?[17]

Eliot encloses echoes of whole words within others — 'gout' in 'dégoute', 'd'égout' — and reiterates similar phonetic formations across differing phrases — 'fait des vers' in 'faits divers' — to emphasize and consolidate the material sound of these words. He arranges the physical body of the language, however, inside a highly elaborate apparatus of syntactical ratiocination — that very French array of rhetorical negatives, antithetical conjunctions, subordinate and relative clauses. But the discriminating thinking that this rationalistic syntax fosters in standard French has turned into a sheer mouthful of Gallic bread and cheese. And the sauerkraut — 'choucroute' — to which Eliot's speaker refers worriedly gestures toward the local prompt for this new conceit of reason-seeming nonsense — in the civilian culture of the war, which proscribed this stereotypically German food. Further evidence of this political pressure comes in the next stanzas, where he adapts the format of the 'questionnaire', in which 'redacteurs' or newspaper editors aim enquiries at a civilian populace as menacing as the answers provided are nonsensical, contradicting any question–response logic but echoing all too audibly to the dominant quality of rationalistic inanity in the political journalism of the war.

---

[16] Eliot's antipathy to the premises and methods of modern Liberalism, the majority power in literary and political London in 1914, may be thought of as one source of his shutting down poetically when he arrived in Britain in August 1914. His complex interaction with the cultural infrastructures of Liberalism, and the strongly negative attitude he expressed toward the premises of pan-European liberalism, are surveyed by Vincent Sherry, *The Great War and the Language of Modernism* (Oxford: Oxford University Press, 2003), esp. 157, 162–3, 171, 351 n. 13.

[17] Eliot, *Inventions of the March Hare: Poems 1909–1917*, ed. Christopher Ricks (London: Faber, 1996), 86. Much of the poetry Eliot wrote between 1917 and 1919 is also included in this volume. The various drafts, with Ricks's extensive critical commentary, give the best picture of Eliot's development in this crucial interim.

This initiative extends into English literary idiom for Eliot in a poetic form for which his French interlude has also refreshed his attention: the quatrain stanza, modelled for him (as for Pound) by Théophile Gautier. In late spring 1917, Eliot composed at least five poems in this new measure.[18] This considerable surplus of productivity witnesses the release of energies pent up for several years, but it also registers the stimulus of his discovering a shape most particularly cadenced, a rhythm quickening to presentiments that have been forming in his verbal imagination over several years of this ongoing war. Within its tightly maintained structure of alternately rhyming lines, a regimen that translates into a stiffly disciplined metric, Eliot's stanzas develop a semi-discursive syntax and vocabulary to convey an impression of well-regulated thought that dissolves constantly, however, into preposterousness.

The familiar instances of this literary wit include the extravagantly rationalistic inanities or opacities of 'Mr. Eliot's Sunday Morning Service' and 'Whispers of Immortality'. The liturgy of the first of these opens thus:

> Polyphiloprogenetive
> The sapient sutlers of the Lord
> Drift across the window-panes.
> In the beginning was the Word.

> In the beginning was the Word.
> Superfetation of τὸ ἕν,
> And at the mensual turn of time
> Produced enervate Origen.[19]

The archly declarative, apparently reasonable syntax consorts and contrasts magnificently with the wholly fugitive sense of the Latin and Greek formations. Archaism? Yes, but indulged only to recover and characterize the remoteness from sense in the current political idiom that stirs so restively behind this new voice.

This historical origin may be recovered through the archaeology of one of Eliot's earliest efforts in the quatrain prosody. Not a very good poem at all, 'Airs of Palestine, No. 2' offers, nonetheless, some direct evidence of the incentive this new quatrain measure takes from current political lingo. It takes as its target and point of critical mimicry Sir John Spender, editor of the Liberal *Westminster Gazette*: 'God from a Cloud to Spender spoke', the poem opens joco-seriously,

> And such as have the skill to swim
> Attain at length the farther shore
> Cleansed and rejoiced in every limb,
> And hate the Germans more and more.

---

[18] A good record of Eliot's extraordinary productivity at this time comes in a letter of 30 Apr. 1917 from Vivien Eliot to his mother, in *The Letters of T. S. Eliot, i: 1898–1922*, ed. Valerie Eliot (London: Faber, 1988), 178.

[19] The original typescript version is commented on by Pound, whose revisions are accepted by Eliot and incorporated here, in 'Mr. Eliot's Sunday Morning Service', in *Inventions of the March Hare*, 377.

> They are redeemed from heresies
> And all their frowardness forget;
> And scales are fallen from their eyes
> Thanks to the Westminster Gazette.[20]

Where scriptural references and religious diction mingle with the rhythm of a barrack-room ballad, the odd tonality serves at once to echo and characterize the moral rationales for the war, that doggerel logic, which Spender's paper and its partisan likes have tirelessly offered. This tone also offers a rough-but-ready replica of the mock-sententiousness and pseudo-reasonableness that the later, more polished quatrains will smooth out.

The conceit of Eliot's quatrain art finds its signature piece in 'Sweeney Among the Nightingales'. In keeping with the counter-rhythm of his new poetics, the stanzas work equally to invite and defy an impression of considered or even consistent significance. On (most of) its surface, the piece presents a topical satiric caricature, featuring the habitués of a seedy London bistro as a contemporary bestiary, a virtual zoology of pseudo-human types: there is 'Apeneck Sweeney', there is 'the silent vertebrate in brown', while another personage 'tears at the grapes with murderous paws'.[21] This little misanthropic comedy can be scripted to a narrative of cultural history, a dominant mythology, one in which Eliot is usually assigned a primary part: the 'Lost Generation' of the first post-war moment (*The Waste Land* will provide its namesake location). This rootless, pan-European and trans-Atlantic vagabondage finds its *dramatis personae* in the poem's international cast of characters: the Irish 'Sweeney', the Slavic Jew 'Rachel *née* Rabinovitch', and so on. The establishing circumstance of the recent war is also imaged cryptically but vividly in the visage of Sweeney himself. The 'zebra stripes along his jaw' may reflect the creases cut into his neck by the stiff collar of the dress uniform worn by military personnel in the Great War—Sweeney is the soldier, returned to London from the Front. Just so, however, the poem opens on to another level of potential significance, which its imaginative apparatus makes every evident effort of rhetoric and gesture to claim. The majestic cadenza of the final quatrains—

> The host with someone indistinct
> Converses at the door apart,
> The nightingales are singing near
> The convent of the Sacred Heart,
>
> And sang within the bloody wood
> When Agamemnon cried aloud
> And let their liquid siftings fall
> To stain the stiff dishonoured shroud.

---

[20] Eliot, 'Airs of Palestine, No. 2', ibid. 84–5.
[21] Eliot, 'Sweeney Among the Nightingales', in *The Complete Poems and Plays of T. S. Eliot* (London: Faber, 1969), 56.

—includes, in the reference to Agamemnon, a closural event prepared in advance by the Greek epigraph, which Eliot has taken from Aeschylus's tragedy *Agamemnon*. There the soldier returning from the Trojan War cries out as he is stabbed by his scheming wife Clytemnestra—a feminine menace that Eliot also reflects in his poem in the threat that these various 'nightingales' (the word, in French, is slang for prostitutes) present to the male protagonist. Could Agamemnon really be the heroic prototype of Sweeney?[22] His ape neck might equip him with a gift for simian mimicry, but it hardly enables him to resemble the Hellenic hero credibly.

Why devise this parallel *manqué*? The meaning of Eliot's framing action may lie not in the content it organizes but in the gesture it represents—specifically, in the empty gesture it presents, where the epigraph and last stanza join to promise a formal logic that is not embodied in the poem's central *mise-en-scène*. This absence is amplified through the rhythm particular to the quatrain, which appears driven, inexorably as ever, but by a premiss as contradictory as Sweeney's claim to heroic fame. Yet the Home Front to which this soldier has returned also preserves a memory of equally compromised rationales for the nobility of that military enterprise, a failure Eliot echoes and answers through the ramifying irony of the poem's structural conception.

The culmination of Eliot's direct engagement with the historical and political event of the war comes in the poem he composed at the moment of its official conclusion. 'Gerontion' took shape through July 1919.[23] This was the month during which the 'peace' treaty was being finalized at Versailles, an event to which the poem makes several decisive references.

Eliot's speaker represents the substance of the monologue disquisition in its conclusion as 'small deliberations'—*small*, presumably, because *Gerontion* means, specifically, a *little* old man. Where he expands these 'small deliberations', in his mind's eye, to 'multiply variety | In a wilderness of mirrors', however, the poet is conveying a larger circumstance as the framing occasion of the poem's event. He is imaging the scene in which the 'deliberations' of (supposedly) 'great men' have recently taken place—in the Great Hall of Mirrors of the Trianon Palace at Versailles. If the 'wilderness of *mirrors*' secures this allusion, an irony special to the history being inscribed at Versailles lies in that otherwise unlikely figure of '*wilderness*'. This royal estate stood originally as a monument to Enlightenment civilization, since its reflecting halls and formal gardens mapped a scheme of metred and reasoned degree to the rationalist-deist plan of the universe. The emblematic edifice of this first Age of Reason is overshadowed now by the

---

[22] The late addition of the Greek epigraph—it is not included in the penultimate draft of the poem—suggests that the heroic parallel comes to Eliot as a second thought, which he includes to complicate the hermeneutic of Sweeney; see the summary of the manuscript evidence by Ricks in *Inventions of the March Hare*, 381.

[23] Eliot, 'Gerontion', in *Complete Poems and Plays*, 37–9. Eliot mentions the poem as 'this new one, "Gerontion"', on 9 July 1919, in a letter to John Rodker, in *Letters of T. S. Eliot*, i. 312.

consummation of the second, in the rituals of savage, retributive justice just conducted at Versailles.

Other references to this event provide the orienting points for the speaker's long, central meditation on 'History', which, in this representation, 'has many cunning passages, contrived corridors | And issues'. As in the Great Hall of Mirrors at Versailles, the image of 'History' repeats in a receding frame, playing a trick of substance and multiple reflections. This mirage-like prospect seems especially and even wilfully deceptive, however, the illusion peculiarly shrewd, in so far as these 'passages' are 'cunning', the 'corridors' being 'contrived'—presumably, around the 'issues' being argued, which include the guilt the Allied powers officially imposed on Germany and the war reparations plan that this manoeuvre authorized. Eliot's current work in the Colonial and Foreign Department at Lloyd's Bank certainly alerted him to the worst consequences of this economic punishment. The critical emphasis in his representation falls on the insidiousness of the case making, moreover, a stress that echoes back to the sort of devious reasoning that was familiar to him from the discourses of the Liberal war. And it is this specifically English sensibility that Eliot puts on the rhetorical line in the poem's character-in-voice.

Eliot's aged speaker belongs to the senescence of contemporary British Liberalism, a generation that has authored in words a war that its old men have not fought in body. Gerontion makes this admission in the opening moment of the poem, in the oblique case of his citation of classical mythology:

> I was neither at the hot gates
> Nor fought in the warm rain
> Nor knee deep in the salt marsh, heaving a cutlass,
> Bitten by flies, fought.

Establishing his membership in the particular generation and partisan class of aged Liberals, Gerontion also performs that identity, orienting himself toward the reality of the war in a verbalist rite that is well rehearsed, if badly performed. The clausal construction projects the progressive discriminations of verbal reason—'neither/Nor/Nor'—as its stipulative spirit, its motivating action, but the ambitious plan of a thrice-suspended period turns into the wreckage that its phrasal sequence actually makes of it. This masterfully awkward contortion of rationalist syntax speaks as the spasm of the master language of English Liberalism at war. And Eliot extends the sensibility of his speaking character to its revealing extreme in the central meditation on 'History'.

'Think now', his speaker proposes to open this deliberation, and repeats the same injunction several times,

> Think now
> She gives when our attention is distracted,
> And what she gives, gives with such supple confusions
> That the giving famishes the craving . . .

>   Think
> Neither fear nor courage saves us. Unnatural vices
> Are fathered by our heroism. Virtues
> Are forced upon us by our impudent crimes . . .
>
>   Think at last
> We have not reached conclusion, when I
> Stiffen in a rented house. Think at last
> I have not made this show purposelessly . . .

Verging compulsively on some deliberated significance—'Think now', 'Think |
Neither', 'Think at last', 'Think at last'—the speaker proceeds to a 'conclusion',
however, which 'We have not reached'. The logic is promissory at best, really only
hortative. Eliot seizes this conceit of meaning-seeming nonsense as a poetics, as
witnessed especially near the end of the main passage, where he turns the words of
progressive and logical proposition into a composite of contradictions. How is it,
after all, that an '*Unnatural* vice' can be biologically '*fathered*', and a vile unreal thing
begotten from a natural good? Whose 'impudent *crimes*' are capable of generating
'*Virtues*'? These disparities seem unapparent to the speaker, who talks through them
with every pretence of reasonable and coherent meaning. The inverse ratio and
particular power of this verse show thus in its capacity to outsize its own rationalist
measures, reaching through the sense it feigns to the illogic it really means, where
the emotion that is released grows in ratio to its overwhelming of an older Reason.
This complex effect is the meaning that recent 'History' has revealed to the critical
imagination of the modernist, who, like Pound, distinguishes his art by the special
faculty he manifests for tapping this awareness and providing the extraordinary
moment of history the answering echo of a new imaginative language.

IV

Yeats's literary commitments and political engagements during the years of the
Great War suspended him, as it were, in the middle of the Irish Sea. While his centre
of operations shifted continually between London and Sussex, Dublin and Sligo,
he seemed nonetheless to centre his attention, wilfully perhaps but also rhetorically
and forcefully, far to the side of the English war. Absence or denial of this event
appears as the posture the poet wishes to strike. This dismissal represents an attempt
to keep his focus on the Irish front, as though he resented the English distraction.
But it is of course the global cataclysm and crisis that helped foment the Irish Rising
and compel subsequent developments. And so the poetry witnesses a sort of double
vision, or contrary insistence, at once resisting the signal event of this European
war and registering its effects in ways little and large.

His poetic disengagement with the war is conducted most memorably for most
readers with the poems he was driven to compose on the death of Major Robert

Gregory, the son of his collaborator-patron Lady Augusta Gregory, who died in service in the Royal Irish Air Corps in Italy early in 1918. As the speaking character of 'An Irish Airman Foresees His Death', Gregory notably disclaims any imaginative part in the campaigns or causes that will have eventuated in his death. He takes the occasion instead as incentive for acts that locate a significance of entirely personal and private type, as some forerunner of Hemingway's twentieth-century, existentialist hero:

> Nor law, nor duty bade me fight,
> Nor public men, nor cheering crowds,
> A lonely impulse of delight
> Drove to this tumult in the clouds.[24]

And in the more formally explicit elegy, the Spenserian eclogue of 'In Memory of Major Robert Gregory', there is virtually no specificity of location or context for the title-subject's demise. Were it not for the beauty of the representations, or perhaps through the very beauty, one might read a nearly pathological aplomb in the feigned but wilful ignorance of actual circumstance and history, say, in objecting that 'Our Sidney and our perfect man | Could share in that discourtesy of death'.[25] The strained polity here echoes to the language of the Georgian poets in the opening moments of the war, when a vocabulary of classical pastoral was elaborated as an illusion screen on the emergent horror of modern atrocity. Denial of the same kind appears as the motive and aim of Yeats's own poetic idiolect here.

Acknowledging of course the validity and primacy of Yeats's Irish commitments, one may read his resistance to admit the major significance of this World War as one measure of the very immensity of that development. The landmark work of poetic imagination that Yeats started to consider in 1917, *A Vision*, revels in the dimensionality of this unprecedented event of World War. A model of world history that is based upon periodic crisis and conflagration, imaging a framework of historical action on the grandest scale of cosmic years and universal types, it draws the force of catastrophic gigantism from the close spectre of total war and its unprecedented destruction. The horrific extremity of the day-by-day events on the Continent, some of their colossal novelty and atrocity, shows in the schemes and tropes of grandiose disaster in the prose book, in the rhetoric and emphases of breathless sublimity in the poetry it helps to generate:

> Turning and turning in the widening gyre
> The falcon cannot hear the falconer;
> Things fall apart, the centre cannot hold;
> Mere anarchy is loosed upon the world,

---

[24] W. B. Yeats, 'An Irish Airman Foresees his Death', in *The Poems*, ed. Daniel Albright (London: Dent, 1990), 184.
[25] Yeats, 'The Wild Swans at Coole', ibid. 182.

> The blood-dimmed tide is loosed, and everywhere
> The ceremony of innocence is drowned.[26]

If modernism denotes a sensibility attentive to the extremities of its own historical moment, Yeats has gathered the sense of world-altering world endings into a poetic language remarkably adequate to the manifold crisis of this exceptional time. This sense of ramifying fracture from the past may be apprehended as a difference from the traditions of heroic literature, as by Jones; or as a disruption in the mainstream conventions of Public Reason in liberal modernity, as by Pound and Eliot; or as the apocalyptic convulsion that Yeats envisions as the true shape of the contemporary chaos. Each of these instances comprises a prime type of the modernist Now, the enabling condition of the newest—and most durable—poetry of the extraordinary moment of this Great War.

[26] Yeats, 'The Second Coming', ibid. 235.

CHAPTER 11

A WAR OF FRIENDSHIP: ROBERT GRAVES AND SIEGFRIED SASSOON

FRAN BREARTON

By wire and wood and stake we're bound,
By Fricourt and by Festubert,
By whipping rain, by the sun's glare,
By all the misery and loud sound,
By a Spring day,
By Picard clay.

Robert Graves, 'Two Fusiliers' (1917)

In a recent essay on reimagining the Great War, Sharon Ouditt observes that Pat Barker, in the best-selling novel *Regeneration*, 'acknowledges her sources with the integrity of one who wishes to make available to her readership the extent to which she has imagined the material, and to which it draws on scholarly research. Those familiar with Graves and Sassoon . . . will easily spot those resonances.' Barker, she concludes, 'in combining fact and fiction, is contributing to the postmodern genre of "faction"'.[1] Joint readings by Barker, and by one of Graves's biographers, Miranda Seymour, in the mid-1990s, contributed to a package deal of interwoven 'fact' and 'fiction'. Praised for its 'authenticity' and its 'vivid evocation[s]', *Regeneration* has since become an educational resource, and has been made into a successful film, its shaping of the relations between Graves, Sassoon, and Owen now one of the primary sources of information for a generation discovering the 'war poets' for the first time.[2] Whether it is deemed a work of postmodern brilliance, or of authentic, realist representation (a divergence in critical responses not easily reconciled), it is too often assumed to offer a reliable insight into the historical figures at its centre. It contributes, too, to a tendency to bring to the war poets a critical perspective not so readily accepted outside what is seen to be their 'special' case: that is, the extent to which their poetry is to be judged against the uniquely terrible circumstances of its production.

   In this essay, I will suggest ways in which the relation between Graves and Sassoon may be reinterpreted (and in the process question the 'integrity' as well as the implications of imaginative appropriations and critical evaluations of the war poets). To rethink the terms of their relationship, and of their habitual quarrels—which resulted in a complete breakdown of the friendship in 1933—is also to rethink the significance of their contribution to, or revision of, a genre of 'war poetry', and to an English tradition of poetry more generally. The wartime friendship of Graves, Sassoon, and Owen has become the stuff of myth—and not myth in its Gravesian sense ('reliable enough as history') but in the more popular sense of the mythical as 'fanciful' or fictional that Graves eschews.[3] Yet that 'myth' of the war poets sometimes omits consideration of what was central to the friendships and, in the case of Graves and Sassoon, to the disintegration of that friendship: that is, their aesthetic similarities and differences. As Adrian Caesar notes, in his important study *Taking It Like a Man*, 'different artistic directions' as well as political and sexual issues are vital in understanding the strained relations between the two.[4] Yet the 'one size fits all' approach to war poetry still found in circulation (war poetry is soldier poetry; war poetry is always anti-war poetry; war poetry is experiential; war poetry, if it is to be any good, speaks from disillusionment, not patriotism; war poetry is meant to shock the complacent public; the war poets have some kind of shared agenda) tends to obscure the fact that, in the years following the First

---

[1] Sharon Ouditt, 'Myths, memories, and monuments: reimagining the Great War', in Vincent Sherry (ed.), *The Cambridge Companion to the Literature of the First World War* (Cambridge: Cambridge University Press, 2005), 249.

[2] See reviews quoted in Pat Barker, *Regeneration* (London: Penguin, 1991).

[3] See Robert Graves, *The White Goddess*, 4th edn. (London: Faber, 1999), 9.

[4] Adrian Caesar, *Taking It Like a Man: Suffering, Sexuality and the War Poets* (Manchester: Manchester University Press, 1993), 207.

World War, Sassoon and Graves fought a rather different battle with each other about developments in modern poetry. Many of their overt arguments concern factuality, sexuality, and money—all deemed private matters; yet those arguments submerge within them a running debate about poetic form, literary modernism, and, in Graves's phrase, 'the use or function of poetry'.[5]

Graves's account, in *Goodbye to All That* (1929), of his first meeting with Sassoon is as follows:

I went to visit C Company where a Third Battalion officer whom I knew was commanding. The C's greeted me in a friendly way. As we were talking I noticed a book lying on the table. It was the first book (except my Keats and Blake) that I had seen since I came to France that was not either a military text-book or a rubbish novel. It was the *Essays of Lionel Johnson*. When I had a chance I stole a look at the fly-leaf, and the name was Siegfried Sassoon. I looked round to see who could possibly be called Siegfried Sassoon and bring *Lionel Johnson* with him to the First Battalion. He was obvious, so I got into conversation with him, and a few minutes later we were walking to Béthune, being off duty until that night, and talking about poetry. Siegfried had, at the time, published nothing except a few privately-printed pastoral pieces of eighteen-ninetyish flavour and a satire on Masefield which, about half-way through, had forgotten to be a satire and was rather good Masefield. . . . At this time I was getting my first book of poems, *Over the Brazier*, ready for the press; I had one or two drafts in my pocket-book and showed them to Siegfried. He told me that they were too realistic and that war should not be written about in a realistic way. In return he showed me some of his own poems. One of them began:

> Return to greet me, colours that were my joy,
> Not in the woeful crimson of men slain . . .

This was before Siegfried had been in the trenches. I told him, in my old-soldier manner, that he would soon change his style.[6]

Typically, this account is both a mythologizing of the encounter and a demytho-logizing of perceptions of the war poets consequent, in part, on the posthumous publication in 1920 of Wilfred Owen's *Poems* (an edition introduced by Sassoon). In Graves's staging of the event, Graves is the young generation Romantic (Keats and Blake), Sassoon the languorous 1890s romantic parody (Johnson). Yet the genera-tion roles are also reversed: Sassoon's privately printed verse presents him as lagging behind the younger poet's accepted-for-publication status. Graves deliberately reminds us of two further things: first, and correctly, that his own war experience outstripped that of any other soldier-poet (Sassoon's being, by comparison, rel-atively limited); second, that the now well-known story of Sassoon precipitating Owen into his 'realistic' anti-war mode during their months at Craiglockhart in 1917 has, as far as Graves is concerned, an earlier chapter—the story of his own similar role as regards Sassoon in 1915–16. As with most of his autobiographical

---

[5] Graves, *White Goddess*, 10.
[6] Graves, *Goodbye to All That: An Autobiography* (London: Jonathan Cape, 1929), 224.

and critical writings, there is a self-serving element here, a desire on Graves's part, which was never to leave him, to affirm his own importance as poet against anyone and everyone else; but there is also an element of Sassoon and Graves as poets *contra mundum*, an implied solidarity against the philistine environment of the army. As Graves observes in 1916, 'S.S. and I have great difficulty in talking about poetry and that sort of thing together as the other officers of the battalion are terribly curious and suspicious. If I go into his mess and he wants to show me some set of verses, he says: "Afternoon Graves, have a drink . . . by the way, I want you to see my latest recipe for rum punch." . . . We are a disgrace to the battalion and we know it.'[7]

Sassoon's account of their meeting, in his fictionalized *Memoirs of an Infantry Officer* (1930), is rather different:

Returning from an after dinner stroll I found that several Second Battalion officers had come to visit us. . . . Among them, big and impulsive, was David Cromlech [Robert Graves], who had been with our Battalion for three months of the previous winter. As I approached the group I recognised his voice with a shock of delighted surprise. He and I had never been in the same Company, but we were close friends, although somehow or other I have hitherto left him out of my story. On this occasion his face was only dimly discernible, so I will not describe it, though it was a remarkable one. An instinct for aloofness which is part of my character caused me to remain in the background for a minute or two, and I now overheard his desperately cheerful ejaculations with that indefinite pang of affection often felt by a detached observer of such spontaneous behaviour . . . [N]either of us really wanted to talk about the Somme battle. . . . We knew that this might be our last meeting, and gradually an ultimate strangeness and simplicity overshadowed and contained our low-voiced colloquies. We talked of the wonderful things we'd do after the war; for to me David had often seemed to belong less to my war experience than to the freedom which would come after it. He had dropped his defensive exuberance now, and I felt that he was rather luckless and lonely—too young to be killed up on Bazentin Ridge.[8]

Significantly, 'David Cromlech' does not enter the story until 'George Sherston' (Sassoon) has had his share of 'the horrors of war' and been awarded the Military Cross, almost a year after their first meeting. The Graves figure here is more obviously recognizable as the one-dimensional Graves of *Regeneration*—on the surface full of bungling good will, tactlessly public-schoolboyish. The narrative structure of Sassoon's *Memoirs* thus sets his older voice of experience against the youthful symbol of hope, a voice already tainted, in 1928, by the sense that the post-war world, and Graves too, had failed to live up to his expectations—personally and poetically. It establishes a counter-myth which has become dominant: Sassoon as the embittered protest-poet and mentor, Graves the 'too young' victim who could do little more than put on a good show ('desperately cheerful', defensively exuberant) in accordance with the precepts in which he had been trained. The

---

[7] Graves to Edward Marsh, 15 Mar. 1916, in *In Broken Images: Selected Letters of Robert Graves 1914–1946*, ed. Paul O'Prey (London: Hutchinson, 1982), 42.

[8] Siegfried Sassoon, *Memoirs of an Infantry Officer* (1930), repr. in *The Complete Memoirs of George Sherston* (London: Faber, 1972), 354–5.

affinity here is not so much 'we poets' as it is 'we soldiers' in trying times, the tone evocative of Sassoon's profoundly sentimental feelings towards his men.

Of course, neither account is entirely to be trusted, although there are some consistencies between the late 1920s memoirs and the relevant letters and diary entries from the wartime period, since both versions are coloured by the experiences of the 1920s. In addition, both poets have been the subject of several biographies which illuminate, from different angles, a peculiarly fraught relationship, in a detail which needs no reiteration here. Similarly, Adrian Caesar's work sheds considerable light on some of the sexual tensions at work between the two.[9] But Sassoon chose, in later years, to reorientate his perceptions of a network of poetic and personal relations—gradually placing Owen centre-stage—and critical responses have tended to follow him in devoting attention primarily to the Sassoon-Owen axis.[10] Robert Graves is entirely written out of Sassoon's second Great War memoir from 1945, *Siegfried's Journey*, a non-fictionalized (and yet, through such omissions, entirely fictionalized) account of the period from 1916 to 1920. (In a thought-provoking parallel, Graves reacts similarly to Laura Riding, who is written out of the 1957 edition of *Goodbye to All That*, whilst Sassoon remains a central figure.) Hence also, perhaps, Graves's marginalized and simplified representation in a work such as *Regeneration*. But this is not the picture which emerges at the time, or from the poetry.

On one level, then, the relationship is personal, and the closeness of the friendship is probably unique among the soldier-poets of the Great War. In a letter to Sassoon in 1933, Graves talks of 'imagining back to a time when I knew and liked you—loved you was more like it'.[11] Yet it is much more than personal, given the extent to which they were entangled with each other's writing: Graves proposed revisions to Sassoon's 'To Any Dead Officer'; Sassoon did some editing of *Goliath and David*; they both convalesced at Harlech in the autumn of 1916, working on getting new collections in order.[12] More importantly, evident in Graves's letters from 1917 is his sense that he, Sassoon, Robert Nichols, and, 'when we've educated him a trifle more',[13] Wilfred Owen, are the four who will transform English poetry in the future: 'we have lit such a candle as by God's grace will set the whole barn alight'.[14]

Literary history does not now tend to tell it that way, inasmuch as Eliot and Pound have a greater claim to have 'set the whole barn alight' and revolutionized

---

[9] To what extent the friendship was tinged with a homoerotic element remains a moot point, although it seems clear that Sassoon's feelings, and probably also Graves's, were feelings of love to a degree unusual even in the close male bonding found in trench life. For a fuller discussion of these issues, see Caesar's study, *Taking It Like a Man*. Graves has so far been the subject of three biographies—by Martin Seymour-Smith, Richard Perceval Graves, and Miranda Seymour. See also biographies of Sassoon by Jean Moorcroft Wilson, John Stuart Roberts, and Max Egremont.

[10] See e.g. Arthur E. Lane, *An Adequate Response: The War Poetry of Wilfred Owen and Siegfried Sassoon* (Detroit: Wayne State University Press, 1972).

[11] Graves to Siegfried Sassoon, n.d. [Sept. 1933], *In Broken Images*, 228.

[12] See *In Broken Images*, 60, 66, 71.   [13] Graves to Edward Marsh, 29 Dec. 1917, ibid. 90.

[14] Graves to Robert Nichols, n.d. [Nov. 1917], ibid. 89.

poetry in the post-war years. That said, given the sometimes negative perceptions of Georgianism that took on currency in the 1920s, it is worth remembering that Graves praised Sassoon's poems for becoming 'much freer and more Georgian'[15]—two things more often treated as mutually exclusive. The aspiration to write, in Graves's phrase, 'the New Poetry' is evident in the verse letters written by Graves and Sassoon in 1916; but also implicit in the poems are the reasons for their failure to do so—at least in the collective sense of which Graves dreamed.

Sassoon's 'A Letter Home (To Robert Graves)' was written at Flixécourt in May 1916. It contains those elements which made Sassoon, in the months that followed, into the satirical protest poet, with its 'Clockwork soldiers in a row'.[16] It serves also to indicate what may be seen as stylistic weaknesses in Sassoon, with its tendency towards the over-adjectival ('web-hung woods', 'hornbeam alleys', 'glowworm stars') and its occasionally obtrusive rhyming couplets: 'He's come back, all mirth and glory, | Like the prince in fairy story. | Winter called him far away; | Blossoms bring him home with May.' Sassoon's penchant for perfect rhyming, either in couplets or cross-rhyme quatrains, sometimes works to intensify a poem's effect, as in 'The Kiss', sometimes to lessen it. There are also moments here of what Graves called the 'eighteen-ninetyish' Sassoon, moments which may incline a reader to sympathy with the Imagists' later objections to the forced syllabic and metrical regularities of pre-war verse. In 1917, Graves outlined his ideal diction as one in which the poet uses 'common and simple words [and] make[s] the plain words do the work of the coloured ones': the poet, he writes, pre-empting Keith Douglas's later desire to make 'every word work for its place in a line',[17] should strive towards 'clarity of expression', something which Sassoon, he implies, only intermittently achieves.[18] An elegy for David Thomas, who had been killed in March 1916, Sassoon's 'A Letter Home' is not a poem which bitterly refuses traditional consolation, in a manner we have come to associate with the Owenesque Great War protest elegy, but one which, as with many of Sassoon's poems, indulges Marvellian pastoral and seeks out Miltonic 'pastures new' for the dead:

> Now he's here again; I've seen
> Soldier David dressed in green,
> Standing in a wood that swings
> To the madrigal he sings.

Yet it is also a poem of aesthetic idealism, in a manner that we have come to associate more with Graves the Muse poet than with Sassoon the protest poet—'I know | Dreams will triumph, though the dark | Scowls above me where I go'—and

---

[15] Graves to Edward Marsh, 15 Mar. 1916, ibid. 44.

[16] Siegfried Sassoon, 'A Letter Home (To Robert Graves)', in *Collected Poems 1908–1956* (London: Faber, 1984), 37–9.

[17] Keith Douglas to J. C. Hall, 10 Aug. 1943, in *The Letters*, ed. Desmond Graham (Manchester: Carcanet, 2000), 295.

[18] Graves to Sassoon, 13 Sept. 1917, in *In Broken Images*, 83.

it reiterates the sense of a poetic alliance: 'War's a joke for me and you | While we know such dreams are true!'

Sassoon's 'A Letter Home' is a poem which implies the need for an imagined home in the future, a letter to home which seeks to find home. Graves's reply, the 'Familiar Letter to Siegfried Sassoon (*From Bivouacs at Mametz Wood, July 13th, 1916*)', brings that need into central focus. It envisages, to a degree which makes for poignant reading now, given the collapse of their relationship, a shared (pastoral) idyll for two peacetime poetic adventurers. Yet it also uncannily pre-empts their very different futures, in which Graves in 1929 said 'goodbye to all that' and 'resolved never to make England my home again', and Sassoon purchased, in 1933, a Georgian country estate, his own 'English paradise', a part of England's past.[19] Graves's imagined life in the poem is one in which, after recuperation in the mythical hills of Wales, 'Until we feel a match once more | For *anything* but another war . . . we'll . . . sail away across the seas | (The God of Song protecting us) | To the great hills of Caucasus', where:

> Robert will learn the local *bat*
> For billeting and things like that,
> If Siegfried learns the piccolo
> To charm the people as we go.
>
> .   .   .   .   .   .
>
> Perhaps eventually we'll get
> Among the Tartars of Thibet,
> Hobnobbing with the Chungs and Mings
> And doing wild, tremendous things
> In free adventure, quest and fight,
> And God! what poetry we'll write![20]

'[W]hat poetry we'll write!' Graves's assumption here might more usefully now be reread as a question about what *kind* of poetry they would write. Home and tradition, it is evident as early as 1916, mean different things—or matter in different degrees—to Graves and Sassoon, in spite of a projected poetic alliance. That ambiguity in relation to 'home' is also a measure of different attitudes towards poetic form and tradition. Sassoon was repelled in the 1920s by certain forms of literary experimentation, an anti-modernist stance which was to intensify as the years went on. Much of his later poetry bears this out, holding on, as it does, to traditional diction, forms and images, and more often than not with an incurable nostalgia: 'Time, whose lost siren song at evening blows | With sun-flushed cloud shoreward on toppling seas; | Time, arched by planets lonely in

---

[19] See Graves, *Goodbye to All That*, 2nd edn. (London: Penguin, 1960), 279. The comment is not made explicitly in the 1929 edition, though the original Epilogue to Laura Riding makes the same point implicitly. See also Max Egremont, *Siegfried Sassoon: A Biography* (London; Picador, 2005), 389.

[20] Graves, *The Complete Poems*, ed. Beryl Graves and Dunstan Ward (Harmondsworth: Penguin, 2003), 37–9.

the vast | Sadness that darkens with the fall of day.'[21] In that sense, Sassoon's war poems—abrasive, and, as suggested below, often experimental in style and form—can seem an aberration in his *œuvre*, as if the time away from home in the Great War is mirrored by his temporary occupation of a stylistic 'elsewhere'. In Graves's early poems, on the other hand, a more ambiguous relation to his time and place, and a certain anti-authoritarianism, are already in evidence. In the pre-war poem 'In Spite', his mischievous rhythms take issue with a late Victorian form and idiom: 'My rhymes no longer shall stand arrayed | Like Prussian soldiers on parade | That march | Stiff as starch, | Foot to foot, | Boot to boot.' 'How petty', he concludes, to take a rhyme, 'Pleat it with pleats, | Sheet it with sheets | Of empty conceits.... And weld it into a uniform stanza.'[22] Only a few years later, in 1917, he makes what appears to be the opposite case in 'To an Ungentle Critic':

> Must winds that cut like blades of steel
> And sunsets swimming in Volnay,
> The holiest, cruellest pains I feel,
> Die stillborn, because old men squeal
> For something new: 'Write something new:
> We've read this poem—that one too,
> And twelve more like 'em yesterday'?
>
> No, no! my chicken, I shall scrawl
> Just what I fancy as I strike it,
> Fairies and Fusiliers, and all.
> Old broken knock-kneed thought will crawl
> Across my verse in the classic way.[23]

As these poems suggest, Graves can play the Yeatsian patriarch as much as the *enfant terrible*. Yet in fact both poems argue for the same thing, and with a consistency he was to retain throughout his career: the freedom to write without reference to the literary establishment, or to literary fashion, or to the prevailing political and cultural *Zeitgeist*. As with Sassoon, there may be anger with 'old men' in evidence; but where Sassoon's anger is directed at life (military authorities), Graves's is aimed at literature (authoritarian critics).

Graves's 'Familiar Letter to Siegfried Sassoon' is written in octosyllabic rhyming couplets, thereby drawing on what Douglas Dunn, in another context, describes as 'a solid seventeenth-century pedigree in Ben Jonson, Marvell and Milton', and a tradition in which 'Public statements have often been disguised as private epistolary poems'.[24] The wartime epistolary exchange between Sassoon and Graves has its descendants too, in the work of Auden and MacNeice on the eve of the Second

---

[21] Sassoon, 'A Prayer to Time', in *Collected Poems 1908–1956*, 255.
[22] Graves, 'In Spite', in *Complete Poems*, 9–10.   [23] Graves, 'To an Ungentle Critic', ibid. 29.
[24] See Douglas Dunn, 'Longley's Metric', in Alan J. Peacock and Kathleen Devine (eds.), *The Poetry of Michael Longley* (Gerrards Cross: Colin Smythe, 2000), 21.

World War, or more recently in the verse letters written by Michael Longley and Derek Mahon in the context of the Northern Irish 'Troubles'. In all these instances, the exchange of verse letters fulfils a need in the poet to affirm artistic integrity at a time when poetry is seen to be under threat—its 'use and function' surely at their most questionable. Yet perhaps there is a further critical perspective to be inferred, since in each case the verse letters attempt to posit shared aesthetic principles, but on the whole serve to expose aesthetic differences. Auden and MacNeice's very different responses to the outbreak of the Second World War are a case in point, given Auden's ambiguous 'poetry makes nothing happen' in his 1939 elegy for W. B. Yeats,[25] and MacNeice's counter-argument in *The Poetry of W. B. Yeats*; or we might remember the quarrel between Mahon and Longley in the December 1971 *New Statesman* following the publication of Longley's 'Letter to Derek Mahon'. In the case of Graves and Sassoon, the surface affection of the 1916 verse letters elides aesthetic differences that were to surface later; yet they may now be read in similar terms. As much as they propose unity, they also obliquely suggest that the wartime poetic alliance is likely to prove temporary; the hopes and aspirations outlined in these poems may be a necessary survival tactic for the present moment, but they are not, in the end, a blueprint for the future.

Hopes and dreams aside, the verse letters are not themselves poems which find a new wartime music for the lyric voice, in spite of Sassoon's belief in what he calls that 'Secret Music' which 'No din this side of death can quell'[26]—which is another version of the 'dreams' that will 'triumph'. Sassoon's poems show one obvious debt to 1890s decadence in their preoccupation with music, and his habitual association of music with transcendence, joy, and redemption. The early poem 'To Victory', quoted by Graves above, longs for a 'Return, musical, gay with blossom and fleetness, | Days when my sight shall be clear and my heart rejoice'.[27] 'A Mystic as Soldier' wills 'music' to 'sound again';[28] 'The Poet as Hero' claims 'absolution' in his 'songs';[29] 'France' has its 'harmonies as might | Only from Heaven be downward wafted— | Voices of victory and delight'.[30] The close of 'Secret Music', in which 'music dawned above despair', ultimately finds its fulfilment in Sassoon's superb celebration of the Armistice, 'Everyone Sang': 'O, but Everyone | Was a bird; and the song was wordless; the singing will never be done.'[31] The poem, according to Sassoon, was written in April 1919 without apparent effort in only a few minutes; its

---

[25] W. H. Auden, 'In Memory of W. B. Yeats', in *The English Auden: Poems, Essays, and Dramatic Writings 1927–1939*, ed. Edward Mendelson (London: Faber, 1977), 242.

[26] Sassoon, 'Secret Music', in *Collected Poems 1908–1956*, 29.

[27] Sassoon, 'To Victory', ibid. 12.   [28] Sassoon, 'A Mystic as Soldier', ibid. 13.

[29] Sassoon, 'The Poet as Hero', in *The War Poems*, ed. Rupert Hart-Davis (London: Faber, 1983), 61.

[30] Sassoon, 'France', in *Collected Poems 1908–1956*, 11.

[31] Sassoon, 'Everyone Sang', ibid. 114.

'free form ... spontaneous, and unlike any other poem I have written'.[32] It may be seen as the culmination of a belief sustained through the war years in the return of poetry as beauty, and Sassoon's more traditional forms and images as a stay against the violence being wrought on the lyric mode.

Yet, ironically enough, and whatever the merits of these lyrical poems, a different, and more powerful 'music' is found instead in those poems which are discordant, not only in sentiment, but in rhythm. In that sense, the poems which register the shock of lyric disruption simultaneously affirm lyric survival. 'Base Details', for instance, opens in an iambic pentameter whose disturbing jauntiness is achieved through its monosyllabic regularity:

> If I were fierce, and bald, and short of breath,
> I'd live with scarlet Majors at the Base,
> And speed glum heroes up the line to death.[33]

In contrast to this rhythmical speeding up (of) the line are the ponderous dactyls which are the hallmark (cue pantomime entrance) of the Base Major 'Guzzling and gulping ... Reading the Roll of Honour'. In the poem's rhythmic shifts are embedded its mockery. Similarly, the triple rhythm of 'The General'—' "Good-morning; good morning!" the General said | When we met him last week on our way to the line'[34]—is evocative of advertising jingles or nursery rhymes. (During the 'cannonading cataclysm' of the 1916 June bombardment on the Somme, Sassoon describes 'the following refrain ... running in my head: *They come as a boon and a blessing to men,* | *The Something, the Owl, and the Waverley Pen* ... an advertisement which I'd often seen in smoky railway stations'.[35] The nursery rhyme element in his satires also owes a debt to Graves, whose interest in nursery rhymes—which often contain within them surreal images of violence—is evident through his poems of the 1910s and 1920s, and who argued that the best of them are 'nearer to poetry than the greater part of *The Oxford Book of English Verse*'.[36]) The poem's mnemonic rhythmical qualities encourage a kind of complacency in the reader which renders all the more shocking the reversal in the final lines of the expectations set up by rhythm and tone: 'But he did for them both by his plan of attack'. In a sense, the poem's own stylistic 'plan of attack', with its triple feet, its brevity, and its form (it comprises one six-line stanza, followed by a single line) puts paid to the reader's own forward march.

---

[32] Sassoon, *Siegfried's Journey, 1916–1920* (London: Faber, 1945), 140–1. He also notes that 'No one has ever said a word against it', though Robert Graves was less than generous a few years later when he introduced the following comment into the 2nd edn. of *Goodbye to All That* (228): 'Siegfried's famous poem celebrating the Armistice began: *Everybody suddenly burst out singing* ... [sic]. But "everybody" did not include me.' (The correct line is 'Everyone suddenly burst out singing'.)

[33] Sassoon, 'Base Details', in *Collected Poems 1908–1956*, 68.

[34] Sassoon, 'The General', ibid. 69.   [35] Sassoon, *Complete Memoirs of George Sherston*, 331.

[36] Graves, quoted in Iona and Peter Opie (eds.), *The Oxford Dictionary of Nursery Rhymes* (Oxford: Oxford University Press, 1952), 2.

In another of Sassoon's best-known poems, 'Blighters', the relentless hammering out of unambiguous stresses turns the poem on one level into a parody of 'the prancing ranks | Of harlots' who 'shrill the chorus, drunk with din',[37] and on another, into an ironic comment on the ranks of soldiers who die in the 'din' of warfare, who fall in rows like the 'tier beyond tier' of the music-hall audience. Seemingly crude in both form and theme, 'Blighters' is a poem in which the obtrusive becomes a measure of its subtlety. The 'crammed' House of the music-hall is also obliquely evocative of the centre of political power, as if the theatre of war is itself a 'Show' for their amusement. The 'prancing ranks' suggest the cavalry in earlier forms of (glorified) warfare. The audience's 'grin | And cackle' become disturbingly ironic in the final line, since as the poem protests against the 'jokes . . . To mock the riddled corpses round Bapaume', it also puns on 'riddled' to make its own double (triple) entendre: the corpses are riddled with bullets, riddled by being the subject of 'jokes', and the line glances back to the image of the tank coming 'down the stalls', itself riddling—in the sense of pervading and permeating—the body of people watching the show. In two senses, then, the poem is guilty of what it derides, making capital out of its own riddling qualities, turning war and suffering into art (and therefore presumably entertainment), countering violence with violence—the 'Lurching' tank as 'drunk' in its own way as the chorus girls it is meant to silence.

In contrast to Sassoon, whose reputation now rests primarily on these satirical poems, as well as on the more sustained achievements of 'Repression of War Experience' or 'Counter-Attack', and who promoted himself through the 1920s as a war poet, Graves in later years suppressed much of his early work, and almost all of his war poems. His judgement in such suppressions is not always to be trusted, since by the 1960s he had cut from his *Collected Poems* some of the finest achievements of his career. Yet in the case of the early war poems, his scruples are more understandable. It is hard to claim for any of the poems in *Over the Brazier* (1916) or *Fairies and Fusiliers* (1917) a status equivalent to either Owen's or Sassoon's best poems from the same period. In that sense, Graves, however famous he may be as memoirist, is not a recognizably important war poet—or at least not of the soldier-poet variety habitually associated with the Great War. That said, some of the early war poems deserve to be better known, both in and of themselves, and in terms of their influence on Sassoon and Owen. They also show some of the qualities which were to turn Graves into such an exceptional poet in mid-career, from the 1930s to the 1960s.

Over the Brazier contains poems written while Graves was still at school, from 1910 to 1914, and a handful of early war poems from 1915. (As noted above, the book was in preparation for press when Graves first met Sassoon.) Unlike some of his contemporaries, Graves does not, in his 1914–15 poems, idealize war, or

---

[37] Sassoon, 'Blighters', in *Collected Poems 1908–1956*, 19.

distance poetry from war; rather, in 'A Renascence', he suggests a (problematical) link between poetic flowering and violence (as many were later and controversially to suggest in relation to the violence in Northern Ireland), writing of the 'fighting men' that 'of their travailings and groans | Poetry is born again'.[38] That poetry is born out of torment is an idea that Graves retains, although the cause of the torment changes—from war to his cruel Muse—and in 'Limbo', may be found all the images later associated with the hard-hitting war poems of both World Wars:

> After a week spent under raining skies,
>   In horror, mud and sleeplessness, a week
> Of bursting shells, of blood and hideous cries
>   And the ever-watchful sniper: where the reek
> Of death offends the living . . . but poor dead
>   Can't sleep, must lie awake with the horrid sound
> That roars and whirs and rattles overhead
>   All day, all night, and jars and tears the ground;
> When rats run, big as kittens: to and fro
>   They dart, and scuffle with their horrid fare . . .[39]

Those images do not, here, find their most adequate expression: 'horrid sound' detracts from 'horrid fare', for instance; the 'roars and whirs and rattles' lack the onomatopoeic force that gives Owen's later poems their density of meaning; and 'rats . . . big as kittens', however accurate it may be, inadvertently brings to mind the small-scale, fluffy, and harmless, rather than the horror the lines are meant to express. That said, the poem marks out Graves's differences from Sassoon in 1915, in his urge to evoke, not evade, the 'reality' of war. It is also a precursor to Alun Lewis's Second World War poem 'All Day It Has Rained', in imagery and intention, if not in effect.

More impressive in *Over the Brazier* is the collection's title-poem (rather than the frequently quoted 'It's a Queer Time'), in which imagined structures—which by implication include the poem itself—are brought down: 'Idyllic dwellings—but this silly | Mad War has now wrecked both, and what | Better hopes has my little cottage got?'[40] The question—what better hopes does this poem have?—lurks here too. Its simplicities of tone and diction and its lullaby rhythms ('What life to lead and where to go | After the War, after the War?') reinforce the poignancy of its close, in a manner suggestive of those poems in which Graves's deliberately childlike idiom takes on a more sinister aspect—as in the 'Nursery Memories' of 'The First Funeral', or 'A Child's Nightmare'. Other poems in *Fairies and Fusiliers* may be read as if in dialogue with some of Sassoon's habitual preoccupations: in 'To R. N.', 'Cherries are out of season, | Ice grips at branch and root, | And singing birds are mute.'[41] 'Two Fusiliers', whilst it does not idealize war, does pre-empt

---

[38] Graves, 'A Renascence', in *Complete Poems*, 13–14.   [39] Graves, 'Limbo', ibid. 14.
[40] Graves, 'Over the Brazier', ibid. 20–1.   [41] Graves, 'To R. N.', ibid. 31.

some of Owen's homoerotic, perhaps masochistic celebrations of male bonding in wartime: 'Show me the two so closely bound | As we, by the wet bond of blood, | By friendship blossoming from mud, | By Death: we faced him, and we found | Beauty in Death, | in dead men, breath.'[42] Owen described Graves's technique in *Fairies and Fusiliers* as 'perfect'.[43] 'I should never stop if I started to rejoice over these poems,' he wrote to Sassoon in November 1917: 'You read many to me: but, wisely, not the best:—or the most charming.'[44] This is not to make claims for Graves's early war poems beyond their merits, but to note that his presence and influence complicate the wartime picture in ways not always fully acknowledged. Graves's poetic voice in the war years is by no means as easily identifiable as Sassoon's satirical one; nor does it have at this stage the maturity of Owen's. But it was a familiar voice to both Owen and Sassoon, one that both pre-empts some of their thematic concerns and finds some stylistic echoes in their poems.

In the decades after 1918, Graves became a major (if eccentric) poetic figure, whose influence on British and Irish poetry has been far-reaching. Sassoon, on the other hand, has remained trapped in the mode of 'war poet', at least in terms of critical reception, the Georgian who was temporarily shell-shocked into satirical mode, and whose new lyrical poems from the 1930s to the 1950s cast few ripples on the water. Perhaps the reason, as Adrian Caesar has suggested, lies in their different attitudes to the war, and the differences these engendered in a post-war aesthetic. The quality of Graves's war poems is by no means consistent, but his inconsistencies are not those of attitude towards the war. War may be, for Graves, 'silly' or 'Mad'; but soldiering is a contract entered into that cannot be questioned. In 'The Next War', a poem in which history is seen to repeat itself without end, the speaker describes the men as 'bound' by 'fate' to 'serve'. His advice, therefore, is: 'So hold your nose against the stink | And never stop too long to think. | Wars don't change except in name; | The next one must go just the same.'[45] The poem bears out Graves's later claim that he was 'both more consistent and less heroic than Siegfried', who is famously described by Graves as alternating 'between happy warrior and bitter pacifist'.[46] It is in the tension between these two modes that Sassoon's best—because most ambiguous—poems come to rest. They are poetic modes too, as the satirical meets the lyrical Sassoon. Alongside 'Blighters', with its apparent certainties and underlying tensions, we might also set such poems as 'The Kiss', which could be interpreted as an ironic comment on the 'homicidal eloquence' of the training Sassoon received, as he describes it in *Memoirs of an Infantry Officer*,[47] but which aesthetically cannot but delight in its weaponry ('She glitters naked,

---

[42] Graves, 'Two Fusiliers', ibid. 31.

[43] Wilfred Owen to Leslie Gunston, 8 Jan. 1918, in *Collected Letters*, ed. Harold Owen and John Bell (London: Oxford University Press, 1967), 526.

[44] Owen to Siegfried Sassoon, 27 Nov. 1917, ibid. 511.

[45] Graves, 'The Next War', in *Complete Poems*, 46.   [46] Graves, *Goodbye to All That*, 339.

[47] Sassoon, *Complete Memoirs of George Sherston*, 289–90.

cold and fair'[48]). Graves argues that 'it comes off whichever way you read it'—as intended seriously or as satire.[49] The poem, read as both simultaneously, becomes a measure of Sassoon's ambiguity towards war (and an oblique study of his own ambiguous sexuality).

Their different perceptions of war—and implicitly therein of poetry—also help to illuminate the famous episode of 1917 when Sassoon issued his 'Declaration against the War' with the intention of provoking a court martial. The story is told differently by Sassoon and Graves in their memoirs, and the differences of perspective were never resolved. Both agree about the justice of Sassoon's complaint against 'the political errors and insincerities for which the fighting men are being sacrificed', although Sassoon, in retrospect, questions how qualified they were to make that judgement. Yet, while Graves agreed in theory with Sassoon's comments, he never approved of the protest ('he's quite right in his views but absolutely wrong in his action'[50]), and in a letter to Sassoon in October 1917, written shortly before Sassoon requested a return to active service, his arguments point up key differences between the two:

You can only command their [the soldiers'] respect by sharing all their miseries as far as you possibly can, being ready for pride's sake to finish your contract whatever it costs you, yet all the time denouncing the principles you are being compelled to further. . . . I believe in keeping to agreements when everybody else keeps them and if I find myself part to principles I don't quite like, in biding my time till I have a sporting chance of rearranging things. One must bow in the house of Rimmon occasionally. Your conscience is too nice in its discernment between conflicting forces.[51]

Perhaps there may be some irony now in reading such a comment by Graves, from whose vocabulary, it is tempting to suggest, the word 'compromise' seemed in later life to be expunged. Yet unconsciously, and in what sounds like the viewpoint of the stereotypical upper-class English gentleman, he also outlines two different modes of writing. Sassoon, caught between, and acutely conscious of, conflicting forces in himself, and in his situation as poet and soldier simultaneously, produces out of such conflicts some of his best work. But we might also remember Graves's intense dislike of the later Yeats, and of Yeatsian rhetoric. Uncannily paralleling his 1917 arguments, Graves's own poetic principles as formulated thirty years later rest on a contradiction—'I am', he writes in The White Goddess, 'nobody's servant'; and yet the Goddess 'demands either whole-time service or none at all'[52]—but they do not rely on the outward expression of a quarrel with oneself.

In the years that followed, their different attitudes here became less important than, though not unrelated to, a bitter debate about 'truth'. According to Sassoon, 'David' [Graves] 'swore on an imaginary Bible that nothing would induce them

---

[48] Sassoon, 'The Kiss', in Collected Poems 1908–1956, 14.   [49] Graves, Goodbye to All That, 339.
[50] Graves to Edward Marsh, 12 July 1917, in In Broken Images, 77.
[51] Graves to Sassoon, 27 Oct. 1917, ibid. 85–6.   [52] Graves, White Goddess, 10–11.

to court martial me and that I should be treated as insane', and so he gave way. But it was, he writes, a 'successful lie. No doubt I should have done the same for him if our positions had been reversed.'[53] Graves recalls it differently: 'I made it plain that his letter had not been given and would not be given the publicity he intended; so, because he was ill, and knew it, he consented to appear before the medical board.'[54] The particular instance seems of limited importance, but the quarrel over the factuality, or otherwise, of the war memoirs was to bring the friendship to an end. On 7 February 1930, Sassoon wrote to Graves protesting about the numerous inaccuracies he found in *Goodbye to All That*: the 'inaccuracies', he observes, 'are not noticeable to "the general public", but they are significant to those who shared your experiences'.[55] Graves's reply, which counters the accusations, also contains a comment, of sorts, on Sassoon's most recent collection of poems, *The Heart's Journey*:

Your *Heart's Journey* which I have not seen yet but only read in reviews and in already published fragments, appears to . . .

no . . . no . . ..[56]

The acrimony continues through two further letters, and the correspondence ceases thereafter. (There are some further letters in the spring of 1933, old wounds opened by a request from Graves to Sassoon for money, after which all communication ended. They were 'reconciled' at a meeting in Cambridge in 1954.)

In the breakdown in relations in 1930, three related issues are of particular note: first, the fraught relation between public and private; second, the perception of the war as a 'shared experience'; third, the problem of perspective and representation—as regards both literature and history. Even before the acrimonious correspondence about *Goodbye to All That* began, Sassoon had insisted on alterations to the text (necessitating the withdrawal and reissue of the first edition), since Graves, without permission, had included Sassoon's 'Letter to Robert Graves', written during Sassoon's convalescence in 1918. The poem was unpublished, and Sassoon tried to retrieve it from Graves during a quarrel in 1922 (Graves returned only a copy). But Graves did not merely quote the poem, he also edited it by omitting several lines, including the following:

> Yes, you can touch my banker when you need him.
> Why keep a Jewish friend unless you bleed him?
> .   .   .   .
> O Rivers please take me. And make me
> Go back to the war till it break me.

---

[53] Sassoon, *Complete Memoirs of George Sherston*, 512–13.
[54] Graves, *Goodbye to All That*, 324.
[55] Sassoon to Graves, 7 Feb. 1930, in *In Broken Images*, 200.
[56] Graves to Sassoon, 20 Feb. 1930, ibid. 203. 'The dots', O'Prey notes, 'are not omission marks, but Graves's "comment" on *The Heart's Journey* book of poems.'

> Some day my brain will go BANG,
> And they'll say what lovely faces were
> The soldier-lads he sang
> Does this break your heart? What do I care?
>   Sassons.[57]

The omissions, Graves claimed, were due to lack of space; but this may be disingenuous. Graves both treats the poem as public property and cuts those moments in it which are highly personal, and which reflect directly on the nature of his relationship with Sassoon (financial dependence among them). Yet if the inclusion (and omissions) are seen as a betrayal of the private, a contradiction becomes evident which typifies debates surrounding war memoirs in the late 1920s.

In the preface to his own war memoir, *Undertones of War*, Edmund Blunden (whose own friendship with Graves ended with the publication of *Goodbye to All That*) claimed that 'no one will read it who is not already aware of all the intimations and discoveries in it . . . by reason of having gone the same journey. No one? Some, I am sure; but not many. *Neither will they understand*—that will not be all my fault.'[58] Implicit here is the sense outlined by Sassoon that the experiential Great War writer can speak for and to those who 'shared . . . experiences', who have 'gone the same journey'. It is perhaps on these grounds that in *Regeneration*, Barker places, unacknowledged, Wilfred Owen's account of going over the top in a letter of 14 May 1917 into the mouth of her fictional working-class officer Billy Prior, although with some anachronistic modifications of language: 'It felt', says Prior, 'sexy . . . You keep up a kind of chanting. "Not so fast. Steady on the left!" . . . I looked back and saw the ground was covered with wounded. Lying on top of each other, writhing. Like fish in a pond that's drying out. I wasn't frightened at all. I just felt this . . . amazing burst of exultation.'[59] This, however, is Owen:

There was an extraordinary exultation in the act of slowly walking forward, showing ourselves openly. . . . I kept up a kind of chanting sing-song: Keep the Line straight!

> Not so fast on the left!
> Steady on the Left!

. . . When I looked back and saw the ground all crawling and wormy with wounded bodies, I felt no horror at all but only an immense exultation at having got through the Barrage.[60]

To an extent, the 'borrowing' assumes that 'experience' of war is transferable: that it is shared regardless of age, class, sexuality, ideological perspective, pre-war experience. The desire to get the story right, as in the return to 'primary' sources

---

[57] See the withdrawn 1st edn. of *Goodbye to All That*, 341–3. The complete poem was published after Sassoon's death in *War Poems*, 130–2.
[58] Edmund Blunden, *Undertones of War* (Harmondsworth: Penguin, 1982), 7; italics original.
[59] Barker, *Regeneration*, 78–9.
[60] Owen to Colin Owen, 14 May 1917, in *Collected Letters*, 458.

in *Regeneration*, or in Sassoon's insistence on accuracy, may obscure the more evident truth from debates surrounding war memoirs, letters, diaries, or poems: that 'shared experience' is itself something of a myth. When Sassoon protests about Graves's inaccuracies, he claims to be 'testing your book as a private matter between you and me';[61] yet it is an awareness of public consumption that causes him to withdraw 'Letter to Robert Graves', an awareness of the dangers of leaving one voice in narrative control of another, of sharing, or transferring subjective material.

Graves closes the first edition of *Goodbye to All That* with the observation that he 'learned to tell the truth—nearly', a wry acknowledgement of the book's fictional qualities, in which he has 'leading and subsidiary characters', and which includes 'most of the usual storybook things'.[62] So whilst Graves tends to suggest that 'truth' is fictional, Sassoon, in the Sherston memoirs, claims for his fiction a degree of 'truth' lacking in Graves's work. The difference implied here reverberates in both poets' relations to modernism's stylistic experiments in the post-war period. In an illuminating discussion of the quarrel between Graves and Sassoon in 1930, Allyson Booth exposes some of the inconsistencies in Sassoon's position, since he 'berate[s] Graves for his perversion of factuality', and yet in his own *Memoirs* 'makes a point of addressing the problems of producing an accurate account of the war'. In that sense, both poets illustrate the validity of Booth's argument that 'The magnitude, the violence, and the intensity of World War I made impossible the adoption of a position from which anything like "factuality" might have been delineated.' The literary strategies which emerged in the 1920s respond to that impossibility. Yet, as she also notes:

Modernists were committed to and exhilarated by that project of invention, the results of which we now identify as a privileging of private and psychological facts over public and concrete ones. But when the experiences in question are rapes or wars, the difficulty of determining factuality is transformed from an interesting aesthetic problem into a heart-breakingly physical one, and the elusiveness of factuality becomes deeply disturbing, both emotionally and politically.[63]

Graves, more than Sassoon, is exhilarated by the 'staged' and fictional qualities of *Goodbye to All That*; the first edition of the book delights in subversion of official documents and records, and its lack of respect for 'authority' is in keeping with its casual attitude towards the 'facts'. Likewise, in the 1930s and 1940s, his 'autobiography' is told, he suggests, in his poems, and in a manner which also privileges the private and psychological over the 'facts'. As he writes in 1951: 'A volume of collected poems should form a sequence of the intenser moments of the poet's spiritual autobiography.... Such an autobiography, by the way, does not

---

[61] Sassoon to Graves, 7 Feb. 1930, in *In Broken Images*, 200.

[62] Graves, *Goodbye to All That* (1929), 439–41.

[63] Allyson Booth, *Postcards from the Trenches: Negotiating the Space between Modernism and the First World War* (Oxford: Oxford University Press, 1996), 85 and 87.

always keep chronological step with its historical counterpart: often a poetic event anticipates or succeeds the corresponding physical event by years.'[64]

Graves is not necessarily seen as central to a modernist project; but nor is he remote from it, and as the author with Laura Riding of *A Survey of Modernist Poetry* in 1927 (a book he was originally to write with T. S. Eliot), and of some of the early psychological readings of literature, he has considerable critical importance in understanding the developments of modernism. Sassoon, on the other hand, felt repelled, and ultimately marginalized, by modernism. Not least of the ironies of Barker's *Regeneration*, of course, is that as it reimagines Sassoon in the Great War, it does so through unacknowledged dependence on some of the 'modernist' texts that Sassoon believed had sidelined his own aesthetic values, with its echoes and paraphrases of Eliot's *The Waste Land*, Hemingway's *Farewell to Arms*, and so on. In that sense, the novel stands perhaps inadvertently as testament to Sassoon's lack of influence on post-war modes of writing. One consequence of Sassoon's marginalized feeling was the increasing stress he placed on the importance of his wartime poetic relation with Owen. As Max Egremont writes:

He missed what Owen might have become—a constant ally amid Sassoon's broken literary friendships with Bob Nichols, Graves, Turner, the Sitwells. Wilfred had been 'a kindred poet', although 'of more powerful intellectual genius'. Together, they might have defeated the Eliot school: a recurrence of Sassoon's fantasy.[65]

Probably only Owen's death permitted the fantasy of modernism's defeat at Owen's hands to remain intact, but its recurrence is a measure of Sassoon's felt literary isolation by the 1940s. In his diary in 1948 he writes: 'I have, more and more, believed that he [Owen] would have been incalculably valuable to me. His death made a gap in my life which has been there ever since.'[66] A year later, Graves takes the opposite stance, celebrating his distance from 'the caprices of a world in perpetual flux', claiming to be free from 'the frantic strain of swimming against the stream of time'.[67]

Given their early collaborative instincts, there is a certain irony to the fact that what Sassoon and Graves most obviously shared in the 1940s and 1950s was isolation from 'the stream of time' as much as from each other. In Graves's case, this is a willed distance from national, political, and literary canons which served to liberate his mature poetic voice; in Sassoon's case, it is the consequence of a nostalgia for a lost England, lamented in part through his regret for Owen's lost years. The journey through Sassoon's poems can feel like a journey backwards rather than forwards in time, from 'Died of Wounds' or 'The Hero' in the First World War to his Second

---

[64] Graves, 'Foreword to *Poems and Satires 1951*', in *The Complete Poems*, ii, ed. Beryl Graves and Dunstan Ward (Manchester: Carcanet, 1997), 345–6.

[65] Egremont, *Siegfried Sassoon*, 466.   [66] Sassoon, quoted ibid. 452–4.

[67] Robert Graves, *The Common Asphodel: Collected Essays on Poetry 1922–1949* (London: Hamish Hamilton, 1949), p. x.

World War poem 'Silent Service': 'let Britain's patient power | Be proven within us for the world to see . . . In every separate soul let courage shine— | A kneeling angel holding faith's front-line.'[68] In a reverse scenario, it is possible to argue that not until the 1940s does Graves write war poems that equal the best of Owen's or Sassoon's Great War trench lyrics—even if to say so is to stretch the genre of 'war poetry' beyond usual expectations.[69] In different ways, neither Graves nor Sassoon could ever claim to be free of the war which both made and—one might also argue—marred them as poets. 'And have we done with War at last?', asks the speaker in the opening line of Graves's 'Two Fusiliers'. For good or ill, in terms of their poetic development, the answer for these two Fusiliers must surely be no.

---

[68] Sassoon, 'Silent Service', in *Collected Poems 1908–1956*, 238.

[69] Those poems which articulate Graves's devotion to the Muse may also be read in terms of the First World War. See 'To Juan at the Winter Solstice' and 'The White Goddess', in *Complete Poems* (2003), 405 and 428, and discussion of these poems in Fran Brearton, *The Great War in Irish Poetry* (Oxford: Oxford University Press, 2000), ch. 3.

'EASTER, 1916': YEATS'S FIRST WORLD WAR POEM

MARJORIE PERLOFF

> When Pearce summoned Cuchulain to his side,
> What stalked through the Post Office? What intellect,
> What calculation, number, measurement, replied?
>
> W. B. Yeats, 'The Statues'

'How does the war affect you?', wrote W. B. Yeats's old friend and fellow occultist Florence Farr from Ceylon in October 1914. At first Yeats shrugged it off: in Ireland, he told Farr, the war seemed more remote than in England, making it easier to concentrate on other things.[1] But in London some months later, he complained to his American friend and benefactor John Quinn that '[the war] is merely the most expensive outbreak of insolence and stupidity the world has ever seen, and I give it as little of my thought as I can. I went to my club this afternoon to look at the war news, but read Keats's Lamia [*sic*] instead.'[2] This air of studied indifference characterizes Yeats's irritable little lyric of February 1915, 'On Being Asked for a War Poem':

> I think it better that at times like these
> A poet's mouth be silent, for in truth

---

[1] Florence Farr to W. B. Yeats, 3 Oct. 1914, in *Yeats Annual*, ix, ed. Deirdre Toomey (Basingstoke: Macmillan, 1992), 242–3. Farr was then headmistress of Ramanathan College in Ceylon.

[2] Yeats to John Quinn, 24 June 1915, quoted in Roy Foster, *W. B. Yeats: A Life*, ii: *The Arch-Poet* (Oxford: Oxford University Press, 2003), 5.

> We have no gift to set a statesman right;
> He's had enough of meddling who can please
> A young girl in the indolence of her youth,
> Or an old man upon a winter's night.[3]

The request had come from Henry James, who was helping Edith Wharton bring out a collection of war poems to raise money for the Belgian refugees in Paris.[4] The poem, first called 'To a friend who has asked me to sign his manifesto to the neutral nations' and then 'A Reason for Keeping Silent', inspired an angry response from the strongly anti-German Quinn, who told Yeats, 'those five or six lines were quite unworthy of you and the occasion.... I do not believe in divorce between letters and life or art and war.'[5]

The divorce persisted, however, during the winters with Ezra Pound at Stone Cottage, where in 1914–15 Yeats studied and adapted the stylized rituals of the Noh drama and completed the first volume of his autobiography, *Reveries over Childhood and Youth*. Pound, as James Longenbach notes, was becoming increasingly caught up in the war fever, especially after the death at the Front of his great artist friend Henri Gaudier-Brzeska in June 1915. But Yeats remained aloof: his own Noh play, *At the Hawk's Well*, designed by Edmund Dulac and danced by Michio Ito, a disciple of Nijinsky from the Ballet Russe, had its first performance (4 April 1916) at Lady Cunard's at what turned out to be, ironically enough, a war charity affair.[6] Having launched *At the Hawk's Well*, Yeats set off for Sir William Rothenstein's idyllic cottage in the Cotswolds to spend the Easter holiday. Sir William had planned to paint Yeats's portrait.

It was here on Easter Monday (24 April) that Yeats received word of the Rising. The rebellion moved him as no account of the Battle of the Somme or Verdun ever could, for the principals were mostly people he knew personally, and his own future hung in the balance. The Rising was the first decisive event to threaten Yeats's ability to advance the Irish cause from his base in London, where he had lived a large part of his life, ever since his schooldays. It was in London, after all, that Yeats's early writings were published, in London that he founded the Irish Literary Society (1891), the Gaelic League (1893), and so on. Even if he complained of being a stranger in London, Yeats held the privileged position of the Protestant Anglo-Irish Ascendancy. 'The loose federation of personalities Yeats gathered around himself', Declan Kiberd notes, 'was one of the very first groups of decolonizing intellectuals to formulate a vision of their native country during a youthful sojourn in an

---

[3] Yeats, 'On Being Asked for a War Poem', in *The Poems*, ed. Daniel Albright (London: Dent, 1990), 205.

[4] See James Longenbach, *Stone Cottage: Pound, Yeats and Modernism* (Oxford: Oxford University Press, 1988), 118.

[5] John Quinn, quoted in Albright, 'Notes to *Poems*', in Yeats, *Poems*, 579.

[6] See Foster, *W. B. Yeats*, ii. 40.

imperial capital.'[7] From his perch in London, Yeats could do many things to further the Irish cause, the downside being that the poet's Ireland, at this stage, was largely invention, an imaginary homeland, characterized, in Kiberd's words, by its mix 'of Celticism and Peter Pannery'.[8] Indeed, the poet's real literary roots were planted firmly in the English Romantic tradition, especially that of Blake and Shelley.

Ironically for Yeats, it was the British engagement in the Great War, an engagement he had derided as a great nuisance and distraction, that brought about the Easter Rising. The Irish Home Rule Bill, first introduced into Parliament by Gladstone in 1893 and passed by the House of Commons in 1912, requiring only the expected endorsement of the Lords to become law, was summarily tabled in Parliament. The new leader of the Irish Party, John Redmond, accepted this state of affairs. Indeed, Home Rule, in Kiberd's words, 'was to be the post-war reward for Redmond's support for England and for "plucky Catholic Belgium". Tens of thousands of Irishmen volunteered to fight (as they saw it) for the rights of small nations; other members of the Irish Volunteers felt in all conscience that this was not their war.'[9] These latter now flocked to the IRB (Irish Republican Brotherhood) as well as to Arthur Griffith's Sinn Féin ('ourselves alone') movement.

The scene was thus set for the Easter Rising, but neither Yeats nor Lady Gregory and her circle expected it; indeed, they reacted with shock to the news that on Easter Monday some 700 members of the IRB, led by Patrick Pearse, had occupied first the Post Office and from there the centre of Dublin, and proclaimed the founding of an independent Irish State. The Rising lasted less than a week: Pearse, appalled by the slaughter of civilians, surrendered on the Saturday after Easter; by then, more than 300 citizens had been killed, as well as more than 130 British soldiers and 70 rebels. British retaliation was severe. Between 3 and 12 May, fifteen rebel leaders were executed, 'despite', as Kiberd tells us, 'a strong consensus that they should have been treated as prisoners-of-war. Martial law was imposed and 3,500 people were arrested, more than twice the number which had actually taken part in the Rising.'[10]

Yeats's reaction can be traced in his correspondence with Lady Gregory, his sisters, and various friends. Despite initial suspicion of the rebels, Yeats sympathized with most of the principals: Thomas MacDonagh, a university lecturer and literary critic, had dedicated a book to him; Joseph Plunkett came from an affluent, cultured Dublin family; James Connolly was an actor at the Abbey Theatre; Constance Markiewicz had been born a Gore-Booth; she and her sister Eva represented, for Yeats, the country house gentry near Sligo. Most important: John MacBride was Maud Gonne's estranged husband. At the same time, Yeats disliked Pearse—'a man made dangerous by the Vertigo of Self Sacrifice'[11]—and had contempt for

---

[7] Declan Kiberd, *Inventing Ireland: The Literature of the Modern Nation* (Cambridge, Mass.: Harvard University Press, 1995), 100.

[8] Ibid. 113.   [9] Ibid. 192–3.   [10] Ibid. 193.

[11] Yeats to Lolly Yeats, n.d., quoted in Foster, *W. B. Yeats*, ii. 46; see also Longenbach, *Stone Cottage*, 56.

Arthur Griffith, the leader of Sinn Féin. Accordingly, his initial stance was one of caution: 'There is nothing to be done but to do one's work and write letters.'[12] And he remained in his London flat, detached from the turmoil.

But by May, reports came in of the murder, by the British police, of the pacifist Francis Sheehy Skeffington, a popular Dublin figure, well known to Yeats. Furthermore, the wholesale execution of the rebels aroused the sympathy of Lady Gregory as well as the entire Yeats family. Those hitherto regarded with bemusement and some contempt joined the visionary company of the great nineteenth-century Irish patriots Robert Emmet and Wolfe Tone. Yeats now became sharply critical of the English government. In an important letter to Lady Gregory, he wrote:

> If the English conservative party had made a declaration that they did not intend to rescind the Home Rule Bill there would have been no rebellion. *I had no idea that any public event could so deeply move me*—and I am very despondent about the future. At this moment I feel that all the work of years has been overturned, all the bringing together of classes, all the freeing of Irish literature & criticism from politics. . . . I do not yet know what [Maud Gonne] feels about her husband's death. Her letter was written before she heard of it. Her main thought seems to be 'tragic dignity has returned to Ireland'. She had been told by two members of the Irish Party that 'Home Rule was betrayed'. She thinks now that the sacrifice has made it safe.[13]

And he adds, 'I am trying to write a poem on the men executed—"terrible beauty has been born".'

It is interesting to observe how contradictory even this letter is. When Yeats notes that 'all the work of years has been overturned', he is not referring to the drive for Irish freedom but, on the contrary, to his old Gaelic League effort to 'free' Irish literature from all politics—an effort already made futile by the events themselves. As for the 'bringing together of classes', one senses that Yeats is more eager to find himself at one with the class above him, the aristocracy, than to befriend the members of the working class. And as for Maud Gonne's aphorism on tragic dignity, it is not at all clear that Yeats agrees with it. But he could not bring himself to cross her. Indeed, after a brief visit to Dublin in early June, Yeats decided to spend the summer in Normandy, where Maud Gonne was living with her children, with the stated intention of proposing marriage to her once again. When Gonne—predictably—refused, he turned to her daughter Iseult, proposing to her as well, and again being refused. The neurotic relationship with both women dragged on until, at the end of August, Lady Gregory summoned Yeats back to Ireland and took him straight to Coole Park for a much-needed rest. It was at Coole on 25 September that Yeats finished 'Easter, 1916'.

I detail this material, much of it familiar to Yeats students, so as to help the reader understand that a political poem like 'Easter, 1916'—or, for that matter,

---

[12] Yeats to Lolly Yeats, n.d., quoted in Foster, *W. B. Yeats*, ii. 46.

[13] Yeats to Lady Gregory, 11 May 1916, in *The Letters of W. B. Yeats*, ed. Allen Wade (London: Rupert Hart-Davis, 1954), 612–13; my italics.

Yeats's later 'Nineteen Hundred and Nineteen' and 'Meditations in Time of Civil War'—responds to particular situations in all their ambiguity. Today, when 'anti-war poems' are usually written by those whose knowledge of the war in question is largely derived from the media and whose positions are usually both simple and clear-cut (for example, 'The Iraq war was motivated by the lust for Middle Eastern oil'), the political complexity of modernist war poetry must come as a great surprise.

It is the common wisdom that modernism was 'aestheticist', that its autonomous art was far removed from 'life', and that this 'great divide', as Andreas Huyssen called it in his book of that title, must be broached by a *rapprochement* between 'high' and 'low' art, between art and popular culture. But the more one studies the great modernist poets and fiction writers, the more dubious this postmodernist proposition seems. Indeed, Yeats's writing demonstrates—as does that of Eliot and Pound—how readily so-called ideological positions are contaminated by extraneous factors, in Yeats's own case, by his lifelong passion for Maud Gonne, herself a fiery revolutionary, so devoted to the Irish Nationalist cause that, in later life, she condoned Hitler's actions, declaring that at least the Germans hated the English as much as she did. Gonne was also virulently anti-Semitic.[14]

Yeats, in any event, tried to write a poem on the Rising that Gonne might admire even as it would also satisfy the Dublin public and convey his own ambivalence toward the events of 1916. As a poet, moreover, whose readership in England and the United States was at least as large as that in his native Ireland, Yeats faced the difficult challenge of presenting as tragedy an event that, given the larger war picture of 1916, was hardly considered to have major import. On 1 July, after all, the Battle of the Somme began, a battle best remembered for its first day, on which the British suffered 60,000 casualties (20,000 deaths). It was the bloodiest day in the history of the British Army, and the battle, dragging on till November, produced over 460,000 casualties altogether. How to process the horror of such a set of circumstances? 'Things fall apart; the centre cannot hold,'[15] as 'The Second Coming' has it, but how and why?

Yeats was a great mythographer. The Sligo countryside, as literary tourists know, is hardly beautiful or even especially distinctive, but Yeats manages, throughout his poetry, to transform it into one of poetry's Sacred Places even as he makes readers long to see Lissadell (the home of the Gore-Booth sisters), Ben Bulben, and Coole Park. In 'Easter, 1916', the trick is to immortalize the rebels, not as heroes in the abstract, but as agents of *change*—change by no means all positive, but dramatic in the mere fact of its taking place. And drama is the key word here, for Yeats presented

---

[14] See Foster, *W. B. Yeats*, ii. 344–5, 468–9. 'Gonne, years after the post-war revelations of genocide, was still saying that if she had been German, the only thing that would have stopped her becoming a Nazi was their exclusion of women from positions of power; she also boasted of telling Richard Ellmann ("a young American Jew") that, compared to Hiroshima and Nagasaki, Hitler's death-camps were "quite small affairs".'

[15] Yeats, 'The Second Coming', in *Poems*, 235.

his characters as actors playing out a script largely beyond their control, actors caught up in a street theatre in which their individual identities are subordinated to a larger communal drive, Easter itself symbolizing the power and possibility of wholesale renewal.

Numerology plays an important part in the poem. 'Easter, 1916' has four stanzas of 16, 24, 16, 24 lines respectively, covertly embodying the Rising's date—the twenty-fourth day of the fourth month of the year 1916—even as its metre offsets these multiples of four with a trimeter or, more properly, a three-stress line, the number of syllables varying between six and nine.[16] Yeats makes his trimeter dramatic by introducing regular trochaic substitutions, as in

> Coming with *vivid faces*

as well as overstressing his lines and introducing caesurae—

> *All changed, || changed utterly*

—where only one of the six syllables receives no stress, creating the effect of an insistent drumbeat. The use of fricatives and voiced and voiceless stops in the refrain makes these heavily stressed syllables even more emphatic:

> All *changed, changed utterly*:
> A *terrible beauty* is *born*.

And the rhyme, *ababcdcd*, reinforces the four-part structure of the poem, its sense of eternal recurrence in the midst of seeming change.

Within this elaborate formal structure, the colloquial dominates, at least in the poem's opening, which begins, not with an account of the Rising itself—indeed, that tale is never told—but with the word 'I', placing the poet, and his attempt at understanding what has happened, at centre-stage:

> I have met them at close of day
> Coming with vivid faces
> From counter or desk among grey
> Eighteenth-century houses.
> I have passed with a nod of the head
> Or polite meaningless words,
> Or have lingered awhile and said
> Polite meaningless words,
> And thought before I had done
> Of a mocking tale or a gibe

---

[16] This structure was first noticed by one of Helen Vendler's students, Nathan Rose. See Vendler, 'Technique in the Earlier Poems of Yeats', in *Yeats Annual*, viii, ed. Warwick Gould (Basingstoke: Macmillan, 1991), 20 n. 4; cf. Terence Brown, *The Life of W. B. Yeats* (Oxford: Blackwell, 1999), 233–4. I have discussed the verse form and structure *vis-à-vis* Matthew Arnold's 'Haworth Churchyard', in 'Yeats and the Occasional Poem: "Easter 1916" ', *Papers on Language & Literature*, 4/3 (Summer 1968), 308–28.

> To please a companion
> Around the fire at the club
> Being certain that they and I
> But lived where motley is worn:
> All changed, changed utterly:
> A terrible beauty is born.[17]

'The power of [Yeats's] poem', writes Declan Kiberd, 'derives from the honesty with which he debates the issue, in the process postponing until the very last moment his dutiful naming of the dead warriors: this had been, of course, the practice of bards after a battle, in which they invariably claimed that the land had been redeemed by the sacrifice. Yeats's entire lyric is a sequence of strategies for delaying such naming.'[18] The delay of naming—the almost contemptuous use of 'them' in the opening lines—has another effect: it brings the reader squarely into the poet's radius of discourse, as if to say, 'You know who these guys are, better than I do.' Their 'vivid faces' stand out against the backdrop of the twilight, like actors on a darkened stage. In line 3, Yeats designates their status with the economical synecdoche of 'counter or desk'—shop or office. And those shops and offices—ordinary workplaces—are what the elegant 'Eighteenth-century houses' of Dublin have come to house. Ordinary people coming home from ordinary jobs: the poet recalls exchanging no more than 'polite meaningless words' with these Dubliners, later making fun of their remarks to his friends at the club, 'Being certain that they and I | But lived where motley is worn'—motley, the fool's variegated garment.

In his 1915 letter to Quinn cited above, Yeats talks of retreating to his London club and reading Keats's *Lamia* rather than listening to the war news. The English–German War, he repeatedly insisted, was not his concern. But ironically, in inuring himself from the Great War, Yeats had also remained aloof from the recent Irish troubles: at Stone Cottage, the Pound–Yeats curriculum was heavily weighed to such exotic arts as the Noh theatre, the irony being that war looms large in precisely these Japanese plays. 'All changed, changed utterly': however the Rising was to be judged, its sudden intrusion into the daily round of Dublin life, captured by the 'round' of the rhyming trimeter stanza, marks a momentous change—a cataclysm oddly mirroring what was happening on the Western Front, unanticipated as the deadly trench warfare of 1916 had been in the idyllic summer when war broke out.

In the second stanza, Yeats dramatizes the complex meaning of the Rising in a roll-call of four of its yet unnamed 'heroes':

> That woman's days were spent
> In ignorant good-will,
> Her nights in argument
> Until her voice grew shrill.

---

[17] Yeats, 'Easter, 1916', in *Poems*, 228–30.   [18] Kiberd, *Inventing Ireland*, 213.

> What voice more sweet than hers
> When, young and beautiful,
> She rode to harriers?
> This man had kept a school
> And rode our winged horse;
> This other his helper and friend
> Was coming into his force;
> He might have won fame in the end,
> So sensitive his nature seemed,
> So daring and sweet his thought.
> This other man I had dreamed
> A drunken, vainglorious lout.
> He had done most bitter wrong
> To some who are near by heart,
> Yet I number him in the song;
> He too has resigned his part
> In the casual comedy;
> He, too, has been changed in his turn,
> Transformed utterly:
> A terrible beauty is born.

Yeats's roll-call is carefully calculated. Of the seven men who actually signed the Proclamation of the Republic—Padraic Pearse, Thomas MacDonagh, James Connolly, Eamon Ceannt, Joseph Mary Plunkett, Sean MacDermott, and Thomas Clarke—only the first two figure here. Pearse, however fanatical Yeats took him to be, was something of a poet, and his transformation from sideline spoiler to leader of the rebellion certainly merited attention. MacDonagh was more sympathetic: the poem pays tribute to his literary gift and his sensitivity, although Yeats had earlier suggested that Ireland gave MacDonagh no breathing room, that he should have moved to England in order to realize his potential.[19]

But it is the first and fourth actors who get the most attention: Constance Markiewicz, *née* Gore-Booth, once a beautiful, aristocratic young horsewoman, whose grace and charm, so the poet posits, have been destroyed by revolutionary zeal, is, as Elizabeth Cullingford has noted, a stand-in for Maud Gonne, whom Yeats regularly castigated for her 'shrill' and all-consuming political activism.[20] Gonne, living in France, could not be listed since she played no actual role in the

---

[19] In his 1909 diary 'Estrangement', Yeats writes, 'Met MacDonagh yesterday—a man with some literary faculty which will probably come to nothing through lack of culture and encouragement. . . . In England this man would have become remarkable in some way, here he is being crushed by the mechanical logic and commonplace eloquence which give power to the most empty mind because, being "something other than human life", they have no use for distinguished feeling or individual thought' (Yeats, *Autobiographies* (London: Macmillan, 1966), 488).

[20] Elizabeth Cullingford, *Gender and History in Yeats's Love Poetry* (Cambridge: Cambridge University Press, 1993), 121–5. The Gore-Booth sisters are the subject of one of Yeats's great elegies, 'In Memory of Eva Gore-Booth and Con Markiewicz', which I discuss in my 'Spatial Form in Yeats's "Lissadell" Poems', *PMLA*, 82 (Oct. 1967), 444–54. Markiewicz's death sentence was commuted

Rising, but it is Gonne whose 'terrible beauty' is Yeats's concern. And here that 'drunken, vainglorious lout' John MacBride comes in. Neither a major figure in the Rising, nor, like Markiewicz, Pearse, and MacDonagh, a symbol of tragically wasted potential, MacBride has a purely personal significance for Yeats: he was the man Maud Gonne eloped with in 1903, the estranged husband who 'had done most bitter wrong', so Yeats felt, to the woman he himself adored (and possibly to her daughter Iseult as well).[21] MacBride is thus the one person here whose transformation has evidently been for the better: 'he too has resigned his part | In the casual comedy'. Yeats's 'Yet I number him in the song' is meant to be an expression of generosity, calculated, no doubt, to impress Gonne with the poet's fair-mindedness, the irony being that MacBride could only be 'Transformed utterly' by giving up his life. The 'terrible beauty', in other words, is that of death itself. The roll-call thus ends on a high dramatic note, more theatrical than accurate. Were documentary truth the aim of 'Easter, 1916', Yeats would have omitted Con Markiewicz and John MacBride in favour of such unexpected casualties of the Rising as Francis Skeffington or Roger Casement, the latter condemned to death for his part in the Rising—he had tried to enlist German support for the Irish cause—despite his last-minute opposition to the Easter events.[22]

More mythography than 'realistic' document, the poem abruptly shifts ground in the third stanza from narrative to nature imagery—specifically, the imagery of stone and stream:

> Hearts with one purpose alone
> Through summer and winter seem
> Enchanted to a stone
> To trouble the living stream.
> The horse that comes from the road,
> The rider, the birds that range
> From cloud to tumbling cloud,
> Minute by minute they change;
> A shadow of cloud on the stream
> Changes minute by minute;
> A horse-hoof slides on the brim,
> And a horse plashes within it;
> The long-legged moor-hens dive,
> And hens to moor-cocks call,
> Minute by minute they live:
> The stone's in the midst of all.

because of her sex. The poems devoted to Maud Gonne's 'unfortunate' political radicalism are too many to name; a whole series is found in *The Green Helmet* (Churchtown, Dundrum: Cuala Press, 1910).

[21] See *The Gonne–Yeats Letters 1893–1938*, ed. Anna MacBride White and Norman Jeffares (New York: Norton, 1994), 161–2.

[22] See Foster, *W. B. Yeats*, ii. 51–2.

The great feat of this stanza is to introduce a concept of *change* entirely different from that commemorated in the refrain of the first two stanzas. Change in nature is gradual, 'Minute by minute', a 'shadow of cloud on the stream'. In the natural world, birds, horses, and streams are in perpetual free motion: there is constant sliding, plashing, and mating as 'hens to moor-cocks call'. 'In the midst of all' this Heraclitean flux sits the stone symbolizing the 'enchanted' or betrayed 'heart', frozen so as 'To trouble the living stream'. The stone deflects the stream's flow, changing its course irrevocably.

Is this a good or a bad thing? 'The changes of cloud, birds and riders seem more vital than the unchanging stone,' writes Declan Kiberd, 'but they only "seem" so, for without that stone in its fixity no ripples could vibrate at all.'[23] This is certainly the case, and readers have often argued that the stone symbolizes the firmness of purpose and strength of mind of the patriots, that the 'troubling' of the revolution is necessary if there is ever to be real 'change' in the life of the nation. Natural change, by this argument, is all very well, but if human beings do not interfere with nature, there can be no civilization, and certainly no progress. But the difficulty is that the imagery of cloud and stream has nothing if not positive connotations, and that the next stanza begins with the lines 'Too long a sacrifice | Can make a stone of the heart'. Kiberd gets around this emphatic assertion by arguing that 'the poet, with scrupulous exactitude, claims only that sacrifice "can" make a stone of the heart', not that it necessarily does so, and he suggests that 'By refusing to change the rebels have, in fact, changed everything, even if in that recognition the poet is still not convinced that they were right.'[24] There is no way of being certain how the poem wants us to judge the role of the 'troubl[ing] stone'.

When we read Yeats's stanza in the context of his correspondence and related writings, the overall picture becomes no clearer. True, Maud Gonne herself gives the following account:

Standing by the seashore in Normandy in September 1916 [Yeats] read me that poem ['Easter, 1916']; he had worked on it all the night before, and he implored me to forget the stone and its inner fire for the flashing, changing joy of life; but when he found my mind dull with the stone of the fixed idea of getting back to Ireland, kind and helpful as ever, he helped me to overcome political and passport difficulties and we travelled as far as London together.[25]

Here the meaning of 'stone' is quite clear, as it is in the 'The Death of Synge' (1909), where Yeats refers to a politically radical woman of his acquaintance as one who has taken up 'an opinion as if it were some terrible stone doll', and declares that the flesh of such women 'becomes stone and passes out of life'.[26]

---

[23] Kiberd, *Inventing Ireland*, 214.   [24] Ibid.

[25] Maud Gonne, 'Yeats and Ireland', in Stephen Gwynn (ed.), *Scattering Branches: Tributes to the Memory of W. B. Yeats* (London: Macmillan, 1940), 31–2.

[26] Yeats, 'The Death of Synge', in *Autobiographies*, 504.

But in the poem itself there is no such clarity. The order of nature—birds, plashing horse, clouds, stream—with its minute-by-minute change is all very lovely, but it is not, after all, the poet's order, as the first two stanzas have made only too clear. The voices of hens calling to moor-cocks do not grow 'shrill', and no 'polite meaningless words' are exchanged. Accordingly, when, in the fourth and final stanza, the assertion 'Too long a sacrifice | Can make a stone of the heart' is followed by the burning question 'O when may it suffice?', we have to take the poet's perplexity wholly at face value. Whatever Yeats may have said to Maud Gonne, whatever he may written about 'stone dolls' in his *Autobiographies*, in 'Easter, 1916' the presence of the stone 'troubl[ing] the living stream' remains ambivalent, the one reality being that the two kinds of change presented are antithetical.

Bards, in any case, can't solve the problem: 'O when may it suffice?' is answered by the words 'That is Heaven's part', 'our part' being merely 'To murmur name upon name, | As a mother names her child | When sleep at last come | On limbs that have run wild'. But this display of stoic acceptance will not quite do either. And so we move to the climax:

> What is it but nightfall?
> No, no, not night but death;
> Was it needless death after all?
> For England may keep faith
> For all that is done and said.
> We know their dream; enough
> To know they dreamed and are dead;
> And what if excess of love
> Bewildered them till they died?
> I write it out in a verse—
> MacDonagh and MacBride
> And Connolly and Pearse
> Now and in time to be,
> Wherever green is worn,
> Are changed, changed utterly:
> A terrible beauty is born.

The nightfall of the rebels is not that of the peacefully sleeping child of lines 62–4. The insistent 'No, no, not night but death' explodes that image and leads to the terrifying question, 'Was it needless death after all?' This is the question asked of all revolutions and wars: was the death 'worth it'? The poet is here debating with himself, asking himself whether it isn't just possible that 'England may keep faith | For all that is done and said'. And there's the rub.

Studies of the Easter Rising, including Charles Townshend's recent definitive *Easter 1916: The Irish Rebellion*, suggest that it was less the original rebellion than the public outcry about the English suppression of that rebellion that led to later IRB initiatives—initiatives that may have hastened the passage of the Home Rule Act of 1920. Then again, as Yeats worries, by then the English might have acted anyway.

Who can tell? And there is still another question on the poet's mind: 'what if excess of love | Bewildered them till they died?' Here Yeats seems to be thinking of his own excessive love for Maud Gonne—a love that certainly clouded his judgement for years. In a similar sense, the rebels' excess love for their cause, their fanaticism, may have 'bewildered them', hastening their noble but empty gesture and thus their death.

'O when may it suffice?' Only after his fourth nervous, staccato question, does Yeats step back and memorialize the patriots, now for the first time naming them. The ending of 'Easter, 1916' has been justly praised for its drama: 'I write it out in a verse', the poet declares, paving the way for those famous but previously withheld names and the now thrilling repetition of the refrain, where 'Pearse' rhymes so memorably with 'verse'. What has been 'born' is indeed a 'terrible beauty'—sublime, awful, irreconcilable, as critics on both the Left and the Right have frequently remarked. 'The paradox of "Easter, 1916"', writes David Lloyd, 'is that the achievement of such politically symbolic status, the transformation of lout or clown into martyr which brings about the foundation of the nation, is seen to produce not reconciliation but a troubled tension.'[27] Or, in the words of Donald Davie:

The most impressive thing about the whole poem is that the 1916 leaders are mourned most poignantly, and the sublimity of their gesture is celebrated most memorably, not when the poet is abasing himself before them, but when he implies that, all things considered, they were, not just in politics but in human terms, probably wrong.[28]

Here, then, is a poem commemorating a controversial revolutionary moment that satisfied readers of the most varying persuasions. Or almost: Maud Gonne did not like it. 'My dear Willie', she wrote on 8 November 1916, 'No, I don't like your poem, it isn't worthy of you & above all it isn't worthy of the subject . . . you who have studied philosophy & know something of history know quite well that sacrifice has never yet turned a heart to stone though it has immortalized many & through it alone mankind can rise to God.' And she goes on to praise MacDonagh and Pearse as 'men of genius', insisting that even 'my husband' (MacBride) 'has entered Eternity by the great door of sacrifice which Christ opened and has therefore atoned for all'.[29] For Gonne, a great public poem, one that 'our race would treasure & repeat', must have a clear message, a clarion call to action. Perhaps this is why she herself was not capable of writing poetry, whereas Yeats understood that 'We make out of the quarrel with others, rhetoric, but of the quarrel with ourselves, poetry.'[30]

[27] David Lloyd, 'The Poetics of Politics: Yeats and the Founding of the State', in Jonathan Allison (ed.), *Yeats's Political Identities: Selected Essays* (Ann Arbor: University of Michigan Press, 1996), 393.

[28] Donald Davie, ' ' "Michael Robartes and the Dancer" ', in Denis Donoghue and J. R. Mulryne (eds.), *An Honoured Guest: New Essays on W. B. Yeats* (New York: St Martin's Press, 1966), 87.

[29] Gonne to Yeats, 8 Nov. 1916, in *Gonne–Yeats Letters*, 284–5.

[30] Yeats, 'Per Amica Silentia Lunae', in *Mythologies* (London: Macmillan, 1962), 331.

The great poem cannot take sides: its endurance depends precisely on its suspension of disbelief, allowing for such disparate critics as Lloyd and Davie to praise 'Easter, 1916' as a major work.

But to return to the writing of the First World War. The oxymoron 'terrible beauty', to which Yeats subscribed, explains why he could not endorse the English 'war poets'—Wilfred Owen, Isaac Rosenberg, Siegfried Sassoon, and so on—whom he dismissed in his introduction to the *Oxford Book of Modern Verse* (1936) in a notorious comment:

I have a distaste for certain poems written in the midst of the Great War; they are in all anthologies, but I have substituted Herbert Read's *End of a War* written long after. The writers of these poems were invariably officers of exceptional courage and capacity . . . but felt bound . . . to plead the suffering of their men. In poems that had for a time considerable fame, written in the first person, they made that suffering their own. I have rejected these poems for the same reason that made Arnold withdraw his *Empedocles on Etna* from circulation; *passive suffering is not a theme for poetry*. In all the great tragedies, tragedy is a joy to the man who dies; in Greece the tragic chorus danced.[31]

Few contemporary readers will approve of that last sentence: the notion that 'tragedy' can breed 'joy'—an idea that Yeats makes much of in his late poem 'Lapis Lazuli'—seems callous in the face of what was happening in Europe in 1936, not to mention the horrors of trench warfare, as experienced by Owen (who died in one of the last battles of the war in 1918) and Sassoon. Nevertheless, Yeats's comment about 'passive suffering' not being 'a theme for poetry' points to something important. Elegy, after all, is traditionally a form in which lament is balanced by consolation. Without the latter, the lament, whether personal or public, can seem merely lugubrious. Yes, we say, it is very sad that X was shot dead yesterday, but what is the larger context in which we are to understand that death?

A great elegist himself, whether mourning and commemorating a special friend (Robert Gregory), a great house (Coole Park), or a public event (the Easter Rising), Yeats had difficulty not only with the young war poets, but especially with Sean O'Casey's 1928 play *The Silver Tassie*. O'Casey's earlier plays for the Abbey Theatre dealt with material closely related to Yeats's own 'Easter, 1916', and the poet had staunchly defended *The Plough and the Stars*, even though many Irish critics found the play too irreverent toward the Nationalist cause.[32] But *The Silver Tassie*, which turned its attention from Ireland to the Great War and was written in London, where O'Casey had come into contact with Expressionist theatre, struck Yeats as mere programmatic didacticism. The 28 April letter he sent O'Casey, rejecting *The Silver Tassie* on behalf of the Abbey, is vitriolic.

Yeats begins by praising Act I (in which the exploits of the hero, a simple young football star who joins the infantry, are juxtaposed with the ominous news of war

---

[31] Yeats, 'Introduction', in Yeats (ed.), *The Oxford Book of Modern Verse, 1892–1935* (Oxford: Clarendon Press, 1936), p. xxxiv.

[32] See Foster, *W. B. Yeats*, ii. 304–9.

deaths in France), but he dislikes the abstract, Expressionist turn in Act II, where the speeches are largely choral commentaries on the horrors of war. And so he argues:

You were interested in the Irish Civil War, and at every moment . . . wrote out of . . . your sense of its tragedy . . . and you moved us as Swift moved his contemporaries.

But you are not interested in the great war, you never stood on its battlefields or walked its hospitals and so write out of your opinions. You illustrate those opinions by a series of almost unrelated scenes as you might in a leading article, there is no dominating character, no dominating action, neither psychological unity nor unity of action. . . . The mere greatness of the world war has thwarted you, it has refused to become mere background and obtrudes itself upon the stage as so much dead wood that will not burn with the dramatic fire. . . . Among the things that dramatic action must burn up are the author's opinions.[33]

This letter, coming as it did from Yeats the Senator and Nobel prize winner, caused a huge *brouhaha* in Irish literary and political circles and marked O'Casey's furious departure, not only from the Abbey but from Dublin; he never lived in Ireland again.

For our purposes here, the issue is not whether Yeats's estimate of *The Silver Tassie* was right or wrong—certainly, the play has had its persuasive defenders[34]—but whether Yeats's argument itself has any merit. The answer, I think, is twofold. The reproach that 'you never stood on its battlefields' seems obviously misguided; indeed, Yeats had criticized Owen and Sassoon for precisely the opposite—for being themselves on the battlelines and hence sentimentalizing 'passive suffering'. Yeats knew perfectly well that a poet need not witness a particular event in order to write about it. The charge that 'the mere greatness of the world war has thwarted you' is more serious. If there have been few great poems dealing directly with the First World War (or the Second World War, for that matter), it is surely because the significance and import of such large-scale events cannot be readily digested—especially not into the lyric fabric. Describing the horrors of war, the poet is too often left with nothing to do but point to its hapless victims and find someone to blame.

Perhaps this is why Yeats himself chose such smaller-scale subjects as the Easter Rebellion and the subsequent civil war. For one thing, the Dublin family drama, involving those that poet and reader know so well they need not be named, served as a displacement for that other or 'Great' War, too overwhelming to write about, except by mythologizing it as Yeats does with subtle indirection in 'The Second Coming' or in 'Nineteen Hundred and Nineteen'. What makes 'Easter, 1916' such

---

[33] Yeats to Sean O'Casey, 20 Apr. 1928, in *Letters of W. B. Yeats*, 740–2.

[34] Declan Kiberd, e.g. finds O'Casey's achievement in *The Silver Tassie* 'of a high order'. 'O'Casey', he writes, 'demonstrates with rare empathy, how the demobbed soldiers hated returning home, because they were tortured by their inability to describe the war to relatives. . . . [Harry's] isolation is an eerie continuation of his condition in the war-zone, where each soldier stood on a spookily silent set and "only flashes are seen. No noise is heard"' (Kiberd, *Inventing Ireland*, 244).

an important representative of its genre is that it takes into account the inevitable ironies that even the most 'tragic' events produce. While, for example, the 'heroes' are meeting their death, their elegist is using the occasion to rekindle a lost romance. Certainly this was Yeats's case in his response to Maud Gonne's conviction that 'tragic dignity has returned to Ireland'. No memorial poem, in short, is ever entirely disinterested.

Ulterior motives, however, do nothing to destroy the poem's integrity *qua* poem. 'Easter, 1916' dramatizes Yeats's own genuine ambivalence towards the rebel cause, his own admiring but troubled assessment of the value of the Rising. He knew only too well that the issue was prickly, so he allowed only twenty-five copies of 'Easter, 1916' to be printed in 1917, and these were for private circulation. In the interval between its composition and its publication in *Michael Robartes and the Dancer* in 1921, the Great War ended, and the outlook for the end of colonial rule in Ireland became brighter, even as factionalism in Ireland itself became more extreme. By 1922, a year after the publication of *Michael Robartes*, Home Rule became a reality, but no sooner had the Irish Free State been created than the country descended into the abyss of civil war. Yeats wrote eloquently about that conflict in the poems of *The Tower* (1928), but perhaps never again quite as stringently as he had in 'Easter, 1916'. The questions posed in that elegy remained, in any case, the pressing ones: 'O when may it suffice?', and especially 'Was it needless death after all?' Great war poetry always asks these questions, but can never quite answer them.

PART III

ENTRE DEUX GUERRES

'WHAT THE DAWN WILL BRING TO LIGHT': CREDULITY AND COMMITMENT IN THE IDEOLOGICAL CONSTRUCTION OF 'SPAIN'

STAN SMITH

PRIVATE BATTLES

' "I am your choice, your decision. Yes, I am Spain" ', declared an oracular life force in Auden's 1937 pamphlet-poem, called, simply and sufficiently, *Spain*.[1] It was enough in the 1930s to say that one word, it seemed, for everyone to know exactly

---

[1] W. H. Auden, *Spain* (London: Faber, 1937), 9; the poem is reprinted in revised form as 'Spain 1937' in Auden's *Another Time* (London: Faber, 1940), 103–6. The original text, and a list of revisions, can be

what was meant. The Civil War which began in July 1936 with General Franco's military revolt against the newly elected Popular Front government rapidly became an icon focusing all the contradictions and conflicts of the era. Rex Warner's poem 'The Tourist Looks at Spain', first published in the Spain-dominated fourth issue of John Lehmann's journal *New Writing*, in Autumn 1937, summed up the way in which 'Spain' had galvanized British writers:

> What we saw dead was all the time alive,
>   and what we see is living.
> It is over our own eyes that the mist holds.
> Say clearly: Spain has torn the veil of Europe.[2]

The Civil War here replaces the clichés of 'what every tourist knows' about Spain with a new revelation. Just as Auden's life force substitutes itself for the volunteers whose choices it defines, so Warner's poem enters a second and third remove of address to invoke a collective commitment: ' "the same words spoken by many different voices: | 'There is a world to win: we know the oppressors.' " ' In the same vein, Nancy Cunard's 1937 poem 'Yes, it is Spain', derivative of Auden's poem, asks rhetorically, 'What else could you do but go?', making Spain the untranscendable horizon of contemporary consciousness: 'You think this is something new? No; this too becomes Spain, | All of it, all of it's Spain.'[3] Like Auden and Warner, Cunard feels compelled to externalize the rhetoric, attributing the poem's final summons to a historic tribunal composed of her favourite writers and painters from Dante to Zola, who command, in concert: ' "Every man to his battle, child; this is yours, understand it, | In that desert where blood replaces water—Yes, it is Spain." ' The 'words from the Pacific Americas, words of Antillean temper, | Coming together, comrades, words from Finland to Abyssinia',[4] of her unpublished 'Sequences from a Long Epic on Spain' claim a similar polyphonic authority, as does her 1937 collective manifesto, *Authors Take Sides on the Spanish War*.

The coming together of individual commitment and collective action lies at the ideological core of Civil War poetry. 'Our generation', Stephen Spender recollected

---

found in Valentine Cunningham (ed.), *The Penguin Book of Spanish Civil War Verse* (Harmondsworth: Penguin, 1980), 97–100 and 461–2.

  [2] Rex Warner, 'The Tourist Looks at Spain', in *New Writing IV* (Autumn 1937), ed. John Lehmann (London: Lawrence & Wishart, 1937), 229. The issue also included three poems by the recently dead John Cornford, together with Margot Heinemann's elegies, 'A Madrid Diary' by the German writer Alfred Kantorowicz, a translation of a poem by Lorca ('deliberately murdered by the fascists soon after the outbreak of the Civil War', the contributors' notes report), and a short play by a young Spanish writer, Rafael Dieste. It closed with Spender's 'Notes on the International Congress' held in Valencia in the summer of 1937, 'Spain Invites the World's Writers'. Among other writings of and about the war, the journal regularly published translations of the ballad 'Romances' which flourished in Spain during this period.

  [3] Nancy Cunard, 'Yes, it is Spain', in *Poems of Nancy Cunard from the Bodleian Library*, ed. John Lucas (Nottingham: Trent Editions, 2005), 45–6.

  [4] Cunard, 'Sequences from a Long Epic on Spain', ibid. 53–9.

half a century later, 'was conscripted into politics by Hitler': young writers espoused communism as the only way to fight fascism, innocently accepting 'the Marxist interpretation of history' and believing that 'Communism would lead to the freedom of oppressed people, to a world of social justice, and to a depoliticised egalitarian anarchist utopia'.[5] Auden's poem fused individual and collective commitments by depicting the volunteers converging on the Spanish peninsula in some vast natural migration in which 'All presented their lives'. John Lehmann, Spender's co-editor in 1939 of the anthology *Poems for Spain*,[6] recalled in his 1955 memoir *The Whispering Gallery* that Spain merged literary and political preoccupations, presenting 'an opportunity that appeared at the same time as an imperative. I wanted, I felt it absolutely necessary, to make *New Writing* mirror this latest crucial phase of "a new life breathing through the old", and become the place where whatever imaginative writing came out of the Spanish experience should naturally be published.'[7] Lehmann, too, envisaged commitment to the Spanish cause in a metaphor of pseudo-scientific determinism: 'everything, all our fears, our confused hopes and beliefs, our half-formulated theories and imaginings, veered and converged towards its testing and its opportunity, like steel filings that slide towards a magnet suddenly put near them.'[8] He later concluded, however, that the war 'dragged us all deeper into the morass of ideological conflict, putting to the sharpest test the idealism that the advance of fascism in Central Europe had awakened in us'.[9]

The idea of a test recalls Christopher Isherwood's conviction in *Lions and Shadows* (1938) that his and Auden's generation, which missed the Great War, had to confront its own personal test of manhood, 'a complex of terrors and longings connected with the idea "War"': '"War", in this purely neurotic sense, meant The Test. The Test of your courage, of your maturity, of your sexual prowess: "Are you really a Man?" Subconsciously, I believe, I longed to be subjected to this test; but I also dreaded failure.'[10]

Rupert John Cornford, the scion of a distinguished Cambridge academic family, so named in honour of his parents' friend Rupert Brooke, that earlier poetic casualty of war, joined the Communist Party in 1935. He was killed on the Cordoba front in December 1936. In his major poem of the war, 'Full Moon at Tierz: Before the Storming of Huesca', Cornford spoke explicitly of Spain as the place where 'our testing has begun', a testing which involved not just external action but also what the poem called the 'private battle with my nerves'.[11] His poem 'As Our Might

[5] Stephen Spender, 'Diary', *London Review of Books*, 9 Apr. 1992, 25.

[6] Stephen Spender and John Lehmann (eds.), *Poems for Spain* (London: Hogarth Press, 1939); hereafter abbreviated in the text as *PS*.

[7] John Lehmann, *The Whispering Gallery* (London: Longmans, Green, 1955), 279.

[8] Ibid. 273.   [9] Ibid. 332.

[10] Christopher Isherwood, *Lions and Shadows* (London: Methuen, 1979; 1st pub. 1938), 46.

[11] John Cornford, 'Full Moon at Tierz: Before the Storming of Huesca', in *Understand the Weapon, Understand the Wound: Selected Writings of John Cornford*, ed. Jonathan Galassi (Manchester: Carcanet, 1976), 39.

Lessens',[12] written while he was still at Cambridge, was posthumously transformed by Lehmann into a poem about the Spanish 'Test' when he published its first three sections, along with Margot Heinemann's elegies, in *New Writing IV*. The poem is centrally, if somewhat abstractly, concerned with confronting the test of action, while acknowledging the fear that 'haunts us all', that 'Flesh still is weak'. 'The living thought must put on flesh and blood', it asserts, discovering in action 'New ways of love, new ways of feeling' which give 'nerve and bone and muscle to the word'. Action alone 'creates new ways of living, | Shatters the old ideas of loving'. The intellectual can no longer retreat into introspection, but must 'regain the name of action' by willed engagement with the external, political world. If 'Black over Europe falls the night, | The darkness of our long retreat', he has an existential responsibility for the future: 'what the dawn will bring to light, | Victory or fresh defeat, | Depends on us until the nightmare's over.' This responsibility is all the more overwhelming because of one's recognized weakness and vulnerability. Flesh is weak, bone brittle, the poem argues, but 'Our sinews must be hard as metal'. Strength can be found only in a collective engagement which acknowledges no frontiers of class or nation: 'Our home, our job, is everywhere,' and 'freedom must be won, not bought'. A growing part of 'the Test', however, was the internal struggle to maintain faith in the cause of Spain even though it was increasingly corroded by brutality and *realpolitik* in one's own ranks, a struggle which required deepening complicity in what Auden in *Spain* notoriously designated 'conscious acceptance of guilt in the necessary murder'.[13]

For, as Lehmann observed:

Long before the Nazi–Soviet pact, the last stages of that war had seen the turning of the tide: volunteers and political workers home from Spain told stories of Communist ruthlessness, cynicism and intolerance towards minorities and minority opinion, or any opinion that did not square with the Party line, that we found it difficult to credit at first, but less and less easy to excuse as they accumulated.[14]

Victor Gollancz, the fellow-travelling publisher of the Left Book Club, turned down George Orwell's *Homage to Catalonia* (1938) because of its inadmissible revelations about the Communist suppression of POUM and Anarchist workers in Barcelona in May 1937. Orwell's revelations, those of a 'disillusioned revolutionary', Lehmann later commented, 'broke the last resistance of many who had been desperately holding out against the shock of truth'; but 'it was better late than never to realize that we had been walking beside someone whose features we had never clearly discovered until then; to see after all that we had to choose between D. H. Lawrence's change of heart and a revolution engineered by forces that did not, would never speak the language we recognized as our own'.[15]

---

[12] Cornford, 'As Our Might Lessens', ibid. 32–5.   [13] Auden, *Spain*, 11.
[14] Lehmann, *Whispering Gallery*, 332.   [15] Ibid. 333.

As the war progressed, the contradictions between illusion and reality became more obvious, but they had been inscribed in the discourse of Spain from the start, and lived out in innumerable private battles with the nerves. Auden himself fell silent after returning from Spain in 1937, explaining later, 'Nobody I know who went to Spain during the Civil War who was not a dyed-in-the-wool Stalinist came back with his illusions intact.'[16] By the time his revised 'Spain 1937' appeared in *Another Time* (1940), the Nazi–Soviet Pact of 1939 had permanently redefined the ideological maps of the 1930s. Malcolm Muggeridge's instant obituary for that decade, in 1940, struck the new note of world-weary cynicism:

the International Brigade fought valiantly, attracting to itself the adventurous, the idealistic, and sometimes the despairing, from all parts of the world. These at any rate had managed, to their own satisfaction, to make explicit a conflict they felt was implicit in the circumstances of their lives. Fortunate, perhaps, those who died; not living on to doubt again, and wonder if blood shed in Spain had truly served the cause they had at heart.[17]

'Such doubts came, if at all, later,' Muggeridge observed, for 'While the Spanish Civil War was in progress, it seemed certain that in Spain Good and Evil were at last joined in bloody combat.' The anonymous *TLS* reviewer of *Poems for Spain* in 1939 had already registered the nature of the dilemma:

The tragic conflict in Spain cannot be evaded by the modern poet. Whether or not it compels him to direct expression, it must haunt his mind with painful questions and torture his imagination. For here, as in a theatre but with the appalling realism of indiscriminate slaughter, the discord at the heart of our civilization is nakedly displayed.[18]

But, in his opinion, what 'makes the conflict so peculiarly tragic' is that, 'believing that in supporting the Spanish republic they are defending the very life-principle of civilization', they do so 'with weapons that inevitably deny the very values they wish to affirm'.

Characteristic of such writing, he wrote, was 'a stark impassioned utterance' in which the poet steeled himself for the struggle. John Cornford's poems, for example, 'seem, as Mr Spender remarks, to be written by the will rather than from the sensibility, to be indeed the calculated acts of a fighter determined in vindicating his creed to be "invincible as the strong sun, | Hard as the metal of my gun"'. Herbert Read displays 'the same muscular concentration, enriched by a subtler and maturer sensibility'. The collection was epitomized by 'this quality of clenched brevity'—the adjective eliding the Communist clenched fist salute and the clenched teeth of John Buchan's public school heroes. This emphasis

---

[16] Auden, 'Authority in America', *Griffin*, 4 Mar. 1955, 9.

[17] Malcolm Muggeridge, *The Thirties: 1930–1940 in Great Britain* (London: Hamish Hamilton, 1940), 248–9.

[18] [Hugh l'Anson Fausset], 'Left Wing Poets and Spain', *Times Literary Supplement*, 4 Mar. 1939, 131.

on a muscular physicality is symptomatic of an age in which the clash of masculinities was central to the political discourse. (Heinemann's elegies, praised for being 'particularly poignant for their clear mental focus', obviously unsettled the reviewer's gender stereotypes.) But, he concluded, 'there is little time for the maturing of poetry in minds which are violent and unsettled, and little hope . . . of imagination reaching out to embrace the human reality which unites the combatants'.

SINKING THE EGO

Those private battles with the nerves were not simply struggles to overcome the fear of personal death; they also involved convincing oneself to continue believing in and justifying the cause itself. Communist poets steeled themselves by submitting their allegedly fallible subjectivity to the iron discipline of a party line which, though endlessly mutating, claimed to offer the only accurate interpretation of the 'objective' movement of history. Louis MacNeice's autobiography, *The Strings Are False*, confessed that, in the 1930s, 'The strongest appeal of the Communist party was that it demanded sacrifice; you had to sink your ego.'[19] Spender's autobiography, *World within World*, was candid about the 'subjective' motivations for submitting to a rigid ideology:

Communism seemed to offer a way out of my dilemma. It suggested to me that after all I was not myself. I was simply a product of my bourgeois circumstances. By 'going over to the proletariat' and entering a different set of circumstances I could become another kind of social projection. I would be 'on the side of history' and not 'rejected' by it.[20]

Montagu Slater, the Communist editor of *Left Review*, summed up the orthodox position in his poetic puppet play 'Old Spain', performed by the Binyon Puppets at the Mercury Theatre, London, in July 1938, with music by Benjamin Britten. Three kneeling women in black call from 'an invaded country' to a young man asleep, urging him to 'Think of Spain as the limit of | Your private love'.[21] Fearing that he can bring only loss and failure to their aid, he speaks respectfully of a friend whom 'We called . . . sectarian | Inhuman and abstract, | Too human and not | English enough yet', who, nevertheless, was 'ready | With one more body' to see 'all history | Fulfilled in his gesture' of commitment. Another whose 'English life | Turned sour in his mouth' likewise opted to give his life for Spain, confirming the second woman's assertion that 'A revolutionary | Has a duty to die.' That these are puppets speaking does not seem to be an intended irony.

---

[19] Louis MacNeice, *The Strings Are False: An Unfinished Autobiography* (London: Faber, 1965), 146.
[20] Stephen Spender, *World within World* (London: Hamish Hamilton, 1951), 311.
[21] Montagu Slater, 'Old Spain', in *Peter Grimes and Other Poems* (London: Bodley Head, 1946), 71–5.

In Spain, Auden wrote, 'our thoughts have bodies'.[22] Communist ideology, reinforced by the continuous proximity of death, induced in many poets a way of looking at the self as simply a physical body in a world of material objects, a fulcrum for action rather than a thinking and feeling subject. The handful of poems written by the Irish Communist Charles Donnelly before his death at Jarama in February 1937 exemplifies the literary consequences of sinking the ego. The first-person singular almost disappears from Donnelly's poems. Linguistic tricks learnt from the early Auden reduce the self to the status of an object among objects in a landscape, perceived primarily through the eyes of others. 'The Tolerance of Crows' imagines his own death with inhuman detachment, deploying abstract conceptual nouns which objectify the self in a language of quantity, dispositions, angles of elevation and direction, casting war as a simple question of 'solved | Problems on maps' (PS, 50–1). Renouncing the personal pronoun, the poem reduces the self to a physical body, flesh and nerves, and an impersonal 'mind that cuts | Thought clearly for a waiting purpose', brutally redefining 'love' as a physical function that 'impales' itself on any flesh. Other poems of Donnelly's, published in *Ireland Today*, exhibit the same depersonalizing idiom. 'Heroic Heart' belies the Romantic subjectivity that its title ironically implies, speaking instead of the disinterestedness of a 'plasmic soil | Where things ludicrously take root',[23] where the human exists primarily as matter, dissociated head, muscle, mouth, organs which 'Waste down like wax', jawbones that 'find new way with meats, loins | Raking and blind, new way with women', reducing sex to mechanical process. 'Poem' offers perceptions without a subject, a 'will' that seems to flicker autonomously as 'simple action only', 'Between rebellion as a private study and the public | Defiance'.[24] A figure in a landscape, addressed in the second person as 'you', the self is objectified as a target for the 'sniper [who] may sight you carelessly contoured' on the skyline, or, dead, becomes simply a 'name, subject of all-considered words' in a public discourse of political martyrdom.

Similar strategies are discernible in the poems of the British Communist Tom Wintringham, who survived Spain to fight in the Second World War. 'The Splint' explores being wounded without ever evoking an experiencing 'I', diminishing the subject to an imposture, 'powers | And pretences that are yourself' (PS, 94–5). The self here is dispersed into bodily processes, 'the eyes' | Leap, pulse-beat, thought-flow', so that even 'the jerked wound . . . the pain's throb' are objectified, and 'Hours creep at you like enemy | Patrols'. The nearest the poem comes to acknowledging personal weakness lies, significantly, not in pain but in 'fear of pain, sin | Of giving in'. The will has to be steeled to 'keep mind and mouth shut'. Ego must be sunk in the collectivity, 'These men [who] | Count you a man', whose comradeship validates

---

[22] Auden, *Spain*, 10.

[23] Charles Donnelly, 'Heroic Heart', in Cunningham (ed.), *Penguin Book of Spanish Civil War Verse*, 104.

[24] Donnelly, 'Poem', ibid. 108–9.

the externalized 'you' of the last stanza, the self realized as an other to those others. Wintringham's 'British Medical Unit—Granien' begins at a level of generality, its vocatives addressed to an apparently impersonal other which turns out to be a projection of the self. It moves, in its final stanza, to a first-person plural in which individual identity both finds and loses itself in a shared commitment defined, initially, only in contradistinction to its antagonist: 'Our enemies can praise death and adore death; | For us endurance, the sun' (PS, 41). Identifying with the waning light of the surgeon's electric torch, the enfeebled self then in a sudden reversal finds renewal in a shared allegiance: 'We are allied with | This light.' His 'Barcelona Nerves' likewise begins among objects and events in a 'Dynamo-driven city waiting bombers' (PS, 29–30), to which the collective 'we' comes late. In a world beset on all sides by a repetitive death, life is a matter of 'breaking | By own hardness, and a held hand, out | From fury, frustration, fear', the depersonalized synecdoche of comradeship (unqualified by the possessive adjective 'our') gesturing towards that grammatical collectivity which emerges in the last words of the poem: 'We make what can wreck others into our gaining, | Into our choice.' Collectivized, as in Auden's *Spain*, 'choice' resurrects the submerged ego as a historical agent.

Cornford's 'Full Moon at Tierz' reveals a more complicated, less doctrinaire reality.[25] The image of the full moon rising on friend and foe alike ('the same night falls over Germany', and 'England is silent under the same moon') recalls both Edward Thomas's Great War poem 'The sun used to shine' and Auden's 'Out on the lawn', in both of which the moon shines down on Europe, indifferent to the partisan allegiances that divide the continent. The 'testing' announced by the barren hills of Aragon is not only of courage in the fight with an external fascism. It refers also to an internal moral struggle with one's bourgeois self, to maintain loyalty to the party amidst misgivings about its policies and practice. The dilemma is expressed at length in a long, rambling letter that Cornford wrote to Margot Heinemann in which, speaking of his sense of solidarity with 'German comrades', he nevertheless noted that several of them had left the party 'because they genuinely believe the C.I. [Communist International] has deserted the revolution'. He, however, was 'beginning to find out how much the Party and the International have become flesh and blood of me. Even when I can put forward no rational argument, I feel that to cut adrift from the Party is the beginning of political suicide.'[26]

If he really did have no doubts, of course, cutting adrift would not have crossed his mind. The struggle to discipline the self into the iron resolve of the unquestioning cadre is clearest in the paradoxical union of solidarity and solitude at the heart of the poem: 'Now with my Party, I stand quite alone.' This is the subject steeling itself to a commitment that remains abstract and hortatory, a wish and a prayer, rather than a reality:

---

[25] Cornford, 'Full Moon at Tierz', 38–40.
[26] Cornford, quoted in *Understand the Weapon, Understand the Wound*, 180.

> Then let my private battle with my nerves,
> The fear of pain whose pain survives,
> The love that tears me by the roots,
> The loneliness that claws my guts,
> Fuse in the welded front our fight preserves.

A careless reading might attribute to the poet the closing exhortation to 'Raise the red flag triumphantly | For Communism and for liberty.' But the strident affirmation is in fact imaginary, projected into an uncertain future when 'the workers of all the world' will gather on the plain of Huesca to raise the red flag and 'Swear that our dead fought not in vain' (which recalls the earlier anxious desire to 'prove the agony was not in vain'). The poem's real climax comes at the start of this last stanza, in the acknowledgement that 'Freedom is an easily spoken word | But facts are stubborn things.' The poem is riddled with doubt, detectable in the heretical hesitation about 'what the Seventh Congress said, | If true, if false', in the celebration of 'the impartial beauty of the stars' and the indifference of 'the unfeeling sky', or in the references to the 'Crooked . . . road that we must tread', 'freedom's crooked scars', and the 'innocent mask' concealing that 'our freedom's swaying in the scales'. The poem's harrowingly dramatic power derives from the way it enacts the very processes by which the isolated individual steels himself rhetorically to sink his ego in a 'welded front'. 'What the dawn will bring to light', however, remains genuinely unresolved.

The last poem Cornford wrote, 'A Letter from Aragon', assumes a quite different tone, suggested by the refrain, 'This is a quiet sector of a quiet front', combining the pathos and bathos of personal death. Ruiz, we are told, was buried in a shroud that 'was too small and his washed feet stuck out'; the 'stink of his corpse' came through the 'clean pine boards'.[27] 'Death was not dignified', but unheroic, insignificant: 'You could tell from our listlessness, no one much missed him.' The last words of the poem seem to return to a more familiar rhetoric. But this is deceptive, for they present not the poet's own feelings but those of an Anarchist worker, a fellow patient in the hospital, urging him to ' "Tell the workers of England | This was a war not of our own making" '. As in 'Full Moon at Tierz' the dramatic distancing authenticates, but also relativizes, an appeal that is more plaintive than histrionic.

The lyric understatement of Cornford's 'To Margot Heinemann', published in *New Writing IV*, conceals a similar complexity. The sentiments are strangely conflicted, for the thought of the loved one here is not sustaining, but a debilitating wound, the pain at his side and the shadow that chills his view, tempting the poet to weakness and fear. If he is afraid to lose her, he is also afraid of this fear, as if he needs to subdue that sense of loss to the revolutionary undertaking. The last mile to Huesca is 'The last fence for our pride';[28] but the possessive

---

[27] Cornford, 'A Letter from Aragon', ibid. 41.
[28] Cornford, 'To Margot Heinemann', ibid. 40.

adjective refuses to specify its referent: is it the romantic hubris of the two lovers, or the proper pride of the revolutionary in the 'welded front' he shares with his comrades? The whole poem is a personal address to its dedicatee, and the pronouns 'I' and 'you' are insistently reiterated at strategic points at the start and end of lines, while 'my' recurs six times in sixteen lines; yet it is precisely this personal love which, it appears, has to be renounced. The ambiguity persists into the final appeal not to forget his love, which seems to sink romantic attachment into the greater solidarity of the cause, for 'love' of which he is prepared to lose his life. This ambivalence explains the poem's opening co-option of Marx's thoughts on religion in his 'Contribution to the Critique of Hegel's Philosophy of Right'. Like 'the wretchedness of religion', romantic love is 'at once an expression of and a protest against real wretchedness . . . the sigh of the oppressed creature, the heart of a heartless world and the soul of soulless conditions'. This, presumably, is why such love is negatively conceived as 'the pain at my side', for, as Marx continues, 'The abolition of . . . the illusory happiness of the people is a demand for their real happiness. The call to abandon illusions about their condition is the call to abandon a condition that requires illusions.'[29] By implication, the illusory happiness of romantic attachment, which brings with it grief and separation, must be subsumed into the authentic mutuality of a transformed social reality.

ANTI-HEROIC NOTES

For John Lehmann, writing on 'The Influence of Spain' in 1939, the value of Stephen Spender's earlier Civil War poems was that 'they struck an independent, anti-heroic note' in many ways representative of those 'who felt that the adjustment of original enthusiasm to the realities of modern warfare and modern political struggle was a much more complex and painful process than was generally admitted, while their loyalty to the anti-fascist cause never wavered'.[30]

Spender's 'Thoughts during an Air Raid' sets the pattern for most of the 'Poems about the Spanish Civil War' in Part 4 of his 1955 *Collected Poems*. A kind of proleptic elegy for himself, it attempts to imagine his own death from the outside, as seen by others, as impersonally as he must view other people's deaths. The poem's depersonalizing of selfhood is reinforced in the 1955 version by the substitution, for the repeated 'I' of Spender's earlier version in *The Still Centre* (1939), of the impersonal pronoun 'one', except in a single dismissive reference to 'this thing

[29] Karl Marx, 'A Contribution to the Critique of Hegel's "Philosophy of Right": Introduction', in *Critique of Hegel's 'Philosophy of Right'*, trans. Annette Jolin and Joseph O'Malley, ed. Joseph O'Malley (Cambridge: Cambridge University Press, 1970), 131.
[30] Lehmann, 'The Influence of Spain', in *New Writing in England* (New York: Critics Group Press, 1939), 20.

"I"...propped up' in bed.[31] 'Of course', the poem begins, 'the entire effort is to put oneself | Outside the ordinary range | Of what are called statistics,' making the idea of a bomb diving right through this bed an 'obscene' thought. A hundred people may be killed in the outer suburbs, but 'one' carries on, unable really to imagine a world from which one is absent, though 'there are many | For whom one's loss would illustrate | The "impersonal" use indeed'. In a world dispersed into isolated, self-absorbed individuals, where 'no one suffer[s] | for his neighbour', the horror is postponed for each until, in an artful sudden summoning of the third-person pronoun, death 'settles on him', reducing the subject to object status.

Spender's Civil War poems are haunted by the bullet's arbitrary power instantaneously to translate a living subject into a dead object. 'The Coward' deploys the myth of Narcissus transformed into a flower 'which is a wound', to suggest that, in death, there is little difference between 'the heroes' sunset fire' and this one who 'died, not like a soldier' but in 'rings of terror'.[32] For hero and coward alike, 'All the bright visions in one instant | Changed to this fixed continual present.' 'A Stopwatch and an Ordnance Map' sees time and space, history and geography, converge to fix for ever at five o'clock the 'blank time' of this man's death under the olive trees, so that he now stays 'faithfully in that place', split from his living comrade by the divisive bullet which 'Open[s] wide the distances | Of his final loneliness'.[33]

'Ultima Ratio Regum' likewise speaks of 'the boy lying dead under the olive trees' as 'too young and too silly' to have been 'notable to [the] important eye' of the guns, 'a better target for a kiss' who 'too lightly...threw down his cap | One day' (PS, 42–3). The casual erasure of this life as 'intangible as a Stock Exchange rumour' makes one ask why, when only one bullet in a thousand kills a man, this youth was so arbitrarily chosen; ask, too, whether so much expenditure could be justified 'On the death of one so young, and so silly'. Spender's poem sets the decent silliness of a life 'valueless | In terms of employment' against the indecency of systems that define human beings in economic terms, whether capitalist or Communist.

In a snide footnote, Malcolm Muggeridge claimed that Spender, 'in the course of a poem, remarked that in Spain there was a bullet addressed to him. If so, it was not delivered.'[34] An insert slip in the book adds that 'Mr. Stephen Spender wishes to deny the accuracy of the author's statement regarding him.' Muggeridge's remark involves a wilful misreading of the opening three lines of the poem 'War Photograph', published in The New Statesman in June 1937, as autobiography rather than dramatic monologue:

---

[31] Stephen Spender, 'Thoughts during an Air Raid', in Collected Poems 1928–1953 (London: Faber, 1955), 96.

[32] Spender, 'The Coward', ibid. 102–3.

[33] Spender, 'A Stopwatch and an Ordnance Map', ibid. 100.   [34] Muggeridge, Thirties, 248.

> I have an appointment with a bullet
> At seventeen hours less a split second
> —And I shall not be late.[35]

Perhaps in response to Muggeridge's mockery, Spender omitted this stanza from *The Still Centre* and subsequent printings of the poem, continuing to revise the text until it was finally reduced to three three-line stanzas under the title 'In No Man's Land' in the 1955 *Collected Poems*, before being omitted entirely from the 1985 *Collected Poems*.[36] The poem alludes to Robert Capa's widely distributed photograph 'Loyalist Militiaman at the Moment of Death, Cerro Muriano, September 5, 1936', snapped as the soldier leapt from his trench, unaware that within a split second he would be dead. The instant that 'lurks | With its metal fang planned for my heart | When the finger tugs and the clock strikes' is both the trigger of the gun that kills him and the lens of the camera that 'shoots' this death. The place 'Where inch and instant cross' is the real time and place of death and also the 'flat and severed second on which time looks' of the photograph itself, which will remain unchanged throughout the coming years, 'As faithful to the vanished moment's violence | As love fixed to one day in vain'. The 'No Man's Land' of the poem's final version is both that terrain between warring camps where men die in earnest, and the perpetually frozen chronotope of the 'War Photograph' itself, where the doomed man endlessly 'launches his rigid continual present', the instant before death fixed for ever by the camera. It is the photograph, not the dead man, that speaks of an appointment with a bullet always a 'split second' in the future, at that five o'clock in the afternoon when the clock strikes, completing a mechanical trinity with rifle trigger and camera shutter. For this 'No Man's Land' is, too, the unbridgeable gap between the actual life, for ever not yet dead, and the photographic image of it. The actual remains of Federico Borrell García[37] are lost to history on the rocky hillside. His only surviving 'corpse [is] a photograph taken by fate'.

Confronting the intimacy of death, Spender's poem exhibits a cool scrupulous impersonality effected in part by the echoes of Keats's 'Ode on a Grecian Urn', which also reflected, at a second aesthetic remove, on the way in which a work of art translates the lives of wasting generations into an abiding image, the photograph's 'I shall remain' directly recalling the Ode's 'Thou shalt remain, in midst of other woe'.[38] But the site of this death suggests also a less consoling idea of art's

---

[35] Spender, 'War Photograph', repr. in Cunningham (ed.), *Penguin Book of Spanish Civil War Verse*, 413.

[36] Curiously, Valentine Cunningham's indispensable *Penguin Book of Spanish Civil War Verse*, in which most of the poems discussed in this essay can be found, prints both texts without noting their relation.

[37] Richard Whelan, 'Proving that Robert Capa's "Falling Soldier" is Genuine: A Detective Story', <http://www.pbs.org/wnet/americanmasters/database/capa_r.html>; see also Richard Whelan, 'Robert Capa's Falling Soldier: A Detective Story', *Aperture*, 166 (Spring 2002), 48–55.

[38] John Keats, 'Ode on a Grecian Urn', in *The Complete Poems*, ed. John Barnard (Harmondsworth: Penguin, 1973), 345.

depersonalizations, recalling the 'cold hillside' on which Keats's knight-at-arms lies dying in 'La Belle Dame sans Merci'.[39]

One of Spender's most powerful poems, 'Fall of a City', generalizes death and defeat in the vision of an urban wilderness emptied of its inhabitants, the once potent rhetorics which inflamed its passions now reduced to torn posters, scattered leaflets, 'mutilated, destroyed, or run in rain, | Their words blotted out with tears', the badges and salutes torn from lapels and hands, 'thrown away with human sacks they wore', the names of heroes who once enthralled crowded public halls, 'FOX and LORCA claimed as history on the walls', surviving now only as 'deleted' graffiti (PS, 85–6). Lehmann commended 'Fall of a City' for exploring 'the special horror of a modern warfare between opposing ideologies, when a whole population must in a few hours . . . switch over to the hypocrisy of an imposed creed to protect themselves from annihilation'.[40] He praised another poem, 'At Castellon', for 'vividness of imagery and depth of feeling' and 'a simplicity . . . rare in [Spender's] work since the early poems'. 'At Castellon', unusually for Spender, presents a narrative without subjective interior. This account of being passed on at night from village to village to ultimate safety confines itself to external things, the glint of light reflected in the unlit headlamps of mysterious parked trucks, the 'small false ember' of cigarettes in the dark, their smokers anonymous, unseen (PS, 30–1). Even the 'working man' awoken to guide them is no more than eyes that gleam and relapse into their dream. His torch is a 'gliding star of light', as if conducting them through the underworld, while, on the road behind them, bombers unload their 'Cargoes of iron and of fire | To delete . . . | The will of those who dared to move | From the furrow, their life's groove'. The poem, that is, translates the moment into an ancient mythic pattern, reinforced by casting the bombers as 'winged black roaring fates', brutally generalizing the deaths of real, unknown people to the same clinical verb—'delete'—deployed in 'Fall of a City'.

'Two Armies' likewise creates a generalized allegory of warfare on a frozen plain where 'No one is given leave | On either side, except the dead, and wounded' and the combatants are held to their commitment now only by a 'discipline drilled once in an iron school' which holds them at gunpoint.[41] Ideology has evaporated into frosty breath on these infernal plains, and now, nervous and cold, 'each man hates the cause and distant words | That brought him here' more than the enemy, as, between the sleeping armies, 'a common suffering | Whitens the air with breath and makes both one | As though these enemies slept in each other's arms'.

The poem calls up echoes familiar to a generation reared on the poetry of the Great War, in particular, Wilfred Owen's 'Anthem for Doomed Youth' (as in its

---

[39] Keats, 'La Belle Dame sans Merci', ibid. 335.   [40] Lehmann, 'Influence of Spain', 21.
[41] Spender, 'Two Armies', in Collected Poems 1928–1953, 97–8.

reference to 'The inexhaustible anger of the guns'[42]) and 'Strange Meeting'. In his *London Review of Books* memoir, Spender wrote that the latter 'imagines a conversation between an English and a German soldier, soon after which both are dead, each one having killed the other. Their dialogue is more that of lovers than of enemies.'[43] The recurring homoerotic impulse of Spender's Civil War poems can be explained by the reason he gives in this memoir for his own generation's fascination with the young men of the Weimar Republic: 'Between individuals, the German and the English rapprochement had a strongly sexual aspect, perhaps because the public murder of nation by nation which is war may be secretly compensated for by attraction between individuals of each side—an assertion of the private love which lies at a deeper level of truth than the public hatred.' Far from being the robotic machinery of violence, as in Wintringham and Donnelly, corporeality is reborn in Spender's Civil War elegies which are also love poems, merging Eros and Thanatos, as the utopian site of human renewal and the transcendence of ideology, figured in the carnal, sexual body which is 'a better target for a kiss'.[44]

LANDSCAPES OF ACHERON

The vulnerability of the subject, whose living breathing body can so easily be translated into a lifeless object, animates Spender's 'Port Bou', first published in *New Writing* in Autumn 1938. The poet's 'I' intrudes obsessively throughout the poem, exhibiting the same fear of personal death that infects 'Thoughts during an Air Raid'. If, with an excess of solipsism, he casts himself as 'the exact centre' of this stage-scenery background, he feels for this very reason 'solitary as a target' for the guns that open up across the harbour mouth, not reassured by the thought that it is only practice (*PS*, 89–90). Escape from encirclement is a motif of the poem. The harbour, embracing but not enclosing the sea, is compared to a small coiled animal in a child's arms, staring out through the gap to 'outer freedom in animal air', and both images become implicit figures of his own state of mind, his circling arms resting on a newspaper, fearful of the war beyond the 'surrounding' (in *New Writing*, 'circling') hills. 'Embrace' is here a deeply ambivalent word, combining, like the child clutching the animal that wants to escape, both security and imprisonment. So, too, in the 'warm' but 'waving flag-like' faces of the militiamen, 'the war finds

---

[42] Wilfred Owen, 'Anthem for Doomed Youth', in *The Complete Poems and Fragments*, i: *The Poems*, ed. Jon Stallworthy (London: Chatto & Windus, Hogarth Press, and Oxford University Press, 1983), 99.

[43] Spender, 'Diary', *London Review of Books*, 9 Apr. 1992, 25.

[44] Were it not that *Collected Poems 1928–1953* included 'The Room above the Square' among 'Poems about the Spanish Civil War', it might seem a merely personal lyric of separation and abandonment by a lover who once 'stayed in the high room for me', now departed for 'sunbright peninsulas of the sword', as 'Torn like leaves through Europe is the peace | That through us flowed' (p. 95).

peace', in an image of comradeship which nevertheless fails to console a mind that is 'paper where dust and ink falls'.

Spender can envisage the larger war only in mythic, abstract terms. Port Bou, just inside the Spanish frontier, the point of transit between a France at peace and the war zone, becomes thus a liminal space internalizing frontiers simultaneously real and symbolic. The mythology of passage, picking up the familiar Thirties trope of crossing the frontier, is apparent in his *New Writing* report a year earlier, 'Spain Invites the World's Writers':

Port Bou itself makes the strangest impression . . . impressing us with that peculiar feeling of a war, that the people are not so much living in the town as haunting it; they are spirits obsessed by their idea, easily transferable to some other scene of war; and their relation to their homes, their material surroundings, is very slight.[45]

'Haunting' is the significant word: the living are already, it seems, recruits to the underworld of death, to which Port Bou is the point of entry.

As might be expected, the motif of a descent into the underworld recurs in the poetry of the Civil War. Rex Warner's 'Storm and War' speaks of the 'faceless ghosts' of those 'hurled away by war' passing in procession through the mountain valleys, observing, like Spender's 'The Coward', that 'bully, hero, saint or simpleton' are all alike 'indifferently rolled' in the storm.[46] Not referring to the frontier of the Pyrenees by name, Warner deploys a generalizing narrative to transcend localized and partisan rhetoric. Sylvia Townsend Warner achieves a similar effect by combining classical allusion with a cool clinical distance which depopulates the landscape she depicts. Her 'Waiting at Cerbere' [*sic*], set in the village of Cerbère, just inside the French frontier opposite Port Bou, like Spender's poem, merges actual and symbolic border crossings, describing what may be either a literal or a metaphorical village of the dead on the opposite hillside, where no one stirs in the streets or comes out of the dark doorways, and only the cicada strums at the tavern of the Black Cross. Below the headland, only the foam of the sea suggests a living force, rising and falling 'Like a quickened breath' (*PS*, 86–7), while a deserted road zigzags to the frontier. The name of the village recalls Cerberus, the dog which in classical mythology guards the entrance to the underworld. The near-Imagist stasis of the poem suggests a liminality that eludes the partisanship of life and death, crossing the frontier or descending into Hades. Her 'Benicasim', about a brief pause at a rest-home for the war-wounded, develops the classical motif. The landscape of semi-tropical trees and cactus, bright villas perched like macaws, and an 'air heavy with sun and salt and colour', predominates over both the transient observers and the equally transient wounded, seen in the distance wandering along the beach, 'the risen-from-the-dead', being repaired to return to battle (*PS*, 87–8). This place of 'the recaptured sun' affords only a narrow space for recovery. Inland

---

[45] Spender, 'Spain Invites the World's Writers', 245.
[46] Warner, 'Storm and War', in *Poems* (London: Boriswood, 1937), 46.

are the mountains where death waits, 'close at hand', to be coped with only by mythologizing experience, evoking the river the dead have to cross in Greek myth: 'And it seems to me we have come | Into a bright-painted landscape of Acheron.'

With the notable exceptions of George Barker's surrealist histrionics in *Calamiterror* (1937) and *Elegy on Spain* (1939), and the self-aggrandizing vitriolic satire of the Franco-supporting Roy Campbell's *Flowering Rifle: A Poem from the Battlefield of Spain* (1939), most poetry of the non-combatant but committed observer dwelt on the pathos of civilian death with ostensibly dispassionate deliberation. Herbert Read's 'A Song for the Spanish Anarchists', for example, is a succinct, impersonal lyric celebrating a world where 'no man is a slave' (*PS*, 93); less abstract and remote is 'The Heart Conscripted', which speaks of the deaths of 'Lorca . . . killed, singing' and Ralph Fox, 'who was my friend', singers in 'the song which has no end' (*PS*, 39–40). His 'Bombing Casualties in Spain', however, turns dispassion to harrowing effect, contrasting the rosiness of dolls' faces with the 'wanly waxen' pallor of dead children, 'their eyes not glass but gleaming gristle', 'laid out in ranks | like paper lanterns', their human corporeality slowly fading into the inhuman thinness of wasps' nests, 'extinct in the dry morning air' (*PS*, 41–2).

Edgell Rickword's impassioned indictment, 'To the Wife of A Non-Intervention Statesman', warns that the Western democracies' non-intervention in Spain prepares the way for a future where 'In Hitler's frantic mental haze | already Hull and Cardiff blaze', the bombing of Guernica prefiguring that of 'Oxford's dreaming spires' and 'Paul's grey dome' (*PS*, 74–7). Cecil Day Lewis's 'Bombers' closes with a similar message, but works towards it through the premonition of an approaching air raid, heard vaguely at first, by a heart preoccupied with other things, as no more than 'A deep in air buried grain of sound' which 'Starts and grows, as yet unwarning', until, still only imagining loss, the bombers arrive, 'carrying harm' (*PS*, 82–3). The description of their approach grows and expands like the 'grain of sound' until it overwhelms the poem, casting bombers whose wombs 'ache to be rid of death' as the 'heavy angels' of a new and brutal Annunciation. Artfully interweaving internal rhymes and half-rhymes which undercut with unexpected connections the narrative's syntagmatic thrust, the poem amplifies a continuous analogy between the 'grain of sound' and the 'seed that grows for ruin, | The iron embryo conceived in fear' which sooner or later will be 'delivered' (picking up the ambiguity of 'carrying'). The vocative final stanza calls on the British public, for whom Spain has been a faraway country, to 'Choose between your child and this fatal embryo.' Like an Old Testament prophet, it casts this choice in the form of a question, the internal rhymes of 'guilt' and 'built', 'want' and 'haunt', underlining the personal immediacy, the macabre pun on bearing arms and bearing children adding insult to the rebuke:

> Shall your guilt bear arms, and the children you want
> Be condemned to die by the powers you paid for
> And haunt the houses you never built?

'Newsreel', which appears only a page after this in *Overtures to Death*, deploys an unexpected imagery of conception and gestation to rebuke those movie-goers who leave history at the door of the cinema's 'dream-house'.[47] The silver screen converts the public sphere into the banal stereotypes of the newsreel, so that even footage of the 'iron seed' of big guns, 'erected | To plant death in your world's soft womb', fails to trouble a 'watery, womb-deep sleep'. The conclusion spells out the import of these somewhat strained Freudianisms, insisting that such supposed 'exotics' will soon

> Grow nearer home—and out of the dream-house stumbling
> One night into a strangling air and the flung
> Rags of children and thunder of stone niagaras tumbling,
> You'll know you slept too long.

The sense that it will all eventually come home to roost in our own sheltered island is, perhaps, the most pervasive of poetic conventions in the later 1930s. Louis MacNeice first considered Spain in his 'Eclogue from Iceland', the country he was visiting with Auden in 1936 when they heard the news of Franco's insurrection. In that poem, the character Craven reports that 'This Easter I was in Spain, before the Civil War, | Gobbling the tripper's treats, the local colour,' but 'The comedy of the bootblacks in the cafés', the architecture, bullfights, and the 'scrawled hammer and sickle' were to him 'all copy—impenetrable surface', so that he 'did not look for the sneer beneath the surface'.[48] MacNeice's *Autumn Journal*, written in the last months of 1938, and published in May 1939 after the fall of the Spanish Republic, certainly penetrates that surface, though critics have overlooked the extent to which what 'Spain' signified in this period informs the whole narrative, and not just the section in which it is most obviously addressed. Cunningham, for example, reprints section VI of the poem but not the two closing sections (XXIII and XXIV), in which a return to Barcelona in December 1939, as the Republic faltered and died, prompts reflections on what this implies for the whole future of Europe.

Beginning with personal delight in the sunshine, exclaiming that 'To-day was a beautiful day', section V of the poem homes in at once on newspaper posters urgently headlining Hitler and 'the dull refrain of the caption "War" | Buzzing around us'.[49] Admitting to being one of those who, in Day Lewis's phrase, had slept too long, MacNeice here acknowledges that now 'The bloody frontier | Converges on our beds.' We can't, he says (recalling Christ's moment of weakness and vacillation in Gethsemane), ask at this hour for the cup to be taken from us, 'Having helped to fill it ourselves'. The section closes, however, by restoring that opening 'To-day' to the anxious public world. The insomniac poet finally drifts off as dawn

---

[47] C. Day Lewis, 'Newsreel', in *Overtures to Death* (London: Jonathan Cape, 1938), 17.
[48] Louis MacNeice, 'Eclogue from Iceland', in W. H. Auden and Louis MacNeice, *Letters from Iceland* (London: Faber, 1937), 126–7.
[49] MacNeice, *Autumn Journal*, in *Collected Poems*, ed. Peter McDonald (London: Faber, 2007), 109.

breaks, wondering 'what the morning | Paper will say . . . for the morning already | Is with us, the day is to-day'.[50] The words recall, inevitably, Auden's reiterated formula in *Spain*, 'to-day the struggle', but also Cornford's concern with 'What the dawn will bring to light'. The section thus prepares the moral ground for the words with which section VI opens: 'And I remember Spain | At Easter ripe as an egg for revolt and ruin.'[51] Section VI, however, recalls this pre-war visit to Spain not in affirmation of commitment but as one more instance of liberal backsliding and evasion. Annoyed by the rain, noticing only obliquely the 'writings on the walls— | Hammer and sickle, Boicot, Viva, Muerra', and the cripples and children begging, all in the insistent 'And . . . And' of childish narration, it admits, 'that, we thought to ourselves, was not our business; | All that the tripper wants is the *status quo* | Cut and dried for trippers'. He departed for home not remembering but wilfully 'forgetting Spain, not realising'

> That Spain would soon denote
>   Our griefs, our aspirations;
> Not knowing that our blunt
>   Ideals would find their whetstone, that our spirit
> Would find its frontier on the Spanish front,
>   Its body in a rag-tag army.[52]

Less histrionically than in Auden's *Spain*, here thoughts have bodies, the menacing shapes of the English fever become precise and alive, and private friendship blossoms into a people's army. The penultimate section XXIII of the poem recounts a return to a different Spain, in the last days of December 1938, leaving London snow and personal problems behind. Previously beset by nostalgia, the poem now, in the depth of the Republic's impending defeat, speaks of hope, the future. As the road ran downhill into Spain, it reports, the issues were plain:

> We have come to a place in space where shortly
>   All of us may be forced to camp in time:
> The slender searchlights climb,
>   Our sins will find us out, even our sins of omission.[53]

Despite the desolation of Barcelona, the people still manage to laugh, revealing that life is more than 'merely the bare | Permission to keep alive and receive orders', and humanity 'more than a mechanism | To be oiled and greased and for ever unaware | Of the work it is turning out'.[54] MacNeice, who wrote, in a sceptical aside on Communist pretensions in a prefatory note to the sequence, that 'I refuse to be "objective" or clear-cut at the cost of honesty', nevertheless sees in the embattled Republic evidence that 'Here at least the soul has found its voice'. Just as section V had called up echoes of Christ's momentary doubts in Gethsemane, on the eve

---

[50] MacNeice, *Autumn Journal*, 111.
[51] Ibid. 112.   [52] Ibid. 114.   [53] Ibid. 158.   [54] Ibid. 159.

of the Crucifixion, so section XXIII recalls that moment of backsliding betrayal after it, asking himself whether the cocks crowing in the new year constitute 'the heart's reveille or the sour | Reproach of Simon Peter'. [55] Finding his own 'niggling equivocations' shamed by the 'matter-of-fact faith and courage' of these 'stubborn heirs of freedom', he struggles to come to terms with the disillusion of which Lehmann and Muggeridge write, contrasting 'We who play for safety' with 'these people [who] contain truth, whatever | Their nominal façade', praying to 'make their half-truth true'.[56] MacNeice sees that commitment to what the *Times Literary Supplement* reviewer calls 'the human reality' does not preclude, but may even demand, partisanship. The section ends with an aubade which is also a challenge like that which Peter faced: 'the cock crowing in Barcelona'. These 'antinomies in which we live' are then resolved in the poem's concluding section XXIV, which announces that 'night's cocoon will open | When day begins'. The aubade is also a cradle-song, prefiguring an 'earnest of the real | Future when we wake', the prospect of 'a possible land | Not of sleepwalkers, not of angry puppets', where 'the individual, no longer squandered | In self-assertion, works with the rest'.[57] Though 'The New Year comes with bombs', MacNeice's utopian vision, in a commitment beyond doubt and credulity, transforms the plangent cadences of Auden's *Spain*, insisting that, still, 'the choice is yours to make, | The mortgage not foreclosed, the offer open'. A liberal-humanist socialist never deluded by the grandiloquent lies of Stalinism, MacNeice the classical scholar rejects the melancholy analogies with the landscapes of Acheron with which History consoles the defeated, recalling instead another historic turning-point. The running water 'To-morrow to be crossed' is 'no river of the dead or Lethe'. The defeat of the Republic heralds yet another triumph for Hitler and fascism; but the defiance of its defenders provides a model for the greater struggle yet to come, for 'To-night we sleep | On the banks of Rubicon.'[58] *Autumn Journal*, that is, far from being an autumnal lament for a world that has been lost, looks toward a future yet to be won. And that, perhaps, is the abiding significance of Spain.

---

[55] Ibid. 159.   [56] Ibid. 161.   [57] Ibid. 163.   [58] Ibid. 164.

This essay is part of a research project supported by the Spanish Ministry of Science and Technology (BFF 2002–02842), the Comunidad Autonoma of La Rioja (ANGI–2002/05), and the University of La Rioja, Logroño, Spain (API–02–35).

....

CHAPTER 14

UNWRITING THE GOOD FIGHT: W. H. AUDEN'S 'SPAIN 1937'

....

RAINER EMIG

If one considers the fact that war has been offering literature one of its most fertile subjects, and that it has accompanied the history of poetry from the heyday of the epic, it is remarkable that few literary texts, and few poems, seriously engage with the difficulties of writing about war. Auden's 'Spain 1937' is one of the exceptions. It is exceptional not only in showing an awareness of the problems of its subject, but also because it translates this awareness into its own structures—to the extent of endangering its form and meaning. It is no coincidence that the poem was rewritten and ultimately withdrawn from the Auden canon. The present essay will attempt to show why these revisions represent more than mere biographical and ideological turns in the *œuvre* of one of the most challenging poets writing in English in the twentieth century. 'Spain 1937'—this is the gist of what is to follow—represents an attempt to write and unwrite war at the same time, and the price that has to be paid for the endeavour.

War poems generally fall into two categories. They either try to depict the perceived reality of war, the experience of boredom, fatigue, anxiety, fear, suffering, but also discipline, comradeship, bravery, heroism, and relief. Or they assess war retrospectively (or, more rarely, prospectively) as a historical event, inevitable or avoidable development, tragedy, or triumph. The poets of the First World War, the important literary models for Auden, did both. But what does one do with a war that is only just about to become one, the civil strife in Spain that was at the same time an internecine Spanish struggle for political supremacy and an international conflict that attracted fighters from all over the world, and many renowned ones from Britain? The international dimension of what could easily have been a minor military coup in a then backward region of the world emerged out of the symbolic view that the world outside Spain took of the conflict. To many, right- and left-wingers alike, it seemed to spell the beginning of the final polarization of world politics into fascism versus communism. To many British, and to many British writers and artists, it appeared to put an end to the frustrating stalemate of British politics, which, after a traumatic General Strike in 1926, had veered neither towards the Left nor towards the Right, but remained stuck in what appeared like middle-class complacency.

Auden, together with many others, now felt the need to rally round his new flag of communism by not merely writing about the Spanish conflict from afar, but by actually being there and becoming involved in it. It is one of many ironies in Auden's life that what had started out as an attempt at action once again quickly led into writing. Useless as an ambulance driver, Auden's services to the Republican cause outside Valencia from mid-January to March 1937 were quickly utilized for propaganda. Indeed, his very departure for Spain made it into the news pages of the British press.[1] Recruited for radio broadcasts promoting the Republican cause (he also wrote articles for the *New Statesman*), he nonetheless quickly became disaffected with the situation and returned to Britain after only a few weeks, having initially intended to stay until summer.[2]

'Spain 1937', quickly published by Faber in pamphlet form (as *Spain*) in May 1937 with the explicit aim of raising money for Medical Aid for Spain,[3] is thus from the start in an ambivalent position as a statement on the Spanish Civil War. It hovers between specific propagandistic aim, general assessment, and personal note. This complexity, if not confusion, has baffled not only its readers and critics.[4] It also caused Auden's own disaffection with the text and its subsequent disappearance from the Auden canon. In what follows I will try to analyse in some depth how contradictions and complexities emerge in the text—and whether they may be regarded only as flaws or also as interventions in a debate on war that emerges from the specific Spanish situation, but has implications beyond it.

The first aspect that strikes the reader of Auden's poem is the surprising specificity of its title. Its exact location in space and time is understandable in a poem that aims

---

[1] See Humphrey Carpenter, *W. H. Auden: A Biography* (London: Allen & Unwin, 1981), 208: '"FAMOUS POET TO DRIVE AMBULANCE IN SPAIN", announced the *Daily Worker* on 12 January 1937.'

[2] Carpenter states that Auden was already on his way back to Britain on 2 Mar. 1937 (ibid. 215).

[3] See Rupert Davenport-Hines, *Auden* (London: Minerva, 1996), 166.

[4] Even the apologetic Edward Mendelson calls the poem an example of 'irresolution, set in a political context' with 'damaging consequences' (Edward Mendelson, *Early Auden* (London: Faber, 1981), 79).

partly at a propagandistic statement on a topical conflict, yet it contrasts markedly with the common generalizations in titles of Auden's early poems ('A Bride in the 30s' would already be a quite specific one). It also stands in opposition to the poem's introduction, which is neither about Spain nor about the 1930s, but rather irritatingly covers nothing less than the history of civilization. The initial statement is as brusque as it is tautological and hyperbolical at the same time: 'Yesterday all the past' is as plausible as it is a double exaggeration.[5] The comprehensiveness of the claim declares nothing less than the end of history—or at least its relegation to the storehouse of cultural memory. This would divorce the present from its influence and make it in fact ahistorical.

That this is by no means the case is already indicated by its accompanying statement, which, rather obscurely, alludes to the language of size. Constructions of the type 'the x of y' are common in Auden's early poems, and are often used for sheer preciousness and with vague connotations ('the varied action of the blood' from the 1929 poem 'Watch any day his nonchalant pauses' is such an example[6]). Yet here this language of size is identified as 'Spreading', and therefore not containable, as the preceding statement makes the past appear. Further emphasis is placed on 'Spreading' by making it one of only two verbs in the initial six stanzas, which are identified as related by their opening words 'Yesterday' (it opens the first line of five of them, forms the closing line of three, and appears twice in all six). The only other verb in these six four-line stanzas (which are, like all twenty-three stanzas of the poem, organized as two five-stress lines interspersed with a three-stress line followed by another five-stress one) is 'eyeing'. It too is a participle, thus stressing duration and continuation rather than momentary action. Its significance will be discussed below.

Language spreads, while it simultaneously demarcates—size as much as territory. The China to which the language of size spreads is, of course, an anachronism and did not exist at the time of counting-frame and cromlech (cromlechs being prehistoric standing stones). Although the Chinese detour also has topical significance (the Sino–Japanese war was another prelude to the Second World War and one that Auden, together with Isherwood, would soon inspect at close range for their joint project *Journey to a War* only one year later, in 1938), the gap between specific moment and general history remains. That history is indeed in the sights of the poem from the start, however, is already implied in its specific title, which—through its tellingly unpoetic form—can also be read as an entry in a history book, another structure through which continuity is turned into an inventory.

History in Auden is never an easy subject, and it does not take until the later poems 'Homage to Clio', 'Makers of History', and 'The History of Truth' for the

---

[5] W. H. Auden, 'Spain 1937', in *The English Auden: Poems, Essays, and Dramatic Writings 1927–1939*, ed. Edward Mendelson (London: Faber, 1977), 210–12.

[6] Auden, 'Watch any day his nonchalant pauses', ibid. 31.

reader to understand that it is never an unproblematically given array of facts.[7] Neither is it an ontological or teleological force of the Hegelian kind, a sort of spirit driving humankind along. In Auden's poems history is always at least partly a construction, even a poetic one. Yet it is a construction with real consequences for those who construct it and those who are constructed by it. As I have argued in greater detail elsewhere,[8] it resembles a concept formulated in the 1960s and 1970s by the French philosopher Michel Foucault: that of a discursive formation. By this he means systems constructed by humans as integral parts of their culture, which, in turn, construct more systems, until, in the final consequence, they appear inevitable, 'natural', and self-determined.[9] 'Spain 1937' shows both the construction of such systems, or 'truths' as Foucault somewhat provocatively calls them, and their eventual effect as almost metaphysical Truths with a capital 'T', now seemingly removed from, if not in control of, human existence.

The initial stanzas of 'Spain 1937' engage in a pronouncedly pedestrian construction of history through pedantic references to its factual and material frameworks and requisites, such as trade routes, measuring instruments, and defence works. They also play jokingly with the ambivalence of material reality and anecdote, science and superstition. Reckoning with shadows might as much refer to sundials as it could refer to the story of Diogenes asking Alexander the Great to stop blocking the sun. Assessing insurance by cards sounds surprisingly contemporary, but appears to refer to fortune-telling.

Yet into this sometimes playful and sometimes serious materialist or at least largely factual framework, the poem already inserts 'Truths', the Western teleological conception of history as moving from antiquity via the Middle Ages to the Enlightenment, the Industrial Revolution and even colonialism and imperialism. What hovers over all these developments (and what is granted the only other verb in the introductory section) in the manner of the many airmen in Auden's early poems, with their detached and simultaneously endangered and dangerous overviews, is a fortress.[10] As a military structure, it remains the poem's only overt reference to conflict, until in the fourth stanza a trial and feuds appear, and eventually the term 'struggle', which then takes over the poem together with its contrastive epithet (contrastive to 'yesterday'), 'to-day'. Its equally important, though more submerged, function is that of doubling the perspective the poem has exhibited so far. Significantly, the text lacks a lyrical I, and instead presents its overview of the

---

[7] Stan Smith goes as far as regarding 'Homage to Clio' as a belated response to 'Spain 1937' (Stan Smith, *W. H. Auden* (Oxford: Blackwell, 1985), 171).

[8] See Rainer Emig, *W. H. Auden: Towards a Postmodern Poetics* (London: Macmillan, 2000), 92–3 and 111–14.

[9] See Michel Foucault, *The Archaeology of Knowledge*, trans. A. M. Sheridan Smith (London: Tavistock, 1974); and *idem*, *The Order of Things*, trans. A. M. Sheridan Smith (London: Tavistock, 1974).

[10] Carpenter calls the perspective 'hawk-like, Hardyesque' in *W. H. Auden*, 217.

history of civilization from an all-seeing elevated perspective, seemingly untouched by events and changes, yet in a position of authority that is here, for the first time, also marked as a threat. The supposedly neutral perspective of impersonal universal history contains at least the potential for violence, while it may at the same time be a defence.

It is telling that the first occurrence of words related to struggle happens in the context of religion, first of heresy, then of tavern feuds concerning theology. Into this idea of history as a line of events, 'Spain 1937' places a turning-point in the guise of the Reformation. This is not merely a personal reference point for Auden's lifelong struggle with his religious affiliation. It also provides an interesting analogy to the Spanish Civil War as a supposed turning-point in the (then still budding) history of the twentieth century, a turning-point towards either communism or fascism, as many—including Auden—regarded it.[11] Nonetheless, religion also means religion, even and particularly in the context of Auden's view of the Spanish conflict. It is well documented that he was shocked by the aggression towards the Church, its representatives and symbols, a reaction that strongly attested to his ultimately bourgeois world-view, in which the Establishment (as the typically British conglomerate of politics, patriotism, and Anglicanism) also stood for certainty.[12] In Spain, however, the (Catholic) Church had more visibly and blatantly than in Britain become associated with the deprivation and exploitation of the lower classes, especially landless peasants. Yet, while Spain is shockingly enough nowhere in sight in the opening six stanzas of 'Spain 1937', the specifically British upper-middle-class values that shaped Auden and many of his generation, often promoted by lectures on (precisely) universal history and universal values, often leading straight to 'the adoration of madmen', are exposed, ridiculed, and seemingly discarded. Yet who can speak in their stead—and from what position?

It is striking that after its rather histrionic and impersonal opening the poem suddenly introduces the figure of the poet, and a very Romantic poet at that, alone among pines near waterfalls and a leaning tower. Auden generally disliked the Romantics (except Byron), especially in their expression of political claims for poetry, like Shelley. It is therefore not surprising that the poet in 'Spain 1937' does not have a poetic answer to the dichotomy between yesterday's past and today's struggle. Instead he narcissistically prays to his vision and wishes for 'the luck of the sailor', which means for a safe escape from the mess that surrounds him.

The poet is not alone in making demands, rather than offering positions and action. He is accompanied in the subsequent stanzas by an investigator, by the poor, and even by the nations. All of them address a higher force, an even more elevated one than the poet's self-centred vision. This is none other than an upper-case

---

[11] See Norman Page, *The Thirties in Britain* (Basingstoke: Macmillan, 1990), 82–105, esp. 87.

[12] Auden mentions his shock at the closure of churches and the absence of priests in James Albert Pike (ed.), *Modern Canterbury Pilgrims: The Story of Twenty-Three Converts and Why They Chose the Anglican Church* (London: A. R. Mowbray, 1956), 41.

History, Time described as operator and organizer (in Auden's typically clinical language). From this History the investigator demands answers, the poor relief, and the nations intervention. In the four stanzas that outline these attitudes, the Spanish Civil War eventually moves closer, though it is still represented in general and generalizing shapes. Regional demarcations and factionalism, even machismo, are alluded to as a background to the conflict in the investigator's stanza. Yet although he looks at the local, the small, and the large, his concern is with something that will become central in the rest of the poem: 'the lives of my friends'. The poor understandably represent deprivation and social injustice as one cause of the Civil War. The nations once again stand for the outside perspective (including class-bound British views), and are consequently treated less respectfully when they request (in a typical conglomerate of conventional religiosity, Freudian patriarchal authoritarianism, and naive trust in progress and technology) the intervention of a *deus ex machina* in the form of 'a dove or | a furious papa or a mild engineer'.[13] The three positions are, moreover, analogous to conservative appeasement, fascist authoritarianism, and socialist technophilia.

The nations also bundle the individual perspectives of poet, investigator, and poor. Auden's view of nationhood is here again an entirely pragmatic one. He sees its role not so much as historical destiny or mission, but as a shaping of individual needs and an ordering of individual anxieties. Different types of nation are represented through animal symbolism. The sponge is associated with the city-state, and might refer to antiquity and the Middle Ages, when being a citizen meant to be free and (at least theoretically) equal. Shark and tiger are associated with the violent territorialism, expansionism, and competitiveness of military empires. Finally, the quaint robin is used as an emblem of the 'plucky canton', a Swiss-style form of nation that thrives on its homeliness and relative inertia, yet looks strangely helpless when put side by side with the predators of the preceding image. What is important in this list is that it shows nationhood in its varieties as the equivalent of ecological niches, not as historical inevitabilities, but as adaptations and reactions to circumstances. This also colours the exchange of positions between nations (as ordering instruments by and for individuals) and abstract universal History and Time. It is an uneven—indeed, a paradoxical—exchange, since all the positions from which the requests to History and Time are made are generated by individual decisions, or at least by individual responses, not by a higher superhuman force.[14]

It is therefore not illogical that what answers the requests and demands of poet, investigator, poor, and the nations is not an impersonal History. It is 'the life', specific and lower-case, and its answer is a possibility, not a certainty. This is the crucial move of 'Spain 1937'. This life represents the only explicit lyrical 'I' of the

---

[13] See Michael O'Neill and Gareth Reeves, *Auden, MacNeice, Spender: The Thirties Poetry* (Basingstoke: Macmillan, 1992), 209–10.

[14] Justin Replogle summarizes the poem's concern in the neat formula 'freedom-necessity-choice' (*Auden's Poetry* (London: Methuen, 1969), 44).

poem, and all the later controversial statements of the poem are attributed to it. It is at first cleverly introduced as a quasi-Romantic entity, when its answer comes 'from the heart', before the enjambment pluralizes it into eyes and lungs, and then depersonalizes it into 'the shops and squares of the city'. It is a collective speaker, not an impersonal one. It is a speaker that is already enmeshed in civilization, *civis* representing the citizen, not the individual, the family, the tribe, and not the nation either (this supranational view will strongly colour Auden's post-Second World War poetry). It is therefore also not an organic life force, and is cultural, rather than 'natural'.

It is not merely its identity and speaking position that are surprising, but also its reply. It denies any request to act as an alleviating or redemptive force. Indeed, it says 'no' to the demands of individuals and the collective—for the sheer reason that it cannot act as a distant saviour and authority for them, because it *is* them. Relegation of responsibility to an elevated and potentially transcendental force is denied by the eloquent 'life' of the poem, since all it can do is accept whatever decision individuals forming a collective as citizens make. It states that it is not the Prime Mover of the so-called Cosmological Argument, Thomas Aquinas's interpretation of Aristotle, which has recently been resurrected by American campaigners against evolution and for a supposed 'intelligent design'. Instead of false transcendental grandeur, this 'life' presents itself in decidedly low-key manifestations, as 'Yes-man, the bar companion, the easily duped'. Ultimately it represents whatever individual and collective *do*, not what they *are*, nor what they believe in.

Auden opens a radical debate here. He outlines a concept of ethics that defines itself strictly through acts and decisions, and beyond any thinking in identities, be they personal, collective (such as political party, class, or nation), or transcendental. All these identities inform and influence actions and decisions, as can be seen by the range of examples that encompass naive moral vow, the telling of funny stories, business attitudes, and even marriage, but then move on to more radical ideas, such as the Augustinian idea of a Just City and full circle back to the poet figure of the seventh stanza, suicide pact and Romantic death-wish. All of these are equally acceptable to life, since it does not judge, but merely performs what individuals and collective decide. Auden—and this is typical of all his poetry—does not offer a metaphysical way out of the quandary of decision-making. Neither does he show a political escape route.

When the voice of 'life' therefore neatly brackets off its sermon—which it started with a sequence of 'no' and 'not'—with a surprising 'yes', and adds the poem's most pathos-laden statement, 'I am Spain', the reader cannot help but shudder in confusion. A poem that, lest we forget, bears 'Spain 1937' as its title, and is an ostensible response to the Spanish Civil War, mentions Spain for the first time in its fourteenth stanza out of twenty-three. And when it mentions it, its most pronounced speaker (a rhetorically much stronger one than poet, investigator, or nations) now claims to represent Spain.

The shocking assertion only makes sense when it is reread through the discussion that the life that makes this claim has undertaken before it reaches this conclusion. It does not claim that there is an essence behind itself (as in 'I represent everything that is Spanish'); neither does it insist on a firm political status (as in 'I am the voice of the Spanish Republic'). This Spain is the many, and often conflicting, positions of its individuals and collectives, including the Spanish nation and even Franco's Falange. They are held together in an odd merger of an organic and a technological image sketched in stanza 12 as heart, eyes, lungs, but also shops and squares of 'the city': in short, by being citizens. This collective civic identity does not submerge individual desires, anxieties, and weaknesses, but it challenges them to arrive at ethically correct and responsible actions and decisions—without the promise of an ultimate elevation to or salvation in a greater transcendental identity, such as that of an eternal Spanishness. Ultimately, one could even argue, the Spain of Auden's poem potentially includes anyone who associates with the necessary decisions concerning Spain's citizens, even the international fighters and supporters of either side of the conflict, be they on Spanish territory or not.

This non-essentialist interpretation of 'Spain' in Auden's poem is the only reading that overcomes an otherwise insurmountable logical flaw between the poem's insistence on generalizations, historical and cultural networks, and the entanglement and mutual generation of private and public. That 'Spain' is defined not only as *a* choice and *a* decision, but as '*your* choice, *your* decision' (my italics) supports the inclusive character of the appeal. It may read like propaganda, but it is a rhetoric that is self-undermining and therefore critical, since it stands on its own, without a clear definition of who 'you' is, and no easy identification of a common goal or enemy either.

The strong rhetorical stress on the declaration of 'Spain' is coupled with equally powerful hints that, whatever choices and decisions are made, the outcomes might be tragic. These hints of the poem are structural, and they play with genre conventions. The poem's twenty-three stanzas fall neatly into six 'Yesterday' ones and six that outline the ethical argument sketched above and are connected by 'As' and 'And'. These represent the two initial acts of a traditional five-act play, exposition (the poem's general history) and dramatic build-up (its ethical argument and self-identification), and it is not difficult to figure out that this play is not going to be a comedy, but a tragedy. The next two stanzas represent the dramatic climax of the third act, in which for the first time a lyrical 'I' appears. The 'Spain' declaration marks the highlight and end of this third act.[15] It is followed by three anti-climactic stanzas focusing on collectives in the shape of the many, them, and finally us, which form the fourth act. The fifth act consists of five stanzas starting with 'To-morrow' and then 'To-day'. Finally there is a one-stanza epilogue.

[15] Samuel Hynes even states: 'In terms of my metaphor of the 'thirties as a tragic drama, Auden's "Spain" is about the third act' (*The Auden Generation: Literature and Politics in England in the 1930s* (London: Faber, 1976), 253).

In keeping with the ethics of doing and the relegation of responsibility to the individual, the short three central stanzas are concerned with the 'Many' and with 'They'. These nameless and faceless collectives are by no means a strange depiction of the Spanish population (which would be more than condescending), yet they include it, too. On 'remote peninsulas', 'sleepy plains, in the aberrant fishermen's islands', and even in the corrupt city, the demanding voice of 'Spain' is heard in stanza 15. Spain is, of course, itself a peninsula, but remote only for the traditional British onlooker or foreign volunteers in the Civil War. The poem carefully floats its imagery between symbolic possibility and metaphoric imprecision, precisely to avoid an all-too-easy ascription of identities and, ultimately, sides. Sleepy plains and corrupt cities are certainly something one can find in Spain in the 1930s. But they never become exclusive images. Instead, they retain their universality. This is true even for the puzzling 'aberrant fishermen's islands', which might be an oblique reference to Tenerife, where Franco started his military coup in 1936.

After all the careful balancing acts between individuality, collectivity, and universality, however, one has to admit that, after the introduction of the local and international collective affected by the demand to decide and act, the poem contains its first serious logical flaw. In a regression to the Romantic imagery that was ridiculed in stanza 7, it now describes the acts of the 'Many' in images of migrating gulls and flower seeds. These are beautiful similes; yet they contradict the ethical prerequisite of choice, since gulls migrate instinctively and flower seeds spread randomly. The subsequent two verses are more in line with the imagery of Auden's early poetry—and more appropriate to the ethical argument developed in the third section of 'Spain 1937'. They describe clinging to express trains moving through the night and through a tunnel, fitting images both for the actual mode of reaching Spain for many volunteers and for the symbolic uncertainty and obscurity of their future and that of the country for which they had come to fight. Walking over passes is a further appropriate image, while floating over the oceans (both in stanza 16) is not.[16] Yet even the problematic stanzas 15 and 16 finally return to the question of decisions and actions in their final verse. It once again reads so simply as to smack of propaganda, and yet represents the logical consequence of the most radical decision-making process one could envisage. Challenged by their lives to decide and act, the unnamed many who have decided to become involved in the struggle in Spain present nothing less than these lives, which enabled them to make this decision in the first place.

It is perhaps the uncertainty and confusion that emerge from this decision to invest one's entire existence for a cause, which lead to the feverish imagery and temporary loss of logic in the anti-climactic fourth part of 'Spain 1937'. First the poem makes a brief return to the ironical detachment of its universalist

---

[16] John R. Boly also criticizes these sections in his *Reading Auden: The Return of Caliban* (Ithaca, NY: Cornell University Press, 1991), 171.

opening stanzas. Now it describes Spain rather condescendingly in geographical and meteorological terms, and indeed as a part of Africa that is only 'soldered' to Europe, without, however, naming it. Its name tellingly appears only once in the corpus of the text, in the declaration of 'the life'. The fourth part of the poem then concludes with a strange statement that, for the first time, involves an implicit 'we': 'Our fever's menacing shapes are precise and alive.'

The voice of the text has shifted again. After the impersonal start and the limited perspectives of poet, investigator, and the poor, the nation that combined them, and the challenging voice of 'the life' addressing a 'you', the subtle and sudden implied 'we' looks temptingly like a possible solution. Yet, like the illogical drift into Romantic natural imagery of stanzas 15 and 16, it is a problematic response. Fever once again does not agree with ethical choice. It might stand for passion, yet also for the loss of a clear view. And indeed the fever here produces delusions, only that the text calls them—paradoxically—'precise and alive'. The precision claimed for passionate (or sick) fantasies appears very much like clutching at straws.[17] Yet the 'alive' quality of the desperate perspective regains some motivation by being connected to the lives that are presented as a potential sacrifice and the life that enables the collective to arrive at such a choice. Nonetheless, the verse remains warped, and it is certainly no coincidence that it is followed by the bathos of the first line of the concluding fifth section of the poem, which declares the future to be a mere possibility of tomorrow, a 'perhaps'.[18]

While the poem's rather bombastic opening was certain that all the past could be relegated to yesterday, the claim concerning the future that forms its mirror-image is now hesitant and comes across as feeble. Indeed, stanza 18 replicates many of the images of the poem's beginning. It also includes movement, exploration, and expansion. Yet this time it is not continents and trade routes that are charted, but very individual issues, such as fatigue, consciousness, diet, breathing (only radiation stands out as both abstract and non-individual). It is as if the grand gesture of the poem's universal start has crash-landed on the final realization of one's individual life and the consequences of its decisions and actions.

This is not to say that the images of the stanza and those that follow are completely pessimistic. They appear small and even tired, as if the mere decision to become involved in the struggle has already been too much of an effort. The entire section does not contain a single verb, as if to emphasize its inertia. Yet, as the anaphoric repetition of 'To-morrow' signals, the section also looks towards an aftermath of the struggle, an aftermath that, again, seems to take place as much in Spain as anywhere (including a very middle-class Britain). There, in this uncertain and

---

[17] I am not convinced by Stan Smith's reading, which suggests that 'In *Spain 1937* the alien landscape of the peninsula is a place where we find what has been gripping *our* unconscious' (Smith, *W. H. Auden*, 95). There is neither a collective unconscious in Freud nor an identification of the implicit 'we' in Auden's 'Spain 1937'; nor can their thoughts easily be translated.

[18] See Hynes, *Auden Generation*, 253.

only potentially likely future, one finds again the reform movements that were so influential in the late nineteenth and early twentieth century, all of them aiming for the good life, a small-scale ethics of goodness compared to the decision necessary for the poem's struggle. Even romantic love is rediscovered, but placed only on the same scale as the symbolically slightly disconcerting 'photographing of ravens', traditionally portents of ill omen.

Politically, too, a rather ambivalent scenario opens up when what is predicted for this possible future is 'fun' under the authoritarian shadow of a capitalized 'Liberty'. The term 'master' that appears twice in stanza 19 (once in 'masterful') is always a critical one in Auden's early poems, since authority generally stands for the dubious one of tradition or 'the old gang'. Here, its attachment to freedom could signal an ironic nod in the direction of the world power that has most ostensibly written liberty on its flag, the United States of America, soon to be Auden's home. Yet 'Liberty' could also be merely an ironic oxymoron in connection with 'masterful', one that acknowledges that, whatever outcome the struggle may have, freedom will only ever be imaginable inside authoritarian power structures. This would go back to the poem's discussion of life as choice, and choice as responsibility and challenge, and to the insistence that life, choice, and ethics are only imaginable as part of a civic identity (and not a romantic individual or equally romantic collective one—such as communism or fascism). It would also, perhaps grudgingly, declare that even the ideal of a democratic citizenship that combines individual desires, anxieties, weaknesses, and injustices is not free from, but indeed rests on, power, and power demands institutions, authority, and ultimately repression.

Pageant master and musician as theatrical organizers of the embellishments of such political structures are, nonetheless, ironically juxtaposed to the terrorist-like poets in the subsequent stanza. Yet these 'poets exploding like bombs' (an image that reiterates 'bombs of conspiracy | In arm-pit secrecy' from an early poem called 'Will you turn a deaf ear'[19]) are said to be there 'for the young'. Such thinking in terms of individual resistance against inevitable institutions and power is qualified as immature and naive. Anarchy, a strong movement with military forces of its own in the Spanish Civil War, is thus dealt with very critically. Auden's poem positions itself against communism and against anarchism and in favour of a pragmatic acceptance of some form of liberal democracy—at a time when Auden was ostensibly fighting, or at least writing for the global Left in its struggle against, Spanish fascism![20] It is hard to believe that it was not this implicit political

---

[19] Auden, 'Will you turn a deaf ear', in English Auden, 35–6.

[20] Peter C. Grosvenor is one of the few critics to see this clearly when he writes: 'In fact, it is an error to conclude from his use of the fashionable language of the decade that he was ever in any meaningful sense a Marxist at all. Auden seems to have been a moderate in both political and religious terms, temperamentally suited to social liberalism and Anglicanism at a time when liberalism appeared spent and the Church of England was part of the larger English establishment that had been discredited by the trauma of the Great War' (Grosvenor, 'Auden, "Spain", and the Crisis of Literary Popular

positioning, but other statements made in 'Spain 1937', that caused controversy. The reason for overlooking its complex stance and its even more complex and quasi-philosophical underpinning with an ethical argument certainly lies in the poem's dense and often ambivalent, if not contradictory and paradoxical, imagery.

In all its complexity, though, the poem never forgets that it is a balancing act when it comes to taking sides. The possible future under a liberal-democratic authority is kitted out in nostalgic and very British middle-class images of walks, bicycle races, and suburbia. There is even a lower-case 'communion', which implies both an E. M. Forster-like message of 'only connect' and a vague return to religiosity. That such visions of a potential future as regressive dreams of an idealized past are a distraction in the present situation, however, is quickly made clear when the last verse of stanza 20 reminds the reader that today is the time of struggle.

Stanza 21 of the poem attracted the most vociferous criticism, most famously from George Orwell, for its line 'The conscious acceptance of guilt in the necessary murder'[21] (although Orwell also praised 'Spain 1937' as 'one of the few decent things that have been written about the Spanish war'[22]). One can argue that Orwell's attack—on the grounds that this statement could only come from someone who has never been in the position to kill another human being, in short, a poet rather than a fighter—smacks of machismo. Indeed, it is a line in a poem in poetic diction, and its superficial scandalousness rests in the fact that it describes something seemingly unpoetic (although killing has fed innumerable poems) and, worse, describes it neutrally. Yet when one goes back to the tone of the poem's initial section, whose emphasis on 'Yesterday' forms a structural bracket with the 'To-morrow' and 'To-day' of its penultimate fifth part, one simply finds the same typically Audenesque attempt at detached and objective analysis. The scandal of the second line of stanza 21 diminishes even further when one sees it as a follow-on from its first line, which talks about the chances of death deliberately increasing (amended to an inevitable increase later), a statement that is simply realistic.

Yet one can (and should) go further than that—and further than Auden himself did, when he half-heartedly first changed the controversial expression in the second verse to 'the fact of murder' (a revision that was retained by Auden's editor Edward Mendelson when he reprinted the poem in the posthumous collection *The English Auden*) and then dropped 'Spain 1937' from his canon altogether. As part of the poem's intense discussion of ethics as a question of decisions and actions (rather

---

Frontism', in David Garrett Izzo (ed.), *W. H. Auden: A Legacy* (West Cornwall, Conn.: Locust Hill Press, 2002), 240.

[21] Auden, *Spain* (London: Faber, 1937), 11.

[22] George Orwell famously wrote: 'Mr Auden's brand of amoralism is only possible if you are the kind of person who is always somewhere else when the trigger is pulled' (Orwell, 'Inside the Whale', in *The Collected Essays, Journalism and Letters of George Orwell*, i: *An Age Like This, 1920–1940*, ed. Sonia Orwell and Ian Angus (Harmondsworth: Penguin, 1970), 516). It first appeared as a booklet of its own entitled *Inside the Whale* (London: Victor Gollancz, 1940). In this text, he expands an earlier attack made in *The Adelphi*, in Dec. 1938. See Mendelson, *Early Auden*, 321.

than of essential or transcendental certainties and guarantees), the decision to kill (which even in war is clearly called 'murder') leads to guilt. This guilt must be consciously accepted if the decision is to be an ethical one. Making a decision to kill here does not mean being good or acting ethically; it is merely called 'necessary'—in the same way that an authoritarian liberty is not seen as desirable and utopian, but as the only likely outcome of the struggle, despite its drawbacks. The supposedly irresponsible propagandist statement is part of a careful debate, and it never presents itself as ideal. On the contrary, like most statements in 'Spain 1937', it is tinged not only with a feeling of fatigue, but also with irony. Among its intertextual ancestors is Lenin's supposed description of Western intellectuals who excuse the excesses of the Russian Revolution as useful idiots in the struggle to achieve communism. Considering that 'Spain 1937' implicitly views a communist position as untenable, because it wrongly releases the individual and the collective from responsibility, the 'necessary murder' is as ironic as it is ethically complex.

Even the revised term 'the fact of murder' retains this complexity. A fact, etymology tells us, is that which is made, not that which is given or inevitable. It thus results from the same ethical choice as the 'necessary murder', only its seemingly more 'objective' rhetoric cleverly disguises this fact. Auden himself clearly felt that neither term was eventually adequate to express the dilemma he wanted 'Spain 1937' to convey. That the concluding two verses of the controversial stanza talk about spent powers, a boring meeting, and—most importantly—'the flat ephemeral pamphlet' is more than telling. 'Spain 1937' was originally published in pamphlet form. The text declares its own impotence, and even potential failure. Yet it does not end there, and this is important. In the same way as doubts about the possible outcome of the struggle for the Spanish Republic do not free the individual or the collective from the responsibility to make decisions on this struggle and take action, the poem is not allowed to conclude in a complacent lament on its own insignificance.

The images that dominate its twenty-second (and penultimate) stanza and the last one of its fifth part—traditionally the catastrophe of a tragedy—are all concerned with inadequacy, and expressed in terms like 'makeshift', 'scraping', 'Fumbled', and 'unsatisfactory'. But they are also concerned with community—more precisely, and now less abstractly, with comradeship. Consolation is what starts off this stanza, a term that could also represent a less regressive and nostalgic outlook on a possible aftermath of the conflict than the British middle-class fantasies of the previous stanzas. Consolation is, of course, a highly ethical affair, and one that works only by deciding and acting, never by insisting on selfhood or higher truths. Sharing is the second ethically loaded term introduced by the penultimate stanza of 'Spain 1937'. Although it is part of a rather clichéd wartime scenario of cigarettes and card games in a candlelit barn, it also stands for justice and the fair distribution of wealth, whose absence was one of the causes of the Spanish conflict.

After accusing Orwell of machismo, one also has to identify Auden as a mongerer in clichés of male friendship which pander both to his homosexuality and to traditional ideals of war. His manly jokes and fumbling, but ultimately unsatisfactory, embraces are as much part of homosocial as of homoerotic traditions. They are particularly inappropriate for the Spanish Civil War, in which many women fought on the side of the Republicans. This is one of several moments in the poem when one feels that Auden hardly came close to the realities of fighting—or Spain—during his short stay. Another is his naive assumption earlier on in stanza 9 that the poor, though they have no fire in their homes, still read the evening paper. Yet the poem never forgets its serious message, even when it drifts into inappropriate fantasies. All its macho behaviour is merely a prequel to 'hurting'. Out of community does not necessarily evolve harmony. This would be another utopian delusion. In fact, comradeship, even friendship, can also be the prelude to hurting one another, and the hurt can be emotional as well as physical. In the case of war, and particularly a civil war, it is generally both, a fact attested by the observation that many people in Spain to this day are still at pains to make sense of the Spanish Civil War, even (or exactly) when it affects them only indirectly through their parents and grandparents.

The sombre word 'hurting' thus forms the appropriate finale of the poem's tragic catastrophe. Yet it is not its final word. There is a short epilogue, much as in traditional Shakespearean tragedies. It is indeed *Hamlet* that most readily comes to mind as a point of comparison here, not only in the sense that Shakespeare's drama can also be read as a play about decisions, the problematic ethics of choice, and its catastrophic consequences, which leave only an external power as the new master. Much of the melancholy of Prince Hamlet's monologues (and of his dying words, 'the rest is silence'[23]) is also found in the last four lines of Auden's poem. Universal statements such as that declaring the stars to be dead or the indifference of animals to human suffering have an apocalyptic ring. But, as with the penultimate stanza, resignation is not what 'Spain 1937' can permit itself, if it wants to stay true to its demanding ethical message.

The stars are indeed dead—and have always been. Animals have never cared for human joy or pain (despite the well-intentioned projections of animal lovers). Any attempt to find consolation—and thus relief—in higher powers or in lower ones, religion or astronomy, biology or anthropology, is futile. 'We are left alone with our day,' the poem declares, and insists on returning us to 'the life' that is all we are, but also continues to demand decisions and actions from us. Time, our individual time as well as historical time during a volatile military and political conflict, is of the essence, and limited. And when 'History' appears one last time and speaks to the defeated, it has little to say but 'Alas'. Help or pardon, the poem's final terms, are within the grasp of humans, not at the disposal of abstract higher forces. Despite Auden's rejection of especially this final stanza as 'wicked doctrine', it by no means 'equates goodness with success', as he himself wrongly came to

---

[23] William Shakespeare, *Hamlet*, v. ii. 337.

believe.[24] Responsibility, also for hurting and killing and making decisions, including wrong ones, is what in the final consequence makes us human. Our ethical task, Auden's poem argues in the context of an unpredictable civil war, which attracted as many egotistical investments as it stimulated utopian hopes and dreams, is to turn this human potential into attempts at civilized and humane lives.

[24] Auden, 'Foreword', in *Collected Shorter Poems 1927–1957* (London: Faber, 1966), 15.

CHAPTER 15

···

WAR, POLITICS, AND DISAPPEARING POETRY: AUDEN, YEATS, EMPSON

···

JOHN LYON

W. H. Auden's 'poetry makes nothing happen'[1] is one of the most discussed and interpreted phrases in twentieth-century poetry, the subject of discriminations which are—depending on one's point of view—ever more exacting or ever more exquisite.[2] The phrase's seductiveness for readers and critics lies in its gnomic

---

The author of this essay is gratefully indebted to Peter McDonald and to my colleague, George Donaldson.

[1] W. H. Auden, 'In Memory of W. B. Yeats', in *The English Auden: Poems, Essays, and Dramatic Writings 1927–1939*, ed. Edward Mendelson (London: Faber, 1977), 242.

[2] A far from complete gathering of such critics includes Louis MacNeice, *The Poetry of W. B. Yeats* (London: Faber, 1967), esp. 192; Samuel Hynes, *The Auden Generation: Literature and Politics in England in the 1930s* (London: Faber, 1976), 349–53; Lawrence Lipking, *The Life of the Poet: Beginning and Ending Poetic Careers* (Chicago: University of Chicago Press, 1981), 151–60; Edward Callan, *Auden: A Carnival of Intellect* (Oxford: Oxford University Press, 1983), esp. 146–53; Lucy McDiarmid, *Saving Civilization: Yeats, Eliot and Auden between the Wars* (Cambridge: Cambridge University Press, 1984), *passim*; idem, *Auden's Apologies for Poetry* (Princeton: Princeton University Press, 1990), *passim*; Michael O'Neill and Gareth Reeves, *Auden, MacNeice, Spender: The Thirties Poetry* (Basingstoke: Macmillan, 1992), 159–61; Stan Smith, 'Persuasions to Rejoice: Auden's Oedipal Dialogues with

quality, its apparent directness and absoluteness, the simplicity of its wording, its assurance of profundity and certainty. Yet it is a phrase which eludes our attention, shifting sands already becoming apparent when we ask where we are to put the emphasis. '*Poetry* makes nothing happen?' 'Poetry *makes* nothing happen?' 'Poetry makes *nothing* happen?'[3] The simplicity of the individual words also proves elusive. 'Nothing' is especially problematic: at least since Shakespeare the word has been something of a riddle. And the vagueness of 'things' is writ large in English verse from Wordsworth's 'a sense sublime | Of something far more deeply interfused', his 'All thinking things', and his 'rolls through all things',[4] getting vaguer and more negative, through Tennyson's 'something more, | A bringer of new things' and his 'something ere the end',[5] to Geoffrey Hill's sinister 'Things marched . . .' and 'Things happen'.[6] The latter of Hill's phrases also suggests that 'happen'—one thinks too of 'happenstance', the colloquial 'Stuff happens' and its vulgar variant, 'Shit happens'—also writes vagueness into the phrase: 'happen' simply acknowledges that events have occurred but withholds explanation, not least explanation in terms of causation. Already a disjunction is appearing in the Auden phrase between its resonance and its meaning: it sounds good, but sense slips between one's fingers, leaving 'memorable speech'[7]—Auden's characterization of poetry—but also memorable opacity. To borrow the words of another of Auden's speakers, 'What does it mean? What does it mean? Not what does it mean to them, there, then. What does it mean to us, here now? It's a facer, isn't it boys?'[8] A facer? Or a teaser? John Keats knew that 'Beauty is truth, truth beauty'—a comparably

W. B. Yeats', in Katherine Bucknell and Nicholas Jenkins (eds.), *W. H. Auden: 'The Language of Learning and the Language of Love', Uncollected Writing, New Interpretations*, Auden Studies 2 (Oxford: Clarendon Press, 1994), 155–63; Peter McDonald, *Mistaken Identities: Poetry and Northern Ireland* (Oxford: Clarendon Press, 1997), 189–216; Michael O'Neill, *Romanticism and the Self-Conscious Poem* (Oxford: Clarendon Press, 1997), 263–65; and Rainer Emig, *W. H. Auden: Towards a Postmodern Poetics* (Basingstoke: Palgrave, 2000), 107–9. Anthony Hecht expresses his frustration at the extensive discussion: 'And now comes a little phrase that has raised as many hackles as nearly anything else Auden ever wrote. An awful lot of foolish commentary has been devoted to, mainly attacking, Auden's claim that "poetry makes nothing happen"' (Hecht, *The Hidden Law: The Poetry of W. H. Auden* (Cambridge, Mass.: Harvard University Press, 1993), 144). Yet Hecht cannot resist joining in (see esp. pp. 140–4 and 147–9), any more than the writer of the present essay: in the latter's defence, however, foolishness or nonsense forms a substantive part of the argument advanced here. The fullest treatment of Auden's four words, a whole book which grows from them, is undoubtedly Peter Robinson's *Poetry, Poets, Readers: Making Things Happen* (Oxford: Clarendon Press, 2002).

 [3] This point has been made by George Myerson in conversation with the present writer and by McDonald, *Mistaken Identities*, 197.

 [4] William Wordsworth, 'Lines written a few miles above Tintern Abbey', in *William Wordsworth*, ed. Stephen Gill (Oxford: Oxford University Press, 1984), 134.

 [5] Alfred Tennyson, 'Ulysses', in *The Poems of Tennyson*, i, ed. Christopher Ricks, 2nd edn. (London: Longman, 1987), 617.

 [6] Geoffrey Hill, 'September Song' and 'Ovid in the Third Reich', in *Collected Poems* (Harmondsworth: Penguin, 1985), 67 and 61.

 [7] Auden, 'Introduction to *The Poet's Tongue*', in *English Auden*, 327.

 [8] Auden, 'Address for a Prize-Day', ibid. 61.

gnomic utterance with a comparably complex critical reception—emanated from a Grecian urn with the distinctive power to 'tease us out of thought'.[9]

Let us try putting it another way. In November 2004, giving his inaugural lecture as Professor of Poetry at the University of Oxford, the distinguished critic Christopher Ricks chose the occasion to mount a defence of prose, his implied point being that such a defence in such a context was precisely not impertinent.[10] Ricks is right to resist and to disprove by example any general declaration for the superiority of poetry over prose. He knows, too, that there is a third term at the party, 'verse' ('This may be verse but it isn't poetry'), and that 'poetry' as a term of value may be unhitched from the requirements of verse or even of observing line endings and stretched to encompass prose—or even stranger things, as was the case with Wilfred Owen's pity, which we shall recall below. But might we for a moment entertain an inverted heresy—that on *some* occasions and in *some* respects poetry may be inferior to prose? That poetic licence can license tendentiousness, sleight of hand, the evading of the requirements of coherent, consecutive, and argued prose? The question of poetry's relation to historical and political events is always with us, but it becomes especially acute when history and politics are *in extremis*—in times of war, for example. The value of some such poetry for readers—its power to move us and impress itself on our memories—might lie less in the truths it articulates than in the extremity of the situation from which it is in flight, an extremity implied in its evasiveness and opacity, its fugitive sense. As William Empson, another poet writing in the 1930s, has it, 'The safety valve alone || Knows the worst truth about the engine.'[11]

It is evident that returning Auden's 'poetry makes nothing happen' to its immediate context does not make it any clearer. The phrase comes in 'In Memory of W. B. Yeats',[12] a poem which elegizes one of the twentieth century's most important poets. Auden's elegy also marks the end of the 1930s, the decade of 'the Auden Generation', in Auden's own words 'a low dishonest decade',[13] and a decade which had seen most hope that art might prove politically efficacious. Recording the then present European nightmare in which 'the living nations wait, | Each sequestered in its hate', Auden's poem anticipates a dark future and stands on the brink of the Second World War. Poetry's escape clause occurs in the second of the elegy's three sections:

> You were silly like us: your gift survived it all;
> The parish of rich women, physical decay,

[9] John Keats, 'Ode on a Grecian Urn', in *The Complete Poems*, ed. John Barnard (Harmondsworth: Penguin, 1973), 345–6.

[10] An edited extract from Professor Ricks's lecture was published as 'All praise to proper words' in the *Times Literary Supplement*, 25 Feb. 2005, 13–15.

[11] William Empson, 'Your Teeth are Ivory Towers', in *The Complete Poems of William Empson*, ed. John Haffenden (Harmondsworth: Penguin, 2000), 67.

[12] Auden, 'In Memory of W. B. Yeats', in *English Auden*, 241–3.

[13] Auden, 'September 1, 1939', ibid. 245.

> Yourself; mad Ireland hurt you into poetry.
> Now Ireland has her madness and her weather still,
> For poetry makes nothing happen: it survives
> In the valley of its saying where executives
> Would never want to tamper; it flows south
> From ranches of isolation and the busy griefs,
> Raw towns that we believe and die in; it survives,
> A way of happening, a mouth.[14]

Figuratively we are in a landscape in which poetry itself is imagined as a river which 'flows south', issuing in 'a mouth'. (The mouth, however, also relates back to the 'mouth of the dying day' of Yeats's death and to the 'mourning tongues' reciting his poems in the first section of the elegy.) There is an escapism here, not only in the metaphor of travelling across an *American* landscape—'ranches', '*Raw* towns'—which leaves Ireland and Europe behind, but also a loosening of meaning. Hence the American feminist poet Adrienne Rich, engaged in a battle of her own and intent on loosening the patriarchy's grip on language, and on the word 'lonely' in particular, was responding profoundly to the way in which Auden's (nonetheless anti-political) poem works when she borrowed Auden's landscape and cadence:

> You want to ask, am I lonely?
> Well, of course, lonely
> as a woman driving across country
> day after day, leaving behind
> mile after mile
> little towns she might have stopped
> and lived and died in, lonely
>
> If I'm lonely
> it must be the loneliness
> of waking first . . . [15]

Moreover, in Auden we arrive finally and starkly at 'a mouth': poetry does not issue *from* a mouth but rather *in* a mouth. Retrospectively, literature has modified this final phrase rather cruelly in the 'guts of the living', since the most famous mouth in literature is now the incessant babble of 'Mouth' in Beckett's *Not I*. Hamlet, too, has something to say about the politics of making mouths, since it was in such terms that he simultaneously admired the warring Fortinbras and wondered at his folly and presumption:

> Witness this army of such mass and charge,
> Led by a delicate and tender prince,
> Whose spirit, with divine ambition puff'd,

---

[14] Auden, 'In Memory of W. B. Yeats', 242.
[15] Adrienne Rich, 'Song', in *Diving into the Wreck: Poems 1971–1972* (New York: Norton, 1973), 20.

> Makes mouths at the invisible event,
> Exposing what is mortal and unsure
> To all that fortune, death, and danger dare,
> Even for an eggshell.[16]

In the Auden passage there is a suggestion of a self-protective, self-inwoven phrasing ('it survives | In the valley of its [own] saying'), and a tendency to verbal nouns—'saying', 'happening'—which keeps the emphasis on poetry as process, distracting our attention from the ends of poetry, from poetic consequences, from the invisible events to which poetry might give rise. Auden tells us that 'poetry makes nothing happen', that it 'survives | In the valley of its saying', that it is 'a way of happening', that it is 'a mouth'. How are we to put these varying characterizations together? Are we dealing with an accumulation: 'poetry makes nothing happen' *and* it 'survives | In the valley of its saying' *and*...? Or are we seeing a revisionary process of thinking which discards thoughts as it goes along, a stripping of meaning, or a case analogous to what deconstructionists call writing under erasure, where words score a line through themselves even as they are written or spoken? Illogical though it seems, the answer appears to lie somewhere between those two opposed possibilities. We do not seem to be reading a stringent and searching process of negation and rejection which pares itself down to settle on the smallness of those two final syllables, 'a mouth'. But nor do the lines add up into some large coherence: in particular, 'poetry makes nothing happen' and 'A way of happening' seem, if pressed, likely to issue in contradiction. Such coherence as there is seems to exist at the level of figures rather than argument. Auden's lines have what Stephen Booth—arguing more generally for literature as 'precious nonsense'—describes as 'a feel of coherence ... [an] ideationally insignificant coherence [which] often takes the place of, does the job of, the ordinary, substantive, syntax-borne coherence that we expect, demand, and do not notice is absent'.[17] This is the Auden, we remind ourselves, whose long association with Christ Church, Oxford, was something he had in common with Lewis Carroll, the Auden who had an enduring enthusiasm for nonsense and light verse. Moreover, as the editor of *The Chatto Book of Nonsense Poetry* reminds us, 'nonsense may be a liberating way of dealing with the intolerable.'[18]

The promise of coherence which 'In Memory of W. B. Yeats' makes its readers is a limited one: the poem is divided into sections, and its publication history is of shape shifting.[19] A variant of its first line excepted, the second section including 'poetry makes nothing happen' did not appear in the first version of the elegy, published

---

[16] William Shakespeare, *Hamlet*, IV. iv. 47–53.

[17] Stephen Booth, *Precious Nonsense: 'The Gettysburg Address', Ben Jonson's Epitaphs on his Children, and 'Twelfth Night'* (Berkeley and Los Angeles: University of California Press, 1998), 6–8.

[18] Hugh Haughton, 'Introduction', in *idem* (ed.), *The Chatto Book of Nonsense Poetry* (London: Chatto & Windus, 1988), 8.

[19] For a brief account of the poem's textual history, see *English Auden*, 426.

in the *New Republic*, 8 March 1939, but was in the second published version in the *London Mercury* in April of the same year. Around this time Auden was also writing a prose piece, 'The Public v. the Late Mr. William Butler Yeats', for the Spring 1939 number of *Partisan Review*. Though critics contest the priority of the relation,[20] this prose work and the second section of the elegy are intimately bound up with one another. Yet readers seeking the clarity of an exposition in discursive prose are disappointed: in 'The Public v. the Late Mr. William Butler Yeats' Auden divides his voice between that of a Public Prosecutor and a Counsel for the Defence, staging an imaginary court-room drama.[21] Such a division of voice suggests that thinking for Auden, rather than being a matter of holding a problem in the mind in all its complexity and complication, typically involves a process of striking contrary (and simplifying) attitudes: hence the either/or campery ('Shall I pluck a flower, boys, shall I save or spend?'[22]) of Empson's affectionate 'Just a Smack at Auden' remains one of the most important documents in Auden's critical reception. The argumentative acumen of neither of Auden's lawyers inspires much confidence. It is not entirely clear that they are contesting the same case, and the fictional context only partly excuses the loose knockabout quality of the 'exchanges': this is a very casual court-room. For all the exactness of some of the characterizations of Yeats which may be plucked from it—Yeats's 'feudal mentality', for example—the tendentiousness of the Public Prosecutor's case is crudely parodic. So the first brief paragraph begins with a disclaimer that it is the work, not the man, that is to be judged, and then proceeds immediately to drive the *ad hominem* attack home: 'I must only remind you that there is usually a close connection between the personal character of a poet and his work, and that the deceased was no exception.' While conflating man and poet, the Public Prosecutor does at least have the merit of concentrating on Yeats. By contrast, a master of *non sequitur*, the Counsel for the Defence jumps around in altogether more general, loftier regions. At one point he is asking—apparently rhetorically—'He [the Public Prosecutor] has sneered at the deceased for not taking arms, as if shooting were the only honourable and useful form of social action. Has the Abbey Theatre done nothing for Ireland?' Yet such a question is not allowed to trouble the most famous passage, the passage most intimately related to the middle section of the Yeats elegy: within a paragraph Auden, as Counsel for the Defence, is declaring,

For art is a product of history, not a cause. Unlike some other products, technical inventions for example, it does not re-enter history as an effective agent, so that the question whether art should or should not be propaganda is unreal. The case for the prosecution rests on the fallacious belief that art ever makes anything happen, whereas the honest truth, gentlemen, is that, if not a poem had been written, not a picture painted, not a bar of music composed, the history of man would be materially unchanged.

[20] For a discussion of the differing views, see Robinson, *Poetry, Poets, Readers*, 42.
[21] Auden, 'The Public v. the Late Mr. William Butler Yeats', in *English Auden*, 389–93.
[22] Empson, 'Just a Smack at Auden', in *Complete Poems*, 81.

This is nonsense, albeit memorable nonsense. Yet to start adducing specific contrary cases (the Abbey Theatre, perhaps?) to refute the Defence's claim is to mistake the kind of game being played. Such a resonant assertion is more thoroughgoingly nonsensical. '[M]aterially' writes a considerable leeway into the assertion of unchangeability: just what kind of matter matters? More importantly, without the arts a large part of what Auden calls 'the history of man' would have gone unrecorded. But, most extremely, the 'history of man', *so defined*, ceases to be intelligible as the history of man, and 'history' and 'man' in such a context become nonce-words. Again, history and politics seem to be exerting a pressure on art, and on writings about art, which puts sense, self-protectively, to flight.

Sense and efficacy are, however, welcomed back in the third and final section of Auden's elegy for Yeats—but more in religious rather than political terms. In this the poem participates in a lengthy tradition in the English elegy—Gray's 'Elegy Written in a Country Churchyard' is perhaps the best-known example—where acceptance and consolation, or at least their appearance, are achieved by means of an equivocation between politics and religion. Now less conversational and consciously imitative of Yeatsian verse, Auden's poem can talk of time's capacities for worship, forgiveness, and pardon; and the poet is again accorded very considerable powers:

> Follow, poet, follow right
> To the bottom of the night,
> With your unconstraining voice
> Still persuade us to rejoice;
>
> With the farming of a verse
> Make a vineyard of the curse,
> Sing of human unsuccess
> In a rapture of distress;
>
> In the deserts of the heart
> Let the healing fountain start,
> In the prison of his days
> Teach the free man how to praise.

This final attitude appears as an extraordinary fusion or confusion of Nietzschean tragic gaiety—which W. B. Yeats himself endorsed, most particularly in 'Lapis Lazuli'—and Christianity. Auden's espousal of Christianity in 1940 is incubating here, shadowing the larger shift in commitments as we move from earlier to later Auden. There is something quasi-biblical—suggestive of swords turned to ploughshares—in the turning of the curse into wine, and the springing up of oases in deserts. Moreover, ideas of imprisonment and freedom—man in the prison of his mortal flesh—are held loftily at metaphorical or metaphysical height, necessarily keeping at a distance more troubling, more literal, and more political senses of these ideas. The move away from the political is further underlined with the removal,[23]

---

[23] For an account of this textual change, see Robinson, *Poetry, Poets, Readers*, 48.

from later versions of the third section of this shape-shifting poem, of three stanzas which culminate in the politically problematic examples of Kipling and Claudel:

> Time that is intolerant
> Of the brave and innocent,
> And indifferent in a week
> To a beautiful physique,
>
> Worships language and forgives
> Everyone by whom it lives;
> Pardons cowardice, conceit,
> Lays its honours at their feet.
>
> Time that with this strange excuse
> Pardoned Kipling and his views,
> And will pardon Paul Claudel,
> Pardons him [Yeats] for writing well.

Politics, rather than being addressed, is being written out of this poem in the interests of higher, vaguer, and more suspect 'things', things that poetry apparently can make happen.

The context of Auden's life affords an excess of contradictory explanations of why Auden is in flight from politics in this way. Thus the *non serviam* of 'poetry makes nothing happen' is seen to arise from a concession of the failure of the Republican effort in the Spanish Civil War and a recognition of the shabbiness of the Republican doings in that war. Alternatively, it is seen as excuse making subsequent to the callow irresponsibility of the line in 'Spain 1937' regarding 'The conscious acceptance of guilt in the necessary murder', a line famously criticized by George Orwell, and a line which Auden revised in later versions of that poem.[24] There is also, perhaps, embarrassment at what Auden and Christopher Isherwood had once regarded as 'a war all of our very own',[25] the Sino–Japanese War, a war which they had gone on to treat merely as a touristic frivolity. Critics, then, seem to divide, either castigating Auden for his pretension and presumption in ever supposing that poetry could have a political impact or chastising him for his irresponsibility in failing to make effective use of what is held to be poetry's political power. And when the critics look to what was then the future, in particular the looming Second World War, the contradictory pattern repeats itself. Critics quote with disapproval, and go on to offer counter-examples of, Auden's assertion that 'I know that all the verse I wrote, all the positions I took in the thirties, did not save a single Jew.'[26] Others, especially when Hitler is included in Auden's assertion, find

---

[24] This paragraph offers an incomplete summary of the differing views of the critics cited in n. 2 above. For an account of the original line in 'Spain 1937', its change and Orwell's criticism, see Mendelson's editorial note in *English Auden*, 425.

[25] Auden's words to Christopher Isherwood, quoted in Humphrey Carpenter, *W. H. Auden: A Biography* (London: Allen & Unwin, 1981), 225.

[26] Auden, quoted in Robinson, *Poetry, Poets, Readers*, 54.

it altogether more difficult to refute: 'Nothing I wrote against Hitler prevented one Jew being killed. Nothing I wrote made the war stop a minute sooner.'[27]

The *immediate* context—Auden having so recently left Europe, then on the brink of war, for America—has, like Auden's own poem, a strong element of nonsense. It is difficult to imagine a more serious recognition of the poet and his political responsibility than the question asked of Auden's seeking refuge in the United States by Sir Jocelyn Lucas, MP, in the House of Commons on 13 June 1940. Yet, in a bizarre misprision of *Henry V*, the government minister, in his reply, thought he was being asked about the sportsman H. W. ('Bunny') Austin, currently representing Oxford abroad at tennis.[28] The situation resembles something out of *Alice*: anyone for tennis?

The other context for Auden's elegy is, of course, the life and works of Yeats, the poet who, according to the first line of Auden's poem, himself 'disappeared in the dead of winter'. Yeats's long writing career managed nearly every possible view of the relation between poetry and politics. The elusive ambiguity of his account of 'Easter, 1916', with its oxymoronic refrain memorializing a 'terrible beauty',[29] provoked Auden's Public Prosecutor to note sarcastically that 'To succeed at such a time in writing a poem which could offend neither the Irish Republican nor the British Army was indeed a masterly achievement.' In seeming contradiction of such a stance, late in his life Yeats was wondering, 'Did that play of mine send out | Certain men the English shot?'[30] Yeats, moreover, was the writer who made poetry literally disappear: when in 1936 he published his notorious *Oxford Book of Modern Verse 1892–1935*, the poets of the Great War, pre-eminently Wilfred Owen, were not there. More oddly and accurately, they were both there and not there, since a goodly portion of Yeats's 'Introduction' was given over to a discussion of their absence: following Matthew Arnold in the nineteenth century, Yeats asserted that 'passive suffering is not a theme for poetry'. And Yeats went on to offer this most extraordinary anecdote in defence of tragic joy:

Florence Farr returning third class from Ireland found herself among Connaught Rangers just returned from the Boer War who described an incident over and over, and always with loud laughter: an unpopular sergeant struck by a shell turned round and round like a dancer wound in his own entrails. That too may be a right way of seeing war, if war is necessary; the way of the Cockney slums, of Patrick Street, of the *Kilmainham Minut*, of *Johnny I hardly knew ye*, of the medieval *Dance of Death*.[31]

It may be; by whatever class and way one travels, it may not.

---

[27] Auden, quoted in Charles Osborne, *W. H. Auden: The Life of a Poet* (London: Eyre Methuen, 1980), 291.

[28] The incident is recounted in Carpenter, *W. H. Auden*, 291–2.

[29] W. B. Yeats, 'Easter, 1916', in *The Poems*, ed. Daniel Albright (London: Dent, 1990), 228–30.

[30] Yeats, 'Man and Echo', ibid. 392.

[31] Yeats, 'Introduction', in *idem* (ed.), *The Oxford Book of Modern Verse, 1892–1935* (Oxford: Clarendon Press, 1936), pp. xxxiv and xxxv.

The political and ethical controversies surrounding Auden's relation to the conflicts of the Thirties and to the Second World War are, then, as nothing compared to the contentions regarding Yeats and the Great War. The full complexities of this latter relation have been fully elaborated by critics, most recently in the brilliant accounts by Peter McDonald and Fran Brearton.[32] The less ambitious and more particular focus of this essay is on the illogicalities, contradictions, tricks, voiced silences, loquacious reticences, and sleights of hand which the extremities of human violence can cause poetry to enact. It is impossible—and indeed insulting—to separate the Irish Troubles from the First World War, and it is true that, whatever Yeats's own claims to the contrary, Yeats did write a number of poems which addressed the First World War, 'An Irish Airman Foresees his Death' being an obvious, if problematic, example. Yet the poem which most directly addresses the issue is a masterpiece of illogicality, its very existence contradicting its own argument:

> **On being asked for a War Poem**
> I think it better that in times like these
> A poet's mouth be silent, for in truth
> We have no gift to set a statesman right;
> He has had enough of meddling who can please
> A young girl in the indolence of her youth,
> Or an old man upon a winter's night.[33]

Yeats's alternatives—pleasing young girls and cheering old men—are trundled out too often and too automatically in his verse to be anything other than camp sentimentalities. Was the silent mouth of Yeats's poem in Auden's mind when he reduced poetry in his elegy to a mouth? The self-unwriting of Yeats's poem had begun earlier in a previously published version (that version had the more demotic 'We poets keep our mouths shut' in place of 'A poet's mouth be silent') with its then title 'A Reason for Keeping Silent',[34] and 'silent' is something of a signature in poems that are profoundly unhappy with their own existence and uncomfortable with the matter they are seeking—or not seeking—to address. For all his dislike of Wilfred Owen, Yeats had something in common with Owen in the way they both tied themselves in logical and linguistic knots in trying to describe the relation between poetry and war:

---

[32] See Peter McDonald, *Serious Poetry: Form and Authority from Yeats to Hill* (Oxford: Clarendon Press, 2002), esp. 'Yeats and Remorse', 17–50; and Fran Brearton, *The Great War in Irish Poetry: W. B. Yeats to Michael Longley* (Oxford: Oxford University Press, 2000), esp. 43–82.

[33] Yeats, 'On being asked for a War Poem', in *Poems*, 205.

[34] This version of the poem appeared in Edith Wharton (ed.), *The Book of the Homeless* (New York: Charles Scribner's, 1916), 45.

> Above all I am not concerned with Poetry.
>
> My subject is War, and the pity of War.
>
> The Poetry is in the pity.[35]

Again, in this extract from Owen's famous preface, we have the ostensible clarity and absoluteness of aphorisms, their grandeur further emphasized by the capital letters and by the gnomic utterances each being set apart in individual paragraphs. But when these statements are taken together, 'Poetry' slips out and in—now you see it, now you don't—of the argument which Owen appears to be pursuing, and we are left with something more like a riddle than a syllogism, a riddle in which the meaning of 'Poetry' withdraws into figurative vagueness and all but disappears.

As Auden's elegy with its meticulously recorded date reminds us, Yeats did not live to see the Second World War, but, like so many others, he foresaw it, not least in 'Lapis Lazuli', a poem written in 1936, the same year which saw the publication of his *Oxford Book of Modern Verse*. And 'Lapis Lazuli' is an extraordinary poem, thoroughly contrived, wilfully artificial, piling artistic example upon artistic example, and—though it mangles logic and language to say it—raising tendentiousness to a poetic principle. Because 'Lapis Lazuli' is a difficult poem in the frequent and familiar sense that readers require notes, explanations, and contextualization, critics have failed fully to register that it is undoubtedly a virtuosity of trickery and—arguably—a poem of extraordinary offensiveness: contrariwise, Yeats's biographer, R. F. Foster, records Yeats's own view that this poem was 'almost the best I have made of recent years'.[36] Like Auden's elegy for Yeats, 'Lapis Lazuli' is a poem divided into sections, so that the promise of coherence it makes to its readers is a circumscribed one, something less than—or other than—the sustained and consecutive coherence of a prose argument. Its beginning has particular women in mind—Laura Riding, Margot Ruddock, and, pre-eminently perhaps, the passionately political Ethel Mannin[37]—and Yeats is writing at an earlier stage of the women's movement when there was even less self-consciousness about the offensiveness of misogyny than there is today. Nonetheless, the poem's opening is extraordinarily aggressive, intent on taking no prisoners, a vehemently combative statement of a non-combatant position:

> I have heard that hysterical women say
> They are sick of the palette and fiddle-bow,

---

[35] Wilfred Owen, 'Preface', in *The Complete Poems and Fragments*, ii: *The Manuscripts and Fragments*, ed. Jon Stallworthy (London: Chatto & Windus, Hogarth Press, and Oxford University Press, 1983), 535.

[36] Yeats, quoted in R. F. Foster, *W. B. Yeats: A Life*, ii: *The Arch-Poet 1915–1939* (Oxford: Oxford University Press, 2003), 550.

[37] Ibid.

> Of poets that are always gay,
> For everybody knows or else should know
> That if nothing drastic is done
> Aeroplane and Zeppelin will come out,
> Pitch like King Billy bomb-balls in
> Until the town lie beaten flat.[38]

The poet then immediately shifts to invoke the example of Shakespeare, perhaps the most ill-judged argumentative move in the history of poetry. Invited into 'Lapis Lazuli' as an ally, Shakespeare does damage from which the poem can never recover:

> All perform their tragic play,
> There struts Hamlet, there is Lear,
> That's Ophelia, that Cordelia;
> Yet they, should the last scene be there,
> The great stage curtain about to drop,
> If worthy their prominent part in the play,
> Do not break up their lines to weep.
> They know that Hamlet and Lear are gay;
> Gaiety transfiguring all that dread.
> All men have aimed at, found and lost;
> Black out; Heaven blazing into the head:
> Tragedy wrought to its uttermost.
> Though Hamlet rambles and Lear rages,
> And all the drop scenes drop at once
> Upon a hundred thousand stages,
> It cannot grow by an inch or an ounce.

They 'Do not break up their lines to weep': here one concedes that Yeats is concentrating on the endings of the plays and is expressing a preference for certain styles of acting, a preference he expressed many times. He valued 'the noble art of oratory' over 'the poor art of acting'; he valued highly stylized, 'musical' 'half-chant', rather than actors speaking naturalistically 'as if they were reading something out of the newspapers'.[39] But *who* 'Do not break up their lines to weep'? The actors? Or the characters? The uncertainty is not an inadvertence on Yeats's part but a deliberately cultivated conflation or confusion, 'a blurred semantic space' as Jahan Ramazani characterizes it,[40] a manifestation of this poem's high Yeatsian trickery. We do not expect actors to burst into tears in performance. But characters often do, especially in Shakespeare. Yeats's assertion, then—'[They] Do not break up their lines to weep'—would seem to achieve the illogical distinction of being simultaneously true and false.

---

[38] Yeats, 'Lapis Lazuli', in *Poems*, 341.

[39] Yeats, 'The Theatre', in *Essays and Introductions* (Basingstoke: Macmillan, 1961), 168.

[40] Jahan Ramazani, *Yeats and the Poetry of Death: Elegy, Self-Elegy, and the Sublime* (New Haven: Yale University Press, 1990), 88.

Thinking of characters rather than actors, we have to recognize that again and again in Shakespeare iambic pentameter lines are left incomplete as words give way to weeping. Weeping is often explicitly discussed—for example, when Lear, reconciled with his daughter, asks Cordelia 'Be your tears wet?'[41] All the Shakespearean examples Yeats cites weep. In picking his poetic quarrel with those 'hysterical women', Yeats perhaps had the example of Lear pre-eminently in mind:

> O, how this mother swells up toward my heart!
> *Hysterica passio*, down, thou climbing sorrow,
> Thy element's below.[42]

But to keep Lear on side, Yeats had not merely to keep hysteria, 'the Mother', down, as Lear himself attempts—less than successfully—to do here; Yeats also had to make the rest of the play disappear from readers' minds, for throughout *King Lear* the King is repeatedly in tears and finds himself 'bound | Upon a wheel of fire that mine own tears | Do scald like molten lead'.[43]

In Yeats's poem, there is Hamlet, there is Lear, there is Ophelia, there is Cordelia. But where is the great soldier, Caius Martius, whose eyes, at the climax of his play, are made 'to sweat compassion'?[44] Where, above all, is *Macbeth*, the manliest and bloodiest of plays, the play much admired by Nietzsche, whose notion of tragic joy underlies Yeats's poem, the Nietzsche who had an especial admiration for *Macbeth*? Thus Nietzsche writes in *Daybreak*:

Whoever thinks that Shakespeare's theatre has a moral effect, and that the sight of Macbeth irresistibly repels one from the evil of ambition, is in error: and he is again in error if he thinks Shakespeare himself felt as he feels. He who is really possessed by raging ambition beholds this its image with *joy*; and if the hero perishes by his passion this precisely is the sharpest spice in the hot draught of this joy. Can the poet himself have felt otherwise? . . . This would be to stand the poets on their head: they, and especially Shakespeare, are enamoured of the passions as such and not least of their *death-welcoming* moods—those moods in which the heart adheres to life no more firmly than does a drop of water to a glass.[45]

Yet perhaps Yeats must exclude *Macbeth* from his catalogue of Shakespearean tragic heroes because that play offers the most eloquent refutation of the Yeatsian posture. Told of the murder of his wife and children, Macduff is counselled by Malcolm to 'Dispute it like a man'. Macduff's reply, in its humane simplicity, is unanswerable: 'I shall do so; | But I must also feel it as a man.'[46]

---

[41] Shakespeare, *King Lear*, iv. vii. 71.   [42] Ibid. ii. ii. 249–51.   [43] Ibid. iv. vii. 46–8.
[44] Shakespeare, *Coriolanus*, v. iii. 200.
[45] Friedrich Nietzsche, *Daybreak: Thoughts on the Prejudices of Morality*, trans. R. J. Hollingdale (Cambridge: Cambridge University Press, 1982), 140; italics original. For more general views of Nietzsche's influence on Yeats, see Erich Heller, 'Yeats and Nietzsche: Reflections on a Poet's Marginal Notes', in *The Disinherited Mind: Essays in Modern German Literature and Thought*, 4th edn. (London: Bowes and Bowes, 1975), 329–47; and Otto Bohlmann, *Yeats and Nietzsche: An Exploration of Major Nietzschean Echoes in the Writings of William Butler Yeats* (London: Macmillan, 1982).
[46] Shakespeare, *Macbeth*, iv. iii. 219–21.

We have conceded that actors, unlike dramatic characters, do not 'break up their lines to weep'. But even here, Shakespeare, enlisted for the counsel for the Yeatsian defence, in fact provides strong evidence for the prosecution: at Hamlet's request, declaiming the account of the slaughter of Priam, the First Player provokes Polonius to interrupt that declamation in wonder: 'Look whe'er he has not turned his colour and has tears in's eyes.'[47] A few moment later Hamlet himself describes the actor—'his visage wann'd, | Tears in his eyes, distraction in his aspect, | *A broken voice*'[48]: here, then, is an actor who does 'break up his lines to weep'.

The final line of the Shakespearean section of 'Lapis Lazuli' is self-sparingly vague: 'It cannot grow by an inch or an ounce.' What exactly does 'It' designate here? Hindsight has cruelly 'modified' Yeats's vague little word 'in the guts of the living' . . . and in the guts of the dead. For if 'It' has come to refer to the Second World War, 'It' has come to refer to a war unprecedented in the vast *scale* of its suffering and destruction; moreover, talk of not growing 'by an inch or an ounce' proves hard to countenance or even to contemplate in the context of the destructions and deprivations of that war's concentration and death camps.[49]

But Yeats's poem has at least one further trick up its sleeve. Turning to the piece of carved lapis lazuli which was given to Yeats by Harry Clifton and which, in turn, gives Yeats's poem its title, the poet writes,

> Two Chinamen, behind them a third,
> Are carved in Lapis Lazuli,
> Over them flies a long-legged bird
> A symbol of longevity;
> The third, doubtless a serving man,
> Carries a musical instrument.
> Every discoloration of the stone,
> Every accidental crack or dent,
> Seems a water-course or an avalanche,
> Or lofty slope where it still snows
> Though doubtless plum or cherry-branch
> Sweetens the little half-way house
> Those Chinamen climb towards . . .

Time has evidently not served this art object well, leaving it variously damaged. Yeats's poetic imagination transforms this damage into 'natural' phenomena or 'natural' disasters: cracks and dents become watercourses and avalanches; and the blurring of the carving is transformed into snow. (The words 'natural' and

---

[47] Shakespeare, *Hamlet*, ii. ii. 520–1.   [48] Ibid. ii. ii. 554–6; my italics.

[49] Placing this line in the context of our nuclear age, inaugurated by the nuclear bombing of Japan at the end of the Second World War, Jahan Ramazani makes a related but more extreme point: 'We may grant Nietzsche's and Yeats's tragic spectators that death is a part of the "eternal condition of things", but it is harder to grant that each war is as well; the possibility of nuclear annihilation—all the drop scenes dropping at once, never to rise again—has made it even harder' (Ramazani, *Yeats and the Poetry of Death*, 90).

'artificial' tend to blur into each other in discussing this poem, and what seems a commonplace opposition threatens to become a nonsense.) Yet Yeatsian artifice is not content to leave matters there. Thinking of the 'little half-way house' which is the Chinamen's imagined spring-time destination, the product purely of the poet's own fancy, Yeats in his imagination withdraws even further from—the oxymoron is inescapable—the reality of the art object before him:

> and I
> Delight to imagine them seated there;
> There, on the mountain and the sky,
> On all the tragic scene they stare.
> One asks for mournful melodies;
> Accomplished fingers begin to play.
> Their eyes mid many wrinkles, their eyes,
> Their ancient, glittering eyes, are gay.

Here artifice is piled upon artifice as, amidst music, imagined cracks in stone or imagined wrinkles of age on human faces are finally transformed into laughter lines. For one critic, Richard Ellmann, 'Under the tremendous pressure of the poet's mood, the lapis lazuli is made to yield the message of affirmation which he must have.'[50] An alternative—indeed, opposed—view is that this poem is as crazed or as crazy or as crafty as the carved lapis lazuli which it first contemplates and then artfully withdraws from, making even the reality of that art object disappear. On such a view, the poem plays on the reader, and on the troubled Thirties world in which its first readers must live, a sick and inhumane joke or trick or contrivance. Henry James (writing of Flaubert) says what perhaps can best be said on either side of the argument when he notes: 'Style itself moreover . . . never *totally* beguiles; since even when we are so queerly constituted as to be ninety-nine parts literary we are a hundredth part something else.'[51]

William Empson, distinguished poet though he was, was considerably less than 'ninety-nine parts literary'. On occasion, to the chagrin of readers and critics of poetry, public events, the forces they exert, and the non-poetic demands they make on writers can cause poets simply to stop writing—in the words of William Empson's poem, first published in 1949, a poem about stopping writing perhaps for fear of, or in the face of, madness, to 'Let it go'.[52] Empson's tendency to write (or a least to publish) very little poetry after the 1930s has been an enduring vexation and puzzle to his admirers. To one of the greatest of these, Christopher Ricks, Empson wrote in 1975:

I think you credited me with strong family feelings, and said I stopped writing because I married. There was much else which was a positive comfort to have said, but I had already

---

[50] Richard Ellmann, *The Identity of Yeats* (London: Faber, 1964), 187.

[51] Henry James, 'Gustave Flaubert', in *Literary Criticism: French Writers; Other European Writers; The Prefaces to the New York Editions* (New York: The Library of America, 1984), 340; italics original.

[52] Empson, 'Let it go', in *Complete Poems*, 99.

thought it a gap, a limitation in your mind that you cannot imagine a man taking a real interest in public affairs. I hope I have a normal amount of domestic piety and affection, and I wish now that I had more children—I respect you for having so many. But I dropped all my literary interests, even reviewing, because I got absorbed in the war; I thought the defeat of Hitler so important that I could do nothing else (it was a time of great happiness, looking back, and anyway considerable pleasure, but I have just a steady trickle of mental productiveness, and it was then all directed into propaganda). I still think the war was quite important enough for that, and a good deal of my previous poetry had been concerned to say so; it could not be called a betrayal of my deeper interests. I remember being scolded briefly by a journalist in a pub near the BBC, on his way out, near the end of the war, because I had dropped all my literary work so completely—'just left us cold', he said, assuming there was nothing else I was good at really; I was startled by an attack from such an unexpected quarter.[53]

Poetic silence or poetic nonsense, then, both seem common responses to the nonsense of the violence of war, but neither response should be confused with quietism nor berated as irresponsibility. It is the verse which promises to make sense of war, to keep or get things in proportion, that we should, perhaps, mistrust.[54]

[53] Empson, 'On stopping Poetry: an extract from a letter to Christopher Ricks', in *Complete Poems*, 126–8.

[54] The tendency which I have been describing here for poetry in the face of the extremities of war to 'disappear', to pursue evasiveness or trickery or even nonsense, is by no means limited to the verse of the late 1930s, anticipating the Second World War. Andrew Marvell, a major poet of the English Civil War, currently being (mis)appropriated, less than persuasively, by critics and editors as a politically committed poet, evinces such characteristics. Writing of Marvell, S. L. Goldberg describes this well: 'The only resolution the poems offer is the one they achieve as poems. And [Marvell] also recognizes what this implies: not only that as a man he has to maintain a difficult balance between equally possible but conflicting kinds of fulfilment, but that keeping such a balance is almost impossible—almost indeed, a kind of trick...This doesn't mean that his poems are politically or morally indecisive, however; his subtleties are not a way of evading choice or action. But they do delicately insist on the gap between the poet's activity and the activities he is writing about, between their own protean awareness and the limiting action forced on us in ordinary life. Usually...they insist on the loss as well as the gain involved in their own imaginative creation' (S. L. Goldberg, 'Marvell: Self and Art', in John Carey (ed.), *Andrew Marvell* (Harmondsworth: Penguin, 1969), 166–7).

Turning to the Irish 'Troubles' of the later decades of the twentieth century, we find Derek Mahon, at the beginning of 'The Last of the Fire Kings' (in *Poems 1962–1978* (Oxford: Oxford University Press, 1979), 64), intent on escape and poetic trickery:

> I want to be
> Like the man who descends
> At two milk churns
>
> With a bulging
> String bag and vanishes
> Where the lane turns,
>
> Or the man
> Who drops at night
> From a moving train
>
> And strikes out over the fields
> Where fireflies glow,
> Not knowing a word of the language.

> Either way, I am
> Through with history . . .

Again, as we have seen with Yeats above, there is the self-contradicting claim for silence—'Not knowing a word of the language'. 'Either way' signals that 'Through with history' is ambiguously contradictory, and we may read that ambiguity back into the previous stanzas of seemingly innocent escapist fantasy: what, in this Irish context, might those 'milk churns' contain or conceal? In the supposed beauty of the night, there is violence in 'strikes' and fire. And what does that bulging bag contain? In life, a string bag is distinguished by the fact that one can see through it, and when 'bulging', its contents are overt and obvious. In Mahon's poem, poetic trickery withholds such information and insight from us.

The Northern Irish poet Paul Muldoon has engaged overtly with Auden's 'poetry makes nothing happen' in his poem '7, Middagh Street', in *Poems 1968–1998* (London: Faber, 2001), 175–93, and in discursive mode has declared how in his poetry he does 'quite often engage in leading people on, gently, into little situations by assuring them that all's well and then—this sounds awfully manipulative, but part of writing is about manipulation—leaving them high and dry, in some corner of a terrible party, where I've nipped out through the bathroom window' (An Interview with Paul Muldoon', by Clair Wills, Nick Jenkins, and John Lanchester, *Oxford Poetry*, 3/1 (Winter 1986/7), 19–20). For a critical discussion of how Muldoon's verse evades interpretation, see John Lyon, ' "All That": Muldoon and the Vanity of Interpretation', in Tim Kendall and Peter McDonald (eds.), *Paul Muldoon: Critical Essays* (Liverpool: Liverpool University Press, 2004), 110–24.

PART IV

THE SECOND WORLD WAR

'OTHERS HAVE COME BEFORE YOU': THE INFLUENCE OF GREAT WAR POETRY ON SECOND WORLD WAR POETS

DAWN BELLAMY

'Why', Keith Douglas asked in 1943, 'are there no poets like Owen and Sassoon who lived with the fighting troops and wrote of their experiences while they were enduring them?'[1] Looking back towards his First World War poetic predecessors,

---

[1] Keith Douglas, 'Poets in This War', in *The Letters*, ed. Desmond Graham (Manchester: Carcanet, 2000), 352.

aware of the dual burdens of public expectation and personal anxiety, he answers the 'Where are the War Poets?' cry thus:

There are such poets, but they do not write. They do not write because there is nothing new, from a soldier's point of view, about this war except its mobile character. There are two reasons: hell cannot be let loose twice: it was let loose in the Great War and it is the same old hell now. . . . Almost all that a modern poet on active service is inspired to write, would be tautological.[2]

Despite his desire to avoid repetition and to write something new, Douglas is unable wholly to deny the influence of the soldier-poets of 1914–18. Their legacy is an inevitable part of the consciousness of an aspiring Second World War poet. Alun Lewis, similarly, links himself with Edward Thomas, for, as John Pikoulis puts it, 'like Thomas the war has become an integral part of his life experience, not a violent thought-slaying wound as it was to Owen'.[3] And John Jarmain begins his pre-war sonnet 'Thinking of War' with the words 'If I must die', echoing Brooke's diction in 'The Soldier'—'If I should die'—but ultimately advocating personal forgetfulness as opposed to national remembrance.[4] The influence of the First World War manifests itself in a variety of ways in the soldier poetry of 1939–45, ranging from the naming of specific Great War poets to the presence of symbols which acquired a new literary significance during the war of 1914–18. In *The Great War and Modern Memory* (1975), Paul Fussell identifies the emergent iconography of twentieth-century war literature, and explores those aspects of poetry which either originated in the poetry of the time or took on a new significance during the conflict, such as floral imagery, references to crucifixion and sacrifice, and homoeroticism. His investigation of that iconography's influence since 1918 is based on his theory that 'At the same time the war was relying on inherited myth, it was generating new myth, and that myth is part of the fibre of our own lives.'[5]

   The most distinct icon of the First World War is the poppy, with its connotations of bloodshed and remembrance. Immortalized by such poems as Isaac Rosenberg's 'Break of Day in the Trenches' and John McCrae's 'In Flanders Fields', its presence has a range of associations. McCrae portrays the flower as a symbol of remembrance—'In Flanders fields the poppies blow | Between the crosses, row on row, | That mark our place'[6]—whereas Rosenberg's 'Break of Day in the Trenches' makes explicit the connection between the flowers' redness and the colour of blood: 'Poppies whose roots are in man's veins | Drop, and are ever dropping.'[7] Nourished

---

   [2] Keith Douglas, 'Poets in This War', 352.
   [3] John Pikoulis, *Alun Lewis: A Life* (Bridgend: Poetry Wales Press, 1984), 115.
   [4] John Jarmain, 'Thinking of War', in *Poems* (London: Collins, 1945), 43; Rupert Brooke, 'The Soldier', in *The Poetical Works of Rupert Brooke*, ed. Geoffrey Keynes (London: Faber, 1960), 23.
   [5] Paul Fussell, *The Great War and Modern Memory* (Oxford: Oxford University Press, 1975), p. ix.
   [6] John McCrae, 'In Flanders Fields', in Jon Silkin (ed.), *The Penguin Book of First World War Poetry* (Harmondsworth: Penguin, 1979), 85.
   [7] Isaac Rosenberg, 'Break of Day in the Trenches', in *The Poems and Plays of Isaac Rosenberg*, ed. Vivien Noakes (Oxford: Oxford University Press, 2004), 128.

by the constant flow of blood from dying soldiers, the poppies fall, but are constantly replaced to drop again, as countless men become victims of 'the shrieking iron and flame | Hurled through still heavens'. Conspicuous by its absence in the poetry of the Second World War, the poppy, as a floral image, is often replaced by the lily. An exception to this is Lewis's 'The Sentry', but even here, the poppy is not the traditional scarlet symbol of the First World War:

> I have begun to die
> And the guns' implacable silence
> Is my black interim, my youth and age,
> In the flower of fury, the folded poppy,
> Night.[8]

Lewis maintains the First World War connection between the poppy and death, enacting the persona's resignation to his own death in the alliterative pattern of the penultimate line. The repeated fricatives hint at the presence of a tension which contradicts the composed acceptance of the recurrent 'I have begun to die'; yet the poppy, despite its 'fury', is 'folded' in on itself, hiding its redness and seeming to return to its pre-1914 associations of sleep. The poppy is outwardly detached from its 1914–18 myth, but by depicting his 'youth and age, | *In* the flower of fury' (my italics), Lewis's persona alludes to the all-consuming nature of the poppy, recalling Rosenberg's image of poppies rooted in man's veins. The poppy's bloody symbolism is only partially denied.

The presence of the lily in Second World War poetry is not only indicative of the conflict's different topography, but also evokes images of purity and innocence, as associated with the flower's Christian symbolism.[9] For the recruits of 1939, a knowledge of the horrors of the First World War was unavoidable, but still they enlisted, an action apparently in direct opposition to the anti-war message which emerged from some of the poetry of the earlier conflict. The lily in Second World War poetry can be interpreted as a motif of innocence, of the combatants' wish not to be seen as endorsing through repetition the bloodshed of 1914–18. Besides, theirs was a vastly different conflict, with a known enemy and a defined cause which, for many, underwrote their participation. Douglas, for instance, told Edmund Blunden that 'For me, it is simply a case of fighting *against* the Nazi regime'.[10] Begun in 1938 and revised in 1941, Lewis's 'Threnody for a Starry Night' alludes directly to the biblical image of 'the lilies of the field', connecting the past with the present through an image of communal darkness: 'We were the daylight but we could not see.'[11] The lilies and the 'glittering tree' are the only things able to 'endure | This

---

[8] Alun Lewis, 'The Sentry', in *Collected Poems*, ed. Cary Archard (Bridgend: Seren, 1994), 28.

[9] See Matt. 6: 28–9. The lilies of the field are cited as an example of simplicity and purity; their natural beauty is effortless.

[10] Douglas to Edmund Blunden, n.d. [Mar./Apr. 1944], in *Letters*, 328; italic original.

[11] Alun Lewis, 'Threnody for a Starry Night', in *Collected Poems*, 43.

silence ever'; immune to the sins of humanity, the natural world lives on amid the surrounding destruction. The resilience of the lilies here is comparable with that of the First World War poppies. However, their essential purity enables them to remain untainted by the 'mass rearming', an image which aligns the flowers with the soldiers' hope not to be tarnished by the only previous example of twentieth-century worldwide warfare. The lilies in Jarmain's 'El Alamein', conversely, are not a means of separating the Second World War soldier from the bloodshed of the past. Instead, they are a surviving symbol of the incommunicable nature of front line warfare, thus separating the combatant experience from that of the non-combatant:

> Others will come who cannot understand,
> Will halt beside the rusty minefield wires
> And find there—flowers.[12]

Jarmain reiterates the response of those First World War poets who believed that those who did not fight could not possibly understand the atrocities the soldiers faced. This similarity is undermined, though, by the discrediting of an alternative myth which was adopted by his soldier-poet predecessors, that of regeneration. Poppies often represented dead men. Jarmain's lilies do not:

> those that come to view that vacant scene,
> Where death remains and agony has been
> Will find the lilies grow—
> Flowers, and nothing that we know.

The lilies' presence is not an emblem of ongoing life. Instead, they exist as an inappropriate symbol of purity in a place where once stood 'the tanks, the guns, the trucks, | The black, dark-smoking wrecks'.

In contrast, Sidney Keyes retains the consolatory trope of regeneration, but does not return specifically to the floral imagery of First World War poetry. 'Cervières', written in 1940, makes a pessimistic prophecy:

> Soon an invader will be taking more than cherries:
> They'll be stealing our dreams or breaking up
> Our history for firewood.[13]

The damaged cherry trees and their stolen fruit are symbols of a more sinister form of destruction to follow as Keyes's persona imagines a future characterized by loss, but death remains implicit. The traditional consolation of regeneration, however, is explicit as Keyes enacts the conventional movement towards optimism: 'their despoiling is a kind of sowing'. Concluding that 'Somewhere our loss will plant a better orchard', the speaker comforts the crying children and, at the same time, reassures himself that the war is as much about life as it is about death. The elegiac

---

[12] Jarmain, 'El Alamein', in *Poems*, 21.
[13] Sidney Keyes, 'Cervières', in *Collected Poems*, ed. Michael Meyer (Manchester: Carcanet, 2002), 10.

tone of 'Cervières' demonstrates Keyes's need to find some measure of justification for the War; the hope of a 'better orchard' exists as compensation for the grief that Keyes predicts.

Douglas's self-elegy, 'On a Return from Egypt', offers and requests no consolation; he relished the opportunity to participate in the conflict, thinking of Alamein as 'an important test, which [he] was interested in passing'.[14] His final poem features both the poppy and the lily, but Douglas removes the floral imagery of war poetry from one aspect of its traditional mythology, and recasts it in an atmosphere of 'depleted fury'.[15] Douglas presents a reflective persona; separated temporarily from battle, he has a sense of connection to a more distant past, and thus to an implicit future:

> the specimens, the lilies of ambition
> still spring in their climate, still unpicked:
> but time, time is all I lacked
> to find them, as the great collectors before me.

These floral symbols are neither innocent nor regenerative in the traditional way, and although resilient in their continued springing, they are almost a mirage, a distant prize that remains just out of reach. Douglas's reflection on the lilies does not allow for nostalgia or issue a call for remembrance. His persona reveals that 'cold is an opiate of the soldier', gesturing towards, yet transforming the poppy in, an allusion to opium. The flower has been replaced. Its presence-in-absence acknowledges the earlier conflict, whilst suggesting that the poignancy of its role in the 1914–18 war is redundant for a soldier about to participate in the Normandy landings.

As he prepared for the events of 6 June 1944, Douglas believed that he was being 'fattened up for more slaughter'.[16] His choice of phrase has sacrificial implications: he presents himself as a potential offering to the enemy on behalf of the English Army. During the First World War, the sheer multiplicity of the deaths interpreted as sacrificial offerings resulted in the creation of a new mythology specific to the context of that war. In Hilda D. Spear's words, 'the symbolic sacrifice of the One is redefined: it is no longer symbolic; it is no longer a single sacrifice.'[17] However, this new mythology is not simply context-specific to the war of 1914–18; it is also resonant within the work of some soldier-poets of the Second World War. Lewis, for instance, in 'Lines on a Tudor Mansion', writes of the soldiers' inescapable knowledge:

> *We* know
> Violence terrible and degrading,
> Beauty disfigured,

[14] Douglas, *Alamein to Zem Zem*, ed. Desmond Graham (London: Faber, 1992), 15.

[15] Douglas, 'On a Return from Egypt', in *The Complete Poems*, ed. Desmond Graham (London: Faber, 2000), 132.

[16] Douglas to Edmund Blunden, n.d. [Mar./Apr. 1944], in *Letters*, 328.

[17] Hilda D. Spear, *Remembering, We Forget: A Background Study to the Poetry of the First World War* (London: Davis-Poynter, 1979), 103.

> And the coward cruel brute
> Shaping us in his image.[18]

With its allusion to Genesis 1:26–27, the end of this stanza registers the persona's cynicism.[19] God has somehow failed man by allowing such violence, by condoning the single sacrifice which has, it now seems, failed to prevent a series of subsequent deaths similarly intended to be for the good of mankind. Instead of strengthening faith in eternal life, all that these deaths have achieved is to separate a generation from the 'storied past':

> Only the fleeting sunlight in the forest,
> And dragonflies' blue flicker on quiet pools
> Will perpetuate our vision
>
> Who die young.

The poem was published in Lewis's first collection, *Raiders' Dawn* (1942), which pre-dated his posting to India by several months. His lack of military experience, however, does not prevent him from revisiting the sentiments of those First World War poets who questioned the role of a wartime God. In 'Last Pages of a Long Journal', Lewis writes:

It is a slow and endless mission. Often it will be too much, as the 1914–18 war was too much for Wilfred Owen; there was too much against him, and he was too much alone with his love of humanity and his hatred of the authorities who legalized the crucifixion.[20]

Spear argues that Christian myth was reformulated during the First World War:

Jesus the Son was accepted and loved because He was a suffering victim, whereas God the Father was rejected and often hated because he was willing to sacrifice Jesus. This willingness was no longer seen as a personal and supreme sacrifice on the part of God the Father, but as an act of harsh and selfish egoism. . . . The soldier victims were identified with Jesus; His lot was theirs: they suffered agony, bore their crosses, frequently endured a cruel and undeserved death; the older generation were identified with God and the Pharisees; they believed in the need for sacrifice and by their acts enforced it, yet it seemed not to touch them personally.[21]

Lewis, aware of this shift in belief, explores his predecessors' thinking in 'Lines on a Tudor Mansion', placing it in the context of his own fears about the violence demanded by war. He posits an alternative view in 'Finale', which was published in the same 'Poems in Khaki' section of *Raiders' Dawn*. Here, Lewis abandons his questioning, and is more easily aligned with the religious iconography of those First World War poets who perceived the soldiers' sacrifices as glorious:

[18] Lewis, 'Lines on a Tudor Mansion', in *Collected Poems*, 33; italics original.
[19] 'And God said, Let us make man in our image, after our likeness. . . . So God created man in his *own* image' (Gen. 1: 26–7).
[20] Lewis, 'Last Pages of a Long Journal', quoted in Pikoulis, *Alun Lewis*, 99.
[21] Spear, *Remembering, We Forget*, 101–2.

> Today he struck a final gesture,
> Arms akimbo against the sky,
> Crucified on a cross of fire
> With all the heroic age magnificent in him.[22]

The soldier's crucifixion here serves the common good through its magnification of a generation's heroism. There is a sense of triumph and glory in this man's death. Similarly, Keyes, in 'The Foreign Gate', writes of glorious deaths, not alluding explicitly to sacrifice and crucifixion, but attesting to their struggle and their role in 'the future's keeping' in his insistence that 'A soldier's death is hard' and that 'the death | Of these is different, and their glory greater'.[23]

In 'Lines on a Tudor Mansion' and 'Finale', Lewis explores the polarities of the sacrifice iconography which emerged from the poetry of the First World War. He neither focuses exclusively on the vision of a soldier's crucifixion as a triumphant end which creates another saviour, nor wholly adheres to the belief that a careless older generation continues willingly to sacrifice its sons without noticing that such offerings fail to affect the course of history. However, in a later poem, 'The Crucifixion', he emphasizes the futility of a 'surrender of self to a greater statement', concluding,

> he knew this awful hanging
> Obscene with urine, sagging on a limb,
> Was not the End of life, and improved nothing.[24]

Here, his proximity to the spiritually disillusioned poets of the First World War is at odds with the fact that he was writing without direct experience of battle. Inevitably though, prior to his departure for India, Lewis reflects on life and death, and these reflections are manifestly influenced by his awareness of what his soldier-poet predecessors experienced.

Douglas approaches the imagery of sacrifice and crucifixion from a different perspective, trying neither to justify the War, nor to explore its impact on an established system of belief. His war poetry insists on the inextricability of life from death, and persistently presents imagery of death's finality, suggesting that Douglas would not endorse the possibility of a worthy sacrifice: if, as in 'Dead Men', the dead are 'not capable of resurrection',[25] then it is unlikely that death, even in wartime, is able to serve some greater purpose. As early as 1935, in 'Famous Men', Douglas envisages the buried dead:

> And think, like plates lie deep
> licked clean their skulls,
> rest beautifully, staring.[26]

Such portrayals of death become more brutal eight years later in 'Dead Men': 'All that is good of them, the dog consumes.' Intensified by the War, these images leave

---

[22] Lewis, 'Finale', in *Collected Poems*, 36. [23] Keyes, 'The Foreign Gate', in *Collected Poems*, 63.
[24] Lewis, 'The Crucifixion', in *Collected Poems*, 107.
[25] Douglas, 'Dead Men', in *Complete Poems*, 100. [26] Douglas, 'Famous Men', ibid. 10.

scant space in Douglas's poetry for any consideration of the regenerative power of sacrificial offerings. Still, Douglas does not fail to recognize and address the mythology, if only to voice a denial of the notion of good emerging from evil. In 'The Offensive 2' he asserts: 'after the death of many heroes | evils remain'.[27]

Douglas articulates the worthlessness of the heroic death: evil cannot be eradicated, even by the sacrifice of so many men. What Douglas discovers moves him beyond those predecessors whose Christian beliefs were shaken by the realization that Jesus's death was not the final sacrifice. Owen's 'The Parable of the Old Man and the Young', for instance, while based predominantly on the story of Abraham and Isaac (Genesis 22), depicts the War as a sequence of consecutive ritual killings: 'the old man . . . slew his son | And half the seed of Europe, one by one.'[28] Despite their uncertainty, First World War poets continued to hope that exposing the truth would act as a warning to future generations. Owen states, in his 'Preface', 'All a poet can do today is warn.'[29] Douglas, by contrast, suggests in 'The Offensive 2' that others should search for their own answers, choosing experience over didacticism: 'take as long as you like to find | all our successes and failures are similar.'

In 'Landscape with Figures 1' Douglas addresses the issue of doubt: 'But you who like Thomas come . . . find monuments, and metal posies.'[30] Christ's presence in the poetry of the First World War was not necessarily indicative of righteousness and glory: some soldiers experienced the crisis of doubting their faith in response to the horrors that they were witnessing. In a letter to Osbert Sitwell in July 1918, Owen aligns his soldiers with the betrayed and condemned Christ: 'For 14 hours yesterday I was at work—teaching Christ to lift his cross by numbers, and how to adjust his crown; and not to imagine he thirst till after the last halt.'[31] Believing that 'pure Christianity will not fit in with pure patriotism',[32] Owen's religious faith underwent a profound change during the war. He claimed to 'have comprehended a light which will never filter into the dogma of any national church: namely that one of Christ's essential commands was: Passivity at any price!'[33] His experiences led him to question his faith, and although he argued that 'I am more and more Christian as I walk the unchristian ways of Christendom,' the searing of his conscience distilled his understanding of what Christianity really means.[34] Taking his biblical point of reference from the aftermath of the Crucifixion, a moment of spiritual doubt,

---

[27] Douglas, 'The Offensive 2', ibid. 98.

[28] Owen, 'The Parable of the Old Man and the Young', in *The Complete Poems and Fragments*, i: *The Poems*, ed. Jon Stallworthy (London: Chatto & Windus, Hogarth Press, and Oxford University Press, 1983), 174.

[29] Owen, 'Preface', in *The Complete Poems and Fragments*, ii: *The Manuscripts and Fragments*, ed. Jon Stallworthy (London: Chatto & Windus, Hogarth Press, and Oxford University Press, 1983), 535.

[30] Douglas, 'Landscape with Figures 1', in *Complete Poems*, 109.

[31] Owen to Osbert Sitwell, ? July 1918, in *Collected Letters*, ed. Harold Owen and John Bell (London: Oxford University Press, 1967), 562.

[32] Owen to Susan Owen, [?16] May 1917, ibid. 461.   [33] Ibid.

[34] Ibid. Owen writes: 'am I not myself a conscientious objector with a very seared conscience?'

Douglas nevertheless keeps the iconography as a peripheral feature in 'Landscape with Figures 1': instead of dead soldiers approximating Christ crucified, he writes of 'vehicles | squashed dead . . . stunned | like beetles'. He continues to defeat the reader's expectation: the doubters in Douglas's text do not, like Thomas, find evidence of resurrected life. On the contrary, the anti-pastoral imagery, similar to that at the end of 'Cairo Jag', intensifies the denial of regeneration. William Scammell suggests that 'The Doubting Thomas who comes to "poke fingers in the wounds" is perhaps the poet himself as much as it is the reader, fascinated to know what death looks and feels like';[35] like Thomas, Douglas seeks confirmation of death's immutability. Whereas Thomas is confronted by the miracle of resurrection, Douglas is rewarded with a less complicated answer. According to George Parfitt, in First World War poetry, 'If the soldier is actually identified with Christ, he has "put on the armour of God" and is fighting to save mankind. His death will be followed by resurrection and victory.'[36] The Christ figure is absent from Douglas's poem, and the possibility of rebirth is denied in a world in which the natural and the unnatural form a destructive partnership.

The soldier poetry of the First World War led the reading public to expect a certain response from combatant poets between 1939 and 1945.[37] Although very different in nature, in landscape, and in weaponry, the two conflicts inevitably have points of contact, some of which are reflected in the re-emergence, in Second World War soldier poetry, of these aspects of the poetic iconography (flowers, crucifixion) of 1914–18. Such images maintain a sense of continuity with the past; the war poetry genre, altered by the experiences of the soldiers in the trenches, remains recognizable in spite of the Second World War's difference from the First. One aspect of the iconography, however, is almost entirely absent from the poetry of the later conflict: homoeroticism. Fussell, recognizing this absence, asks:

Were writers of the Second War sexually and socially more self-conscious than those of the First? Were they more sensitive to the risks of shame and ridicule? Had the presumed findings of Freud and Adler and Krafft-Ebing and Stekel so diffused themselves down into popular culture that in the atmosphere of strenuous 'democratic' uniformity dominating the Second War, one was careful now not to appear 'abnormal'?[38]

These questions, which remain unanswered in *The Great War and Modern Memory*, form an important basis for an exploration of how homoeroticism manifests itself

[35] William Scammell, *Keith Douglas: A Study* (London: Faber, 1988), 171–2.
[36] George Parfitt, *English Poetry of the First World War: Contexts and Themes* (London: Harvester Wheatsheaf, 1990), 89.
[37] See Cyril Connolly, 'Why Not War Writers? A Manifesto', *Horizon*, 4/22 (1941), 236–9. Articles such as this illustrate the weight of expectation exerted by British magazine and newspaper editors. Questions were raised when writers did not respond in the same way as those involved in the First World War, and solutions were proposed: '*Creative writers should be used to interpret the war world so that cultural unity is re-established and war effort emotionally co-ordinated*' (p. 237, italics original).
[38] Fussell, *Great War and Modern Memory*, 280.

in the poetry of the Second World War. 'No one turning from the poetry of the Second War back to that of the First', writes Fussell, 'can fail to notice there the unique physical tenderness, the readiness to admire openly the bodily beauty of young men, the unapologetic recognition that men may be in love with each other.'[39] The role of psychology in the apparent suppression of homoeroticism is seen by Gregory Woods as only part of the explanation:

[I]n its attitudes to horror as well as to beauty, the poetry of the First World War is more concerned with physical detail than that of the Second . . . . One reason for this may be the static nature of the First World War . . . . Intact or broken, perforce, the next man's flesh took up a large percentage of the view. Furthermore, the Second World War involved all generations and both sexes directly. So, able-bodied young men lost some of the attention.[40]

The change identified by Woods is reflected in the hetero-eroticism of Lewis's poetry; it is not only testament to his own relationships with women but also represents the very different nature of the Second World War in terms of its locations and personnel. Both 'Raider's Dawn' and 'All Day It Has Rained' present heterosexual images which draw attention to the destruction and separation caused by the war—issues which affected Lewis personally, as he shows in 'Goodbye': 'So we must say Goodbye, my darling, | And go, as lovers go, for ever.'[41] The final stanza of 'Raider's Dawn' describes a 'necklace left | On a charred chair' which 'Tells that Beauty | Was startled there'.[42] Lewis's feminine image depicts chaos.

The domesticity disrupted by the War is also alluded to in 'All Day It Has Rained', in which the men stretch out in their tents, smoking, darning, and reading. Listing their activities, the persona recalls, 'And we talked of girls, and dropping bombs on Rome,'[43] a juxtaposition which again highlights the magnified relationship during wartime between love and death. A common feature of homoeroticism, the link between sex and violence, is not exclusively associated with relationships between men, as Woods explains: 'male homo-erotic themes in literature share many of the characteristics of the wider (hetero-erotic, but male-dominated and phallocentric) tradition.'[44] Lewis not only links sex with violence in a heterosexual dimension but also establishes a different link between the two which is particularly pertinent to the wartime environment: the violence is inflicted by those outside the relationship and, instead of connecting this violence with eroticism, his poetry demonstrates how the war changed the nature of sexual feeling.[45]

---

[39] Fussell, *Great War and Modern Memory*, 279–80.
[40] Gregory Woods, *Articulate Flesh: Male Homo-eroticism and Modern Poetry* (New Haven: Yale University Press, 1987), 69–70.
[41] Lewis, 'Goodbye', in *Collected Poems*, 110.   [42] Lewis, 'Raider's Dawn', ibid. 22.
[43] Lewis, 'All Day It Has Rained', ibid. 23.   [44] Woods, *Articulate Flesh*, 1.
[45] See Woods's discussion of the impotence depicted in Lewis's war poetry: 'the mere fact of being in uniform—generally considered such a fillip to a man's sexual appeal—seems to place one beyond the bounds of amorousness' (Woods, *Articulate Flesh*, 57).

Lewis's poetry from India makes clear that women were part of the soldiers' environment; a man's gaze was not necessarily directed constantly towards his comrades. 'The Journey', written about a trip between Aksa and Bhiwandi,[46] describes repetitive nights and days:

> Daylight had girls as tawny as gazelles,
> Beating their saris clean in pools and singing.
> When we stopped they covered up their breasts;
> Sometimes their gestures followed us for miles.[47]

Drawing on his surroundings, Lewis also revisits and inverts one of the homoerotic traditions of First World War poetry: a focus on soldiers bathing.[48] F. T. Prince's Second World War poem 'Soldiers Bathing'[49] also inverts this tradition: as the persona watches his 'band | Of soldiers', he is most forcibly struck by what Fussell terms 'a renewed appreciation of the Crucifixion', rather than by 'youthful beauty and potency'.[50] The overt religious tone of Prince's poem—'some great love is over all we do'—ensures that the naked men are symbols of the 'freedom' granted by Jesus's sacrifice:

> Because to love is frightening we prefer
> The freedom of our crimes. Yet, as I drink the dusky air,
> I feel a strange delight that fills me full,
> Strange gratitude, as if evil itself were beautiful,
> And kiss the wound in thought, while in the west
> I watch a streak of red that might have issued from
> Christ's breast.

Lewis in 'The Journey', however, is not spiritually motivated. Instead of watching men swimming, and thus contemplating the eroticism and, in Fussell's words, 'awful vulnerability of mere naked flesh',[51] Lewis's persona is confronted by women who choose to cover themselves, and whose vulnerability is not at stake. It is the soldiers who question their own mortality: 'There was also the memory of Death | And the recurrent irritation of our selves.' Even the potential hetero-eroticism is partially denied by the women's propriety, as if Lewis's persona, as Woods points out, is somehow desexualized by his experiences as a soldier. Similarly, in 'Indian Day', Lewis describes a 'supple sweeper girl',[52] allowing his persona's appreciative gaze to fall briefly on her body. She is merely glimpsed as she 'goes by | Brushing the dung of camels from the street', and remains a part of the wider landscape rather than becoming an object of sexual desire. The women with sexual potential in Lewis's poetry are kept at a distance; they are wives and lovers from whom his personae

---

[46] See Pikoulis, *Alun Lewis*, 202–3.   [47] Lewis, 'The Journey', in *Collected Poems*, 133.
[48] See Fussell, *Great War and Modern Memory*, 299–309.
[49] F. T. Prince, 'Soldiers Bathing', in *Collected Poems 1935–1992* (Manchester: Carcanet, 1993), 55.
[50] Fussell, *Great War and Modern Memory*, 307.   [51] Ibid. 299.
[52] Lewis, 'Indian Day', in *Collected Poems*, 142.

are separated while taking on their new, and temporary, identities as soldiers. Since the women his personae encounter as part of their military experiences are predominantly a reminder of difference, their presence works in opposition to the homoeroticism of First World War poetry. The focus on male flesh and its vulnerability in wartime enabled First World War soldier-poets, such as Sassoon, vicariously to acknowledge, via a sense of similarity, their own mortality. In 'The Dug-Out', Sassoon's persona addresses a sleeping comrade: '*You are too young to fall asleep for ever;* | *And when you sleep you remind me of the dead.*'[53] This reminder is not only of others' deaths, but also of the possibility of the persona's own. The glimpses of female flesh in Lewis's poetry, on the other hand, emphasize his difference; they make inescapable his distance from home, from his wife, and perhaps even from his previous sense of himself, thus compounding his awareness of his own fragility.

Like Lewis, Jarmain alludes to distant women, to those left behind by the soldiers. Their lives will inevitably be affected by the experience of war, despite their physical separation from the men who actively 'go out and sow this burning rose'.[54] Although in 'Sleeping on Deck' and 'Soldiers' Prayer' the lover's identity is not revealed, this is not ambiguity designed to conceal, as was common practice for some.[55] Jarmain sent both poems to his wife in his letters home from the desert, not only imbuing them with a personal dimension to complement their universality, but also hinting at the identity of the person to whom he appeals at the end of 'Sleeping on Deck': 'O, my heart has need of you here, | And the hollow of your arm to lay my head.'[56] Ironically, the predominant echo here is of Auden's 'Lay your sleeping head, my love',[57] a poem which conceals the identity of its addressee *because* of the text's sexuality.[58] In 'Fear', Jarmain's persona urges him to 'Think of easy and pleasant things' in order to overcome his realization that 'In all this sand a man's very small after all.'[59] However, when his thoughts immediately turn to a loved one, he reacts sharply, 'No, not of her; not of things too dear—.' The double caesura conveys his panic at having thought of something which increases his fear—thoughts of a loved one intensify the sense of what could be lost—and it is only when he turns to

---

[53] Siegfried Sassoon, 'The Dug-Out', in *Collected Poems 1908–1956* (London: Faber, 1984), 94; italic original.

[54] Jarmain, 'The Innocent Shall Suffer', in *Poems*, 38.

[55] See Alan Ross, *Blindfold Games* (London: Collins Harvill, 1986). Ross discusses his enjoyment, during the Second World War, of the work of Antoine de Saint-Exupéry, and expresses his surprise at learning of the writer's homosexuality. He explains: 'Until well after the war had finished, ambiguity in the description of relationships, or more often disguise, was the usual and almost unavoidable practice' (pp. 290–1).

[56] Jarmain, 'Sleeping on Deck', in *Poems*, 19.

[57] W. H. Auden, 'Lay your sleeping head, my love', in *The English Auden: Poems, Essays and Dramatic Writings*, ed. Edward Mendelson (London: Faber, 1977), 207.

[58] See Michael Schmidt, *Lives of the Poets* (London: Phoenix, 1999), 827: 'He masked the origins of his verse. . . . Thus to his main audience he remained a high priest, to his friends an impossible and wonderful queen.'

[59] Jarmain, 'Fear', in *Poems*, 29.

more mundane things that he is able to regain his self-control. In comparison with Lewis's personae, Jarmain's do not engage overtly with the sexual potential of the women from whom they are separated, and there is, in general, a lack of human physical detail in Jarmain's work.

One poem in which Jarmain does allow himself to engage, very briefly, with physical appearances is 'Prisoners of War'.[60] His opening simile—'Like shabby ghosts down dried-up river beds | The tired procession slowly leaves the field'—alludes to Owen's 'Dulce et Decorum Est': 'Bent double, like old beggars under sacks, | Knock-kneed, coughing like hags, we cursed through sludge.'[61] Owen's text continues its focus closely on the physical; Dominic Hibberd draws attention to its homoeroticism when he links it with 'Disabled' and writes that 'Both describe beautiful youths who are now in hell. The gas victim is said in a preliminary draft to have had a head "like a bud, | Fresh as a country rose"'.[62] In contrast, Jarmain allows the men to 'file away'. His persona envisages the imprisoned men as 'safe' now that 'They are quit of killing and sudden mutilation; | They no longer cower at the sound of a shell in the air.' Eschewing the homoerotic alignment of sex and violence, Jarmain distances the prisoners from the brutality, and in another Owen-like image, describes them as 'herded'.[63] Just as Lewis uses the foreignness of the women he encounters to prompt explorations of the vulnerability of his own position, so Jarmain's sighting of the 'Dazed and abandoned' prisoners provides him with the opportunity to reflect on the continuing danger of his own situation. He writes almost exclusively of their experience, and parenthesizes the only two self-referential lines; but the real concerns of Jarmain's persona lie in what remains unsaid. If the prisoners are safe at a remove from the battlefield, the implication is that those who remain at the mercy of the shells are constantly at risk.

The absence of images of 'physical tenderness' does not prevent the soldier-poets of the Second World War from being generally concerned with the same questions of mortality as were posed by their Great War precursors. What is significantly different in the case of homoeroticism is that Second World War poets such as Lewis and Jarmain do not make explicit use of the iconography which became so recognizable during the First World War. Whereas their references to other aspects of that war's literary iconography, such as flowers and images of sacrifice, form part of a conscious continuation of the soldier-poet tradition in which they place themselves, they turn away from the homoerotic imagery of their predecessors. In some cases, this is directly replaced by images of hetero-eroticism, possibly because it was deemed more socially acceptable, or simply because women were more visible as part of the war effort in 1939–45. In general, the shift away from a focus on the

---

[60] Jarmain, 'Prisoners of War', ibid. 37.
[61] Owen, 'Dulce et Decorum Est', in *Complete Poems and Fragments*, i. 140.
[62] Dominic Hibberd, *Wilfred Owen: A New Biography* (London: Weidenfeld & Nicolson, 2002), 277.
[63] Jarmain alludes to Owen's 'Anthem for Doomed Youth': 'What passing-bells for these who die as cattle?' (Owen, *Complete Poems and Fragments*, i. 99).

physical in Second World War poetry, as identified by Woods, means that images of the body occur less frequently, and therefore, that eroticism, whether homo- or hetero-, tends not to be a predominant feature of the work.[64]

In contrast to his contemporaries' engagement with the homoerotic iconography of First World War poetry, the presence of homoerotic imagery in Douglas's work is a more complex issue. Douglas frequently aligns love and death, and in doing so, he acknowledges the long-established link between sexuality and war. However, he resists any associations of comfort which might be attributed to such a link. Fussell explains:

What we find . . . especially in the attitude of young officers to their men, is something . . . like the 'idealistic', passionate but non-physical 'crushes' which most of the officers had experienced at public school. . . . What inspired such passions was—as always—faunlike good looks, innocence, vulnerability, and 'charm'. The object was mutual affection, protection, and admiration. In war as at school, such passions were antidotes against loneliness and terror.[65]

In the eroticism of Douglas's poetry, no such antidotes exist.

Douglas's '*Vergissmeinnicht*' is a poem rich with sexual connotations. Woods, in his study of homoeroticism and modern poetry, not only explores the connection between the wartime act of looting and male homoeroticism, but also considers the link between eroticism and violence, tracing its development as the nature of warfare changed: 'With the transition to fire-arms, the ballistics of sexual intercourse soon increase in deadliness.'[66] Both the homoeroticism of looting and the sexual connotations of firearms are resonant in Douglas's text. For Scammell, 'The dream of love [in '*Vergissmeinnicht*'] turns into the "nightmare ground" of naked appetite; sexual organs become nothing more than weapons or wounds; lovers are transmogrified into necrophiliac "combatants" whose courtship results only in death.'[67] What the poem's homoerotic elements exemplify is Douglas's departure from expectation in terms of the literary homoeroticism of the First World War. Characterized, in the opinions of Fussell and Spear, by its chastity and spirituality, the poetry of 1914–18 explores the connection between sex and violence within the context of the destructive consequences of the war's effect on loving relationships.[68] Douglas, however, in '*Vergissmeinnicht*', exploits more intensely the sado-masochistic associations of eroticism; the soldier is 'mocked at by his own equipment | that's hard and good when he's decayed'.[69]

---

[64] There are, inevitably, exceptions to such generalizations. Poets such as Dan Davin in 'Cairo Cleopatra' (p. 66), and Melville Hardiment in 'Holed-Up Cyclops' (p. 292), make explicit sexual references, and C. P. S. Denholm-Young's 'Dead German Youth' (p. 69) describes one whose 'face was woundless' and whose 'hair | Drooped forward and caressed his boyish brow', before continuing in what seems more like a paternal, than an erotic, manner; in Victor Selwyn (ed.), *Poems of the Second World War: The Oasis Selection* (London: Dent, 1987).

[65] Fussell, *Great War and Modern Memory*, 272.   [66] Woods, *Articulate Flesh*, 51.

[67] Scammell, *Keith Douglas*, 105.

[68] See Fussell, *Great War and Modern Memory*, 272; and Spear, *Remembering, We Forget*, 73–4.

[69] Douglas, '*Vergissmeinnicht*', in *Complete Poems*, 118.

The effect of the War on this dead soldier's relationship with his lover, a reminder of a First World War poetic concern, is simply one element among many within the sexual compass of '*Vergissmeinnicht*'. Blending homo- and hetero-eroticism, Douglas explores the complexity of coupling even on a formal level, with the inconstancy of the rhyme scheme presenting different pairings of *a* and *b* rhymes in stanzas 1, 2, and 3 before settling into a more regular *abab* pattern in the final three stanzas. It is pertinent that the loot discovered by Douglas's persona is 'the dishonoured picture of [the dead German's] girl', so that in taking this 'spoil', the persona claims not only the dead soldier but also his lover: the poem's sexuality is thus resistant to categorization.

The persona's lack of pity for his victim, and the interposition of Steffi between observer and observed, leave little space for camaraderie. Instead of mourning the loss of a beautiful boy, and finding consolation in thoughts of the similarity between observer and observed, Douglas's persona reaches a more pragmatic and infinitely less comforting conclusion. The degradation of the dead soldier, despite his lover's attempts at idealized permanence, is presented with the emphasis on the visual, as photographic evidence. By engaging our vision, Douglas shows us the battlefield's truth, a truth which ultimately has no regard for the division between lover and warrior. If the homoeroticism of such poets as Owen and Sassoon establishes an idealized love for one's comrades, Douglas's eroticism refuses to acknowledge love as a consolatory defence against a brutal killing: 'death who had the soldier singled | has done the lover mortal hurt.'

The homage paid to the First World War soldier-poets by the poetry of Lewis, Jarmain, and many of their contemporaries is indicative of their awareness of a sense of tradition. The details may change according to context and individual philosophies, but the sentiments espoused frequently resemble those conveyed in the poetry of 1914–18. The mythology which emerged from that conflict is sustained as the poets integrate features of the iconography visible in the work of poets such as Owen, Sassoon, and Rosenberg, men whose responses to their wartime experiences are repeatedly charged with having 'transformed' the role of the war poet.[70] Seemingly reluctant to challenge their preconceived role, many poets of the Second World War avoided the anxiety of influence experienced by Douglas by being unafraid of accusations of tautology.[71] Douglas, in contrast, makes no secret of his ambivalent relationship with the past, and although he makes explicit his attempts at disconnection, he is unable to deny completely his links with his predecessors; simply by being a soldier-poet of the Second World War he becomes part of a specific genre. That Douglas is not selective about the iconography—the eroticism of his poetry, for instance, sets him apart from his contemporaries—implies an unconscious, internalized

---

[70] See Andrew Motion, 'Afterword', in Matthew Hollis and Paul Keegan (eds.), *101 Poems Against War* (London: Faber, 2003), 136.

[71] See Douglas, 'Poets in This War', 352.

dimension to his use of the Great War's mythology. The vastly different nature of the conflict meant that the soldier-poets of 1939–45 would not be saying exactly the same things as their predecessors; yet their sense of themselves as part of a larger literary tradition enables them to transpose the mythology of the previous conflict so that the past remains resonant in the present. 'Almost all that a modern poet on active service is inspired to write, would be tautological.' But within Douglas's '*Almost* all' (my emphasis) is the space for the poets of the Second World War to write of their own experiences, influenced, rather than silenced, by those others who had come before.

CHAPTER 17

....

'DEATH'S PROLETARIAT': SCOTTISH POETS OF THE SECOND WORLD WAR

....

RODERICK WATSON

The conflict of 1939–45 came to be known as 'the people's war'. The ambiguity of this phrase, with its hints of a democracy that so many found only in death, has a special resonance for the Scottish poets in this account.

Reviewing G. S. Fraser's collection *Home Town Elegy* for the third of his annual *Poetry Scotland* anthologies in July 1946, Maurice Lindsay considered Fraser's 'somewhat defeatist philosophy', which he saw as reflecting

the terrible malaise which settled upon his generation (and mine, although I came in at the tail end of it) during the years before the war. It was a loss of belief in the worth of humanity, bred from the certain knowledge that we were growing up for war, that war was an evil and ultimately a useless thing, and that its arrival on top of us was as certain as tomorrow's dawn. Seen in retrospect, that feeling does not now seem so false as it might have done if victory in conflict had been achieved without the advent of the atomic bomb![1]

[1] Maurice Lindsay, untitled review of G. S. Fraser and Nicholas Moore, in Maurice Lindsay (ed.), *Poetry Scotland: Third Collection* (Glasgow: William McLellan, 1946), 63.

Fraser's early poems do reflect something of this spirit, showing the influence of Eliot and Auden in their rather sophisticated and world-weary tone. The young poet recognizes and defuses the debt by way of a self-deprecatingly ironic pose:

> Strange that so young I should carry only
> A civil mask and a handful of talents.
> Strange that the 'I' should have done so soon.
>
> No wonder the mask and the handful are lonely.
> No wonder I wander, a crazy loon,
> By the shining pavements and the duller moon,
> Seeking a poem for my handful of talents.
>
> 'What will you write about? Trees, politics, women . . .'[2]

In his poem 'To My Friends' on leaving university, Fraser reflected that his generation was 'born too late, in this unlucky age' and 'Must watch heroic honour rant alone; | And yet we have controlled our politic rage | And argued, sometimes, in an easy tone.'[3] His later work, especially the poetic 'letters' home from North Africa, would use this carefully calculated 'easy' tone to great effect.

Fraser was well aware of the political issues of the 1930s, and indeed the socialist manifesto he published as student editor of the *St Andrew's University Magazine* led to that edition being suppressed. Yet, in the poem 'To Hugh MacDiarmid' he reflected that 'mine was never the heroic gesture', and while he admired the older poet's 'thought that burns language to a cinder, | Your anger, and your angry poet's joy', he admits that there can be no 'Scottish Muse' for himself. Seeing himself as 'Convention's child', Fraser values the 'human or the personal' over any more inflated talk of cause, nation, or race, and regards MacDiarmid's 'Keltic mythos' with a shudder.[4] In 'A Letter to Anne Ridler' he reflected on his own weariness as a working journalist in Aberdeen and 'a poet of this century | Pursued by poster-strident images | And headlines as spectacular as a dream', suffering 'a headache from the endless drum, | The orator drumming on his private anger, | And the starved young in their accusing group'.[5] Nevertheless, when war was finally declared, Fraser immediately volunteered and joined the Black Watch at the age of nearly 25. His journalistic training and his physical awkwardness soon brought him to the Company Office, followed by a transfer to the RASC. In 1941 he was posted to Cairo to work on Army publications, followed in 1942 by a move to Eritrea as editor of the *Eritrean Daily News*, and then back to Cairo in 1944 as a warrant officer and staff writer for the Ministry of Information. Fraser's best poems of the war come from these years.

In an army that was to be greatly extended through conscription, George Sutherland Fraser was part of an increasingly educated and literate body of men

---

[2] G. S. Fraser, 'Problems of a Poet', in *Poems of G. S. Fraser*, ed. Ian Fletcher and John Lucas (Leicester: Leicester University Press, 1981), 19.

[3] Fraser, 'To My Friends', ibid. 36.   [4] Fraser, 'To Hugh MacDiarmid', ibid. 38.

[5] Fraser, 'A Letter to Anne Ridler', ibid. 45.

and women caught up in world events that would bring troops from Canada, Australia, South Africa, India, and the remotest parts of the United Kingdom to fight together side by side. Looking back to the poets of this time, Hamish Henderson remembered that he, like them, 'grew for war'. Henderson was four years younger than Fraser—'I was eighteen at the time of the Munich crisis, and nineteen when war was declared'—and, looking back from 1987, he reckoned that the Battle of El Alamein 'was one of the major formative events of [his] life':

The citizen army which was gradually built up in the Middle East to face Rommel was a literate army, its soldiers the beneficiaries of the 1918 Education Act. In this it certainly differed greatly from the set-up a quarter of a century earlier which their fathers had known. In the First World War the voice of the ordinary swaddy was the soldier's folk-song, documented in collections such as John Brophy and Eric Partridge's *The Long Trail*, and although the Second World War also produced quite a copious folk-song, the striking new thing was an amazing flowering of written poetry, some of it of quite a high standard. And of this poetry, a good deal of the most interesting undoubtedly emerged from the historic crossroads of the Middle East.[6]

Henderson was to make a major contribution to this output and was himself the anonymous author of songs and barrack-room ballads that satirized army life from the perspective of the 'ordinary swaddy'. In fact, in 1947 he edited a bawdy collection of soldiers' poems (including three of his own) as *Ballads of World War II*.[7] Nor was he alone in this endeavour, for a key anthology of army poetry called *Oasis* had been published in Cairo in 1943. Henderson remembered that the collection was produced by 'three volunteer editors whose highest rank was corporal', and went on to observe that 'Cairo saw an astonishing proliferation of poetry magazines and booklets during the war; others were *Citadel*, *Orientations* and *Personal Landscape*.'[8] The proliferation was indeed remarkable, for the *Oasis* editors had to choose from more than 3,000 poems submitted by 800 contributors.[9] Looking back on such work forty years later, one of those editors remembered 'a literate and aware generation' and reflected on the 'grass roots nature of World War

[6] Hamish Henderson, 'The Poetry of War in the Middle East, 1939–1945', in *Alias MacAlias: Writings on Songs, Folk and Literature* (Edinburgh: Polygon, 1992), 295.

[7] See Henderson to Hugh MacDiarmid, n.d. [1947], in *The Armstrong Nose: Selected Letters of Hamish Henderson*, ed. Alec Finlay (Edinburgh: Polygon, 1996), 13.

[8] Henderson, 'Poetry of War in the Middle East, 1939–1945', 295.

[9] These three soldier-editors were Victor Selwyn, David Burk, and the South African poet Denis Saunders. In 1976 Selwyn founded the Salamander Oasis Trust as a registered charity to publish and archive poems and diaries from the Second World War. An advertisement for such material produced the Poetry London edition *Return to Oasis* (1980), which included material from the original wartime volume. This anthology of known and unknown poets was so successful that it was followed by *The Schools Oasis* (1982) and *From Oasis into Italy* (1983), the Everyman Dent *Poems of the Second World War* (1985), and *More Poems of the Second World War* (1989). Finally, a selection from all these volumes appeared as *The Voice of War* (Harmondsworth: Penguin, 1996). Victor Selwyn, MBE, died in 2005.

Two'.[10] The anthologist Brian Gardner has also commented on a shift of emphasis in the 1940s towards a wider and less eclectic literary audience, with publications such as the *Penguin New Writing* series: ' "Leave this book at a Post Office when you have read it, so that men and women in the services may enjoy it too," was the advice of *New Writing*.'[11] Nor did Fraser lose touch with the literary scene at home, for even in the Army he corresponded with other poets. In 1941, for example, he contributed to, and wrote an influential introduction for, *The White Horseman*, an anthology of the 'New Apocalypse' group, edited by fellow Scot J. F. Hendry and Henry Treece. (Fraser was serving in Perth at the time, but his work had little in common with the movement, and he soon disavowed it.)

The remarkable literary contribution of the desert war in particular (one has only to think of Keith Douglas, Vernon Scannell, Sidney Keyes) is all the more striking for the fact that so many of the leading Scottish poets of that generation (and virtually everyone mentioned in this essay) found themselves in the same theatre of action. Fraser was posted to North Africa in 1941. In the same year Hamish Henderson arrived with the 51st Highland Division as an intelligence officer; Robert Garioch and Sorley MacLean were posted to Egypt with the Royal Signal Corps; while 21-year-old Edwin Morgan was on his way in a troopship, trained as a stretcher-bearer for the RAMC. In June 1942 Garioch was captured outside Tobruk; MacLean was wounded that November at the Second Battle of El Alamein; and George Campbell Hay arrived to serve with the RAOC in Algiers and Tunisia. Henderson survived the desert to take part in the invasion of Sicily and to follow the War the length of Italy. Hay also saw service in Italy and then Greece before being invalided home from Macedonia in 1944. (It never happened, but it is not too difficult to imagine a moment when all six of them might somehow have met on leave—perhaps in some Cairo café with Fraser presiding. Certainly they all knew each other, or knew of each other by mutual friends or correspondence.)

The theatre of the 1939–45 conflict was truly global, and its literature, lacking the single traumatic focus of the Great War's trenches, was to prove equally disparate. While poems were written about the heat of battle, many more invoke the boredom or misery of training, the weather, the delights and discomforts of military routine, cooking, camping, missing home, travel to far-flung places, or the social mix to be found in a citizen army scattered across the turning world. So it was that thousands of letters on such subjects were posted home, and Victor Selwyn—remembering the 800 contributors to his *Oasis*—proposed that this soon led to 'writing articles

---

[10] Victor Selwyn, 'Introduction', in *idem* (ed.), *The Schools Oasis* (1982), quoted in <http://www.salamanderoasis.org/news/obituary-selwyn-victor.html>.

[11] Brian Gardner, 'Introductory Note', in *idem* (ed.), *The Terrible Rain: The War Poets 1939–1945* (London: Methuen, 1999), p. xviii. *Penguin New Writing* was edited by John Lehmann. For a dense and fascinating account of the literary scene and the proliferation of small magazines in wartime Britain in the 1940s, see Andrew Sinclair, *War Like a Wasp: The Lost Decade of the 'Forties* (London: Hamish Hamilton, 1989), esp. ch. 7.

for unit wall newspapers, service magazines and poetry. The creative bug was born. The writing skill developed.'[12]

Some of Fraser's most effective poems from North Africa chose the convention of writing home. 'Christmas Letter Home', addressed to his sister in Aberdeen, allows the poet to remember his youthful awkwardness in the presence of girls called Bunny and Sheila and Rosemary (who also featured in an earlier poem called 'Social Pleasures': 'I smile, I say, "May I?" She smiles faintly, | We move off stiffly'). From the perspective of desert war and news of slaughter in Russia, however, such memories are 'Drifting and innocent and sad like snow'. Yet there may be strength here too:

> And Bunny and Sheila and Joyce and Rosemary
> Chattering on sofas or preparing tea,
> With their delicate voices and their small white hands
> This is the sorrow everyone understands.
> More than Rostov's artillery, more than the planes
> Skirting the cyclonic islands, this remains,
> The little, lovely taste of youth we had:
> The guns and not our silliness were mad,
> All the unloved and ugly seeking power
> Were mad, and not our trivial evening hour
> Of swirling taffetas and muslin girls.[13]

In poems such as 'Exile's Letter' and 'A Winter Letter' (again to his sister), Fraser reflects on how the separations of war 'with its swoop and its terror | That pounces on Europe and lifts up life like a leaf' may be no more than a rehearsal for the 'exile' of life itself—born of the perpetual unattainability of desire and the impossibility of ever returning to 'home' as we remember it; tainted, too, with the bittersweet taste of nostalgia:

> And last night I dreamt I returned and therefore I write,
> Last night my train had drawn up at a black London station,
> And there you were waiting to welcome me, strange but the same,
> And I shook your gloved hands, kissed your light-powdered cheek, and was waiting
> To see your new flat, and your books, and your hats, and your friends,
> When I suddenly woke with a lost lonesome head on my pillow,
> And black Africa turning beneath me towards her own dawn,
> And my heart was so sore that this dream should be snapped at the prologue
> That I send you my soreness, dear heart, for the sake of this dream.[14]

In 'Exile's Letter' he reflects that 'exiled from ourselves we live | And yet can learn to forgive | The past that promised us so much | And ends, alas, my dear, in such, | Such

---

[12] Selwyn, 'Introduction', in *idem* (ed.), *The Voice of War*, p. xxiii.
[13] Fraser, 'Christmas Letter Home', in *Poems of G. S. Fraser*, 56.
[14] Fraser, 'A Winter Letter', ibid. 83.

chatter in an exile's town'.[15] Cairo was just such a town, and poems like 'The Streets of Cairo', 'Egypt', 'Three Characters in a Bar', and 'Letter from Asmara, May 1943' all recall the louche gatherings of colonial exiles, displaced writers, and lonely soldiers that Fraser found in wartime North Africa:

> I write from one of those strategic places
> Where history, not love or verse, is made,
> And where men sigh for Aberdeen or Parma
> As endless pointless poker games are played,
>
> The winnings to be spent on lime-and-whisky
> (A new and barbarous colonial taste):
> These evening sessions tend to be repeated:
> These days repeat each other, with no haste.
>
> It would be futile, in this air, like you
> To sculpture verse or crystallise a myth;
> A shabby myth himself the traveller;
> Who once had lovers; who remembers kith,
>
> Who notes how women in this climate dry,
> But chatters bad French to a Syrian
> Dropped in his sex like pebbles in a tarn
> Making small circles: sex takes what it can.
>
> .   .   .   .
>
> The soldier is a cosmopolitan,
> You cannot trust his habits or his tastes:
> He likes to hear the news from home in letters,
> But readily returns towards his wastes.[16]

One man's weariness is another's excitement, and Edwin Morgan was to remember the separation and disruption of war as a kind of liberation, allowing him to recognize and realize his own homosexuality, away from the repressions of his native Glasgow, among like-minded men, or at least among lonely men who were willing to make a generous accommodation. In poems written more than thirty years later, Morgan remembers the happiness of comradeship in 'the troopship . . . pitching round the Cape in '41' ('The Unspoken'),[17] and, in an interview with Christopher Whyte, he agreed that 'The New Divan', a long poem of 100 irregular stanzas from 1977, was 'really largely about the war, though it goes back in time, into prehistory in fact. It's not just one thing, but to me, it's my war poem.'[18] His memories of Egypt are especially evident in the last fourteen sections of 'The New Divan', and stanza 95 reimagines the desert with great vividness:

---

[15] Fraser, 'Exile's Letter', ibid. 73.   [16] Fraser, 'Letter from Asmara, May 1943', ibid. 79–80.
[17] Edwin Morgan, 'The Unspoken', in *Collected Poems* (Manchester: Carcanet, 1990), 182.
[18] Morgan, 'Power from Things Not Declared', interviewed by Christopher Whyte, in *Nothing Not Giving Messages: Reflections on Work and Life*, ed. Hamish Whyte (Edinburgh: Polygon, 1990), 148.

Slowly tawny, slowly ashy, the desert and the day
suddenly gulp the plum of darkness. Rays
of indigo spill down the wadis. Tents are cheerful
with lights-out laughter but the round of things is the
night. On guard, I climb the water-tower. Strengthening
stars are thick in absolute black. Who ever mourned
the sun? A universe unbroken
mends man and the dark. No northern mists envelop
me . . .[19]

There is a certain liberation in distance and darkness as Morgan recalls the 'buzz' of Cairo—'Domes, shoeshines, jeeps, glaucoma, beads—' (stanza 97)—and the friendship of comrades and lovers. Here, as in all his work, the credo is: 'There is no other life, | and this is it.'[20] But other memories are not so kind. He 'dreaded stretcher-bearing . . . my muscles not used to the strain', but—

The easiest trip of all I don't forget,
In the desert, that dead officer
Drained of blood, wasted away,
Leg amputated at the thigh,
Wrapped in a rough sheet, light as a child.[21]

In the evocation of an urbane Cairo 'full of characters', G. S. Fraser can still sometimes lose his ironic composure: 'And Europe stinks | Of the perverted human will, is tortured | Just as our guts are tortured by our drinks. || And Europe spews up Europe, as we spew | Cairo on Cairo . . . .'[22] News of the winter war in Russia and the Battle of Rostov was particularly disturbing. Over more than two years that city was to be defended, lost, and retaken by the Russians against the German Army's efforts to break through to the oilfields of the Caucasian plains. In the opening onslaught alone, at the end of 1941, the Wehrmacht was turned back with losses of 14,000 at the cost of more than 140,000 Russian lives. The utter ruthlessness of the Soviet sacrifice, of death 'hammering, hammering, hammering home', moved Fraser to produce his most powerful war poem, 'Rostov', a cry of anguish at the terrible slaughter:

That year they fought in the snow
On the enormous plain, the rivulets
Thick with the yellow thaw, and darker, dark
With what at distance might be blood or shadows:
Everything melted, everything numbed, broke.
Every hand was pawing at desolation
And the huge, stupid machine felt a shudder.
It did not matter about all the dead

---

[19] Morgan, 'The New Divan', in *Collected Poems*, 328.   [20] Morgan, 'London', ibid. 251.
[21] Morgan, 'New Divan', 329–30.
[22] Fraser, 'Monologue for a Cairo Evening', in *Poems of G. S. Fraser*, 113.

> For what better than death in battle
> (The sick voice said in the belly,
> 'What better than death in battle?')
> And the heart had been numbed long ago.[23]

In complete contrast to Fraser's sense of melancholy exile—of exile even from himself—Hamish Henderson's poetry has a dynamic engagement with the dust and confusion of a modern mobile war. His work is wholly in keeping with a soldier's experience on the back of a lorry or under the stars at night, with irreverent army songs and barrack-room bawdry, with a direct hatred of fascism, yet a grudging respect for the human enemy over the horizon. All of this is reflected in Henderson's forthright ballads and in the large scale and almost epic address of his free verse 'elegies' from the desert.

As a child brought up by his mother and grandmother, Henderson was steeped in traditional Scottish and Gaelic culture and the oral wealth of the berry-pickers and travellers around his home in Blairgowrie, Perthshire. This inheritance was never to leave him, for he was lifelong socialist, an early translator of Antonio Gramsci's 'Prison Letters', and a political activist on behalf of the common folk.[24] After the war Henderson became a pre-eminent scholar and collector of Scotland's oral culture, one of the first members of the School of Scottish Studies in Edinburgh, and a leading light in the folk-song revival (working with Alan Lomax) in the 1950s and 1960s. Henderson's mother died when he was only 12, and, as a gifted child, he was sent to boarding schools in the South and eventually went to Cambridge in 1938 to study European languages and literature. When war broke out, he immediately volunteered, and his service began with the Pioneer Corps, building coastal defences in the South of England:

> From Spain return the Clyde-red brave Brigadiers.
>   I clench my fist to greet the red flag furled.
> Our hold has slipped—now Hitler's voice is rasping
>   From small square boxes over all the world.
>
> There's fog. I climb the cobbled street of Oldham
>   With other conscripts, and report to one
> Who writes with labour, and no satisfaction
>   That I've turned up.—From now, my boyhood's done.[25]

Henderson's interest in the folk-song tradition led him to collect popular songs of the day and to write broadside verses about the horrors, alternately comic and

---

[23] Fraser, 'Rostov', ibid. 54.

[24] Henderson discovered Gramsci's work while he was with Italian partisans in the War. He returned to Italy to study Gramsci further in 1948, but was repatriated by the authorities worried about his possible communist sympathies. His version of the *Prison Letters* was finally published in 1974.

[25] Henderson, 'Ballad of the Twelve Stations of my Youth', in *Collected Poems and Songs*, ed. Raymond Ross (Edinburgh: Curly Snake Publishing, 2000), 24.

grim, of army life: 'We get gobbets of meat, and veg to eat | That taste like sweaty socks, | And when we shit, we're afraid to sit | For fear of getting the pox.'[26]

He carried this practice into the desert war, often on a more serious note, and collected soldiers' songs from the enemy camp whenever he met Italian or German POWs. Henderson had a distinguished and unusual war career. As an intelligence officer attached to the 51st Highland Division, he saw action throughout the desert war, taking part in the invasion of Sicily and going on to operate in the mainland of Italy in liaison with communist partisans. (In the 1980 BBC television programme 'The Innocent and the Dead', he remembered entering Rome on his own in a jeep well ahead of the Allied forces.) Songs such as 'The 51st Highland Division's Farewell to Sicily' and poems like 'Ballad of Snow-White Sandstroke' and 'Ballad of the Simeto (For the Highland Division)' are eloquent testimony to an event-filled war and the poet's capacity to mix English and Scots idiom in robust verse reportage—as is 'Anzio April', with its villanelle-like recurring refrain:

> Kenny's bomb-happy: I'm a ruddy poet.
> By Christ, my case is worse and that's a fact.
> Maybe I'm nuts. Maybe I'll start to show it.
> Sometimes I think that all the rest are cracked.
> They're on the spot, and hell they hardly know it
> . . . Or so you'd think, the damfool way they act.
> > Spud's writing home, and Eddie thinks he's Bing.
> > *Over the grave all creatures dance and sing.*
>
> Snap out of that. Brigades of battered swaddies
> Have got to stay and shoot—or lose their pants;
> While strange to say our Jocks (the muckle cuddies)
> Have still an inclination to advance.
> Down Dead-end Road, and west among the wadis
> They'll pipe and make the Jerries do the dance.
> > Next month the race. Today we run the heats,
> > *And numskull death his little tabor beats.*[27]

Henderson's finest achievement, however, is the sequence of ten poems, *Elegies for the Dead in Cyrenaica*, which were written between Autumn 1942 and December 1947, and first published complete by John Lehmann Ltd. in 1948.[28] This long poem, more than any other in the literature of the period, catches something of the strangely spectral nature of the desert war. In his Foreword to the 1948 edition, the poet reflected on the genesis of the sequence, and since the North African campaign

---

[26] Henderson, 'Pioneer Ballad of Section Three', ibid. 37.

[27] Henderson, 'Anzio April', ibid. 110.

[28] 'First Elegy' was first published in the winter of 1943–4 as 'Fragment of an Elegy' in *New Writing and Daylight*, ed. John Lehmann. In a letter to Henderson from Cairo on 1 Jan. 1945, G. S. Fraser admired this poem, recognizing something of its loose and expansive force: 'like Whitman, the whole thing will be even more impressive when you have it in bulk. It's like a broad river carrying a lot of gravel along with it' (Fraser, in *The Armstrong Nose*, 6).

features so largely among the poets in this essay, Henderson's thoughts are worth quoting at length:

It was the remark of a captured German officer which first suggested to me the theme of these poems. He said 'Africa changes everything. In reality we are allies, and the desert is our common enemy.'

The troops confronting each other in Libya were relatively small in numbers. In the early stages of the desert war they were to a large extent forced to live off each other. Motor transport, equipment of all kinds and even armoured fighting vehicles changed hands frequently. The result was a curious 'doppelgaenger' effect, and it is this, enhanced by the deceptive distances and uncertain directions of the North African wasteland, which I have tried to capture in some of the poems.

After the African campaign had ended, the memory of this odd effect of mirage and looking-glass illusion persisted, and gradually became for me a symbol of our human civil war, in which the roles seem constantly to change and the objectives to shift and vary. It suggested too a complete reversal of the alignments and alliances which we had come to accept as inevitable. The conflict seemed rather to be between 'the dead, the innocent'—that eternally wronged proletariat of levelling death in which all the fallen are comrades—and ourselves, the living.[29]

This specular sense can also be linked to Henderson's lifelong socialist sympathies ('Stripes are shed and ranks levelled | in death's proletariat'[30]) as he recognizes that the ordinary soldiers had little cause to celebrate the imperial conflicts that had brought them to their end in the sand:

> There were our own, there were the others.
> Their deaths were like their lives, human and animal.
> There were no gods and precious few heroes.
> What they regretted when they died had nothing to do with
>   race and leader, realm indivisible,
> laboured Augustan speeches or vague imperial heritage.
> (They saw through that guff before the axe fell.)
>   Their longing turned to
> the lost world glimpsed in the memory of letters:
> an evening at the pictures in the friendly dark,
> two knowing conspirators smiling and whispering secrets;
>   or else
> a family gathering in a homely kitchen
> with Mum so proud of her boys in uniform.[31]

The Cyrenaica elegies invoke a freezing and scorching landscape, steeped in history and dust; yet this paradoxically empty space is a symbolic stage where the

---

[29] Henderson, 'Foreword to the 1948 Edition', in *Elegies for the Dead in Cyrenaica* (Edinburgh: EUSPB, 1977), 59.
[30] Henderson, 'Third Elegy: Leaving the City', in *Collected Poems and Songs*, 55.
[31] Henderson, 'First Elegy: End of a Campaign', ibid. 52.

metaphysical and the material come together, in the shade of Pharaohs, Greeks, and Romans, in a war of trucks, jeeps, and perpetual movement. The 'Fourth Elegy: El Adem', echoes the language of the Bible—appropriately enough in such a bitter place, with more than an echo of Scottish Calvinist fervour: 'The sons of man | grow and go down in pain: they kneel for the load | and bow like brutes, in patience accepting the burden, | the pain fort and dour.'[32] In other poems Henderson uses snatches of Scots, Gaelic, Italian, and German, quoting from Sorley MacLean, Cavafy, Dante, Goethe, and Hölderlin, while his register moves from soldiers' slang to a high-reaching rhetorical address, not far from the passionate strain to be found in the poets of the New Apocalypse, as in these closing lines from the last elegy:

> Run stumble and fall in our desert of failure,
> impaled, unappeased. And inhabit that desert
> of canyon and dream—till we carry to the living
> blood, fire and red flambeaux of death's proletariat.
> Take iron in your arms! At last, spanning this history's
> apollyon chasm, proclaim them the reconciled.[33]

The final effect can be as stark and uncompromising as the landscape it evokes; but perhaps the most memorable and successful poems are those that bring this epic vision closest to the everyday evolution of the troops on both sides. In a poem that can stand alongside Keith Douglas's '*Vergissmeinnicht*' and Sorley MacLean's 'Glac a' Bhàis', Henderson's 'Seventh Elegy: Seven Good Germans', imagines the lives and last hours of seven dead troopers. Or another day in the desert is captured in the terse free verse of the 'Second Elegy: Halfaya':

> At dawn, under the concise razor-edge
> of the escarpment, the laager sleeps. No petrol fires yet
> blow flame for brew-up. Up on the pass a sentry
> inhales his Nazionale. Horse-shoe curve of the bay
> grows visible beneath him. He smokes and yawns.
> Ooo-augh,
>   and the limitless
> shabby lion-pelt of the desert completes and rounds
> his limitless ennui.[34]

Reviewing these elegies for the *New Statesman* in 1949, Giles Romilly remarked on the 'distinctive power and clarity' of such poems from the desert campaign. 'The simplicity of the scene, the sense of space, the presence of a manageable number of objects—can one doubt these set the poet free? . . . The desert was like the stain

[32] Henderson, 'Fourth Elegy: El Adem', ibid. 57. 'Peine fort et dur' was a medieval torture reserved for those who would plead neither 'guilty' nor 'not guilty'. Rocks were piled upon them until they succumbed—one way or the other.

[33] Henderson, 'Tenth Elegy: The Frontier', ibid. 72. Apollyon is a demon of the bottomless pit in Rev. 9: 11.

[34] Henderson, 'Second Elegy: Halfaya', ibid. 53.

of dye with which a scientist colours a piece of matter before looking at it under a microscope. It allowed detail to stand out and take on symbolic value.'[35]

The same intensity can be found in the work of Gaelic poet Sorley MacLean, who was born and brought up, the son of a tailor, on the island of Raasay, between Skye and the Scottish mainland. He was still more ambivalent than Henderson about fighting for an empire and an English-speaking hegemony that had, in effect, done much to marginalize (and at one time to suppress) his own native language and culture. The relationship between Highland Scotland and 'Great Britain' had been a complex one ever since the Jacobite uprisings in 1715 and 1745—the last civil wars to be fought on British soil. These conflicts had Scots fighting on both sides and then, with the formation of the frontier-guard Black Watch in 1725, the start of a military tradition that saw Highland regiments recruited to fight for the glory of the British Empire in battlefields all round the globe. Henderson saw the paradoxes of this situation, and viewed the Highland soldiers with a romantic eye: 'conscripts of a fast vanishing race, on whom the dreadful memory of the clearances rests, and for whom there is little left to sustain them in the high places of the field but the heroic tradition of *gaisge* (valour)'.[36] Sorley MacLean was more brutally pragmatic, at least with what seemed like the certainties of the 1930s:

My fear and hatred of the Nazis [is] even more than my hatred of the English Empire. My only hope is that the British and German Empires will exhaust each other and leave the Soviet the dominating influence on the oppressed people of all Europe including Britain and Germany.... The only real war is the class war and I see my own little part merely as one that contributes to the mutual exhaustion of the British and German Empires. I support the British Empire because it is the weakest and therefore not as great a threat to Europe and the rest of the world as a German victory.[37]

MacLean disliked what he saw as the 'vile, cast iron, bourgeois class rule in the British army',[38] but his anxieties about the rise of fascism had been clear since the 1930s, when he had agonized about whether to volunteer for the International Brigade to fight against Franco in Spain. The emotional upheaval that MacLean underwent in the struggle between his socialist principles, painful family commitments, and a series of intensely complex love affairs produced the *Dàin do Eimhir* sequence, which many critics regard, along with Christopher Whyte, as arguably the major achievement of Scottish Gaelic poetry in the twentieth century. These love poems to 'Eimhir' were written between 1931 and 1941 before being collected and published in 1943.[39] They take the name of Cuchulainn's

---

[35] Giles Romilly, quoted in Henderson, *Elegies for the Dead in Cyrenaica*, 63.

[36] Henderson, 'Foreword to the 1948 Edition', 60.

[37] Sorley MacLean to Hugh MacDiarmid, 8 Mar. 1941, quoted in Joy Hendry, 'Sorley MacLean: The Man and his Work', in Raymond J. Ross and Joy Hendry (eds.), *Sorley MacLean: Critical Essays* (Edinburgh: Scottish Academic Press, 1986), 27.

[38] MacLean to Douglas Young, 27 Oct. 1940, ibid.

[39] Sorley MacLean, *Dàin do Eimhir* (Glasgow: William MacLellan, 1943). Critics have argued that this should be regarded as the definitive edition, although the volume contained only forty-nine out of

wife as the symbolic beloved in a series of intensely painful and passionately conscience-stricken meditations, exaltations, and bitter complaints that struggle to find a balance between love and war, passion and politics, selfish and social values, obsession and reason:

> Dè bhiodh pòg do bheòil uaibhrich
> mar ris gach braon den fhuil luachmhoir
> a thuit air raointean reòta fuara
> nam beann Spàinnteach bho fhòirne cruadhach?
>
> What would the kiss of your proud mouth be
> compared with each drop of the precious blood
> that fell on the cold frozen uplands
> of Spanish mountains from a column of steel?[40]

On the outbreak of war MacLean also started to write 'An Cuilithionn'/'The Cuillin', a long and fervently political poem which took the spectacular mountain range on Skye as a metaphor of striving and almost unattainable ideals, surrounded by broken ground and a global morass of human pain and misery, including the history of the Clearances and his own people:

> and until the whole red Army comes
> battle-marching across Europe,
> that song of wretchedness will seep
> into my heart and my senses.
> The warriors of the poor mouldering
> rotting carcases in Spain,
> and the hundreds of thousands in China.[41]

The work was never completed to the poet's satisfaction, and his disillusionment with Stalin's Russia after the War led him to leave it unpublished until its appearance in the 1987–8 issue of *Chapman* magazine. He continued to work on the *Dàin do Eimhir* sequence, however, while he was serving in North Africa, writing the uncollected short lyric 'Knightsbridge, Libia' in June 1942: 'Though I am to-day against the breast of battle | not here my burden and extremity; not Rommel's guns and tanks, | but that my darling should be crooked and a liar.'[42] Yet the fatigue of war and the reality of battle led to doubts about his writing, if only for the moment, as he confessed in a letter to Hugh MacDiarmid that he was 'very much ashamed

---

sixty-nine poems that were written in a series of creative bursts over a period of ten years. The complete poems and an extensive account of their history can be found in Somhairle MacGill-Eain/Sorley MacLean, *Dàin do Eimhir*, ed. Christopher Whyte (Glasgow: ASLS, 2002).

[40] Maclean, 'IV', in *Dàin do Eimhir*, 48; later titled 'Gaoir na h'-Eòrpa'/'The Cry of Europe'. All English translations by the poet himself.

[41] Maclean, 'An Cuilithionn'/'The Cuillin', in *From Wood to Ridge: Collected Poems in Gaelic and English* (Manchester: Carcanet, 1989), 75.

[42] Maclean, 'Knightsbridge, Libia', in Maurice Lindsay (ed.), *Poetry Scotland: Second Collection* (Glasgow: MacLellan, 1945), 42.

of [his] preoccupation with [his] own private troubles'.[43] Nevertheless, MacLean continued to work on the collection while he was recovering in hospital from the wounds that sent him home from the War with shattered feet, helped by Douglas Young, with whom he had kept in touch since his student days in Edinburgh. (Young had introduced him to MacDiarmid then.) In hospital he began to remove some of the lyrics of more personal complaint, to reveal the leaner and more universalized sequence that was eventually published in 1943.

It was the clarity of the desert itself that led MacLean to write about his experiences in his most direct and effective war poetry. In 'Dol an Iar'/'Going Westward' he goes 'westwards in the Desert | with my shame on my shoulders, | that I was made a laughing-stock | since I was as my people were'.[44] He reflects on the far-flung nature of the conflict from the bombing of Glasgow and Prague, from Guernica to Belsen; yet in a moment of insight akin to Henderson's vision of the common soldier's lot, he recognizes that 'there is no rancour in my heart | against the hardy soldiers of the Enemy, | but the kinship that there is among | men in prison on a tidal rock.' Nevertheless, 'this is the struggle not to be avoided, | the sore extreme of human-kind', and he will find renewed strength by calling on 'the big men of Braes', and 'the heroic Raasay MacLeods' from the very ancestry that he was once made to feel ashamed of. The poem ends on a rhetorical question, but not without an ambivalent note called up by the word 'ruinous': 'the men of my name—who were braver | when their ruinous pride was kindled?' Indeed, that same tradition of Highland pride is subtly called into question once again in the poem 'Curaidhean'/'Heroes' in which he remembers an English soldier who died at his post: 'A poor little chap with chubby cheeks | and knees grinding each other, | pimply unattractive face— | garment of the bravest spirit.' The poem ends:

> Chunnaic mi gaisgeach mór á Sasuinn,
> fearachan bochd nach laigheadh sùil air;
> cha b' Alasdair á Gleanna Garadh—
> is thug e gal beag air mo shùilean.

> I saw a great warrior of England,
> a poor manikin on whom no eye would rest;
> no Alasdair of Glen Garry;
> and he took a little weeping to my eyes.[45]

There is no irony in this praise, except perhaps to reflect on the inadequacy of all such vaunting, and on the vanity that lies behind the 'big men' and the colourful heroes of battlefield legend. The poet's understatement sees the anonymity of modern war in a plainer light, for 'Word came to him in the bullet shower | that he should be a hero briskly, | and he was that while he lasted | but it wasn't much

[43] MacLean to Hugh MacDiarmid, 15 Mar. 1942, Edinburgh University Library, MS 2954.13.
[44] MacLean, 'Dol an Iar'/'Going Westward', in *From Wood to Ridge*, 205.
[45] MacLean, 'Curaidhean'/'Heroes', ibid. 210.

time he got.' The poem's conclusion establishes a kinship in grief for this 'poor manikin' by echoing the last lines of a formal lament for the Jacobite Alasdair Dubh MacDonell, the 11th chieftain of Glengarry, written by Cicely MacDonald in 1721: 'Thug thu 'n diugh gal air mo shùilibh' ('You brought tears to my eyes today'). The reference is further complicated, however, by the fact that the 15th chief of Glengarry, also called Alasdair, is remembered as a flamboyant and vain character, swathed in tartan and immortalized in a famous portrait by Raeburn. Proud of his ancestry and touchy about his status, he was not averse to 'improving' his estate and clearing his tenants off the land. In either case, MacLean's chubby Englishman with his 'ugly high-pitched voice' is less, and also more, than these romantic icons from a warlike Highland past. The poet's tone is equally muted in 'Glac a' Bhàis'/'Death Valley', thinking of a dead German boy, 'with his forelock down about his cheek'. He may have been an abuser of the Jews, but perhaps he was also a member of that greater band—'led, from the beginning of generations, | unwillingly to the trial | and mad delirium of every war | for the sake of rulers?' In any case, 'he showed no pleasure in his death | below the Ruweisat Ridge'.[46]

These few poems by Sorley MacLean are among the most memorable of the desert war. Their matter-of-fact tone is completely different from the passionate address of 'The Cuillin' or 'Poems to Eimhir', yet there is emotional and conceptual complexity here, as the poet negotiates the double-edged references to his own Gaelic heritage. Thus 'Latha Foghair'/'An Autumn Day' remembers lying all day on a slope under an artillery bombardment with six dead men:

> Ris a' ghréin 's i cho coma,
> cho geal cràiteach;
> air a' ghainmhich 's i cho tìorail
> socair bàidheil;
> agus fo reultan Africa,
> 's iad leugach àlainn.
>
> Ghabh aon Taghadh iadsan
> 's cha d' ghabh e mise,
> gun fhoighneachd dhinn
> có b' fheàrr no bu mhiosa.
>
> In the sun which was so indifferent,
> so white and painful;
> on the sand which was so comfortable
> easy and kindly;
> and under the stars of Africa,
> jewelled and beautiful.
>
> One Election took them
> and did not take me,

[46] MacLean, 'Glac a' Bhàis'/'Death Valley', ibid. 211.

without asking us
which was better or worse.[47]

MacLean's ironic reference to 'Election' takes the poet back to his early upbringing in the Free Church, with its Calvinist emphasis on the 'elect' as those who are already saved—a doctrine he resisted even as a boy. In a letter to Douglas Young in 1941, he recalled his sense of injustice at a faith in which so many are born to be inevitably damned, and he reflected that 'perhaps my obsession with the "cause" of the unhappy, the unsuccessful, the oppressed comes ultimately from this'.[48]

In the barrenness of the desert MacLean, like Henderson, can indeed confront larger causes than those of the immediate conflict. Nor was he alone in this wider sense of human life and social injustice, for it is also the characteristic position of his fellow Gael, George Campbell Hay. If MacLean and Henderson have compassion for the German dead, Hay was to be terribly haunted by the sufferings of the native Arab population, caught up in another culture's war and openly despised by both sides. In fact, Hay's hatred of what he saw as English racism and imperialism and his strong Scottish nationalist sympathies had led him to appeal against conscription as a conscientious objector, and when his appeal failed, he took to the hills of his native Argyll to escape arrest.

Hay was not alone among Scots writers in resisting the War, although each had his own and different reasons. The novelist Robin Jenkins and the poets George Bruce and Norman MacCaig expressed profoundly held moral objections to the taking of life and were accepted as conscientious objectors—although MacCaig had to serve a short prison sentence for refusing to take civilian work that directly supported the military effort. Edwin Morgan had felt the same, before accepting service in the Royal Army Medical Corps. On the other hand, Douglas Young refused conscription in order to raise a legal argument about the sovereignty of Scotland and the precise status of the 1707 Treaty of Union. He made his political point but—not surprisingly—lost the case and served a term in jail.[49]

The reluctance of what Fraser saw as his 'unlucky generation' to give way to expressions of patriotic fervour is hardly surprising after the horror of the Great War and the economic and spiritual depressions that followed it. C. Day Lewis caught the spirit of the times (at least in his circle) with his poem about defending 'the bad against the worse' when asked to speak for freedom by a capitalist establishment notable only for its folly and greed.[50] Socialist disaffection was even more marked in Scotland, where the post-war decline of heavy industry, urban decay, and mass unemployment had reached truly crisis levels in the 1930s. Following from John

[47] MacLean, 'Latha Foghair'/'An Autumn Day', ibid. 215.
[48] MacLean, quoted in *Dàin do Eimhir*, 141.
[49] For his own account of this affair, see Douglas Young, *Chasing an Ancient Greek* (London: Hollis and Carter, 1950), ch. 10, esp. pp. 56–66.
[50] C. Day Lewis, 'Where are the War Poets?', in *Collected Poems of C. Day Lewis* (London: Jonathan Cape with Hogarth Press, 1954), 228.

Maclean and the 'Red Clydeside' of the 1920s, such conditions produced rising Scottish support for the ILP under James Maxton and Tom Johnston. The Home Rule question began to stir again, and support for Scottish nationalism actually grew stronger in the 1930s and the early years of the War. (Under the impetus of Hugh MacDiarmid, after all, the Scottish literary renaissance had produced its finest work in the years between 1923 and 1939 in a movement that had always insisted on the marriage of cultural and political issues.) Now further tensions were generated as English workers came north to staff Scottish factories (despite still widespread local unemployment), while the Ministry of Labour caused even more resentment by conscripting thousands of young Scottish women and sending them south to work in munitions factories in the Midlands.[51] Tom Johnston, who became Secretary of State for Scotland in 1941, spoke for Home Rule by citing the shocking disparities between Scotland and England in matters of industrial investment, slum renewal, unemployment, and infant mortality.

Such were the considerations that had fuelled the socialism of MacDiarmid, Henderson, and Sorley MacLean, and which gave a particularly anti-English bias to the nationalism of young George Campbell Hay, now working as a teacher in Edinburgh after graduating from Oxford with a degree in classics.[52] Hay's refusal to serve was not to be sustained, however, and after his arrest he was inducted into the Royal Army Ordnance Corps. According to Sorley MacLean, who met him at that time, Hay had come to recognize that the Nazis were 'the greatest curse to small nations'.[53]

Hay was the son of John MacDougall Hay, a church minister best remembered as the author of *Gillespie* (1914), a grim novel of commercial greed and spiritual doubt in a small Scottish town. Hay was only 4 when his father died, and he was brought up in Edinburgh by his mother, spending many summers with his father's relatives in Tarbert, Loch Fyne. The boy proved to be a gifted linguist, and soon learned Gaelic from the old folk and the local fishermen there. He is one of the few Scottish poets of the time to write in Scots, English, and Gaelic with equal facility, and indeed he was later to become competent in ten other languages, including Norwegian, Croatian, Icelandic, French, Italian, Modern Greek, and Arabic. During

[51] See Tom Devine, *The Scottish Nation, 1700–2000* (London: Allen Lane, 1999), ch. 23 ('War and Peace'), pp. 548–9. Devine notes that Britain was the only country on either side to conscript young women in this way. The SNP did well in the War, and Robert MacIntyre, the first nationalist MP, was elected to Westminster in 1945.

[52] Hay met Douglas Young in Oxford. Young was a regular correspondent with both Hay and MacLean. Hay introduced MacLean to MacDiarmid and translated some of the *Eimhir* poems into Scots. MacLean shared a small booklet of poems in Gaelic Scots and English with Robert Garioch: *17 Poems for 6d* (Edinburgh: Chalmers Press, 1940).

[53] MacLean, quoted in *Collected Poems and Songs of George Campbell Hay*, ed. Michael Byrne, 2 vols. (Edinburgh: Edinburgh University Press, 2000), ii. 29. This is the definitive account of Hay's life and times. The first volume is a notable scholarly edition of all his poems. The cited English translations are by the poet himself.

the War he sought a better use for his gifts by asking for a transfer to the Intelligence Service, but his early record and his nationalist sympathies made him unacceptable to the authorities. So it was that he found himself stacking supplies and acting as an unofficial interpreter when his company landed in North Africa at the end of 1942.

Hay loved the bustle and ethnic diversity of native life, reflecting in a letter to Douglas Young that the local people 'show qualities here which would greatly benefit Western Europe, but W. Europe having all the machine guns doesn't worry about unmaterial qualities. She peers thru the sights and sees nothing beyond but phosphates, cork, cheap labour and what not.'[54] Such sympathies were soon to cost him dear, but in fact his best war poetry was inspired by the fate of the local population, caught up in the machinery of colonial rule and conflict. These themes and his North African experience came back to him with particular force in 1944 in the south of Italy, where his unit was stationed in the aftermath of the Allied invasion. The poem 'Atman' is titled after an Algerian peasant in hard times who was condemned by a comfortable magistrate and whipped and imprisoned for stealing. Faced with the complacencies of power, Hay identified with this man of humble origin, not so different from crofting folk in Scotland: 'I know you Atman, | the woman of your house and your five youngsters, | your little clump of goats and your ass, | your plot of rye and your cow.'[55] The same interest led him to write the Gaelic poem 'Meftah Bâbkum es-Sabar?' addressed to an Arab friend, the title of which is taken from an Arabic proverb meaning 'patience [is] the key to your door'. Hay sympathized with the spiritual aspects of Islamic culture, but could not agree with its requirement to submit to Providence as the will of God. Thinking almost certainly of his own Gaelic inheritance, he counselled resistance, and ended the poem with a cry to rediscover

> the book where we will write new poetry below the last verse
> put in it by the poets of old—
> such will be our land. Or if there be no struggle,
> a mean thing of no account, hidden away in a corner,
> which another people drained dry and forgot.[56]

The Gaelic poet's identification with Arab life reached its greatest expression in his long, although uncompleted, narrative poem 'Mochtàr is Dùghall'/'Mokhtâr and Dougall'. Using a bardic 'keening' metre in more than 1,000 remarkably empathetic lines, Hay imagines the Arabic cultural inheritance via a family history over three generations encompassing trade, exploration, violence, and philosophy, but all leading to young Mokhtâr's death, killed by a German mortar bomb in a minor desert encounter. The 'Dougall' section was to do the same from a Scottish perspective, leading to Dougall's death in the same skirmish and drawing on Hay's

---

[54] Hay to Douglas Young, 20 Apr. 1943, ibid. 32.
[55] Hay, 'Atman', in *Collected Poems and Songs*, i. 163.
[56] Hay, 'Meftah Bâbkum es-Sabar?', ibid. 195.

own love for the fishing communities of Loch Fyne. But the Scottish section stalled after barely 200 lines, and the poem was laid aside until rediscovered and published in 1982. Hay did write the epilogue, however, which is a bitter passage on 'An Duine agus an Cogadh'/'Man and War', in which he reflects that 'A world apart is each son of man, | a living world in himself is every person.'[57] And with a properly Highland sense of genealogy he imagines that the chain of generations is alive in each of us, so that the voice of a man long dead 'will be heard, | when the grandson of the grandson whom he never saw is speaking'. All men are 'storehouses' of such links, containing gems and rubbish, 'ancient heirlooms virtues and vices'. The poem's last lines are a howl of anguish at the scale of the loss when Mokhtâr and Dougall are united in the democracy of death:

> Two complex priceless worlds
> were blotted out forever before they had attained
> the fullness of their being . . .
> Murder of the dead, murder of the children
> never begotten—the end of two worlds.

Hay was haunted by the end of many more such worlds when he witnessed the bombardment of Bizerta. As the main seaport of Tunis under French colonial rule, this ancient city (founded by the Phoenicians around 1000 BC) was strategically vital to the retreating Germans who held it as their last access to the sea. After the Allied break-out at El Alamein, Bizerta became a vital staging post towards the invasion of Sicily, and the British and American forces directed all their effort against the city in April and May 1943. On sentry duty, miles away, Hay saw the silent flickering blaze that marked the work of the bombers and inspired one of the finest poems of the conflict—not least because it marks the true nature and the true cost of 'total war' from London to Berlin and Tokyo:

> C'ainm nochd a th'orra,
> na sràidean bochda anns an sgeith gach uinneag
> a lachsraichean 's a deatach,
> a sradagan is sgreadail a luchd thuinidh,
> is taigh air thaigh ga reubadh,
> am broinn a chèile am brùchdadh toit' a' tuiteam?
> Is cò a-nochd tha 'g atach
> am Bàs a theachd gu grad 'nan cainntibh uile,
> no a' spàirn measg chlach is shailthean
> air bhàinidh a' gairm air cobhair, is nach cluinnear?
> Cò—nochd a phàigheas
> seann chìs àbhaisteach na fala cumant?

> What is their name to night,
> the poor streets where every window spews

---

57 Hay, 'Mochtàr is Dùghall'/'Mokhtâr and Dougall', ibid. 159.

> its flame and smoke,
> its sparks and the screaming of its inmates,
> while house upon house is rent
> and collapses in a gust of smoke?
> And who to night are beseeching
> Death to come quickly in all their tongues,
> or are struggling among stones and beams,
> crying in frenzy for help, and are not heard?
> Who to-night is paying
> the old accustomed tax of common blood?[58]

The rhetorical formality of this Gaelic utterance gives an added power to the poet's vision, although he explained that the unusual metre of 'Bisearta' was taken from a medieval Italian poem by the Dominican reformer and radical preacher Savonarola—a man whose beliefs took him to his own fiery stake. Hay saw no end to such suffering, and in 'Truaighe na h-Eòrpa'/'Europe's Piteous Plight' he imagined all of Europe in similar straits, with 'ancient carvings . . . split and stained with gore'.[59]

For what is perhaps his most outspoken condemnation of what the modern world had come to, Hay turned to English. The title 'Esta Selva Selvaggia' ('This Savage Wood') echoes lines from Canto 1 of Dante's *Inferno*: 'Ah, how painful it is to speak | of this wood, so savage and harsh and brutal, | and the very thought of which rekindles my fear.'[60] The poem switches metres constantly, using couplets, Dante's tercets, full rhyme, half-rhyme, and a polyphony of other languages to invoke a vision of global hatred and suffering in a terrible succession of rhythmic vignettes:

> The swaying landmines lingering down
> between Duntochter and the moon
> made Scotland and the world one.
> At last we found a civilisation
> common to Europe and our nation,
> siren, blast, disintegration.
>
> The house has buried sister, mother.
> Sheer chance—a direct hit. Another
> near Bou Arâda buried brother.
> None was left, and no one mourned.
> The telegram has been returned
> undelivered, scrapped and burned.
>
> .   .   .   .
>
> Chopping sticks below the prickly pears;
> turban, hook nose, cheeks hollow with his years.
> He drew his lips back, said: 'There comes a day

---

58 Hay, 'Bisearta', ibid. 177.
59 Hay, 'Truaighe na h-Eórpa'/'Europe's Piteous Plight', ibid. 215.
60 See Byrne's editorial notes, ibid. ii. 158.

when the *Fransâwi* will be swept away.'
Jabbing the earth he twisted his cleaver round—
'Just as I grind this cleaver in the ground,
kilêb, kelbât—dogs, bitches—where we find them,
—*hakdha, hakdha*—thus we will grind them.'

  ·   ·   ·   ·   ·   ·   ·

This father, hunched up on the parapet,
peddles his daughter with sly, beaten eyes;
finding no hirer, begs a cigarette.

  ·   ·   ·   ·   ·   ·

'*Haus kaput*—*maison finie*—
kaput—*capito?*—*familie.*
Alles ist kaput. Compris?'

Once again, it is the destruction of tradition, the cutting short of generations, the death of 'yesterday', that seems the cruellest cut of all to Hay. The 'old men' have betrayed their own history and the continuity they were supposed to protect, and the poem ends with an insistently repeated rhyme on 'grey' and 'day' in a darkly lyrical passage prophetic of only travail to come:

Yesterday? We saw it die.
And yet unburied see it lie
rotting beneath a sultry sky.

Where the east pales bleak and grey,
to-morrow is it, or yesterday?
Ask the old men. Can they say?

Yesterday made them. On its walls
they write its end: and down it falls
in blood and pacts and protocols.

We, having seen our yesterday,
blasted away, explained away,
in darkness, having no to-day,
guess at tomorrow dawning grey,
tighten our packstraps for the way.[61]

This was the madness that Sydney Goodsir Smith characterized in 'October 1941' as a 'Deevil's Waltz' across the globe in his 1946 collection of that name: 'As the frantic rammage Panzers brash on Moscow toun— | *An the leaves of wud October, man, are sworlan owre the warld.*'[62] He too shared something of Hay's feeling for the humble dispossessed, and his long poem 'The Refugees: A Complaynt' (written in October–November 1940) reflects on a Europe now suddenly mobilized in misery—something he must have heard directly from the Polish troops to whom

---

[61] Hay, 'Esta Selva Selvaggia', i. 211–14. *Fransâwi* refers to the French colonial rulers of Tunis.
[62] Sydney Goodsir Smith, 'October 1941', in *Collected Poems 1941–1975* (London: John Calder, 1975), 52.

he was teaching English. If Smith's Scots diction seems overly strained in this early poem, his later lyrics manage a plainer lament in poems such as 'El Alamein' and 'The Mither's Lament':

> what care I for the leagues o sand
> The prisoners and the gear they've won?
> My darlin liggs amang the dunes
> Wi mony a mither's son.[63]

George Campbell Hay survived the desert, but his war came to an end in Macedonia in 1946. By this time he was serving as a sergeant in the Education Corps, and his unit was posted to Kavalla, a remote place where the ruling right-wing Greek nationalists were in brutal conflict with communist guerrillas. This struggle for power was further compounded by recent enmity and ancient feuds between Greeks, Turks, ex-Fascist Armenians, and Bulgar warlords. It was a dangerous place for someone with both socialist and nationalist convictions; nevertheless, and as always, the linguist Hay mixed and talked freely with local working-class people. The Army disapproved, but more worryingly he came to the attention of the right-wing factions who took him for a communist agitator. It was in these particularly tense circumstances that the poet suffered the first of several mental breakdowns, brought on, perhaps, by a violent personal attack at the hands of Greek nationalists, and he was invalided home in the summer of that year. Hay continued to write after the War and produced fine poems, but he spent many years in and out of psychiatric hospitals undergoing treatment, including insulin shock treatment for schizophrenia, and struggling with an alcohol problem. His heart-breaking vision of the War, as a 'world' war in the truest sense, remains one of the most powerful and affecting literary testaments of the time.

Nor did it really end in 1945, for many of those who survived still had poems to make, just as they had to live with their memories for years to come. So the War comes back in surprising places—as in a story told in a pub to a young American brought up in Glasgow and living and working in Scotland. A trained marine biologist, James Hyman Singer—Burns Singer—became a freelance writer in London in the mid-1950s and published his first collection of verse as *Still and All* in 1957. This volume contained 'In Memoriam Keith Douglas' dedicated to G. S. Fraser, but is most notable for a long narrative poem, 'The Transparent Prisoner', which recounts another man's war experiences in an act of vivid imaginative transference. Captured in the desert war, the speaker describes his experiences as a POW and then as a slave labourer in a German coal-mine where the most extreme physical deprivation underground leads him to an overpoweringly spiritual vision of 'transparency'. The poem has a wholly conversational opening tone:

> They took me somewhere sleeping in the desert
> Up middle of a minefield near Benghazi;

---

[63] Smith, 'The Refugees: A Complaynt', ibid. 53.

> ...It was the Germans—you'd hardly call them Nazi—
> Polite and battle-hungry happy men
> —O I would like to meet those chaps again.

It then makes an extraordinary journey in fifty-five stanzas to the intensity of a moment that will haunt him, and leave him paradoxically unfulfilled, for the rest of his life:

> I saw the moments and the seasons swim
> Precisely through me and I saw them show
> Huts, hills and homes, and distance, and my dream
> Of little footsteps shrieking in the snow
> As they tip into darkness, all grow bright
> And smother everything in transparent light.
> I watched. A tender clarity became
> That moment mine, as clear as through a hand
> Bones shadow out into a candle's flame.[64]

'The Transparent Prisoner', like Campbell Hay's war poetry, speaks for the wider reaches of the conflict and its aftermath, reminding us of the fate of thousands—in Stalin's Gulags, for example, or in the concentration camp of memory itself—whose suffering did not end with the declaration of peace.

Not all of those who took part could write about it straightaway. Thirty-three-year-old Robert Garioch Sutherland, in the Royal Signal Corps, was captured in charge of an electricity generator outside Tobruk in 1942, and spent the rest of the War as a POW, being moved from camp to camp in Africa, Italy, Austria, and Germany. Published thirty years later, his memoir *Two Men and a Blanket* (Edinburgh: Southside, 1975) is a low-key testament to how to survive the real enemies in such captivity: namely, perpetual hunger, boredom, and most of all, the cold (hence the book's title). It all comes back to him years later, sitting at the seaside:

> Cantie in seaside simmer on the dunes,
> I fling awa my doup of cigarette
> whaur bairns hae biggit castles out of sand
> and watch the reik rise frae the parapet.
>
> Suddenlike I am back in Libya;
> yon's the escarpment, and a bleizan plane.[65]

Or again, in 'The Prisoner's Dream' written in 1955, Garioch remembers a winter's night in captivity and the rare treat of eating a whole onion—it may have been Christmas or New Year—followed by a strange dream of returning to Edinburgh

---

[64] Burns Singer, 'The Transparent Prisoner', in *Collected Poems*, ed. James Keery (Manchester: Carcanet, 2001), 141 and 148.

[65] Robert Garioch, 'During a Music Festival', in *Complete Poetical Works*, ed. Robin Fulton (Edinburgh: Macdonald, 1983), 67.

only to be assailed there, in his familiar home surroundings, with an overwhelming sense of choking guilt and responsibility. Waking up in prison again is a huge relief. He cannot fathom where such a dream came from unless, he reflects, it was because of the onion he ate. It is not a convincing explanation. The fine lyric 'Letter from Italy' remembers the stars as a point of contact between the poet and a loved one at home, concluding:

> Perimeters have bounded me,
> sad rims of desert and of sea,
> the famous one around Tobruk,
> and now barbed wire, which way I look,
> except above—the Pléiades.[66]

Like Henderson before him, Garioch had contributed to the Army ballad tradition with 'Kreigy Ballad' about the POW experience, but the most profound—if indirect—response to his wartime experiences can be found in three long poems written in the 1950s: 'The Bog', 'The Wire', and 'The Muir'. All share the sense of choking guilt and oppression felt in 'The Prisoner's Dream' and a sense, too, of anonymous crowds held in a vast perimeter of common captivity.

'The Bog' takes a distinctively Scottish wasteland of water, peat, and mist to envisage us all mired together in slime, holding on to dreams of heaven or conquest, while 'Thae men that fetch us bombs frae yont the seas, | heich in their Heinkels, ken the same despair'. The poet remembers the agonizing end to Beethoven's piano sonata, the 'Appassionata', and imagines the exhilaration and terror of total disruption as 'The causey street we staun on shaks and shogs, | freestane fowre-storey houses flee in air'. Yet the bog is where he is and where he stays. If he keeps his head down, he can tolerate it, content perhaps with his own tiny portion of gold at the end of a grim rainbow with 'colours braw as onie shroud: | broun and dark broun, black and mair black.'[67]

The poet returns to this bleak metaphor in the longest of these poems, 'The Muir', which is an extended meditation on the evolution of science and a pursuit of knowledge that led to nuclear physics and Hiroshima. Dense with literary and scientific references from many periods, the poem is haunted by the fate of the eighteenth-century Scottish poet Robert Fergusson who died young in a madhouse, gripped by a horror of damnation. Garioch reflects that this was no melancholy Romantic pose, but a genuine kind of understanding:

> yon skeelie makar, aince articulat,
> . . . howled like a cuddy his falsetto bray
> wi no wrocht artifice of poesy
> or music; here was truth, and it was wae.[68]

66   Garioch, 'Letter from Italy', ibid. 70.   67   Garioch, 'The Bog', ibid. 48.
68   Garioch, 'The Muir', ibid. 61.

'The Wire' draws more directly on Garioch's wartime captivity, with an allegorical vision of the world as a vast moor crowded with people, webbed with barbed wire and surrounded by guard towers:

> A man trips up; the Wire gaes ding,
> Tins clash, the guaird lifts up his heid;
> Fu slaw he traverses his gun
> And blatters at him till he's deid.[69]

Only a few in the most remote parts of the moor manage to survive, by finding an eerie joy in 'pure despair' as they shrink their life to the tiniest, almost invisible spark:

> Outwardly they seem at rest,
> binna the glint of hidden fires.
> Their world shaks, but they bide still
> as nodal points on dirlan wires.

Such was the survival strategy of the camps. It is a terrible oppression.

These are among the darkest of Garioch's poems, quite at odds with the modest and dryly sceptical spirit of most of his work, which tends to reflect on the pretensions of the world in the persona of an ordinary working man, or the schoolteacher that he became, standing on the sidelines of high culture and low ambition alike. Garioch lost his copy of Jaroslav Hašek's *The Good Soldier Schweik* when he was captured at Tobruk; his later work shares something of Schweik's disingenuous but canny instinct for survival. Yet 'The Bog', 'The Muir', and 'The Wire' come from another place altogether, a place visited, alas, by thousands of people in a uniquely global conflict, a place prophetic, even, of threats to come in the post-war atomic age. Behind the symbols of precious victory, behind the bells ringing and the ticker-tape parades, lie the long shadows of the death camps, total war, mass conscription, millions dead, and cities in flames around the world. The poets were there to see it and to speak it, not without despair, not without hope:

> And aye the reik bleeds frae the warld's rim
> As it has duin frae Babylon and Troy,
> London, Bonn, Edinbro, time eftir time.
> And great Beethoven sang a Hymn to Joy.[70]

---

[69] Garioch, 'The Wire', ibid. 50.   [70] Garioch, 'During a Music Festival', 67.

CHAPTER 18

OCCUPYING NEW TERRITORY: ALUN LLYWELYN-WILLIAMS AND WELSH-LANGUAGE POETRY OF THE SECOND WORLD WAR

GERWYN WILIAMS

'Most Welsh language poets of my generation ignored the whole business as though it had nothing to do with them or with Wales—a negative reaction which was surely very strange even for civilians':[1] writing in 1973, this is how Alun Llywelyn-Williams

I wish to acknowledge the help and advice of Professor Emeritus Gwyn Thomas in preparing this article.

Unless otherwise stated, when a quotation appears in English from a source referred to in Welsh, it is my own translation.

[1] Alun Llywelyn-Williams, 'Alun Llywelyn-Williams', in Meic Stephens (ed.), *Artists in Wales*, ii (Llandysul: Gomer Press, 1973), 174.

(1913–88) summed up Welsh-language poets' reaction to the Second World War.[2] Among those who did respond to the War at the time, R. Meirion Roberts (1906–67) provides a chaplain-poet's perspective in an understated and subdued collection of verse; Elwyn Evans (1912–2004) offers a Middle East soldier-poet's response in a limited but important body of work; and T. E. Nicholas (1878–1971) provides the most prolific response as a communist prisoner of war in the most considered and least agitprop poems he produced. However, for literary ambition and intellectual depth, the only real contender to Alun Llywelyn-Williams himself is Waldo Williams (1904–71): writing on the Home Front as a conscientious objector, he produced a substantial body of work, both poetry and prose, containing a nationalist and pacifist response to the war.[3] As confirmed by the belated anthology of Welsh poetry regarding the Second World War, *Gwaedd y Lleiddiad* (1995), the study of Welsh poetry of the Second World War is essentially a democratic and comprehensive assignment, taking into account a variety of responses by combatants and civilians, men and women who experienced the War and those responding as members of a post-war generation.[4] Certainly as far as the combatants' response to the War is concerned, Alun Llywelyn-Williams reigns supreme and unchallenged among Welsh poets.[5]

No other Welsh poet was better placed than Llywelyn-Williams, geographically and culturally, to face the literal and figurative new territory represented by the Second World War. In contrast to the clichéd perception of Welsh men of letters, he had not climbed from the semi-rural and underprivileged ranks of the *gwerin*, but was brought up as a doctor's son in a middle-class urban household in Cardiff. As a university student in the city of his birth, from 1935 to 1939, he established and edited the left-wing journal *Tir Newydd* ('New Territory') which sought to counter what he regarded as the ruralism and medievalism dominating much contemporary Welsh literature. 'The city and college of Cardiff is this journal's birthplace,' he proudly announced in his first editorial; 'this is where we saw that a new territory

---

[2] For Wales and the Second World War, see John Davies, *A History of Wales* (Harmondsworth: Penguin, 1994), 597–611.

[3] All four poets cited are discussed in my survey of Welsh literature and the Second World War: Gerwyn Wiliams, *Tir Newydd: Agweddau ar Lenyddiaeth Gymraeg a'r Ail Ryfel Byd* (Caerdydd: Gwasg Prifysgol Cymru, 2005), 100–28.

[4] Alan Llwyd and Elwyn Edwards (eds.), *Gwaedd y Lleiddiad: Blodeugerdd Barddas o Gerddi'r Ail Ryfel Byd 1939–1945* (Llandybïe: Cyhoeddiadau Barddas, 1995), is a pioneering anthology that includes more than 200 poems; it follows a similar anthology of First World War poems by the same editorial partnership, *Gwaedd y Bechgyn: Blodeugerdd Barddas o Gerddi'r Rhyfel Mawr 1914–1918* (Llandybïe: Cyhoeddiadau Barddas, 1989).

[5] An entry for Alun Llywelyn-Williams is included in Meic Stephens (ed.), *The New Companion to the Literature of Wales* (Cardiff: University of Wales Press, 1998), 467–8; and his friend and former colleague Elwyn Evans provides an introduction to his life and works in *Alun Llywelyn-Williams* (Cardiff: University of Wales Press, 1991). See in addition Dafydd Glyn Jones, 'The Poetry of Alun Llywelyn-Williams', *Poetry Wales*, 7/1 (Summer 1971), 14–24. Joseph P. Clancy has translated all his published poems as well as a selection of his prose in *The Light in the Gloom: Poems and Prose by Alun Llywelyn-Williams* (Denbigh: Gee and Son, 1998).

awaits us in Wales, to be discovered and cultivated and claimed, so as to extend the boundaries of Welsh culture.'[6] His was an unashamedly modernizing agenda as he sought to locate the discussion of Welsh literature within the wider context of current developments in architecture, visual arts, music, theatre, and cinema, as well as influential scientific matters. His approach was combative rather than defensive: only three years after Saunders Lewis's gesture of cultural separatism which saw him defining and promoting a Welsh literary canon in his *Braslun o Hanes Llenyddiaeth Gymraeg* ('An Outline of the History of Welsh Literature') (1932), Llywelyn-Williams had no qualms about suggesting that contemporary Welsh poetry had a lot to learn from contemporary English poetry, and in particular the left-wing verse of W. H. Auden, Stephen Spender, C. Day Lewis, and Rex Warner. He was highly critical of the direction in which current Welsh poetry seemed to be going—towards conservatism, classicism, and medievalism: 'classicism has throughout the ages been associated with conservatism and reactionism and oppression and intolerance.'[7] This put him at odds full-frontally with the highly influential right-wing vision of Saunders Lewis, whose survey of Welsh literature had drawn to a close in 1536; one of its opening claims had been that 'For a Welsh writer today the Middle Ages, and primarily the period between the twelfth and the sixteenth century, are significant for him, they have an effect on him and they steer his work, in a manner that a writer in France or Germany or England could not comprehend.'[8]

But Llywelyn-Williams's promotion of the Auden generation should not be interpreted as part of an Anglocentric vision, for *Tir Newydd*'s outlook was positively internationalist, and this was another attitude that would help him as a soldier-poet involved in the War on mainland Europe. The fact that Llywelyn-Williams was in Berlin following its downfall in 1945 placed the Welsh language in a challenging position; in his poetry, it was forced to face up to a situation of immediate and immense political, social, and historical importance beyond its usual geographical and cultural concerns. This in itself invests his war poetry with a significance which extends beyond the scope of Second World War studies.

When war finally broke out, the wartime rationing of paper meant that *Tir Newydd* could not survive. Its modernizing mission, however, was in many respects continued by Llywelyn-Williams in his life and works. He was in his mid-20s in 1939 and employed, at the time, by the BBC in Cardiff as a member of the pioneering

---

[6] Llywelyn-Williams, '"Tir Newydd"' ('New Territory'), *Tir Newydd*, 1 (Summer 1935), 1. He repeats a similar sentiment in *Gwanwyn yn y Ddinas: Darn o Hunangofiant* ('Spring in the City: A Fragment of Autobiography') (Dinbych: Gwasg Gee, 1975), the opening sections of which are translated by Joseph P. Clancy in *The Light in the Gloom*, 37–8: 'I was proud of Cardiff city. I believed it was the most beautiful and interesting city in the world, and I dreamed of ways to improve it and make it more and more beautiful and increase its fame.'

[7] Llywelyn-Williams, 'Gwaith ac Adwaith: Rhai Sylwadau ar Farddoniaeth Gyfoes Cymru', *Tir Newydd*, 8 (May 1937), 24.

[8] Saunders Lewis, *Braslun o Hanes Llenyddiaeth Gymraeg* (Caerdydd: Gwasg Prifysgol Cymru, 1986; 1st pub. 1932), 1.

team of the recently established Welsh Region. In September 1939 he was relocated to London as part of the corporation's centralized news service: as radio announcer, he faced the pressing creative challenge of satisfying the demands put on the Welsh language by a modern-day broadcasting organization.[9] Around 2,920 people registered as conscientious objectors in Wales during the Second World War, and the Welsh Nationalist Party advocated a neutral stance for Wales.[10] The nationalist opposition to war had in fact been galvanized by the events surrounding the burning in 1936 of a proposed bombing school in the Llŷn Peninsula by three prominent Welshmen, amongst them Saunders Lewis. This event seems to have had a greater impact and influence upon Welsh-language writers than the Second World War.[11] Neither neutralism nor pacifism were viable options for Llywelyn-Williams; he increasingly felt a moral duty to join the military fight against fascism and Nazism. As a Welshman he could not regard himself divorced from the immediate threat facing civilization on an international plane. Together with fellow broadcasters and writers like Elwyn Evans and Geraint Dyfnallt Owen, as well as 300,000 other Welshmen, and in contrast to the dramatist John Gwilym Jones and the poet Waldo Williams, who represented the nationalist and pacifist minority opposition to war, Llywelyn-Williams joined the Royal Welsh Fusiliers in November 1940. By July 1942 he was a lieutenant stationed at Brecon, in charge of training new recruits, but such was the obligation he felt to take part in active combat against the enemy that he volunteered to serve abroad, and therefore experienced the War in Germany and Belgium from November 1944 onwards.

CIVILIAN

Llywelyn-Williams was never a prolific poet: his collected poems, published in 1979 in *Y Golau yn y Gwyll* ('The Light in the Gloom'), total eighty-five; three-quarters of them belong to the period 1934–56. Although most of Llywelyn-Williams's poetic responses to the Second World War are included within the section entitled 'War' in *Pont y Caniedydd* ('The Songster's Bridge', 1956), his first volume—*Cerddi*

---

[9] Llywelyn-Williams refers to some of the challenges he faced in *Gwanwyn yn y Ddinas*, 162–3. See also John Davies, *Broadcasting and the BBC in Wales* (Cardiff: University of Wales Press, 1994), 128: 'The bulletins gave Llywelyn-Williams the opportunity to put into practice his ideas about the dignity of broadcast Welsh, and many of his coinages, particularly those for war terms—the word *awyren* (aeroplane), for example—became incorporated into the language.'

[10] See D. Hywel Davies, 'The War Years', in *The Welsh Nationalist Party 1925–1945: A Call to Nationhood* (Cardiff: University of Wales Press, 1983), 223–59.

[11] This is certainly Gwyn Thomas's suggestion in 'Cofio Alun Llywelyn-Williams', *Barn*, 307 (Aug. 1988), 45: 'Welsh poetry has on the whole confined her attention to this side of the War as it were, and Penyberth and what happened there is the major experience in Welsh literature.' See also 'Penyberth', in Stephens (ed.), *The New Companion to the Literature of Wales*, 581.

1934–1942 ('Poems 1934–1942') (1944)—includes at least ten poems written during his service as a soldier in Sandhurst, Weymouth, and Brecon and also whilst on
leave in Cardiff. In addition to those which deal directly with the War, he managed
to capture in the whole collection some of the nervousness and anxiety of the
1930s as the world, for the second time in the twentieth century, moved inevitably
towards war.

'The poetry I attempted to wrest from this sorry state of affairs immediately
before and during the years of the war was a poetry of despair,' said Llywelyn-
Williams; 'my own personal despair, my despair for Wales helplessly entangled in
the cataclysm, and my despair for the whole of human civilization.'[12] In 1936—the
year in which Hitler won 99 per cent of the vote in German elections and the
Spanish Civil War began—Alun Llywelyn-Williams wrote 'If the Rain Would Stop,
Friend'. One senses a sinister threat, although at this stage it is unidentified and
referred to in mythological and symbolic terms: 'Friend, we cannot wait | and see
the wolf roaming a Cardiff street.'[13] The tone is already urgent and apprehensive:
'if we could free ourselves . . . from the fear, from the terror, | from the nightmare
of our world— | but almost everyone is an enemy.' The paranoia and uncertainty
increase in 'On the Threshold of War', written the following year: 'they say that
the war has broken out, | but who our enemies are has not been revealed, || We'll
find that from tomorrow's paper.'[14] Nothing is certain or dependable: in 'After
Listening to the Doctor's Advice' the previous reference points have lost their
relevance, and uncertainty has spread like a disease among people and infected the
mutual understanding that helped society function: 'the old map is not correct, the
roads | are strange, the old signs silent.'[15] The brave new world that he had greeted
as recently as 1935, the civic topography and industrial landscape of Cardiff that he
had promoted with confidence and pride in *Tir Newydd* as a powerhouse for a new
Wales, is abruptly turned into a dystopia of disillusionment.

Llywelyn-Williams was overwhelmed by political disillusionment. Neville Chamberlain's appeasement policy in his dealings with Hitler and Mussolini led to the
Munich Conference in September 1938, where the Sudetenland was yielded to
Germany in the misguided assumption that Hitler's territorial aims would be
satisfied. Two months later *Kristallnacht* occurred, one of the definitive events of
the Holocaust: synagogues were burnt, houses ransacked, shops looted, nearly 100
people killed, and over 20,000 transported to concentration camps. Surely it is
the British Prime Minister and his fellow politicians whom Llywelyn-Williams had
in mind when he referred to the amateurs in a newsreel in 'Lounge on the Hill':
'let us watch, while we can, in the ample seats, | the film slip across the light of

[12] Llywelyn-Williams, 'Alun Llywelyn-Williams', 173–4.
[13] Llywelyn-Williams, 'If the Rain Would Stop, Friend', trans. Clancy, in *Light in the Gloom*, 113.
[14] Llywelyn-Williams, 'On the Threshold of War', trans. Clancy, ibid. 116.
[15] Llywelyn-Williams, 'After Listening to the Doctor's Advice', trans. Clancy, ibid. 117.

the screen, | and marvel more and more at the bad acting'.[16] He employs similar imagery in 'Blaen Cwm Gwdi', which refers to 'a flaw | in the grey actors' fluent speech'.[17] Years later he would recall this period in unambiguous terms:

There was cause enough for us to protest and rebel when I was a youth, more so than in any other period, because the years between the two world wars signified one of the most shameless and turbulent periods that we had witnessed in our history. These were years of wide-scale economic recession with thousands of unemployed people suffering indescribable poverty and adversity, and the governments in power among the most weak and ineffective and despicable in their foreign and domestic policies that had tormented any country, no-one in authority showed they had the faintest idea how to manage things, and some were profiting barefacedly from the wretchedness.[18]

'It had come at last' was how Llywelyn-Williams refers in his autobiography to Chamberlain's long-awaited announcement on 3 September 1939 that Britain had declared war on Germany.[19] Relocated from Cardiff to London, he was placed near the very centre of things: as John Davies commented, 'In 1940, London was the place to be, and clearly the Welsh broadcasters enjoyed themselves hugely.'[20] So Llywelyn-Williams was presented with a rare opportunity to record the mood and condition of the wartime capital; he did so in nine poems written during the year that he spent there, the period of the Phoney War that came to a head with the Battle of Britain between July and October 1940.

In 'Here in the Tranquil Fields' Llywelyn-Williams strikes a rather idealized note as he refers to the War:

> No use being angry at the interfering,
> at the rush of the war's machines;
> the corrupt society is ending, ending,
> and the sorrow and sadness is the accompaniment, and the final sigh.[21]

'I believed that the society was corrupt and the sooner it was destroyed the better and men provided with an opportunity to build a better city in its place'[22]—that is how Llywelyn-Williams summed up his feelings, in retrospect. This was a war to purge the old contaminated world, the long-expected conclusion to what Auden famously called a 'low dishonest decade'.[23] The same conviction, that war would improve matters, prevails in 'The World that Vexes Us'—'the trial will strengthen

---

[16] Llywelyn-Williams, 'Lounge on the Hill', trans. Clancy, ibid. 118.
[17] Llywelyn-Williams, 'Blaen Cwm Gwdi', trans. Clancy, ibid. 129.
[18] Llywelyn-Williams, 'Holi: Alun Llywelyn-Williams', in Gwyn Thomas (ed.), *Mabon*, 4 (1971), 17–18.
[19] Llywelyn-Williams, *Gwanwyn yn y Ddinas*, 160.
[20] John Davies, *Broadcasting and the BBC in Wales*, 129.
[21] Llywelyn-Williams, 'Here in the Tranquil Fields', trans. Clancy, in *Light in the Gloom*, 120.
[22] Llywelyn-Williams, 'Holi: Alun Llywelyn-Williams', 18.
[23] W. H. Auden, 'September 1, 1939', in *English Auden: Poems, Essays and Dramatic Writings 1927–1939*, ed. Edward Mendelson (London: Faber, 1977), 245.

you, and the destruction for a time'—and 'The Airman' refers enthusiastically to the pilot who 'will loose his great blessing to the earth, and shatter the world!'[24] As far as the love he and his wife, Alis, had for each other, it too—according to 'When Freely We Stroll Again'—would be stronger following a period apart: 'Sweet every yearning when we are home together, | purified by the dead, silent months.'[25] Yet there was nothing to suggest that either of them would survive the War: when peace would eventually return, when the 'purer city rises hereafter, | there will be a strange couple in our old home'.[26] As Llewelyn-Williams stated elsewhere, 'When the war came at last, I wasn't convinced that my friends and I would survive, and I believed that Cardiff and such places would be burnt to ashes in next to no time.'[27] There is therefore nothing contrived in the astonishment at having survived that he later expresses in 'After the Conflict' and 'The First Christmas of Peace', the closing poems of the 'War' section in *Pont y Caniedydd*.

He continues to diagnose the sickness that characterized the period in 'Cui Bono?', and not for the first time employs medical imagery: 'despite expecting, like an invalid, the wise verdict | and the sure advice; the medicines are terror | and the doctor's books merely cultivated lies.'[28] He had listened 'to the doctor's advice'[29] in a previous poem, but could no longer depend upon that advice. As in the case of the later poem 'Exploring the Land', 'Cui Bono?' brings to mind '1914–1918: Yr Ieuainc wrth yr Hen' ('1914–1918: The Young to the Old'), W. J. Gruffydd's vitriolic indictment of the older generation, written after he had survived his term of duty on board a minesweeper during the First World War:

> More blind than the blind, the sight that has seen the dying
> of the faith that was dulled by the tricks of the world,
> truth turning untrue, and the soft word harsh,
> every creed a disgrace, and every poem silent.[30]

But whilst Gruffydd had contrasted the corrupt elders with the honourable young, the older generation having betrayed the younger generation's trust in them by leading them into war, Llewelyn-Williams offers a more bitter truth: as he sees matters, the younger generation are infected with the cynicism of the old. Gruffydd had claimed that the old had not in their 'sad life' any 'hope', 'faith', or 'love';

[24] Llywelyn-Williams, 'The World that Vexes Us' and 'The Airman', trans. Clancy, in *Light in the Gloom*, 123 and 128.

[25] Llywelyn-Williams, 'When Freely We Stroll Again', trans. Clancy, ibid. 124.

[26] Llywelyn-Williams, 'Here in the Tranquil Hills', trans. Clancy, ibid. 120.

[27] Llywelyn-Williams, 'Holi: Alun Llywelyn-Williams', 17.

[28] Llywelyn-Williams, 'Cui Bono?', trans. Clancy, in *Light in the Gloom*, 121.

[29] Llywelyn-Williams, 'After Listening to the Doctor's Advice', 117.

[30] W. J. Gruffydd, '1914–1918: Yr Ieuainc wrth yr Hen' ('1914–1918: The Young to the Old'), trans. Robert Minhinnick, in Menna Elfyn and John Rowlands (eds.), *The Bloodaxe Book of Modern Welsh Poetry: Twentieth-Century Welsh-Language Poetry in Translation* (Tarset: Bloodaxe, 2003), 53–4. Such was his admiration of Gruffydd that Llywelyn-Williams prepared a special issue of *Tir Newydd* in his honour in May 1938.

Llywelyn-Williams's concern in 'Nothing Will Save Us but Our Hearts' is that 'there's no love today | in the bosom of this senseless generation'.[31] In all three poems belonging to 1940, Llywelyn-Williams presents a generation disillusioned and frustrated, their feelings fuelled by the seeming impasse of the Phoney War.

But 'Cui Bono?' also touches upon a theme of Second World War literature that originated in the 1930s: namely, the progression of lies and deceit, as described by Piers Brendon:

[T]he Depression years witnessed the dissemination of falsehood on a hitherto unprecedented scale. Never had science and art so combined to promote earthly powers. Goebbels and others developed novel techniques of thought control. New media such as radio and talking pictures were mobilised to sway the masses. Leaders used aircraft to grab the limelight and they emblazoned their messages on the sky. Dictators imposed their version of the truth by means of dogma and terror . . . . Facts were moulded like plasticine into the approved shape, whether Communist, Aryan, Fascist or imperial.[32]

'[V]ain the asking, and the answer will never come,' says Llywelyn-Williams in 'Cui Bono?' Previously in *Tir Newydd* he had complained about 'the old trick of playing with terminology, by saying, for example, that "National Socialism" had triumphed in Germany (Hitler made much of that title)'.[33] 'The Airman' also refers to 'the diverse lies of the peevish speeches | delivered beneath the banners' seal', and in an elegy to his friend, Raymond Atcheson, who had introduced Alun Llywelyn-Williams to the Auden generation but who had died in 1938, he refers to him 'denying the fellowship | before the lie overflowed'.[34] The dishonesty that Auden had identified as defining the period seemed to have contaminated language itself, the poet's most basic material, a realization that Llywelyn-Williams would creatively exploit in his later poems.

Auden had also insisted that 'no one exists alone. . . . We must love one another or die.'[35] Llywelyn-Williams saw matters in a similar light: 'because there's no love today | in the bosom of this senseless generation . . . nothing will save us but our hearts'.[36] Significantly, *Cerddi 1934–1942* is framed by love poems: the collection opens with 'Cefn Cwm Bychan', written in 1934, and closes with 'Love's Unity', written in 1942, by which time the lovers had formally acknowledged their commitment through marriage in 1938. The different perspectives contained within the poems is revealing. The opening poem emphasizes their insignificance as mere mortals: 'you and I, girl, who are we | that God should remember us, or

---

[31] Llywelyn-Williams, 'Nothing Will Save Us but Our Hearts', trans. Clancy, in *Light in the Gloom*, 122.

[32] Piers Brendon, *The Dark Valley: A Panorama of the 1930s* (London: Jonathan Cape, 2000), p. xvi.

[33] Llywelyn-Williams, 'Nodiadau'r Golygydd', *Tir Newydd*, 10 (Nov. 1937), 3.

[34] Llywelyn-Williams, 'Remembering a Friend', trans. Clancy, in *Light in the Gloom*, 125.

[35] Auden, 'September 1, 1939', in *English Auden*, 246.

[36] Llywelyn-Williams, 'Nothing Will Save Us, 122.

man our song?'[37] One hears allusions to the fatalistic rhetorical questions posed by
T. H. Parry-Williams in 1923: 'Beth ydwyt ti a minnau, frawd . . . ?' ('What are we,
brother, you and I . . . ?') and 'Beth fyddi dithau, ferch, a myfi . . . ?' ('And what will
you be, my girl, and I . . . ?').[38] But by the closing poem eight years later, love had
matured into a less passive and more assertive force: already in 'Since Death is Close
By' Llywelyn-Williams claims that 'never can he [death] ravage love's unstinted
joy | that was snatched by us from his eternal terror';[39] but by the time that he came
to compose 'Love's Unity', the love is presented in deliberately exaggerated terms:

> Beware of the jealous in us: the fortified place
> that does not wish to reveal our close-kept secrets,
> the kingdom that keeps its bare borders pure
> from the ardent surge of the waves on the beach.
>
> My darling, listen, as we lie here together,
> side by side, close, thigh to thigh,
> do you hear the two proud, sovereign kingdoms
> intertwining and fusing into one?[40]

In those troubled times, the unifying love that acts as a bond between the poet and
Alis assumes an urgent and universal significance; it represents an ideal of trust
and meaning, mutual understanding and respect, honesty and truthfulness. This
is a more personal version of the concept of understanding between people that
Waldo Williams promoted in the aftermath of war in 1946 as the 'Only balm to
the world' in his homage to the community living around the Preseli mountains
in north Pembrokeshire.[41] As Llywelyn-Williams was to state years later—and
one imagines that Waldo Williams would have no difficulty accepting these words
either—'Making whole the relationship between different individuals is the starting
point of all goodness for me, and the only practical basis for properly reforming
society and civilization.'[42]

Soldier

Cerddi 1934–1942 may be read as poetic reportage on the period referred to in the
title of Llywelyn-Williams's book: the material is organized chronologically, and the

[37] Llywelyn-Williams, 'Cefn Cwm Bychan', trans. Clancy, ibid. 111.
[38] Originally written in 1923, 'Yr Esgyrn Hyn' was included by T. H. Parry-Williams in his slim
though highly influential volume *Cerddi*, in 1931; Joseph P. Clancy provides a translation, 'These
Bones', in his *Twentieth Century Welsh Poems* (Llandysul: Gomer Press, 1982), 62–3.
[39] Llywelyn-Williams, 'Since Death is Close By', trans. Clancy, in *Light in the Gloom*, 123.
[40] Llywelyn-Williams, 'Love's Unity', trans. Clancy, ibid. 129.
[41] See Waldo Williams, 'Preseli', trans. Tony Conran, in Elfyn and Rowlands (eds.), *Bloodaxe Book
of Modern Welsh Poetry*, 125–6.
[42] Llywelyn-Williams, 'Holi: Alun Llywelyn-Williams', 20.

year and place of composition systematically noted at the end of every poem. It is not so easy to locate the poems contained within the 'War' section in *Pont y Caniedydd* and relate them to a specific time and place. Llywelyn-Williams's review of Jon Silkin's study of First World War poetry, *Out of Battle*, is of interest in this context: 'It's not so much the social backgrounds or even the cultural stimulus that matters. In the last resort, the poems that come out of the battle must be judged as poetry like any other poems for the imaginative quality of their testimony and for the lasting significance of their achievement.'[43] In the war poems contained within his second book of poems, Llywelyn-Williams appears to be distancing himself somewhat from temporary situations, especially in his most mature compositions—although some of them had been written during or immediately after the War. After all, eleven years separated the end of the War and the date of publication of *Pont y Caniedydd*. Together, the 1942 and 1956 volumes offer the best of both worlds: on the one hand, the 'immediacy of expression' demanded by the intensity of the experience that he referred to whilst discussing the English war poets of 1914–18; on the other hand, the 'more considered interpretation of the war' which he identified in the responses of Herbert Read and David Jones.[44]

The 'War' section opens with 'In Night Battle', a short poem containing two stanzas and reminiscent, both metrically and thematically, of 'Y Blotyn Du' composed by Hedd Wyn, the soldier-poet killed during the First World War.[45] The relationship between Hedd Wyn and Llywelyn-Williams is confirmed in the second stanza which, by referring to 'garw waedd y lleiddiad' ('the harsh cry of the killer'), brings to mind 'gwaedd y bechgyn' (literally, 'the cry of the lads') from Hedd Wyn's 'Rhyfel' ('War'), the Welsh poem relating to the First World War most often alluded to by subsequent writers.[46] The connection with previous Welsh war poetry is strengthened further by the reference to 'briwgig yn y baw' ('broken flesh in the muck') which reminds one of 'A gwedy boregat briwgic' ('And after morning's fray, torn flesh') from Taliesin's graphic description of war dating back

---

[43] Llywelyn-Williams, untitled review of Jon Silkin's *Out of Battle: The Poetry of the Great War*, *Poetry Wales*, 8/3 (Winter 1972), 102.

[44] Ibid. 102 and 103.

[45] Hedd Wyn's 'Y Blotyn Du' is translated as 'The Black Blot' by Gillian Clarke in Elfyn and Rowlands (eds.), *Bloodaxe Book of Modern Welsh Poetry*, 67.

[46] Llywelyn-Williams, 'In Night Battle', trans. Clancy, in *Light in the Gloom*, 133. Gillian Clarke's translation of Hedd Wyn's 'Rhyfel' ('War') in *The Bloodaxe Book of Modern Welsh Poetry*, 67, is rather unsatisfactory: it misleadingly translates the two contrasting nouns 'gwaedd' ('cry') and 'gwaed' ('blood') in the final couplet as synonyms ('blood'). D. Tecwyn Lloyd's earlier translation is quoted in Gerwyn Wiliams, 'The Literature of the First World War', in Dafydd Johnston (ed.), *A Guide to Welsh Literature c.1900–1996* (Cardiff: University of Wales Press, 1998), 27; and Alan Llwyd provides an alternative translation in David Lister, 'Wales awaits poetic justice', *Independent on Sunday*, 13 Mar. 1994. The claim regarding the allusions to the poem is substantiated in my survey of Welsh poetry regarding the First World War: Gerwyn Wiliams, *Y Rhwyg: Arolwg o Farddoniaeth Gymraeg ynghylch y Rhyfel Byd Cyntaf* (Llandysul: Gwasg Gomer, 1993), 158.

to the sixth century. Taliesin's heroic poetry is firmly established as a cornerstone of the Welsh literary canon.[47]

This was not the first occasion for Llywelyn-Williams to allude to early Welsh poetry: 'Men of Catraeth' is dated 1938, the year that Ifor Williams's scholarly edition of *Canu Aneirin*, referring to the heroism of the Britons at Catraeth (Catterick), had appeared;[48] 'Lounge on the Hill' alludes to *Canu Llywarch Hen*, also edited by Ifor Williams, three years after an edition of this early Welsh saga poetry had been published.[49] The availability and accessibility of this ancient war poetry can be regarded as one advantage that Second World War poets had over their First World War counterparts: it enriched their range of reference and intensified their emotional impact and literary creativity. And as the references to W. J. Gruffydd and Hedd Wyn suggest, they could also turn to the poetry of 1914–18 for precedents on how, artistically, to approach the challenges of recent warfare. But the allusions to early Welsh war poetry are conscious and intentional rather than occasional or accidental in *Pont y Caniedydd*. Consequently, whilst the war poems in *Cerddi 1934–1942* and *Pont y Caniedydd* forge a thematic link, the manner by which they approach their subject-matter sets them apart.

Llywelyn-Williams enlisted in the Army with a certain amount of idealism in 1940, initially convinced that the war represented an opportunity to establish a new order and to rid the world of evil. His early enthusiasm does not seem to have lasted long. 'The Counter-Attack', the second poem in the 'War' section, suggests the laboriousness, the monotony, and the futility of the work in which he was involved:

> After clearing this forest, warily probing
> each innocent bush and each tidy glade . . .
> after conquering the broken streets, trampling hearths
> once handsome, plundering their pretty rooms.[50]

And although it follows 'In Night Battle', which is annotated with the background details '1 March 1945, outside the town of Weeze in northwest Germany', the poem did not evolve from a military experience abroad: it was originally written in August 1943 while Llywelyn-Williams was based at Brecon, and later published in the April

---

[47] The translation quoted comes from Joseph P. Clancy, 'The Battle of Gwen Ystrad', in *idem*, *Medieval Welsh Poems* (Dublin: Four Courts Press, 2003), 39.

[48] Ifor Williams's *Canu Aneirin* (Caerdydd: Gwasg Prifysgol Cymru, 1938) is a scholarly edition of the heroic poetry attributed to the sixth-century poet Aneirin, who wrote *Y Gododdin*. For accessible translations, see Clancy, *Medieval Welsh Poems*, 45–76. David Jones alludes to the poem in his modernist classic, *In Parenthesis* (1937), which Alun Llywelyn-Williams regarded as 'the only poetic masterpiece to emerge from the [First World] war'; see Llywelyn-Williams, untitled review of Silkin's *Out of Battle*, 104–5.

[49] Ifor Williams's *Canu Llywarch Hen* (Caerdydd: Gwasg Prifysgol Cymru, 1935) is a scholarly edition of early Welsh saga poetry dating back to the ninth or tenth century and contains within it *englynion* associated with the historic character Llywarch Hen. For accessible translations, see Clancy, *Medieval Welsh Poems*, 76–104.

[50] Llywelyn-Williams, 'The Counter-Attack', trans. Clancy, in *Light in the Gloom*, 133.

1944 issue of the Welsh quarterly *Y Traethodydd*. It is easy to understand, however, why Gwyn Thomas mistakenly associated the poem with the following description of the destruction that Llywelyn-Williams witnessed in Germany:

I was with other soldiers there toward the end of the war. I remember going through the Reichswald—around the winter and spring of 1945—going there to fight. As we came out of a forest near a place called Goch we came across a regiment of the SS. . . . I remember going around the outskirts of the forest after the battle; this was the only time when I saw lads who had been killed. One of my friends was among them: he had been set out tidily but was completely dead, the poor fellow.[51]

Be it a premonition or not, here were the 'fruitless marks of the bitter slaughter's anguish', the destruction caused by him and his fellow combatants, and the only indication that his humanity has not ceased to function is his troubled conscience:

> . . . comes upon us the harder, more hazardous battle of dealing
> with the grace that chills the blood of the seething heart.
> Vile, furtive underminer; against this,
> tank, or bomb, or gunshot is of no avail.[52]

In the actual experience of war, his hopefulness is dimmed, and the earlier doubts he had harboured in Brecon are validated. All mention of 'shatter[ing] the world' in order to create 'a new world' cease:[53] they sound in retrospect like the slick sloganeering of the politician and propagandist. Llywelyn-Williams's innocent perception of war has been corrected by the reality. He was forced to face up to his experience and be true to himself: 'I could only offer a direct affirmation of my own experience as a combatant.'[54] And that, after all, is all a poet can do, according to Wilfred Owen: 'That is why the true Poets must be truthful.'[55]

But the truth hurt: although six of the war poems included in *Pont y Caniedydd* were more or less complete by 1946, three years went by before he began composing the first of the five remaining poems based upon his experiences. They are significant years for him as a poet: as he suggests in a letter sent to his wife in July 1945, he considered himself at an artistic crossroads. Although he would eventually return to work for the BBC, at this stage he had no wish to do so:

Features would entail too much creative work, and despite the good reception that my poems had, I feel now that whatever artistic energy I may have once possessed, it has all been knocked out of me by the war. I have said what I wanted to say, and now since being in Germany, I have seen it all come true, to say it again would be absurd. To see civilization

---

[51] Llywelyn-Williams, 'Sgwrs ag Alun Llywelyn-Williams', *Llais Llyfrau* (Winter 1986), 6. Gwyn Thomas's comment appears in his *Alun Llywelyn-Williams* (Caernarfon: Gwasg Pantycelyn, 1987), 36.

[52] Llywelyn-Williams, 'Counter Attack', 133.

[53] Llywelyn-Williams, 'The Airman', 128, and 'Since Death is Close By', 123.

[54] Llywelyn-Williams, 'Alun Llywelyn-Williams', 174.

[55] Wilfred Owen, 'Preface', in *Complete Poems and Fragments, ii: The Manuscripts and Fragments*, ed. Jon Stallworthy (London: Chatto & Windus, Hogarth Press, and Oxford University Press, 1983), 535.

come to an end, as one feared it would, even if it hasn't happened in one's own country, is a pretty shattering experience, and doesn't exactly augur well for the future.[56]

It was as if the experience of war—what one might venture to call the existentialist appeal of war that he had at one stage desired—now nauseated him.[57] Indeed, the experience seems nearly to have destroyed him, so much so that he felt that he no longer had anything to say as a poet. And according to his biographer, Non Indeg Evans, 'When the war ended he did not wish to share any of his experiences in Europe with his family and friends, and Alis Llywelyn-Williams confirms that remembering the day when he was injured (and his driver killed) frightened him for the rest of his life.'[58] However, rather than yielding to the nihilism and anarchy that he witnessed all around him, Llywelyn-Williams eventually managed to discover a new significance in art.

SURVIVOR

If he witnessed signs of nihilism and anarchy anywhere, he did so in Berlin in August 1945. By the beginning of May 1945, Berlin had been conquered by Stalin's Red Army, Hitler had committed suicide, and Germany had accepted defeat. The sequence of three poems, 'In Berlin—August 1945'—the 'most honest' poems that he ever composed according to his own description in conversation toward the end of his life[59]—is the best testimony available in Welsh, from the perspective of an eyewitness, of the destruction wrought upon the German capital at the end of the War. After being injured on St David's Day 1945, in an explosion that killed his driver, he was hospitalized for more than two months in Belgium before being assigned to 'a public relations unit, so to speak—an excellent job—taking war

---

[56] Llywelyn-Williams to Alis Llywelyn-Williams, 24 July 1945, English-language letter quoted in Non Indeg Evans, 'Bywyd a Gwaith Alun Llywelyn-Williams' (unpublished Ph.D. thesis, University of Wales, Bangor, 1995), 185.

[57] Llywelyn-Williams had been led into the Army convinced of the moral case for war. However, the semi-autobiographical unpublished novel 'Gwŷs i'r Gad' ('A Call to Arms') quotes the response of the protagonist, Gareth, to a letter received in May 1944 from his friend, the BBC wartime correspondent Wynford Vaughan Thomas, who was at the time located in Anzio, Italy. Warned to stay put on the Home Front for his own well-being, Gareth struggles to deny the attraction of war: 'It would be foolish and repugnant to wish to leave the peace and quiet of Brecon in order to take part in the destruction that was sweeping through Italy and the whole of Europe. Certainly, he didn't wish to do so. He loathed such an irrational and dangerous attraction. And yet . . . and yet. . . .' The letter received from Wynford Vaughan Thomas was a factual document, translated from the original English and incorporated within the novel; four months after receiving it, Llywelyn-Williams would be venturing abroad. An edited version of 'Gwŷs i'r Gad' appears as an appendix to Evans's doctoral thesis, 'Bywyd a Gwaith Alun Llywelyn-Williams'.

[58] Evans, 'Bywyd a Gwaith Alun Llywelyn-Williams', 85.

[59] Llywelyn-Williams, 'Bardd y Mis: Alun Llywelyn-Williams', *Barddas*, 51 (Apr. 1981), 1.

reporters around'.[60] Through the words of Llywelyn-Williams the Welsh language bore witness to one of the twentieth century's major landmarks. Llywelyn-Williams's was not a war reporter's response, recording the first copy of history, but rather a poet's response, that of one who allowed the experience to settle before giving it artistic expression. And this contrasted with his work for what was, in essence, a propaganda unit offering quick interpretations and immediate answers at the time. At least three years went by before he wrote the Berlin sequence: it appears that he wrote 'Lehrter Bahnhof' and 'Theater des Westens' in 1949 and 'Zehlendorf' in December 1951.[61] Years later he recalled 'the destruction' which was 'terrible': 'That's what made the greatest impact upon me, not the killing.'[62] In 1952, in a radio broadcast, he described the experience that formed a basis for the opening poem:

I remember going one evening in August 1945 to a Berlin station, a station not far from the Tiergarten and the garden where Hitler had spent his remaining hours a few weeks previously. The main hall was a reservoir, for the underground pipes had been burst by the bombing, the roof was smashed, and the platforms piled with mud and filth and shattered glass and steel: and the rain that night constantly falling.[63]

In another letter of September 1945 he refers to himself as 'a sort of impersonal onlooker on to the destruction, too, but that does not make the lovely things to which I belonged any more real—music and poetry, and love of the mountains; one feels numb and paralysed, and there is only an ache of *hiraeth*, ever so deep and strong'.[64] Yet, the fact that several years lay between the original experiences and the later poems guarantees a certain amount of distance and objectivity as well as ensuring that the poet is not restricted by the temporary details of the event. The Berlin poems form a retrospective sequence written by a survivor-poet rather than a soldier-poet. In fact, one is immediately directed to Wales, rather than Germany, by the opening reference to 'Heledd' in 'Lehrter Bahnhof'.[65] Heledd was a princess in exile from the court of Pengwern in seventh-century Powys, and a principal character in early Welsh saga poetry, and in the poem she is identified with the homeless Inge in twentieth-century Berlin; as well as being a proper noun in German, 'ing' is a common noun in Welsh meaning 'pain, agony, affliction'.[66]

---

[60] Llywelyn-Williams, 'Sgwrs ag Alun Llywelyn-Williams', 6.

[61] See Evans, 'Bywyd a Gwaith Alun Llywelyn-Williams', 396, where composition dates for the poems are presented, based on a list found among the poet's private papers.

[62] Llywelyn-Williams, 'Sgwrs ag Alun Llywelyn-Williams', 6.

[63] Llywelyn-Williams, 'Yr Ail Rwyg', 9 Nov. 1952, a radio broadcast quoted in Evans, 'Bywyd a Gwaith Alun Llywelyn-Williams', 192.

[64] Llywelyn-Williams to Alis Llywelyn-Williams, 21 Sept. 1945, English-language letter quoted ibid. 176.

[65] Llywelyn-Williams, 'Lehrter Bahnhof', trans. Clancy, in *Light in the Gloom*, 140–1.

[66] See the entry for 'ing, yng', in *Geiriadur Prifysgol Cymru: A Dictionary of the Welsh Language: Cyfrol II G-LLYYS* (Caerdydd: Gwasg Prifysgol Cymru, 1968–87), where it is translated as 'strait(s), extremity, press of battle, crisis, distress, dire adversity, affliction; anguish, excruciating pain, agony, pang'.

'[T]he years play tricks with us,' says the poet: despite the fact that many centuries separate Heledd and Inge, they are drawn together by their common experience as victims of war. This suggests a continuous history, an ongoing tradition of warfare, as Llywelyn-Williams establishes himself at the outset as the latest Welsh poet over a thousand years to bear witness to war. The station is caught in limbo: a bullet had 'ripped the fingers [of the clock] away | that appointed the coming and going | of the harsh wheels' stately bustle'. The fact that there is no timetable operating in a train station—of all places—emphasizes the sense of anarchy. But this timeless state also helps to underline the poem's relevance and extend its significance.

Contemporary descriptions of the destruction in Berlin—'The whirlwind went by— | and from the cleft in the wall, from the crack in the pavement, | the water pours without echoing the song of the brook. | The night drips around us'—are interlaced with allusions to *Canu Llywarch Hen*: 'let us . . . praise the hearth's purity beneath the grey lichen's blight'; 'Sharp is the breeze'.[67] This modern-day Heledd is a fallen princess: 'concealed on the handy bed of the rubble, | as a gift for savouring the cigarette, for sucking the chocolate, | you can extend your love to the lonely conqueror.' In the face of such a cheapened and debased existence, the third and final stanza asks when will order be reinstated, but also closes with a sobering thought:

> This was always a gross, pompous city
> and fit to be ruined;
> have you heard, Heledd,—no, wounded Inge,—
> the greedy eagle's fierce laughter,
> have you seen, in his half-shut eyes,
> the preordained image of all our fragile cities?

Ifor Williams saw signs of 'Fate and arrogance reaping destruction' in *Canu Llywarch Hen*;[68] Llywelyn-Williams sees history repeating itself and hubris destroying other Pengwerns and other Berlins in the future.

In the second poem of the sequence, 'Zehlendorf'—'a suburb on the south-western border of the city . . . [through which] the Russians . . . made their final attack on the city'—Inge appears again, but this time in a public park leaning over an unidentified gravestone: 'do not give him a name'.[69] This again emphasizes the universal and symbolic significance of recent historical events already seen in the opening poem of the sequence: the gravestone signifies the death of millions during the war itself, the omnipotent, unavoidable, and ever-present death 'that mercifully climbs to our bed at the long day's end, | that awaits us on the farthest corners of our consciousness, | on Everest's highest peak, there to greet our strength'. The

---

[67] Compare Jenny Rowland's translation of 'Aelwyd Rheged', in her *Early Welsh Saga Poetry* (Cambridge: D. S. Brewer, 1990), 482, which contains the line 'This hearth—grey lichen hides it'; see also her translation of a line from 'Llym Awel', ibid. 501: 'Sharp is the wind, bare the hill.'

[68] Ifor Williams, 'Rhagymadrodd', in Williams (ed.), *Canu Llywarch Hen*, p. lxix.

[69] Llywelyn-Williams, 'Zehlendorf', trans. Clancy, in *Light in the Gloom*, 141–2.

same death also defeated 'the guardian of the ford, the defender of the border' centuries before: the reference here is to another major character from early Welsh saga poetry, namely Gwên ap Llywarch.[70] It is then suggested that the 'anonymous cross' may belong to a victim running for his life, one overtaken by hopelessness, or an internee at Belsen. The mood is depressing and sombre, and nature itself does not seem to offer any hope for the future: above the grave, 'the prophetic trees will not venture to promise | that spring will come back in its turn'.

The prospects remain gloomy at the beginning of the third and final poem within the sequence, 'Theater des Westens':

> It keeps on raining. Somewhere in the roof
> the hidden pool overflows at the tip of a crack,
> and through the captive darkness, the steady unhappy
> drops trickle to soak the slack carpet.[71]

The same rain had greeted the protagonist at the end of Llywelyn-Williams's unpublished novel 'Gwŷs i'r Gad' ('A Call to Arms'), when his military aircraft touched down on the European mainland: 'The first part of the journey was over. And it was raining';[72] the rain is a source of misery in 'If the Rain would Stop, Friend', and the same oppressive, monotonous rain was immortalized by the most prominent Welsh writer in English associated with the war, Alun Lewis, in 'All Day It Has Rained'.[73] But despite the rain leitmotif, creativity and artistry are seen challenging the inevitability and negativity of death in Llywelyn-Williams's poem:

> Let us be content to watch Inge dancing,
> dancing where the harsh electric light is focussed;
> stronger than the fear that lurks in the rain's pulsations
> is the music that fosters the assurance of her supple arms.

Llywelyn-Williams later referred to the genesis of this poem in the experience of 'seeing for the first time in my life (more's the pity) some of the glory of the ballet' and hearing the musicians whom he praised 'for persevering so gallantly amidst such destruction, and maintaining such a high standard'.[74] Art is identified as a civilizing life force. But once more, the literal experience is filtered through the poet's literary inheritance, and the fatalistic Heledd is superseded by an allusion to Olwen, another female character from early Welsh literature, for whom Culhwch

---

[70] See Jenny Rowland's translation of 'Gwên ap Llywarch', in *Early Welsh Saga Poetry*, 468, which contains the line 'I intend to keep watch on the ford'.

[71] Llywelyn-Williams, 'Theater des Westens', trans. Clancy, in *Light in the Gloom*, 142.

[72] Llywelyn-Williams, 'Gwŷs i'r Gad', in Evans, 'Bywyd a Gwaith Alun Llywelyn-Williams', 394.

[73] M. Wynn Thomas compares and contrasts the writers in his *Internal Difference: Twentieth-Century Writing in Wales* (Cardiff: University of Wales Press, 1992), 49–67; Greg Hill sheds further light on the matter in 'A Oes Golau yn y Gwyll? Alun Llywelyn-Williams ac Alun Lewis', in M. Wynn Thomas (ed.), *DiFfinio Dwy Lenyddiaeth Cymru* (Caerdydd: Gwasg Prifysgol Cymru, 1995), 120–44.

[74] Llywelyn-Williams to his parents, 19 Aug. 1945, quoted in Evans, 'Bywyd a Gwaith Alun Llywelyn-Williams', 191.

was forced to perform around forty *anoethau* or extremely difficult tasks before winning her as his bride.[75] The dazzling creativity and imagination which characterize *Culhwch ac Olwen* as a prose tale inject new energy and optimism into the poetic sequence and provide Llywelyn-Williams with hope for the future: 'let the mother again be joyful'; 'there is a garden to be tended' and 'strength in the green shoots'. Inge is now seen dancing, and her creativity is a counterpoint to the gloom and pessimism of the previous two poems. Dance is seen as an ancient art-form, and here it symbolizes man's ability throughout the ages to rise above his material environment and liberate himself through the strength of his imagination:

> Because the training has been long, and her instruction thorough
> in many an ancient city; and many an age
> has fashioned her delicate art, the craft that incarnates
> the spinning of the notes, that purifies the primal wound.

'To see civilization come to an end' may not 'augur well for the future': however, in retrospect, the activity which Llywelyn-Williams witnessed in 'the only playhouse in the sector of Berlin under control of the British forces which was comparatively undamaged'[76] seemed to challenge the doomed sense of finality he had previously expressed in July 1945. The humanitarian Llywelyn-Williams finds new grounds for hope, a source of personal solace, in the rejuvenating power of art. This realization presented him with a future for his own art and enabled him to reinvent and redefine himself as a poet.

Written in 1954, 'Ballad of the Phantoms' and 'On a Visit' are poetic statements of reconciliation which represent Llywelyn-Williams's last attempt to take control and make sense of his war experiences. Although the gloss 'A wartime conversation' appears in the *Pont y Caniedydd* edition of 'Ballad of the Phantoms', nothing in the poem itself would seem to link it exclusively to the Second World War. The wartime conversation recounted is between two strangers, a female bartender and a male combatant, both of whom have witnessed a fellow human being killed at close range. At least, that is what one deduces from the references to 'Girl', 'boy', 'lad', and 'husband':[77] the use of common rather than proper nouns ensures that the characters are representative types and that the poem has a universal significance. The location could just as easily be 1970s Hanoi or 1990s Sarajevo as Brussels during the winter of 1944–5. With poise and dignity, the poem moves towards its conclusion: 'We are comrades in suffering. | It's the saddest mystery in the world; | And our cheer is in its sharing.'

---

[75] *Culhwch ac Olwen*, a medieval prose tale, is a primary example of Welsh Arthurian literature; see *Culhwch and Olwen: An Edition and Study of the Oldest Arthurian Tale*, ed. Rachel Bromwich and D. Simon Evans (Cardiff: University of Wales Press, 1992).

[76] See Llywelyn-Williams, 'Notes', trans. Clancy, in *Light in the Gloom*, 205.

[77] Llywelyn-Williams, 'Ballad of the Phantoms', trans. Clancy, ibid. 134.

A similar emphasis on the common suffering caused by war is found in the poem which immediately follows, 'On a Visit'.[78] Besides the sequence of three poems that constitute 'In Berlin—August 1945', this elegant and balanced narrative poem—it consists of seventy-two lines subdivided into twelve six-line stanzas—is the longest war poem written by Llywelyn-Williams, and he explores thoroughly within it all aspects of the situation he presents. He measured First World War poetry by these criteria—'an appreciation of how wholly was the experience perceived and expressed, how complex the admission of truth, how compassionate the poet's view of man's condition'[79]—and measured by his own standards, 'On a Visit' must be regarded as a classic poetic meditation on war.

A retrospective, reconciliatory tone is established from the outset:

> Peace has surely come by now to heal it completely
> and turn the sicken house to a home of joy once more;
> if I could return some winter twilight
> and walk again through the noiseless lane's silent snow
> to where I once was, there would be a change in time and a new
> order, and I would not know a world as strange as summer.

The starting point is the 'new | order' of the present, not wartime, and the positive attributes of 'Peace' and 'joy'. The voice is experienced, middle-aged, and responsible—Llywelyn-Williams was 41 in 1954. He also ensures that enough time has lapsed between the past he is about to discuss and his own present, and at the start of the second stanza goes as far as to suggest that 'perhaps it was a dream'. Throughout the poem one is convinced of its authenticity by the precision and care with which the situation is described. Yet, one senses that Llywelyn-Williams's main interest lies not in the concrete details he seems to be recalling, but rather in the moral significance of his tale. The basic predicament—a man seeking refuge in a strange house from a snowstorm—appears rather prosaic, but it is presented in a way that injects the commonplace with extraordinary resonance. The poem is essentially an 'epiphany' as that word is defined by David Lodge: a 'descriptive passage in which external reality is charged with a kind of transcendental significance for the perceiver. In modern fiction an epiphany often has the function performed by a decisive action in traditional narrative, providing a climax or resolution to a story or episode.'[80] It is, therefore, appropriate that Llywelyn-Williams attempts to rise above the material reality of war in this, one of the two last poems he wrote about the War.

---

[78] Llywelyn-Williams, 'On a Visit', trans. Clancy, ibid. 135–7. An alternative translation of 'Ar Ymweliad', entitled 'The Visit', is provided by R. S. Thomas in *Modern Poetry in Translation*, new series no. 7 (Spring 1995), 157–9. It is one of six poems chosen and translated by Thomas to represent modern Welsh verse, and the fact that it immediately follows a translation of 'In Two Fields' by Waldo Williams supports the claim that Alun Llywelyn-Williams and Waldo Williams represent between them the two premier, though contrasting, Welsh poets of the Second World War.

[79] Llywelyn-Williams, untitled review of Jon Silkin's *Out of Battle*, 105.

[80] David Lodge, *The Art of Fiction* (Harmondsworth: Penguin, 1992), 147.

The first words uttered by 'the Baron' and the householder are in French, but are followed by the formality and antiquity of 'ffrwst' (literally: hurry, haste, rush), 'diriaid' ('dreadful'), and later 'ffrewyll' ('whip'), three words that date back to at least the twelfth century. '[N]y at duw da y diryeit' ('God does not allow good for the *diriaid*, that is, 'ill-fated') appears in 'Claf Abercuawg' in *Canu Llywarch Hen*, and the rather archaic syntax employed by the baron, 'gwae ni o'r graith' ('we sorrow for the scar'), calls to mind a common syntax, 'gwae hi oe thynghet' ('Woe to it for its fate'), in the early Welsh saga poetry.[81] The rapport with *Canu Llywarch Hen* is reinforced by the reference to 'fate's joke on all cordiality', a central theme in the saga poetry, and the simile 'fel claf anhyblyg' ('like a stubborn patient') calls to mind the decrepit and diseased character of Claf Abercuawg and also Llywarch Hen, who lost his twenty-four sons in battle. As Heledd had long ago wandered in 'Stauell gyndylan ys tywyll heno' ('The hall of Cynddylan is dark tonight'), so the narrator bears witness to the destruction of war as he is led 'o stafell i stafell' ('from room to room') 'yn yr hanner gwyll' ('in the half-darkness').[82]

The deliberate choice of words—'lleufer' ('light') in the eighth stanza reminds one of the ruthless reference to 'kyscit lloegyr llydan nifer | a lleuuer yn eu lly-geit' ('Asleep is Lloegr's broad war-band | with light upon their eyes') in one of Taliesin's war poems, and 'llamsachus' ('leaping') calls to mind the horses of the *Mabinogi*—confirms the impression of resonating antiquity as the poem nears its emotional climax.[83] By this stage, both men have been joined by the baron's wife, and just as the two strangers in 'Ballad of the Phantoms' had occupied the common ground of suffering, so the three players in 'On a Visit' are 'comrades in suffering': it is eventually disclosed that the husband and wife have lost their son in war and have kept their loss to themselves, but by the means of the unexpected visitor—the 'clumsy fool' as he describes himself for accidentally offending them—they are provided with an opportunity, if not to shed their burden of grief that threatens to overwhelm them, then at least to share it. Their son had been an accomplished pianist, and the baron's piano playing proves a source of empathy and therapy and emotional release:

> then the gracious melodies
> flowed from his hand, prelude and dance and song so bitterly sad,
> so carelessly joyful, and gentle and full of compassion—
> till the sound grew soft, a communion where angels walked,
> honouring our wound and setting our captive hours free.

---

[81] See Jenny Rowland's translations of 'Claf Abercuawg' and 'Cân yr Henwr', in *Early Welsh Saga Poetry*, 499 and 475.

[82] See Jenny Rowland's translation of 'Stafell Gynddylan', ibid. 484.

[83] The lines appear in 'Marwnat Owein', in *Canu Taliesin*, ed. Ifor Williams (Caerdydd: Gwasg Prifysgol Cymru, 1960), 12, and the poem is translated by Clancy as 'Lament for Owain ab Urien', in *Medieval Welsh Poems*, 44. '[L]lamsachus' appears in 'Pwyll Pendeuic Dyuet', in *Pedeir Keinc y Mabinogi*, ed. Ifor Williams (Caerdydd: Gwasg Prifysgol Cymru, 1930), 12.

However challenged and discredited the concept may be—the way music was abused in the Nazi death camps is probably the worst example—his belief in the redeeming qualities of music provided Llywelyn-Williams with a source of personal and artistic salvation.[84]

Llywelyn-Williams was able to reassess his role as a poet after the fundamental doubts that assailed him as a result of the trauma of war. Just as he had celebrated his having survived the war in 'The First Christmas of Peace', the final poem of the 'War' section in *Pont y Caniedydd*, so he expressed his belief, in 'The Poet of the World as it Is', that poetry in general should celebrate the fact that 'Life goes on, and God requires of a poet | praise of life's wonder and its mystery.'[85] In another poem in which he explicitly addresses the function of the poet, 'The Poet's Penance', he claims that 'dreams are at the heart of the world' and that 'God has laid upon the poet | the pain of living them in words'.[86] As in the case of 'Ballad of the Phantoms' and 'On a Visit', both 'The Poet of the World as it Is' and 'The Poet's Penance' belong to that prolific year, 1954, and in an essay published during the same year he again attempted to define the role of the poet and reassert his own creative function: 'The poet attends on mystery. . . . That's what is common to major poets at all times in every civilization and every religion, that they bear witness to the continuous and permanent cycle of life's destruction and renewal.'[87]

This shift in emphasis, away from the topical and toward the timeless, as seen in particular in the most mature war poems contained in *Pont y Caniedydd*—as opposed to *Cerddi 1934–1942*— helps explain the greater awareness of the Welsh poetic canon in the later poems. The allusions were occasional in the 1942 volume, but by 1956 they are regular and intentional, and point towards his substantial development as a poet. Llywelyn-Williams's relationship with his indigenous literary tradition ultimately helped to defend him from nihilism by providing him with a wider historical and cultural context within which to locate his experience of the horrors of war; as Greg Hill has pointed out in his comparative study of both poets, the absence of a similar resource for Alun Lewis placed him in a far more precarious

---

[84] His former friend and colleague Dyfnallt Morgan expressed his reservation about Llywelyn-Williams's belief in 'Cofio Alun Llywelyn-Williams', in Tomos Morgan (ed.), *Rhywbeth i'w Ddweud: Detholiad o Waith Dyfnallt Morgan* (Llandysul: Gwasg Gomer, 2003), 221–2: 'Out of a civilization that elevated the fine arts . . . arose the abhorrence of totalitarianism. We have heard of extermination camp guards in Germany coming home after a day of butchering to enjoy a night in their cosy homes reading Goethe, weeping over Rilke's poems, intoxicated by Schubert's music. . . . I cannot for the life of me take comfort in man's creativity. The other side of the coin is his ability and tendency to destroy. Like the Jewish writer, George Steiner, I can only think of a means of redemption for man from his wretched condition in transcendental terms.'

[85] Llywelyn-Williams, 'The Poet of the World as it Is', trans. Clancy, in *Light in the Gloom*, 153.

[86] Llywelyn-Williams, 'The Poet's Penance', trans. Clancy, ibid. 147.

[87] Llywelyn-Williams, 'Diwedd y Byd', in *Nes Na'r Hanesydd? Ysgrifau Llenyddol* ('Closer than the Historian? Literary Essays') (Dinbych: Gwasg Gee, 1968; essay 1st pub. 1954), 150.

situation, vulnerable to the nihilism which finally defeated him.[88] Whereas previously in the 1930s, in *Tir Newydd* and *Cerddi 1934–1942*, Llywelyn-Williams had seen fit to criticize Welsh literature for its apparent failure to respond to modern society, he now seemed to be advocating the perennial relevance of its antiquity.

But although he repositioned himself as a poet, aligning himself with his indigenous literary tradition and distancing himself from the Auden generation, Llywelyn-Williams maintained much of his independence as a poet.[89] The form he employed in the majority of his poems was *vers libre*, a foreign import that had not received universal acceptance within conservative literary circles. Part of the Welsh compromise with *vers libre* resulted in a meeting of opposites, between the free spirit *vers libre* and the home-bird *cynghanedd*, and the tension-wrought arranged marriage named *vers libre cynganeddol*; this was seen most notably in the poems written by T. Gwynn Jones in 1934–5.[90] Llywelyn-Williams's adoption of the form underlined his own cosmopolitan and internationalist outlook, and also helped authenticate *vers libre* as a valid form for Welsh poetry.[91] Another indication of his independent stance involves his relationship to social causes. Even in his most socially committed phase during 1934–42, one suspects that he had certain reservations, and was not uncritically convinced: in retrospect he played down his early political leaning, describing himself as 'some sort of Marxist' who had 'very crude' socialist ideas.[92] After 1936, when the burning of a proposed bombing range in the Llŷn Peninsula led to a whole generation of Welsh writers publicly committing themselves to the nationalist cause, Llywelyn-Williams again guarded his independence by disregarding the new orthodoxy.[93] His own experience had made him wary, alerting him to

---

[88] Hill, 'A Oes Golau yn y Gwyll? Alun Llywelyn-Williams ac Alun Lewis'.

[89] Dafydd Glyn Jones, 'The Poetry of Alun Llywelyn-Williams', 14, referred to 'his comparative independence of the tradition . . . although professionally . . . Alun Llywelyn-Williams is much involved in the Welsh literary community, I have always felt that as a poet and critic he has stood somewhat apart from it'.

[90] A major figure in the Welsh literary revival at the start of the twentieth century, T. Gwynn Jones was a master of reinvention, and originally published his poems in *vers libre cynganeddol* under a pseudonym in 1934–5; they were later republished in *Y Dwymyn* (Aberystwyth: Gwasg Aberystwyth, 1944).

[91] Even the most determined critics of Welsh *vers libre* have tended to single out Alun Llywelyn-Williams's poetry as the exception that proves the rule: see, in particular, D. Tecwyn Lloyd, 'Y Wers Rydd a'i Hamserau', in *Llên Cyni a Rhyfel a Thrafodion Eraill* (Llandysul: Gwasg Gomer, 1987), 169: 'I would suggest that Alun Llywelyn-Williams is one of the very very few [Welsh] poets who has managed to treat *vers libre* successfully.'

[92] Llywelyn-Williams, 'Sgwrs rhwng Alun Llywelyn-Williams a Bedwyr Lewis Jones', in J. E. Caerwyn Williams (ed.), *Ysgrifau Beirniadol*, i (Dinbych: Gwasg Gee, 1965), 123; and idem, *Gwanwyn yn y Ddinas*, 98.

[93] It is interesting to note that Cardiff station director, E. R. Appleton, prevented Llywelyn-Williams from getting a permanent post with the BBC in 1935 on the grounds that he was ' "an ardent young Nationalist" '; quoted in John Davies, *Broadcasting and the BBC in Wales*, 72. Appleton was almost certainly overstating the case: Llywelyn-Williams's membership of the Welsh Nationalist Party in the 1930s was unenthusiastic and short-lived, due to his critical response to what he regarded as its right-wing, reactionary tendencies.

the potentially catastrophic results of writers promoting political ideology, and language, as a consequence of this, becoming debased. As George Steiner memorably put it, the fate of the German language offers the most extreme case in point:

Gradually, words lost their original meaning and acquired nightmarish definitions. *Jude, Pole, Russe* came to mean two-legged lice, putrid vermin which good Aryans must squash, as a party said, 'like roaches on a dirty wall'. 'Final Solution', *endgültige Lösung*, came to signify the death of six million human beings in gas ovens.

The language was infected not only with these great bestialities. It was called upon to enforce innumerable falsehoods, to persuade the Germans that the war was just and everywhere victorious. As defeat began closing in on the thousand-year Reich, the lies thickened to a constant snowdrift. The language was turned upside down to say 'light' where there was blackness and 'victory' where there was disaster.[94]

The personality presented in the war poems of Llywelyn-Williams is that of a responsible, self-composed, experienced man; his is the muse of reason contained within meticulously crafted poems. The poet's calling was not a source of particular pleasure to him: 'I must admit that I have never got much pleasure whilst trying to write poetry. I do not like, in the first place, the painful process of writing.'[95] He refers on more than one occasion to the creative conflict. His comment that 'every poem is a battle between the poet and words and syntaxes, an attempt to achieve complete and appropriate expression of a specific experience or feeling'[96] echoes what T. S. Eliot in 'East Coker' described as 'the intolerable wrestle | With words and meanings'.[97] His words suggest that Llywelyn-Williams certainly did not take his calling as a poet lightly: he was only too aware of the social importance—in a non-partisan and universal sense—and seriousness attached to such a calling. He could quite easily have agreed with Eliot on another occasion, when he wrote in 'Little Gidding' in 1942 that 'our concern was speech, and speech impelled us | To purify the dialect of the tribe'.[98] Llywelyn-Williams's war poems—unhysterical, balanced, objective—represent his attempt to reclaim for the language some of its purity and integrity and help establish trust in it once more in the twentieth century.

---

[94] George Steiner, 'The Hollow Miracle', in *Language and Silence: Essays 1958–1966* (London: Faber, 1967), 122–3.
[95] Llywelyn-Williams, 'Holi: Alun Llywelyn-Williams', 21.
[96] Llywelyn-Williams, 'Sgwrs rhwng Alun Llywelyn-Williams a Bedwyr Lewis Jones', 120.
[97] T. S. Eliot, 'East Coker', in *The Complete Poems and Plays* (London: Faber, 1969), 179.
[98] Eliot, 'Little Gidding', ibid. 194.

....

CHAPTER 19

THE MUSE
THAT FAILED:
POETRY
AND PATRIOTISM
DURING
THE SECOND
WORLD WAR

....

HELEN GOETHALS

At first sight, 'poetry' and 'patriotism' might seem an unlikely juxtaposition of terms; indeed, in the context of the Second World War, 'poetry *or* patriotism' might have been a more conventional title. But it is precisely the conventional view that will be challenged in this article, since the apparent antithesis rests on certain assumptions that continue to hamper our understanding of both the poetry and the politics of the Second World War.

'War poetry' is an inherently historicizing term, postulating a relationship between the historical events of, and the poetic response to, a given period of war. Both the events and the poems are assembled by historians and literary critics into related historical and literary narratives of the war, a process which necessarily involves a selection of what are perceived as significant events and poems. Because our perception of the significant past is determined by the preoccupations of the present, in an infinite succession of present moments, the selections will inevitably vary over time. While it could be argued that the burgeoning number of anthologies of the poetry of the First World War has broadly kept pace with the changing and increasingly complex historical understanding of that war, the same could scarcely be said of the Second.

The popular perception of the war was established more than a generation ago, by Angus Calder's *The People's War* (1969) and Arthur Marwick's *Britain in a Century of Total War* (1970), social histories which argued that the War in Britain had been fought in every sense defensively. They were followed by two now classic works of literary criticism, Robert Hewison's *Under Siege* (1977) and A. T. Tolley's *The Poetry of the Forties* (1985), and reinforced by such remarkable recent works as Paul Fussell's *Wartime* (1989), Studs Terkel's *The Good War* (1997), and Joanna Burke's *An Intimate History of Killing* (1999). According to these accounts, the ordinary soldier- or civilian poet was unable (and perhaps unwilling) to see the full picture, and his role was thus reduced to scribbling sardonic footnotes to the official history of the War. The poetry of the period is barely in print, and mainly mediated through the anthologies. The only one of these still easily available is also the earliest, Brian Gardner's *The Terrible Rain*, first published in 1966, and consisting of poems chosen, according to the introductory note, 'because they seemed to express genuine and relevant attitudes to the war'.[1] Catherine Reilly's *Chaos of the Night* (1984), the four *Oasis* anthologies published in the 1980s, and Desmond Graham's *Poetry of the Second World War: An International Perspective* (1995) all made useful additions to Gardner's original canon, but did not fundamentally alter his historical and critical perspective.

Sixty years after the cessation of hostilities, what is urgently needed is an enlargement of the canon, one which takes into account not merely the military and social history of the War, but also its diplomatic, economic, ideological, and cultural aspects. A wider view would build on such critical works as Adam Piette's *Imagination at War* (1995), Mark Rawlinson's *British Writing of the Second World War* (2000), and W. G. Sebald's *On the Natural History of Destruction* (2003), in order to make a selection from the entire range of responses to war, those of Idris Davies and Philip Larkin being seen as 'genuine and relevant' as are those of Keith Douglas and Alun Lewis. In such an approach the relationship between poetry and patriotism would be viewed not as a simple, fixed contradiction in terms, but as a changing and complex—indeed, a deadly—struggle between private conscience and public enterprise.

A wider angle might well reject the thematic organization of Second World War anthologies so far and, in the manner of Jon Silkin's *Penguin Book of First World War Poetry*, offer instead a closer chronological parallel between the progress of the

---

[1] Brian Gardner, 'Introductory Note', in *idem* (ed.), *The Terrible Rain: The War Poets 1939–1945* (London: Methuen, 1977), p. xvii.

War and the progress of poetry. The chronological framework of the War would not be confined to the outbreak and cessation of hostilities between Britain and Germany, but redrawn to include the poetic and political events of the period 1938–48, from Munich to the Berlin airlift. The War would then be seen not so much as a belated attempt to redress the European imbalance of power, but rather as one of several stages of the conflict that dominated the twentieth century, the struggle between capitalism and socialism. In such a perspective, and by way of broad example, the three assumptions implied in the term 'patriotic poetry' will be seen to correspond to three distinct periods of the War.

During the first period, stretching from the Munich agreement in September 1938 to the fall of the Chamberlain government in May 1940, the dominant assumption was that poetry could and should be kept entirely separate from politics, because political poetry was necessarily propaganda, and propaganda was necessarily a Bad Thing. This assumption, widely held in 1939, stemmed from well-documented reactions to two previous wars: the anger of the First World War poets against the dishonest reporting of the battlefields, and the use of poetry to drive lambs to the slaughter of the trenches, and the disillusionment of the Thirties poets after the betrayal of the Left during and after the Spanish Civil War. Both Wilfred Owen's 'Dulce et Decorum Est' and Yeats's 'Lapis Lazuli' contributed to the radically new tone of Charles Causley's 'Recruiting Drive':

> Under the willow
> I heard the butcher-bird sing,
> Come out you fine young fellow
> From under your mother's wing.
> I'll show you the magic garden
> That hangs in the beamy air,
> The way of the lynx and the angry Sphinx
> And the fun of the freezing fair.
>
> .   .   .   .   .   .
>
> You must take off your clothes for the doctor
> And stand as straight as a pin,
> His hand of stone on your white breast-bone
> Where the bullets all go in.
> They'll dress you in lawn and linen
> And fill you with Plymouth gin,
> O the devil may wear a rose in his hair
> I'll wear my fine doe-skin.[2]

In John Lehmann and Stephen Spender's anthology *Poems for Spain* (1939), poetry had been willingly pressed into the service of propaganda, but as the Republican cause was betrayed and lost, so too was the poets' belief in the soundness of political

---

[2] Charles Causley, 'Recruiting Drive', in Desmond Graham (ed.), *Poetry of the Second World War* (London: Pimlico, 1988), 29.

poetry in general. George Orwell, in his attack on Auden's *Spain*, pointed out the harm that poetry could do to politics; Louis MacNeice denounced the damage that politics could do to poetry:

Art, though as much conditioned by material factors as anything else, is a manifestation of human freedom. The artist's freedom connotes honesty because a lie, however useful in politics, hampers artistic vision. Systematic propaganda is therefore foreign to the artist in so far as it involves the condoning of lies. Thus, in the Spanish Civil War some English poets were torn between writing good propaganda (dishonest poetry) and honest poetry (poor propaganda). I believe firmly that in Spain the balance of right was on the side of the government; propaganda, however, demands either angels or devils. This means that in the long run a poet must choose between being politically ineffectual and poetically false.[3]

The idea of art as 'a manifestation of human freedom' became in itself liberating for the British poets waiting to be called up, unwilling 'prisoners of war' looking for a way, not so much out of the War, as through it. George Orwell in 'Inside the Whale', after warning against any direct meddling in politics, recommended a clear mental and moral separation between the unavoidable patriotic action of the citizen and the necessary individual thought of a writer. The writer should see himself in the situation of Jonah inside the whale, caught up in the collapse of Western civilization, in a world whose historical movement he had not been able to—indeed, could not—control. He would be well-advised to follow the example of Henry Miller, spokesman for 'the ordinary man',[4] content with recording merely the individual point of view, assuming a 'glorious irresponsibility' which would be liberating for both the artist and his art.

Orwell's advice was brilliantly in tune with the mood of the threatened and Phoney War, both poetically and politically. Poetically, it coincided with a change in taste: an interest in surrealism, in the psychoanalytical theory of Jung, and a rediscovery of the work of D. H. Lawrence and W. B. Yeats. The poets were in no mood to add any more strident voices to the 'drum's discordant sound'.[5] Politically, the early period of the War was marked by the failure of appeasement and the ideological void created by the Germano–Soviet Pact of August 1939. The role of poet as 'ordinary man' was widely adopted, though it took on a variety of forms.

In the all-too-conspicuous absence of Auden and other unacknowledged legislators of the 1930s, given the geographical dispersion of the poets once conscripted, and the varied regional and Commonwealth origins of the soldier-poets, the isolationist stand appeared the only one available. Under duress, poets 'did their bit' as inclination and opportunity presented themselves. Some were recruited into civilian jobs,

---

[3] Louis MacNeice, 'The Poet in England To-day: A Reassessment', in *Selected Literary Criticism*, ed. Alan Heuser (Oxford: Oxford University Press, 1987), 113.

[4] George Orwell, 'Inside the Whale', in *The Collected Essays, Journalism and Letters of George Orwell*, i: *An Age Like This, 1920–1940*, ed. Sonia Orwell and Ian Angus (Harmondsworth: Penguin, 1970), 548.

[5] John Scott of Amwell (1730–83), 'The Drum', in Jon Stallworthy (ed.), *The Oxford Book of War Poetry* (Oxford: Oxford University Press, 1988), 68.

and those not stationed abroad threw themselves into the bohemian life of literary London, so well described in the memoirs of Julian Maclaren-Ross, Derek Stanford, and others. For those who could not avoid call-up, the conflict between patriotic and poetic duty was resolved by separating action and thought. It is for this reason that Henry Reed's 'Naming of Parts' remains so emblematic of the War. By juxtaposing two voices, the strident, public voice of the war instructor and the private *sotto voce* of the ordinary sensual man, it enacts that very outward acquiescence and inner resistance that Orwell had predicted would be liberating for poetry:

> To-day we have naming of parts. Yesterday,
> We had daily cleaning. And to-morrow morning,
> We shall have what to do after firing. But to-day,
> To-day we have naming of parts. Japonica
> Glistens like coral in all of the neighbouring gardens,
>   And to-day we have naming of parts.[6]

The individual, sensual point of view became not only the liberating postulate of poetry, but could even be seen, as here by Francis Scarfe, to fulfil a patriotic function:

The greatest change war produced in me was to help me towards writing, with deeper feeling and sensual appreciation, lyrics about ordinary things and people. I regard these not only as a means of self-preservation, but also as a necessary part of a writer's job in a war: the preservation of all that is permanent and moving and simple in human life.[7]

More importantly, the normal circumstances of war appeared to absolve the poet from performing what had until recently been seen as one of his main functions, that of telling the truth. In wartime, either the truth was not known or, if known, could not be told, lest the information fall into the hands of the enemy: 'Careless talk costs lives.' If the poet could not be truthful, he would at least be honest, offering the reader only the evidence of his own senses. To paraphrase Browning, rather than lend his mind out, he would lend his eyes and ears out. The truth about the War would be the aggregate of the poets' honest observations. As one soldier-poet remarked: 'Although no one is likely to confine the sprawl of this war in a single poem, the collected work should form a mosaic of the responsibility, the purpose, the feel, the look of it, and the human being in it, that may possibly be new.'[8] Far from being new, it was a fundamentally conservative point of view. The deliberate short-sightedness of the poets challenged neither the post-Romantic view of poetry as essentially lyrical—turning on a single emotion—nor the post-Romantic view of war as the continuation of politics by other means. The poets of the Second

---

[6] Henry Reed, 'Naming of Parts', in *Collected Poems*, ed. Jon Stallworthy (Oxford: Oxford University Press, 1991), 49.

[7] Francis Scarfe, *The Liberation of Poetry 1930–1941* (London: George Routledge & Sons, 1942), 198.

[8] Oscar Williams, 'Comments by the Poets', in *idem* (ed.), *The War Poets* (New York: John Day, 1945), 28.

World War, like those of the First, were focusing not on War but on the conduct of the War, and not on the function of poetry, but on its nature.

The self-imposed division between patriotic action and poetic thought created a crisis of integrity, in the sense that it compromised the social integration of the poet and, later, his individual integrity. The individual stance fatally underestimated the importance of poetry in time of war. The lessons of the First World War had been learnt in the 1930s by the readers of Sassoon, Owen, and Rosenberg, and those readers now looked to the poets to clarify their own response to war. The famous question 'Where are the War Poets?', asked in the *Times Literary Supplement* and actually raised in Parliament, reflected a variety of expectations of poets, but at the very least it showed that they had an essential role to play in public life. Poets with their 'still, small voices', confined their contribution to 'tossing ink grenades at the Goliath of War'[9] and, by their self-mocking irony, brought back into the limelight not poetry, but the poet. But by taking up the position of the marginal, powerless poet, they were in fact maintaining the notion that poetry itself was powerless and marginal, a position which was later to have grave repercussions for both poetry and politics.

The individual stance also encouraged internal divisions between warring schools of poetry, with poets ranging themselves on either side of the somewhat obscure line dividing the 'classical' from the 'romantic'. This unedifying battle of the books further weakened the cause of poetry, by distracting attention from a more important dogmatic division: the self-created split within the poet, between the private and the public self. The split was based partly on the ideas of Yeats, particularly his much-approved distinction that 'We make out of the quarrel with others, rhetoric, but of the quarrel with ourselves, poetry.'[10] Thus it happened that the 'memorable speech' of the Second World War turned out to be that of Churchill and Priestley. The idea that, as one soldier-poet put it, 'The truest statements about war are made under one's breath, and the most false on public platforms',[11] was to encourage poets to leave the new media (radio and, after the war, television) to the politicians and journalists, thus ignoring the very outlets that offered a return to the essentially vocal nature of their art, and perhaps a return to their original functions in society.

This fatal split between the public and the private was masked by the events of the second stage of the War, which temporarily forced the poets into the public arena. For a brief time, from May 1940 to November 1942, when Britain 'stood alone', patriotic poetry was not seen as a contradiction in terms. For a brief space, poets responded to the call Orwell had made, in *The Lion and the Unicorn*, for a patriotism reunited with intelligence. They began by subscribing to some rather loose distinctions between German and British notions of patriotism. For Orwell,

---

[9] Charles Hamblett, 'Introduction', in *idem* (ed.), *I Burn for England* (London: Leslie Frewn, 1966), 15.

[10] W. B. Yeats, 'Per Amica Silentia Lunae', in *Mythologies* (London: Macmillan, 1962), 331.

[11] Williams, 'Comments by the Poets', 16.

it was the defensive nature of (British) patriotism that made it acceptable in a way that (German) nationalism was not:

Nationalism is not to be confused with patriotism . . .. By 'patriotism' I mean devotion to a particular place and a particular way of life, which one believes to be the best in the world but has no wish to force on other people. Patriotism is of its nature defensive, both militarily and culturally. Nationalism, on the other hand, is inseparable from the desire for power. The abiding purpose of every nationalist is to secure more power and more prestige, *not* for himself but for the nation or unit in which he has chosen to sink his own individuality.[12]

E. M. Forster preferred to distinguish between the governmental culture of Germany and the national culture of England:

Germany is not against culture. She does believe in literature and art. But she has made a disastrous mistake; she has allowed her culture to become governmental, and from this mistake proceed all kinds of evils. In England our culture is not governmental. It is national: it springs naturally out of our way of looking at things, and out of the way we have looked at things in the past. It has developed slowly, easily, lazily; the English love of freedom, the English countryside, English prudishness and hypocrisy, English freakishness, our mild idealism and good-humoured reasonableness have all combined to make something which is certainly not perfect, but which may claim to be unusual.[13]

Both defensive and unusual patriotism needed to be distinguished from the home-grown variety of jingoism, the belligerent songs which had been born in the music-hall during the Crimean War and had grown up to taunt the Boers and the Huns. John Masefield, the Poet Laureate, was careful to title his first public poem of the War 'Some Verses to Some Germans'. Behind Herbert Read's 'To a Conscript of 1940' lay a new and more open variation on the theme of patriotism, as expressed by George Orwell:

If whole armies had to be coerced, no war could ever be fought. Men die in battle—not gladly, of course, but at any rate voluntarily—because of abstractions called 'honour', 'duty', 'patriotism' and so forth. All that this really means is: that they are aware of some organism greater than themselves, stretching into the future and the past, within which they feel themselves to be immortal. 'Who dies if England live?' sounds like a piece of bombast, but if you alter 'England' to whatever you prefer, you can see that it expresses one of the main motives of human conduct.[14]

[12] Orwell, 'Notes on Nationalism', in *Collected Essays, Journalism and Letters of George Orwell*, iii: *As I Please, 1943–1945*, ed. Sonia Orwell and Ian Angus (Harmondsworth: Penguin, 1970), 411; italics original. For an updated, and American, philosophical discussion of the term 'patriotism', see Igor Primoratz (ed.), *Patriotism* (Amherst, NY: Humanity Books, 2002).

[13] E. M. Forster, 'Culture and Freedom', in *Two Cheers for Democracy* (New York: Harvest Books, 1977), 31. But see also Robert Hewison, *Culture and Consensus* (London: Methuen, 1995), for evidence of governmental control of culture since 1940.

[14] Orwell, 'Notes on the Way', in *Collected Essays, Journalism and Letters of George Orwell*, ii: *My Country Right or Left, 1940–1943*, ed. Sonia Orwell and Ian Angus (Harmondsworth: Penguin, 1970), 32.

'Whatever you prefer' was to be constructed on two levels, the one political, the other mystical. On the political level, Churchill's government insisted that the first objective was simply to win the War, by whatever means, and continued to define war aims negatively, in the simple and unobjectionable terms of resisting fascism. What would happen once the War had been won—indeed, the entire question of whether the end would justify the means—was conveniently left open. In this way every point of view—except those of the pacifists and the revolutionary Left—could be rallied, even the apolitical, anarchist points of view, as argued in Herbert Read's *Politics of the Unpolitical* (1943) and D. S. Savage's *The Personal Principle* (1944) and exemplified in the poetry of the neo-Romantics.

Poets on the Right could see the defence of England as literally and figuratively a defence of her 'green and pleasant land'. 'Deep England', as Angus Calder in *The Myth of the Blitz* (1991) and Robert Hewison in *Culture and Consensus* (1995) have pointed out, was a patriotic theme common to many forms of propaganda throughout the 1940s, but poetry had certain advantages over other art-forms. The visual arts could give only a limited expression to the theme, for the Old Masters were safely stored away for the duration of the War, and so the actual evidence of a national tradition of landscape art was rarely on view. Poetry, on the other hand, was widely published and conveniently portable. Moreover, contemporary artists were hampered by the actual scene before their eyes—landscapes defaced by bombs, factories, training camps, and other effects of war. They tended to take refuge in oblique approaches: John Piper, for example, in abstraction, and Graham Sutherland in surrealism.

The poet's eye was able to look beyond the present chaos to a more serene past and future, hence one of the recurrent images of the 1940s, that of the 'poet in a landscape'. It was a point of view which formed a bridge between the neo-Romantic and the classical schools, involving a return to the pre-industrial age and conjuring up in words an imaginary landscape, created out of the circumstances of war, which often produced an exacerbated sensitivity to the phenomenal world. The political could be written in the form of the personal and the universal, the poet drawing on inner landscapes, in which feelings for his native land were enriched by personal memory and an acute awareness of the essential exile of the human condition. For this reason, celebrations of Welsh and Scottish landscapes were read as no less patriotic than the more familiar English pastoral.

In addition, poetry had the advantage of being demonstrably part of a tradition and one, moreover, that could help to define 'the English spirit'. According to the historians writing at the time, poetry provided a kind of silver thread running through English history. *The English Spirit*, A. L. Rowse's popular, portable history which argued that the only vice of the English was to be too peaceful and accommod-ating a people, was peppered with quotations from English poetry, and the historical narrative of G. M. Trevelyan's highly influential *Social History of England* was organized in chapters centred on the 'English' poets. The patriotic aspect of literary history lent itself well to cinematic treatment, as evidenced in films such as Humphrey Jennings's *Words for Battle* (1941) and Michael Powell's *A Canterbury Tale* (1944).

The Oxford Book of English Verse had been conceived during the Boer War, it had pervaded the poetic atmosphere of the First World War, and the poems between its covers were now pressed into service for the Second. The preface to the 1939 edition explained how the long tradition of poetry in the English language offered evidence of the peculiar stoicism of the English:

The reader, turning the pages of this book, will find this note of valiancy—of the old Roman 'virtue' mated with cheerfulness—dominant throughout, if in many curious moods. He may trace it back, if he care, far behind Chaucer to the rudest beginnings of English Song. It is indigenous, proper to our native spirit, and it will endure.[15]

A backward-looking view was not incompatible with a forward-looking one. The same preface defined the role of poetry in wartime as to 'hearten the crew with auspices of daylight'. This became the self-appointed task of poets on the Left, particularly with the advent of a national government which included Labour and the entry of the Soviet Union on the side of the Allies. Socialism, by definition, implied the notion of brotherhood, and tended to express itself in choral work, an idea to be found in John Jarmain's poem, 'Embarkation, 1942':

Then in a callow dawn we stood in lines
Like foreigners on bare and unknown quays,
Till someone bravely into the hollow of waiting
Cast a timid wisp of song;
It moved along the line of patient soldiers
Like a secret passed from mouth to mouth
And slowly gave us ease;
In our whispered singing courage was set free,
We were banded once more and strong.
So we sang as our ship set sail,
Sang our own songs, and leaning on the rail
Waved to the workmen on the slipping quay
And they again to us for fellowship.[16]

The theme of *The Old World and the New Society*, the title of a Labour Party policy statement published in February 1942, was given many a poetic variation, most famously in John Pudney's elegy 'For Johnny':

Fetch out no shroud
For Johnny-in-the-cloud;

[15] Sir Arthur Quiller-Couch, 'Preface to New Edition', in *idem* (ed.), *The Oxford Book of English Verse 1250–1918* (Oxford: Oxford University Press, 1940), p. xiii.

[16] John Jarmain, 'Embarkation, 1942', in Victor Selwyn (ed.), *More Poems of the Second World War* (London: Dent, 1989), 74.

> And keep your tears
> For him in after years.
>
> Better by far
> For Johnny-the-bright-star,
> To keep your head,
> And see his children fed.[17]

In fact, by 1945 Oscar Williams's anthology of war poetry was able to argue that war poetry should be read as part of an ongoing struggle for democratic social reform:

> The true modern poets are poets of compassion. The pity that Owen so deeply felt for the soldier in the trenches has been extended by them into compassion for all who suffer everywhere, not only in combat, but from the evils of poverty and social pressures intolerable to human beings.[18]

On the other hand, potentially conflicting political viewpoints could be avoided altogether by defining 'England' and 'Englishness' in quasi-mystical terms. This approach led to an emphasis on the sacred character of poetry, a return to the notion of the poet as bard and seer. It was a response to the very obvious need for the beautiful and the transcendent, which poetry seemed peculiarly able to provide. The difficult, mad mystical poets of the late eighteenth century came back into fashion and were reread in the context of the 1940s: Christopher Smart, William Blake, William Cowper, John Clare. The crucifixion became a central image of tribute to a generation which had made a collective sacrifice. Neo-Romantic poets cast themselves into the role of sacrificial victim, in poems like Sidney Keyes's 'War Poet', in which the poet's face becomes 'a burnt book | And a wasted town'.[19] Poets far from the battlefields—Edith Sitwell, Dylan Thomas, H. D., David Gascoyne—could present death as an entrance into a transcendent world. The poet's vision turned the unbearable sights of war into symbolic images, icons. The visual power of images of churches in flames fed into a religious mood, later strikingly evoked by Stephen Spender:

> There was a feeling of incandescent faith that never quite took fire. It was present in Eliot's *Four Quartets*, Edith Sitwell's *Still Falls the Rain*, Dylan Thomas's *Refusal to Mourn the Death, by Fire, of a Child in London*, in John Piper's drawings of churches burning, in Henry Moore's drawings of people in air-raid shelters, and in the apocalyptic paintings of buildings on fire and of blast furnaces, by Graham Sutherland. . . . The mood was compounded of seriousness through constant confrontation with death and destruction, of the sense of belonging to a community where all classes were drawn together in sympathy, of the phoenix-like rebirth of the English past from the ashes of burning cities, and of awe at the

---

[17] John Pudney, 'For Johnny', in Gardner (ed.), *Terrible Rain*, 77.
[18] Williams, 'Introduction', in *idem* (ed.), *War Poets*, 3.
[19] Sidney Keyes, 'War Poet', in *Collected Poems*, ed. Michael Meyer (Manchester: Carcanet, 2002), 70.

terror and grandeur of history endured. These attitudes meet in the idea of the sacred, that England itself was sacred.[20]

The idea that 'England itself was sacred' strikes a new patriotic note, one which was to have malignant consequences during the third and last stage of the War. It drew on definitions of nationalism that saw its roots as pre-political, pre-rational, on ideas developed by German Romanticism, which were much closer to the Fascist mystique of nationalism. It was a more malignant form of nationalism, which included ethnic and racial distinctions, which could deny to some people, such as the Japanese, the benefit of universal human rights. In addition, and for the first time, patriotism placed 'England' above criticism, for to criticize the sacred was to commit sacrilege. God was on the Allied side. The ideological shift was all the more dangerous for occurring at the very moment when Allied strategy was most open to criticism, as it quietly moved from a modestly defensive to a massively offensive stage of the War.

One aspect of the Dunkirk spirit had been the focus on the spectacular courage of the RAF pilots who, under Brooke's English heaven, had defended Britain from invasion in the summer of 1940. Forgetting the warnings of W. H. Auden and drawing instead on the Nietzschean joy of Yeats's poem 'An Irish Airman Foresees his Death', poets joined the general chorus of praise for the element that was indeed to distinguish this war from all previous wars, the war in the air. The Battle of Britain was history made straight into myth, from Churchill's well-publicized speeches to the HMSO pamphlet that sold 300,000 copies on the first day that it was published in March 1941. For the victims of the Blitz, it was not a war poet, but Richard Hillary, the brave fighter pilot and iconoclastic author of *The Last Enemy* (1942), who became the hero of the hour.

But the war *in* the air was also the war *from* the air. From the spring of 1942, the decision was taken to use the strategy of area bombing to paralyse German industry and demoralize her civilian population. The start of the campaign was the 1,000-bomber attack on Cologne in May 1942. From the first, the strategic bombing campaign was questionable, both in military and in human terms. Research soon after the events showed that industry recovered quickly, and civilian morale, far from being shaken by the bombing, was all the more determined to resist. The campaign was extremely costly to the Allies themselves in terms of the loss of expensive aircraft and aircrew. Moreover, the sheer scale of the civilian casualties raised moral questions. To give just a few figures: the area bombing of Germany cost the lives of some 100,000 British and American aircrew, and resulted in the death of between 750,000 and a million Germans. More French and Italian citizens than Britons were killed by bombing. The strategic bombing *before* Hiroshima caused 800,000 casualties, including 300,000 dead, and rendered more than 8.5 million homeless. In Hiroshima

---

[20] Stephen Spender, *The Thirties and After: Poetry, Politics, People 1933–1975* (London: Macmillan, 1978), 96.

the atomic bomb killed 118,661 people outright, and injured some 80,000 others; in Nagasaki more than 73,000 were killed outright, and nearly 75,000 were injured.[21]

These appalling figures are to be set against the 60,595 killed, 86,182 injured, by bombs in Britain. The mythology of the Blitz and the stoicism of 'Britain Can Take It' masked the far greater extent to which Britain and her allies were inflicting it. Of course, the figures were not known at the time; of all the propaganda campaigns during the War, the one concealing the aims and results of the strategic bombing war waged by the Allies was by far the most successful.[22] But even at the time, the morality of the bombing of Hamburg in July 1943 (in which more than 45,000 civilians were killed by a firestorm) was questioned, both in the press and at greater length in pamphlets such as *Seed of Chaos*, written by Vera Brittain and issued by the Bombing Restriction Committee in 1944. Strategic bombing turned the War into one of grim aggression, and moreover one which in its later stages pitted the strong against the weak, the armed against the unarmed. To such criticism, 'Bomber' Harris replied that he did not consider 'all the remaining cities of Germany as worth the bones of one British Grenadier'.[23]

What were the poets' responses to this new phase of the War? All too few still, small voices were raised in protest, though one pacifist poet, Alex Comfort, did insist on the moral symmetry involved in the very notion of universal human rights: 'Acquiescence in the murder of the population of Lidice is as evil as acquiescence in the murder of the population of Hamburg.'[24] Most poets were guilty of 'white propaganda': not actually telling any lies, but not telling the whole truth either. They continued to focus on their own side, continued to spin what Charles Hamblett later called 'the thin-skinned texture that precariously holds together the bubble of our collective imagination'.[25] It was not so much that they were fiddling while Rome was burning, as that they were writing about ruined churches while in Germany and Japan the jaws of hell gaped wide.

The short-sighted honesty of the first stage of the War now prevented them from even searching for the truth, from questioning too closely the motives and methods of their own side. The poets who had answered the call of 'My Country Right or Left' now relapsed into the blindly patriotic obedience of 'my country right or wrong', as George Orwell bitterly pointed out:

Actions are held to be good or bad not on their own merits but according to who does them, and there is almost no kind of outrage—torture, the use of hostages, forced labour,

---

[21] Figures taken from I. C. B. Dear and M. R. D. Foot (eds.), *The Oxford Companion to World War II* (Oxford: Oxford University Press, 1995).

[22] See Philip M. Taylor, *British Propaganda in the Twentieth Century* (Edinburgh: Edinburgh University Press, 1999), 187.

[23] Arthur Harris, quoted in Dear and Foot (eds.), *Oxford Companion to World War II*, 312.

[24] Alex Comfort, *Art and Social Responsibility* (London: Falcon, 1946), 30. Edith Sitwell, in *The Shadow of Cain* (London: John Lehmann, 1974), addressed the question of the atomic bombings in religious terms.

[25] Hamblett, 'Introduction', 14.

mass deportations, imprisonment without trial, forgery, assassination, the bombing of civilians—which does not change its moral colour when it is committed by 'our' side.[26]

The moral colour-blindness was often a question of distance, 'judging distances', as the title of a poem by Henry Reed very suggestively put it. Whatever the reasons for the fight, hand-to-hand combat could always be justified as self-defence, but how to judge the actions of 'an aircraft waging war | Inhumanly from nearly five miles height?' What about 'this damn inhuman sort of war', in which 'A man who is too squeamish to kill a rabbit can launch a rocket'?[27]

Keith Douglas, in his much-discussed poem 'How to Kill', did address this central moral question:

> Now in my dial of glass appears
> the soldier who is going to die.
> He smiles, and moves about in ways
> his mother knows, habits of his.
> The wires touch his face: I cry
> NOW. Death, like a familiar, hears
>
> and look, has made a man of dust
> of a man of flesh. This sorcery
> I do. Being damned, I am amused
> to see the centre of love diffused
> and the wave of love travel into vacancy.
> How easy it is to make a ghost.[28]

But even here, though the war poet is brutally honest, he is not telling the truth about the War. The injunction 'and look' involves the reader in the moral question, but the soliloquy form of the poem inhibits judgement by focusing attention on the doer, not the deed. As so often in the poetry of the Second World War, the staging of a theatre of war makes the action of the play seem inevitable. The poet manœuvres the reader into feeling that the plot cannot be altered, it can only be watched with a kind of helpless fascination.[29] What is being enacted in words—however finely—is the poet's psychological state of mind. The tragic-comic figure of the murdering poet is not an actor in the play, but part of the audience, and the murderous act he would denounce remains forever off-stage. W. H. Auden, whose physical distance from the war led to his being branded 'unpatriotic', was acutely aware of this moral danger: 'It is terrifying to realize that even great and real suffering can be turned into a theatre and so be no help.'[30]

---

[26] Orwell, 'Notes on Nationalism', 419.

[27] R. N. Currey, quoted in Ian Hamilton, *The Poetry of War 1939–45* (London: Alan Ross, 1965), 161.

[28] Keith Douglas, 'How to Kill', in *The Complete Poems*, ed. Desmond Graham (London: Faber, 2000), 119.

[29] For a study of Keith Douglas's 'extrospective style', see Tim Kendall, '"I see men as trees suffering": The Vision of Keith Douglas', *Proceedings of the British Academy*, 117 (2002), 429–43.

[30] W. H. Auden, quoted in Edward Mendelson, *Later Auden* (London: Faber, 1999), 244.

In the final stages of the War, the feeling that war was somehow 'unreal' combined with the poets' sense of powerlessness, to produce a poetry which was fatally self-regarding. Alun Lewis's 'All Day It Has Rained' is often quoted to illustrate the feeling of depression that overcomes the deracinated and disorientated recruit in a training camp, but it becomes a far more frightening poem if it is read as an expression of the extent to which training for war effects the extinction of all fellow-feeling:

> And we talked of girls and dropping bombs on Rome,
> And thought of the quiet dead and the loud celebrities
> Exhorting us to slaughter, and the herded refugees;
> —Yet thought softly, morosely of them, and as indifferently
> As of ourselves or those whom we
> For years have loved, and will again
> Tomorrow maybe love; but now it is the rain
> Possesses us entirely, the twilight and the rain.[31]

Like Tolkien's elves, a whole generation of poets was retreating into the twilight, into a private self-referential world which absolved their writing from the need for moral judgement and political action. Poetry was not only to be written, but also read, in an autarkic world of splendid isolation. New Criticism—a critical trend begun before the War—returned in triumph in 1947, with Cleanth Brooks's *The Well-Wrought Urn*. Clear moral judgement was to be replaced by *ambivalence*, *ambiguity*, *tension*, *irony*, and *paradox*, all words which theorized the refusal to take a moral stand. In the face of the moral problems posed by the terrifying new discoveries of science, the non-interventionist position of the poets contributed to the moral vacuum denounced by C. P. Snow in *The Two Cultures* (1959) and Al Alvarez in his preface to *The New Poetry* (1962).

The poets' silence has often been excused by the argument that the sheer magnitude of the pain caused by the Second World War beggared description. Ronald Blythe in the introduction to his anthology *The Components of the Scene* (1966) expressed it thus: 'Perhaps the uniquely barbarous way in which World War II ended—Belsen and the atom bomb—suddenly drove the whole subject beyond . . . the artist's comment.'[32] The convoluted style of this sentence hides the plain truth expressed in its punctuation. Belsen and the bomb were put between dashes, as things which, because they had not been known, were unknowable, because they had not been comprehended, were therefore incomprehensible. But that very separation, the barriers carefully constructed by nationalist governments and the intelligentsia who support them, are in fact the problem. In the first two

---

[31] Alun Lewis, 'All Day It Has Rained', in *Collected Poems*, ed. Cary Archard (Bridgend: Seren, 1994), 23.

[32] Ronald Blythe, 'Introduction', in *idem* (ed.), *The Components of the Scene* (Harmondsworth: Penguin, 1966), 24.

stages of the War, Orwell had argued that a sense of community would provide the connection between the individual and the rest of humanity:

People sacrifice themselves for the sake of fragmentary communities—nation, race, creed, class—and only become aware that they are not individuals in the very moment when they are facing bullets. A very slight increase of consciousness and their sense of loyalty could be transferred to humanity itself, which is not an abstraction.[33]

But the transfer did not occur, either poetically or politically. The end of the Second World War shaded into the Cold War; belief in the individual and loyalty to fragmentary communities became barriers to any real sense of common humanity.

'Only connect': E. M. Forster's words resonate throughout the history of the twentieth century, reminding us that failure to connect with others leads to war and man-made death. The 'terrible rain', the 'rain of ruin', that characterized the last phase of the War was not heaven-sent but, as Auden pointed out, a human tragedy, resulting from a series of entirely human choices:

> For the present stalks abroad
> Like the past and its wronged again
> Whimper and are ignored,
> And the truth cannot be hid:
> Somebody chose their pain,
> What needn't have happened did.[34]

'What needn't have happened did': Auden continued to write (though in England he was little read) because, with Emerson, he believed that 'There is no calamity which right words will not begin to redress.'[35] The wronged—civilians in Japan or Iraq—suffer because no one connects with their suffering. During and after the Second World War, the poets did not make enough political and poetic connections. They gave the War a number of local habitations, but they failed to give it a name.

---

[33] Orwell, 'Notes on the Way', 32.

[34] Auden, 'A Walk After Dark', in *Collected Poems*, ed. Edward Mendelson (London: Faber, 1976), 346.

[35] Ralph Waldo Emerson, 'Eloquence', in *Complete Works*, vii, ed. Edward Waldo Emerson (Cambridge: Riverside Press, 1903), 64.

CHAPTER 20

....

LOUIS MACNEICE'S WAR

....

PETER MCDONALD

When Louis MacNeice disembarked from the liner *Samaria* in Liverpool at the end of 1940, he came to England as, in his own term, 'an ex-expatriate'.[1] For ten months, the poet had been resident in the USA; and before then, at the very beginning of the War, he had been based briefly in Ireland. The England to which MacNeice decided to return was now one more fully immersed in the realities of war than it had been in late 1939: in the poet's absence, the catastrophic reversal at Dunkirk had taken place, and the bombing of British cities had begun in earnest; the Home Front had become something more than a metaphor. As things were to turn out, MacNeice would spend the War largely in London, working for the BBC as a features author and producer, with much of his professional effort given over to the broadcasting of (very broadly conceived) 'propaganda'. He would also publish two full-length volumes of poetry during this time—*Plant and Phantom* (1940) and *Springboard* (1944)—containing the poems that preceded, accompanied, and followed his decision to spend the War in England, rather than in Ireland or the United States. While the experience of wartime remained a significant element in all of MacNeice's subsequent poetry, most effectively perhaps in his last collection *The Burning Perch* (1963), his poems written during the War itself make up a distinctive body of work, recording and giving original shape to the pressures and complexities of living in and through intense global conflict.

[1] Louis MacNeice, 'Traveller's Return', *Horizon*, 3/14 (Feb. 1941); repr. in *Selected Prose of Louis MacNeice*, ed. Alan Heuser (Oxford: Clarendon Press, 1990), 83.

MacNeice's decision to return to Britain in 1940, however, had nothing to do with the plotting of his writing career, still less with any ambitions to become a war poet. In one sense, it was part of a determination to submerge his life as a writer in a situation which could end his life altogether. Shortly after the War was declared, MacNeice put things bluntly in a letter to his older mentor, Professor E. R. Dodds:

The tiresome corollary of all this from my point of view is that, *if* it is my war, I feel I ought to get involved in it in one of the more unpleasant ways. Ignoring the argument that writers are more use writing. No doubt they are. But writers also unfortunately seem to be expected to express opinions on these subjects, & if, *qua* writer, one were to say that one was pro-War, then one ought to be prepared to accept the nastier parts of the war just as much as anyone else.[2]

But a lot of weight, in November 1939, was still attaching itself to that '*if*': and indeed, MacNeice would in a matter of weeks board ship for America, and an academic appointment at Cornell University. Nevertheless, there was no doubt for the poet that commitment to the War was something quite distinct from any supposedly literary form of commitment. By August 1940, he was writing to Dodds from America of how 'By this stage I am on for doing anything—cleaning sewers or feeding machine guns, but preferably nothing too intelligent.'[3] In fact, one of the poet's first actions on his eventual arrival in the England of December 1940 was to attempt to enlist in the Royal Navy—unsuccessfully, in the event, though on account of his recent operation for (life-threatening) peritonitis, rather than any notion that his literary gifts were of too great national value to be put at risk.

Nevertheless, the process of understanding MacNeice's war needs to begin with an awareness of how pressing, in 1939, was the question of '*if* it is my war'. For a start, MacNeice, who considered himself Irish, was writing then from Belfast (where his father and stepmother lived, and to whose guardianship he was about to entrust his young son Dan), to Dodds, another Irishman whose career was in England. Eire was (and was to remain) neutral in the conflict; but even Northern Ireland (both Dodds's and MacNeice's home ground), despite its fierce official loyalty to the Crown, did not introduce conscription in the course of the War. MacNeice might easily have remained in either Northern Ireland or Eire; and there are grounds to suppose that he hoped to be appointed to the Chair of English Literature at Trinity College, Dublin, in late 1939. Certainly, MacNeice was not going to make the war his in the belief that it was a war in the interests of the British Empire. Even when writing as a returned 'ex-expatriate' for a British audience in 1941, he reminded his readers that 'I have never really thought of myself as British; if there is one country I feel at home in, it is Eire', adding that 'As a place to write in or live in I prefer the USA to England and New York to London.'[4]

[2] MacNeice to E. R. Dodds, 10 Nov. 1939, Bodleian Library, MS Dodds fol. 53ᵛ; italics original.
[3] MacNeice to E. R. Dodds, 18 Aug. 1940, Bodleian Library, MS Dodds fol. 70ᵛ.
[4] MacNeice, 'The Way We Live Now', *Penguin New Writing*, 5 (Apr. 1941); repr. in *Selected Prose*, 82.

While MacNeice was keenly aware of what it might mean, as an Irishman, to 'take the King's shilling' in the War, he could not identify either with the apparent indifference, real or affected, of some of the Irish people he met in the long autumn of 1939.[5] In the autobiographical manuscript of 1940–1, which was published after his death as *The Strings Are False*, MacNeice remembered the day of Germany's invasion of Poland, when he 'was alone with the catastrophe', and 'spent Saturday drinking in a bar with the Dublin literati; they hardly mentioned the war but debated the correct versions of Dublin street songs'.[6] 'Dublin was hardly worried by the war', he continued, 'her old preoccupations were still preoccupations'; and while '[t]he intelligentsia continued with their parties', others were ready to give the old imperial enemy their tacit support: 'A young man in sports clothes said to us: "Eire of course will stay neutral. But I hope the English knock hell out of Hitler." '[7] The detached bemusement of such recollections was to deepen, in the course of the War, into something more trenchant for MacNeice; but whatever the significance of Eire's neutrality for the poet, it is worth remembering that protracted stays in the country marked the end, as well as the beginning, of his war. While the autumn of 1939 was spent between Dublin, the West of Ireland, and Belfast, MacNeice chose to spend the three months after VE day in Ireland too, with a bout of intense creativity which included his verse-play *The Dark Tower*—a poetic meditation on the meaning of the War which complements the poetry written in 1939, before 'my war' had properly got under way.

A sequence of ten poems written in August and September of 1939, 'The Coming of War', was MacNeice's first significant artistic reaction to the public and personal crises of the newly declared hostilities. The poet was travelling through Ireland in the company of his friend, the scholar Ernst Stahl, just before the invasion of Poland: part of their time had been spent with MacNeice's family in the County Antrim coastal village of Cushendun, and the rest motoring from Dublin to the West of Ireland, and finally back to Dublin, to see Stahl off on his return journey to an England by now officially at war. The poems are haunted, obviously, by the

---

[5] See MacNeice's letter to E. R. Dodds from Dublin, 13 Oct. 1939, Bodleian Library, MS Dodds fols. 48^{r-v}: 'Down here one gets quite de- (or dis)orientated. It all sounds like a nightmare algebra which you have to change back into people being killed. It is all very well for everyone to go on saying "Destroy Hitlerism" but what the hell are they going to construct? I am now falling into a sort of paradox which is:—if the war were a rational war leading somewhere, I should want to stay out of it in order to see where it led to: but if it is a hopeless war leading nowhere, I feel half inclined to take the King's shilling & escape—more likely than not—the frustration to come. The motives in each case of course being selfish.' Commenting on this letter, Terence Brown claims that MacNeice 'reckons he has a perfectly honourable choice in this matter', adding that 'he understands that from the nationalist point of view the war is England's war' (Brown, 'Louis MacNeice and the Second World War', in Kathleen Devine (ed.), *Modern Irish Writers and the Wars* (Gerrards Cross: Colin Smythe, 1999), 167). Nationalist though he might have considered himself, MacNeice did not share 'the nationalist point of view' on this matter.

[6] MacNeice, *The Strings Are False: An Unfinished Autobiography* (London: Faber, 1965), 212.

[7] Ibid. 213 and 212.

international situation; but they are also haunted by something much more personal in nature, which helps further to explain MacNeice's uncertainty about whether or not the imminent war would be his. Eleanor Clark, a young American writer whom MacNeice had met and fallen in love with on his first visit to the USA, represented a very powerful reason for the poet's wishing to leave his life and work in London; and her presence in 'The Coming of War'—especially in its original, ten-poem form—is just as important as any political or cultural considerations in MacNeice's general sense of ambivalence about the War itself.[8] Clark's strong political commitments (she was part of a circle of left-wing writers in New York) meant that her view of the European war was just as detached as those of the partying literati of Dublin, if for very different reasons. In this sense, her place in 'The Coming of War' is doubly interesting: Eleanor embodies a possible romantic fulfilment which would take MacNeice out of Europe and its conflicts; at the same time, she is a figure whose political thought (which goes completely unmentioned) would interpret the War in ways remote from anything of which MacNeice felt himself capable.[9]

'The Coming of War' has some of the unevenness of lived experience, and is short on the certainties of hindsight. As a travelogue, of sorts, the sequence takes stock of a country which is both attractive and, for MacNeice, impossible: in 'Dublin', the opening poem, there is 'the air soft on the cheek | And porter running from the taps | With a head of yellow cream', but also 'Nelson on his pillar | Watching the world collapse'.[10] The journey takes the first-person voice through a place which has many of the characteristics of Limbo: it is caught between two states, each of which seems to be an unreality. One unreal state is that of Ireland, which is rendered unreal by the imminent cataclysm; another is the War itself, unknowable and unimaginable in the newly arriving future. In the welter of conflicting unrealities, Eleanor Clark figures as a reality now *absent*:

> O my darling if only you were with me
> And the old rhythms could be made to work
> And the new horror that is the old redoubled

---

[8] 'The Coming of War (Dublin, Cushendun, the West of Ireland, and Back)' appeared as ten poems in MacNeice's short volume *The Last Ditch* (Dublin: Cuala Press, 1940). It was shortened to seven poems for *Plant and Phantom* (London: Faber, 1941), and cut to five for *Collected Poems 1925–1948* (London: Faber, 1949), when the overall title was changed to 'The Closing Album'. The 1940 version is printed in full in *The Collected Poems of Louis MacNeice*, ed. Peter McDonald (London: Faber, 2007), appendix 3.

[9] See MacNeice to Eleanor Clark, n.d. [Apr. 1939], quoted in Jon Stallworthy, *Louis MacNeice* (London: Faber, 1995), 245–6: 'I have been thinking about this War question. You say, quite rightly, darling, that it will be just a dirty war of power politics, so what am I doing in it? All you are interested in is "The Revolution" & you say that, if one is going to take action, the only thing to do is to foment the revolution directly. But look! If a war with Germany starts, it will be no damn good having an immediate revolution at home or a mutiny at the front . . . . It seems to me that the only hope in this War (if it happens) is for the people of England to enter into it on certain terms with the government (i.e. that it shall be terminated as quickly as possible by negotiation & with no Versailles nonsense).'

[10] MacNeice, 'Dublin', in *Collected Poems*, 680.

> Were not there waiting in the dark.
> The bulletins and the gladiators beset me
> Casting a blight on the Irish day.
> And you beyond the clamour of Manhattan
> Are terribly far away.[11]

'The new horror that is the old redoubled' contains a deliberate blankness, part of its sense of determinism about the oppressive force of the 'old'. While 'the old rhythms'—of life and love, as well as poetry—seem no longer capable of being made to work, the old 'horror', about to return 'redoubled', is something that has been waiting to come back. Whereas Eleanor is 'terribly far away', the 'horror' 'waiting in the dark' has been there all along. MacNeice's metaphor, when he says that 'The bulletins and gladiators' are 'Casting a blight on the Irish day', risks—and probably falls foul of—insensitivity, conflating as it does the depression of a young man in autumn 1939 with a word, 'blight', of mortal significance for the Ireland of a century before. However, MacNeice is concerned with a 'horror' close to a different home, for the returning nightmare here is the 'blight' of the Great War, ready again to infest a generation.

The sense of unreality and strangeness in Ireland is the same as that which MacNeice had recorded the previous year, in *Autumn Journal*, where

> posters flapping on the railings tell the fluttered
> World that Hitler speaks, that Hitler speaks
> And we cannot take it in and we go to our daily
> Jobs to the dull refrain of the caption 'War'
> Buzzing around us as from hidden insects
> And we think 'This must be wrong, it has happened before,
> Just like this before, we must be dreaming...'[12]

The dazed thought that 'we must be dreaming' is present also in 'The Closing Album', but now there is to be no reprieve from the return of nightmare, such as that represented by the Munich agreement in *Autumn Journal*. It is Eleanor Clark's America which is 'A dream that has come untrue' for the poet, since 'now, my love, there is more than the Atlantic | Dividing me from you'.[13] Ireland, for its part, is stuck in a dream-world, part shabby and part glamorous, as in Galway, with 'The hollow grey houses, | The rubbish and sewage, | The grass-grown pier', but also with 'a hundred swans | Dreaming on the harbour'. Driving with Stahl back to Dublin from the West, MacNeice crossed the River Shannon; his version of this in *The Strings Are False* makes the journey one between dreaming and waking states:

Ernst wanted to catch a boat that night but we thought we had time to visit Clonmacnois which lies on the east side of the Shannon. The Shannon in Ireland is a division between two worlds. Once you have crossed it to the east you have left behind the world of second sight,

---

[11] MacNeice, 'The Coming of War', ibid. 683.   [12] MacNeice, *Autumn Journal*, ibid. 109.
[13] MacNeice, 'The Closing Album', ibid. 683.

re-entered the world of common or commercial sense. The Shannon itself is unlike the rivers of the mountains. Today it was a broad dull silver band, placid in drizzling rain. The tombs and broken towers of Clonmacnois were grey and placid too. Expecting nothing again.[14]

When this material is taken up for the seventh poem in 'The Closing Album', Ireland itself, with the monastic ruins of Clonmacnois as its symbol, is a place locked into a dreaming state, while the travellers face the reality of a reawakened horror from the past:

> Eastward again, returning to our so-called posts,
> We went out of our way to look at Clonmacnois—
> A huddle of tombs and ruins of anonymous men
> Above the Shannon dreaming in the quiet rain.
>
> You millenarian dead, why should I arraign,
> Being a part of it, the stupidity of men
> Who cancel the voices of the heart with barbarous noise
> And hide the barren facts of death in censored posts?[15]

The second half of the poem is a mirror of the first, where the distortions of the present transform the landscape and dream of the first quatrain. The rhyme scheme's chiasmus (*abcddcba*) offers its own kind of 'second sight', as the second stanza partially repeats the rhyme words of the first, but in the light now of that 'world of common or commercial sense' on the other side of the Shannon (a river which begins to feel here like either Lethe or the Styx, though it may in fact be closer, in the circumstances, to the Rubicon). Thus, 'Clonmacnois' is overlaid by 'barbarous noise', and 'anonymous men' by 'the stupidity of men', while 'the quiet rain' gives way to the question 'why should I arraign'—to which, of course, no answer will be forthcoming. Unsettlingly, the mention of 'our so-called posts' in a wartime Britain is finally refracted to become the 'censored posts' containing 'the barren facts of death'—a reference with powerful resonances of the Great War. Leaving one past behind them, MacNeice and his companion are on their way to a past that would not leave them behind.

In fact, MacNeice himself made the choice to leave Europe for the USA and Eleanor Clark. In doing so, he seemed to be joining writers like W. H. Auden and Christopher Isherwood, who had already made the journey; and like them, he was subject to a good deal of disapproving comment from those who were carrying on with the literary life in wartime Britain. Here, of course, biography and literary history blur into one another, and become difficult to distinguish: MacNeice's worries about whether or not the War was his cannot be disentangled from his hopes, in 1939–40, that Eleanor Clark might be his instead. The biographical fact that, although Eleanor and Louis were close throughout his stay in the USA in 1940, they did not become lovers, carries a decisive force in MacNeice's life, and is

---

[14] MacNeice, *The Strings Are False*, 212.
[15] MacNeice, 'The Closing Album', in *Collected Poems*, 685.

certainly an important part of his decision, by the middle of the year, to leave again for Britain. In a last letter before leaving, MacNeice told Eleanor that 'perhaps, darling, we ought to call it a day', and explained that 'I have tried to softpedal the sex business but the more I softpedal it, the more it obsesses me . . . . I can't go back to Europe, especially with so much death about, & try to keep up a troubadourish relationship with you.'[16] (Perhaps MacNeice's curious simile, in describing his arrival in New York in 1940, when 'the sky was a candid blue like the eyes of a frigid woman', was in fact an indication of trouble to come.[17]) Yet the ten months in the USA, which effectively separated MacNeice from wartime Britain, were also a time of intense literary activity, when many of the poems in *Plant and Phantom* were composed, and when the practice of his art—as well as the influences of personal and public events—helped him to reach a point of commitment, or at least of decision. As MacNeice phrased this, as early as March, 'freedom means Getting Into things & not getting Out of them.'[18]

Talk of 'freedom' in such contexts is revealing. The word was, of course, much bandied about in connection with the War and its reasons, and MacNeice would have been fully aware of its currency. But the time spent in the USA was also, for the poet, a time of brooding over the meaning of different kinds of freedom—personal, political, and artistic. Near the time of his departure, MacNeice composed a foreword to his *Poems 1925–1940*, the precociously hefty volume published by Random House in New York early in 1941. 'I write poetry', MacNeice insisted, 'because it is my road to freedom and knowledge'; but he also announced an unavoidable change:

When a man collects his poems, people think he is dead. I am collecting mine not because I am dead, but because my past life is. Like most other people in the British Isles I have little idea what will happen next. I shall go on writing, but my writing will presumably be different.[19]

By this point, MacNeice wanted to be identified as someone soon to be back in the British Isles, but the self-presentation here is also that of a man in Limbo—a man who, while not actually (or at least not as yet) dead, is patrolling death's vicinity, and is dead already to his own past.

Some of the poems written in the USA make use of this perspective, and MacNeice writes often from a vantage-point that sees events, as it were, *sub specie mortis*.

---

[16] MacNeice to Eleanor Clark, 19 Nov. 1940, quoted in Stallworthy, *Louis MacNeice*, 285.

[17] MacNeice, 'American Letter', *Horizon*, 1/7 (July 1940); repr. in *Selected Literary Criticism of Louis MacNeice*, ed. Alan Heuser (Oxford: Clarendon Press, 1987), 75. The same phrase occurs in *The Strings Are False*, 21, where MacNeice also reports: 'As for the women of New York, they are more outspoken perhaps, but they appear on the whole when it comes to practice less sexy than the women of London' (p. 23).

[18] MacNeice to Mrs E. R. Dodds, 22 Mar. 1940, Bodleian Library, MS Dodds fol. 67[v].

[19] MacNeice, 'Foreword', in *Poems 1925–1940* (New York: Random House, 1941); repr. in *Collected Poems*, 791.

In 'Plant and Phantom', for example, written in September 1940, the War can be felt behind the poet's abstractions in the long series of definitions of man:

> Whose life is a bluff, professing
> To follow the laws of Nature,
> In fact a revolt, a mad
> Conspiracy and usurpation,
> Smuggling over the frontier
> Of fact a sense of value,
> Metabolism of death,
> Re-orchestration of world.[20]

'Metabolism of death' has the packed feeling of a riddle, in common with the rest of this (rather too mysterious) poem, but it conveys in part MacNeice's sense of his own life as something either preparing for or in league with its own death, and the deaths of many others, in the near future. The 'mad | Conspiracy' of being alive catches something of the 'bout of irrationality'[21] which MacNeice saw his American life (and love-life) as representing: it is a conspiracy against most of the logical conclusions—about himself, the War, and his future actions—which MacNeice felt himself able to draw. 'Entirely', written in March, figures life as 'a mad weir of tigerish waters | A prism of delight and pain', and its central stanza makes the spring into a (possibly *Waste Land*-inflected) foresuffering of conflict, even in the presence of love:

> If we could find our happiness entirely
>   In somebody else's arms
> We should not fear the spears of the spring nor the city's
>   Yammering fire alarms
> But, as it is, the spears each year go through
>   Our flesh and almost hourly
> Bell or siren banishes the blue
>   Eyes of Love entirely.[22]

There is a conscious echo here of MacNeice's earlier love poem, 'The Sunlight in the Garden' (from *The Earth Compels*, 1938), in which love could defy 'the church bells | And every evil iron | Siren and what it tells'.[23] Now, 'the blue | Eyes

---

[20] MacNeice, 'Plant and Phantom', ibid. 170.

[21] MacNeice to E. R. Dodds, 5 Feb. 1940, Bodleian Library, MS Dodds fols. 65^r–66^v: 'Don't ask me what's going to happen next because I don't know. I think maybe it's about time I had a bout of irrationality. I feel I've been fitting myself into patterns for so long & (though you may be sceptical about 'romance'?) it is so exciting to find oneself timelessly happy; also I am going to write (at least I hope so) quite new kinds of poems. After which, no doubt, the deluge but I can't think about that now.'

[22] MacNeice, 'Entirely', in *Collected Poems*, 171.

[23] MacNeice, 'The Sunlight in the Garden', ibid. 58.

of Love' are parts of an imperfectly accommodated life, in which happiness is to be compromised by a state of emergency. The voice in this poem is itself subject to an uneasy accommodation, as MacNeice's use of run-on lines pulls against the metrical regularity of the rhyming stanzas. This is most apparent in the closing lines, when the poet considers the situation 'if the world were black and white entirely':

> We might be surer where we wished to go
> Or again we might be merely
> Bored but in brute reality there is no
> Road that is right entirely.

MacNeice's ability to counterpoint a highly musical stanza form with an almost flat speaking voice develops some of his 1930s practice; now, however, something more than poetic style is at stake. The defeated effort to 'get the hang of it entirely' is becoming almost defiant in its rejection of absolute or clear solutions; and the residual Americanism of 'get the hang of it' has its part to play in the poem's sense of time and place.[24]

One image which recurs in MacNeice's poetry of 1940 is that of the stylite, the holy man whose asceticism drives him to separate himself from the world by taking up residence on a pillar. In 'Stylite', of March 1940 (like the other poems in *Plant and Phantom*, the poem is carefully dated by the author on its volume publication), this figure combines different kinds of isolation, that of the visionary and that of the hermit:

> The saint on the pillar stands,
> The pillar is alone,
> He has stood so long
> That he himself is stone;
> Only his eyes
> Range across the sand
> Where no one ever comes
> And the world is banned.[25]

The presence of Tennyson's St Simeon Stylites is discernible here, providing the figure with an element of the grotesque; so too is the idea of the intellectual ensconced in his ivory tower (with which MacNeice was later to engage directly, when the term was applied by Virginia Woolf to his own generation of British writers).[26] In so far as this pillared saint represents the poet himself in 1940, he

---

[24] 'Get the hang of it', originally an Americanism, was still sufficiently novel in English to merit quotation marks from H. G. Wells in his *Work, Wealth, & Happiness of Mankind* (1932): 'Never before has there been this need and desire to "get the hang" of the world as one whole' (as cited in *OED*, 'hang', *n.*, 3).

[25] MacNeice, 'Stylite', in *Collected Poems*, 168.

[26] See MacNeice, 'The Tower that Once', *Folios of New Writing*, 3 (Spring 1941); repr. in *Selected Literary Criticism*, 119–24.

is a character for whom time is almost up, and seems to be under sentence of death: 'Round his neck there comes | The conscience of a rope, | And the hangman counting.' The poem ends—puzzlingly perhaps—with a glimpse of another pillared figure, 'A white Greek god', who is both 'Confident' and has his 'eyes on the world'. While MacNeice does not want to be the ascetic stylite, he knows that he cannot become the Apollonian figure of commitment and achievement; like so much else written by him in 1940, this is the record of an unresolved dilemma. In a poem MacNeice published in America, 'Coming from Nowhere', the stylite makes another appearance, 'Hunched on the rock | A pillared saint | With knees drawn up | And vacant eyes'.[27] Here, it is 'Love' which 'Makes him alone | Cut off from men', as 'He sits and waits | Till time erodes | The walls of thought, | The thoughts of self.' The poem ends, like 'Stylite', by envisaging a resolution which its whole tenor has already rendered (at the very least) wishfully unconvincing:

> Until from nowhere
> Again the sun
> Unrolls a carpet;
> Then he leaves
> His rock and with
> Deliberate feet
> On golden water
> Walks the world.

Perhaps the unlikelihood of a happy resolution to his affair with Eleanor matches here the implausibility of the saint's serenely confident return to the world, in a Christ-like walking on the waters. In fact, the only water on which the poet was to 'walk' was that of the Atlantic Ocean, on the perilous trip back to Britain, under constant threat of U-boat attacks, which he made at the end of the year.

The perils of the voyage (a record of which survives as the opening chapters of *The Strings Are False*) were foreseen by MacNeice, and were not perhaps entirely unwelcome. A number of the 1940 poems return to images of death for their resolution, and their author, who already regarded his past life as dead, was inclined to invoke suicidal alongside other impulses. In an American poem of May 1940, 'The Death-Wish', in which 'people, over-cautious, contrive | To save their lives by weighting them with dead | Habits, hopes, beliefs', the idea of suicide is on a continuum with sexual desire:

> it is not surprising that
> Some in their impatience jump the rails,
> Refusing to wait the communal failure, preferring
> The way the madman or the meteor fails,
> Deceiving themselves to think their death uncommon,

---

[27] 'Coming from Nowhere' was included in *Poems 1925–1940*, where it is dated Feb. 1940; repr. in *Collected Poems*, 761–2.

> And mad to possess the unpossessable sea
> As a man in spring desires to die in woman.[28]

'Failure' is the inevitability here; the individual's refusal 'to wait the communal failure' (in a tellingly American turn of phrase) aligns him with 'the meteor or the madman', but does nothing to make his death any less 'uncommon'. 'Every-where', as MacNeice had written in an earlier poem, 'the pretence of individuality recurs';[29] yet this acknowledgement of self-deceit does not entirely draw the sting of individuality's desire, its drive to 'possess the unpossessable'. The poem has a self-consciously Freudian cast, but it represents nevertheless an accurate and powerful report on MacNeice's own feelings in 1940, for which the War was one way in to 'the deep sea that never thinks' of death. In contemplating his own individuality, MacNeice was determined to harbour no illusions about its special status: and his return voyage, through the so-called Atlantic Tunnel, was one away from illusion, even if it was more difficult to say what it was a journey *towards*. Nothing, from now on, could presume to think itself 'uncommon', least of all possible death.

These thoughts are given shape at the end of the third chapter of *The Strings Are False* (which is also the end of the manuscript material, written on shipboard, which Dodds, as posthumous editor, placed as the opening of the work):

So I got on to this boat and here I am, fitted with a gas-mask, carrying my lifebelt from cabin to lounge to dining-room . . . . It is, as I said, the same boat that brought me over. That was in January 1940 and this is December 1940. But before all that? I am 33 years old and what can I have been doing that I still am in a muddle? But everyone else is too, maybe our muddles are concurrent. Maybe, if I look back, I shall find that my life is not just mine, that it mirrors the lives of the others—or shall I say the Life of the Other? Anyway I will look back. And return later to pick up the present, or rather to pick up the future.[30]

The element of 'muddle' is significant: MacNeice was far from sure about what claims the purely personal might have from now on, upon either his art or his actions. Besides the composition of some of the autobiographical material in *The Strings Are False* itself, 1940 had seen some of the poet's most searching and powerful personal writing—including the anguished and painfully clear-sighted poem 'Autobiography'. A return to the War might be effectively a decision to sink the self in some common effort over which it could have no real control, and this seems to have appealed to MacNeice at the time, even if it represented an impulse which he was capable of regarding as an ultimately selfish kind of death-wish. But there was also, already, another impulse at work in MacNeice's thinking: this is towards 'the lives of others' (a phrase instantly deflated by the ironically portentous 'Life of the Other'), in which some meaning for the life of the individual might now be found. Here, in the hope that 'muddles' might somehow prove 'concurrent', MacNeice found a location for a good deal of his subsequent wartime writing. Work for the BBC was, almost by

---

[28] MacNeice, 'The Death-Wish', in *Collected Poems*, 200.
[29] MacNeice, 'An Eclogue for Christmas', ibid. 5.   [30] MacNeice, *The Strings Are False*, 35.

definition, an exercise in providing material of common interest, intended to bind together a listening public in a common purpose; but how the writing of poetry could be made to fit into such a pattern was necessarily a more problematic matter.

Like his contemporaries, MacNeice had by 1941 long distanced himself from 'propaganda' poetry (and had, indeed, always been much further from such a thing than many). The poems composed on his return to England, then, were never likely to be examples of any officially minded or approved 'war poetry'. In fact, the pieces that were to be collected as *Springboard* (with its carefully precise subtitle, *poems 1941–1944*) resist most of the more obvious orientations for writing from the Home Front. Like MacNeice's war itself, they are given momentum by a literal baptism of fire, in the London of the Blitz: poems such as 'Brother Fire', 'The Trolls', 'Troll's Courtship', and 'Whit Monday' provide *Springboard* with a foundation of first-hand experience, in which the strengths of documentary-like directness are brought together with a vivid, almost surrealist, disregard for 'message' or conclusive argument.

MacNeice's experiences of the major air raids on London were, of course, in many respects experiences shared with the larger community under nightly bombardment. But for the poet, these events were also in some sense bracing and creatively empowering; the ungovernable individualist in MacNeice could find in the Blitz an environment in which he could be—however strangely—at the same time self-involved and communally committed. 'Brother Fire', with its concluding address to the 'delicate walker, babbler, dialectician Fire', the 'enemy and image of ourselves', asks an apparently odd question:

> Did we not on those mornings after the All Clear,
> When you were looting shops in elemental joy
> And singing as you swarmed up city block and spire,
> Echo your thought in ours? 'Destroy! Destroy!'[31]

This concentrates attitudes which find their expression in some of MacNeice's journalism of the time. In one of his five 'London Letters', contributed to the American journal *Common Sense* in 1941, MacNeice reports on how 'to walk along a great shopping street . . . on the morning after a blitz, far from being depressing, is almost exhilarating', and adds immediately that 'this may shock you but many people share my experience'.[32]

Writing for a large home audience, in the pages of *Picture Post*, MacNeice recounted his experiences during one of the biggest raids (on the night of 16–17 April 1941), and admitted that 'it was—if I am to be candid—enlivening', and recorded 'a voice inside me which (ignoring all the suffering and waste involved) kept saying, as I watched a building burning or demolished: "Let her go up!" or

---

[31] MacNeice, 'Brother Fire', in *Collected Poems*, 217.
[32] MacNeice, 'London Letter: Reflections from the Dome of St Paul's', *Common Sense*, 10/7 (July 1941); repr. in *Selected Prose*, 131–2.

"Let her come down. Let them all go. Write them all off. Stone walls do not a city make." [33] Again, the element of intensely individual—even aesthetic—perception is mingled with one of communal solidarity:

The hoses were playing on a big store from the street and from the buildings opposite; the shifting pattern of water and smoke and flame was as subtle as the subtlest of Impressionist paintings; the jets from the hoses, I noticed with surprise, were a deep mauve, but this richness of colouring faded as the day grew brighter . . . . I was gazing into a shop of fancy goods that were open to the air and coated with powdered plaster. 'You can take one now,' a man shouted to me, 'price has gone down.' Wisecracks among the ruins; wisecracks and greetings and stories of the night—stories that in peacetime you'd think a bit tall, but which now are a matter of course and often an understatement.

MacNeice's apparently abstracted, aesthetically tinged vision of the fire is being aligned here with a shared perception of the events as potentially absurd; in this surreal environment, the oddness and tangential nature of a detached individual is, paradoxically, something which Londoners have in common. So the thought 'Destroy! Destroy!', echoed in 'Brother Fire', is not *mine* (as it were), but rather 'ours'. In terms of 'propaganda' content, this is the very opposite of defeatist thinking for MacNeice; but it still adds something like the thrill of the anarchic to his presentation of the situation.

The German bombers, which are transformed by MacNeice into figures of mythic comedy as 'Trolls,' who 'ramble and rumble over the roof-tops', 'humming to themselves like morons', threaten the population with a death that (the poet implies) holds few terrors. In the third section of 'The Trolls', MacNeice adapts the painfully self-conscious meditations on death which had filled his poetry written over the past year in the USA to the first-person plural of the Blitz:

> Death has a look of finality;
> We think we lose something but if it were not for
> Death we should have nothing to lose, existence
> Because unlimited would merely be existence
> Without incarnate value. The trolls can occasion
> Our death but they are not able
> To use it as we can use it.
> Fumbling and mumbling they try to
> Spell out death correctly; they are not able. [34]

How to 'use' death is at the heart of the matter for MacNeice; and the language of his poetry here combines the abstract with the grotesque, insisting on the 'we' who undergo this part-physical, part-metaphysical trial together in a bombed London. At stake is 'existence' and its 'incarnate value', and it is the force represented

---

[33] MacNeice, 'The Morning after the Blitz', *Picture Post*, 2/5 (3 May 1941); repr. in *Selected Prose*, 118.

[34] MacNeice, 'The Trolls', in *Collected Poems*, 218.

by the trolls—something above and beyond, or even below and aside from the *Luftwaffe*—which makes its comically inadequate challenge to this sense of worth. Death, now in the current events of London, is providing exactly the sharpening of perception and crystallization of human value which an isolated and unhappy poet had imagined it bringing in his poems of the year before. When the troll speaks, in 'Troll's Courtship', it cannot begin to understand the death it might bring:

> Because I cannot accurately conceive
> Any ideal, even ideal Death,
> My curses and my boasts are merely a waste of breath,
> My lusts and lonelinesses grunt and heave
> And blunder round among the ruins that I leave.[35]

The epigraph which MacNeice gave to the first section of *Springboard*—George Herbert's line, 'Even poisons praise thee'[36]—helps explain the place the trolls occupy in the poet's parables of the London Blitz. At the same time, it provides another kind of puzzle: *whom*, exactly, are these poisons praising? One answer seems to be 'ideal Death', presented often in the light of religious address—and nowhere more so than in the poem 'Prayer in Mid-Passage', and its invocation of 'Thou my meaning, thou my death.'[37]

In a series of prose notes headed 'Broken Windows or Thinking Aloud', dating from 1941–2 and possibly intended to form the basis of an article or broadcast, MacNeice touched repeatedly on the conjunction of death and meaning in the War and writing—with the characteristic rider 'Not that my primary concern at the moment is writing':

The War has thrown us back upon life—us & our writing too. But we were less alive than our art because more negative . . . . The 'message' of a work of art may appear to be defeatist, negative, nihilist; the work of art itself is always *positive*. A poem in praise of suicide is an act of homage to life.[38]

MacNeice's 'Novelettes' sequence (begun in Ireland and completed in the USA) had included poems like 'Suicide' and 'The Expert', both of which the poet subsequently abandoned, and neither of which quite justifies the claim of 'a homage to life'. The subject of 'The Expert' is given to 'soft-pedalling desire' (the phrase MacNeice himself used in his fraught correspondence with Eleanor Clark), and ends up 'Drunk and alone among the indifferent lights | In stark unending streets of granite and glass':

> He ducked his head to avoid illusory stalactites
> And fell, his brain ringing with the noise of brass

---

[35] MacNeice, 'Troll's Courtship', ibid. 219–20.
[36] George Herbert, 'Providence', in *The Works of George Herbert*, ed. F. E. Hutchinson (Oxford: Clarendon Press, 1941), 119. (The line is 'Ev'n poisons praise thee'.)
[37] MacNeice, 'Prayer in Mid-Passage', in *Collected Poems*, 234.
[38] MacNeice, 'Broken Windows or Thinking Aloud', in *Selected Prose*, 138.

> Captions; the groundswell of the pavement, steady
> As fate, rose up and caught him, rolled him below
>
> A truck—this ex-professor who had already
> Outlived his job of being in the know.[39]

The poem in fact consigns its subject to a suicidal end, almost scornfully, in the assumption that all expert knowledge of the world has become redundant, and that the rules of engagement with life have now changed fundamentally. In London, MacNeice felt able to see more clearly the possibility of something 'more *positive*' for art in the death which was now all around as well as within his thoughts. In 'Broken Windows', this finds expression:

Death in its own right—as War does incidentally—sets our lives in perspective. Every man's funeral is his own, just as people are lonely in their lives, but Death as a leveller also writes us in life. & Death not only levels but differentiates—it crystallizes our deeds.[40]

'We did not need a war to teach us this,' MacNeice goes on, 'but war has taught us it'; 'Before the war', he concludes, 'we wore blinkers.' There is something a little disconnected about these notes, as though MacNeice is trying to make up in epigrammatic economy for gaps of argument and evidence. It is possible that Auden influenced MacNeice here, in particular the Auden of *New Year Letter* (1941) and its 'Notes'; nevertheless, the determination to be affirmative on the subject of death is seriously declared, and it shapes MacNeice's war poetry in a decisive way.

As he composed the poems of *Springboard*, MacNeice was working towards patterns of affirmation to be drawn from the reality of loss, damage, and uncertainty. Inevitably, this was sometimes a precarious business. A lengthy sequence, 'The Kingdom', fails to rescue its subjects from the over-determined framework of significance to which MacNeice subjects them, as parts of 'the Kingdom of individuals'. The influence of BBC propaganda writing has not been properly worked through in these poems, so that the poetic voice becomes merely brisk and obvious:

> these are humble
> And proud at once, working within their limits
> And yet transcending them. These are the people
> Who vindicate the species. And they are many.[41]

The bathos is irredeemable, and the very length of the sequence seems to make matters more explicit, and worse. Similarly, the short poem entitled 'Convoy' (based on MacNeice's experiences while briefly attached to a Royal Navy ship to gather material for a radio feature) announces that 'All is under control and nobody need shout, | We are steady as we go, and on our flanks | The little whippet warships

---

[39] 'Suicide' appeared amongst the 'Novelettes' poems in *Last Ditch*; 'The Expert' in the same sequence as printed in *Poems 1925–1940*. The poems are reprinted in *Collected Poems*, 579 and 762–3.
[40] MacNeice, 'Broken Windows or Thinking Aloud', 142.
[41] MacNeice, 'The Kingdom', in *Collected Poems*, 242.

romp and scurry about', and then delivers the observation that 'This is a bit like us', comparing the 'destroyers and corvettes' to 'pragmatic | And ruthless attitudes' which protect the individual's 'course for all his soul's more basic needs'.[42] In ways its author cannot have intended, the poem is truly an exercise in the art of sinking.

As MacNeice pointed out in a prefatory note to the book, *Springboard* contains a number of titles which 'have the definite article, e.g. "The Satirist", "The Conscript"' (as well as 'The Mixer' and 'The Libertine'); as the poet goes on to insist, 'any such individual seems to me to have an absolute quality which the definite article recognizes.'[43] Yet there is one individual in the volume whose 'absolute quality' was more vividly and intimately known to MacNeice—this is the subject of the poem 'The Casualty' (the opening poem in the book's second section), Graham Shepard, who died on active service in the Atlantic in 1942. In the elegy he composed for his closest friend, MacNeice broke out of the over-definite and slightly glib tone of his weaker war poems, and found another register, in which the strangeness and shock of actual loss are not compromised by the imposition of larger patterns of significance. The idea of death at sea strikes echoes of *The Tempest* and *Lycidas*, but MacNeice adds a disconcerting note to the underwater scene:

> So now the concert is over, the seats vacated,
> Eels among the footlights, water up to the roof
> And the gilded cherubs crumbling—and you come in
> Jaunty as ever but with a half-frustrated
> Look on your face, you expect the show to begin
> But you are too late and cannot accept the proof
>
> That you are too late because you have died too early
> And this is under sea.[44]

The moment of Shepard's 'instantaneous' death, which is one 'Congealing the kaleidoscope at Now', throws time out of joint, both for the imagined dead man and for the imagining poet. The confusion between 'too early' and 'too late', which Shepard is made to experience, sits close to the harrowing refrain of MacNeice's 1940 poem 'Autobiography' (*Come back early or never come*),[45] and anticipates by twenty years the romantic misalignments of his late love poem 'The Introduction' ('And she frightened him because she was young | And thus too late . . . And he frightened her because he was old | And thus too early').[46] The undersea stage set adds an incongruous glamour, and MacNeice makes sure that Shepard's character is celebrated as one of largely incongruous individuality, of irreverence and unpredictability. The impossibility of containing Shepard's character in definition or generalization is enacted by MacNeice's ability to play off the stanzaic form of his elegy against the straying and multiplying energies of syntax—a syntax itself

---

[42] MacNeice, 'Convoy', ibid. 221.   [43] MacNeice, prefatory note, ibid. 804–5.
[44] MacNeice, 'The Casualty', ibid. 237–8.   [45] MacNeice, 'Autobiography', ibid. 200.
[46] MacNeice, 'The Introduction', ibid. 593.

generated by the continually augmented nature of the information and recollection that flood through the rhymed form, resulting in a headlong rush of sentences across line and stanza breaks. If the stanzaic grandeur and formality of occasion in 'The Casualty' seem to recall Yeats, its hurrying cadences and informality of register pull the poem in an altogether different direction. Shepard himself is presented as an individual beyond the reach of generalization, and 'spilling across the border | Of nice convention'; MacNeice's poem, too, spills across conventional lines of demarcation, determinedly refusing to point any morals, and saying nothing whatsoever about the War in which Shepard loses his life.

The subject which is at the centre of the poem's exotic and packed stage is death; but even this is hedged about with irony and inaccessibility. As MacNeice approaches this, the voice speeds up further, and the snappy, somewhat clipped lines confront death's horizon with both loneliness and perplexity:

> How was it then? How is it? You and I
> Have often since we were children discussed death
> And sniggered at the preacher and wondered how
> He can talk so big about mortality
> And immortality more. But you yourself could now
> Talk big as any—if you had the breath.
>
> However since you cannot from this date
> Talk big or little, since you cannot answer
> Even what alive you could, but I let slip
> The chance to ask you, I can correlate
> Only of you what memories dart and trip
> Through freckling lights and stop like a forgetful dancer.

The movement here, from the enjambed rhyme words of 'slip' and 'trip' to the internal half-rhyme of 'stop', culminates in a puzzled stopping short; the 'forgetful dancer' transposes Yeats's dancers, perhaps, into an image of interruption and uncertainty. There can be no question of MacNeice's 'talking big', even (or especially) on Shepard's behalf, and the whole poem, which is gripped and propelled by the particularity and loving detail of memory, makes an eloquent case for the realities of life rather than the abstractions of 'Any ideal, even ideal Death' (as the warmongering Troll puts it in 'Troll's Courtship').[47]

'The Casualty' makes it clear that MacNeice did not approach the losses of the War in a shallowly journalistic spirit; on the contrary, he saw those losses as presenting a profound challenge to any writing which prioritized factual content over larger questions of meaning. At the same time, 'meaning' was not to be quickly or cheaply achieved, and was certainly distinct from the conclusions of even MacNeice's own variety of wartime propaganda. The death of MacNeice's father in 1942 occasioned

---

[47] MacNeice, 'Troll's Courtship', ibid. 219.

the only powerful section of 'The Kingdom', but here the Christianity is simply contemplated, and perhaps admired, rather than shared or understood:

> All is well with
> One who believed and practised and whose life
> Presumed the Resurrection. What that means
> He may have felt he knew; this much is certain—
> The meaning filled his actions, made him courteous
> And lyrical and strong and kind and truthful,
> A generous puritan.[48]

The impenetrably abstract noun of 'the Resurrection' is translated into human adjectives by MacNeice, whose distance from his father's beliefs remains marked. In the context of his wartime writing, however, it is the assertion that 'The meaning filled his actions' which does most work here, aligning Bishop MacNeice with those other individuals in *Springboard* who translate values of belief or instinct into the facts of being and action. Thus, it is the poem 'Prayer before Birth' which stands at the head of this death-possessed collection, and its pleas for freedom of thought and action which—however precariously—set the scene for the various encounters between belief and obligation which the whole volume contains. The first-person voice of this poem knows that the death of the self is only one—and perhaps the least—of the mortal risks of living in time of war:

> I am not yet born; forgive me
> For the sins that in me the world shall commit, my words
>   when they speak me, my thoughts when they think me,
>   my treason engendered by traitors beyond me,
>   my life when they murder by means of my
>   hands, my death when they live me.[49]

Even the communal dangers and solidarity of the Home Front cannot disguise the fact here, that in war the losses taken are only part of the costs incurred; the other part, which it requires a degree of moral imagination to accept, are the losses inflicted—as the poem puts it, 'my life when they murder by means of my | hands'. MacNeice does not confine this awareness to any narrowly religious interpretation, though he does on occasion find that religious imagery is adequate to the purpose, as at the end of 'Thyestes', where 'such are we . . . Messmates in the eucharist of crime | And heirs to two of those three black crosses on the hill'.[50]

It would be a mistake to think that there is something distinctively 'modern' about the awareness that war involves even the individual who is not in active service in a degree of (perceived or actual) guilt; and the experience of living in Britain through the Second World War threw up no moral or ethical dilemmas that had not occurred in the past. Nevertheless, MacNeice's darker poetry of the Home

---

[48] MacNeice, 'The Kingdom', ibid. 247–8.
[49] MacNeice, 'Prayer before Birth', ibid. 213.   [50] MacNeice, 'Thyestes', ibid. 233.

Front looks harder and more searchingly at issues of complicity and guilt than much of the writing of its time (including writing from the theatres of war themselves) was able to do. And *Springboard* did seem unnecessarily and perplexingly dark to a number of its contemporary readers: one American reviewer, for instance, complained that 'These are not poems to rally resistance but are poems of shared guilt.'[51] MacNeice's initial uncertainties about whether or not the War was to be 'my war', and the comparative slowness of his decision to commit himself to work in Britain as part of the War, perhaps enabled him to feel less certain of the inherent virtues of the enormous, world-shattering enterprise in which he was committed to playing a tiny part. *Springboard*'s most sombre poem, however, is concerned with levels of guilt and complicity which MacNeice, like his readers since, found painfully complex in terms of politics, history, and culture. This is 'Neutrality', a short lyric which addresses (on the surface at least) the neutral status in the War of Eire, 'The neutral island facing the Atlantic', and concludes with apparent reproach:

> But then look eastward from your heart, there bulks
> A continent, close, dark, as archetypal sin,
> While to the west off your own shores the mackerel
> Are fat—on the flesh of your kin.[52]

Certainly, there is a level of anger here; just as certainly, there is also a level of complexity, making a point about matters of complicity in the context of a deeper awareness of how far complicity might run. 'Sin' is paired with the rhyme of 'kin', and MacNeice's poem does not shy away from the whole issue of what it is to be 'Messmates in the eucharist of crime', to be kin—whether deliberately or not, and whether knowingly or not, with the 'archetypal sin' of an evil world.

On a political level, there is much to say about the meaning, intention, and reality of Irish neutrality: it may well be that (as in fact MacNeice believed) De Valera's policy was a near inevitability, given the political and economic conditions of the time; and the country's official neutrality should not be confused with any failure on the part of the Irish people to play a significant role in the Allied war effort, since many Irishmen fought and died, regardless of the diplomatic realities. To take account of all this is not to debunk MacNeice's poem as a piece of crude rhetoric or propaganda—this would be a risky misreading. Ireland is put alongside 'The neutral island in the heart of man', and both of these places or states are 'bitterly soft reminders of the beginnings | That ended before the end began'. The power of 'bitterly soft'—two words locked in a contradiction that can only be resolved by thinking in Irish terms, of the 'soft' weather of the West of Ireland, perhaps, in conjunction with the bitterness of historical and cultural politics of the Island as a whole—fuels the riddle of beginnings and ends, so that the first stanza creates a state of paradox and puzzle within which the rest of the poem does its work.

---

[51] Coleman Rosenberger, *Poetry* (Chicago), 68/1 (Apr. 1946), 48.
[52] MacNeice, 'Neutrality', in *Collected Poems*, 224.

Here, the reader (who is not—and certainly not *only*—an Irish one) is told twice to 'Look into your heart', and there finds a Yeatsian Sligo and Knocknarea, as well as the 'intricacies of gloom and glint' with 'ducats of dream and great doubloons of ceremony'. All of this inward looking reveals, not an actual Ireland, but an Ireland of the mind, a kind of inveterate Romanticism and wishfulness which insists on the possibility of distancing itself from 'archetypal sin'. 'Neutrality' declares the wishes false; but it implicates all concerned, including its author. If there is anger in the concluding lines, there is also distress, and a measure at least of self-accusation.

'Neutrality' acts according to the principle, which MacNeice was forming during the war, that the individual—whether as a mind or as an imagination—can be willingly subsumed in both a common purpose and a common peril. *Springboard* works best when the poet finds images for this, and is at its weakest when he attempts to explain or discuss the situation. The over-explicitness which hampers some poems in the volume was to remain as a dangerous current, by which a good deal of MacNeice's writing in the immediately post-war years was dragged down. But MacNeice's best poetry—notably that of his last two collections, *Solstices* (1961) and *The Burning Perch* (1963)—was prefigured by the strongest and most intensely pressurized poems of the war years. 'The Springboard' itself is among these, and its central figure epitomizes the problems—of conflicting duty and desire, individuality and common purpose—with which MacNeice's imagination, at its most resilient, was able to deal. A man's form, like that of a diver, 'High above London, naked in the night | Perched on a board',[53] gives to the poem a quasi-surrealistic immediacy, which is also that of MacNeice's Blitz writing. At the same time, metaphysical questions are absorbed almost casually into the poem's fabric, while 'His blood began to haggle over the price | History would pay if he were to throw himself down.' The situation combines the implied public scrutiny in a sense of duty with the private agony of suicidal despair—both things which MacNeice knew plenty about by 1942. The figure seems paralysed by both his own 'unbelief' and a more general scepticism, in the knowledge that 'His friends would find in his death neither ransom nor reprieve | But only a grain of faith—for what it was worth.' Yet MacNeice ends the poem with the jump itself:

> And yet we know he knows what he must do.
> There above London where the gargoyles grin
> He will dive like a bomber past the broken steeple,
> One man wiping out his own original sin
> And, like ten million others, dying for the people.

In the first of these lines, when the meaning and argument are at a point of maximum strain, MacNeice has the courage to risk flatness, in a statement of monosyllabic exactness. The climactic dive into extinction is something in which

---

[53] MacNeice, 'The Springboard', ibid. 236.

'we' and 'he' prove to be interdependent: the poetry spells out an intricate series of consequential knowledges—self-knowledge and the knowledge of what is needed, as well as the knowledge of action. The religious imagery does not serve any necessarily religious meaning; rather, it becomes a powerful element of the poem's logic—a metaphor, perhaps, for what happens when a man understands that his actions, as well as his identity, are themselves metaphorically charged with meaning. The same lesson might be implied, on a national scale, in 'Neutrality'. But, like the hero of MacNeice's *The Dark Tower*, the figure on the springboard must will his own extinction in order to prove the reality of a free will.[54]

The story of MacNeice's war is in part that of the relationship, both uneasy and deeply creative, between the artist's personal circumstances and the larger world in which these had their being. That world was a World War; but it was also a world of ideas and beliefs, and of ethical, moral, and religious problems, in the midst of which an actual life conducted itself, with degrees of both muddle and coherence. Having been careful in dating all the poems in *Plant and Phantom*, MacNeice was much more sparing in affixing dates to those of *Springboard*. There are two exceptions: one is the air raid poem 'Whit Monday' (dated 1941), and the other is the last poem in the book, 'Postscript', with its closing assertion of the need for 'a new | Shuffle of cards behind the brain | Where meaning shall remarry colour'.[55] MacNeice's new wartime marriage (to Hedli Anderson) is partly behind the buoyancy and hope of the poem; but personal happiness is not the whole story, as MacNeice's appended date for the poem perhaps implies: for the last words in *Springboard* are '*June, 1944*'.

---

[54] See MacNeice, *The Dark Tower* (broadcast 1946, composed 1945): 'I Roland, the black sheep, the unbeliever— | Who never did anything of his own free will— | Will do this now to bequeath free will to others' (in *Selected Plays of Louis MacNeice*, ed. Alan Heuser and Peter McDonald (Oxford: Clarendon Press, 1993), 148).

[55] MacNeice, 'Postscript', in *Collected Poems*, 250.

C H A P T E R   2 1

....

SIDNEY KEYES IN HISTORICAL PERSPECTIVE

....

GEOFFREY HILL

Sidney Arthur Kilworth Keyes, born on 27 May 1922, was killed in action, in Tunisia, on 29 April 1943, a few weeks short of his twenty-first birthday. At the time of his death he was the author of one small book of verse, *The Iron Laurel*, published in the summer of 1942, and of a second book ready for the press, *The Cruel Solstice*, which appeared posthumously, late in 1943 or in early 1944.[1] Subsequently two further posthumous volumes were put into print: the *Collected Poems* of 1945 and *Minos of Crete,* a book of plays and stories, with excerpts from letters and his notebook (1948). The publisher in all four instances was Routledge, at that time under the literary guidance of a courageous fighting poet of the First World War, thereafter a mild philosophical anarchist, Herbert Read, DSO, MC. Read had begun to take an interest in Keyes's work as early as spring 1941 when he accepted for publication an anthology of poems by eight Oxford undergraduates that Keyes co-edited with Michael Meyer. Apart from Keyes himself, the most significant contributor was Keith Douglas, whose name must inevitably be threaded through this appraisal because his achievement is now so patent and secure.[2] Keyes has still to be fought

---

[1] I take the year 1943 from *The National Union Catalogue: Pre 1956 Imprints*, ccvcv. 44. 'Late' is my conjecture. I possess two copies of *The Cruel Solstice*. One imprint page (a) reads *1943 Reprinted 1944*; the other (b) has *First published January 1944 Reprinted April 1944, Reprinted June 1944*. Both title-pages give 1944. Volume (b) misspells the name of the dedicatee; volume (a) spells it correctly.

[2] Keyes's name occurs three times in Douglas's surviving papers. None of these is at all laudatory. One has to do with business ('Sidney Keyes of The Cherwell will know about this'), one bestows

for, as I propose to do here; so has Drummond Allison, killed in Italy in 1943, whose Fortune Press volume *The Yellow Night*, containing three or four poems of distinction, is his sole literary legacy.

Most descriptions of Keyes present him as a gothic pastoralist.[3] Those who see him in this way can certainly present supporting evidence. A few weeks before he was killed, Keyes stated: 'I think I should have been born in the last century in Oxfordshire or Wiltshire, instead of near London between two wars, because then I might have been a good pastoral poet, instead of an uncomfortable metaphysical without roots.'[4] My purpose in the present essay is to explore this contention as fully as possible while withholding final assent from the conclusion to which it points. There are uncomfortable moments throughout Keyes, but he is in the end a more confident metaphysician than he suggests, as well as being a pastoral poet of impressive, if intermittent, power.

Among the handful of literary historians and general readers who are aware of him, Keyes is exclusively a poet of the private world. Michael Meyer, his first editor and biographer, set the tone in his early sketch of his friend, a brief memoir published in 1944 in the W. H. Heinemann journal *The Windmill* and subsequently expanded as the editorial preface to *The Collected Poems of Sidney Keyes* of 1945:

faint praise ('Sidney Keyes . . . technically quite competent . . . [has] no experiences worth writing of'), the third occurs when Douglas is trying out possible titles for his own projected book ('The Iron Trees . . . this sounds as if its aping Sidney Keyes . . . though'). See Keith Douglas, *A Prose Miscellany*, ed. Desmond Graham (Manchester: Carcanet, 1985), 83, 119, 147.

[3] See e.g. Michael Meyer, *The Windmill*, ed. Reginald Moore and Edward Lane (London: Heinemann, 1944), 57–9: 'This, then, is the world of Sidney Keyes: a Kent garden, inhabited by firelight shadows. Fear and guilt ruled him from the first. In the ordinary course of events, he would have been an esoteric poet, a haunted countryman like John Clare. But the chance that destroyed him made him the spokesman of a generation . . . . The world of his imagination merged into the world of reality'. See also Meyer's 'Memoir', in Keyes, *Collected Poems*, ed. Michael Meyer (Manchester, Carcanet, 2002), 116–24: 'Isolated with his nurse in the great house, except for the relations he saw at meals, he had to create a world of his own to survive' (p. 116). Where would English poetry and fiction be, one wonders, without the isolated child in the great house? We can amuse ourselves, if so inclined, by thinking of the child Sidney Keyes as a counterpart to Kay Harker, isolated in the big house, Seekings, in Masefield's two marvellous books for children, *The Midnight Folk* and *The Box of Delights*. Like Keyes, Kay Harker possesses 'an almost supernatural power over animals' (Meyer, *Windmill*, 57), as does Kipling's 'Mowgli'. I am not saying that the figure of the isolated child, having to create a world of its own to survive, doesn't have a significant minor role in European culture and literature. Nor do I deny to Keyes his rightful place in that company; his affinity with them must be acknowledged in any attempt to come to terms with his art. In one aspect of his orientation he strikes me as being a belated scion of the twentieth-century 'great house' poets—the Sitwells of Renishaw, Lady Dorothy Wellesley at Penns in the Rocks, Vita Sackville-West of Sissinghurst Castle, and, by adoption, Eliot of Garsington, Yeats of Coole Park, and Rilke of Duino. At his death Keyes's estate was assessed at £7,000 (*Oxford Dictionary of National Biography*, (Oxford: Oxford University Press, 2004), xxxi. 476), a generous sum for 1943, that perhaps represents his share of his grandfather's legacy. In the same source Douglas's estate is described as 'negligible'.

[4] Keyes, quoted in Meyer, 'Memoir', 118 n.

The creative artist in him never came into contact with human beings, but lived in the crazy haunted country of a child. All artists perhaps remain imaginatively at one age, and Keyes was always three or four. He retained the distorting eye which transforms everything that excites it into something grotesque and macabre.[5]

I don't understand what is meant here by the 'distorting eye' except as a device put to occasional specific use in particular poems. Cinema photography held a considerable fascination for Keyes; he especially admired German Expressionist films of the 1920s, such as *The Cabinet of Dr. Caligari*, on which he based his poem 'Holstenwall'.[6] But this was a generational thing: Keith Douglas also enjoyed *The Cabinet of Dr. Caligari*—'His taste for films', we are told, 'was insatiable and catholic.'[7]

Keyes's great friend and fellow undergraduate at Queen's College, Oxford, John Heath-Stubbs, has claimed that he had

a particular admiration for certain minor poets who occupy a curious little trough between the end of the high Romantic movement . . . and the beginning of high Victorian poetry . . . . These poets were Thomas Lovell Beddoes, George Darley and John Clare. He also admired the serious poems of Thomas Hood. . . . These might be regarded as a generation of English *poètes maudits*.[8]

Beddoes killed himself, Clare was confined in what used to be called lunatic asylums from 1836, when he was aged 43, until his death in 1864 when he was 70.

The suggestion can be risked that Keyes was drawn to Clare less by his fate as a *poète maudit* (though there is a hint of that in the poem 'A Garland for John Clare') than by the cogent particularity of Clare's style: 'And sees the snow in feathers pass | Winnowing by the window glass'; 'And wisdom gossipd from the stars | Of politics and bloody wars' (the reference is to peasants busily consulting *Old Moores Almanack*); or:

> The shepherd too in great coat wrapt
> And straw bands round his stockings lapt
> Wi plodding dog that sheltering steals
> To shun the wind behind his heels . . .
> While in the fields the lonly plough
> Enjoys its frozen sabbath now.[9]

With due respect to Heath-Stubbs's insights and analyses of the writers of that period, I have to say that poetry of such fertile economy does not arise from any

---

[5] Meyer, *Windmill*, 57. See n. 3 above.
[6] Keyes, 'Holstenwall', in *Collected Poems*, 40. See also Meyer's note on the poem, 132.
[7] Desmond Graham, *Keith Douglas 1920–1944: A Biography* (London: Oxford University Press, 1974), 85.
[8] John Heath-Stubbs, *Hindsights: An Autobiography* (London: Hodder & Stoughton, 1993), 111.
[9] John Clare, *The Shepherd's Calendar*, ed. Eric Robinson and Geoffrey Summerfield (London: Oxford University Press, 1973), 1, 2, 3.

'curious little trough'. Clare is Thomson's and Cowper's proletarian inheritor, and beats them hollow (with the exception of 'The Olney Hymns', 'The Cast-away', and the poem about a hare, that is).

Where Meyer refers to the 'distorting eye', Keyes could be better seen as working to achieve and put to use the enabling eye. Douglas's eye is frequently confronted by distortion, because he is a battleground poet in a way that Keyes is not. Keyes is a war poet only by accident, or 'by misadventure',[10] as David Jones expresses it.

> On scrub and sand the dead men wriggle
> in their dowdy clothes. They are mimes
> who express silence and futile aims
> enacting this prone and motionless struggle
> at a queer angle to the scenery.[11]

Here, Douglas's own eye is one that is now enabled to transmit, as if directly, the 'famous attitudes of unconcern',[12] 'the dust upon the paper eye | and the burst stomach like a cave'.[13] Douglas saw intense but intermittent action from early November 1942 to mid-January 1943, at which point he was wounded.[14] During convalescence he had time to complete a number of his best-known battlefield poems. The battlefield is a mass, or a scatter, of queer angles, and Douglas's eye is set to record them. Keyes is reported to have written poems during his two weeks in action, but these have not survived.[15] Douglas was a militarist through and through; Keyes was a conscript civilian poet who underwent death in battle. The manner of his death, obscured for so long by missing or conflicting evidence and by hearsay and rumour, was itself one of the queer angles of the North African campaign.[16]

It is time that we took account of Keyes's enabling eye and ear: 'A caterpillar | Measures with looping back a mulberry leaf'; 'Buzzard drops down the sky and shadows straddle | Longer on grass and rock'; 'Plovers crouch in the rain between the furrows | Or wheel club-winged and tumble across the wind'; 'Remember the weasel questing down the hedge'; 'As tulips gulp the sun'; 'The fine rain speckles | My windowsill'; 'Contending with the landscape, arguing | With shrike and shrewmouse'; 'the elder's curdled flowers'; 'the cryptic swift performing | His ordered evolutions through our sky'; 'but breaking of the fine-tipped willow buds'; 'spawned on the rocks of Galway | Among the dried shark-eggs and the dirty froth'; 'the curlews' | Insatiable crying'; 'raftered halls | Hung with hard holly . . . Decked with the pale and sickled mistletoe'; 'Between the frost's pale foliage and the

---

[10]   David Jones, 'Preface', in *In Parenthesis* (London: Faber, 1963; 1st pub. 1937), p. xvii.
[11]   Keith Douglas, 'Landscape with Figures 2', in *The Complete Poems*, ed. Desmond Graham (London: Faber, 2000), 110.
[12]   Douglas, 'Sportsmen', ibid. 157.   [13]   Douglas, *Vergissmeinnicht*, ibid. 118.
[14]   See Graham, *Keith Douglas, 1920–1944*, 163–84.
[15]   See James Lucas, 'Memoir', in Keyes, *Collected Poems*, 125.
[16]   John Guenther, *Sidney Keyes: A Biographical Inquiry* (London: London Magazine Editions, 1967), 197–219, esp. ch. 10 ('The Quest for Keyes'). But see Lucas, 'Memoir', 127.

bright | Leaves of the fire'; 'Or when the summer flashed and rocketed | Between green sedges like a kingfisher'; 'the wild thyme splayed against the paving stones'; 'the talk | Of rain among the gutters, or at dawn | The sentry's feet striking the chilly yard'; 'At the field's border, where the cricket chafes | His brittle wings among the yellow weed, | I pause to hear the sea unendingly sifted | Between the granite fingers of the cape'; 'Among their horses' big-eyed skulls in the meadow'; 'The yellow charlock scratches at her door'; 'I note the greenfly working on the rose'; 'the may was knobbed with chilly buds'.[17]

As previously stated, my purpose, at this point in my argument, is to present as full a case as I can for the agrarian nature of Keyes's imagery and arguments, while holding back from the conclusion that he is to be read throughout as a pastoralist or a pastoral poet *manqué*. It is true that he frequently highlighted the affinity between himself and Clare. In a letter of 29 December 1941, he wrote: 'This morning I went for a walk by the stream; there was a hard frost and bits of ice were hanging on twigs by the water—"Like fishes' eyes" as John Clare said.'[18]

And in the beautiful early poem 'A Garland for John Clare' he recalls:

> Mad John Clare, the single timeless poet.
> We have forgotten that. But sometimes I remember
> The time that I was Clare, and you unborn.[19]

John Heath-Stubbs has also written, however, that 'Sidney Keyes had a strong belief in the philosophical or metaphysical mission of the poet.'[20] David Wright's contrasting opinion was that Keyes's 'best poems are about living creatures he had observed'—for example, 'Pheasant' and 'The Buzzard'.[21] One needs to try to find some way of explaining why Keyes's work is not split down the middle, into 'philosophical or metaphysical' writings on one side and poems of nature observation on the other. The observation of nature *is* the metaphysics; and it is so, again, by means of word placing that is neither language at the bidding of concept nor language subservient to the natural phenomenon. Take the sonnet—Keyes conceived it as one of a number of proposed 'Rilkean' sonnets[22]—'William Wordsworth':

> No room for mourning: he's gone out
> Into the noisy glen, or stands between the stones

---

[17] Keyes, *Collected Poems*, 9, 10 ('The Buzzard'); 13, 14 ('Sour Land'); 19 ('Poem for May the First'); 19 ('Poem for Milein Cosman'); 23 ('Ploughman'); 25 ('A Garland for John Clare'); 26 ('Neutrality'); 29 ('Extracts from "A Journey through Limbo"'); 31–2 ('The Glass Tower in Galway'); 41 ('The Bards'); 59 ('The Foreign Gate'); 69 ('Lament for Harpsichord: The Flowering Orchards'); 74 ('Images of Distress'); 75 ('The Uncreated Images'); 76 ('Two Offices of a Sentry, I'); 77 ('Design for a Monument'); 78 ('The Gardener'); 81 ('The Kestrels').

[18] Keyes to Milein Cosman, 29 Dec. 1941, in *Minos of Crete: Plays and Stories*, ed. Michael Meyer (London: Routledge, 1948), 171.

[19] Keyes, 'A Garland for John Clare', in *Collected Poems*, 25.   [20] Heath-Stubbs, *Hindsights*, 69.

[21] David Wright, 'Keyes's Poetry', *London Magazine*, new series, 7 (Nov. 1967), 162.

[22] See Keyes, *Collected Poems*, 131: Meyer's notes to 'William Wordsworth' and 'All Souls: A Dialogue'.

Of the gaunt ridge, or you'll hear his shout
Rolling among the screes, he being a boy again.
He'll never fail nor die
And if they laid his bones
In the wet vaults or iron sarcophagi
Of fame, he'd rise at the first summer rain
And stride across the hills to seek
His rest among the broken lands and clouds.
He was a stormy day, a granite peak
Spearing the sky; and look, about its base
Words flower like crocuses in the hanging woods,
Blank though the dalehead and the bony face.[23]

'Blank', like 'blind', 'naked', and 'wild', is for Wordsworth a word of focus, its range covering several forms of desolateness and uncomprehending: 'o'er my thoughts | There hung a darkness, call it solitude | Or blank desertion'.[24] 'Oh, blank confusion',[25] 'By a blank sense of greatness passed away',[26] 'Blank misgivings of a Creature | Moving about in worlds not realized'.[27] Keyes's 'Blank though the dalehead and the bony face' uses the northern (Cumbria, North and West Yorkshire) word for the upper portion of a river valley (the lower part being the dale-end) (*OED*). The line occurred to Keyes, I imagine, somewhat in this manner: bareness of things is not necessarily barrenness of things; bleakness of vision (the appearance of the rocky dalehead) correlates with a bleakness of certain forms of visionary insight. Not all forms of vision; there are crocuses in the stony landscape, there are colour and light in the language that springs from even the bleakest outlook; the physiognomy of Wordsworth the man is bony, the physiognomy of Wordsworth's deepest seeings has often the appearance—to him as well as to us—of blankness. According to an editorial note in Keyes's *Collected Poems,* the sonnet was suggested by the photograph of Wordsworth's death-mask, a photograph used as the frontispiece to Herbert Read's book about the poet. Keyes is reported as saying, 'Isn't that fine! *That* is everything which I mean by Wordsworth'; but he then said, 'Even so, it is, in a way, a sheep-like old face.'[28] This is the range of inference embodied in the word 'blank'. Death-masks necessarily have a blank look; it has something to do with the appearance of the eyes; a sheep's face looks blank in a somewhat different way. The word hovers between the features of majestic rigour and the gaze of incomprehension.

What is striking about this sonnet is that it is neither, on the one hand, descriptively agrarian, nor on the other, philosophical or metaphysical. It is these

[23] Keyes, 'William Wordsworth', ibid. 30.

[24] William Wordsworth, *The Prelude or Growth of a Poet's Mind*, ed. E. De Selincourt (London: Oxford University Press, 1932), 25; I. 394–5 (1850 text).

[25] Ibid. 256; VII. 695 (1805 text).   [26] Ibid. 300; VII. 592 (1805 text).

[27] Wordsworth, 'Ode ("There was a time")', in *William Wordsworth*, ed. Stephen Gill (Oxford: Oxford University Press, 1984), 301.

[28] Keyes, quoted in *Collected Poems*, 131.

several things at once: and it is this ability to compound and complicate and simplify in an instant that is one of the signs of potential greatness in a poet.

Some of the best appreciations of this kind of blankness in Wordsworth—of being at once a *tabula rasa* for unpremeditated impressions and unable to take in, to make anything of, the manifold perplexities of the world—are to be found in the writings of Charles Williams, in particular *The English Poetic Mind* of 1932.[29] Williams was a poet, novelist, theologian, and historian, who worked for many years as an editor in the London office of Oxford University Press. Editions of Hopkins and Kierkegaard were produced under his aegis. At the beginning of the Second World War the London office of the Press was evacuated to Oxford, where Williams met, and was taken up by, C. S. Lewis and the 'Inklings'. He was invited to lecture in the wartime English School, and did so with great success.[30] Perhaps the best short study of his work is that written for the British Council by John Heath-Stubbs, who attended the lectures as an undergraduate.[31] Williams died in Oxford in 1945.[32]

A few months before he was killed, Keyes wrote to a correspondent interested in his work: 'The only living writers whom I can accept entirely are Eliot, Charles Williams, Graves (to some extent), my great friend John Heath-Stubbs . . . and a few others—very few.'[33]

Although there is no doubt in my mind that Keyes at 20 was at least as good a poet as Williams was in his mid-fifties, nonetheless it is Williams on poets and poetry who most illuminates for me the essentials of what I want to say about Keyes. Here are a few of Williams's observations:

Poetry has to do all its own work; in return it has all its own authority.[34]

These things [images in poetry] are not merely pictures; they have something else in them. They awaken some sort of capacity—for motion, for separation, for solitude, for different life . . . . I have wondered whether this communication is of the sense which poetry has of its own vigil before its own approaching greatness.[35]

It is surely true that the chief impulse of a poet is, not to communicate a thing to others, but to shape a thing, to make an immortality for its own sake.[36]

These three statements all appeared in print in 1932, and could have been known to Keyes, though I do not say that they were. What matters—or so my argument maintains—is not so much 'accessibility' as power. But inaccessibility does not

---

[29] Charles Williams, *The English Poetic Mind* (Oxford: Clarendon Press, 1932).

[30] See Alice Mary Hadfield, *Charles Williams: An Exploration of His Life and Work* (Oxford: Oxford University Press, 1983), 188–9; and Humphrey Carpenter, *The Inklings* (Boston: Houghton Mifflin, 1979), 118–19, 148 ff., 187, 188.

[31] Heath-Stubbs, *Hindsights*, 64.

[32] See Hadfield, *Charles Williams*, 235; and Carpenter, *Inklings*, 199–200 and 203–4.

[33] Keyes to Richard Church, ? Jan. 1943, quoted in Meyer, 'Memoir', 122; see also Guenther, *Sidney Keyes*, 153.

[34] Williams, *English Poetic Mind*, 167.   [35] Ibid. 198.   [36] Ibid. 5.

deny 'communication'; the 'authority' of poetry is its 'communication'; to 'shape a thing' is to 'communicate' in a way that is not the same thing at all as conveying information. 'The call of poetry in word and thought is to be final', Williams wrote in a private letter which Keyes could not possibly have seen.[37] Nonetheless, I would say that he strove for finality—or that approximation to finality which is the equipoise of technical mastery and the finally untameable nature of language.

As already pointed out, Wordsworth has a number of focusing, or tuning, words—'blind', 'naked', 'wild', 'blank'; to these should be added the word 'power'—Williams lists some of them in the second chapter of *The English Poetic Mind*.[38] In *The Prelude* 'our simple childhood' is particularly associated with something 'That hath more power than all the elements'.[39] And at the end of the same book Wordsworth writes (and again Williams marks the passage):

> Visionary Power
> Attends upon the motions of the winds
> Embodied in the mystery of words.
> There darkness makes abode, and all the host
> Of shadowy things do work their changes there,
> As in a mansion like their proper home.[40]

There is a deeply moving penultimate entry in Keyes's 1942–3 Notebook: 'I am thankful that my intellect is not strong enough to master my passions, nor my passions my intellect: for this is the true condition of creation. I am thankful that I can see myself as funny and ineffective, but not my powers.'[41] The crux, then, is *power*, or *powers*. Keyes, like all poets, desires to transform language into power. We judge poets to a considerable extent by their ability—or inability—to effect such a transformation.

My only reservation about those who knew Keyes well and who wrote about him—Heath-Stubbs, Meyer, among others—is that they do not always take care to chart the difference between strangeness of personality and the strange aloofness that is the particular power of achieved poetry. Even Heath-Stubbs, in his elegy for Keyes, 'The Divided Ways', focuses excessively on the goblin-like elements in his personality:

> But now, at last, I dare avow my terror
> Of the pale vampire by the cooling grate;
> The enemy face that doubled every loved one;
> My secret fear of him and his cold heroes.[42]

The arbitrary power of the achieved poem is a quite other power.

---

[37] Williams, quoted in Hadfield, *Charles Williams*, 133.
[38] See Williams, *English Poetic Mind*, 11.
[39] Wordsworth, *The Prelude*, 163; V. 509 (1850 text).
[40] Ibid. 168; V. 595–600 (1850 text).
[41] Keyes, 'Notebook: 1942–43', in *Minos of Crete*, 165.
[42] Heath-Stubbs, 'The Divided Ways', in *The Divided Ways* (London: Routledge, 1946), 56.

If war poetry is conceived of narrowly as poems about fighting, the appellation does not fit Keyes. His battalion landed in North Africa on 10 March 1943, and saw action for the first time towards the end of April. Keyes was killed on 29 April. 'He wrote some poetry while we were on Oued Zarga,'[43] that is, in the front line, but this, it seems, perished with him, though his notebook survived. At the same time he was consistently a poet of war as history and history as war ('The Foreign Gate', 'Schiller Dying', 'Dunbar, 1650') and of wartime separation as the foe of love ('War Poet', 'To Keep Off Fears', 'A Hope for Those Separated by War', 'Ulster Soldier', 'Two Offices of a Sentry', 'Moonlight Night on the Port'). There is scarcely any shift of style between the poems of history and those of personal grief and loss. Some might see this as a mark of immaturity, but I do not, taking my bearings from some remarks of Ezra Pound on the nature and function of poetry:

The first difficulty in a modern poem is to give a feeling of the reality of the speaker, the second, given the reality of the speaker, to gain any degree of poignancy in one's utterance.

The supreme test of a book is that we should feel some unusual intelligence working behind the words.

...the feeling of poignancy Gourmont was able to create by a constantly felt dramatic voice.[44]

What one senses in Keyes's poems is the presence of this constantly felt dramatic voice (he also wrote plays) that contrives its own poignancy, and that is the semantic record of an unusual intelligence: 'The golden sun revolves | On the invisible radius of time'; 'Rain strikes the window. Miles of wire | Are hung with small mad eyes. Night sets its mask | Upon the fissured hill'; 'Fear was Donne's peace; to him, | Charted between the minstrel cherubim, | Terror was decent'.[45]

We have by now moved some way from our original sense of Keyes as a belated nineteenth-century pastoralist; but I have not minutely charted our progress (if that is what it is), and some further explanation is owed the reader. There are two passages in Keyes's prose writings which, placed in mutual opposition, mark the antipodes of his thinking about the nature and craft of poetry. One has already been cited—the late letter in which he laments that he was not born in the nineteenth century, and consequently did not fulfil his destiny, that of being 'a good pastoral poet'.

One needs, to counteract that sigh of regret, to study the implications of a paragraph from 'The Artist in Society', his essay contributed to the symposium *The Future of Faith*, published in 1942.[46] The essay is in the intelligentsia style

---

[43] Lucas, 'Memoir', 125.

[44] Ezra Pound, quoted in Ronald Bush, *The Genesis of Ezra Pound's Cantos* (Princeton: Princeton University Press, 1976), 159, 168, 160.

[45] Keyes, *Collected Poems*, 9 ('The Buzzard'), 72 ('Ulster Soldier'), 38 ('Time Will Not Grant').

[46] Percy Colson (ed.), *The Future of Faith* (London: Hurst & Blackett, 1942).

of the day. A good place to look for parallels to it would be in *Transformation Two*, edited by Stefan Schimanski and Henry Treece, published in 1944,[47] or in *Focus One*, edited by B. Rajan and Andrew Pearse, published in 1945.[48] These volumes were issued from such London publishing houses as Lindsay Drummond and Denis Dobson; one might even say that the contributors shared a house style. It is a small but not unuseful corrective to the image of Keyes as a kind of poetic throw-back to see him as sharing, albeit briefly, in the intellectual petty commerce of the day.

'The Artist in Society' is a significant document, and not only for readers of Keyes's poetry. It is made unnecessarily opaque because he fixes one of his crucial points with a quotation from a poem in German for which no source is given and which is also left untranslated. It is in fact four lines from Rilke's ninth *Duino Elegy* and, in the 1939 translation by Leishman and Spender, reads as follows:

> *Here* is the time for the Tellable, *here* is its home.
> Speak and proclaim. More than ever
> the things we can live with are falling away, and their place
> being oustingly taken up by an imageless act.[49]

It is not an exaggeration to state that the poetic craft of Sidney Keyes works toward a speaking and proclaiming that is obscured neither by a demand for documentary realism nor by a cult of art for art's sake.

For Rilke the 'home' of the 'Tellable' is the world unsubdued by utilitarian sanctions, simply itself irradiated by the vision of the Rilkean seer. In Keyes's own words, the poet 'is neither propagating a doctrine, nor "expressing himself"; rather, he is letting the world express him and giving himself entirely to something outside himself'.[50] This is striking in its pure Rilkean tone, though at the same time it is reminiscent of certain phrases in Yeats's great eulogy for the dead J. M. Synge: 'he gave his country what it needed, an unmoved mind where there is a perpetual last day, a trumpeting and coming up to judgement.'[51]

In the present cultural climate, there are going to be two sharply divided views among the literary public: one, that such claims and statements are obnoxiously esoteric; the other, that they are uncannily on target. I have to declare my position among those who would maintain the latter view. Speak and proclaim. But I am getting ahead of myself and must recapitulate.

---

[47] Stefan Schimanski and Henry Treece (eds.), *Transformation Two* (London: Lindsay Drummond, 1944). One might note here, Richard Church, 'Strength for Tomorrow' (pp. 131–6). Keyes wrote an important letter to Church, setting out his poetic aims. See John Guenther, *Sidney Keyes*, 152–3.

[48] B. Rajan and Andrew Pearse (eds.), *Focus One* (London: Denis Dobson, 1945). Here one might consider D. J. Enright, 'The Muse in Confusion' (pp. 86–9), and Julian Symons, 'Of Crisis and Dismay' (pp. 90–111).

[49] Rainer Maria Rilke, *Duino Elegies*, ed. and trans. J. B. Leishman and Stephen Spender (London: Hogarth Press, 1939), 84–5.

[50] Keyes, 'The Artist in Society', in *Minos of Crete*, 146.

[51] W. B. Yeats, *The Cutting of an Agate* (London: Macmillan, 1919), 129.

What I propose to call 'the Rilke connection' is of the utmost significance in our consideration of Keyes's poetic craft and of its place in the development of twentieth-century British poetry. It is a connection that I am by no means the first to have noticed.[52] And when Keyes reviewed, very favourably, *Beauty for Ashes*, a book-length poem by Morwenna Donnelly, for the wartime periodical *Kingdom Come*, he wrote that, despite certain flaws, her poem succeeds in Rilkean terms: 'like Rilke, she is finally answered, and accepts the revelation. That is the important fact.'[53] Here, it is the Rilkean ontology that is paramount; throughout Keyes's work, however, one is also conscious of a Rilkean note to the language itself. What he takes from the German poet, and from other Germans such as Hölderlin and Schiller, is a sense that poetry is to be conceived of and confirmed in its quality as heroic elegy. Keith Douglas also admired Rilke, whom he read both in German and in English.[54] The difference is that Keyes grounded himself in Rilke—it is the source of his strength and of his vulnerability to later British critics—and that Douglas did not. Keyes's recurrent note is the cry that opens the *Duino* sequence: 'Wer, wenn ich schriee . . .?'[55] No style of modern or postmodern poetry in English is now more out of fashion.

Keyes's 'The Foreign Gate', which takes up twelve of the thirty-nine pages of verse in *The Iron Laurel*, is headed by a quotation from Rilke's sixth *Duino Elegy*, which he leaves in the original, but which Leishman and Spender translate: 'Yes, the Hero's strangely akin to the youthfully dead. / . . . Fate, . . . enraptured all of a sudden, | sings him into the storm of her roaring world.'[56] The style of this long poem is a twentieth-century heroic style: suppose that Yeats had uncharacteristically translated Rilke into a form of loose Pindaric and that a nineteen-year-old Oxford undergraduate had modified this with the rhetoric of a poem by the locally celebrated Charles Williams. Keyes writes:

> Once a man cried and the great Orders heard him:
> Pacing upon a windy wall at night
> A pale unlearned poet out of Europe's
> Erratic heart cried and was filled with speech.
> Were I to cry, who in that proud hierarchy
> Of the illustrious would pity me?
> What should I cry, how should I learn their language?
> The cold wind takes my words.[57]

The measure of this is overwhelmingly Rilkean, though 'What should I cry . . . ?' also echoes the King James Bible.[58] The 'man' and the 'windy wall' are Rilke at Duino;

[52] See e.g. Heath-Stubbs, *Hindsights*, 69 and 76; Michael Hamburger, *String of Beginnings* (London: Skoob Books, 1991), 97.

[53] Keyes, review of Morwenna Donnelly's *Beauty for Ashes*, *Kingdom Come*, 3/12 (Autumn 1943), 44–5. By the time this review appeared, Keyes was already dead.

[54] See Graham, *Keith Douglas 1920–1944*, 222 n. 1.   [55] Rilke, *Duino Elegies*, 24.

[56] Ibid. 64–7.   [57] Keyes, 'The Foreign Gate', in *Collected Poems*, 64.   [58] Isa. 40: 6.

lines 5–6 are a close paraphrase of the first *Elegy*'s opening declamation.[59] But
two other poets are also present, adumbrated, in such phrasings as 'Pacing upon
a windy wall at night', which could as easily be taken to represent learned Yeats
on his tower, or perhaps Williams's learned Taliessin, the Arthurian warrior-poet,
pacing the ramparts of Logres on the very outskirts of empire. Keyes read widely
and deeply, a characteristic that has been held against him by critics who fancy that
books are not a part of real life.

We have, coexisting in Keyes's poetry, three types or aspects of reality: the mind's
registering of what is immediately before it ('A caterpillar | Measures with looping
back a mulberry leaf'; 'at dawn | The sentry's feet striking the chilly yard'), the
so-called reality of wartime fame and success (as in the poem 'Timoshenko'), and
a third aspect that has to do with Rilke's allusion to the 'imageless act' which he
associates with the baneful mechanics of contemporaneity. Keyes's poetry is itself
an affirmation of the image, not for the sake of illustration or pedagogy, but as
a rebuttal of all that Rilke means by the 'imageless'. That is to say, for Keyes the
image-making is very often present as an act of public recall; or as a statement of
the fact that in history things as they were cannot be called back, though we are not
thereby released from the moral and emotional burden of recalling them:

> 'Remember the torn lace, the fine coats slashed
> With steel instead of velvet. Künersdorf
> Fought in the shallow sand was my relief.'
> 'I rode to Naseby' . . . 'And the barren land
> Of Tannenberg drank me. Remember now
> The grey and jointed corpses in the snow,
> The struggle in the drift, the numb hands freezing
> Into the bitter iron . . .'[60]

Keyes later referred to 'The Foreign Gate' as one of his 'nearest-misses';[61] John
Guenther calls it 'Auden's "fair notion fatally injured"', and goes so far as to say
that 'Certainly [Keyes] should not have published it.'[62] I think that he is wrong.
In 'The Foreign Gate', as in 'Schiller Dying', Keyes is vindicating the historical
imagination in a very particular sense.

Keyes's vision, in short, is a vision of 'a European catastrophe of the spirit',[63] and
in his poetry he makes, I believe, a deliberated choice of words, metres, and rhythms
in order to accommodate this vision. 'Schiller Dying', of November 1941, is one of
the most significant literary inventions of its period. Here it is as if Keyes were taking
on the style of Romantic-heroic, late eighteenth-century German poetry; but, in this
case, to reverse its conclusions. The whole tenor of Schiller's correspondence with

---

[59] Rilke, *Duino Elegies*, 24–5.   [60] Keyes, 'The Foreign Gate', 62.
[61] Keyes, quoted in Guenther, *Sidney Keyes*, 153.   [62] Ibid. 75.
[63] Erich Heller, *The Artist's Journey into the Interior and Other Essays* (San Diego: Harcourt Brace
Jovanovich, 1976), 47.

Goethe, and of the poetry he returned to after his seven-year silence, is alien to this portrayal of his dying. It is also alien to the description of his deathbed published by his sister-in-law.[64] This 'wheezing red-nosed ghost'—compacting in one phrase the offices of valetudinarian and clown—is an invention much in excess, not only of the official hagiography, but also of Schiller's own philosophy and poetic aura.

> Joy is waylaid and slain. It was my joy
> They murdered on the Rhenish roads, and left
> A wheezing red-nosed ghost to end the journey.
> My joy is murdered, tumbled in the ditch
> With Rousseau and Wallenstein, a black blood-welter.
> Joy, my Adonis, rise; now I can meet you
> Unmasked in all your violence, dry blood
> Hanging about your eyes, your beauty punished.[65]

Schiller's political aesthetic, whether we read that as 'joy' or 'freedom', has been pitched into the 'black blood-welter' of European *Realpolitik*; he is as much adrift as is that other major figure in Keyes's political iconography, the dispossessed peasant of the enclosures acts.[66] Keyes's view of Schiller's work and influence (changed here to catarrhal effluence) anticipates to some degree the critical attitude, expressed 'not so long after the Second World War', by the historian Erich Heller:

Friedrich Schiller is the name of a poetical disaster in the history of German literature, a disaster, however, of great splendour. His work—a lifework of considerable genius, moving single-mindedness, and great moral integrity—is a striking instance of a European catastrophe of the spirit: the invasion and partial disruption of the aesthetic faculty by unemployed religious impulses.[67]

It is not that writing about politics makes a poet significant; but when a poet as significant as Keyes chooses as his recurrent theme public and private dispossession, a new light is directed on to and against certain features of European Romanticism. He is confronting the idea of poetry as the home of the 'Tellable' by the European reality of the domain of the Unspeakable. Keyes knew about Dachau as early as May 1941.[68] In his article commissioned for the symposium *The Future of Faith* his argument is less than perfectly clear, but he appears to be saying that a reader who supposes the 'prime purpose' of the artist is 'primarily to give information about the world' is narrow-minded or short-sighted. In 1942, of course, information was deemed essential to the national well-being (for example, 'Ministry of Information'). But for Keyes the 'true artist' 'enlarges the experience

---

[64] Friedrich Schiller, *Friedrich Schiller: An Anthology for Our Time, with an Account of his Life and Work by Frederick Ungar* (New York: Frederick Ungar, 1959), 179–84.

[65] Keyes, 'Schiller Dying', in *Collected Poems*, 49.

[66] Keyes, 'Ploughman', 'A Garland for John Clare', 'Death and the Ploughman', ibid. 23, 24–6, 90–2.

[67] Heller, *Artist's Journey into the Interior and Other Essays*, 47.

[68] See Keyes, 'Europe's Prisoners', stanza 5, in *Collected Poems*, 21–2.

of his audience in a way impossible by any other means.' 'He is neither propagating a doctrine nor "expressing himself"; rather he is letting the world express him and giving himself entirely to something outside himself.' Nonetheless, by so doing, 'the artist is . . . directly contributing not only to the growth of the individual spirit, but to the efficiency of society.'[69]

We must endeavour to weigh the poetry of Keyes and Douglas, and Allison and Alun Lewis, all four killed in 1943–4, with and against the priorities of the Second World War and of the 1930s which culminated in that war. For instance, both Keyes and Allison wrote poems in 1942 celebrating the Soviet general Timoshenko.[70] John Guenther, in his compact biography of Keyes, refers to Timoshenko's name being 'in the newspapers'[71] during September 1942, and there is an editorial note confirming this fact and date in the Orwell–Angus edition of George Orwell's writings.[72] Whatever brief *réclame* Timoshenko enjoyed in the British newspapers, it was, it seems, a seven days' wonder. I cite it here as a counterweight to the notion discussed above that Keyes is prevailingly a poet of the private world.

Keyes's 'Timoshenko', a poor poem that cannot surmount its own hyperbole and is coarsened by the obvious and inert ('His eyes grew cold as lead'), is significant only in that it shows Keyes attempting to project an image in cinematic terms ('He turned, and his great shadow on the wall . . . '). The poem, dated September 1942, goes for the symbolically projected decisive moment: what we call fate, destiny, issuing from the solitary act of decision. It shows, also, a young poet taking his bearings from the public domain, a *Daily Mail* or *News of the World* type of newsworthiness. It is as if Keyes were seeking to emulate the public oratory of British poetry of the Spanish Civil War. Rather than talking of his 'distorting eye', it might be closer to the mark to suggest that he tried briefly to blend Expressionism with Socialist Realism, and that the attempt failed. 'Timoshenko' has always struck me as a somewhat naive hymn to Soviet 'efficiency', and to that extent entirely characteristic of public eulogy of its period. It needs to be added that in certain conditions distortion is normative, and that in such poems as 'Schiller Dying' and 'The Foreign Gate', among others, Keyes accepts this as given and is happy (I mean technically happy) to record it.

Desmond Graham has noted that Keith Douglas, shortly before his death, was 'once again acting out the conflict between too much and too little feeling'.[73] This is well said, and gives us a way into reading such early and late poems as 'The Poets', 'An Exercise Against Impatience', the 'Songs', 'This is the Dream', 'On a Return

[69] Keyes, 'Artist in Society', 146.

[70] See Keyes, 'Timoshenko', in *Collected Poems*, 85; Drummond Allison, *The Yellow Night: Poems 1940–41–42–43* (London: The Fortune Press, 1945), 24 ('For J. G.', final phrase—'Christ and Timoshenko share his fears').

[71] Guenther, *Sidney Keyes*, 133.

[72] George Orwell, *The Collected Essays, Journalism and Letters of George Orwell*, ii: *My Country Right or Left, 1940–1943*, ed. Sonia Orwell and Ian Angus (Harmondsworth: Penguin, 1970), 499 n. 3.

[73] Graham, *Keith Douglas 1920–1944*, 244.

from Egypt', and numerous others. The conflict in Keyes needs to be defined in other terms, though obviously there are several points at which their individual tangents intersect. It is as if Keyes is obeying Pound's injunction to achieve some 'degree of poignancy in one's utterance' while, at the same time, 'giving a feeling of reality to the speaker':

> 'At Dunkirk I
> Rolled in the shallows, and the living trod
> Across me for a bridge . . . '[74]

Douglas might say that Keyes is not entitled to write this, because he was not at Dunkirk, and because the dead do not speak. He might expect us to contrast Keyes to Rosenberg, whom Douglas so justly admired.

> The wheels lurched over sprawled dead
> But pained them not, though their bones crunched.[75]

Or he might wish to put forward his own.

> The eye and mouth of each figure
> bear the cosmetic blood and hectic
> colours death has the only list of.[76]

One can praise Douglas's poetry without agreeing that such an objection would be valid. Rosenberg succeeds because he finds the precisely callous verb—'crunched'; Douglas succeeds because he finds the tellingly vacuous epithet—'cosmetic'—and the nonchalant syntax—'death has the only list of'; Keyes succeeds because the phrase 'the living trod | Across me' itself treads across the end of one line and plants itself in the next; and because the poignancy is achieved by an extreme form of emotionally drained matter-of-factness.

It is good that one can describe the achievements of all three poets through attention to matters of detail such as I have here listed. One can also cite a broader field of comparison. The varied distinction of Douglas, Rosenberg, and Keyes stands out by contrast with a quantity of verse written by servicemen, in North Africa and other spheres of war, who were not poets but who wished to communicate sincerely and memorably their experiences of battle or of base camp. I quote some lines by an exact contemporary of Douglas in the desert campaign; like Douglas serving in tanks with the rank of captain:

> She falls to earth.
> And there's a breathless hush upon the land
> For death is near.

---

[74] Keyes, 'The Foreign Gate', 62.
[75] Isaac Rosenberg, 'Dead Man's Dump', in *The Poems and Plays of Isaac Rosenberg*, ed. Vivien Noakes (Oxford: Oxford University Press, 2004), 139.
[76] Keith Douglas, 'Landscape with Figures 2', 110.

> Her grave stands open to the sky;
> And there she lies together with
> The shattered limbs and bleeding mouths
> And eyes that nevermore shall see.[77]

This is a good try, but no more. It is necessary to quote it because it is 'people's poetry' as Rosenberg's and Douglas's and Keyes's is not; and People's Poetry is at present heavily and polemically called upon in denunciations of élitism. In the context of this demand, Private Rosenberg, the small-statured poverty-stricken East End Jew, is almost certainly an élitist; as Keyes and Douglas also are.[78]

Michael Schmidt writes that Douglas's rhythms 'are original in the way they advance speaking and are not betrayed into singing cadences'.[79] But this is unfair to the singing cadence. There is more to it than 'betrayal'; in any case, the speaking voice has its own systems of betrayal, as is demonstrated by many poets from 'Movement' to Mersey Sound.[80] Historically, of course, these are the voice rhythms that have won out over the style of Keyes, which is essentially one of elegiac declamation. It is appropriate to return here to Charles Williams's 'the sense which poetry has of its own vigil before its own approaching greatness'. I would describe most of Keyes's poems as vigils, and vigils that are aware of an approaching greatness, even if Keyes did not live long enough to fulfil his quest. Keyes's 'vigil' poems occur throughout his work, and include 'Nocturne for Four Voices', 'Lament for Dead Symbolists', 'Elegy for Mrs. Virginia Woolf', 'Europe's Prisoners', 'A Garland for John Clare', 'All Souls: A Dialogue', 'Schiller Dying', 'The Foreign Gate', 'Lament for Adonis', 'Lament for Harpsichord: The Flowering Orchards', 'Two Offices of a Sentry', 'The Expected Guest', 'Actaeon's Lament', and 'The Wilderness'.

---

[77] Major Robert Crisp, 'The Shell', in *Brazen Chariots* (New York: Bantam Books, 1978), 186–7. The verses are attributed by the author to Captain Browne, Royal Tank Regiment.

[78] Rosenberg to Ruth Löwy, in *The Collected Works of Isaac Rosenberg*, ed. Ian Parsons (London: Chatto & Windus, 1979), 185: 'Nothing is rarer than good poetry—and nothing more discouraging than the writing of poetry. One might write for pleasure but I doubt[,] if there is no stronger motive[,] whether one would be incited to ambitious work.'

Keyes, 'Artist in Society', 149: 'It is no use giving "art to the people" while the structure of society, which prevents the mass of people from appreciating good art, remains unchanged. In an insecure, unplanned society such as ours, no one has a right to complain that art is obscure or out of touch with the people.'

Douglas, 'Poets in This War', in *The Letters*, ed. Desmond Graham (Manchester: Carcanet, 2000), 351: 'So far I have not mentioned the name of a poet "of the present war". I might refuse to on the grounds that it is unnecessary: for I do not find even one who stands out as an individual . . . . There have been desperately intelligent conscientious objectors, R.A.M.C. orderlies, students. In the fourth year of this war we have not a single poet who seems likely to be an impressive commentator on it.'

[79] Michael Schmidt, *Lives of the Poets* (London: Weidenfeld & Nicolson, 1998), 801.

[80] See e.g. Robert Conquest (ed.), *New Lines* (London: Macmillan, 1956), *passim*, uses of 'yet', 'but', 'so', 'we', 'our'. See also *The Mersey Sound*, Penguin Modern Poets, 10 (Harmondsworth: Penguin, 1983; 1st pub. 1967), *passim*.

One notices in this list the frequent occurrence of the word 'Lament': it is the equivalent of Pound's 'poignancy'. In his foreword to *Eight Oxford Poets*, Keyes wrote of himself and his fellow authors:

We seem to share . . . the feeling that we cannot save ourselves without some kind of spiritual readjustment, though the nature of that readjustment may take widely differing forms. In technique there is also some similarity between us; we are all . . . *Romantic* writers, though I mean little more than that our greatest fault is a tendency to floridity; and that we have, on the whole, little sympathy with the Audenian school of poets.[81]

Let us consider first the phrase 'some kind of spiritual readjustment'. In 1987 the military historian James Lucas, who as Private Lucas was Keyes's runner in the battle for Oued Zarga, contributed invaluable details to our knowledge of the poet's last hours. Lucas concluded his memoir with the valediction 'he was a gallant Christian gentleman who sacrificed himself for the men under his command.'[82] I think Keyes would have shrugged off the title 'Christian gentleman'. It is true that two of his poetic mentors—Eliot and Williams—were devout High Churchmen, and that Keyes was 'immensely impressed' by Williams's *The Descent of the Dove*; but he also read with interest Maud Bodkin's Jungian *Archetypal Patterns in Poetry*.[83] My sense is that Christianity was for him a richly available myth on a par with *The Golden Bough* or the mystical cosmos of Jung or Yeats. He read Jung,[84] and he might, had he lived, have become in middle age a familiar kind of Jungian Christian; but the point he had reached at the time of his death could better be described as stoic:

We walked together through the gloom of the brief twilight, the smoke of the explosions and the dust. He pointed at something on the ground and told me that it was the German sign marking a mine field. We were, therefore, crossing one.[85]

We might look next at the suggestion of 'a tendency to floridity'. Keyes's poetry sometimes suggests floridity (for example, 'Lament for Harpsichord: The Flowering Orchards', a vigil under the aegis of Couperin); that is to say, in one case he equates his imagery with the flowers of nature and of rhetoric as they were conceived by late seventeenth-century French harpsichordists. It is a style of extended troping. However, when Keyes uses the term 'Romantic' as if it is inevitably the source merely of 'floridity', he does his own work less than justice. The tradition in which he writes, the quality to which he aspires, is that of the self-sufficiency of the achieved poem. His criteria, knowingly or not, derive from the crucial tenets of Romanticism and Romantic Modernism—from Schiller, through the heavily indebted Coleridge, to Riding and Graves:

---

[81] Keyes, quoted in Herbert Read, 'Preface', in Keyes, *Collected Poems* (New York: Henry Holt, 1947), p. ix.

[82] Lucas, 'Memoir', 127.   [83] See Heath-Stubbs, *Hindsights*, 86–7.

[84] See Guenther, *Sidney Keyes*, 153.   [85] Lucas, 'Memoir', in Keyes, 126.

Beauty can be evaluated according to an objective criterion. An object is beautiful when it appears free and independent of natural causes.[86]

... nothing can permanently please, which does not contain in itself the reason why it is so, and not otherwise.[87]

As a matter of fact all that has happened is that he [the writer] has made the poem out of the poem itself: its final form is identical with its preliminary form in the poet's mind, uncorrupted by hints to the reader, familiar asides to make it less terrifying.[88]

Some will call this opinion; I venture to call it an acute perception of the nature of all major poetry: the eloquence growing out of, and returning to, itself, a claim that can be demonstrated, by practical criticism, in the case of Shakespeare's dozen or so great sonnets, *Paradise Regain'd*, *The Dunciad*, 'Ode to a Nightingale', 'Sunday Morning', the 'Byzantium' poems, and numerous others. Keyes's 'William Wordsworth' has something of this kind of power, as do a number of Douglas's finest poems, and Drummond Allison's 'The Brass Horse':

> Never presume that in this marble stable
> Furnished with imitation stalactites,
> Withheld from any manger and unable
> To stamp impatient hooves or show the whites
> Of eyes whose lids are fixed, on sulky nights
> He asks himself no questions, has no doubt
> What he a brazen engine is about.
>   .   .   .   .
> We cannot guess what thoughts of combination
> With the decaying cayman on the wall
> Or the snow leopard blinded by elation
> Trouble him in his Brahmin-carven stall,
> For what Arabian mares and ribboned manes
> He writhes his motionless metallic reins.[89]

Allison, Douglas, and Keyes are all without 'hints to the reader' as Riding and Graves intend the phrase, whereas Elizabeth Jennings, say, cannot do without them. This is not the same thing as suggesting that public attitudes towards accessibility do not feature in the work of these three young war poets. They feature, but as a kind of contingent factor or force by which to gauge the integrity and independence of the individual voice.

---

[86] Schiller, *Friedrich Schiller: An Anthology for Our Time*, 67.

[87] Samuel Taylor Coleridge, *Biographia Literaria*, ed. James Engell and Walter Jackson Bate, in *The Collected Works of Samuel Taylor Coleridge*, vii (London and Princeton: Routledge and Princeton University Press, 1983), ii. 12.

[88] Laura Riding and Robert Graves, A *Survey of Modernist Poetry* (London: William Heinemann, 1929), 142.

[89] Allison, 'The Brass Horse', in *Yellow Night*, 22.

It cannot be stated too strongly that the pressure of expectation in the reading public, or, rather, the force of that expectation as ventriloquized by 'leading' critics, is enormous. It requires confidence in one's own integrity of voice to withstand what I have just referred to as contingent factors. It is one of the tragedies of late Wordsworth and late Tennyson that in old age their individual voices became increasingly less able to distinguish themselves from the voice of expectation. The poetry of late Auden is manifestly the work of a thoroughly tamed poet; and *About the House* is a nicely house-trained book. It is not necessarily an advantage to die young: one knows more than one poet satisfactorily broken in by the time of her or his first pamphlet.

Keyes, in 'The Artist in Society', remarks that at the turn of the nineteenth–twentieth centuries there were 'two possible ways out of [the] impasse. The artist could either secede entirely from society, and retire to a world of personal symbols and values; or he could become a painstaking recorder of the physical world.'[90] I take 'impasse' to refer to matters outlined in this and the preceding paragraph. Douglas, at first impression, is more the painstaking recorder of the physical world; Keyes, on first acquaintance, more engrossed in 'a world of personal symbols'—but this leaves us with the awkward verbs 'retire' and 'secede'; and I would strongly rebut the suggestion that Keyes is any kind of secessionist. The poet who, for the space of a single poem, seems to hold the alternatives in exquisite balance is Drummond Allison in 'The Brass Horse'. With Keyes, again, it seems more a case of taking public responsibility for one's personal symbols:

For Milein, l.xii.41

Talk stopped, and the five-fingered hand of sense
Crouched like a creature. Your amazing eyes
Swung inward suddenly, pulling me down
Among the debris of my broken gestures.
And there were lives perversely otherwise
Than ours, yet like; and possible
Solutions to the fearsome riddle
That ravished my mind's country. There was Chartres
Reeling with insult; my own vanity
Of clockwork bird and painted loneliness
Rubble upon that place, rabble upon
The guarded stairs of your mind's secret place.
And there were pictured rivers unexplored
By us; and unmapped forests we could tame
With my hard hand and your bright eyes to guide it.
There were the foundling hours now wandering
Homeless and eager for our saving friendship.
There was a lake, Mozart beside a lake

---

[90] Keyes, 'Artist in Society', 142–3.

Plucking the bitter-fruited orange Fame;
Long ways of hopeful windows; the old year
Stretching its straitjacket of ice and crying
For us to rescue summer. All these images
Lay in that place.
                        Words fell between the picture
And its projection, as your face changed quickly.
Rilke a moment wandered between our eyes
Gazing in each, seeing in separation
A central unity: the whitestone angel standing
Between us irrefutably, teaching our world
Humility and peace. Our peace, our poem.[91]

This is an uneven work, in contrast to 'William Wordsworth', which seems to me totally *au fait* with itself. Nonetheless, it possesses within its imperfection several of the qualities to which I have previously pointed. The poem in fact ends (the concluding seven lines) as if it were indeed a perfectly achieved thing: this is largely due, as in poems noted in this discussion, to the intermingling of intensity and sobriety that results from the rapid change of image 'shots' contained by Keyes's characteristically measured verse paragraphing. The flaws are merely local irritants (*why* 'five-fingered hand of sense'? Surely the 'five' is redundant because everyone knows about the five senses?), and are outweighed by the numerous felicities ('Your amazing eyes', 'the old year | Stretching its straitjacket of ice', 'Homeless and eager for our saving friendship'). 'Your amazing eyes' is not a mere cliché of mid-twentieth-century Petrarchism. Elsewhere in the poem it might have been: it is all a question of careful placing. Coming as it does in the second line, the quality of *being* amazing in oneself infiltrates or diffuses into the rest of the poem, which is a poem of amazement that anything can survive such débâcles as the fall of France ('Chartres | Reeling with insult'), the more intimate débâcle of passionate, wholly unrequited love, and the petty inevitabilities and inadvertences of contingent circumstance ('And there were lives perversely otherwise | Than ours, yet like'). No one but a young maestro could have placed the line 'Homeless and eager for our saving friendship': syntactically it is the 'foundling hours' of shared experience that will not now take place which are predicated by the phrase; in Keyes's symbolic grammar it is the entire experience of their close, frustrated encounter, it is themselves who are to be saved by friendship amazingly won from rejection by an act of making. So that, finally, friendship in separateness achieves the other separateness, the other finality, which is the poem.

To turn to further details of placement and cadence: since my discussion has throughout remarked the presence of Rilke, we observe his presence in this poem also; and perhaps an allusion to Mörike—his novella *Mozart on the Way to Prague*.[92]

---

[91] Keyes, 'For Milein, l.xii.41', in *Collected Poems* (2002), 108–9.
[92] Eduard Mörike, *Mozart on the Way to Prague*, trans. Walter and Catherine Alison Phillips (New York: Pantheon Books, 1947), 41–8, 73–9.

And Yeats is also here, in the clockwork bird.[93] Secondly, among the felicities of detail, the fact that the angel is of 'whitestone': there is a full ambience evoked by that epithet, whether of Chartres or the graveyard of St Peter's in the East, Oxford, where Keyes walked and talked with Milein Cosman.[94] Equally well tuned is the pitch of 'And there were lives perversely otherwise | Than ours', where 'perversely' is both a specification for obtrusive circumstance so much an Other that it appears malign, and also the voicing of a kind of solipsistic petulance that resents the presence of others at all. And 'irrefutably' is both the nature of the obstruction and the saving obduracy of the 'poem', the irrefutable nature of the 'peace' arrived at only because this particular poem is its vehicle.

Judging by the work that survives, I believe the following conclusion has to be drawn: that Keyes is a minor poet but with a potential for greatness, whereas Douglas is a major poet though on a small scale. To say this is not to dispute the validity of Jeffrey Wainwright's own summing up: that Keyes's poems 'written through the summer of 1942 . . . are a great achievement. Their mythological and historical sweep befits a time of world war, and along with this external awareness is psychological insight into the tortuous interactions of love and destructiveness.'[95]

A final word on historical perspective. I have known Keyes's poetry for almost sixty years, since I discovered his 1945 *Collected Poems* at the age of 16 or 17 in a Scarborough bookshop. During all that time he has never ceased to move, delight, and instruct me. I owe him an immense debt that I cannot repay, except, most inadequately, in this present tribute.

---

[93] See Yeats, 'Sailing to Byzantium', in *The Poems*, ed. Daniel Albright (London: Dent, 1990), 239–40.

[94] See Milein Cosman, 'Memoir', in Keyes, *Collected Poems* (2002), 115.

[95] Jeffrey Wainwright, 'Introduction', ibid. p. xiv.

PART V

CONTINUITIES IN MODERN WAR POETRY

CHAPTER 22

ANTHOLOGIZING WAR

HUGH HAUGHTON

I

In 2003, on the eve of the US-led invasion of Iraq, Sam Hamil published *Poets Against the War*, selected from 11,000 poems posted on <poetsagainstthewar.org>. According to the editor, 'Never before in recorded history . . . has a single-theme anthology of this proportion been assembled.'[1] The poets include big names like Robert Creeley and Adrienne Rich, and, while the instant chorus is inevitably rhetorical, it is sometimes powerful. Sherman Pearl makes the claim that 'The Poem in Time of War' should 'carry the news that men | die miserably for lack of', be a 'paper megaphone | for the voices of the dead', and steal from 'forebears' like 'Sassoon's doomed diary and Auden's call to love'.[2] 'All the war poems', she says, 'could be sewn together | into a vast thick quilt' to 'keep us warm.' The war anthology, on this model, is simultaneously political protest and comforting expression of solidarity in time of national crisis. On the other side of the Atlantic, Matthew Hollis and Paul Keegan made a comparable, smaller-scale intervention with *101 Poems Against War*.[3] Such books indicate the political as well as poetic currency of the war anthology.

Sherman Pearl's poem invokes Sassoon and Auden, English poets associated with the two World Wars, recalling the intimate alliance between war and poetry forged in the twentieth century. Sewing poems together is what anthologies do,

---

[1] Sam Hamil, *idem* (ed.), *Poets Against the War* (New York: Thunder Mouth Press, 2003), p. xvii.
[2] Ibid. 172.
[3] Paul Keegan and Matthew Hollis (eds.), *101 Poems Against War* (London: Faber, 2003).

and anthologies have played a central role in the construction and reconstruction of the 'war poem' and 'war poet'. Though war, like love, has been the subject of poetry since the Bible and classical epic, 'war poetry' is a largely twentieth-century invention. It is only in our time that Mars, the god of Battles, has joined Venus as presiding deity of anthologies.

In the 1920s Robert Graves, a poet who figured in several First World War anthologies, co-wrote (with Laura Riding) *A Pamphlet Against Anthologies*, a caustic attack on anthologies of all kinds, and particularly the 'anthology poem'. It came out the same year as *Goodbye to All That* (1928), and alludes to 'Living-Poet' compilations which deal in 'marketable sentiment' aroused by public events such as 'the Outbreak of War' or 'Victory', but it avoids war poetry.[4] The war anthology, however, represents one of the most marketable, though contentious, literary institutions of our time. It is a place where potentially opposed notions of patriotism and idealism are fought out, but also different models of the role of poet and poetry in terms of aesthetic and political values.

Were it not for the immense investment in war poetry as 'marketable sentiment' in newspapers and anthologies, it is unlikely that we would have the First World War poems of Owen, Sassoon, Rosenberg, and Gurney, or even the Second World War poems of Keith Douglas, Randall Jarrell, and Auden. It was during the middle of the First World War that the 'soldier-poet' first appeared on the scene, testing the poetic rhetoric of the past against the realities of modern warfare. In *The Missing of the Somme*, Geoff Dyer argues that the image of Owen as war poet, like the War Memorial, was one of the war's enduring symbolic legacies: 'our memory of the Great War depends', he says, 'on two ostensibly opposed coordinates: the Unknown Soldier and the poet everyone knows'.[5] Like the memorials and the tomb, however, it was largely constructed in the wake of the conflict. Apart from Rupert Brooke, Thomas Hardy, Julian Grenfell, and Alan Seeger, whose 'anthology poems' 'The Soldier', 'Men Who March Away', 'Into Battle', and 'I Have a Rendezvous with Death' were represented in anthologies then as now, the poets we see as typical of the war—Owen, Rosenberg, Edward Thomas, Ivor Gurney, David Jones, and Edmund Blunden—were largely absent from contemporary compilations. Even late in the war, the popular anthologies contained few of the poets or poems that make up the canon, and plenty of names that are now forgotten. As Edgell Rickword said, 'for the most part, the valuable war books were written after the Armistice,' and 'it was not until after the war that the fighting soldier could get square with his bitterest enemy, the journalist.'[6] Owen published only five poems during the war, while the best war poetry of Gurney, Jones, Blunden, and others

---

[4] Laura Riding and Robert Graves, *A Survey of Modernist Poetry and A Pamphlet Against Anthologies*, ed. Charles Mundye and Patrick McGuinness (Manchester: Carcanet, 2002), 239.

[5] Geoff Dyer, *The Missing of the Somme* (Harmondsworth: Penguin, 1995), 29.

[6] Edgell Rickword, 'War and Poetry (1914–1918), Part 2: From Rhetoric to Realism', *Life and Letters Today*, 35 (July 1940), 26.

post-dated it. The posthumous collections of Owen (1920) and Rosenberg (1922) were complemented by the post-war memoirs, Blunden's *Undertones of War* (1928), Graves's *Goodbye to All That* (1929), and Sassoon's *Memoirs of an Infantry Officer* (1930). It was these that forged the figure of the archetypal 'war poet' as a battle-traumatized soldier writing in protest against it. The first anthology to represent this was Frederick Brereton's *An Anthology of War Poems* (1930). It had an introduction on 'The Soldier Poets' by Edmund Blunden, opposing the writers in the trenches to the 'melodious patriots, seated at their customary tables',[7] and it identified the appearance of the 'war poet' with Sassoon, 'the first man' who 'described war fully and exactly', closely followed by Owen.

In an essay on 'The Poets of World War II', Robert Graves observed that 'war poet' and 'war poetry' were 'terms first used in World War I and perhaps peculiar to it'.[8] 'In previous wars', he went on, 'there had been patriotic verse and poems written in time of war, and even occasional poems written by soldiers on campaign', but not 'war poems in the now accepted sense'. He thought that the 'war poetry boom' following the death of Rupert Brooke gradually developed from conventional expressions of patriotic feeling to the expression of 'war neurosis' and critique, culminating in ferocious documentary works like Owen's 'Dulce et Decorum Est' and Sassoon's 'Does it Matter?' Looking back from the Second World War, he argued that such war poetry was unlikely to be produced again, given that conscription had done away with the recruiting imperative and the support for the war against Nazism. Like Graves, the poets and editors of the Second World War inevitably took their bearings from the literature of the First World War, but were engaged in a very different mechanized global war in the new literary climate of the age of Auden. In the earlier war the soldier-poet had displaced the civilians, but in the Second World War the line between the field of battle and ordinary life broke down, and the catastrophic effects of aerial bombardment, Nazism, and the Holocaust affected everyone, not only the armed forces. The question 'Where are the War Poets?' was repeatedly raised in poems and newspapers, but there was no shortage of poets or anthologies, and the real questions were '*Who* are the war poets?' and 'What is a war poem?'. Keidrich Rhys's *Poems from the Forces* (1941) argued fiercely for the work of the 'poet in uniform',[9] while Tambimuttu's *Poetry in War-time* (1942) operated with a notion of 'war-time' rather than 'war' poetry.[10] In fact, as with the First World War, it was only in retrospect that the scale and nature of the new war poetry came to be recognized (and even written), and that poets such as Keith Douglas, Hamish Henderson,

---

[7] Edmund Blunden, 'The Soldier Poets of 1914–1918', in Frederick Brereton (ed.), *An Anthology of War Poems* (London: W. Collins & Son, 1930), 13–14.

[8] Robert Graves, 'The Poets of World War II', in *The Common Asphodel: Collected Essays on Poetry 1922–1949* (London: Hamish Hamilton, 1949), 307.

[9] Keidrich Rhys, 'Introduction', in *idem* (ed.), *Poems from the Forces: A Collection of Verses by Serving Members of the Navy, Army, and Air Force* (London: George Routledge & Sons, 1941), p. xiv.

[10] See M. J. Tambimuttu (ed.), *Poetry in War-time: An Anthology* (London: Faber, 1942).

Alun Lewis, and Randall Jarrell were acknowledged as the dominant voices. The pioneering anthology here was Oscar Williams's *The War Poets: An Anthology of the War Poetry of the 20th Century* (1945), to be followed twenty years later by a new wave of anthologies in the 1960s and after, operating with very different models of the war canon. The twentieth century was defined by catastrophic global wars, and the late-century multiplication of war anthologies clearly reflects that, while providing an index of changing views of what Geoffrey Hill calls 'History as Poetry'.[11]

II

Catherine Reilly records at least fifty wartime anthologies in her *English Poetry of the First World War: A Bibliography*, a sign of the role poetry played in constructing Britain as an 'imagined community'[12] in response to the unprecedented mass war and its massive casualties overseas. As early as 1914, *Poems of the Great War* appeared, with poems by Newbolt, Kipling, Binyon, and Chesterton, alongside *Songs and Sonnets for England in War Time: A Collection of Lyrics by Various Authors Inspired by the Great War,* and Foster's *Lord God of Battles: A War Anthology,* with much the same patriotic cast. Foster's book opened with a call to arms from the Poet Laureate Robert Bridges ('Stand, England, for honour | And God guard the right'[13]), but mainly recycled patriotic ammunition from Shakespeare's *Henry V* to Wordsworth's 'Happy Warrior' via 'Rule Britannia'. In contrast, *Songs and Sonnets* claimed that, while there were anthologies of 'poems of war without number', it was 'unique' in being 'formed during the conflict itself'.[14] Its poets were members of the peacetime poetry establishment, and reflected the journalistic currency of the war poem in civilian Britain rather than 'in the conflict itself'.

Other patriotic anthologies included W. J. Haliday's *Pro Patria: A Book of Patriotic Verse* (1915), C. F. Forshaw's *One Hundred Best Poems of the European War by Poets of the Empire* (1915), and MacDonald and Ford's *A Crown of Amaranth: A Collection of Poems to the Memory of the Brave and Gallant Gentlemen who have Given their Lives for Great and Greater Britain* (1917). Such patriotic garlands and crowns were more various than they sound. *Pro Patria*, a chronological anthology running from medieval ballads to the present, included patriotic poems of other countries, including Russia, the USA, and Ireland. Ending with the national anthems of Allied countries, it even made room for anti-British patriotic songs like 'The Shan Van

---

[11] Geoffrey Hill, 'History as Poetry', in *Collected Poems* (Harmondsworth: Penguin, 1985), 84.

[12] Benedict Anderson, *Imagined Communities* (London: Verso, 1983), 9 ff.

[13] Robert Bridges, 'Stand, England, for honour', in A. E. Manning Foster (ed.), *Lord God of Battles: A War Anthology* (London: Cope & Fenwick, 1914), 8.

[14] 'Publisher's Note', in *Songs and Sonnets for England in War Time* (London: John Lane, The Bodley Head, 1914), p. viii.

Vocht' and 'A Nation Once Again'. By contrast, C. F. Forshaw's *One Hundred Best Poems on the European War by Poets of Empire* (1915) and its sequel, *One Hundred Best Poems on the European War by Women Poets of the Empire* (1916), represented writers with a relentlessly imperial and militaristic agenda. One poem called out 'Come Forward, Sons of Britain', another invoked 'Great England, Scotland—ay, and Erin too', while everywhere 'The Empire's Call Rings Out!' 'A Call to Arms' has as its chorus 'Briton, play the man', embodying a lethal combination of coercive masculinity and recruiting slogan. Another is directed against the Hun and 'ruthless Goth', while invoking the 'Alliance between Valour, God and Right, | A triple union that our Shakespeare sung'. Yet another asserts that 'Trafalgar and Waterloo | Were won by what we call the Crowd'. Such historic rhetoric was clearly directed to the modern crowd, as confirmed by the Revd. J. G. Gibson's 'Soldier Boy's Last Letter': 'It's not hard for me to die— | I'm dying for you all. | Ask all the boys to come and fight | At your boy's dying call.'[15] This is the poem as recruitment poster.

Such anthologies for the home market were complemented by collections of soldiers' songs. A poignant example is Stephen Gwynn and T. M. Kettle's *Battle Songs of the Irish Brigades* (1915), including Kettle's 'Paddy', which gives Kipling's 'Tommy' a nationalistic Irish accent: 'We ain't no saints or scholars much, but fightin' men and clean; | /We've paid the price, and three times thrice, for Wearin' o' the Green.'[16] Kettle was a nationalist who threw himself into the Irish recruitment campaign, and paid with his death in France for wearing the khaki. More typical was F. T. Nettleingham's *Tommy's Tunes* (1917), subtitled 'A comprehensive collection of soldiers' songs, marching melodies, rude rhymes and popular parodies, collected and arranged on active service with the B.E.F.'[17] Such songs were designed to keep up the morale of soldiers, and combine regimental swagger, irreverence, and a ballad sense of history. Their cheerfully vernacular tone and down-to-earth imagery are a breath of fresh air after the fusty solemnity of civilian verse.

'Among the minor results of the Great War is a vast output of war literature', wrote the Canadian Carrie Holman introducing *In the Day of Battle: Poems of the Great War* (1916), the poems of which were marked not by 'the bugle note of actual conflict' but by 'the deeper chord of their intense and ideal patriotism which alone can justify war'.[18] Her anthology drew on fifty-seven non-combatants, sixteen of whom were women, and included poems like Mary Booth's 'The Women of Belgium to the Women of England' and Marion Smith's 'St Jeanne of France', reflecting an international as well as a feminine perspective. The same is true of

[15] In Charles F. Forshaw (ed.), *One Hundred Poems of the European War by Poets of the Empire* (London: Elliott Stock, 1915), 9, 68, 141, 92, 92, 154, 180, 79.

[16] T. K. Kettle, 'Paddy', in Stephen Gwynn and T. K. Kettle (eds.), *Battle Songs of the Irish Brigades* (Dublin: Maunsel, 1915), 26.

[17] For further details, see Catherine Reilly, *English Poetry of the First World War: A Bibliography* (London: George Prior, 1978).

[18] Carrie Ellen Holman, 'Foreword', in *idem* (ed.), *In the Day of Battle: Poems of the Great War* (Toronto: William Briggs, 1916), 7.

A Crown of Amaranth, a collection of heroic elegies for 'brave and gallant gentlemen of all ranks' culled from journals and newspapers from *The Times* to *The Woman at Home*, designed to offer 'heartease to those who proudly mourn', like the 'earliest tribal bards', but with a 'loftier' sense of patriotism.[19] Twelve of the forty-one poets represented were women, including Katharine Tynan and Alice Meynell, veterans of many anthologies. A poem called 'The Women' asserts the patriotism of those who 'give our dearest to be food | For lyddite, shrapnel, mitrailleuse and shell', and affirms, 'Not they who die, not they alone, but we, | Uphold the Flag against the constant stars.'[20] It is hard not to read such poems in the light of Sassoon's 'Glory of Women', with its ferocious rebuff that 'You love us when we're heroes home on leave',[21] but such poems remind us that the war represented an unprecedented crisis of solidarity and mourning for women. As Claire Buck notes, 'of the more than 2,000 poets publishing during these years a quarter were women. By contrast soldiers on active service wrote less than a fifth of the total output.' This is not, she observes, 'recorded in later anthologies or criticism'.[22]

The soldier-poet arrived, in patriotic dress, with Galloway Kyle's *Soldier Poets: Songs of the Fighting Men* (1916) published in a special 'Trench edition'. It included poems on 'Givenchy Field' and 'No Man's Land' which anticipate now familiar verse by Sassoon and Owen, as well as poems addressed 'To the Rats' and on 'A Lark above the Trenches', which point towards Rosenberg. Nonetheless, *Songs of the Fighting Men* and its follow-up, *More Songs of the Fighting Men* (1917), combine realism with patriotism in ways very different from them. There are two poems entitled 'Dulce et Decorum est Pro Patria Mori', for example. In one, dead soldiers gain 'a name of lasting glory' in 'the People's narrative', while in the other we hear 'If England calls to-day— | The last long call of all, | Valhalla's trumpet call'.[23] These are soldier poems which embody just the kind of patriotic bugle-work that Owen's poetry was trying to combat in his poem with the same title.

E. B. Osborn's *The Muse in Arms* (1917) was designed, according to the editor, 'to show what passes in the British Warrior's soul when, in moments of aspiration

[19] See Erskine MacDonald and S. Gertrude Ford, 'Editorial Note', in *idem* (eds.), *A Crown of Amaranth: Being a Collection of Poems to the Memory of the Brave and Gallant Gentlemen who have Given their Lives for Great & Greater Britain, MCMXIV–MCMXVII* (London: Erskine MacDonald, 1917), n.p.

[20] B. M. Hetherington, 'The Women', ibid. 39.

[21] Siegfried Sassoon, 'Glory of Women', in *Collected Poems 1908–1956* (London: Faber, 1984), 72.

[22] Claire Buck, 'British Women's Writing of the Great War', in Vincent Sherry (ed.), *The Cambridge Companion to the Literature of the First World War* (Cambridge: Cambridge University Press, 2005), 87.

[23] Sydney Oswald, 'Dulce et Decorum est pro Patria Mori', in Galloway Kyle (ed.), *Soldier Poets: Songs of the Fighting Men* (London: Erskine MacDonald, 1916), 69; Harold John Jarvis, 'Dulce et Decorum est Pro Patria Mori', in Kyle (ed.), *More Songs of the Fighting Men: Soldier Poets: Second Series* (London: Erskine MacDonald, 1917), 73.

or inspiration . . . he has glimpses of the ultimate significance of warfare'.[24] Far from warning of the pity of war, this late war book aimed to illustrate the warrior's 'singular capacity for remembering the splendour and forgetting the squalor' of his 'dreadful vocation'. Selecting only work by 'the new soldier poet'—of which he says 'There has been nothing like it before in the history of English literature'—he presents his anthology as 'the first coherent picture of the British warrior's moods and emotions in war-time', therefore 'more valuable than the huge harvest of war poetry by civilian verse-makers'. Dismissing the work of German soldiers as of 'less value than Zulu war-chants', he praises the 'modern Sidneys and Raleighs' who 'keep to conventional forms' and 'the traditional currency of thought'. Robert Graves called it a 'typical anthology' of the time, with 'authors drawn from almost every regiment', 'all very gallant and idealistic but with hardly a poet among them'.[25]

Setting the mould for later anthologies, *The Muse in Arms* is divided into broadly chronological thematic sections. Starting with 'The Mother Land', it graduates to 'Battle Pieces' and on to 'In Memoriam' and 'The Future Hope' by way of 'The Christian Soldier', 'School and College', and 'The Chivalry of Sport'. Though it prints three poems by Gurney and Graves, including 'David and Goliath', there are only two by Sassoon, the uncharacteristic early 'Absolution', which affirms 'We are the happy legion', and the tougher 'The Rear-Guard', which speaks of 'Unloading hell behind him step by step'.[26] The 'happy legion' falls easily into place in Osborn's anthology, with its happy allegiance to the classical past, Christian Church, and public school. In 'The Road', Gordon Alchin equates modern soldiers with 'Caesar's legions', while Alexander Robertson sees in Gallipoli 'what once was partly hid, | The splendid pageant of the Aeneid'. W. N. Hodgson's 'Before Action' prays 'Make me a soldier, Lord', and soldiering and Christianity go hand in hand, as in W. E. Littlejohn's 'Holy Communion Service, Suvla Bay', which opens with a shot of 'A battered corned-beef box, a length of twine | An altar-rail of twigs and shreds of string', and ends with a Christian tableau of 'kneeling soldiers in God's battle-line, | A line of homage to a mightier King'. Robert Nichols's 'Comrades' offers a comparable staged finale for a dead soldier: ' "Lift me." They lifted him. | He smiled and held his arms out to the dim, | And in a moment passed beyond their ken, | Hearing him whisper, "Oh my men, my men!" '[27] Though devoted to soldier-poets, *The Muse in Arms* represents a muse enlisted in the service of the State, Church, and British Army.

---

[24] E. B. Osborn, 'Introduction', in *idem* (ed.), *The Muse in Arms: A Collection of War Poems, for the Most Part Written in the Field of Action, by Seamen, Soldiers and Flying Men who are Serving, or who have Served, in the Great War* (London: John Murray, 1918), pp. v–xxi.

[25] Graves, 'Poets of World War II', 308.

[26] Sassoon, 'Absolution', and 'The Rear-Guard', in Osborn (ed.), *Muse in Arms*, 31 and 68–9.

[27] Gordon Alchin, 'The Road'; Alexander Robertson, 'The New Aeneid'; William Noel Hodgson, 'Before Action'; W. H. Littlejohn, 'Holy Communion Service, Suvla Bay'; Robert Nichols, 'Comrades'; in Osborn (ed.), *Muse in Arms*, 45, 44, 22, 171, 52.

Even George Clarke's massive *Treasury of War Poetry* (1918), published at the end of the war, represents conventional patriotic views of war and poetry, throwing into relief the resistance represented by the best poetry of Owen, Rosenberg, Sassoon, and Graves. Of these, only Sassoon, with 'The Troops' and 'Trench Duty', and Graves, with 'The Last Post', figure at all, and their poems scarcely ruffle its monumental surface. Again, lots of the poems come from newspapers, and the poets with the biggest representation continue to be Henry Newbolt (exemplified by 'The Vigil'), Lawrence Binyon (typified by 'For the Fallen'), and Katherine Tynan (represented by 'The Mother', with its vision of boys 'Homing like pigeons to her door'[28]). Clarke argues against the view that 'the soldier-poet' has 'more authentic power as an interpreter of war' than his 'non-militant fellow',[29] calling on 'the history of war poetry' from Drayton's *Agincourt* to Hardy's *The Dynasts* in support. 'The first duty of the war poet', he says, is 'to discover the timeless and the placeless in the momentary and parochial.' A modern reader would welcome more of the 'momentary and parochial,' and less of the 'timeless and placeless', and fuller representation of what the editor calls the 'Realist' as against 'Romantic' poetry of war. Herbert Asquith's sonnet 'The Volunteer' is symptomatically caught between the two. It opens in a vein of realism: 'Here lies a clerk who half his life had spent | Toiling at ledgers in a city grey', 'With no lance broken in life's tournament.'[30] The sestet switches to a Romantic key, reporting that 'From twilight to the halls of dawn he went' and now 'lies content | With that high hour', having gone 'to join the men of Agincourt'. The Prime Minister's son's 'timeless' Agincourt seems a jarring epitaph for a modern clerk who has exchanged a city desk for death in the trenches.

Far from being 'placeless', the anthology is organized in terms of places, with poems on 'England', 'Scotland', 'Ireland', and 'Australia', moving on to 'Belgium', 'France', and 'America', then 'Liège', 'Ypres', 'Verdun', and (incongruously) 'Oxford'. These geographical categories remind the reader of the participation of forces from across the Empire, as well as confirming 'Oxford' as poetic capital (there is no section on London). Later sections include 'Poets Militant', 'Auxiliaries', and 'The Airmen', before the anthology concludes with 'The Wounded', 'The Fallen', 'Women and the War', and finally 'Peace'. The poems on 'Airmen', 'Auxiliaries', and 'Keeping the Seas' foreground people not usually represented in war poetry, and the extended one on 'Women and the War' draws mainly on women poets. In fact, the role of women goes far beyond that, with at least thirty-five represented, including Katharine Tynan, Edith Wharton, and Amy Lowell. Introducing a more recent anthology of women's war poetry, Catherine Reilly had a point when she argued that in previous anthologies 'contributions were largely by men', but that was not true in the war itself.[31]

[28] Katherine Tynan, 'The Mother', in George Clarke (ed.), *A Treasury of War Poetry* (London: Hodder & Stoughton, 1918), 408.
[29] George Clarke, 'Introduction', ibid. 33–41.   [30] Herbert Asquith, 'The Volunteer', ibid. 275.
[31] Catherine Reilly, *idem* (ed.), *The Virago Book of Women's War Poetry and Verse* (London: Virago, 1997), p. vii.

The modern reader is likely to see such anthologies through the eyes of Owen and Sassoon as embodiments of the assembly-line poetry of war they needed to dismantle. Nevertheless, they represent a range of poetic responses greater than the now routine opposition between patriotic rhetoric and realistic anti-war verse allows, documenting the ideological fantasies and patriotic myths invested in the war as well as the hideous challenge it presented to poets, at home and in the trenches, who wanted to be consoled, uplifted, or left with faith intact. If the bulk of the poets, with their routine Agincourts and Golgothas, fail, this is not surprising, given the scale of the catastrophe and the obsolete nature of their poetic equipment. *A Treasury* includes embarrassing poems such as 'The Cricketers of Flanders', telling 'How Britain's fighting cricketers | Helped bomb the Germans out of France', but also Gilbert Frankau's 'Ammunition Column', with its documentary-style glimpse of planes '*strafing* an empty sky; | Puff and flash on the far-off blue round the speck one guesses a plane'. And if there is 'Cambrai and Marne' celebrating 'the day | When Marne so well avenged Cambrai', there is also James Knight-Adkin's 'No Man's Land', with its re-creation of the moment when 'the "rapid", like fireflies in the dark, | Flits down the parapet spark by spark, | And you drop for cover to keep your head | With your face on the breast of the four months dead'.[32]

The first anthology to be directed against 'the false glamour of war' also came out in 1918: Bertram Lloyd's *Poems Written during the Great War 1914–1918*. Quoting a German poem saying 'The glamour from the sword is gone', it sets itself against 'our newspaper-warriors', 'The Cheerful Patriotic Citizen', and 'professional diplomatists, politicians and statesmen', speaking of the 'increasing stream of recruits' who swell 'the ranks of the Iconoclasts of Military Glory'.[33] Recruiting A. E., Israel Zangwill, and Eva Gore-Booth, as well as German, French, and Russian poets, for its iconoclastic cause, it includes a couple of poems by W. W. Gibson and five by Sassoon, including 'Does it Matter?' The editor takes his bearings from 'the tragic irony' of Sassoon, and, though much of its rhetorical idiom is dated, his is the earliest anthology to anticipate the post-war view of war poetry. He followed it with *The Paths of Glory: A Collection of Poems Written during the War, 1914–18* (1919), which, under its ironic title, included more Sassoon poems as well as work by Richard Aldington, Herbert Read, and Eleanor Farjeon.

Jacqueline Trotter's post-war *Valour and Vision: Poems of the War, 1914–18* (1920) was the first anthology to include, among the usual poetic personnel, Wilfred Owen and Edward Thomas. Organized year by year, its 'primary object' was 'to present the poet as the historian' by illustrating 'the different aspects and phases of the war by contemporary poetry': first the initial 'chorus of patriotic verse',

---

[32] James Norman Hall, 'The Cricketers of Flanders'; Gilbert Frankau, 'Ammunition Column'; Charles G. D. Roberts, 'Cambrai and Marne'; James H. Knight-Adkin, 'No Man's Land'; in Clarke (ed.), *Treasury of War Poetry*, 286, 294, 310, 272.

[33] Bertram Lloyd, 'Preface', in *idem* (ed.), *Poems Written during the Great War 1914–1918: An Anthology* (London: Allen & Unwin, 1918), 5–10.

then 'the advent of the soldier-poets in 1915', the appearance of a 'sterner note' in 1917, then the 'turning of the tide' and 'victory'.[34] The soldier poet's 'sterner vision' remains rather minimally represented, with just Graves's 'Two Fusiliers' in 1916, Sassoon's 'Dreamers' and Gibson's 'The Ragged Stone' in 1917, while it is left to W. H. Davies, de la Mare, and Lord Dunsany's 'Dirge for Victory' to represent 1918. The expanded 1923 edition took in May Sinclair's 'Field Ambulance in Retreat', Sassoon's 'Attack' and 'Remorse', and Owen's 'Anthem for Doomed Youth' and 'Greater Love'. Though Trotter claimed that 'all the most famous war poems are to be found in this book', a modern reader will be surprised to see only a handful of poems by Owen and Sassoon together, and nothing by Rosenberg, Gurney, or Blunden. Designed to 'recall our Nation's purpose in the Great War', it still excludes what came later to be 'the most famous war poems'.

As noted, it was not until Frederick Brereton's *An Anthology of War Poems* (1930) that something like the now accepted view of war poetry emerged. Arranged in alphabetical order, and prefaced by Blunden's account of the 'soldier poets', it took on board Binyon's 'For the Fallen', Brooke's 'The Soldier', and Kipling's 'For All We Have and Are' to represent the 'official' verse culture of the time, but its main line goes through Aldington, Blunden, W. W. Gibson, Robert Graves, Ivor Gurney, Ford Madox Hueffer, Wilfred Owen, Rosenberg (including 'Killed in Action', and 'Dead Man's Dump'), Sassoon, and Edward Thomas. The women poets have largely dropped out of the picture, and the main cast is comparable to that in the most influential modern anthologies. It was only more than a decade after the Armistice that Wilfred Owen finally became the representative war poet, and the war poem a record of 'the pity of war'.[35]

III

There is a certain irony in the fact that once 'Iconoclastic' war poetry gained the ascendancy, the poets of the 1930s and 1940s were thrown into writing of wars they by and large supported—the Republican cause in Spain, the Chinese fight against Japanese invaders, and the battle against Nazism. John Lehmann and Stephen Spender's *Poems for Spain* (1939) reintroduced an idealistic, pro-war poetry that represented the international Left's response to the Spanish Civil War. Indeed, it was described as a 'literary parallel' to the 'International Brigade' by its editors.[36]

---

[34] Jacqueline Trotter (ed.), *Valour and Vision: Poems of the War, 1914–18* (London: Longmans, Green & Co., 1920), pp. vii–xi.

[35] Wilfred Owen, 'Preface', in *The Complete Poems and Fragments*, ii: *The Manuscripts and Fragments*, ed. Jon Stallworthy (London: Chatto & Windus, Hogarth Press, and Oxford University Press, 1983), 535.

[36] Stephen Spender and John Lehman (eds.), *Poems for Spain* (London: Hogarth Press, 1939), 7.

Though the introduction is haunted by Owen's claim that 'all a poet can do to-day is warn',[37] it says the poets now have a 'different warning to give', that it is 'necessary for civilization to defend and renew itself'. The anthology embodies not anti-war feeling but commitment to the Republican cause, and, we are told that the 'essential quality' of the poems is that they are 'written from *inside* Spain', 'close to the experience' of battle. It includes Spanish and German poems as well as English ones, and is organized under headings such as 'Action', 'Death', and 'Romances', documenting the work of poets such as Spender, Louis MacNeice, Francis Cornford, and Sylvia Townsend Warner, and ending with poems on the death of Lorca. Public response to the anthology was politically mixed, and Valentine Cunningham's brilliant, retrospective *Penguin Book of Spanish Civil War Verse* (1980) can be read as a historical response to its tendentiousness. Though the poems are almost uniformly pro-Republican, the anthology is a reminder that war poetry is often propagandist, whether from the Left or the Right, and inherently divisive.

With the declaration of the Second World War, debates about war and poetry returned, along with new war anthologies, now built around the intertextual shadow of First World War poetry. There was no return to the obsolete patriotic rhetoric of 1914, but, though Keith Douglas wrote 'Rosenberg I only repeat what you were saying',[38] no return to the iconoclastic mode either. A number of new anthologies looked back from one war to the other, including George Herbert Clarke's a more recent achronistic *New Treasury of War Poetry: Poems of the Second World War* (1943) and the veteran J. C. Squire's *Poems of Two World Wars* (1940), dedicated to the Prime Minister Winston Churchill, reminding us that it was Churchill who in wartime speeches and post-war prose forged the patriotic rhetoric of the new conflict. Even Edmund Blunden, introducing Patricia Ledward's *Poems of this War by Younger Poets* (1942), said that 'this time as last, war has not silenced the Muses in England', who are now 'armed and embattled'.[39] In 1943 Robert Nichols, another survivor from many First World War anthologies, produced *Anthology of War Poetry 1914–18*, prefacing fifty pages of poems with a long introduction in the form of a dialogue between 'The Anthologist' and a young man who received his call-up in 1940. The book is effectively a conversation between soldiers from the two wars, an equivalent of Herbert Read's poem, 'To a Conscript of 1940'. It opens with Flecker's 'The Dying Patriot' and Brooke's sonnets, but follows this with a diet of Graves (including 'Recalling War'), Sassoon, and Owen (including 'Spring Offensive' and 'Anthem for Doomed Youth'). Recalling war was clearly a way of galvanizing the poets of the new war. Field Marshal Lord Wavell's hugely popular *Other Men's Flowers* (1944), was another 'war baby', conceived

---

[37] Owen, 'Preface', 535.

[38] Keith Douglas, 'Desert Flowers', in *The Complete Poems*, ed. Desmond Graham (London: Faber, 2000), 108.

[39] Edmund Blunden, 'Introduction', in Patricia Ledward (ed.), *Poems of this War by Younger Poets* (Cambridge: Cambridge University Press, 1942), p. vii.

'during campaigns in the East', though it largely steers clear of 'war poetry'.[40] Its military editor thought war 'a dull business' which did not 'tend to inspire poetry in those who practise it', and the section on 'Good Fighting' included traditional historical pieces by Scott, Kipling, and Shakespeare and only four 'anthology poems' from the First World War (typified by 'Magpies in Picardy'). Only Sassoon's 'The General' (1917) might have given the serenely anti-modernist Field Marshal pause.

Julian Symons's *Anthology of War Poetry* (1942) was another retrospective wartime anthology, aiming to 'make a little history of war poems, reflecting in miniature . . . the history of the wars of the British Isles'.[41] Only twenty-two of its 188 pages are devoted to the poets of the First World War (with Hardy, Owen, Sassoon, and Graves, supported by Yeats and Ford), while it travels through the French and Napoleonic Wars (via the Romantics), the nineteenth century (with Clough, Housman, and Hopkins), and on to the Spanish Civil War and Sino-Japanese War (drawing on Auden, Spender, and their generation), concluding with nine poets from the Second World War, mainly from the Auden gang. In his introduction, Symons notes that there are 'many poems about war by living writers', but that 'war poets' as such 'do not exist'. 'War poetry is not a special department of poetry,' he says, but 'the poetry . . . of people affected by the reality of war.'

Apart from such retrospective compilations, there were also a number of influential anthologies of new war poems. In her *English Poetry of the Second World War: A Bibiography*, Catherine Reilly concludes that while the First World War 'produced some outstanding poetry by a relatively small number of poets', the Second 'produced a great deal more good poetry'.[42] Of the wartime anthologies she lists, however, relatively few were of war poetry as such. They include a number of anthologies of verse for the forces, led by Keidrich Rhys's *Poems from the Forces*: (1941) and *More Poems from the Forces* (1943). Rhys's combative introduction opened with the question 'asked by our Sunday newspapers', 'Where are the war poets?', and his answer was 'Under your nose'.[43] Objecting to the 'pre-war, editorial-chair attitude of *Horizon*'s editor' that 'war is the enemy of creative activity', and that 'the soldier-artist of the type of Wilfred Owen or David Jones' was fundamentally 'pacifist', Rhys collects an impressive selection of work by 'the man in uniform'. Calling the anthology 'an act of faith' begun in the wake of Dunkirk, he says that the 'poet in uniform' finds himself 'in a thankless position', born into the wrong times, accepting conscription with grace, with a bunch of tame versifiers on one side and on the other 'the intellectuals of the depression' who have 'betrayed him'.[44] He calls the war 'the most justified in history', and his alphabetically organized anthology

---

[40] A. P. Wavell, 'Preface to Revised Edition' (April 1947), in *idem* (ed.), *Other Men's Flowers* (Harmondsworth: Penguin, 1960; 1st pub. 1944), 19.

[41] Julian Symons (ed.), *An Anthology of War Poetry* (Harmondsworth: Penguin, 1942), p. vii.

[42] Reilly, (ed.), *English Poetry of the Second World War: A Bibliography* (London: Mansell, 1986), p. xiv.

[43] Rhys, 'Introduction', p. xiii.   [44] Ibid. pp. xx–xxi.

represents an impressive harvest of 'the most interesting younger war-poets'. They include most of those now recognized as significant: Keith Douglas ('Soissons 1940'), Gavin Ewart, Roy Fuller, Alun Lewis ('All Day It Has Rained'), John Manifold ('The Recruit'), Patricia Ledward, F. T. Prince ('Soldiers Bathing'), Henry Reed ('Naming of Parts'), and Henry Treece. As an instance of the Muse in Arms, it is actually more impressive than any of the First World War anthologies, combining support for the war with real aesthetic sophistication.

Other Forces anthologies include John Pudney and Henry Treece's *Air Force Poetry* (1944) and *Poems from Italy: Verses by Members of the Eighth Army in Sicily and Italy* introduced by Siegfried Sassoon (1945), most of which draw on little-recognized poets. Two were devoted exclusively to women, Peter Ratazzi's *Little Anthology: The First Girl Writers in Battledress* (1944), which included work by Ledward, and *Poems of the Land Army: An Anthology of Verse by Members of the Women's Land Army*, with a foreword by Vita Sackville-West (1945). This included verse by eight poets, including the talented Alice Coats, who is represented by her wittily satirical 'Monstrous Regiment' and a jarring wartime pastoral called 'October, 1940' ('To-day I gather from the orchard grass | Apples and shrapnel'[45]). The quality of such anthologies varied wildly from routine compilations representing soldiers who wrote rather than writers in uniform, to quality literary collections such as *OASIS: The Middle East Anthology of Poetry from the Forces* (1943), which printed work by Hamish Henderson and G. S. Fraser (though not Keith Douglas, curiously), and Patrick Dickinson's *Soldiers' Verse* (1945), a distinctively literary, if rather upbeat selection which, despite its title, mixed combatants and non-combatants, setting work by W. H. Auden, T. S. Eliot, Sidney Keyes, Alun Lewis, and Dylan Thomas side by side. Perhaps the most original of these was *Personal Landscape: An Anthology of Exile* compiled by Robin Fedden (1945), which printed work by civilians and soldiers from Egypt. English writers included Keith Douglas (with five poems, including 'Cairo Jag', '*Vergissmeinnicht*', and 'Desert Flowers'), Lawrence Durrell, Olivia Manning, and Bernard Spencer, but there were also poems by the Greek writers Seferis and Papadmitriou and an essay on Cavafy. 'Landscape' and 'exile' move beyond the conventional terms of war poetry. In fact, the North African campaign generated an astonishing poetic harvest, though it was not until Victor Selwyn's retrospective *Return to Oasis: War Poems and Recollections from the Middle East* (1980), that the scale of literary invention in this particular theatre of war could be fully documented.[46] It included some of the definitive poems of the Second World War, such as Douglas's 'How to Kill' and 'Cairo Jag', Henderson's 'End of a Campaign', F. T. Prince's 'Soldiers Bathing', and Sorley MacLean's 'Death

---

[45] Alice Coats, 'Monstrous Regiment', in *Poems of the Land Army: An Anthology of Verse by Members of the Women's Land Army*, with a foreword by Vita Sackville-West (London: 'The Land Girl', 1945), 33.

[46] See Victor Selwyn, Erik De Mauny, Ian Fletcher, G. S. Fraser, and John Waller (eds.), *Return to Oasis: War Poems and Recollections from the Middle East 1940–1946* (London: Shepheard-Walwyn, 1980).

Valley'. As with the First World War, the post-war anthology is poetically richer than anthologies produced in the heat of battle.

Tambimuttu's *Poetry in War-time* (1942), sponsored by Poetry London, was published under the aegis of T. S. Eliot as a collection of 'the best poems written since the beginning of the war—some of which are also "war poems" '.[47] Reviewing it in the *Listener*, a critic argued that 'most wartime anthologies of poetry will survive, if they survive at all, merely as historical or sociological documents', but thought *Poetry in War-time* a 'brilliant exception'.[48] Most wartime anthologies are indeed 'historical or sociological documents', yet Tambimuttu's anthology of poems written between September 1939 and 1942 stands up remarkably well. With poets published in alphabetical order rather than groupings, it does justice to an eclectic collection of individual writers. It prints Read's fraught 'To a Conscript of 1940' and a war poem by each of the leading poets of the Thirties: Auden's 'September 1, 1939', MacNeice's 'Bar-Room Matins' (with its chilling refrain, 'Die the soldiers, die the Jews, | And all the breadless homeless queues, | Give us this day our daily news'[49]), Day Lewis's 'Stand-to', Spender's 'Poets and Airmen', and William Empson's 'Aubade' ('Only the same war on a different toe. | The heart of standing is you cannot fly'[50]). It mixes these with poems by New Apocalypse writers, including George Barker's 'Sonnets from America', Treece's 'Confessions in Wartime', David Gascoyne's wonderful 'Wartime Dawn', the underrated Nicholas Moore's 'The Ruin and the Sun', Dylan Thomas's 'Deaths and Entrances', and W. R. Rodgers' 'Summer Holiday', with its reflections on 'what will be left of us then but our faces | In albums, our names on war's memorials'.[51] Of enlisted poets, there is a run of poems by Alun Lewis (including 'All Day It Has Rained'), an Audenesque piece by Roy Fuller, and a couple of poems by Gavin Ewart and Terence Tiller. There is no Keith Douglas, however. Just as First World War anthologies had nothing by Owen, so anthologies of the Second have almost nothing by the great soldier-poet of the war, whose reputation post-dated his death. Though the New Apocalypse poets have fallen out of vogue, the resistant quality of the best poems is remarkable, and, in opening the boundary between wartime and war poems, this anthology includes some of the best poems written by British civilians and combatants during the war years.[52]

At the war's end Oscar Williams published *The War Poets: An Anthology of the War Poetry of the 20th Century*, probably the most important wartime anthology. After six years of war, it was still dedicated to Wilfred Owen, and opened with his preface stating 'All a poet can do today is warn'.[53] Though it spans the two World

---

[47] Tambimuttu (ed.), *Poetry in War-time*, cover blurb.   [48] *Listener*, 10 Sept. 1942, 344.

[49] Louis MacNeice, 'Bar-Room Matins', in Tambimuttu (ed.), *Poetry in War-time*, 99.

[50] William Empson, 'Aubade', ibid. 191–2.   [51] W. R. Rodgers, 'Summer Holiday', ibid. 141.

[52] See Holga Klein, 'Tambimuttu's *Poetry in War-time*', in Ian Higgins (ed.), *The Second World War in Literature* (Edinburgh and London: Scottish Academic Press, 1986), 1–18.

[53] Oscar Williams, 'Introduction', in *idem* (ed.), *The War Poets: An Anthology of the War Poetry of the 20th Century* (New York: John Day, 1945), 3.

Wars and the Spanish Civil War, it opens with forty-five pages of First World War verse dominated by Owen and Sassoon. The core is devoted to 'Poems by the Men in the Armed Forces of England and America', with poets given name and rank. The biggest allocations go to Trooper Julian Symons (eleven), Flight Lieutenant Henry Treece and the Australian Captain John Manifold (nine), followed by Sergeant Randall Jarrell (eight), Lieutenant Roy Fuller, and Sergeant Karl Shapiro with six each. It offers a strong selection of fifty-eight US and British poets, though a modern reader will be struck by the under-representation of Alun Lewis and the absence of Douglas, Henderson, and MacLean. The last section on 'War Poems by the Civilian Poets' is almost as substantial, opening with Yeats's 'The Second Coming' and enlisting a wide range of poets from both sides of the Atlantic. The forty-one civilians include five women poets and such important figures as Barker, Berryman, Frost, Marianne Moore, MacNeice, Spender, Dylan Thomas, Wallace Stevens, and Muriel Rukeyser. Williams argues plausibly, on the basis of 'Spain', 'August for the people and their favourite islands', and 'September 1, 1939', that Auden is 'the major war poet of the first half of this century', and it is the 'civilian section' which the editor thought contained the poems which will best 'communicate the realities of war to the generations to come'.[54] The impressive introduction maintained that the popular press's hand-wringing about the lack of war poets was really a sign of the 'resistance to true poetry' that was 'still contemporary'. It also printed a series of thoughtful statements on war and poetry by twenty poets, which includes Richard Eberhart's claim that 'in a dialectical sense, all poetry is war poetry' and Selden Rodman's variation that 'All serious war poetry is anti-war poetry'. Quoting Berryman's remark that 'The poet's poem has always outlived the names of battles, generals and statesmen', the editor argues that 'our war poetry as a whole is perhaps the document of our time that will outlive the rest'. The anthology substantiates the claim remarkably well.

The same year saw *War and the Poet: An Anthology Expressing Man's Attitudes to War from Ancient Times to the Present*, edited by Richard Eberhart and Selden Rodman (1945). This offered a reassessment of war poetry in longer perspective. Not predominantly a record of contemporary writing, it is a transhistorical and international collection, returning to ancient Egypt, the Bible, Homer, and the Greek tragedians, while also drawing on poets from other countries, such as Bashō, Rimbaud, Nicolai Gumilev, Rilke, and Alexander Blok. One section, however, is devoted to mainly non-combatant contemporaries like Auden, George Barker, and Dylan Thomas beside a sprinkle of combatants such as Roy Fuller, Alan Lewis, and the Australian John Manifold, as well as American poets. Though there is no Brecht, nothing on the Holocaust, and no Douglas or Louis Simpson, this is a highly cosmopolitan, historically rich anthology, using the War to reflect on the changing relationship between war and poetry across time.

[54] Ibid. 6–9.

After the War, according to G. S. Fraser, 'the public fairly rapidly lost a wide interest in war poetry'.[55] In fact, it would be more than twenty years before anthologists took up the challenge laid down by these two American anthologies. Many of Oscar Williams's questions about war poetry return to haunt later anthologies of Second World War verse, and whereas the canon of First World War poetry is relatively stable, that of the Second remains much less clear-cut, as we shall see.

IV

In the 1960s war poetry returned to the agenda, with republication of the poems of Douglas and Lewis, a return to war in poems and essays by contemporary poets such as Geoffrey Hill and Ted Hughes,[56] and a new wave of anthologies of both World Wars.

Brian Gardner led the way with *Up the Line to Death: The War Poets 1914–1918* (1964), followed by I. M. Parsons with *Men Who March Away* (1965), another First World War anthology with a preface by the indefatigable Blunden.[57] Both are organized in terms of roughly chronological categories from Declaration to Armistice, with Parsons taking us from 'Visions of Glory' to 'The Bitter Truth', and Gardner from 'Prelude' and 'Happy is England Now' through 'Death's Kingdom' to 'At Last, At Last!' In setting up chronological and thematic headings, they were following in the footsteps of the earliest anthologists, as well as establishing a precedent for later ones. Neither included poems by women or poets writing in other languages.[58] The Second World War poetic canon was being reshaped at the same time along similar lines, with Ian Hamilton's *Poetry of War* (1965), Brian Gardner's *Terrible Rain* (1966), and Charles Hamblett's *I Burn for England: An Anthology of the Poetry of World War II* (1966) coming out in quick succession.[59] Though the last was organized alphabetically, Hamilton and Gardner grouped poems under headings, with Hamilton taking us through 'Simplify me When I am Dead' and 'War Poet' to 'History's Thread', and Gardner from 'Yes, We are Going to Suffer' through 'The Desert', 'Cruel Sea', and 'The Jungle', on to 'Victory'. Once again, none of these

---

[55] G. S. Fraser, 'War Poetry and *Oasis*', in Selwyn *et al.* (eds.), *Return to Oasis*, p. xxxi.

[56] Keith Douglas, *Selected Poems*, ed. Ted Hughes (London: Faber, 1964); *idem*, *Collected Poems*, ed. John Waller, G. S. Fraser, and J. C. Hall (London: Faber, 1966); Alun Lewis, *Selected Poetry and Prose*, ed. Ian Hamilton (London: George Allen & Unwin, 1966).

[57] Brian Gardner (ed.), *Up the Line to Death: The War Poets 1914–18* (London: Methuen, 1964); I. M. Parsons (ed.), *Men Who March Away* (London: Chatto & Windus, 1965).

[58] Gardner does include an extract from Edith Sitwell's 'The Shadow of Cain'.

[59] Ian Hamilton (ed.), *The Poetry of War 1939–45* (London: Alan Ross, 1965); Brian Gardner (ed.), *The Terrible Rain: The War Poets 1939–45* (London: Methuen, 1966); Charles Hamblett (ed.), *I Burn for England: An Anthology of Poetry from World War II* (London: Leslie Frewin, 1966). The same year, Ronald Blythe edited *Writing in a War: Stories, Poems and Essays 1939–1945* (Harmondsworth: Penguin, 1966).

represented foreign-language poets, and, while Charles Hamblett included five women, Gardner's and Hamilton's selections were exclusively male. In this respect, the 1960s anthologists packaged war poems from both wars in the same way.

In the competition between the wars the First World War continued to win. Jon Silkin's *The Penguin Book of First World War Poetry* (1979), following his critical study of the war poets, *Out of Battle* (1972), was part of a wider intellectual revaluation that culminated in Paul Fussell's *The Great War and Modern Memory* (1975). As poet and combative editor of *Stand*, Silkin presented his anthology less as a 'historical' work than as an embodiment of an embattled poetics, akin to Alvarez's *The New Poets* (1966). Steering clear of the prevalent thematic slant, Silkin organized the material by poets, offering a substantial selection of poems by his major figures—Edward Thomas, Blunden, Gurney, Sassoon, Read, Owen, and Rosenberg, supplemented by the modernists David Jones, T. E. Hulme, and F. S. Flint. The book is prefaced by a long, strenuously argued introduction, which takes its bearings from the 'exploratory' work of Rosenberg, and stresses the aesthetic integrity and complexity of the material. Silkin insisted on 'judging poetry as poetry', not as historical or sentimental documents, and though he included a small number of 'anthology poems' by Brooke and Grenfell for 'historical' rather than aesthetic reasons, he gave them a health warning in the form of an asterisk.[60] Though he included no poems by women, he takes the small but crucial step of making room for twenty-one translated poems by Trakl, Apollinaire, and others. Despite a lot of competition, Silkin's anthology remains the most influential representation of the poetry of the First World War, and has gone through three editions, with revisions which tell us something about the changing critical climate. In the second edition (1982), he expanded the number of translated poems, and in the third (1996), he finally addressed the exclusion of women, adding five new female poets, including Mina Loy, explaining his change of heart in a defensive prefatory note.[61] These later revisions do not significantly change its complexion, but underline the ways the canon was changing in what Edna Longley tendentiously calls the 'anthological third wave that subordinated aesthetics to social history rather than patriotism or protest'.[62]

Like that of Silkin, the First World War anthologies of the third wave had their own battles to fight, all offering revisionist readings of the familiar English canon. Catherine Reilly launched *Scars Upon My Heart: Women's Poetry and Verse of the First World War* (1981) to counter the fact that 'anthologies of both wars' were 'largely' stocked with poetry by men.[63] In it Judith Kazantzis argued that 'the

---

[60] Jon Silkin, 'Introduction', in *idem* (ed.), *The Penguin Book of First World War Poetry* (Harmondsworth: Penguin, 1979), 72.

[61] Silkin, 'A Note on the 1996 Edition', in *idem* (ed.), *The Penguin Book of First World War Poetry*, 3rd edn. (Harmondsworth: Penguin, 1996), 13–14.

[62] Edna Longley, 'The Great War, History, and the English Lyric', in Sherry (ed.), *Cambridge Companion to the Literature of the First World War*, 59.

[63] Reilly, 'Introduction', in *idem* (ed.), *Scars Upon My Heart*; repr. in *idem* (ed.), *Virago Book of Women's War Poetry and Verse*, p. vii.

invisibility' of 'women's poetry on the Great War' stemmed from 'deep in the patriarchal mind' and the 'atavistic feeling that war is man's concern'.[64] It contains conventional poems of mourning and patriotic grief, and pieces like Vera Brittain's 'Lament for the Demobilised' and Sinclair's 'Field Ambulance' recording women's experiences of war. Some of the poems, like Ruth Comfort Mitchell's 'He Went for a Soldier', have something of Sassoon's anger; others, like Margaret Postgate Cole's 'Veteran', something of Owen's empathy; while Eleanor Farjeon's 'Easter Monday' (in memoriam Edward Thomas) offers an eerie complement to Thomas's vernacular resilience ('There are three letters that you will not get'[65]). Arranged by author rather than theme, the anthology brings back many of the female figures from the wartime anthologies later airbrushed out. If they do not, as Kazantzis acknowledges, match the 'furious magnificence of the soldier poets' or their linguistic resistance, the anthology at least put them back on the map. Martin Taylor's Lads: Love-Poetry of the Trenches offers a complementary revisionist view. Building on the recognition that 'much of the best First World War poetry is characterized by a strong homo-erotic element',[66] Taylor's scholarly introduction contests traditional mappings, challenging not only the canon of war poetry but that of 'love poetry'. The format is traditional, with sections on 'Killed in Action', 'The Dead', and 'Aftermath', and even 'Mates' and 'Youth in Arms', having a conventional ring. The anthology, though, re-frames even familiar texts. Owen's 'Arms and the Boy' appears alongside R. D. Greenaway's 'Soldiers Bathing', addressed to a 'lad of April', and F. S. Woodley's Housman-style elegy 'To Lieut. O'D', which asks Death, 'Could you not have aimed untruly, | Spared for me the boy I loved?'[67] The tenderness of the anthology invites the reader to reflect again on the homosexual orientation of Owen and Sassoon and to view the trenches as a strange meeting-place between war and love.

Tim Cross's monumental Lost Voices of World War I: An International Anthology of Writers, Poets & Playwrights (1988) effects a different corrective view. It resurrects a different set of lost voices, offering a broader and deeper international coverage than other anthologies, and setting Russian, German, French, and Italian writers (with translations) beside both familiar and unfamiliar English-speaking writers (Tom Kettle included). A multilingual, multi-generic compilation, it represents work by sixty writers, foregrounding German poets like Trakl and Stamm and French poets like Apollinaire and Charles Péguy, and draws a complex international map of war literature that has no precedent. Prefaced by biographical and introductory essays, and illustrated with portraits and pictures, this is a historical anthology which transformed the entire field, making others seem parochial.

---

[64] Judith Kazantzis, 'Preface', in Reilly (ed.), Scars Upon My Heart, repr. in Reilly (ed.), Virago Book of Women's War Poetry and Verse, pp. xxi and xxix.

[65] Eleanor Farjeon, 'Easter Monday', in Reilly (ed.), Virago Book of Women's War Poetry and Verse, 36.

[66] Martin Taylor, 'Introduction', in idem (ed.), Lads: Love-Poetry of the Trenches (London: Constable, 1989), 16.

[67] F. S. Woodley, 'To Lieut. O'D', ibid. 134.

There have been numerous other anthologies, though none has changed the canonic map so drastically.[68] Among them is the Poet Laureate Andrew Motion's *First World War Poems* (2003), where he says, 'It's easy and difficult' to make an anthology of First World War poetry—'easy because the best poems are well known, and difficult for the same reason: what new is there to show?'[69] Arguing that the archetypal poems of the war 'risk becoming less and less intimate as poems' and more like 'state furniture', he sets out to 're-present the poems as living things'. It is hard to do this in a modest-scale book, but, while he puts the spotlight on the familiar verse of Thomas, Sassoon, Owen, and Gurney, he also pulls in work by the modernists Yeats, Eliot, and Pound, a handful of popular songs by 'Anon.', and, following Catherine Reilly, women poets like Postgate and Farjeon. All this reflects the changing consensus. More challengingly, he includes a sequence of late twentieth-century First World War poems by Philip Larkin, Ted Hughes, Michael Longley, and others, which shows that the long march of that war's poetry continues with new poems as well as new anthologies engaging with what Ted Hughes, reviewing one, called the 'National Ghost'.[70]

V

Though the ghost of the First World War still dominates the anthology market, Gardner's and Hamilton's 1960s anthologies of Second World War verse reopened the debate about the literature of that very different war. Gardner and Hamilton included many of the same poets, grouped under comparable headings, but with different criteria in play. Hamilton, as poet and pugnacious editor of *The Review*, used his anthology to offer not only a retrospect but an epitome of the tough, realistic poetry he was championing at the time. Its purpose was to 'do justice' to 'poets who did not rush to extremes' but attempted 'to confront a disintegrating world in personal terms'.[71] He restricted himself to British poets in the Services—Alun Lewis, Roy Fuller, Keith Douglas, Bernard Gutteridge, and Alan Ross—but ended with a short selection of Americans, including Jarrell, Louis Simpson, and Richard Wilbur. The overall impression is of formally tight, journalistic *Review*-style verse of

---

[68] These include Dominic Hibberd and John Onions (eds.), *Poetry of the Great War: An Anthology* (Basingstoke: Palgrave, 1986); Martin Stephen (ed.), *Never Such Innocence Again: A New Anthology of Great War Verse* (London: Buchan and Enright, 1988); David Roberts (ed.), *Minds at War: Essential Poetry of the First World War in Context* (Burgess Hill: Saxon, 1998); and George Walter (ed.), *In Flanders Fields: Poetry of the First World War* (Harmondsworth: Penguin, 2004).

[69] Andrew Motion, 'Introduction', in *idem* (ed.), *First World War Poems* (London: Faber, 2003), p. xi.

[70] Ted Hughes, 'National Ghost', in *Winter Pollen: Occasional Prose*, ed. William Scammell (London: Faber, 1994), 70.

[71] Hamilton, 'Introduction', in *idem* (ed.), *Poetry of War 1939–45*, 1.

high quality but little range (there are no Scots, for example). By contrast, Gardner includes 119 poets with 'genuine and relevant attitudes to the war', including civilians like Auden, MacNeice, and Gascoyne, as well as the best war poets from the Forces, mixed in with 'lesser known and forgotten' poets.[72] Though it offers a broader sample, the best poems get diluted by acres of neat, middle-of-the-road documentary-style poems, robbing them of some of their force. The two anthologies play out the familiar contest between 'wartime' and 'war' poems, civilians and combatants, while dramatizing the endemic conflict between commitment to the historically 'representative' and the aesthetically important. Hamilton's highly selective record of combatant verse was later countered by two indispensable anthologies, *Return to Oasis* (1980), a dazzling record of the poetry written by British poets from the Forces in just one of the theatres of war, the North African desert, and Victor Selwyn's more wide-ranging *The Voice of War: Poems of the Second World War* (1996), which draws on the work of the British Forces more generally, arranged thematically in terms of the different theatres of operation (such as 'The Middle East', 'The Mediterranean', 'Normandy to Berlin', 'South-East Asia and the Pacific').

A corrective to the overwhelmingly masculine constitution of these books was again provided by Catherine Reilly with her *Chaos of the Night: Women's Poetry and Verse of the Second World War* (1984), reinforced by Anne Powell's *Shadows of War* (1999). Though limited to women poets from the British Isles, they draw attention to systematic under-representation. Reilly's fifty poets include the eccentric voices of Edith Sitwell (with 'Still Falls the Rain') and Stevie Smith (with 'Voices against England in the Night'), as well as Sylvia Townsend Warner, Naomi Mitchison, and Anne Ridler, but most are little known. Some of the sharpest poems offer snapshots of ordinary Britain at war, including Ruth Pitter's 'To a Lady, in a Wartime Queue' and Patricia Ledward's 'Air-Raid Casualties: Ashridge Hospital', while others speak directly from a woman's viewpoint, including Ackland's '7 October 1940', with its sardonic hymn to fertility ('Reflect! There is no need for grief nor gloom, | Nature has ever another in Her womb'), and E. J. Scovell's maternal aubade 'Days Drawing In' ('Sweet the grey morning and the raiders gone').[73] By restricting the number of poems by genuine poets such as Scovell, Smith, and Ackland in the name of coverage, the book is of greater documentary than poetic interest. The same can be said of Anne Powell's chronologically organized *Shadows of War: British Women's Poetry of the Second World War*, but, with its larger scale, fuller cast, and wider range of styles, it has a higher proportion of hits as well as misses, including some fine squibs by 'Sagittarius' such as 'The Passionate Profiteer to his Love' and Alice Coats's 'The Monstrous Regiment', with its ironic 'War lends a spurious value to the male'.[74]

---

[72] Gardner, 'Introductory Note', in *idem* (ed.), *Terrible Rain*, p. xvii.

[73] Valentine Ackland, '7 October, 1940', and E. J. Scovell, 'Days Drawing In', in Reilly (ed.), *Virago Book of Women's War Poetry and Verse*, 131 and 241.

[74] Alice Coats, 'The Monstrous Regiment of Women', in Anne Powell (ed.), *Shadows of War: British Women's Poetry of the Second World War* (Stroud: Phoenix Mill, 1999), 83.

Another corrective view was offered by three international anthologies: Daniel Weissbort's *The Poetry of Survival: Post-War Poets of Central and Eastern Europe* (1991), Desmond Graham's *Poetry of the Second World War: An International Anthology* (1995), and Hilda Schiff's *Holocaust Poetry* (1995).[75] They remind us that all the major contemporary poets of Russia and Eastern and Western Europe wrote important poetry about the War and the Holocaust, and that this catastrophic global conflict reshaped literature in all the war-torn and Occupied countries of Europe. Czesław Miłosz recalls that in Poland, for example, 'poetry was the main genre of underground literature', and mentions a 1,912-page anthology called *Poetry of Fighting Poland* (1972). Though he relegates most of this to 'documentary' status, he roots the work of the great poets of his own generation, including Herbert, Różewicz, and Wat, in the 'twentieth-century hell' of the War and the Holocaust.[76] Readers miss the scale of the radical, far-reaching impact of the Second World War on poetry if looking from an exclusively anglophone perspective.

Desmond Graham's *Poetry of the Second World War* spreads the net wider than any earlier anthology, drawing on translations from many languages and poets from many countries in Europe, America, Russia, and Asia. Setting anglophone poems in dialogue with translations chosen for their poetic force and intellectual authority, this is an anthology that radically altered the way we perceive the poetry of the Second World War. Refusing to be bound by received notions of war poetry, Graham sees it as 'an anthology of poems where the experience of the war is apparent and central'. Organized in chronological, thematic sections with headings such as 'Speechless you testify against us', it sets major foreign poets like Akhmatova, Celan, Herbert, and Radnoti beside British poets such as Auden, Douglas, and Lewis, and Americans like Jarrell and Nemerov, resulting in a 'communal effort, with poems from about twenty countries and by a hundred and thirty poets'.[77] The product of a genuinely international outlook and literary discrimination, the anthology is a massive cross-cultural lyric exhibition based on the most powerful poems of the Second World War. Hilda Schiff's *Holocaust Poetry* has a narrower focus, but it, too, gathers poets of many nationalities and languages who have written about Nazi genocide. Organized in chronological and thematic sections ('Persecution', 'Destruction', 'Afterwards'), it creates a choric multi-authored sequence of poems by sixty or so poets from Brecht, Auden, Celan, and Sachs to Sylvia Plath, Geoffrey Hill, and James Fenton. As in Desmond Graham's anthology, many of the most powerful poems are retrospective, though a few are first-hand reports written

---

[75] Daniel Weissbort (ed.), *The Poetry of Survival: The Post-War Poetry of Central and Eastern Europe* (London: Anvil, 1991); Desmond Graham (ed.), *Poetry of the Second World War: An International Anthology* (London: Chatto & Windus, 1995); Hilda Schiff (ed.), *Holocaust Poetry* (London: HarperCollins, 1995).

[76] Czesław Miłosz, *The Witness of Poetry* (Cambridge, Mass.: Harvard University Press, 1983), 79–80.

[77] Desmond Graham, 'Introduction', in *idem* (ed.), *Poetry of the Second World War*, p. xviii.

from the heart of the horror, including those by Pavel Fridemann, an inmate of Theresienstadt, and Primo Levi, a survivor of Auschwitz-Birkenau, bearing witness, as Wilfred Owen did, to the horror of war. If these are not war poems in the usual sense, they are instances of poetry as history, taking on the challenge laid down by Theodor Adorno that 'To write poetry after Auschwitz is barbaric'.[78]

More recently, Harvey Shapiro's *Poets of World War II* (2003), building on Oscar Williams, offers a needed corrective to the British-weighted English-language anthologies, drawing on the work of sixty-two American poets, and arguing that they 'produced a body of a work that has not yet been recognized for its clean and powerful eloquence'.[79] He says that most of the book is 'work by writers who saw service during the war', and 'as many of the poems as possible were written directly out of the experience of war', recording 'the sights, sounds, and emotions of the war'. The anthology is an important record of literary responses to the war in the USA, and includes a range of compelling poems not found anywhere else, including Woodie Guthrie's 'The Blinding of Isaac Woodward' and Gwendolyn Brooks's 'Negro Hero'. There are poems by big names familiar from other contexts—Pound, Moore, Oppen, Zukofsky, Lowell—as well as the more usual crew of war poets, Randall Jarrell, Louis Simpson, Anthony Hecht, and Lincoln Kirstein. This is another pioneering book that changes the map of war poetry in English, with Eberhard's 'Instruments after the War', Ciardi's 'Elegy Just in Case', James Tate's 'Lost Pilot', and Hecht's eerie 'Still Life' important additions to the canon. Writing post-9/11, Shapiro notes that 'we seem, at this writing, to be caught in the drama of the American Century now', arguing that the poems of 'a war fought more than half a century ago continue to speak to the present moment'. The 'present moment' was the year of *Poets Against the War*, reminding us that war anthologies are always shaped by the present as much as the past.

This is not the place to discuss my own *Poems of the Second World War* (2004), which, while building on its predecessors, also attempts to rethink the canon of war poetry.[80] From the outset, I was keen to follow Oscar Williams in including poems by civilians as well as combatants, and, like Graham and Schiff, poems in translation. I also initially wanted to include some of the modern war poetry of Geoffrey Hill and others, but for reasons of space had to restrict myself to a handful of poems by contemporary poets with childhood memories of wartime. Having considered arranging the material chronologically, or thematically (like Graham), or dividing it up in terms of nationality (like Weissbort), or in terms of English-language and foreign poets, I eventually opted to put the poets in alphabetic order (like Brereton's First World War anthology), beginning by setting the great Russian poet Akhmatova

---

[78] Theodor W. Adorno, 'Cultural Criticism and Society', in *Prisms*, trans. Samuel and Shierry Weber (Cambridge, Mass.: MIT Press, 1981), 34.

[79] Harvey Shapiro, 'Introduction', in *idem* (ed.), *Poets of World War II* (New York: Library of America, 2003), p. xx.

[80] Hugh Haughton (ed.), *Poems of the Second World War* (London: Faber, 2004).

after the lesser-known Valentine Ackland, and concluding with the Japanese poet Ei Yamaguchi following the Australian Judith Wright. In the end this seemed the least tendentious way of representing the astonishing range of poetic responses to the War across places, languages, and poets, and ensuring that individual poets were recognized. Mixing American and British, civilians and combatants, foreign and English-language poets, I was keen to represent the modernists T. S. Eliot, Ezra Pound, and H. D., all of whom wrote major sequences about the War, and demonstrate that the Second World War produced a compelling body of poetry in English and other languages, on a far greater scale and range than the First. My brief was to include powerful, distinctive, and various poems that respond, directly or indirectly, to the challenge both of Second World War and their chosen medium. Like the recalcitrant war poems of Douglas and Henderson, the eclogues of Miklos Radnoti, Anna Akhmatova's 'Wind of War', Brecht's Svenborg poems, and Paul Celan's *Deathfugue* are major modern war lyrics, and an indispensable part of the literary witness to what Joanna Bourke calls 'the greatest cataclysm in modern history'.[81]

I have scarcely touched on general anthologies of war poetry. The first anthologies to represent war verse across history were in fact thrown up by the First World War, as I have shown, while others were generated during the Second, including those of Symons (1940), Williams (1945), and Eberhart and Rodman (1945).[82] Two recent examples are Jon Stallworthy's *Oxford Book of War Poetry* (1984) and Kenneth Baker's *The Faber Book of War Poetry* (1996), one taking a chronological, author-based approach, and the other a thematic one.[83] Stallworthy gives only 150 or so of his nearly 340 pages to poetry written before the First World War, confirming Robert Graves's argument. His own view, as the editor and biographer of Owen, is that most 'war poetry has been implicitly, if not explicitly, anti-war'.[84] The anthology largely confirms this, but by excluding drama and epic, it cuts out Shakespeare, Spenser, and Milton, the major English poets to write about war, giving a strange tilt to the historical record. Nevertheless, running from Homer and the Bible to Heaney and Fenton, it offers a thoughtful chronological sample of poetry of war in English, interspersed with scattered translations from other languages. It does not necessarily convince us there is a singular entity called 'war poetry'. Kenneth Baker's miscellaneous *Faber Book of War Poetry*, by contrast, ignores history, arranging the material under headings such as 'Killing', 'Nursing and Medicine', and 'Old Battlefields Revisited'. While impressively eclectic, Mrs Thatcher's Minister for Education is interested in 'The Patriotic Imperative' and 'the Britishness of the

---

[81] Joanna Bourke, *The Second World War: A People's History* (Oxford: Oxford University Press, 2001), 2.

[82] Symons (ed.), *Anthology of War Poetry*; Williams (ed.), *War Poets*; Richard Eberhart and Selden Rodman (eds.), *War and the Poet*.

[83] Jon Stallworthy (ed.), *The Oxford Book of War Poetry* (Oxford: Oxford University Press, 1984); Kenneth Baker (ed.), *The Faber Book of War Poetry* (London: Faber, 1996).

[84] Jon Stallworthy, 'Introduction', in *idem* (ed.), *Oxford Book of War Poetry*, p. xix.

British nation'.[85] The drawback of his miscellaneous scatter-gun approach is that it confuses literary and military history. Under 'Artillery and Big Bombs' we find Milton, Dibdin, and Kipling rubbing shoulders with MacNeice and Apollinaire, while under 'Climate' Alan Ross rubs shoulders with Shakespeare and Aeschylus. It is not clear what this tells us about anything.

What Eric Hobsbawm has called *The Age of Extremes* has been understandably preoccupied with the catastrophic impact of war, and there is a great deal at stake in anthologies of war poetry. They represent our current ideologies of poetry and war, but also exemplify the capacity of individual poets, working in the most intimate grain of the language, to do what Wallace Stevens said modern poetry must do: 'It has to think about war | And it has to find what will suffice.'[86]

---

[85] Kenneth Baker, 'Introduction: The Purple Testament of Bleeding War', in *idem* (ed.), *Faber Book of War Poetry*, p. xxv.

[86] Wallace Stevens, 'Of Modern Poetry', in *Collected Poems* (London: Faber, 1955), 240.

CHAPTER 23

WOMEN'S POETRY OF THE FIRST AND SECOND WORLD WARS

SIMON FEATHERSTONE

Despite the twenty-five years that have passed since the publication of Catherine Reilly's innovative First World War anthology *Scars Upon My Heart* (1981), women's poetry remains a problem for critics of war poetry. Whilst that anthology and its companion volume of Second World War women's poetry, *Chaos of the Night* (1984), remain standard points of reference, they have not led to a thorough debate about what 'women's war poetry' might mean beyond a body of war poetry not by men. There persists a lack of attention to women's poetry of both wars, despite the recovery and revaluation of a range of women's prose writing from these periods. In the present collection, for example, only two essays concentrate solely on women writers, and that imbalance is typical of the field. Whilst Virginia Woolf, Vera Brittain, Rebecca West, Elizabeth Bowen, Rose Macaulay, and other writers of fiction and autobiography are securely placed in any account of First and Second World War writing, no comparable figure has emerged as a representative female war poet.

In one sense, the reason for the continuing uneasiness about women's war poetry is clear enough. Of all literary genres, war poetry is the one most insistently defined by the voices and experiences of men. Predicated initially upon the heroism and sacrifice of the masculine body during the early years of the First World War, and latterly upon sceptical appraisals of such values, war poetry allowed for little more than a peripheral female space, and that defined by men. The archetypal woman's war poem is, perhaps, Vera Brittain's 'To My Brother', the opening line of which gives Reilly's first anthology its title. It is a poem about a woman's response to male experience. 'Your battle-wounds are scars upon my heart,'[1] it begins, appropriating the marks of war but subordinating the writer's experience to that of the soldier. Borrowed knowledge was always a weakness in a poetry validated like no other by actually having *been there*. The misogyny in the work of Wilfred Owen and Siegfried Sassoon was not only an expression of personal antipathy, but was also part of a developing politics and poetics of exclusive knowledge. Extreme experience became a pre-condition of writing war poetry, and the primacy of action and military involvement established by the most influential poets of the Great War has never quite been shaken off. War poetry anthologists might agree that there should be something like a balanced representation of gender, but the persistent descriptors of their subject-matter tend to mean that women are at best reservists in the final draft.

Scholars of women's war writing contested this aesthetic of combat by emphasizing a body of work that explored the changes in women's social experience during wartime—what Claire Tylee calls their 'entry into that exclusive part of the national culture which had previously been forbidden to women'.[2] For these critics, women's war writing describes and reflects the ways in which the social and cultural changes of the First and Second World Wars made available 'all that area of public privilege and power to which men had access, and women did not, such as politics, the professions, skilled industrial work, sexual adventure'.[3] The 'entry' of that writing into a reorganized canon of war literature was a means by which that national culture could be seen whole, and not as exclusively defined by the aesthetic of male trauma that had so emphatically shaped a public sense of war poetry in anthologies, editions, and school textbooks after the Second World War. Yet women's poetry remained stubbornly resistant to this process of reappraisal. Whilst Reilly's and other anthologies were useful in suggesting the extent and variety of women's verse, they finally lacked poets as challenging as Wilfred Owen, David Jones, or Keith Douglas, or, indeed, as prose writers like Virginia Woolf or Elizabeth Bowen. They

---

[1] Vera Brittain, 'To My Brother', in Catherine Reilly (ed.), *Scars Upon My Heart: Women's Poetry and Verse of the First World War* (London: Virago, 1981), 15.

[2] Claire Tylee, *The Great War and Women's Consciousness: Images of Militarism and Womanhood in Women's Writing, 1914–64* (Basingstoke: Macmillan, 1990), 14.

[3] Ibid. See also Dorothy Goldmann (ed.), *Women and World War 1: The Written Response* (Basingstoke: Macmillan, 1993); Agnès Cardinal, Dorothy Goldman, and Judith Hattaway (eds.), *Women's Writing on the First World War* (Oxford: Oxford University Press, 1999); Angela K. Smith, *The Second Battlefield: Women, Modernism and the First World War* (Manchester: Manchester University Press, 2000).

provided ample evidence of women's poetic activity during the wars, but response to that activity, on the whole, was limited to an acknowledgement of its presence rather than a sustained engagement with the poetry itself.

This essay takes a different tack, and argues that women's war poetry requires a revision of the category of war poetry itself. Its most challenging poems are at odds with the conventions of male war poetry, and, because of that, they often don't seem to be war poetry at all. The First World War work of the emigrée writers Mina Loy and Gertrude Stein, and the Second World War poetry of E. J. Scovell, are formally very different, the first pair determinedly avant-garde, and the latter part of an English lyrical tradition. All three, though, reject a public poetry of 'women's war experience'. Their work is not *about* war in the way that a poem by Wilfred Owen or Keith Douglas or, indeed, Vera Brittain is about war. Each refuses the subordination of poetic discourse to male experience. Instead, their work articulates an exploratory aesthetics and politics that develop through unexpected, often understated experiences of wartime change. The different strategies of these poets have value, in part, in their very divergence from the norms that Reilly's influential anthologies implicitly accept. Stein, Loy, and Scovell suggest that the project for critics of women's poetry of both World Wars should involve a questioning of the assumption that war poetry is necessarily concerned with extreme personal experience on the one hand or the politics of national culture on the other.

Gertrude Stein's 'Lifting Belly' is a useful starting-point because of its quirky, provocative challenge to the norms of a war poetry of experience. Stein began the poem in the summer of 1915 in Majorca, where she stayed for a year after leaving Paris when the city was threatened by German attack. On first reading it seems an elusive private dialogue between lovers, a text that dwells upon mundane details of life on the island and contains some of Stein's most winning evocations of domestic and sexual intimacy. The title phrase, which is repeated throughout the text, comes to mean variously, sometimes simultaneously, a belly in the act of raising another person, a swelling (consuming, pregnant) body, having sex, and, in the childish love-talk of the piece, a name for one or both of the lovers. The childlike malleability of language and body, and the delight it both evokes and expresses, are at the centre of the odd dialogue. War and refugee experience seem the last things on its speakers' minds as they play their sensual and linguistic games. Yet the First World War does make a brief appearance in the first part of the poem:

> Dare I ask you to be satisfied.
> Dear me.
> Lifting belly is anxious.
> Not about Verdun.
> Oh dear no.
> The wind whistles that means it whistles just like any one. I thought it was a whistle.

Lifting belly together.
Do you like that there.[4]

A conversation about emotional and physical satisfaction is interrupted by the Battle of Verdun, mentioned tentatively by one voice as a potential source of anxiety, but quickly dismissed as such by the other. The verse paragraph returns to mutual pleasure and sexual experiment as war is subsumed within personal and island life. Yet Verdun's intrusion into, and rapid expulsion from, this intimate text is a marker not of a neglect of war, but of a radically different way of dealing with it.

The exaggerated casualness of the dismissal of a battle in which there were 700,000 casualties[5] (the voice does not just reply 'No', but 'Oh dear no') demands attention in a text that is otherwise negligent of much beyond local events. In one sense, it seems to emphasize the distance between the brutal realities of European war and a personal aesthetic of delight pursued out of reach of the guns. Yet this apparent frivolity, the refusal to talk *about* the war ('Oh dear no'), also poses a question to assumptions about what constitutes war writing in the first place. There is actually quite a lot of war in 'Lifting Belly'—Verdun's appearance in the text is later complemented by the intrusions of disruptive male characters called Caesar (who have a hard time coping with the talkative lesbian lovers) and by references to that war-ridden national anthem 'The Star-Spangled Banner'. The treatment of these representatives of male warfare is disconcerting and (knowingly, punningly) disarming. War does not know its place in a text that refuses to engage with it in the terms of a 'national experience' of change. 'Lifting Belly' cannot be reclaimed for the canon on those grounds, because it is a poetry exiled from both nation and battle, though conscious of both. But the terms of its refusal, far from being frivolous, can be seen instead as revealing and insisting upon alternative discourses of engagement. Lifting belly, with all its curves, intimacies, ambiguities, and potential, is an act and a state embodying everything that the relentless destructiveness of Verdun and the monophonic power of Caesar are not.

Stein's war writing is not concerned with articulating a response to war, but with playing out alternative possibilities to the obsessions that the war itself has established. It is a different kind of war poetry, in which personal lives, sensibilities, and pleasures are preserved in tacit opposition to a totalizing force. For a critic of war poetry, it serves as a reminder of the variousness and possibilities of the genre if he or she can think outside the ideological constraints embedded within it. Stein was no ordinary polemicist, but 'Lifting Belly' stresses that the canon of war poetry doesn't just need to be expanded to 'include' women's experience, but needs to be reconfigured *as a result of* women's experience. The main body of this essay is about the work of two writers different from Stein and different from each

---

[4] Gertrude Stein, 'Lifting Belly', in *Bee Time Vine and Other Pieces, 1913–1927*, ed. Carl Van Vechten (New Haven: Yale University Press, 1953), 71.
[5] See Malcolm Brown, *Verdun 1916* (Stroud: Tempus, 2003), 159–60.

other. But Stein's provocative questioning of the exigencies of response in times of political and military crisis is relevant to a reading of the work of the still relatively marginal figures of Mina Loy and E. J. Scovell. Mina Loy's sequence 'Songs to Joannes' (1915–17), written in Italy in the early years of the First World War, is an exploration of female sexuality through an oblique, fragmentary account of a failed love affair. Scovell's collection *Shadows of Chrysanthemums* (1944) explores themes of domesticity, motherhood, and the natural world. Like Stein, neither poet seems to write much 'about' war, and, like Stein again, that very indirection suggests new kinds of distinctively female war poetries.

MINA LOY

Mina Loy's wartime work is an aggressively, self-advertisingly avant-garde poetry the main topic of which is sex (she wrote to the critic Carl Van Vechten that she knew 'nothing about anything but life—& that is generally reducible to sex!'[6]). It developed its style and gained its focus through Loy's relationships—intellectual and sexual—with the Italian Futurists Filippo Marinetti and Giovanni Papini. Living in an unhappy marriage in Florence in the years before 1914, Loy initially responded to her encounter with the rhetorically adventurous and personally extravagant Marinetti with ingenuous enthusiasm. Yet, as her poetry developed, she began to register and explore the contradictions within Futurist theory and practice. These revolved around a conflict between the celebratory modernism and revolutionary aesthetics of the movement, and the deeply conservative forces of aggressive and unproblematized masculinity, nationalism, and militarism that were embedded within such apparently radical positions. A 'love of danger and violence, patriotism and war, the sole hygiene of the world',[7] as Marinetti termed it in 'The Second Political Manifesto of Futurism' (1911), underpinned the assault upon what he saw as the moribund traditions of European art and politics. As Loy came to realize, such passions allowed no space for the development of a distinctive female contribution to the revolutionary programme.

Loy's work attempted a polemical and poetic practice that harnessed the energies and adventure of Futurism to an exploratory feminine politics. Her 'Aphorisms on Futurism' (1914), for example, has much of the bombast, but none of the gendered ferocity of Marinetti's manifestos. 'DIE in the Past / Live in the Future'[8] is orthodox

---

[6] Mina Loy to Carl van Vechten, n.d., quoted in Carolyn Burke, *Becoming Modern: The Life of Mina Loy* (Berkeley: University of California Press, 1996), 191.

[7] Filippo Marinetti, quoted in Günter Berghaus, *Futurism and Politics: Between Anarchist Rebellion and Fascist Reaction, 1909–1944* (Oxford: Berghahn Books, 1996), 69.

[8] Mina Loy, 'Aphorisms on Futurism', in *The Lost Lunar Baedeker*, ed. Roger L. Conover (Manchester: Carcanet, 1997), 149.

Futurism all right, but the concomitant nationalism and militarism that were inevitable in the Italian's work are absent. 'Feminist Manifesto' (1914) went further. Despite gratuitous Marinetti-like gestures such as the recommendation for 'the *unconditional* surgical *destruction of virginity* through-out the female population at puberty',[9] the text lays the ground for her wartime poetry's main preoccupation: the search for a means of expressing a distinctively female consciousness of modernity that does not entail the revocation of female heterosexual desire. 'Leave off looking to men to find out what you are *not*,' she counsels; 'seek within yourselves to find out what you *are*'. In the context of her intimacies with Futurism, she sets herself to understand the attractions of a man like Marinetti and of his ideas and discourses, even as she tries to adjust the imbalance of power within that alliance and to create an independent means of expression. 'Women must destroy in themselves, the desire to be loved,' she asserts. That act of destruction came increasingly to be involved with the wider political crisis of the First World War.

In her private statements on the war, Loy tended to combine the rhetoric of Futurist militarism characteristic of Marinetti with the often naive projection of experience that is found in some of the poems collected in *Scars Upon My Heart*. 'My masculine side longs for war,' she wrote to the pacifist Mabel Dodge, in the period before Italy joined the conflict in late spring 1915. She asked Carl Van Vechten at the same point, 'don't you sense — what wonderful poems I could have written — round about a battle field!'[10] Loy claimed to have taken up nursing in a Red Cross hospital 'entirely devoid of sentiment — *entirely* on the chance of getting near a battlefield & hearing a lovely noise!' 'I'm so wildly happy among the blood & mess,'[11] she enthused. Her poetry of the period resists this rhetorical giddiness, however. Instead of pursuing Marinetti's poetic strategy of creating militarist performance epics such as *Zang-tumb-tumb* with its drum accompaniment to represent noises of battle, Loy began writing poems about sex and birth. The gaucheness that characterizes Loy's letters about war disappears in a difficult poetry that explores the territory of gendered conflict which Futurism ignored. By the time that Italy entered the war, her biographer Carolyn Burke suggests, 'the European war and the "sex war" were . . . so thoroughly entwined [for Loy] that one combat suggested the other'.[12] This was no easy metaphorical transference, however. 'Songs to Joannes' develops a radically strange discourse that is quite unlike received ideas of First World War poetry.[13] The sequence of thirty-four lyrics is an often obscure, extravagant, and argumentative dialogue about the failures of a love affair. At the same time, though, it is poetry that suggests — both rawly and allusively — the ways in which human intimacy was invaded by the forces and the language of a new kind of violence in Europe.

---

[9] Loy, 'Feminist Manifesto', in *The Lost Lunar Baedeker*, 155.
[10] Loy, quoted in Burke, *Becoming Modern*, 185 and 187.
[11] Loy, quoted ibid. 187.   [12] Ibid. 184.
[13] Loy, 'Songs to Joannes', in *Lost Lunar Baedeker*, 53–68.

The first section of the first lyric confronts the reader with the uncompromising poetic strategy that will define the sequence and which is to perform a thoroughgoing deconstruction of the language and ideology of sexual love in wartime:

> Spawn   of   Fantasies
> Silting the appraisable
> Pig Cupid   his rosy snout
> Rooting erotic garbage
> "Once upon a time"
> Pulls a weed   white star-topped
> Among wild oats   sown in mucous-membrane[14]

Sexual desire is immediately dehumanized as 'spawn' of romantic illusions and as silt that clogs rational processes. Cupid becomes an uncherubic, phallic pig, and the sexual act is a casual penetration of 'mucous-membrane', the customary signifier of the nasal passage. The erotic lyric does not get more debunked than this. Yet, in a characteristic shift of direction, the next stanza acknowledges a contrary impulse in the poem and in the sequence as a whole, and celebrates the very desire that has just been denigrated: 'I would   an   eye in a Bengal light | Eternity in a sky-rocket.' Aspirations to bliss are still heading skywards, even if the stanza ends with 'a trickle of saliva' and a return to the mucous of the opening.

The battles of desire and scepticism and of man and woman, and the struggle to find a language to explore these conflicts, are two concerns of the poems. A third is the context of these conflicts in wartime, and 'Songs to Joannes' provides a sophisticated critique of the cruder wartime excitements expressed in Loy's letters. Instead of those lurid fantasies of military experience, the songs demonstrate the effect of war upon sexual intimacy, recalling the strategy, if not the tone, of 'Lifting Belly'. As the 'Songs' progress, the struggles—sexual and discursive—intensify, the experience of desire is rendered through the discourse of the battlefield, and the war enters the apparently distant world of the lovers. Song XII begins:

> Voices break on the confines of passion
> Desire   Suspicion   Man   Woman
> Solve in the humid carnage
>
> Flesh from flesh
> Draws the inseparable delight
> Kissing at gasps   to catch it[15]

The ambiguity of tone and act is irresolvable here. The 'confines of passion' might represent passion as either positively private or negatively restrictive; the voices might be intrusive, or they might themselves be broken by the intensities of a sexual act ('the inseparable delight') resistant to the pressures of the outside world. As usual, the syntax is undetermined by punctuation, and this allows the key phrase, 'Solve in

---

[14] Loy, 'Songs to Joannes', in *Lost Lunar Baedeker*, 53.   [15] Ibid. 57.

the humid carnage', to float free, grammatically unanchored and tonally ambiguous. '[C]arnage' seems to hold to its archaic definition of mingled bodies (Loy was never without an etymological dictionary, it often seems), and hence prompts an erotic solution to gendered opposition and 'suspicion' (the 'suspect places' of sexual relationships). But it also alerts us to the real war that surrounds and infects the poem and its subjects, the queasy description of sex acting as a reminder of the hospital where, Loy said, she enjoyed being 'among the blood & mess'. 'Human' carnage is displaced to become 'humid carnage', sex offering both a disturbing reminder of slaughter elsewhere and a celebration of the intensity and authenticity of sweating, desiring bodies (the sequence as a whole never loses its appreciation of such carnality, no matter how cynical its attitude might otherwise seem). But war, for the first time, has been explicitly brought to bed. The song acknowledges that its horrors—and its perverse attractions—have entered and shaped sexual relationships.

The fusion of modern war and modern sex is intensified by the sequence's recurring references to conception. As Paul Peppis has argued, Loy's demands for women's sexual freedom always took place in a context of what he terms 'the ideal of free loving maternalism'.[16] In 'Songs to Joannes' this aspiration is expressed, but seems disturbingly thwarted. The fourth song presents a nightmarish vision of 'an unimaginable family', 'Bird-like abortions | With human throats | And Wisdom's eyes'. One of these owlish abortions is itself carrying a baby 'In a padded porte-enfant | Tied with a sarsenet ribbon | To her goose's wings' in a grotesque parody of Mother Goose, that sentimental evasion of the 'carnage' of sex and childbirth. 'I would have lived | Among their fearful furniture | To teach them to tell me their secrets', the poem goes on, an admission, perhaps, of the temptations of the bourgeois family, 'Before I guessed | —Sweeping the brood clean out'.[17] Quite what is guessed is unclear, though the contrast between the egotistical demands of sexual desire and the social consequences of productive sex and settled relationships is a favourite theme of Loy's work. She is always alert to the contradictions of an urgent sexual desire that produces children in a context of the conventions of family and child-bearing that then go on to frustrate the sources of that desire. In the previous lyric there is a moment of wistfulness when the speaker ponders that 'We might have given birth to a butterfly'. Characteristically, though, this musing is rapidly qualified by an image that heralds the avian abortions of the next song. The butterfly has 'the daily news | Printed in blood on its wings'; it is not free and natural, but a marked, damaged thing. Such 'daily news' seems to be in direct conflict with the possibility of sexual desire being both fulfilling and life-giving; the blood of war's casualties transforms the child-butterfly into the aborted bird-Cupid of Song IV.

Loy had long connected the experience of pregnancy with such rhetoric of war. During an unhappy confinement in 1908, she wrote of her body as 'given up

---

[16] Paul Peppis, 'Rewriting Sex: Mina Loy, Marie Stopes, and Sexology', MODERNISM/ modernity, 9/4 (2002), 571.
[17] Loy, 'Songs to Joannes', 54–5.

entirely to the growth of invasion',[18] and her poem 'Parturition' (1914) is a startling evocation of childbirth as prolonged, bitter struggle. The link continued into the First World War. Loy told the writer Neith Boyce in August 1914 that she planned to 'go to Milan and get a child by [Marinetti] before he goes to war—she says there is nothing else . . . to do in war-time'.[19] In 'Songs to Joannes' the theme of conception seems to recur obliquely in Song XIII which begins:

> Come to me   There is something
> I have got to tell you   and I can't tell
> Something taking shape
> Something that has a new name
> A new dimension[20]

As usual, the precise subject of the dialogue is obscure. A suggestion of the speaker's pregnancy—that 'Something taking shape'—could equally be a sense of the rebirth of a sexual relationship. Yet, as the song goes on, the speaker seems intent upon breaching the entrenched positions and egotism that have seemed to define their interactions. 'Let us be very jealous', she says sarcastically,

> Very suspicious
> Very conservative
> Very cruel
> Or we might make an end of the jostling of aspirations
> Disorb inviolate egos
>
> Where two or three are welded together
> They shall become god

Whilst 'welded' is a tough Loyan verb that harks back to the debunking sexual discourse of the first song, the mention of 'three' is a striking innovation in a text that has been remorselessly dualistic. Is there a tentative sense of the confrontational discourse of 'inviolate egos' being 'disorbed' by productive sex? Nothing comes of it. Seven dashes indicate the lover's silence or his physical denial of the possibility, and the song ends in bitter, one-sided argument that restores the sequence's dominant dualism.

The sexual war that the songs dramatize and narrate reaches its climax in the next four poems of the sequence. Songs XIV—XVI are short lyrics defined by simultaneous regret and equivocal surviving passion. In XIV, for example, the speaker brings 'the nascent virginity of | —Myself' to the man. 'No love   or the other thing', she notes laconically,

> Only the impact of lighted bodies
> Knocking sparks off each other
> In chaos[21]

---

[18] Loy, quoted in Burke, *Becoming Modern*, 115.   [19] Neith Boyce, quoted ibid. 174.
[20] Loy, 'Songs to Joannes', 57.   [21] Ibid. 58–9.

This Futurist evocation of the percussive body animated by sex, by argument, by violence (by war?) is followed by a wry evaluation of the very Futurist masculinity that attracts her. 'Trying for Love', she comments, 'Fantasy dealt them out as gods.' The appeal of these fantastic gods is immediately questioned, however. 'I had to be caught in the weak eddy | Of your drivelling humanity | To love you most,' she asserts, softening the hardness of the 'lighted bodies' and reintroducing the debasing discourse of mucous that began the sequence. The most wistful lyric of the series follows this reduction of the 'Superhuman' to 'drivelling humanity'. 'We might have lived together / In the lights of the Arno,'[22] she muses, imagining games, a lullaby, and talk that suggest a return to the fantasy of intimacy and family that appeared in Songs III and IV. But this moment of romance is ended by the most disturbing poem of the sequence.

Song XVII is the central lyric in the series of thirty-four. It returns to Song IV's room and 'fearful furniture' and to an explicit acknowledgement of war as an invasive force in personal life. It begins with despair and hallucination: 'I don't care | Where the legs of the legs of the furniture are walking to | Or what is hidden in the shadows they stride.' This eerie passage of domestic paranoia leads to an even more disturbing vision:

> Red   a warm colour on the battle-field
> Heavy on my knees as a counterpane
> Count counter
> I counted   the fringe of the towel
> Till two tassels clinging together
> Let the square room fall away
> From a round vacuum
> Dilating with my breath[23]

War and the battlefield now occupy the bed not as metaphor but as blood, a tangible, '[h]eavy' covering jarringly described as a domestic counterpane. Maeera Shreiber and Eric Murphy Selinger have argued that the lyric alludes to an illicit abortion, a loss which, like Song XVII itself, lies at the heart of the 'Songs to Joannes'.[24] The bed, the body, breath, and the touch of fingers, earlier signifiers of consuming, if ambivalent passion, here return as markers of absolute loss. The 'round vacuum' occupies the centre of the space, mouth and uterus, dilating in a parody of birth, and creating a centrifuge from which the sequence never quite escapes. 'I am the centre | Of a circle of pain | Exceeding its boundaries in every direction,' Loy had begun her earlier poem 'Parturition'. In a '[v]acuum interlude' in that evocation

---

[22] Loy, 'Songs to Joannes', 58–9.   [23] Ibid. 60.

[24] Maeera Shreiber, ' "Love is a Lyric | of Bodies": The Negative Aesthetics of Mina Loy's *Love Songs to Joannes*', in *idem* and Keith Tuma (eds.), *Mina Loy: Woman and Poet* (Orona, Me.: National Poetry Foundation, 1998), 101–5; Eric Murphy Selinger, 'Love in the Time of Melancholia', ibid. 31–2.

of birth pains, Loy comments, 'I should have been emptied of life'.[25] In the later poem, it seems that its speaker has been.

'Songs to Joannes' performs a difficult dialogue with a silent lover in a context of war. Like Gertrude Stein, Loy is not interested in evoking or reacting to distant events; instead, she explores the ways in which the conflict insinuates itself within private experience. The sequence is not about war, but about a sexual life within war, and about the limits and possibilities of a woman's poetic language and technique as it engages with and emerges from those tensions. A later poem, 'Der Blinde Junge' (c.1922), perhaps Loy's best-known piece, can be read as a post-war coda to these preoccupations. Its evocation of a blinded war veteran playing a mouth-organ on the streets of Vienna has a more specific social context than the earlier sequence, but the exploratory rhetoric and the fascination with the relationship of war, sex, and birth remain. It begins in terms reminiscent of the first lyric of the 'Songs', as human sex is rendered animal:

> The dam Bellona
> littered
> her eyeless offspring
> Kriegsopfer
> upon the pavements of Vienna[26]

The young veteran is here both an 'offspring' of the Roman war goddess and a sacrificial animal ('Kriegsopfer') to the war that his mother embodies. 'Pig Cupid' has become a violent dam that destroys her young, and throughout the poem the soldier is conceived as animal before, in the final section, he becomes a 'thing'. Birth, long-drawn-out in 'Parturition', frustrated in 'Songs to Joannes', is profligate here, as war herself delivers her damaged young on to the city streets of Europe. Yet 'Der Blinde Junge', like all Loy's best work, combines brutal statement with an intelligent, wry adaptation of Futurism's amoral celebration of energy. The boy might be a 'purpose-less eremite', but, as in the central lyric of the earlier sequence, private anguish and vulnerability embody a hidden connection between twentieth-century war and the normalcy of a civilized city apparently distant from barbarism. The poet demands that the sighted citizens of Vienna listen to 'How this expressionless "thing" | blows out damnation and concussive dark || Upon a mouth-organ'. War has invaded the boy; he is its product, and 'damnation' is within him. However, in a knowing parody of the militarist performance poetry of Marinetti and the Futurists, the boy is shown to express its dark energy and transform the light of the normal morning through his other, exclusive knowledge. Like the anonymous speaker of the 'Songs', he is a distanced witness, victim, and performer of the extremities of the First World War.

Mina Loy, true to her Futurist credentials, does not seek resolution or deliverance in her war poetry. 'Songs to Joannes' ends with a typically wry and sceptical appraisal

---

[25] Loy, 'Parturition', in *Lost Lunar Baedeker*, 4–6.   [26] Loy, 'Der Blinde Junge', ibid. 83.

of the process of procreation that has haunted the affair ('Proto-plasm was raving mad | Evolving us'),[27] and the veteran of 'Der Blinde Junge' is not redeemed from horrors by his music. As Thom Gunn has suggested, Loy was a hard woman—as she put it herself, 'rather pugnacious'.[28] Hers was a hardness that produced war poetry outside the borders of the male genre or of any later process of a critical 'recovery' of women's war writing. She was an extremist. 'Men & women are enemies', she wrote in 'Feminist Manifesto'. But, as the polemic goes on to suggest, such enmity is performed through passionate engagement, not emotional withdrawal or ultimate accommodation: 'The only point at which the interests of the sexes merge—is the sexual embrace.'[29] Her tough, oblique war poetry is a product of such 'carnage' in all its implications, and of a testy aesthetic committed to an uncompromising examination of the personal consequences of war for women.

E. J. SCOVELL

E. J. Scovell's collection *Shadows of Chrysanthemums* (1944) is in many ways very different from Loy's sequence, in terms of both poetic strategy and subject-matter. As Peter Scupham puts it, Scovell wrote with 'a reticent candour, a clean exactitude of phrasing, a most observant eye and a warm heart'[30]—none of which can be said of Loy. The poetry is scrupulous in form and modest in its range, consisting mostly of lyrics that return to favourite scenes and objects: flowers, light, domestic interiors, family, and nature in an urban landscape. Detailed observation forms the basis for slow meditation and the drawing-out of implication. Like Loy's and Stein's work, though, her poems' insistence upon the intimate and the ordinary, and their inattention to the public rhetoric of wartime are instructive. Few are readily identifiable as 'war poetry'—Catherine Reilly selects only one four-line piece from *Shadows of Chrysanthemums* in *Chaos of the Night*. 'Home, house and household, the *domus*, are where her imagination starts,'[31] Scupham suggests; but, whilst Scovell's household might be very different from those of the older modernists, like them she uses its enclosed world to map a new sense of the places and experiences of wartime.

Two recurring themes of *Shadows of Chrysanthemums* suggest how this war poetry is developed—a series of 'still lives' about cut flowers (one of which gives the collection its title) and a set of poems about marriage and children. 'The Azalea by the Window' is the first of the flower poems. It is typical of the careful domestic

---

[27] Loy, 'Songs to Joannes', 67.

[28] Thom Gunn, 'Three Hard Women: H. D., Marianne Moore, Mina Loy', in *Shelf Life: Essays, Memoirs, and an Interview* (London: Faber, 1993), 33–52; Mina Loy, 'Interview with Paul Blackburn and Robert Vas Dias', in Shreiber and Tuma (eds.), *Mina Loy*, 207.

[29] Loy, 'Feminist Manifesto', 154.

[30] Peter Scupham, 'E. J. Scovell', *PN Review*, 26/3 (Jan.–Feb. 2000), 26.   [31] Ibid. 28.

rapture that characterizes Scovell's work, evoking the flower as it 'draws to itself the sparse | World-wide light' before rendering it back, 'a fountain, to the dark'.[32] Like Edward Thomas's 'Lad's Love' or 'The Path', perhaps the only kind of 'male' war poetry with which Scovell's work has anything in common, 'The Azalea by the Window' complicates the immediate observation of the natural world, developing a kind of tense metaphysics through its syntax. The household flower is transformed by the poem into a strange and powerful force ('enhanced, | Possessed') which itself 'holds like a cup' a moment of tension and darkening. As with Thomas's poetry, though with even more reticence, only gradually does this intense privacy of vision begin to accrue a distinct, if distant, political reference. The 'World-wide light' intimates the way in which Scovell's interiors will be asked to hold greater meanings as the loosely chronological sequence of poems progresses to wartime. This becomes clear a few pages later, in 'A Room at Nightfall'. Here another scene of dusk and flowers, where the 'narcissus-white' table lamp represents the flower that is 'Last to bloom | Of all lights',[33] is located more precisely. The poem begins with the clause 'As England's earth moves into dark', the previously implied Englishness of place now being made overt. A potentially cosy domestic scene is later destabilized as the perspective shifts from interior to exterior. 'We inside', she writes, 'Seem to hang in a domed pearl where light with shadow, | Shadow is interfused with light.' The personal safety of the couple in the lighted room becomes fragile, the domestic place suspended in darkness rather than illuminating the night outside. That fragility, it is implied by reference back to the first line, is national as well as personal.

The tentative politics of these early interiors is developed in two poems in the second half of the collection. 'Mid-Winter Flowers' again establishes a national as well as a local setting in 'curtained English rooms' where '[f]lowers brought out of darkness' bloom.[34] The jonquils, hyacinths, and freesias once more emphasize the fragility of a room poised in light against mid-winter snow and darkness. They 'tell our year's midnight | And turn our thoughts to east with scent and cold of dawn', Scovell again allowing a domestic environment to register national unease at eastward dangers with a dawn that offers little relief. The title-poem, also the final poem in the collection, concludes this sequence of still lives. 'Shadows of Chrysanthemums' explores the imagery of darkness and light through a detailed observation of flowers at dusk. Here, though, the shadows of the chrysanthemums achieve an intensity that 'outshine[s]' the actual flowers. In the second stanza, the poet evokes a half-world of ghosts, stars, and unfathomable distance as, once more, the domestic interior is opened up and made strange by the natural world that has been brought inside:

[32] E. J. Scovell, 'The Azalea by the Window', in *Shadows of Chrysanthemums* (London: Routledge, 1944), 21.

[33] Scovell, 'A Room at Nightfall', ibid. 23.   [34] Scovell, 'Mid-Winter Flowers', ibid. 29.

> But space in that shadow world lengthens, its creatures
> Fall back and distance takes their features;
> The shadows of the flowers that lean away
> Are blurred like milky nebulae;
> And faint as though a ghost had risen between
> The lamplight and the wall, they seem divined, not seen.[35]

The household is disturbed, and the observer senses an uncanny and unmanageable presence in the room. The 'dying, wild chrysanthemums' intensify their negative presence 'where deep | Is set on deep, and pallors keep | Their far-off stations'. There seems to be no war here, and yet, as with the apparently casual mention of England in the earlier poems in the collection or, indeed, of Verdun in Stein's 'Lifting Belly', the meditation on chrysanthemums is troubled and informed by a wider darkness hinted at in the phrase 'far-off stations'. That 'other' world is at once metaphysical, material, and military, the poet's anxiety both mysterious and urgently contemporary. Dying winter flowers summon all of these forces into the middle-class urban drawing-room.

The poems of *Shadows of Chrysanthemums* also chart the progress of a relationship. This is no Loyan sex war but, like 'Songs to Joannes', it is a sequence that is attentive to the ways in which a private world, of marriage in this case, is invaded by other 'carnage'. Two sonnets, 'Marriage and Death' and 'Love's Immaturity', initiate the theme, and these are followed immediately by the first poem about motherhood, 'The Poor Mother'. From then on a series of poems weaves together themes of sexual and familial love. 'A Wife' reviews a year of marriage, with the speaker, 'born here a second time',[36] becoming a child even as her own time for childbirth approaches. The characteristic quiet bliss of these love poems is offset by an equally characteristic sense of the fragility of such connections. The first of the sequence is called 'Marriage and Death', and a later sonnet, 'Time for Sleeping', introduces the particular mortal threat of war for the first time. Looking down at her sleeping husband, the speaker confesses 'I think of war and death', marking an invasion of intimacy similar to that evoked by the flowers that enter and change the domestic space in other poems. 'Barbara', one of the weaker poems in the collection, is an account of a marriage stalled by war: 'Her husband the young soldier . . . | (No children till the war is over)'.[37] However, this poem of hiatus heralds the longest poem in the collection, a set of eleven lyrics about what it means to bear a child in wartime.

'The First Year' is a poem that expresses the rapture of motherhood ('I am absorbed and clouded by a sensual love | Of one whose soul is sense and flesh the substance of | Her spirit').[38] In a way oddly comparable to 'Lifting Belly', it insists upon the delight of intimate involvement and exclusive contact in 'an imaginary world | Where I speak to my baby in English words'. Implicit in this,

---

[35]   Scovell, 'Shadows of Chrysanthemums', in *Shadows of Chrysanthemums*, 44.
[36]   Scovell, 'A Wife', ibid. 31.
[37]   Scovell, 'Barbara', ibid. 35.   [38]   Scovell, 'The First Year', ibid. 38.

though, is a question of the nature of the relationship between the 'imaginary world' and a world war that is barely, but significantly, registered by 'the woman's maternal-bound | Thought':

> The days fail: night broods over afternoon:
> And at my child's first drink beyond the night
> Her skin is silver in the early light.
> Sweet the grey morning and the raiders gone.

This uneasiness which, as in the flower poems, is located precisely at dusk, balances domestic urgency with an ambivalent, eerie description of her daughter's silver skin, a tone associated both with the new day and the perils of the night. As the year progresses in the poem, so does the perspective of the mother begin to withdraw from the absolute intimacy of the first months. By the end, the baby is seen as still miraculously strange but also resolute and able to survive a dangerous world by being an 'established citizen of earth'. Describing the child asleep on a double bed in the final lines of the poem, Scovell sees her as 'a sleeping sea-bird, guarded best | By yielding to the sea, wild sea its friend and nest'. The 'established citizen', a surprising political phrase in this poem of motherhood, suggests to the poet a means of enduring war and of connecting the intimacy of her experience to the threatening national context that is only once referred to overtly in the poem.

Scovell was—and remained—an undemonstrative, reticent writer. Unlike Mina Loy, she was not a theorist or polemicist; unlike Gertrude Stein, she was not an experimenter. Nevertheless, one poem in *Shadows of Chrysanthemums* does suggest explicitly a strategy for women's wartime writing that brings together the work of these three unlikely war poets. 'An Elegy', the penultimate poem in the collection, evokes a winter world of urban nature, a park in 'this city still unraided'.[39] The distance of war is explicitly registered this time, as is a need for finding a means of engagement with the consequences of violence and death elsewhere. 'It befits us who live on | To consider and to mourn,' she asserts. What is at issue in the poem is the means by which such distanced mourning and engagement could take place:

> How can I make a rite of these
> To mourn the pang I do not know,
> Death fastened on the life of man?
> Sorrow uses what it can.
> Take as my rite this winter tune:
> The child's walk in the darkening afternoon.

It is not one of Scovell's better poems, perhaps because of its very articulation of questions that are normally only implied by her work, but it articulates clearly the need to confront problems of 'response' and of rhetoric. The necessity to engage with war is at once obvious and difficult, the distance of experience shaping the

---

[39] Scovell, 'An Elegy', ibid. 43.

meditation upon it. Scovell's solution is to assert the domestic and the local as central to that engagement, and to render these not as comforting escapes from catastrophe, but as necessary parts of the wider experience of that catastrophe—the afternoon, as so often with this poet, is 'darkening'. Like Gertrude Stein's passionate articulation of an alternative world to Verdun ('Kiss my lips. She did. | Kiss my lips again she did'[40]) and Mina Loy's wartime meditation on 'incognitoes | In seismic orgasm',[41] Scovell's poetry fashions a way of thinking through war's experience and rhetoric by dealing with women's, not men's, bodies and experiences. 'Sorrow uses what it can', and that sense of a pragmatic attention to the exigency of experience beyond both combat and social change offers new possibilities, not just for the expansion of the canon to include women's war poetry, but also for its re-definition in the light of that poetry.

[40] Stein, 'Lifting Belly', 80.   [41] Loy, 'Songs to Joannes', 66.

CHAPTER 24

WAR PASTORALS

EDNA LONGLEY

I

By 'pastoral' I mean any poem that concerns the natural world or the human footprint on that world, including the poem itself. I take the pastoral field to encompass 'anti-pastoral'. In *Pastoral and the Poetics of Self-Contradiction*, Jane Haber argues that pastoral has always been a reflexive 'mode that work[s] insistently against itself, problematizing both its own definition and stable definitions within its texts'. From the genre's inception, 'presence, continuity, and consolation have been seen as related to—indeed as dependent on—absence, discontinuity and loss'.[1] In the 'war pastorals' considered here—from the First World War, the inter-war years, and the Northern Irish conflict—self-awareness or intertextual awareness often goes deep. Thus in 'Bog Cotton' (1979), Michael Longley speculatively aligns an Irish plant with Isaac Rosenberg wearing a poppy 'behind his ear' and Keith Douglas's 'thirstier desert flowers'.[2] This vista questions the remedial capacities of poetry, as well as pastoral: bog cotton is 'useless . . . though it might well bring to mind | The plumpness of pillows, the staunching of wounds. . . . As though to make a hospital of the landscape'. Has modern war overwhelmed the traditional resources of pastoral, figured by 'making a hospital of the landscape'? Or have poets been able to exploit and extend the pastoral repertoire? The issue is not confined to pastoral's elegiac aspect, but it seems relevant that, in Jahan Ramazani's study

---

[1] Jane Haber, *Pastoral and the Poetics of Self-Contradiction* (Cambridge: Cambridge University Press, 1994), 1.

[2] Michael Longley, 'Bog Cotton', in *Collected Poems* (London: Jonathan Cape, 2006), 136–7.

of modern elegy, his 'narrative of generic dislocation [has] a subplot of generic perpetuation'.[3]

As reflexive 'war pastoral', 'Bog Cotton' helps to perpetuate the genre of 'eclogue'. In his *Eclogues* Virgil obliquely comments on Roman affairs by creating a stylized rustic landscape where 'shepherds' and 'goatherds' occupy themselves with dialogues, love-songs, and singing contests. 'Bog Cotton' sets up a conversation between poets, co-opts landscape for a meditation on war and poetry, and is voiced at a certain distance from the natural scene and scenes of war. In heading two sections of this essay 'Interrupted Georgics' and 'Marginal Eclogues', I try to distinguish the broadly perspectival bias (and more radical reflexivity) of 'eclogue' from the broadly situational bias of 'georgic', as derived from Virgil's switch of focus to ploughshares and idiosyncratic discourse on agriculture. The 'georgic' section centres on poems by First World War combatants: principally Edward Thomas, but also Ivor Gurney and Edmund Blunden. The speakers of these poems are immersed in natural or rural environments that implicate war, or war environments that implicate nature or agriculture. Ultimately, as I indicate in Thomas's case, there is no clear line between eclogue and georgic (equally 'artificial' in Virgil's hands): modes that represent poles of the lyric poem itself. The final section, 'A Pastoral Peace?', looks at poems of the Northern Irish 'peace process'.

Not all pastoral poetry is anti-war. Not all war poetry is anti-pastoral. As regards poetry of modern war, the first proposition may seem more self-evident. In First World War verse, rural images knowingly serve pro-war propaganda; or they well up, unexamined, from the literary-patriotic unconscious. Both impulses unite in the calculated vagueness of Rupert Brooke's appeal to 'the autumnal earth', 'the colours of the earth', 'that rich earth'.[4] Hence the anti-pastoral streak in protest poetry, exemplified by Wilfred Owen's satirical citation of Shelley's 'I shall be one with nature, herb, and stone' in 'A Terre'.[5] But there might be less problematic ways in which pastoral intersects with patriotism (Brooke simply elides them), just as there might be ways in which 'war poetry' uses, rather than abuses, pastoral. Paul Fussell says of 'Arcadian Recourses':

Recourse to the pastoral is an English mode of both fully gauging the calamities of the Great War and imaginatively protecting oneself against them. Pastoral reference, whether to literature or to actual rural localities and objects, is a way of invoking a code to hint by antithesis at the indescribable; at the same time, it is a comfort in itself, like rum, a deep dug-out, or a woolly vest. The Golden Age posited by Classical and Renaissance literary pastoral now finds its counterpart in ideas of 'home' and 'the summer of 1914'.[6]

---

[3] Jahan Ramazani, *Poetry of Mourning: The Modern Elegy from Hardy to Heaney* (Chicago: University of Chicago Press, 1994), 10.

[4] Rupert Brooke, 'Safety', 'The Dead', 'The Soldier', in *The Poetical Works of Rupert Brooke*, ed. Geoffrey Keynes (London: Faber, 1960), 20, 22, 23.

[5] Wilfred Owen, 'A Terre', in *The Complete Poems and Fragments*, i: *The Poems*, ed. Jon Stallworthy (London: Chatto & Windus, Hogarth Press, and Oxford University Press, 1983), 179.

[6] Paul Fussell, *The Great War and Modern Memory* (Oxford: Oxford University Press, 1975), 325.

Perhaps the most complex war pastorals work by antinomy rather than 'anti-thesis'—which merely reverses Brooke's elision. The unstable generic boundaries of both 'pastoral' and 'war poetry' prevent 'war pastoral' (or 'battle-field') from being inevitably oxymoronic. Indeed, as Haber stresses, pastoral is a symbiotic outcrop of the original war poetry: epic. The counterpoint between 'bucolic' and 'heroic' in Theocritus's *Idylls* (which includes bucolic's role as critique of the heroic) dramatizes 'the relationship that exists between a limited present and a heroic past.... The "bucolic" perspective in the *Idylls* is repeatedly implicated in its opposite.'[7] Similarly, Virgil's *Eclogues* and *Georgics* belong to, and criticize, civil war: 'Since there'll be bards in plenty desiring to rehearse | Varus' fame, and celebrate the sorrowful theme of warfare [*tristia . . . bella*], | I shall take up a slim reed-pipe and a rural subject' (*Eclogues* VI).[8] One context for the *Eclogues* was the transfer of farms to war veterans. While the 'heroic' may become the sorrowful or pitiful, the violently destructive or painfully imperative, the symbiosis continues. It is epitomized and thematized by poems such as Thomas Hardy's 'In Time of "The Breaking of Nations"' (1915), Edward Thomas's 'As the team's head brass' (1916), Henry Reed's 'Judging Distances' (1943), and Paul Muldoon's 'Ireland' (1980): poems in which war impinges on a rural landscape with lovers. The effects range from Hardy asserting the staying power of his 'maid and her wight' ('War's annals will cloud into night | Ere their story die')[9] to Muldoon regretting that love is less likely to prevail than war:

> The Volkswagen parked in the gap,
> But gently ticking over.
> You wonder if it's lovers
> And not men hurrying back
> Across two fields and a river.[10]

As the title 'Judging Distances' suggests, the symbiosis between epic and pastoral is a matter of background becoming foreground, or vice versa. In Hardy's poem, 'War's annals' finally enter the scene only to be occluded; in Muldoon's 'Ireland', the explosive prospect of 'men hurrying back | Across two fields and a river' displaces the alternative image of 'lovers' and fills the view. The main speaker of 'Judging Distances', like that of Reed's better-known 'Naming of Parts', is a military instructor. 'Naming of Parts' pivots on ironic dissonance between the language of weaponry and the language of poetic pastoral: an eclogue-like contest in which the latter proves equal to the battle:

[7] Haber, *Pastoral and the Poetics of Self-Contradiction*, 13–15.

[8] Virgil, *The Eclogues · The Georgics*, trans. C. Day Lewis (Oxford: Oxford University Press, 1983), 25.

[9] Thomas Hardy, 'In Time of "The Breaking of Nations"', in *The Complete Poems*, ed. James Gibson (London: Macmillan, 1976), 543.

[10] Paul Muldoon, 'Ireland', in *Poems 1968–1998* (London: Faber, 2001), 82–3.

> And this you can see is the bolt. The purpose of this
> Is to open the breech, as you see. We can slide it
> Rapidly backwards and forwards: we call this
> Easing the spring. And rapidly backwards and forwards
> The early bees are assaulting and fumbling the flowers:
>   They call it easing the Spring.[11]

In 'Judging Distances' too, Reed reverses expectations that the language of war will be more 'real' than the language of pastoral. The poem begins:

> Not only how far away, but the way that you say it
> Is very important. Perhaps you may never get
> The knack of judging a distance, but at least you know
> How to report on a landscape.[12]

The military version of pastoral—'report on a landscape'—requires 'three kinds of tree, three only, the fir and the poplar, | And those which have bushy tops too'. And it corrects 'under the swaying elms a man and a woman | Lie gently together' to: 'under some poplars a pair of what appear to be humans | Appear to be loving'. When the speaker concludes that 'between me and the apparent lovers . . . is roughly a distance | Of about one year and a half', the poem's spatial dynamics disclose their temporal axis.

In Thomas's 'As the team's head brass', history meshes more intricately with the pastoral fabric. The speaker, presumably in uniform to invite the question 'Have you been out?', is 'Watching the plough narrowing a yellow square | Of charlock'.[13] This places—perhaps criticizes—him as a spectator of rural England, unlike the ploughman, who leans 'Upon the handles to say or ask a word, | About the weather, next about the war'. But he, too, is distanced from the absent figure who connects and haunts ploughman and implied soldier-poet: the former's dead 'mate':

> The blizzard felled the elm whose crest
> I sat in, by a woodpecker's round hole,
> The ploughman said. 'When will they take it away?'
> 'When the war's over.' So the talk began—
> One minute and an interval of ten,
> A minute more and the same interval.
> 'Have you been out?' 'No.' 'And don't want to, perhaps?'
> 'If I could only come back again, I should.
> I could spare an arm. I shouldn't want to lose
> A leg. If I should lose my head, why, so,

---

[11] Henry Reed, 'Naming of Parts', in *Collected Poems*, ed. Jon Stallworthy (Oxford: Oxford University Press, 1991), 49.

[12] Reed, 'Judging Distances', ibid. 50.

[13] Edward Thomas, 'As the team's head brass', in *Collected Poems*, ed. R. George Thomas (London: Faber, 2004), 115–16.

I should want nothing more . . . Have many gone
From here?' 'Yes.' 'Many lost?' 'Yes, a good few.
Only two teams work on the farm this year.
One of my mates is dead. The second day
In France they killed him. It was back in March,
The very night of the blizzard, too. Now if
He had stayed here we should have moved the tree.'
'And I should not have sat here. Everything
Would have been different. For it would have been
Another world.' 'Ay, and a better, though
If we could see all, all might seem good.'

This poem's lovers, who 'disappeared into the wood', now emerge:

                                                    Then
            The lovers came out of the wood again:
            The horses started and for the last time
            I watched the clods crumble and topple over
            After the ploughshare and the stumbling team.

If the lovers again signify peace and life, their semi-detached return falls short
of Hardy's assurance that erotic or agricultural 'business as usual' will be
resumed. Thomas leaves the ending ambiguously open to history. He underscores the lovers' reappearance with the poem's only rhyming couplet; but the
internal rhyme ('crumble', 'stumbling') has disturbing metaphorical nuances,
and the final consonantal rhyme—'time'/'team'—hints that the former may
run out for the latter. Thomas thought of calling the poem 'The Last Team'.[14]
'[F]or the last time' also shadows the speaker's future by adding him to the
scene's absences.

   War talk, including proleptic talk of dismemberment, destabilizes the poem's
blank-verse rhythms. Here Thomas exploits a formal corollary to the symbolism
whereby sword is taking over from ploughshare. The poem begins: 'As the team's
head brass flashed out on the turn'. 'Verse', as a line of poetry, derives from
the ploughman's 'turn' (versus), an origin that enters the poem's structures. On
the rhythmic front, as war penetrates pastoral, turns of the line become more
jagged. But the plough itself, like Andrew Marvell's destructive 'Mower', violates
the earth: it 'flashes', 'scrapes', 'screws'. At one point the speaker envisages the
ploughman 'treading me down'. Thomas reminds us that the plough—and, by
analogy, the poem—do not really belong to 'another world' from that which killed
the ploughman's mate: *alter ego* of both speakers.

---

[14] Thomas to Eleanor Farjeon, n.d. [June 1915], quoted in Eleanor Farjeon, *Edward Thomas: The
Last Four Years* (Stroud: Sutton Publishing, 1997), 144: 'I don't know about a title for the blank
verse. . . . What about "The Last Team"?' Farjeon misdates the letter.

II INTERRUPTED GEORGICS

'As the team's head brass' proves the capacity of pastoral to take the epistemological shock of the First World War. It might be a model for 'interrupted georgic': that is, for the poem in which war or latent epic infiltrates an agricultural scenario. Perhaps 'interrupted georgic' also applies to Edward Thomas's life. The war had largely suspended his occupation as writer of country books (and of reviews, biography, and criticism). Yet, when he started to write poems in December 1914, after nearly two decades devoted to prose, the war became a paradoxical Muse of his poetic pastoral. In 'As the team's head brass' it adds a further dimension to the aesthetic strategy that Thomas shared with Robert Frost: speech rhythms played against verse pattern. At every level, the poem has its ear to the ground of wartime upheaval in rural England, whether war or technology dooms the 'team'. To quote Caroline Dakers: 'teams of plough horses . . . had been taken for service in France . . . in the wake of the newly invented tank, tractors and steam ploughs belched and rumbled across English fields. . . . All this was a long way from the vision of an unchanging pastoral landscape under attack from invading rapacious Germans.'[15]

Thomas's pre-war prose had already absorbed radical changes to the rural economy and rural society. Since the 1880s, when the government refused to raise tariff barriers against North American wheat, the scale and power of English agriculture had diminished (especially in the south). As English people became the most town-based in Europe, there was a surge of cultural compensation: a back-to-nature movement; renewed attention to all forms of folk tradition; ideological investment in country life, 'village England', and the vanishing farm-labourer as bearers of national identity. Thomas belonged to this cultural tendency. His prose sometimes anatomizes the plight of displaced rural workers; sometimes idealizes their qualities. Aspects of Thomas's *The South Country* (1909) bear out Alun Howkins's observation in *The Death of Rural England*: 'The landscape of Englishness, in stark contrast to the landscape of Romanticism, was a southern landscape—the world of village England.'[16] Thomas's poem 'Lob' (1915), at one level the wartime apotheosis of compensatory ruralism, pivots on an elusive old Wiltshireman who personifies qualities 'English as this gate, these flowers, this mire'.[17]

Yet, just as the *Georgics* attach what Virgil values in Roman civilization to the anachronistic figure of the independent farmer, so 'Lob' is more than a nostalgic backward look. Richly intertextual, as in its neo-Chaucerian couplets, the poem asks how tradition—the sum of relations between natural environment, cultivation,

---

[15] Caroline Dakers, *The Countryside at War 1914–1918* (London: Constable, 1987), 19.

[16] Alun Howkins, *The Death of Rural England: A Social History of the Countryside since 1900* (London: Routledge, 2003), 26.

[17] Thomas, 'Lob', in *Collected Poems*, 59.

community, folklore, language, and literature—might survive or metamorphose in the conjoined contexts of war and modernity: 'One of the lords of No Man's Land, good Lob . . . He never will admit he is dead | Till millers cease to grind men's bones for bread.' Steeped in the actuality, traditions, and literature of rural England, Thomas was the deepest contemporary thinker about these matters, and his thinking led him to read landscape through historical and ecological (eco-historical) lenses. He was thus uniquely equipped to internalize the volatile situation on the cusp of war. In Howkins's words:

When rural England and Wales went to war in 1914, it still had many traditional social and cultural parts to its character. . . . There had been changes in agricultural production, but agriculture's methods were far behind those of the New Worlds of the USA, Canada and Australia. . . . Above all, the countryside remained firmly regional in its loyalties just as much as its dialects, and this was based on real differences in social and geographical structures.[18]

I have argued elsewhere that, partly as a subtle form of cultural defence, Thomas's poetry tests historical structures of the English lyric.[19] Given his imaginative world, this has special implications for the pastoral lyric from folk-song to the Romantics and beyond. Although overage, Thomas enlisted in July 1915. During that month he wrote several poems that obliquely ponder his decision in terms of pastoral tropes, in terms that alter pastoral tropes by historicizing them. In 'Aspens' and 'A Dream', 'known' rural landscapes are permeated by omens from wild nature. Wind, rain, and other waters often symbolize Thomas's sense that human beings do not control their environment, cannot read it, cannot control themselves (the 'blizzard' in 'As the team's head brass' spans weather and war). Thus he questions high-Romantic images of the poet's relation to nature. In 'Aspens', Coleridge's 'Aeolian Harp' and Shelley's appeal to the west wind to 'Make me thy lyre, even as the forest is'[20] become Thomas's Cassandra-like self-image as 'aspens': 'Above the inn, the smithy, and the shop, | The aspens at the cross-roads talk together | Of rain.'[21] In 'turn[ing] the cross-roads to a ghostly room', the 'talk' projects 'village England' as an emptied landscape. 'A Dream', another proleptic 'interrupted georgic', forebodes a landscape emptied of the speaker himself: 'Over known fields with an old friend in dream | I walked, but came sudden to a strange stream. | Its dark waters were bursting out most bright | From a great mountain's heart into the light.'[22] This underground stream (whose symbolism seems psychological as well as historical) recalls the 'deep romantic chasm' in Coleridge's 'Kubla Khan', from

---

[18] Howkins, *Death of Rural England*, 26.

[19] See my essay 'The Great War, History and the English Lyric', in Vincent Sherry (ed.), *The Cambridge Companion to the Literature of the First World War* (Cambridge: Cambridge University Press, 2005), 57–84.

[20] Percy Bysshe Shelley, 'Ode to the West Wind', in *Poetical Works*, ed. Thomas Hutchinson (Oxford: Oxford University Press, 1967), 579.

[21] Thomas, 'Aspens', in *Collected Poems*, 84.   [22] Thomas, 'A Dream', ibid. 82.

which 'A mighty fountain momently was forced', and also the sacred river's 'mazy motion'.[23] Thomas blends these 'waters' with Coleridge's 'voices prophesying war': 'So by the roar and hiss | And by the mighty motion of the abyss | I was bemused, that I forgot my friend.' The dreamer awakes, 'Saying: "I shall be here some day again"'.

A second pair of poems, 'Haymaking' and 'The Mill-Water', move from quintessential pastoral to pastoral's negation. As 'Haymaking' reflects on constructions of rural life, including its own, Thomas reaches back through English literary and visual traditions to agricultural origins:

> All was old,
> This morning time, with a great age untold,
> Older than Clare and Cobbett, Morland and Crome,
> Than, at the field's far edge, the farmer's home,
> A white house crouched at the foot of a great tree.
> Under the heavens that know not what years be
> The men, the beasts, the trees, the implements
> Uttered even what they will in times far hence—
> All of us gone out of the reach of change—
> Immortal in a picture of an old grange.[24]

Another ambiguous ending faces into history. 'Immortal' and 'out of the reach of change' subliminally suggest that what the poem 'utters' or 'pictures' could represent the last of—not only English—pastoral. In 'The Mill-Water' the word 'changelessly' obliterates mankind. A site of rural dereliction, which also encodes wartime depopulation, has been taken over by wild nature. Uncontrolled water marks the absence of cultivation, cognition, and utterance: 'All thoughts begin or end upon this sound, || Only the idle foam | Of water falling | Changelessly calling, | Where once men had a work-place and a home.'[25]

First World War pastoral does more than 'hint by antithesis at the indescribable', to quote Fussell. The process may work the other way: the interruption may define the georgic. As the founding poetry of civilization, pastoral potentially clarifies what the 'indescribable' throws into question: 'a work-place and a home'. The most interesting patriotic pastorals are predicated on a distinction between official 'England', British war aims or war conduct, and a felt relation to specific countryside. One of Charles Sorley's sonnets hauntingly equates war with the Wiltshire uplands: 'A homeless land and friendless, but a land | I did not know and that I wished to know.'[26] Thomas writes more positively: 'Something, I felt, had to be done before I could look again composedly at English landscape, at the elms

---

[23] Samuel Taylor Coleridge, 'Kubla Khan', in *Samuel Taylor Coleridge*, ed. H. J. Jackson (Oxford: Oxford University Press, 1985), 102–4.

[24] Thomas, 'Haymaking', in *Collected Poems*, 82.   [25] Thomas, 'The Mill-Water', ibid. 85–6.

[26] Charles Sorley, 'Two Sonnets', in *The Collected Poems of Charles Hamilton Sorley*, ed. Jean Moorcroft Wilson (London: Cecil Woolf, 1985), 87.

and poplars about the houses, at the purple-headed wood-betony.'[27] In a mostly dismissive essay on 'war poetry', he praises Coleridge's 'Fears in Solitude' as 'one of the noblest of patriotic poems' because written by 'a solitary man who, if at all, only felt the national emotions weakly or spasmodically'.[28] Coleridge's declaration that 'There lives nor form nor feeling in my soul | Unborrowed from my country!'[29] influenced Thomas's most directly patriotic poem, 'This is no case of petty right or wrong'. Having said, 'Beside my hate for one fat patriot, | My hatred of the Kaiser is love true', the speaker calls England 'all we know and live by'.[30] Thomas, with his superior credentials, surely sought to reclaim 'England' from Brooke, whose sonnets he thought self-publicizing.[31] His anthology *This England* (1915), into which he inserted 'Haymaking' and 'The Manor Farm', 'excludes professedly patriotic writing because it is generally bad'.[32] But there was already a gap between 'The Manor Farm' (December 1914), which affirms an English 'season of bliss unchangeable',[33] and the shakier time frame of 'Haymaking'.

One difference between Thomas and Ivor Gurney is Thomas's pastoral eclecticism, and the extent to which his poems take shape as an unsettled journey. Thomas's 'summer of 1914' poem is 'The sun used to shine' (May 1916), an eclogue in which conversations with Frost are both proleptically and retrospectively shadowed by war: 'We turned from men or poetry || To rumours of the war remote.'[34] The poem's setting matters less than its complex historical locus between 'the to be | And the late past'. Thomas's 'localism' is generally a function of structure rather than theme. It becomes theme or concept in 'Home' (April 1915), where the speaker, who has 'come back' to an unnamed place 'somehow from somewhere far', recognizes: ''Twas home; one nationality | We had, I and the birds that sang, | One memory.'[35] The dynamics between poet-speaker, birds, and a passing 'labourer' pioneer a local and ecological model of 'nationality' as 'home'. For Gurney, 'home' is Gloucestershire and the Cotswolds: 'I praised Gloucester city as never before—and lay | By Tilleloy keeping spirit in soul with the way | Cooper's comes over from Eastward, sees Rome all the way' ('The Poets of My Country').[36] This is borne out

---

[27] Thomas, 'This England', in *The Last Sheaf* (London: Jonathan Cape, 1928), 221.

[28] Thomas, 'War Poetry', in *A language not to be betrayed: Selected Prose*, ed. Edna Longley (Ashington and Manchester: MidNag/Carcanet, 1981), 132.

[29] Coleridge, 'Fears in Solitude', in *Samuel Taylor Coleridge*, 97.

[30] Thomas, 'This is no case of petty right or wrong', in *Collected Poems*, 92.

[31] Thomas to Robert Frost, 13 June 1915, in *Selected Letters*, ed. R. George Thomas (Oxford: Oxford University Press, 1995), 111: '[T]hose sonnets about him enlisting are probably not very personal but a nervous attempt to connect with himself the very widespread idea that self sacrifice is the highest self indulgence'.

[32] Thomas, prefatory note, in *idem* (ed.), *This England: An Anthology from her Writers* (London: Oxford University Press, 1915), p. iii.

[33] Thomas, 'The Manor Farm', in *Collected Poems*, 20.

[34] Thomas, 'The sun used to shine', ibid. 114.   [35] Thomas, 'Home', ibid. 64.

[36] Ivor Gurney, 'The Poets of My Country', in *Collected Poems*, ed. P. J. Kavanagh (Manchester: Carcanet, 2004), 257.

by 'First March', in which ordinary 'home-talk' fails to assuage the mind's 'circling greyness'.[37] But the poem ends:

> Suddenly a road's turn brought the sweet unexpected
> Balm. Snowdrops bloomed in a ruined garden neglected:
> Roman the road as of Birdlip we were on the verge,
> And this west country thing so from chaos to emerge.
> One gracious touch the whole wilderness corrected.

A shimmering vulnerability makes Gurney's remembered Cotswold landscapes unbearable. As 'Balm', they represent 'nerves soothed [that] were so sore shaken' ('After War'),[38] but the shaking continues. Yet, like the shared 'Romanness' of Gloucester and France, like his allusions to music, Gurney's landscapes also represent Europe as civilization: their 'gracious touch' a corrective to 'chaos' and 'wilderness'. The Cotswolds figure as a kind of cultivated wilderness, even if cultivated only by the intensity of his inner gaze. And his 'England', like Thomas's, depends on art. Noting that his collection *Severn and Somme* (1917) lacks 'the devotion of self sacrifice' necessary for popularity, Gurney says:

though I am ready if necessary to die for England, I do not see the necessity; it being only a hard and fast system which has sent so much of the flower of Englands [*sic*] artists to risk death, and a wrong materialistic system; rightly or wrongly I consider myself able to do work which will do honour to England. Such is my patriotism.[39]

Gurney and Thomas validate Howkins's stress on the regionality of the Britain that went to war. In Gurney's 'Billet', a private in the Gloucesters who 'wishes to bloody hell' he were enjoying various Gloucestershire recreations 'spoke the heart of all of us'.[40] Gurney both finds himself at 'home' with, and registers difference from, Scottish pipers, 'a Welsh colony . . . whispering consolatory | Soft foreign things', and the tragic 'Silent One' on the wire who had 'chattered through | Infinite lovely chatter of Bucks accent'.[41] But in 'Crickley Hill', perhaps Gurney's most rapturous expression of local patriotism, thoughts of the 'orchis, trefoil, harebells [that] nod all day, | High above Gloucester and the Severn Plain' cause the speaker to ignore another soldier's home-talk.[42] That is, until: ' "Crickley" he said. How I started | At that old darling name of home! And . . . | Fell into a torrent of words'. Early in the war, Thomas discovered the localized nature of its reception when he 'travelled through England, from Swindon to Newcastle-on-Tyne, listening to people . . . talking about the war and the effects of it'.[43] This engendered his idea—or aesthetic—that 'England is a system of vast circumferences circling

---

[37] Gurney, 'First March', in *Collected Poems*, 144.   [38] Gurney, 'After War', ibid. 145.

[39] Gurney to Marion Scott, 27 July 1917, in *Collected Letters*, ed. R. K. R. Thornton (Ashington and Manchester: MidNag/Carcanet, 1991), 288.

[40] Gurney, 'Billet', in *Collected Poems*, 127.

[41] Gurney, 'Crucifix Corner', 'First Time In', 'The Silent One', ibid. 135, 149, 250.

[42] Gurney, 'Crickley Hill', ibid. 39.   [43] Thomas, 'England', in *Last Sheaf*, 111.

round the minute neighbouring points of home'. 'Home' exemplifies this idea; ' "Home" ' (March 1916), the word now hedged by quotation marks, suggests how Thomas's army experience has both confirmed and darkened it. In ' "Home" ' the opposite situation to 'Crickley Hill' similarly marks the point at which affiliations become incommensurable. Three soldiers leave training camp for a country walk:

> Fair was the morning, fair our tempers, and
> We had seen nothing fairer than that land,
> Though strange, and the untrodden snow that made
> Wild of the tame, casting out all that was
> Not wild and rustic and old; and we were glad.[44]

Thomas sets the soldiers' collectivity in the pristine landscape of pastoral, 'wild and rustic and old'. But, as they approach 'the cold roofs where we must spend the night', an ironical reference to the camp as 'home' introduces history and geography: 'Between three counties far apart that lay | We were divided and looked strangely each | At the other.' The shared 'strangeness' of the land has turned into estrangement: 'we knew we were not friends/But fellows in a union that ends | With the necessity for it, as it ought.' The poem itself ends with the speaker self-estranged. Unable to go behind 'the word . . . | "Homesick" ', he fears that the war will make him 'Another man'. In ' "Home" ' the original pastoral paradigm, together with 'home' as a locally precise concept, questions the national 'union' imposed by the 'necessity', also questionable, of the First World War.

Not only urban-modernist texts manifest the cognitive dislocations produced by the war. The instability of 'home' in 'interrupted georgic' dramatizes epistemological as well as historical shifts. Only in 'The Manor Farm' does Thomas evoke what Dakers calls 'an unchanging pastoral landscape'. In 'Two Houses', an enlistment poem, a 'smiling', unreachable farmhouse is set against a trench-like tumulus representing 'the dead that never | More than half hidden lie'.[45] Between 30 January 1917, when he arrived in France with the Royal Artillery, and his death at Arras on 9 April, Thomas wrote no poetry, although his 'War Diary' mixes impressions of French landscape, war reports, and nature notes. But France underlies and defamiliarizes his England as England underlies France in poems by Gurney and Blunden.

In First World War pastoral, the *heimlich* and *unheimlich* are contiguous: often unresolvably so, as in 'Two Houses' or Owen's 'Spring Offensive'. Soldier-poets were disturbed as well as given 'Balm' by snowdrops in ruined gardens, by similarities between northern France or Flanders and southern England. In 'Vlamertinghe' Blunden quotes Keats's 'Ode on a Grecian Urn', and dwells on the English pastoral trope of flowers: 'This must be the floweriest place | That earth allows.'[46] The poem ends with a soldier's voice saying of the 'million' poppies there: 'But if you ask me, mate, the choice of colour | Is scarcely right; this red should have been duller.'

---

[44] Thomas, ' "Home" ', in *Collected Poems*, 104.   [45] Thomas, 'Two Houses', ibid. 88.
[46] Edmund Blunden, *Undertones of War* (Harmondsworth: Penguin, 1982), 256.

Blunden, who virtually terms himself a war pastoralist in the last phrase of his memoir *Undertones of War* ('a harmless young shepherd in a soldier's coat'[47]), is at his best in poems shocked by the disjunction between a farming countryside and its devastation or appropriation by war. 'Rural Economy' ironically conflates sword and ploughshare by portraying enemy artillery as a 'thoughtful farmer': 'The field and wood, all bone-fed loam, | Shot up a roaring harvest home.'[48] A battered 'House in Festubert', identified with the human body ('itself one wound'), has 'blossoming trees robed round', although now a British gun post: 'Home! Their home is ours.'[49] The poem ends with images of 'steel-born bees, birds, beams', and the question: 'Could summer betray you?' A key motif of Blunden's is 'Deceitful Calm' (subtitle of 'Gouzeaucourt'). It shapes his most *unheimlich* poem 'Illusions', which begins: 'Trenches in the moonlight, allayed with lulling moonlight, | Have had their loveliness'; and moves towards 'the nemesis of beauty': 'Death's malkins dangling in the wire | For the moon's interpretation'.[50] Blunden's intermittent power to stand back and strip away deceit may have influenced Keith Douglas's desert pastoral.

Gurney's poetry, whether set in France, England, or some disturbed hybrid of Severn and Somme, does not change its bearings in 1918. He carries the *unheimlich* over into post-war poems where georgic remains forever interrupted. Like his strange syntax, this cannot be discounted as only an effect of his mental illness. 'The Mangel-Bury', perhaps Gurney's finest poem and one of his several poetic tributes to Edward Thomas, brings the trenches back home by updating Thomas's 'Swedes': 'it was February; the long house | Straw-thatched of the mangels stretched two wide wings; | And looked as part of the earth heaped up by dead soldiers.'[51] The poet helps a farmer to load a cart with the mangels, and hopes to learn local lore from him. However, war complicates this rural conversation too: 'But my pain to more moving called | And him to some barn business far in the fifteen acre field.'

Edward Thomas is the major exponent of First World War pastoral, because he absorbs war into a larger metaphysic: an eco-historical long view, as much post- as pre-industrial.[52] His 'earth', like his 'England', is not Brooke's. Thomas's eco-centric perspective offers no more 'consolation' or commemorative reassurance than do Owen's 'elegies'. His proleptic vision extends pastoral elegy to humanity's obsolescence as an 'inhabitant of earth' ('The Other'), and hence to pastoral itself. His houses and dwellings, from 'a woodpecker's round hole' to 'the farmer's home' to poetry, symbolize the fragility of earthly habitats and memorials. All this makes Thomas's war pastoral 'marginal eclogue' as well as 'interrupted georgic', if its marginality is wholly temporal. Between August 1914 and departure for France, he had time to think.

---

[47] Edmund Blunden, *Undertones of War* (Harmondsworth: Penguin, 1982), 242.
[48] Blunden, 'Rural Economy', ibid. 254.   [49] Blunden, 'A House in Festubert', ibid. 245.
[50] Blunden, 'Illusions', ibid. 247.   [51] Gurney, 'The Mangel-Bury', in *Collected Poems*, 263.
[52] See my essay ' "The Business of the Earth": Edward Thomas and Ecocentrism', in *Poetry & Posterity* (Tarset: Bloodaxe, 2000), 23–51.

III Marginal Eclogues

'Inter-war pastorals' are eclogues by definition, reflective and highly reflexive. Here my texts are Yeats's 'A Prayer for my Daughter' (1919), poems from *Letters from Iceland* (1937) by W. H. Auden and Louis MacNeice, and MacNeice's lyric sequence 'The Closing Album' (1939). None of these poets might spring to mind as a 'pastoralist', especially if admiration for Wordsworth is any criterion. Yeats attacks Wordsworth for subjectively 'finding his image in every lake and puddle';[53] MacNeice has stylistic objections to 'the Wordsworthian exclusive crusade for homespun';[54] and Auden's 'Letter to Lord Byron', linchpin of *Letters from Iceland*, defines its own bearings by means of an anti-Wordsworth philippic: 'I'm also glad to find I've your authority | For finding Wordsworth a most bleak old bore.'[55] Auden's political ground for preferring Byron, the 'good townee', is the mystificatory use of nature worship: 'We can't, of course, invite a Jew or Red | But birds and nebulae will do instead.' But the priority of art over nature, or city over country, is a premiss of eclogue, whether its parabolic landscapes are Arcadian or dystopian. Yeats owed Wordsworth more than he pretended;[56] and 'Letter to Lord Byron' names Thomas as Auden's poetic first love. Further, all three poets are imaginatively attached to ancestral countrysides in ways that complicate pure eclogue.

As the poets meditate from the sidelines—sometimes on the sidelining of poetry—1914–18 shapes the prospect of other wars. Yeats can be as in denial of the war as of Wordsworth, both denials having sources in Irish politics. In *The Great War in Irish Poetry* Fran Brearton shows how Anglocentric paradigms, together with Irish reluctance (until recently) to confront Ireland's full involvement in the war, have prevented critics from recognizing that the 'way in which Yeats negotiates with the Great War provides a context for and a contrast to his approach to the Rising and the Civil War: the responses to all three events in his poetry may be seen as inextricably linked'.[57] A crucial context for 'A Prayer for my Daughter', as for 'The Second Coming', is less the First World War itself than the Russian Revolution. In declaring 'The ceremony of innocence is drowned',[58] 'The Second Coming' echoes Burke on the French Revolution. The millennial advent that Yeats now expects is neither cosmic revelation nor the apotheosis of Irish nationhood, but the triumph of the 'Marxian criterion of values as . . . the spear-head of materialism

---

[53] W. B. Yeats, 'Dr. Todhunter's Latest Volume of Poems', in *Letters to the New Island: A New Edition* (London: Macmillan, 1989), 89.

[54] Louis MacNeice, *Modern Poetry* (Oxford: Oxford University Press, 1968), 43.

[55] W. H. Auden, 'Letter to Lord Byron', in W. H. Auden and Louis MacNeice, *Letters from Iceland* (London: Faber, 1937), 99.

[56] See my essay 'Pastoral Theologies', in *Poetry & Posterity*, 90–133.

[57] Fran Brearton, *The Great War in Irish Poetry: W. B. Yeats to Michael Longley* (Oxford: Oxford University Press, 2000), 49.

[58] Yeats, 'The Second Coming', in *The Poems*, ed. Daniel Albright (London: Dent, 1990), 235.

and leading to inevitable murder'. He particularly dreaded that 'Ireland . . . (under the influence of its lunatic faculty of going against everything it believes England to affirm)' might give itself to 'Marxian revolution'.[59] In 'Prayer' this fear coalesces with more valid fears, encrypted into the refrain of 'Easter, 1916': 'A terrible beauty is born'.[60] Maud Gonne, anti-type of the poem's female ideal, was then in Holloway jail. Sinn Fein's success in the UK election of December 1918 had boosted the first phase of the IRA's guerrilla offensive. Attacks on the police were increasing. Thus Yeats's daughter magnetizes other births: revolutionary Russia; an Irish 'terror'; or, alternatively, an Irish state fit for 'innocence and beauty'.

'Prayer' moves in a contrary gyre to that of 'The Second Coming'—from apocalypse to pastoral utopia—starting where its precursor leaves off:

> Once more the storm is howling, and half hid
> Under this cradle-hood and coverlid
> My child sleeps on. There is no obstacle
> But Gregory's wood and one bare hill
> Whereby the haystack- and roof-levelling wind,
> Bred on the Atlantic, can be stayed;
> And for an hour I have walked and prayed
> Because of the great gloom that is in my mind.[61]

West-of-Ireland weather and landscape allow Yeats to bring wild nature and human settlement, anarchy and security, into emblematic opposition. 'Howling' (which mobs do) and 'levelling' have political implications. Later, a sea-wind 'screams upon the tower', and Gonne's 'opinionated mind' produces 'an old bellows full of angry wind'. While 'Prayer' sets Gonne against Yeats's wife, it does not simply advise women to exchange 'opinions' for marriageable 'glad kindness'. Rather, Yeats dramatizes a quarrel in (and about) his own 'mind': political rhetoric (screaming sea-wind), which distorts more than voice, versus poetry (the tower, a linnet's song). This dialectic enquires how Yeats's poetry might negotiate 'the future years', projected as a kind of Bacchanalian war dance: 'Dancing to a frenzied drum'. The way in which the poem modulates its own rhetoric, and conceives a utopian counter-aesthetic, depends upon a mustering of pastoral resources.

Virgil's *Eclogues* was a point of reference for Yeats. Behind 'Prayer' we may discern the Fourth Eclogue (of which more below) in which a dynastically significant birth heralds a second 'golden age'. Classical pastoral characterizes the golden age as earth pouring forth its abundance without need of cultivation. Whereas the goddess-like Gonne has 'undone' 'the Horn of Plenty' by abusing her gifts, the poet prays that his daughter may become 'a flourishing hidden tree | That all her thoughts may like the linnet be, | And have no business but dispensing round | Their magnanimities

---

[59] Yeats to George Russell (A. E.), ? Apr. 1919, in *The Letters of W. B. Yeats*, ed. Allan Wade (London: Rupert Hart-Davis, 1954), 656.

[60] Yeats, 'Easter, 1916', in *Poems*, 228.   [61] Yeats, 'A Prayer for my Daughter', ibid. 236.

of sound'. By translating Golden Age fertility into great-souled creativity, Yeats symbolically heals his (and others') 'dried up' mind. If, in terming the tree a 'laurel', he invokes Daphne and Apollo, in terming the bird a 'linnet' he invokes Wordsworth. Further, the daughter's ideally 'hidden' life 'Rooted in one dear perpetual place' (a localist touch here) recalls Wordsworth's 'Lucy'. Yeats again unexpectedly summons Romantic English 'nature' to his aid when he proposes that: 'All hatred driven hence, | The soul recovers radical innocence | And learns at last that it is self-delighting, | Self-appeasing, self-affrighting'. In Coleridge's 'Dejection' Ode: 'From the soul itself must issue forth | A light, a glory'.[62] Then Yeats balances Romantic nature with English Renaissance pastoral, which values cultivated nature: gardens, architecture (contrast Thomas's 'homes'). His last stanza parallels the climax of Marvell's 'Upon Appleton House', a post civil-war pastoral in which the hopes of the Fairfax dynasty are pinned upon the beauty, innocence, quiet virtue, and marriage of the young 'Maria': 'heaven's centre, Nature's lap | And paradise's only map'.[63] The poem's accumulated pastoral resources enable Yeats to reaffirm 'the ceremony of innocence'. And, in fusing pastoral's poles of art and nature, he models both a powerful aesthetic and an ideal polity:

> And may her bridegroom bring her to a house
> Where all's accustomed, ceremonious;
> For arrogance and hatred are the wares
> Peddled in the thoroughfares.
> How but in custom and in ceremony
> Are innocence and beauty born?
> Ceremony's a name for the rich horn,
> And custom for the spreading laurel tree.

Letters from Iceland directly and indirectly alludes to the First World War. 'Letter to Lord Byron' reports the death of the 'swaggering bully' John Bull, who 'passed away at Ypres and Passchendaele'.[64] In 'Eclogue from Iceland' MacNeice evokes 'the hero | With his ribbons and his empty pinned-up sleeve | Cadg[ing] for money', and celebrates 'that dancer | Who danced the war' (the disturbed Nijinsky).[65] Just as the Easter Rising and the war curbed—for a time, at least—Yeats's Nietzschean enthusiasm for heroes and heroines, so the tendency of *Letters* is anti-heroic and mock-heroic. With regard to 'Ypres and Passchendaele', it exudes a 1930s mix of survivor guilt, inferiority complex, and belated protest. Yet the poets do not espouse the alternative heroics of 'Marxian revolution'. Perhaps the literary chemistry between Auden and MacNeice works differently from that between Auden and Auden's English poetic hero-worshippers. Perhaps, too, Iceland provided the conditions for anti-heroic aesthetics and politics.

---

[62] Coleridge, 'Dejection: An Ode', in *Samuel Taylor Coleridge*, 114.
[63] Andrew Marvell, 'Upon Appleton House', in *The Complete Poems*, ed. Elizabeth Story Donno (Harmondsworth: Penguin, 1972), 99.
[64] Auden, 'Letter to Lord Byron', 55.   [65] MacNeice, 'Eclogue from Iceland', ibid. 128 and 131.

To go there at all was to create the artificial landscape appropriate to eclogue. Yet distance from mainland Europe lands Iceland metaphorical conviction as 'perspective', while its status as an island lands it conviction as contemplative retreat. If most of the generically hybrid *Letters* is 'pastoral' only in this broader sense, Icelandic terrain is always on the horizon—a terrain part familiar as well as foreign. For Auden, Iceland both activated and modified a deep-laid myth. In *The Idea of North* Peter Davidson terms Auden's North 'a complex structure made up of obsessions with mining and geology, Icelandic sagas, Old English poetry, personal experience of the north of England'.[66] MacNeice plays on the double euphony of Iceland/island with 'Ireland', and can situate Iceland in imaginative proximity to western Ireland, to Yeats's western pastoral and his own.

Letters relativizes constructions of 'Iceland'. Auden's 'Journey to Iceland' reviews the different maps and 'hopes' of the traveller, lover of islands, and so on. Also an exorcism of his own Romantic templates, the poem recognizes that 'the fabulous | Country' is 'impartially far'.[67] Its ultimate Nordic image is 'a blinding snowstorm' as 'some writer | Runs howling to his art'. Thus Auden does not transfer to Iceland the parabolic war games of his 'northern' *juvenilia*, but takes it as it comes—or, as in his seemingly casual address to Byron, advances an aesthetic of taking it as it comes. The poets set their own representations among other 'Sheaves from Sagaland', often absurd. There are politics behind the book's relativism. Auden says in his first 'Letter' to Erica Mann: 'The Nazis have a theory that Iceland is the cradle of the Germanic culture. Well, if they want a community like that of the sagas they are welcome to it. I love the sagas, but what a rotten society they describe, a society with only the gangster virtues.'[68] But Icelanders may disappoint Nazi tourists in search of Aryan purity, since they have effectively swapped epic for pastoral. Addressing Christopher Isherwood, Auden says: '[The Icelander] is unromantic and unidealistic... I can't picture him in a uniform... [He] is seldom irresponsible, because irresponsibility in a farmer or fisherman would mean ruin.' Icelanders lack 'fanatical patriotism' and 'hysterical nationalism'.[69] As generically reflexive eclogue, the poets' 'travel book... thrown together in gaiety'[70] inscribes Icelandic landscape with fissures between an epic past and a pastoral present. Yet they do not fence off 'georgic' Iceland from dark politics. Auden says of whale butchering: 'It gave one an extraordinary vision of the cold controlled ferocity of the human species.'[71]

'Eclogue from Iceland'[72] belongs to a series of poems in which MacNeice adapts classical eclogue to commentary on 1930s Britain and Ireland. 'Eclogue' depicts the

---

66 Peter Davidson, *The Idea of North* (London: Reaktion Books, 2005), 85.

67 Auden, 'Journey to Iceland', in *Letters from Iceland*, 27.

68 Auden, 'W. H. A. to E. M. A.—No. 1', ibid. 119.

69 Auden, 'Journey to Iceland', 29–30.

70 MacNeice, *The Strings Are False: An Unfinished Autobiography* (London: Faber, 1965), 164.

71 Auden, 'W. H. A. to 'E. M. A.—No. 2', in *Letters from Iceland*, 148.

72 MacNeice, 'Eclogue from Iceland', 124–135.

poets ('Ryan' and 'Craven') conversing with 'Grettir Asmundson', a ghost from the sagas. Here (as in 'Prayer') aesthetic, ethical, and political issues interpenetrate. MacNeice's dialectics ask how, on the likely verge of European war, anti-heroic liberalism might translate into poetry and action. Just as First World War veterans must 'cadge for money', so Ireland since the Rising figures as 'a nation | Built upon violence and morose vendettas'. One 'hero' of the Rising, the socialist James Connolly, is 'Vilified now by the gangs of Catholic Action'. And, where Yeats deplores 'an old bellows full of angry wind', MacNeice terms fascism 'the wall | Of shouting flesh'. Grettir serves as a role model because, like Yeats's model woman, he lacks extreme gifts: 'the wisdom of Njal or the beauty of Gunnar'. He represents himself as saved by misfortune from the temptations of power: 'I was the doomed tough, disaster kept me witty'. As an 'outlaw', he symbolically negotiates Iceland's mixed terrain: 'Fording the gletcher, ducking the hard hail, | And across the easy pastures, never stopping | To rest among celandines and bogcotton'. Like the poem's artist-heroes, Nijinsky and Chekhov, whose 'haemorrhages drove him out of Moscow', Grettir personifies persistence and resistance against the odds. 'Eclogue' ends with MacNeice putting a more abstract version of these qualities (also an *ars poetica* that prefigures *Autumn Journal*) into Grettir's mouth: 'Minute your gesture but it must be made— | Your hazard, your act of defiance and hymn of hate.' This parallels Auden's attack, in 'Letter to Lord Byron', on the inertia that props up 'Each dying force of history'.[73] In their 'Last Will and Testament', another *ars poetica*, the poets 'pray' for the power to assume 'the guilt | Of human action'.[74]

Letters from Iceland can be classified as 'literature of preparation'. Certain physical features qualify Iceland to embody 1930s 'waiting for the end':[75] to generate apocalyptic omens of war. Glaciers, geysers, and volcanoes suggest first and last things. In Auden's 'Letter to R. H. S. Crossman', 'the Markafljót... | Wasting these fields, is no glacial flood | But history, hostile'.[76] MacNeice's 'Epilogue', which records 'Down in Europe Seville fell', remembers 'Watch[ing] the sulphur basins boil,/Loops of steam uncoil and coil,/While the valley fades away | To a sketch of Judgment Day'.[77] On MacNeice's psycho-cultural map, 'North' (the rigours of an Ulster childhood) is a bleaker compass point than 'West' (he conceives his ancestral Connemara as a lost 'home'). In 'Iceland' geology puts humanity and poetry in its place: 'The glacier's licking | Tongues deride | Our pride of life, | Our flashy songs.'[78] Here last things are more than symbolic, since all will 'Relapse to rock/Under the shawl | Of the ice-caps'. Yet the poem's northern rigour implicitly prepares the speaker and his poetry for war. Similarly, MacNeice's 'Letter to Graham and

[73] Auden, 'Letter to Lord Byron', 58.

[74] Auden and MacNeice, 'Auden and MacNeice: Their Last Will and Testament', ibid. 258.

[75] William Empson, 'Just a Smack at Auden', in *The Complete Poems*, ed. John Haffenden (London: Penguin, 2000), 81–2.

[76] Auden, 'Letter to R. H. S. Crossman, Esq.', in *Letters from Iceland*, 91.

[77] MacNeice, 'Epilogue', ibid. 260.   [78] MacNeice, 'Iceland', ibid. 230.

Anne Shepard' represents 'The obscure but powerful ethics of Going North' as a pilgrimage to 'mortify | Our blowsy intellects'.[79]

If MacNeice's North is purgative, his West is palliative but deceptive. In problematically bringing him back 'home', 'The Closing Album' reinstates history. Initially called 'The Coming of War', this poetic memoir of an eve-of-war trip to Ireland begins with 'Dublin', which epitomizes Irish–British history: 'Nelson on his pillar, | Watching his world collapse'; 'The Four Courts burnt' (an image from the Irish Civil War).[80] The poem does not ignore power dynamics, but its valedictory salute questions Irish nationalism too: 'Fort of the Dane, | Garrison of the Saxon, | Augustan capital | Of a Gaelic nation . . . .' Perhaps this also attaches the 'neutral' Free State to Europe. MacNeice tells Dublin: 'You poise the toppling hour.' It does so by 'Appropriating all | The alien brought' on a site where architecture and nature symbolically interpenetrate: 'Grey stone, grey water'. The poem works as a snapshot, freezing history and war. It also sets up oppositions that will run through the sequence: MacNeice's Irish and English affiliations, city and country, peace and war, forgetting (Dublin 'days are soft | . . . enough to forget | The lesson better learnt') and remembering, MacNeice and Yeats. In 'Dublin' images of violence ('The bullet on the wet | Streets') part-echo, part-demystify 'Easter, 1916'. Then, in 'Sligo and Mayo' and 'Galway', MacNeice follows Yeats by inscribing western Ireland with World War. But, unlike Yeats, he does not disguise the fact:

> The night was gay
> With the moon's music
> But Mars was angry
> On the hills of Clare
> And September dawned
> Upon willows and ruins:
> The war came down on us here.

Ireland, like Iceland, is time and space out. MacNeice's 'album' stores memory with pre-war images. But, because the end is really nigh, the west becomes wilder and more *unheimlich*; pastoral images mutate into war images: turfstacks 'Like the tombs of nameless kings'. Meanwhile, eclogue mutates into interrupted georgic. In the last, 'nameless', open-ended poem, the speaker's prospective involvement in war pervades his mental landscape. Water now represents history on the move. As war encroaches on the architecture of civilization, doom lapping like Yeats's storm howling, it encroaches on poetry. The sequence is revealed to be a love poem, cancelled by war: 'And why, now it has happened, | And doom all night is lapping at the door, | Should I remember that I ever met you— | Once in another world?' 'Another world' recalls Thomas in 1916.

---

[79] MacNeice, 'Letter to Graham and Anne Shepard', ibid. 32.
[80] MacNeice, 'The Closing Album', in *Collected Poems*, ed. Peter McDonald (London: Faber, 2007), 178–82.

IV A Pastoral Peace?

If war and pastoral cannot always avoid oxymoron, peace and pastoral conversely attract. Of course, most war poems are peace poems too; but the balance tilts when 'home' comes home. The original anti-war poem, Tibullus I. x, identifies 'peace' with farm life: 'I would like peace to be my partner on the farm, | Peace personified: oxen under the curved yoke; | Compost for the vines, grape-juice turning into wine . . .'.[81] In reaching for pastoral images, 'end of war' or 'aftermath' poems affirm pastoral's return. In Gurney's 'The Valley Farm' a 'weapon' is productively used by a wood-chopper who 'moves with such grace peace works an act through him; | Those echoes thud and leave a deeper peace'.[82] Of course, there are also Gurney's perpetually interrupted georgics. And Blunden's poem on 'The Rebuilding of Ypres' contrasts false and true memorial uses of pastoral: the official 'mild desire Arcadian' as against the claims of dead soldiers, which powerfully revise Shelley and Brooke:

> but I
> Am in the soil and sap, and in the becks and conduits
> My blood is flowing, and my sigh of consummation
> Is the wind in the rampart trees.[83]

The 'war pastoral' of Northern Ireland since 1969 is a huge topic. Fran Brearton suggests its complexity when she begins her discussion of First World War allusion in Seamus Heaney's *Field Work* (1979) by noting that 'field works' is a military term. She counters the view that Heaney has scaled down his vision by showing that '[his] field is also a field of war from which respite is gained only with difficulty'.[84] Indeed, Heaney's ambiguous title might be a synonym for 'war pastoral', 'war pastoral' a synonym for Northern Ireland. The conflict exemplifies the territorial imperative of any civil war—war on 'home' ground—at work within a predominantly rural area. And this war, like the cultural codes it engages, derives from land history bound up with archipelagic and European wars. 'City' poetry of the 'Troubles' does not exhibit notably different dynamics. In 1950 John Hewitt published a poem celebrating 'Ulster Names'. In 1984 he wrote a 'Postscript':

> Now with compulsive resonance they toll:
> Banbridge, Ballykelly, Darkley, Crossmaglen,
> summoning pity, anger and despair,
> by grief of kin, by hate of murderous men

---

[81] 'Peace', trans. Longley, in Longley, *Collected Poems*, 134–5.
[82] Gurney, 'The Valley Farm', in *Collected Poems*, 67.
[83] Blunden, 'The Rebuilding of Ypres', in *Undertones of War*, 274.
[84] Brearton, *Great War in Irish Poetry*, 243.

till the whole tarnished map is stained and torn,
not to be read as pastoral again.[85]

'Not to be read as pastoral'—but perhaps to be written as war pastoral. Within the field of 'place-name poems' itself, Heaney's *Wintering Out* (1972) makes precisely that transition. Northern Irish poets pick and mix from many traditions of war poetry, pastoral poetry, and both together, from Tibullus to Thomas and Frost, from Homer to Douglas, from Marvell to MacNeice. They also mix Irish pastoral genres: Yeats's western eclogue, Patrick Kavanagh's inland georgic. Muldoon recasts the Irish poem of rural community as a social psychology of conflict.

Poems of the 'peace process' years repeatedly seek to expel war from pastoral. Heaney's 'Tollund' (1994), written just after the IRA ceasefire, revisits the Danish landscape that, in 'The Tollund Man', he had made surrogate for Northern Ireland's fratricidal parishes. Now: 'It could have been a still out of the bright | "Townland of Peace", that poem of dream farms | Outside all contention.'[86] ('Townland of Peace' is an idyllic utopian section of John Hewitt's regionalist poem 'Freehold', written during the Second World War.) But peace is a long haul, and it remains unclear whether 'war poetry' has been stood down. Poems in Heaney's *Electric Light* (2001), Muldoon's *Moy Sand and Gravel* (2002), and Longley's *Snow Water* (2004) continue to offer pastoral models (rather than assurances) of peace. Longley's sonnet 'War & Peace' exploits a Homeric passage in which georgic interrupts epic. The narrative of Achilles pursuing Hector around the walls of Troy encompasses a flashback to pastoral domesticity, focused by 'double well-heads' 'Where Trojan housewives and their pretty daughters | Used to rinse glistening clothes in the good old days, | On washdays before the Greek soldiers came to Troy'.[87] Longley also maintains double vision in 'Edward Thomas's Poem', part of an 'aftermath' sequence that uses First World War images to reflect on art, peace, and the arts of peace. The poem does not resolve the doubts of 'Bog Cotton': 'The nature poet turned into a war poet as if | He could cure death with the rub of a dock leaf.'[88] Muldoon's 'Whitethorns', a parable of conflict resolution, alludes to Frost's 'Mending Wall' and Kavanagh's 'Innocence' ('I cannot die | Unless I walk outside these whitethorn hedges'[89]). Another doubled poem, but with a utopian thrust, 'Whitethorns' recalls a time when 'we would tap paling posts into the ground... | hammering them home then with a sledge... to keep our oats from | Miller's barley'.[90] In the second quatrain, rhymed with the first, the divisive posts become:

---

[85] John Hewitt, 'Postscript', in *The Collected Poems*, ed. Frank Ormsby (Belfast: Blackstaff, 1991), 388.

[86] Seamus Heaney, 'Tollund', in *Opened Ground: Poems 1966–1996* (London: Faber, 1998), 443.

[87] Michael Longley, 'War & Peace', in *Collected Poems*, 310.

[88] Longley, 'Edward Thomas's Poem', ibid. 307.

[89] Patrick Kavanagh, 'Innocence', in *Collected Poems* (London: Allen Lane, 2004), 183.

[90] Paul Muldoon, 'Whitethorns', in *Moy Sand and Gravel* (London: Faber, 2002), 28.

maxed-out, multilayered whitethorns, affording us a broader, deeper shade
than we ever decently hoped to know
so far-fetched does it seem, so far-flung from the hedge
under which we now sit down to parley.

Pastoral, like all poetry, can only offer symbols or templates, whether it figures
peace as 'dream farms'; as resumed wine making or wood chopping or laundry; as a
flourishing laurel or multilayered whitethorn; as conversation ('parley') or poetry.
Perhaps what links such natural/rural images of peace, or of 'civilisation' as war's
true 'opposite',[91] is the desire to bring human faculties or energies into a lost balance,
to reinstate the earthly 'Horn of Plenty'. But, like earlier peace pastoral, Northern
Irish versions know that war forgotten is war renewed. And, despite violence having
largely ceased, aspects of the 'peace process' can be construed as war by other
means. Three poems in the collections cited above revisit Virgil's Fourth Eclogue
(overlaid by Yeats's 'Prayer'), and thus highlight the utopian dimension of eclogue
as a mode of political thought. The protective-visionary poem about a child is a
peculiarly urgent way of imagining the future. Longley's 'The Leveret', Heaney's
'Bann Valley Eclogue' and Muldoon's 'At the Sign of the Black Horse' all involve
babies and mention prams.

In 'The Leveret', a western eclogue, reminders of violence linger. The poet's
visiting grandson is hailed as 'little hoplite',[92] his pram called a 'chariot', and the
landscape contains a stoat with 'a shrew in his mouth'. But such reminders are
set within a mainly peaceable kingdom of cultivation, wild nature, and young
creatures. This finally pivots, not on Yeats's ceremonious unity, but on a more
humbly reflexive symbol that befits a 'cottage': 'I have picked wild flowers for
you, scabious | And centaury in a jam-jar of water | That will bend and magnify the
daylight.' Heaney's *Electric Light* contains three deliberate 'eclogues', all of which
end on an upbeat pastoral note. 'Bann Valley Eclogue', a dialogue between 'Poet'
and 'Virgil', loosely based on the Fourth Eclogue and set in mid-Ulster, evinces
a powerful sense of millennial occasion. Virgil prophesies 'a flooding away of all
the old miasma': a prophecy given weight by the rhythms of the Poet's messianic
conclusion:

> Child on the way, it won't be long until
> You land among us. Your mother's showing signs,
> Out for her sunset walk among big round bales.
> Planet earth like a teething ring suspended
> Hangs by its world-chain. Your pram waits in the corner.
> Cows are let out. They're sluicing the milk-house floor.[93]

[91] Michael Longley's poem 'All of these People' begins: 'Who was it who suggested that the opposite
of war | Is not so much peace as civilisation?' (in *Collected Poems*, 253).
[92] Longley, 'The Leveret', in Ibid. 327.
[93] Heaney, 'Bann Valley Eclogue', in *Electric Light* (London: Faber, 2001), 11–12.

Perhaps to balance 'Whitethorns', Muldoon's 'At the Sign of the Black Horse' represents history as still in dangerous, rather than salutary, flood. After Hurricane Floyd, the poet's family perches outside their house above a flooded American road, while the baby sleeps in an 'old Biltrite pram'. Relocating Yeats's storm as the hurricane, Muldoon entwines an intertextual critique of 'Prayer' with metaphorical flotsam of the years since 1919—flotsam largely determined by his child's Irish-Jewish heritage: 'Asher slept on, his shawl | of Carrickmacross lace, his bonnet tied with silk reputed to come from Samarkand.'[94] The Holocaust is among the reasons why the speaker recurrently doubts that 'the soul' will 'recover radical innocence' anytime soon. Nonetheless, the future sleeps in the child. Set between history and home, Muldoon's poem is another marginal eclogue, another war pastoral that defines peace or civilization by contraries. Its relation to 'A Prayer for my Daughter' underlines how war pastoral builds up civilization by building upon its own history.

[94] Muldoon, 'At the Sign of the Black Horse', in *Moy Sand and Gravel*, 77.

CHAPTER 25

....

THE POETRY
OF PAIN

....

SARAH COLE

About suffering they were never wrong, the Old Masters . . .

W. H. Auden, 'Musée des Beaux Arts'

Does suffering have a voice? Wilfred Owen wrote, from somewhere on the Western Front in 1917, that it is the poet's business to express the pain of his own hurting body, a palsied rhythm set 'to music of the world's eternal wail': 'If', he postulates in 'The Poet in Pain', 'my remorseless ache | Be needful to proof-test upon my flesh | The thoughts I think, and in words bleeding-fresh | Teach me for speechless sufferers to plain, | I would not quench it.'[1] One could almost say that Owen revels in pain in these lines, for the driving imperative of his verse—'for speechless sufferers to plain'—seems to demand such empathetic struggle. Indeed, the poem makes an urgent statement about the way in which the poet's own suffering and the success of his poetry sustain one another, proclaiming all at once that the world's eternal wail (here war) represents a constant strain throughout history; that war generates forms of agony which deprive its participants of language; that the poet works to articulate in words the primal groan of a world in crisis; and that to create an artefact which can somehow crash through the culture's wall of silence and ignorance relies on the writer's own willingness to feel pain. Trauma, as Cathy Caruth has postulated in her influential study *Unclaimed Experience*, 'is always the story of a wound that cries out, that addresses us in the attempt to tell us of a reality

---

[1] Wilfred Owen, 'The Poet in Pain', in *The Complete Poems and Fragments*, i: *The Poems*, ed. Jon Stallworthy (London: Chatto & Windus, Hogarth Press, and Oxford University Press, 1983), 111.

or truth that is not otherwise available'.[2] The speaking wound, an image Caruth borrows from Freud (who in turn is reaching back to Tasso, in a literary-historical chain whose structure may be symptomatic of the way in which pain has often been articulated), resonates in part because it returns a fundamental productivity to the sufferer, in the form of his/her urgent storytelling. In the case of Owen, the idea that trauma can be productive in a literary sense, that the possibility of narrative might even be endemic to the violent experience, is both resonant and problematic. Himself shell-shocked, his texts often read like articulations of a deep and shared wounding, and many of his poems were either composed or revised while he was in psychological treatment at the mental facility Craiglockhart; at the same time, Owen acknowledges, in a work like 'The Poet in Pain', that his personal pain must be deliberately revived and re-created, that his work as spokesperson in a sense requires that he be constantly, if imaginatively, re-wounded. The conscious poetic processes may mime the speaking wound, but from a position of some considered distance.[3]

Owen played an important role in setting the tone for British war poetry in the later twentieth century, and the sentiments expressed in 'The Poet in Pain' about the intertwined relationship between language and suffering run very deep in his work—and also, I will suggest, in a broader twentieth-century project of writing about war. During the First World War, it was the soldier's person that most directly endured the bludgeon of history, and for Owen, the language to emerge from that configuration, if it was to express war's visceral power and elemental facts, must hew very closely to the soldier's torturous, embodied life in the specific landscape of combat.[4] Though he notably disclaimed any interest in poetics ('Above all I am not concerned with Poetry. My subject is War, and the pity of War. The Poetry is in the pity'),[5] Owen's poems do, in fact, point towards an aesthetics of suffering,

---

[2] Cathy Caruth, *Unclaimed Experience: Trauma, Narrative, History* (Baltimore: Johns Hopkins University Press, 1996), 4. I borrow loosely from Caruth, whose notion of the 'speaking wound' is resonant for my purposes, but I do not, in this essay, attempt to think seriously about trauma as a central structure for mediating the relation between poetry and war.

[3] This structure in a certain sense recalls Wordsworth's 'emotion recollected in tranquility', a connection which is not as disjunctive as it seems, given the powerful influence of English Romanticism on many First World War poets, including Owen. For discussion of Romanticism and Owen, see Jennifer Breen, 'Wilfred Owen: "Greater Love" and Late Romanticism', *English Literature in Transition (1880–1914)*, 17 (1974), 173–83; and Alan Tomlinson, 'Strange Meeting in a Strange Land: Wilfred Owen and Shelley', *Studies in Romanticism*, 32/1 (Spring 1993), 75–95.

[4] This essay takes its cues and examples, in large part, from combatant poetry, though I hope, in my analysis, to suggest broader poetic tendencies that need not be defined by military service. Indeed, it is problematic to restrict one's focus to combatant poetry, a practice that has tended to marginalize other voices (civilians and women, most obviously), and to grant an extreme sense of authenticity and truth-value to the soldier-poet. For a helpful critique of this tendency, see James Campbell, 'Combat Gnosticism: The Ideology of First World War Poetry Criticism', *New Literary History: A Journal of Theory and Interpretation*, 30/1 (Winter 1999), 203–15.

[5] Owen, 'Preface', in *The Complete Poems and Fragments*, ii: *The Manuscripts and Fragments*, ed. Jon Stallworthy (London: Chatto & Windus, Hogarth Press, and Oxford University Press, 1983), 535.

and his short lyrics, with their vivid moments of access to both bodies and psyches ripped by war, have reverberated with readers throughout the century. If Owen became a favourite of 1930s English poets, and later influenced generations of war writers, this reclamation in part stemmed from an attraction to the sound, echoing throughout his work, of the hurt human being. Indeed, as one departs from the realm of Owen's work, or even the broader category of combatant poetry, one finds among many civilian poets a persistent reckoning with the felt experience of modern war, as the effort to make known war's pains has taken on a sense of cultural urgency, and the panoply of voices contributing to that project has expanded and diversified.

In what follows, I propose to delineate several shared points among an array of British war poems, aiming to shed light, above all, on one salient feature: the searing pain that cuts through war verse. I am not attempting, in this essay, to provide a study of the many rich contexts for this poetry—personal, historical, and cultural forces that powerfully contributed to the development of war poetics—but to offer, instead, an overarching discussion of some of the shared motifs and principles traversing a spectrum of war poetry. It may be impossible to historicize pain; but we can trace its poetic forms, and this is my interest here.[6] Elaine Scarry has famously made the case for a profound barrier dividing the realm of pain, which silences, from that of language, which speaks. As she writes in *The Body in Pain*:

[O]ne of two things is true of pain. Either it remains inarticulate or else the moment it first becomes articulate it silences all else: the moment language bodies forth the reality of pain, it makes all further statements and interpretations seem ludicrous and inappropriate. . . . But the result of this is that the moment it is lifted out of the ironclad privacy of the body into speech, it immediately falls back in. Nothing sustains its image in the world; nothing alerts us to the place it has vacated.[7]

Scarry's central paradox is a structural one: the body in pain entails a fundamental inexpressibility, and to change that situation, if such is even possible, requires a large-scale commitment to constructing forms of language appropriate to pain, and devoted to its alleviation.[8] Yet, for all the haunting brilliance of Scarry's claim about pain's inarticulacy, literature has, in fact, developed strategies and forms

---

[6] A word on methodology: this essay is written in a reflective spirit; it is literary-historical in both tone and aims, tending to draw connections among disparate writers, historical periods, and, to some degree, national affiliations. I draw especially heavily from First World War poetry, in part because of my own familiarity with that material, in part because it was that body of verse which in many ways set the stage for later war poets of the century. Finally, in keeping with the structure of this collection, I have focused primarily on English, and some Irish, war poems, though I have also included discussion of several American works.

[7] Elaine Scarry, *The Body in Pain: The Making and Unmaking of the World* (Oxford: Oxford University Press, 1985), 60.

[8] Such a commitment would involve vital changes in consciousness which might be registered, e.g. in terms of medical advances, changed cultural standards for war, and a revised understanding of the structure of torture.

for 'bodying forth the reality of pain'. Often halting, oblique, and fragmentary, sometimes taking recourse to a kind of primal expressionism, indebted to literary traditions like the elegy and the war epic, those texts that consider pain, and modern war poetry in particular, might be said to generate their own aesthetics. I hope, in this brief discussion, to develop the lineaments of such an aesthetics, or, if we invoke the conventional metaphor of song, to listen to the melody of pain sung—perhaps quietly, sometimes angrily, at times with a sense of deep futility—in war verse.[9]

In considering how and where and in what form that pain is figured, I will turn to a canonical site of origin for Western literary conceptions of war, Homer's *Iliad*. To make such a move from history to literary history as a guiding discourse is, of course, a consequential choice, yet one, I hope, that will open up some interesting perspectives on modern war verse. Auden's gesture towards the Old Masters in my epigraph poem, 'Musée des Beaux Arts',[10] is a serious one that we might consider: if his particular suggestion is that Breughel's painting of Icarus falling into the sea demonstrates how suffering occurs as a matter of indifference to the rest of humankind, a broader insight embedded in the poem is that aesthetic monuments from earlier periods have something essential to teach the modern viewer/reader about the vulnerable body's place in the world. The point in invoking Homer, I want to stress, is not to recapitulate and revalidate the canon, nor to search for literary allusions and references in the twentieth-century poetry that is our primary concern in this volume, but rather to recognize that Homer's epic mined the experience of war in such depth and detail as to provide a rich and complex template for a study of war's literary products.[11] Though modern war literature has often taken shape precisely in opposition to the classical ideal—with its emphasis on leadership and glory, its heroizing and celebrating of military masculinity, and its narrating of war as the central fulcrum for consolidating national and cultural values—the aesthetic principles of modern war verse nevertheless converge in illuminating ways with Homer. Indeed, this fact alone warrants reflection: ideology and descriptive power appear to be able to move in opposite directions in war narratives, as if the figuration of bodily experience at times slips out of the seemingly totalizing belief structures underlying the works. Literary engagements with combat seem to generate special properties, and it is these properties, which we might think of as

---

[9] For discussion of the representation of pain in the visual arts, see Nigel Spivey, *Enduring Creation: Art, Pain, and Fortitude* (Berkeley: University of California Press, 2001); and Susan Sontag, *Regarding the Pain of Others* (New York: Farrar, Straus & Giroux, 2003).

[10] W. H. Auden, 'Musée des Beaux Arts', in *The English Auden: Poems, Essays and Dramatic Writings 1927–1939*, ed. Edward Mendelson (London: Faber, 1977), 237.

[11] A number of contemporary writers—critics and scholars, as well as poets and novelists—have found in Homer a rich source for contemplating war in the modern world. For especially rewarding examples, see Christopher Logue, *Logue's Homer: War Music* (London: Faber, 2001); and James Tatum, *The Mourner's Song: War and Remembrance from the* Iliad *to Vietnam* (Chicago: University of Chicago Press, 2003).

large-scale reckonings with pain, writ across bodies, communities, and landscapes, that interest me here. War's pain demands expression; this is a premiss of my discussion. Poetry works to articulate that pain, in a variety of forms that we can trace; this will be a central line of inquiry. That articulation often hearkens back to the *Iliad*; this is where we can locate our unifying terms. In what follows, I will isolate in the *Iliad* four consolidating elements, in an escalating scale, and these features, in turn, will ground and orientate my analysis of modern lyrics: the energizing duality of anger and grief, two sides of war's emotional spectrum; an aesthetics of rest, which grows out of the expression of grief; and, overseeing the whole operation, the fact of force.[12]

It is no secret that the *Iliad* takes anger as a primary human and martial category, given its celebrated opening invocation, 'Sing, goddess, the anger of Peleus' son Achilleus' (1. 1), and its encyclopedic accounting for a nearly infinite range of human and divine forms of anger.[13] As scholars remind us, the poem contains no fewer than thirteen different words that convey the concept of anger, and its attention to the diversity of anger's instantiations in the setting of war is correspondingly nuanced. Thus we have, for example, a specific form of wrath that accrues to the death of friends in battle, which calls forth the ferocious instinct of revenge; another that attaches to the problem of prideful language; anger defined in terms of its specific temporality versus anger that carries a tendency to smoulder; and so on.[14] In terms of the poem's dramatic action, Homer elaborates extended formulations of fury, not only in the opening conflict between Achilles and Agamemnon, but also in such climactic passages as the return of Achilles to combat, when his violent energy has a boundlessness that justifies such epithets as 'godlike' and 'insatiate of battle'. This bloody sequence (in which Achilles slaughters hundreds of Trojans, confronts nature itself in the form of the inflamed river, and finally kills Hector) culminates in the desecration of Hector's body in view of the citizens of Troy, who watch aghast from the city walls. All of this follows from Achilles' fury at Hector as a person (rather than, say, from the ordinary enmities of war), an individual who 'will pay in a lump for all those | sorrows of my companions you killed in your spear's fury' (22. 271–2). It is nearly tautological, indeed, to say that for Homer, war and anger have something important to do with one another; every element in

---

[12] For a short essay, one must make choices: it is impossible to account for all elements in such a broad rubric as 'the poetry of pain'. I hope that my four categories—anger, grief, peace, force—help to establish a varied language of pain; but they are not meant to be comprehensive. So, e.g. I give scant attention to several important topics that I would, ideally, consider in more detail: shell-shock and its literary manifestations, the often tortuous operations of memory and commemoration, graphic and gruesome depictions of the mutilated body (these are especially important for contemporary poetry), and dynamics of gender that are often complex and contradictory.

[13] Homer, *The Iliad*, trans. Richard Lattimore (Chicago: University of Chicago Press, 1961). I use Lattimore's translation (the canonical choice) throughout this essay.

[14] See Thomas R. Walsh, *Fighting Words and Feuding Words: Anger and the Homeric Poems* (Lanham, Md.: Lexington Books, 2005).

the war rubric, from its cause to its leading characters to its culminating events, is understood in terms of human rage.

No less important and complex in the *Iliad* is grief, and here, too, the spectrum is wide, with such passionate spectacles as Achilles' histrionic mourning for Patroclus (which comprises several days, the immolation of twelve Trojan prisoners, and a lavish funeral befitting Achilles perhaps more than his beloved friend) sharing the stage with quiet moments of mourning such as the meeting between Achilles and Priam, after Hector's death:

> So [Priam] spoke, and stirred in the other a passion of grieving
> for his own father. He took the old man's hand and pushed him
> gently away, and the two remembered, as Priam sat huddled
> at the feet of Achilleus and wept close for manslaughtering Hektor
> and Achilleus wept now for his own father, now again
> for Patroklos. The sound of their mourning moved in the house.
>
> (24. 507–12)

Justly famous for its portrayal of a grief that, in its spirit of gentleness and pity, momentarily dismantles fundamental organizing structures of war (friend and enemy, victor and victim, battlefield and home, the present and the past), the passage suggests not only that grief is one of war's inescapable attributes, but, more radically, that it is one of war's greatest accomplishments. Such transcendent moments of human intimacy, amidst a ravaged world, in a sense bespeak a whole panoply of civilian values to which the *Iliad* can only gesture, often via its similes. Yet the scene between Priam and Achilles resonates precisely because it isolates a magnificent moment of human suffering and community *within* war—one that could, in a sense, only be a product *of* war.

This moment is not alone; the *Iliad* offers a sustained reflection on the particular forms of peacefulness that attend war. Often books will end at nightfall, as quiet and rest descend—'and each slow dusk a drawing down of blinds', as Owen would put it 2,000 years later.[15] The rhythms of war in the *Iliad* include formal structures of slowdown and recuperation, not only at night, but also during the various truces that occur periodically, and these pauses have their poetic correlatives.[16] For example, at the close of book 8, a representatively bloody book, the tone shifts to one of tense, yet wondrous, rest:

> So with hearts made high these sat night-long by the outworks
> of battle, and their watchfires blazed numerous about them.
> As when in the sky the stars about the moon's shining
> are seen in all their glory, when the air has fallen to stillness,

[15] Owen, 'Anthem for Doomed Youth', in *Collected Poems and Fragments*, 99.
[16] Despite the general tendency to end fighting with the end of daylight, this pattern is not absolute in the *Iliad*; most memorably, the night raid in book 10, in which Odysseus and Diomedes slay a number of sleeping Trojans, represents a powerful counter-example.

and all the high places of the hills are clear, and the shoulders out-jutting,
and the deep ravines, as endless bright air spills from the heavens
and all the stars are seen, to make glad the heart of the shepherd;
such in their numbers blazed the watchfires the Trojans were burning
between the waters of Xanthos and the ships, before Ilion.
A thousand fires were burning there in the plain, and beside each
one sat fifty men in the flare of the blazing firelight.
And standing each beside his chariot, champing white barley
and oats, the horses waited for the dawn to mount to her high place.

(8. 553–65)

War moves rhythmically, it has its formal patterns. Here the rhythm is of pause, as the mood of watchfulness, waiting, and quiet approaches the majestic.

Among war's movements, however, perhaps the most important overarching principle is not the pause or rest, but its very converse: what we might, following the French philosopher Simone Weil, call 'force'. Weil, writing during the Nazi occupation, developed a notion of sweeping power in Homer's epic, in which violence operates on and through individuals, transfiguring them as it mutilates the landscapes of peace, driving the action, in effect restructuring all elements in the radius of war. Here is Weil, in her essay on the *Iliad*:

> The true hero, the true subject, the center of the *Iliad*, is force. Force employed by man, force that enslaves man, force before which man's flesh shrinks away. In this work, at all times, the human spirit is shown as modified by its relations with force, as swept away, blinded, by the very force it imagined it could handle, as deformed by the weight of the force it submits to. For those dreamers who considered that force, thanks to progress, would soon be a thing of the past, the *Iliad* could appear as an historical document; for others, whose powers of recognition are more acute and who perceive force, today as yesterday, at the very center of human history, the *Iliad* is the purest and the loveliest of mirrors. . . . To define force—it is that *x* that turns anybody who is subjected to it into a *thing*.[17]

These opening lines establish the essay's generating idea: the hero and centre and subject of the *Iliad* are not a person or even an emotion (such as anger), but rather the enormous principle that she calls force. Such a configuration helps to re-frame the discussion from a characterological one, in which we consider the motivations and experiences of this or that character, to a format in which war is the one and only constant in the narrative, with its all-encompassing, often hideously transformative effects on people, places, relationships, and culture. What makes the idea of force particularly illuminating in Weil's account is its quality of linkage and unification across seemingly fixed boundaries: it connects the past (of Homer, himself imagining a war 400 years in the past) with the present (of fascism, and a war ravenously under way at the moment); internally, it brings together the

---

[17] Simone Weil, *The Iliad, or The Poem of Force*, trans. Mary McCarthy (Wallingford, Pa.: Pendle Hill, 1956), 3.

various participants in the Trojan War (or in the Second World War, or in any war); and, even more minutely, it aligns the implements of war with the bodies of its participants (the armour and spears and chariots with the very sinews of the fighter's limbs). It is not that war, in Weil's rendering, eliminates ethical boundaries and differences, but that the regime of force transforms all the players into actors in its own drama; it marks, dominates, and dictates, and yet in restructuring the world, it remains aloof from any given subject, any given death. As Weil has it, 'violence obliterates anybody who feels its touch. It comes to seem just as external to its employer as to its victim.'[18]

There are many ways to conceptualize force in the *Iliad*. Weil herself is particularly drawn towards images of victimization and mercilessness—war as a kind of cosmic executioner. One might turn, too, to the hundreds of ruined bodies that litter the plain of Troy, killed in stunning plethora and exactitude. Are there this many ways, one might well ask, for the body, armed and shielded, carefully arrayed by artists no less than bronze-smiths, to be penetrated and destroyed? To give just a few of the myriad forms of dying in the *Iliad*:

> and Pallas Athene guided the weapon
> to the nose next to the eye, and cut on through the white teeth
> and the bronze weariless shore all the way through the tongue's base
> so that the spearhead came out underneath the jawbone.
> He dropped then from the chariot and his armour clattered upon him,
> dazzling armour and shining, while those fast-running horses
> shied away, and there his life and strength were scattered.
>
> (5. 290–6)

> He bent dropping his head to one side, as a garden poppy
> bends beneath the weight of its yield and the rains of springtime;
> so his head bent slack to one side beneath the helm's weight.
>
> (8. 306–8)

> It was Sarpedon's companion in arms, high-hearted Epikles,
> whom he struck with a great jagged stone, that lay at the inside
> of the wall, huge, on top of the battlements. A man could not easily
> hold it, not even if he were very strong, in both hands,
> of men such as men are now, but he heaving it high threw it,
> and smashed in the four-sheeted helm, and pounded to pieces
> the bones of the head inside it, so that Epikles dropped
> like a diver from the high bastion, and the life left his bones.
>
> (12. 379–86)

With the scale of bodily dismemberment so vast, it is remarkable that no death is left without its vibrant narrative moment, its instant of visible incarnation. The

---

[18] Simone Weil, *The Iliad, or The Poem of Force*, 19.

fact, too, that a hiatus is taken, mid-epic, literally to clean the field of the dead, to bury and burn the abandoned bodies, gives a sense of the narrative's own stunned and distraught reaction to the scale of its events. Or perhaps the notion of force is best characterized by one of the text's many images of the armies swept forwards and backwards, like rushing water or swirling wind or stampeding herds—as the similes so robustly convey—such as this one:

> Now as these advancing came to one place and encountered,
> they dashed their shields together and their spears, and the strength
> of armoured men in bronze, and the shields massive in the middle
> clashed against each other, and the sound grew huge of the fighting.
> There the screaming and the shouts of triumph rose up together
> of men killing and being killed, and the ground ran blood.
> As when rivers in winter spate running down from the mountains
> throw together at the meeting of the streams the weight of their water
> out of the great springs behind in the hollow stream-bed,
> and far away in the mountains the shepherd hears their thunder;
> such, from the coming together of men, was the shock and the shouting.

(4. 446–56)

The idea of force captures an essential feature of war literature, what we might generalize as the experience of being swept up in a storm of violence. This storm entails not only the individual's helpless victimization, his bodily vulnerability, but also the frenzied energy of combat, the lust to injure and kill one's opponents, and, in a quite different spirit, a kind of awed reverence for war's sheer power.[19] As we turn to modern war poetry, this conception of force will provide the pivotal, defining quality, characterizing and at times enfolding the other Homeric features I have outlined (anger and grief, the aesthetics of peace-in-war). By stressing the centrality of force in modern renderings of war—a way of reading this material that emphasizes, among other things, the body's complete, often unimaginably painful participation in combat, yet also acknowledges the crucial fact that the category of force is ideologically neutral, encompassing reverence as much as abhorrence, exultation along with victimization—I hope ultimately to suggest that Owen's effort 'for speechless sufferers to plain' does, in fact, partially define the broad enterprise of war writing. The imperative, that is, to make audible and visible war's particular forms of pain represents one rendering of the Homeric principle that war is force. In Tim O'Brien's *The Things They Carried*, a work of fiction (as he calls it) which is also very much a theorizing and reflection on the nature of war writing, O'Brien gives a compelling description of something like the idea of force I am developing here, and his account offers a helpful transition from Homer into modern war:

---

[19] The subject of killing in war—its pleasures and seductions, its own ethics and aesthetics—has arisen recently as a subject of scholarly interest, part of the revision of the Fussellian thesis of war as victimization. See esp. Joanna Bourke, *An Intimate History of Killing: Face-to-Face Killing in Twentieth-Century Warfare* (London: Granta, 1999).

How do you generalize?

War is hell, but that's not the half of it, because war is also mystery and terror and adventure and courage and discovery and holiness and pity and despair and longing and love. War is nasty; war is fun. War is thrilling; war is drudgery. War makes you a man; war makes you dead.

The truths are contradictory. It can be argued, for instance, that war is grotesque. But in truth war is also beauty. For all its horror, you can't help but gape at the awful majesty of combat. You stare at tracer rounds unwinding through the dark like brilliant red ribbons. You crouch in ambush as a cool, impassive moon rises over the nighttime paddies. You admire the fluid symmetries of troops on the move, the harmonies of sound and shape and proportion, the great sheets of metal-fire streaming down from a gunship, the illumination rounds, the white phosphorus, the purply orange glow of napalm, the rocket's red glare. It's not pretty, exactly. It's astonishing. It fills the eye. It commands you. You hate it, yes, but your eyes do not. Like a killer forest fire, like cancer under a microscope, any battle or bombing raid or artillery barrage has the aesthetic purity of absolute moral indifference—a powerful, implacable beauty—and a true war story will tell the truth about this, though the truth is ugly.[20]

Owen's poem 'Spring Offensive' might be read as a poetic rendition of just this kind of concession: a recognition that war is 'astonishing', and that for all its destructive terror, it rivets the soldier with its 'awful majesty of combat' and 'powerful, implacable beauty'. 'Spring Offensive' is a poem about the intimate perception of war's power, an attempt to capture first the sublimity of the pause-in-war, in the Homeric sense, and later the form of wordless wonder that battle engenders. In its opening lines, the poem establishes a particular time, place, and mood: 'Halted against a shade of a last hill | They fed, and eased of pack-loads, were at ease; | And leaning on the nearest chest or knees | Carelessly slept.'[21] Ease (used twice), carelessness, rest—as the regiment comes to its halt, it would seem to be characterized by a deep repose, an almost animal unconcern ('they fed'), but this sense gives way immediately to a reflection on the aesthetics of the world at the moment before battle:

> But many there stood still
> To face the stark blank sky beyond the ridge,
> Knowing their feet had come to the end of the world.
> Marvelling they stood, and watched the long grass swirled
> By the May breeze, murmurous with wasp and midge;
> And though the summer oozed into their veins
> Like an injected drug for their bodies' pains,
> Sharp on their souls hung the imminent ridge of grass,
> Fearfully flashed the sky's mysterious glass.
>
> Hour after hour they ponder the warm field
> And the far valley behind, where buttercups

---

[20] Tim O'Brien, *The Things They Carried* (New York: Broadway Books, 1990), 86–7.
[21] Owen, 'Spring Offensive', in *Complete Poems and Fragments*, i. 192.

> Had blessed with gold their slow boots coming up;
> When even the little brambles would not yield
> But clutched and clung to them like sorrowing arms.
> They breathe like trees unstirred.

Paul Fussell and other critics have stressed the motif, in British First World War writing, of a nostalgic reverence for the pastoral English landscape.[22] But what 'Spring Offensive' insists is that the landscape is coded entirely by war, where the tramping boots are not so much intruders as the defining features of the flowered fields, and where the familiar—those English 'buttercups', the 'May breeze'—is rendered not only unfamiliar, or 'uncanny' in Freudian terms, but 'mysterious' also in a religious sense. This is not a landscape of nostalgia but of war's own strange beauty, whose vibrancy and vitality is generated by the hyper-presence of its very nemesis, death. The sensorium is activated in this awe-filled universe, the body itself is the receptacle of the energy that circulates in an atmosphere defined by violence (yet here supplicating and yielding to the soldier). After the pause, when the 'upsurge' comes, when the men race over the hill 'Exposed', this mood of majestic wait becomes the crash of force: 'And instantly the whole sky burned | With fury against them; earth set sudden cups | In thousands for their blood; and the green slope | Chasmed and deepened sheer to infinite space.' Like the cups that rush to catch the soldiers' blood, Owen's language breathlessly works to capture the incomparable sense of those who 'breasted the surf of bullets', to reach with words towards the horror of combat in its full, burning excess. In a final crescendo of survival, 'there out-fiending all its fiends and flames | With superhuman inhumanities', the men who have somehow remained alive crawl 'slowly back', 'regain[ing] cool peaceful air in wonder', the sheer other-worldliness of their experience destroying the possibility of communication. If Owen concludes with a question about this silence—'Why speak not they of comrades that went under?'—the thrust of the poem has been, in a sense, to suggest that only silence can follow from the soldiers' direct reckoning with force.

'Spring Offensive' represents a particularly layered reflection on the nature of force in war, stressing, as it does, the ferocity of battle, as well as the moment of pause, the awe-inspiring immensity of war's reach, and the quality of beauty in all of this; but it is only one among a great number of war poems that zero in on some aspect of these features of war. Randall Jarrell's 'The Death of the Ball Turret Gunner' (1945), a poem that differs in almost every respect from Owen's, can also be said to reflect on force; indeed, its ironic voice-from-the-dead becomes a very precise and jarring emblem of the body obliterated by war. In its entirety, the poem reads:

> From my mother's sleep I fell into the State,
> And I hunched in its belly till my wet fur froze.

---

[22] See Paul Fussell, *The Great War and Modern Memory* (Oxford: Oxford University Press, 1975), esp. ch. 7, 'Arcadian Resources'.

> Six miles from earth, loosed from its dream of life,
> I woke to black flak and the nightmare fighters.
> When I died they washed me out of the turret with a hose.[23]

The poem's last line epitomizes force in its most extreme and blunt manifestation; so complete is its triumph that the poem itself seems to cower from it, to take recourse in the womb-like or marsupial refuge of its own metaphorics, before such possibilities are rendered embarrassingly insufficient. It is force, too, that David Jones repeatedly chronicles in his 1937 epic *In Parenthesis*, in bursts of destruction, but also in a sense of sustained, exhaustive continuity, that which made the First World War seem to many an infinitely extended restructuring of the world by violence. So, for instance, we have the protagonist John Ball's final encounter with battle, before his death:

> But you seek him alive from bushment and briar—
> > perhaps he's where the hornbeam spreads:
> he finds you everywhere.
> Where his fiery sickle garners you:

fanged-flash and darkt-fire thrring and thrrung athwart thdrill a Whimshurst pandemonium drill with dynamo druv staccato bark at you like Berthe Krupp's terrier bitch and rattlesnakes for bare legs; sweat you on the sudden like masher Bimp's back-firing No. 3 model for Granny Bodger at 1:30 a.m. rattle a chatter you like a Vitus neurotic, harrow your vertebrae, bore your brain-pan before you can say Fanny—and comfortably over the open sights:

> the gentleman must be mowed.

And to Private Ball it came as if a rigid beam of great weight flailed about his calves, caught from behind by ballista-baulk let fly or aft-beam slewed to clout gunnel-walker below below below.[24]

If Jones's manically experimental linguistic energy contrasts with the hyper-brevity of Jarrell's poem, passages like this one from *In Parentheses* nevertheless showcase a similar encounter with the furious violence that reduced the ball turret gunner's body to liquid. The language works wildly to express that violence, and even when it abruptly changes tone, it never changes focus. 'Below below below': the line, with its mantra-like incantation of the slow downward pull engendered by force, suggests in its bodily way the gravitational nature of war's ultimate onslaught (to the ground). Or we might take a line like this one from Siegfried Sassoon's 'Autumn', which again figures the spectacle of force as a principle—the guiding principle—in the universe of war: 'Their lives are like the leaves | Scattered in flocks of ruin, tossed and blown | Along the westering furnace flaring red.'[25] Force is the centre-piece, too, of

---

[23] Randall Jarrell, 'The Death of the Ball Turret Gunner', in *The Complete Poems* (New York: Farrar, Straus & Giroux, 1981), 144.

[24] David Jones, *In Parenthesis* (London: Faber, 1963; 1st pub. 1937), 182–3.

[25] Siegfried Sassoon, 'Autumn', in *Collected Poems 1908–1956* (London: Faber, 1984), 81.

Sean O'Casey's soldiers' songs in *The Silver Tassie* (1929), an embittered play about the corrosive effects of the First World War on young and (formerly) idealistic volunteers. In a characterization of the Front, anonymous soldiers sing of force in motion:

> 3rd Soldier:
> Where hot with the sweat of mad endeavour
> Crouching to scrape a toy-deep shelter,
> Quick-tim'd by hell's fast, frenzied drumfire
> Exploding in flaming death around us.
>
> 2nd Soldier:
> God, unchanging, heart-sicken'd, shuddering,
> Gathereth the darkness of the night sky
> To mask his paling countenance from
> The blood dance of His self-slaying children.[26]

For O'Casey, God is spared blame for the storm of destruction that is war; it is not he but humans who have created 'hell's fast, frenzied drumfire'. But force is returned to the divine, taking simultaneously modern and classical shape, in Christopher Logue's contemporary reimagining of the *Iliad*. Here, for instance, is the death of Patroclus:

> APOLLO
>   who had been patient with you
> Struck.
> His hand came from the east,
> And in his wrist lay all eternity;
> And every atom of his mythic weight
> Was poised between his fist and bent left leg.[27]

Such a visceral personification of the gods provides Logue with a particularly resonant form for imagining and representing force, the enormity and shock of which are most potently evoked in that single line: 'Struck.' Or, finally, we hear the scream of force in this stanza from Isaac Rosenberg's 'Dead Man's Dump':

> Maniac Earth! howling and flying, your bowel
> Seared by the jagged fire, the iron love,
> The impetuous storm of savage love.
> Dark Earth! dark Heavens! swinging in chemic smoke,
> What dead are born when you kiss each soundless soul
> With lightning and thunder from your mined heart,
> Which man's self dug, and his blind fingers loosed?[28]

In these lines, it is the erotics of force that most startles: the 'iron love' or 'savage love' are metaphors for a force experienced in terms of the sexualized intimacy of the

---

[26] Sean O'Casey, *The Silver Tassie*, in *Collected Plays*, ii (London: Macmillan, 1950), 53.
[27] Logue, *Logue's Homer*, 169–70.
[28] Isaac Rosenberg, 'Dead Man's Dump', in *The Poems and Plays of Isaac Rosenberg*, ed. Vivien Noakes (Oxford: Oxford University Press, 2004), 141.

body with war. The fact that people create the materials of their own annihilation in no way lessens the affective resonance of a universe that seems itself to explode at humanity's expense. More generally, the attempt to find language that might match the 'impetuous storm' of 'Maniac Earth' in uproar, to register the experience and aesthetic features of force at its most compellingly destructive, seems a nearly ubiquitous feature of twentieth-century verse about combat.

Paradoxically, to perceive force is also, as we have seen, to encounter the peacefulness that attends war. W. D. Ehrhart, an American poet who served in the Vietnam war, captures the paradox with precision. 'One Night on Guard Duty', for instance, posits the image of a quiet calm that enfolds within it shrieking chaos:

> The first salvo is gone before I can turn,
> but there is still time to see the guns
> hurl a second wave of steel against the dark.
>
> The shells arc up,
> tearing through the air like some invisible hand
> crinkling giant sheets of cellophane among the stars.
>
> The night waits, breathless,
> till the far horizon erupts in brilliant
> pulsing silence.[29]

There it is, the silence, coded by terror but also by beauty, the breathless waiting of the night, following the anthropomorphization of the gigantic war, with its invisible hand;[30] yet the sense of eerie beauty in the scene is deeply troubling, since the 'brilliant pulsing silence' on the viewer's side must, on that 'far horizon', mean a ferocity of crushing force for those being attacked. And Ehrhart of course knows this; his poem turns on the various contradictions that force distils (O'Brien: 'the truths are contradictory'), as, for instance, the bodies on the watching side of an artillery raid being linked, through the night itself, to those waiting to be destroyed on the other. Indeed, as we think of how the very elements (night, sky, silence) simultaneously extend a sense of deep peace and terrible destruction in this poem, we might turn to a very different kind of lyric, one that also imagines the soldier in a state of rarefied, distanced calm, where the quality of tranquility depends entirely on the facts of impending death (but this time it is the speaker's own death that he imagines), W. B. Yeats's 'An Irish Airman Foresees his Death'.[31] The second half of the poem runs as follows:

---

[29] W. D. Ehrhart, 'One Night on Guard Duty', in *To Those Who Have Gone Home Tired* (New York: Thunder's Mouth, 1984), 7.

[30] The 'invisible hand' is an obvious reference to Adam Smith. Its usage here suggests not only that economic principles might be silently guiding the war, but also, more surprisingly, that the invisible hand of the market-place might also have something to do with war poetry. What this does to the position of the partially passive observer in the poem is an open question.

[31] W. B. Yeats, 'An Irish Airman Foresees his Death', in *The Poems*, ed. Daniel Albright (London: Dent, 1990), 184–5. The poem, along with several others, was written in honour of Robert Gregory, who was killed in the war. Gregory was the son of Yeats's long-time associate and friend, Lady

> Nor law, nor duty bade me fight,
> Nor public men, nor cheering crowds,
> A lonely impulse of delight
> Drove to this tumult in the clouds;
> I balanced all, brought all to mind,
> The years to come seemed waste of breath,
> A waste of breath the years behind
> In balance with this life, this death.

One striking feature of Yeats's poem is the stress on the idea of balance, a formal as well as a thematic emphasis: notice, for instance, how the rhyming words function essentially as a series of counterbalancing or oppositional properties, here fight/delight, crowd/clouds, mind/behind, and especially breath/death. The repeated term 'balance', that is, works in consort with the poem's structure to embed a deep sense of harmony into the poem's depiction of the death-drive that is war. If politics plays no part in the occasion of war for the airman ('Those that I fight I do not hate | Those that I guard I do not love'), war itself does fundamentally create the situation of the poem—the metaphysical situation, the nature of its 'delight', the 'tumult' of its 'clouds'. One ought not, that is, to mistake the poem's distancing of the war's loyalties for a distancing of war: it is only in war that this kind of paradoxical lightness can be imagined (here defined by the new technology of flight, whose extreme dangers are not eclipsed by its romance). And a last instance of a paradoxical tranquillity animating the contemplation of death in war comes in Keith Douglas's 'How to Kill', a poem rife with irony about the power of one person to cause the death of another. In its final stanza, 'How to Kill' considers what we might, following Kundera, term the unbearable lightness of being:

> The weightless mosquito touches
> her tiny shadow on the stone,
> and with how like, how infinite
> a lightness, man and shadow meet.
> They fuse. A shadow is a man
> when the mosquito death approaches.[32]

If moments of quiet reflection in war—or, better, the quiet reflection that is specific to war—have an important place in war verse, so too does grief, again a grief that is construed as specific to war. As we have seen, the most telling instance in Homer of a form of mourning particular to war involves the meeting of Achilles and Priam, where mourning represents a cultural achievement as much as

---

Augusta Gregory, and his death was a source of grief within their community. For all its personal specificity, the poem makes its own contribution to the raging debate about Ireland's position in the war, its metaphysics in a sense standing in for the tense political divisions that accompanied the Irish participation in the war effort.

[32] Keith Douglas, 'How to Kill', in *The Complete Poems*, ed. Desmond Graham (London: Faber, 2000), 119.

a regrettable consequence. More generally, though, the *Iliad* figures grief in terms of the loss of friends in combat, and this male/male structure of love and loss, which is at once homoerotic, devastating, and productive, generated a powerful afterlife in British war literature, particularly in the poetry of the First World War.[33] Indeed, comradeship in war, with its high valorization in English culture, its complex erotics, and its connection with bereavement, represents a broad category in cultural history, and one with especially strong literary affiliations. More than the other motifs on which I have focused up to now, that is, the topic of grief in war comes with a long literary pedigree for English poets, in the form of the elegy for the dead male beloved, a tradition with such canonical high points as Milton's *Lycidas*, Shelley's 'Adonais', and Tennyson's *In Memoriam*. Many twentieth-century war poets recognized, and at times imitated, these important literary precursors; yet they also worked to articulate a sense of uniqueness in the characterizing of war losses, and these efforts to construct a field of loss particular to war recall the structure of the Achilles/Priam example as much as the Achilles/Patroclus one, in the sense that the exposure of modes of grief that challenge cultural norms and break apart war's sustaining oppositions represents a potentially innovative development of war.[34] As Robert Graves declared of war intimacies, 'there's no need of pledge or oath | To bind our lovely friendship fast, | By firmer stuff | Close bound enough' ('Two Fusiliers');[35] such war-charged masculine bonds, when broken by death, created an opening for an intricate language of grieving.

Let me isolate three aspects of this language, which are particularly germane to the larger poetics of pain at issue here: an emphasis on the corpse, a will to forget, and a spur to anger. The corpse, it need hardly be said, is an ever present and at times traumatizing reality in war, and its permeation of war's landscape takes many shapes, many forms. It may arouse disgust, horror, terror, pity, anger, a blank impassivity, or all of these. But from the point of view of grieving, the dead body becomes a precious site, the very ground of memorialization. In

---

[33] For discussion of the theme of friendship and loss in First World War literature, see my *Modernism, Male Friendship, and the First World War* (Cambridge: Cambridge University Press, 2003), esp. ch. 3.

[34] The subject of mourning practices in war is a rich one for cultural historians, especially with reference to the First World War, out of which many of the century's commemorative conventions were developed. A canonical starting-point for many critics is Freud's discussion in 'Mourning and Melancholia' (1917) and later in *The Ego and the Id* (1923). For discussion of mourning in the First World War, see David Cannadine, 'War and Death, Grief and Mourning in Modern Britain', in Joachim Whaley (ed.), *Mirrors of Mortality: Studies in the Social History of Death* (New York: St Martin's Press, 1981), 187–242; Thomas Laqueur, 'Memory and Naming in the Great War', in John Gillis (ed.), *Commemorations: The Politics of National Identity* (Princeton: Princeton University Press, 1994), 150–67; and Jay Winter, *Sites of Memory, Sites of Mourning: The Great War in the European Imagination* (Cambridge: Cambridge University Press, 1995). Accounts of mourning in later wars of the century have tended to merge with the burgeoning fields of trauma and memory studies, and are hence too numerous for inclusion here.

[35] Robert Graves, 'Two Fusiliers', in *The Complete Poems*, ed. Beryl Graves and Dunstan Ward (London: Penguin, 2003), 32.

'Futility', Owen turns his attention to a corpse, a body whose anonymity takes shape, ironically, at the very moment of the poem's creation, and he offers it what little he can: the poem's attention, its solace, its compassion. If this is an elegy, it is an elegy for the body itself, not for the person, whose history seems to be slipping away as we read; what remains is the most physical of matter—'sides | Full nerved, still warm'—which the poet can, nevertheless, cherish and mourn.[36] He does so with the most simple of gestures, in the most simple of terms: 'Move him into the sun.' This opening line, whose powerful iambs drum a spare poetic heartbeat, in essence performs the poem's wider duty of attending to the corpse, embalming it with its empathy. If that empathetic cry is one of universal waste and uselessness ('O what made fatuous sunbeams toil | To break earth's sleep at all?'), the poem's connection with the corpse remains arresting, as if that first gesture of solidarity with the still-warm body is never surpassed. Other poems, too—or even just momentary glances within a poem—look at corpses with a range of emotions, from sympathy and warmth to horror and disgust, and these forms of attention at times represent a refusal of both the consolations and the strictures of mourning conventions. In some cases, the dead body of an enemy will make for a momentary salute, since the mangled dead of war often seem distressingly indistinguishable. For Keith Douglas, in 'Vergissmeinnicht', the corpse of a German may not be cause for line-crossing solidarity ('We see him almost with content | abased, and seeming to have paid . . . '), but it does invite reflection. Considering the 'dishonoured picture of his girl' strewn alongside the enemy body, the speaker meditates:

> For here the lover and killer are mingled
> who had one body and one heart.
> And death who had the soldier singled
> has done the lover mortal hurt.[37]

Not exactly an epitaph, these lines nevertheless give the corpse its moment of meaning and provocation; they make the body matter, so to speak, at least in passing (literally, as the troops will soon move past the scene).

As Douglas suggests in his depiction of the way death collapses distinctive spheres, to linger on the corpse invites a confusion and a complication of various categories, including, above all, the desire to remember, the need to forget. So Ivor Gurney will ask to be allowed to forget, in a plea which functions as almost the exact inverse of Owen's focus in 'Futility', on the corpse as an act of defiant grief and unconventional memorializing:

> Cover him, cover him soon!
> And with thick-set

---

[36] Owen, 'Futility', in *Complete Poems and Fragments*, i. 158.
[37] Douglas, 'Vergissmeinnicht', in *Complete Poems*, 118.

> Masses of memoried flowers—
> Hide that red wet
> Thing I must somehow forget.[38]

Flowers may do the conventional work of memory, but the process is spectacularly compromised by 'that red wet | Thing'; when the life of the person, like the ball turret gunner, is reduced to liquid, ordinary assumptions about how grieving works are simply wiped out, blown away along with the bodily integrity that is a fundamental basis of identity. Indeed, to consider the corpse, especially the mutilated corpse on the battlefield, is, almost instinctively, to rebel against it, and many poetic accounts of dead soldiers share more with Gurney's 'red wet | Thing' than with the elegiacally attended corpse in 'Futility'. A striking case, from the contemporary poet Michael Longley, is a poem entitled 'Mole', which hearkens back to the First World War via its dedication to Edward Thomas. Thomas had wondered, in his diary, 'Does a mole ever get hit by a shell?', and Longley's response focuses on the mole's decaying body, an obvious stand-in for its human counterpart:

> Who bothers to record
> This body digested
> By its own saliva
> Inside the earth's mouth
> And long intestine . . .[39]

There is a great deal of digestion at work in these grisly lines, a whole chain of envelopment and absorption that might, too, be read in terms of literary history, or indeed colonial history, as Longley considers the First World War from the vantage-point of Northern Ireland in the 1970s. If the corpse in war is a site of the traumatic will to forget, but also, at times, of elegiac compassion, here Longley seems to have very little empathy for it at all. Those rotting moles have been swallowed up not only by the ground, but by a half-century of bloody history, and this history, jarringly, changes the tone.

From the corpse to historical consciousness; from grief to defiance, as in the *Iliad*—to consider the figuration of grief in modern war poetry points us back to where we began, with anger. Siegfried Sassoon has centre-stage when the subject is rage; his lyrics burn and bristle with fury. In 'The Poet as Hero', he depicts his own form of Achillean wrath, his state of bloody-mindedness after the death of his friend (some say, lover) David Thomas,[40] which he justifies according to the emotional compass of war:

---

[38] Ivor Gurney, 'To His Love', in *Collected Poems* (Manchester: Carcanet, 2004), 21.

[39] Michael Longley, 'Mole', in *Collected Poems* (London: Jonathan Cape, 2006), 104.

[40] For discussion of Sassoon's homosexuality in relation to his war poetics, see Adrian Caesar, *Taking It Like a Man: Suffering, Sexuality and the War Poets* (Manchester: Manchester University Press, 1993).

For lust and senseless hatred make me glad,
And my killed friends are with me where I go.
Wound for red wound I burn to smite their wrongs;
And there is absolution in my songs.[41]

The image of the poet as burning with the desire to kill may not always be a
comfortable one, even for Sassoon, but the diffusion of war poetry's angry energy
recurs in many works. For F. T. Prince, writing during the Second World War, such
anger belongs to history: as he contemplates a group of naked soldiers bathing in
the sea, he is reminded of a Renaissance painting in which awful violence had been
figured as pure rage:

Another Florentine, Pollaiuolo,
Painted a naked battle: warriors, straddled, hacked the foe,
Dug their bare toes into the ground and slew
The brother-naked man who lay between their feet and drew
His lips back from his teeth in a grimace.

They were Italians who knew war's sorrow and disgrace
And showed the thing suspended, stripped: a theme
Born out of the experience of war's horrible extreme
Beneath a sky where even the air flows
With lacrimae Christi. For that rage, that bitterness, those blows
That hatred of the slain, what could they be
But indirectly or directly a commentary on the Crucifixion?[42]

The speaker seems distant from any such emotional maelstrom ('I feel a strange
delight that fills me full, | Strange gratitude, as if evil itself were beautiful'), his
Christianity taking what he sees as a more benign, reflective turn. The rage that
fuels war, for Prince, belongs to a past whose passions have attenuated, and to
a geographical sphere (Catholic Italy) where such rage, if it still exists, might
be ascribed to its otherness ('even the air flows | With lacrimae Christi'). Yet the
poem's conjuring of that other/earlier linkage of war with wrath is never quite
dispelled or re-contained, and the 'streak of red that might have issued from
Christ's breast', which closes the poem, seems a bloody swath, painted over a
contemporary landscape defined, every bit as much as fifteenth-century Europe, by
horrendous slaughter.

Prince points to something anachronistic in defining the ferocity of war in terms
of the anger of its participants, but the idea of rage as a *response* to war, especially as
a response from its soldiers, is a common motif in modern war poetry. To return to
'The Poet as Hero', Sassoon describes himself in that poem as 'scornful, harsh, and

---

[41] Siegfried Sassoon, 'The Poet as Hero', in *The War Poems*, ed. Rupert Hart-Davis (London: Faber,
1983), 61.
[42] F. T. Prince, 'Soldiers Bathing', in *Collected Poems 1935–1992* (Manchester: Carcanet, 1993), 55.

discontented', his 'ecstasies changed to an ugly cry', and this characterization of the speaking personae who populate his lyrics as harsh and abrasive is an accurate one. Sometimes Sassoon's anger has a clear direction, as in 'Glory of Women', in which he attacks both English and German women as sinister in their ignorance, colluding to victimize men, perpetuators not only of war, but of war's biggest and most dangerous myths: 'You love us when we're heroes, home on leave | Or wounded in a mentionable place. | You worship decorations; you believe | That chivalry redeems the world's disgrace.'[43] Sassoon's misogyny is recruited, in 'Glory of Women', into a broader project of creating a poetry of protest. Anger is what politicizes, what gives cultural potency, and other war poets, too, who may opt for a less strident tone, also at times develop a form of anger to suit the political urgency of their work. For Owen, the poetry is meant to be in the pity, but the politics, we might say, is in the anger; his poems, like Sassoon's, often spit furiously in the reader's face. Indeed, the direct turn against the reader—the 'you' which ironically recalls the famous posters of avuncular figures pointing fingers at those who have not volunteered for service—was a common move in First World War poems and has strong tonal consequences, creating a dissonance between reader and writer that is meant to open up the space for accusation. Equally vengeful as 'Glory of Women', though less objectionable to a contemporary readership, is a poem like 'To the Warmongers', in which Sassoon again directs his acid tongue at those he holds responsible for the war:[44]

> I'm back again from hell
> With loathsome thoughts to sell;
> Secrets of death to tell;
> And horrors from the abyss.
> Young faces bleared with blood,
> Sucked down into the mud,
> You shall hear things like this,
> Till the tormented slain
> Crawl round and once again,
> With limbs that twist awry
> Moan out their brutish pain,
> As the fighters pass them by.[45]

'To the Warmongers' is not the only poem to imagine the dead rising in protest against the complacency and cynicism of civilian culture. The dead are imagined in such lyrics as full of fury, their horrifying re-embodiment rendering them into

[43] Sassoon, 'Glory of Women', in *Collected Poems 1908–1956*, 72.

[44] To discuss protest in conjunction with Sassoon is to invoke his more literal protest: a statement of dissent written in 1917, read before the House of Commons and printed in *The Times*, an act of defiance that Sassoon knew could have resulted in court martial. For his own description of the episode in his autobiography, see Sassoon, *The Complete Memoirs of George Sherston* (London: Faber, 1972), 471–514.

[45] Sassoon, 'To the Warmongers', in *War Poems*, 77.

a kind of army in support of the poet, a disfigured and terrifying community in angry defiance, with its own revolution in mind.

At the basis of that revolution is pain. The slain in 'To the Warmongers' are 'tormented', their limbs twist like infernal bodies, and their voices—the very crux of protest—'moan out their brutish pain'. The idea that pain might be an activating rather than debilitating condition is a startling and important one, and it brings us back to where we began, with Owen's imperative to write a poetry with deep roots in the suffering body. If 'The Poet in Pain' provided one version of the theory of the 'speaking wound', we now encounter a wound that shouts, where the need to witness has modulated into a more focused desire to effect political change. Modern war poetry might be said to operate along this spectrum, from articulating pain as a shuddering cry to articulating pain as a defiant provocation. In both cases, we seem to have migrated far from Homer, for whom war ultimately belonged to the sphere of cultural achievement, a showcasing of what is triumphant in the human realm; for twentieth-century war literature, by contrast, war belongs to the sphere of cultural destruction, a showcasing of what has failed in modern civilization. Yet are these divergences as great as they seem? What I have attempted to show in this essay is that the intertwined elements of anger, grief, rest, and force in the *Iliad* also help to organize later war poetry; but when they are reborn in the lyrics that document warfare in the twentieth century, they become attached to a poetics of pain. It is that function, more than the content of war as it is expressed in these works, that generates their political sting. To speak from and for a position of pain is to challenge all that is comfortable, stable, and ordinary. Yet, as Owen wrote in 'Miners', a poem that imagines an expanded political context for war's victims—an alliance of all those men with 'muscled bodies charred' who are the casualties of industrial modernity—the comfortable world will never be dislodged. A politicized imperative to sing of pain thus gives way to a sense of futility, an angry voice is muted back into silence, and those who have been killed in war, or in other violent endeavours of the modern world, become no more than the elemental stuff of the earth:

> Comforted years will sit soft-chaired,
>> In rooms of amber;
> The years will stretch their hands, well-cheered
>> By our life's ember;
>
> The centuries will burn rich loads
>> With which we groaned,
> Whose warmth shall lull their dreaming lids,
>> While songs are crooned;
> But they will not dream of us poor lads,
>> Left in the ground.[46]

---

[46] Owen, 'Miners', in *Complete Poems and Fragments*, i. 135–6.

CHAPTER 26

'DOWN IN THE TERRACES BETWEEN THE TARGETS': CIVILIANS

PETER ROBINSON

While justifying an absence of First World War poetry from his *Oxford Book of Modern Verse 1892–1935*, W. B. Yeats notoriously wrote that 'passive suffering is not a theme for poetry . . . some blunderer has driven his car on to the wrong side of the road—that is all'.[1] In 'Lapis Lazuli', first published in March 1938, he declares his theme by contrasting certain unnamed 'hysterical women' with his interpretations of Hamlet and Lear, Ophelia and Cordelia. He also sets their tragic deaths on the artistic stage against some latest developments in the theatre and art of war:

> For everybody knows or else should know
> That if nothing drastic is done

---

[1] W. B. Yeats, 'Introduction', in *The Oxford Book of Modern Verse 1892–1935*, ed. W. B. Yeats (Oxford: Clarendon Press, 1936), p. xxxiv. For his epigrammatic refusal of the genre, 'On being asked for a War Poem', see *The Poems*, ed. Daniel Albright (London: Dent, 1990), 205. This epigram may also be a quarrel with himself in that he would go on to write poems occasioned by war and its consequences, especially for civilians.

> Aeroplane and Zeppelin will come out,
> Pitch like King Billy bomb-balls in
> Until the town lie beaten flat.[2]

This old man's sardonic anachronism occasions the idea that though 'All perform their tragic play', his theatrical characters, 'If worthy their prominent part', will not succumb and 'break up their lines to weep'. Yeats contrasts tragic stage figures that embrace their fates with a clear-eyed *sangfroid* to those who die as chance would have it, unawares, like the 'accident and incoherence that', as Yeats has it elsewhere, 'sits down to breakfast'.[3] His lines, and his anthology comment too, are themselves a protest against a mechanized world in which stoic heroism and aesthetic poise might be imagined as outmoded. Yet what Yeats also glimpsed were the changing conditions in which other conceptions of the heroic or the humanly significant would be obliged to make their way. In what follows, I glance back at Yeats's remark in the light of difficulties in attributing meaning to the foreseeable accidental deaths, the collateral damage, produced by total war, and attempts by poets to find meaning in the fates of those who can only stand and wait.

First, though, no suffering should be dismissed as merely passive. With instinctive energy, the hurt body and mind fights, to the extent of its capacity, to minimize pain and promote recovery. Further, passivity of a dedicated or committed kind has provided classic poems with a concluding focus. Yeats will not have been unaware of Milton's line, 'They also serve who only stand and wait',[4] or, probably, of Hopkins's curiously similar lines in which 'there went | Those years and years of world without event | That in Majorca Alfonso watched the door'.[5] Since poems in their energizing shapes are not passive either, there seems no earthly reason why patience and endurance cannot be a poem too. But can clumsy ineptitude or calculatedly casual killing? Whatever the circumstances, though, the suffering of victims will be active, as the remorse of agents can be; and enduring both may well require as much focused energy as is available. Even weeping and crying are part of a human confrontation with losses that are likely to be felt as wrongs—as indeed they tend to be when 'Aeroplane and Zeppelin' pitch their 'bomb-balls in'. At scenes where there are many casualties, those not crying out are the ones the medical personnel must fear for most.

In his anthology introduction, Yeats rides his hobby-horse about how 'tragedy is a joy to the man who dies'. Yet he too had written some protest poetry—as when, in lines from 'Nineteen Hundred and Nineteen', 'a drunken soldiery | Can leave

---

[2] Yeats, 'Lapis Lazuli', in *Poems*, 341.

[3] Yeats, 'A General Introduction for my Work', in *Essays and Introductions* (Basingstoke: Macmillan, 1961), 509.

[4] John Milton, 'Sonnet 16', in *John Milton*, ed. Stephen Orgel and Jonathan Goldberg (Oxford: Oxford University Press, 1991), 81.

[5] Gerard Manley Hopkins, 'In Honour of St. Alphonsus Rodriguez', in *Poems and Prose*, ed. W. H. Gardner (Harmondsworth: Penguin, 1953), 67.

the mother, murdered at her door, | To crawl in her own blood, and go scot-free'.[6]
Not much tragic joy for the 'mother, murdered', it would seem; yet this is also
Yeats's implication, for, as a later poet wrote about the Vietnam War, which did
involve the aerial bombardment of civilian populations, 'all joy' is 'gone'.[7] One way
to dismiss Yeats's comment is by attributing it to Maud Gonne's silly Willy who
did not understand his times; but I prefer to credit the poet with a defensible point.
Death in itself is not the issue, nor is being killed. The poetry of war has to give
a meaning to the events it presents for attention. The meaning can't simply be a
given, because then it will not be art. In poetry the occasion has to generate, or at
least convincingly appear to generate, its unique meaning. The difficulty with aerial
bombardment is that too many of the co-ordinates for evoking such significance
within the event would appear to be missing. By contrast, in Yeats's example of the
'scot-free' soldiers, it is the breakdown of law and the punishment for murder that
give his occasion its anguished and angry sense.

During the twentieth century, focus shifted from the plight of badly led soldiers
in a technologically novel morass, to the consequences when military personnel are
relatively protected from danger, but various blunderers, including the institutions
of war-making themselves, have done their worst. In the cases I am considering,
it is not Tennyson's 600 riding into the valley of death, though Yeats may even
have 'The Charge of the Light Brigade' in mind when he echoes 'someone had
blundered'[8] with 'some blunderer'. The 'passivity' of military personnel who obey
orders is a complex one, especially when death is the all but inevitable consequence.[9]
The notion that civilians are bombed by accident, because they are not specifically
targeted, as may happen when military personnel are engaging each other, is one of
the polite fictions we allow. In strategic bombing the intention is usually to shock
and awe, spreading fear through inevitable, and thus tacitly discriminate, killing
of anyone who happens to be unluckily in the way.[10] The strategic argument that
shocking and awing civilian populations will lead to the collapse of the enemy's
will to fight is, at best, unproven—and especially where a country's leaders do not

---

[6] Yeats, 'Nineteen Hundred and Nineteen', in *Poems*, 253.
[7] Robert Lowell, 'Waking Early Sunday Morning', in *Collected Poems*, ed. Frank Bidart and David
Gewinter (London: Faber, 2003), 386. For Lowell's objection to the aerial bombardment of civilians, in
which he cites 'the razing of Hamburg, where 200,000 non-combatants are reported dead', see Lowell,
'To President Roosevelt', in *Collected Prose*, ed. Robert Giroux (London: Faber, 1987), 367–70. For
a philosophical investigation of the moral questions and judgements involved in the area bombing
of civilians during the Second World War, see A. C. Grayling, *Among the Dead Cities* (London:
Bloomsbury, 2006). Grayling takes the 1943 fire-bombing of Hamburg as his crucial example.
[8] Alfred Tennyson, 'The Charge of the Light Brigade', in *The Poems of Tennyson*, ii, ed. Christopher
Ricks, 2nd edn. (London: Longman, 1987), 511–13.
[9] Such passivity is addressed in Vittorio Sereni's prose memoir about his war experiences, 'Ventisei'.
For an English translation, 'Twenty-six', see *Selected Poetry and Prose of Vittorio Sereni*, ed. and trans.
Peter Robinson and Marcus Perryman (Chicago: University of Chicago Press, 2006), 375–87.
[10] For the conclusion to the section on 'Civilians' in the US Strategic Bombing Survey (Europe) of
Sept. 1945, see <http://www.anesi.com/ussbs02.htm>

recognize complaints about the plight of civilians as anything other than treason. The 'blunderer' who lets his bombs fall where they will, even when aiming as best he can, may appear to be doing his job.

William Empson, whose eldest brother had been killed in an RFC flying accident before the Great War, went to prep school at Folkstone in 1915, and so must be among the first British poets to have experienced air raid warnings (the school master's whistle) and dashes for a bomb shelter.[11] Some twenty years later he commented on Japanese bombings of China in 'Autumn on Nan-Yüeh' (1938), a poem with Yeats as its presiding genius:

> So far I seem to have forgot
>   About the men who really soar.
> We think about them quite a bit;
>   Elsewhere there's reason to think more.
> With Ministers upon the spot
>   (Driven a long way from the War)
> And training camps, the place is fit
>   For bombs. The railway was the chore
> Next town. The thing is, they can not
>   Take aim. Two hundred on one floor
> Were wedding guests cleverly hit
>   Seven times and none left to deplore.[12]

'The thing is, they can not | Take aim': in notes on the poem John Haffenden prints two related prose passages by the author. In the first he observes that 'the Japanese give one of their chivalrous announcements that they mean to give the railway a thorough bombing'. Elsewhere Empson reported a conversation with some British Air Force men in Hong Kong concerning the fact that 'Month after month went by and still the Japanese airmen couldn't get a bomb on the bridges'. Their response is reported as: ' "It's disgusting. They're letting the whole show down." The Show was the profession of bombing, in which they were engaged.'[13] We can differentiate disgusts here. The profession of bombing in itself might prompt revulsion and horror, let alone inept bombing. Yet it could be said that if the ability to aim effectively allows aerial bombardment to contribute to attacks on enemy positions, or the destruction of infrastructure without civilian casualties, it is attempting to preserve the profession of arms from inroads upon military traditions of the politically motivated concept of total war. Empson's poem, whatever the fig-leaves of 'chivalrous announcements', versifies, in a blankly dismayed style, the consequences for a civilian wedding of those pilots' inability

---

[11] See John Haffenden, *William Empson*, i: *Among the Mandarins* (Oxford: Oxford University Press, 2005), 67.

[12] William Empson, 'Autumn on Nan-Yüeh', in *The Complete Poems*, ed. John Haffenden (Harmondsworth: Penguin, 2001), 95.

[13] Empson, quoted in 'Notes', ibid. 391 and 392.

to take aim. Empson's method is to declare the fact in flatly prosaic rhymes and then pass on. It is as if the occasion cannot bear the weight of its own desperate meaninglessness.[14]

We might further distinguish between the hapless contributions of blunderers to the totalizing of warfare and the decided policy of bombing enemy towns, as in the January 1945 decision to switch from the high-altitude precision bombing of Japan to night-time area bombing with incendiaries and anti-personnel weapons. In the 1937 raid on Guernica there was no reconnaissance flight to identify targets, and the heavy bomb loads including incendiaries ruled out even attempted precision targeting. Here the profession of arms, and the conscription of civilians into the armed forces, further complicate the picture. The price paid by the French civilians of Normandy in the bombardments prior to the landings on 6 June 1944 that would liberate their graves were also practical measures to reduce casualties among the invading armies.[15] One justification of the use of the atomic bombs on 6 and 9 August 1945 was to forestall the losses to the invading forces predicted on the basis of the battle for Okinawa. The history of warfare in the last century shows a decided tendency to protect military personnel at the tacit expense of civilians. Arthur 'Bomber' Harris's campaign against the German cities took place at night so as to reduce losses among RAF aircrews. They were to aim their bombs at areas which pathfinder flares had marked out also by being dropped in darkness. The American 8th Airforce flew daylight raids against specified targets of military significance for high-altitude precision bombing. Before the development of long-range fighter escorts, they suffered heavy losses. There appear, as a consequence, to be many more poems about the American flyers.

In a total war where distinctions between combatants and non-combatants are set aside, the ability to stand off the target so as to preserve the safety of your own side produces the shift from the soldier as the focus of war, and its pity, to the civilians. The logical development of the German losses sustained in the Battle of Britain was the V1 flying bomb and the V2 rocket. In two of the most notorious sorties of the mid-century—those against Guernica and Hiroshima—there was no loss of life among aircrews. Theodor Adorno's analysis of the disappearance of 'strategy' with the methods of the blitzkrieg coincides with the development of the

---

[14] For an emotive attempt to evoke significantly the bombing of civilians by the Japanese, see W. H. Auden, 'In Time of War', sonnets XIV and XV, in *The English Auden: Poems, Essays, and Dramatic Writings 1927–1939*, ed. Edward Mendelson (London: Faber, 1977), 256–7. Auden was a major in the US Army, serving with the Morale Division of the Strategic Bombing Survey in Germany during 1945. 'We asked them if they minded being bombed. We went to a city which lay in ruins and asked if it had been hit,' he recalled in 1963. See Humphrey Carpenter, *W. H. Auden: A Biography* (London: Allen & Unwin, 1981), 335.

[15] 'Between 15,000 and 20,000 French civilians were killed, mainly as a result of Allied bombing.' See <http:www.ddaymuseum.co.uk> The casualty figures for the Allies on D-Day itself are estimated at 10,000, of which 2,500 were killed.

'strategic bomber'.[16] As the dangers for the combatants delivering the weaponry has diminished to all but zero (the ultimate case being nuclear submarine crews with nowhere to return to after their mission), so the subject of war poetry has also shifted. In the age of the long-range missile with nuclear warhead, there are military men such as Lord Carver who have in effect agreed with Adorno that when human conflict has reached such a state of self-alienation, we are all defenceless, and the profession of arms is at an end.

There appear to be hardly any famous poems about the air war during the 1914–18 conflict. The poets were mostly soldiers, and officers too. Again, Yeats would seem to be an exception. His 'An Irish Airman Foresees his Death' bears some resemblances to the mythologies that grew up around the air aces of the war—fighters whose exploits could be accommodated into conventions derived from chivalric romance. There are survivals of such thinking in the writings of Antoine de Saint-Exupéry.[17] Robert Gregory, the tacit subject of the 'Irish Airman' poem, is praised in an elegy for him as 'Soldier, scholar, horseman, he'.[18] Here too his motivation and fate are sketched in the most idealized of terms: 'A lonely impulse of delight | Drove to this tumult in the clouds.'[19] The airman is conceived as poetically detached, from those he euphemistically kills and kill him, from those he defends, and even his country and countrymen. The reasons for this can be intuited by comparing this work to the uncollected 'Reprisals' in which Yeats, in his own voice, is directly critical of the airman's lack of interest in the fate of those left behind on the ground: 'Half-drunk or whole mad soldiery | Are murdering your tenants there.'[20] Though Yeats's airman poems are not principally about *that* war at all, being more concerned with the survival of an Irish aristocratic family and its traditions, he nevertheless draws attention to the dubious analogy between the air aces and chivalric honour codes, to how such falsely applied codes conceal a failure of aristocratic responsibility to the ordinary people below, and how, in short, flyers are likely to have to be detached from the consequences of their actions down there on the ground. 'Those that I fight I do not hate,' the airman ventriloquistically asserts—foreshadowing as he does Adorno's observation that 'Consummate inhumanity is the realization of Edward Grey's humane dream, war without hatred.'[21]

The most pressing reason for that detachment was, in the first place, survival. Geoffrey Hill's poem 'To the Nieuport Scout' depends for its imagistic pathos upon

---

[16] See Theodor Adorno, 'Uninformed Opinion', in *Minima Moralia: Reflections from Damaged Life*, trans. E. F. N. Jephcott (London: NLB, 1974), 107.

[17] See Antoine de Saint-Exupéry, *Pilote de guerre* (1942), in *Œuvres* (Paris: Gallimard, 1959), 263–385.

[18] Yeats, 'In Memory of Major Robert Gregory', in *Poems*, 183.

[19] Yeats, 'An Irish Airman Foresees his Death', ibid. 184.

[20] Yeats, 'Reprisals', in *The Variorum Edition of the Poems*, ed. Peter Allt and Russell K. Alspach (New York: Macmillan, 1971), 791.

[21] Adorno, 'Out of the firing-line', in *Minima Moralia*, 56. Sir Edward Grey was the British Foreign Secretary at the outbreak of the 1914–18 War.

our recalling the flimsy planes in which the pilots, without parachutes to encourage pluck (though parachutes were issued to those who manned artillery observation balloons), flew their sorties.[22] The high percentage of losses and the fact that they are not ground-attack planes help occasion the poem's frail lament—and Hill's piece might itself be responding to the lack of poetry about these losses. War poetry is, in this sense, dependent upon there being serious risk for the combatants. Poems about fighter pilots in the Battle of Britain dwell upon the equal fates of friend and enemy, deaths by fire trapped in tiny cockpits, and in this respect repeat the antique epic encounter, though at further distance, of Owen's 'Strange Meeting'.[23] Among the memorable poems written about the crews of the American 8th Airforce, perhaps the best known is Randall Jarrell's 'The Death of the Ball Turret Gunner', in which the individual humanity of the flyer is established by the association between a mother's womb and the ball turret of a B17 where the gunner is crouched like a foetus. There he wakes 'to black flak and the nightmare fighters', and his death is treated as one might deal with a miscarriage: 'When I died they washed me out of the turret with a hose.'[24] Jarrell is able to focus this single fate precisely because, again, we have a military encounter—a battle between the gunner and the nightmare fighters. Another poem, a memoir text called 'World War II' by Edward Field, begins: 'It was over Target Berlin the flak shot up our plane | just as we were dumping bombs on the already smoking city.' This eloquently blunt account of their purpose and predicament is also plainly reiterated at the end:

> This was a minor incident of war:
> two weeks in a rest camp at Southport on the Irish Sea
> and we were back in Grafton-Underwood, our base,
> ready for combat again,
> the dead crewmen replaced by living ones,
> and went on hauling bombs over the continent of Europe,
> destroying the Germans and their cities.[25]

It is less difficult to make poems about the fates of individuals than about 'the Germans and their cities'. When Geoffrey Hill first touched on the topic, alluding to 'Christmas Trees', the flares dropped by British pathfinder bombers, he did it by focusing attention on the fate of Dietrich Bonhoeffer in a German prison.[26] Richard Eberhardt's 'The Fury of Aerial Bombardment' names two individuals in its final

---

[22] Geoffrey Hill, 'To the Nieuport Scout', in *Canaan* (Harmondsworth: Penguin, 1996), 27.

[23] See e.g. John Pudney, 'Combat Report', in Brian Gardner (ed.), *The Terrible Rain: The War Poets 1939–1945* (London: Methuen, 1966), 76–7.

[24] Randall Jarrell, 'The Death of the Ball Turret Gunner', in *The Collected Poems* (New York: Farrar, Straus & Giroux, 1981), 144. The evocative positioning of the ball turret gunner evidently inspired the poet, though the waist gunner of a B17 was twice as likely to be killed. For Jarrell's poems about 'Children and Civilians', see ibid. 189–96.

[25] Edward Field, 'World War II', in Harvey Shapiro (ed.), *Poets of World War II* (New York: Library of America, 2003), 195 and 200.

[26] Geoffrey Hill, 'Christmas Trees', in *Collected Poems* (Harmondsworth: Penguin, 1985), 171.

verse, both of them dead bomber crew, but does not name any killed on the ground: 'Of Van Wettering I speak, and Averill . . . who late in school | Distinguished the belt feed lever from the belt holding pawl.'[27] It would be left to a poet and pilot eloquently to address the retrospective distress, though focused on similarly anonymous victims, of those dropping the incendiaries. James Dickey's 'The Firebombing' recalls destroying people's homes in order to attack their 'will to fight' when what they were called upon to do without complaint was suffer, endure, and die:

> The enemy-colored skin of families
> Determines to hold its color
> In sleep, as my hand turns whiter
> Than ever, clutches the toggle—
> The ship shakes   bucks
> Fire hangs   not yet fire
> In the air above Beppu
> For I am fulfilling
> An 'anti-morale' raid upon it.[28]

Dickey's poem is performing one of the importantly new roles created by the mechanical reproduction of death: the preservation of shared humanity and responsibility—even when caught in the unenviable position of having to do one's patriotic duty. It does this by leaning towards the modernist modes of simultaneously presented multiple perspectives which had been adapted to war contexts during the 1914–18 conflict by poets associated with the Cubists in Paris. 'Nuit' by Pierre Reverdy includes two lines referring to the end of an air raid on the French capital: 'Les avions de feu sont presque tout passé | A travers les signaux d'alarme' ('The warplanes have almost all gone by | Through the air-raid sirens').[29] Later in the century the modernist enthusiasm for multiplicity of viewpoint would be obliged to address by means of such techniques the more anguished and intractable issues arising from moral conflict and multiple perspective in wartime.

Writing during the 1950s of the fire raids that had burned so much of the old wooden architecture in Japanese cities, Noriko Ibaragi resorted to a child's wonder at the heavens in 'Dialogue' and to a survivor's sardonic irony in 'When I was at my Most Beautiful'.[30] When writing about the bombing of Milan in 1943, Salvatore Quasimodo equally refrained from direct criticism of the raids as such.[31]

---

[27] Richard Eberhardt, 'The Fury of Aerial Bombardment', in Shapiro (ed.), *Poets of World War II*, 31.

[28] James Dickey, 'Firebombing', ibid. 157.

[29] Pierre Reverdy, 'Nuit', in *Plupart du temps 1915–1922* (Paris: Gallimard, 1969), 244.

[30] Noriko Ibaragi, 'Dialogue' and 'When I was at my Most Beautiful', in *When I was at my Most Beautiful and Other Poems*, trans. Peter Robinson and Fumiko Horikawa (Cambridge: Skate Press, 1992), 23 and 32–3.

[31] Salvatore Quasimodo, 'Milano, Agosto 1943', in *Poesie e Discorsi sulla poesia* (Milan: Mondadori, 1971), 134. Ezra Pound, though, lamented the damage to the Italian cultural heritage done by air attacks in 'The Pisan Cantos'; see *The Cantos* (London: Faber, 1986), 459 and 497. The Tempio Malatestiano in Rimini had been hit by Allied bombing on 28 Dec. 1943 and 29 Jan. 1944.

It is worth noting, in this light, the degree to which the modes of war poetry are shaped by perceptions of a war's justification and outcome—even when the civilian populations of countries bombarded can barely be held accountable for either the declaration of war or the means by which it is conducted. The shames of being on the side of the unjustified aggressor, or of suffering unimaginable defeat, or the modern criminalizing of the defeated in war trials will inevitably leave marks on the war poetry of their surviving civilians and children. This is affectingly true of Peter Huchel's expressive poem spoken in the voice of a German pastor lamenting the destruction of his parish in a fire-storm.[32]

While touching on poetry from the viewpoint of pilots and aircrews, I have been tacitly outlining what some civilian-related poems had to struggle with in order to count as war poetry. Combatants have a more focused sense of risk and danger. They can know their enemy and love him as themselves—or not. Being in military units, they have the support of comradeship and the attendant possibilities for specific mourning of individuals killed in action. This is even true, for example, of Mairi MacInnes's two mature poems occasioned by the death in a flying accident of her pilot love. She was serving in the WRENS at the time of her loss.[33] Poet-combatants who survive may be equipped with narrative memories and roles as involved witnesses. But as Empson noted in his poem about the Chinese bombed at a wedding, when there are no survivors, no witnesses, and no mourners, poetry has little ground upon which to locate itself. Yeats's words in the introduction to his anthology were to keep the Great War poets out of his book; and yet, looking back, it was just those excluded poets who had set the mould for what war poetry would be taken to be. In the case of aerial bombardment, in which cities are beaten flat, it is as if all there can be is anonymous death and hysterically weeping women.

However, despite the accelerating shift from the suffering of the fighting forces to that of the civilian populations, the place of civilian death in war is still an anomalous one. Being non-combatants, their deaths are not always counted as losses, or necessarily remembered on memorials. Their helplessness makes them prone to being used for artistic protests; their contribution to such protests is as providers of graphic spectacle. Yeats's anthology appeared in the year that the Spanish Civil War broke out. This was the war that gave us the first of the series of names synonymous with the discriminate bombing of civilians: Guernica. At the

---

[32] Peter Huchel, 'Bericht des Pfarrers vom Untergang seiner Gemainde' ('The Vicar's Report on the Destruction of his Parish'), in Patrick Bridgewater (ed.), *Twentieth-Century German Verse* (Harmondsworth: Penguin, 1968), 220–2. For an English poem on this subject, see James Fenton, 'A German Requiem', in *The Memory of War and Children in Exile: Poems 1968–1983* (Harmondsworth: Penguin, 1983), 9–19.

[33] See Mairi MacInnes, 'The Old Naval Airfield' and 'Passion', in *The Pebble: Old and New Poems* (Urbana and Chicago: University of Illinois Press, 2000), 35–6 and 106–7. For her generation's 'memory of bombs', see MacInnes, 'Hardly Anything Bears Watching' (ibid. 13–14). MacInnes's wartime recollections are in *Clearances: A Memoir* (New York: Pantheon, 2002), 52–74.

focal centre of the creative outcry against this act are Picasso's weeping women.[34] Guernica is a key symbol not least because, as mentioned above, the Condor Legion that bombed the city supported by Italian planes on the 26 April 1937 suffered no losses, and the city they attacked had no air defences.[35] Among the many poems about this act of total war, two of the most famous are Paul Eluard's 'La victoire de Guernica'[36] and the Basque-born Blas de Otero's 'Caniguer'—its title a scrambling of the town's three syllables.[37] J. F. Hendry's 'Picasso: for Guernica', and 'Guernica' by A. S. Knowland, are two English-language pieces from the time.[38] This is the first war in which there was sustained bombing of civilian targets, the first war in which there could have been a 'Song of the Antiaircraft Gunner' by Miguel Hernandez,[39] and certainly the first war to harvest a crop of poems about aerial bombardment.[40] The Spanish War is significant also because it is the first modern war in which, because of the development of media news, there could be organized public outcries and a public protest poetry that arose in direct response to it.

Some of the difficulties for making art from the mass killing of civilians can be identified by considering Picasso's famous painting. Stephen Spender wrote about the work when it was on display in London: 'So long as a work of art has this explosive quality of newness it is impossible to relate it to the past.'[41] This may be a fair assessment of a recent work that aims to make a telling statement, but it can hardly be true of Picasso's work on the painting. Recent research proposes that the artist drew consciously on the style of antique friezes.[42] Spender also associates the painting mimetically with the experience that it evokes. The painting is 'explosive'. This is a case of the journalistic low mimetic, and underlines the fact that Spender is also engaging in propaganda on behalf of the Spanish Republic: 'People who say that it is *excentric* [*sic*] . . . are only making the gasping noises they might make if they were blown off their feet by a high-explosive bomb.'[43] Later, he interprets the picture both as a response to second-hand experience and as highly suggestive of what it is like to be in an air raid. The largely monochrome picture evokes 'despair of the darkness because it is too complete and you are lost;

---

[34] See Elizabeth Cowling, *Picasso: Style and Meaning* (London: Phaidon Press, 2002), 591–603.

[35] For an account of the raid, see Russell Martin, *Picasso's War: The Destruction of Guernica and the Masterpiece that Changed the World* (New York: Plume, 2002), 31–45.

[36] Paul Eluard, 'La victoire de Guernica', in William Rees (ed.), *French Poetry 1820–1950* (Harmondsworth: Penguin, 1990), 715–18.

[37] Blas de Otero, 'Caniguer', in *Con la inmensa mayoría* (Buenos Aires: Losada, 1960), 170–1.

[38] J. F. Hendry, 'Picasso: For Guernica', and A. S. Knowland, 'Guernica', in Valentine Cunningham (ed.), *The Penguin Book of Spanish Civil War Verse* (Harmondsworth: Penguin, 1980), 418 and 167.

[39] Miguel Hernandez, 'Song of the Antiaircraft Gunner', in *The Selected Poems of Miguel Hernandez*, ed. and trans. Ted Genoways (Chicago: University of Chicago Press, 2001), 218–21.

[40] See the 'Junker Angels in the Sky' section of Cunningham (ed.), *Penguin Book of Spanish Civil War Verse*, 157–71.

[41] Stephen Spender, 'Guernica', ibid. 419.

[42] For a recent account of Picasso's work, see Cowling, *Picasso*, 571–89.

[43] Spender, 'Guernica', 419. André Gide had commented on the painting's eccentricity.

despair of the light because it is too complete and you are revealed to the enemy raiders'.

That Guernica was bombed during daylight, for two hours and forty-five minutes in the late afternoon, watched by Lieutenant-Colonel Wolfram von Richtofen from the summit of Monte Oiz, hardly lessens the point of Spender's comments—though they are, strictly speaking, relevant to other such atrocities, and go to underline how Picasso's painting is a generalized statement of shocked outrage at such bombing, and not a report on this particular attack. According to Juan Larrea, the Republican government was 'so disappointed by Picasso's open-ended, universalizing approach to *Guernica* that they debated removing the mural' from the Spanish pavilion at the 1937 International Exposition in Paris, and 'only fear of adverse publicity deterred them'.[44] We can perhaps sympathize with the reaction of the Republican government, which correctly noted that, however much the expressivity of the painting had come from the painter's response to the event, the imagery which gave meaning to Picasso's work was not occasioned by the bombing raid itself. The painting also includes no 'Junker angels' of death, to adapt George Barker's flailing phrase.[45] There is no represented enemy. Its significance is gained by symbolism, analogy, distortion, and painterly techniques.

Spender, writing about the mural when it was displayed at the New Burlington Gallery, London, might be thinking about his own Civil War poem 'Thoughts during an Air Raid', one in which he speculates on an understandable lack of *esprit de corps* among those alone below the bombers:

> Yet supposing that a bomb should dive
> Its nose right through this bed, with one upon it?
> The thought's obscene. Still, there are many
> For whom one's loss would illustrate
> The 'impersonal' use indeed.[46]

However much people pull together in such circumstances, once the events are over, civilians not in communal air raid shelters may have no organized sense of their fates as shared or actively faced. Again, this does not prevent the writing of plausible, or better than plausible, poems; but it does recall the perceptiveness, however wrong-headed, of Yeats's assertion that poetry cannot be made out of passive suffering.

If we turn now to poetry occasioned by sustained bombing as experienced from the ground, we can see how it is responding to the problem that Yeats effectively, though negatively, points to in his introduction. The absence of the enemy and of fellow-combatant witnesses precipitates the poetic occasion into something that, in

---

[44] Juan Larrea, quoted in Cowling, *Picasso*, 589.
[45] George Barker, 'Elegy on Spain', with a 'Dedication to the photograph of a child killed in an air raid on Barcelona', in Cunningham (ed.), *Penguin Book of Spanish Civil War Verse*, 157–61.
[46] Spender, 'Thoughts during an Air Raid', ibid. 350. The poet later italicized the 'one': see Spender, *Collected Poems 1928–1985* (London: Faber, 1985), 47.

war poetry terms, is troublingly 'meaningless'. There does not seem to be anyone exactly to hate, for the pilots and bomb-aimers are faceless, gone, and possibly themselves in mortal danger. Milton and Hopkins again seem to be the ones who have the last word. A solution to this during the Blitz was to bring religious symbolism to bear as a way of attributing meaning to this mechanized routine of fairly randomly scattered death. The high danger of such a poetic tactic—whether by prompting charges of opportunism or by inviting the question of why we have been forsaken—can be seen in the ending to Stephen Spender's 'Air Raid across the Bay at Plymouth'. Its third section attempts to catch the moment when two searchlights chase down an enemy plane: 'Two beams cross | To chalk his cross.' This image is then given its straining Christian elaboration in the poem's fifth and final part:

> Jacob ladders slant
> Up to the god of war
> Who, from his heaven-high car,
> Unloads upon a star
> A destroying star.
>
> Round the coast, the waves
> Chuckle between the rocks.
> In the fields the corn
> Sways, with metallic clicks.
> Man hammers nails in Man,
> High on his crucifix.[47]

The conceit of the poem stretches credibility, and is metaphysical in Samuel Johnson's critical sense of 'heterogeneous ideas . . . yoked by violence together'.[48] When Spender republished his Collected Poems 1928–1985, he reduced this section to the first four lines of the second verse. If he saved his poem thus from the false sublime, it may have been only to reduce it to the inconsequentially imagistic. Therein lies its problem. The represented occasion and the attributed meaning will not stick together. This poem is about a 'phoney' war in Adorno's sour sense: human meaning cannot be properly attributed to it.[49]

T. S. Eliot famously weds occasion and significance in the 'familiar compound ghost' section of 'Little Gidding'. That he does it with greater tact than Spender in his Plymouth air raid poem is thanks to a paraphrastic ambiguity of reference which does not prevent the 'dark dove with flickering tongue' from condensing—though not without strain of its own—a Christian symbol with a *Luftwaffe* bomber, or the 'dead leaves' which 'still rattled on like tin' and the 'metal leaves' to combine a Dantean image with bits of bomb fragment, or have the concluding 'blowing of the

---

[47] Spender, 'Air Raid across the Bay at Plymouth', in Gardner (ed.), *Terrible Rain*, 61; see Spender, *Collected Poems 1928–1985*, 121–2.

[48] Samuel Johnson, 'The Life of Cowley', in *Johnson's Lives of the Poets: A Selection*, ed. J. P. Hardy (Oxford: Clarendon Press, 1971), 12.

[49] Adorno, 'Out of the firing-line', 55.

horn' call up a memory of, say, Browning's 'Childe Roland to the Dark Tower Came' and, simultaneously, an air raid siren sounding the all-clear.[50] Eliot's achievement, to various later poets' dismay, is achieved by means of a purified diction. He does not let the immediate circumstances derail his concerns, but mediates them with an all but euphemistically allusive language into vehicles for those themes.

That Eliot succeeded in yoking together occasion and themes with less violence and more cunning can be shown by comparing his passage with the superficially similar Edith Sitwell poem 'Still Falls the Rain', subtitled 'The Raids, 1940. Night and Dawn':

> Still falls the rain—
> Dark as the work of man, blind as our loss—
> Blind as the nineteen hundred and forty nails
> Upon the Cross . . .[51]

Sitwell signals her occasion in the subtitle, and then, in effect, stays with the thematic incantation. That this is less flawed than Spender's effort is a matter of her rhythms and loose associations having practically no traffic with any material details of the Blitz. Yet, as with the title of Brian Gardner's anthology, *The Terrible Rain: The War Poets 1939–1945*, the meaning of the title heavily underlined by two Boeing B29 Superfortresses dropping their payloads, 'rain' itself provides a naturalistic and euphemistic poeticism. The Christian generality also effaces all social facts of the Blitz, and in this it echoes the propagandistic use of the photo of St Paul's Cathedral rising above the fires. Difficulties in these poems can be related back to Picasso's *Guernica*. The relationship between the events barely described and the significances attributed to them by the use of stock symbols instances modernism's overwhelming artistic stretch, at the expense of its early ambitions to concrete responsiveness. The event can come to seem almost incidental to the massive piece of cultural saying that the mature modernist artist brings to bear. The nervy abstracted meditations of H. D.'s late work might exemplify a related dilemma.[52]

A similar approach is to bring images of natural cycles to bear on these special circumstances. Laurence Binyon's 'The Burning of the Leaves' has been called by Kenneth Allott 'a "blitz" poem in the same restricted sense as parts of Eliot's "Little Gidding" '.[53] Yet it occasions an evocation of hope and survival by transposing its reflections to a generic autumnal scene, provider of what has been termed 'aromatic

---

[50] T. S. Eliot, 'Little Gidding', in *The Complete Poems and Plays* (London: Faber, 1969), 191–8. See also Eliot's 'Defence of the Islands' (p. 201) and 'A Note on War Poetry' (p. 202).

[51] Edith Sitwell, 'Still Falls the Rain', in John Hayward (ed.), *The Penguin Book of English Verse* (Harmondsworth: Penguin, 1956), 444–5.

[52] See H. D., 'The Walls Do Not Fall', in *Complete Poems 1912–1944*, ed. Louise L. Martz (New York: New Directions, 1983), 507–43. See also Wallace Stevens, 'The Immense Poetry of War' and 'Flyer's Fall', in *Collected Poetry and Prose* (New York: Library of America, 1997), 251 and 295.

[53] Laurence Binyon, 'The Burning of the Leaves', in Kenneth Allott (ed.), *The Penguin Book of Contemporary Verse* (Harmondsworth: Penguin, 1962), 49.

consolation'.[54] Only through the possible implications of the words 'smoke' and 'ruin' does the poem, as anthologized, link itself to the Blitz. 'That world which was ours is a world that is ours no more,' the poet writes at the end of his third verse, and then adds:

> They will come again, the leaf and the flower, to arise
> From squalor of rottenness into the old splendour,
> And magical scents to a wondering memory bring;
> The same glory, to shine upon different eyes.
> Earth cares for her own ruins, naught for ours.
> Nothing is certain, only the certain spring.[55]

Here too, 'one of the major lyrics of the home front'[56] gains a general applicability to human catastrophes and the passage of time, at the expense of being able to address its specific occasion in the experience's terms—and all but states as much in its penultimate line. Without Kenneth Allott's remarking that it is 'in a restricted sense' about the bombing of London, a reader is unlikely to understand it as so restricted.

Dylan Thomas's three bombing poems essay different approaches to using natural imagery for art prompted by mechanized warfare. 'Among Those Killed in the Dawn Raid was a Man Aged a Hundred' signals the thematic point with its title. The text then takes the circumstance as an occasion to contrast ideas of natural and unnatural deaths: 'O keep his bones away from that common cart, | The morning is flying on the wings of his age.'[57] 'Ceremony after a Fire Raid' is an elaborated response that attempts to set the poet's techniques at full stretch ('A child of a few hours | With its kneaded mouth | Charred on the black breast'[58]) for the enormity of his subject, in a manner comparable to Louis MacNiece's 'The Trolls' ('a last | Shake of the fist at the vanishing sky, at the hulking | Halfwit demons who rape and slobber',[59]) or his 'Brother Fire' with its calculatedly complicit close:

> Did we not on those mornings after the All Clear,
> When you were looting shops in elemental joy
> And singing as you swarmed up city block and spire,
> Echo your thoughts in ours? 'Destroy! Destroy!'[60]

The best of Thomas's three, and one of the most memorable poems about an air raid casualty, 'A Refusal to Mourn the Death, by Fire, of a Child in London', appears

---

[54] Logan Pearsall Smith, quoted in John Hatcher, *Laurence Binyon: Poet, Scholar of East and West* (Oxford: Oxford University Press, 1995), 289.

[55] For the full text, see Laurence Binyon, 'The Burning of the Leaves: Five Poems', in *The Burning of the Leaves and Other Poems* (London: Macmillan, 1944), 1–6.

[56] Hatcher, *Laurence Binyon*, 90.

[57] Dylan Thomas, 'Among Those Killed in the Dawn Raid was a Man Aged a Hundred', in *Collected Poems 1934–1952* (London: Dent, 1952), 127.

[58] Thomas, 'Ceremony after a Fire Raid', ibid. 121–3.

[59] Louis MacNeice, 'The Trolls', in *The Collected Poems of Louis MacNeice*, ed. Peter McDonald (London: Faber, 2007), 219.

[60] MacNeice, 'Brother Fire', ibid. 217.

not to have been completed until 1945—and so may have been prompted by the V-bomb raids during the last year or so of the War:

> Deep with the first dead lies London's daughter,
> Robed in the long friends,
> The grains beyond age, the dark veins of her mother,
> Secret by the unmourning water
> Of the riding Thames.
> After the first death, there is no other.[61]

Unlike MacNeice's, Thomas's poetic language all but bypasses the fire raid's actual scene. The task of grounding the texts in contemporary events is left to his titles, which have an explanatory length fairly unusual for this poet. Thomas focuses the 'absence of meaning' problem by bringing in Christian sacrifice and atonement too, but his imagery also mythically metamorphoses the events into archetypal patterns. His poems are particularly concerned with grief and mourning, which may again be because of the absence of an enemy—though this does not prevent MacNeice from picturing a fist shaken at the 'vanishing sky' in 'The Trolls'. Thomas's poems are stoically muted. There is little raging against the dying of the light in these less personal instances.

Norman Nicholson's 'Bombing Practice' also resorts to natural imagery to evoke the Futurism-derived theme of war as spectacle:

> The swinging aeroplane drops seed through the air
> Plumb into the water, where slowly it grows
> Boles of smoke and trees
> Of swelling and ballooning leafage,
> Silver as willows
> Or white as a blossoming pear.[62]

Nicholson's imagery of trees might be a conscious attempt to grant meaning to an event in the industrialization of warfare. The idea of the bombs as seeds—which points towards a final line where they 'plant their germs of pain in the limbs of men'—is a painfully false step; yet it consciously wrestles with the problem in finding the explosion of bombs in water harmlessly beautiful. The spectacle of warfare as an aesthetic pleasure recalls Walter Benjamin's criticism of the Futurists who had made humanity's destruction the apotheosis of art for art's sake.[63] Here is a further problem for the civilian poet, whose relation to modern warfare, if luckily at a distance, is likely to be one of waiting and watching. There is a doubling of

---

[61] Thomas, 'A Refusal to Mourn the Death, by Fire, of a Child in London', in *Collected Poems 1934–1952*, 94.

[62] Norman Nicholson, 'Bombing Practice', in *Collected Poems*, ed. Neil Curry (London: Faber, 1994), 28.

[63] Walter Benjamin, 'The Work of Art in the Age of Mechanical Reproduction', in *Illuminations*, trans. Harry Zohn, ed. Hannah Arendt (London: Jonathan Cape, 1970), 244.

such civilian experiences of war in another of Nicholson's poems from his 1944 collection *Five Rivers*, a mass observation piece called 'Evacuees'.[64]

Geoffrey Hill does not seem to have been evacuated, but shocked and awed as a little boy—and then to have lived through the war-long blackout. In *The Triumph of Love*, he recalls the spectacle of Coventry's destruction in an aesthetic mode that may consciously recall Benjamin's criticism of the Futurists. Hill's entire *œuvre* speaks against succumbing to such a confusion of values—though his plush local effects can be similarly and not only self-critically spectacular:

> A stocky water tower built like the stump
> of a super-dreadnaught's foremast. It could have set
> Coventry ablaze with pretend
> broadsides, some years before the armoured
> city suddenly went down, guns
> firing, beneath the horizon; huge silent whumphs
> of flame-shadow bronzing the nocturnal
> cloud-base of her now legendary dust.[65]

Hill's particular anger and resentment as a war child are here brought to focus with 'Ingratitude | still gets to me, the unfairness | and waste of survival; a nation | with so many memorials but no memory'.[66] In the earlier *Mercian Hymns*, Hill had conjured the life of the boy in the Blitz with a greater inwardness and a memorialization all the more indelible for its lack of clamour: 'At home the curtains were drawn. The wireless boomed | its commands. I loved the battle-anthems and the gregarious news.' Hill's poem then moves to 'the earthy shelter' where the speaker huddles with 'stories of dragon- | tailed airships and warriors who took wing'.[67] Elaine Feinstein similarly escaped in her Leicester bomb shelter: 'and yet at night | erotic with the | might-be of disaster | I was carried into | dreaming with delight.'[68] These two examples also instance the likely solitariness of the civilian's relationship to peril in wartime. The generation of poets who had been children during the Blitz were enabled, thus, not to write poems about the significance of the events they lived through, but about their own survival tactics—which had involved fictionalizing, or dreaming, identifying with warfare emptied of its grim banality.

Though Hill describes Britain as a 'nation | with so many memorials but no memory', for aerial bombardment and civilian casualties the future of the past may in fact be aggravated by a lack of *adequate* memorials. This is the burden of Joe Kerr's 'The Uncompleted Monument: London, War, and the Architecture of Remembrance'.[69] The great difficulty with official remembrance is that the history

---

[64] Nicholson, 'Evacuees', in *Collected Poems*, 53.
[65] Geoffrey Hill, *The Triumph of Love* (Harmondsworth: Penguin, 1999), 2–3.
[66] Ibid. 40.   [67] Hill, 'XXII', in *Mercian Hymns*, in *Collected Poems*, 126.
[68] Elaine Feinstein, 'A Quiet War in Leicester', in *Selected Poems* (Manchester: Carcanet, 1994), 61.
[69] Joe Kerr, 'The Uncompleted Monument: London, War, and the Architecture of Remembrance', in Iain Borden, Joe Kerr, Jane Rendell, with Alicia Pivaro (eds.), *The Unknown City: Contesting Architecture and Social Space* (Cambridge, Mass.: MIT Press, 2001), 69–89.

being publicly acknowledged can be ambiguously blurred in the appropriation. Does the memorialization of military sacrifice truly contribute to the arts of peace, or does it serve as a tacit justification for continued use of force to protect our interests via the arts of war? The recollection of civilian casualties may be less ambiguous; or, rather, it may be less easy to see the political advantage in remembering some randomly scattered unlucky deaths that, far from occasioning the acknowledgement of our heroic endeavours in the field, serve rather to draw attention to the limits of governmental concern with the conditions of its civilian populations. Kerr concludes his essay by citing Roy Fuller's 'Soliloquy in an Air-Raid':

> Ordered this year:
> A billion tons of broken glass and rubble,
> Blockage of chaos, the other requisites
> For the reduction of Europe to a rabble.[70]

As this reaching for an apt quotation underlines, it may well be in works surviving in collections and anthologies to one side of the official culture of memorialization that words which helpfully attempt to integrate truth and remembrance may be found. The difficulties of memorialization as also demonstrated by war poetry in relation to the bombing of civilians have been directly linked to what has been called 'the death of meaning'.[71] Yet this slogan too may be a form of enactive fatalism that achieves by its recognition what the technology it protests against had haphazardly produced. Rather, what mechanized and technologized total war and its ambiguous relationship to mass democracy have done is put to death one idea of heroic or tribal meaning. It has done nothing to reduce or destroy, and it may even have emphasized, by contrast, the meanings generated by civilians themselves in the attempted continuance of their daily lives.

As we have seen, the poetry of aerial bombardment had to confront difficulties created by the lack of key elements in early twentieth-century war poetry. These might be summed up by the fact that the protagonists are even more separated than Yeats's blunderer in his car and the victim who is hit by it. Roy Fisher's poem 'The Entertainment of War' is a significant document, not least because it explores an experience of these missing elements. As in the verse from Empson's poem of the Sino–Japanese War, 'Autumn on Nan-Yüeh', since there are neither survivors nor witnesses, the people seem absent from their own deaths. None of the victims' fates are experienced, and there is no enemy at all. An aunt, an uncle, two cousins, and 'a woman from next door' have been killed in an air raid on Birmingham:

---

[70]   Roy Fuller, 'Soliloquy in an Air-Raid', in Charles Hamblett (ed.), *I Burn for England: An Anthology of the Poetry of World War Two* (London: Leslie Frewin, 1966), 131.

[71]   See Kerr, 'Uncompleted Monument', 75–8.

These were marginal people I had met only rarely
And the end of the whole household meant that no grief was seen;
Never have people seemed so absent from their own deaths.[72]

In the remainder of the poem, Fisher reports how 'This bloody episode of four whom I could understand better dead | Gave me something I needed to keep a long story moving', and adds that 'had my belief in the fiction not been thus buoyed up | I might, in the sigh and strike of the next night's bombs | Have realized a little what they meant, and been for the first time afraid'. His child's-eye view of the bombing occasions the effective disappearance of both the victims and the enemy—yet perhaps in this he is only underlining something that is the case for 'the Home Front'. Most of the time you are not eye-deep in corpses, and if you are, then you are likely to be one of them; most of the time the enemy is nowhere to be seen.

When Fisher revisits the topic in 'Wonders of Obligation', he fills in the missing elements, by taking a more historically and culturally perspectival view of the events. He had seen 'the mass graves dug | the size of workhouse wards' which had been made 'ready for most of the people | the air-raids were going to kill', and explains:

> Once the bombs got you
> you were a pauper:
> clay, faeces, no teeth; on a level
> with gas mains,
> even more at a loss than before
> down in the terraces between the targets,
> between the wagon works
> and the moonlight on the canal.[73]

The phrases 'down in the terraces' and the 'moonlight on the canal' quietly switch the perspective in the passage from the civilians and their mass grave to the implied pilots and bomb-aimers up in their planes, seeking out the indicators of their targets. In doing this, Fisher underlines both the banal industrialization of such death delivery, and also the way in which industrialized death is an analogue, at the very least, for the peacetime treatment of its workforce. Total war reveals class structure in the forms of domestic architecture, because the factory targets are surrounded by the poor accommodation built for the working people. Collateral damage to civilians is likely to have an uneven distribution over a nation's social strata.[74] Here Fisher is presenting as a considered point what Field had revealed with his word 'dumped'.

---

[72] Roy Fisher, 'The Entertainment of War', in *The Long and the Short of It: Poems 1955–2005* (Tarset: Bloodaxe, 2005), 33–4.

[73] Fisher, 'Wonders of Obligation', ibid. 14–15.

[74] Joe Kerr reports a campaign *c.*1995–7 in the East End of London to erect a monument to the 2,193 local civilian casualties of the Blitz, noting that this was 'the most heavily bombed area of any British city'. See Kerr, 'Uncompleted Monument', 86.

The poet deftly brings together the two sides of this theatre where both are players, but players with little or no agency in their fates. Many aspects of the civilians' war didn't get into the poetry at all—for reasons connected with cunning, petty criminality, and survival, as revealed some fifty years later, by Fisher's poem 'Item'.[75]

There have been a great many wars since 1945, which have included the sustained bombing campaigns against the North Koreans and the North Vietnamese, as well as briefer air attacks on such cities as Tripoli, Belgrade, and Baghdad, on refugee camps, insurgent strongholds, on towns and villages, with incalculable and certainly uncalculated civilian casualties. What with the invention of the Internet, the writing of protest poems against such horrors as are reported on the news media has become a part of our contemporary scene.[76] When such writing aspires to be memorably significant war poetry, it faces difficulties only too similar to those outlined in looking at work from the mid-twentieth century's wars—ones that have been aggravated by the familiarity of the spectacle in newsreel and television footage. This can be emblematically illustrated by John Tranter's 'Guernica', written during the 1970s:

> Take the Stuka staking out the air
> with banshee breath; the bombing pilot
> has a dark complexion, and his thumb on the button
> is very easily dealing death.[77]

The assonance and alliteration in these lines ('Take the Stuka staking') suggest a theme practically pre-packaged for poetry. Tranter's poem is not so much a protest poem as a poem protesting the pointlessness of protest: 'There's no use questioning', it begins. 'Guernica' ends, though, by reversing its perspective—not the dive-bomber pilot with his finger on the button, but the anti-aircraft gunner with his on the trigger: 'The blasting Oerlikon executes a rhyme | and strips the pilot from his sight.' A similarly ready-made fluency infects the pun on 'sight': both eyesight and gun-sight. The poem concludes by returning to its protest against complaint: 'There's no use cornering the gunner in his grief. | His finger rests along the ring of night.' And the poem, too, has executed a rhyme. Tranter's is a poetry of belatedness; here he effectively addresses difficulties with such belatedness in the poetry of war.

Adorno foresaw something of this, writing about the counter-productive result of inventing the term 'genocide': 'the unspeakable has been cut down to size at the very moment that it is protested against'.[78] Sensing something of the like in the social demand for emotive response in art, Donald Davie's 'Rejoinder to a Critic' retorts:

---

[75] Fisher, 'Item', in *The Long and the Short of It*, 256–8. There are some poems of the 'Home Front' in Gardner (ed.), *Terrible Rain*, 125–34.

[76] See the 'Poets Against War' website at <www.poetsagainstwar.net> and the instant anthology: Todd Swift (ed.), *100 Poets Against the War* (Cambridge: Salt Publications, 2003).

[77] John Tranter, 'Guernica', in *Selected Poems* (Sydney: Hale & Iremonger, 1982), 45.

[78] Adorno, 'The Paragraph', in *Can One Live after Auschwitz?: A Philosophical Reader*, trans. Rodney Livingstone, ed. Rolf Tiedemann (Stanford, Calif.: Stanford University Press, 2003), 60.

> 'Alas, alas, who's injured by my love?'
> And recent history answers: Half Japan!
> Not love, but hate? Well, both are versions of
> The 'feeling' that you dare me to. . . . Be dumb!
> Appear concerned only to make it scan!
> How dare we now be anything but numb?[79]

The poem, deploying a metaphysical conceit that contains the large in the small, argues a point about feeling in poetry by aligning its position with an opposition to the gratuitously unlimited killing of civilians in the fire-bombing of the Japanese cities and the nuclear attacks on Hiroshima and Nagasaki:

> Donne could be daring, but he never knew,
> When he inquired, 'Who's injured by my love?'
> Love's radio-active fall-out on a large
> Expanse around the point it bursts above.

Yet there is ghastly 'daring' in Davie's conceit as well. Like Adorno in his perceptiveness, he can appear to be collaborating with, by succumbing to, the very dehumanization against which he is protesting. In response, poets have been driven to ever more subtle modes of indirection. As Elizabeth Bishop, punning on the brass of the Air Force Band and of the 'top brass', put it: 'The gathered brasses want to go | *boom—boom*.'[80] When all's said, we have taken great strides in the business of 'man thinning out his kind'[81] since Yeats imagined that 'Aeroplane and Zeppelin' would 'Pitch like King Billy bomb-balls in | Until the town lie beaten flat'; but whether we have made any moral progress on the sanctity of civilian life in wartime since the poet's death in January 1939 must, as I write, be painfully in doubt.

---

[79] Donald Davie, 'Rejoinder to a Critic', in *Collected Poems*, ed. Neil Powell (Manchester: Carcanet, 2000), 67–8.

[80] Elizabeth Bishop, 'View of the Capitol from the Library of Congress', in *The Complete Poems 1927–1979* (London: Chatto & Windus, 1983), 69.

[81] Lowell, 'Waking Early Sunday Morning', 386.

....

CHAPTER 27

THE WAR REMAINS OF KEITH DOUGLAS AND TED HUGHES

....

CORNELIA D. J. PEARSALL

In his 1964 introduction to the poems of Keith Douglas, killed in 1944 at Normandy at the age of 24, Ted Hughes points to what he sees as a central insight of this Second World War poet: 'The truth of a man is the doomed man in him or his dead body. Poem after poem circles this idea, as if his mind were tethered.'[1] Hughes's deeply appreciative account of Douglas's work attempted to reinvigorate the reputation of this widely overlooked poet, at a point when Hughes's own life was becoming untethered: his writings on Douglas (articles in 1962 and 1963; the introduction to a volume of Douglas's selected poems in 1964) straddle the suicide of Sylvia Plath in February 1963. Born just a decade after Douglas, Hughes was, like him, the son of a distinguished veteran of the First World War, and he learned much not only about war but also about poetry from this insufficiently examined precursor.[2] This essay

---

[1] Ted Hughes, 'Introduction', in Keith Douglas, *Selected Poems*, ed. Ted Hughes (London: Faber, 1964), 13.

[2] Edna Longley notes that 'studies of Hughes—far more abundant than of Douglas—make little room for an obvious ancestor and inspiration', in ' "Shit or Bust": The Importance of Keith Douglas', in *Poetry in the Wars* (Newcastle-upon-Tyne: Bloodaxe, 1986), 94. Longley herself offers insightful comparative discussion in this chapter, as does William Scammell in his *Keith Douglas: A Study* (London: Faber, 1988), *passim*.

begins with letters of Plath and Hughes describing the poetic and personal impact on them of reading Douglas in 1962, and ends with Hughes's critical return to Douglas a quarter-century later, the intensity of his engagement undiminished. Both men represent, in their persons and their poetry, the human wreckage of the European wars, which include the dead but also what Hughes suggests are the equally pitiable survivors. The identities (the 'truth of a man') of the quick and the dead lie everywhere exposed in the detritus of war, and this essay's three parts follow the stripping down of the remains, moving from the battlefield litter of loot and corpses in the first part, to the skeletal in the second, and then finally to disarticulated bones in the third. Each of these remnants serves as a figure—for Douglas, and, following him, Hughes—for the materialization of poetic practice itself.

Both Hughes and Plath are explicit regarding the profound impact on them of reading Douglas. Hughes's letter to his sister Olwyn Hughes, written in early June 1962 from Court Green, the home he shared with Plath in Devon, captures his personal and professional excitement over this discovery:

Do you know Keith Douglas' poetry? . . . A wonderful poet—utterly neglected. So I wrote a BBC programme, enthusing, & received a letter from his mother . . . she's 75, & living from job to job as an old lady's companion, and was pathetically interested to hear if my broadcast encouraged anybody to notice her son's poetry. Anyway, Hutchinson's wrote, & asked if I would write a foreword, if they republished his collected poems. . . . He's a very fine poet, & must have been an admirable sort of bloke. Infinitely the best of that 1920 generation, & one of the best ever, to say he was killed at 24![3]

Plath's account, from a letter to her mother, Aurelia Plath, from Court Green the same week, dated 7 June 1962, recounts similar information:

Ted did a beautiful [BBC] program on a marvelous young British poet, Keith Douglas, killed in the last war, saying how shocking it was no book of his was in print. In the next mail he got grateful letters and inscribed books from the poet's 75-year-old, impoverished mother and a suggestion from a publisher that Ted write the foreword to a new edition of the book. Both of us mourn this poet immensely and feel he would have been like a lovely big brother to us. His death is really a terrible blow and we are trying to resurrect his image and poems in this way.[4]

Both letters tell the same story of Hughes's efforts on radio and potentially in print to promote Douglas's reputation. Hughes places Douglas's work in literary-historical contexts, first among other Second World War poets ('that 1920 generation'), then among all poets ('one of the best ever'). Yet, while he historicizes Douglas, he also personalizes him, positing that he 'must have been an admirable sort of bloke.' Plath, whose equal fervour for Douglas is omitted in her husband's account, intensifies

---

[3] Hughes to Olwyn Hughes, n.d. [June 1962], Olwyn Hughes Papers (MSS 980), Manuscript, Archives, and Rare Book Library, Emory University.

[4] Sylvia Plath to Aurelia Schober Plath, 7 June 1962, in *Letters Home: Correspondence 1950–1963*, ed. Aurelia Schober Plath (London: Faber, 1992), 456.

this assumed familiarity, articulating a personal longing for the deceased poet. Her terms reflect what appears to have been for her the immediacy of the shock of his death: 'Both of us mourn this poet immensely'; 'His death is really a terrible blow.' Plath's letter conveys her sense that securing a posthumous reputation for Douglas is a joint commitment: '*we* are trying to resurrect his image and his poems'. If so, it was among the last of their shared marital projects. Within a month of these June letters, Plath learned of Hughes's burgeoning affair with Assia Wevill, and their separation and the dissolution of the marriage had begun.

The letter to Hughes from the poet's mother, Marie J. Douglas, to which the letters of both Hughes and Plath refer, has proved elusive (it may have been destroyed in Plath's bonfire of Hughes's papers after he left Court Green), but Hughes's letters to Marie Douglas are preserved in the Douglas Papers in the British Library. Writing from Devon, in a letter postmarked 10 June 1962, he describes the evolution of his admiration for her son's poetry, beginning with his discovery of it in an anthology:

And I then procured a copy of his Collection, with great difficulty, from an American book dealer. Since then, I've become as familiar with his poetry as with any, and it seems to me to get better and better. I had hoped, by this broadcast, to urge somebody to re-publish his poems, but I shall not stop at a broadcast. I think your son must have been a kind of man one looks for in vain among the survivors, and even among much of history.[5]

Hughes's intimacy with Douglas's poetry spanned the remainder of his own career. In 1987 he published a lengthy introduction to a new edition of Douglas, in which his admiration had if anything increased, the poems having continued, in the intervening twenty-five years, to 'get better and better'. In his 1962 letter to his sister he proclaims Douglas 'one of the best [poets] ever', given his early death, while in unpublished notes for his 1987 introduction to another Douglas collection he calls him 'one of the most purely gifted poets ever born in England'.[6] His letter to Douglas's mother refers to the poet in as personal a cast as had Plath's letter to her mother; his intimate knowledge of the poetry, with which he is 'as familiar . . . as with any', extends to an assumption of intimate knowledge of the man. Douglas comes to Hughes after having been searched for, having been 'look[ed] for in vain among the survivors', not only of the most recent war but 'among much of history'.

LOOT

Ted Hughes did not need to look far to find European war 'survivors'. His poetry periodically recurs to the burden shouldered by his family of the extraordinary

---

[5] Hughes to Marie J. Douglas, n.d. [June 1962], British Library Manuscripts, Add. 59833.
[6] Hughes, Ted Hughes Papers (MSS 644), Manuscript, Archives, and Rare Book Library, Emory University.

military service of his father, Billie Hughes, who survived the battlefields not only of Gallipoli but also of France and Flanders. Hughes's poem 'Out' dates from 1962, a period of intensive engagement with Douglas's poems (he recorded it on 29 August 1962). It was published in *Wodwo* (1967), his first collection after his wife's death and after his production of editions of Douglas (1964) and of Plath (1965). An explicitly autobiographical poem, 'Out' falls into three sections. I focus here on the first, entitled 'The Dream Time':

> My father sat in his chair recovering
> From the four-year mastication by gunfire and mud,
> Body buffeted wordless, estranged by long soaking
> In the colours of mutilation.
>   His outer perforations
> Were valiantly healed, but he and the hearth-fire, its blood-flicker
> On biscuit-bowl and piano and table-leg,
> Moved into strong and stronger possession
> Of minute after minute, as the clock's tiny cog
> Laboured and on the thread of his listening
> Dragged him bodily from under
> The mortised four-year strata of dead Englishmen
> He belonged with. He felt his limbs clearing
> With every slight, gingerish movement. While I, small and four,
> Lay on the carpet as his luckless double,
> His memory's buried, immovable anchor,
> Among jawbones and blown-off boots, tree-stumps, shell-cases and craters,
> Under rain that goes on drumming its rods and thickening
> Its kingdom, which the sun has abandoned, and where nobody
> Can ever again move from shelter.[7]

In 'Out' we enter the company of a house-bound father as fixed and inactive as the furniture he sits on: he 'sat in his chair recovering', as if he were woven into the upholstery, less recovering himself than recovering the chair. While the piano stands silent, the 'clock's tiny cog' beats metronomic accompaniment to the reverie it produces. So small a sound is all that is necessary to bring on the grinding of the guns, and the inexorable martial downbeat of the 'rain that goes on drumming its rods'. The clock's diminutive beating, what Hughes a moment later calls its 'slight, gingerish movement', draws the sitter back into 'gunfire and mud', its tinny syncopation at once plunging him back into the trenches and dragging him out. The layers of the dead are called 'mortised', an adjective signifying they are intricately joined, as with a mortice and tenon; an appropriate term, given that after his return from the war Billie Hughes worked in carpentry as a joiner. The men 'He belonged with' are also *mort*-ized, made dead, and yet it appears to be Billie Hughes who is mortified, stiffened, and silenced by his own survival.

---

[7] Hughes, 'Out', in *Collected Poems*, ed. Paul Keegan (London: Faber, 2003), 165–6.

Billie Hughes was awarded Britain's Distinguished Conduct Medal, the nation's second highest honour, after the Victoria Cross, for heroism in action, for repeatedly carrying the wounded at Ypres from the battlefield back to the trenches. Yet, while he and the blood-flickering fire 'Moved into strong and stronger possession | Of minute by minute', the passage of time in 'The Dream Time' renders the father's actions passive, ineffectual. The clearing of his limbs, dramatized formally by the poem's insistent enjambment, is directly associated with the 'slight, gingerish movement' of the clock, so that his hands and feet appear to move with its faintness and caution. Although he had again and again dragged the wounded away from battle, clearing their limbs, the distinguished veteran is here depicted as dragged away himself, a body incapable of physical volition or self-propelled momentum.

Billie Hughes is all too literally demobilized, the term used for discharged soldiers after the First World War. (We recall the snatch of pub conversation in *The Waste Land*: 'When Lil's husband got demobbed'.[8]) While the poet's father ultimately made his way home from the front lines, there to be passively subjected to recovery and 'valiant' healing, his son is now paralysed by the war. 'Small and four', as diminutive a time-keeper as the 'clock's tiny cog', his identity may be more directly associated with the war than that of his father. Certainly, the time he keeps to is wartime, as his four years are coterminous with the 'four-year mastication by gunfire and mud', and the 'four-year strata of dead Englishmen' he belongs to still more than his father. The child is felled by his father's military action, and can only lie on the carpet, 'buried, immovable', abandoned, unlike his father's comrades, amid the wreckage of the battlefield. The father is associated with functional domestic objects (hearth-fire, biscuit-bowl, piano, table-leg), the son with the spent and useless debris of war, sprawled out 'Among jawbones and blown-off boots, tree-stumps, shell-cases and craters'. His father's immobility is contagious and inescapable, as all his family now inhabit a place and condition in which 'nobody | Can ever again move from shelter'.

Part of what Keith Douglas offers Hughes is a precise and energetic antidote to paralysis. While his father inhabits a 'Body buffeted wordless', Hughes sees in Douglas a body buffeted into graceful and effective articulation. The physical movement of the poetry itself was much remarked by Ted Hughes. In his 1964 introduction, Hughes calls Douglas's language 'extremely forceful . . . a feat of great strength', while 'As for technique', 'there is nothing numb or somnambulist in it.' Hughes admires especially in Douglas 'the essentially practical cast of his energy, his impatient, razor energy'.[9] And mobility is what Douglas himself found distinctive about his own war, which he considered otherwise a grim repetition of the previous World War. In his essay 'Poets in This War' (1943), Douglas poses a question asked by others, then and since, 'Why are there no poets like Owen and Sassoon?', and

---

[8]   T. S. Eliot, *The Waste Land*, in *The Complete Poems and Plays* (London: Faber, 1969), 65.

[9]   Hughes, 'Introduction', 11.

offers this answer: 'because there is nothing new, from a soldier's point of view, about this war except its mobile character'.[10] The quality of energetic momentum that Hughes hears in Douglas's verse is attributed by Douglas to the distinctive characteristic of the War itself.

In June 1962 Hughes wrote to Marie Douglas, 'Thank you for so kindly writing out the copy of [Douglas's essay] "The Nature of Poetry". Thank you, too, for offering me a copy of his book. If you would sign it, I would count it among my most valuable possessions.'[11] Douglas's brief manifesto, 'On the Nature of Poetry', written while an undergraduate at Oxford and about a page long, begins: 'Poetry is like a man, whom thinking you know all his movements and appearance you will presently come upon in such a posture that for a moment you can hardly believe it a position of the limbs you know.'[12] Douglas explains that by this he means that poetry inevitably moves beyond any limits one attempts to set for it, but his own poetry is everywhere shaped by the mobility of unexpected masculine postures, in both its form and its content. Already in 1964 Hughes considers himself to know Douglas's limbs, in their energy and grace; his enthusiasm for this muscular poetics has, if anything, gained momentum in his 1987 'Introduction', in which he lauds the 'the naked physique of the poetry', its 'tensile strength'.[13]

'It is still very much alive, even providing life,'[14] Hughes declares of Douglas's poetry in 1964, and indeed, while his own father's war service immobilizes the household, Douglas's poetry is so life-giving that it has the ability even to animate the dead. For Douglas, the dead are dynamic—perhaps more so, during war, than the living, whose movements are everywhere conscripted and checked, whether by the enemy or by the military superiors from whom Douglas repeatedly courted court marshalling for his openly insubordinate responses to their authority, as with, as Edna Longley puts it, his 'desertion *to* the battle of Alamein'.[15] Enjoying an easy mobility, the dead are understood to be active and ongoing participants in the War, as corpses 'dispose themselves' companionably,[16] while the living, as Hughes observes in his 1987 introduction to Douglas, 'are hardly more than deluded variants of the dead'.[17]

This consistent and deliberate confusion between the living and the dead is a central pattern of *Alamein to Zem Zem*, Douglas's memoir of his combat in the desert war in North Africa, which was published posthumously. (Marie Douglas sent Hughes a copy after his broadcast, and Hughes wrote in gratitude, 'I've been

---

[10] Keith Douglas, 'Poets in This War', in *The Letters*, ed. Desmond Graham (Manchester: Carcanet, 2000), 352.

[11] Hughes to Marie J. Douglas, n.d. [June 1962], British Library Manuscripts, Add. 59833.

[12] Douglas, 'On the Nature of Poetry', in *The Complete Poems*, ed. Desmond Graham with an introduction by Ted Hughes (London: Faber, 2000; 1st pub. by Oxford University Press, 1987), 133.

[13] Hughes, 'Introduction', in Douglas, *Complete Poems*, pp. xix and xxix.

[14] Hughes, 'Introduction', in Douglas, *Selected Poems*, 11.

[15] Edna Longley, '"Shit or Bust"', 95.   [16] Douglas, 'Aristocrats', in *Complete Poems*, 117.

[17] Hughes, 'Introduction', ibid. p. xxiii.

trying to get hold of 'From Alemain [*sic*] to Zem-zem' for three years.'[18]) The living resemble corpses, as is the case with the first dead body Douglas encounters in *Alamein to Zem Zem*: peering into the 'murk' of a trench, he sees what he calls an 'object . . . as long as a man and in a pose which suggested limbs. I stretched a tentative and reluctant hand down into the pit, wondering whether I should touch a stiffened arm, shoulder or leg.'[19] But the dead body escapes his grasp, as his reluctant hand fastens instead on what is simply another soldier's bedding. His first dead body is a living man's kit. While the living resemble the dead, the dead are like the living in their capacity for movement. What really is the first corpse Douglas sees assumes the easy posture of the ambient, appearing merely as 'a man in black overalls who was leaning on the parapet'. The shape of the duffle which Douglas had mistaken for a corpse reclines 'in a pose which suggested limbs', while corpses array themselves in various postures, one 'leaning on the parapet', another 'taking up his position'.[20] Displaying an inexhaustible capacity for lyric self-positioning, these corpses and variants of corpses stand, and move, as figures of incarnate poetry, as Douglas had defined it—that is, like a man whose movements and appearance had been familiar, now rendered unfamiliar, perhaps even suddenly unknowable, by an unexpected shift in the position of his limbs.

Hughes's 'Out' catalogues the dismayingly littered ground of a domestic battle-field, with its 'jawbones and blown-off boots', but in Douglas anything that remains has value—not surprisingly, perhaps, given Douglas's numerous lively accounts of the necessity and serendipity of battlefield looting. 'Loot is one of the most important things,' Douglas asserts, in the last collected letter he wrote before his death. 'It is the thing that makes all that exhilaration in fighting . . . simply rumma-ging in the glorious brantub provided by any battlefield.'[21] The battlefield detritus so overwhelming to the submerged 4-year-old of the Hughes household is what exhilarates or at least temporarily compensates survivors. In 'Enfidaville', Douglas writes of displaced townspeople, 'already they are coming back; to search | like ants, poking in the débris, finding in it | a bed or a piano and carrying it out'.[22] Viewing this retrieval of objects (bed, piano) connoting sensuous and sensual pleasures of the sort the war has interrupted, the poet asks of the scavengers, 'Who would not love them at this minute?' All residue may be reclaimed, which is to say looted, as human or material remains remain and find new uses. 'Dead Men' describes how from the 'shallow graves' of the buried soldiers 'the wild dog | discovered and exhumed a face or a leg | for food'.[23] The poet comes to find this scavenging image consolatory, as the dead remain, after their fashion, vital presences. Douglas reflects, 'the wild dog finding meat in a hole | is a philosopher'. The pariah is a philosopher, and also

---

[18] Hughes to Marie J. Douglas, n.d., British Library Manuscripts, Add. 59833.
[19] Douglas, *Alamein to Zem Zem*, ed. Desmond Graham (London: Faber, 1992), 31.
[20] Ibid. 34 and 38.   [21] Douglas to Jocelyn Baber, 28 Apr. 1944, in *Letters*, 342.
[22] Douglas, 'Enfidaville', in *Complete Poems*, 116.   [23] Douglas, 'Dead Men', ibid. 100.

a poet, who in the same fashion roams the battlefield, searching remorselessly for what he can plunder. All war poetry is loot.

'Out' follows Hughes's intensive reading of Douglas in the early Sixties; another poem regarding his father's war service, 'For the Duration', published in 1989, follows his return to Douglas for a new 1987 edition of his poems. Hughes's father's martial activities have not gained in energy or force in the intervening quarter-century. Hughes describes his father at war: 'again and again | Carrying in the wounded | Collapsing with exhaustion', then being thrown by a 'shell-burst' 'Before you fell under your load into the trench'.[24] The son recalls of the shrapnel that hit his father 'how it spun you' and remarks, too, the 'traversing machine-gun that tripped you'. Billie Hughes appears to have stumbled gracelessly across many battle-fronts, 'collapsing', falling, being 'spun' and 'tripped', his physical ineptitude seeming itself to have contributed to his inexplicable survival.

In his 1987 'Introduction' Hughes pursues an extensive comparison of Douglas with Wilfred Owen in ways that illuminate these lyric portraits of his father. According to Hughes, Owen's 'empathy with the wounded and killed suggests a supine figure', drawing us back to the motionless father and prostrate child in 'Out', overwhelmed and laid low by domesticated empathy. Meanwhile, Douglas's poetry exhibits 'a masculine movement, a nimble, predatory attack, hard-edged, with a quick and clean escape'. Hughes offers a historical analysis, contrasting 'the punished, mobilized experience' of the Second World War and 'the helpless, immobilized innocence' which he recognizes in retrospect is in fact a personal analysis.[25] In a 1988 letter he recollects that after he had written that piece, he realized that Owen 'grew to represent my father's experience', and Douglas came to represent that of his brother Gerald, '(who was in North Africa through the same period). So that pattern of antithetical succession was prefigured, for me, and quite highly charged.'[26] But a sense of urgency, while unacknowledged, comes across in a 1964 letter from Hughes to his brother, who had moved to Australia, and to whom he had sent his new edition: 'Did you get the Keith Douglas poems, Gerald? Answer this.'[27] And Plath had recognized this fraternal relationship to Douglas as well, when she wrote of his effect on her and Hughes, 'Both of us . . . feel he would have been like a lovely big brother to us.'

Tacitly admitting to Douglas's mother his disappointment in his own heroic father, Hughes writes to her that her 'son must have been a kind of man one looks for in vain among the survivors, and even among much of history'. But perhaps summoning the 'razor energy' that Hughes so admires in Douglas's poetry

---

[24] Hughes, 'For the Duration', in *Collected Poems*, 760.

[25] Hughes, 'Introduction', in Douglas, *Complete Poems*, pp. xxvii, xxv–vi, xxiii.

[26] Hughes to William Scammell, 2 Feb. 1988, 'Postscript 1: Douglas and Owen', in Hughes, *Winter Pollen: Occasional Prose*, ed. William Scammell (London: Faber, 1994), 215.

[27] Hughes to Gerald Hughes, n.d. [postmarked 14 July 1964], Gerald Hughes Papers (MSS 854), Manuscript, Archives, and Rare Book Library, Emory University.

is harder for the luckless survivors who themselves constitute war's remains, himself included. In the third part of 'Out', subtitled 'Remembrance Day', Hughes demands of corpses he may suspect are more effectual than any living person: 'You dead bury your dead.' As Hughes surveys the scattered wreckage of his inherited battlefields, as he turns in the early 1960s from editing the poetry of Douglas to editing the poetry of Plath, he acknowledges that one's only hope *is* that the dead, whose quickening remains still the demobilized survivors, may indeed bury the dead, because the living, as philosophical scavengers, never can.

SKELETAL POETICS

'Will you look up SKELETAL in a dictionary (I haven't one) and find out if it exists and means like a skeleton': so Douglas wrote in a letter to Betty Jesse from the Front in March 1944, the privations of combat including the absence of dictionaries.[28] The word exists, and does indeed mean, according to the *OED*, 'part of or resembling a skeleton'. Douglas's inquiry was prompted by his use of the word in 'Mersa', referred to in the poem as 'the skeletal town'.[29] Just past the town, he joins some 'cherry-skinned soldiers' on the 'white beach'. The fruitful adjective 'cherry' indicates that the soldiers are sunburned, but suggests also that they are edible, and indeed the poem moves at the end to the eating away of this red flesh. As he stands in the water, looking down at his feet, 'The logical little fish | converge and nip the flesh | imagining I am one of the dead.' But of course it is the poet himself who most aggressively imagines not only the death of his body, but the inexorable logic of its degustation. In Douglas's 'Dead Men', unearthed soldiers are now simply 'a casual meal for a dog, nothing but the bone | so soon'. In 'Time Eating', digestion is 'Ravenous' Time's most aggressive function: 'Time's ruminative tongue will wash | and slow juice masticate all flesh.'[30] To imagine being dead is to imagine being fed upon—by fish, dogs, time itself—but while the flesh is consumed, the bone is what for a time remains.

Edna Longley comments that Douglas produced 'Not skeletal poetry, but poetry with no superfluous flesh, fighting fit, the cadence of energy.'[31] But in Douglas all flesh can appear superfluous, as war renders into visibility the stony, hardened interior of the doomed man. What is skeletal is not easily reducible, as the hard, dense substance is the most enduring part of a dead body, potentially unassimilable either to life or to death. The skeletal takes sharp if often shifting definition in Douglas's war poetry, not only as a recurrent image throughout his *œuvre*, but as a figuration for poetic survival. 'Simplify me when I'm dead' is one of the Douglas's

---

[28] Douglas to Betty Jesse, 26 Mar. 1944, in *Letters*, 327.
[29] Douglas, 'Mersa', in *Complete Poems*, 99.   [30] Douglas, 'Time Eating', ibid. 71.
[31] Longley, ' "Shit or Bust" ', 111.

most frequently anthologized poems, and thus itself an example of at least that form of literary survival. Though a poem about death and decay, for Hughes it suggests life itself; he declares of the poem in notes in the Emory University archives, 'I know very little poetry as utterly alive and invigorating as this.'[32] Douglas posits that 'the processes of earth' will 'strip off the colour and the skin: | take the brown hair and blue eye | and leave me simpler than at birth'.[33] While the skin is simplified by time's eating, the skeleton can be subjected to assessment, however limited: 'Of my skeleton perhaps | so stripped, a learned man will say | "He was of such a type and intelligence," no more.' Though perhaps leaving 'no more' to be said, the skeleton nevertheless leaves a substance that may be exposed to the judgement of posterity. Hughes wrote on the flyleaf of Desmond Graham's biography of Keith Douglas, 'Poets and pigs are only valued when they're dead,'[34] a comparison that is not necessarily despairing. While poets and pigs are dissected and subjected to calculated appraisal after their deaths, they may also appreciate in value. In Douglas's poems, skeletal remains do not simplify, but instead complicate the dead; desiccated, eaten by dogs, strangely indissoluble, bones demand the discrimination of the living.

In an undated four-page letter to Olwyn Hughes that, given its internal references, must have been written in the period soon after the epistolary exchanges of Hughes and Plath with which this essay began, we can witness the reach of Douglas's skeletal hand. Hughes writes while in the midst of separating from Plath (about whom he tells his sister, 'as soon as I clear out, she'll start making a life of her own, friends of her own, interests of her own'). He recounts what we might consider a Second World War anxiety dream ('I dreamed Hitler came to me, furious, demanding that I carry out the commands instantly'), but does not connect this apparition of the Führer either to his infuriated wife or to the war poet whose editing project he was embarking upon. He writes with a kind of breezy confidence about this project and what it might portend: 'Faber's commissioned me to edit a selection of Keith Douglas' poems, of which I'm very fond. With an introduction. I'll gradually become the guiding taste at Faber's, when Eliot retires—it would be an amusing coup. I suggested they do Douglas.'[35] We can hear the ways in which the mention of the Douglas edition is bound together with a larger, only partly facetious, ambition to replace T. S. Eliot—who, as it happens, had written Douglas a highly encouraging letter in 1941, calling his poems 'extremely promising', and telling him, 'you have definitely an ear'.[36]

But Douglas's influence in this period is reflected still more in Hughes's poetic ambitions than in his editorial ones. Several poems in *Wodwo*, Hughes's first volume of poetry after publishing his editions of Douglas and Plath, are littered

[32] Hughes, Ted Hughes Papers (MSS 644).
[33] Douglas, 'Simplify me when I'm dead', in *Complete Poems*, 74.
[34] Hughes, quoted in Desmond Graham, 'An Unwilling Biographer', *PN Review* 47, 12/3 (1985), 23.
[35] Hughes to Olwyn Hughes, n.d., Olwyn Hughes Papers (MSS 980).
[36] T. S. Eliot to Keith Douglas, 15 Feb. 1941, in Douglas, *Letters*, 164.

with skeletons that are figurations for his own poetic practice. In the last page of this letter to his sister, Hughes includes what he calls a 'lyrical' poem, 'not very extreme, about Heptonstall of course'. The poem 'Heptonstall', which takes its title from the West Yorkshire town where his parents lived and Plath would be buried, describes the town as a 'Black village of gravestones', composed of an accretion of skulls: 'Skull of an idiot', 'Skull of a sheep', 'Skull of a bird'.[37] In the poem 'Gog', which, Hughes told an interviewer, began as a description of a German military assault, a 'jaguarish' creature takes its clearest identity from its aggressive calcification: 'My great bones are massed in me': 'I listen to the song jarring my mouth | Where the skull-rooted teeth are in possession. | I am massive on earth. My feetbones beat on the earth.'[38] The creature of Hughes's 'Gog' takes his powers of articulation from bone itself: its song is composed from 'skull-rooted teeth', its metrical rhythms are beaten out by 'feetbones'. These poems take not only their content but their form from a pained commitment to a stony, stripped down, skeletal poetics.

Hughes considers Douglas's poetry to have arrived at 'a very essential, irreducible self', thus characterizing the stripping down to the elemental that is the hallmark of Douglas's lyrical style. The skeletal is that which accommodates yet resists death, and thus is an apt figure for Douglas's poetic ambition. Recovering from shrapnel wounds in 1943 at the No. 1 General Hospital in El Ballah, Palestine, Douglas, according to his biographer Desmond Graham, 'wrote the first of the war poems on which his reputation was to rest', and indeed it appears that his reputation especially exercised him in his convalescence.[39] Douglas could not have been firmer in his purpose; Lt Col. John Stubbs, who spent much time in Douglas's company at the hospital, reports him saying repeatedly, 'I insist, I am going to be a major poet come what may.'[40] To become skeletal is to become a figure for death, but it is also to cheat it, since the skeletal is what for a duration can survive even bodily decay. In 'How to Kill', Douglas's speaker witnesses, as he shoots a German soldier, Death make 'a man of dust | of a man of flesh', becoming in an instant a 'ghost'.[41] The weightless man is the truly dead; this is how to kill, by leaving no bone. Thus an ambition to produce skeletal poetry constitutes an ambition to become canonical, to create poetry that remains. Echoing a line in '*Vergissmeinnicht*' (a German soldier, dead for three weeks, is 'mocked at by his equipment | that's hard and good when he's decayed'),[42] Roger Garfitt comments perceptively on this poet's enduring appeal in similar terms: 'Douglas created a poetry that would be hard and good when he's decayed.'[43]

While his war experience intensified the development of his skeletal poetics, Douglas's lyric commitment pre-dates his mobilization. 'The Poets', written around 1940, while Douglas was still at Oxford, refers to 'we [who] are already phantoms;

---

[37] Hughes, 'Heptonstall', in *Collected Poems*, 170–1.   [38] Hughes, 'Gog', ibid. 162.
[39] Desmond Graham, 'A Soldier's Story: Keith Douglas at El Ballah', *PN Review* 47, 12/3 (1985), 26.
[40] Douglas, quoted by Graham, ibid. 27.   [41] Douglas, 'How to Kill', in *Complete Poems*, 119.
[42] Douglas, '*Vergissmeinnicht*', ibid. 118.
[43] Roger Garfitt, 'Keith Douglas', *Poetry Nation*, 4 (1975), 111.

boneless, substanceless, wanderers',[44] suggesting that the ceaseless search for calcareous structure is the fate of poets. And in 'Famous Men', written when he was 15 and included as the second poem in Hughes's 1964 edition, accomplished figures now 'lie deep, | licked clean their skulls, | rest beautifully, staring'.[45] The poem insists, 'The quick movement of dactyls | does not compensate them,' but we can hear how skeletal materiality itself becomes associated with the quick physicality attributed by Hughes to Douglas's versification. The abiding ambition we find throughout this poetry is the ambition to abide, as poems themselves constitute the poet's skeletal remains, challenging death with dactyls like skulls.

Lyric Front Lines

In the autumn of 1941, Douglas was stationed at a convalescent depot at Nathanya, in Palestine. The cause was a severe ear infection he had acquired in Cairo, but the acuity of his ear, already praised by T. S. Eliot, seems to have developed in the course of this posting; while there he wrote a handful of poems that reflect closely on his poetic practice, and specifically on his distinctive form of lineation. At Nathanya he spent his days exploring some four miles of deserted beach along the Mediterranean coast, writing to his friend Jean Turner, 'Well I have been walking beside the sea waves and have rather unoriginally been inspired, presumably by the waves etc, to produce 3 rather unoriginal poems,'[46] a facetious assessment with which critics have tended sharply and quite reasonably to disagree. He tells his mother in a letter of 26 October 1941, 'I usually walk several miles along the sands,' and the three poems he wrote ('The Hand', 'Adams', and 'The Sea Bird') owe as much to the lines his steps made in the sand as to the breaking of the waves.[47] The originality of these poems is in some measure a function of their line breaks, as epistolary commentaries written by Hughes in 1988 on two of the poems demonstrate. In these letters Hughes is struck anew, and in some sense clearly also as if for the first time, by what in his 'Introduction' the previous year he characterized as the nimble balancing act performed by Douglas's writing: 'Each line gives a strong impression of acrobatic balance involving the whole body.'[48] We have seen already how Hughes, like Douglas before him, associates the movement of a man's limbs (active, nimble) with the kind of poetry each admired; these poems go still further in aligning the lineaments of body and verse, limbs and lines.

[44] Douglas, 'The Poets', in *Complete Poems*, 50.   [45] Douglas, 'Famous Men', ibid. 10.
[46] Douglas to Jean Turner, n.d. [postmarked 20 Nov. 1941], in *Letters*, 203. Desmond Graham asserts that 'The poems certainly did not merit his dismissive comment' (Graham, *Keith Douglas, 1920–1944: A Biography* (London: Oxford University Press, 1974), 131). William Scammell concurs: 'his flippant judgement couldn't have been further from the truth' (Scammell, *Keith Douglas*, 110).
[47] Douglas to Marie J. Douglas, 26 Oct. 1941, in *Letters*, 201.
[48] Hughes, 'Introduction', in Douglas, *Complete Poems*, p. xix.

Sidelined by his ear on his way to the front lines of the Western Desert, Douglas found himself reflecting on lines in poetry. 'Negative Information', the poem he wrote just before producing the three at Nathanya, begins:

> As lines, the unrelated symbols of
> nothing you know, discovered in the clouds
> idly made on paper or by the feet of crowds
> on sand, keep whatever meaning they have
>
> and you believe they write, for some
> intelligence, messages of a sort;
> these curious indentations on my thought
> with every week, almost with each hour come.[49]

These lines radically disjoin the formal element of the line from any necessary content, as lines are symbols that are 'unrelated' to one another or to any intelligible meaning. '[Y]ou believe they write', but the contrails of the clouds, marks on the paper, or footprints in the sand are illegible. Meant for some other 'intelligence', with more understanding of their relation, the lines nevertheless inexorably trace 'curious indentations' on the poet's 'thought'. The image of lines made by feet in the sand recurs in the first of his Nathanya poems, 'The Hand', which ends by imagining 'the tracks of [the mind] at liberty | like the geometry of feet | upon a shore, constructed in the sand'.[50] The 'tracks' of the mind parallel the 'indentations' of 'thought' in the previous poem, as acts of cognition resemble footprints 'on sand' or 'upon a shore'. In the first stanza of 'The Hand' he observes admiringly of this body part, 'the bone retains its proportion in the grave,' as the geometrical precision associated with lines formed by feet in the sand is recognized as a quality of digital bone as well.

Geometrical precision is critical to verse making ('the geometry of feet'), Douglas had already determined in 'On the Nature of Poetry' (his 1940 essay which his mother copied by hand for Ted Hughes), in which he declares that a poet must not 'waste any more words' in his work 'than a mathematician: every word must work for its keep'.[51] Several years later, in August 1943, Douglas wrote to J. C. Hall in a letter widely taken to be his final poetic manifesto: 'my object (and I don't give a damn about my duty as a poet) is to write true things, significant things in words each of which works for its place in a line.'[52] His duty as a poet is homologous to his duty as a soldier: the object in either profession is to maintain the disciplined order of the line. Exploring the properties and proportions of lines, not so much in their lengths (often highly variable in Douglas) but in the *work* that words do within and between themselves, is a significant object of the two richly overlapping poems he wrote next, 'The Sea Bird' and 'Adams', both of which commence with steps in the sand.

[49] Douglas, 'Negative Information', in *Complete Poems*, 81.
[50] Douglas, 'The Hand', ibid. 83.   [51] Douglas, 'On the Nature of Poetry', 133.
[52] Douglas to J. C. Hall, 10 Aug. 1943, in *Letters*, 295.

'The Sea Bird' unfurls itself as one long sentence, which begins,

> Walking along beside the beach
> where the Mediterranean turns in sleep
> under the cliffs' demiarch
> through a curtain of thought I see
> a dead bird and a live bird
> the dead eyeless, but with a bright eye
>
> the live bird discovered me
> and stepped from a black rock into the air—
> I turn from the dead bird to watch him fly . . . [53]

The poet describes two birds he catches sight of on the Mediterranean coast, one living and one dead. Douglas's title plays on the homophonic 'see' and 'sea', setting up the baffling matter of the sight of the sea birds. The 'eyeless' dead bird seems to share the 'bright eye' of the live bird, so much so that when we read the line 'I turn from the dead bird to watch him fly' we are not certain which bird is actually ascendant. The continuity from tercet to tercet is achieved by radical use of enjambment, so that many lines are pivotal, and frequently a clause might refer to the syntactical unit that precedes or follows it: the 'bright eye' that arrests the poet's eye, for example, could refer to 'the dead eyeless' bird or the live one. The enjambment continues until the bird steps into the air, and the dash that follows appears to represent its movement off the edge of the line itself. The bird rises, until in the poem's conclusion the live bird 'escapes the eye, or is a ghost | and in a moment has come down, | crept into the dead bird, ceased to exist'. Whether this is the eye of man or bird (and which bird?), we are again confounded. Yet the live bird in its mobility is less palpable than the dead one on the beach, being 'a ghost'.

That the poem achieves its most intense effects from the figuration of its lines is dramatized in an extended extemporaneous response to the poem by Hughes in a 1988 letter to William Scammell:

I see the impalpably painfully real thing, in 'The Sea Bird', as the real identity of the live bird and the dead one—an image of his sense of his own death having somehow already happened, of himself alive being already in his own death and corpse in some abnormal degree of awareness. In 'The Sea Bird' so many of the lines superimpose the two

> a dead bird and a live bird

not differentiated in place

> the dead eyeless, but with a bright eye

(the empty eyesocket has a bright eye in it)

> the live bird discovered me

---

[53] Douglas, 'The Sea Bird', in *Complete Poems*, 86.

(rumbled me as an eyeless corpse)—(as Adams, in fact) even

and stepped from a black rock into the air

(stepped out of a sarcophagus—like a ghost)

I turn from the dead bird to watch him fly

(I shift focus from the vision of him as a corpse to the vision of him as a live bird, though still watching the same bird).[54]

Pursuing a line-by-line reading that proceeds for a few more lines of this poem, Hughes interrupts Douglas's words with his own riff on each line, producing a rhythmic syncopation that seems in effect to create another poem. Hughes observes that 'so many of the lines superimpose the two' birds, even as he moves into a superimposition of his own lines that is also, given their placement in parentheses, a subordination of them. This letter is reprinted in *Winter Pollen*, although Jane Feaver, the volume's editor at Faber, suggested that it be omitted and instead published some day in a collection of Hughes's correspondence. But Hughes saw the value of what he himself considered an unusual exchange, less between himself and Scammell than between himself and Douglas, and indeed between himself and the birds. Writing to Feaver from Court Green in a letter of 23 April 1993, Hughes explains, 'really, I would like to keep [it]. And no, I don't usually go on like that in letters: those were lucky moments where I caught a bird or two as they went over.'[55]

Hughes's spontaneous interlineal commentary underscores the linear superimposition that constitutes one of Douglas's most distinctive formal signatures: in a sense, his lyric front lines. The superimposition of the birds upon one another is an ocular effect achieved by the superimposition of one line upon another. Hughes comments on the 'turn' (appropriately, given the poem's opening image of a sea that 'turns in sleep') by which we 'shift focus' while 'still watching the same bird', and this applies to the form of the poem itself, in which a line might modify the line before, yet also turn or shift focus to modify the line that follows. The alternate meanings are superimposed upon one another, like mortized strata, which leads Hughes to marvel: 'Interesting to see how the same binary system strobes away down through almost all the lines—fascinating how tightly and precisely he brings it off.'[56] And we must ourselves be struck by the way in which, in the mortized strata of Douglas's and Hughes's lines, the dead poet and the living poet, like the dead and living birds, become also confounded.

'The Sea Bird', as an autonomous text, is itself confounded by the poem 'Adams', to which in some respects it bears close resemblance. Though both follow the prints

[54] Hughes to William Scammell, 8 May 1988, 'Postscript 2: "Adams" and "The Sea Bird"', in *Winter Pollen*, 217–18.

[55] Hughes to Jane Feaver, 23 Apr. 1993, Ted Hughes Papers (MSS 644).

[56] Hughes, 'Postscript 2', 218.

of Douglas's feet in the sands of Nathanya, it is not entirely certain which poem was written first. In general, later versions of Douglas's poems are sharply edited and shorter, but Graham suggests that 'The Sea Bird' pre-dates 'Adams', the longer and 'more hazardously ambitious' of the two; Hughes reads 'Adams' as 'a gloss' on 'The Sea Bird'.[57] While one may hold chronological priority over the other, we should see them nevertheless as simultaneous, coexistent. The relation between the two poems, which are nearly identical in their first four and a half stanzas and at the same time strikingly divergent, parallels the relation of divergent coexistence between the dead and live birds in each poem.

Douglas's goal as a poet is 'to write true things, significant things in words each of which works for its place in a line', and the first line of 'Adams' shows how hard each word works to command its place: 'Walking alone beside the beach'.[58] The poet walks alone but also along with the beach, at once solitary and accompanied, alongside as if his feet in the sand trace parallel lines not only in but with the shore. These steps extend to the first line of the second tercet, which reads, 'walking thinking slowly I see'. The adverb 'slowly' works so assiduously for its place that it may modify 'walking', 'thinking', or 'I see', as the line draws together varied acts of attempted cognition.

The likeness of the living and the dead bird in 'The Sea Bird' is axiomatic, but in 'Adams' the resemblance between man and bird must be established:

> Adams is like a bird
> alert (high on his pinnacle of air
> he does not hear you, someone said);
>
> in appearance he is bird-eyed,
> the bones of his face are
> like the hollow bones of a bird.

The tercets adumbrate the simile 'Adams is like a bird' only to confound the very notion of similitude by illustrating how the trope of simile can function itself by way of lineal superimposition. Adams is so 'like' the bird that it is impossible to distinguish them, since the lines that immediately follow make it impossible to tell if the 'he' who is at once 'alert' and inattentive ('he does not hear you', the poet says, having heard, and now said, what 'someone said') is Adams or the bird. By the last stanza of the poem, it is the poet who seeks to superimpose himself on the bird, which he accomplishes, as had Adams, by the superimposition of clauses in lines that pivot upon one another: 'Till Rest, cries my mind to Adams' ghost; | only go elsewhere, let me alone | creep into the dead bird, cease to exist.' The word 'alone', returning from the poem's opening line, works fiercely for its place in the two final lines, signifying, at least: let me alone creep into the dead bird, while you cease to exist; let me alone, while you creep into the dead bird and cease to exist; let me

[57] Graham, *Keith Douglas*, 133; Hughes, 'Postscript 2', 217.
[58] Douglas, 'Adams', in *Complete Poems*, 84.

alone creep into the dead bird and thus cease to exist. Although the poet seeks to enter a likeness to the bird as extreme as Adams's, in the end it is the poet and the Adamic man who are superimposed on one another.

Reading 'Adams' again in 1988, Hughes is drawn to compare the poem less to 'The Sea Bird' than to another work, a list drawn up by Douglas in March 1944 enumerating the qualities of what he called his 'Bête Noire', or the beast on his back. Hughes asks Scammell,

Don't you think there's something about

> Adams is like a bird
> he does not hear you, someone said
> in appearance he is bird-eyed

reminiscent of

> He is a jailer.
> Allows me out on parole
> brings me back by telepathy
> is inside my mind.[59]

Although Adams and the 'Bête Noire' are clearly both ominous figures, most striking in both texts, as Hughes's ear discerns, are the strong rhythms of their linear structures. Hughes pulls lines out of context from 'Adams', thus demonstrating how autonomous each line is, though so densely entrenched in the poem itself. Musing in his 1988 correspondence with Scammell on his 1987 Douglas 'Introduction', Hughes admits that he struggled and may have failed 'to define something', explaining, 'This something is whatever it is that inhabits the curious electrified inflection of his each line.'[60] Hughes suggests that the most distinctive feature of this verse is a lineal force whose electricity might itself seem a function of what Hughes in 1964 called the poet's 'energy, his impatient, razor energy'. With each return to them, Douglas's lines seem to have appeared to Hughes (to paraphrase Douglas) like the limbs of a man whose movements and appearance he knew, ever capable of moving into alignments that for a moment he can hardly believe a position of the limbs, or lines, he knows.

'Strange figure, that Adams,' Hughes writes to Scammell; 'Odd how he sticks in the mind, so jagged and disturbing—Douglas's old Adam!'[61] While 'Adams' in 1988 seems to him unshakeable, Hughes had omitted 'Adams' from his 1964 edition of Douglas, a decision regretted by Geoffrey Hill, who in a review of the volume calls it 'by far the finer of the two poems'. Hill posits: 'It is conceivable that Douglas composed "Adams" first; and, for reasons best known to himself, decided later to break this almost-perfect poem down.'[62] If he is right, Douglas in essence

---

[59] Hughes, 'Postscript 2', 217.   [60] Hughes, 'Postscript 1', 216.
[61] Hughes, 'Postscript 2', 219.
[62] Geoffrey Hill, ' "I in Another Place": Homage to Keith Douglas', *Stand*, 6/4 (1964/5), 11 and 12.

looted from the poem to produce 'The Sea Bird', and also, as Hill notes, the 1943 poem 'Words'. 'I lie in wait' for words, the poet confesses in 'Words', before noting examples of other 'ways of catching'[63] fugitive language:

> For instance this stooping man, the bones of whose face are
> like the hollow birds' bones, is a trap for words.
> And the pockmarked house bleached by the glare
> whose insides war has dried out like gourds
> attracts words.

Adams is entrapped by this later poem, drawn, just like the words he had seemed not to hear, to what is hollowed out, emptied. When he enquired of his friend the meaning of 'SKELETAL', Douglas may have learned from her that it means 'dried up', 'withered', just as this damaged house has been 'dried out', bleached white, like the bleached beach in 'Mersa'. Words are attracted to the skeletal, bone being, as Douglas consistently shows, the articulate remnant of the disarticulated body. Hughes, though reluctantly ensnared by the detritus of his father's war, must have learned this lesson from all that lured him to Keith Douglas's war remains: bones, birds, words.

---

[63] Douglas, 'Words', in *Complete Poems*, 107.

CHAPTER 28

....

'FOR ISAAC ROSENBERG': GEOFFREY HILL, MICHAEL LONGLEY, CATHAL Ó SEARCAIGH

....

TARA CHRISTIE

Isaac Rosenberg was killed at the Western Front, near Arras, France, on the morning of April Fool's Day, 1918, while on dawn patrol. His body was never recovered. The Anglo-Jewish poet, painter, playwright, and First World War soldier from the East End of London left behind a considerable *oeuvre* for an artist whose life was cut short at the age of 27. Yet we can still say today what Rosenberg scholar and biographer Joseph Cohen said 45 years ago—namely, that Rosenberg's admirers are 'practically unanimous in lamenting' his 'continued lack of status among the modern poets', and that 'so little has been said about Isaac Rosenberg that one hardly knows where to begin'.[1] Since the emergence

---

[1] Joseph Cohen, unpublished notes, 'Isaac Rosenberg: From Romantic to Classic', held in an as yet unprocessed folder in the Joseph Cohen archive, Rare Books and Special Collections Department, Thomas Cooper Library, University of South Carolina.

of three biographies in 1975,[2] very little has been said or written of Rosenberg, and for most of the last thirty years, 'The Forgotten Poet of Anglo-Jewry' (as he was dubbed by Jon Silkin)[3] has spent more time out of print than in it.[4] For the first time in twenty years, Rosenberg is back in print with Jean Moorcroft Wilson's *Selected Poems of Isaac Rosenberg* (2003), Jean Liddiard's *Selected Poems and Letters of Isaac Rosenberg* (2003), and Vivien Noakes's Variorum edition of *The Poems and Plays of Isaac Rosenberg* (2004)—three recent publications which may signal a new trend towards the recovery of this poet.[5] For, as with any writer whose works have long been out of print, Rosenberg has not been the focus of much literary scholarship, nor has he been allotted considerable (if any) space in anthologies of modern poetry, or taught in many classrooms. All the instruments agree: with Rosenberg, we still don't know 'where to begin'.

Rosenberg does not fit into the well-worn, ready-made category of 'war poet'. This is not simply because (as Ian Parsons points out) the great majority of Rosenberg's poems are either not about, or were written before, the war,[6] but also because in our attempts to define war poetry, we rely perhaps too heavily upon terminology redolent of Owenesque pity. For Rosenberg's poetry is not in the pity, but takes a colder, more impersonal stance on the suffering of war.[7] Marius Bewley writes:

---

[2] Joseph Cohen, *Journey to the Trenches: The Life of Isaac Rosenberg, 1890–1918* (New York: Basic Books, 1975); Jean Liddiard, *Isaac Rosenberg: The Half Used Life* (London: Gollancz, 1975); Jean Moorcroft Wilson, *Isaac Rosenberg: Poet and Painter, A Biography* (London: Cecil Woolf, 1975).

[3] Jon Silkin, 'The Forgotten Poet of Anglo-Jewry', *Jewish Chronicle*, 26 Aug. 1960, 17.

[4] Since his death in 1918, Rosenberg has only rarely been in print. *Poems by Isaac Rosenberg* (London: Heinemann, 1922) appeared with an introductory memoir by Laurence Binyon, but it soon went out of print, and is today an extremely rare book. Rosenberg's *Collected Works* (Chatto & Windus, 1937) also went quickly out of print. Rosenberg remained out of print until Ian Parsons brought out an edition in 1979, now itself long out of print.

[5] *The Selected Poems of Isaac Rosenberg*, ed. Jean Moorcroft Wilson (London: Cecil Woolf, 2003); *Selected Poems and Letters [of Isaac Rosenberg]*, ed. Jean Liddiard (London: Enitharmon Press, 2003); *The Poems and Plays of Isaac Rosenberg*, ed. Vivien Noakes (Oxford: Oxford University Press, 2004). In November 2005, the first fictional novel about Rosenberg was published. Entitled *Beating for Light: The Story of Isaac Rosenberg* (Milverton: Amolibros/Juniper Books, 2005), Geoff Akers's novel weaves the facts of Rosenberg's biography, letters, and poems, into a fictional account of Rosenberg's life and times from his early days at Whitechapel to his last days at the Front.

[6] Ian Parsons, 'Introduction', in *The Collected Works of Isaac Rosenberg*, ed. Ian Parsons (Oxford: Oxford University Press, 1979), p. xviii.

[7] It is worth noting that Owen's statement, 'The Poetry is in the pity', has been so widely used as to be misused. Jahan Ramazani argues that Owen's statement is itself a problematic summation of Owen's own poetry, and has misled critics to overlook the integral complexities of Owen's poetry: 'Owen states only half of his paradoxical aesthetic when he writes: "My subject is War and the pity of War. The Poetry is in the pity". "Pity" is Owen's term for emotional identification with the victims of war. But Owen's poetry suggests that "pity" cannot erase the boundary that separates victim from onlooker ... His subject is also the incomprehensibility of war; the poetry is also in the alienation. Having roused pity, Owen often forces the reader back, warning that pity cannot bridge the chasm separating spectator and victim' (Ramazani, *Poetry of Mourning: The Modern Elegy from Hardy to Heaney* (Chicago: University of Chicago Press, 1994), 4).

Rosenberg's poetry does not stop short of the pity and tenderness in Owen's, but passes beyond it into something new. He is aware that the suffering of war is too great to be comforted, and he cannot mistake pity for succour; in his poetry, suffering achieves something like classical composure . . . his victims have a heroic moral strength, a stoicism which invites the mind not to the frustrating pity of helplessness, but to something like the re-creative pity of the ancient stage.[8]

Whereas Owen writes out of the Romantic tradition, Rosenberg's work is profoundly influenced by the Metaphysical poet John Donne, whom Rosenberg began reading in 1911, and whose poems he packed into his haversack when he headed for the Front in October 1915.[9] The influence of the Metaphysicals on Rosenberg's early verse and later 'trench poems' plays an important though overlooked role in his outsider status within popular critical accounts which have emphasized the war poets' exclusive inheritance of the Romantic tradition.[10] W. B. Yeats dismissed Rosenberg's poetry as 'all windy rhetoric'[11] much as he dismissed Owen as 'all blood, dirt & sucked sugar stick'.[12] 'All' is the operative word, for had Yeats not already committed himself to a categorical exclusion of war poetry from his *Oxford Book of Modern Verse* (1936), he might have admired the 'heroic moral strength' and 'stoicism' of Rosenberg's speakers, their almost Yeatsian embrace of the 're-creative pity of the ancient stage'.[13]

---

[8] Marius Bewley, *Masks & Mirrors: Essays in Criticism* (New York: Atheneum, 1970), 289–90.

[9] In addition to Donne's poems, Rosenberg packed one other book into his haversack: the seventeenth-century prose masterpiece *Religio Medici*, written by Donne's junior contemporary Sir Thomas Browne. We do not yet know for certain which Donne edition Miss Winifreda Seaton gave to Rosenberg in 1911; the book, like Rosenberg's body, was never recovered. The 1896 Muses' Library edition of Donne (which Edgell Rickword had with him in the trenches in France) was reprinted in both 1901 and 1904, and is a likely guess, since Rosenberg clearly seems to have acquired his copy of Donne prior to the publication of H. J. C. Grierson's 2-vol. 1912 edition. It is possible that Rosenberg, who was reading Walter Pater at the time, was drawn to Browne's *Religio Medici* by Pater's commentary on Browne's work in *Appreciations, with an Essay on Style*, 4th edn. (London: Macmillan, 1901). He might also have been a part of the growing interest in Browne at the Slade School of Art. Fellow classmates Gwen Raverat and Stanley Spencer showed a great deal of interest in Browne at this time. In 1910, Raverat did two woodcuts of Browne, and Spencer's letters reveal that he was so inspired by Browne's *Urn Burial* that in 1912 he buried several of his drawings in a tin in the earth off Mill Lane in Cookham, thinking often of them lying underground when he travelled into London each day to go to the Slade.

[10] Identifying the all too 'familiar ground in tracing links between the war poets and their Romantic ancestors', Christopher Martin insists that there are 'other points to make'. See Martin, 'War Poets', *Essays in Criticism*, 30/3 (July 1980), 270.

[11] W. B. Yeats, quoted in Fred D. Crawford, *British Poets of the Great War* (Cranbury, NJ: Associated University Presses, 1998), 202.

[12] Yeats to Dorothy Wellesley, 21 Dec. 1936, in *The Letters of W. B. Yeats*, ed. Allan Wade (London: Rupert Hart-Davis, 1954), 874.

[13] Rosenberg, who was himself writing 'Moses', a play in dramatic verse, wrote to Mrs Herbert Cohen from the trenches: 'We are on a long march and I'm writing this on the chance of getting it off; so you should know I received your papers and also your letter. . . . I am glad Yeats liked your play: His criticism is an honour. He is the established great man and it is a high thing to receive praise from him' (Rosenberg to Mrs Herbert Cohen, n.d., in *Collected Works*, 237).

Yeats's judgement notwithstanding, Rosenberg has remained an important and continuing influence on twentieth-century English and Irish poets. In 1975, Jean Liddiard remarked that 'Rosenberg has been something of a poet's poet, admired—if I am not mistaken—by Geoffrey Hill, Charles Tomlinson, C. H. Sisson, Jon Silkin, Ted Hughes and many others.'[14] In this essay, I will be discussing three poems entitled 'For Isaac Rosenberg', written by contemporary poets: the English poet Geoffrey Hill (b. 1932), the Northern Irish poet Michael Longley (b. 1939), and the Irish poet Cathal Ó Searcaigh (b. 1956). If Rosenberg's death on April Fool's Day was befitting a poet whose 'whole life was permeated by the ridiculous' and whose 'luck was forever bad',[15] then it is worth noting that these three dedicatory poems have suffered a decidedly Rosenbergian fate: Hill's 'For Isaac Rosenberg' (1952) was never collected, Longley's 'For Isaac Rosenberg' (1983) changed its title to 'No Man's Land' prior to publication, and Ó Searcaigh's 'For Isaac Rosenberg' (1997) is written not in English but in Gaelic. These three poems represent an obscured but enduring heritage of contemporary poets reading and writing about Rosenberg in ways that expose new and invigorating points of entry into this poet's work. Hill engages with Rosenberg as a Metaphysical poet, Longley's Rosenberg represents the larger omission of Anglo-Jewish life stories from family and literary history, and Ó Searcaigh identifies with the marginalization of Rosenberg while also confronting his own non-combatant status. The similarities and dissimilarities between these three dedicatory poems are a vivid testament not only to the complexity of Rosenberg's verse but also to the notion that, as Jacob Isaacs stated in 1937, Rosenberg 'could receive no greater recognition than the influence he now exerted on contemporary poetry, and on writers of to-day'.[16] Setting Rosenberg's critical neglect against his prominence among three contemporary poets, we shall see that the poets are responding to what the criticism has so far missed, and that Rosenberg emerges as a vital figure for contemporary British and Irish poets attempting to write in and about a troubled world in which 'the open wounds of history'[17] left by the two World Wars and the Northern Irish Troubles continue to press upon the poetic imagination.

In 1952, in the small poetry journal *Isis*, Geoffrey Hill, then a student of English literature at Keble College, Oxford, published the following little-known and as yet uncollected poem, 'For Isaac Rosenberg':

> Princes dying with damp curls
> In the accomplishment of fame

---

[14] Jean Liddiard, 'Introduction to Rosenberg and Commentary on Letter', *European Judaism*, 9/2 (1975), 25.

[15] Cohen, *Journey to the Trenches*, 5–6.

[16] Jacob Isaacs, then a lecturer in English Literature at London University, is paraphrased in 'Isaac Rosenberg: Memorial Exhibition of Paintings and Drawings', *Jewish Chronicle*, 25 June 1937, 41.

[17] Fran Brearton, *The Great War in Irish Poetry* (Oxford: Oxford University Press, 2000), 258.

> Keep, within the minds of girls,
> A bright imperishable name—
> And no one breaks upon their game.
>
> Yet men who mourn their hero's fall,
> Laying him in tradition's bed—
> With high-voiced chantings and the tall
> Complacent candles at his head—
> Still leave much carefully unsaid.
>
> When probing Hamlet was aware
> That Death in a worn body lay
> Cramped beneath the lobby-stair—
> (Whose mystery was burnt away
> Through the intensity of decay)—
>
> It followed, with ironic sense,
> That he himself, who ever saw
> Beneath the skin of all pretence,
> Should have been carried from the floor
> With shocked, tip-toeing drums before.
>
> With ceremony thin as this
> We tidy death; make life as neat
> As an unquiet chrysalis
> That is the symbol of defeat:
> A worm in its own winding-sheet . . . [18]

Hill recently recalled that he was first introduced to Rosenberg's verse through a review of *The Collected Poems of Isaac Rosenberg* (1949) in the short-lived literary magazine *Nine*.[19] Entitled 'A Robust Poet', Ralph Houston's review addresses the general neglect of Rosenberg's verse and names T. S. Eliot, in particular, as one of Rosenberg's rare 'influential admirers':

Isaac Rosenberg was killed in France in 1918. Since then he has had a fit audience, though few, and some of his influential admirers have done much to draw the public's attention to him. The original 'mention in despatches' by Mr. Eliot was followed by an excellent article by Denys Harding . . . and a review of the complete works by Dr. Leavis. . . . Despite these efforts, however . . . Rosenberg is seldom mentioned in discussions of poetry today. But if

---

[18] Geoffrey Hill, 'For Isaac Rosenberg', *Isis*, 11 (Oxford: The Fantasy Press, 1952); quoted by permission of Geoffrey Hill. After writing to Hill in 2003, I am pleased to report that Hill has granted permission for the poem to be reprinted on 'The Geoffrey Hill Server', a website devoted to Hill's work. The poem can now be found at <http://www.unicaen.fr/mrsh/anglais/geoffrey-hill/english/poems.php?id=Rosen>

[19] In a letter to the author (27 Feb. 2004), Geoffrey Hill's assistant, Ellen Wrigley, writes: 'Professor Hill asked that I let you know that he discovered Isaac Rosenberg through a review in the magazine *Nine*, of which about twelve issues appeared in the early 1950s in the United Kingdom. The editor/publisher of the magazine is Peter Russell.' The Rosenberg edition that Houston reviewed was edited by Gordon Bottomley and Denys Harding and published in London by Chatto & Windus in 1949.

the public still considers that it can get along very well without good poetry, I am sure that contemporary poets need Rosenberg's assistance, an assistance he gives us by example.[20]

Given the fact that Eliot was not a commander on the battlefield, Houston's use of the military phrase is perhaps not without irony in its lament for Rosenberg's lack of recognition. Not unlike a 'mention in despatches' drowned out by higher-priority military reports in a time of war, Eliot's praise of Rosenberg in 1920 (quoted below) would go virtually unheard amidst other clarion calls for modern poetry:

During the last few years an enormous mass of verse has been printed.... There are three or four poets whose verse is worth reading.... Let the public... ask itself why it has never heard of the poems of T. E. Hulme and Isaac Rosenberg, and why it has heard of the poems of Lady Precocia Pondoeuf and has seen a photograph of the nursery in which she wrote them. Let it trace out the writers who are spoken well of because it is to no one's interest to take the trouble to disparage them.[21]

Henry Hart has suggested that Hill's 'For Isaac Rosenberg' mocks 'sentimental rites of remembrance' and 'grandiose public funerals' by showing how his 'two princes'—namely, Rosenberg and Hamlet—'succumb to the formalities they denounce'.[22] While I agree with Hart, I want to suggest that Eliot is the third ghost in the poem, and that the more elusive implications of Hill's 'For Isaac Rosenberg' are not realized until we consider Eliot's role in the poem. Like Houston's review, Hill's poem makes its own remark about Eliot's interest in Rosenberg and pays powerful homage to the First World War poet about whom 'much' has been left 'carefully unsaid'. Hill's casting of Rosenberg in the role of Hamlet,[23] 'who ever saw | beneath the skin', triggers the well-known opening lines of Eliot's wartime poem on the Metaphysicals, 'Whispers of Immortality' (1918):

> Webster was much possessed by death
> And saw the skull beneath the skin;
> And breastless creatures under ground
> Leaned backward with a lipless grin.
> Daffodil bulbs instead of balls
> Stared from the sockets of the eyes!

---

[20] Ralph Houston, 'A Robust Poet', *Nine*, 3/1 (Dec. 1950), 78.

[21] T. S. Eliot, 'A Brief Treatise on the Criticism of Poetry', *Chapbook*, 2 (Mar. 1920), 1–2.

[22] Henry Hart, *The Poetry of Geoffrey Hill* (Carbondale, Ill.: Southern Illinois University Press, 1986), 21–2.

[23] Hill draws from a history of comparisons between Donne and Hamlet. Joseph Duncan explains: 'The emphasis upon the unfathomable mystery of Donne's personality led almost inevitably to a comparison with Hamlet. As early as 1880 Minto compared Donne, weak-willed, contemplative, and despondent, to Shakespeare's puzzling hero. Sanders declared that as W. E. Henley had written of Robert Louis Stevenson, there was in Donne, "much Antony, of Hamlet most of all." Rupert Brooke later observed that "Hamlet, with his bitter flashes, his humour, his metaphysical inquisitiveness, and his passion, continually has the very accent of the secular Donne, but that he is an avenger, not a lover. To Ophelia he must have been Donne himself." ' (Duncan, *The Revival of Metaphysical Poetry* (Minneapolis: University of Minnesota Press, 1959), 117).

> He knew that thought clings round dead limbs
> Tightening its lusts and luxuries.[24]

When we stop to ask why Hill would allude to Eliot's 'Whispers of Immortality' in a poem for Isaac Rosenberg, we see that it is in part because Hill identifies Rosenberg as a Metaphysical poet, 'who', like Webster and Donne, 'ever saw [the skull] | Beneath the skin'. Over time, Hill would continue to identify the Metaphysical strain in Rosenberg's poetry; in a lecture delivered in 1998, for example, Hill referred to Rosenberg's 'knowledge of and appreciation of Donne' when he complained that Rosenberg's work was still 'among the exotica, not within the canon'.[25]

Yet Hill's allusion to Eliot may have less to do with Donne's influence on Rosenberg, and more to do with Rosenberg's influence on Donne. Rosenberg's poems, particularly those written in the trenches, attest to the ways in which Metaphysical poetry was appropriate to the *mise en scène* at the Western Front. In one of Rosenberg's most widely known and anthologized poems, 'Break of Day in the Trenches' (1916), Donne's 'The Flea' is invoked by the soldier-speaker who reaches up to pull a 'parapet's poppy' and encounters, not a flea, but a 'queer sardonic' trench rat:

> The darkness crumbles away.
> It is the same old druid Time as ever,
> Only a live thing leaps my hand,
> A queer sardonic rat,
> As I pull the parapet's poppy
> To stick behind my ear.
> Droll rat, they would shoot you if they knew
> Your cosmopolitan sympathies.
> Now you have touched this English hand
> You will do the same to a German
> Soon, no doubt, if it be your pleasure
> To cross the sleeping green between.[26]

Having first 'touched this English hand' on its way to do 'the same to' a German soldier's hand, the rat reminds us that the poet (Private Rosenberg, 3rd Platoon, King's Own Royal Lancaster Regiment) was sitting in the trenches and reworking the opening lines from Donne's 'The Flea':

> Marke but this flea, and marke in this,
> How little that which thou deny'st me is;
> It suck'd me first, and now sucks thee;
> And in this flea, our two bloods mingled bee . . .[27]

---

[24] Eliot, 'Whispers of Immortality', in *The Complete Poems and Plays* (London: Faber, 1969), 52.

[25] Hill, 'Isaac Rosenberg, 1890–1918', *Proceedings of the British Academy: 1998 Lectures and Memoirs*, 101 (Oxford: Oxford University Press, 1999), 213.

[26] Rosenberg, 'Break of Day in the Trenches', in *Poems and Plays*, 128.

[27] John Donne, 'The Flea', in *The Complete English Poems*, ed. C. A. Patrides (London: Dent, 1985), 47.

Drawing on Donne's 'The Flea' and 'Break of Day', Rosenberg's poem re-contextualizes Donne's famous arguments for love where or when love is least likely to occur (by way of a flea, or at daybreak, which threatens to separate night-time lovers) and stretches them to new outlandish levels by arguing for love at break of day *in the trenches*, at the very moment when the fighting is to begin. In the midst of the shock, trauma, and violence of the trenches, Rosenberg's poems deliberately call upon the Metaphysical Donne to help render the kind of experience made intelligible only through what Samuel Johnson called the 'far-fetched' and 'outlandish' Metaphysical conceit.[28] For a discussion of Hill's poem, the critical converging point between Rosenberg and Eliot is this: that Rosenberg's 'Break of Day in the Trenches' (1916) reveals the ways in which Donne was reimagined and reinterpreted at the Front, and that Eliot's 'Whispers of Immortality' (1918) suggests the ways in which the deathscape at the Western Front shapes the lens through which Eliot contemplates the Metaphysical *ars moriendi* of Webster and Donne. It was not lost on Eliot that the imagery found in Webster and Donne was appropriate to the imagery of war—and that poets like Rosenberg were engaging with Donne and the Metaphysicals in an attempt to handle images of outlandish horror witnessed at the Front. In unpublished drafts of 'Whispers of Immortality', we see the great trouble Eliot had with the final lines. The change from the first-person voice, 'But I must crawl between dry ribs | To keep my metaphysics warm',[29] to the collective first-person voice, 'But our lot crawls between dry ribs | To keep our metaphysics warm',[30] may hint towards Eliot's non-combatant guilt that, even as he penned the lines, soldiers like Rosenberg were literally crawling between dry ribs to keep their metaphysics warm.

Hill's allusion to 'Whispers of Immortality' in 'For Isaac Rosenberg' uncovers a way to read Rosenberg back into the narrative we tell about the early twentieth-century revival of Metaphysical poetry, and a way to recover Rosenberg as an under-appreciated anticipatory figure of a literary phenomenon that would be propagated as Eliot's post-war Metaphysical revival. If Hill's poem forges a critical revaluation of Rosenberg's work, it is (claims Jeffrey Johnson) because Hill's poetry attempts to give voice to the voiceless, lost, and marginalized figures from the past. According to Johnson, Hill

stands...with a small guard of like-minded scouts, watching the horizon of the setting sun and sifting the remnants left by the careless and bloody parade of history. He not only watches and reconstructs meaning for the sake of history, he also observes with regret and distress what has been left behind and lost.[31]

---

[28] Samuel Johnson, 'The Life of Cowley', in *Johnson's Lives of the Poets: A Selection*, ed. J. P. Hardy (Oxford: Clarendon Press, 1971), 12.

[29] 'Whispers of Immortality', draft [A–B], lines 19–20, quoted in T. S. Eliot, *Inventions of the March Hare: Poems 1909–1917*, ed. Christopher Ricks (London: Faber, 1996), 365.

[30] Eliot, 'Whispers of Immortality', in *The Complete Poems and Plays*, 53.

[31] Jeffrey Johnson, *Acquainted with the Night: The Shadow of Death in Contemporary Poetry* (Cambridge, Mass.: Cowley Publications, 2004), 48 and 50.

In 'For Isaac Rosenberg', Hill digs up the forgotten remnants left by the careless and bloody parade not just of history, but of literary history. In this poem, Hill speaks 'for Isaac Rosenberg' since Rosenberg—like millions of young soldiers who died at the Front—could no longer speak for himself.

Geoffrey Hill has had a career-long interest in Rosenberg, Eliot, and the Metaphysical poets,[32] and although 'For Isaac Rosenberg' was omitted from his first volume, *For the Unfallen* (1959), Rosenberg is a tangible presence in the volume. *For the Unfallen* parodies the title of the well-known First World War elegy etched on countless war memorials, 'For the Fallen' (1914), written by the Georgian poet Laurence Binyon,[33] Rosenberg's friend and literary advisor. In his introductory memoir to the first collected edition of Rosenberg's *Poems* (1922), Binyon wrote that Rosenberg 'endured the inhuman horror of modern war with a great heart' and, admitting that Rosenberg 'would not have liked to be called a hero', still insisted that 'his fortitude was truly heroic.'[34] In 'For the Fallen', Binyon penned the well-known lines:

> Solemn the drums thrill; Death august and royal
> Sings sorrow up into immortal spheres,
> There is music in the midst of desolation
> And a glory that shines upon our tears.
>
> .   .   .   .   .   .
>
> They shall grow not old, as we that are left grow old:
> Age shall not weary them, nor the years condemn.
> At the going down of the sun and in the morning
> We will remember them.[35]

It is precisely with this type of war commemoration poem that Hill takes issue in 'For Isaac Rosenberg'. For Hill, it 'followed, with ironic sense' that Rosenberg would have thus been mourned when he himself, like the young Hamlet, would have objected to a 'ceremony' as 'thin as' that fallen soldier's tribute delivered by Fortinbras over Hamlet's dead body:

---

[32] Hill's review essay on Eliot's *The Varieties of Metaphysical Poetry*, ed. Ronald Schuchard (London: Faber, 1993), is entitled 'Dividing Legacies,' and is found in Hill's *Style and Faith* (New York: Counterpoint, 2003), 141–62. While critics have traced Hill's repeated allusions to the Metaphysicals, I want to suggest that Hill's own poetry and critical prose—as well as his interest in Rosenberg—create alternative stories of twentieth-century engagement with the Metaphysical poets. Although Henry Hart's *The Poetry of Geoffrey Hill* deftly points out many of Hill's allusions to Donne and Crashaw, Hill has (since the publication of Hart's book) further developed, both in his poetry and in his critical prose, his career-long Metaphysical engagement, a subject about which there seems still significant critical work to be done.

[33] Laurence Binyon was a poet and art critic who took an early and active interest in Rosenberg's poetry in 1912, when Rosenberg was a student at the Slade. Binyon corresponded with Rosenberg about his poetry until Rosenberg's death.

[34] Laurence Binyon, 'Introductory Memoir', in *Poems by Isaac Rosenberg*, 11.

[35] Binyon, 'For the Fallen', in George Herbert Clarke (ed.), *A Treasury of War Poetry: British and American Poems of the World War* (Boston: Houghton Mifflin Company, 1917), 126.

> Let four captains
> Bear Hamlet like a soldier to the stage,
> For he was likely, had he been put on,
> To have proved most royal; and for his passage
> The soldiers' music and the rite of war
> Speak loudly for him.
> Take up the bodies. Such a sight as this
> Becomes the field, but here shows much amiss.
> Go, bid the soldiers shoot.[36]

Hill's elegy for Rosenberg shares the anger and bitterness of Sassoon's anti-commemoration poem 'On Passing the New Menin Gate' (1937):

> Who will remember, passing through this Gate,
> The unheroic dead who fed the guns?
> Who shall absolve the foulness of their fate,—
> Those doomed, conscripted, unvictorious ones?
>   Crudely renewed, the Salient holds its own.
>   Paid are its dim defenders by this pomp;
>   Paid, with a pile of peace-complacent stone,
>   The armies who endured that sullen swamp.
>
> Here was the world's worst wound. And here with pride
> 'Their name liveth for ever,' the Gateway claims.
> Was ever an immolation so belied
> As these intolerably nameless names?
> Well might the Dead who struggled in the slime
> Rise and deride this sepulchre of crime.[37]

Like Sassoon's poem, Hill's 'For Isaac Rosenberg' rejects the prideful pomp of complacent and tidy commemoration songs sung by high-voiced chanters.

A brief (and by no means exhaustive) survey of the poetry and critical prose of Hill testifies to his continued devotion to Rosenberg. In 1959, Hill reviewed the Isaac Rosenberg Exhibition at Leeds University;[38] a few years later in his review of Ted Hughes's edition of the *Selected Poems of Keith Douglas* (1964), Hill discussed at length Douglas's affinity with Rosenberg.[39] In *Speech! Speech!* (2000), a single poem in 120 stanzas, Hill writes stanza 27 about Rosenberg[40]—27 being Rosenberg's age when he was killed at the Front. In the Dantean ecologue, *The Orchards of Syon* (2001), Hill writes of

> well-tended ground
> ripe for laying waste, the Great War.

---

[36] William Shakespeare, *Hamlet*, v. ii. 374–82.

[37] Sassoon attended Belgian King Albert's inauguration of the Menin Gate on 24 July 1927. The next day in his hotel room he wrote this poem, which was not published until after his death. Siegfried Sassoon, 'On Passing the New Menin Gate', in *Collected Poems 1908–1956* (London: Faber, 1984), 173.

[38] Hill, 'Isaac Rosenberg Exhibition, at Leeds University', *New Statesman*, 6 (June 1959), 795.

[39] Hill, '"I in Another Place": Homage to Keith Douglas', *Stand*, 6/4 (1964/5), 6–13.

[40] Hill, *Speech! Speech!* (Washington: Counterpoint, 2000), 14.

> Lawrence's Eastwood, Rosenberg
> in Stepney and Whitechapel—I'm
> ordered to speak plainly, let what is
> speak for itself . . . [41]

On 'The Geoffrey Hill Study Centre', an educational website dedicated to 'the English poet, essayist and teacher, Geoffrey Hill', Rosenberg is one of three figures to have his own separate hyperlink page.[42] There is, in short, further critical work to be done on Hill's Rosenberg. And what 'For Isaac Rosenberg' shows is not only Hill's high estimation of Rosenberg's place in literary history, but also Hill's first attempt to pay homage to a poet who remains, in spite of the critical neglect, a vital and continuing presence in twentieth-century poetry.

In 1998, Hill returned to Keble College, Oxford—the very place in which he had penned 'For Isaac Rosenberg' in the early 1950s—to deliver his Warton Lecture on English Poetry, 'Isaac Rosenberg, 1890–1918', which concluded:

Even after seventy years Rosenberg does not have the kind of acceptance that comes with various forms of recognised accessibility; but the intrinsic value of his work was recognised immediately [and] it became known and has been so recognised ever since:

> Living in a wide landscape are the flowers—
> Rosenberg I only repeat what you were saying—

These words, by one of the two outstanding British poets of the Second World War, Keith Douglas, serve as a fitting conclusion. Douglas, of course, does not *only* repeat what Rosenberg was saying: the words of his tribute are those of an indebtedness in which there is no mere repetition, no transiency; nothing redundant.[43]

Keith Douglas's 'repetition' of Rosenberg in the poem 'Desert Flowers' (1943) is a fitting segue to a discussion of the Northern Irish poet Michael Longley. In the poem 'Bog Cotton' (1979), Longley reaches back to Rosenberg by way of Keith Douglas and 'nearly repeat[s]' Douglas repeating Rosenberg:

> Let me make room for bog cotton, a desert flower—
> Keith Douglas, I nearly repeat what you were saying
> When you apostrophised the poppies of Flanders
> And the death of poetry there: that was in Egypt
> Among the sandy soldiers of another war.
> .   .   .   .
> You saw that beyond the thirstier desert flowers
> There fell hundreds of thousands of poppy petals
> Magnified to blood stains by the middle distance

---

[41] Hill, *The Orchards of Syon* (Washington: Counterpoint, 2002), 18.
[42] 'The Geoffrey Hill Study Centre': <http://www3.sympatico.ca/sylvia.paul/ghill_archives.htm>
[43] Hill, 'Isaac Rosenberg, 1890–1918', 228.

Or through the still unfocused sights of a rifle—
And Isaac Rosenberg wore one behind his ear.[44]

Endeavouring to 'make room' for what has been shut out of popular literary and historical narratives, Longley's poetry self-consciously writes from within—and into—the Rosenberg–Douglas tradition of war poetry overlooked by the academy.[45] Like his wife, the critic Edna Longley, he is keen to recover marginalized figures such as Rosenberg in accounts of literary modernism. In his interview with John Brown in 2000, Longley said:

Pound and Eliot are not among my favourite poets.... How many people in the world actually enjoy them? ... Really great English poets like Edward Thomas and Wilfred Owen and Isaac Rosenberg who died in the trenches would have made it more difficult for Pound and Eliot, more complicated.... The war poems of Owen and Rosenberg ring out in my ears like modern versions of Sophocles and Aeschylus. Utterly modern. Huge. Who cares if they're 'Modernist'?[46]

Perhaps more so than any other living poet, Longley is a devotee and literary successor of the war poets. In his introduction to *Cenotaph of Snow: Sixty Poems about War* (2003), a chapbook collecting poems written over four decades, Longley is so embedded in the tradition of British war poetry that he feels the need to put some distance between himself and the label 'war poet':

These are poems about war, not war poems. You have to be a war poet to write war poems. I am a non-combatant drawn to the subject of war for a number of reasons, including: 1) my father fought in the First World War, was decorated for bravery and—an old-fashioned patriot—joined up again in 1939; 2) my native Ulster has been disfigured for thirty years by fratricidal violence; 3) I revere the poets of 1914–1918 (Owen, Rosenberg, Sassoon, Sorley, Blunden, Thomas, Jones) and their successors of 1939–1945 (Douglas, Lewis); 4) in my forties I rediscovered Homer, first the *Odyssey* and then the *Iliad* which is the most powerful

---

[44] Michael Longley, 'Bog Cotton', in *Collected Poems* (London Jonathan Cape, 2006), 137.

[45] Longley's tentative plea to 'make room' is made manifest in the long parenthetical section in the middle (the second and third stanzas) of the four-stanza poem, in which Longley describes bog cotton:

> (It hangs on by a thread, denser than thistledown,
> Reluctant to fly, a weather vane that traces
> The flow of cloud shadow over monotonous bog—
> And useless too, though it might well bring to mind
> The plumpness of pillows, the staunching of wounds,
>
> Rags torn from a petticoat and soaked in water
> And tied to the bushes around some holy well
> As though to make a hospital of the landscape—
> Cures and medicines as far as the horizon
> Which nobody harvests except with the eye.)

[46] Longley, interviewed by John Brown, in John Brown, *In the Chair: Interviews with Poets from the North of Ireland* (Cliffs of Moher: Salmon Publishing, 2002), 90.

of all war poems as well as being the greatest poem about death. . . . These, then, are the preoccupations behind *Cenotaph of Snow*.[47]

For Longley's audience, this recent declaration of reverence for 'the poets of 1914–1918' is more a synthesis in retrospect than a new-found conclusion. In *The Great War and Modern Memory* (1975), Paul Fussell identified Longley as 'Another to whom the Great War established an archetype for subsequent violence—as well as a criticism of it'.[48] In 1980, Paul Durcan claimed: 'The First World War (which was the beginning of the Irish tragedy as indeed it was the beginning of every other convulsion in the western world in the 20th century) has been the primal landscape of Longley's poetry from the start.'[49] Most recently in *The Great War in Irish Poetry* (2000), Fran Brearton has explained that 'the title "war poet" is attributed to [Longley] perhaps even more frequently than to Heaney, even if Heaney, as the more popular figure, has been exposed to greater "war poet" pressures from the public'.[50]

   Longley's unfaltering devotion to, and deep-seated identification with, the British war poets raises several questions about what is at stake in this self-proclaimed literary lineage. The hybridity of Longley's Anglo-Irish identity politics poses certain challenges. In the Irish poetic tradition, Longley is marginalized for his Englishness, for what is often interpreted as his Protestant literary Unionism, his poetry's cultural, political, aesthetic, and literary ties to mainland Britain. Longley himself recalled that as a child he 'walked out of an English household on to Irish streets' and felt that he was 'schizophrenic on the levels of nationality, class and culture'.[51] Yet in the English poetic tradition, Longley—like Louis MacNeice before him—is marginalized for his Irishness. Like Rosenberg, Longley does not fit into ready-made categories. Brearton points out that Longley is

obviously involved in an Irish tradition but he also builds on an English tradition. In fact he is in the tradition of dealing with tensions between traditions. He is constantly talking about Englishness and Irishness, urban and pastoral. . . . It was much easier to recognise Heaney as a rural Irish Catholic. . . . And even someone like [Derek] Mahon was more easily identifiable with his urban Belfast angst. Longley didn't fit either of those patterns and so it made it more difficult for him to find a niche.[52]

Given Longley's admiration for Rosenberg, we might question to what extent Longley's quest for a place within the complicated fracture points of a hybridized

---

[47] Longley, title-page, *Cenotaph of Snow: Sixty Poems about War* (London: Enitharmon Press, 2003), 2.
   [48] Paul Fussell, *The Great War and Modern Memory* (Oxford: Oxford University Press, 1975), 324.
   [49] Paul Durcan, 'Poetry and Truth', *Irish Press*, 20 Mar. 1980, 6.
   [50] Brearton, *The Great War in Irish Poetry*, 261.
   [51] Longley, 'Strife and the Ulster Poet', *Hibernia*, 7 Nov. 1969, 11.
   [52] Brearton, quoted in Nicholas Wroe, 'Middle Man', *The Guardian*, 21 Aug. 2004; <http://books.guardian.co.uk/poetry/features/0,12887,1287473,00.html>

British literary tradition draws him to a figure such as Rosenberg, whose own hybrid Anglo-Jewish identity politics put similar pressures on British literary canon formation.

If we now turn to Longley's poem for Rosenberg—entitled 'For Isaac Rosenberg' in the unpublished manuscripts,[53] though eventually published under the title 'No Man's Land'—we encounter a poem about marginalization and identity politics in family and literary history. In 'Bog Cotton', Longley's reaching back through Keith Douglas to Rosenberg illustrates the way in which the poets of the two World Wars 'provided' Longley, as he said in one interview, 'with a map and compass when I began to contemplate our own sordid little conflict'.[54] But in Longley's 'For Isaac Rosenberg' (hereafter referred to by its final title, 'No Man's Land'), 'Longley's family and literary ghosts . . . converge,'[55] and Rosenberg is reimagined as both a literary and a familial father—a theme which resonates with Longley's statement in one interview that the 'two World Wars were part of my family history before they became part of my imaginative landscape. Sometimes I listen to Owen and Rosenberg as though they were my dad's drinking and smoking companions, sharing a Woodbine behind the lines during a lull.'[56] In 'No Man's Land', Longley not only envisions Rosenberg as one of his father's comrades but also connects Rosenberg's Anglo-Jewish ancestry to his own. In 'Granny', an early version of the first half of 'No Man's Land' (1976),[57] Longley pays tribute to the forgotten life (and death) of Longley's 'Jewish granny', the late Jessica Abrahams, who, Jim Haughey writes, 'disappeared from family history after her premature death at twenty'.[58] Longley's desire to recover the memory of his Anglo-Jewish grandmother (marginalized in family history) prompts the poet's turn to Anglo-Jewish Rosenberg (marginalized

---

[53] The unpublished manuscripts and typescripts to Longley's poem are printed here with permission from the author, and are held in the Michael Longley archive (Co. No. 744, Box 21, folder 35), Manuscripts, Archives, and Rare Books Library (MARBL), Robert W. Woodruff Library, Emory University.

[54] Longley, interviewed by John Brown, in Brown, *In the Chair*, 94.

[55] Brearton, *Great War in Irish Poetry*, 271.

[56] Longley, interviewed by John Brown, *In the Chair*, 94.

[57] Longley, 'Granny', in *Man Lying on a Wall* (London: Victor Gollancz, 1976), 36. It is worth pointing out that Longley's book of poems was published by Victor Gollancz, the Anglo-Jewish, London-born publisher and nephew of Rabbi Professor Sir Herman Gollancz. Gollancz not only served in the British Army in the First World War, but also married Ruth Löwy, Rosenberg's fellow classmate at the Slade School of Art in London before the War. Ruth Löwy's mother, Mrs E. D. Löwy, was one of Rosenberg's patrons, and it has been suggested that Rosenberg was in love with Ruth Löwy at the time of her marriage to Victor Gollancz. Rosenberg did a red chalk study of 'Ruth Löwy's head, reclining on a pillow, curls cascading down on either side, eyes closed in a delicately subdued rapture'. See Cohen, *Journey to the Trenches*, 63 and 76. For a reproduction of Rosenberg's chalk study, see 'Ruth Löwy as the Sleeping Beauty. Sanguine' (1912), in *Collected Works*, 97, fig. 6(b). Gollancz also published Jean Liddiard's *Isaac Rosenberg: The Half Used Life*.

[58] Jim Haughey, *The First World War in Irish Poetry* (Lewisburg, Pa.: Bucknell University Press, 2002), 246.

in literary history). The subsequent, more expanded version of 'No Man's Land', dedicated '*in memory of Isaac Rosenberg*', juxtaposes Jessica's oblivion (part I) with that of Rosenberg (part II):

I

Who will give skin and bones to my Jewish granny?
She has come down to me in the copperplate writing
Of three certificates, a dog-eared daguerreotype
And the one story my grandfather told about her.

He tossed a brick through a rowdy neighbour's window
As she lay dying, and Jessica, her twenty years
And mislaid whereabouts gave way to a second wife,
A terrible century, a circle of christian names.

II

I tilt her head towards you, Isaac Rosenberg,
But can you pick out that echo of splintering glass
From under the bombardment, and in No Man's Land
What is there to talk about but difficult poems?

Because your body was not recovered either
I try to read the constellations of brass buttons,
Identity discs that catch the light a little.
A shell-shocked carrier pigeon flaps behind the lines.[59]

Commemorating those who have been abandoned in a 'terrible' anti-semitic 'century', Longley stands alongside Hill in 'watching the horizon of the setting sun and sifting the remnants left by the careless and bloody parade of history'.

Longley's role as the scrappy collector of discarded war relics is made clear in the poem's manuscripts. In cancelled stanzas of the poem (then entitled, 'A Broken Wing: For Isaac Rosenberg'), Longley imagines the 'shellshocked carrier pigeon' with a broken wing, unable to fly home from the Front with lists of dead and missing soldiers:

a carrier pigeon on its way back
From the front line, shellshocked, zigzagging.

Has artillery put out its eyes? Its legs
Wear lists of casualties, bad news in splints.
I spread my fingers on that broken wing
And count the dead, and count the missing.[60]

Obliged to 'count the dead, and count the missing', Longley not only takes on the burden of the role of poet-commemorator of unacknowledged victims, but also assumes the role assigned to his 'sad retarded uncle', Lionel, whose job at the Front

---

[59] Longley, 'No Man's Land', in *Collected Poems*, 157; quoted by permission of Michael Longley.
[60] Longley, 'A Broken Wing: For Isaac Rosenberg', Michael Longley archive.

was to go 'over the top slowly behind the stretcher parties | And, as a park attendant where all hell had broken loose, | [Collect] littered limbs until his sack was heavy'.[61] In other cancelled lines of 'No Man's Land', we see Longley's struggle with this obligation to be the gatherer and recorder of the odds and ends left out in No Man's Land. In the following, the poet stumbles across Rosenberg's 'identity disc':

> Must I be the looter, souvenir hunter,
> Pickpocket of death out in No Man's Land
> Who spots among Lugers and brass buttons
> His identity disc face down in the mud?[62]

Troubled by the omission of certain life stories from public and personal history, and compelled to write such stories out, 'No Man's Land' also implicates Longley's grandfather, who tells only 'one story' about his first wife Jessica—and that story is ultimately much less about her than about him, in his rage, tossing the brick through the neighbour's window as his wife 'lay dying'. Longley's poem expresses the tragedy of Jessica's short life being reduced to a single story, her words modified in the guts of the living husband.

More troubling still is the poem's connection between the missing narrative and the missing body. In this, Longley's intention is clear: 'Because your body was not recovered either | I try to read the constellations of brass buttons'. In tilting Jessica's head towards Rosenberg, Longley not only affirms the corporeality of people whose bodies have gone missing, but also envisions a more intimate connection between the poet and his grandmother (in unpublished drafts of the poem the line reads: 'I would introduce her to Isaac Rosenberg'). By playing the matchmaker, Longley imagines himself a familial as well as literary heir of Rosenberg. The silence surrounding these figures from the past—Jessica Abrahams, Isaac Rosenberg, even Longley's father, who for a long time kept his experiences in the First World War to himself[63]—compels Longley to 'try' to piece their stories (and their bodies) back together. Not unlike the child-narrator in Seamus Deane's *Reading in the Dark*,

---

[61] Longley, 'Master of Ceremonies', in *Cenotaph of Snow*, 14.

[62] Longley, Michael Longley archive.

[63] Longley recalls: 'Having lived through so much by the time he was thirty, perhaps my father deserved his early partial retirement. At the age of seventeen he had enlisted in 1914, one of thousands queuing up outside Buckingham Palace. He joined the London-Scottish by mistake and went into battle wearing an unwarranted kilt. A Lady from Hell. Like so many survivors he seldom talked about his experiences, reluctant to relive the nightmare. But not long before he died, we sat up late one night and he reminisced. He had won the Military Cross for knocking out single-handed a German machine-gun post and, later, the Royal Humane Society's medal for gallantry: he had saved two nurses from drowning. By the time he was twenty he had risen to the rank of Captain, in charge of a company known as "Longley's Babies" because many of them were not yet regular shavers. He recalled the lice, the rats, the mud, the tedium, the terror. Yes, he had bayoneted men and still dreamed about a tubby little German who "couldn't run fast enough. He turned around to face me and burst into tears." My father was nicknamed Squib in the trenches. For the rest of his life no-one ever called him Richard, (Longley, *Tu'penny Stung: Autobiographical Chapters* (Belfast: Lagan Press, 1994), 18).

Longley puts an extraordinary amount of pressure on himself to commemorate and remember when the act of remembering is, literally, a re-membering of body parts, a *giving* of 'skin and bones' to those whose bodies were not granted proper burial, whose bodies and legacies are misplaced.[64]

Longley's 'No Man's Land' also pays homage to Rosenberg as an author of 'difficult poems' ('and in No Man's Land | What is there to talk about but difficult poems?'). In one letter to R. C. Trevelyan, who was just one of many to confess that they found Rosenberg's poetry 'difficult', Rosenberg justified the complexity of his poetry by pointing to the environment in which it was written: 'I know my faults are legion; a good many must be put down to the rotten conditions I wrote it in—the whole thing was written in the barracks, and I suppose you know what an ordinary soldier's life is like.'[65] The manner and mode in which Longley's poem is written testify to Rosenberg's complex modernist experiments in poetry. Creating meaning out of otherwise arbitrary connections between the two long-forgotten Anglo-Jewish figures from the East End of London, Longley's poetic imagination draws parallels between Jessica and Rosenberg that are not unlike those which Virginia Woolf draws between Clarissa Dalloway and Septimus Warren Smith. After drawing our attention to Jessica's 'dog-eared daguerreotype', Longley describes the familiar daguerreotype of Rosenberg dressed in khaki uniform with gleaming 'brass buttons' that 'catch the light a little'.[66] Because the bodies of Jessica and Rosenberg were never recovered, their daguerreotypes become larger-than-life relics as the last remaining testaments to the presence of the once-living flesh.

Yet 'No Man's Land' is no Victorian relic poem; Longley's Rosenberg is an 'utterly modern' poet who wrote 'difficult' modern poetry in the trenches. Like the sight of Molly Bloom's arm throwing a coin out of the window to the one-legged sailor in Joyce's *Ulysses*, a single event—here, the sound of broken glass—becomes Longley's way to connect the otherwise disparate strands of simultaneous human experience. Citing the 'one story' told of Jessica—that of his grandfather tossing 'a brick through a rowdy neighbour's window'—Longley turns to ask Rosenberg if he is able to 'pick out that echo of splintering glass | From under the bombardment' in No Man's Land. Longley's apostrophe to Rosenberg—'I tilt her head towards you, Isaac Rosenberg'—demonstrates that 'No Man's Land' is a poem not only written 'in memory of Isaac Rosenberg' but also written *directly to* Isaac Rosenberg. Longley's anxiety over the direct address to Rosenberg (perhaps tinged with a bit of non-combatant guilt?) is revealed in the unpublished manuscripts, in which 'your body' (Rosenberg's) reads 'his body', and the line, 'I tilt her head towards you, Isaac

---

[64] See Longley's poem, 'Pipistrelle', which begins: 'They kept him alive for years in warm water, | The soldier who had lost his skin' (*Cenotaph of Snow*, 47).

[65] Rosenberg to R. C. Trevelyan, n.d. [postmarked 15 June 1916], in *Collected Works*, 235.

[66] See the dog-eared daguerreotype included in Rosenberg's letter to Sydney Schiff (dated Oct. 1915) and another printed along with Rosenberg's letter to Edward Marsh (dated late Dec. 1915), in *Collected Works*, 220 and 228.

Rosenberg', reads: 'I would show her tilted head to Isaac Rosenberg'.[67] As readers of this poem, we are asked to consider the connectedness of that tragic fate shared by Jessica and Rosenberg—a fate which led not only to early death (both died in their twenties) but also to obscurity, be it in family or in literary history.

Longley's attentiveness to Rosenberg's 'difficult poems' brings us to one final connection between them. It has been said that 'Rosenberg, the more "difficult" and unEnglish of the . . . [war] poets . . . had the greater impact on the young [Keith] Douglas'.[68] The same might be said of Longley. For if not 'greater' than that of Owen and Edward Thomas, Rosenberg's impact on Longley is certainly different from that made on him by Owen's poetry of pity and Thomas's wartime pastoral poetics. It is Rosenberg's refractory and impersonal stance on war's suffering that Longley loves and looks for in Rosenberg. Christopher Gillie writes:

Rosenberg did not hate the war less than Owen did, but he accepted it impersonally as—inhuman as it was—a world of experience which could be assimilated into his poetic consciousness and enlarge it. Unlike Owen, he did not see a vocation in war poetry as such, but the war was the fact, and as a fact it had to be lived through.[69]

Objecting in one letter to 'Rupert Brooke's begloried sonnets', Rosenberg claimed that the war 'should be approached in a colder way, more abstract, with less of the million feelings everybody feels; or all these should be concentrated in one distinguished emotion'.[70] Longley writes with Rosenberg's self-containment, his withholding of sentimentalism, his extinction of poetic personality, and his conscious abstraction of personal experience in order for it to speak universally:

> He was preparing an Ulster fry for breakfast
> When someone walked into the kitchen and shot him:
> A bullet entered his mouth and pierced his skull,
> The books he had read, the music he could play.
>
> .   .   .   .
>
> They rolled him up like a red carpet and left
> Only a bullet hole in the cutlery drawer:
> Later his widow took a hammer and chisel
> And removed the black keys from his piano.[71]

The Irish poet Cathal Ó Searcaigh sees the role of the poet as 'archivist . . . recording and registering what is past or passing'.[72] Ó Searcaigh feels the obligation to sift through and reconstruct meaning out of the 'remnants left by the careless and

---

[67] Longley, Michael Longley archive.
[68] William Scammell, *Keith Douglas: A Study* (London: Faber, 1988), 27.
[69] Christopher Gillie, *Movements in English Literature: 1900–1940* (Cambridge: Cambridge University Press, 1975), 73–4.
[70] Rosenberg to Mrs Cohen, n.d., in *Collected Works*, 237.
[71] Longley, 'The Civil Servant', in 'Wreaths', in *Collected Poems*, 118.
[72] Cathal Ó Searcaigh, interviewed by John Brown, in Brown, *In the Chair*, 257–8.

bloody parade of history' and to observe 'with regret and distress what has been left behind and lost'. Writing often of his birthplace in the rural Gaeltacht at the foot of Mount Errigal in County Donegal, an area of the world celebrated more in the (disappearing) oral tradition of the Gaeltacht than in the written tradition, Ó Searcaigh elaborates upon his role as poet-archivist:

I have become the collector of its oral traditions, the archivist of its memories and myths, the narrator of its stony maps. In this role, I am like the Gaelic poets of the past, recording and registering what is past or passing. Poetry for me is a means of making memorable what is being forgotten . . . . The challenge for all of us who belong to minority cultures is to find ways of creating a collaboration between our past and our present.[73]

Perhaps drawn to more obscure and overlooked poets of the past for some of the same reasons that he is drawn to forgotten customs and ways of life in the Gaeltacht and abroad, Ó Searcaigh identifies with Rosenberg not only as a poet who resists the ready-made categories available to him, but also as a marginalized poet belonging to a 'minority culture'. Light-heartedly referring to himself in a recent interview as 'the unknown Irish poet', Ó Searcaigh speaks of a certain devotion to Rosenberg *because* he is under-appreciated, unknown, misunderstood, and marginalized:

Speaking Gaelic . . . being gay . . . makes me a marginalized figure as a poet. . . . The act of repossession is vitally important to me. Thomas Kinsella's *Poems of the Dispossessed* [*An Duanaire: 1600–1900, Poems of the Dispossessed* (1981)] was an important book of poetry . . . from the dark ages of the Irish psyche. I believe that my own book of Irish poetry should be called *Poems of Repossession*, and would begin in the 1940s onward. We [Gaelic poets] have repossessed our tradition in the Irish language, in the way that Isaac Rosenberg repossessed his own heritage in his poetry.[74]

Ó Searcaigh has spoken elsewhere of his *dúchas*—an Irish word which he loosely translates as 'the cultural endowment that we receive from our people's past'[75]—and given the long-standing tradition of Irish writing engaged with Jewish literature and history, it is interesting to think of the Anglo-Jewish Rosenberg as part of Ó Searcaigh's *dúchas*. Recent examples of this tradition include *The Gossamer Wall: Poems in Witness to the Holocaust* (2002) by the Gaelic poet Michael Ó Siadhail,[76] and Paul Muldoon's recent poem 'The Grand Conversation', in which an Irish 'He' and a Jewish 'She' play a 'game of ancestral persecution one-upmanship'.[77]

Ó Searcaigh's poem, 'Do Isaac Rosenberg'/'For Isaac Rosenberg' (trans. Frank Sewell) was first published in *Human Rights Have No Borders* (1998), a poetry

---

[73] Ó Searcaigh, 'Cultures of Ulster/Rhythms of Ulster', n.d.; <http://www.culturesofulster.com/CathalOSearcaighaddress.htm>

[74] Ó Searcaigh, telephone interview with Tara Christie, 29 June 2005.

[75] Ó Searcaigh, 'Cultures of Ulster/Rhythms of Ulster'.

[76] Michael Ó Siadhail, *The Gossamer Wall: Poems in Witness to the Holocaust* (Newcastle-upon-Tyne: Bloodaxe, 2002).

[77] Jenny Ludwig, 'As If Washing Might Make it Clean', *Boston Review* (Summer 2003); <http://www.bostonreview.net/BR28.3/ludwig.html>

anthology edited by Kenneth Morgan and Almut Schlepper. A second translation appeared in 2004 by Denise Blake,[78] but I here quote in full only Sewell's translation because it is, on the whole, the more attentive to Rosenberg's poetry and is, as such, the more fruitful version for this discussion. For example, Sewell writes:

> Then I thought of you, Isaac Rosenberg
> war-weary in the 'torn fields of France'

—lines which immediately invoke—and in fact quote from—Rosenberg's 'Break of Day in the Trenches' (1916):

> Strong eyes, fine limbs, haughty athletes,
> Less chanced than you for life,
> Bonds to the whims of murder,
> Sprawled in the bowels of the earth,
> The torn fields of France.[79]

Blake's translation reads:

> With that, I think of you, Isaac Rosenberg
> war-worn on the overthrown fields of France.

There is of course the inherent danger of what is lost—or, in this case gained—in translation. Yet, as the author of this 'poem of repossession', Ó Searcaigh would seem to be concerned more with giving voice to 'people trapped helplessly by social or historical forces'[80] than with the problems of his translation into English. In this poem, giving voice to the voiceless Rosenberg—in whatever language will be by others heard most clearly—seems just as (if not more) important to Ó Searcaigh as finding *le mot juste*. Sewell's translation in its entirety reads:

> At dawn, we gave up our courting
> out in the wilderness. Larks soared
> from the bog-holes and hollows of Prochlais.
>
> Then I thought of you, Isaac Rosenberg,
> war-weary in the 'torn fields of France',
> stunned by the siren larks, one dawn
>
> as you returned to your camp over the ruined
> bones of friends, shaken, with bombs
> pouncing on the red and black battlefield.
>
> The larks' joy between air and water
> brought your poems across eternity's barricade, line
> by line, stutteringly, scared, like soldiers in battle,

---

[78] Denise Blake, 'For Isaac Rosenberg', in *Take a Deep Breath* (Cladnageeragh: Summer Palace Press, 2004), 63–4.

[79] Rosenberg, 'Break of Day in the Trenches', 128.

[80] Ó Searcaigh, interviewed by John Brown, *In the Chair*, 257–8.

and they stopped me in my tracks with horror:
the dark pits of trenches, youth's smashed-up
hopes, the carnage wracked my conscience,

I who was never within an ounce of my life,
who never had to pile over the top and into battle,
who never lost out in any of the bloodshed,

I who never saw young soldiers torched
and dumped in an open field of slaughter,
their blighted bodies stinking with death,

I who was never plunged in the mud and mire,
never shell-shocked or stung by a bullet
sucking out my life like some crazy bee honey . . .

O, don't mind me, Isaac Rosenberg, calling you
from here, my safe-house of love poems,
while Europe still eats its heart out;

only mine was light with joy, my lover
beside me in all his glory, every limb,
joint, rim, every bit of him tempting me

to believe that we're safe together,
that life is for feasting
and love wards off trouble.

The larks tell me what they told you,
before you were blown to pieces—
that love and music beat war and empire;

and though I've never been in action,
though I've had a safe, ordinary life,
looking after my own and keeping out of it,

I want to assure you, poet whose truth
was bared to the bones in World War 1,
I too am on the side of light, and of life.[81]

We might first ask what prompts Ó Searcaigh's turn to Rosenberg in this poem. As with Longley, Ó Searcaigh's primal tap-root into the First World War is through his own family history. As a child, Ó Searcaigh was 'mesmerized' by the sepia-coloured military photograph of his father's uncle, John Gallagher, a 'young, very handsome man in army dress. . . . I always kept looking at it . . . because of that photo alone, I think I became more fascinated with the First World War than the Second.'[82] But Ó Searcaigh's turn to Rosenberg is precipitated not by meditating on the war, but rather by hearing the singing of larks early one morning after a night of 'courting | out

---

[81] 'Do Isaac Rosenberg'/'For Isaac Rosenberg', trans. Frank Sewell, *Human Rights Have No Borders*, ed. Kenneth Morgan and Almut Schlepper (Dublin: Marino Books, 1998), 139–42; quoted by permission of Cathal Ó Searcaigh.
[82] Ó Searcaigh, telephone interview with Tara Christie, 29 June 2005.

in the wilderness'. Crediting the larks with bringing Rosenberg's 'poems across eternity's barricade' to him, Ó Searcaigh invokes Rosenberg's 'Returning, we hear the larks' (1917), in which a war-weary soldier is (as Ó Searcaigh writes) suddenly 'stunned by siren larks':

> Sombre the night is.
> And though we have our lives, we know
> What sinister threat lurks there.
> Dragging these anguished limbs, we only know
> This poison-blasted track opens on our camp—
> On a little safe sleep.
>
> But hark! joy—joy—strange joy.
> Lo! heights of night ringing with unseen larks.
> Music showering on our upturned list'ning faces.
>
> Death could drop from the dark
> As easily as song—
> But song only dropped....[83]

Feeling grateful for the larks' song showering down upon him because he knows all too well 'What sinister threat lurks there', Rosenberg's soldier-speaker finds joy and comfort even in the most threatening and dangerous of places.

Awed by Rosenberg's ability to interpret the lark's song as a sign that one should celebrate life even in the midst of so much death, Ó Searcaigh confronts his own non-combatant guilt as the 'I who never'. The insistent repetition of that phrase represents Ó Searcaigh's increasing anxiety about aligning himself with Rosenberg. It is as if, by a sheer act of will, inspired by and no less heroic than Rosenberg's own, Ó Searcaigh overcomes the guilt and can, at the end of the poem, stand with Rosenberg and say to him: 'I want to assure you, poet whose truth | was bared to the bones in World War 1, | I too am on the side of light, and of life.'

---

[83] Rosenberg, 'Returning, we hear the larks', in *Poems and Plays*, 138–9.

CHAPTER 29

THE FURY
AND THE MIRE

JON STALLWORTHY

'My subject is War, and the pity of War. The Poetry is in the pity.'[1] That was Wilfred Owen in 1918. *My* subject, many wars later, is 'War and the fury of War. The Poetry is in the fury.'

Poetry is notoriously difficult to define. 'Of the many definitions', said W. H. Auden, 'the simplest is still the best: "memorable speech".'[2] To be worth writing, and reading, it must be memorable—as so much so-called poetry is not. And what do we mean by 'War Poetry'? Logically, this category—to my mind, this unsatisfactory category—should embrace any poem about any aspect of war: it should include Eliot's *The Waste Land* and 'Little Gidding'; it should include Yeats's 'The Second Coming'. Each has a World War at its centre, and in the field—the battlefield—of poetry it is hard to think of speech more memorable. But when we speak of 'war poetry' we normally mean battlefield poems, and my subject in this essay is the controlled fury of battlefield poems. These, too, can be difficult to define, but we know them when we see—and hear—them: Owen's 'Dulce et Decorum Est', for example. What does that poem do? First of all, it persuades us that it is true; secondly, that its truth is shocking; and thirdly, that we should do something about it. Owen offers us what a medieval rhetorician would call an *exemplum*, an

---

[1] Wilfred Owen, 'Preface', in *The Complete Poems and Fragments*, ii: *The Manuscripts and Fragments*, ed. Jon Stallworthy (London: Chatto & Windus, Hogarth Press, and Oxford University Press, 1983), 535.

[2] W. H. Auden, 'Introduction to "The Poet's Tongue"', in *The English Auden: Poems, Essays, and Dramatic Writings 1927–1929*, ed. Edward Mendelson (London: Faber, 1977), 327.

example, an illustration of a man choking to death on poison gas; that followed by a *moralitas*, a moral coda of passionate indignation.

> If in some smothering dreams you too could pace
> Behind the wagon that we flung him in,
> And watch the white eyes writhing in his face,
> His hanging face, like a devil's sick of sin;
> If you could hear, at every jolt, the blood
> Come gargling from the froth-corrupted lungs,
> Obscene as cancer, bitter as the cud
> Of vile, incurable sores on innocent tongues,—
> My friend, you would not tell with such high zest
> To children ardent for some desperate glory,
> The old Lie: Dulce et decorum est
> Pro patria mori.[3]

The victim's fate is pitiful, but to my ear the poetry is in the controlled fury of the final twelve-line sentence, rather than in the pity.

Almost twenty years later, a young Cambridge Communist, John Cornford, set off for the Spanish Civil War, carrying the pistol his father had carried through the Great War and, in his head, Owen's 'Dulce et Decorum Est'. We know that because his 'Letter from Aragon' takes its structure from Owen's poem. First, the *exemplum* (or, to be exact, three *exempla*):

> This is a quiet sector of a quiet front.
>
> We buried Ruiz in a new pine coffin,
> But the shroud was too small and his washed feet stuck out.
> The stink of his corpse came through the clean pine boards
> And some of the bearers wrapped handkerchiefs round their faces.
> Death was not dignified.
> We hacked a ragged grave in the unfriendly earth
> And fired a ragged volley over the grave.
>
> You could tell from our listlessness, no one much missed him.
>
> This is a quiet sector of a quiet front.
> There is no poison gas and no H.E.
>
> But when they shelled the other end of the village
> And the streets were choked with dust
> Women came screaming out of the crumbling houses,
> Clutched under one arm the naked rump of an infant.
> I thought: how ugly fear is.
>
> This is a quiet sector of a quiet front.
> Our nerves are steady; we all sleep soundly.

---

[3] Owen, 'Dulce et Decorum Est', in *The Complete Poems and Fragments*, i: *The Poems*, ed. Jon Stallworthy (London: Chatto & Windus, Hogarth Press, and Oxford University Press, 1983), 140.

> In the clean hospital bed, my eyes were so heavy
> Sleep easily blotted out one ugly picture,
> A wounded militiaman moaning on a stretcher,
> Now out of danger, but still crying for water,
> Strong against death, but unprepared for such pain.
> This on a quiet front.[4]

Cornford's 'Letter from Aragon', like Owen's memory of the Somme, persuades us that it is true, shocking, and a call for action. The soldier's fury builds in his refrain, the repeated echo of the Great War's most famous book title, *All Quiet on the Western Front*, and the reference to poison gas offers another link to Owen's poem. Cornford's coda, his *moralitas*, is again a direct address to his reader:

> But when I shook hands to leave, an Anarchist worker
> Said: 'Tell the workers of England
> This was a war not of our own making
> We did not seek it.
> But if ever the Fascists again rule Barcelona
> It will be as a heap of ruins with us workers beneath it.'

Cornford did not leave Spain. He was killed on his twenty-first birthday, or the day after, in the battle for Madrid.

As many people had foreseen, the Spanish Civil War proved to be the curtain-raiser for a second World War. It is a truth universally acknowledged, as Jane Austen would say, that, unlike the First World War, the Second produced no poetry of importance. This truth is no more truthful than the one mocked by Austen or that attacked by Owen as 'the old Lie'. There are wonderful, terrible poems of the later war, too little known on this side of the Atlantic because half are American; too little known in America because half are British.

To illustrate this point, my third *exemplum* is an American poem as strong—as pity-full, as furious—as any by Owen or Sassoon: Louis Simpson's 'The Heroes'. Simpson served with a glider-infantry regiment of the 101st Airborne Division in France, Holland, Belgium, and Germany. In combat he was a runner. He carried messages. In Holland he was wounded by a shell, and at Bastogne his feet were frost-bitten; but he survived. After the War, however, he had a nervous breakdown and was taken into hospital suffering from amnesia. The War was blacked out in his mind, as were episodes in his life *before* the War. When he was discharged from hospital, he found that he could hardly read or write. In a contributor's note to an anthology, Simpson says:

Before the war I had written a few poems and some prose. Now I found that poetry was the only kind of writing in which I could express my thoughts. Through poems, I could release

---

4 John Cornford, 'Letter from Aragon', in *Understand the Weapon, Understand the Wound: Selected Writings of John Cornford*, ed. Jonathan Galassi (Manchester: Carcanet, 1976), 41. H.E. is High Explosive.

the irrational, grotesque images I had accumulated during the war; and imposing order on those images enabled me to recover my identity. In 1948, when I was living in Paris, one night I dreamed that I was lying on the bank of a canal, under machine-gun and mortar fire. The next morning I wrote it out in the poem 'Carentan O Carentan', and as I wrote I realized that it wasn't a dream, but the memory of my first time under fire.[5]

Simpson's experience bears a striking resemblance to Wilfred Owen's: both suffered from neurasthenia, or shell-shock. Owen lost his memory, but only after he was forced to relive the horrors of battle in those dreams that are a principal symptom of shell-shock was he able to write about the Western Front.

Simpson's first dream poem, 'Carentan O Carentan', appeared in his first book, *The Arrivists* (1949), and has a dreamlike distance from experience. The poems of his second book, *Good News of Death* (1955), show reality emerging from the dream:

The Heroes

I dreamed of war-heroes, of wounded war-heroes
With just enough of their charms shot away
To make them more handsome. The women moved nearer
To touch their brave wounds and their hair streaked with gray.

I saw them in long ranks ascending the gang-planks;
The girls with the doughnuts were cheerful and gay.
They minded their manners and muttered their thanks;
The Chaplain advised them to watch and to pray.

They shipped these rapscallions, these sea-sick battalions
To a patriotic and picturesque spot;
They gave them new bibles and marksmen's medallions,
Compasses, maps and committed the lot.

A fine dust has settled on all that scrap metal.
The heroes were packaged and sent home in parts
To pluck at a poppy and sew on a petal
And count the long night by the stroke of their hearts.[6]

The title signals a line of descent from a poem of the previous war, Sassoon's 'The Hero', which begins:

'Jack fell as he'd have wished,' the Mother said,
And folded up the letter that she'd read.
'The Colonel writes so nicely.'[7]

Simpson follows Sassoon in contrasting civilian illusion with military reality, as revealed in their two linguistic registers (the civilian's 'patriotic and picturesque spot' unspoilt by the military 'scrap metal'). The heroes' 'brave wounds' echoes the

---

[5] Louis Simpson, quoted in Ian Hamilton (ed.), *The Poetry of War, 1939–1945* (London: Alan Ross, 1965), 171–2.

[6] Louis Simpson, 'The Heroes', in *Selected Poems* (London: Oxford University Press, 1966), 20.

[7] Siegfried Sassoon, 'The Hero', in *Collected Poems 1908–1956* (London: Faber, 1984), 26.

Mother's consolation that her son had been 'so brave', and prepares for the chilling irony of the poem's concluding stanzas. Sassoon's hero, 'cold-footed useless swine', had tried 'To get sent home' and 'died, | Blown to small bits'. Simpson's heroes are, arguably, more fortunate—'packaged and sent home in parts', albeit not to a heroes' welcome but to a workbench at which to assemble poppies, like the veterans of the previous war. The Sassoon template, like Simpson's savagely ironic choice of comic rhymes (rapscallions/battalions) in a tragic context, deepens the fury that gives his poem its propellent power.

No one, I think, would deny that these are powerful war poems, but of course most (like most poems) are less potent, and many are altogether impotent. To demonstrate the qualitative range of poems prompted by warfare—and to suggest why many fail—I propose to move on to a brief case-study of the poetry of the Vietnam War.[8] This falls, more starkly than the poems of any earlier conflict, into two principal categories: those written by so-called Stateside poets, who never left America, and those of the 'Vets', the veterans, who did.

The Stateside poems can themselves be divided into two categories: first, the poetry of first-hand witness to the moral and other effects of the war on *America*—poems by Alan Ginsberg, for example; second, the poetry of second-hand witness to the war in *Vietnam*—too much of it like this:

Women, Children, Babies, Cows, Cats

> 'It was at My Lai or Sonmy or something,
> it was this afternoon . . . We had these orders,
> we had all night to think about it—
> we was to burn and kill, then there'd be nothing
> standing, women, children, babies, cows, cats . . .
> As soon as we hopped the choppers, we started shooting.
> I remember . . . as we was coming up upon one area
> in Pinkville, a man with a gun . . . running—this lady . . .
> Lieutenant LaGuerre said, "Shoot her." I said,
> "You shoot her, I don't want to shoot no lady."
> She had one foot in the door . . . When I turned her,
> there was this little one-month-year-old baby
> I thought was her gun. It kind of cracked me up.'[9]

This was written by a great poet—Robert Lowell—but I cannot be alone in thinking it is not a great poem. In fact, I think it embarrassing in its blend of black demotic ('I don't want to shoot no lady') with the literary ('we hopped the choppers', and the coy 'Lieutenant LaGuerre'). The speaker does not persuade me that he mistook

---

[8] For a comprehensive critical and contextual study, see Subarno Chattarji, *Memories of a Lost War: American Poetic Responses to the Vietnam War* (Oxford: Clarendon Press, 2001).

[9] Robert Lowell, 'Women, Children, Babies, Cows, Cats', in *Collected Poems*, ed. Frank Bidart and David Gewanter (London: Faber, 2003), 596.

the baby (so neatly foreshadowed in his orders) for a gun; or that 'It kind of cracked [him] up'. Certainly, the poem does not crack *me* up. It would tell us—even if we did not know that Lowell never served in Vietnam—that his testimony is second-hand. In this, it is strikingly unlike his poignant and powerful poem 'Fall 1961', that bears first-hand witness to a father's fear in the midst of the Cuban missile crisis:

> All autumn, the chafe and jar
> of nuclear war;
> we have talked our extinction to death.
> I swim like a minnow
> behind my studio window.
>
> Our end drifts nearer,
> the moon lifts,
> radiant with terror.
>   .   .   .   .
> A father's no shield
> for his child . . . [10]

If, like me, you feel more for the American father and his child than for the Vietnamese mother and baby, it might be that the poet felt more. Few parents can feel as much pity and terror for a mother and baby seen in a newspaper or a television screen as for a threatened child of their own.

It does not follow, however, that a poem of first-hand witness will necessarily be better—more moving because more focused—than one of second-hand witness. Tennyson did not see the Charge of the Light Brigade other than with his mind's eye, but his lifelong absorption in Arthurian legend and chivalry enabled him to take his place, imaginatively, with the 'Noble six hundred'. He feels—and enables us to feel—fury, and horror, and pity, and amazed admiration:

> Cannon to right of them,
> Cannon to left of them,
> Cannon behind them
>   Volleyed and thundered;
> Stormed at with shot and shell,
>   While horse and hero fell,
> They that had fought so well
> Came through the jaws of Death,
> Back from the mouth of Hell,
> All that was left of them,
>   Left of six hundred. [11]

[10] Lowell, 'Fall 1961', ibid. 329.
[11] Alfred Tennyson, 'The Charge of the Light Brigade', in *The Poems of Tennyson*, ii, ed. Christopher Ricks, 2nd edn. (London: Longman, 1987), 511–13.

Thomas Hardy did not see the Boer War burial party 'throw in Drummer Hodge, to rest | Uncoffined—just as found', but his lifelong absorption in the little world of Wessex enabled him to take his place, imaginatively, at the boy's graveside:

> Young Hodge the Drummer never knew—
> > Fresh from his Wessex home—
> The meaning of the broad Karoo,
> > The Bush, the dusty loam,
> And why uprose to nightly view
> > Strange stars amid the gloom.[12]

There is no fury in Hardy's poem, but only profound pity and sadness—as for the son he never had. These poems of second-hand witness have an immediacy and power equal to any of first-hand witness, being the work of great poets, each with a lifelong imaginative investment in his subject. But such poems are rare. The second-hand testimony of lesser poets, lacking such investment, is seldom impressive and sometimes embarrassing.

For demographic and social-historical reasons, the ratio of poets to other servicemen and -women serving in Vietnam was less than in either World War. Most American intellectuals disapproved of the Vietnam War, and men of military age—particularly white men of military age—could avoid conscription by signing up for university education. And many did. The ratio of Stateside poets to battlefield poets was, therefore, greater than in either World War. There were hundreds of armchair poets pretending, like Lowell, to first-hand witness and/or degrees of moral commitment to which they were not entitled. Few were as good as Lowell, and collectively they deserved the savage rebuke offered by a front-line veteran of the Second World War, Anthony Hecht. He wrote of one such (fortunately unidentified) armchair poet:

> Here lies fierce Strephon, whose poetic rage
> Lashed out on Vietnam from page and stage;
> Whereby from basements of Bohemia he
> Rose to the lofts of sweet celebrity,
> Being, by Fortune, (our Eternal Whore)
> One of the few to profit by that war,
> A fate he shared—it bears much thinking on—
> With certain persons at the Pentagon.[13]

The knock-out punch of the last line should not blind us to the lightning jab of the first: 'Here *lies* fierce Strephon'. Is he lying in the grave or telling lies, or both? The fury driving this poem is directed, I assume, not at a Stateside poet bearing

[12] Thomas Hardy, 'Drummer Hodge', in *The Complete Poems*, ed. James Gibson (London: Macmillan, 1976), 90–1.

[13] Anthony Hecht, 'Here lies fierce Strephon', quoted in *Anthony Hecht in Conversation with Philip Hoy*, ed. Philip Hoy (Oxford: Between the Lines, 1999), 76.

true witness to the impact of the war on America, but one pretending to first-hand witness of combat in Vietnam.

Hecht's rebuke comes with the moral authority of a poet burdened with the responsibility of bearing witness to the ultimate brutality of the Second World War. He served with the Infantry Division that discovered Flossenbürg, an annex of Buchenwald. As he writes:

When we arrived, the SS personnel had, of course, fled. Prisoners were dying at the rate of 500 a day from typhus. Since I had the rudiments of French and German, I was appointed to speak, in the hope of securing evidence against those who ran the camp. Later, when some of these were captured, I presented them with the charges levelled against them, translating their denials or defences back into French for the sake of their accusers, in an attempt to get to the bottom of what was done and who was responsible. The place, the suffering, the prisoners' accounts were beyond comprehension. For years after I would wake shrieking. I must add an important point: after the war I read widely in Holocaust literature, and I can no longer separate my anger and revulsion at what I really saw from what I later came to learn.[14]

After the War, his Jewish imagination seared with what he had seen and read, Hecht discharged his responsibility to the dead, to history, in one of the War's most powerful poems, 'More Light! More Light!' (supposedly the last words of the poet Goethe as he lay dying in Weimar). This opens with a graphic account of a sixteenth-century atrocity, committed in the name of religion: a Christian martyr's burning at the stake. The smoke from his pyre mingles with that from a later and greater atrocity committed not in the name of religion, but against an entire religious community:

> We move now to outside a German wood.
> Three men are there commanded to dig a hole
> In which the two Jews are ordered to lie down
> And be buried alive by the third, who is a Pole.
>
> Not light from the shrine at Weimar beyond the hill
> Nor light from heaven appeared. But he did refuse.
> A Lüger settled back deeply in its glove.
> He was ordered to change places with the Jews.
>
> Much casual death had drained away their souls.
> The thick dirt mounted toward the quivering chin.
> When only the head was exposed the order came
> To dig him out again and to get back in.
>
> No light, no light in the blue Polish eye.
> When he finished a riding boot packed down the earth.
> The Lüger hovered lightly in its glove.
> He was shot in the belly and in three hours bled to death.
>
> No prayers or incense rose up in those hours
> Which grew to be years, and every day came mute

---

[14] Hecht, interviewed by Philip Hoy, ibid. 24.

> Ghosts from the ovens, sifting through crisp air,
> And settled upon his eyes in a black soot.[15]

There can be no immediate first-hand experience here, but what Hecht had seen and heard in Flossenbürg galvanized his imagination with a shock of such high voltage that his poem passes it on to its readers. Obviously the voltage is reduced when it reaches us—as it must be in 'Dulce et Decorum Est' and any such poem—but 'More Light! More Light!' shocks an exposed nerve. This is its function and its value, and, in this, it has something in common with the reporting of a first-class war-correspondent like Robert Fiske. The difference—a crucial difference—is that we can hold 'Dulce et Decorum Est' and 'More Light! More Light!' in our memory, as we cannot retain the front line journalism of a Fiske—or, for that matter, the front line letters of an Owen.

The charge against a poem like Lowell's 'Women, Children, Babies, Cows, Cats' is that, far from shocking an exposed nerve, it has the numbing effect of second-hand journalism, thereby contributing to the insensitive apathy that enables us to turn, unmoved, from our newspaper's coverage of disaster to that of a football match. Hecht's rebuke to 'fierce Strephon' points up the further disturbing fact that many of those protesting against the war made money from appearances on 'page and stage'. The situation and the poetry of the combatant 'Vets' could not have been more different. Their poems of first-hand experience often have a raw power, but I know of none that lives in the memory like 'More Light! More Light!' A problem for many American poets then aspiring to be war poets was that, rightly perceiving it to be an unjust war, they chose not to participate as servicemen or -women; and lacking first-hand experience, could not write convincingly of the war 'on the ground'.

Given some of their trumpeted expressions of moral commitment to the anti-war cause, it is perhaps surprising that none of them felt strongly enough to follow the example of W. H. Auden, who, in January 1937, prompted a banner headline of the *Daily Worker*: 'FAMOUS POET TO DRIVE AMBULANCE IN SPAIN'.[16] Explaining his decision to a friend, he wrote: 'I shall probably be a bloody bad soldier but how can I speak to/for them without becoming one?'[17]

One American poet *did* follow Auden's example. John Balaban went to Vietnam, but not as an ambulance driver. He went as a conscientious objector to work in an orphanage (for children orphaned by his country's war), learnt Vietnamese, and stayed after the war to teach in a Vietnamese university. His poems of those years have a fine grain, a specificity of detail, rare in the many poems bearing first-hand witness to an armchair reading of newspapers or the watching of television news.

[15] Hecht, 'More Light! More Light!', in *Collected Earlier Poems* (New York: Alfred A. Knopf, 1990), 64–5.

[16] See Humphrey Carpenter, *W. H. Auden: A Biography* (London: Allen & Unwin, 1981), 208: '"FAMOUS POET TO DRIVE AMBULANCE IN SPAIN", announced the *Daily Worker* on 12 January 1937.'

[17] Auden, quoted in E. R. Dodds, *Missing Persons: An Autobiography* (Oxford: Clarendon Press, 1977), 133.

As with the war poems of earlier wars, many of Balaban's best were written after the guns had fallen silent, for example:

In Celebration of Spring

Our Asian war is over; others have begun.
Our elders, who tried to mortgage lies,
are disgraced, or dead, and already
the brokers are picking their pockets
for the keys and the credit cards.

In delta swamp in a united Vietnam,
a Marine with a bullfrog for a face,
rots in equatorial heat. An eel
slides through the cage of his bared ribs.
At night, on the old battlefield, ghosts,
like patches of fog, lurk into villages
to maunder on doorsills of cratered homes,
while all across the U.S.A.
the wounded walk about and wonder where to go.

And today, in the simmer of lyric sunlight,
the chrysalis pulses in its mushy cocoon,
under the bark on a gnarled root of an elm.
In the brilliant creek, a minnow flashes
delirious with gnats. The turtle's heart
quickens its raps in the warm bank sludge.
As she chases a frisbee spinning in sunlight,
a girl's breasts bounce full and strong;
a boy's stomach, as he turns, is flat and strong.[18]

Balaban's opening has disturbing vibrations for readers in 2004: 'Our Asian war is over; others have begun.' As for Owen and Sassoon, the guilty men are the old men who sacrificed the young—'Our elders who tried to mortgage lies'. Scavenging vermin in America—'the brokers'—anticipate the somehow more attractive scavengers in Vietnam—the bullfrog and the eel. The controlled fury of the speaker's first stanza is followed by pity for the dead of both sides, and for the living dead. There is not much celebration 'on the old battlefield' or 'across the U.S.A.', but with the third stanza, spring returns and the natural cycle of generation begins again: the 'chrysalis *pulses*', 'a minnow *flashes*', 'the turtle's heart | *quickens*'. And not only the turtle's heart: 'a girl's breasts bounce full and strong; | a boy's stomach, as he turns, is flat and strong'. Adam and Eve are in their garden again. Finally, as at the end of Owen's 'Dulce et Decorum Est' and Cornford's 'Letter from Aragon', Balaban turns from his *exempla* to address his reader directly:

---

[18] John Balaban, 'In Celebration of Spring', in *Locusts at the Edge of Summer: New and Selected Poems* (Washington: Copper Canyon Press, 1997), 108–9.

> Swear by the locust, by dragonflies on ferns,
> by the minnow's flash, the tremble of a breast,
> by the new earth spongy under our feet;
> that as we grow old, we will not grow evil,
> that although our garden seeps with sewage,
> and our elders think it's up for auction—swear
> by this dazzle that does not wish to leave us—
> that we will be keepers of a garden, nonetheless.

Balaban spoke of 'Our Asian war', and, of course, it *was* an American war, but not all of its poets were American. Britain had its 'Stateside' contingent of armchair witnesses, and one—so far as I am aware, only one—poet-witness to the war on the ground: James Fenton. In the 1970s, he was a freelance reporter in Indochina and a foreign correspondent in Germany for the *Guardian*. Like Hecht, a poet of the School of Auden, his German experience fuelled one of the great English-language poems of the Holocaust, 'A German Requiem'.[19] This was first published in 1981, the same year as one of the great English-language poems of the South-east Asian wars, his 'Dead Soldiers'. The power and poignancy of each derives from Fenton's first-hand experience of human suffering, but the poignancy is sharpened by his deployment of grimly comic detail and a refusal to lapse into mawkish solemnity. The seeming solemnity of his poem's title is subverted by what follows:

Dead Soldiers

> When His Excellency Prince Norodom Chantaraingsey
> Invited me to lunch on the battlefield
> I was glad of my white suit for the first time that day.
> They lived well, the mad Norodoms, they had style.
> The brandy and the soda arrived in crates.
> Bricks of ice, tied around with raffia,
> Dripped from the orderlies' handlebars.
>
> And I remember the dazzling tablecloth
> As the APCs fanned out along the road,
> The dishes piled high with frogs' legs,
> Pregnant turtles, their eggs boiled in the carapace,
> Marsh irises in fish sauce
> And inflorescence of a banana salad.
> On every bottle, Napoleon Bonaparte
> Pleaded for the authenticity of the spirit.
> They called the empties Dead Soldiers
> And rejoiced to see them pile up at our feet.

---

[19] James Fenton, 'A German Requiem', in *The Memory of War and Children in Exile: Poems 1968–1983* (Harmondsworth: Penguin, 1983), 9–19.

> Each diner was attended by one of the other ranks
> Whirling a table-napkin to keep off the flies.
> It was like eating between rows of morris dancers—
> Only they didn't kick.[20]

This most curious of war poems begins on a battlefield, but, as in Greek tragedy, the violence takes place off-stage. Instead of blood-stained battledress, we see a white suit, a dazzling (presumably white) tablecloth, and whirling (presumably white) napkins. A poet who has seen a battlefield gives his poem a narrator who remembers the menu rather than the body count.

> 'one eats well there', I remark.
> 'So one should,' says the Jockey Cap:
> 'The tiger always eats well,
> It eats the raw flesh of the deer,
> And Chantaraingsey was born in the year of the tiger.
> So, did they show you the things they do
> With the young refugee girls?'

The casual brutality of this passes with no more comment from the narrator than his earlier report on the only casualties he notices: 'They called the empties Dead Soldiers | And rejoiced to see them pile up at our feet.' The insensitive speaker has none of Fenton's own knowledge of Cambodian politics, and depends for his information on a dubious source (one hesitates to call 'intelligence'). Pol Pot's brother

> tells me how he will one day give me the gen.
> He will tell me how the prince financed the casino
> And how the casino brought Lon Nol to power.
> He will tell me this.
> He will tell me all these things.
> All I must do is drink and listen.

He drank, listened, predicted, and was 'always wrong'. He is no wiser now:

> I have been told that the prince is still fighting
> Somewhere in the Cardamoms or the Elephant Mountains.
> But I doubt that the Jockey Cap would have survived his good connections.
> I think the lunches would have done for him—
> Either the lunches or the dead soldiers.

And so the poem comes full circle—back to its title. But at this (their third) appearance, the dead soldiers are no longer capitalized, metaphorical, but actual dead soldiers.

What do these and other war poems achieve? In that their subject is tragedy, they can—when made with passion and precision—move us (as Aristotle said) to pity

---

[20] Fenton, 'Dead Soldiers', ibid. 26–8. APCs are Armoured Personnel Carriers.

and terror; also, I suggest, to a measure of fury. And just as we go to a performance of Shakespeare's *King Lear* or Britten's *War Requiem* for pleasure, we return (or at least I return) to 'Dulce et Decorum Est' or 'The Heroes' for the wonder and pleasurable satisfaction a masterpiece affords.

In the short term, I doubt whether the poems about Vietnam had any significant effect on the course of the war. Certainly the (much better) poems of 1914–18 and 1939–45 had no significant effect on the course of the two World Wars. In the longer term, however, war poems *have* through history had a significant effect in shaping their societies' attitudes to warfare. The epics of heroic ages—the *Iliad*, *Beowulf*—encouraged the pursuit of glory with their celebration of courage and skilful sword-play. Over the centuries, all that changed. More British poems of the First World War confirmed 'The old Lie: Dulce et decorum est | Pro patria mori' than challenged it; but, with few exceptions, they have been relegated to the dustbin of history. The poets whose work has survived sing a very different song: one that has played a significant part in introducing subsequent generations to the realities of modern warfare.

The poems of the Second World War have had less impact—not because they were less good, but because the reading public has become increasingly attuned to prose, and because the Word (prose as well as verse) has increasingly lost ground to the Image. Today, our knowledge of the war in Iraq probably derives as much from newspaper and television images as from the spoken or written word. I have yet to see a poem about 'our [latest] Asian war' that is worth the paper it is written on, but all the precedents suggest that we should not expect to see one yet. As and when we do, I think it is more likely to come from the hand of a doctor or war correspondent than from an armchair witness or a serving soldier. And while there may be poetry in the pity, I would bet that there will be more in the fury.

PART VI

POST-WAR POETRY

'THIS IS PLENTY. THIS IS MORE THAN ENOUGH': POETRY AND THE MEMORY OF THE SECOND WORLD WAR

GARETH REEVES

Most of the poetry discussed in this essay is by non-combatants, those too young to have been directly involved in the Second World War, but whose world was irrevocably altered by the conflict and its aftermath. This in itself raised, and raises, questions of conscience and responsibility. What right have non-participants to speak of agonies they have not experienced directly? Yet to maintain silence is an act of wilful ignorance, to be blind to the altered terrain one finds oneself inhabiting, is to be, however unknowingly, complicit. Yet again, to dwell on past atrocity, to keep its memory alive, however meant as an act of humility and homage to the dead ('lest we forget') can, on the contrary, turn into an affront to the dead ('what right have you?'), or into a mangling of the past, or into an act of hubris, or—and this in some contexts is the most pernicious danger—into a way to 'make germinate', in

Seamus Heaney's phrase,[1] the very conflict to be appeased and laid to rest—or into a fearsome concoction of some or all of these possibilities. The first half of this essay will address the issue of war memory through a discussion of some strategically chosen poets and poems, treated in roughly chronological order, culminating in an account of Geoffrey Hill's 'September Song', a breath-taking distillation of poetry's dilemma in the aftermath of conflict. The second half will dwell on James Fenton's poetry up to and including 'A German Requiem', in the present writer's opinion one of the finest, and most disturbing, English-language poems to have addressed civilian response to war—that is to say, since we all live in a world of conflict or post-conflict, to have addressed the heart, and heartlessness, of civilization itself.

Keith Douglas *was* a combatant, killed in conflict (commanding a tank troop in the main assault on Normandy in 1944), whose poetry comes back to us speaking with the authority of the dead, one of Eliot's 'dead . . . tongued with fire beyond the language of the living'.[2] Because the position of Douglas's poem 'How to Kill' (1943) in relation to the War is diametrically opposed to that of most of the poetry to be discussed in this chapter, it provides, paradoxically perhaps, an illuminating perspective on the central issues. One might think that his poem, with a title like that, would be incapable of demonstrating the tragic moral perspective of, say, 'The Shield of Achilles' (1952), Auden's elder-statesmanlike poem of synoptic wisdom, with its long historical perspective that judges all history and finds it wanting. But, on the contrary, 'How to Kill' demonstrates an absolute sense of right and wrong from a startlingly shocking perspective. With powerful irony it speaks with the voice of one of the damned, but sees with double vision, both panoptically and microscopically. Although the speaker is someone within history, taking on the voice of a killer, he is able at the same time to stand outside history and show that he knows that what he is doing is evil. The voice both judges and is judged. 'Death, like a familiar, hears.'[3] This condemned Doctor Faustus, possessed by something impersonal, watches his own damnation with cool detachment: 'This sorcery | I do. Being damned, I am amused.' Part of the poem's implied statement is that its experience is an adjunct of the modern world, part of 'growing up'; hence its initial parallel between childish ball-games and the adult '*gift designed to kill*' (Douglas's italics). Initiation into adulthood, being-in-the-world, insulates one from the humanity of others, from the fact that they too have their individual histories: the target of the speaker's bullet 'moves about in ways | his mother knows, habits of his'. The speaker recognizes from his own experience what he is about to kill. There is a dehumanizing moral suicide therefore in this death, in this witnessing of 'love travel[ling] into vacancy'.

---

[1] Seamus Heaney, 'The Tollund Man', in *Opened Ground: Poems 1966–1996* (London: Faber, 1998), 65.

[2] T. S. Eliot, 'Little Gidding', in *The Complete Poems and Plays* (London: Faber, 1969), 192.

[3] Keith Douglas, 'How to Kill', in *The Complete Poems*, ed. Desmond Graham (London: Faber, 2000), 119.

In the words of Michael Schmidt, Douglas 'extended poetry into one of the extreme areas of modern experience. Yet he penetrates that extreme area without hysteria—as it were dispassionately. That is the wonder of his verse: it is the world which is extreme, the strategy for survival and for witness is a kind of neutrality.'[4] That was to be one way forward for poetry in the aftermath of conflict—although, arguably, it is the opposite, a retreat. How after the horrors of World War could poetry, could any art, rise—or lower itself—to the occasion? Theodor Adorno's famous statement that 'To write poetry after Auschwitz is barbaric',[5] does not mean, as many think, that, in John Banville's words, 'writing poetry after Auschwitz is to be forbidden, or impossible'.[6] Banville goes on to say that Adorno was arguing that the Holocaust presented poetry with an unprecedented challenge which should not be ducked by resorting to a 'murky neo-primitivism', but should be faced with 'clear-sighted modernity'; art should not 'evad[e] existentialist man's duty to confront his own times in all their complexity and atrociousness'. In their different ways some of the finest post-war poets live up to Adorno's challenge, if only by acknowledging with various degrees of complexity, sinuosity, at times even deviousness, the near impossibility of so doing. And if silence was not a viable option, then you might opt for the caution of humility. This was the strategy adopted by Donald Davie, who based his case against the poetic expression of extreme feeling on the premiss that such extremity underlies the violence unleashed in conflict. Blake Morrison makes the apt connection with Douglas, who during the War wrote prophetically that 'to be sentimental or emotional now is dangerous to oneself and to others'.[7] Morrison rightly argues that this is 'very similar' to the view expressed in Davie's poem 'Rejoinder to a Critic' (1957),[8] which argues that both love and hate are extremities of emotion, and the one, love, implies the possibility of the other, hate. Against those who, like the 'critic' of the title, find Davie's poetry emotionally frigid, it must be insisted that this poem is not against intensity of emotion as such, only against its being put on display, in particular in poetry. 'Be dumb!' in the poem means 'don't speak about it', not 'don't feel it'. The poet, the poem says, should '*Appear* concerned only to make it scan!'[9] Even so, the poem ends by more than hinting that such an attitude does indeed require at some level the denial of feeling,

---

[4] Michael Schmidt, 'Introduction', in *idem* (ed.), *Eleven British Poets: An Anthology* (London: Methuen, 1980), 3. Schmidt also makes the parallel with Doctor Faustus.

[5] Theodor W. Adorno, 'Cultural Criticism and Society', in *Prisms*, trans. Samuel and Shierry Weber (Cambridge, Mass.: MIT Press, 1981), 34.

[6] John Banville, 'Beyond Good and Evil', *The Nation*, 31 Jan. 2005, 11.

[7] Douglas to J. C. Hall, 10 Aug. 1943, in *The Letters*, ed. Desmond Graham (Manchester: Carcanet, 2000), 295.

[8] Blake Morrison, *The Movement: English Poetry and Fiction of the 1950s* (London: Methuen, 1980), 107.

[9] Donald Davie, 'Rejoinder to a Critic', *Collected Poems* (Manchester: Carcanet, 1990), 74; my italics.

that not to express emotion is to run the danger of negating it: 'How dare we now be anything but numb?' Aftermath entails a deliberate emotional retreat.

It was against this background that ten or so years later Charles Tomlinson (Davie's friend and poet-in-arms against what they considered to be the rhetorical extravagance and neo-Romanticism of poets of the previous generation, especially Dylan Thomas) wrote his poem 'Against Extremity' (which contains the sentence 'The time is in love with endings'[10]), amongst whose targets is Sylvia Plath, some of whose poems famously, or notoriously, locate their emotions in imagery drawn from the Holocaust. For Tomlinson and like-minded readers, such a strategy was to misappropriate horrific public memories for private gratification. For critics such as George Steiner and Al Alvarez, it was to tap into material which had hitherto been squeamishly excluded from poetry. Alvarez's anthology *The New Poetry* made available to British readers American post-war poetry (including Plath's) that went 'beyond the gentility principle' endemic to much contemporary British poetry. His introduction explicitly invokes the new conditions of the War's aftermath and refers to 'the forces of disintegration which destroy the old standards of civilization. Their public faces are those of two world wars, of the concentration camps, of genocide, and the threat of nuclear war.'[11] Alvarez goes on to argue that war's atrocity is, uniquely in world history, now universal, involving not just the military but civilians on a mass scale, and 'concentration camps run scientifically as death factories'. Arguments like this can be used to justify Plath's practice in poems such as 'Lady Lazarus' and 'Daddy' (both written in 1962): to internalize wartime atrocity poetically as part of an emotional strategy is legitimate because it taps into what has become a universal imagery of trauma.

But however one reacts to these arguments, the tide of poetic opinion was turning. Already there was setting in a reaction to the caution of the 'Movement' poets (among whom were Davie and Tomlinson), usefully summarized by Ted Hughes (an admirer of Douglas's poetry):

One of the things those poets [of the Movement] had in common I think was the post-war mood of having had enough . . . enough rhetoric, enough overweening push of any kind, enough of the dark gods, enough of the id, enough of the Angelic powers and the heroic efforts to make new worlds. They'd seen it all turn into death-camps and atomic bombs. All they wanted was to get back in civvies and get home to the wife and kids and for the rest of their lives not a thing was going to interfere with a nice cigarette and a nice view of the park. . . . Now I came a bit later. I hadn't had enough. I was all for opening negotiations with whatever happened to be out there.[12]

---

[10] Charles Tomlinson, 'Against Extremity', in *Collected Poems* (Oxford: Oxford University Press, 1987), 163.

[11] A. Alvarez, 'The New Poetry or Beyond the Gentility Principle', in *idem* (ed.), *The New Poetry: An Anthology* (Harmondsworth: Penguin, 1966), 26.

[12] Ted Hughes, 'Ted Hughes and *Crow*', interviewed by Egbert Fass, *London Magazine*, Jan. 1971, 10–11; quoted in Morrison, *The Movement*, 244.

All this, one may feel with some justification, is mere poetic politics, one fashion reacting to the previous. But it indicates something of the issues at stake: how was it possible to react poetically to what was perceived as an experience unprecedented not only in intensity but also in scope? Even Hughes himself, never one for reticence or indirection, found that the readiest route was indirectly via the First World War. As Neil Corcoran writes, 'The First World War, the war of the father, does duty in Hughes, as it were, for the rest of the horrors of the century.'[13] Quoting from Part I of Hughes's poem 'Out' (1967),[14] which evokes the poet's father as victim and guilty survivor of trench warfare and the son as 'his luckless double', Corcoran comments that it is as though the poet 'has inherited that war genetically'. Part II of 'Out' is a remarkable version of the Beckettian theme, 'astride of a grave and a difficult birth',[15] in which 'the dead man' suffers a rebirth, 'gazing around with the eyes | Of an exhausted clerk', into a seemingly dead world. The remarkable anti-Remembrance Day Part III (called simply 'Remembrance Day') begins in bitter anger ('The poppy is a wound, the poppy is the mouth | Of the grave . . . | | A canvas-beauty puppet on a wire | Today whoring everywhere'), goes on to attempt to get out from under the dead weight of his father's war experience, and, bidding 'goodbye to that bloody-minded flower' and to a whole era ('the remaindered charms of my father's survival'), concludes with a plangent dismissal of his country and all it fought for: 'Let England close. Let the green sea-anemone close.'

Hughes's poem may be a late flowering of the First World War, but its very bitterness is due in part to the powerful pull of the poetry produced by that war. First World War 'trench' poetry set an awesome precedent. Arguably this situation was responsible for the fact that some of the finest poetry to show the effects of the Second World War took longer to germinate than its First World War counterpart, at any rate in Britain (although a notable exception is David Jones's In Parenthesis, published nineteen years after the end of the First World War). On this point Douglas, again, was prophetic: '[T]he soldiers have not found anything new to say. Their experiences they will not forget easily, and it seems to me that the whole body of English war poetry of this war, civil and military, will be created after the war is over.'[16] The issue is not merely that memorial and elegy need the lapse of time before they can be composed; it is whether memorial and elegy are appropriate or even possible.

This complex of emotions—guilt, complicity, inadequacy, humility, hubris—is itself the subject of Geoffrey Hill's most emotionally and intellectually challenging poetry. Its hard theme is that to write poetry about, even to create great art out of, mass extermination is to feed off and thus perpetuate it. 'Arrogant acceptance from which song derives | Is bedded with their blood, makes flourish young | Roots in

[13] Neil Corcoran, English Poetry since 1940 (London: Longman, 1993), 115.
[14] Ted Hughes, 'Out', in Collected Poems, ed. Paul Keegan (London: Faber, 2003), 165–6.
[15] Samuel Beckett, Waiting for Godot (London: Faber, 1965), 90.
[16] Douglas, 'Poets in This War', in Letters, 353.

ashes.'[17] These lines (from the first of 'Two Formal Elegies: For the Jews in Europe') intensely involve despair and exhilaration: syntactically, what is 'bedded' is both acceptance of violence and also the song made possible by that acceptance. This is Swiftian satire at its most biting and truth telling: our highest achievements are the bright side of darkest human nature. Hill's poetry would give voice to the silent dead, but is all the time conscious that in so doing it relives and resurrects the atrocity buried with them. 'Artistic men prod dead men from their stone' ('Of Commerce and Society 4');[18] and the Auschwitz death camp continues to have a fantasy half-life in the way it is remembered and memorialized: 'a fable | Unbelievable in fatted marble', where 'unbelievable' mixes scornful irascibility and colloquial disbelief in a way that comprehends the gamut of incredulity, in a dense utterance characteristic of Hill's poetry (marble monument, marbled flesh). Both the story and its memorial are beyond comprehension.

Davie accused Hill's poetry of 'set[ting] up an equation in which one side cancels out the other, leaving us with an ironic zero';[19] but the antithesis of an ironic zero is an ironic plenitude, and that is just as true of Hill's poetry. The plain, even stark, style of Hill's 'September Song' (1968) contains a knotted and knotty message. Acutely reticent at the same time as acutely confessional, it is inscrutable in its locked-in emotions. It accuses itself of getting poetic mileage out of its subject even as it does so; it is self-indulgent even as it reprimands itself for self-indulgence; it scrutinizes its own conscience. The victim 'deported'—and in the context this word conjures up 'departed'—to the death camp was born in the same year, 1932, as Hill, but the poet is still alive to write the poem. The speaker's consequent guilt comes across in the central but ostentatiously parenthetical sentence '(I have made | an elegy for myself it | is true)'[20]—central in its position in the poem, and central to the poem's emotional complex, parenthetical because bracketed and parenthetical to what the poem is supposed to be about: not the poet, but the victim. That sentence, seemingly forthright, is, like every other phrase in the poem, double-edged: 'In making this elegy I please myself merely,' and 'I have made an elegy that turns out to be anticipating my own death'—not just because the poet shares the same birth year as the victim, but because all elegies have this about them. They all say, 'it could have been me'; they all imply the poet's own mortality (as one of the greatest English elegies, Milton's *Lycidas*, demonstrates). But 'it | is true' not only that the poet has written all these guilt-ridden things, but also that in so writing, in so confessing, he has written truly: it is a true poem because it implicates the elegist in the elegy he is writing. It is also true in its chillingly unsentimental evocation of the mechanical efficiency of the mass slaughter. But to describe death from the perspective of one

---

[17] Geoffrey Hill, 'Two Formal Elegies 1', in *Collected Poems* (Harmondsworth: Penguin, 1985), 30.
[18] Hill, 'Of Commerce and Society 4', ibid. 49.
[19] Davie, *Under Briggflatts: A History of Poetry in Great Britain 1960–1988* (Manchester: Carcanet, 1989), 247.
[20] Hill, 'September Song', in *Collected Poems*, 67.

of its perpetrators in thrall to impersonal forces, as in 'How to Kill', is one thing, however spine chilling; to do so as an outsider not directly caught up in the conflict, as someone therefore achieving a poetic *frisson* in spite of himself, is quite another. The sentence 'As estimated, you died' may conjure up the coldly calculating efficiency of the Nazi death machine, but even to utter that sentence, chilling in its presumption, is to savour insensitivity. At its conclusion, the poem would seem to be retreating to the sort of world, with 'a nice view of the park', that, Hughes claimed, many embraced after the War. Thus the poem ends, with apparent low-key contentment, 'This is plenty. This is more than enough.' This is more than enough said by this poem you have just read; and if one looks at what *has* been said, it does indeed turn out to be more than enough, for this quasi-pastoral retreat cannot ward off the sinister: 'Harmless fires' inevitably calls up the harmful death camp fires which the speaker would erase from his mind; and in the context 'fattens' and 'flake' take on highly sinister overtones. The description is indeed more than enough, in that it comes loaded with more even than what the poet bargained for. The poem becomes, in spite of itself, in spite of the attempt to put aside what the speaker himself never experienced and therefore is not licensed to describe, knowingly melodramatic in the way it makes poetic capital out of the Holocaust. The attempt to retreat from self-indulgence results only in another turn of the self-indulgent screw. Even retreating into silence is culpable. To say anything is more than enough said.

Into this arena of culpability, guilt, and silence, James Fenton's 'A German Requiem' entered in 1981 with an aplomb resulting, it would appear, on the one hand from his time as a political journalist in Indochina (especially as a war correspondent in Cambodia) and Germany, and on the other from an apprenticeship in postmodernist poetics—although, like all postmodernists worthy of the name, he is wary, to the point of scorn, of all such labels. A highly assured but reticent performance—assured because reticent—the poem reads as if waiting to be written, as if the Holocaust were listening out for this memorial to the impossibility of memorial, of what is now glibly called 'closure'. And it is as if the poet too, as poet, had been preparing for the moment when inscrutability would find its best subject. Though some of Fenton's poetry courts the danger of turning early Audenesque portentousness into postmodernist affectation, 'A German Requiem' takes on a haunting depth. He has created an ideal poetic vehicle for expressing, not just the inexpressible, but the fact of inexpressibility. His most characteristic, and most penetrating, poetry neither reveals nor conceals, but gives voice to the pervasively oppressive presence of concealment. And if it encourages the reader to come up with such a response, that is in part the point: all attempts at explanation are doomed to mere style, but in the handling of that style lies a minimal but human salvation. Perhaps to say something, to make a poem, is, after all, worth the effort. It does at the very least attest, it is hoped, to our humanity. In 'A German Requiem' postmodernism's evasions and indeterminacies are brought to brilliant focus, in a style that combines clarity of statement with opacity. It is underspoken, stunning and stunned, a style befitting a civilization, and finally the poet-witness, silenced.

That style began to emerge in the early 'Terminal Moraine', which begins with a bald declaration that the ensuing poem has to do with inscrutability: 'It's simple but I find it hard to explain | Why I should wish to go from the moraine.'[21] If Auden's 'The Watershed' hovers on the brink of turning its post-industrial terrain into a psychological arena of frustrated anxiety and blockage, Fenton's poem goes over the brink. But it does so with an explicitness that belies turbulent undercurrents: 'every sudden breeze || Is amplified for my benefit. I listen and in the deep | Of the night, when I am alone, I landscape my sleep.' The poem does what it says, 'give[s] shape to thought', rather than makes thought out of shapes. The poet 'become[s] a thing | Of caves and hollows, mouths where the winds sing', possessing the caves and hollows and winds, rather than being possessed by them. The neat transposition in the final couplet, where heart turns into car, says it all with a clarity of utterance gainsaying the psychological opacity: 'But when a car is on the road I hear | My heart beat faster as it changes gear.'

A similar procedure is apparent in the later, more sophisticatedly mysterious, 'A Vacant Possession' with its ominously stark Audenesque diagnostic detail, though diagnosing what is carefully obscured: 'Look how you can scrape the weeds from the paving stones | With a single motion of the foot,'[22] near the start of the poem, sounds rather like Auden's oft-quoted 'look there | At cigarette-end smouldering on a border' near the start of 'Consider this and in our time',[23] an unspecified addressee being commanded to look at a minute particular. But if Auden's poem intimates psychic ills amidst threatening landscape, Fenton's gets there faster if more spookily. In the third stanza, 'she leans against | A mossy water-butt in which, could we see them, | Innumerable forms of life are uncurving': the pseudo-precise, pernickety way of putting it—'could we see them', 'uncurving'—masks vaguely ominous depths.

The technique came into its own with Fenton's experiences as a war correspondent. His poem 'Cambodia' sounds as if written in defiant acknowledgement of the 'voice without a face' which 'Proved by statistics that some cause was just' in Auden's 'The Shield of Achilles'.[24] The voice of 'Cambodia' starkly declares the numbers game in five end-stopped couplets, almost entirely composed of monosyllabic words (there are five disyllabic words, but none longer). It is as if Hill's sentence 'As estimated, you died' has chillingly infected Fenton's diction, for the poem sounds calculated to convey the riddlingly incalculable incomprehension of both victim

[21] James Fenton, 'Terminal Moraine', in *The Memory of War and Children in Exile: Poems 1968–1983* (Harmondsworth: Penguin, 1983), 92.

[22] Fenton, 'A Vacant Possession', ibid. 47.

[23] W. H. Auden, 'Consider this and in our time', in *The English Auden: Poems, Essays and Dramatic Writings 1927–1939*, ed. Edward Mendelson (London: Faber, 1977), 46.

[24] Auden, 'The Shield of Achilles', in *Collected Poems*, ed. Edward Mendelson (London: Faber, 1976), 597.

and, in the end, perpetrator: 'One man shall wake from terror to his bed. | Five men shall be dead. || One man to five. A million men to one. | And still they die. And still the war goes on.'[25] Fenton's speakers often sound like this, as though they are getting a bitter kind of consolation out of turning their bewilderment into lapidary statement—statement that invites decoding in proportion to its opacity.

A sustained instance of this procedure is the poem 'In a Notebook', which acts out a bewildered and bewildering incomprehension on the part of both speaker and reader. The poem enacts the process by which event becomes memory, and in so doing demonstrates the fact that to recall the past necessarily involves the act of recording it; for the scene remembered in the poem reaches the reader only, explicitly, as writing, as a piece of text. In spite of the bewilderment, or perhaps because of it, that text has a distant, controlled, and riddling quality, gained in large part from the rhythmically steady, trance-like iambs unvaried by caesurae. Hence the line unit takes precedence, a stylistic feature which is cunningly deployed. The first three, italicized stanzas (of this five-stanza poem) are evidently lines by the poet, later happened upon by him 'in a notebook', describing the eve of battle. But they are already distanced from the events and scene they describe: we are witness not to a war correspondent's immediate impressions but to past-tense poetic description whose artful composition reflects the poet-reporter's voyeuristic role from a perspective already looking to the future: 'And I sat drinking bitter coffee wishing | The tide would turn to bring me to my senses | After the pleasant war and the evasive answers.'[26] When the tide does turn, and he has supposedly come to his senses, it is only to realize that, 'reading this passage now' from the notebook, all that remains of the scene is the text, the (memorable) lines of poetry, that he penned there. Hence the first of the two non-italicized stanzas, presumably written in the 'present' of the poem, is largely composed of some of the (formerly italicized) notebook lines, with the implication that all that can be retrieved of the ravaged civilization, the 'villages [that] are burnt' and 'the cities void', is the poetry which the poet-reporter, guiltily, even conspiratorially, made out of them: not even memories of that civilization, but only memories as transformed into a necessarily stylized record. Or, to put it another way, memory always distorts; there is no such thing as pure recall. Our pasts, individual and collective, are what we were then. Hence the conclusion, which puts aside all attempt at embellishment, poetic or emotional: 'And I'm afraid most of my friends are dead.' This line, with its less regular, almost stumbling rhythm, represents a small emotional jolt right at the end of the poem, all the more arresting for its under-spokenness. It seems to break through the poem's trance-like state into a very English-sounding idiom, laconic, tight-lipped, conversational, curiously polite, but heartfelt.

[25] Fenton, 'Cambodia', in *Memory of War and Children in Exile*, 23.
[26] Fenton, 'In a Notebook', ibid. 24.

Fenton's baffled speakers often take refuge in style as a defence against their bafflement. 'Dead Soldiers' depends on our knowing, we feel, as much, or as little, about the murderous Pol Pot regime as does the poet: namely, that it was murderous, which is to know more than enough. Being closer to it produces nothing other than sinister wit revolving around that knowledge, which is nearly but never uttered: 'inflorescence of a banana salad'; 'They called the empties Dead Soldiers | And rejoiced to see them pile up at our feet'; 'The frogs' thighs leapt into the sad purple face | Like fish to the sound of a Chinese flute.'[27] This is the self-consciously knowing style of one who self-confessedly knows little, and who makes a stylistic point of cultural alienation and incomprehension with Audenesque public school phrases like 'Slipped away with the swag', and with comically precise but off-centre similes: 'Each diner was attended by one of the other ranks | Whirling a table-napkin to keep off the flies. | It was like eating between rows of morris dancers— | Only they didn't kick.' The poem ends with the speculation that Pol Pot's brother ('the Jockey Cap') was 'done for', 'Either [by] the lunches or the dead soldiers'—if in acknowledgement of possible remorse on the part of the brother, the reader cannot tell, and nor, one suspects, can the poem's speaker.

With 'A German Requiem' it is remarkable how Fenton's experience as a war correspondent and political journalist climaxes in an achievement whose very *raison d'être* is lack of experience, is precisely not having been present at the horrors that are the poem's absent subject.[28] As Corcoran writes, 'apparently entirely simple in diction and syntax and straightforward in technique . . . it is in fact a poem preoccupied with opacity . . . the literally "unspeakable" Nazi past is the pressure behind every line.'[29] The poet has found the perfect subject for his cryptically menacing style. The poem presents the two complementary roles of an investigative reporter, looking for clues and presenting the evidence, which translate on the personal and private level as trying to remember and wanting not to forget—though tugging beneath the surface are the opposed impulses of trying to forget and wanting not to remember. The syndrome is hinted at in a difficult passage from Hobbes's *Leviathan* used as an epigraph to the poem, in which '*Imagination*' must compensate for the '*decaying sense*' of forgetfulness, 'So that *Imagination* and *Memory* are but one thing . . .'.

Alan Robinson helpfully explains that the poem's 'displaced subject—the Holocaust—is a perceptual absence, literally in the devastated urban landscape that has disappeared without trace, metaphorically in the reticent conspiracy of silence of the Germans who lived through it, and accessible to the poet only through conjecture'.[30] Perceptual absence and conspiracy of silence come together in that arresting combination of clarity and opacity which, I have been arguing, is a prime characteristic of Fenton's style. In the opening section, syntactic transparency screens murky

---

[27] Fenton, 'Dead Soldiers', in *Memory of War and Children in Exile*, 26–27.

[28] Fenton, 'A German Requiem', ibid. 9–19.   [29] Corcoran, *English Poetry since 1940*, 248.

[30] Alan Robinson, *Instabilities in Contemporary British Poetry* (Basingstoke: Macmillan, 1988), 3–4.

depths; stylistic plainness, meaningful complexity. The simple pronominal clause 'It is', recurring nine times in the first six lines, becomes dense with significance and signification, begging the poem's central question, 'what is?' 'It' becomes the poem's subject, all that is unspeakable, as well as the fact of unspeakability. 'It' turns into silence, the act of forgetting, as well as that which is forgotten, into memory and denial of memory. 'It is not the streets that exist' almost says that the absence of streets exists, which is given a further twist in the rest of the line, 'It is the streets that no longer exist'. Similarly with 'It is not your memories' and 'It is not what you have written down'. The not-memories, what have been wilfully forgotten, and the not-written, the unrecorded, are what 'is'. This way of putting it reifies absence. The poet would write down the absence, would 'discover a ritual' parallel to that of the unspecified (at this point in the poem) addressee(s), a ritual to enable 'go[ing] on forgetting all your life'. Here passive forgetfulness turns into the activity of forgetting, denial into confirmation. The speaker thus early in the poem finds himself in mysterious collusion with his subject, as the stunned style testifies, and as becomes explicit by the end of the poem.

But for the time being, the 'you' are war widows, and the 'ritual' is 'the Widow's Shuttle', the visit 'once or twice a year' to 'the eloquence of young cemeteries', where it is 'comforting' 'To get together and forget the old times'—an acutely underspoken collocation of 'get' and 'forget' that turns the act of forgetting into a conspiracy. The collocation is part of the scenario in which, as Robinson again explains, the visit to the cemetery is fused 'with a recreation of the euphemistic fictions with which Jewish deportations to the gas chambers were veiled by the Nazis'.[31] Nazi victim and contemporary war widow merge in lines that, with cryptic poise, conflate the deceptive 'routine'—to use Hill's word from 'September Song'—of present-day Germany with that of the Holocaust:

> Here comes the driver, flicking a toothpick into the gutter,
> His tongue still searching between his teeth.
> See, he has not noticed you. No one has noticed you.
> It will pass, young lady, it will pass.

Sinisterly uncaring nonchalance hovers over the toothpick and the searching tongue, the latter detail just missing metaphorical euphemism for the speaker's, and the reader's, enquiry. And, with masterful economy, the sentence 'See, he has not noticed you' captures the visible absence, or the invisible presence, of the past from which contemporary society has barely emerged. The 'it' that floats back into the poem here—'It will pass, young lady, it will pass'—encompasses resentment, memory, conspiratorial silence, the fact of the Holocaust, and the whole gamut of emotions belonging to victim, perpetrator, and onlooker. The lines are the mirror image of the sentence in 'September Song': 'Not forgotten | or passed over at the proper time.'[32]

---

[31] Ibid. 4.   [32] Hill, 'September Song', 67.

As the poem says later, 'But come. Grief must have its term? Guilt too, then', but with how much conviction, or collusion, is impossible to say. Who is the speaker of 'But come', who the addressee? Is the poet-enquirer asking for, or being asked for, indulgence; is the reader? Is this deception or self-deception? As the next line puts it, 'there is no limit to the resourcefulness of recollection'. And the poem ends where it began, but with the silence more absolute and more conspiratorial, encompassing not just the society that perpetrated the Holocaust, but all who attempt to bear witness, to 'enquire':

> His wife nods, and a secret smile,
> Like a breeze with enough strength to carry one dry leaf
> Over two pavingstones, passes from chair to chair.
> Even the enquirer is charmed.

Even as he admits to this enchantment, the poet-enquirer is himself charmed into writing these seductively conspiratorial lines, and the reader into relishing the conspiracy. The precision is fake, or at any rate precise only verbally: 'one leaf, two pavingstones', sounds better than 'one leaf, three pavingstones', for instance. It is a question of style. But then, as Fenton's poetry demonstrates again and again, style means so much more than itself: even the reader is charmed. At the end of the poem, that impersonal pronoun returns with renewed emphasis and inscrutability, reinforced by the entirely monosyllabic context:

> It is not what he wants to know.
> It is what he wants not to know.
> It is not what they say.
> It is what they do not say.

The fact of silence becomes the absolute of this poem. What is known and what is said, and what is not known and what is not said, by enquirer and by those enquired of, by poet, by speaker, and by reader, are reduced to an absolute conundrum whose only certainty is this 'it' that refuses to yield up anything other than its own intransigence—and the poetry which, seductively, conveys that intransigence.

'A German Requiem' makes remarkable play of the fact that 'when so many had died, so many and at such speed, | There were no cities waiting for the victims'. Here literal displacement provides ample material out of which the poet can work up metaphorical parallels for social and psychological displacement. 'The eloquence of young cemeteries' is literally, as well as emotionally, true, for under these circumstances identities could, it seems, be preserved only in a macabrely literal fashion: 'They unscrewed the name-plates from the shattered doorways | And carried them away with the coffins.' One can sense Fenton's quirky imagination homing in on such a fact. It becomes the occasion for ingenious, but at the same time disorientatingly plangent, sardonic humour: an 'uncle's grave informed you that he lived on the third floor, left. | You were asked please to ring, and he would come down in the lift'—at which point the poem performs a remarkable change of register, from grimly comic to sombre, which, like Marvell's 'The grave's a fine and private place, | But none I think do there embrace',[33] gives graveyard humour a new lease of life. The poet picks up the phrase 'he would come down' and extemporizes on it in a brief section all to itself:

> Would come down, would ever come down
> With a smile like thin gruel, and never too much to say.
> How he shrank through the years.
> How you towered over him in the narrow cage.
> How he shrinks now . . .

The scenario retains an ominous mysteriousness, the relationship between uncle and niece (if they are indeed still the two figures here) unclear but silent and evidently distant, 'the narrow cage', literally the lift, taking on a sinister post-Holocaust inflection, the man's Third Reich employment unspoken and no doubt unspeakable. But the expression of all this is arrestingly haunted, a lyric space in the poem comparable to that created by 'Death by Water' in *The Waste Land*. The physical 'shrinking', which mutates into temporal, psychological, and judgemental diminishment, is accompanied by the haunting diminuendo of the reiterated 'how' which prevents, or rather transcends, the partisan. Bewilderment and sympathy here mingle in our recognition of the woman.

Mention of *The Waste Land* brings home the fact that the poetry of 'A German Requiem' insists, as does Eliot's poem, on being *heard*—even if only by the mind's ear. In this respect it represents a retreat from postmodernism to high modernism, many of whose practitioners wrote poetry as if they wanted to believe that its lyricism could resist, even as it demonstrated, the radical uncertainties of contemporary life, a belief nowhere more prevalent than in *The Waste Land*. Fenton's poem is able to rescue from the memory of war and its eloquent cemeteries nothing more, but also nothing less, than such plangent and vertiginous utterances as 'Would come down, would ever come down', a fragment shored against the ruins of the Second World War as haunting as, for instance, the sentence from *The Waste Land*'s 'Death by Water', 'A current under sea | Picked his bones in whispers',[34] which Eliot shored against the First. If Fenton's approach teeters on the edge of being 'more than enough', that is something the poetry knows and therefore guards against. The poetry gives a voice to the inscrutability of history without letting it become anything other than inscrutable. For this reason 'A German Requiem' is the great poem of its age, just as *The Waste Land* is of its.

---

[33] Andrew Marvell, 'To his Coy Mistress', in *The Complete Poems*, ed. Elizabeth Story Donno (Harmondsworth: Penguin, 1972), 51.
[34] Eliot, *The Waste Land*, in *Complete Poems and Plays*, 71.

CHAPTER 31

....

BRITISH HOLOCAUST POETRY: SONGS OF EXPERIENCE

....

CLAIRE M. TYLEE

In the twentieth century, the mass, indiscriminate slaughter facilitated by industrialized warfare provoked a crisis in representation: obscene terrains of filthy, traumatized humans living with the moribund amongst the putrescent remains of unsanctified corpses challenged the basic decorum of civilization. Artistic conventions and discourses cultivated to transmit civilized values were themselves tainted and incapacitated for dealing with such abject areas of experience. As the American-Israeli historian Omer Bartov has expressed it, such places resist even the appellation 'hellish'. Hell is conceived of in the Western tradition as ruled by strict laws and divine logic to be a punishment for sinners: 'The landscapes of World War One and the Holocaust, on the other hand, are the domain of the innocent, inhabited by souls who never expected to end up in them, and conforming to no rational plan or logic decipherable by their victims.'[1] The problem of

---

[1] Omer Bartov, 'The European Imagination in the Age of Total War', in *Murder in Our Midst: The Holocaust, Industrial Killing, and Representation* (New York: Oxford University Press, 1996), 33. Confirming the continuity that Bartov identifies between the First World War and the Holocaust, the historian Jay Winter argues that 'what the 1914–18 war did was to make [those] crimes against humanity possible...the war opened a doorway to brutality' through which men such as the commandant of Auschwitz 'willingly passed' (Winter, *The Great War and the Shaping of the Twentieth Century* (Harmondsworth: Penguin, 1996), 399).

finding adequate forms of expression itself became a theme of writing about the Western Front in the First World War. Poets tried to express the inchoate horrors paradoxically or ironically. Any elevated or metaphorical language was called into question by poets like Wilfred Owen, Siegfried Sassoon, and Edmund Blunden, who sarcastically opposed the use of classical war rhetoric.[2] The whole linguistic crisis, exacerbated by wartime propaganda, was eloquently summed up by Ernest Hemingway in *A Farewell to Arms*. There Lt Henry is 'embarrassed by' abstract words such as 'glory', 'honour', and 'sacrifice', which are themselves what he finds *obscene* 'beside the concrete names of villages, the numbers of roads, the names of rivers, the numbers of regiments and the dates'.[3]

The crisis worsened in the course of the century. We use concrete names such as 'Passchendaele', 'Guernica', 'Hiroshima', 'Auschwitz', 'Mai Lai', or 'Szrebrenica' to stand baldly for atrocious facts that are incommensurate with either the language of everyday experience or the exalted oratory of war. Nevertheless, as postmodern theorists such as Lyotard have argued, we must remember such events if we are to have an adequate sense of humanity and cultural identity. Yet the events of the Holocaust alluded to by the words 'Auschwitz' or 'Treblinka' are said to present a specific dilemma. According to survivors like Elie Wiesel, the *univers concentrationnaire* created by Nazism was unique and incomprehensible: 'Auschwitz defies imagination and perception; it submits only to memory.... Between the dead and the rest of us there exists an abyss that no talent can comprehend.'[4] That abyss cannot be bridged. Primo Levi agreed: 'We the survivors are not the true witnesses.... We survivors are only an anomalous minority who did not touch bottom. Those who did, who saw the Gorgon, have not returned to tell about it.'[5] If that world was indecipherable to its victims, and unseen by its survivors, it would seem even more impossible for outsiders to re-create it in art or translate its experience into language. This appears to justify Theodor Adorno's dictum that to attempt to write lyric poetry after Auschwitz would itself be a kind of barbarism.[6]

Nevertheless, to remain silent about the Holocaust would not only confirm the exclusion of its victims from European culture, and thus be complicit with Nazi policies; silence would risk repetition of the evil. In 1995 Andreas Huyssen cited Primo Levi to support his view that, since 'the Third Reich waged an obsessive war

---

[2] See John Silkin (ed.), *The Penguin Book of First World War Poetry* (Harmondsworth: Penguin, 1979) for examples of relevant poems by Wilfred Owen, Edmund Blunden, and Siegfried Sassoon, especially Sassoon's 'The rank stench of their bodies haunts me yet' (pp. 123–4).

[3] Ernest Hemingway, *A Farewell to Arms* (London: Penguin, 1929), 143–4.

[4] Elie Wiesel, *From the Kingdom of Memory: Reminiscences* (New York: Summit, 1990), 194. See also Andreas Huyssen, *Twilight Memories: Marking Time in a Culture of Amnesia* (London: Routledge, 1995), 257.

[5] Primo Levi, *The Drowned and the Saved*, trans. R. Rosenthal (New York: Vintage, 1989), 63–4.

[6] Theodor W. Adorno, 'Cultural Criticism and Society', in *Prisms*, trans. Samuel and Shierry Weber (Cambridge, Mass.: MIT Press, 1981), 34. Adorno later modified this stance; having read Paul Celan's work, he allowed for the necessity of poetry to express suffering.

against memory, practicing "an Orwellian falsification of memory, falsification of reality, negation of reality"... fifty years after the notorious Wannsee Conference at which the Final Solution was first given political and bureaucratic shape, the Holocaust and its memory still stand as a test case for the humanist and universalist claims of Western civilization'.[7] As Wiesel admitted, 'The holocaust in its enormity defies language and art, and yet both must be used to tell the tale, the tale that must be told.'[8] Echoing Hemingway, the Holocaust survivor Ruth Kluger has claimed that we must 'start with what is left: the names of places';[9] these are like the concrete piers of a destroyed bridge, all that remains to enable us to connect with the past and the dead. But now that even such signals as names risk collapse into clichés, how can we renew their significance? Poetry aims to restore meaning by provoking its readers to construct imaginary connections.

Thus in 1971, Harold Fisch ignored Adorno's viewpoint in his discussion of 1950–1960s Holocaust poetry by two British Jews.[10] One, Nathaniel Tarn, had responded with Hasidic inspiration in such poems as 'The Master of the Name in his Privy'. The other is the better-known Emanuel Litvinoff. Fisch quotes from Litvinoff's 1952 poem 'To T. S. Eliot' to demonstrate how 'partly due to the memory of the Holocaust which has seared itself into the consciousness of all, the non-Jew is now called to judgement'. Claiming Bleistein as his relative, in a parody of Eliot's anti-Semitic poetry, Litvinoff delivered what Fisch called 'an angry but dignified rebuke', imagining himself walking there when

> the smoke drifting over Treblinka
> reeked of the smouldering ashes of children,
> I thought what an angry poem
> you would have made of it, given the pity.[11]

By 1995, Hilda Schiff was able to compile an international anthology of Holocaust poetry. Her introduction acknowledged the problems. The aesthetics of traditional poetry could not cope, could it? Certainly, 'Beauty was *not* truth, as Keats had

---

[7] Huyssen, *Twilight Memories*, 251. Huyssen quotes Levi, *The Drowned and the Saved*, 31.

[8] Wiesel, quoted in Herbert Muschamp, 'Shaping a Monument to Memory', *New York Times*, 11 Apr. 1993, sect. 2, 1.

[9] Ruth Kluger, *The Landscape of Memory: A Holocaust Girlhood Remembered* (London: Bloomsbury, 2003), 74–5.

[10] Harold Fisch, *The Dual Image: A Study of the Jew in English Literature* (London: World Jewish Library, 1971), 108–9.

[11] Emanuel Litvinoff, 'To T. S. Eliot', in Peter Lawson (ed.), *Passionate Renewal: Jewish Poetry in Britain since 1945: An Anthology* (Nottingham: Five Leaves Press, 2001), 235–6. Lawson repeats (pp. 17–20) the story that surrounds this poem, which Litvinoff wrote for an ICA event in 1952 after Eliot had republished in *Selected Poems* his early anti-Semitic poetry of the 1920s, including 'Burbank with a Baedeker: Bleistein with a Cigar'. Litvinoff had just started to read 'To T. S. Eliot' when Eliot entered the room. Dannie Abse recalled Eliot 'putting his head down' afterwards. In the 1990s Michael Rosen ridiculed George Macbeth's defence of Eliot's anti-Semitism as normal for its period in 'English Literature': 'Our lives are so much the richer | For reading English literature' (in Lawson (ed.), *Passionate Renewal*, 272).

averred, nor was truth beauty.'[12] Furthermore, like British Great War propaganda, Nazism itself seemed to have voided metaphorical discourse of meaning when, for instance, in a notorious speech Himmler urged his SS officers to remember that the slaughter of the innocent was 'a glorious page' in Germany's history.[13] Yet, agreeing with Lyotard, Schiff also forcibly stated the case for our need of poetry if we are to 'reach out imaginatively to the experience of other individuals', or at the very least to bear witness.[14] This is a view that has been seconded by other critics such as Inga Clendinnen, who refers to the philosopher Richard Rorty for support.[15] Schiff's anthology can be regarded as primary evidence for the continuing debates as to whether Holocaust poetry is or is not possible, what kinds of response it can accommodate, and how our sensibilities may fail when confronted with such enormity as the systematic dehumanization of whole peoples, including women and children.

So, what might we mean by 'Holocaust poetry'? This will certainly depend on what is now meant by the sign, 'The Holocaust'. Although many Holocaust poems are included in anthologies of Second World War poetry,[16] the two concepts are not coterminous in space or time. Not only did the field of the Second World War extend, as far as the British were concerned, to North Africa and South-East Asia, but the racist and political policies that were fundamental to Nazism and to the Holocaust commenced as soon as Hitler came to power in 1933. Holocaust literature therefore rightly includes poetry written about events before Britain declared war in 1939, such as W. H. Auden's 'Refugee Blues'.[17] Furthermore, although we might say that the subject-matter of poetry written about the Second World War would extend beyond the liberation of the Nazi extermination camps in early 1945, spread to the Far East and to the defeat of Japan later in 1945, and

---

[12] Hilda Schiff, 'Introduction', in *idem* (ed.), *Holocaust Poetry* (London: Harper Collins, 1995), p. xx.

[13] Heinrich Himmler, speech to SS-Gruppenführer in Posnan, 4 Oct. 1943, in Steve Hochstadt (ed.), *Sources of the Holocaust* (Basingstoke: Palgrave, 2004), 163–5.

[14] Schiff, 'Introduction', pp. xiv and xxii.

[15] Inga Clendinnen, *Reading the Holocaust* (Cambridge: Cambridge University Press, 1999), 163–4.

[16] e.g. Ronald Blythe (ed.), *Writing the War: Stories, Poems and Essays of 1939–45* (Harmondsworth: Penguin, 1966), contains Sidney Keyes's poem 'Europe's Prisoners' and Stephen Spender's 'Memento'; Catherine Reilly's anthology of poetry from the First and Second World Wars, *The Virago Book of Women's War Poetry and Verse* (London: Virago, 1997), contains Holocaust poems by Audrey Beecham, Karen Gershon, Lotte Kramer, Erica Marx, Evangeline Paterson, and Elizabeth Wyse; Hugh Haughton (ed.), *Second World War Poems* (London: Faber, 2004), includes Paul Celan's 'Death Fugue', Nelly Sachs's 'Oh the Chimneys', Lura Krugman Gurdus's 'Majdanek', and poems by Primo Levi, Dan Pagis, Janos Pilinsky, Miklos Radnoti, and Tadeusz Różewicz. One poem each by Gershon and Kramer appear in Anne Harvey (ed.), *In Time of War* (London: Blackie, 1987).

[17] In an attempt to display the roots of the Holocaust in anti-Semitism, *The Holocaust for Beginners* follows Raul Hilberg in his 3-vol. *The Destruction of the European Jews* (New York: Holmes and Meier, 1985) by tracing the Holocaust back at least to the Crusades of 1096. See Haim Bresheeth, Stuart Hood, and Litza Jansz, *The Holocaust For Beginners* (Cambridge: Icon, 1994), 5–7. Martin Gilbert traces 'the first steps to iniquity' to Martin Luther's 'Honest Advice' in 1543 (Gilbert, *The Holocaust and the Jewish Tragedy* (London: Collins, 1986), 19).

could include the Nuremberg trials of 1945–6, the subject-matter of Holocaust poetry also includes the Eichmann trial in Jerusalem in 1961. (So Schiff includes Denise Levertov's startling poem 'During the Eichmann Trial', but also Elaine Feinstein's 'Annus Mirabilis 1989' when the Berlin Wall came down, as evidence that anti-Semitism, that 'old monster', was still flourishing behind the Iron Curtain in 1979.[18]) By bringing to the surface of public consciousness what had been largely concealed during the War and repressed afterwards, the kidnapping and trial of Adolf Eichmann informed a new generation about Nazi war crimes and led to a reconceptualization of the War in Europe and of 'crimes against humanity'. In particular, it drew attention away from the *concentration* camps liberated by the Allies in the West, such as Dachau and Belsen, which were horrific enough, to the hidden *extermination* camps that the Russians had liberated in the East, such as Auschwitz. (Like the ghettos and labour camps, they were, of course, all death camps.) Until then, the term 'holocaust' (from the Greek for 'whole burnt offering') had been newly used to indicate fear of nuclear destruction; from then on it came to imply genocide, especially the 'Final Solution' of eradicating Jews from Europe by gassing and cremating them. Taking place in the new State of Israel, the trial empowered Jews in the diaspora to investigate the nature of anti-Semitism and the near eradication of European Jewry, particularly as they affected Britain.[19]

New histories made clear that, apart from political opponents, the particular target of Nazism was people defined as Jewish, and therefore subhuman, to be exterminated like vermin. Other groups were also systematically defined, persecuted, and murdered, including Gypsies, homosexuals, political opponents, and people categorized as being deficient in various ways. Slavs were considered inferior, and were shot or condemned to slow death through slave labour. However, if it is a feature of Romany culture that the past should be forgotten, it is almost a defining feature of Jewish culture that the past should be recorded.[20] Whereas we have next to no literature concerning the mass murder of at least 250,000 Gypsies in Europe, there has been a huge effort to document the genocide of more than 6 million Jews (about two-thirds of the European total), for which the Hebrew term Shoah ('a terrible wind') has been reserved by Jews themselves. Furthermore, as Michael R. Marrus concludes, 'the Nazis' assault upon Jewry differed from the campaigns against other peoples and groups', since Nazi ideology required the total extirpation of the Jews and of their culture. He quotes Goebbels: 'The Jews are no people like any other people, but

[18] Levertov's poem bears comparison with Primo Levi's 'For Adolf Eichmann', in Haughton (ed.), *Second World War Poems*, 146, and Michael Hamburger's 'In a Cold Season', in Lawson (ed.), *Passionate Renewal*, 117–20. See also Audrey Beecham, 'Eichmann', in Reilly (ed.), *Virago Book of Women's War Poetry and Verse*, 147.

[19] See e.g. Gilbert, *Holocaust and the Jewish Tragedy*; Tony Kushner, *The Holocaust and the Liberal Imagination* (Oxford: Blackwell, 1994); and David Cesarani, *Arthur Koestler: The Homeless Mind* (London: Heinemann, 1998).

[20] See James E. Young, 'Introduction', in Thomas Riggs (ed.), *Reference Guide to Holocaust Literature* (London: St James' Press, 2002), p. xxxi; and Clendinnen, *Reading the Holocaust*, 6–8.

a pseudo-people welded together by hereditary criminality. . . . The annihilation of Jewry is no loss to humanity, but just as useful as capital punishment.'[21]

It is thus inevitable that a study of Holocaust poetry should centre on writing by Jewish authors. A sense of personal identification with Jewish victims of the Holocaust might even be said to characterize post-war Jewish ethnicity in Britain. The poet Dannie Abse expressed this in his poem, 'The White Balloon': 'Auschwitz made me | more of a Jew than Moses did.'[22] We might expect a difference between poems by Jewish and by non-Jewish authors, who were and are not threatened in the same way, or at least in the reception of their writing by Jewish and non-Jewish readers. The context for our response to the English Protestant poet Geoffrey Hill is different from the context of responses to the British-German poets of Jewish descent Michael Hamburger or Karen Gershon. That difference goes some way to explain the controversy over the use of Holocaust imagery by Sylvia Plath, an Anglo-American of German Protestant descent.

British poetry finds itself in a peculiar situation *vis-`a-vis* the Holocaust.[23] The authenticity of personal testimony is highly regarded in Holocaust literature.[24] Yet, apart from deportation and slave labour camps in the occupied Channel Islands or the bombing of civilian populations, there and on the mainland, the major Nazi atrocities did not take place on British soil. They were directly witnessed by few people who were or who became British. A notable exception is the British writer Mervyn Peake, who was present at the liberation of Belsen as a war artist. He wrote about the inadequacy of his immediate reaction of using aesthetics as a shield from the merciless reality, in his poem 'The Consumptive, Belsen 1945'.[25] There are notable British Holocaust prose memoirs by Kitty Hart-Moxon, Hugo Gryn, and Anita Lasker-Wallfisch, all survivors of Auschwitz (and there have been attempts to re-create Holocaust experience in fiction written at second hand by, for instance,

---

[21] Joseph Goebbels, quoted in Michael R. Marrus, *The Holocaust in History* (Harmondsworth: Penguin, 1993), 24–5.

[22] Dannie Abse, 'The White Balloon', in *Selected Poems* (Harmondsworth: Penguin, 1994), 209–10; compare this with his earlier 'Red Balloon' (p. 40). Elaine Feinstein also stated that she really became a Jew and her sense of security was exploded 'once and for all' when she learned about the Holocaust (Feinstein, 'Elaine Feinstein Writes', in *The Bloodaxe Book of Contemporary Women Poets: Eleven British Writers*, ed. Jenni Couzyn (Newcastle-upon-Tyne: Bloodaxe, 1985), 114).

[23] The situation in 1992 was discussed by Jon Harris, 'An Elegy for Myself: British Poetry and the Holocaust', *English*, 41 (1992), 213–33. Harris appends a list of Holocaust poetry.

[24] This is partly because of the continuance of Holocaust denial perpetrated by pseudo-historians like David Irving, but patiently challenged by researchers such as Deborah Lipstadt. As I prepared this paper in November 2005, Irving was being prosecuted in Austria for the crime, and a leading German Holocaust denier, Ernst Zündel, had been extradited from Canada to go on trial in Germany for racial hatred.

[25] Mervyn Peake, 'The Consumptive, Belsen 1945', in Alan Sinclair (ed.), *The War Decade: An Anthology of the 1940s* (London: Hamish Hamilton, 1989), 268–9. The importance of that experience to Peake's fictional writing has been widely discussed; see e.g. Alice Mills, 'Holocaust Peake', *Peake Studies*, 5/4 (1998), 28–42.

Bernice Rubens, D. M. Thomas, and Caryl Phillips).[26] However, we have no British camp survivors who have written as eloquently of their suffering in either poetry or prose as the German Jew Paul Celan, the French resistance fighter Charlotte Delbo, the Italian scientist of Jewish descent Primo Levi, the Romanian Jew Dan Pagis, or the Hungarian-Jewish teenager Elie Wiesel. Indeed, Harold Bloom has claimed that whereas writers such as Celan, Wiesel, and Nelly Sachs 'can touch the horror with authority . . . British and American writers need to avoid it, as we have no warrant for imagination in that most terrible of areas'.[27]

We need to expand our notion of what constitutes Holocaust poetry beyond such authoritative, first-hand witness of the camps if we are to include many of the writings selected by Schiff. It may be that British poets cannot claim the close personal responsibility felt by, for instance, the Russian Yevgeni Yevtushenko over the massacre at Babii Yar—'I am | each old man | here shot dead'[28]—or Bertolt Brecht over the destruction of German culture, or the Pole, Tadeusz Różewicz, at the museum in Auschwitz. That does not mean that British poets have felt no responsibility to bear secondary witness. Quite the contrary. Nor was the trauma of the Holocaust restricted to those who were confined on the Continent. During the 1930s, Britain took in refugees. In particular, the *Kindertransport* rescue scheme brought 10,000 children to Britain in the last ten months before the War. Novels, plays, and memoirs have been written about their experience of Nazism, especially the traumatic loss of their parents and family in Europe, presenting that as an integral part of Holocaust cruelty.[29] For Jewish *Kinder*-poets such as Karen

---

[26] Kitty Hart, *Return to Auschwitz* (London: Sidgwick & Jackson, 1981; 1st pub. as *I Am Alive*, 1961); Hugo Gryn, *Chasing Shadows* (London: Penguin, 2001); Anita Lasker-Wallfisch, *Inherit the Truth, 1939–1945* (London: Giles de la Mare, 1996); Bernice Rubens, *Brothers* (London: Hamish Hamilton, 1983); D. M. Thomas, *The White Hotel* (Harmondsworth: Penguin, 1981); Caryl Phillips, *The Nature of Blood* (London: Faber, 1997). And see the study by Sue Vice, *Holocaust Fiction* (London: Routledge, 2000), for the controversy surrounding Thomas's use of authentic Holocaust testimony in his novel.

[27] Harold Bloom, quoted in Susan Gubar, *Poetry after Auschwitz: Remembering What One Never Knew* (Bloomington, Ind.: Indiana University Press, 2003), 9. Despite Bloom's opinion, the Jewish-German poet Nelly Sachs spent the war in Sweden, so might be judged to have no more first-hand authority than Litvinoff.

[28] Yevgeni Yevtushenko, 'Babii Yar', trans. George Reavey, in Schiff (ed.), *Holocaust Poetry*, 92–4.

[29] That number was less than 1 percent of the 1.5 million Jewish children who were slaughtered by the Nazis. There is now an extensive literature about the *Kindertransport*, including Karen Gershon's ground-breaking collective memoir, *We Came as Children* (London: Gollancz, 1966); Lore Segal's autobiographical novel, *Other People's Houses* (New York: New Press, 1991); fictional novels by Anita Brookner, *Latecomers* (London: Jonathan Cape, 1988), and Caryl Phillips, *Higher Ground* (New York: Viking, 1989); and Diane Samuels's play, *Kindertransport* (London: Oberon, 1995); as well as various documentary films. For longer bibliographies, see Peter Lawson, 'Karen Gershon', in S. Lillian Kremer (ed.), *Holocaust Literature: An Encyclopedia of Writers and their Works* (London: Routledge, 2001), 415–19; and in the same book, Claire M. Tylee, 'Diane Samuels' (pp. 1082–5), and 'Lore Segal' (pp. 1135–7). For a discussion of Gershon's prose about refugee experience, see Christophe Houswitschka, ' "What I was going to be I already was: a writer": Karen Gershon and the Collective Memory of the Kindertransport', in Ulrike Behlau and Bernhard Reitz (eds.), *Jewish Women's Writing of the 1990s and beyond in Great Britain and the United States* (Mainz: WVT, 2004), 73–85.

Gershon (*née* Käthe Löwenthal), Lotte Kramer, Gerda Mayer, and Anne Ranasinghe (*née* Annelise Katz), it is their major theme. To Michael Hamburger, who escaped to Britain with his German-Jewish parents in 1933, we are indebted for not only his own poetry but the magnificent translations of major Holocaust poets such as Paul Celan and Nelly Sachs. Other Jewish poets born in Britain such as Dannie Abse, Elaine Feinstein, and Denise Levertov, like Litvinoff, write as survivors who would surely have perished if Germany had invaded. Emanuel Litvinoff might speak for all these British-Jewish writers when he says, 'My parents' flight from Russia saved me, my seven brothers and one sister, from the holocausts of famine and Nazism. I am connected to these tragedies with the guilt and obsession of a survivor and they inform almost everything I have written.'[30] As Harold Fisch recognized, the sense of being a survivor (even if at one remove) does give such poets authority and a right to speak. Some have felt it to be an obligation.

Non-Jewish British poets, too, who lived through the time, have written in response to the Holocaust as politically engaged observers, such as W. H. Auden, whose long-term partner was Jewish and who, like Stephen Spender, witnessed Nazi Germany in the 1930s.[31] Edward Bond, whose wife is Austrian, claims in 'How We See' that 'after Treblinka' we see racism differently, and in 'If' he invites us to imagine 'if Auschwitz had been in Hampshire', in order to argue that 'We must create a new culture'.[32] Alongside such bystanders are other poets who have alluded to the Holocaust extensively. Notorious amongst these is Sylvia Plath, whose work has given rise to one of the major controversies concerning the (mis)appropriation of Holocaust imagery for other purposes. Tony Harrison has also been criticized for insensitivity, whereas Geoffrey Hill, like Peter Porter and Thom Gunn, appears to have enabled readers to 'reach out imaginatively' in insightful ways, as Schiff demanded.[33]

Poets of the next generation, born after the War, seem to have regarded their obligations differently. For instance, James Fenton and Tom Paulin have each produced a sequence of poems that approach the Holocaust circumspectly.[34] Though remarkably different in tone—Fenton's poetry being calm and detached, Paulin's iconoclastic and at times scurrilous—they share similar aims. Fenton's epigraph from Hobbes's *Leviathan* indicates what they have in common:

After great distance of time, our imagination of the Past is weak; and wee lose . . . many particular Circumstances. This *decaying sense*, when we would express the thing it self,

[30] Litvinoff, cover of *Journey through a Small Planet* (London: Clark, 1993).
[31] History has caught up with his 1930s sonnet XVI of 'In Time of War', in which the places Auden points to as real examples of 'Where life is evil now', are 'Nanking. Dachau' (in *The English Auden: Poems, Essays and Dramatic Writings 1927–1939*, ed. Edward Mendelson (London: Faber, 1977), 257).
[32] Edward Bond, quoted in Schiff (ed.), *Holocaust Poetry*, 155 and 156.
[33] Poems by Porter, Gunn, and Hill appear in Schiff's anthology. Harrison is extensively discussed in Antony Rowland, *Tony Harrison and the Holocaust* (Liverpool: Liverpool University Press, 2001) and again in *idem*, *Holocaust Poetry* (Edinburgh: Edinburgh University Press, 2005).
[34] James Fenton, 'A German Requiem', in *The Memory of War and Children in Exile: Poems 1968–83* (Harmondsworth: Penguin, 1983), 9–19; Tom Paulin, *The Invasion Handbook* (London: Faber, 2002).

(I mean *Fancy* it selfe,) wee call *Imagination*, as I said before: But when we would express the *decay*, and signifie that the Sense is fading, old, and past, it is called Memory. So that *Imagination* and *Memory* are but one thing.

Fenton's 'A German Requiem' (1983) is concerned with the collective rituals of oblivion whereby Germany was keeping recollection of the Holocaust at bay, and dramatizes that wilful amnesia. Paulin's *The Invasion Handbook* (2002) tries to reveal the processes of deception and evasion at work in the British collective memory of what led from the First World War to the Battle of Britain, paying due regard to the quiet force of anti-Semitism. If early on, the problem lay in breaking silence in order to raise people's awareness of what the Holocaust involved, to engage their imaginative sympathies, by the 1990s, as Andreas Huyssen demonstrated, the major problem had become the hackneyed use not only of names and places but of Holocaust iconography, especially in films and on television, with the consequent danger of vacuous trivialization.[35] As racism surfaced again in Europe, Fenton and Paulin were trying to find new ways to refresh our culture.

Although so many British poets have written in response to the Holocaust, perhaps the term 'British Holocaust poet' should be reserved for the Jewish poets who directly suffered persecution under the Nazis and who came to terms with their trauma through their poetry: the *Kindertransport* poets Karen Gershon, Lotte Kramer, and Gerda Mayer.[36] Nevertheless, in order to characterize their verse, it is helpful to place it against the poetry written by Gentiles and by Jewish writers who were also survivors, but in a secondary sense, since they were born in Britain. It is plausibly argued that other British poets have been influenced by the Continental Holocaust poetry they may have read or even translated, particularly Celan; yet this does not seem to be true of the *Kindertransport* poets. Rather, their models belong to an anglophone tradition, and it is interesting to speculate why.

Obviously we cannot deal here with every English poem related to the Holocaust. However, there are two poets born between the wars like the *Kinder*-transportees, who have written extensively in profound response to the Holocaust and whose poetry has created critical controversy: Sylvia Plath and Geoffrey Hill. I want to place alongside Plath's feminist rage and Hill's humanist compassion the cynical Marxist work of a poet born after the war, Tom Paulin. Paulin's writing has responded to the postmodern condition of the early twenty-first century when the Holocaust has been commercially exploited almost to the point of triviality. Like Walter Benjamin's Angel,[37] Paulin looks back at the wreckage of European history from the Treaty of Versailles onwards to 1941, and situates his own response to the Jewish genocide

---

[35] See Huyssen, *Twilight Memories*, 251–2.

[36] I take the term from Peter Lawson's article 'Three Kindertransport Poets: Karen Gershon, Gerda Mayer and Lotte Kramer', in Behlau and Reitz (eds.), *Jewish Women's Writing of the 1990s and Beyond*, 87–94.

[37] Walter Benjamin, 'Theses on the Philosophy of History', in *Illuminations*, trans. Harry Zohn, ed. Hannah Arendt (London: Jonathan Cape, 1970), 259.

within a polyphony of cultural conflict. The poetry of these three writers, Plath, Hill, and Paulin is loud, confident, public verse, and they are concerned to comment on, and take issue with, a common Western culture, especially their Christian background, and they self-consciously wrestle with their poetic heritage in order to do so. By contrast, the writing of the British-Jewish Holocaust poets is low-key, deeply personal, revealing individual experience and grief, and, I would argue, it tends to be ambivalent about English culture rather than frankly critical of it. They vary from each other, of course, but share a common straightforwardness that at first appears almost naive by comparison with the company in which they find themselves in the anthologies compiled by Schiff and Lawson. Whilst they display less overt difficulty or sophistication than the three better-known poets, it is interesting to investigate how far their unassuming stance might be said deliberately to conceal their difference but still constitute an implicit reproach to their host country.

Despite the fact that Harold Bloom's view that British and American writers should avoid the Holocaust might have been used as an alibi, such writers are nevertheless confronted with Arthur Koestler's stinging charges in 1943–4 that 'matter-of-fact unimaginativeness has become a kind of Anglo-Saxon racial myth',[38] and that 'there is no excuse for you—for it is your duty to know and to be haunted by your knowledge. As long as you don't feel, against reason and independently of reason, ashamed to be alive while others are put to death and guilty, sick, humiliated, because you were spared, you will remain what you are: An accomplice by omission.'[39] Sylvia Plath (who, unlike Hill, is pointedly excluded from S. Lillian Kremer's encyclopaedia, *Holocaust Literature*, although included in Hilda Schiff's anthology) was among the first English-speaking poets to take up Koestler's gauntlet. Refusing to be an ignorant accomplice, she poured out a stream of impassioned poetry inspired by Holocaust imagery in the months before her suicide. In a BBC interview in 1962, she claimed her right to engage with the Holocaust because of her German and Austrian background, which made her concern with the camps 'uniquely intense'.[40] This avowal took courage. The hostility to Germans and Austrians which German-speaking Jewish refugees remembered encountering in England during the War did not cease on VE day in 1945. The revelations of the war trials in Nuremberg and Jerusalem seemed to justify a wholesale anti-German prejudice which has continued to be reinforced by the dissemination of negative stereotypes through Second World War films right up to the present day.

As Tim Kendall points out, Plath was writing shortly after the Eichmann trial in 1961–2; just as the Rosenberg trial informed the imagery of her novel *The Bell Jar*,

---

[38] Arthur Koestler, 'On Disbelieving Atrocities' (1944), in *The Yogi and the Commissar and Other Essays* (London: Jonathan Cape, 1945), 96.

[39] Koestler, 'Answer to Some Inquiries', *Horizon*, 8/48 (Dec. 1943), 433. The background to this correspondence in *Horizon* is given in Mark Rawlinson, 'This Other War: British Culture and the Holocaust', *Cambridge Quarterly*, 25/1 (1996), 1–25.

[40] Sylvia Plath, in Peter Orr (ed.), *The Poet Speaks* (London: Routledge, 1966), 169.

so the poems in *Ariel* are freighted with the horror of the Eichmann revelations, long before they became clichés.[41] The most (in)famous is 'Daddy', where the addressee is a 'Panzer-man' who speaks an obscene language—German—which is an engine 'chuffing me off like a Jew. | A Jew to Dachau, Auschwitz, Belsen'.[42] The other poem widely cited in condemnation of Plath's (mis)appropriation of Holocaust imagery is 'Lady Lazarus'. In that poem Plath's poetic persona manages terrifyingly to resurrect herself, displaying her body to an indifferent audience, her 'skin | Bright as a Nazi lampshade' but crawling with worms 'like sticky pearls'. It might seem that all that would have been left in the ashes of her burnt body is Holocaust detritus: 'A cake of soap, | A wedding ring, | A gold filling'; but she warns that she will rise again, 'with my red hair | And I eat men like air'.[43] Critics of this work cite one of the instigators of the debate about Plath, George Steiner, who in 1965 wrote that artists 'commit a subtle larceny when they evoke the echoes and trappings of Auschwitz and appropriate an enormity of ready emotion to their own private design'.[44] The critical debate is now lengthy, but it depends largely on whether Plath is taken to be writing personal, confessional poetry, and means her claim to 'be a bit of a Jew' literally, or whether it is possible to interpret her poetry as drawing on her own experience to express a political response to the patriarchal ideology that is responsible for the fact that 'Every woman adores a Fascist'.

The second of the two critical extremes is exemplified in a feminist anthology edited by Sandra M. Gilbert and Susan Gubar, *The Norton Anthology of Literature by Women*: 'The mythologizing of self and family that energizes Plath's later poems has led to much critical misunderstanding. The problem with . . . a good many attacks that have been mounted against Plath is that the literary figure of "Daddy" in the poem of that name (like the father figure in *The Colossus*) is not identical with, but rather *generalized* from, Plath's literal father.'[45] The opposite extreme is to be found exemplified in a recent article by Leah Keren in *The Jewish Quarterly*, which angrily accuses Plath of 'Holocaust envy': not only did Plath appropriate Jewish suffering as a literary subject, 'in her suicide, she appropriated the Holocaust mode of death—a gas oven. . . . A powerful imagination may give Plath the right to write about the Holocaust but it does not give her the right to consider herself a Jew.'[46] Nevertheless, Keren concedes that Plath was writing at a time when Holocaust survivors were only just beginning to speak, and 'her speech, especially in the first person, made

---

[41] Tim Kendall, *Sylvia Plath: A Critical Study* (London: Faber, 2001) 55–6, 169–71.

[42] Plath, 'Daddy', in *Collected Poems*, ed. Ted Hughes (London: Faber, 1981), 222–4.

[43] Plath, 'Lady Lazarus', ibid. 244–7. The contrast with Paul Celan's 'Death Fugue' ('your golden hair Margarete | your ashen hair Shulamith') is surely no accident, nor that Plath presents her persona as a female *Luftmensch*; this is not an elegy, but a cry of rage.

[44] George Steiner, 'Dying is an Art', in *Art and Silence* (London: Faber, 1967), 324–34.

[45] Sandra M. Gilbert and Susan Gubar, in *idem* (eds.), *The Norton Anthology of Literature by Women: The Tradition in English* (New York: Norton, 1985), 2024–5.

[46] Leah Keren, 'Trying to be "A bit of a Jew": Sylvia Plath and the Holocaust Controversy', *Jewish Quarterly*, 192 (Winter 2003/4), 63–5.

other speech possible. This is not to be undervalued.' Furthermore, in Keren's opinion, few authentic Holocaust testimonies qualify as 'Art', capable of achieving more than 'mere history' by moving readers to relate emotionally to evidence of the ghettos, cattle-trucks, and camps as Plath's highly dramatic poetry does.

Susan Gubar side-stepped the issues of either Jewish or feminist identity politics in her appraisal of just what has been achieved by 'Plath's adaptation of the voices of the imagined, absent dead', pointing out that this rhetorical device of prosopopoeia (or impersonation) has been widely used in 'some of the most powerful poems about the Shoah'. Gubar argues that this tactic allows authors such as Nelly Sachs 'to conceive of subjectivity enduring beyond the concentration camp, and thereby to suggest that the anguish of the Shoah does not, and will not, dissipate'.[47] Gubar points out that in anglophone poetry this representation of a dead voice is a double conjuring trick, since English was one of the few European languages not spoken on the trains chuffing off to Auschwitz. What she does not say is that Plath's voice in 'Daddy'and 'Lady Lazarus' is a shriek of vengeance, reminding blood-sucking torturers and murderers that social retribution awaits them, as indeed it did at the Nuremberg and Eichmann trials, and prophesying (through her allusion to Coleridge's 'Kubla Khan'—'Beware, beware'[48]) that they will also be condemned through art, which they cannot ultimately destroy. This, of course, is demonstrated as true every time Plath's poetry is read. It expresses not only an undissipated anguish, but a mythological, self-replenishing fury.[49]

Plath wrote two further poems informed by Holocaust imagery: 'Mary's Song' and 'Getting There'. In the first, a young mother, like Plath herself, identifies with Mary, Mother of the Lamb of God, to envisage the holocaustal fate in store for her child. In the second, the poem's persona endures a long, nightmarish journey that impels her across Europe to an unknown destination. Using the driven experience of a woman in labour, Plath constructs an apparent allegory for poetic creation during the bewildering onrush of twentieth-century history which gave birth to her as a new poet. Gubar persuasively interprets 'Getting There' through the lens of the forced deportations by cattle train and death marches that translated the Nazis' prisoners to the new universe of the camps, where they arrived stripped of their old identity. Tim Kendall disagrees that 'Getting There' is a Holocaust poem: 'The subject of the poem is holocaust in general, not one particular holocaust.'[50] Yet in a critical study devoted to Plath he sympathetically explores her use of Holocaust

[47] Susan Gubar, 'Prosopopoeia and Holocaust Poetry in English: Sylvia Plath and her Contemporaries', *Yale Journal of Criticism*, 14/1 (2001), 192.

[48] Samuel Taylor Coleridge, 'Kubla Khan', in *Samuel Taylor Coleridge*, ed. H. J. Jackson (Oxford: Oxford University Press, 1985), 103.

[49] The continued emphasis on the pain of the victims and the grief of the survivors tends to obscure their heroic resistance (e.g. in the Warsaw Ghetto) and their retaliation once they had the chance; see e.g. the photos taken by Lee Miller at the Liberation of Dachau of the guards beaten up by the prisoners.

[50] Kendall, *Sylvia Plath*, 177.

iconography in 'Mary's Song'. He argues that in this poem 'Plath's cosmology implicates everything—the vast panorama of human history [including the burning of heretics and the extermination in the camps]—in one universal holocaust.'[51]

Antony Rowland takes issue with this in his book *Holocaust Poetry*. Accusing Plath of lacking rigour and of 'theological muddle', he finds that ' "Mary's Song" constitutes a confusion of images that does not question the ethics of representation, and its Christian framework'.[52] He justifies this by taking exception to Plath's image of the Jews' 'thick palls' that float over Poland and Germany. A normal reader would recognize the ideas latent in this phrase to be both a dark pall of smoke and the pall or funeral cloth that covers a coffin, hearse, or tomb. That cloth is a way of making sacred the taboo object of the dead body whilst symbolically hiding it from sight, so Plath's phrase implies that Poland and Germany are one huge, appalling graveyard still overshadowed by the past burning of the Jews. It seems to me perverse of Rowland to suggest that the phrase is ascribing to the Jews a Catholic priest's shoulder band (what on earth could that mean?). Rather, I hear a latent allusion to Blake's poem 'London', where he castigates this so-called Christian city for its treatment of the weak: 'the Chimney-sweeper's cry / Every black'ning Church appalls'.[53] It was surely appropriate for Plath similarly implicitly to condemn a so-called Christian country for its indecent treatment of Jewish bodies and blatant disregard of the Commandments. Her poem breathes meaning into the phrase that Gershon uses ironically when she says, ' "the appalling Jewish experience" was my own'.[54]

However, Rowland does give Plath faint praise for her 'camp poetics' (a facetious pun which implies that she is 'camping it up'), claiming that her satire in 'Lady Lazarus' is 'moving in the direction of the more self-reflexive, awkward poetics to be found in the work of Geoffrey Hill and Tony Harrison', although Rowland still confesses himself 'sometimes unclear where the unreflective reproduction of Holocaust icons ends and the satire begins' in her work.[55] 'Awkward poetics' is an aesthetic technique that Rowland defines in the course of his book as partly involving 'a self-critique which emphasizes that the post-Holocaust poet can only write self-consciously as a secondary witness of historical events in Europe'.[56] Whilst admitting that poetry always comprises 'subtle irregularities to inaugurate creative tensions', Rowland claims that, cognizant of Adorno's warning, yet recognizing the impossible necessity of representing the Holocaust, 'post-Holocaust aesthetics utilize these self-conscious moments to emphasize the specific difficulties of engaging with an event

[51] Kendall, *Sylvia Plath*, 127.   [52] Rowland, *Holocaust Poetry*, 79 and 52.
[53] William Blake, 'London', in *Complete Writings*, ed. Geoffrey Keynes (Oxford: Oxford University Press, 1966), 216.
[54] Karen Gershon, 'To My Children', in *We Came as Children* (Basingstoke: Macmillan, 1989), 176. In 'On Reading Karen Gershon's "Poems on Jewish Themes" ', Gerda Mayer teases herself about not being able to follow Gershon down into the pit of desolation, but remaining clowning about at its lip, lest she should 'NOT appal...those decent English' (Mayer, *Monkey on the Analyst's Couch* (Sunderland: Ceolfrith Press, 1980), 22).
[55] Rowland, *Holocaust Poetry*, 29.   [56] Ibid. 66.

so resistant to artistic representation'.[57] His taxonomy of awkward poetics includes embarrassed rhetoric, incongruity, paradox, the anti-redemptive, the anti-elegiac, and anti-objectivism.[58] It is particularly exemplified in the Holocaust poems of Geoffrey Hill, such as 'September Song', a work notable for its compression.[59] The power of Rowland's thesis is demonstrated by the fact that it can be fruitfully applied to poetry he does not consider, such as 'Shirking the Camps', 'Kristallnacht', and other poems in Tom Paulin's *The Invasion Handbook*.[60] Paulin's poem itself enacts the displacement activities that 'you' would distract yourself with rather than 'sing a song of Belsen'.[61] He tries to share the anger of a *Kristallnacht* survivor, but then the broken glass recalls the 'murder, theft, danger' of his own culture's history of iconoclasm. His voice trails off as he suspects 'something complicit' with fascism.[62]

As Paulin, hailing from Northern Ireland Protestantism, recognizes, it is almost impossible not to be complicit with thuggery merely by using the English language, which was imposed by force throughout the British Empire. Plath, as a nascent feminist, parodies language's bullying power by exaggerating what Gubar calls her 'Mother Goose rhymes'.[63] Yet even self-consciously 'awkward poetics' such as parody cannot altogether avoid the colonizing implications of English and its Anglican baggage. So I think Rowland's judgement that Plath's thought needs to be more rigorous is spurious. Her compression of meanings (the implicit yoking together of apparently disparate ideas in vivid imagery, as in the example discussed above) is precisely what gives her work its disturbing power. In fact, although Kendall calls Alan Sinfield's defence of Plath's poetry 'dubious' and reductive, I would agree with Sinfield's view that (amongst other aims) Plath was struggling to bring into consciousness ideas not yet fully articulated in her period,[64] particularly to understand what came to be sloganized as 'the personal is the political'. Plath's Holocaust poetry belongs to that generation of literary and theoretical writings of the 1960s and 1970s by authors such as Margaret Atwood, Eva Figes, Betty Friedan, Germaine Greer, Kate Millett, Adrienne Rich, and Fay Weldon, that gave birth to the Second Wave of the Women's Movement. The Movement not only stressed

---

[57] Ibid. 11. For a test case of Rowland's theory, a poem that does not utilize awkward poetics but attempts universalizing moral authority, and does not appear in Holocaust anthologies, see Alan Bold's 'June 1967 at Buchenwald', in Edward Lucie Smith (ed.), *British Poetry Since 1945* (Harmondsworth: Penguin, 1971), 321–4.

[58] For a full list, see Rowland, *Holocaust Poetry*, 12.

[59] Hill has published a number of poems connected with the Holocaust, including 'Of Commerce and Society', repr. in *Collected Poems* (Harmondsworth: Penguin, 1985), 46–51, and his recent *The Triumph of Love* (Harmondsworth: Penguin, 1999). These are analysed by Rowland in *Holocaust Poetry*, ch. 2, where he acknowledges the criticism by Paulin amongst others that Hill risks complacency and obscurity. Hill discussed his views on Holocaust writing in an interview with Caryl Phillips, 'The Art of Poetry LXXX', *Paris Review*, 154 (Spring 2000), 270–99.

[60] Paulin, *Invasion Handbook*, 140–1.   [61] Ibid. 40.   [62] Ibid. 131.

[63] Gubar, 'Prosopopoeia and Holocaust Poetry in English', 205.

[64] Kendall, *Sylvia Plath*, 170–1, referring to Alan Sinfield, *Literature, Politics and Culture in Post-War Britain* (Oxford: Blackwell, 1989), 224.

the political power of language itself over consciousness. It also promoted the importance of imagination and of group political consciousness raising through self-revelation. On the one hand it scrutinized the ideology implicit in popular culture such as folk-tales and fairy stories; on the other hand, it demonstrated the need to break the silence maintained over sexual abuse, taboo memories, and repressed anger, if women's decolonization was to be achieved. Feminist psychoanalytic criticism has specifically related sexual trauma to war trauma and Holocaust trauma.[65]

The repression of Holocaust experiences and of women's personal feelings was doubly stultifying for Jewish women. Despite the success of early Holocaust literature by women,[66] this was followed by a prolonged silence. Holocaust scholarship paid women's experience very little attention until Jewish feminist scholars broke ranks and started to explore gender differences in Holocaust experience and writing, and ethnic difference in feminist analysis.[67] In this respect I agree with Kerner that Plath's example of 'hysterical writing'[68] is empowering for Jewish women poets, since Plath made so clear that the subordinated and abused figure she was theatrically impersonating could be seen and heard as both Jewish and a woman. Her divided identity as both a German- and an English-speaker in 'Daddy' may have provided an especially empowering model for German-Jewish refugees. However, as with other persecuted ethnic minorities, the importance of the family to individual survival would make it difficult for Jewish women to identify with Plath's attack on 'the Father', especially since he is figured as a Nazi. That would obviously be particularly distasteful to refugees orphaned by the Nazis. Thus it is significant that none of the three *Kinder*-poets started to publish poetry about their state of alienation until well into their middle age—more than twenty years after

---

[65] See e.g. Cathy Caruth (ed.), *Trauma: Exploration and Memory* (Baltimore: Johns Hopkins University Press, 1995), and Kalí Tal, *Worlds of Hurt: Reading the Literatures of Trauma* (Cambridge: Cambridge University Press, 1996).

[66] Anne Frank's *Diary of a Young Girl* (1952) is a perennial best-seller. Early Holocaust memoirs by women include Olga Lengyel's *Five Chimneys: A Woman Survivor's True Story of Auschwitz* (1947). The silencing of Holocaust memory, particularly in Britain, and its deleterious effect on survivors, and even on the next generation, has been detailed by Anne Karpf, *The War After* (London: Heinemann, 1996).

[67] The ground-breaking study was Esther Katz and Joan Miriam Rangeley (eds.), *Proceedings of the Conference: Women Surviving the Holocaust* (New York: Institute for Research in History, 1983). The bibliography of the field is now lengthy, but see also Marlene Heinemann, *Gender and Destiny: Women Writers and the Holocaust* (Westport, Conn.: Greenwood Press, 1986), and Dalia Ofer and Lenore J. Weitzman (eds.), *Women in the Holocaust* (New Haven: Yale University Press, 1998). For an account of Jewish feminisms, see Adrienne Baker, *The Jewish Woman in Contemporary Society: Transitions and Traditions* (Basingstoke: Macmillan, 1993).

[68] I use the technical term 'hysterical writing' to indicate the productions of 'the woman writer who must speak the discourse of the hysteric, who both refuses and is totally trapped within femininity', as in Juliet Mitchell's exegesis of Julia Kristeva's feminist psychoanalytic theories in *Women: The Longest Revolution* (London: Virago, 1984).

their exile and orphaning: Gershon was the earliest, aged 36, Mayer was 43, and Kramer was 50.[69]

As Bryan Cheyette has complained in his studies of Jewish prose writers, Jewish authors in Britain are oppressed by a sense of the dominating culture: 'It is almost as if Jewish writers in Britain had to combat an all-encompassing Englishness'; but he identifies narrative strategies that they have developed 'to resist an overbearing Englishness fixed in [a particular conception of] the past'.[70] Eva Figes and Lore Segal, both child refugees from Nazified Europe, have left autobiographical accounts of the repressive effects of their English education. The native-born Elaine Feinstein overcame her problems with the English poetic tradition by learning from Ahkmatova and other Russian poets whose work she translated. However, German was the mother tongue for the majority of the *Kinder*-transportees (who tended to be assimilated Jews and not fluent in Yiddish or Hebrew). This created particular problems for them both because of the Holocaust and because of the anti-German prejudice they encountered in Britain. Kramer wrote of first being branded 'Jew' in Germany and then sneered at as 'German' in England, an experience reported by other child refugees such as Eva Figes and Sylvia Rogers.[71] As Gershon reflected in 'The Children's Exodus': 'being taught | to hate what we had loved in vain | brought us lasting injury.'[72] They were not only bound by a sense of gratitude to Britain (as Gershon mentions in the Foreword to her collective autobiography and Kramer expresses in such poems as 'Dover Harbour'[73]); they were also constrained by the dominant representations of their exile to Britain as a heroic tale of rescue and escape, rather than of irretrievable loss.[74] The English master-narrative of the war actually did them harm.

Thus, at first sight their poetry may seem unadventurously English almost to the point of inertia. All three *Kindertransport* poets draw on popular English traditions for their verse forms: where Gershon mainly employs lines which end-stop and have the four strong stresses and mid-rhymes of Anglo-Saxon verse, Mayer's simple

[69] To take examples of prose *Kinder* memoirs, Lore Segal was aged 36 when she published *Other People's Houses* in 1964, and Eva Figes was about 40 when she wrote *Little Eden: A Child at War* (London: Faber, 1978).

[70] Bryan Cheyette, 'Introduction', in *idem* (ed.), *Contemporary Jewish Writing in Britain and Ireland: An Anthology* (Lincoln, Nebr.: Nebraska University Press, 1998), p. xxxv; my interpolation.

[71] Kramer, 'Equation', in Lawson (ed.), *Passionate Renewal*, 213; Figes, *Little Eden*; Sylvia Rogers, *Red Saint, Pink Daughter* (London: André Deutsch, 1996).

[72] Gershon, 'The Children's Exodus', in *We Came as Children*, 171.

[73] Kramer, 'Dover Harbour', in Lawson (ed.), *Passionate Renewal*, 216.

[74] For a discussion of representations of the *Kindertransport* experience in film that celebrate it as a tale of redemptive rescue, see Beate Neumeier, 'Kindertransport: Childhood Trauma and Diaspora Experience', in Behlau and Reitz (eds.), *Jewish Women's Writing of the 1990s and Beyond*, 61–70; and for a discussion of dominant narratives of escape in British Second World War literature, see Mark Rawlinson, 'British Culture and the Holocaust', *Cambridge Quarterly*, 25/1 (1996), 1–25. Gershon's prose concerning the *Kindertransport* experience is discussed by Christoph Houswitschka, '"What I was going to be I already was: a writer"'.

rhyming quatrains resemble hymns, nursery rhymes, and the ballads adapted by Blake, Coleridge, and Wordsworth, and Kramer tends to sonnet form. They share a surface politeness of tone. It is notable how unhistrionic their verse is, especially when compared with Plath's; they do not make their own pain spectacular. On the contrary, Gershon's unpunctuated lines often feel distinctly flat. Yet this apparent emotionless of form indicates a public carapace hiding private responses that shock against the expectations of normal decorum. So it is not surprising to discover that Gershon claims Wilfred Owen and Siegfried Sassoon as her English mentors: 'I feel as if I had always known them.'[75] This, I think, is partly because of their sympathy for the grief and pain caused by war, but more because they had found ways to reveal shocking, repressed emotional memories in a plain language. The very numbness of her writing is an indication of the trauma.

For instance, Gershon's joyless poem 'A Jew's Calendar'[76] starts with a date in 1941 when 'all remaining German Jews | were exiled to the Russian Front', gradually to recount that nothing else is sure about the fate of this Jew's parents. In 1945, she checked the Red Cross lists that name the German Jews 'not dead', and when she could not find their names, 'so glad was I'. Why on earth is this? It is because she will not have to compensate them for their suffering. This makes her glad, so that 'I did not grieve for them'. The perversion of feeling is expressed through a linguistic inversion that recalls a similar shock in Blake's poem 'A Poison Tree'—'glad I see | My foe outstretch'd beneath the tree'[77]—but there that thrill of revenge at least seems naturally human. It is left for the reader to judge that the unthrilled blankness expressed by Gershon is unnatural, yet one more result of Nazism.

On the other hand, in her more famous poem 'I Was Not There', she complains that she was not there when her parents set out from home for the last time and, although there was nothing she could have done to save them, 'I must atone because I live'.[78] The poem rhymes and assonates with the words 'home', 'camps', and 'death', and the third stanza ends with the apparently irrelevant line 'the ground is neutral underneath'. This picks up an earlier claim that the day her parents left, the dawn 'was neutral was immune'. Similarly, an impatient, rejecting response to what the precise facts were—'what difference does it make now'—is echoed in the final line of the poem, that it is no defence to say 'it would have made no difference' even had she been there. The apparent immunity to any feeling other than guilt contrasts with traditional elegies in English that the poem summons up, such as Wordsworth's Lucy poems—'Oh! | The difference to me!'—where the dead loved one is now 'Rolled round in earth's diurnal course, | With rocks, and stones, and

---

[75] See Lawson, 'Three Kindertransport Poets', 88, where he cites the foreword to Gershon's *Collected Poems* (London: Gollancz, 1990), 2, and her unpublished memoir, 'A Tempered Wind' (1992), 163–4.

[76] Gershon, 'A Jew's Calendar', in Reilly (ed.), *Virago Book of Women's War Poetry and Verse*, 177–8.

[77] William Blake, 'A Poison Tree', in *Complete Writings*, 218.

[78] Gershon, 'I Was Not There', in Schiff (ed.), *Holocaust Poetry*, 133–4.

trees', at home in the natural world rather than alienated from the neutral ground and dawn.[79] Gershon seems to be expressing what David Brauner, in 'the Jewish Anti-Pastoral', has identified as a fundamental difference between Jewish writers in Britain (such as Linda Grant and Howard Jacobson) and other writers in the English tradition. He suggests that because of their legacy of historical suffering, 'and in particular, for post-war Jews the oppressive omnipresent consciousness of the Holocaust, Jews cannot subscribe to a pastoral worldview predicated on the notion of harmony between man and his environment, or between man and his fellow man'.[80]

Whereas this cosmological insecurity is tragic in Gershon's writing, Gerda Mayer's poetry treats it with humour. For instance, in her Blakean 'Children with Candles', the speaker is filled with wonder, yet impossibly anxious lest the storm 'blow their voices out'.[81] This is an anxiety only too comprehensible in the light of Nelly Sachs's 'A Dead Child Speaks'.[82] More bitter is the humour in Mayer's 'God Wot', where the dying flowers which are the object of a still-life painting class in 'God-wottery' intrusively remind her of a carriage travelling east, 'And wave thin hands, and fight for fetid air'.[83] However, breaking rhythm and line length, she claims that she lacks the nerve to depict them in this shocking way, even though she knows 'their names; though I know their faces and their names'. That paradox ends with a poor play on words: 'Forgetmenot . . . rendered anonymous'. (The fact that this flower is 'Vergissmeinnicht' in German uncomfortably recalls Keith Douglas's more famous Second World War poem of that title, an elegy for a dead German soldier, which ends with an idea suppressed in Mayer's poem, that death 'has done the lover mortal hurt'.[84]) Such intrusiveness of overwhelming ideas is another indication of trauma.

Similarly, in Mayer's 'The Agnostic's Prayer', which parodies lines of Anglican hymns by thanking God 'for your grace and favour', an ambiguity in the sound of the lines praying God to keep her own and her neighbour's cats safe reads as if she is asking God to keep her *neighbours* 'from each other's throats'.[85] The bathos of poor jokes re-creates precisely the sinking disharmony of Mayer's attempt to fit in with English jollity. To my mind it casts a harsh light on Hill's awkward poetics in 'September Song': his very first play on words, putting 'deported' instead of 'departed' after 'born' in the heading epigraph, strikes me as unfeelingly facetious rather than imaginative, as do the puns in 'patent terror'.[86] But that is a matter of

[79] William Wordsworth, 'Song ("She dwelt among the untrodden ways")' and 'A slumber did my spirit seal', in *William Wordsworth*, ed. Stephen Gill (Oxford: Oxford University Press, 1984), 147–8.

[80] David Brauner, *Post-War Jewish Fiction: Ambivalence, Self-Explanation and Transatlantic Connections* (Basingstoke: Palgrave, 2001), 111–12.

[81] Mayer, 'Children with Candles', in Lawson (ed.), *Passionate Renewal*, 257.

[82] Nelly Sachs, 'A Dead Child Speaks', in Schiff (ed.), *Holocaust Poetry*, 67.

[83] Mayer, 'God Wot', in Lawson (ed.), *Passionate Renewal*, 253.

[84] Keith Douglas, 'Vergissmeinnicht', in *The Complete Poems*, ed. Desmond Graham (London: Faber, 2000), 118.

[85] Mayer, 'The Agnostic's Prayer', in Lawson (ed.), *Passionate Renewal*, 251.

[86] Hill, 'September Song', in *Collected Poems*, 67.

personal response; as Hill says, he wrote this pastoral elegy for himself. By contrast, it is the hollow jauntiness typical of Mayer's adult verse that marks her difference from the convivial norms of English society and amateur poets to which, on the surface, her poetry belongs. Her peculiar humour has been likened by Peter Porter to Stevie Smith's, where a carefree surface of near-doggerel suddenly splits to reveal the insecurity beneath (where the reader is suddenly given to understand that the poet's waving indicates that she, too, is in danger of drowning). Porter says that, like Smith, Mayer 'writes children's rhymes for grownups'.[87]

In fact, Mayer's use of poetic forms that echo nursery rhymes[88] and hymns in their simple metre and stanza length comes nearer to real horrified terror than Smith's. This is particularly marked in 'Grandfather's House', a poem that starts with a glorious image of her parents as children sliding down the banisters. It continues apparently like a nursery rhyme with actions, such as 'Jack and Jill' or 'When the Bough Breaks' or 'Here we go round the mulberry bush', as 'down fell all. | Down, down, down, and beyond recall'.[89] The poem unexpectedly moves into a thoughtful cynicism, claiming that it is better not to have been born 'than to have seen what I have seen', before pulling itself back to end with a masking folk-song injunction to 'deck their graves with meadow-green'. In a way that is reminiscent of the German children's tales of the Brothers Grimm, threats lurk near the carefree surface. For instance, in the grotesque parody of fairy story which is entitled 'In his orchard' and written in the ballad form of Blake's songs, near where 'Lieschen and Gretchen were dawdling', the wind blows away the *stench* from 'the little ripe corpses' that the Giant is growing in an orchard fenced with skeletons.[90]

A similar combination of fairy-tale, the Gothic, and Blake's *Songs of Innocence and Experience* figures in Eva Figes's revisionary memoir *Tales of Innocence and Experience*. In an essay on theatre and film representations of the *Kindertransport*, including Diane Samuels's play *Kindertransport*, Beate Neumeier remarks on their use of the fairy-tale and the Gothic. Whilst the pre-Holocaust childhood world of the past is represented as fairy-tale, 'reality is expressed as a gothic nightmare', where 'the gothic motif of the return of the repressed' recalls the 'childhood trauma of separation and annihilation'.[91] The Gothic is one of European culture's most important strategies for dealing with taboo issues, particularly our horror of death and dead bodies and our fear of threats to the integrity of the self. The Holocaust poetry of the *Kinder*-poets requires us to deal with those taboos, contemplating both that horror and that fear. They draw on and combine both English and German

---

[87] Peter Porter, 'The Muse in the North East', *The Observer*, 15 Mar. 1981, 33.

[88] On Mayer's use of nursery rhyme metre, see Elaine Feinstein, 'Sparkling Mildew and Doubt', *Jewish Quarterly*, 43/1 (1996), 74.

[89] Mayer, 'Here we go round the mulberry bush', in *Bernini's Cat: New and Selected Poems* (North Shields: Iron Press, 1999), 34.

[90] Mayer, 'In his orchard', ibid. 32; my italics, to draw attention to the echo of Sassoon, 'The rank stench of those bodies haunts me still'.

[91] Neumeier, 'Kindertransport', 66.

literary sources associated with childhood to structure that return of repressed childhood trauma.

What Peter Lawson calls Mayer's 'ghastly playfulness'[92] masks a more astringent bitterness than is to be found in either Gershon's or Kramer's poetry. Yet all three poets adapt English verse forms to show what is hidden behind the mask of self-controlled Englishness adopted by British Jews. In Gershon's 'I Was Not There', the speaker's mind 'refuses to conceive | the life the death' her parents must have experienced. Here the absence of punctuation suggests that her persona's imagination balks at the living death, or life-in-death of the camps, but recognizes what she is averting her mind from. Yet the very next poem in the sequence, 'Race', claims that every living Jew has 'in imagination seen | the gas-chamber the mass grave | the unknown body' that was their own.[93] That distinguishes her state of mind from that of the *Kind* analysed in Lotte Kramer's sonnet 'Cocoon', whose 'willed amnesia' is guaranteed by her husband 'to stifle terror, exile, fear'.[94] The tweedy English husband has turned her into an 'English wife', through a love which is implied to be as stultifyingly destructive as it is protective, since it prevents her from metamorphosing into a full human being. Paranoia, too, is revealed. In Gershon's 'Home', the German-Jewish woman who is like one of 'them' in England is nevertheless terrified of them as 'potential enemies', remembering that her childhood playfellows would have killed her if she had stayed in Germany.[95] Yet the masquerade of Englishness that hides a German past does not only stifle fear and pain. Alongside the threat, the pogrom of daily life, as Gershon calls it, were also instances of extreme kindness and joy. They too can be rediscovered through a poetry that draws on the German children's story tradition. Lotte Kramer's 'The Shoemaker's Wife' recounts the story of a witch-like German woman who secretly defied her anti-Semitic husband and sons to come at night with mended shoes.[96] In 'The Town', Gershon alludes to the story of the Pied Piper. She returns to the place that drove her family out and unexpectedly 'my own crippled childhood broke | from streets and hillsides like a dancer'.[97]

Nevertheless, despite their potentially dramatic material, Kramer's sonnet 'Scrolls' explains the refusal to make spectacular the terror, exile, and fear, which motivates the distancing of all the British Holocaust poets. In a poem that predates the founding of the Holocaust Exhibition at the Imperial War Museum, she imagines a scenario 2,000 years into the future.[98] Just as the discovery of the Dead Sea Scrolls has unearthed evidence associated with the mass suicide that ended the Battle of Masada and the Jewish revolt against the Romans, sacred in Jewish

[92] Lawson, 'Three Kindertransport Poets', 91.
[93] Gershon, 'Race', in *We Came as Children*, 178.
[94] Kramer, 'Cocoon', in Lawson (ed.), *Passionate Renewal*, 220.
[95] Gershon, 'Home', ibid. 253.
[96] Kramer, 'The Shoemaker's Wife', in Schiff (ed.), *Holocaust Poetry*, 7.
[97] Gershon, 'The Town', in *We Came as Children*, 175.
[98] Kramer, 'Scrolls', in Reilly (ed.), *Virago Book of Women's War Poetry and Verse*, 201.

history for 2,000 years, so in the future scrolls might be discovered in Poland, or burnt clothing, a letter, or 'some scraps of verse', preserved in the mud. Then she envisages the prurience of the researchers, curators, and exhibition crowds, that will result in a 'book of dredged tears', an exhibition room cluttered with 'sores', and the queues of bored people vicariously 'poaching' emotion off the backs of other people on Sunday afternoons. The final couplet is condensed, but it suggests that she burns uselessly with hidden rage at this profane cultural wasteland, identifying herself with the victims of the massacre who fall blazing from their wailing wall.

The sonnet is compressed, and the very difficulty of unpacking it suggests that it is an example of what Rowland would term 'awkward poetics'. Neither the Jews nor the Holocaust are directly identified, and some knowledge of Jewish culture is required to decipher the allusions. The final image, for me, conjures up photos of the Warsaw Ghetto Uprising, when some of the rebels leapt to their death in the burning city rather than surrender to the Nazis. However, the point I wish to make is that the difficulty here is not to do with the aesthetic problem of how to represent the Holocaust itself, but with the political problem of how to represent it to a culture where it is so alien, and where that alienates the poet. The self-consciousness comes from that sense of alienation. Kramer is uncompromising. Yet she, like the other Holocaust poets, has revealed her inner thoughts honestly to an English public, however unpalatable they may be, and in so doing has testified to her survival in the face of persecution.

Lest that should appear to give this essay a redemptive ending, remember that the *Kinder*-poets have stressed the costs of their survival: their sense of guilt, loss, loneliness, and alienation, and the traumatic ideas they cannot expunge. (It was not by chance that Gershon's chosen pen-name means 'stranger in a strange land'.) Like Plath's, Hill's, and Paulin's, their poetry is a testament to the Holocaust, but their poems are seldom pleasurable, and they are hard-won. Gershon characterizes her own artistic legacy in 'Afterwards'. This implicitly alludes to a poem about women's creativity by another Jewish woman writer, Adrienne Rich in 'Aunt Jennifer's Tigers'. There, like women of the past, Aunt Jennifer has endured the terrifying ordeal of her marriage by embroidering imaginative tapestries. The poem ends by predicting that, 'When Aunt is dead' and her trials are over, 'the tigers in the panels that she made | Will go on prancing, proud and unafraid'.[99] By contrast, Gershon prophesies that, 'When I am dead my orphaned memories | will squat about the world like refugees'.[100] What I have tried to do in this essay is to take these discomforting *Kindertransport* poems in, and to welcome them as an integral part of the canon of British war poetry, of no less worth than the war poems by more widely known poets such as Hill, Paulin, and Plath.

---

[99] Adrienne Rich, 'Aunt Jennifer's Tigers', in Gilbert and Gubar (eds.), *Norton Anthology of Literature by Women*, 2025.
[100] Gershon, 'Afterwards', in *Grace Notes* (Basingstoke: Macmillan, 2002), 9.

CHAPTER 32

QUIET AMERICANS: RESPONSES TO WAR IN SOME BRITISH AND AMERICAN POETRY OF THE 1960S

ALAN MARSHALL

Graham Greene's novel *The Quiet American* (1955) deals with the period shortly after the Second World War when it became clear that imperial power was in new hands. Set in Indochina at the beginning of the Vietnam War, it concerns the decline and retreat of the old European colonial powers, Britain and France, and the emergence of the United States as the major Western power. Greene realized that this was to be a different kind of imperial power: a 'quiet' empire, as the novel has it, too modest to call itself an empire at all. This empire would (in keeping with its quietness) be fought for surreptitiously, by lending a hand to indigenous democratic movements, and with a little underhand weaponry thrown in as and when—the modern cloak-and-dagger of exploding cigars. The empire of the free world would be secured not in the name of empire, naturally, but of democracy—which by the 1950s had become another word for anti-communism. Greene also foresaw that things would not be quiet for long. Vietnam would blow up right across American television screens: 'An event as ordinary | As a President. | A plume of smoke, visible at a distance | In which people burn'.[1]

This essay takes Greene's novel as offering a framework for looking at how some British poets responded to this change in the balance of power and at the crisis of identity, as it has been characterized, that Britain underwent as a result of it. I will begin by trying to establish one or two points of contrast with some contemporary American poets. Here too I want to use Greene's novel, and to draw on certain binaries, certain conventional contrasts, and even national stereotypes, at the risk of over-simplification, which is what Greene himself appears to have risked, in order, hopefully, to get at deeper patterns and truths. For Greene's novel is also an essay in the messy continuance and development of Henry James's famed international theme, its passage from innocence to experience, and the strange persistence of British insularity at the frontiers of colonial violence.

As it happens, *The Quiet American* is also, among other things, a book about poetry: about the kind of poetry one reads and the kind of people who read it. In the first few pages alone, the narrator has quoted Baudelaire; the quiet American is reported to have said that he does not like poetry, is discovered nonetheless to have a selection of American poetry on his shelves, and there are references to Shakespeare, Augustan verse, and a Vietnamese accountant who loves Wordsworth. More importantly, however, Greene raises explicitly the question of the kind of language a writer is to use in respect of the condition the world was in just ten years after the triumph of 1945—where war is over and yet ongoing, where it is 'Cold' but overheated, and where politics are, simultaneously, post-colonial and imperial. Through its protagonist, a reporter, the novel asks whether it is possible to use plain language, to speak directly and not obliquely, to be in earnest and not ironical, sincere and not deceitful—in a word, whether Wordsworth's notion of poetry as a man speaking to men still holds up.

One model of plain-speaking, direct, straightforward language that the novel examines is 'reportage': 'My fellow journalists called themselves correspondents; I preferred the title of reporter,' the English narrator Fowler tells us. 'I wrote what I saw. I took no action—even an opinion is a kind of action.'[2] Leave aside the rather too obvious question about where poetry stands in relation to this axiom (is it another way of sitting on the fence, not getting involved, expressing no opinion, and

---

[1] George Oppen, 'Of Being Numerous' (1968), in *New Collected Poems*, ed. Michael Davidson (New York: New Directions, 2002), 173.

[2] Graham Greene, *The Quiet American* (Harmondsworth: Penguin, 1974; 1st pub. 1955), 28.

avoiding action, like the narrator's Baudelairean opium?). The notion of reportage is more historically specific than that. For by the time Greene wrote his novel, it suggested a very American take on the world: the plain laconic diction of writers schooled in the dramatic conjunction of war, photography, and journalism, the legend of the foreign correspondent. Ernest Hemingway was the master (though the novel makes a sarcastic reference to Stephen Crane—who wrote about war without ever seeing one). The 'quiet American' himself may even have been named after one of the most renowned American correspondents—Ernie Pyle, who like the fictional Pyle, died 'in action' in the Far East. Fowler tries to distance himself from the notion of the 'foreign correspondent'—just as he tries to distance himself from the conflict. But neither position is entirely convincing, as the novel demonstrates. And then Greene's writing, for all its debts to Conrad, had learned something from the directness, the unfussiness, even, on occasion, the hard-boiled worldliness, of Hollywood-inflected English.

It is important that the quibbling power of the novel's title be permitted to resonate a little. For Greene invites us to consider the quietness of his American alongside the more subtle quietness of his English narrator: a quietness composed of quietism on the one hand (this determination not to be 'involved') and a complex dishonesty on the other. The problem with quietism, as Greene knows, is that it allows us to end up on the right side of history anyway, alongside the victors, without having to declare ourselves (the problem with declaring ourselves, on the other hand, is where it allows us to imagine that we could step free of our historical complicity and cross to the other side).

In an essay about the position of the narrator in the contemporary novel, which is really an essay about modernism generally, Theodor Adorno wrote: 'Just as painting lost many of its traditional tasks to photography, the novel has lost them to reportage and the media of the culture industry, especially film.'[3] Greene's novel records this shift in power, just as it shrewdly accommodates it. Following Adorno, we may think of modernism as an attack not just on realism (where we share 'aesthetic distance' from a shared real world), but also on the notion of the meaningfulness of plain speech: the Wordsworthian situation of one person communicating straightforwardly and realistically with another. The two World Wars compounded and confirmed this faithlessness. 'One need only note', Adorno writes, 'how impossible it would be for someone who participated in the war to tell stories about it the way people used to tell stories about their adventures.'[4] Experience is too complicated, the individual subject too divided and attenuated. Writing that wants to 'tell how things really are', Adorno argues, 'must abandon a realism that only aids the façade in its work of camouflage by reproducing it'.[5]

---

[3] Theodor Adorno, 'The Position of the Narrator in the Contemporary Novel', in *Notes to Literature*, trans. Shierry Weber Nicholsen, ed. Rolf Tiedemann, i (New York: Columbia University Press, 1991), 31.

[4] Ibid.   [5] Ibid. 32.

Nevertheless, there is, I think, in Adorno's writing, if I understand it correctly, an intuition that experimental literature had not just found a way of expressing this latest stage of the human condition—it was strangely and unavoidably complicit in it. For modernism abandons the individual subject in the attempt to give it expression; abandons the ordinary, to express the ordinary. There are modernist poets in the Anglo-American tradition who seem to bear this intuition out, if not necessarily after a fashion of which Adorno would have approved, since for him there could be no way back: the doubly negative knottedness of modernism could not simply be untied. For Adorno, as for the German-language poet Paul Celan (reworking the words of Bertolt Brecht), '*ein Gespräch | beinah ein Verbrechin ist*' ('a conversation | is almost a crime').[6] Whereas, in the work of an exemplary modernist like Ezra Pound, we can detect, in the desolation of Pisa, at the end of the Second World War, an extraordinary longing to speak plainly again—to say something simple, to converse. The poetry is full of attentions and recognitions, commonplace things, snatches of dialogue recalled or overheard, the grace, as Georg Lukács called it,[7] of the ordinary:

> In the spring and autumn
>   In 'The Spring and Autumn'
>   there
>   are
>   no
>   righteous
>   wars[8]

The simplicity of this is of course hard-earned and deceptive—but it is indubitably there: for example, in the highly subjective but straightforward judgement (wars are wrong), whose subjectivity is all the more exposed in that it is presented apropos of nothing, and in that it seems to reflect damningly on Pound's own role in Mussolini's war. The simplicity is complicated for a moment by the bookish allusion to the Confucian classic, *The Spring and Autumn Annals*[9]—but it is bared again by the strangely unreasonable nature of what is being said; as who should say, there might be righteous wars in summer and winter. The repetition of the phrase 'in the spring and autumn' suggests someone deliberately gathering emphasis—or, alternatively, someone stammering. At any rate, one man trying to speak with another.

---

[6] Paul Celan, 'A Leaf, Treeless', in *Poems of Paul Celan*, trans. Michael Hamburger (London: Anvil, 1988), 330–1. Celan's poem is a response to Brecht's stupendous feat of self-exoneration, 'An die Nachgeborenen' ('To Posterity').

[7] Georg Lukács, *The Theory of the Novel*, trans. Anna Bostock (London: Merlin Press, 1971; 1st pub. 1920), 50.

[8] Ezra Pound, *The Cantos* (London: Faber, 1986), 497.

[9] See Carroll F. Terrell, *A Companion to the* Cantos *of Ezra Pound* (Berkeley: University of California Press, 1993), 422.

Within the experimental modernist tradition, it is the Americans who, after 1945, seem more able to meet the Wordsworthian understanding of the poet's role, and who can marry poetry and reportage. The work of George Oppen, for instance, owes a great deal to the innovations of Pound and William Carlos Williams. A communist activist during the 1930s, Oppen was awarded a Purple Heart for his military service in the Second World War, and his life and career have some striking parallels with those of the English poet Basil Bunting. In one of his greatest poems, the fourteen-part sequence 'Route' (1968),[10] Oppen tells exactly the kind of story about the experience of war that Adorno feels ought to be impossible; he repeatedly tells us that 'all this is reportage'; and he conspicuously casts the poet as an earnest but baffled conversationalist ('One man could not understand me because I was saying simple things; it seemed to him that nothing was being said'). The story itself is like the kind of story Walter Benjamin might have cited in his essay on Nikolai Leskov, and concerns the dilemma of the French in Alsace during the occupation:

Pierre told me of a man who, receiving the notification that he was to report to the German army, called a celebration and farewell at his home. Nothing was said at that party that was not jovial. They drank and sang. At the proper time, the host got his bicycle and waved goodbye. The house stood at the top of a hill and, still waving and calling farewells, he rode with great energy and as fast as he could down the hill, and, at the bottom, drove into a tree.

The point is that the story Oppen tells, which is a story that was told to him, is so morally and experientially fraught that it can be told only as a story: any attempt to break off from it, in order to arrive at a moral, would detract from its simplicity and its complexity.

Another American poet at work in the 1960s, whose allegiances were also experimental (to Whitman and Melville), who was prepared to say what Oppen calls 'simple things', at the risk of being misunderstood, was Muriel Rukeyser, author of one of the most succinct testimonies of the twentieth century:

> I lived in the first century of world wars.
> Most mornings I would be more or less insane,
> The newspapers would arrive with their careless stories,
> The news would pour out of various devices
> Interrupted by attempts to sell products to the unseen.
> I would call my friends on other devices;
> They would be more or less mad for similar reasons.[11]

This is breath-taking, simply, in its uninhibited summoning of the century; exhilarating in its economical rendition of one's impotent subjection to what had become, by 1968, the same old same old. As Oppen wrote: '—They await | War,

---

[10] Oppen, 'Route', in *New Collected Poems*, 192–202.
[11] Muriel Rukeyser, 'Poem' (1968), in *The Collected Poems*, ed. Janet E. Kaufman and Anne F. Herzog, with Jan Heller Levi (Pittsburgh: University of Pittsburgh Press, 2005), 430.

and the news | Is war | As always.'[12] The poet as one person trying to speak with another is at the mercy of the newspapers, the radio, the television, the telephone, these 'various devices' that variously bear witness to the unvarying news of war. Though the rhythms may be different, Rukeyser took some of her inspiration, the power of that free 'strong voice',[13] from Walt Whitman—poet, war poet, and of course journalist—as Allen Ginsberg also did. And different as Ginsberg may be from Rukeyser or Oppen, we note in him too, in such a representative and magnificent poem as 'America' (1956), for instance, a freedom and simplicity of address (though without any lack of poignant lyric wit), that seems to be a function of an almost existentialist situating of the self *vis-à-vis* the first century of World Wars: as if confronting the way in which one might be implicated in those wars were only a matter of existential courage, expressed linguistically.

It seems, at any rate, that the freedoms of American experimental modernism in the 1960s, as already pioneered by Williams on the one hand and Whitman on the other, and as expressed in the poetry of war, were not felt by the most gifted of the British poets in dialogue with modernism. There seem to be two general reasons for this: first, in Britain the dominant modernist presence was still T. S. Eliot, not Williams or even Pound; secondly, for the British poet, poetry as an act of what I want to call, albeit unsatisfactorily, linguistic existentialism held few meaningful attractions for poets for whom the present was somehow less the present than it was just the latest, the most recent stage of the past; and for whom the latest wars made little sense without reference to the nation's historical immersion in war.

Basil Bunting, Geoffrey Hill, and J. H. Prynne are all poets whose work demonstrates a significant engagement with the terms of international modernism, whether as represented by Pound or Celan, and which may be said to exist in some sort of tension with Wordsworth's conversational paradigm. This tension was exacerbated after 1945 by the peculiarities of Britain's situation—a warlike nation living more or less at peace, but largely defined by and in thrall to its wars, and, like some soon to be decommissioned battleship, floating uneasily, unsure of its moorings, in a world still full of smaller wars. The poets had also to contend, as I have said, with the masterful presence of T. S. Eliot, and the suffocating terms of Eliot's own war poem, 'Little Gidding', the last of his *Four Quartets*. All three of them can be seen, in their very different ways, to be responding critically to Eliot—whereas this was just what their experimentally inclined American contemporaries had been spared, either by Williams's repudiation of Eliot or else by the prodigiously fertile example of Whitman.

'But few appearances are like this.'[14] It would be hard to think of a work less like reportage than Geoffrey Hill's second book, *King Log* (1968). There are no ironic

---

[12]   Oppen, 'Of Being Numerous', in *New Collected Poems*, 174.
[13]   Rukeyser, 'Searching/Not Searching', in *Collected Poems*, 484.
[14]   Geoffrey Hill, 'Funeral Music 3', in *Collected Poems* (Harmondsworth: Penguin, 1985), 72.

Larkinesque references to the swinging Sixties here. It is, however, a book full of dates—but it is conspicuous that none of the dates accompanying the poems falls later than 1945 (excepting the 'penitential exercise' included in the 'postscript'[15]), giving it an instantly memorial quality. At the centre of it is 'Funeral Music', Hill's vision of the Wars of the Roses—not as they were but as they must appear—which is also a vision of the dead and dying of two World Wars—in relation to the precise agonies of any instant of which 'all echoes are the same'.[16] In this respect it could be said to recall Orson Welles's virtually contemporaneous staging of the Battle of Shrewsbury in *Chimes at Midnight* (1966), in which even the lovable Falstaff looms unrecognizably towards us encased in metal like some hideous autochthonous First World War tank.

All through the book the poet stares fixedly behind him, as if forced despite himself to emulate Walter Benjamin's Angel of history—then catching himself, with his mouth open, in that now grotesque pose. 'If the ground opens, should men's mouths | open also?', he asks (in 'Four Poems Regarding the Endurance of Poets',[17] the first of which bears the title 'Men Are a Mockery of Angels'). In poem after poem, poets or poetry (I list some of Hill's verbs) 'regard', 'survey', 'recognize', 'gaze at', 'look down' upon (or try 'not to look down' upon), are variously 'dazzled by' and 'bear witness' to the innumerable 'strange-postured dead', as if these 'had *Finis* on their brows'; as if dying *were* an art; and as if tragedy were not 'Feasting on this, reaching its own end'.[18] The book plays endlessly on the rich array of similarities and differences between being finished as a human being, finished off, before you feel you are finished ('Crying to the end "I have not finished"',[19] in the formidable closing line of 'Funeral Music'), dying while your life feels as though it is still in mid-sentence, or, if you're a poet, before your pen has glean'd your teaming brain, and the way works of art are finished—the way a poem is moved 'grudgingly', for instance, to its 'extreme form'.[20] The poet is warmed by the sight of the dead, he flatters himself that he is animated by it: 'It seemed I stared at them, they at me';[21] whereas he is not so much animated as, as he said, unfinished. So when, in his inauthentic way, the poet 'gaze[s] at the authentic dead',[22] he is treating them like works of art, as if they had had some say in how all this came to pass, like John Tiptoft whom he imagines creating 'the tableau of his own death'.[23] 'So these dispose themselves,' he writes in 'Funeral Music'.[24] But as this baroquely self-conscious poetry constantly reminds us, the dead have as much right as the living to be recognized for what they mostly are: inauthentic, bastardized, given up,

---

[15] Hill, 'In Memory of Jane Fraser', in *King Log* (London: André Deutsch, 1968), 69–70.
[16] Hill, 'Funeral Music 8', in *Collected Poems*, 77.
[17] Hill, 'Four Poems Regarding the Endurance of Poets', ibid. 78–81.
[18] Hill, 'Tristia: 1891–1938', ibid. 81.   [19] Hill, 'Funeral Music 8', 77.
[20] Hill, 'Three Baroque Meditations 2', ibid. 90.   [21] Hill, 'Funeral Music 7', ibid. 76.
[22] Hill, 'A Letter from Armenia', in 'The Songbook of Sebastian Arrurruz', ibid. 99.
[23] Hill, 'Funeral Music: An Essay', ibid. 200.   [24] Hill, 'Funeral Music 1', ibid. 70.

indisposed. One ending, then, is at odds with another. 'This is plenty,' but 'This is more than enough.'[25] This is this: the same pronoun, the same quantity seen in a different light.

It has been noted before that in the steady allusions to music and silence, *King Log* is conducting some kind of argument with Eliot's *Four Quartets*.[26] With consummate skill (which can be gauged by the consternation the poem has provoked among both poets and critics ever since), and 'With an equable contempt for this World' ('Funeral Music'),[27] Eliot subsumed the 'grunts and shrieks' of history ('Funeral Music: An Essay')[28] in the abstract temporality of music, or rather, in the elaborate dead ends of language musically conceived. The matter of history became mere temporality, and temporality was turned into music and silence. The effect was to take the 'dung and death' out of dung and death.[29] It is by means of dung and death, therefore, or rather shrieks, grunts, and blasphemous jokes, that Hill takes the argument back to Eliot, and attempts to rattle his post-Symbolist cage. What gives authority and bite to what may be called, then, in contradistinction to Eliot's post-Symbolist music of time, Hill's 'noise of time' is his comparable ear for poetry's mesmerizing power—its power, one wants to say, to stop you dead; to make you feel as though it stopped you dead. As Emily Dickinson is reported to have said, in the spirit of the Earl of Worcester: 'If I feel physically as if the top of my head were taken off, I know *that* is poetry.'[30]

The war to which 'Little Gidding' obviously refers is the English Civil War of the seventeenth century, though Lyndall Gordon points out that Eliot contemplated blending it with the Battle of Bosworth and the Wars of the Roses.[31] As far as I am aware, what has gone unremarked is that the image of the 'broken king' in 'Little Gidding' also recalls *Richard II*, Shakespeare's extraordinary study in 'the deposing of a rightful king' (thereby seeming to transform him into a prototype of Eliot's Caroline martyr), and Richard's grievous sense that 'time is broke' (punning on the name of the usurper Bolingbroke), and the paradoxical way in which Richard, despite his sense of the disorder thereby visited on 'the music of men's lives', makes his own majestic music of it, as he reconciles himself to that 'pattern | Of timeless moments', as Eliot calls it, 'the death of kings'.[32] That Shakespeare's history plays seem to resonate after a fashion in *Four Quartets* is important, because of the very different way in which they are left to resonate in *King Log*. The repetition of

---

[25] Hill, 'September Song', in *Collected Poems*, 67.

[26] See e.g. Gabriel Pearson, '*King Log* Revisited', in Peter Robinson (ed.), *Geoffrey Hill: Essays on his Work* (Milton Keynes: Open University Press, 1985), 34.

[27] Hill, 'Funeral Music 1', in *Collected Poems*, 70.   [28] Hill, 'Funeral Music: An Essay', ibid. 199.

[29] T. S. Eliot, 'East Coker', in *The Complete Poems and Plays* (London: Faber, 1969), 178.

[30] Emily Dickinson, quoted in T. W. Higginson to Mrs Higginson, 16 Aug. 1870, in *The Letters of Emily Dickinson*, ed. Thomas H. Johnson (Cambridge, Mass.: Belknap Press, 1986), 474.

[31] Lyndall Gordon, *Eliot's New Life* (Oxford: Oxford University Press, 1988), 137.

[32] Eliot, 'Little Gidding', in *Complete Poems and Plays*, 191; William Shakespeare, *Richard II*, v. i. 50, v. v. 43, v. v. 44; Eliot, 'Little Gidding', 197; Shakespeare, *Richard II*, iii. ii. 156.

'England' in 'Little Gidding' recalls the patriotic rhetoric of *Henry V* (which does not mean that this Anglophile quiet American wasn't leading his readers, in true Symbolist fashion, up the garden path), but Hill takes us closer to the blood-strewn worlds of *Henry IV* and *Henry VI*. In this world all wars are civil. Death and suffering are things we inflict on one another, on the human being who is next to us, not on a bunch of foreign extras.

In this context, Hill's shrieks, grunts, jokes, and blasphemies are also, crucially, an approximation, amid so much pompous elaboration, to poetry as a Wordsworthian speech-act. Here is a man who would be speaking to a man if he were not 'gasping "Jesus"'; if he were not in the middle of being slaughtered on a battlefield and 'Dragged half-unnerved out of this worldly place'.[33] Even the jargon of the history primer, of the TV commentator ('Oh, that old northern business . . .'[34]) can, if you come across it at the right moment, seem to speak on behalf of history, especially against a background of poetry, which is to say a background of silence. It is within these limits that Hill manages, as few poets writing in English have managed since, to splice together accessible commonplace speech, language that seems to talk to us, and the difficult radiance of self-conscious modernism, language that seems to talk to itself: 'A field | After battle utters its own sound | Which is like nothing on earth, but is earth.'[35] Whereas Eliot's punning conjunction of 'England and nowhere' is meant to vaporize the earth (a battlefield becomes something as nebulous as a 'field of action'),[36] Hill's several puns on 'nothing' would bring us back down to it: they confront us with the earth, with something like insistence ('but is earth'). The book's constant images of earth and fields, too close in sometimes, rubbing our noses in it, or the language of it, seem bound to recall the trenches, still vivid to us from the poetry of the First World War. And just as the trenches became identified with poppies, so in *King Log* the air seems to be thick, almost heavy, with a profusion of plants and flowers, far in excess of Eliot's scentless rose.

Basil Bunting's career might have been dreamed up in the pages of a Graham Greene novel. He finished school towards the end of the First World War, but as a Quaker, he refused to be drafted and was incarcerated, as a conscientious objector, in Wormwoods Scrubs. Between the wars he knocked about Europe, studied languages, wrote poetry, raised a family, learned sailing. By the time the Second World War broke out, he was eager to enlist. Because of his knowledge of Persian, he was eventually shipped out to Iran, where he worked with the RAF and British Intelligence. He was at Tripoli; he helped prepare Eisenhower's warroom in Sicily; he was made British Vice-Consul in the city of Isfahan, and then after the war he became, for a time, Chief of Political Intelligence in the Middle East. He

---

[33] Hill, 'Funeral Music 8', 77.   [34] Hill, 'Funeral Music 3', in *Collected Poems*, 72.
[35] Ibid.
[36] Eliot, 'Little Gidding', 192 and 195. For Eliot's punning here, see Alan Marshall, 'England and Nowhere', in A. David Moody (ed.), *The Cambridge Companion to T. S. Eliot* (Cambridge: Cambridge University Press, 1994), 106.

smoked opium with the tribal chieftains. Then he married an Iranian woman and became foreign correspondent for *The Times*.[37]

Bunting's contrasting experiences of twentieth-century wars are correspondingly reflected in his poetry. In 'The Well of Lycopolis' (1935) he rattles off the expectations of the average British Tommy in the First World War:

> Join the Royal Air Force
> and See the World. The Navy will
> Make a Man of You. Tour India with the Flag.
> One of the ragtime army,
> involuntary volunteer,
> queued up for the pox in Rouen. What a blighty!
>
> Surrendered in March. Or maybe
> ulcers of mustard gas, a rivet in the lung
> from scrappy shrapnel,
> frostbite, trench-fever, shell-shock,
> self-inflicted wound,
> tetanus, malaria, influenza.
> Swapped your spare boots for a packet of gaspers.
> Overstayed leave.
> Debauched the neighbor's little girl
> to save two shillings ... [38]

This has the hard-edged satiric grimness, the contempt for imperial wars, for the carnage visited on the 'involuntary volunteer[s]' of the 'ragtime army', the poor, the 'uneducated workingmen' ('(The day being Whitsun)'[39]), that is common to poetry in the 1920s and 1930s—though it is expressed with a rhythmical and syntactical variety and control that are exceptional. If it makes us think of *The Waste Land*, as it is perhaps bound to, then that is because it is inclined to overstate the shallowness of human experience.

In 'The Spoils' (1951), by contrast, a poem that deals directly with the Second World War, the sense of the vividness of things, the strange intensity of reality, precludes any such presumption. Cynicism is inadequate—though not irony. 'We marvelled':

> Broken booty but usable
> along the littoral, frittering into the south.
> We marvelled, careful of craters and minefields,
> noting a new-painted recognisance
> on a fragment of fuselage, sand drifting into dumps,

[37] Information about Bunting's life is taken from Keith Alldritt's satisfyingly spare biography, *The Poet as Spy: The Life and Wild Times of Basil Bunting* (London: Aurum Press, 1998).

[38] Basil Bunting, 'The Well of Lycopolis', in *Complete Poems* (Newcastle-upon-Tyne: Bloodaxe, 2000), 44.

[39] Bunting, '[The day being Whitsun we had pigeon for dinner]', in 'First Book of Odes', ibid. 103.

a tank's turret twisted skyward,
here and there a lorry unharmed
out of fuel or the crew scattered;
leaguered in lines numbered for enemy units,
gulped beer of their brewing,
mocked them marching unguarded to our rear;
discerned nothing indigenous, never a dwelling,
but on the shore sponges stranded and beyond the reef
unstayed masts staggering in the swell,
till we reached readymade villages clamped on cornland,
empty, Arabs feeding vines to goats;
at last orchards aligned, girls hawked by their mothers
from tent to tent, Tripoli dark
under a cone of tracers.
Old in that war after raising many crosses
rapped on a tomb at Leptis; no one opened.[40]

The sense of the marvellous is conveyed through rich detail and unexpected apt vocabulary: 'frittering', for instance, which can mean things being worn away or being fried, whether from desert heat or from enemy fire. '[N]ew-painted recognisance' suggests military identification and reconnaissance, but also art's own preoccupation with the shock of recognition—the news that stays news ('new-painted'). The archaism 'leaguered' means beleaguered, besieged—but also evokes the arbitrariness, and archaism, of leagues, tribes, of those national, ethnic, or ideological associations between whom wars are waged. The details are choice: a 'lorry unharmed' (but what about the crew? The military eye is utilitarian, practical); 'a tank's turret twisted skyward' (spiralling vainly heavenwards); 'Arabs feeding vines to goats'—an inversion, surely, of the fructuous order of things (wherein Arabs might drink wine from goatskins). The poem marvels at war, at what it makes and unmakes, but it marvels just as much at that baffling power of dissociation that is able to combine aesthetic observation with adroit survival skills ('careful of craters and minefields'), the contemplative and the purposive. As that other veteran, Oppen, put it, 'There is a simple ego in a lyric, | A strange one in war.'[41] Bunting here demonstrates as vividly as any poet writing in English during the twentieth century the Tolstoyan truth of these great words and the tremendous ambivalence which they allow. Nevertheless, in such passages the poem comes close to reportage—and perhaps only the studied nature of the language prevents its being so.

However, it is in his masterpiece of the 1960s, *Briggflatts*, named after a Quaker meeting-house, that Bunting presents his most profound coming to terms with what war means and has meant to him and to us. The poem is presented as 'an autobiography' and was written by a poet who found himself caught up in two

---

[40] Bunting, 'The Spoils', ibid. 56.
[41] Oppen, 'Blood from the Stone', in *New Collected Poems*, 53.

World Wars. But the wars about which he writes date back a millennium or more, and there is not a passage of reportage anywhere in it. It seems that for Bunting here, as for Hill, the mere reporting of reality or recent history is not enough.

Yet if reportage is one inadequate handle on time, so is the poetry of Eliot, the twentieth-century poet who perhaps had most to say about it. For the Hill of *King Log*, as we saw, English identity is not a supreme fiction, as Eliot so equably has it; it is a muddied thing or mess of things—for example, a thing of wars. For Eliot time is mainly metaphysical; for Hill it is mainly historical. Bunting can also be seen in terms of an ongoing argument with Eliot; and *Briggflatts*, with its five sections and musical structure, its cosmopolitanism on the one hand and its sense of place on the other, readily invites comparison with *The Waste Land* and *Four Quartets*. But, contrary to Eliot's broad or airily Platonic bent, Bunting insists on the ungainsayable specificity, the complex simplicity, of the productions of time: a piece of music, the origin of species, the motion of the planets, the death of one soldier at the hands of another, and so on.

There are of course important differences between the ways in which *Briggflatts* and *King Log* address the past. Both make a case for the common nature of a given experience (for example, suffering in battle or in love), based on our common humanity, but whereas *King Log* gestures toward the distinctiveness of a particular historical event not by specifying it at length but rather by repeatedly drawing attention to the way in which he, the poet, is ultimately restricted to his own history ('I have made | an elegy for myself'; or 'I believe in my | Abandonment, since it is what I have'; or 'I would have preferred | You to them' while being 'too late' for either[42]), a solipsism that is not a million miles away from the Eliot of *The Waste Land*, Bunting tries to make a more sustained attention to historical detail part of the constitutive action of the poem.

The poet weaves together several histories, including passages from his own life. In the magnificent first section he presents an episode of youthful love, and then commemorates the abrupt desertion of that love by the boy-poet who heads south and turns up, in the second section, in the Tottenham Court Road. Before that, on the moors, the youth recalls the life and death of the Viking Eric Bloodaxe, who in the middle of the tenth century had been king of Norway but then fled to Britain rather than do battle with his rebellious brother. After he arrived, Eric held sway as and where he could: 'king of Orkney, king of Dublin, twice | king of York'.[43] But it was, thinks Peter Makin, in his fine querulous book, the makeshift life of a pirate: 'He was trying to live out the glory of a Viking, when he had abandoned the premiss (ruthlessness) on which it was based.'[44] This is partly true, but only partly. For kingliness also figures in the poem, as it does in Shakespeare, as an image of the

---

[42] Hill, 'September Song', 67; 'Funeral Music 6', 75; 'Tristia: 1891–1938', 81; in *Collected Poems*.
[43] Bunting, *Briggflatts*, in *Complete Poems*, 69.
[44] Peter Makin, *Bunting: The Shaping of his Verse* (Oxford: Clarendon Press, 1992), 173.

truculent ego, in all its embattled pompous authority, now brittle, now resilient. Heavy is the head that wears that crown—as what head, finally, does not?

> Where we are who knows
> of kings who sup
> while day fails? Who,
> swinging his axe
> to fell kings, guesses
> where we go?[45]

The poem implies that at some time or other all boys are kings with a small k.

The Sagas tell us that Eric was slain at Stainmore. Later on, the poem will bring his death hard alongside the battle of nearby Catterick, thought to have taken place some 350 years earlier, when the Anglian invaders butchered the warriors of Northumbria. Their deaths were, as Bunting says, 'celebrated in the Cymric language' by the bard Aneurin.[46]

> Grass caught in willow tells the flood's height that has subsided;
> overfalls sketch a ledge to be bared tomorrow.
> No angler homes with empty creel though mist dims day.
> I hear Aneurin number the dead, his nipped voice.
> Slight moon limps after the sun. A closing door
> stirs smoke's flow above the grate. Jangle
> to skald, battle, journey; to priest Latin is bland.
> Rats have left no potatoes fit to roast, the gamey tang
> recalls ibex guts steaming under a cold ridge,
> tomcat stink of a leopard dying while I stood
> easing the bolt to dwell on a round's shining rim.
> I hear Aneurin number the dead and rejoice,
> being adult male of a merciless species.
>   .   .   .   .   .   .
> I see Aneurin's pectoral muscle swell under his shirt,
> pacing between the game Ida left to rat and raven,
> young men, tall yesterday, with cabled thighs.
> Red deer move less warily since their bows dropped.
> Girls in Teesdale and Wensleydale awake discontent.
> Clear Cymric voices carry well this autumn night,
> Aneurin and Taliesin, cruel owls
> for whom it is never altogether dark.[47]

'This is where English poetry has got to,' wrote Donald Davie, of this evocation of 'autumn twilight over an ancient battlefield in the Yorkshire dales'.[48] Aneurin's 'numbering' of the dead suggests, in this poem full of musical allusions, rhythmical

---

[45] Bunting, *Briggflatts*, 81.   [46] Bunting, 'Notes', in *Complete Poems*, 226.
[47] Bunting, *Briggflatts*, 75.
[48] Donald Davie, 'English and American in *Briggflatts*', in *The Poet in the Imaginary Museum: Essays of Two Decades*, ed. Barry Alpert (Manchester: Carcanet, 1977), 291–2.

counting—the scanning of the dead. '[N]ipped' suggests quick movement (nipping along), which in turn suggests life, muscular Aneurin, 'pacing' (in contrast to the men 'tall yesterday'). It also suggests pinched and pained; and, vitally, that which pinches and gives pain—the sharp tooth of the 'merciless species'. ('[G]amey tang' and 'tomcat stink' might recall Leopold Bloom relishing his kidney breakfast. 'Latin is bland' because it is too mild in the mouth.) Mourning and rejoicing at the same time (for poets, as for owls, it is 'never altogether dark'), the whole passage is a vivid example of Bunting's Darwinian pantheism: images of hunters and hunted, and of hunters who have themselves been hunted: the dead warriors are 'game', a leopard is 'dying'—out-hunted—as the poet interposes recollection of an expedition in Isfahan, where during the War (when else?) he learned to hunt ibex.[49] We are invited, by this image of him lingering at the door, looking out, to look with him. The conceit, often used to striking effect in the cinema (John Ford's *The Searchers* comes to mind), also reactivates the contrast of warm hearth and great outdoors which is such a part of the emotional tonality of the opening section of the poem ('No one here bolts the door, | love is so sore'[50]). The reference to girls who will 'awake discontent' gives expanding depth and resonance to the crisis of the boy walking out on the girl in the first part of the poem, and evokes the situation in which so many women found themselves following the cutting down of whole generations of the 'adult male' in the two twentieth-century World Wars.

When Bunting writes 'I hear Aneurin number the dead and rejoice, | being adult male of a merciless species', he is establishing the terms of his acceptance of man's most brutal instincts—specifically here his innate aggression. But what *Briggflatts* also does—and I struggle to think of a modern poem of any length that is quite so intent on the connection—is to put this on the table alongside that other brutal instinct, the sexual instinct, about which its feelings appear to be more guilty and ambivalent. Thus the ecstatic acceptance of the battlefield, rejoicing in the species as species, has its analogue in the earlier description of Pasiphae: 'nor did flesh flinch | distended by the brute | nor loaded spirit sink | till it had gloried.'[51] The whole poem in fact begins in consciousness of this problematical, aggressive-competitive, nonetheless charming, maleness of the male: 'Brag, sweet tenor bull . . . Ridiculous and lovely.'[52] By such male stuff is the next generation made and unmade. And so the poem moves, in its first part, from the skittishness of the bull to that of the boy dreaming of warriors, arriving, through a series of luminous images, at something like the truth of Melville's words: 'All wars are boyish, and are fought by boys.'[53]

Somewhere in Bunting's pictures of war there seems always to be this sneaking sense of sexual guilt. Note that the long quotations above from both 'The Well of

---

[49] Makin, *Bunting*, 183.   [50] Bunting, *Briggflatts*, 61.   [51] Ibid. 70.   [52] Ibid. 61.
[53] Herman Melville, 'The March into Virginia Ending in the First Manassas (July, 1861)', in *Collected Poems of Herman Melville*, ed. Howard P. Vincent (Chicago: Packard, 1947), 10.

Lycopolis' and 'The Spoils' come to rest on images of young girls (not women) 'debauched' or 'hawked'. The male reproductive instinct is implicitly figured as rapine, warlike, rather than consensual—and of course as unreliable: always going off to fight. 'Guilty of spring | and spring's ending'.[54] Bunting's image for the unreliability of the male is brilliantly paradoxical: the fickle warrior is 'an unconvinced deserter'.[55]

In the 1920s Bunting was Ford Madox Ford's amanuensis while the latter was working on the first book of his great sequence of novels about the First World War, *Parade's End* (1924–8). One wonders to what extent this tale of another ambivalent warrior, or unkinged king, the Yorkshire aristocrat Christopher Tietjens, with its sense of the lumpishness of the male, his insistent Northernness, his protracted absence when he goes off fighting, leaving wartime girls to 'wake discontent', and its startling set-piece evocations of sexual longing, guilt, and yet at the same time idyllic consummation (the two works feature two of the most memorable journeys by horse and cart in English literature), may have lingered in Bunting's unconscious memory. And then there are the larks. *Briggflatts* watches them rise and fall—enacting the fateful male principle: 'Painful lark, labouring to rise': 'Breathless lark | drops to nest'. In Ford's *A Man Could Stand Up*, Tietjens corrects his sergeant's sentimentalizing of the skylarks that were such an obstinate feature of the battlefield, their 'Woner'ful trust in yumanity! Woner'ful hinstinck set in the fethered brest by the Halmighty!':

Tietjens said mildly that he thought the sergeant had got his natural history wrong. He must divide the males from the females. The females sat on the nest through obstinate attachment to their eggs; the males obstinately soared above the nests in order to pour out abuse at other male skylarks in the vicinity.[56]

Thus for Ford, as for Bunting, the sexual division of labour and the origin of wars.

I want to end by looking at J. H. Prynne's *Kitchen Poems* (1968). Although the five related poems that comprise the book are not war poems in the usual sense, they deal in original and sophisticated ways with Britain's situation after 1945. This is post-war poetry specifically addressed to the nation's post-imperial condition. On the one hand Prynne takes his aesthetic bearings, as is well known, from American poets such as Charles Olson and William Carlos Williams, with their post-Imagist emphasis on dynamic syntax (mimetic of the human being as breathing, walking, doing—mentally and physiologically *on the move*) and highly particularized language, without (to use the familiar Imagist formulae) superfluous ornament, metre, or rhyme. But he brings to the proceedings a glowing enigmatic irony, as the prized particularity of things gives way to, or is obscured by, the specialization of discourse. By integrating such discourse into his verse, he can extend the practice of defamiliarization on which art, especially modernist art,

---

[54] Bunting, *Briggflatts*, 64.   [55] Ibid. 67.
[56] Ford Madox Ford, *A Man Could Stand Up*, in *Parade's End* (London: Everyman, 1992), 591.

thrives—and at the same time he can ironize, and even humanize, that discourse; he can cut it down to size. Ultimately perhaps, he can also bring us back, albeit circuitously (the circuitous way is the only way left) to a world of things. For example:

> the prime joy of
> control engineering is what they please
> to denote (through the quartzite window) "self-
> optimising systems", which they like
> to consider as a plan for the basic
> living unit.[57]

The 'basic-living unit' is the individual human being in the jargon of the control engineer, whose advanced biological perspectives are juxtaposed with the consistently basic appetite for pleasure ('prime joy', 'please', 'like'), which in turn makes a mockery of all our 'plans'. Despite the evidence that has been adduced for Wordsworth's influence on Prynne,[58] the Wordsworthian conversational paradigm, the idea of the poet as a man speaking to men is more comprehensively imperilled here than it is in either Hill's work or Bunting's. Needless to add, reportage once again is out of the question.

It is when we attend to how the poems address England's post-war condition that Eliot comes into the picture. For Prynne undercuts Eliot's canny mythologizing of English history in *Four Quartets* ('as now in England'[59]), and satirizes in his gently pointed way the Symbolist paraphernalia that dovetails in the latter's poems with Christian other-worldliness. I mean by this that Prynne seems to show up Eliot's symbolism as a kind of paraphernalia, whose 'idea of the end'—in my beginning is my end, and so on—'is a neat | but mostly dull falsity'.[60] The 'white heat of technology', as Harold Wilson called it, brings Eliot's musical analogies roughly up to date: 'The | English condition is now so abstract that | it sounds like an old record; the hiss and | crackle suborns the music.'[61] The five poems that make up the book recall, like Bunting's *Briggflatts*, the five sections of Eliot's *Waste Land* and the five movements of each of the *Four Quartets*. However, at stake are two very different interpretations of Britain's situation in the aftermath of the Second World War. Eliot was an unashamed apologist for imperialism, as Frank Kermode was among the first to spell out, but an apologist with a rather wonderful alibi, a metaphysical get-out clause: for the British Empire was, for Eliot, but a shadow of the Roman

---

[57] J. H. Prynne, 'Die a Millionaire', in *Poems* (Newcastle-upon-Tyne: Bloodaxe, 1999), 13.

[58] See e.g. N. H. Reeve and Richard Kerridge, *Nearly Too Much: The Poetry of J. H. Prynne* (Liverpool: Liverpool University Press, 1995); Birgitta Johansson, *The Engineering of Being: An Ontological Approach to J. H. Prynne* (Umea: Umea University Press, 1997); and Alan Marshall, '"Drift," "Loss," and "Return," in the Poetry of J. H. Prynne, from *Kitchen Poems* to *The White Stones*', *Études britanniques contemporaines*, 27 (Dec. 2004), 137–52.

[59] Prynne, 'Die A Millionaire', 14.   [60] Prynne, 'A Gold Ring Called Reluctance', in *Poems*, 21.

[61] Ibid. 22.

Empire, which was itself but a prelude to the Holy Roman Empire, which was itself but a shadow of the Platonic Christian other world.[62] In 'Little Gidding' the embattled Empire of Britain under siege is resplendent with this eschatological light, like the blinding glare of midwinter spring.

The more refracted light produced by Prynne's thickening of discursive perspectives affords an opportunity to consider the history of sovereign nations and patrolled borders in relation to, and as just one aspect of, the history of different kinds of movement, alongside, for example, the atomistic movement of biological cells, the body as the site of 'glandular riot', the traffic of goods and wares, the circulation of money, the currency of language, the movement of individual persons, and ultimately the 'molecular friction' of whole peoples drifting precariously across the earth's for the most part also invisibly moving crust (our 'drifting lives' are themselves 'underlaid by drift in the form of *mantle*'[63]). The poet plays spectacularly with scale: what becomes of a people or tribe if you see it as merely the sum of its atoms? To look at history in such terms is to demythologize nationhood and imperialism:

> Imperialism was just
> an old, very old name for that
> idea, that what you want, you by
> historic process or just readiness
> to travel, also "need"—and
> need is of course the sacred daughter
> through which you improve, by
> becoming more extensive. Competitive
> expansion: if you designate a
> prime direction, as Drang nach Osten
> or the Western Frontier, that's to
> purify the idea by recourse to History
>
> *before* it happens. Envisaging the chapter-
> head in the historical outline as "the
> spirit (need) of the age"—its primary
> greed, shielded from ignominy by the
> like practice of too many others.
>
>   That
> of course is *not* expansion but acquisition
> (as to purchase the Suez Canal was merely
> a blatant example): the true expansion
> is probably drift, as the Scythians
> being nomadic anyway for the most part
> slipped sideways right across the Russian
> steppes, from China by molecular friction
> through to the Polish border.[64]

[62] See e.g. Frank Kermode, 'Introduction', in *Selected Prose of T. S. Eliot*, ed. Frank Kermode (London: Faber, 1975), 21.

[63] Prynne, 'Numbers in Time of Trouble', in *Poems*, 17.   [64] Prynne, 'Die a Millionaire', 13–14.

Here imperialism has, as it were, lost its idea—has lost touch with its roots, and its roots, in a sense, were perfectly simple: the hapless confusion of want and need, or greed and hunger ('How definitely glad I am that greed is | an alternative to hunger'[65]), in people who could not sit still for moving around. We think of imperialism as a function of the 'Competitive | expansion' (economist-speak for warmongering) of the nation-state, which in turn undermined the nation-state:[66] but what happens if we see it instead as a function of our inherently nomadic tendencies, our tendency to move and be moved, to expand on this or that, to ruminate, to drift—as poets drift ('I wandered lonely as a cloud...')? Then it becomes a clue to a way of life that might be existentially prior to the nation-state: a mild state of anarchy, or even euphoria. Imperialism might then be seen, in ironic and utopian terms, as the product of the corruption of our anarchic tendencies by the acquisitive nation-state which preys off our insecurities, our unfortunate need to belong, with its tribalism and biologism ('the genetic links are everywhere claimed'[67]); as well as our shambolic need to piece together our identities out of our belongings ('we give the name of | our selves to our needs. | We want what we are'[68]). This chronic need, in a word, to have and be had.

Nevertheless, even as Prynne causes the scales to fall from (or is it dance before?) our eyes, the poetry is loaded with allusions to what Rukeyser called 'this century of World Wars'. 'Western Frontier' might be a reference both to Frederick Jackson Turner's famous essay on 'The Significance of the Frontier in American History' (1893), published in the early days of American empire, and to Erich Maria Remarque's celebrated novel of the Great War, *All Quiet on the Western Front* (1929); 'Drang nach Osten' evokes Germanic expansion eastwards into the Slavonic and Baltic states since the Middle Ages, but above all Hitler's disastrous invasion of the Soviet Union; 'the Polish border' was the flashpoint in Britain's declaration of war in 1939; Russia and China suggest the Red Menace and the onset of the Cold War; and Suez, of course, refers to the humiliating invasion of Egypt in 1956, when the United States pulled the rug on the undying imperial pretensions of Britain and France.

What Prynne opposes to our imperial antics and the lofty paternalism with which we cling to the spoils ('We want | too much for the others. | We must shrink... our

---

[65]   Prynne, 'A Gold Ring Called Reluctance', 23.

[66]   'Imperialism was born when the ruling class in capitalist production came up against national limitations to its economic expansion... Of all forms of government and organizations of people, the nation-state is least suited for unlimited growth because the genuine consent at its base cannot be stretched indefinitely, and is only rarely, and with difficulty, won from conquered peoples', writes Hannah Arendt. 'How a competition between fully armed business concerns—"empires"—could end in anything but victory for one and death for the others is difficult to understand. In other words, competition is no more a principle of politics than expansion' (Hannah Arendt, *The Origins of Totalitarianism* (New York: Harcourt Brace, 1979), 126).

[67]   Prynne, 'A Gold Ring Called Reluctance', 21.

[68]   Prynne, 'Sketch for a Financial Theory of the Self', in *Poems*, 20.

pains are too earnest'[69]) is patience, discretion, hesitation, slowness. This is figured in 'The Numbers' as a retreat into the locality of place, the tentative adjustment to where we are:

> The whole thing it is, the difficult
> matter: to shrink the confines
> down. To signals, so that I come
> back to this, we are
>   small | in the rain,
>   open or without it,
>   the light in de-
> light, as with pleasure amongst not merely
> the word, one amongst them; but the
> skin over the points, of the bone.
> That's where we have it & should
>   diminish: I am no
>   more, than custom.[70]

The difficulty consists, after so much folly, in coming back to ourselves: in recognizing that we are 'small | in the rain' (as if the rain could shrink us); in recognizing that we are, among the multitudes of the earth, just 'one amongst them'. At which point, 'I am no | more '—or as the feint in the line suggests, it could almost seem so. The whole process is figured, as so often in Prynne's poetry, as Wordsworthian adjustment to the local weather: 'Only watch the weather | as the sky does change, | or the seasons in | quick-slip succession.' Here politics is about getting inside our own skins ('the | folds of our intimate surface'), not measuring others by them. 'The politics, therefore, is for one man, | a question of skin, that he ask | of his national point no more, in | this instance, than brevity.' The repetition of that phrase 'no more' is typical of Prynne's quiet style, but it is in fact a clarion call and vibrates with the moral-political energy of the book as a whole, its brilliant, sometime comical evocation of another kind of Englishness, which might be essentially, temperamentally, anti-imperial: hesitancy, discretion, slowness. This is particularly clear in the final poem, 'Gold Ring': 'Competitive | expansion' isn't always necessary because 'We can eat | slowly'. Which brings us to the significance of the book's title, its reversion to the small, to the scraps, to the kitchen. 'Have | you had enough? Do have a little more? | It's very good but, no, perhaps I won't.'[71]

---

[69] Prynne, 'The Numbers', ibid. 11.   [70] Ibid. 10.
[71] Prynne, 'A Gold Ring Called Reluctance', 21.

CHAPTER 33

POINTING TO EAST AND WEST: BRITISH COLD WAR POETRY

ADAM PIETTE

I will be looking at two rival topics in British post-war poetry, the courting of America and the engagement with poets from Eastern Europe, in order to map the co-ordinates of a specifically British poetry of the Cold War. The anti-Americanism and anti-communism of the Movement poets, the neo-Marxist 'Trotskyite' attachments of the Cambridge school, the Alvarez pro-American cringe, the migration of poets to the States after Auden (notably Thom Gunn), the engagement in translation as a means of solidarity with dissident poets in the Eastern bloc (notably Hughes and Silkin), the deflected image of the superpowers in the poetry of the Troubles: these are just some of the Cold War-inflected matters crucial to a proper understanding of post-war poetry. The topics will be focused through consideration of post-imperial, anti-American resentments, nuclear anxieties, polarized political standpoints, the issue of CIA funding and British poetry (Spender *et al.*), and the ways in which definitions of the avant-garde and of what constitutes 'formal' poetry were conditioned by Cold War assumptions.

The British Cold War was fought on a variety of fronts, principally at the new Yalta frontiers of continental Europe (Vienna, Berlin) and at the decolonizing periphery of empire—Burma, Malaya, Kenya, and so on—and was conducted as a struggle for the hearts and minds of foreign powers who might misconstrue such interventions as old imperial or neo-colonial acts of retrenchment. The principal observer being courted was of course the United States: Churchill's Fulton speech outlining the responsibilities of the 'special relationship' in the era of the Iron Curtain had made this perfectly explicit from the outset. But propaganda and policy were also levelled at the Soviet and later the Chinese communist regimes, ensuring a hard and fast stance against their global ambitions. This gaze east and west was not always a mere poodle's pawing at the feet of a superpower. Historians have come to agree in recent years that it was primarily the British in the early post-war years who succeeded in convincing the Americans to assume responsibility for the Cold War, first in Europe (by outlining the threat to Berlin and by forcing the Americans' hand by withdrawing from Greece and Turkey), and then in Asia and Africa (through propaganda drives against Sino-Soviet expansion in favour of US/UK decolonization and informal empire). And it was British intelligence and lobbying that first outfaced the Soviet Union's global propaganda machine in the form of the Foreign Office's formidable Information Research Department.

The illusion of influence was not to last, however, as the US spurned British requests for a sharing of nuclear knowledge, as British post-war bankruptcy forced the government to assume the posture of Marshall Plan beggar, as the rapid series of crises in Europe culminating in the Berlin airlift led the UK government to welcome US bombers and then missiles on to sovereign soil. The propaganda battle against the Soviets, too, was less lost so much as ceded to the Americans, especially with the advent of the CIA and its new intelligence-gathering machine—US condescension towards the British can be dated to its assumption of control over Operations Silver and Gold, the intercept tunnels under Vienna and Berlin.

Starved of funds and unable to interest the US in a proper exchange of nuclear technology after the spy crises of the 1940s and 1950s, the UK rocket programme, Blue Streak, was eventually run down to nothing. The limit of humiliation was reached with Suez, with Eden standing down his forces as the US and USSR issued threats and embargoes on the old colonial powers. Face was saved with the startling success of British counter-insurgency in Malaya and Kenya, successes which contrasted with the US's costly stalemate in Korea and later its bungled attempt to imitate British and French counter-insurgency in Vietnam. Nevertheless, the die was cast. Despite the independent nuclear deterrent, despite the 'third force' potential of the Commonwealth, and despite the continuation of the special relationship in all its forms, the UK had to learn to abandon the high table of atomic and thermonuclear diplomacy.

Peter Hennessy has shown, in *The Secret State*, how successive Prime Ministers attempted to twist the special relationship their way—that is, to protect British interests (the UK, after all, was in the front line of Soviet missile attack) and to limit the potential for US 'Dr Strangelove' mistakes and 'forestalling' nuclear warfare: in Macmillan's words, to have 'enough nuclear power to prevent some foolish decisions being made to our detriment on the other side of the Atlantic'.[1] For that, the logic told the Prime Ministers, from Attlee to Macmillan, the UK needed atomic, then thermonuclear capability. But when they got it, they could not compete with Soviet and American technological developments in order to sustain it—everything fell apart when the US dropped Skybolt, when the V-force of thermonuclear bombers became obsolete, when the UK had meekly to follow NATO commands and take on Polaris.

For British citizens, poets included, the contraction of empire which the War's costs had accelerated, with the independence of India, Burma, and others, the shock of the austerity programmes, the wealth and prestige of the new superpower partner, constructed what is now a very familiar set of gripes and muffled resentments. It is a commonplace to argue that the Movement poets, with their Little Englander Anglo-Saxon attitudes, retreated into contemplation of small-scale domestic issues and the ventriloquizing of a middling, middle-brow, semi-defeated, suburban type. That this 'Larkinian' figure was miming the contracted post-imperial nation is unquestionable. That that figure might also be a Cold War projection is less often conceived.

If Larkin admires Betjeman for being out of step with modernity, for his 'insular' and 'regressive' themes,[2] this has partly to do with the decision to concentrate on a reduced post-imperial Englishness. As Jed Esty has argued in A Shrinking Island, it was the loss of empire which led to this insular regressiveness, as though England had to be reconceived as a limited region rather than a centre of a global network.[3] It is typical of Larkin's style here to defend Betjeman not only against the modernizing welfare planners, but specifically against a hypothetical American reader: 'I can well imagine the American demurring, however.'[4] Larkin knows that the contraction of the Empire must entail a relation of dependency upon the US. The planners, Larkin would say, were modernizing the island in order to offer England up as trophy to American power.

Larkin's poetry consistently aligns the depredation of old England with American values. The 1961 'Here' imagines some neglected edge of England harbouring 'removed lives', just beyond 'the poppies' bluish neutral distance'.[5] Old England, in other words, is lost in a beyond more distant than a dream of the First World War, suspended in some impossible neutral zone beyond foreign encroachment. The empire remains as a free power beyond America's Cold War containment ('unfenced existence'), but only in the unreal form of an illusionary memory

[1] Harold Macmillan, quoted in Peter Hennessy, The Secret State: Whitehall and the Cold War (London: Penguin, 2003), 62.

[2] Philip Larkin, 'It Could Only Happen in England', in Required Writing: Miscellaneous Pieces 1955–1982 (London: Faber, 1984), 206.

[3] See Jed Esty, A Shrinking Island: Modernism and National Culture in England (Princeton: Princeton University Press, 2005).

[4] Larkin, 'It Could Only Happen in England', 215.

[5] Larkin, 'Here', in Collected Poems, ed. Anthony Thwaite (London: Faber, 1990), 136.

located as mirage on a horizon offshore. The real political spaces of England are colonized, defeated, second-rate. If Larkin's subject is the abandoned nation-state, the slow dying of old England half-allegorized as neglected monument, absent space, or devious old man ('Nothing to be said', 'MCMXIV'), then the correlative of this is American ascendancy—captured in the glib assumptions of Jake Balakowsky in 'Posterity'—and the abandonment of old colonies and Europe to the Russian sphere of influence ('Homage to a Government' and 'When the Russian tanks roll westward'). The attitude to the US is exemplified in the famous attack on Auden in America. Auden's irreparable decline involved the conversion of 'a tremendously exciting English social poet' into 'an engaging, bookish American talent, too verbose to be memorable and too intellectual to be moving'.[6]

Whilst Larkin articulated the resentments buried beneath the Cold War special relationship, other Movement poets looked west for (nuclear) comfort. Thom Gunn espoused the Beat-anarchic freedoms that American youth culture afforded poets, then moved permanently over there. But the freedom is articulated through fake combat readiness, through Gunn's ironic admiration for the military culture of the new superpower, captured in the title of his first collection, *Fighting Terms*. For him, American sexiness had something to do with the homoerotic appeal of the raw cold warrior: the freedoms of the young warrior male, the tough on his motorbike ('Lines for a Book', 'On the Move') posing in Presley's 'posture for combat' ('Elvis Presley').[7]

Donald Davie, though intent on a liberated idea of Europe, and keen to attend to the particularities of English culture, joined him. His act of expatriation is partly an act of exasperation, created by the stripping of power from the UK:

> British is what we are
> Once an imperial nation,
> Our hands are clean now, empty,
> Cause for congratulation.[8]

That stripped-down status has had a knock-on effect on the language, for Davie. The English language feels itself 'too poor | Spirited', broken by 'Humiliation, corporate and private', by fear of 'the inauthentic | Which invades it on all sides | Mortally', the English poet dreaming of expatriation as a release.[9] The move, crucially, is towards superpower. Writing to an American friend, the Yeats scholar Curtis Bradford, Davie admits as much, envying America's 'manifested copiousness':

> [I] envy you out of England. Man with man
> Is all our history; American,
> You met with spirits.[10]

---

[6] Larkin, 'What's Become of Wystan?', in *Required Writing*, 127 and 123.
[7] Thom Gunn, 'Elvis Presley', in *Collected Poems* (London: Faber, 1993), 57.
[8] Donald Davie, 'From the New World', in *Collected Poems* (Manchester: Carcanet, 1990), 147.
[9] Davie, 'To Enrique Caracciolo Trejo', ibid. 163–5.
[10] Davie, 'A Letter to Curtis Bradford', ibid. 99.

Dressed up as a quest for the old British energies in the ex-colony, Davie's envy is in truth an attraction to the 'spirits' of twentieth-century power. In a late poem to Thom Gunn, Davie reflects on their common status as transatlantic poets: 'We are mid-Atlantic people, | You and I,' he imagines Gunn saying. No, Davie demurs, Gunn is 'mid-Pacific', living close to the 'pacific | Ocean, the peacemaker'. Yet that American peace is a blind for the true source of US attraction, Cold War weapons of mass destruction, concealed in the Californian silos near Gunn's adopted home, as Davie goes on to surmise:

> Over your head the flying lizard
> Sprung from its Lompoc silo, Vandenberg Airforce Base,
> Tracks high across mid-ocean to its target.
> Ignore it, though a tidal wave will rage
> From where it plunges, flood Japan
> And poison Asia.[11]

The Movement, then, could be seen as a movement towards the edge of the Cold War, either the wistful shoreline where Larkin's visions of old England appear as mirages impossibly beyond American influence, or radically towards the edges of the States themselves, the end of the world from where the end of the world will be unleashed: 'This is the end of the world. At the end, at the edge,' writes Davie, of Gunn's Pacific shores of nuclear America.

Another Movement poet to relocate west was the biggest cold warrior of them all, Robert Conquest. After working for the Foreign Office's Information Research Department for ten years gathering information about Soviet camps and disseminating proof of the Gulag as propaganda to interested parties, Conquest left, first, to advocate the Orwellian poetic credo of the Movement, as outlined in the preface to the 1957 anthology *New Lines*. For Orwellian, read Cold War liberal: '[One might] say that George Orwell with his principle of real, rather than ideological, honesty, exerted, even though indirectly, one of the major influences on modern poetry.'[12] Conquest then went to work in America, vanguard for him of the freedom of the West. To follow Auden was no longer to abandon British culture, but to defend it, under the wings and missiles of the American eagle. The US harboured the nuclear sublime, the heart of Cold War technology, the power of rockets like 'a wave to break across the sky' from 'deep in the larger landmass'.[13] This was the country which made the science fiction (which Conquest liked to write) come true, homeland of the Cold War, 'this dangerous peace'.[14]

---

[11]   Davie, 'To Thom Gunn in Los Altos', in *Collected Poems*, 294–5. Vandenberg saw the first Thor intermediate range ballistic missile (IRBM) launch in 1958, hosted the CORONA spy satellite program, Atlas missile tests and silos, then Titan and Minuteman ICBM test launches.

[12]   Robert Conquest, 'Introduction', in *idem* (ed.), *New Lines* (London: St Martin's Press, 1956), p. xvi.

[13]   Conquest, 'To Launch the Satellites', in *New and Collected Poems* (London: Hutchinson, 1988), 55.

[14]   Conquest, 'A Girl at Sea', ibid. 67.

For an Orwellian cold warrior, the 'vicious winter' of the Cold War 'grips its prey less tightly' in the warmth of the United States.[15] It is from the vantage-point of superpower that light verse about love and travel can be generated without guilt, and the occasional broadside launched against Soviet propaganda and the evils of socialist realism: 'Barren and burnished | The air clangs angry | Above the political city.'[16] It takes an ex-propagandist to write so well against propaganda.

So influential did the Movement become that it effectively silenced the neo-Romantic opposition in British culture, despite the resistance of groups such as the 'Dionysian' Mavericks.[17] The struggle for ascendancy led to what Silkin called the 'sentimental tyranny' of Movement rationalism[18]—which had everything to do with the close fit between the Movement and Cold War imperatives. Conquest set the style for the ascendancy by stating that the Movement '[submitted] to no great systems of theoretical constructs nor agglomerations of unconscious demands',[19] thus equating surrealist and neo-Romantic poetry with the Marxist enemy, and the rational 'new lines' with Orwellian vigilance and power.

The Movement's secret attachment to the nuclear comforts of the United States emerges in symptomatic form as envy of the securities and largesse of American poets, Davie's admiration for Olson and Pound being the obvious example. It had also to do with the gaze east, towards the dissident poets behind the Iron Curtain. Again Davie is typical here (despite Amis's and Auden's dismissal of foreign languages and cities) with his admiration for Pasternak, Mickiewicz, and Mandelstam. His fine elegy 'Mandelstam, on Dante' makes a sweet Dantescan fetish of the tortures suffered in Lubyanka and Voronezh:

> You are not to be thought of apart from the life you lived
> And what Life intends is at once to kill and caress
> That thus the distress which beat in on your ears, on your eyes
> And the sockets of your eyes, be Florentine.[20]

Torture pains are imitated here, stress and beat of verse dedicated to the blows received in the interrogation chambers of the enemy creed. This admiration for dissident poetry is a prominent feature of the work of many British Cold War poets. The engagement in translation as a means of solidarity with poets in the Eastern bloc is a powerful factor in the poetry of Michael Hamburger, Ted Hughes, and Jon Silkin—but used, significantly, to wrest British poetry from the stranglehold of Movement sweet reasonableness.

Silkin's *Stand* was proud of its commitment to Eastern bloc poets, from Blok to Brodsky. It published Alex Miller's translation of *The Twelve*, Elaine Feinstein's

---

[15] Conquest, 'George Orwell', ibid. 91.   [16] Conquest, 'Socialist Realism', ibid. 135.

[17] See Howard Sergeant and Dannie Abse (eds.), *Mavericks* (London: Editions Poetry and Poverty, 1957).

[18] Jon Silkin, 'Introduction', in *idem* (ed.), *Poetry of the Committed Individual: A Stand Anthology of Poetry* (Harmondsworth: Penguin, 1973), 18.

[19] Conquest, 'Introduction', p. xiv.   [20] Davie, 'Mandelstam, on Dante', in *Collected Poems*, 280.

versions of Marina Tsetayeva, Edwin Morgan's translations of Voznesensky and Yevtushenko (notably 'Stalin's Heirs'), Ian Milner's versions of Miroslav Holub. Translation, for Silkin, was an act of listening, to gauge 'what the sensuous powers and moral entrapments feel like' in other cultures, in order to help us in the UK 'not to preserve but freely to practise our own [culture]'.[21] But in terms of Cold War engagements, the reading of translations from the USSR is an act of humbling proxy witness, supplementing the loss of innocence brought on by the cumulative shock of the Holocaust: 'The experience of concentration camps, and totalitarianism, has been diffused throughout consciousness and we have lost what little innocence we might have possessed.'[22]

For Silkin, the best English poets are those who have allowed the terror of that knowledge to diffuse throughout the textures of their poetry in English, poets like Geoffrey Hill—for his imaginary staging of totalitarian holocaust in England (re-creating Towton in the 'Funeral Music' sequence)—or Roy Fisher, whose still images of ordinary objects like chairs are 'frightening, not because of what they are (seen as), but for what they have been made to do'[23] in the terror camps of totalitarian countries:

> Here are the schoolroom chairs on which
> the ministers, in the playground,
> Sat to be shot.[24]

Such acts of translation brought the horrors of Cold War totalitarianism abroad back home on to British soil, in a nightmarish and uncanny deictics of the here and now.

More acutely, the example of dissident writers also quite simply affirmed the power of poetry in ways the West had forgotten. As George Reavey wrote in his introduction to his fine translations of Yevtushenko:

There is something about the poet and his poetic utterance that has a terrifying effect on some Russians, and especially on the Authorities, be they Tsarist or Soviet. It is as though poetry were an irrational force which must be bridled and subjugated and even destroyed. If the critics cannot do it, then the police must try.[25]

Translation and imitation of Russian dissident poetry gave poets in the West a surrogate sense of that irrational force, not only as though preserved within the Russianized English of the poems, but also as though half-relishing the bridling subjugation of those brutal 'authorities' in an 'age of rockets'.[26]

Michael Hamburger, German-Jewish émigré poet writing in English, saw translation as a means of forcing British culture to feel more deeply the hard necessities

---

[21] Silkin, 'Introduction', 20.   [22] Ibid. 37.   [23] Ibid. 36.

[24] Roy Fisher, 'Seven Attempted Moves', in Silkin (ed.), *Poetry of the Committed Individual*, 70.

[25] George Reavey, 'Yevtushenko: Man and Poet', in *The Poetry of Yevgeny Yevtushenko*, ed. and trans. George Reavey (London: Calder & Boyars, 1969), p. vii.

[26] Yevgeny Yevtushenko, 'Rockets and Carts', ibid. 89.

of the Cold War, specifically a form of core solidarity with East European suffering under censorship, as transformed by the 'absolute poetry and absolute politics' of European Symbolism.[27] A similar forcing characterized the efforts of *Modern Poetry in Translation*, founded by Daniel Weissbort and Ted Hughes in 1966. The coded meanings of translation can be gauged from Hughes's description of the little magazine's editorial policy: 'we saw our editorship as something like an airport for incoming translations, an agency for discovering new foreign poets and new translators, who then might pass inland to more permanent residence in published books.'[28] To be both an airport and an agency is to rival, at a psychic level, the state from which the incoming missile-missives depart. The first issue of *Modern Poetry in Translation* was largely devoted to Eastern Europe (Zbigniew Herbert, Miroslav Holub, and Vasko Popa), and the kinds of experience Hughes was interested in—violent, psychosexual-political, shamanic-somatic—come equipped with a special Cold War lustre in the translation work.[29]

Recalling his sense of solidarity with mid-European poets in 1989, the year the Wall fell, Hughes makes this clear:

Circumstantial proof that man is a political animal, a state numeral, as if it needed to be proved, has been weighed out in dead bodies by the million. The attempt these poets have made to record man's awareness of what is being done to him, by his own institutions and by history, and to record along with the suffering their inner creative transcendence of it, has brought their poetry down to such precisions, discriminations and humilities that it is a new thing.[30]

Such circumstantial proof locks Hughes's own poems into the same Cold War frames, revealing their obsession with the hardware of lethal technology as a new figure for the killer instincts within unconscious species drives: the pike as nuclear submarine ('submarine delicacy and horror. | A hundred feet long in their world'[31]); thrushes like strike aircraft ('attent sleek thrushes on the lawn, | More coiled steel

---

[27] Michael Hamburger, *The Truth of Poetry: Tensions in Modern Poetry from Baudelaire to the 1960s* (London: Weidenfeld & Nicolson, 1969), 81.

[28] Hughes, quoted on *Modern Poetry in Translation* website through King's College, London: <http://www.kcl.ac.uk/humanities/mpt/issu.html>

[29] Other poetry translation projects which sustained Cold War-inflected links with dissident poets in the Eastern bloc include *Delos*, with translations of Mandelstam and Pasternak, and Oxford University Press's list: e.g. Oxford University Press published Pasternak's *In the Interlude: Poems, 1945–1960*, trans. Henry Kamen in parallel text (1962), and Andrei Voznesenky's *Antiworlds*, trans. Auden *et al.*, ed. Patricia Blake and Max Hayward (1967).

[30] Ted Hughes, 'Vasko Popa', in *Winter Pollen: Occasional Prose*, ed. William Scammell (London: Faber, 1994), 220–1.

[31] Hughes, 'Pike', in *Collected Poems*, ed. Paul Keegan (London: Faber, 2003), 85. The first nuclear submarine was the USS *Nautilus*, authorized by Congress in July 1951, built, at the Electric Boat Shipyard in Groton, Conn., between 1952 and 1954, launched on 21 Jan., commissioned as first nuclear powered vessel 30 Sept., 1954. 'Pike' was published by the Gehenna Press in 1959, and then in *Lupercal*, Mar. 1960. The submarine was in the news in 1959 following a series of fires, leaks, and flooding incidents, which prompted fear of nuclear sabotage. See<http://navysite.de/ssn/ssn571.htm>

than living'[32]). If the male poet harbours such beasts within his psychosomatic system, as well as outside in the silos and bases of the Cold War, then every relationship is similarly translated into something rich and dangerous by the fact of the nuclear threat between East and West. Married to an American woman and poet, translating male poets from the Communist East, Hughes felt the Cold War rock his house with something approaching exhilaration. In 'Wind', every house is subject to the 'wind' of nuclear holocaust ('the brunt wind that dented the balls of my eyes'), which, paradoxically, makes the domestic space sing as though under aesthetic pressure: 'The house || Rang like some fine green goblet in the note | That any second would shatter it.' Under threat of Mutually Assured Destruction (or MAD), every man and wife is under the surveillance of a savage eye of death, figuring the murderous arguments of the sex war: 'wind wielded | Blade-light, luminous and emerald, | Flexing like the lens of a mad eye.'[33] Again it is the Cold War which helps to lift the self-consciousness of a couple's paranoia into the transcendent realm of art and war technology, the absolute poetry and politics of the 'M.A.D. eye' nuclear sublime. Under the psychotically introjected dual gaze of 'Russia and America', who 'circle each other' in 'A Woman Unconscious', lies the sacrificial victim of the Cold War, the citizen imagination troped as a Plath figure dying in 'the white hospital bed'.[34]

The Cold War acted as a form of double pressure, then, on poets in the 1950s and 1960s, subjecting them to the blandishments and dependency resentment of the special relationship to the west, and aligning them with the suffering and example of dissident poets to the east. Both forms of pressure had a dispiriting effect on the morale of poets on these islands. The American example produced the infamous A. L. Alvarez introduction to the 1962 anthology *The New Poetry*, accusing British poets of craven gentility, inveighing against the negative examples of late Auden, Dylan Thomas, and the Movement controlling the machinery of British poetry.[35] To the east, the example of the dissidents was palpable in the high profile of poets such as Yevtushenko and Brodsky in sales and on the poetry circuit (for example, the popularity of the Penguin Modern Poets and Penguin Modern European Poets series). The net effect was to invite British poets to relocate, in real and imaginary terms, to the States or Europe and beyond, to adopt an itinerant lifestyle or writing style that renounced and redeemed UK provincialism and its gentility principle. Heading west: Christopher Middleton to the University of Texas; Lee Harwood publishing in New York alongside the New York school, then writer-in-residence in San Francisco; Ken Smith teaching creative writing at Clark University, his first collection coming out from Chicago's Swallow Press in

---

[32] Hughes, 'Thrushes', in *Collected Poems*, 82. Both 'Thrushes' and 'Pike' were written whilst Hughes was working in the US (Spring 1958–Dec. 1959).

[33] Hughes, 'Wind', ibid. 36.   [34] Hughes, 'A Woman Unconscious', ibid. 63.

[35] A. L. Alvarez (ed.), *The New Poetry* (Harmondsworth: Penguin, 1962). See also Alvarez's *Under Pressure: The Writer in Society: Eastern Europe and the U.S.A* (Harmondsworth: Penguin, 1965).

1972;[36] John Ash relocating to New York in the early 1980s, an Ashbery disciple gnomically trashing British culture. Heading east: Edwin Morgan with his trips to Russia and Eastern Europe, his wonderful translation work;[37] Duncan Bush, who shuttled between Wales and Europe, and wrote the prose-verse novel *The Genre of Silence* (1988) about the disappearance of the Soviet poet Victor Bal in Stalin's purges. Victor Bal is fictional, but it is an indication of the depth of identification of poets such as Bush with their dissident counterparts that the 'imitation' of Bal's poetry is so uncannily realistic. Bal perishes in the terrible purges of writers after 1937, and leaves manuscripts of poems addressed to fellow victims (Mandelstam, Babel), to the poisonous and self-destructive Writers' Union ('sheep | milling for the microphone | like wolves'[38]), and, most pertinent to the Cold War, addressed to all writers caught up in the imagining of totalitarian forces: 'We lie awake at night and dream | the knocking at the door through which | we'll disappear for ever.'[39] What Bush captures so deftly is the constant hum of paranoia within all minds composing poetry during the Cold War, a fantasy of persecution ('the times' | skulduggery and paranoia') generated by sympathy for poets to the east with their *samizdat* poems—'self-seeding, || perennial, unkillable as thistle'.[40]

Still, the overwhelming influence was from America, boosted by the special relationship's occult and hypnotic sway even and inevitably over movements set up in opposition to Cold War militarization. In Cold War Britain, as the New Left rose to prominence in the wake of anti-nuclear protests in the late 1950s, a very special relationship developed between British poets opposed to the arms race and their seniors in the Beat (particularly Ginsberg and Burroughs) and Black Mountain schools (Olson above all, alongside Creeley and Duncan). The British Poetry Revival in particular was largely shaped by the example of the resistance of American poets and writers to the nuclear warfare state. Gael Turnbull's Migrant Press bridged the UK and US, linking poets with the American avant-garde. Stuart Montgomery's Fulcrum Press brought the voices of Snyder, Zukovsky, and Duncan into relationship with the resuscitated English modernism being practised by Roy Fisher and Basil Bunting. Significantly, Fisher ended up teaching on an American Studies programme, as did Eric Mottram.[41] And many of the Revival poets joined

---

[36] In Cold War terms, see also Ken Smith's documentary *Berlin: Coming in from the Cold* (Harmondsworth: Penguin, 1991). His poem 'Secret Police' imagines them singing praises to the God of Paranoia.

[37] See Edwin Morgan, *Collected Translations* (Manchester: Carcanet, 1996). This includes Mayakovsky done into Scots, translations of Voznesensky, Pasternak, and Vinokurov.

[38] Duncan Bush, 'Night, Day', in *The Genre of Silence* (Ogmore-by-Sea: Poetry Wales Press, 1988), 38.

[39] Bush, 'Writers' Union Building, Moscow, 1937', ibid. 31.

[40] Bush, 'The Age of Rust', ibid. 37.

[41] Indeed, it was the fact that Mottram printed too many Americans in the *Poetry Review*, which he edited during the 1970s, which led to his dismissal by the Poetry Society, a sacking which still resonates today in the split between mainstream and so-called Linguistically Innovative Poetry.

Ginsberg in the June 1965 Albert Hall Poetry Incarnation partly inspired by the anti-Vietnam protest meetings occurring in the States. Underlying many of the more arcane oppositional interests and concerns of the Revival were very powerful and intense reflections on the nuclear sublime, a theorizing of the Cold War as a global, militarizing, 'closed' system of controlling discourses.[42] Bob Cobbing's experiments in permutation and chance in the generation of text begin with an acknowledgement of the ways in which culture is being driven by the Cold War's computerized systems of prediction, game play, and feedback. Similarly, Eric Mottram's interest in open field poetics came into being partly through his sense of the alarming fit between nuclear culture in the States and modes of mind control in provincial dependants like the UK. His 1974 Kent Journal, reflecting on May 1970 when the National Guard opened fire on Kent State University students protesting against Cold War culture in all its ramifications, identified the enemy's ideology of armoured power and policed boundaries with radioactive assault on the body's cell walls, as Allen Fisher has argued.[43] Mottram's 1989 collection *Peace Projects and Brief Novels* puzzled over the deeper dynamics of Cold War paranoia: 'according to Darwin | only the most paranoid survive'.[44] That paranoia was based on the fantasy construction, by the paranoid system itself, of an East–West division in the citizen imagination: 'history makers propelled you east | further fantasy orders'; 'with absurd leaders hung with fantastic offerings from craving to be abject in the West'.[45]

J. H. Prynne, in his ground-breaking 1969 collection *The White Stones*, inaugurated an Olsonian poetics of dissent through a compromised perceptual withdrawal from the discourses of power, figured most insistently as the splicing, radioactively insinuative language of nuclear control. The poems interrogate the disjunctions of the Cold War in a series of semi-occult and abstract-riddling moves which foreground the global geopolitics of an East–West division. 'The Western Gate' reimagines the earth as subject to the Cold War's 'turning & failing metaphysic', the false gleam of history, the formal circuits of power, reducing the dissident poet's role to redundant ecology or bankrupt Eliotic custodianship of language ('I dedicate the results | to the fish of the sea and the purity of | language'[46]). The line of poetry itself is 'taut with | strain' under nuclear threat ('The explosion | is for all of us'),

---

[42] See e.g. Michael Horovitz, 'Afterwords', in *idem* (ed.), *Children of Albion: Poetry of the Underground in Britain* (Harmondsworth: Penguin, 1969), 369: 'We're weaving our own several embroideries . . . on the sublime nuclear bing-bang loom inherited from Corso and Voznesenky and Kops, who blow up the bomb in the best blast blessible—outlining its look & boom in haphazard mosaics of words which locate the explosions in their psyche, to express them—creatively.'

[43] Allen Fisher, 'Æsthetics and Ethics: An Aspect of Eric Mottram's 1974 Kent Journal'; <http://www.albany.edu/mottram/emmag1af.html>

[44] Eric Mottram, 'Peace Project 2', in *Peace Projects and Brief Novels* (King's College, London: Talus Editions, 1989), 4.

[45] Mottram, 'Peace Project 3', ibid. 5.

[46] J. H. Prynne, 'The Western Gate', in *Poems* (Newcastle-upon-Tyne: Bloodaxe, 1999), 48.

and all citizens, psychically and politically, are co-opted into the waiting game of deterrence, recruited to the 'western gate' as military watchmen in fear of NATO's sky and horizons. Other poems offer a less symptomatic view, a neo-Romantic desire for some non-aligned trumping of the Cold War's geopolitics: 'the life of the heart | and the grace which is open to both east and west' of 'Moon Poem'.[47] But even here it is difficult to disengage the lines of hope from the infections and inflections of the other side's discourses, as though the very environment to which a post-Romantic might hold allegiance has already been polluted by nuclear ideology. 'On the Matter of Thermal Packing' imagines the subject slushing through the 'meltwater' generated by a thaw in the Cold War's ice, 'frozen water' which stands as a dream trope for the special relationship binding the UK to US nuclear policy (coded as associating 'New England' with 'English localism').[48] But the meltwater is toxic, radioactive, alive with the paranoia built into the Cold War's fear and hate system, its hold on minds, its infiltration of bodies, the 'eloquence' of its propaganda:

> The days a nuclear part
> Gently holding the skull or
> Head, the skin porous to the
> Eloquence of . . .

The Cold War may not be happening in quite the live way in which the World Wars were fought. Nevertheless, poets, as all citizens, 'must live in compulsion', Prynne's striking phrase for Cold War subjection in 'Star Damage at Home'. That subjection is a compulsion both to feel and fear the nuclear sublime ('the mortal cloud . . . the idea of blood | raised to a final snow-capped abstraction') and to be forced politically to participate in the American superpower's divisions (over civil rights, over Vietnam), understood as a re-enactment of the Civil War ('Fix the eye on | the feast of hatred forcing the civil war | in the U.S.'[49]). The special relationship, Prynne argues, is just such an amalgam of compulsions at the level of the imagination.

Ian Hamilton Finlay's extraordinary concrete constructs in the Rousseauist 'Little Sparta' garden in Lanarkshire ponder the intrusion of nuclear technology and death into an aestheticized *fasciscant* Romano-Anglo-American *imperium* haunted by a corrupt/decadent dream of the French Revolution. Nuclear and military tropes are wedded to seemingly decorative classical garden design (the aircraft carrier birdbath, the temple with its inscription 'To Apollo, His Music, His Missiles, His Muses', the dryad statues in camouflage) to create a radical and witty concrete poetry of the Cold War as post-Enlightenment ideology. By the wee loch in the garden, Lochan Eck, protected by seven machine-gun turrets, is the most striking

---

[47] Prynne, 'Moon Poem', ibid. 54.
[48] Prynne, 'On the Matter of Thermal Packing', ibid. 85.
[49] Prynne, 'Star Damage at Home', ibid. 109.

of his sculptural pieces, the ebony shark's fin in the Arcadian field, wittily and frighteningly summoning the shape of a nuclear submarine's conning tower into the garden of revolutionary delights, hence its title 'Nuclear Sail' (the croft and garden at Stonypath in the Pentland hills is only a short drive away from Holy Loch where the United States based Polaris nuclear submarines).

Poetry, the Revival seemed to be saying, has a superpowerful rival in the fictionalizing language games of the Cold War's discursive field—the only proper response is to go underground for the duration, organizing networks of resistance in small presses, reading spaces, and poetry zones (Prynne's rooms in Cambridge, Mottram's in King's, Hamilton Finlay's Spartan garden), mimicking the codes, intelligence cells, and secrecies of a Pynchonesque counter-culture.

If the Cold War only looked like it was just a war of words—it actually killed thousands in the 'Third' World, Korea, Vietnam, Afghanistan, and so on—it was nevertheless a war which was waged as a form of words as well, with its own systems of propaganda and persuasion. And poets were recruited to its causes and fronts too, most usefully if they remained unaware of the sources of their support. The covert funding of cultural institutions by the CIA hit the newsstands with the revelation in 1967 that *Encounter* had had funds channelled into it by the Congress for Cultural Freedom (CCF), a front organization run by Michael Josselson and other CIA *apparatchiks*. Though it was being edited by Frank Kermode and Melvin L. Lasky when the news broke, the real victim in the public eye was the old stalwart of 1930s poetry, Stephen Spender, who had edited it at the height of the Kennedy Cold War and was still its corresponding editor from the States. Poetry and poets of a liberal kind were favourite targets for the CCF, since the anti-Communist propaganda drive could most easily counter totalitarian Zhdanovite socialist realism with a formal, apolitical display of complex feeling identified with the New Critical lyric—the CCF's first port of call was the New Criticism temple, the *Kenyon Review*. The *Encounter* revelation and the consequent suspicion thrown on Spender's naive good-will did a lot to break down the hegemony of New Critical liberal poetics in the universities and bookshops. It also reaffirmed the class conflict implicit in the Cold War division between hawks and doves, as Stewart Home's typical Revival spin on events implies: 'Auden fled to America, Spender stayed here, where, as editor of *Encounter*, he was the leading beneficiary of the underwriting of English publishing by the CIA. Along with the Cambridge spies, English poetry proves conclusively that the Oxbridge system devours intelligence and spews out shit.'[50] What the Congress's shady dealings also suggested, just as menacingly for the conspiracy theorists, was that a domestic poetry of complex feeling might very well be the most (disguisedly) political discourse of them all. Only a paranoid counter-cultural poetics could succeed in the secret cold war of words within British culture.

---

[50] Stewart Home, 'Sixty Years of Treason', in Iain Sinclair (ed.), *Conductors of Chaos: A Poetry Anthology* (London: Picador, 1996), 166.

However much Spender and company might deny knowledge of the Congress slush fund, the very fact that the CIA had been so ready to fund the so-called non-Marxist Left in the cause of anti-communism was enough for the Revivalists to veer sharply to extremes. The Cold War, in other words, polarized British poetry along ideological lines, mainstream versus underground, however non-committal or even non-aligned the poet might explicitly be. The nasty turf wars of the 1970s and 1980s in Reaganite/Thatcherite Britain were more than typical Grub Street scuffles, but militant mimicry of the conflicts occurring in the broader spectrum of nuclear politics. The splits and fissures in the poetry world were a Cold War in miniature, coded, secretive, vicious, the mainstream seemingly in hock to Cold War funding, be it CCF or British Council, the underground fascinated by power and systems and technologies of death, issuing obscure chapbooks and broadsides like secret service memos and directives to a tiny counter-intelligence network.

The truth of the matter is not so dark—many poets functioned perfectly well in polite ignorance of the superpolitical world. More interestingly, significant groupings of poets operated in the twilight zone between East and West, a non-aligned space neither in truck to the nuclear sublime nor in paranoid counter-cultural reverse imitation of its power structures. Poets like Peter Robinson, associated with the Cambridge school as editor of *Perfect Bound*, moved into the 'third space between' after conflicts with the school over politics. His measured, reflective poetry ponders Britain's role as Cold War player and target, setting against the control towers of its surveillance of culture the intimate bonds and allegiances of lovers. In an early poem, 'Finding the Range', Robinson compares poetry's art of peace with the world of the military running the landscapes of Europe. Cycling inadvertently near a NATO shooting range on 'dutch brakeless bikes', two lovers fall asleep after picnicking in a copse offering 'cover', whilst listening to the 'crackle of automatic rifle fire', glimpsing 'the men | with twigs stuck in their hats'. The poet watches the clouds pass by in the sky above the Army Corps, 'the forest and the plain | and us', and quips: 'watching them | I might be counting sheep'.[51] The joke has its own reserve and caution, but resonates with crackling energy nevertheless. The clouds as sheep judge the anti-pastoral forces playing soldiers on the plain below. NATO has taken over the landscapes of poetry, turning copses into 'cover', forests of pine into 'salient feature', stripping the land of the grazing sheep, banishing them to the realm of the puffy ideal. The Armed Forces stretch from the 'shallow horizon' of England over the sea to the front lines in Germany: 'an army corps | practises combat deployment | 36 hours from its allotted front line.' Yet the pastoral art of peace which poetry deploys, with its own front lines and range, can offer a comic rebuff of its own to the heartless military appropriations

---

[51] Peter Robinson, 'Finding the Range', in *Overdrawn Account* (London: The Many Press, 1980), 45. See also Robinson's extraordinary 1980s poem collocating domestic argument with imminent nuclear apocalypse, 'Pressure Cooker Noise', in *Selected Poems* (Manchester: Carcanet, 2003), 25.

of territory, public and private. 'Finding the Range' argues for poetry's peace whilst acknowledging, through edgy satire, the Cold War's grip on its own landscapes. The men with their rifles may chance upon the lovers, may even have poetry in their sights: but the art of peace has taken due cover in the copse, and dares to please itself with an Aristophanic joke about the weird games the powers that be may play. Their rehearsal of the game of war is judged and betrayed by the rival art, even at the risk of a counter-energy accusing the poet of sleeping on duty, sheep-like, drifting, insubstantially dreaming behind the lines of the 'peace'-keeping Cold War.

Robinson describes himself explicitly in an interview as non-aligned, equating his position between mainstream and underground camps with the non-aligned countries of the Cold War.[52] Similarly unrecruitable, yet opposed to the dual gravitational draw of East and West, were the feminist writers who emerged with voices liberated by the women's movements of the 1960s and 1970s, and who were also temperamentally allergic to the Cold War's male power games and militarization of culture. Liz Lochhead's 'Dreaming Frankenstein' tropes the relation between women writers and Cold War male violence as that between Mary Shelley and the monster: 'She said she | woke up with him | in her head, in her bed. | Her mother-tongue clung to her mouth's roof | in terror, dumbing her, and he came with a name | that was none of her making.'[53] The penetration of the imagination by male violence and military ideology is here troped as a rape and possession of the sleeping writer. The Campaign for Nuclear Disarmament (CND) attracted women poets into strategic non-aligned positions of protest, as with the poems and novels of Zoë Fairbairns (as well as her poetry editorship of *Spare Rib*).[54] Pat Arrowsmith, organizer of the first Aldermaston march, arrested eleven times for CND protests, brought out in 1981 a collection of anti-war poems, *On the Brink*. Best in the collection is 'View from Orford Castle', which places the castle's war-scarred history of 'suffering and slaughter' in proximity with one of the nuclear establishment's 'modern forts', Orford Ness Atomic Weapons Research Establishment testing site glimpsed on the horizon ('those mounds are filled | with deadly gadgets that could tear | the earth to bits').[55] The historical perspective shifts into the future, and Arrowsmith can register the 'taint || of strontium poison permeat[ing] the air'. She

---

[52] Peter Robinson, interviewed by Ted Slade, 'The Poetry Kit Interviews Peter Robinson', *The Poetry Kit* (1999): 'the non-aligned formal eclecticism I picked up as a student writer has stayed with me.' Available at <http://www.poetrykit.org/iv/robinson.htm>

[53] Liz Lochhead, 'Dreaming Frankenstein', in Douglas Dunn (ed.), *The Faber Book of Twentieth-Century Scottish Poetry* (London: Faber, 1992), 345–6.

[54] Fairbairns's works were concerned with resistance to the patriarchal thinking behind overtly male technology. As she put it in an essay on the women's peace movement, they represented a 'way of thinking that confronts, subverts and turns away from the deadly ejaculatory intellectualizing of the war movement, symbolised so neatly in its own creation, the cruise missile' (Zoë Fairbairns, 'Taking it personally', in *Peace Moves: Nuclear Protest in the 1980s: Photographs by Ed Barber*, with text by Zoë Fairbairns and James Cameron (London: Chatto & Windus, 1984), 31).

[55] Pat Arrowsmith, 'View from Orford Castle', in *On the Brink* (London: CND, 1981), 13.

wrote the poem in 1975 on the thirtieth anniversary of Hiroshima—a picture of devastated Hiroshima is on the facing page of the CND edition.

Denise Levertov's poem 'Talk in the Dark' takes an anarchist view of the jostling between nuclear powers and doves and hawks, here in the poem as rival arguing voices in dialogue; it appears on the excellent Peace Pledge Union Poetry and War website:[56]

> Now it's to be a mass death.
> Mass graves, says one, are nothing new.
>
> No, says another, but this time there'll be no graves,
> all the dead will lie where they fall.
>
> .   .   .   .
>
> I want to live, says another, but where can I live
> if the world is gone?

Keyed in to the important sub-genre of American nuclear poetry,[57] Levertov's poems speak from the impossible post-mortem perspective of post-nuclear holocaust, rewriting the afterlife codes of the morbid lyric. Where can the 'I' live after such a man-made apocalypse of mass death? As nuclear criticism of the 1980s attempted to argue, such a point of view is an impossible subject position, beyond archive, beyond readership, post-culture, post-human, without the 'world' of subjectivity.[58]

An Essex girl who emigrated to the States to become an American poet, Levertov writes with the directness and anger of a writer who has been absorbed by the US West, yet preserves the distance, both critical and gendered, which helps generate a poetics of dissent which can speak out loud without fear, angry at the ways in which the Cold War—and its hot version in Vietnam—have infiltrated the imagination and made it theirs:

> The same war
> continues.
> We have breathed the grits of it in, all our lives,
>
> our lungs are pocked with it,
> the mucous membrane of our dreams
> coated with it, the imagination
> filmed over with the gray filth of it.[59]

---

[56] See <http://www.ppu.org.uk/learn/poetry/poetry_nuclear4.html> It is accompanied on the website in the section on nuclear war by Alison Fell's 'August 6, 1945', which imagines a post-nuclear victim of radiation blast, like a napalmed girl on the road: 'she will walk the dust, a scarlet girl | with her whole stripped skin | at her heel, stuck like an old | shoe sole or mermaid's tail.' See Fell's collection *Kisses for Mayakovsky* (London: Virago, 1984) and her poems 'Women of the Cold War' and 'The Hallowe'en Witch (for the wire-cutters of Greenham Common)'.

[57] For history, background and reviews of key 'nuclear' texts, see *Nuclear Texts and Contexts*, all issues 1988–92 online at <http://www.wsu.edu/~brians/ntc/>

[58] For nuclear criticism, see the special 1984 issue of *diacritics* (14/2); and Richard Klein, 'The Future of Nuclear Criticism', *Yale French Studies*, 77 (1990), 76–100.

[59] Denise Levertov, 'Life at War', in *The Sorrow Dance* (London: Jonathan Cape, 1967), 79.

The white space of the printed page, identified since Dickinson with the spectral afterlife of the voice after death, is 'gray' now with the Cold War's polluting influence, the poet's page gritted, pocked, and filmed over with the other more sinister continuities of the endless, 'background' wars of Levertov's generation: 'The same war || continues.'

Anarchist-pacifist feminism was an important field of energy at the key site of resistance to the special relationship's most hated and feared secret: the Trident bases. And it was at Greenham Common where that field of energy took form, especially after the 'Embrace the Base' action on 12 December 1982, when more than 30,000 women converged on the base and linked hands to encircle the nine-mile perimeter fence (also linking the nine camps at the nine gates—code-named after the colours of the rainbow). The peace camp's song-book is a touching memorial of the camp's collective songs of protest. Activist artists joined the camp at crucial times to offer their support—an example being the Irish artist Alanna O'Kelly, who gave a live performance of her ballad 'Chant Down Greenham', which mixed the sounds of protest and peace chants with sounds from the base. The song may not be very impressive as a poetic text: '35 thousand Women for peace, | Embracing the base | So there'll be no more War.'[60] It is as a document of the *performance* of anti-nuclear protest that it still has affectionate power.[61] It is such performances which constitute the true core resistance to the Cold War called for by anti-war leaders such as Edward Thompson.[62]

The third group of poets occupying the intermediate zone between the East and West nuclear poles were the poets of Northern Ireland. The Troubles may have been a continuation of the liberation struggles of Ireland, but they were nevertheless importantly inflected by Cold War considerations. Funded partly by American money, drawing ideological support from the Marxist decolonizing liberation movements in the Third World, the IRA had revolutionary appeal at its hard left core which drew directly on Cold War energies. Conversely, the British government deployed in Northern Ireland the tactics and counter-intelligence

[60] Alanna O'Kelly, 'Chant Down Greenham'. See the São Paolo Bienal website on O'Kelly: <http://www1.uol.com.br/bienal/23bienal/paises/ipie.htm> The Greenham Common song-book is online through the Danish Peace Academy website: <http://www.fredsakademiet.dk/abase/sange/greenham.htm>

[61] Greenham Common also convinced male writers to change their tune: witness Ian McEwan's libretto written for Michael Berkeley's 1983 oratorio, *Or Shall We Die?*, which he published in *The Comfort of Strangers*, and which sings of 'womanly times' against the Cold War and a rainbow embrace around the whole of the UK: 'Make a circle round this land | Shall There Be Womanly Times or shall we die? | Join heart and hearts and hand in hand | There will be womanly times, we will not die' (McEwan, *Or Shall We Die?: Words for an Oratorio Set to Music by Michael Berkeley* (London: Jonathan Cape, 1983)).

[62] Edward Thompson, quoted in Nicholas Humphrey and Robert Jay Lifton (eds.), *In a Dark Time* (London: Faber, 1984), 151: 'We can match this crisis only by a summoning of resources to a height like that of the greatest religious or political movements of Europe's past. I think, once again, of 1944 and of the crest of the Resistance.'

operations which it had honed in Burma, Kenya, and Malaya. The Troubles, in other words, had all the hallmarks of a Cold War colonial war brought back 'home' within the UK. The poetry of the Troubles, from Fiacc to Muldoon, takes the strangeness of this on board, partly as though registering the pressure of English reading eyes.

Padraic Fiacc in his 'Enemy Encounter' gazes at a 'British Army Soldier', comically young (could be his daughter's boyfriend), encountered in the street. He says 'something bland to make [the soldier] grin', but the boy stares past with glass eyes, terrified, for 'I am an Irish man | and he is afraid | That I have come to kill him.'[63] His 'The British Connection' recites a litany of the concealed weapons in the people's houses ('Screws, bolts, nuts, Belfast confetti'), whilst 'Soldiers' records the intense social propaganda aimed at young boys to become warriors in the struggle, the 'Anna Magnani voice' screaming: '"We are the poor | And the poor have to be 'soldiers".'[64] The bizarre and sinister brutal comedy of the poems comes from the disconcerting fact that this war has all the features of the wars the British were normally fighting abroad in the long Cold War for hearts and minds in the decolonizing Third World: popular Marxist uprising against the invader ('"the poor have to be 'soldiers"'), homemade weaponry and bombs, secret paramilitary training and ideology, racist encounters ('I am an Irish man | and he is afraid').

Seamus Deane foregrounded in coded form the pressure of the Cold War on Northern Irish lives in 'A Schooling': 'Ice in the school room, listen, | The high authority of the cold'. The cold of the Cold War is ingested as ideology through the 'Government milk' Deane remembers drinking in 1940s Northern Ireland:

> the Government milk
> I was drinking and my world
> All frost and snow, chalk and ice.[65]

The 'History Lessons' at the same allegorical school turn to a dream of Moscow, Deane remembering watching a film of the burning of Moscow during the Second World War, again troped as a Cold War education: 'the sunlight | Stealing over frost, houses huddled up in | Droves, deep drifts of lost || People.'[66] The long gulp in the mouth as the voice moves from 'lost' to 'People' across the stanza break mimes the shock of the young boy Deane as he recognizes his own people in the Moscow story. The history of the Russian struggle against fascism and the Cold War allure of the USSR is colouring the dream of the Troubles, the 'Elections, hunger

---

[63] Padraic Fiacc, 'Enemy Encounter', in Frank Ormsby (ed.), *Poets from the North of Ireland* (Belfast: Blackstaff, 1990), 94–5. See also Fiacc's edited anthology *The Wearing of the Black: An Anthology of Contemporary Ulster Poetry* (Belfast: Blackstaff, 1974).

[64] Fiacc, 'The British Connection' and 'Soldiers', in Ormsby (ed.), *Poets from the North of Ireland*, 93–4 and 92–3.

[65] Seamus Deane, 'A Schooling', ibid. 157–8.

[66] Deane, 'History Lessons', in *History Lessons* (Dublin: Gallery, 1983), 10–11.

strikes and shots', the burning of the houses, the raids ('Men on ladders | Climbed into roselight'). The dream, for Deane, concentrates down to a single fixed image, signifying the 'Russian' interpretation of the Troubles: 'a burning | In the heart of winter and a boy running'. The boy running might stand as a figure for the imagination trying to escape from the ideological forces of the cold's high authority, forces which translate Belfast into Moscow, the warfare in Northern Ireland into an anti-Fascist struggle, the people lost in the deep drifts of the propaganda bedevilling all Cold War-inflected conflicts.

That boy running represents most of the poets sickened by the violence meted out against and by their people in the ferocious war. If the Cold War was secretly underpinning the fanaticisms on the ground in Northern Ireland, from the Marxist-revolutionary wing of the IRA to the counter-insurgency psyops deployed by the Special Forces, the poets took their cue from the non-aligned dissident communities in the Soviet Union and America properly to disengage themselves from the ideological quagmire. Seamus Heaney learns the pacifist mantra, '*The end of art is peace*',[67] from a dream of pre-industrial Ireland, but the true source of his neutral stance in the Troubles is the example of fellow poets enfranchising themselves from the wars of the twentieth century: 'I am neither internee nor informer,' Heaney tells us in 'Exposure', but an 'inner émigré, grown long-haired | And thoughtful; a wood-kerne || Escaped from the massacre'.[68] The code-word for the resistance to Hitler and Stalin, 'inner émigré', is stitched together with the protective and survivalist instincts of the Irish peasantry against English incursions. This is Deane's boy running, just as Heaney himself could be said to have escaped the massacre with the 1972 resignation of his Queen's University Belfast lectureship and move to the woods of County Wicklow in the South.

It is also an escape to the decolonized territory of Eire, outside the zone of wartime propaganda. In a poem addressed to Deane, 'The Ministry of Fear', Heaney recalls an encounter with a British soldier, rifling through his letters at a road-block. The poet realizes there and then that the poetic tradition is closed to the Irish Catholic:

> Ulster was British, but with no rights on
> The English lyric: all around us, though
> We hadn't named it, the ministry of fear.[69]

The propaganda machine of the British Government of the Second World War is everywhere in Northern Ireland, because this is an ideological war (with its own cultural apparatus) of a similar magnitude, closing off the subject people's access to the traditions of the language.

---

[67] Seamus Heaney, 'The Harvest Bow', in *Opened Ground: Poems 1966–1996* (London: Faber, 1998), 184. The source of Heaney's line is Coventry Patmore.
[68] Seamus Heaney, 'Exposure', ibid. 144.   [69] Heaney, 'The Ministry of Fear', ibid. 136.

The escape is partly an escape from all involvement in war poetry because of the risk of the accusation of vulturism, as 'The First Flight' admits: 'I was mired in attachment | until they began to pronounce me | a feeder off battlefields.'[70] That attachment to the Catholic community tied Heaney up into a necessarily sentimental attitude to the spectacle of violence: the voice of his shot cousin in 'Station Island' accuses him of having 'saccharined my death with morning dew'.[71] But equally, Heaney, like Deane, identifies escape as the inner emigration or flight of the imagination because of its prehistory in dissident writing from the Soviet Union, the boy running from the cities burning in Cold War's winter. This is partly the point of his essay on Mandelstam in *Preoccupations*,[72] as well as the Mandelstam reference in 'Exposure': 'As I sit weighing and weighing | My responsible *tristia*. | For what? For the ear? For the people?'[73] But unlike the cold warriors who managed their allusions to Soviet dissident poetry to screw up their courage in the unreal war, here Heaney leans on Mandelstam both to identify the Northern Irish predicament as a version of the Cold War fought abroad, but also for support for the act of exile from the war as such (as into a space where all political questions are blank—'For the people?'). Mandelstam's internal and real exile to Voronezh becomes a governing trope to justify disengagement.

Disengagement of a very different kind seems to be the convoluted point to Muldoon's poetry about the Cold War connection. In 'Cuba', Muldoon remembers the news breaking of the Cuban missile crisis, and the ways it was communicated to the Irish Catholic home, his father pounding the table, using the threat of ' "the world at war, if not at an end" ' to scare his daughter into submission, boasting of Kennedy as ' "nearly an Irishman" ', but only in so far as this means ' "he's not much better than ourselves" ', therefore capable of blurting out Armageddon (' "And him with only to say the word" '), so say your prayers. Whilst the young Muldoon ponders his father's politics and the end of the world, his sister May is forced to go into details when confessing to a mild sexual encounter 'from beyond the curtain'.[74] The whole episode is draped in disguising, trivializing comedy, yet sparkles with suggestion of the impact of the wider world of geopolitical warfare upon the domestic power games within the Northern Irish family unit. The pressure of the patriarch on the family may be theologically bullying and sexually prurient: its real power is modelled on the presidential power of the casual destructive word, Cold War apocalypse as interpellative back-up to the father's voice. More insinuatingly, the episode functions as a tiny allegorical drama. The Cold War is, the poem

[70] Heaney, 'The First Flight', ibid. 274.   [71] Heaney, 'Station Island', ibid. 261.
[72] Heaney, 'Faith, Hope and Poetry: Osip Mandelstam', in *Preoccupations: Selected Prose 1968–1978* (London: Faber, 1980), 217–20.
[73] Heaney, 'Exposure', 144.
[74] Muldoon, 'Cuba', in *Poems 1968–1998* (London: Faber, 2001), 78–9. First published as 'Cuba, 1962' in 1978. Tim Kendall, quoting a 1982 interview, notes that 'Muldoon has laconically recalled that during the Cuban missile crisis the queue for the confessional in his local church was longer than ever' (Kendall, *Paul Muldoon* (Bridgend: Seren, 1996), 75).

tells us, a policing operation, boosting local reactionary power bases over subject cultures.[75] The way the boosting works is a screwing in of the Cold War's destructive energies into those cultures' systems of menace and surveillance. Superpower shores up micropower; Cuba props up Belfast table-thumping. Muldoon's cool and comic scrutiny of the process is admirable in its way; it is also as clearly an act of Dedalus-like disengagement. But that disengagement is not peace-seeking and dissident-exiled as Heaney's is. It has its own lucid ruthlessness too, coldly analytical as well as wry. It judges the Cold War ('from beyond the [iron] curtain') through imitation of the voices running it as a system of control (over women, Catholics, Irish poets) down at the level of the local, of the family voices in each citizen's head.

If the disengagement of the Northern Irish poets from the Cold War is important, it is as the end-game of the larger political process, which also terminated itself with the fizzling out of the old colonial wars of independence and the trumping of Cold War systems by the ordinary people 'from beyond the curtain' in *perestroika* and the break-up of the Soviet Union. It also marked the end-game of British Cold War poetry, from its compromised beginnings as Movement solidarity with the cold warriors, through imitation of US counter-culture and Soviet dissidents, pointing to east and west, towards recognition of the real battlegrounds of the Cold War, the decolonizing cultures at the world's margins. The high authority of the cold, as Deane and Muldoon noted, intricately involved all exercise of power in the provinces of the new world order. Muldoon's solidarity with his sister(s), however cool and disengaged, effectively creates a bridge between the folk memory of the Cold War (which will always centre on the Cuban missile crisis) and engagement with the anarchist-pacifist resistance of the anti-nuclear women's movements. Such bridges are the essential story of Cold War British poetry, for they demonstrate, as if by imitative praxis, the ways in which the Cold War was finally withstood and lived over and out at the level of the imagination, however 'filmed over with the gray filth of it', a dream of truce which made the truce *happen* in the end.[76]

---

[75] See also the sonnet sequence 'Armageddon, Armageddon' from the 1977 collection *Mules*, where the local civil war is keyed in to the larger Cold War 'zodiac' of supranational divisions: e.g. the vision of poisoned wells and fish in Sonnet V, with the 'Gemini' forces of the Cold War above: 'Twin and Twin at each other's throats' (Muldoon, 'Armageddon, Armageddon V', in *Poems 1968–1998*, 70).

[76] See Muldoon, 'Truce', in *Poems 1968–1998*, 86–7.

CHAPTER 34

'DICHTUNG UND WAHRHEIT': CONTEMPORARY WAR AND THE NON-COMBATANT POET

DAVID WHEATLEY

In his almost unreadably brutal 1979 poem 'Dichtung und Wahrheit', Allen Curnow ponders the role of our finer aesthetic sensibilities as we respond to horror. The horror in question is at a far remove from the speaker: it comes from 'a man I know [who] wrote a book about a man he knew', but even in mediated form retains its power to shock:

> and this man, or so he the man I knew said, fucked
> and murdered a girl to save her from the others
> who would have fucked and murdered this girl
> much more painfully and without finer feelings,
> for letting the Resistance down and herself be fucked

> by officers of the army of occupation, an oblation
> sweet-smelling to Mars and equally to porn god Priapus.[1]

Not even pausing to reassure her that she is the 'less deceived' of the two, her killer insists that death at the hands of a sensitive soul is preferable to murder at the hands of a local barbarian. Just as the killer distances himself from the local 'bunch | of scabby patriots', the tale of the woman's death passes through layer upon layer of moral distancing, as when 'the man I know who knew this man or some other | man' decides to write a book describing 'what a better educated man' than the killer would have done in his place. This man, in Curnow's description, worries that the experience has been lost on the killer: 'What can you do, with nothing but a cock | and a knife and a cuntful of cognac, | if you haven't got the talent? || A big one!' The further we get from the actual murder the more obscene the act becomes, even as the speakers congratulate themselves on their distance from the inarticulate brutes below them. Condemnation and relish shade into one, and the more articulate the speaker, the more disturbing the relish becomes.

The poem is book-ended by two silences: that of the killer and that of the poet. It is always someone else doing the killing and pornographically relishing the results. Yet the poem is anything but evasive: if we condemn the poet for his self-protective standpoint, we are not repudiating but repeating the strategy of the poem; we too play the game of competitively finer feelings and install ourselves at the top of the self-deluding pyramid of sensitive souls. If we admire the poem, our position is hardly less uncomfortable: if this is enough, or 'more than enough', to paraphrase Geoffrey Hill's 'September Song',[2] are we too succumbing to the equivalence of aesthetics and morals proposed by the poem's last speaker? Does the poet have the phallically 'big' talent to make successful art out of appalling subject-matter? The question is itself obscene. The poem seems to invalidate any successful way of reading it, turning us into both perpetrators and queasy bystanders as we struggle for the right reading. If not exactly a poem to love, 'Dichtung und Wahrheit' strikes a warning note that should resonate through any discussion of contemporary poetry and its response to warfare and atrocity.

Curnow was born in 1911, and spent the Second World War as a journalist in New Zealand. Although that war was not without its share of poets who saw active service, 'Dichtung und Wahrheit' is a war poem written out of the experience of non-involvement, and both exemplifies and interrogates the condition of the non-combatant poet. The invasions of Afghanistan and Iraq and online anthologies such as *Poets Against the War* and *nthposition.com* have renewed the debate about poetry and politics, but while the technology has changed since the days of *Authors Take Sides on the Spanish Civil War*, in many ways the debate has remained the

---

[1] Allen Curnow, 'Dichtung und Wahrheit', in *Early Days Yet: New and Collected Poems 1941–1997* (Manchester: Carcanet, 1997), 111.
[2] Geoffrey Hill, 'September Song', in *Collected Poems* (Harmondsworth: Penguin, 1985), 67.

same. Should writers take a stand, and how? What constitutes a political poem? How do we measure its success? A good place to start any search for answers is Robert Duncan's correspondence with Denise Levertov, which stages one of the great confrontations of the sceptical and *engagé* imaginations in twentieth-century writing. Both came to prominence as Black Mountain poets in Donald Allen's *The New American Poetry* (1960), but after many years of friendship and mutual support, they quarrelled over Levertov's anti-Vietnam poems of the late 1960s. With his Blakean, anarchist temperament, Duncan is unable to conceive of war as, in itself, a bad thing: the search for justice and truth is a state of conflict, not rest. The poet's function, he insisted, is 'not to oppose evil, but to imagine it'.[3] When Levertov describes the apolitical privilege of rich young women in her poem 'Tenebrae' with the phrase 'They are not listening', Duncan surprisingly finds all the coercion and violence on Levertov's side: 'It is the poem itself that is not listening, that has turned to the vanity that all moralizing is in order to evade the imminent content of the announced theme.'[4] In the era of flower power and nationwide anti-war protests, Duncan writes with antinomian fury against the artist as political spokesman. What he objects to principally is the instrumentalization of poetic language for non-literary ends, not just for artistic reasons but because he denies any transference from literary to non-literary discourse:

When [protest] is directed towards a *means-end*, it is either futile or, succeeding, belongs to a complex of political meanings that can have no 'truth in itself.' This is of the nature of all acts in so far as they are *means*, i.e. not identical with their own intent.... [W]e do not say something by means of the poem but the poem is itself the immediacy of saying—it has its own meaning.[5]

A poem which offers itself up to the 'means-end' of political protest has ceased to be a poem. Their stand-off slowly killed Duncan and Levertov's friendship, and even today Duncan's implacability represents a challenge to any writer who would equate political righteousness with artistic success. Writing on the Duncan–Levertov correspondence, Marjorie Perloff strikes an apologetic note: 'Is what seems like a one-dimensional and simplistic lyric outburst against injustice or racism to be praised because its author is a member of a minority group and hence not to be subjected to the literary norms of the dominant race and class?'[6] Even to admit the question is to assume that a one-dimensional and simplistic utterance on the right side of any argument is worth having in the first place. Why should it be? In

---

[3] Robert Duncan to Denise Levertov, 19 Oct./3 Nov. 1971, in *The Letters of Robert Duncan and Denise Levertov*, ed. Robert J. Bertholf and Albert Gelpi (Stanford, Calif.: Stanford University Press, 2004), 669. This long letter has two dates on it.

[4] Duncan to Denise Levertov, ibid. 666. For Levertov's 'Tenebrae', see Levertov, *New Selected Poems* (Tarset: Bloodaxe, 2003), 92.

[5] Duncan to Denise Levertov, 28 Oct. 1966 and 19 Oct./3 Nov. 1971, in *Letters*, 558 and 668.

[6] Marjorie Perloff, *Poetry On & Off the Page: Essays for Emergent Occasions* (Evanston, Ill.: Northwestern University Press, 1998), 220.

a literary converse to the Christian injunction to love our enemies, it must also be possible to hate our simple-minded friends. For a conscientious writer on political themes, it is practically a daily duty.

Another memorable statement of the dilemma of *engagé* writing can be found in the work of one of the foremost twentieth-century aesthetic philosophers, Theodor Adorno. Adorno published his essay 'Commitment' in 1962, in response to Jean-Paul Sartre's *What is Literature?*, and had already jousted with Georg Lukács on this theme, defending the political core of modernist writing against Lukács's disgust for its anti-realist nihilism (as he saw it). He had also, in 1949, made his famous declaration on poetry and Auschwitz, still widely misquoted as an assertion that poetry was henceforth 'impossible'. His exact words are more nuanced: 'To write poetry after Auschwitz is barbaric. And this corrodes even the knowledge of why it has become impossible to write poetry today.'[7] The decent thing would be to stop writing poetry after Auschwitz; but this is a barbaric age, and for poetry to do it justice, it must internalize that barbarism, as Adorno thought Kafka, Beckett, and Celan had done. In 'Commitment' he defends this stance against Sartre with a robust attack on the political 'obligation' with which Sartre sought to trump the aesthetic demands of writing: 'motivations are irrelevant'.[8]

With his vision of all-encompassing reification in contemporary society, Adorno sees Sartre's belief in the committed individual as not dissimilar to the Fascist cult of personal sacrifice as an instrument of mystification. Even his long-time antagonist Bertolt Brecht provides Adorno with ammunition against Sartre: 'He once calmly wrote that, to be honest, the theatre was more important to him than any changes in the world it might promote.'[9] Adorno negotiates a way between commitment and art for art's sake by arguing that if Brecht's theatre were simply politics, it would be politically inadequate and untrue, leaving it defensible only on aesthetic grounds. He notes the Western desire to reclaim Brecht from his Communist politics, but condemns that too, refusing to neuter Brecht's work by separating its artistic success from its political dimension. The position of the artist remains paradoxical: if art delivers a voice to the voiceless and some measure of aesthetic justice, it does so only by commodifying suffering for the benefit of an amnesiac culture:

The moral of this art, not to forget for a single instant, slithers into the abyss of its opposite. . . . Even the sound of despair pays its tribute to a hideous affirmation. Works of less than the highest rank are also willingly absorbed as contributions to clearing up the past. When genocide becomes part of the cultural heritage in the themes of committed literature, it becomes easier to continue to play along with the culture which gave birth to murder.[10]

---

[7] Theodor W. Adorno, 'Cultural Criticism and Society', in *Prisms*, trans. Samuel and Shierry Weber (Cambridge, Mass: MIT Press, 1981), 34.
[8] Adorno, 'Commitment', trans. Francis McDonagh, in Ernst Bloch *et al.*, *Aesthetics and Politics* (London: NLB, 1977), 181.
[9] Ibid. 185.   [10] Ibid. 189.

What Adorno distrusts most of all is a naive trust in dissent to rise above our 'administered society', unaware of how it is mediated and managed by the forces it opposes. His solution is not political quietism, but a form of wounded autonomous art, leaking political awareness and import from its own despairing inadequacy: 'This is not a time for political art, but politics has migrated into autonomous art, and nowhere more so than where it seems to be politically dead.'[11]

A list of contemporary poets who have braved the dilemmas of commitment and quietism to write about conflict would include Galway Kinnell, Rita Dove, Marilyn Hacker, Adrienne Rich, Sharon Olds, Carolyn Forché, Harold Pinter, Tony Harrison, Andrew Motion, Paul Muldoon, and Sean O'Brien. While a dwindling band of living writers has first-hand experience of combat (Richard Wilbur, Louis Simpson), most write as civilians and bystanders. Yet, as the example of one of the best-known contemporary 'war' poems shows, the distinction between combatant and bystander is no longer what it was. In Jo Shapcott's 'Phrase Book', written during the First Gulf War, the enemy is no closer to the Allied pilot, on his fighter plane's computer screen, than to the poet's speaker, covering the war as a reporter. To be 'lost in the action' might mean crashing behind enemy lines or channel-surfing on satellite television:

> I'm standing here inside my skin,
> which will do for a Human Remains Pouch
> for the moment. Look down there (up here).
> Quickly. Slowly. This is my own front room
>
> where I'm lost in the action, live from a war . . . [12]

The First Gulf War was also the occasion of Jean Baudrillard's declaration that 'The Gulf War Will Not Take Place', his title expressing its postmodern doubts about the reality of war (and everything else) by way of Giraudoux's *La guerre de Troie n'aura pas lieu*. In Baudrillard's analysis, the real is evacuated in favour of the spectacle and the simulacrum, and those who would have us believe in a hidden truth behind the media façade are the true deceivers. From an initial position of power as a reporter inside the bubble of a media-packaged reality, the speaker finds herself invaded by what, on one level, appears to be a sexual assault, but on another is the dark side of her euphemism-laden language, as the military acronym 'bliss' (standing for 'Blend, Low silhouette, Irregular shape, Small, | Secluded') prefigures the violence that follows the bliss of a random sexual encounter. As fear overcomes the speaker, she falls back on phrase book-derived cries for help that appeal to a deep-rooted sense of imperialist entitlement: 'What have I done? I have done | nothing. Let me pass please. I am an Englishwoman.' The poem punctures the speaker's assumptions of superiority and exemption from violence, vengefully withdrawing her bystander status, but Keith Tuma identifies its central weakness: the 'boundaries of the self'

---

[11] Ibid. 194.
[12] Jo Shapcott, 'Phrase Book', in *Her Book: Poems 1988–1998* (London: Faber, 2000), 65.

explored by Shapcott are 'altogether permeated by the media', but the effect of this is 'hardly one of disorientation or surprise... the irony of [the speaker's] insistence on her status as an "Englishwoman" is one-dimensional and obvious'.[13] The exposure of this speaker as a sham merely serves to bolster a controlling authorial irony, whose heavily flagged superiority to this outbreak of imperialism under fire the reader can share with minimal effort. The speaker may no longer be a mere bystander, but the reader remains so, all too comfortably.

Nevertheless, Shapcott's poem demonstrates the unease that many contemporary poets have felt with the mediated nature of their subject-matter. Tony Harrison has also written about the role of media representations of war, as well as contributing to the mass media with the poetic dispatches he wrote on the Bosnian war for the front page of the *Guardian*. A large proportion of *Under the Clock* (2005) is devoted to political poems, making no apology for their ephemerality in the cause of savage indignation at the expense of Bush, Blair, and their war on terror. Good poetry owes no special allegiance to any one form of politics, but the aesthetic strategies entailed by Harrison's desire to take a stand make an excellent test case for the intersection of poetry and politics today.

The BBC comedy series *I'm Alan Partridge* ought to provide an unlikely intertext for a Tony Harrison poem, but in 'Watership Alan' the hapless local DJ is making a promotional film for barge holidays when farmers antagonized by his comments on the BSE crisis drop a dead cow on him from a bridge. An airborne dead cow features in Harrison's 'Species Barrier' too, with all the incongruity of *I'm Alan Partridge* but slightly less comedy. This dead cow is from a press photograph of Afghanistan, which accompanied the poem's first publication in the *Guardian*; the poet wonders sarcastically whether it might be a 'food-aid drop' without a parachute.[14] E. M. Forster urged us to 'only connect', and as Harrison warms to his theme, he connects the turmoil of post-invasion Afghanistan to other contemporary crises with greedy but dubious enthusiasm. The year 2001 was also that of the foot-and-mouth crisis, and in Harrison's surreal conjunction the dead Afghan cow becomes a victim of the contiguous culls in which all British animals near an infected farm were slaughtered and burned. By extension, there is a 'species barrier' between the Coalition bombers and the Afghan peasant farmers far below them. If so, Harrison does nothing to dismantle it with the (perhaps deliberately) offensive comparison in stanza 3, when the carcass becomes a 'maggot Mecca crescendoing with prayer' that 'will never feed the hungry folk who pass'. Humanitarian aid in the service of an invading army is scarcely less violent than a bombing raid; the Afghans may as well be maggots for all the Coalition understands their culture. In pursuit of his satirical quarry, however, Harrison too performs an act of imaginative violence on his Afghan

---

[13] Keith Tuma, *Fishing by Obstinate Isles: Modern and Postmodern British Poetry and American Readers* (Evanston, Ill.: Northwestern University Press, 1998), 198–9.

[14] Tony Harrison, 'Species Barrier', in *Under the Clock: New Poems* (Harmondsworth: Penguin, 2005), 9.

scene. What, in reality, do the invasion of Afghanistan and the foot-and-mouth crisis have in common? Not very much, if truth be told. The juxtaposition of slaughtered healthy animals in Britain and the disastrous loss of 'An Afghan's total herd' makes a powerful image, even as the comparison is strained; but rather than ponder the tenuousness of the connection, Harrison can only force it home in lines remarkable for their clogged alliteration and bumptious failure to scan. This is Brechtian *plumpes Denken* as crude as any Middle-Eastern oil:

> An Afghan's total herd like some gunned stray
> from culled Cumbria dumped on Kabul,
> the colluding cabinet of the hooked UK
> still committing its 'contiguous cull'.

In his poem 'Laureate's Block', written after the death of Ted Hughes in 1998, Harrison pre-emptively rejects the laureateship, though his spurning of a job he had not in fact been offered could not help but seem tetchily self-righteous. This rhetorical short circuit, as his indignation pre-empts a more complex reality with which the poem might otherwise have to engage, is a constant feature of Harrison's anti-war work. *Under the Clock* begins with a series of quatrains, 'The Krieg Anthology', whose one-note satire consists of lurid, shrieking atrocity coupled with *Spitting Image*-style portraits of Bush and Blair. Poems about bombs dropped on children can hardly be expected to observe Augustan proprieties, but it should at least trouble the reader that Iraqis feature in these poems as dead babies, bomb victims, and nothing else. It is a literally infantilizing picture. Nor should a satirist be expected to deliver balance; but the fact that Saddam Hussein does not feature at all in these poems (even as a West-supported stooge) only adds to the leftist orientalism of Harrison's project, not unlike that of Michael Moore's *Fahrenheit 9/11*.

If Western aggressors are omnipresent in 'The Krieg Anthology', '11 September 2001', dedicated to the poet's son 'in Cyprus', is entirely free of any sense of agency, of what has happened to whom or why, contenting itself with a passing reference to British army manœuvres on Cyprus and 'an island divided | by bankrupt religions | both bred in the desert'.[15] His 'curse on both your houses' even-handedness is an attractive proposition from the comfortable distance of a Mediterranean island (even one as conflict-torn as Cyprus), but the impossibility of such a style carrying over to 'The Krieg Anthology' exposes a painful limitation in Harrison's political verse. Not for nothing is his other poem on September 11 entitled 'Gaps', with its closing image of a photograph of the poet's son and father taken in New York:

> bright New York winter sun between two showers
> shining on both of them, and in between
> the World Trade Center's unbombarded towers.[16]

---

[15] Harrison, '11 September 2001', ibid. 19.   [16] Harrison, 'Gaps', ibid. 12.

The irony here is that, even as Harrison comes up against his inability to depict a terrorist attack in the same cartoon style he reserves for Blair and Bush, 'Gaps' is in fact, and possibly for that very reason, a far superior poem to most of the rest of *Under the Clock*.

Harrison reaches his nadir in the longest poem in 'The Krieg Anthology', 'Holy Tony's Prayer', in which a humbug Prime Minister complains that Ali Ismail Abbas (the Iraqi boy who lost his arms and legs in a bombing raid) is a 'sick Iraqi PR coup,' and suggests putting about the story that he has been deliberately mutilated by his own people. Tony Blair's oily religiosity is not an attractive trait, but Harrison's depictions of it barely rise above the sub-adolescent: 'I unleash terror without taint | a sort of (dare one say it?) saint! | Miraculous! No moral mire | soils my immaculate attire.'[17] The grain of truth to Harrison's outrage is undeniable: the mutilated Iraqi boy is being abused a second time over in providing the Western media with a sentimental good news story. There was, presumably, no such sop to Iraqi Kurds' feelings after Saddam Hussein's gas attack on Halabja, and the difference that this suggests between naked fascism and the more PR-conscious type might form the basis for an interesting political poem. But this is emphatically not it. In (Harrison's) Blair's fantasies of the Iraqis mutilating the boy themselves there is almost a desire for the Coalition to be even more ruthless and bloodthirsty than it is, the better to absorb the full extent of the poet's projections of absolute evil. In this he dovetails neatly with the Pinter of 'American Football': if the target is not quite malign enough, then the poet must make it so. The resulting poems are deeply flawed, not because they contain too much politics but, among other reasons, because they contain too little. Harrison has confused explicitness and effect, doggerel artlessness and accessibility, his enemy's evil and his own righteousness.

Mention of Pinter here leads to the other most prominent contemporary British anti-war poet. The genius of Pinter plays such as *The Caretaker* and *The Birthday Party* is their studied yet vague menace: what has Stanley Webber done, in *The Birthday Party*, to merit his terrifying ordeal at the hands of Goldberg and McCann? It is impossible to say, yet therein lies the strength of the play. Pinter's poetry, by contrast, could not be more peremptory in its certainties. Poems such as 'God Bless America', 'Democracy', 'American Football', and 'The "Special Relationship"' conjure a vision of yee-haw apocalypse mandated by religious bigotry and blood-lust. The mysterious sadism of *The Birthday Party* becomes very unambiguous US triumphalism:

> Praise the Lord for all good things.
>
> We blew their balls into shards of dust,
> Into shards of fucking dust.

---

[17] Harrison, 'Holy Tony's Prayer', in *Under the Clock: New Poems*, 4.

We did it.

Now I want you to come over here and kiss me on the mouth.[18]

To attempt a critique of this poem's shortcomings, its feeble sarcasm and psycho-sexual *frisson*, in isolation from its politics is probably futile. While 'American Football' spells out its topicality with the subtitle 'A reflection upon the Gulf War', other poems wear date-lines as badges of their journalistic immediacy, as in the grotesque 'Democracy' ('The big pricks are out').[19] How much better or worse this poem is made by its explanatory '*March 2003*', it may be beyond the power of criticism to say. To attack these poems for being partisan or lacking in balance is beside the point: even if the politics of these poems were beyond argument, they are *too* right for their own good.

In his short book *Welcome to the Desert of the Real*, Slavoj Žižek ponders a basic trope of much contemporary reflection on conflict, known during the Northern Irish Troubles as 'whataboutery'. In a debate that attempts to analyse a single atrocity such as the September 11 attacks, one side can always shift the focus by pointing out America's many misdeeds and asking, But what about . . . ? As Žižek writes, however: 'The moment we think in the terms of "Yes, the WTC collapse was a tragedy, but we should not fully solidarise [*sic*] with the victims, since this would mean supporting US imperialism", the ethical catastrophe is already here: the only appropriate stance is unconditional solidarity with *all* victims.'[20] In one of his Lacanian formulations, Žižek insists that 'the truth is always monstrous', and for an act of literary solidarity to carry any force, it too must contain something monstrous, in the Curnow rather than the Pinter vein of monstrosity, turning our satisfaction with its moral stance vengefully back on the reader. It is a test that Pinter's 'God Bless America' fails miserably. Americans are hawkish religious bigots, and the 'others' are their perennial nameless victims. Yet precisely in the act of asking 'what about'—what about the victims of American aggression?—Pinter succeeds only in dehumanizing them even further ('The gutters are clogged with the dead | The ones who couldn't join in | The others refusing to sing'[21]). A Pinter poem that turned on itself and its certainties, and allowed the 'other' even the possibility of being a hawkish religious bigot, if he so wished, would mark a huge advance over the cartoon victimhood that this poem chooses to peddle instead.

While Harrison and Pinter are merely two of its best-known names, the anti-war movement has inspired a significant number of anthologies, from Faber's *101 Poems Against War* and Todd Swift's *100 Poets Against the War* to the *Poets Against the War* and *nthposition* websites. Their number may be all that is significant about them, to

---

[18] Harold Pinter, 'American Football', in *Various Voices: Prose, Poetry, Politics 1948–2005* (London: Faber, 2005), 260.

[19] Pinter, 'Democracy', ibid., 258.

[20] Slavoj Žižek, *Welcome to the Desert of the Real* (London: Verso, 2002), 51.

[21] Pinter, 'God Bless America', in *Various Voices*, 256.

judge from Swift's memorably dire collection, in which the reader is offered endless artless variations on the badness of war. Marcus Moore's 'Killer' marches along to a rhythm as stiff as any goose-step: 'a rich man owns the mill | he has an iron will | he sits behind the till | he likes to watch the coffers filling | selling arms gives him a thrill.' 'The news had been one-sided as usual', begins a potted media studies seminar by Neeli Cherkovski. By the time we reach Ken Waldman's pleas to 'make the world more | open for children, to share understanding', only a bed-in by John and Yoko could make our ecstasy of righteous narcissism any more complete.[22] Much of the rhetoric associated with anti-war poetry is pitched at a level that even Georg Lukács would call vulgar Marxism. Here is Fred Johnston bewailing the quietism of Irish poetry:

Why isn't Irish poetry engaged, and ferociously, with the socio-political events of its time? . . . If Adorno argued that no poetry was possible after Auschwitz, what sort of poetry can be written after the deaths by sanctions . . . of over half a million children in Iraq? Why aren't we, as poets, screaming?[23]

The argument could hardly be more programmatic or patronizing: the writer must engage, on the level of content, with 'socio-political events', 'scream' in protest and—beyond this things get hazy. The true point of Johnston's polemic is less the political content of any protest poem than the fact of protest itself; that is enough. Johnston's own protest seems addressed primarily to other poets and the fact that, unlike him, they are not outspoken enough to protest about their fellow poets' cowardice.

Faced with Pinter's and Harrison's failure, it is important to insist that there are reasons for objecting to their anti-war poems other than apolitical revanchism. Launching the anti-war anthology *enough* in 2003, Charles Bernstein examined the nature of poetry as public speech in a time of war:

If we are to talk of 'poets' against the war, then what is it in our poems—as opposed to our positions as citizens—that does the opposing? Perhaps it might be an approach to politics, as much as to poetry, that doesn't feel compelled to repress ambiguity or complexity nor to substitute the righteous monologue for a skeptic's dialogue. At this trying time we keep being hectored toward moral discourse, toward turning our work into digestible messages. This too is a casualty of the war machine, the undermining of the projects of art, of the aesthetic. Art is never secondary to moral discourse but its teacher.[24]

One notable example of contemporary British poetry that fails to succumb, as Harrison and Pinter do, to the blandishments of moral righteousness is David Harsent's *Legion* (2005). The volume's opening sequence is a series of despatches

[22] Marcus Moore, 'Killer'; Neeli Cherkovski, *'from* After the Anti-War March'; Ken Waldman, 'Where there's war'; available at <http://www.nthposition.com/100poets.pdf>

[23] Fred Johnston, 'Longing for Readings', *Poetry Ireland Review*, 85 (Feb. 2006), 95.

[24] Charles Bernstein, launch talk at the Bowery Poetry Club, 9 Mar. 2003; posted on the Buffalo poetics 'listserv', 10 Mar. 2003:<http://listserv.buffalo.edu/archives/poetics.html>

from an unnamed war zone, and eyewitness accounts of ethnic cleansing of the kind associated with Bosnia and Kosova. The phrase 'ethnic cleansing' falls under the heading of what Geoffrey Hill has called 'atrocities of the tongue',[25] in the violence it repeats and enshrines under the cover of media-sanctioned cliché; but rather than dwell on the violence behind such phrases, Harsent refers almost breezily to a 'facility for widows' (the implication being that if the women do not enter as widows, they certainly emerge as such), as though he meant a social welfare office: here violence is taken as read, as is the futility of the theatrical indignation indulged by Harrison and Pinter. Not that *Legion* is not brutal and graphic. 'Chinese Whispers' flits from unvarnished atrocity to atrocity in a series of quatrains:

> How's this for a tale of slaughter:
> a man who slew his herd, then drew a hood
> over the trembling head of each blonde daughter
> and shot them where they stood?[26]

Even here though, Harsent makes much of his detached narrative perspective, calmly asking us 'How's this for a tale of slaughter', aware of the competition elsewhere in the same poem, insisting on the rhyme of 'slaughter' and 'daughter', and pausing uneasily on small details such as the blondness of the slaughtered girls' hair. Elsewhere, the sequence is framed by a series of italicized 'Despatches' that offer first-hand but fragmentary descriptions of combat, as though we were listening in on intercepted radio transmissions. The closer to the bone the experience described gets, the more resistant the texture of the writing becomes, as though safeguarding its opacity against the voyeuristic reader who, like the speaker of Shapcott's 'Phrase Book', would presume to be 'lost in the action' too. This is writing that takes active care to circumvent the reader keen to 'rampage . . . permissively in the history of other people's sorrows',[27] as Seamus Heaney once accused Sylvia Plath's Holocaust-inflected poetry of doing. A series of 'Snapshots' displays the forensic immediacy of a pathologist's report, delivered entirely without authorial commentary ('Troopers dead in a trench and a river of rats || . . . Lovers dead in bed and a shift of maggots'[28]). Observation becomes data retrieval, as in 'Ghost Archaeology', where the bland bureaucratic language of 'the reels | of thirty-five mill, the buckram-bound ledgers . . . the data'[29] conveys perfectly well what the nature of those 'data' might be.

Two decades before *Legion*, Christopher Reid published *Katerina Brac*, a volume written in the voice of a fictional Eastern European writer that made much of its opportunities for cultural ventriloquism while also satirizing the vogue among Western poets for writing from the old Eastern bloc, amounting almost to envy

[25]   Hill, 'History as Poetry', in *Collected Poems*, 84.
[26]   David Harsent, 'Chinese Whispers', in *Legion* (London: Faber, 2005), 21.
[27]   Seamus Heaney, 'The Indefatigable Hoof-Taps: Sylvia Plath', in *The Government of the Tongue: The 1986 T. S. Eliot Memorial Lectures and Other Critical Writings* (London: Faber, 1988), 165.
[28]   Harsent, 'Snapshots', in *Legion*, 15.   [29]   Harsent, 'Ghost Archeology', ibid. 16.

of its quality of authentic witness and suffering. *Legion* is similarly non-specific in its references, keeping its local colour purposely vague, from its obscure-sounding saints, suggestion of religion cross-bred with blood-lust ('Our Lady of Retribution'), to evocation of inscrutable peasant ceremonies, as when men file to the cairn of what might be a murder victim, 'some in their wedding suits'.[30] Even in its vagueness, however, there remains an element of risk: why set the book in Central or Eastern Europe if not to trade on that region's stereotypical associations with primitivism and never-ending ethnic strife? How different would those poems look if Harsent had chosen to set them in a conflict closer to home, such as the Northern Irish Troubles? John McAuliffe expresses his misgivings when he notes that Harsent refuses 'any engagement with the dialectics of war, of history, or its relation to specific national communities', and how instead 'the war seems motiveless, generic and irremediably foreign',[31] which sounds uncomfortably close to Seamus Heaney's *North*, or some critics' versions of Heaney's *North*, in which the reality of conflict, why it happens, and who is to blame, are elided for the sake of a tableau of mythologized bloodshed and death.

In its defence, the vagueness of *Legion* is more than the alibi of a lazy Westerner watching the horrors of the Bosnian war on the news; its lack of specificity turns the focus back on the reader, forcing us to confront the inadequacy of the images it supplies and fill in its gaps for ourselves. In 'Chinese Whispers' no tale of atrocity is without its surrounding haze of doubt and unreliability ('They told us about . . . ', 'News arrived of . . . ', 'This one's got legs . . . '), tempering our outrage with reminders of the role of inflammatory disinformation in war. If elsewhere Harsent shows no emotion in describing real atrocities, any indignation we show here might turn out to be for massacres that never were. In 'Sniper' he adopts the persona of a gunman concealed in a church tower, 'kneeling up but looking down, like a man at prayer'.[32] The sniper surveys a very local theatre of conflict, remembering the café where he drank coffee and played pin-ball, and 'the girl with Madonna's face | until she showed her teeth', her actual ugliness doing double duty for the 'neighbourly murder[s]'[33] (to invoke Seamus Heaney again) waiting to expose the ugly side of small-town life. As in Keith Douglas's 'How to Kill', also written from the perspective of a sniper, the speaker offers no justification for his actions, and is not about to be deflected from his purpose by excessive humanizing of his targets:

> The night-sky floods then clears, flagging a single star,
> and the city settles to silence under my peace.
> The woman, the child, the granddad, are nothing . . . or nothing more
> than what history can ignore, or love erase.

[30] Harsent, 'Cairn', in *Legion*, 31.
[31] John McAuliffe, untitled review of Harsent's *Legion*, *PN Review* 168, 32/4 (Mar.–Apr. 2005), 61.
[32] Harsent, 'Sniper', in *Legion*, 32.
[33] Heaney, 'Funeral Rites', in *Opened Ground: Poems 1966–1996* (London: Faber, 1998), 97.

There might be an echo in Harsent's line of Tacitus's mordant observation of the Roman legions, that *ubi solitudinem faciunt, pacem appellant* (where they make a wilderness they call it peace). The poem achieves 'peace', but a killer's peace, and unlike poems of Pinter's written from a similar position, does so without a taint of sarcasm. In *A Vision*, Yeats expressed a desire for his work to 'hold in a single thought reality and justice';[34] and while Harsent's work achieves no such unity, it refuses to relinquish its artistic balance, even as the gross evil of the sniper's crimes discredits any 'justice' on his terms. Obscene as the word 'peace' sounds on his lips, the sniper articulates the trauma of war in a manner that holds reality and artistic justice in a single thought, while leaving us in no doubt as to the actual cruelty and evil the poem embodies.

The true element of the war poem, I would argue, is the shortfall between artistic and actual justice, the justice it does to its own material and the human justice it cannot deliver, a gap the writer can choose to explore with full artistic honesty or evade through self-deception and wish-fulfilment. It has not been my objective to set up Harsent as the exemplary contemporary British poet of conflict: the reality is that the recent wars in Europe and the Middle East have not produced a single self-evident British or Irish 'war poet' for our times, or at least not in the mechanical way that anthologies such as *Poets Against the War* assume war poetry can be produced, to order; and this is to be neither celebrated nor deplored. It is simply the truth of artistic inspiration and artistic choice. More than thirty years of the Northern Irish Troubles, it is worth remembering, produced a negligible tally of poems on that subject by writers from parts of the United Kingdom other than Northern Ireland itself, and it is just as fatuous to condemn British writers for their dereliction of duty as it is to see Mahon, Heaney, and Longley as 'Troubles' poets and nothing else. The sequence on war forms only one of three parts of *Legion*: barbarically, there remain other poems to be written, about standing stones in Devon, and music and paintings, even as Fred Johnston would haul the war poet back to the more important business of screaming.

Perhaps the greatest war poet of our time is Geoffrey Hill, whose remarkable recent sequence of books beginning with *Canaan* in 1996 is haunted by childhood memories of warfare, and the noises off of more recent conflicts too; but from the point of view of *Poets Against the War* these books would hardly qualify as war poetry at all. Other writers deserving an honourable mention include Michael Longley for the sequence of volumes beginning with *Gorse Fires* in 1991, Jorie Graham, whose *Overlord* (2005) returns to the Allied invasion of Europe by way of reimagining the present, and in a more fractured and disorienting vein, Keston Sutherland's *Neocosis* (2005). What is common to all these writers, in the words of Samuel Beckett's radio talk 'The Capital of the Ruins', written out of his post-war experiences with the

---

[34] W. B. Yeats, *A Vision* (London: Macmillan, 1937), 25.

Red Cross in Normandy, is 'a vision and sense of a time-honoured conception of humanity in ruins, and perhaps even an inkling of the terms in which our condition is to be thought again'.[35] If this conception does not extend to a rethinking, in all human humility, of what it means to write poetry too, then no amount of savage indignation will avail our 'poetry against war'. Rather, as Geoffrey Hill finds, pondering his own life as a child of pre-war England, and the many other lives he might have led instead, the true artist writing in fitful peace in the shadow of never-ending conflict finds that 'all have godlike elements | divided among them: such suffering, | you can imagine, driven, murderous, | albeit under notice of grace'.[36]

[35] Samuel Beckett, 'The Capital of the Ruins', in *As the Story Was Told* (London: John Calder, 1990), 27–8.

[36] Hill, *The Orchards of Syon* (Washington: Counterpoint, 2002), 2.

PART VII

NORTHERN
IRELAND

'THAT DARK PERMANENCE OF ANCIENT FORMS': NEGOTIATING WITH THE EPIC IN NORTHERN IRISH POETRY OF THE TROUBLES

PAUL VOLSIK

Any poetry that is concerned with a canonized theme (love, elegy, war) cannot but be in dialogue with the textual space constructed by its canon. The theme of civil violence, if not war, of the sort that confronted Northern Irish poets in the latter part of the twentieth century is thus woven into an intertext which includes many forms—some popular like the western, some, within the genre, massively dominant in the twentieth century, including the standard canon of the work of the poets of the two World Wars. But there are others, like the epic, with a longer and more freighted past.

My analysis of the epic will begin with what may seem a distant issue, but is, I would (with others) argue, an origin: MacPherson's founding pseudo-epic *Ossian*—a text which served to help define the epic, in the Celtic world, in nationalist terms. The essay will then attempt to show how, despite the double, articulated critique of this link both by poets who experienced a war (the First World War) the brutality of which flew in the face of the sentiments and sentimentalities generated by the nationalist reading of the epic and by modernism's radical attack on the aesthetic that incarnated them (notably the dream of a unifying founding 'national' narrative), the model was to survive to haunt the troubles in Northern Ireland. The final, and major, part of this analysis will show how poets sympathetic to a nationalist community involved in armed conflict could find themselves negotiating (ambiguously) with certain of the *topoi* that structured this particular construction of the epic and the aesthetic priorities that were seen as consubstantial with them, while other poets, not always, but often, and not by chance, of Protestant origin, would in some sense be forced to confront more directly the darker sides of this construct and turn away from it in a gesture of refusal, one of whose manifestations would be horror of the dark, apparently endless, violence that it can incarnate.

Constructing and Deconstructing the Nationalist Epic and the Epic Character of Nationalism

At the very outset of the Romantic revolution, in a period when the question of nation was becoming central in poetry, the pseudo-epic *Ossian* (1762–3), which rewrote the Irish Fenian stories, fired the imagination of the whole of Europe. Thus Johann Gottfried Herder in his 'Correspondence on *Ossian* and the Songs of Ancient Peoples' (1773) introduces the song of this 'barbarous' people as 'the gnomic song of the nation',[1] a song that is indissoluble from the war he sees at the heart of the original epic text. Herder hears alliterative Germanic verse forms and the distich line as the incarnation of the 'marching-order of the warrior-band', a call to arms, and the echo of shields clashing. The nation, manliness, a certain violence of language, and warfare are being inextricably mixed. This reading is theorized by Hegel in his *Aesthetics*, which indissolubly links epic and nation, and nation and warfare. All those aspects of the epic that do not fit this reading (humour or the grotesque, for example) are cast into shadow.

---

[1]   Johann Gottfried Herder, 'Correspondence on *Ossian* and the Songs of Ancient Peoples', in David Simpson (ed.), *The Origins of Modern Critical Thought: German Aesthetic and Literary Criticism from Lessing to Hegel* (Cambridge: Cambridge University Press, 1988), 71.

The triumph of this tradition was so complete that it not only came to dominate critical discourse but also, like any *doxa*, provoked criticism. In *Ulysses*, arguably the greatest rewriting of an epic text, written during and after the butchery of the First World War and itself a dialogue with the epic genre and all its aesthetic modulations, Leopold Bloom will encounter an archetypal epic 'Patriot', presented thus:

The figure seated on a large boulder at the foot of a round tower was that of a broad-shouldered deepchested stronglimbed frankeyed redhaired freelyfreckled shaggybearded widemouthed largenosed longheaded deepvoiced barekneed brawnyhanded hairylegged ruddyfaced sinewyarmed hero.[2]

The whole section is a magnificent, intellectually subtle analysis of the difficulty of distinguishing clearly between noble savage and ignoble barbarian, of the fundamentally problematic and hybrid nature of a certain historically determined articulation of nationalism and the epic. It is not just that Joyce here mocks a certain Achillean, Cyclopean patriotism, not just that this patriotism manifests itself as a series of portentous platitudes expressed in a problematic public space—the pub (the fallen version of the 'Great Hall' and its 'mead-benches')—in a 'widemouthed' way, it is not just that in cadging drinks the Patriot is parodying the generosity of the 'ring-giver' leader of war bands; it is also that Joyce draws attention to the fact that, while Nausicaa/Gerty MacDowell in the following section is the voice of the sentimental novel (a genre seen as predominantly feminine), so the Patriot is ventriloquized by the voice of the epic seen as the incarnation of a brutal (and, paradoxically, sentimental) patriotism. In the passage quoted above, what is being 'taken' from the epic (and inflated) is 'hyperbolic' eulogy for the hyper-virile combatant. Here the real 'hero' of Joyce's epic odyssey is not, as the reader knows, the racially pure (redhaired freelyfreckled) Celtic patriot, but the 'impure' and feminized Jewish Bloom. Once again, Joyce mocks a certain popular if not populist late nineteenth century's absurdly inflated enthusiasm for and mix of nationality and virility, and also points, more subtly, to the fact that this discourse of purity is grounded in the 'impure' in a hybridized (not 'Hibernian') text:

From his girdle hung a row of seastones which jangled at every movement of his portentous frame and on these were graven with rude yet striking art the tribal images of many Irish heroes and heroines of antiquity, Cuchulin, Conn of hundred battles, Niall of nine hostages . . . Goliath . . . Charlemagne . . . The Last of the Mohicans . . . The Woman who Didn't . . . Napoleon Bonaparte . . . Dark Rosaleen . . . Patrick W. Shakespeare . . . Arrah na Pogue . . .[3]

Joyce is suggesting in his selection of tribal imagery (the term 'tribal' is itself rightly mocked—indeed, it is a term that has haunted, confused, and envenomed

---

[2] James Joyce, *Ulysses*, ed. Hans Walter Gabler with Wolfhard Steppe and Claus Melchior (Harmondsworth: Penguin, 1986), 243.
[3] Ibid. 244.

discussions of Northern Irish poetry) that nationality is not the space of identity and the distinct, but an extraordinary hybrid space with roots in history and also in history as it is rewritten in many different aesthetic productions. The poetic is mixed with the massively prosaic, an Irished English 'Bard' in dialogue with the patriotic melodramas of the profoundly opportunist Boucicault (Arrah na Pogue), but also incorporating the irrevocably foreign as central to Irishness. Thus that which is of antiquity is linked to that which is of no antiquity at all. It is politically a mix of the tribal, the monarchic, the republican and the imperial, a vision that will enforce gender roles not only for men, but also for women, who are contained in the role of the virginally pure (the opposite of Molly Bloom or of the 'New Woman' of the novel *The Woman who Did*) in a nostalgically mythical incarnation of national identity, embodied as the beautiful, eroticized, and death-haunted Dark Rosaleen:

> 'O, the Erne shall run red,
> With redundance of blood,
> The earth shall rock beneath our tread,
> And flames wrap hill and wood,
> And gun-peal, and slogan-cry
> Wake many a glen serene,
> Ere you shall fade, ere you shall die,
> My Dark Rosaleen!
> My own Rosaleen!'[4]

CONTINUITIES

But Joyce's frontal attack (or that of others like Beckett), did not, of course, stop the continued deployment of and high valuation placed on the epic. For worse and for better—one thinks of David Jones's powerful reworking of *Y Gododdin* as intertext for his *In Parenthesis* or Walcott's *Omeros*—the epic paradigm survives a period that had experienced the trauma of the First World War. Though Yeats did not totally share Pearse's fascination with the purifying sacrificial nature of war, he nevertheless saw in the heroic warrior a pillar of a future renewed Ireland. One has only to look at *The Green Helmet*, which ends with the election of Cuchulain as the champion of Ireland for his possession of the following epic qualities:

> And I choose the laughing lip
> That shall not turn from laughing, whatever rise or fall;
> The heart that grows no bitterer although betrayed by all;
> The hand that loves to scatter; the life like a gambler's throw.[5]

---

[4] James Clarence Mangan, 'Dark Rosaleen', in Thomas Kinsella (ed.), *The New Oxford Book of Irish Verse* (Oxford: Oxford University Press, 1986), 275.

[5] W. B. Yeats, *The Green Helmet*, in *The Collected Plays* (London: Macmillan, 1953), 243.

Yeats's life-long enthusiasm for this type of 'ring-giver'/heroic figure, for whom the ability to hate 'well' is essential, will lead him to refuse to include any of the English combatant poets of the First World War, who are such canonical figures in English anti-epic reading of warfare in the twentieth century, in his *Oxford Book of Modern Verse*. More than purely aesthetic, this decision was, as his introduction showed, a fundamental refusal to see his own heroic and epic vision of warfare questioned by men who, though they fought, chose not go to their death with 'joy' and refused to 'forget their suffering' as Yeats felt they should.[6]

In the thirty years after Yeats's death the epic was pushed to the background as Irish poetry withdrew from the public space into a more lyrical one, but when poets did return to the public arena, Yeats's particular construction of the epic would haunt their work. As Patrick Kavanagh put it in his sonnet 'Epic':

> I have lived in important places, times
> When great events were decided: who owned
> That half a rood of rock, a no-man's land
> Surrounded by our pitchfork-armed claims.
> I heard the Duffys shouting 'Damn your soul'
> And old McCabe, stripped to the waist, seen
> Step the plot defying blue cast-steel—
> 'Here is the march along these iron stones'.
> That was the year of the Munich bother.[7]

We see here how even in the work of poets who were used by the generation of the Troubles as a counterweight against Yeats we find a similar world—the world of the *Iliad*. The sonnet (and this formal choice is no doubt ironically significant) negotiates a series of marches—fought over frontier zones—as well as the militarization of the foreign and domestic space. Kavanagh creates a text in which resonate three different strata of 'iron stones', three different strata of the problem of frontiers: first the local, or, in his terms, the 'parochial'—the boundaries between 'plots'—itself haunted by the close frontier between Eire and Northern Ireland; secondly, the historical (Munich); and thirdly the epic (Homer) as foundational. It is the historical that is, in some ways, the most complex, for in the mention of Munich we have the problem of military violence (Hitler's march on Prague and the need—or not—to confront it through war) manifesting itself in places like the Iron Mountains (Erzgebirge) that separated (in German) Germany from Czechoslovakia, with, pending in the background, the later terrible ethnic cleansing of the Sudeten Germans who had inhabited this area for generations. If 'Epic' echoes the endemic violence of this part of Ireland, it does so in a much larger context, and with a complex system of counterbalancing. But the paradox of this

---

[6] Yeats, 'Introduction', in *idem* (ed.), *The Oxford Book of Modern Verse 1892–1935* (Oxford: Clarendon Press, 1936), pp. xxxiv–xxxv.

[7] Patrick Kavanagh, 'Epic', in *Collected Poems* (London: Allen Lane, 2004), 184.

poem is that it does not in fact question the epic as the epic of war; in some ways, it democratizes Yeats's construction, taking martial violence from the mythical (Troy) not just to Ireland (Ballyrush) but to Northern Ireland (Gortin), yet still accepting that one 'family' can, and perhaps should, wish to 'damn the soul' of the other and that this desire can be the iron foundation stone of significant poetry.

But it was precisely from Northern Ireland that a counter-voice was to appear, a voice that would criticize the fascination with this model and serve as a reference point for many of the younger (especially Protestant) poets of the Troubles. That voice was Louis MacNeice. In a famous passage describing his own ambivalent fascination with Ireland, he characterizes it as a place where one man's hope is

> The other man's damnation:
> Up the Rebels, To Hell with the Pope
>   And God Save—as you prefer—the King or Ireland.
> The land of scholars and saints:
>   Scholars and saints my eye, the land of ambush,
> Purblind manifestoes, never-ending complaints,
>   The born martyr and the gallant ninny;
> The grocer drunk with the drum,
>   The land-owner shot in his bed. [8]

It is this reticence about an 'epic' world of ambushes, about the epic hero turned grocer or the grocer turned epic hero, drunk on the rhythms of the drum, a world where only the 'born martyr' and the 'gallant ninny' can really feel at home that will resurrect again with the coming of the Troubles in a dialogue with the national if not nationalist Yeatsian tradition.

HESITATIONS?

At the heart of the epic is the manifestation of a community united, without hesitation, against a 'foreign' threat. This community, however one names it—tribe, clan, or nation—finds in the epic that which reaffirms gallantry and the meaningfulness of martyrdom, imposes a shared ethical framework, and bestows on the epic poet, as spokesman, an assured place in its heart, in so far as it is he who makes sense of violent and tragic conflicts, records what it considers its formative events, and eulogizes and memorializes its heroes. In so far as this is true, then a poet like Derek Mahon is emblematically an anti-epic poet, a poet whose sense of belonging is limited in the extreme, whose sense of isolation, exile, and solitude is fundamental, whose only nostalgia—and an ironic nostalgia at that—is for the small vulnerable communities in the desolate landscape they inhabit.

---

[8] Louis MacNeice, *Autumn Journal*, in *Collected Poems*, ed. Peter McDonald (London: Faber, 2007), 138.

Mahon's poems express a horror of the values that underpin the dreams of the combative 'families' or tribes. It is such horror that one finds, for example, in his 'The Last of the Fire Kings', in which the poet is 'through with history' and refuses to 'perpetuate | The barbarous cycle'.[9] What the communities want, says the poet, is precisely an epic writing of their world, the trace of the seductive but destructive sound of 'Sirens' where rioters face their enemies with dustbin lids as drums and shields (Davids facing the Goliath of the British Army, but also using a problematic symbol, a quasi-parody of the shield of the epic hero) and block up their own windows, refuse to see, choose to live in a 'darkened' world. For them, far from proposing a civilized elsewhere to the chaos of the present, the poet should 'serve', be the 'creature' of the combatant:

> But the fire-loving
> People, rightly perhaps,
> Will not countenance this,
>
> Demanding that I inhabit,
> Like them, a world of
> Sirens, bin-lids
> And bricked-up windows—
>
> Not to release them
> From the ancient curse
> But to die their creature and be thankful.

One might also draw attention to the apparently secondary but, in fact, strategic aside: 'rightly perhaps'. This interpolation can be read as a means of foregrounding a sense of doubt in a world which apparently knows no doubt. Whereas the epic bard, at least in the nationalist reading of the epic world, shows no doubt, knows very precisely where the 'good' lies, in which violent action it expresses itself and how fate of various sorts makes sense of events, for Mahon there are no such certainties. In this absence of certainty, this inhabiting of a space of radical doubt, Mahon is the inheritor of a twentieth-century tradition of outsiders—Beckett, Camus, Lowry—for whom the notion of 'home' and the dreams of a historical teleology become problematic, but for whom a sense of the radical reality of suffering remains.

What also remains for Mahon is the mass of victims, those who suffer the fall-out of epic projects, the 'survivors' of mass violence, the ghosts who find themselves imprisoned in the limbo of history, the beings whom he inscribes in what is arguably the finest single poem to come out of the Troubles: 'A Disused Shed in Co. Wexford'. In this poem, the mushrooms found in the disused shed come to symbolize multiple incidents of extreme violence—the conquest of Peru, the French Revolution, the Irish civil wars, Treblinka—and enable the poet not just to serve as witness to the intolerable suffering caused but also to pay tribute to the

[9] Derek Mahon, 'The Last of the Fire Kings', in *Poems 1962–1978* (Oxford: Oxford University Press, 1979), 65.

quieter heroism of survival, a survival that is 'human' but perhaps more profoundly the survival of the 'humane' in the face of the abject:

> Magi, moonmen,
> Powdery prisoners of the old regime,
> Web-throated, stalked like triffids, racked by drought
> And insomnia, only the ghost of a scream
> At the flash-bulb firing squad we wake them with
> Shows there is life yet in their feverish forms.
> Grown beyond nature now, soft food for worms,
> They lift frail heads in gravity and good faith.[10]

One might suggest that a similar sense of 'gravity', 'frailty', and 'good faith' informs the work of Michael Longley. As an ex-Classics scholar, he negotiates directly with the violence that he witnessed as a resident of Belfast, but also directly with the poetic tradition of the epic. Longley thus engages with the genre not by simply imitating or mocking, though his 'The Parting'—

> He: 'Leave it to the big boys, Andromache.'
> 'Hector, my darling husband, och, och,' she.[11]

—could be read as just as violent in its attack as Joyce's *Ulysses* in its mockery of the gender specifications which a certain reading of the epic and nationalist conflict set in place.

By reaching into the heart of the tradition, Longley sets up echoes with his private life and also the historical situation in which he finds himself as the Protestant son of an English father who had himself been profoundly marked by his experience of the First World War. The epic attracts him at several levels, not only thematically and formally (Longley is interested, for example, in Homer's articulation of syntax and line length) but also generically, one instance being the way in which he negotiates between the tradition of the Latin love elegy (Tibullus or Propertius) and the classical epic. Thus his historically important translation of Tibullus's 'Peace', with its use of the colloquial—the sort of speech which undercuts the formalities associated with the epic—relates to his translations of certain episodes of the great epic texts. In his poem 'Altera Cithera', Longley rewrites Propertius 'in ballpoint pen', to bring to the ground, not in death but like 'lovers', all those tempted by the 'dreary | Epics of the muscle-bound'.[12] Yet what is paradoxical about Longley is that he is obviously enthralled by the epic—if not perhaps by the 'muscle-bound'. He has stated that he has 'snatched from [Homer's] narrative flow moments of lyric intensity in which to echo [his] own concerns, both personal and political'.[13] This suggests that the epic is not, for Longley, an exotic genre,

---

[10] Mahon, 'A Disused Shed in Co. Wexford', ibid. 80.
[11] Michael Longley, 'The Parting', in *Collected Poems* (London: Jonathan Cape, 2006), 226.
[12] Longley, 'Altera Cithera', ibid. 74.
[13] Longley, quoted at <http://www.teachnet.ie/ckelly/ceasefire.htm>

its violence taking place in a mythical elsewhere (mythic mornings, for example), but a text which deals very precisely with home—Belfast, the place that Longley, unlike many other local poets, never left, the most intimate place, the domestic subject of much of his work. It is therefore not surprising that one of his most successful translations/transpositions of Homer is to be found in his reworking of a passage which follows Odysseus's homecoming and involves the epic hero's 'soiling' of his most intimate space—his massacre of the suitors and (above all) the disloyal servant girls, and his implication of his own son in this frenzied act. The passage is titled 'The Butchers', which echoes the name given to a group of Shankill Loyalists ('The Shankill Butchers') who, in the 1970s, were responsible for the killing of nineteen Catholics. Not only did these assassins kill the Catholics they had abducted, but they also tortured and mutilated them with butcher's knives and axes. Longley is here (with only slight modifications to Homer's text) describing a world in which violence is handed down from father to son as an apparently unrefusable inheritance:

> Odysseus, spattered with muck and like a lion dripping blood
> From his chest and cheeks after devouring a farmer's bullock,
> Ordered the disloyal housemaids to sponge down the armchairs
> And tables, while Telemachos, the oxherd and the swineherd
> Scraped the floor with shovels, and then between the portico
> And the roundhouse stretched a hawser and hanged the women
> So none touched the ground with her toes, like long-winged thrushes
> Or doves trapped in a mist-net across the thicket where they roost,
> Their heads bobbing in a row, their feet twitching but not for long.
> And when they had dragged Melanthios's corpse into the haggard
> And cut off his nose and ears and cock and balls, a dog's dinner,
> Odysseus, seeing the need for whitewash and disinfectant,
> Fumigated the house and the outhouses . . . [14]

RESURRECTIONS?

We have thus seen that, for these Protestant poets, the notion of community is at best problematic, that they hesitate (and the same could be shown of a poet like Tom Paulin) to speak for or even to belong to a group whose origins they refuse to see as heroic, in the way that the Orange Order sees the Battle of the Boyne or the Siege of Londonderry as 'epic' foundational events in the history of their 'nation'. One could argue that this is not true, or not as true, for the Catholic poets of Northern Ireland. For them, the tribe was seen as a microcosm of the nation. This sense of the importance of community could be one reason why Lady Gregory dedicated her

---

[14] Longley, 'The Butchers', in *Collected Poems*, 194.

rewriting of the Cuchulain story to the 'people of Kiltartan'.[15] It was also important that, as Declan Kiberd remarked, the story of Cuchulain had the immense advantage of having taken place in a past that 'was sufficiently remote to be tractable to present agendas . . . to a period before splits into sectarian and political turbulence'.[16] It is this mythic territorial base and space that served poets like Montague and Heaney well when they came to look at the military violence that was so massively present in the Troubles, and it is in the territorial nature of the story that one finds the origin of certain *topoi* that link the sacrifice of the hero to regeneration in a way that *The Golden Bough* had suggested and that Heaney reinvests. This articulation of the political and the geographical is striking in the period's renewed interest in *dinnseanchas*, but it is evident above all in the remarkable work of John Montague, a poet who is an exile returned. It is symptomatic that Montague, notably in his influential collection *The Rough Field*, resurrects an ancestral landscape, marked by 'communal loss',[17] and ends in the violent world of 'A New Siege', where he finds it possible to use Cuchulain to 'ground' his analysis of the sectarian violence—only this time the Protestants become the warrior figures:

> a black Cuchulain
> bellowing against
>   the Scarlet Whore
> twin races petrified
>   the volcanic ash
> of religious hatred.[18]

Much could and should be said about this remarkable sequence and this particular passage. For, as in Heaney, we find here a structuring articulation of place poems, poems that describe rural communities, and poems that deal with violence. But, for both poets, things have changed since the nineteenth century, in that the dream of a period before conflict has become even more distant and mysterious while, in the lines quoted, the use of the word 'races' to qualify the two linked communities—a word which, in the late twentieth century, cannot but have disturbing echoes—renders the idea of a possible community of Catholics and Protestants even more problematic. Take, for example, 'Old Mythologies', a poem from an earlier collection, *Poisoned Lands* (1961), written before the outbreak of the Troubles in Ulster, in which at last 'all proud deeds [are] done':

> a whole dormitory of heroes turn over,
> Regretting their butchers' days.
> This valley cradles their archaic madness

---

[15] This example is interesting in that it raises the complex problem of the articulation (here by a writer of Protestant origin) of the 'parochial' and the 'national'.

[16] Declan Kiberd, *Irish Classics* (London: Granta, 2000), 401.

[17] John Montague, 'The Rough Field', in *The Rough Field 1961–71* (Dublin: Dolmen, 1974), 39.

[18] Montague, 'A New Siege', ibid. 74. The lineation could be seen here as figuring a divide.

> As once, on an impossibly epic morning,
> It upheld their savage stride:
> To bagpiped battle marching,
> Wolfhounds, lean as models,
> At their urgent heels.[19]

This poem is not as dense as those in the later collection, but it involves precisely an emblematic negotiation with 'Old Mythologies'. Though the text contains manifest ironies (like Longley, it sees the heroes as 'butchers', as the victims of 'archaic madness'), the major thrust (unlike Longley) is nostalgic, in that the poem articulates heroism and hedonism ('proud deeds'), Celtic war ('bagpiped battle') and nation, with the 'Wolfhounds, lean as models'. In *Ulysses* the Patriot is accompanied by what the narrator calls 'a bloody mangy mongrel, Garryowen' that 'let a grouse out of him would give you the creeps'.[20] The emblem of the 'grousing' nation in *Ulysses* is as fallen as its owner. In Montague's poem the wolfhound, as emblem of Irishness (though the Irish wolfhound has a more problematic history than it would seem), has apparently found a new life. Those that accompany the heroes are 'lean as models' with a subtle play on 'models'—both iconically fashionable and a template for a certain mode of being. But above all it is the 'impossibly epic morning' that fascinates—because, over and above its stereotypical articulation of origins (morning) and epic warfare, one cannot be sure whether or not the 'impossibly' is to be read negatively (as 'infuriatingly'), mythologically (as 'unbelievably'), or critically (as 'in a way that could not have occurred'), or as all three.

The negotiation with the epic continues in Montague's work and undergoes an interesting modification, perhaps as the ethics of the nationalist cause are challenged when the bombings begin. This might explain the uncertainties of a text like *A Slow Dance* (1975), which contains poems bordering on the pietistically propagandist like 'Falls Funeral', but others which suggest a drawing back, like 'Hero's Portion'. This is a problem which will confront all those who feel a certain fascination with the heroization of conflict and have a strong sense of 'community'. Such a poet is Seamus Heaney.

From the very beginning, one could argue that Heaney's position (and text) was infinitely more complex than Montague's, his work always a subtly dialogic space in which a multitude of languages and intertexts oppose each other and articulate in surprising ways. His ability to function at the frontier between such different poles in carefully weighted binary oppositions (fascination and horror, for example) and to create texts that hybridize subtly different traditions means that one has to be particularly careful when analysing any one of these poles in isolation. The tropism towards the epic, which perhaps counterweighs his tropism towards certain Catholic traditions—for example, Marian devotion—allows Heaney to play pagan against

---

[19] Montague, 'Old Mythologies', in *Poisoned Lands* (Dublin: Dolmen, 1961), 22.
[20] Joyce, *Ulysses*, 242–3.

Christian, consonantal against vocalic, masculine against feminine, a certain construction of the Protestant against Catholic, North against South, narrative against lyric, an Anglo-Saxon tradition against an Irish one in a way that has deep roots in the nineteenth century but reworks this opposition by innovative means. One of the possible readings of this reworking is that, paradoxically, it attempts to create common ground between the different communities in Northern Ireland in a mythical space back beyond the divisions generated by Christianity. But Heaney does this, precisely—and perhaps dangerously—by understanding, rather than by exorcising, a world of seemingly unending tribal violence, a world that is continuously confronted with monsters and the criminal. It is this that makes his poem 'Punishment', which deals with a similar configuration to 'The Butchers' (the punishment of a sexually transgressive young woman), so controversial, particularly its famous ending that states a refusal to criticize 'the exact | and tribal, intimate revenge'.[21]

This essay will here only consider two specific areas in which the epic as a narrative of armed violence haunts Heaney's work: the reappropriation of the diction of Anglo-Saxon or Germanic epic; and his translation of *Beowulf*, its rewriting as an Ulster text, full of the alliterative distich line that had so excited Herder, in some sense the objective correlative of the clash of communities and the continuities within them.

The consonantal/Anglo-Saxon/Viking/Jutish pole of Heaney's work is evident throughout *North*, but perhaps the most telling example is 'Bone Dreams', which works towards a fine erotic encounter between the two poles mentioned above, but begins with a reappropriation of certain English roots, lexical as well as metrical, in a manner not unlike Stephen Dedalus's reappropriation of 'tundish' in *Portrait of the Artist*:

> As dead as stone,
> flint-find, nugget
> of chalk,
> I touch it again,
> I wind it in
> the sling of mind
> to pitch it at England . . .
>
> .   .   .   .   .
>
> I push back
> through dictions,
> Elizabethan canopies.
> Norman devices . . .
>
> .   .   .   .   .
>
> to the scop's
> twang, the iron
> flash of consonants
> cleaving the line.[22]

[21] Seamus Heaney, 'Punishment', in *Opened Ground: Poems 1966–1996* (London: Faber, 1998), 118.
[22] Heaney, 'Bone Dreams', ibid. 107–8.

It is the movement backwards to a grounding 'scop's | twang' that is central. And one cannot help but draw attention to the play on the word 'twang' as both the dialectal, rooted, non-standard, non-RP version of the language but also, more distantly and perhaps provocatively, the Protestant Ulster nasal sound.[23] This fascination with the asperities of a certain variety of English is one of the major thrusts of Heaney's work, and it is one that explains what might otherwise seem the marginal incident or accident of his translation of *Beowulf*—explains, perhaps, how a fascination with the world and word of *Beowulf* is at the genetic heart of his work, as is his engagement with the poetry of Ted Hughes, or indeed the complex overlapping of Christian and pagan that one finds in the Old English epic itself. As Heaney himself suggests in his introduction, he is, in his translation of *Beowulf,* 'mooring' himself in 'that complex history of conquest and colony, absorption and resistance, integrity and antagonism'—with perhaps a play on two meanings of 'moor'.[24]

One of the major characteristics of his translation is the deployment of 'Hiberno-English Scullion-speak'.[25] Heaney nationalizes *Beowulf* by constantly 'Ulsterizing' the language, an aesthetic strategy which is not systematic in his work, as Heaney is far from being a dialect poet like, for example, that other great admirer of things Anglo-Saxon, William Barnes. It is, nevertheless, such rooting in a familial and regional past that one finds in such passages as

> And now he won't be long for this world.
> He has done his worst but the wound will end him.
> He is hasped and hooped and hirpling with pain,
> limping and looped in it.[26]

But of course, however 'English' this might seem (to the point, almost, of pastiche), it is important to recall that the English used in Ulster dialect is not the product or the possession of the (Catholic) nationalist community. It is something Protestants and Catholics share. Whatever one might think about the aesthetic successes or failures of this strategy, its political import and paradox seem to be clear. This language may be rooted in a particular place, but, at the same time, it generates a much larger mythical community: the North, title of one of Heaney's major texts and a space which includes in its turbulent heartland not simply Catholic and Protestant but a certain Ireland and a certain England.

It is thus not surprising that the reader should enter *Beowulf* through a dedication to Ted Hughes, a dedication that places the translation in the shadow or the light of a particular view of language (see Hughes's 'Thistles') and dream of nation. These are inheritances of nineteenth-century nationalism and its reading of *Beowulf,*

---

[23] See the *OED*'s definition: 'The modification of vocal sound by its passage through the nose; nasal, as formerly attributed to the Puritans, now esp. as characterizing the pronunciation of an individual, a country or a locality.'

[24] Heaney, 'Introduction', in *Beowulf* (London: Faber, 1999), pp. xxii and xxx.

[25] Ibid. p. xxvii.   [26] Ibid. 31.

but they are readings which enable Heaney to negotiate the contemporary—the Troubles in Northern Ireland. For *Beowulf* presents him with a world of violence, but a violence that is contained by ritual, the formalities of war bands encountering each other, the 'big talk'[27] about which Longley is so reticent. The epic in this sense becomes the noble face of violence—not only is the goal of the violence acceptable, consensual, but the poem itself ritualizes its content by its formality and symmetries, the manifestations of the courtesies that Heaney has always admired. This does not mean that the sombre side of the epic world is forgotten—far from it. It is the reality and the constant shadow of death and destruction that give epic grandeur to the world in which Beowulf finds himself—a world haunted by creatures of the night and darkness whose violence seems endless and manifests itself both internally within the group and externally without.

But beyond this, and at a more explicitly ideological level, *Beowulf* maps communities, includes and thus excludes, inscribes dreams of homogeneity, and does so through language. The text is a translation in which Heaney has taken a variety of Old English words (*cynn*: 'kind, kin, species, family'; *folc*: 'people, crowd, army, nation'; *leod*: 'people, soldiers, country'; *maeg*: 'kinsman, kin'; *theod*: 'nation, race') and translated them non-systematically. This gives us a poem where words like 'race', 'nation', 'people', 'sept', 'clan', 'tribe', and 'kin' form overlapping ' totalities' whose 'phantasmal boundaries'[28] are necessarily uncertain and whose notional content is extremely plastic. Such words encourage the late twentieth-century reader to read from his or her own historical ground—just as the events described (the process of translation covered many years of conflict) echo contemporary events, generating powerful anachronisms. So, to return to *Beowulf*, if one puts aside the word 'race',[29] the presence of which in Heaney's work deserves to be analysed in detail, one could look briefly at particular occurrences in the introduction, in the translation, of two words: 'sept' and 'nation'.

The word 'sept' occurs in Heaney's translation of *Beowulf* in the lines 'Never need you fear | for a single thane of your sept or nation'.[30] The word 'sept' is traditionally used in English of Ireland—Heaney is here 'Irishing' his text. The *OED* defines 'sept' as 'a division of a nation or tribe; a clan, orig. in reference to Ireland'—a definition which itself uses as apparent synonyms 'nation' and 'tribe'. It is perhaps not surprising that Heaney should do the same, albeit in a historical and aesthetic context (the Troubles in Ulster) fraught with political turbulence, where the word 'nation' is a semantic minefield. Similarly, at the end of *Beowulf*, in that part of the poem which describes the hero's funeral pyre, Heaney writes of the 'keening' of the Geat woman, who sees in the death of the great warrior the beginning of disaster—such is the world of epic, a world where peace is an accidental interlude and the death of the successful warrior a disaster. At the

---

[27] Heaney, *Beowulf*, 31.   [28] Ibid. p. xv.
[29] Ibid. 56 and 95.   [30] Ibid. 54.

very end of his translation, Heaney writes: 'she unburdened herself | of her worst fears, a wild litany | of nightmare and lament: her nation invaded, | enemies on the rampage, bodies in piles, | slavery and abasement.'[31] It would seem that Heaney has himself introduced the phrase 'her nation invaded', which does not appear to be in the original text or in any of the translations I have been able to consult. This underscores the contemporary relevance of the event. Heaney writes in his introduction, as if to prepare the reader:

The Geat woman who cries out in dread as the flames consume the body of her dead lord could come straight from a late-twentieth-century news report, from Rwanda or Kosovo; her keen is a nightmare glimpse into the minds of people who have survived traumatic, even monstrous events and who are now being exposed to a comfortless future.[32]

One could extend Heaney's litany of disasters and suggest that the series would include Rwanda, Kosovo, and his own native Ulster, which raises the inevitable question of who exactly is the victim, and who exactly the invading army (is the British Army functioning like the Hutu militia or the Serb war bands?). One reading might be that the Geat woman becomes a sort of contemporary Dark Rosaleen, but one who is less certain that her nation is destined to triumph. More importantly, this addition suggests retroactively that Ulster is the space of which epics are made, that the world of *Beowulf* is a world that has relevance, and more than simply as a warning, to the contemporary world.

[31] Ibid. 98–9.   [32] Ibid. p. xxi.

CHAPTER 36

'STALLED IN THE PRE-ARTICULATE': HEANEY, POETRY, AND WAR

BRENDAN CORCORAN

Tristes presentimientos de lo que ha de acontecer
'Sad presentiments of what must come to pass'

Francisco Goya, *The Disasters of War*

'Q. and A. come back. They "formed my mind".
"Who is my neighbour?" "My neighbour is all mankind." '

Seamus Heaney, 'The Catechism'

'In the work of mourning, it is not grief that works: grief keeps watch.'

Maurice Blanchot, *The Writing of the Disaster*

After Spanish nationalists rose up against the French puppet government in 1808, only to be brutally quashed as the state consolidated power, Francisco Goya began an extended series of aquatint etchings first published posthumously in 1863 as *Los Desatres de la Guerra* (*The Disasters of War*). The images are small but brutal. The simplicity, honesty, and horrific elegance of these compositions depicting scenes of torture, rape, murder, death, and social collapse eloquently 'denounce war', as

Philip Hofer says, 'by making a telling visual report' of the insurrection that led to the Peninsular War.[1] More poetic than journalistic, these profoundly intimate images present unnamed persons, living and dead, in attitudes of extremity. War in Goya's eyes is people suffering. But in addition, the images are captioned with fragmentary, enigmatic, even oracular declarations. The first of Goya's etchings reads, *'Tristes presentimientos de lo que ha de acontecer'* ('Sad presentiments of what must come to pass'), and presents a lone figure in rags kneeling with arms outspread and hollow eyes upcast amidst a nondescript blackness that appears to be garroting his throat and drawing his hands back into itself. This supplicant before an implacable universe is the obverse of the penitent; the last vestige of shredded hope opens the figure to the cold and indifferent heavens, and he becomes not a pray-er but a seer witnessing through the past that has brought him to this desperate pitch 'sad presentiments of what must come to pass'. Past and future are suspended in this instant in the way the man's outreaching arms are held above a dark abyss. The bleakness of Goya's vision is allayed only by the supplicant's gaze that remains at once apart from and a part of both death and life.

'It was a terrible moment for him, caught between dread and witness,' as Seamus Heaney says in his Nobel Lecture, when describing the horror of a lone Catholic man called out from his Protestant peers by unknown gunmen who then massacred his colleagues, who, in a final squeeze of the hand, had tacitly offered themselves as protection from being singled out presumably for death.[2] While such gunshots are inextricably 'a part of the music of what happens', Heaney points to the squeeze of the survivor's hand by those about to die as the germ 'of the future we desire'.[3] Of course, no one, including the poet, can apprehend the experience of the survivor who will bear this 'instant' of his death as the beginning of the rest of his life.[4] Yet for Heaney, this man's uncanny survival suggests the position of poetry as it addresses war. One terrible predicament of those who survive trauma is that they bear, like Goya's figure, the strange fate of possessing a knowledge of suffering and death that is inadequate to alleviate the dread not only of what happened but of what will happen again elsewhere if not here.[5] Something of death *and* life, for instance, is, transmitted in that squeeze of the hand, but such knowledge is lost to the abyss

---

[1] Philip Hofer, 'Introduction to the Dover Edition', in Francisco Goya, *The Disasters of War*, ed. Philip Hofer (Mineola, NY: Dover, 1968), 1.

[2] Seamus Heaney, 'Crediting Poetry', in *Opened Ground: Poems 1966–1996* (London: Faber, 1998), 456.

[3] Ibid. 457.

[4] Maurice Blanchot explores this predicament of survival in *The Instant of My Death*, analysed at length by Jacques Derrida. Derrida speaks of this 'unbelievable tense', the unimaginable position and temporality of the survivor as witness who gives testimony to death as dying (Maurice Blanchot/Jacques Derrida, *The Instant of My Death/Demeure: Fiction and Testimony*, trans. Elizabeth Rottenberg (Stanford, Calif.: Stanford University Press, 1998), 49).

[5] The awful paradox of this condition is that this knowledge or experience is capable of re-traumatizing the survivor, creating the vicious cycle of traumatic repetition noted by Freud in *Beyond the Pleasure Principle*.

'between dread and witness'. Heaney's elegiac poetics consistently responds in rich and complicated ways to death, including death as a result of historical forces like war. However, where war is concerned, he is interested not only in mourning loss or portraying suffering but in tapping, with poetry, a semblance of the survivor's impossible knowledge so as to map suffering and death in concert with life.[6] In the broadest terms, he boldly aims to generate a productive, as opposed to a palliative, art capable of assisting at 'the birth of the future we desire'.[7]

Heaney's art is hardly as dark as Goya's, but his own poetry since the early 1960s shares with Goya not only a perturbation by war and death but a much-discussed sense of artistic responsibility to his own community and a wider world. The image of the witness to history as a kind of seer is present throughout his work, including each of his major translation projects, and is central to one of his most important sequences, 'Mycenae Lookout'. Yet Heaney's work connects with the Spaniard's in another way: Goya's visionary supplicant could be a model for Heaney's St Kevin, lost in his own extreme 'posture of endurance'.[8] Though there is no evidence to suggest that Goya's supplicant (held in the Prado) seeded Heaney's imagination in the years before St Kevin's emergence in 'St. Kevin and the Blackbird' from *The Spirit Level* (1996), 'Summer 1969', the fourth part of 'Singing School' from *North* (1975), contains a striking encounter with some of Goya's other paintings in the Prado at the very instant the violence in Belfast began to heat up. 'Summer 1969' twists itself around Heaney's guilt (and relief) at *not* being present for the outbreak of sectarian violence. The example of Lorca as poet of the people prior to his murder by Fascists during the Spanish Civil War haunts the centre of Heaney's poem. One voice is even quoted as urging the poet to return home to ' "try to touch the people" '.[9] Fortunately, Heaney ignores this grandiloquent suggestion, though his poetry and prose regularly acknowledge not only the desire but a pressure to respond to the specific violence roiling Northern Ireland. Most tellingly, 'Summer 1969' depicts Heaney's actual response as a 'retreat' (at once strategic and spiritual) into the seeming peace of art. However, the art of the Prado that occupies the lyric gaze is Goya's, and in particular, the 'Shootings of the Third of May' and the terrifying nightmare paintings:

> Dark cyclones, hosting, breaking; Saturn
> Jewelled in the blood of his own children;
> Gigantic Chaos turning his brute hips
> Over the world. Also, that holmgang
> Where two berserks club each other to death
> For honour's sake, greaved in a bog, and sinking.
>
> He painted with his fists and elbows, flourished
> The stained cape of his heart as history charged.

---

[6] This is one way of reading Heaney's idea of redress as a mapping of the 'labyrinth' of 'our given experience' (Heaney, 'The Redress of Poetry', in *The Redress of Poetry: Oxford Lectures* (London: Faber, 1995), 2).

[7] Heaney, 'Crediting Poetry', 457.   [8] Ibid. 458.   [9] Heaney, 'Summer 1969', ibid. 140.

Heaney's ekphrasis offers at once a vision of the past and sad presentiments of the future as the self-annihilating 'berserks' are 'greaved in a bog, and sinking'. Though the berserks in the bog follow from the poem's earlier references to Ireland's violence, Goya's images resist appropriation to just an examination of the Troubles. In his 'retreat to the Prado', Heaney contemplates not only war in Ireland but war as a universal crisis facing the artist or poet. A poem about Ireland and its Troubles, this is also a poem about war. Yet the final image of the furious and committed artist caught in the act of creation, his bodily assault upon his medium, shifts attention away from the artist's vision, to his plight as the violence of history *necessarily* bears down on him. The poem with its striking final image suggests the cost to the artist of such necessary receptivity to history; however, the artist *per se* is not the true subject of the poem. In the image of the artist as matador engaged in a *danse macabre* with history's inexorable drive we find history, the artist, and the work of art bound into a complex relationship. The seemingly quixotic gesture of the artist confronting the inexorable ends *without* the death of bull or man. This suspension by the poem of both figures together in a moment of crisis demonstrates the mechanism which Heaney uses to represent *and* apprehend the relationship of art, the artist, and history.

But what is the purpose of Heaney's portrayal of the artist's confrontation with history? The image concluding 'Summer 1969' and the world-view that underlies it, engage the great question that dogs Heaney's career as truly a poet of conscience: what is art's 'salubrious effect' in the world, and how is it achieved?[10] This question goes beyond the matter of mere representation by poetry of violence, war, or history, as it claims for poetry a positive or productive role in the real world. The boldness of this claim, which will underlie Heaney's formulation of the 'redress of poetry' in the late 1980s, is that it risks sentimentality, facile consolation, or easy aesthetic remedies for the irremediable. A poetry committed to making a difference in the world—'touch[ing] the people', for example—risks being, at worst, untrustworthy, given what we know. The offering of something healthful through art can be earned only by a scrupulous refusal to elide the inconvenient facts of history's brutality. Borrowing words from George Seferis, Heaney insists that poetry must be ' "strong enough to help" '.[11] But, what *is* a 'salubrious effect'? It is important to note that Heaney reins in his expectations of poetry's 'efficacy'; obviously, as he famously says, 'no lyric has ever stopped a tank'.[12] Instead, poetry's 'efficacy' lies within its homeopathic power not to deflect the charge or console in the aftermath of history, but to suspend, albeit momentarily, the pressure of history's ever-ongoing assault. The value of a moment of true reflection is not to be underestimated, for, as Simone Weil says in her seminal essay *The Iliad, or The Poem of Force*, 'Where there is no room for reflection, there is none either for justice

---

[10] Heaney, 'Frontiers of Writing', *The Redress of Poetry*, 191.   [11] George Seferis, quoted ibid.
[12] Heaney, 'The Government of the Tongue', in *The Government of the Tongue: The 1986 T. S. Eliot Memorial Lectures and Other Critical Writings* (London: Faber, 1988), 93.

or prudence.'[13] For all of Heaney's efforts to grasp the effect as much as the efficacy of a poetry that *responds* to the world in all of its traumas, it is Robert Frost's simple yet supremely elegant formulation that Heaney's art most thoroughly espouses: 'the true poem' is one which 'ends . . . in a momentary stay against confusion'.[14] Such poetry helps people not only to enjoy life, but 'to endure it'.[15]

Heaney affirms the idea of poetry functioning as such a 'stay' through his recourse to various figures for endurance, including, most famously, his bog-body poems. St Kevin, however, is a tutelary image because not only is he resolutely 'on the side of life',[16] as Czesław Miłosz says of poetry, he is 'imagined'.[17] 'St Kevin and the Blackbird' displays what Heaney calls, in relation to Dylan Thomas, a 'veteran knowledge',[18] a worldliness evidencing a 'craft [that] has not lost touch with a suffered world'.[19] Heaney's understanding of this story situated in the field of the marvellous—but recounted in the Nobel Lecture as a response to the murderousness of war—emphasizes the poetic and prosaic use of Wilfred Owen's word 'pity' as the monk, 'overcome with pity and constrained by his faith to love the life in all creatures great and small', begins his meditation on immobility, his extraordinary holding action—literally—which suspends and sustains the bird through its nesting cycle.[20] Such suspension of life is, for Heaney, the 'order of poetry':

> And since the whole thing's imagined anyhow,
> Imagine being Kevin. Which is he?
> Self-forgetful or in agony all the time
> From the neck on out down through his hurting forearms?
> Are his fingers sleeping? Does he still feel his knees?
> Or has the shut-eyed blank of underearth
> Crept up through him? Is there distance in his head?
> Alone and mirrored clear in love's deep river,
> 'To labour, and not to seek reward', he prays,
> A prayer his body makes entirely
> For he has forgotten self, forgotten bird
> And on the riverbank forgotten the river's name.[21]

Heaney's Kevin is not Goya's unnamed supplicant and seer, but the two might just as well be held in the same thought, balanced together like so many other binary

[13] Simone Weil, *The Iliad, or The Poem of Force*, trans. Mary McCarthy (Wallingford, Pa.: Pendle Hill, 1956), 14.
[14] Robert Frost, quoted in Heaney, 'Government of the Tongue', 93.
[15] Heaney, 'Counting to a Hundred: On Elizabeth Bishop', in *Redress of Poetry*, 185.
[16] Czesław Miłosz, quoted in Heaney, 'Joy or Night: Last Things in the Poetry of W. B. Yeats and Philip Larkin', ibid. 158.
[17] Heaney, 'St Kevin and the Blackbird', in *Opened Ground*, 410.
[18] Heaney, 'Dylan the Durable? On Dylan Thomas', in *Redress of Poetry*, 135.
[19] Ibid. 137.   [20] Heaney, 'Crediting Poetry', 458–9.
[21] Heaney, 'St Kevin and the Blackbird', 410.

terms crucial to Heaney's understanding of poetry and the world.[22] Both figures witness life and suffering, and both figures remain at their stations *as* visions of what 'must come to pass'. Celebrating Yeats's 'The Stare's Nest by my Window' as an example of a 'completely adequate poetry', Heaney says, in 'Crediting Poetry', that Yeats's poem 'is as tender-minded towards life itself as St Kevin was and as tough-minded towards life itself as Homer'.[23] As the saint loses himself to the holding action he becomes, he figures less an action than a principle: 'poetry's covenant with life'.[24] In the end, the bird, like the self, is irrelevant; what remains is the ideal timelessness of love imagined through or *as* a poem and *its* instant. Obviously, 'St Kevin and the Blackbird' is not a poem about war *per se*, but the blankness of Kevin's mind, like a seer's, models the achievement of an ideal poetry of radical receptivity capable of encompassing simultaneously in local/Irish and global/universal dimensions the brutality of the world and the loving-kindness of the saint.[25] As Heaney says in 'The Catechism': 'Q. and A. come back. They "formed my mind". | "Who is my neighbour?" "My neighbour is all mankind." '[26]

St Kevin also marks Heaney's 'changed orientation' from one of distrusting to one of 'crediting the positive note'.[27] In the *ars poetica* of his Nobel Lecture, Heaney speaks of himself and a late twentieth-century reading culture as being

> rightly suspicious of that which gives too much consolation... the very extremity of our late-twentieth-century knowledge puts much of our cultural heritage to an extreme test.... And when this intellectual predisposition coexists with the actualities of Ulster and Israel and Bosnia and Rwanda and a host of other wounded spots on the face of the earth, the inclination is not only not to credit human nature with much constructive potential but not to credit anything too positive in the work of art.[28]

In this discussion he acknowledges his own years of bearing the knowledge of being 'incapable of heroic virtue or redemptive effect'—though yearning for just such an adequacy—until, as he says, 'finally and happily, and not in obedience to the dolorous circumstances of my native place but in spite of them, I straightened up'. This awakening prompts him 'to try to make space in [his] reckoning and imagining for the marvellous as well as for the murderous'.[29] This statement suggests that Heaney sees his own work for at least the preceding twenty years as

---

[22] St Kevin and Homer occupy opposite pans of the scale wherein we might read other antinomies, including Ireland and elsewhere, the local and the cosmopolitan, now and then. Though at different points in the career one side may appear more weighty than the other, it is crucial for Heaney's poetics that the antinomies exist together, for redress involves keeping them in a state of equilibrium, suspended in the mind and work of the poet not just together but *because* of each other.

[23] Heaney, 'Crediting Poetry', 464.

[24] Heaney, 'Current Unstated Assumptions about Poetry', *Critical Inquiry*, 7/4 (1981), 650.

[25] In a statement fundamental to many Irish poets' thinking about their work, Patrick Kavanagh decares: 'Parochialism is universal; it deals with the fundamentals' (Kavanagh, *Collected Prose* (London: MacGibbon & Kee, 1967), 283).

[26] Heaney, 'The Catechism', in 'Ten Glosses', in *Electric Light* (London: Faber, 2001), 54.

[27] Heaney, 'Crediting Poetry', 457.   [28] Ibid. 457–8.   [29] Ibid. 458.

stemming from a far darker place than many readers would expect. But, as Dillon Johnston demonstrates, Heaney's work has grappled continuously with an interest in and a knowledge of violence, beginning on the farm but expanding much further afield.[30] I would extend Johnston's reading further to say that from the earliest work Heaney is perhaps most continuously focused on death, though not in a maudlin or nihilistic manner. Indeed, as he demonstrates in poems and essays, his is in many ways an Orphic project, which, as he says of Dylan Thomas, 'keeps its gaze firmly fixed on the upward path, and works against the gradient of relapse',[31] the necessity we know through the story to be death's ultimate victory. Of course, after singing out of loss and hope in the depths of death's kingdom, the Orphic poet on the upward path is tormented precisely by the question of his art's efficacy. This image of Orpheus after having momentarily won out over death yet always about to lose his love again and for good serves as yet another image of the stay, of a suspension in which life and death are compassed together.

Seamus Heaney is not a 'war poet'. When introducing *Cenotaph of Snow* (2003), his own collected 'poems about war', Michael Longley, in an echo of Wilfred Owen's draft 'Preface', crucially declares: 'These are poems about war, not war poems. You have to be a war poet to write war poems. I am a non-combatant drawn to the subject of war for a number of reasons.'[32] Longley's distinction is a salutary clarification when considering the relationship of poetry written by poets from Northern Ireland and the sectarian violence—the war that has largely defined the place since 1969. The 'war poet' who writes 'war poems', according to Longley's logic, must be a combatant. Such plain-spoken honesty de-emphasizes the question of identity and instead attends to poetics, which involves not only the means but the subject of lyric representation. Longley's larger point is that many of his poems tackle 'war' as a subject-matter which incorporates but remains *distinct from* its Irish franchise. This conjunction of local and brutal actualities and a universal ineffability has proved irresistible to poets since Homer. Why Heaney, like Longley, is '*drawn* to the subject of war' says much about the poet and, more generally, offers insight into the larger connection between war and poetry.[33]

---

[30] Dillon Johnston, 'Violence in Seamus Heaney's Poetry', in Matthew Campbell (ed.), *The Cambridge Companion to Contemporary Irish Poetry* (Cambridge: Cambridge University Press, 2003), 113–32. Johnston offers a very useful and extensive survey of violence throughout Heaney's *œuvre*.

[31] Heaney, 'Dylan the Durable?', *The Redress of Poetry*, 144.

[32] Michael Longley, *Cenotaph of Snow: Sixty Poems about War* (London: Enitharmon, 2003). Longley's introduction to the book appears at <http://www.enitharmon.co.uk/books/viewBook.asp?BID=74>

[33] Heaney himself states the obvious in 'Crediting Poetry', when, ensconced in the seeming remove of Wicklow as Northern Ireland endured the torsion of war, he recalls 'feeling puny in my predicaments as I read about the tragic logic of Osip Mandelstam's fate in the nineteen-thirties, feeling challenged yet steadfast in my non-combatant status when I heard, for example, that one particularly sweet-natured school friend had been interned without trial' (Heaney, 'Crediting Poetry', 452).

While Irish poets like Longley or Heaney may have been drawn to the subject of war in general and its many attendant issues, they also felt pressure to write about *their* war. But, as Paul Muldoon noted in 1984, 'the trouble with this place [Northern Ireland] is that if you don't engage in it, you're an ostrich (whatever "engage in it" means). If you do engage in it, you're using the situation as a kind of . . . you're on the make, almost, cashing in.'[34] Muldoon identifies the essential paradox that has driven the tempestuous critical debates about the appropriateness of various poets', including Heaney's, responses to war in Ireland. Poets driven to write about war in Ireland or elsewhere must struggle to achieve *adequacy*, a kind of truth telling that interfuses empirical actualities with poetry's capacity to transform and illuminate the subject in question. Such a poetry offers a 'glimpsed alternative [to whatever the predicament is], a revelation of potential that is denied or constantly threatened by circumstances'.[35]

In examining this 'imperative' to produce an adequate poetry, Fran Brearton suggests that 'Heaney reveals a more acute insecurity than either Mahon or Longley about the pressure to respond to the Troubles in some tangible way, for poetry to make something happen, to legitimate its function in the world.'[36] This impulse extends across his career, as Heaney repeatedly interrogates the central idea of *adequacy*, the right relationship between poetry and war, 'beauty and atrocity'.[37] This idea is expressed perhaps most famously in his lines from the 1974 essay 'Feeling into Words', where, grappling with the violence of the summer of 1969, he says that poetry now involves 'a search for images and symbols adequate to our predicament'.[38] He explains: 'I felt it imperative to discover a field of force in which without abandoning fidelity to the processes and experience of poetry . . . it would be possible to encompass the perspective of a humane reason and at the same time grant the religious intensity of the violence its deplorable authenticity and complexity.'[39] Central to this notion of adequacy is the balance, what he will later point to as the goal of a 'transcendent equilibrium' between the resources of poetry itself—its 'humane reason', its beauty or music—and the intense actuality of the violence and its origins.[40] He describes at once 'poetry *as* an answer' in addition to 'the idea of an answering poetry as a responsible poetry'.[41] Poetry's answer lies 'in its own language rather than in the language of the world that provokes it'.[42] Thus, he declares; 'if our given experience is a labyrinth, then its impassability is countered by

---

[34] Paul Muldoon, quoted in Edna Longley, *Poetry in the Wars* (Newcastle-upon-Tyne: Bloodaxe, 1986), 12–13.

[35] Heaney, 'Redress of Poetry', 4.

[36] Fran Brearton, *The Great War in Irish Poetry: W. B. Yeats to Michael Longley* (Oxford: Oxford University Press, 2000), 225.

[37] Heaney, 'The Grauballe Man', in *Opened Ground*, 116.

[38] Heaney, 'Feeling into Words', in *Preoccupations: Selected Prose 1968–1978* (London: Faber, 1980), 56.

[39] Ibid. 56–7.   [40] Heaney, 'Redress of Poetry', 3.

[41] Heaney, 'Frontiers of Writing', 191.   [42] Ibid.

the poet's imagining some equivalent of the labyrinth and bringing himself and the reader through it'.[43] In clarifying his idea of redress, which is fundamental to what Brearton calls his 'poetics of responsibility', Heaney reiterates the notion of poetry as 'an adequate response to conditions in the world at a moment' of crisis.[44] War becomes exemplary of the totality of the human condition *in extremis*. For Heaney, like many of his colleagues in Northern Ireland, an adequate poetry is not a balm, but a salubrious 'stay', a strategic pause wherein a feeling or 'a thought might grow'.[45]

Having entered his work, the Troubles offers yet another lens through which to read Heaney's poetry. However, such a lens risks limiting the poetry so that every poem is seen as in some way a 'Troubles poem' or a poem *about* Ireland.[46] In much the same way that readers have fixated on the Heaney of 'Digging' and 'Personal Helicon'—the poet of boggy, childhood idylls delving into the substrate of his local world—so readers all too often stop at frequently anthologized poems like 'Punishment' or 'Exposure' to register what Ciaran Carson most dreaded as a consoling rationalization of suffering in Northern Ireland: the suggestion that here is an *œuvre* and not just a book (*North*) reflecting 'the Good that can come out of Troubled Times'.[47] Introducing *North* for the *Poetry Book Society Bulletin* in 1975, Heaney writes: 'During the last few years there has been considerable expectation that poets from Northern Ireland should "say" something about "the situation", but in the end they will only be worth listening to if they are saying something about and to themselves.'[48]

Heaney's struggle with the question of adequacy leads him to distrust and actively question not political poetry *per se* but the motivations behind its being written. For example, in 'Exposure' from *North* (1975), he famously writes about 'weighing and weighing | My responsible *tristia*'.[49] Against the backdrop of war, he asks why write about this: 'For what? For the ear? For the people? | For what is said behind-backs?' Later, in 'The Flight Path' from *The Spirit Level* (1996), an ardent Irish nationalist asks: ' "When, for fuck's sake, are you going to write | Something for us?" "If I do write something" ', the poet replies, ' "Whatever it is, I'll be writing for myself." '[50] Of these lines, Heaney says in a 1999 interview:

[43] Heaney, 'Frontiers of Writing', 191.

[44] Brearton, *Great War in Irish Poetry*, 225; Heaney, 'Frontiers of Writing', 191.

[45] Derek Mahon, 'A Disused Shed in Co. Wexford', in *Poems 1962–1978* (Oxford: Oxford University Press, 1979), 79.

[46] Frank Ormsby attempts to define, in the most general and non-prescriptive terms, 'Troubles poetry'. His discussion acknowledges the problematic, identity-dependent notion 'that *any* poem by a Northern Irish poet since 1968, on whatever subject, could be termed a troubles poem, in that it may, consciously or unconsciously, reflect the context in which it was written' (Ormsby, 'Preface', in *idem* (ed.), *A Rage for Order: Poetry of the Northern Ireland Troubles* (Belfast: Blackstaff, 1992), p. xvii).

[47] Ciaran Carson, ' "Escaped from the Massacre?" ', *The Honest Ulsterman*, 50 (1975), 186.

[48] Heaney, in Clare Brown and Don Paterson (eds.), *Don't Ask Me What I Mean: Poets in Their Own Words* (London: Picador, 2003), 102.

[49] Heaney, 'Exposure', in *Opened Ground*, 143.   [50] Heaney, '*from* The Flight Path', ibid. 413.

I was simply refusing to have a poem levied. . . . If you're going to write a poem of political protest, which, let me put on record, is not only an honourable, but a necessary thing, you have to be sure that it's *your* subject, that it's *your* anger, not somebody else's anger. . . . Protest per se isn't a contribution, I don't think, because protest is going on all the time. . . . So-called political poetry, protest poetry, gets on my nerves. Political poetry in Northern Ireland should not be a spectator sport. It should have some purchase on the actual realities of the place.[51]

Despite the risks of writing poems about war, such poems offer not only the 'salubrious' potential resulting from poetry's adequate engagement with war, but a site wherein to address powerful issues that possess simultaneously local and universal dimensions. The poem about war is especially interesting because it often encompasses other types of poems like the elegy. Edna Longley begins her own examination of poetry and war by appreciating this expansive nature of 'war' as she suggests that 'perhaps "war", not "history" or "politics" [or "violence", for that matter], covers the broadest imaginative contingencies'.[52] She asserts that where the human institution of war as a subject of poetry is concerned, 'transcendence and historicity are not as mutually exclusive as structuralism makes out'. And it is at the interface of 'transcendence and historicity' that so many of the pitched critical battles about the *right* relationship between art and war take place.

In a 2003 interview, Heaney acknowledges his own tilt away from the exclusively Irish historical context and towards more 'transcendent' concerns. Upon being asked about whether the reduction of 'political tension in Northern Ireland' since the 1998 Good Friday Agreement had diminished his 'urgency as a poet', Heaney states:

In fact, I sort of jumped the Northern Ireland hurdle four or five years before the ceasefire and all that followed from it. The poems in *Seeing Things*, in particular the 'Squarings' sequence, were a declaration of independence from the matter of Ulster—and they were done in 1988, '89. I felt at that stage that I had to quicken myself, shed some old skin. But now there's a bigger 'chief-woe, world-sorrow', as Hopkins would have said, something that puts Northern Ireland in the shade.[53]

This statement reiterates what he says in 'Crediting Poetry' about 'straighten[ing] up' and sloughing off the weight of the 'murderous' subject of Northern Ireland.[54] This apparent broadening of the poet's gaze also comes in the aftermath not of any political changes on the ground in Northern Ireland, but of the deaths of Heaney's parents in the mid-1980s. His own suffering and consideration of his literal origins prompt a new 'lightening' that, paradoxically, may make the poetry better able to

[51] Heaney, interviewed by Karl Miller, *Seamus Heaney in Conversation with Karl Miller*, ed. Karl Miller (London: Between the Lines, 2000), 23–4; italics original.

[52] Edna Longley, *Poetry in the Wars*, 10.

[53] Heaney, in Seamus Heaney and Jason Koo, 'Citizens of the Republic of Conscience', *Gulf Coast*, 16/2 (2004), 205.

[54] Heaney, 'Crediting Poetry', 458.

bear the strain of 'world-sorrow'. Upon liberating himself from the problems of Ulster in the late 1980s, it is important to note how, for Heaney, war not only does not go away as a theme, but rather increases as a presence in the poetry of *The Spirit Level* (1996). The war in Northern Ireland remains present in and as a subject of his poetry, but the gaze is cast wider; as much as Ireland's Troubles, the timeless threat and universality of loss become the real subjects of his poetry, touched however faintly or powerfully by war. And though when speaking of the new millennium he describes 'a bigger "chief-woe, world-sorrow"', such attentiveness to the global register of suffering may be found throughout his body of work, even as this note defines many poems written since the late 1980s.

Asked in 1988 about the continued relevance of Coventry Patmore's phrase, 'the end of art is peace', quoted by Heaney in 'The Harvest Bow' and then in his epigraph to *Preoccupations* (1980), Heaney replies by inquiring again into the adequacy of the lyric gaze encompassing not Irish pain *per se* but 'world-sorrow':

Can you write a poem in the post-nuclear age? Can you write a poem that gazes at death, or the western front or Auschwitz—a poem that gives peace and tells horror? It gives true peace only if the horror is satisfactorily rendered. If the eyes are not averted from it. If its overmastering power is acknowledged and unconceded, so the human spirit holds its own against its affront and immensity. To me that's what the 'end of art is peace' means and understood in those terms, I still believe it.[55]

Like Auden's statement in his elegy for W. B. Yeats that 'poetry makes nothing happen',[56] the statement by Theodor Adorno that 'to write poetry after Auschwitz is barbaric' is one of modern poetry's most clichéd and misused phrases.[57] Used in common parlance without the rigorous cultural interrogation that the statement is meant to provoke, it signals the worst kind of self-indulgent poetic or critical hand-wringing that elides serious engagement with the risks of insensibility or sentimentality faced whenever poetry deals with history.[58] Fortunately, in a 1965 lecture, Adorno addressed the widespread misapprehension that lingers still:

I once said that after Auschwitz one could no longer write poetry, and that gave rise to a discussion I did not anticipate. . . . I would readily concede that, just as I said that after Auschwitz one *could not* write poems—by which I meant to point to the hollowness of the resurrected culture of that time—it could equally well be said, on the other hand, that one *must* write poems, in keeping with Hegel's statement in his *Aesthetics* that as long as

---

[55] Heaney, interviewed by Rand Brandes, 'Seamus Heaney: An Interview', *Salmagundi*, 80 (Fall 1988), 21.

[56] W. H. Auden, 'In Memory of W. B. Yeats', in *The English Auden: Poems, Essays, and Dramatic Writings 1927–1939*, ed. Edward Mendelson (London: Faber, 1977), 242.

[57] Theodor W. Adorno, 'Cultural Criticism and Society', in *Prisms*, trans. Samuel and Shierry Weber (Cambridge, Mass.: MIT Press, 1981), 34.

[58] Susan Gubar addresses at length these tensions and the limits as the well as resources of poetry *not* to re-member but to register 'discontinuity' and 'keep . . . alive *as* dying' the extreme limits of historical knowledge (Susan Gubar, *Poetry after Auschwitz: Remembering What One Never Knew* (Bloomington, Ind.: Indiana University Press, 2003), 7).

there is an awareness of human suffering among human beings there must also be art as the objective form of that awareness.[59]

'On the side of art', Adorno criticizes not so much poetry as the culture of the West that produced, almost inexorably, the Holocaust. Within such a debased culture, poetry's capacity to witness or testify to 'human suffering' proves valuable so long as this responsibility avoids self-indulgence. But Adorno goes further, inquiring into the real if atrocious question, 'whether one can *live* after Auschwitz'. A pallid derivative of this question is echoed by the graffito in Ballymurphy that Heaney quotes in 'Whatever You Say Say Nothing': 'Is there a life before death?'[60] Adorno refers to a Sartre play in which a character who is tortured 'asks whether or why one would live in a world in which one is beaten until one's bones are smashed'.[61] 'Since it concerns the possibility of any affirmation of life,' Adorno says in the strongest possible terms, 'this question cannot be evaded.' In seeking a poetry 'that gives peace and tells horror', Heaney espouses a poetics that encompasses the question of whether 'any affirmation of life' is possible; the question remains embedded in his response that the 'overmastering power' of horror must be 'acknowledged and unconceded'.[62] Thomas Hardy, from another direction, addresses much the same thing in his still-conditional declaration that, '*if* way to the Better there be, it exacts a full look at the Worst'.[63] Such a gaze into the 'Worst', which interrogates our very reason for living amidst such suffering, forms the core of a poetics of witness. For the poet who occupies 'the solitary role of witness . . . the redress of poetry', Heaney says, 'comes to represent something like an exercise of the virtue of hope as it is understood by Václav Havel,'[64] who describes it as a stance in which 'its deepest roots are in the transcendental, just as the roots of human responsibility are'.[65]

Generally, Heaney refuses to merely transform loss and suffering into the readily *forgotten* loveliness of false consolation, but 'The Strand at Lough Beg' short-cuts the hard work of witnessing for a notoriously resolving or consoling vision. Imaginatively dabbing clean with moss and dew his dead cousin Colum McCartney, killed in a random sectarian attack in Northern Ireland, Heaney's 'The Strand at Lough Beg' concludes consolingly by burying the cousin with the crime of his murder and the travesty of the war itself. When Heaney says, 'With rushes that shoot green again, I plait | Green scapulars to wear over your shroud,'[66] he overreaches as poet, claiming for himself and poetry in general a power and a prerogative that one may *wish* to have, but one cannot claim, especially in the

---

[59] Adorno, *Metaphysics: Concept and Problems*, trans. Edmund Jephcott, ed. Rolf Tiedemann (Stanford, Calif.: Stanford University Press, 2000), 110–11.

[60] Heaney, '*from* Whatever You Say Say Nothing', in *Opened Ground*, 133.

[61] Adorno, *Metaphysics*, 111.   [62] Heaney, interviewed by Rand Brandes, 21.

[63] Thomas Hardy, 'In Tenebris II', in *The Complete Poems of Thomas Hardy*, ed. James Gibson (London: Macmillan, 1976), 168; my italics.

[64] Heaney, 'Redress of Poetry', 4.   [65] Václav Havel, quoted ibid. 4–5.

[66] Heaney, 'The Strand at Lough Beg', in *Opened Ground*, 153.

twentieth century. As a consequence, the dead man, as an emanation of trauma itself, refuses to stay buried (a pattern Heaney is familiar with), coming back to harangue the poet in 'Station Island'. The symbolically achieved mourning fails, and the hubristic claim of truly consolatory or obtusely transformative powers demands revision. Ultimately, Heaney hears the voice of a poem and a grief left unfinished, which must stay unfinished, unburied precisely, as Blanchot says, to 'keep watch'.[67]

In 'Station Island', Heaney keeps this death alive in the same way in which he keeps the wound to the Grauballe man 'cured',[68] and with this paradox Heaney finds his ultimate field of force. McCartney's ghost charges that his cousin the poet 'confused evasion with artistic tact'.[69] The dead man berates the poet for imagining and writing something that emanated from himself and not 'the fact' of the murder—which remains at an unreachable remove from the poet. Significantly, the dead man does not say that the poet should refrain from representing what happened. And indeed, the success of Heaney's revision lies in the fact that the images of the murder and its scene are not 'corrected' or replaced with something more 'accurate'; rather, the 'true' voice of the dead is appended to the 'false', if searching, voice of the living poet. We hear the voice of the unquiet dead out of time not only chastising but refusing the easy burial ordered by the living, and so remaining unburied and present—as a voice—to the poet and the poem. As if becoming a genius of the place, this voice out of time and space replaces any empirical actuality about the place or event, and the purgatorial blinds of forgetting are cast aside for a different kind of remembrance, a haunting, in which the dead and death remain—timelessly—with the living and within the poetry. The two McCartney poems, which must be read as extensions of the same poem, demonstrate how Heaney's poetry witnesses war not as a vast incomprehensibility but within the suffering of a person, living or dead, and bearing a voice that refuses the silence of mere memorialization.

Heaney says, by way of Owen, that 'the "poet as witness" ... represents poetry's solidarity with the doomed, the deprived, the victimized, the under-privileged. The witness is any figure in whom the truth-telling urge and the compulsion to identify with the oppressed becomes necessarily integral with the act of writing itself.'[70] Heaney's work across his career should be categorized as a species of witnessing poetry, still haunted by the presence and example of poets like Owen and Mandelstam.[71] Brearton suggests that Heaney's 'polarized' use of Owen to

---

[67] Maurice Blanchot, *The Writing of the Disaster*, trans. Ann Smock (Lincoln, Nebr.: University of Nebraska Press, 1995), 51.

[68] Heaney, 'Grauballe Man', 115.   [69] Heaney, 'Station Island', in *Opened Ground*, 261.

[70] Heaney, 'The Interesting Case of Nero, Chekhov's Cognac and a Knocker', in *Government of the Tongue*, p. xvi.

[71] In his introduction to an extraordinary small book of translations of 'Anything Can Happen', his poem in response to the September 2001 terrorist attacks in the US, which was translated into twenty-four 'languages of conflict' and published for the benefit of Amnesty International, Heaney yet again addresses the question of 'how exactly art earns its keep in a violent time' (Heaney, *Anything Can Happen* (Dublin: Townhouse, 2004), 19 and 14). With its 'element of surprise' and 'soothsaying force',

figure truth and Mandelstam to embody beauty in their respective responses to horror offers a false 'resolution . . . akin to a state of chronic poetic schizophrenia'.[72] Such an unresolved resolution, 'fostered alike by beauty and by fear',[73] is not a pathology, but a key to Heaney's poetics. His truly antinomial (as opposed to antithetical) poetics of suspension, in which life is necessarily suspended *with* death, depends on a poetic witnessing of a catastrophic world through *both* truth and beauty.[74] This is his aim. Heaney's own work across a career offers an additive poetry of inclusion enduring the knowledge that a salubrious prospect requires a response to the Worst the world might offer.

The Spirit Level, published during Heaney's Nobel year, contains some of his strongest poems in response to the violence of war, including 'The Flight Path', 'Keeping Going', and 'Two Lorries', each of which addresses the Troubles directly. However, the sequence that dominates the volume, 'Mycenae Lookout', while referring discreetly to the crisis at home, casts its gaze back in time and beyond Ireland's borders to the first 'total war' represented by an extremely adequate poetry. Though Heaney has addressed Homer's *Iliad* before, most notably in *The Cure at Troy: A Version of Sophocles' Philoctetes* (1991), any iteration of the *Iliad* by an Irish poet will readily be seen as a response to the Troubles. Yet Homer is valuable as a resource because the world-rupturing intensity of the Trojan War speaks to the denaturing effect of all wars—including the Troubles. Troy is *not* Belfast or Derry, and the Trojan War as the subject of the first great poem in the West allows modern poets to stretch momentarily their fidelity to the parochial so as to confront a figure of universal human crisis.

Freely based on Aeschylus's *Agamemnon*, 'Mycenae Lookout' presents Heaney's vision of war through an indirect witness to the war at Troy. It is precisely his indirect yet intimate knowledge of this war's various costs that allows the gaze of lookout and poem to transcend an exclusively local relevance. Furthermore, 'Mycenae Lookout' is Heaney's *The Waste Land*. Among many similarities, both of these five-part poems are set against the backdrop of global cataclysm that infiltrates their civil societies functioning apart from the dying. Eliot's and Heaney's poems

what Heaney calls 'the indispensable poem . . . arrives from and addresses itself to a place in the psyche that Ted Hughes called "the place of ultimate suffering and decision"'. Explicitly *not* privileging one aggrieved nation, he says that 'we have all been driven to the threshold of that place [by] acts of coldly premeditated terror, carefully premeditated acts of war'. Such witnessing poetry addresses at once the 'assimilable facts of day-to-day life' and 'terrible foreboding' (p. 14). This project, with its local and global dimensions, tries to demonstrate the scope of poetry to sustain suffering with the prospect that something human, as insignificant as a poem even, remains.

[72] Brearton, *Great War in Irish Poetry*, 245, 249–50.

[73] Heaney uses Wordsworth's phrase as the epigraph to 'Singing School', *Opened Ground*, 134.

[74] In 1972, shaken by the violence in Belfast, Heaney says: 'On the one hand, poetry is secret and natural, on the other hand it must make its way in a world that is public and brutal' (Heaney, 'Belfast', in *Preoccupations*, 34).

are both dominated by dread and the metamorphic potential of what Heaney calls a 'life-warp and world-wrong';[75] the power, musicality, and scope of both sequences, as parts of larger lyric visions aimed at sustaining the human image, affirm Eliot's conclusion that 'These fragments I have shored against my ruins'.[76] Heaney and Eliot confront catastrophe not by representing it, but by letting it into their poems, where ruin is momentarily stayed by the resources of poetry and the vision of the poet.

'I was a lookout posted and forgotten,' opens a 'Sweeney Redivivus' poem from 1984.[77] And over a decade later, reprising the part first laid down in 'Oracle' from *Wintering Out* (1972), but now fully realized, Heaney says, 'Me the lookout | The queen's command had posted and forgotten.'[78] Mycenae's lookout is connected by more than shared language to Heaney's version of the *Buile Suibhne* and his own riffs on the life of the fabulous Sweeney. Heaney identifies closely with Sweeney and the lookout as both suffer the metamorphic force of war. Sweeney is literally changed into a peripatetic bird-man by a curse that follows the shock of combat, and the Mycenae watchman comes to see his own life as petrified into a 'silent and sunned . . . esker on a plain', a glacial deposit akin to the 'ridge' that Heaney's defeated Antaeus becomes, 'a sleeping giant, | pap for the dispossessed'.[79] Heaney's 'Mycenae Lookout' is a long time coming, as it embodies over thirty years of intense consideration of poetry's capacity to bear witness to war.

> Some people wept, and not for sorrow—joy
> That the king had armed and upped and sailed for Troy,
> But inside me like struck sound in a gong
> That killing-fest, the life-warp and world-wrong
> It brought to pass, still augured and endured.

Seeing, knowing, and testifying to what transpires is the essential concern of 'Mycenae Lookout', and its first poem, 'The Watchman's War', crucially establishes from the outset the tension of being, albeit from afar, a witness to history's 'abattoir'. The watchman sees the terrible conjunction between 'sorrow' and 'joy' that is war. His humble and trustworthy voice, first conveyed in the martial stability and confidence of the heroic couplet, is immediately undercut by the excruciating paradox, the apt and corrupt rhyming of 'joy' and 'Troy'. Though Clytemnestra and Aegisthus are thrilled to see Agamemnon embark on his bloody mission, the watchman, akin to Goya's supplicant and seer, *feels* in the present 'what must come to pass', but lacking the means or the strength to truly testify, instead *bears* witness the way sound stuck in a struck gong stays and stays within the vibrating bronze. The watchman, like the poem or poet, is an instrument, akin to the water bucket in

---

[75] Heaney, 'The Watchman's War', in 'Mycenae Lookout', in *Opened Ground*, 414.

[76] T. S. Eliot, *The Waste Land*, in *The Complete Poems and Plays* (London: Faber, 1969), 75.

[77] Heaney, 'In the Beech', in 'Sweeney Redivivus', in *Opened Ground*, 271.

[78] Heaney, 'Watchman's War', 414.   [79] Heaney, 'Hercules and Antaeus', ibid. 130.

the scullery of Heaney's childhood home, registering 'in utter silence' the 'passing' of every earth-shaking event.[80]

Heaney describes the originary sensitivity and perspicacity of his 'ahistorical, pre-sexual' self as 'in suspension between the archaic and the modern', connecting times passively if acutely, the way 'the ripple at its widest desired to be verified by a reformation of itself, to be drawn in and drawn out through its point of origin'.[81] Child and adult, then and now, here and elsewhere, interior and exterior, are all suspended and sustained together in this image that defines Heaney's poetics. In a 1999 interview, he says: 'For years I thought of that image of the surface of water shaking while a train passes. . . . I thought of it as an image for lyric poetry—perhaps all art—registering the effect of history. The train passes with a thunder like war. It is not necessary that the poem documents this war, but it registers the vibrations of a state of mind.'[82] The watchman, however, suffers because these vibrations have no release except in horrifying dreams of carnage. 'Posted and forgotten', left to his nightmares and knowledge of 'world-sorrow', the watchman is ultimately stifled by the tension between the scope of the disaster impending (perhaps always) and the desire for some end to it all:

> And then the ox would lurch against the gong
> And deaden it and I would feel my tongue
> Like the dropped gangplank of a cattle truck,
> Trampled and rattled, running piss and muck,
> All swimmy-trembly as the lick of fire,
> A victory beacon in an abattoir.

This is the moment when Ireland, always already a part of Heaney's poetic and personal concerns, enters in the image not of a bog but of the fetid muck of an overflowing cattle truck. This is the image of silent witness to the deaths wrought by history; *not* saying anything about the global or the local devastations—as he suggested in 'Whatever You Say Say Nothing'—also bears a potentially explosive cost for the witness or his community. Curiously, this poem from *North* also bears an image from Troy used to describe Ulster's Catholic community: 'Where half of us, as in a wooden horse, | Were cabin'd and confined like wily Greeks | Besieged within the siege, whispering morse.'[83] By 'Mycenae Lookout', Heaney's gaze, while encompassing the past's atavisms, quite literally has 'concentrate[d] attention out beyond | The city and the border, on that line | Where the blaze would leap the hills when Troy had fallen'.

For the watchman poised and expectant, assigned to await word of what will happen, the war is a bizarre interregnum, literally 'an in-between-times', a temporal

---

[80] Heaney, 'Crediting Poetry', ibid. 447.   [81] Ibid. 447 and 466.
[82] Heaney, interviewed by Luigi Amara, David Huerta, and Julio Trujillo, 'Conversación con Seamus Heaney: La conciencia poética', *Letras Libres*, 1/4 (Apr. 1999), 38; my translation.
[83] Heaney, '*from* Whatever You Say Say Nothing', in *Opened Ground*, 132–3.

no man's land he has to endure with almost geologic fortitude. If for those at Troy the war is the focus of their lives, all else nothing but forethought and afterthought, then for the watchman the war years are a gap. Heaney, who famously says in 'Terminus', 'Two buckets were easier carried than one. | I grew up in between',[84] explains in *The Cure at Troy* that this is precisely the place of poetry. The Chorus at the outset of this play speaks of poetry's role in telling about terrible events. But, echoing 'The Redress of Poetry' and his criticisms of the activist who sees poetry exclusively through its interventionist potential, Heaney, as Chorus member disparaging heroes and victims alike, mocks any individual's or society's conscious self-identification with its wounds:

> Licking their wounds
> And flashing them around like decorations.
> I hate, I always hated it, and I am
> A part of it myself.
>   And a part of you,
> For my part is the chorus, and the chorus
> Is more or less a borderline between
> The you and the me and the it of it.
>
>   Between
> The gods' and human beings' sense of things.
>
> And that's the borderline that poetry
> Operates on too, always in between
> What you would like to happen and what will—
> Whether you like it or not.
>
>   Poetry
> Allowed the god to speak. It was the voice
> Of reality and justice.[85]

In identifying his idea of the 'frontier of writing',[86] Heaney describes a witnessing poetry as a medium, the bridge *or* the gap, in between desire ('destiny') and actuality ('dread').[87] Similarly, he conceives such a poetry as connecting the human and the transcendent, and thus creating the channel through which the god speaks.[88] And this is where Heaney's boldness lies: in his inveterate willingness to allow room for hope in the zone of his own 'veteran knowledge' that, truly, 'no one really escapes from the massacre'.[89] This gets most famously articulated in part of the Chorus's conclusion to *The Cure at Troy*:

---

[84] Heaney, 'Terminus', in *Opened Ground*, 295.

[85] Heaney, *The Cure at Troy: A Version of Sophocles' Philoctetes* (London: Faber, 1991), 2.

[86] Heaney, 'Frontiers of Writing', 190.   [87] Heaney, 'Watchman's War', 415.

[88] In 'The Government of the Tongue', Heaney writes: 'The poet is credited with a power to open unexpected and unedited communications between our nature and the nature of the reality we inherit. The oldest evidence for this attitude appears in the Greek notion that when a lyric poet gives voice, "it is a god that speaks" ' (p. 93).

[89] Carson, ' "Escaped from the Massacre?" ', *The Honest Ulsterman*, 50 (1975), 183.

Human beings suffer.
They torture one another.
They get hurt and get hard.
No poem or play or song
Can fully right a wrong
Inflicted and endured.

History says, Don't hope
On this side of the grave,
But then, once in a lifetime
The longed-for tidal wave
Of justice can rise up
And hope and history rhyme.[90]

Of course, 'hope' does not and never will literally rhyme with 'history'; Heaney expects the miracle of such real rhyming to occur most rarely, if at all. Indeed, the play, as he sees it, is hardly about war.[91] Yet, just as the Trojan conflict forms the back-story for *Philoctetes*, another take on war shadows Heaney's version. Behind *The Cure at Troy* lies the astounding avoidance of full-scale war in South Africa as the apartheid regime was falling and Nelson Mandela was released from prison. Heaney even describes 'the wondrous change and wondrous intervention of Nelson Mandela' as 'the *miraculum*', pointing out that Sophocles' play seemed 'to mesh beautifully with Mandela's return. The act of betrayal, and then the generosity of his coming back and helping with the city—helping the polis to get together again.'[92]

For the watchman of 'Mycenae Lookout', however, no miracle is as yet in sight, though like poetry or the poet, he stands as a plinth, the still centre of a scale of justice, static and powerless to influence the outcome of the weigh-in. His mind and gaze distorted from such static gazing, the watchman describes how

If a god of justice had reached down from heaven
For a strong beam to hang his scale-pans on
He would have found me tensed and ready-made.
I balanced between destiny and dread
And saw it coming, clouds bloodshot with the red
Of victory fires, the raw wound of that dawn
Igniting and erupting, bearing down
Like lava on a fleeing population.

[90] Heaney, *Cure at Troy*, repr. as 'Voices from Lemnos', in *Opened Ground*, 330.

[91] Rather, as he says, it is 'really about someone who has been wounded and betrayed, and whether he can reintegrate with the betrayers or not. Human sympathy says yes, maybe political vengefulness says no, but the marooned man in Sophocles' play helps the Greeks who betrayed him to win Troy' (Heaney, quoted in Shaun Johnson, 'Hope Is Something That Is There To Be Worked For', *The Independent* (London), 31 Oct. 2002, Features, 4).

[92] About Mandela himself, whom he met in Dublin, Heaney says, 'Of all the heroes, he's the great one. There's a great transmission of grace there—and, of course, great stamina to go with it' (Heaney, quoted ibid.).

At this moment of history's charge, the watcher becomes a seer caught between what he knows must, and what he hopes will, come to pass. The witness here occupies a terrible position, helpless before not the 'tidal wave of justice' but the lava flow of injustice bearing down horrifically and inexorably on innocents. 'The Watchman's War' describes seeing and knowing as kinds of trauma parallel to the experience of combat. It presents a remarkably grim situation in which, despite his decency, the watchman's hope—what Heaney in relation to the IRA's 1994 ceasefire calls a 'stoical clarity . . . different from optimism'[93]—finds expression only in the severity of his dread. A witness to catastrophe over the horizon as well as here in the *polis*, the palace, the self, the watchman is left like the shaken tree from 'The Poplar', asking: 'What loaded balances have come to grief?'[94]

'The Watchman's War' portrays a very earthbound witness-as-poet bearing like St Kevin the costs of his oddly privileged knowledge and solitary, in-between perspective. 'Cassandra' is, of course, the true visionary, but on the scale opposite the watchman, she presents the real voice of abjection. In *Agamemnon*, as a witness not to what happens but to what will happen, she speaks truth to the Chorus: 'I tell you, you shall look on Agamemnon dead.' The Chorus begs for silence, and in disgust, as opposed to despair, she says, 'Useless; there is no god of healing in this story.'[95] Whether such a god or principle exists haunts Heaney, who, when in Greece in autumn 1995, made a special point of visiting the temple of Asclepius. In conversation with Vincent Browne in 2001, Heaney speaks of care:

You look at the world and you look at Kosovo, at Africa, at South America, at Russia and you realise that care for the other is a kind of global fundamental obligation almost of our kind, you know. That used to be doctrinally taught in schools as part of the kind of penitential faith that I grew up in. There was a system, a theological, doctrinal system applied to the widest reach of your understanding. It applied to the most intimate crevices of yourself in the examination of conscience.[96]

His interlocutor regrettably says, 'I don't see that reflected in your poetry, that sense of caring for the other, for the broader world?' Heaney replies: 'It's not. The broader world as a content and as a geography is not in my poetry, no . . . [and here he mentions Kosovo in 'The Known World']. But I don't think that's necessarily the way poetry works. It's more a pitch and a tuning, poetry. I think there's something

---

[93] Heaney, 'Cessation 1994', in *Finders Keepers: Selected Prose 1971–2001* (London: Faber, 2002), 47.

[94] Heaney, 'The Poplar', in *The Spirit Level* (London: Faber, 1996), 50.

[95] Aeschylus, *Agamemnon*, in *Aeschylus i*, trans. Richmond Lattimore (Chicago: University of Chicago Press, 1953), ll. 1246 and 1248.

[96] Heaney, quoted in Vincent Browne, 'Still Finding Himself in his Poetry', *Irish Times*, 31 Mar. 2001.

answerable in the poetry, I think there is a sense of being answerable to and for what's going on.'

With 'her soiled vest, | her little breasts, | her clipped, devast- || ated, scabbed | punk head, | the char-eyed || famine gawk',[97] Cassandra embodies the bog-body from 'Punishment': a naked girl with 'shaved head | like a stubble of black corn'.[98] Only now, the bog-body speaks her rage. Is this a revision in the vein of the poems about Heaney's murdered cousin? Or is this a case of a poem, a character, a voice refusing its status as historical? If 'Punishment' looked outwards to Jutland to speak directly to the inner dark of Ulster, 'Cassandra' looks directly into Agamemnon's palace and her death to speak of a far wider world—that also assaults Heaney's bold self-identification in 'Punishment': 'I am the artful voyeur.' 'No such thing | as innocent | bystanding', begins Cassandra. But she continues, turning the same words in on herself as scapegoat: 'No such thing | as innocent.' An anxiety about what happened to such a thing as innocence in the twentieth century underlies her criticism and her own self-identification, just as Philip Larkin's Great War poem 'MCMXIV' haunts the palace at Mycenae: 'Never such innocence again.'[99]

Just as Heaney's Cassandra echoes Larkin on the First World War, his watchman, in the third section of 'Mycenae Lookout', revisits Auden, whose Troy is haunted by the Second World War, cataclysm connecting to cataclysm across the millennia. Cassandra and Agamemnon murdered, 'His Dawn Vision' bears allusions to Auden's seminal poem about war, 'The Shield of Achilles', and returns to the watchman's view at the edge of disaster:

> No element that should have carried weight
> Out of the grievous distance would translate.
> Our war stalled in the pre-articulate.[100]

Here, time is out of joint; we know the killings have taken place, and yet the poem ends not with definitive 'tombs' but with Achilles still 'amorously' pursuing Hector before distraught spectators on Troy's ramparts. This is a vision of catastrophe always already about to befall the human community. Whether 'sad presentiments' or what has always been beneath the veneer of civilization, the watchman envisions 'Cities of grass. Fort walls. The dumbstruck palace'. Beginning with this apocalyptic vision of total war as the obliteration of the city, whether Troy or Hiroshima, the poem, like the sequence, accommodates the distant past and our indeterminate future. Heaney shows the human witness suffering as nothing out there in 'the grievous distance' connects, and language fails to adequately comprehend the

---

[97] Heaney, 'Cassandra', in 'Mycenae Lookout', 415–16.
[98] Heaney, 'Punishment', in *Opened Ground*, 117.
[99] Philip Larkin, 'MCMXIV', in *Collected Poems*, ed. Anthony Thwaite (London: Faber, 1990), 128.
[100] Heaney, 'His Dawn Vision', in 'Mycenae Lookout', 418.

phantasmagoria. Knowledge, then, grounds into a core self where what cannot be told remains with the world it suffuses. At this point, Heaney addresses the limits of testimony, as knowledge of 'our war' is 'stalled' sublingually—or, rather, at the 'pre-articulate' source.[101] The poem suggests that rather than a failure of communication, this butting up against an idea of source *is* testimony about an all-too-real if terrible origin: 'I felt the beating of the huge time-wound | We lived inside. My soul wept'. At the 'pre-articulate', a nadir has been reached in which the weight of silence and testimony are suspended with one another, but something begins to shift as well. Some knowledge of death, a metonymy for war, lies within the self, ensconced without words. But, most significantly, this 'pre-articulate' origin also entertains the hope that language will be accessed, that poetry of adequate witness will result.

The sequence's penultimate poem, 'The Nights', presents life within the 'time-wound' where 'The war [has] put all men mad'.[102] For the watchman, war ends with the derangement of the world inside and outside the *polis*; peace becomes the 'rope-net and . . . blood-bath'. Yet, for Heaney, the business of witnessing involves more than an articulation of things as they are. 'Mycenae Lookout' ends with yet another vision that maps the labyrinth and offers a different way of seeing within the 'time-wound' or 'world-sorrow'. The final poem, 'His Reverie of Water', centres on Heaney's element; the prospect of the *cure* at Troy becomes a vision of the 'future we desire',[103] he salubrious, healing well. Nevertheless, as the hero and killer enters the humanizing bath, we are reminded 'that the far cries of the butchered on the plain || keep dying into . . . the housewalls' behind which the cleansing takes place.[104] Within the poem, no walls dampen these cries; in his bath, the hero, who Homer reminds us must also die, is suspended with his fate. Heaney follows the water, however, towards a further source. The secret well below the Athenian Acropolis becomes a site where invader and invaded, war and peace, past and future, come together indistinguishably, the way 'the treadmill of assault || turned waterwheel'. In this image, the 'time-wound' is 'cured' like 'the vent' of the Grauballe Man's 'slashed throat'[105]—the murderous lies within the marvellous, and vice versa. 'Mycenae Lookout' ends with an image of omphalos; the ultimate source is a circuit completed across this poet's career linking the universal and the local. Traumatic repetition is subsumed within a circuit of hope that specifically requires the language of a witness—or a poem that is as willing to look for the Better as to subsume the Worst. With this poem, Heaney's 'ladder' is sunk not into the 'foul rag and bone

---

[101] Heaney relates the 'pre-articulate' to an idea of poetic source where life and death are nearly comprehensible. In another context, he describes such a place: 'It was just suddenly and solidly there in front of you, like a parent or a pillar, and there it remains to this day, omphalos of the pre-literary and even the pre-literate life, irreducible, undislodgeable and undeniably true' (Heaney, 'Burns's Art Speech', in *Finders Keepers*, 348).

[102] Heaney, 'The Nights', in 'Mycenae Lookout', 421.   [103] Heaney, 'Crediting Poetry', 457.

[104] Heaney, 'His Reverie of Water', in 'Mycenae Lookout', 421.

[105] Heaney, 'Grauballe Man', 115.

shop of the heart',[106] but into the earth itself as source, out of which men emerge, not new-born but more knowledgeable and brutally chastened, 'like discharged soldiers', witnesses to the incomprehensible prospect of at once 'sorrow' and 'joy'.[107]

[106] W. B. Yeats, 'The Circus Animals' Desertion', in *The Poems*, ed. Daniel Albright (London: Dent, 1990), 395.

[107] Heaney, 'Watchman's War', 414.

CHAPTER 37

....

UNAVOWED ENGAGEMENT: PAUL MULDOON AS WAR POET

....

APRIL WARMAN

Paul Muldoon is not a writer for whom the term 'war poet' seems immediately appropriate. The commonest association of the phrase 'war poetry' is with the strong moral drive which appears in Owen's famous 'Preface'—'Above all I am not concerned with Poetry. My subject is War.... All a poet can do today is warn'[1]—or in Seamus Heaney's writings of the 1970s: 'From that moment [the start of the Troubles in summer 1969] the problems of poetry moved from being simply a matter of achieving the satisfactory verbal icon to being a search for images and symbols adequate to our predicament.'[2] As Mark Rawlinson argues, 'In the influential figure of the war poet as it has been constructed since 1914, cultural and moral authority is founded in an agent-centred and engaged perspective on combat.'[3] It is hard to see Muldoon in anything other than an antithetical relation to this model. He has repudiated any moral bent

---

[1] Wilfred Owen, 'Preface', in *The Complete Poems and Fragments*, ii: *The Manuscripts and Fragments*, ed. Jon Stallworthy (London: Chatto & Windus, Hogarth Press, and Oxford University Press, 1983), 535.

[2] Seamus Heaney, 'Feeling into Words', in *Preoccupations: Selected Prose 1968–1978* (London: Faber, 1980), 56.

[3] Mark Rawlinson, *British Writing of the Second World War* (Oxford: Clarendon Press, 2000), 13.

that his poetry may be seen to contain,[4] and explicitly denied having an 'engaged perspective'.[5]

Rawlinson goes on to state, 'The authority of [the war poet's] witness is proportional to its dissociation from administrative objectification and from an aesthetics of detachment.'[6] 'An aesthetics of detachment' is precisely what much of Muldoon's work, especially his early poetry (the volumes up to and including *Quoof* (1983), which were written whilst Muldoon lived in Northern Ireland), is particularly associated with: during his early reception, the word 'hermetic' became a standard descriptor of his poetry.[7]

Far from asking the reader to take certain (ethical) perceptions and arguments from it, far from trying to convince us of certain truths, of the 'authority' of its 'witness', Muldoon's work is celebrated (and sometimes deplored) for its resistance to interpretation. His disorienting procedures are frequently placed in opposition to Heaney's moral stability: 'Where Heaney gives earnest witness, Muldoon the ironist ducks and weaves, endlessly evasive, polyvocal and outlandish';[8] 'Muldoon's... playfulness is in sharp contrast to Heaney's often earnest tone';[9] or, less admiringly, 'Heaney's poetry seems unforced, deep, natural... Muldoon's is tricky, clever, tickled by its own knowingness.'[10] Critics applaud his poetry's ability to forgo referential stability, its eluding of the restrictions that such stability can entail; they celebrate its 'rejection of the notion of stable or univocal origins which... are linked to a conservative politics',[11] or its 'question[ing of] its own authority along with origins, foundations, heritage, precedent, preceptor and pedigree'.[12] The Muldoon suggested by such comments could not be further from claiming Rawlinson's 'moral authority' and 'witness'.

[4] Asked by John Haffenden whether he 'detect[s] a strong moral drive in [his] work', Muldoon responds, 'It's apparent to me as a reader of the poems in *New Weather* [his first collection, from 1973] in particular, many of which I don't like because of exactly that tone' ('Paul Muldoon', interviewed by John Haffenden, in John Haffenden (ed.), *Viewpoints: Poets in Conversation with John Haffenden* (London: Faber, 1981), 135).

[5] Ibid. 137: 'I might appear to be evasive. But I don't have committed beliefs—it's as simple as that.'

[6] Rawlinson, *British Writing of the Second World War*, 14.

[7] See e.g. Heaney, 'The Mixed Marriage', in *Preoccupations*, 212; Dillon Johnston, 'The Go-Between of Recent Irish Poetry', in Michael Kenneally (ed.), *Cultural Contexts and Literary Idioms in Contemporary Irish Literature* (Gerrards Cross: Colin Smythe, 1988), *passim*; John Goodby, 'Hermeneutic Hermeticism: Paul Muldoon and the Northern Irish Poetic', in C. C. Barfoot (ed.), *In Black and Gold: Contiguous Traditions in Post-War British and Irish Poetry* (Amsterdam: Rodopi, 1994), *passim*.

[8] David Wheatley, 'An Irish Poet in America', *Raritan*, 18/4 (Spring 1999), 145–6.

[9] Goodby, 'Hermeneutic Hermeticism', 139.

[10] John Carey, 'The Stain of Words', in *Sunday Times*, 21 June 1987, 56.

[11] Clair Wills, *Improprieties: Politics and Sexuality in Northern Irish Poetry* (Oxford: Oxford University Press, 1992), 194.

[12] Edna Longley, ' "When Did You Last See Your Father?" Perceptions of the Past in Northern Irish Writing 1965–1985', in *The Living Stream: Literature and Revisionism in Ireland* (Newcastle-upon-Tyne: Bloodaxe, 1994), 167.

In fact, both Muldoon's circumstances and his temperament dictate that he cannot be, and certainly does not present himself as, a war poet in the tradition of the influential figure that Rawlinson delineates. Whereas Owen conforms, and contributes, to Rawlinson's model—'Twentieth-century canons of war literature privilege the perspective of the combatant soldier who is engaged in war's central activity of injuring and killing persons'[13] (an experience which Heaney recasts as 'a life so extremely mortgaged to the suffering of others that the tenancy of the palace of art is paid for a hundredfold'[14])—and whereas Heaney himself, though not a combatant, has been, at times, inclined to identify strongly (and controversially)[15] with a traumatized community, Muldoon tends to distance himself from the notion that he can, or would wish to, speak as one who has suffered, or as representative of a suffering community: 'The poems I've written about the political situation [in Northern Ireland] tend to be oblique, and I think properly so.'[16]

This caution is in keeping with the fact that while Muldoon, as a resident of Belfast from 1969 to 1985, lived in a time and place of violence, his involvement was only *in potentia*: until you are the victim of a terrorist attack, you can hardly claim to be a target. He was, like many others, in an indeterminate relation to the violence occurring in sometimes close proximity to him: not a victim by comparison with those actually hurt, killed, or bereaved (or an agent compared with those doing the killing), but not unaffected by comparison with those entirely outside the arena of violence. The conflict in Northern Ireland does feature increasingly in Muldoon's early work, but, as he says, it and the moral responses it evokes feature obliquely, in such a way as to disavow any authority that might accrue to the poet through them. This essay aims to examine how this obliquity functions; how (and how far), despite, alongside, or even through, his famous evasiveness, not only the fact of sectarian violence, but also its felt moral implications for those who experience it (with whatever degree of directness), appear in Muldoon's early poetry.

This obliquity functions in Muldoon's early work principally, I would argue, through the inscrutable attitudes to violence of the poems' personae. Poems that relate to violence (not only specifically Northern Irish violence) are most frequently cast as first-person narrative, but their speakers rarely do more than

---

[13] Rawlinson, *British Writing of the Second World War*, 11.

[14] Heaney, 'The Government of the Tongue', in *The Government of the Tongue: The 1986 T. S. Eliot Memorial Lectures and Other Critical Writings* (London: Faber, 1988), 100. For a corrective to a too hagiographical view of Owen, see Geoffrey Hill's more measured appraisal: 'Owen's sense of his own value as "pleader" for the inarticulate common soldier presupposes his unawareness or inability to comprehend that at least three of the finest British poets of that war, Isaac Rosenberg, Ivor Gurney, and David Jones, had gone, or were still going, as "common soldiers" through all that he describes' (Hill, 'Language, Suffering, and Silence', *Literary Imagination*, 1/2 (1999), 247).

[15] e.g. Edna Longley contends that 'empathy with one Ulster community, such as Heaney's in *North*, might constrain rather than release a poet's imagination' (Longley, 'Poetry and Politics in Northern Ireland', in *Poetry in the Wars* (Newcastle-upon-Tyne: Bloodaxe, 1986), 202).

[16] Muldoon, 'Paul Muldoon', 137.

record unfolding events. Incidents are narrated, or hinted at, but no comment upon, or even reaction to, them is indicated; their moral implications are altogether ignored. Muldoon's approach to violence is, to borrow D. W. Harding's remark on Rosenberg, 'unusually direct', with 'no secondary distress arising from the sense that these things ought not to be'.[17]

Such inscrutability in the poems' personae means that access to the poet's own views on violence is thoroughly obstructed. The common readerly temptation to conflate poet and speaker is unhelpful here: it only adds to the impression that Muldoon himself has nothing he wishes to say on the subject. It is, indeed, what lies behind frustration such as that of Barra O Seaghda, who dismisses Muldoon as a poet who 'plays with politics, but snaps his fingers and disappears, vapour-like, up the postmodern chimney when any reality comes knocking at the door'.[18]

Muldoon's first collection, *New Weather* (1973), contains no direct reference to the Troubles, but its parabolic narratives do raise some of the questions of responsibility that violence evokes. Two poems from it are exemplary of his future attitude to the issues raised by conflict, in their withholding of moral judgement in situations which seem to demand it. 'The Field Hospital' entirely and overtly separates the positions of writer and speaker, voicing dramatically the concerns of the physicians of the hospital of the title. What seems like moral clarity in the physicians, with their rhetoric of self-sufficiency ('with the strength of our bare hands'[19]) and pride in their aloof impartiality before all causes except the saving of lives ('We answer to no grey South || Nor blue North . . . But that hillside of fresh graves'), is abruptly brought into question, and possibly recast as complacency, by the reality of a suffering victim, and their casual, even callous, attitude towards her:

> Would this girl brought to our tents
> From whose flesh we have removed
> Shot that George, on his day off,
>
> Will use to weight fishing lines,
> Who died screaming for ether,
> Yet protest our innocence?

Tim Kendall reads the poem's last stanza as a resolution of this conflict: he sees the

> gigantic, yellow moths
> That brushed right over her wounds,
> Pinning themselves to our sleeves
> Like medals given the brave

as 'connect[ing] her wounds with their [the physicians'] deserved commendation', and the poem as a whole as valorizing the dispassionate: 'a tacit manifesto for the

[17] D. W. Harding, quoted in Seamus Perry, 'Old Druid Time', *Times Literary Supplement*, 25 Nov. 2005, 8.

[18] Barra O Seaghda, quoted in Goodby, 'Hermeneutic Hermeticism', 152.

[19] Muldoon, 'The Field Hospital', in *Poems 1968–1998* (London: Faber, 2001), 33.

poet's role in a divided society'.[20] This is a possible reading, but to present it as the only interpretation the poem affords collapses the ambivalence which is sustained to the last line. It is the voice of the physicians that likens the moths to medals; the value they place on their own impartiality is not itself an impartial viewpoint.

In fact, their language suggests a degree of unease within their self-congratulation: the very act of comparison ('*Like* medals') is based in a recognition of essential difference (not *really* medals: bravery remains unguaranteed). Furthermore, the phrase 'brushed right over her wounds' contains an unpleasant suggestion that the moths, as they are appropriated to the physicians' rhetoric, perform an obscuring or minimizing of the girl's injuries. In this poem, the positions of the healers and of the girl who might be seen as their victim are uneasily juxtaposed: its strength lies precisely in its refusal to endorse either. Essential to a clear reading is an appreciation of the poem's status as dramatic presentation of an unresolved opposition of viewpoints, rather than a vehicle for the poet's views, a 'tacit manifesto'.

'The Field Hospital' does acknowledge that suffering exists, and that it creates moral difficulties, which are made the more immediate by Muldoon's refusal to resolve them. 'Good Friday, 1971. Driving Westwards' is even more indicative of Muldoon's future development, in that it unsettles any factual basis for the exercise of moral judgement. The poem describes a car journey that ends in what may or may not be a hit-and-run accident:

> for a time I lost
> Control and she thought we hit something big
> But I had seen nothing, perhaps a stick
> Lying across the road. I glanced back once
> And there was nothing but a heap of stones.
> We had just dropped in from nowhere for lunch
>
> In Gaoth Dobhair, I happy and she convinced
> Of the death of more than lamb or herring.
> She stood up there and then, face full of drink,
> And announced that she and I were to blame
> For something killed along the way we came.[21]

In making it uncertain whether or not a victim ever actually existed, Muldoon leaves readers unsure whether they are seeing an evasion of responsibility by the narrator or a display of melodramatic (and drunken) self-importance on the girl's part. The narrator's determination to be 'happy' despite the accident, his insistent repetition of the word 'nothing', and his changing version of the harmless things they might have hit—'perhaps a stick' or 'a heap of stones' (itself connotative of a grave-cairn)—suggest that he is protesting too much. On the other hand, the

[20] Tim Kendall, *Paul Muldoon* (Bridgend: Seren, 1996), 31.
[21] Muldoon, 'Good Friday, 1971. Driving Westwards', in *Poems 1968–1998*, 19–20.

wilfulness of the girl's action and the theatricality of 'announced' suggest that she insists on the fact of a death in order to relish her own implication in it. The title's allusion to Donne's enthusiastic self-abasement ('O thinke mee worth thine anger, punish mee'[22]), along with the Christian iconography of 'lamb or herring', reinforces this second interpretation, inviting a reading of the poem involving a critique of Christianity as a religion of guilt and punishment. As with 'The Field Hospital', neither reading is given precedence over the other, but here the lack of a definitive version of events leaves us unable even to begin to make our own moral judgement. With its closing couplet—'Children were warned that it was rude to stare, || Left with their parents for a breath of air'—the most the poem comments on is the general reluctance of those 'implicated simply by being on the sidelines'[23] to confront a morally ambiguous situation.

New Weather, as I remarked, contains no direct reference to the Troubles, but, appearing as it did in a context where it could be felt that 'it is arguable that *any* poem by a Northern Irish poet since 1968, on whatever subject, could be termed a Troubles poem, in that it may, consciously or unconsciously, reflect the context in which it was written',[24] it is inevitable that Northern Irish meaning should be read into its violent parables. Kendall, for example, describes 'The Field Hospital' as 'Set during the American Civil War but clearly analogous to the conflict in Northern Ireland'.[25] In *Mules* (1977), his next volume, Muldoon begins to include the Troubles as subject-matter, but more through their teasingly foregrounded absence than through their presence; he addresses them through knowing play on the expectations for Northern Irish relevance that readers will inevitably, and not unreasonably, bring to his work.

The horrors that are hinted at in the first stanza of 'Bang' ('For that moment we had been the others | These things happen to.... Which of us had that leg belonged to?'[26]) are suddenly left behind as the narrator improbably asserts: 'It brought me back years to that Carnival | In the next parish.' When this reminiscence ends with a girl 'moaning the name of the one who had scored the goal | Earlier that evening', the sexual overtone requires a reassessment of the earlier scenario. If the narrator is 'brought back' to the carnival by the event of the first stanza, then this, which the title, and the expectations created by Muldoon's Northern Irish context, had led us to identify as an explosion, reconfigures itself as a sexual encounter. The unclaimed leg becomes as likely to be tangled indistinguishably with a partner's as severed in a blast. The suggestion of violence is proffered with

---

[22] John Donne, 'Goodfriday, 1613. Riding Westward', in *Complete English Poems*, ed. C. A. Patrides (London: Dent, 1985), 358.

[23] Muldoon, 'Paul Muldoon', 133–4. Muldoon refers to the situation imagined in his poem 'The Country Club'.

[24] Frank Ormsby, 'Preface', in *idem* (ed.), *A Rage for Order: Poetry of the Northern Ireland Troubles* (Belfast: Blackstaff, 1992), p. xviii.

[25] Kendall, *Paul Muldoon*, 31.   [26] Muldoon, 'Bang', in *Poems 1968–1998*, 65–6.

one hand only to be whisked away by the other. The unexpected substitution at once confounds and exposes readerly expectation to be titillated by excitingly contemporary subject-matter.

Again, the preoccupation with Muldoon's native county of the sonnet sequence 'Armageddon, Armageddon' (also from *Mules*),[27] and its allusions to violence (especially internecine violence: 'Were Twin and Twin at each other's throats?'; 'Our father . . . torn between his own two ponies, || Their going their different ways') tempt us to read for veiled commentary on the Ulster situation. References such as that in Sonnet III to 'where the first Orange Lodge was founded, || An orchard full of No Surrenders', explicitly invoke Northern Irish politics. Yet the sequence's unstable mix of ill-defined, semi-fantastic scenarios resists any coherent (let alone political) reading. The seven sonnets cover Mediterranean island hopping, Irish folklore, a kind of tourist's guide to Armagh, a dream vision on a train, and three unrelated, nightmarish scenarios which adumbrate some kind of societal breakdown. As Peter McDonald observes, 'these pieces make up a peculiar kind of sequence, one characterized more by *non sequitur* than connection.'[28] It is impossible to take the specifically Ulster references as clues to a larger political meaning for the poem. Added to this destabilization of Northern Irish (political) reading is the fact that the sequence is narrated with such casual affectlessness that an interpretation which tries to read it as responsible commentary risks appearing faintly ridiculous: in Sonnet IV,

> He [our brother] had guarded our mother bent-double
> Over the kitchen sink, her face in the basin.
> She had broken another of her best dishes,
> We would bury her when we were able.

The speaker bathetically ventriloquizes the mother's probable misplaced reaction, which renders the loss of a best dish as significant as her own undignified death. The casual response to the latter, treating it only in terms of its practical ramifications, refuses to acknowledge the ethical dimensions of cruelty and loss, and thus, also, their potential political significance.

In *Why Brownlee Left* (1980), sectarianism and its consequences start to feature in Muldoon's poetry in a relatively overt and undisrupted way. 'Anseo' famously relates the childhood brutalization of the speaker's classmate. Repeatedly punished at school for lateness, for failing to answer 'Anseo' at roll-call, Joe Ward, now a paramilitary living 'In a secret camp | On the other side of the mountain' where he fights 'for Ireland, || Making things happen',[29] is shown to have internalized the authoritarian mind-set of his school:

---

[27] Muldoon, 'Armageddon, Armageddon', in *Poems 1968–1998*, 67–71.

[28] Peter McDonald, *Mistaken Identities: Poetry and Northern Ireland* (Oxford: Clarendon Press, 1997), 162–3.

[29] Muldoon, 'Anseo', in *Poems 1968–1998*, 83–4.

> every morning at parade
> His volunteers would call back *Anseo*
> And raise their hands
> As their names occurred.

The five-line 'Ireland' laconically implies that terrorism is more expected than love in Northern Ireland, or at least in Northern Irish poetry, as a Volkswagen with its engine ticking over leads 'You' to 'wonder if it's lovers | And not men hurrying back | Across two fields and a river'.[30] This evokes the same confusion of which 'Bang' makes use, substituting a sexual for a violent scenario. But here, in the title's explicit locating of the poem amongst the proliferation of attempts to define 'Ireland', and in the inclusive pronoun 'You' (which attributes the 'wondering' to both first and second persons, poet and reader), Muldoon himself acknowledges the plausibility of such confusion, rather than having it seem a product of the reader's overheated imagination. But in both 'Anseo' and 'Ireland' there is still no narratorial commentary on the state of affairs they portray. Northern Ireland has become an overt focus of attention, but this is an attention which merely records telling incidents and perceptions, and does not offer itself as an interpreter of these. Its neutrality is less disconcerting than that of the fourth sonnet of 'Armageddon, Armageddon', as the events it relates are less close to home, but its affectlessness is still far from what is expected as a response to such malign circumstances. The moral ramifications that inevitably, for readers, attend such subject-matter make the neutrality seem far from truly neutral, but anomalous and mildly disturbing.

Muldoon's next volume, *Quoof*, is even more explicitly concerned with the conflict. As Clair Wills notes, 'Terrorist bombings, army manoeuvres, shootings, murders and reprisals all feature in this volume.'[31] In presenting these, many of the poems share the deadpan response of 'Anseo' and 'Ireland'. 'The Sightseers', for example, contrasts its octave's evocation of a pleasingly symmetrical family ('My father and mother, my brother and sister') and their 'dour best-loved Uncle' with a sestet that relates uncle Pat's experience of sectarian persecution. The family had set out

> not to visit some graveyard—one died of shingles,
> one of fever, another's knees turned to jelly—
> but the brand-new roundabout at Ballygawley,
> the first in mid-Ulster.
>
> Uncle Pat was telling us how the B-Specials
> had stopped him one night somewhere near Ballygawley
> and smashed his bicycle
>
> And made him sing the Sash and curse the Pope of Rome.
> They held a pistol so hard against his forehead
> there was still the mark of an O when he got home.[32]

---

[30] Muldoon, 'Ireland', ibid. 82–3.
[31] Wills, *Reading Paul Muldoon* (Newcastle-upon-Tyne: Bloodaxe, 1998), 88.
[32] Muldoon, 'The Sightseers', in *Poems 1968–1998*, 110–11.

The casual, factual tone, sustained throughout, belies the shocking difference of subject-matter between octave and sestet; as far as the speaker is concerned, it seems that the story of Uncle Pat's victimization makes for as good entertainment as 'the brand-new roundabout'. The other attraction on offer, 'some graveyard', with its connotations of family piety, is rejected: the random multiplicity of mortality cannot hold the attention: '—one died of shingles, || one of fever, another's knees turned to jelly—'. This last in the catalogue of possible deaths in fact sounds far from natural—'knees turned to jelly' suggests 'died of fright', with a possible allusion to the practice of 'kneecapping', infamously associated with Ulster. But if this shadows an alternative fate for Uncle Pat at the hands of the B-Specials, then the narrator, it seems, is not interested. As the poem's title implies, it is entertainment—the uncanny detail of the O on Uncle Pat's forehead—that is valued, not the moral questions raised by such persecution. The affectless tone of this poem is similar to that which appears in the two poems quoted from *Why Brownlee Left*; what is unnerving is how much more concerned we feel the speaker *should* be by the situation he narrates. It may seem plausible to remain unconcerned by the history of a classmate's brutalization by society, but such callousness about the victimization of a 'best-loved uncle' is chilling.

'Mink' does not have this disconcerting blend of intimacy and detachment; it is equally unsettling, however, in that its approach to violence goes beyond the neutrality of 'Anseo' or 'Ireland' to a wilful randomness of response that appears slightly crazed. It makes reference to the murdered IRA infiltrator Robert Nairac not through the medium of political or moral comment on his fate, or even through detached factual narrative, but through the arbitrary and irresponsible connections of rhyme (Nairac/anorak) and material similarity (mink/fur-lined hood). In a poem of just four impassive lines, a mink escaped from its south Armagh mink farm 'is led to the grave of Robert Nairac | by the fur-lined hood of his anorak'.[33] To choose this approach to Nairac is to deny both the political meaning that Nairac's death and disappearance carry in Ulster, and the moral connotations that any murder holds. The indulgence in surrealism suggests a refusal in the narrator to acknowledge normal, social, responsible reactions, an anarchic declaration of independence from the requirements and fixities of morality.

However, the meaning that both these poems, and, to a lesser extent, all the poems I have discussed so far, do carry, inheres in how their determined detachment is itself open to interpretation. Over the four volumes, the discrepancy between the affectless tenor of these poems and their inherently shocking subject-matter becomes increasingly marked, and increasingly requires explanation. Early on, in the parables of *New Weather* and the knowing play on expectations of *Mules*, it simply suggests a writer reluctant to expose himself, through direct statement, to political misappropriation. Later, the increasingly anomalous detachment that

---

[33] Muldoon, 'Mink', *Poems 1968–1998*, 119.

features in *Why Brownlee Left* and *Quoof* suggests a kind of damage in the poems' narrators: to respond to brutality so carelessly, even callously, implies a mind dehumanized by its situation. The speaker comes to seem not just self-protectively remote from his situation, but somewhat crazed by the circumstances which require such self-protection. Muldoon can be read as commenting on Ulster's situation through his dramatized representations of the damaging effects on the psyche of living in a time and place of constantly threatened violence, and constantly demanded moral (which is often twisted towards political) positioning.

'The More a Man Has the More a Man Wants',[34] which ends *Quoof*, is in many ways similar to 'Mink', but its far greater length (forty-nine fourteen-line stanzas) gives its bizarre manœuvres a greater range of possible meaning. It is open to being read dramatically, its sinister, fragmentary narrative suggesting a damaged, even schizoid narrator; but whereas the provocative brevity of 'Mink' virtually ensures such a reading, challenging readers to neutralize its conspicuous incompleteness through reference to the extra-textual notion of a dramatized subjectivity, the extent of 'The More a Man Has' provides such an abundance of material that an appeal to extra-textual factors no longer seems absolutely necessary, or necessarily to account entirely for the poem.

The similarities to 'Mink' lie in the eerily outlandish approach to violence of 'The More a Man Has', and its favouring of imaginative over rational (and, therefore, moral) logic. Its disjunctive story (loosely, of the acts and reflections of a turncoat terrorist on the run) veers from scenario to scenario not through narrative consequence, but through dream logic, ties of equivalence, and arbitrary connection, rather than rational continuity.

The foregrounding in 'Mink' of the material properties of language at the expense of logical coherence (the pre-eminence given to Nairac/anorak) reappears throughout the longer poem: for example, 'skinheads' inappropriately form a 'quorum', largely, it seems, for the sake of the rhyme with 'aquarium'. The imaginative liberty that coolly asserts the relevance of the mink to Nairac appears, for example, when Gallogly, the amorphous protagonist, is transported from the Belfast area to New York via the assertion that he 'has only to part the veil | of its stomach wall | to get right under the skin . . . || of the horse in *Guernica*'. But the significant difference between the two poems lies in the greater length, and thus variety, of 'The More a Man Has'. The single juxtaposition in 'Mink' of brutal subject-matter with bizarre response is here repeated through a number of different registers and scenarios over the course of the poem—indeed, the affectlessness in the longer poem is partly the product of such variety, as the very abundance of proffered responses to violence betrays them all as predetermined and parodic.

---

[34] Muldoon, 'The More a Man Has the More a Man Wants', ibid. 127–47.

Six lines alone, on the shooting of a UDR corporal, demonstrate the unsettling mixture of tones through which the basic contrast between distressing subject-matter and detached reaction is maintained in the poem:

> You could, if you like, put your fist
> in the exit wound
> in his chest.
> He slumps
> in the spume of his own arterial blood
> like an overturned paraffin lamp.

The fundamentally affectless tone is built from rapid, mocking forays into various registers. The first line borrows the affable 'if you like' for a punitively tasteless revitalization of the stock idiom 'You could', used simply to suggest possibility. The reader is discomfitingly implicated by the play on pronouns: the indeterminate 'You could' (used in the sense of 'one could') shifts, through the literalizing emphasis given to the invitation by 'if you like', towards an accusatory second person (the content of the offer casting the reader in the unflattering role of a doubting Thomas). '[E]xit wound' partakes of the semi-official jargon that Muldoon describes as the 'kennings of the hourly news bulletin' (which he 'hoped to purge [him]self of' in the poem),[35] a use of language that works to appropriate and redefine events according to particular interests. The reimagining of 'arterial blood' as the poetic 'spume' suggests, by contrast, an artistically inclined speaker, and a new appropriation of the corporal's death: to creative transformation. The paraffin-lamp simile, however, has a blank neutrality which contrasts with the previous appropriative redescriptions, revealing it to be as unsettling that such an event should be endowed with no meaning, as for its meaning to be skewed. Such an abundance of versions of one event draws attention to the manipulative power of language, rather than the events it describes. The kaleidoscopic mode of 'The More a Man Has', switching unaccountably between scenes, and between different possible perspectives on scenes, drains language of its referentiality, emphasizing instead its creative potency, as unconfined by the demands of objectivity. Whereas the remarkable brevity of 'Mink' works to provoke readers into finding a way to read it referentially, the minute and extended attention to the details of linguistic usage in 'The More a Man Has' may pre-empt this implicit appeal to factors beyond its own activities: its formal preoccupations and play among registers provide plentiful material for speculation in themselves. The potential for a dramatized, referential reading is present, but the poem's uncontainable variety means that no interpretation can be comprehensive, can take into account all possible ways in which it might feasibly be read.

The reception of the poem illustrates this. Even before identification of its meaning begins, its cumulative tonal blankness permits a variety of emphases, even within a single reading. McDonald, commenting on another, similar section of

---

[35] Muldoon, 'Paul Muldoon writes . . .', *Poetry Book Society Bulletin*, 118 (Autumn 1983), 1.

'The More a Man Has', rightly observes the startling discrepancy between register and subject-matter, but he describes the poem's register in two ways, which suggest rather different things about the poem's speaker. 'Part of the shock of this writing', he asserts, 'lies in its playing off verbal and formal *brio* against the brutality of the incident described; rather than a pre-formulated language of description, or of analysis (condemnatory or otherwise), Muldoon deals in a deadpan precision.'[36] McDonald's formulation elides the difference between 'verbal and formal *brio*' and 'deadpan precision'. By equating these, McDonald suggests moral possibilities latent in the ostensible heartlessness of linguistic *brio*. To be 'deadpan' implies that reactions and emotions exist, they are simply being suppressed, and McDonald's pre-emptive, derogatory identification of the alternative to suppression as 'a pre-formulated language of description or . . . analysis' implicitly proposes a converse authenticity and value for such suppression.

The affectlessness of 'The More a Man Has', and of Muldoon's evasive approaches to violence more generally, can be, and frequently are, seen as a cover for a moral sensibility too aware of the inadequacy of language and the dangers of political appropriation to speak directly, but one which, nonetheless, has ultimately ethical aims. For example, Tim Kendall persuasively describes 'The More a Man Has' as a 'brilliant brutal parable for contemporary Northern Ireland', an allegorical embodiment of the moral opacity of the Northern Irish situation: it 'obliquely conveys the terrible "Truth" that in a violent society perspectives quickly become lost, motives and identities obscured'.[37] Edna Longley sees the poem's refusal to be tied to conventional morality as freeing it to explore, through formal innovation, alternative, more productive routes to meaning. She ties such meaning to a break with the over-determined versions of Irish history that she sees it as working in reaction against: 'the poem's political message remains, above all, its medium, and its medium is metamorphic. . . . Muldoon's metamorphoses melt or expand rigid understandings of history; make us experience history as an arbitrary kaleidoscope, a form of mental illness.'[38] I myself read 'The More a Man Has' as having a covert moral dimension: I see its linguistic promiscuity and imaginative liberties, its deadpan affectlessness, as a many-times multiplied version of the chilling depiction of a deranged mind I see in 'Mink', and, to a lesser extent, other poems.

However, to return to McDonald's formulation, 'verbal and formal *brio*', while it can have a 'deadpan' quality read into it, is not identical with such. In itself, it cannot be said necessarily to contain suppressed moral potential. The apparent pleasure in language of 'The More a Man Has', its privileging of the non-referential, *could* be read not as oblique reaction to, and therefore comment on, context, but as simple rejection of responsibility to context, in favour of the freedom of art. Terence Brown, for instance, characterizes Muldoon through his apparent 'freedom from humanist

---

[36] McDonald, *Mistaken Identities*, 67–8.   [37] Kendall, *Paul Muldoon*, 116–17.
[38] Longley, 'Poetry and Politics in Northern Ireland', 210.

moral concern which makes [his] work imaginatively exhilarating when its ostensible subject matter might be reckoned wholly appalling'.[39] Sean O'Brien goes so far as to identify not simply a potential for amoral reading (imaginative exhilaration) in 'some of the grimmer poems of sex and violence in *Quoof*', but a reprehensible writerly attitude: that 'art is . . . an end for which life is simply material'.[40] Anyone wishing to deny the existence of a moral impulse behind the apparent amorality of Muldoon's poems could not be refuted definitively by recourse to textual evidence. The texts refuse moral meanings; it is perfectly possible, even desirable, to interpret that amorality as an oblique gesture towards some more positive impulse; but, as the range of routes to a propitious interpretation of 'The More a Man Has' illustrated above shows, no one such reading can be asserted as definitive or inevitable.

Writing is generally perceived as a moral, humanist endeavour,[41] and such a perception is only heightened when writing is known to come from a situation of conflict in which humanism is endangered. Because of this, the explanation that readers provide for the gap that appears in Muldoon, between shocking subject-matter and affectless response, will almost always take the form of a moral rationale for the apparent amorality. Peter Robinson sees in a later poem, 'Incantata', an elegy for a former lover, an 'attempt . . . to be . . . a reparative emblem', but concedes that 'This is a status the poem cannot claim, nor the poet claim for it, but which readers, in appreciating it, may confer.'[42] Such reparative ambition is less clearly apparent in Muldoon's early poetry, but readers are nonetheless frequently eager to confer reparative status, in relation to Northern Irish violence, upon it.[43]

Louis MacNeice wrote of his collection *Solstices*, 'My own position has been aptly expressed by the dying Mrs Gradgrind in Dickens's *Hard Times*: "I think there's a pain somewhere in the room but I couldn't positively say that I have got it." '[44] Readers tend to assume that the 'pain' of Northern Irish experience is unspoken but somehow contained in Muldoon's early poems; the conclusions they draw on the basis of this assumption are, however, ones for which he need take no responsibility, unconfirmed as they are by the surface content of his work. The poems themselves are devoid of moral content; it is only when they are read that their disengaged stance couples with readers' preconceptions to produce the

[39] Terence Brown, *Ireland's Literature* (Mullingar and Totowa, NJ: Lilliput Press and Barnes & Noble, 1988), 219.

[40] Sean O'Brien, *The Deregulated Muse* (Newcastle-upon-Tyne: Bloodaxe, 1998), 178.

[41] See e.g. Martha Nussbaum's assertion: 'So far as the implied author goes, I think very often there is a claim that the form of desire and attention that is embodied in the text is of superior human value in some way' ('An Interview with Martha Nussbaum', *Cogito*, 10/3 (Nov. 1996), 181–2).

[42] Peter Robinson, *Poetry, Poets, Readers: Making Things Happen* (Oxford: Clarendon Press, 2002), 187.

[43] Longley, e.g. casts Muldoon's poetry as 'midwife to a future not predicated on the past', and 'the labour-pains of progress' (Longley, 'Poetry and Politics in Northern Ireland', 210; and *idem*, '"Varieties of Parable": Louis MacNeice and Paul Muldoon', in *Poetry in the Wars*, 222).

[44] Louis MacNeice, in Clare Brown and Don Paterson (eds.), *Don't Ask Me What I Mean: Poets in Their Own Words* (London: Picador, 2003), 165.

impression of a simultaneity of worthy engagement and equally worthy scepticism of engagement, on which Muldoon's reputation to a great extent rests. The absence of any direct confrontation with the moral implications of violence means that, for readers, their presence is felt on the margins throughout his early volumes, underpinning their apparent evasiveness with a seriousness that is the more unchallengeable because never owned. While more straightforward (or perhaps more cynical) readers simply find, with Helen Vendler, 'a hole in the middle where the feeling should be',[45] others will extrapolate from this absence an unspoken moral awareness all the stronger for its suspicion of the perils of articulation.

Carolyn Forché, editor of *Against Forgetting*, an anthology of the work of 'significant poets who endured conditions of historical and social extremity', stipulates that, for inclusion, 'poets must have personally endured such conditions'. This seems to privilege Rawlinson's model of engaged testimony; however, she also asserts that 'Regardless of "subject matter", these poems bear the trace of extremity within them, and they are, as such, evidence of what occurred. . . . I was interested in what these poets wrote, regardless of the explicit content.'[46] This suggests another way in which war poetry operates, and one which is far more applicable to Muldoon. Alongside the construction of war poetry as explicit, morally motivated witness to horrifying experience, there is a simultaneous assumption that writing from an extreme situation will be marked by that situation, however unapparent such marking might be. Muldoon's poetry and its reception provide an extreme instance of the way in which witness—the location of significance in an artwork's relation to its context in extremity—is a function as much of the way a poem is read, as how it is written.

Around fifteen years after he left Northern Ireland, Muldoon published the long poem 'At the Sign of the Black Horse, September 1999',[47] which includes, amongst many other things, reference to the twentieth century's most evocative, memorialized instance of suffering, the Nazi Holocaust. There are many similarities between 'Black Horse' and 'The More a Man Has': both are end-of-volume long poems, in which disparate subject-matter is drawn together through little more than the poet's apparent whim. 'Black Horse' is loosely set in the aftermath of Hurricane Floyd: the wash of debris down the Delaware and Raritan canal in New Jersey (beside which Muldoon now lives) is reimagined as a deluge of twentieth-century history, as represented by the European- and American-Jewish forebears of Muldoon's new son, Asher. Diverse historic characters and episodes are amassed, without much indication that the speaker, overwhelmed by detail, differentiates much between them: 'the 1920 Studebaker's [earlier identified with Asher's distant

---

[45] Helen Vendler, 'Anglo-Celtic Attitudes', *New York Review of Books*, 6 Nov. 1997, 58.

[46] Carolyn Forché, in *idem* (ed.), *Against Forgetting: Twentieth Century Poetry of Witness* (New York: W. W. Norton, 1993), 30.

[47] Muldoon, 'At the Sign of the Black Horse, September 1999', in *Moy Sand and Gravel* (London: Faber, 2002), 73–90.

relative Arnie Rothstein, 1920s ballgame-fixer and bootlegger] just one step ahead of a Panther tank | nodding approvingly through the ghetto after the Germans have massacred | the Jews of Bialystok'.

As with 'The More a Man Has', critical reception has emphasized the poem's 'technical dexterity'[48] and 'verbal interlacings';[49] Laura Quinney identifies in it exactly the same strategy of 'addressing grim topics in a hard, high-spirited vein'[50] that is so prominent in *Quoof*. The approach to the Holocaust of 'Black Horse' has the same air of affectlessness, of attention to linguistic detail rather than to the moral burden of what its language conveys, as does that of 'The More a Man Has' to the Troubles. For example, the sinister image, 'A tattoo on the left forearm | of some child-kin of my children, a very faint tattoo', stands alone, without comment; the tone of the (frequently repeated) phrase 'child-kin of my children' hovers troublingly between the shockingly sentimental (and vicariously narcissistic) and the alarmingly arch: a morally responsible narrator is absent. However, such similarities of tone conceal a fundamental difference between the two poems, which arises from Muldoon's differing relations to the 'grim topics' each poem addresses. While the Troubles were inescapably part of Muldoon's immediate experience, his relation to the Holocaust is indirect and mediated, his decision to address it voluntary; he has no more authoritative connection to it than his readers do.[51]

'The More a Man Has' deploys a form—narrative—which naturally coheres, and which it is Muldoon's achievement to disrupt and fragment, thereby resisting readerly expectations that would extrapolate from the poem's context and content a coherent moral response to violence within it. The form of 'Black Horse', however, is basically that of a catalogue, a form which is naturally disjunctive,[52] but which it is Muldoon's achievement in the poem to make cohere. The poem contains a number of elements which invite the reader to make connections between its disparate components. One is its reworking of Yeats's 'A Prayer for my Daughter': it paraphrases this profusely, often to nonsensical ends, but sometimes to hint indirectly at a governing meaning for the poem's chaotic miscellany. Near the beginning of the poem the hope is expressed that 'we might bundle a few belongings into a pillow slip | and climb the hill and escape, Please Examine || Your Change, to a place where the soul might recover radical innocence'—this last notion adapts Yeats. But the poem ends less hopefully: Asher's soul is 'less likely than ever to

[48] Michael Kinsella, 'On Being Preposterous', *PN Review*, 29/4 (Mar.–Apr. 2003), 71.

[49] Jenny Ludwig, 'As If Washing Might Make It Clean', *Boston Review*, Summer 2003; <http://www.bostonreview.net/BR28.3/ludwig.html>

[50] Laura Quinney, 'In the Studebaker', *London Review of Books*, 23 Oct. 2003, 20.

[51] The tenuous connections that Muldoon suggests between himself and the Holocaust—the insistent emphasis on his children's ancestry, or the Judaization of the Irish navvies with whom he identifies (they become 'schlemiels' and 'schmucks' who 'keen and kvetch')—serve only to highlight his actual remoteness from the event.

[52] See John Lyon, 'Michael Longley's Lists', *English*, 45/183 (1996), 228–46, for an excellent account of the functions of listing in poetry.

recover radical innocence and learn at last | that it is self-delighting'. The suggestion is that the historical detail which the poem has been accumulating has caused this altered view: the self-sufficiency of Yeats's 'self-delighting, | Self-appeasing, self-affrighting'[53] soul is unattainable to the individual bound up (by, for one thing, ancestry) in the processes of history. The poem can be seen to be about the inevitable implication of even the most innocent individual, like the new-born Asher, in the imperfections of history.

Such a meaning is also furthered by another of the poem's repeated devices, the recurrent intrusion of the language of public injunction into the fabric of the poem, which stylistically enacts the inextricability of private and public spheres. In content, these interjections will, again, often appear nonsensical: the 'Please Examine || Your Change' quoted above seems a meaningless intrusion on an image that is already elusively whimsical. But closer examination of such moments reveals them almost always to bear some relevance to the context in which they appear. When this is the grotesque relevance of 'For Hire' (as of an unoccupied taxi) to 'the morning when Dr Patel had systematically drawn | the child from Jean's womb' (a recent miscarriage is one of the recurring preoccupations of the poem), it adds to the *Quoof*-like affectlessness of the poem's speaker. But 'Please Examine Your Change' reappears later:

> Ton upon ton of clay, hay, hair, shoes and spectacle frames
> made it less and less likely that we would land
>
> on our feet on the Griggstown Causeway any time soon, Ramp Divides,
> Please Examine Your Change As Mistakes Cannot Be Rectified.

The full version of the phrase (combined with the 'less and less likely' that will later be applied to the possibility of recovering 'radical innocence') suggests the irredeemability of the past (clay, hay, spectacle frames, and so on, reappear throughout the poem as a shorthand, with their connotations of the confiscated belongings found in the concentration camps, for the debris of history).

Through such oblique devices, Muldoon draws together the surface incoherencies of the poem towards a single specific theme: the relation of the individual to history. Critics have been quick to notice this: Quinney sees in the poem 'the panic of ... participation in history'.[54] Longley reads Yeats's presence as indicating a Muldoon 'freshly interested in Yeats's manner of moving between public and private worlds'.[55] Robert MacFarlane attributes to the poem 'an examination of the emotional mechanisms by which we come to understand tragedies in which we had no part'.[56] Rather than, as in his early work, resisting a predetermined

---

[53] W. B. Yeats, 'A Prayer for my Daughter', in *The Poems*, ed. Daniel Albright (London: Dent, 1990), 237.
[54] Quinney, 'In the Studebaker', 21.
[55] Longley, 'Twists and Turns', *Poetry Review*, 92/4 (Winter 2002–3), 65.
[56] Robert MacFarlane, 'High and Dry in the Flood', *Times Literary Supplement*, 11 Oct. 2002, 24.

meaning for his poetry, Muldoon, in 'Black Horse', works to engineer meaning, and invite particular interpretations. He has been more than usually eager to guide the reading of this poem, declaring, 'I hope that readers will come to terms with the jagged edges of "At the Sign of the Black Horse, September 1999" ', and explaining (or even excusing) such 'jaggedness' by uncharacteristically prescriptive reference to the 'necessity of modern poetry to reflect our increasingly jagged age'.[57]

In many ways, this new insistence that poetry should engage with history is admirable: Muldoon-the-poet is finally admitting his connection with Muldoon-the-man, tied to, and responsible to, a specific historical moment. MacFarlane praises *Moy Sand and Gravel* as a vindicating exposition of the covert ethicality he has always read into Muldoon's work, a proof that Muldoon has all along had a 'grander plan to . . . bring [his readers] into confrontation with what he calls the "dark matter" of existence'.[58] What I find problematic is that Muldoon continues, in this new context, to deploy devices that distance his speaker from his material, when his relation to such material is already (as it was not in *Quoof*) fairly remote. In choosing to address a broad, if eclectically represented, sweep of twentieth-century history, Muldoon is not subject to the 'improper expectations' that Longley famously identifies as the burden of Ulster poets.[59] A moral evaluation of such history is not an interpretation for which his poems will be read whatever their ostensible content: it is, in fact, one that would not occur to readers had he not raised the subject. In regard to the Holocaust in particular, he, in his distance from the event, is in the same position as his readers: any danger of prurient, predetermined reading comes as much from him as from them.

The *Quoof*-like gap between horrific subject-matter and affectless presentation still appears. It is hard to know what to make of a narrator who announces:

> The red stain on the lint
> that covered whatever it was in the autoclave brought back an afternoon in Poland
> when the smoke would fling and flail itself, Maximum Headroom,
> from a crematorium
> at Auschwitz.

But in 'Black Horse' the disjunction has the effect of appearing to conceal, and thus privilege, a response that is no different, no more in need of protection, than anyone else's. If devices such as deadpan narration and a foregrounding of verbal *brio* function to dramatize a subjectivity damaged into affectlessness by the events it recounts, then Muldoon would appear to be claiming a special sensitivity (and therefore a special licence to apparent callousness) to events that are properly no more damaging to him than to any other individual living in the long aftermath of the Second World War. Muldoon seems himself aware of some indecorum in

---

[57] Muldoon, in Brown and Paterson (eds.), *Don't Ask Me What I Mean*, 195.
[58] MacFarlane, 'High and Dry in the Flood', 24.
[59] Longley, 'Poetry and Politics in Northern Ireland', 185.

the 'jagged' disjunction, citing vindicatory precedent for it: 'The combination of intractable material with intricate formal methods was a particular strength of W. B. Yeats.'[60]

Longley questions the wisdom of Muldoon's addressing the Holocaust: 'The Jewish material may be too much to internalize in the way that the "Prayer for My Daughter" template requires.' She goes on to note that, in this poem, 'Muldoon's comedy and his seriousness are, for once, slightly at odds.'[61] I would suggest that this being 'at odds' results from the fact that both the poem's 'comedy' and its 'seriousness' come across as deliberately intended by Muldoon. He is responsible for both its bizarre juxtapositions and verbal playfulness *and* its attempt seriously to address the issue of the individual's relation to history (unlike in *Quoof*, where only the 'comedy' can be unquestionably attributed to the author). Because readers will not approach 'Black Horse' with preconceived expectations for such an earnest attempt, responsibility for the poem's 'seriousness' cannot be offloaded on to them; the dissonance between the two elements cannot be interpreted as oblique representation of the jarring that occurs when an individual comes up against the preconceptions of the world: it can only be a jarring of his intended meaning against his chosen method of presentation.

In a review of new English poetry, Jeremy Noel-Tod writes: 'The problem with English imitators of Muldoon is that they lack the volatile subtext of the Troubles to give their mental meanderings significance.'[62] While I would by no means demote Muldoon to the status of a self-imitator (judging by the recent *Horse Latitudes*, he clearly retains his potential for self-reinvention), Noel-Tod's comment does indicate how much Muldoon abandons when he exchanges the endlessly volatile (because incontrovertibly private) subtext of his own experience (including his experience of living in a time and place of violence) for the relatively stable (because fundamentally public) investigation of the individual's relation to twentieth-century history, 'our increasingly jagged age'. Muldoon's apparently growing commitment to such an investigation is a brave, as well as a hugely interesting, development; but his singular approach may undergo some adjustment before it can best sustain it.

---

[60] Muldoon, quoted in Brown and Paterson (eds.), *Don't Ask Me What I Mean*, 195.
[61] Longley, 'Twists and Turns', 66.
[62] Jeremy Noel-Tod, 'Poetic Staples', *Poetry Review*, 92/4 (Winter 2002–3), 114.

INDEX